Détente and Confrontation

RAYMOND L. GARTHOFF

Détente and Confrontation

American-Soviet Relations from Nixon to Reagan

THE BROOKINGS INSTITUTION
Washington, D.C.

Copyright © 1985 by
THE BROOKINGS INSTITUTION
1775 Massachusetts Avenue, N.W., Washington, D.C. 20036

Library of Congress Cataloging in Publication Data

Garthoff, Raymond L.
    Détente and confrontation.

    Includes bibliographies and index.
        1. United States—Foreign relations—Soviet Union.
2. Soviet Union—Foreign relations—United States.
I. Title.
E183.8.S65G37   1985   327.73047   84–45855
ISBN 0–8157–3044–6
ISBN 0–8157–3043–8 (pbk.)

9 8 7 6 5 4 3 2 1

THE BROOKINGS INSTITUTION is an independent organization devoted to nonpartisan research, education, and publication in economics, government, foreign policy, and the social sciences generally. Its principal purposes are to aid in the development of sound public policies and to promote public understanding of issues of national importance.

The Institution was founded on December 8, 1927, to merge the activities of the Institute for Government Research, founded in 1916, the Institute of Economics, founded in 1922, and the Robert Brookings Graduate School of Economics and Government, founded in 1924.

The Board of Trustees is responsible for the general administration of the Institution, while the immediate direction of the policies, program, and staff is vested in the President, assisted by an advisory committee of the officers and staff. The by-laws of the Institution state: "It is the function of the Trustees to make possible the conduct of scientific research, and publication, under the most favorable conditions, and to safeguard the independence of the research staff in the pursuit of their studies and in the publication of the results of such studies. It is not a part of their function to determine, control, or influence the conduct of particular investigations or the conclusions reached."

The President bears final responsibility for the decision to publish a manuscript as a Brookings book. In reaching his judgment on the competence, accuracy, and objectivity of each study, the President is advised by the director of the appropriate research program and weighs the views of a panel of expert outside readers who report to him in confidence on the quality of the work. Publication of a work signifies that it is deemed a competent treatment worthy of public consideration but does not imply endorsement of conclusions or recommendations.

The Institution maintains its position of neutrality on issues of public policy in order to safeguard the intellectual freedom of the staff. Hence interpretations or conclusions in Brookings publications should be understood to be solely those of the authors and should not be attributed to the Institution, to its trustees, officers, or other staff members, or to the organizations that support its research.

In order to know what is going to happen,
one must know what has happened.

NICOLO MACHIAVELLI

Foreword

Relations between the United States and the Soviet Union clearly constitute one of the central problems of American policy and world politics. The tension that has characterized the past decade, the evident misunderstanding that contributes to that tension, and the potential destructiveness that could be triggered by U.S.-Soviet confrontation, all encourage an effort to bring the most detailed and careful scholarship to bear on this topic. While it is a formidable undertaking for any one person to deal with such a wide-ranging and contentious subject, there is great advantage in having an integrated analysis by one scholar. Moreover, while judgments on particular issues will inevitably vary, it is important to set a standard for serious, constructive, informed, and objective discussion that any challenging interpretation should seek to meet.

The author of this study, Raymond L. Garthoff, is unusually well qualified. He has long been one of the foremost American scholars of the Soviet Union and has been intimately involved in practical diplomacy as well. He was a key member of the diplomatic team that negotiated the SALT I treaty—the episode that initiates the historical period reviewed in the volume. He continued to serve in the U.S. diplomatic service for much of the period, serving as U.S. Ambassador in Bulgaria before coming to the Brookings Foreign Policy Studies program in January 1980.

The study presents a fine-grained historical review of developments affecting American-Soviet relations. It examines both U.S. and Soviet perspectives and their interaction. This approach demonstrates that each side tends to see itself more as reacting to initiatives of the other side than is actually the case. Indeed, this book yields insights and conclusions not available in the current literature, and often modifies the prevailing impression, sometimes to a startling degree.

The author wishes to express his appreciation to the many people who provided assistance based on their own direct participation in the events discussed, many of whom must remain unnamed. Among those who provided information, comments, or both are David Aaron, A. Doak Barnett, Harold Brown, Zbigniew Brzezinski, Lawrence Caldwell, Alexander Dallin, Nathaniel Davis, Karen Dawisha, Ralph Earle II, Harry Gelman, Alexander L. George, Harry Harding, Jr., Christine M. Helms, Jerry Hough, John W. Huizenga,

ix

William G. Hyland, Spurgeon M. Keeny, Jr., Jan Lodal, Murrey Marder, Michael K. MccGwire, Paul H. Nitze, Vladimir Petrov, William B. Quandt, Dimitri K. Simes, Gerard C. Smith, Helmut Sonnenfeldt, Brent Scowcroft, Marshall D. Shulman, Vladimir I. Toumanoff, Jiri Valenta, Paul C. Warnke, and Herbert C. York. The author also benefited from discussions with many Soviet officials, scholars, and commentators, especially those from the Institute of the U.S.A. and Canada, the Institute of the World Economy and International Relations, the Ministry of Foreign Affairs, the Ministry of Defense, and the Central Committee. He also thanks Mark Koenig for research assistance, in particular on U.S.-Soviet trade and human rights developments; Caroline Lalire and Whitney Watriss for editing the manuscript; Bruce J. Dickson, Christine L. Potts, and Steven Wegren for verifying its factual content; and Karin E. Burchard, Ruth E. Conrad, Maxine Joyner, Jeanie Cline Roberts, and Ann M. Ziegler for typing it. Ward & Silvan prepared the index.

This study was partially supported by the Ford Foundation, the Andrew W. Mellon Foundation, the Carnegie Corporation of New York, the Rockefeller Foundation, and the National Council for Soviet and East European Research. The Brookings Institution gratefully acknowledges the financial assistance of those organizations.

The views expressed are solely those of the author and should not be ascribed to the persons whose assistance is acknowledged above, to the sources of funding support, or to the trustees, officers, or other staff members of the Brookings Institution.

BRUCE K. MACLAURY
President

April 1985
Washington, D.C.

Contents

Détente and Confrontation

1   Setting the Stage: Contexts, Perspectives, and Issues

THE UNITED STATES and the Soviet Union are virtually foreordained to continuing rivalry—but also, short of mutual destruction, to continuing coexistence. In addition to a range of conflicting interests and objectives, the two powers ineluctably share some common interests and aims, of which survival is paramount. Through the harshest tensions and crises of the cold war, and through occasional relaxations of tension, this pattern of competition and coexistence has persisted, and it will do so in the foreseeable future.

The present study investigates the experience of the period from 1969 through 1984. This period was marked first by a relaxation of tensions, or "détente," that prevailed during most of the 1970s. By the latter years of the decade, however, there had been a renewal of tensions and confrontation that has continued into the mid-1980s.

Détente is the term that has come to characterize American-Soviet relations in the period from 1972 through 1979, although it was increasingly weakened, especially after 1975. Today, most Americans probably see détente as a failed or even discredited policy. Yet confrontation, while it may be accepted as a necessity under some circumstances, is not widely favored as an alternative. One question to be addressed is whether the rise and fall of what has sometimes been called "the decade of détente" was a true test of the viability of a policy of détente, or simply a unique turn of the wheel of history. Peace, like war, comes in many different forms.

The purpose of this study is to learn from history as a guide to the future, in particular, to the future of American-Soviet relations. The focus is on the decade-and-a-half beginning, on the American side, with the onset of the presidency of Richard M. Nixon and his call for replacing confrontation with "an era of negotiation" in pursuit of "a structure of peace." It closes with President Ronald Reagan's repudiation of détente and avowal, once again, of a cold war strategy of "direct confrontation," combining a "dialogue from

1

strength" and a "crusade." On the Soviet side, this period happens to span the key years of General Secretary Leonid I. Brezhnev's leadership and the transition through Yury V. Andropov and Konstantin U. Chernenko to Mikhail S. Gorbachev, a period marked by persistent advocacy of détente.[1]

The mix of cooperation and competition in American-Soviet relations makes it difficult to define the period of détente precisely. Despite President Nixon's early call for an era of negotiation, a series of confrontations in the ensuing three-and-a-half years made progress toward that goal slow. Then, in mid-1972, the first Nixon-Brezhnev summit meeting took place, and détente suddenly blossomed. During the next few years, a flood of cooperative ventures was inaugurated, culminating symbolically in 1975 in a joint space rendezvous, and accompanied by a great deal of rhetoric about peaceful coexistence and partnership in building a structure of peace.

Although cooperation developed in a number of areas, particularly from 1972 to 1975, it never supplanted ongoing competition nor offered sufficient guarantee against renewed confrontation. From the American perspective, one important cause of the decline of détente was the active Soviet role in Africa and South Asia after 1975. Growing concern over the strategic balance from 1976 on was an equally important source of disenchantment. From the Soviet perspective, successive U.S. administrations were seen as conducting a vigorous policy of containing and curtailing Soviet influence, especially in the Middle East, from the very beginning of détente. Moreover, the U.S. Congress had dashed expectations for economic benefits promised and even granted by the Nixon administration by making them conditional on unacceptable and humiliating concessions concerning internal Soviet affairs, specifically, escalating demands for Jewish emigration. Finally, in the period from 1977 on, the Soviet leaders perceived a growing American attempt to regain strategic superiority.

Was détente a potential solution to the risks and costs of confrontation, a solution undercut by actions of the Soviet Union, or of the United States, or both? Or did détente exacerbate the problem by providing only a disarming illusion of an alternative? Was détente a Soviet snare to lull American sensitivity to a buildup of Soviet military power and political-military expansion? Did the United States and the Soviet Union ever have a common understanding of détente—or did they hold differing conceptions that were incompatible from the start? Did détente fail? Was it ever really tested?

Many Americans may believe the answers are so clear that these questions need not even be raised. In fact, the questions, to say nothing of the answers, are far more complex than is usually imagined.

---

1. Brezhnev succeeded Nikita S. Khrushchev as head of the Communist party of the Soviet Union in October 1964, but it was not until the period 1969–72, coincident with the development of a policy of détente, that Brezhnev consolidated a dominant position in the Soviet leadership. Following his death in November 1982, he was succeeded by Andropov, he in turn by Chernenko in February 1984, and he by Gorbachev in March 1985.

Contexts and Perspectives

Close study of American-Soviet relations since 1969 in the context of global events and internal American and Soviet politics is needed to provide a basis for answering those questions. The underlying nature of the American-Soviet relationship in this period is complex and requires close scrutiny and detailed analysis. The relationship is an interaction with dynamics of its own. It involves not only the aims of the two powers, but also the policies and actions they employ to serve those (and other) aims. It necessarily involves the perceptions each has of the world and of its own role, and of the role, aims, and capabilities of the other. Defining national interests has long been recognized as involving the subjective political judgments of national decisionmakers. Domestic political interests and factional political maneuvering, the cybernetic and institutional roles of constituencies and interest groups, and the political needs of policymakers may all be as important in shaping actual policy and action in world politics as ideological, geopolitical,[2] world-order, economic, or other foreign policy interests and objectives of those decisionmakers.

Understanding interests, objectives, perceptions, politics, and actions, both Soviet and American, as well as their interaction, is difficult but necessary. The present study seeks to improve such understanding. The making (or historical reconstruction) of just one nation's foreign policy toward its principal rival is itself complex. Inquiry into both sides of the equation is doubly complex. Moreover, even superpowers such as the United States and the Soviet Union cannot frame and carry out their policies toward one another without being heavily influenced by other developments in the world. Many of these developments are partly or totally beyond their control and even their ability to predict. Yet these events provide independent distractions, threats, or opportunities, as well as new arenas for engaging or competing with the principal adversary. As such, they are an important element affecting the policies of the superpowers, and must be an element in the analysis of those policies. The relations of both the Soviet Union and the United States with China have, for example, affected the world scene and their own bilateral relations in important ways. So, too, have developments in Europe, part of which is intimately associated with each superpower, but which also comprises a number of more or less independent actors on the world scene. In particular, a détente in East-West relations centered on Europe began before the American-Soviet détente. And, in contrast to the fate of the American-Soviet détente, European détente

---

2. The term *geopolitical* is used in this study in accordance with general current usage as a synonym for realistic "power political" factors or approaches in international politics, and as an antonym to idealistic or ideological factors or approaches. It thus corresponds closely to the traditional term in historical and political science analysis *Realpolitik*. This is in contrast to the earlier use of the word in English as a translation of the term *Geopolitik*, which represented a particular deterministic geographical-political school that developed in variants in Great Britain and Germany earlier in this century. Henry Kissinger has contributed much to this conversion of the usage.

has lasted on after it. Finally, many different kinds of actions affecting allies and lesser adversaries around the world, and the varying involvement of the superpowers in third world conflicts, played a role in stimulating the American-Soviet détente of the 1970s. Later, such actions played a significant part in undermining that détente.

Generalizations of this broad nature do not suffice. It can, for example, be observed that such events as, say, the Soviet intervention in Afghanistan undercut (some would say violated, or exposed) détente. Whether that conclusion is valid, however, and whether that event should have had that result, are examples of questions that require much deeper analysis of what the two sides thought détente meant, and also of the contexts within which the leaders of the two nations made decisions relative to the situation in Afghanistan. Finally, it also requires study of the evaluations each side made of the motivations of the other.

In order to address the question of the perceptions and purposes of the leaders of the two powers, it is essential to recreate the contexts of their decisions. Doing so requires very detailed reconstruction of events and analysis. Reconstructing accurately what facts and factors were known at the time, and learning retrospectively what actually occurred and why, pose many problems beyond that of access to information. Hazards of studying the very recent past are evident: people think they know and understand events through which they have lived. In fact, contemporary information (and understanding) is often deficient, and remembrance is both selective and influenced by later perceptions. The experience of contemporary history is therefore often deceptive. The challenge of the future requires a better understanding of what actually occurred in the 1970s and first half of the 1980s, as well as of why it happened and what it means. While it is premature to expect definitive history at this early remove, a great deal of information is available for analysis.[3]

American studies of relations between the United States and the Soviet Union are usually, perhaps necessarily, undertaken by students of Soviet affairs. While expertise on the Soviet Union is essential, its emphasis has tended to lead to an overconcentration on *Soviet* motives, objectives, and actions in what is a complex reciprocal interrelationship. For example, such studies customarily identify the subject as Soviet-American relations, unconsciously attributing the focal role to the Soviet Union and usually overstating

---

3. Throughout most of the period under study, until the end of 1979, I was concluding thirty years of official service in the field of American-Soviet relations. This experience provided firsthand exposure and participation in many of the areas covered, and has facilitated access to other active or former officials for interviews. Other sources include declassification of some official documents, and the spate of memoirs by such participants as former Presidents Richard M. Nixon, Gerald R. Ford, and Jimmy Carter, former Secretary of State Henry A. Kissinger, former National Security Adviser Zbigniew K. Brzezinski, former Secretary of State Cyrus R. Vance, and former Secretary of State Alexander M. Haig, Jr., and by a number of less centrally placed participants and observers. In addition, I have made extensive use of published Soviet materials, and interviewed a number of senior Soviet officials.

Soviet initiative. The United States is implicitly assigned a more reactive role. This approach can distort the analysis. Soviet policy in general, and in its relationship to the United States in particular, is often reactive. In addition, from the Soviet perspective, the American role is much more active and initiatory. Moreover, in describing a relationship between adversaries, attribution of the initiative often carries connotations of a more activist, offensive stance, so that even the wording may imply more than is realized. While there is no completely neutral solution, the most satisfactory is probably a "protocol" approach: refer to American-Soviet relations when describing the relationship as approached from the American side, and to Soviet-American relations when describing the relationship from the Soviet side. That is what is done in this study.

There is a natural tendency in most political analyses to focus directly on the subject under study. This approach has merit and is necessary, but it is not sufficient. Time and again essentially extraneous considerations have important effects on perceptions and decisions, whether recognized at the time. For this reason, it is important to trace the overlay and interaction of parallel or intersecting developments. There are many levels of interactions that require correlating wide-ranging aspects of internal political, foreign political, military strategic, and other developments in the United States, the Soviet Union, and the world as they come to bear on individual actions and decisions.

The Historical Context

The United States and the Soviet Union had little active or significant political contact in the prewar period, even after diplomatic recognition of the Soviet Union in 1933, apart from some trade beginning in the 1920s. The turning point was World War II, when a common foe drew the two nations into collaborative alliance. Then, very rapidly following the defeat of the Axis powers that ended the raison d'être for the alliance, their relationship dissolved into mutual suspicion. Joseph V. Stalin's brutal installation of communist rule in Eastern Europe, and communist attempts to extend further into Europe (Czechoslovakia, Berlin), the Near East (Iran, Turkey, Greece), and the Far East (China, Korea) were seen as imposing on a reluctant America the need to assume leadership in a "free (that is, noncommunist) world" in opposing and containing Soviet-led expansionist communism. The cold war was forced upon us. Such is a thumbnail sketch of the development of American-Soviet relations as generally seen through American eyes.[4]

---

4. This image is intentionally outlined here in stark and simple terms, and does not reflect modifications in academic study that have developed through the traditional school of scholarship in the early postwar period, the revisionist challenge of the 1960s, or more sophisticated attempts at synthesis in recent years.

What is the comparable Soviet view? First, the United States is seen as a capitalist state, since 1945 as the leading imperialist power.[5] In addition, the United States had been an active participant in the capitalist attempts to choke the Bolshevik Revolution of 1917: American troops landed in the north of Russia and in Siberia in 1918–19 and aided the unsuccessful White counterrevolution. During the 1920s the United States alone among the major powers had shunned diplomatic relations with the Soviet Union. Later, during attempts in the 1930s to stop Adolf Hitler's Germany, the United States chose to withdraw from an active diplomatic role. When Germany attacked the Soviet Union in June 1941, although the United States did soon begin providing lend-lease aid to the USSR, the spirit in which it did so was expressed by Senator Harry S Truman in an offhand comment cited in dozens of Soviet accounts: "If we see that Germany is winning we ought to help Russia and if Russia is winning we ought to help Germany and that way let them kill as many as possible."[6] Following the war, the United States, itself untouched by the devastation of the war, immediately and abruptly cut off lend-lease and constricted shipment of reparations materials to the USSR from defeated Germany. The Soviets were effectively frozen out of the occupation government of "the Allies" in Italy and Japan. Attempts were made to place anti-Soviet political émigrés back into power in Poland and elsewhere in Eastern Europe. The United States generally sought to establish what it described as positions of strength, from which the Soviet Union would be encircled and neutralized. All this was done under the umbrella of the atomic bomb, which the United States used in Japan principally to intimidate the Soviet Union with its power, and which, through the Baruch Plan, it sought to deny to the Soviet Union. And so on through a perception of the cold war that few Americans could even imagine, much less accept.

The purpose here is not to sort out historical responsibilities and truth. Rather, it is to note the legacy, still very active, of suspicion and fear engendered in both countries by their widely differing perceptions of one another and of the course of international relations. The present study analyzes developments affecting Soviet policy, with the aim of clarifying Soviet perspectives and perceptions, as well as American policy.

The cold war waxed and waned for more than two decades as both sides attempted from time to time to ameliorate the confrontation. The earliest effort at rapprochement, albeit abortive, was the attempt by some Soviet leaders to reduce East-West tensions in the immediate aftermath of Stalin's

---

5. In Marxist-Leninist ideological terms, the designation "imperialist" does not necessarily imply the possession of colonial empires, nor is it an expletive. As defined by Vladimir I. Lenin, imperialism is simply "the highest stage of capitalism."

6. "Our Policy Stated in Soviet-Nazi War," *New York Times*, June 24, 1941. For a recent Soviet reference to Truman's remark, made on the fiftieth anniversary of the establishment of Soviet-American diplomatic relations, see Yu. Molchanov, "Fifty Difficult Years," *Kommunist* [The Communist], no. 16 (November 1983), p. 107.

death in 1953. There were, however, sufficient doubts in the West that the tentative Soviet overtures for reunification of a neutral Germany were rebuffed. The attempt was also undercut by the suppression of a spontaneous uprising in East Berlin in July 1953 and the related weakening of the faction in the Soviet leadership that had advocated a course of relaxing tensions.[7] Nonetheless, Soviet steps to reduce tensions continued. New Soviet flexibility permitted ending the Korean War and attaining a peace treaty that led to the withdrawal of Soviet troops from Austria. The Soviets also unilaterally withdrew and returned their only "overseas" bases: Hanko in Finland, and Darien in Manchuria, both extorted in treaties after the war.

Mutual interest in relaxing tensions spawned the first meeting of East-West leaders in a summit conference at Geneva in 1955. The ensuing "Spirit of Geneva" dissolved in 1956 following the Soviet suppression of the popular uprising in Hungary. Nonetheless, within just a few years a series of high-level reciprocal visits of Soviet and American leaders took place, including three in 1959 (Soviet Deputy Prime Minister Anastas I. Mikoyan, Vice President Richard M. Nixon, and Chairman Nikita S. Khrushchev). A visit by President Dwight D. Eisenhower to the Soviet Union, the first ever by an American president (except for the secret wartime conference at Yalta), was also planned. But that prospective visit, and a multilateral summit meeting in Paris, collapsed in the wake of the interception of an American U-2 reconnaissance airplane near the center of the USSR on May Day 1960.

The next serious bid for détente followed the most intense confrontation of the cold war, the Cuban missile crisis of October 1962. In an effort by both sides to reduce tensions following the resolution of that confrontation, in 1963 the first real arms control agreements were reached—the partial nuclear test ban, the installation of a "hot line" (direct communication link) between Moscow and Washington, and an agreement to ban nuclear weapons in space. Other steps were under consideration, but tapered off as the United States began to engage itself directly in Vietnam in 1964–65.

Prime Minister Aleksei N. Kosygin and President Lyndon B. Johnson did meet in 1967 at Glassboro, New Jersey, but there was no real meeting of minds. In 1968 efforts to move toward a European détente, and toward an American-Soviet summit conference that would launch the ambitious strategic arms limitation talks (SALT), were suspended after the Soviet occupation of Czechoslovakia. The invasion occurred literally on the eve of the planned announcement of a Johnson-Kosygin summit meeting and a start of SALT negotiations. Even after the Soviet occupation of Czechoslovakia and the defeat of his party in the 1968 presidential election, President Johnson attempted to

---

7. For one seasoned observer's later reflection on this possibly missed opportunity, see Charles E. Bohlen, *Witness to History, 1929–1969* (W. W. Norton, 1973), p. 371. See also Coral Bell, *Negotiation from Strength: A Study in the Politics of Power* (Alfred A. Knopf, 1963), pp. 106–13.

arrange a lame duck summit meeting. When, however, President-elect Nixon made clear to the Soviets that he opposed the idea, the Soviets spurned Johnson's proposal.[8]

Such was the background to President Nixon's inaugural call for opening "an era of negotiation." It remained for the conjunction of circumstances, leaders, and events in the early 1970s to produce sufficient progress in collaborative efforts to relax tensions to justify general recognition of a transition beyond the cold war to détente.

The International Political Context

The international political context was of great importance to the development of Soviet-American détente in the key formative years from 1969 to 1972. One important factor in the evolution of the relationship between the two superpowers was the emergence of strategic nuclear parity. But there were other, independent international developments that, while affected by and in turn affecting the strategic balance, also had their own roots and ramifications. Two of particular note were the movement in Europe in the late 1960s toward East-West détente and the development of a more acute Sino-Soviet conflict in parallel with budding Sino-American rapprochement. These developments are examined in later chapters, but it is useful to note here briefly how each contributed to the initiation of American-Soviet détente.

The idea of East-West détente emerged in the mid-1960s. It was advanced in 1966 and 1967 by the Warsaw Pact countries, in 1966 by General Charles de Gaulle, and in 1967 by the North Atlantic Treaty Organization (NATO). This rapprochement was interrupted briefly by the Soviet occupation of Czechoslovakia in 1968, but the year 1969 marked a significant new beginning. The Soviet Union wished to renew Western European consideration of détente following Czechoslovakia, and in March 1969 the Warsaw Pact again proposed a conference on European security and cooperation. The NATO alliance meeting at Reykjavik, Iceland, in June responded positively but cautiously, and prospects for movement on multilateral détente remained clouded. Following the election of Willy Brandt as chancellor of the Federal Republic of Germany (FRG, or West Germany) in October 1969, West Germany undertook an *Ostpolitik* aimed at détente and moved rapidly to sign a

---

8. See Lyndon Baines Johnson, *The Vantage Point: Perspectives of the Presidency, 1963–1969* (Holt, Rinehart and Winston, 1971), pp. 448–90; and Henry Kissinger, *White House Years* (Boston, Mass.: Little, Brown, 1979), pp. 49–50. The fact that the outgoing and incoming administrations carried on separate and uncoordinated talks with the Soviets, leaving the final decision to them, was remarkable. A knowledgeable Soviet official indicated to me the Russians' astonishment.

Non-Aggression Pact with the USSR in Moscow in 1970. West Germany also entered into negotiations that led to treaties with Poland, Czechoslovakia, and the German Democratic Republic (GDR, or East Germany) in the early 1970s. Following in train with the bilateral West German *Ostpolitik*, the United States, Britain, and France in 1971 negotiated with the USSR a Quadripartite Berlin Agreement designed to defuse the perennial flashpoint of Berlin. By 1972 détente was well under way in Europe, and in 1973 a Conference on Security and Cooperation in Europe (CSCE) opened, and talks on mutual and balanced force reductions (MBFR) began.

The year 1969 also marked the eruption of a series of armed clashes on the Soviet-Chinese border, seriously escalating the long-simmering hostility between these two major communist powers. Not coincidentally, the same year saw the first secret steps toward an American-Chinese rapprochement and normalization of relations, following twenty years of unremitting hostility, broken relations, and the undeclared war in Korea. While rapid restoration of relations between the two countries could not be predicted in 1969, the potential was there. After a surprising secret visit by Henry A. Kissinger, assistant to the president for national security affairs, to Beijing in July 1971 and an invitation to President Nixon to visit China early the next year, the process set in motion in 1969 was revealed publicly.

With the sudden sharp worsening of Sino-Soviet relations (not at Soviet instance), the leaders in Moscow saw additional incentives to explore the unexpected new opportunities for a détente with the United States. With exquisite balance, on the very day, October 20, 1969, that the Soviet Union opened talks with China on the border issue, Ambassador Anatoly F. Dobrynin met with President Nixon to advise him of Soviet readiness to begin preliminary strategic arms limitation talks with the United States. And, by coincidence, on the very next day Brandt was elected chancellor of West Germany. A plenary meeting of the Central Committee in Moscow in mid-December 1969 was probably instrumental in turning the party's attention to this course.[9]

In these interrelated developments in the late 1960s and early 1970s, it should be noted that improvements in East-West relations in Europe and in American-Soviet relations developed in parallel and were mutually supporting. Similarly, in its early years the American-Chinese rapprochement of the 1970s evolved parallel to, and in support of, American interests in developing U.S.-Soviet détente. By the late 1970s, however, the pursuit of closer American-Chinese ties contributed to the decline and fall of American-Soviet détente. And the survival and continuation of European détente after the collapse of American-Soviet détente has led to frictions in American–Western European relations.

---

9. The report and proceedings of this Central Committee plenum on international affairs were not published, but knowledgeable Soviet sources have indicated its importance off the record. The new course became clear by the time of the Twenty-fourth Party Congress in March–April 1971.

Of particular importance to American disenchantment with détente was the Soviet involvement in a series of third world conflicts. The first, in the view of many Americans, was the Arab-Israeli War of October 1973. The Soviet-Cuban actions in Angola in 1975–76 and in Ethiopia in 1977–78 represented a more active Soviet commitment and role. The direct Soviet military intervention in Afghanistan at the close of 1979 was seen as the culmination of an aggressive course.

On the other side, the Soviet leaders saw a number of instances of American action over the same period directed against Soviet interests. In particular, there was the skillful American exclusion of the Soviet Union from the Near Eastern peace process and broader curtailment of Soviet influence in the Middle East. At least equally important was the establishment of an American-Chinese geopolitical alignment against Soviet interests in Asia and the third world.

Vietnam played a singularly important role. The central preoccupation of the Nixon administration from 1969 to 1973 was disengagement of the United States from direct military involvement in the war in Indochina. In the late 1970s Vietnam again came to play an important though quite different role in triangular Sino-Soviet-American diplomacy.

Cuba was another factor that entered American-Soviet relations in several ways. In 1970, early in the tentative movement toward improvement in American-Soviet relations, Cuba became the focus of a quiet Soviet-American confrontation over Soviet steps to establish a submarine base on the island. In 1978, with the Soviet Union supplying more modern fighter-bomber aircraft, Cuba again became a focus of American concern. And in 1979, when the United States discovered the presence of a brigade of Soviet ground forces on the island, a psuedo-crisis arose. Of particular importance was Cuba's role in Africa in conjunction with Soviet pursuit of its interests there. By the early 1980s Cuba was supporting Nicaragua and insurgents in El Salvador. All those episodes had a damaging impact on détente.

The effects of these and other developments in the rest of the world had serious and negative effects on American—and Soviet—*expectations* about the advantages of détente. Thus they came to play a significant part in undermining support for it.

These instances of the interplay and reverberation of geopolitical conflicts illustrate the broad international political context in which American-Soviet relations develop. A number of these episodes are examined in some detail in this study because of their important effects on American-Soviet relations.

Domestic Political Contexts

The course of American relations with the Soviet Union, and Soviet relations with the United States, has greatly influenced—and been greatly influenced by—internal political developments in the two countries. This was notably so both in the rise, and in the fall, of détente in the 1970s.

President Nixon's personal advocacy of détente came as a surprise even to many of his supporters and colleagues. While his interest in it was by no means limited to immediate political appeal, this was clearly one consideration of the veteran politician. In fact, Nixon had earlier been not only ambivalent, but erratic, about his approach to relations with the Soviet Union. In his election campaign in 1968 he had made little mention of his proposed policy, and then in fragmented and inconsistent ways. On October 24 he made a notably hard-line speech about an alleged "security gap" that he said was occurring, and asserted that, if elected, he would act immediately to restore a "clear-cut military superiority" over the Soviet Union. Yet two days later, apparently sensing that he had gone too far in one direction, he veered sharply in another, saying that the United States "must move away from confrontations in this nuclear age into a new era—the era of negotiation,"[10] foreshadowing the call in his inaugural address to replace "a period of confrontation" with "an era of negotiation."[11] And in his first press conference as president, in an off-the-cuff comment, he jettisoned the idea of "superiority" in arms for a concept of "sufficiency."[12]

Détente undoubtedly contributed to Nixon's reelection in November 1972. The dramatic summit meeting in Moscow in May of that year that launched détente, while perhaps less immediately relevant than the apparent end of the war in Vietnam, was important. Later, under fire for the cover-up of Watergate, Nixon sought to wrap himself in the banner of détente. But the third summit meeting in June 1974 yielded little, and past successes, including détente, did not offset his ultimate failure as president or shield him from the consequences. Indeed, at the last summit, while Nixon made every effort to tie himself to détente, the Soviets, bewildered by the Watergate political crisis and suspicious that it was a ruse by opponents of détente, carefully avoided Nixon's personal identification with détente in their own statements. Instead, they stressed that détente was a relationship between the two countries and peoples, not merely between their current leaders.

By 1976 détente was under fire from conservative quarters in the primary and election campaigns, and President Gerald R. Ford banished the word from his political lexicon, although to no ultimate avail. By January 1980 (after Afghanistan), and during the 1980 election campaign and thereafter, détente was no longer a positive symbol in American politics. Although President Jimmy Carter never repudiated it as an aim, in practice the inconsistent

---

10. Cited in Robert Walters, "Nixon Bids for Curbs in A-Arms," *Washington Sunday Star*, October 27, 1968.

11. "Inaugural Address of President Richard Milhous Nixon," January 20, *Weekly Compilation of Presidential Documents*, vol. 5 (January 27, 1969), p. 152. (Hereafter *Presidential Documents*.)

12. "The President's News Conference of January 27, 1969," *Presidential Documents*, vol. 5 (February 3, 1969), p. 178.

objectives of his administration, reflected in the shifting influence of the view-points of Cyrus R. Vance, the secretary of state, and Zbigniew Brzezinski, the assistant to the president for national security affairs, during the years 1977–79, raised increasingly serious questions about whether détente was viable. But the concept was never abandoned in those years, even as competition between the two powers completely submerged cooperation by the last year of that administration.

The Reagan administration, on the other hand, did reject the concept of détente from the outset. Secretary of State Alexander M. Haig, Jr., in his activist way, and then Secretary of State George P. Shultz in a more quiet way, did attempt to resurrect in substance, though not in name, a "hard-headed" détente, as former President Nixon now approvingly terms it. But they were unable, at least in the first years of the administration, to surmount President Reagan's penchant for a confrontational stance or the consequences of unleashing a Soviet confrontational response.

The internal political ramifications of détente go well beyond its fluctuating general political popularity. The relation of détente to arms control and hence to military policy and programs is obvious. So, too, is its relation to economic ties and trade. There are, however, other, more subtle relationships.

The conception of détente as initially developed and then managed by Nixon and Kissinger required a central decisionmaker able to control firmly all aspects of policymaking and implementation. A succession of presidents have found that while the powers of the presidency are vast, they are not unlimited. The reason is not only constitutional but bureaucratic. For example, Kissinger's concept of implementing détente called for manipulating incentives and penalties to affect the actions of the other side and to modulate the actions of one's own side in order to signal the other side. Yet even in the heyday of détente, and increasingly in later years, this approach proved difficult and sometimes impossible to carry through. The U.S. Senate denied one incentive (and an important part of the network of enmeshing ties) when in 1974 it overrode the administration and insisted on its own terms of "linkage" for the basic U.S.-USSR Trade Agreement. This linkage, which proved self-defeating, involved the addition of the requirement for an explicit high level of Jewish emigration as part of a finely balanced bilateral economic agreement. Similarly, in 1975 the Senate refused to grant the administration the penalty it sought in continuing covert support for the side in the civil war in Angola that was opposing the side supported by the Soviet Union and Cuba.

Even within the executive branch, the imperative of controlling in order to manage détente reinforced the inclinations of both Nixon and Kissinger to hold more and more closely in their own hands the information, choices, and decisions on a wide range of foreign policy questions. Freezing the government apparatus out of its normal role certainly permitted greater flexibility in making some decisions, but partly as a consequence the decisions were not always the best ones. Nor was it always possible to control and effect the desired results. For example, on occasion Kissinger sought to orchestrate signals by sending precise instructions to American ambassadors in the field (such as to "demonstrate a cold attitude toward all Soviet representatives and curtail social functions") without sharing the reasons or purposes for the actions they were instructed blindly to take. Apart from stimulating some recalcitrance and resentment, such attempts to manage everything centrally in detail, rather than working together as a team, often led to other than the desired effect.

A policy of détente, even one carefully combining incentives and disincentives, does not require that kind of extreme concentration of control. Moreover, any close management of the multitudinous aspects and instruments of policy is impaired by an inability to control completely. Conducting a policy involving a mix of cooperation and competition—of collaborative measures for arms control, while pursuing politically competitive and even antagonistic courses of action in some other areas—is very difficult to explain and to sustain with the public. This is especially so since different domestic political constituencies will wish to emphasize one or the other approach. Moreover, public opinion tends to move toward one or the other, instead of pursuing (and still less, optimally manipulating) both.

In general, the domestic political influence of both the leadership and the public on détente, and the impact of détente on internal developments, are highly important. Indeed, as will be seen, ultimately the fate of the efforts to sustain détente between the United States and the Soviet Union in the 1970s foundered on domestic political considerations in the United States as much as on any other factor.

In Soviet policy consideration, public opinion is not irrelevant, but it plays virtually no role in moving or limiting foreign policy. Domestic policy issues and internal political maneuvering within the leadership, however, can and do play a role, sometimes critical. In the Soviet Union, détente with the United States was adopted precisely in the period from 1969 to 1972 when Brezhnev was establishing his preeminence in foreign relations. That internal political dynamic reinforced other considerations in maintaining a consistently strong support for détente through the Brezhnev period, and it has continued since. This does not mean, of course, that there have been no changes in specific policies to implement détente, which change in response to changes in the international political scene. But since the Twenty-fourth Party Congress in 1971, détente and peaceful coexistence have been established as the general line of the party and government in international affairs.

Despite the virtual collapse of détente and, indeed, of most cooperative contacts between the United States and the Soviet Union since the beginning of 1980 following the Soviet occupation of Afghanistan, the Soviet leaders have continued to insist that pursuit of détente, despite obstacles placed in the way by the United States and increased opposition from influential American circles, remains a central task. Thus Brezhnev's Report of the Central Committee to the Twenty-sixth Party Congress in February 1981 stated: "When thunder clouds gathered on the international horizon at the beginning of the 1980s, the Soviet Union continued to persevere and deepen détente. . . . The USSR wants normal relations with the United States. There is simply no other sensible path from the standpoint of the interests of both of our nations and of mankind as a whole."[13]

Notwithstanding the long Soviet advocacy of détente, there were early challenges to decisions over certain policies, and apparently even to détente itself. Some voices of caution were raised within the Soviet leadership about the general line in the formative period from 1969 to 1972. One aspect of American policy in particular made it difficult, at least for some Soviet leaders, to consider the time then ripe for pressing ahead with contacts with the United States: the Vietnam War. The armed forces of the United States were engaged in direct hostilities with the forces of the Soviet Union's informal communist ally, the Democratic Republic of Vietnam (DRV, or North Vietnam). Another reservation may have arisen from the desire by some to continue trying to drive a wedge between the United States and its allies in Western Europe by seeking détente only with the latter, the line from 1966 to 1970. Conflicting Soviet views also arose over the proper balance of economic ties with the West. But the policy of the Nixon administration persuaded Brezhnev and most of his colleagues to press ahead with the line adopted by the Twenty-fourth Party Congress in April 1971, and to seek détente with the United States.

In May 1972, on the eve of the first Soviet-American summit meeting, at least one Politburo member, Pyotr Ye. Shelest, objected to proceeding with the meeting after the United States suddenly escalated hostilities in North Vietnam by mining the port of Haiphong. He was promptly demoted. The removal later of three other Politburo members—Gennady I. Voronov in 1973, Aleksandr N. Shelepin in 1975, and Nikolai V. Podgorny in 1977—may also have been related to differences over détente policy issues.

Other Soviet discussions of détente have hinted at internal criticism voiced from both the left and the right. For example, a discussion in *Questions of Philosophy*, after noting that the Twenty-fifth Party Congress had given "deep scientific elaboration" to the relationship between détente and the class struggle, criticized unnamed "right opportunists" who proposed working out "rules for peacetime" impinging on Soviet support for the class struggle, and on the other hand "left opportunists" who "as it were would require giving up détente in the name of the class struggle." Less attention was given to the former deviation, although it was attributed to a "revisionist approach" (of which, in Marxist-Leninist parlance, communists would be guilty) as well as to bourgeois circles identifying international peace with class peace. More fire was devoted to the leftist deviation, which is said to have asserted that peaceful coexistence "would in practice mean helping capitalism" by "freezing the status quo." These unnamed critics of détente were sternly reminded by the

---

13. L. I. Brezhnev, "Report of the Central Committee of the CPSU to the XXVI Congress of the Communist Party of the Soviet Union, February 23, 1981," *Pravda*, February 24, 1981.

Twenty-fifth Congress that revolution is dependent on *internal* development in each society, not external (Soviet) actions.[14]

There are of course many domestic implications of détente that need not be considered here. One should, however, be noted. Détente implies, and its implementation involves, much wider and greater outside contact, with consequent impact on Soviet (and other communist) societies. Increased East-West interaction of all kinds posed many questions and challenges for those brought up in a society sheltered from ideological influences different from the enforced official dogma. For example, when, in retaliation for the Soviet occupation of Afghanistan, the United States and a number of other Western countries discouraged attendance at the international Olympic Games in Moscow in 1980, Soviet officials responsible for curbing alien influences were reported to have been much relieved, despite official Soviet encouragement of wide Western attendance. As noted earlier, the Western conception of détente has assumed (and favored) more and more contact among peoples as a part of the development of détente and as a consequence of it. In the Soviet conception of détente, while in principle and generally in practice interaction may be accepted, the main aim is to remove intergovernmental barriers such as trade restraints, rather than curtailing prudent governmental restraints on people. The Soviets have been very wary of the West's use (in their view, abuse) of détente to interfere in their internal affairs and those of the "socialist commonwealth" (Soviet bloc). This attitude is true even for routine expansion of contacts; it has been even more acutely an issue when politically sensitive expansion of contacts has been actively pursued by other states. One key instance was the attempt by the U.S. Congress to make Soviet commitments on the emigration of Soviet Jews a condition of trade normalization. Another was the offensive in support of human rights in the Soviet Union launched by President Carter immediately after assuming office. A third was the strong American support for Solidarity in Poland.

Soviet interest in reviving détente survived the unilateral American repudiation of both the practice of détente after Afghanistan and its advocacy as well under the Reagan administration. By the last weeks of Brezhnev's rule, the Soviet leadership had, however, begun to stress at the same time the need to meet the American challenge of a confrontational stance and military buildup, without jettisoning the aim of détente. General Secretaries Andropov and Chernenko and other Soviet leaders have continued since Brezhnev's death to urge a resumption of détente.

While Brezhnev's departure from the scene (and the deaths of Aleksei N. Kosygin and Mikhail A. Suslov only shortly before) did not lead to a change in the Soviet line, it did mean that a well-established conservative

---

14. For the quoted passages and the reference to the Twenty-fifth Party Congress, see A. S. Milovidov and Ye. A. Zhdanov, "Social-Philosophical Problems of War and Peace," *Voprosy filosofii* [Questions of Philosophy], no. 10 (October 1980), p. 40.

(not to say *immobiliste*) restraint began to pass from the scene. Opportunities for greater flexibility may come now that the interim successions of Andropov and Chernenko have led to the younger Gorbachev. On the other hand, the post-Brezhnev time of transition has meant that all policy decisions have become more political, that is, more susceptible to political challenge and to the need for constant reconfirmation of consensus among the leadership and key institutional constituencies, including the military.

The Strategic Context

By the end of the 1960s, the Soviet Union had acquired strategic intercontinental military forces approaching those of the United States in numbers, if not yet in capability. Moreover, the United States had proposed strategic arms limitation talks and appeared to be prepared to accept a general parity in strategic military power. From the standpoint of the United States, this initiative did reflect a readiness and desire to constrain the arms race, at least quantitatively. From the standpoint of the Soviet Union, the prospective attainment of strategic parity, and acceptance of it by the American leaders, marked an unprecedented advance over the Soviet Union's military inferiority since the Revolution. Moreover, in addition to enhancing Soviet security, it also could represent an important step toward attaining *political* parity as a superpower.

The most immediate and direct effect of the prospective emergence of strategic parity was to make SALT agreements possible. The broader political effect was, however, equally important. Although SALT agreements were reached in 1972, conservative and cautious approaches by both sides led to only limited accords. Intended as but a first step, the limited nature and equivocal public impression of the 1972 interim agreement on strategic offensive arms made it more difficult to attain a second-stage agreement. In addition, political maneuvering in the three years leading up to the first summit meeting and the launching of détente made it clear that, within the constraints of strategic parity, there remained a wide area for continuing political competition.

In the incipient years of détente the strategic context clearly facilitated agreements and the entire détente process. Later, however, as the arms competition continued and SALT faltered, and as the two powers became embroiled in third world conflicts, the strategic context—or, more accurately, perceptions of the strategic balance and its effects—contributed to a deterioration in relations and the decline of détente.

There are other important aspects of the military and strategic relationship between the two powers and their respective alliances. Some of these concern capabilities (and perceptions of capabilities) relevant to regional conflicts and other world developments that involve and affect American and Soviet policies and actions. None have, however, been as central to the overall

American-Soviet relationship as the formation of a rough parity in the global strategic balance—and later fears, in both countries, that that balance would be upset.

Perspectives and Perceptions

International relations comprise the actions and interaction of states and other entitics. States take actions to further their interests as defined and perceived by their leaders. To some extent, leaders base their foreign policy decisions on objective factors—political, economic, military, geographic, and other. They must, however, also make judgments and choices on the basis of their values and perceptions. In international politics, actions and policies are based not only on subjectively perceived national interests and objectives, but also on subjective perceptions of the interests and intentions of others.

Conflicting interests and objectives underlie the adversarial relationship between the United States and the Soviet Union. At the same time, there are also congruent interests, the most fundamental of which is the common interest in survival, that provide a basis for some cooperation. But for a number of deeply rooted reasons, American-Soviet relations have involved rivalry and conflict.

Real conflicts of interest create real problems. These problems, however, frequently have been exacerbated and the differences compounded (and sometimes even created) by two other closely related phenomena: differences in *perspective*, and differences in *perceptions*. Differences in perspective cause various parties to perceive and to interpret phenomena differently. They are one cause of differences in perception. Another is differences in the perceivers, causing varying perceptions among American (and also among Soviet) participants in the policy process, compounding the differences in perspective shared by American or by Soviet participants.

Sometimes differences in perspective simply reflect different interests and roles: the reactions of American and Soviet leaders to any development clearly favorable to one side produce different objective reactions. Often, however, differences in perspective also create divergences that may not be so readily recognized by either side.

Both American and Soviet foreign policies are preeminently directed toward enhancing security, and in this sense they are defensive. Inevitably, in seeking to maximize security, each superpower will pursue some objectives that conflict with the interests or objectives of the other. Beyond that, because of the adversarial nature of the relationship between the two powers, each also seeks—justified, in its own eyes, by defensive purposes—to contain and curtail the influence of the other. In addition, both powers seek to extend their influence for other reasons. During recurrent (usually brief) periods of decreased tension, occasional conflicts of interest may be accepted as signs of competition accompanying cooperation, as in the heyday of the late détente,

1972–75. But in times of increasing tension, as has characterized the period since 1977 and particularly since the end of 1979, such developments are seen by the other side as unmitigated offensive moves reflecting hostile intent.

Undoubtedly, the Soviet leaders saw their move into Afghanistan in 1979 as defensive. Americans, however, saw it as offensive. On the other hand, Americans saw increasingly close U.S. ties with China, based on a common platform of security against the Soviet Union, as defensive, while to Moscow this American-Chinese collusion was clearly a dangerous offensive course directed against its security.

Have Soviet efforts to enter the Middle East been offensive or defensive? Have American efforts to exclude Soviet influence in the Middle East been defensive or offensive? These questions are two sides of the same coin, and the answers depend to a substantial extent on the perspective of the evaluator.

While each nation may be quite convinced that its intent is a defensive enhancement of its own security, to the other many of its actions will appear to be—and sometimes will *be*—offensive. The undulating rise and fall of tension between the two powers has involved many changes in objective factors. It has also included many important changes in *perceptions* (and misperceptions) on both sides. Sometimes the effect of such perceptions has been evident, but often it has been misunderstood or completely unnoticed. On the whole, the effect of perceptions has been negative, aggravating objective (or "real") differences of interest.

Perceptions have only belatedly come to be recognized as a factor affecting international relations. As developments are studied with greater awareness of the perceptual factor, it becomes evident that, while perceptions are but one element in a complex interaction, most, if not all, international problems are affected by perceptions in ways not appreciated in traditional analysis.[15]

Consideration of perceptions in political analysis is not a substitute for attention to other factors, but it adds a dimension often overlooked. For example, studies of bureaucratic politics or of the roles of various interest groups in decisionmaking raise the question of possible differing perceptions of the external world by various competing participants. Put another way, analysis must consider whose perceptions are significant in each case.

Perceptions are especially important because of the tendency for policymakers (and analysts) to assign intentions to others without being aware that they in fact project onto or impute to others perceptions that may differ widely from actual and conscious perceptions.[16] Frequently, people are not

---

15. The best study of this issue, which includes extensive references to other sources on the subject, is Robert Jervis, *Perception and Misperception in International Politics* (Princeton, N.J.: Princeton University Press, 1976).

16. One of the major difficulties in the analysis of perceptions is that an analyst is unavoidably dealing with his own perceptions of the perceptions of others. Whether it is possible to

aware of the extent to which their own perceptions hinge on implicit assumptions about the perceptions of others.

Public perceptions are also factors in the political process and can influence or even determine decisions. Thus decisionmakers may be compelled by political imperatives based on public perceptions to make some decisions they would not make if they could act on the basis of their own perceptions and determinations of national interest. On the other hand, public perceptions can be influenced and manipulated.[17] Nonetheless, public perceptions, for example, of the strategic balance, may constrain and channel political possibilities, even if based in part on officially generated information.

Western governments (and those seeking to influence Western governments) have manipulated public perceptions of the Soviet threat and the strategic balance. On a more massive scale, the Soviet leadership has also manipulated public perceptions. There is a basic asymmetry in terms of the openness and accessibility of Western media to various (including Soviet) influences, as contrasted with the controlled situation in the Soviet Union. This difference affects not only the ability to propagandize; it can also affect the perceptions of leaderships. This is particularly true when official Western sources as well as the media do support themes such as the existence of a growing Soviet military threat.[18]

---

identify correctly the actual perceptions of others is a real question. It is necessary, for example, to filter out manipulated themes expressed in published statements to find real expressions of perception. Questions concerning the validity of perceptions also arise. It is also necessary to exercise care not to judge the accuracy of the perceptions of others through the prism of one's own. Misperceptions are thus doubly difficult to discern and to attribute. Even in a situation that seems clear-cut, a differing perception may not be a misperception, given the vantage point, or the values, of another perceiver.

17. Perceptions have also been used to justify actions or programs actually sought on other grounds. For example, a challenge to the charge that the Soviet Union has gained strategic superiority often leads to a response that even if, objectively, the balance has not yet shifted to Soviet advantage, that is the public and world perception and it is therefore necessary to act on that basis. This line of argument is particularly insidious to the extent that such perceptions have in fact come to exist as a consequence of selective propaganda put out by those who later cite the resulting perception as a reality justifying military programs only weakly supportable on any other grounds. To cite an example from a different quarter, overly simple perceptions of potential overkill based on the raw arithmetic of megatonnage and putative casualties per weapon may be used as an excuse to avoid facing the need for strategic analysis of force requirements for meeting various contingencies.

18. Conclusions about the existence of a threat are subjective matters of perspective and perception to a far greater extent than is usually recognized. Assessment of a threat may, or may not, be valid quite apart from whether the "facts" on which it is based are accurate. Data on military forces, buildups, and capabilities are but one set of elements in that assessment. Another is intention. Intentions are much more difficult to assess realistically—particularly since most intentions are contingent, and many are matters of perspective. For example, an assessment that "Red" is going to attack "Blue" would be valid if Red indeed planned to attack Blue. But a judgment that Red's military forces constituted a "threat" to the interests of Blue would involve many contingent judgments, depending not only on objective factors,

Ideology has continued to play a role, albeit in the judgment of most analysts a declining one, in determining Soviet policy. One important way in which it does affect Soviet policymaking is as a prism influencing Soviet perceptions. At the same time, the United States also has its ideological perceptions, although less formal and doctrinal, that exert a powerful influence on American perceptions.

Virtually for as long as the Soviet Union has existed, there have been analytical arguments in the West over the respective roles of ideology and national interest, of Marxism-Leninism and traditional Russian geostrategic interests, in motivating Soviet political conduct on the world stage. While there are sometimes discernible differences in their influence, on the whole attempts to assign relative weights are unnecessary. Ideology sanctions decisions based on calculations of expedient behavior, and the geopolitical arena of the Soviet empire was inherited from the former Russian empire.

Ideology is obviously of signal importance—Marxism-Leninism is the wellhead of a fundamentally adversarial world view that casts the Soviet Union and the Western capitalist powers on opposite sides of historical barricades. The Soviet leaders, as Marxist-Leninists, continue to believe there is an ineluctable revolutionary social-economic-political dialectical dynamic in history. They also see the Soviet Union as the central entity riding this progressive wave of the future, and the capitalist order, represented by the still exceedingly powerful Western governments, as destined to succumb to this historical process. In practice, many aspects of the communist ideology are submerged by a pragmatic approach, sanctioned by the ideology, that the leaders bring to the making of state policy. Nonetheless, the ideological framework and perceptual lens remain.

To recognize differing perceptions by others does not mean to accept them or to excuse their consequences. Policymakers (and policy analysts) should, however, be more keenly aware of the existence and significance of differences in perceptions. Their judgments about the objectives and intentions of others should be more tentative—and consideration of the basis for their own judgments more thoughtful and reserved. Leaders and political actors do not generally welcome these qualities. Nuances and balanced considerations tend to make it more difficult to rally and mobilize action. Nevertheless, there are important—indeed, potentially critical—benefits to decisionmakers (and to the world at large) in clarifying the *real* factors operating in the world. Perceptions, although sometimes thought of as fluff and not the stuff of politics, are real factors. When considered at all, perceptions of others may be seen as factors to be managed and exploited; rarely are they recognized as important elements in one's own understanding and in political transactions. Yet they are.

---

but also on what Red—and Blue—intended and actually did. Leaders of a state may regard its military forces and capabilities as a deterrent and intend that they serve defensive purposes, but these same forces may be perceived by a rival or adversary as offensive and threatening.

Comprehension of the perceptions of others, especially of adversaries, is not easy. It requires a degree of empathy that, while not the same thing as sympathy, nonetheless requires that one entertain viewpoints and views not only alien, but perceived as adverse, to one's own views—and interests. The very attempt may be misunderstood and the observer maligned. Yet it is essential to look at phenomena as closely as possible from the standpoint of all parties in order to understand the realities of differing perspectives. This effort is important to reducing differences and tensions; it is also important to effectively opposing an adversary on matters where interests do conflict.

This study, in seeking to determine the factors at work in Soviet as well as American policymaking, addresses Soviet as well as American perspectives and perceptions.

Issues and Purpose

In tracing and analyzing the course of American-Soviet relations from 1969 through 1984, the most salient feature to emerge is the significant, if ultimately unsuccessful, effort in the 1970s to develop a lasting détente. The collapse of that effort at the close of the decade was owing in part to its ambitious aims. It also resulted, however, from the failure of both sides to recognize and to reconcile those objectives and actions that, as differently perceived by *both* sides, contravened and eventually submerged the common effort.

The story is not, of course, ended. Present uncertainties and difficulties in American-Soviet relations, marked by less contact and greater confrontation than at any time in two decades, have only eclipsed, but not erased, the continuing need to temper differences and conflicts with resumed cooperation in containing the risks in areas of continuing competition. If the quest for improved relations and relaxation of tensions is to be resumed, if only to reduce the risks of catastrophic confrontation, it is important to learn whatever lessons are to be found in the wreckage of the collapse of the "structure of peace" built in the 1970s.

An era of negotiation was proclaimed by President Nixon in 1969, and a Peace Program was solemnly adopted by the Twenty-fourth Congress of the Communist Party of the Soviet Union in 1971. There were 4 summit meetings in the early and mid-1970s; 11 bilateral commissions were created; and over 150 agreements on subjects ranging from health improvement to strategic arms limitation were reached. Why did all this deteriorate in the middle of the 1970s and collapse as the decade ended? Is there a basis for cooperative regulation of political competition, and for containing and reducing military competition—or only illusion in its pursuit? There is much to learn from the successful steps, and still more from the failures, of the efforts in the 1970s as relations between the two superpowers are shaped in the 1980s.

To understand the developments that led to the American-Soviet détente of the 1970s and to its decline and collapse, it is necessary to analyze a complicated skein of interrelated factors. From the very start there were differences in conceptual approaches and in concrete objectives between the two powers. These became more evident only under the test of experience. Moreover, there were, perhaps necessarily, differences in understanding by leaders and publics. Differences in understanding as well in objectives led to differing expectations. Increasingly over time, these expectations—on both sides—were not met, leading to disillusion with détente or at least with the performance of the other side. Conceptual divergences were compounded by perceptual differences that led the two sides to interpret the same developments quite differently, often with adverse impact on judgments about the motives of the other side. A wide range of developments in the world, whether initiated by the two powers (or, more often, not), came to involve them, or at least so it was perceived. These developments affected judgments and policies important to their mutual relationship. Suspicions grew and fears were generated. The process of reaction in the early 1980s under both the Carter and Reagan administrations, while it may have dispelled some illusions, may have created others. In any event, the renewal of confrontation and jettisoning of détente have not provided a viable alternative.

Finally, internal developments and internal political dynamics have affected judgments about the policy of détente. Even means employed in the pursuit of détente, especially when they were not adequately explained or understood, or were not consistent with requirements for internal political support, have adversely affected domestic understanding and support. More generally, bureaucratic and political conflicts and rivalries in each of the two countries came to affect the conduct of relations between the powers. These internal factors, while they affected both sides, were particularly significant in the United States.

As has been stressed, it is necessary to look closely at the complex web of factors involved in order to understand the process better. Only through a detailed study can the key underlying questions be answered—and often the answers are not those that would have been anticipated and are commonly held.

What actually motivated the two powers to move into détente in the early 1970s? What led to its subsequent deterioration and ultimate collapse by the end of the decade? To what extent were real differences in interests at issue, and to what extent did divergences in perspective and perceptions contribute? To what extent were the *aims* of the two powers compatible? Their policy *objectives*? Their *actions*? Their *reactions* to one another's actions and to other developments?

To what extent were American and Soviet policy aims compatible with achieving and sustaining détente? With deterrence as an aim, with strategic arms limitation as a means, and with acceptance of parity in military power? With nonrecourse to force in situations affecting the interests of the other? With *political* "parity"?

To what extent were policies of the United States, and of the Soviet Union, internally consistent and predictable? To what extent were domestic and foreign policies and practices consistent and compatible?

To what extent were the Soviet Union, and the United States, prepared to live by a "code of conduct" in foreign relations under détente? Were they prepared to curb pursuit of advantages at the expense of the other? To accept a common standard and not to judge the other by a double standard? To perceive the other in an objective way?

To what extent were third party actions instrumental in affecting Soviet and American policies? What impact did such developments have on American-Soviet relations, and to what extent did they undercut the mutual relationship?

What is the range of American and Soviet policy choice between confrontation and détente? To what extent are Soviet and American policies expansionist, and to what extent is each affected by perceived security requirements? (And can that question be answered objectively, or is the answer necessarily subjective?)

These questions illustrate underlying issues addressed in this analysis, especially in the concluding chapters.

In sum, the purpose of this study is threefold: (1) to investigate the course of American-Soviet relations over the decade and a half from 1969 through 1984, seeking to determine what in fact happened and why; (2) to study the factors contributing to the improvement in relations in the détente of the early 1970s, to its decline and collapse in the latter half of the decade, and to the efforts in the 1980s to devise a post-détente American policy toward the Soviet Union; and (3) to draw from this experience observations and conclusions that can be instructive in formulating and conducting American policy and relations with the Soviet Union in the future.

2 American and Soviet Conceptions of Détente

DÉTENTE, and differing American and Soviet conceptions of it, played a crucial role in American-Soviet relations in the 1970s. From 1969 to 1972 the two countries moved slowly and unevenly toward a conjunction of interests that would permit their improving relations. Rather suddenly, that conjunction blossomed at a summit meeting in May 1972. The heyday of the détente between the two powers was, however, short-lived. Virtually as soon as it was established, differences and difficulties reemerged, and there was a progressive deterioration in relations from the mid-1970s to the end of the decade. In the opening days of 1980, the weakened structure of détente collapsed in the aftermath of the Soviet occupation of Afghanistan and the ensuing American reaction. There followed a return to confrontation unmatched in two decades.

Détente, while the shorthand description for the policies subscribed to by both powers in the 1970s, was not a clearly defined concept held in common. It became increasingly evident, beginning even in the early 1970s when détente was at a high point, that Washington and Moscow had very different conceptions of what a détente policy entailed, and had had from the outset. The expectations of both sides in turn differed greatly. And as their respective expectations were not met, disillusionment with the performance of the other side followed. Moreover, in the United States (although not in the Soviet Union) disillusionment with the very idea of détente itself also followed.

It is, however, unavailing to say that détente was tried and failed—or, alternatively, that it was violated or abandoned by one side or the other. It is more useful to see just what each side believed détente represented, and to identify the areas of common and conflicting understanding. In addition, while the present chapter focuses on conceptions of détente—in a sense the theoretical frameworks for policy—there were many other strands to policy action and interaction. These strands naturally reflected and involved a host of concrete

24

political, economic, military, and other considerations that formed the substance of relations, and that are addressed throughout this study.

Détente is a French word that actually means a "relaxation of tension" in a literal way—as with the release of a bowstring. Long ago it came to be used in diplomatic parlance to represent an easing of strained or tense relations between states. It is distinguished from another French word, *entente*, which represents a positive development of close and cooperative relations. Much of the confusion in American understanding seems to have stemmed from a tendency to interpret détente as though it meant entente. The Soviets have used a term of their own, *razryadka napryazhennosti*, or simply *razryadka*, also meaning a lessening or relaxation of tension.

The term détente had been used in the 1960s to describe steps aimed at lessening tension in East-West relations. In particular, it had been used by President Charles de Gaulle in the mid-1960s, and in the North Atlantic Treaty Organization (NATO) in the latter 1960s as one element in an alliance policy calling for balancing defense and détente.[1] The first use of the term to describe the specific efforts launched by President Richard M. Nixon in 1969 (and, in a sense, by the Soviet Union at about the same time) to improve American-Soviet relations is elusive.[2]

Indeed, the Nixon administration went to some lengths to avoid using the word détente. Instead, Nixon and his assistant for national security affairs, Henry A. Kissinger, spoke of "a new era," of substituting negotiations for confrontation, and of pursuing a "structure of peace" through mutual accommodation. By 1973–74, however, détente came to be used in the United States officially as well as popularly as a shorthand term describing the new policy.

The American Conception of Détente

President Nixon entered office with a number of ideas on restructuring American foreign relations, including relations with the Soviet Union.

1. This concept was elaborated in the "Harmel Report," adopted by NATO in December 1967; see the discussion in chapter 4.

2. It is a little easier to trace early official uses of the term. The first instance I have located in which Nixon used the term to describe his policy was in "The President's Address to the 25th Anniversary of the General Assembly [of the United Nations], October 23, 1970," *Weekly Compilation of Presidential Documents*, vol. 6 (October 26, 1970), p. 1435. (Hereafter *Presidential Documents*.)

On the Soviet side, General Secretary Leonid I. Brezhnev used the term generally in several instances in the latter half of the 1960s, most authoritatively in his report to the Twenty-third Party Congress in March 1966. L. I. Brezhnev, *O vneshnei politike KPSS i Sovetskogo gosudarstva: Rechi i stat'i* [On the Foreign Policy of the CPSU and the Soviet State: Speeches and Articles], 3d ed. (Moscow: Politizdat, 1978), p. 40. Brezhnev's first use of the term as applied to Soviet-U.S. policy, with specific reference to Nixon's new policy declarations of 1969, was in a speech in June 1970. Ibid., pp. 137–38.

He believed that while the United States was entering a new era of strategic parity, in which it could not again restore the military superiority it had enjoyed in the 1950s and 1960s, it retained considerable strengths that could be brought to good advantage in negotiating with the Soviet Union. The United States could, Nixon believed, accept the inevitable not only with good grace, but with gain—if it played its cards well. He felt he knew the Soviet Union better than any of his predecessors because of his visits there and his talks with Soviet leaders in 1959 while vice president, and in 1965 and 1967 as a private citizen. He recognized that his credentials as a conservative, Republican, anti-communist political figure would blunt opposition from the right, and thus give him an opportunity that his two Democratic predecessors had not had. If, by recognizing the strategic parity the Soviet Union had sought for so long and was in fact achieving, he could gain Soviet assistance in ending the Vietnam debacle and in resolving some other international disputes, he might be better able to negotiate and implement his broad design for a "structure of peace." Nixon had no illusions that the Soviet leaders would give up either their ideological aspirations or their political objectives, but he believed it might prove possible to engage them in deals that would contain and channel the competition and blunt Soviet interest in attempting to confront the United States and its core allies. As Nixon himself later put it: "The Soviet Union will always act in its own self-interest; and so will the United States. Détente cannot change that. All we can hope from détente is that it will minimize confrontation in marginal areas and provide, at least, alternative possibilities in the major ones."[3] Meanwhile, Nixon also had in mind restoring American relations with China. By strengthening American relations with Europe and Japan as well as building new relations with China and the Soviet Union, he would enhance the political leverage of the United States in the world. Nixon's geopolitical views of the world were reinforced and expanded by the generally similar, if more complex and subtle, approach of Kissinger.[4]

Nixon and Kissinger's approach required a tight centralization of policy in order to "manage" foreign policy actions. These two men sought to shape and wield American policy with minimum contribution or even participation by the other members of the administration; perhaps this stemmed from psychological factors as well as political considerations. This approach of excluding other key members of the executive branch from involvement or

---

3. Richard Nixon, *RN: The Memoirs of Richard Nixon* (Grosset and Dunlap, 1978), p. 941.

4. How Nixon intuitively appreciated this similarity on virtual passing acquaintance is still something of a mystery. Perhaps he merely assumed that Governor Nelson A. Rockefeller's European-born Harvard professor would have the abilities to elaborate and carry out the design he himself sensed but could only articulate awkwardly. It was, in any case, a choice of genius on his part. There now exists a substantial library of books and articles analyzing Kissinger's role and intellectual and psychological motivations. One useful analysis, which uses as its platform Kissinger's memoirs but which draws on the whole literature, is Harvey Starr, *Henry Kissinger: Perceptions of International Politics* (Lexington, Ky.: University Press of Kentucky, 1984).

even awareness of the foreign policy strategy of the White House inevitably created dissonances, but these problems simply confirmed the judgment of Nixon and Kissinger that it was necessary to hold even more tightly the design of policy, and increasingly its implementation as well.

Moreover, Nixon was an intensely political person who had devoted his whole adult life to American politics. While his administration's annual public reports to the Congress on foreign policy established a more self-contained justification for his pursuit of a structure for peace, the now-extensive record bears blunt witness to more mundane driving forces. Nixon wanted and needed identification with an advocacy of peace for his political success and for his place in history, although not enough to end the Vietnam War for four years. He wanted a foreign policy which would place America in a central and manipulative position of power in the world, just as he sought to consolidate a central, manipulative position of power at home within the White House. Personal domestic political and international political motivations were mixed, and it was not always possible to identify which would be (or even, after the event, which had been) dominant.

President Nixon's inaugural address placed a heavy stress on peace and negotiation: "Let us take as our goal: Where peace is unknown, make it welcome; where peace is fragile, make it strong; where peace is temporary, make it permanent. After a period of confrontation, we are entering an era of negotiation. Let all nations know that during this administration our lines of communication will be open. . . . We cannot expect to make everyone our friend, but we can try to make no one our enemy. . . . With those who are willing to join, let us cooperate to reduce the burden of arms, to strengthen the structure of peace." At the same time, Nixon stated the counterpoint: "But to all those who would be tempted by weakness, let us leave no doubt that we will be as strong as we need to be for as long as we need to be," and "I know that peace does not come through wishing for it—that there is no substitute for days and even years of patient and prolonged diplomacy."[5]

As noted, the word détente was nowhere to be found (nor was parity or anything about strategic arms limitation) in these statements. But there was a secret signal in them—one introduced by Kissinger. He has recounted in his memoir that, ever since he had been active in Governor Rockefeller's entourage, he had remained in touch with a KGB contact in the Soviet Embassy, Boris Sedov. As the inauguration approached, Sedov's "major preoccupation" was to have Nixon include in his inaugural address some statement to the effect that he was keeping the lines of communication to Moscow open, a point Sedov said would be well-received there. Kissinger accordingly arranged

---

5. "Inaugural Address of President Richard Milhous Nixon," January 20, *Presidential Documents*, vol. 5 (January 27, 1969), pp. 152–53.

for inclusion of the statement that "during this Administration our lines of communication will be open."[6]

In fact, for some time before his election Nixon had been thinking of improving relations with the Soviet Union through negotiation. He had been planning to say in a speech in March 1968, a speech he never delivered because of President Johnson's sudden announcement of his decision not to run for reelection, that he foresaw "a new era in our relations with the Soviets, a new round of summit meetings and other negotiations."[7]

The Nixon administration was the first (and to date, the only) one to issue a series of annual presidential reports to the Congress setting forth the aims and strategy of foreign policy in much more comprehensive fashion than in the annual State of the Union messages. These documents are very useful to the historian, despite—or because of—their having been formulated to serve a number of political purposes. The series was titled *U.S. Foreign Policy for the 1970's*, with the subtitle of each annual issue emphasizing the theme of peace: *A New Strategy for Peace*, vol. 1 (February 18, 1970); *Building for Peace*, vol. 2 (February 25, 1971); *The Emerging Structure of Peace*, vol. 3 (February 9, 1972); and *Shaping a Durable Peace*, vol. 4 (May 3, 1973).[8] These documents are referred to later in several contexts, but at this point it is worth noting the absence of the term détente in the first three volumes (save for one reference to détente in Europe), and the notably guarded use of the term in the fourth volume in 1973: "Detente does not mean the end of danger. . . . Detente is not the same as lasting peace."[9] Instead, a number of more sweeping phrases were

---

6. Henry Kissinger, *White House Years* (Boston, Mass.: Little, Brown, 1979), p. 50, and see pp. 127–28. Kissinger speculates on Sedov's motives in making the suggestion, but refrains from saying that he himself probably got vicarious satisfaction out of arranging this secret signal as one of his first acts in a White House role.

7. This undelivered speech is revealing in many ways. It is given in full along with a description of Nixon's thinking at the time by the speechwriter who assisted him in drafting it in Richard J. Whalen, *Catch the Falling Flag: A Republican's Challenge to His Party* (Boston, Mass.: Houghton Mifflin, 1972), pp. 131, 140–44.

In this undelivered speech, Nixon conditioned the prospect of improving relations with the Soviet Union on Soviet assistance in American disengagement from Vietnam, a theme important in Nixon's policy in 1969–72. In 1968, however, he saw such a move as directed *against* the Chinese communists, a position he modified substantially in 1969 and thereafter, as he sought successfully to play off the Soviet Union and China in building leverage against Vietnam. See chapter 7.

8. Richard M. Nixon, *U.S. Foreign Policy for the 1970's*, Report to the Congress, vol. 1 (Washington, D.C.: Government Printing Office, 1970); vol. 2 (GPO, 1971); vol. 3 (GPO, 1972); vol. 4 (GPO, 1973). Although presented as reports by the president, they were written by Kissinger's staff and personally reviewed by him; they also were submitted reluctantly for review by a few officials in the Department of State. As one who had this opportunity and experienced the pain provoked by any proposed revision, I can testify to the tight hold Kissinger maintained over them. A fifth volume, for issue in early 1974, was drafted but never finally approved or issued, given the higher priorities of the Watergate struggle then under way.

9. Nixon, *U.S. Foreign Policy for the 1970's*, vol. 4 (1973), p. 233.

used, such as "a new era," "mutual accommodation," building "a structure of peace," and a "durable peace," and later, "peaceful coexistence," a "code of conduct," and "the purpose of this Administration [is] to transform the U.S.-Soviet relationship so that a mutual search for a stable peace and security becomes its dominant feature and its driving force."[10] Thus, the theme of détente was very prominent, even if that term was long eschewed.

A policy of détente had not been clearly developed or even thought through in 1969 or even by 1972.[11] In fact, the policy remained largely ad hoc, as evidenced by President Nixon's readiness even in May 1972 to forgo a summit meeting and Strategic Arms Limitation Talks (SALT) agreement, if that proved to be the price, rather than to give up intensified bombing of North Vietnam. In practice, the development of détente was a gradual and uncertain process even in American policy (and to a considerable extent in Soviet policy as well), to say nothing of the problem of reconciling the contradictory elements in the conceptions and policies of the two sides. Nonetheless, a general conception of détente developed.

Nixon and Kissinger saw détente as a strategy, rather than as an objective; it was a means rather than a goal. At the same time, in order to justify the strategy and mobilize political support, détente was publicly articulated in terms of a lofty goal—a "structure of peace." In his 1970 address to the United Nations General Assembly, in which Nixon first used the term détente, he counterposed it with "power politics," saying that "we must transcend the old patterns of power politics in which nations sought to exploit every volatile situation for their own advantage, or to squeeze the maximum advantage for themselves out of every negotiation."[12] Such statements were especially incongruent with an administration more attuned than most to hardball power politics.

This discrepancy between the private calculation and the public characterization, between the realistic management of power and the promise of "a new era" of "durable peace," ultimately came to haunt détente and undercut popular support, as the excessive expectations it aroused were not realized. Nixon and Kissinger were reacting to what they saw as the conflicting imperatives of an external manipulation and wielding of power, and an internal political dynamic that required a simple and confident avowal of peace rather than education of the public in the complex ways of the world.

---

10. Ibid., vol. 1 (1970), pp. 2, 3, 4–13; vol. 4 (1973), pp. 26, 37; and vol. 3 (1972), p. 16.

11. This point is well made by one of Kissinger's National Security Council (NSC) staff at the time. See William G. Hyland, *Soviet-American Relations: A New Cold War?* R-2763-FFRC (Santa Monica, Calif.: Rand Corp., 1981), pp. 22–25.

12. *Presidential Documents*, vol. 6 (October 26, 1970), p. 1435.

A useful study stressing the rooting of the Nixon-Kissinger détente policy in classical power politics is Robert S. Litwak, *Détente and the Nixon Doctrine: American Foreign Policy and the Pursuit of Stability, 1969–1976* (Cambridge University Press, 1984).

The administration was quite clear that the basic purpose of détente was to reduce the risks of nuclear war: in Kissinger's words, "We are in favor of détente because we want to limit the risks of major nuclear conflict."[13] That, of course, is but a starting point for a foreign policy.

Kissinger also sought to articulate the strategy of détente in terms that he hoped would bridge the gap between two imperatives. In congressional testimony he mused that "the challenge of our time is to reconcile the reality of competition with the imperative of coexistence."[14] He referred to the purpose of détente as moderating conflicts and crises with "restraint."[15] More explicitly in terms of the American aim, he said, "Détente is a means of controlling the conflict with the Soviet Union."[16] Most basically, Kissinger spoke of an American need to "manage the emergence of Soviet power" as "the preeminent problem," a task that could be met by détente.[17]

Management of the emergence of Soviet power to some extent implied adjustment by the United States to the reality of increased Soviet power and strategic parity. But even more it meant a strategy to contain and to harness Soviet use of its increasing power.[18] To this end, Kissinger sought to enmesh the Soviet Union in a web of relationships with the West, and above all with the United States, a web that he would weave. He sought to induce the Soviet leaders to enter into mutually advantageous ties involving increasing interdependence, to build the Soviet stake in maintaining cooperative relationships and in eschewing confrontations that would imperil or disrupt them. Again, to cite his congressional testimony, "By acquiring a stake in this network of relationships with the West the Soviet Union may become more conscious of what it would lose by a return to confrontation. Indeed, it is our expectation that it will develop a self-interest in fostering the entire process of relaxation of tensions."[19] To achieve this objective, Kissinger believed that the United

---

13. Kissinger, "Interview at Peking, November 12," *Department of State Bulletin*, vol. 69 (December 10, 1973), p. 716. (Hereafter *State Bulletin*.)

14. "Prepared Statement of Hon. Henry A. Kissinger, Secretary of State," in *Détente*, Hearings before the Senate Committee on Foreign Relations, 93 Cong. 2 sess. (GPO, 1975), p. 247.

15. Kissinger, *State Bulletin*, vol. 69 (1973), p. 716.

16. "Secretary Kissinger Interviewed for U.S. News and World Report," June 12, *State Bulletin*, vol. 73 (July 7, 1975), p. 17.

17. "Secretary Kissinger's News Conference of December 23 [1975]," *State Bulletin*, vol. 74 (January 19, 1976), p. 70.

18. In Kissinger's terms, as he put it in his memoir, "To expect the Soviet leaders to restrain themselves from exploiting circumstances they conceive to be favorable is to misread history. To foreclose Soviet opportunities is thus the essence of the West's responsibility. It is up to *us* to define the limits of Soviet aims. . . . Coexistence on the basis of the balance of forces should therefore be within our grasp—provided the nature of the challenge is correctly understood." Kissinger, *White House Years*, pp. 119, 120.

19. "Prepared Statement of Hon. Henry A. Kissinger," in *Détente*, Hearings, p. 250. Kissinger reiterated this theme in many statements.

States had to fashion its relations with the Soviet Union in such a way that the Soviet leaders would have "incentives for moderation and penalties for intransigence."[20]

Students of international relations and diplomatic history will readily recognize that Kissinger was adapting the classic technique of the carrot and the stick. One seeks to move a recalcitrant animal by offering mutually reinforcing positive incentives pointed in the desired direction, coupled with negative sanctions if it does not move. More basically, the entire thrust of Kissinger's strategy of détente was one of maneuver in a shifting global balance of power that was becoming increasingly akin to the classical multipolar structure of the eighteenth and nineteenth centuries, albeit now with two predominant powers.

One reason that Kissinger in practice stressed U.S.-Soviet relations was in recognition of the inescapable power of the Soviet Union. Another was to maximize American leverage; Kissinger believed that much greater tactical and even strategic flexibility was possible, both in establishing the net of relationships and in manipulating them, than if decisions were made by a coalition. This point can be illustrated by negative example. In 1980 the United States, wisely or not, sought to impose severe penalties on the Soviet Union after the occupation of Afghanistan, and again in 1982 in response to the imposition of martial law in Poland. Western Europeans, on the other hand, were not prepared to go nearly so far or to jettison détente in Europe. To the extent the United States and Western Europe diverged in their reaction, not only was the American action less effective as a sanction on the Soviet Union, but the development of fissures in American and European assessments and positions gave the Soviet Union new leverage. Another important, perhaps crucial, element in the picture was the opportunity the American leaders saw under détente to gain diplomatic leverage by careful exploitation of the triangular relationship among the United States, the Soviet Union, and China.[21]

The American strategy for détente that Kissinger and Nixon fashioned stressed interrelation. The term most widely used to characterize this interrelation (again, as with détente itself, the term was not used initially by the authors of the strategy) has been *linkage*. Critics, and some proponents,

---

While the network of ties was intended to influence Soviet thinking, it also had unanticipated effects on American opinion. The American public, influenced by the rhetoric of détente, tended to see the growth of a network of functional ties with the Soviet Union as implying shared values and interests to a greater extent than was justified (or reflected in U.S. as well as Soviet policy). This point is well made by Litwak, *Détente and the Nixon Doctrine*, pp. 91–92.

20. Kissinger, *State Bulletin*, vol. 73 (July 7, 1975), p. 17.

21. Coral Bell, in a thoughtful and stimulating analysis, places this element at the core of the American strategy on détente in Bell, *The Diplomacy of Detente: The Kissinger Era* (St. Martin's Press, 1977), especially pp. 3–6. See also chapters 6 and 20 of the present study.

have seen linkage primarily as meaning leverage, as in a linking of one matter to another as a bargaining counter to trade or to levy pressure. And, indeed, this is one meaning and use of linkage, although it may involve an artificial tie established only for leverage: agreement on A, only if the other side will also agree on B, which it presumably otherwise would not do. B may be something that the second party is insufficiently interested in to agree to without the inducement of A, or it may be a concession on another matter at issue, or an agreement to desist from something. Whatever the specific case, the essence of the matter is the same: the first party's agreement to A is conditional on the second party's acceptance of B. An implicit condition is that the second party must want or need A more than the first; another may be that the second party is weaker than the first and therefore makes the concession. For these reasons the Soviet leaders have objected, both in principle and with respect to particular applications, to linkage in American-Soviet détente agreements. They have not wished to concede they have a greater interest in détente or trade or arms control than the United States, or that they would bend to greater American power to meet American terms.

Defenders of the concept of linkage advance several arguments. One is that interrelation (and therefore linkage) is simply a fact of international life. As stated in the first volume of *U.S. Foreign Policy for the 1970's: A Strategy for Peace*, one essential for successful negotiations is "appreciation of the context in which issues are addressed. The central fact here is the interrelationship of international events. We did not invent the inter-relationship; it is not a negotiating tactic. It is a fact of life. This Administration recognizes that international developments are entwined in many complex ways: political issues relate to strategic questions, political events in one area of the world may have a far-reaching effect on political developments in other parts of the globe."[22] While this point is correct, it does not address the real issue.

Kissinger takes the matter one step further in his memoir, when he describes linkage as an attempt "to free our foreign policy from oscillations between overextension and isolation and to ground it in a firm conception of the national interest." To do this, he argues, it is necessary to establish priorities. "A conceptual framework—which 'links' events—is an essential tool. The absence of linkage produces exactly the opposite of freedom of action; policymakers are forced to respond to parochial interests, buffeted by pressures without a fixed compass."[23]

A more frank argument is made by others who recognize that linkage is not merely a "fact of life," or even a conceptual tool. Rather, it is an active tool of policy. As an instrument of policy, linkage is most readily recognized as a tactic to exert bargaining leverage. But it goes beyond serving as a negotiating tool. Under Nixon and Kissinger linkage became the governing

22. Nixon, *U.S. Foreign Policy for the 1970's*, vol. 1 (1970), p. 136.

23. Kissinger, *White House Years*, p. 130.

device for applying and regulating the incentives and penalties that they placed at the center of their concept of diplomatic strategy.[24]

Ultimately the question of the role of linkage depends not on whether it is an admissible instrument of policy, but on whether this instrument is wielded wisely or not, on whether particular linkages are balanced and negotiated or imposed, and on whether they succeed in advancing the purposes of policy or only in stymieing them.

One flaw in the administration's strategy of linkage was its failure to recognize that the ability to control the elements of policy is limited. Particularly in the context of the American political system, Nixon and Kissinger were led increasingly to grasp policymaking and implementation into their own hands in order to control them better. But while they could, at least for a time and at some cost, handle the bureaucracy of the executive branch, they could not always manage and control Congress. More broadly, efforts to manipulate incentives and penalties vis-à-vis the Soviet Union time and again came up against the interests of recalcitrant elements of the government, or the American political and economic community, or the Western alliance. None of these was prepared to ignore its intrinsic interests with respect to arms control, trade, or other areas. In addition, linkage became too much identified with sticks, with too little attention to carrots. Finally, punitive use of linkage may punish the wielder as much as the other side, especially since most transactions (as in trade and arms control) are inherently based on common or congruent interests. At the least, punitive use weakens or destroys the consensus on which a policy dependent upon linkage must be based.

Fundamentally, the American conception of détente in the 1970s represented an attempt not only to reduce the risks of an incalculably devastating nuclear war—the basic motivating force and common security interest of both sides—but also to use this common interest as a springboard for building a network of mutually advantageous relationships. But beyond that, détente would provide leverage for managing the emergence of Soviet power, and in doing so would draw the Soviet Union into de facto acceptance of the existing world order.

A further aspect of the American conception of détente, related directly to linkage and to managing the assimilation of the Soviet Union into the world order, was the drive to gain Soviet acceptance of a "code of conduct" or "rules of the game" for political competition. The idea of recognizing areas of competition and developing agreed rules on permissible actions has an evident appeal. Agreed rules of the game could lead to reducing misunderstandings as to objectives, accepting constraints on kinds of political action, abjuring military and other confrontational means, and developing means of crisis

---

24. See Helmut Sonnenfeldt (a former close associate sometimes called "Kissinger's Kissinger"), "Linkage: A Strategy for Tempering Soviet Antagonism," *NATO Review*, no. 1 (February 1979), pp. 3–5, 20–23. See also Litwak, *Détente and the Nixon Doctrine*, especially pp. 93–96, for a useful discussion.

avoidance and management. To be sure, the promise seems almost too good to be true. And such, indeed, was the outcome.

The reasons for the difficulties and failures of a code of conduct in practice can be attributed both to the process and to perceptions, as well as to behavior on both sides. The problem is much more complex than skeptics at the time or critics later have recognized. Particularly because of the continuing interest in the post-détente 1980s in reestablishing a code of conduct, it is important to analyze the effort in the 1970s to adopt and to maintain one, as is done later in this study. But for immediate purposes, it is sufficient to note that while from the outset the Nixon-Kissinger team had a realistic skepticism about future Soviet performance, there was also a belief that, within limits, the strategy would work, and that it was a low-risk endeavor so long as policymakers did not harbor undue expectations. These policymakers were confident they would not.

There remained, however, an unrealistic element in the whole approach. It was the agreement, stated solemnly in documents by both countries, not to seek unilateral advantage. In practice, both sides continued to do so. Moreover, in times of political competition and rivalry, the détente agreements provided too great a temptation even to political leaders—and all the more to political critics—to lambast the other side for continuing to seek advantages, while turning a blind eye to their own pursuit of them.

The unilateral application of the constraints and restraints of détente only to the actions of the other side constituted a rather large blind spot in the vision of the Americans who designed détente. While subtly and realistically focusing on what could be done to manage *Soviet* behavior in the world, they showed astonishingly little awareness of the potential impact of the process of détente on *American* behavior. A code of conduct was something the American leaders could square with their own perceptions and with justifications for U.S. policy and actions. But of course the Soviet leaders would also apply the standard in terms of their perceptions and justification of their actions. At the same time, leaders and publics on both sides were inclined to apply much more demanding standards in judging behavior by the other side. This double standard would only become evident with time, and even then to very few observers and even fewer leaders. But it would be critical to détente.

Another purpose of détente in the Western conception (more so in the case of Western Europeans than of Kissinger and Nixon) has been to open up Soviet and other communist societies as a natural consequence of the increased contact among peoples that would stem from greatly increased cultural, travel, trade, and other ties. This expectation may indirectly be related to Western European desire to foster a more stable world order, or ascribed simply to a normalization of relations. The Soviet leaders, however, regard it otherwise—as an offensive attempt to promote subversion.

Under the Carter administration, the same basic conception of détente continued to be held. Détente was seen, and was described, as a combination of cooperation and competition. There were, however, differences within the Carter administration. The assistant to the president for national security affairs, Zbigniew Brzezinski, while accepting (and articulating for the Carter administration) that conception of détente, sought to use détente to effect changes within the Soviet system (in the Soviet Union itself and especially in Eastern Europe). In contrast to Nixon and Kissinger, Brzezinski also saw a requirement for more forceful measures to contain Soviet expansion in the third world, and was attracted to playing the "China card." Secretary of State Cyrus R. Vance, on the other hand, while also accepting détente as a mix of cooperation and competition, was more inclined to seek ways to expand the areas of cooperation, and less inclined to see the same measures needed for containment in the third world, or to see value in such moves as playing the China card. President Jimmy Carter himself had mixed inclinations and did not recognize their incompatibility: he wished to pursue détente and peaceful coexistence while waging aggressive competition with (and within) the Soviet system in certain areas. Later, in response to perceived developments in the world, Carter increasingly moved away from Vance's conception to Brzezinski's. By 1980 he was leading not a competitive, but a confrontational, policy, while avowing—and wishing for—a return to détente.

The tensions in this contradiction between avowed aims and actual policy were broken by the election of a new president who clearly rejected détente and who was dedicated to vigorous competition and a stance of confrontation. From the outset the Reagan administration repudiated the very idea of détente, although Secretaries of State Alexander M. Haig, Jr., and George P. Shultz did attempt to resurrect the prospect of a policy of competition and cooperation if the Soviet Union was prepared to accept American terms for such a relationship. At the same time, however, at least from 1981 through 1983, the Reagan administration also pursued a policy of confrontation. It sought, through a campaign of strong political propaganda, and through its own defense buildup and economic constraints and sanctions, to increase pressure on the Soviet Union to compel internal and external policy changes, which the administration assumed would curb what were perceived as aggressive Soviet drives and capabilities. By the end of the first term of the Reagan administration it was unclear whether the president would give priority to a renewed effort at negotiation.

There was another dimension to the American (and Soviet) conceptions of détente: differences between declared (or "declaratory") and actual (or "operative") policies. Neither American nor Soviet leaders express all of their views or aims frankly in public pronouncements. Nonetheless, official policy statements convey at least some real concerns and objectives, and often much of the underlying policy approach. With experience, one learns to read between the lines. Official policy statements not only conceal or prettify some aspects of actual policy; they also present a more rational and idealized depiction than does the underlying reality.

During the period from 1969 to 1972 the stated aim of Nixon and Kissinger's policy was to develop a structure of peace, while they characterized the existing situation as one of competitive coexistence with occasional challenges and crises requiring containment. From 1972 through 1975, the declared policy of Nixon-Ford-Kissinger was détente, whereas the actual policy continued to be competitive coexistence and containment. In 1976 the Ford administration dropped the term détente, and more or less shifted declared as well as actual policy to competitive coexistence.

The Carter administration's declared policy from 1977 through 1979 was détente, while its actual policy was an erratic mix of predominantly détente in 1977 (although not viewed as such in Moscow) and predominantly competitive coexistence in 1978 and 1979. In 1980 Carter's declared position was a sharp move to containment, although with the avowed aim of returning to détente if Soviet behavior permitted it. Actual policy in 1980 was containment heavily tinged with confrontation, including a suspension of most of the elements of détente achieved in the 1970s.

The Reagan administration abjured détente and pursued a policy of containment and confrontation, although it discovered that in practice some elements of competitive coexistence proved politically necessary. While confrontational elements were most prominent in declared policy from 1981 through 1983, in 1984 the declared policy shifted to emphasis on dialogue and negotiation.

The Soviet Conception of Détente

What is détente? What do we mean by that term? Détente above all means overcoming the "cold war" and transition to normal, equal relations among states. Détente means a readiness to resolve differences and disputes not by force, not by threats and sabre-rattling, but by peaceful means, at a conference table. Détente means a certain trust and ability to take into account the legitimate interest of one another.[25]

Such was General Secretary Leonid I. Brezhnev's characterization of détente in a speech keyed to the change in American administrations in 1977. Détente, or the relaxation of international tensions, is also frequently characterized in Soviet discourse as a companion, if not an equivalent, to peaceful coexistence between states with differing social systems. Again to cite Brezhnev, who addressed the subject frequently, the connection between peaceful coexistence, détente, and the renunciation of force in the Soviet conception is clear in this passage from a speech in 1975:

Over recent years conviction in the possibility and, indeed, in the necessity of peaceful coexistence has been confirmed in the thinking of both the peoples and the leaders of most countries. Détente became possible because a new correlation of forces in the world arena has been established. Now the leaders of the bourgeois world can no longer

25. L. I. Brezhnev, *Pravda*, January 19, 1977.

seriously count on resolving the historic conflict between capitalism and socialism by force of arms. The senselessness and extreme danger of further increasing tension under conditions when both sides have at their disposal weapons of colossal destructive power are becoming ever more obvious.

The norms of peaceful coexistence between states are already fixed in many official bilateral and multilateral written commitments. Of course, that did not just happen by itself. In order to do away with the "cold war" and reduce the danger of a new world war tremendous political work was needed. And we can say that the decisive role in achieving détente was due to the combined efforts of the Soviet Union and the other countries of the socialist commonwealth, their consistent struggle against the forces of aggression and war.

Now the world is entering on a period when the task of embodying the principles of peaceful coexistence and mutually advantageous cooperation in daily practice has come to the fore.[26]

While the Soviet adoption and pursuit of a policy of détente was linked to Brezhnev's name and period of rule, it has been a policy of the leadership as a whole, and has continued to be reaffirmed by General Secretaries Yury V. Andropov, Konstantin U. Chernenko, and Mikhail S. Gorbachev, and other Soviet leaders. There have naturally been differences within the Soviet leadership over various aspects and applications of the policy of détente, as the discussion in this study makes clear. It is also relevant that the gradual adoption of a policy and strategy of détente in the late 1960s and early 1970s coincided with Brezhnev's rise and the consolidation of his leading role. Nonetheless, it also has represented a consensus of the collective Soviet leadership under Brezhnev, Andropov, and Chernenko. Thus Andropov, from his first speech as the new leader at Brezhnev's funeral, stressed: "We shall always be loyal to the cause of the struggle for peace, for détente."[27] And Chernenko (who in 1982 had also stressed that "détente is unquestionably the path to peace and cooperation"),[28] after succeeding Andropov, in 1984 continued to state that "the development of events can be turned from confrontation to détente."[29] Restoration of détente has continued to be held as the aim of Soviet policy.

In the Soviet view détente was made possible by the Soviet attainment of a nuclear retaliatory capability in the early 1960s and a rough strategic parity by the 1970s. The Soviet leaders had felt keenly their inferiority in overall and strategic military power, and greatly welcomed this development, which they had long sought. The ebullient Nikita S. Khrushchev had tried, prematurely and unsuccessfully, to bluff his way past Soviet inferiority, but this

---

26. L. I. Brezhnev, *Pravda*, June 14, 1975.

27. "Speech of Comrade Yury V. Andropov," *Pravda*, November 16, 1982.

28. K. U. Chernenko, *Izbrannye rechi i stat'i* [Selected Speeches and Articles], 2d ed. (Moscow: Politizdat, 1984), p. 551.

29. "Speech of Comrade K. U. Chernenko," *Pravda*, April 30, 1984.

approach resulted only in setbacks, most notably in the Cuban missile crisis. By the end of the 1960s, however, his more cautious successors believed that the power of the Soviet Union, and in particular its nuclear deterrent, had contributed to establishing a general correlation of forces between the Soviet Union and the United States, and the Soviet and Western camps overall, sufficient to permit dealing with the West on a basis of equality.

In the Soviet perception, the United States had used its military superiority to build "positions of (superior) strength" and, more directly, to threaten and on occasion to use military power to advance its own interests. It had also sought to prevent comparable Soviet global political presence and influence. This perception accorded with their ideological beliefs as well as their experience, and it was only by strenuous efforts to improve their relative power position that the Soviets had achieved a posture of rough parity. (In fact, as the Soviets well appreciated, in the early 1970s they were still well short of full equality in military power in many respects.)

Accordingly, in the Soviet view, as stated in a key Central Committee resolution in mid-1980, "Détente is the natural result of the correlation of forces in the world arena that has formed in recent decades. The military strategic balance between the world of socialism and the world of capitalism is an achievement of truly historic significance."[30]

The meaning and role of strategic parity are addressed presently, but in the context of the present discussion it is necessary to recognize the key importance of the changed balance of power (including, but not limited to, strategic nuclear military power) from the standpoint of the Soviet conception of détente. The Soviets saw the achievement of general military parity between the two superpowers (and their camps or alliances) as having important political implications.

Détente, as conceived by *Soviet* leaders, would help manage the transition of *the United States* into a changing world, one no longer marked by American predominance but by a political parity of the Soviet Union with the United States that matched their military parity. While in many ways logically parallel to the purposes of détente in the American conception (in a reverse mirror reflection), the Soviet view in practice carried quite different implications. Some of these are fairly obvious, but others are not, as will be seen.

How does détente, as conceived by the Soviet leaders, fit into their ideological view of the world and history?

Marxism-Leninism is based on historical determinism, a belief that socioeconomic forces, through a struggle of *classes*, are the driving dynamic of history. The advent of the Soviet Union as a socialist state raised the issue of war between *states* as a possible form of class struggle. Indeed, to the early Bolshevik leaders, it was the central fact of life. Successive Soviet leaders have

---

30. "On the International Situation and Foreign Policy of the Soviet Union: Resolution of the Plenum of the Central Committee of the CPSU, June 23, 1980," *Kommunist* [The Communist], no. 10 (July 1980), p. 9.

seen the greatest danger to the socialist cause (identified with the Soviet Union) as coming from the imperialist (capitalist) military threat. And the one mortal danger faced during the last half-century of Soviet rule after the victorious conclusion of the Civil War (and defeat of coincident foreign military interventions) was the attack by Germany in World War II. In Soviet eyes, the greatest threat since that war has been the unparalleled destructive power of the American nuclear arsenal.

The primary role of military power is therefore defense of the achievements of world socialism—preeminent of which is the Soviet Union. In addition, Marxist-Leninist ideology sanctions the use of military power (and any other means) available to socialist (Soviet) leaders whenever, but only if, expedient in advancing the socialist cause and not jeopardizing the security of what has already been gained, above all in terms of the security of the Soviet Union. Military power is *not*, on the other hand, seen as the decisive element in advancing the historical process. The progressive revolutionary process will advance through indigenous actions by the rising working class in each society when conditions are ripe.

When a "world revolution" failed to occur after the successful conclusion of the Civil War, the new Soviet state turned to recovery and then to achievement of "socialism in one country." Priority was given to economic development and to assurance of political control. The key role of military power on behalf of world socialism was to guarantee the survival of the first socialist state. Although the term was not then in vogue, *deterrence* of renewed military intervention by the capitalist powers was the underlying strategic concept. Later, when attacked, the role of the armed forces was of course defense and defeat of the attacker. The same concept of deterrence has governed the period since World War II, except that now there is a socialist camp or commonwealth, and military power in the nuclear age is recognized as enormously more dangerous and important.

The principal role of Soviet military power has consistently been to dissuade imperialist powers from resorting to *their* military power against the Soviet Union (and, later, against the other countries of the socialist camp) in an effort to thwart the progressive course of history driven by revolutionary socioeconomic dynamics—not by military conquest. While the Soviets see other important and ideologically sanctioned uses of military force, including support for an active Soviet foreign policy, the basic Marxist-Leninist ideological framework predicates a fundamentally deterrent role for Soviet military power.[31]

To cite again the 1980 Central Committee resolution, détente was further characterized as "a factor deterring the aggressive aspirations of the imperialists." By this time, the Soviet view was that the United States had

---

31. In addition to the very summary discussion in these paragraphs, see Raymond L. Garthoff, *Soviet Military Policy: A Historical Analysis* (Praeger, 1966), pp. 3–28, 65–97, 191–206, 220–38.

"taken the course of upsetting the military balance that has developed in the world in its favor and to the detriment of the Soviet Union" and, of course, also to the detriment of "international détente." The imperialist hopes of upsetting parity were said to be "doomed to failure," but only because the party leadership recognized under these conditions the requirement for "the comprehensive strengthening of the defense capability of our state in order to frustrate the plans of imperialism aimed at attaining superiority and establishing a world *diktat*."[32]

This preview of one aspect of the Soviet perception of the reasons for the decline of détente at the end of the decade helps to place in perspective their conception and their expectations at the outset.

Peaceful coexistence has been a central feature of the Soviet conception of détente. The conception has a long history, originating with the early recognition by the Bolsheviks that the expected world revolution was not going to occur as a single process and therefore that the new Soviet Socialist Republic would have to coexist with the capitalist states for an indefinite period. Peaceful coexistence among states with differing social systems meant no more than that—recognition of the fact of coexisting with an absence of war.

Peaceful coexistence acquired a new emphasis in 1956, when the Twentieth Party Congress rejected the Marxist tenet of the inevitability of war, and declared that the foreign policy of the Soviet Union was based on peaceful coexistence.[33] Again at the Twenty-fourth Congress in 1971 (reaffirmed at the Twenty-fifth in 1976 and the Twenty-sixth in 1981), Soviet policy was said to be based on peaceful coexistence. Indeed, the new Constitution of the USSR adopted in 1977 states that the foreign policy of the USSR is directed "to consistently implementing the principle of peaceful coexistence of states with different social systems."[34]

Skeptics in the West are inclined to regard such pronouncements as propaganda, or even dark deception, while apologists invest them with an undeserved aura of benign and unselfish goodness. Both err by reading into the Soviet pronouncements their own perceptions of Soviet motivation. In fact, while stating their position in the way most favorable to their image (as do all states), the Soviet leaders have tended to lay out their general line of policy

---

32. *Kommunist*, no. 10 (1980), pp. 8, 9, 10. Emphasis added.

33. There are indications that even before the death of Stalin, some of his lieutenants—and later successors—had begun to recognize that in the nuclear age war could no longer be countenanced as inevitable. See Raymond L. Garthoff, "The Death of Stalin and the Birth of Mutual Deterrence," *Survey*, vol. 25 (Spring 1980), pp. 10–16.

34. "The Constitution of the USSR," adopted by the Supreme Soviet on October 7, 1977, *Pravda*, October 8, 1977. The foreign policy of the USSR is also said to be directed at six other objectives, including "supporting the struggle of peoples for national liberation and social progress" and "securing the state interests of the Soviet Union"; these are all consistent in terms of the *Soviet* conception of détente.

forthrightly. They *do* desire to avert war through peaceful coexistence among states. They also believe that a progressive revolutionary movement of history is unfolding inexorably and that the Soviet Union is on the side of history. History is not dependent on the actions of the Soviet Union; the Soviet Union should support and assist the historical process, but without attempting to force its pace. Nor should its support involve actions that could put at risk the historic achievement of the Soviet state. In the nuclear age, war would mean an incalculable disaster for the Soviet Union and setback for world socialism.

The Soviet leaders believe that the imperialists (leaders of capitalist states) have a proclivity to resort to military force and war to extend (and, still more, to preserve) their strategic, political, and economic interests. Hence, as stated in 1969 at the International Conference of Communist and Workers' Parties in Moscow, the Soviet view is that a "struggle to *compel*" the imperialists to accept peaceful coexistence is required.[35] Again, it is not necessary to ascribe sinister motives to a Soviet statement meaning that they see a tough uphill effort to get Western leaders to agree, both in principle and still more in practice, to letting history take its course without resorting to force to try to stop it (as in Vietnam, the Dominican Republic, Guatemala, and many other cases in the 1950s and 1960s). Nor is it necessary to accept the Soviet view of "history." Rather, it is important to understand how *they* perceive history, and therefore world politics.

While aiming to end war and, indeed, imperialist resort to military force anywhere, the Soviets have not only "disclosed" but have insisted loudly that peaceful coexistence among states does *not* mean an end to "the class struggle" or the "national liberation movement" in colonial or neocolonial situations. On the contrary, it is avowed authoritatively and frequently that peaceful coexistence and détente will aid national liberation, progressive, and socialist revolutionary class struggle. This theme was not a new element under détente in the 1970s. In Brezhnev's first major address as party leader, made on the forty-seventh anniversary of the October Revolution in 1964, he had stated that "a situation of peaceful coexistence will enable the success of the liberation struggle and the achievement of the revolutionary tasks of peoples."[36] Brezhnev again made the point clearly in his speech on the fiftieth anniversary of the founding of the USSR seven months after the first summit meeting.[37] This position was held consistently and reiterated frequently as détente developed. For example, Politburo member Fyodor D. Kulakov declared, on the eve

---

35. "Tasks of the Struggle against Imperialism at the Present Stage and the Unity of Action of the Communist and Workers' Parties and All Anti-Imperialist Forces," *Pravda*, June 18, 1969. Emphasis added.

36. L. I. Brezhnev, *Izbrannye proizvedeniya* [Selected Works] (Moscow: Politizdat, 1981), vol. 1, p. 21.

37. L. I. Brezhnev, "On the Fiftieth Anniversary of the USSR," *Pravda*, December 22, 1972.

of the first Brezhnev-Nixon summit meeting, "Peaceful coexistence is the best foundation for practical solidarity with the revolutionaries of the whole world."[38] Moreover, "peaceful coexistence does not mean the end of the struggle between the two world social systems," but represents a struggle which will continue "right up to the complete and final victory of communism on a world scale."[39]

At the key Twenty-fourth Party Congress in March 1971, Brezhnev stated that peaceful coexistence provided the basis for relations with the United States.[40] The decision to seek to improve relations with the United States, which Brezhnev successfully advanced at that congress, had been reached only after overcoming the opposition of many skeptical members of the Central Committee and the Politburo.[41]

Following the first Soviet-American summit meeting in May 1972, many discussions explained to Soviet readers the political and ideological meaning of the new course of détente. It meant that the overall correlation of forces in the world, including the "social, economic and military power of the Soviet Union and other socialist countries," was compelling the United States to undergo an agonizing reappraisal and to change course from pursuing a hegemonic "Pax Americana" that relied on a policy of "positions of strength" to accepting peaceful coexistence.[42]

For the Soviet leaders, the most significant aspect of this changed correlation of forces and the necessity for peaceful coexistence was that the United States and the imperialist powers could no longer count on being able to destroy the Soviet Union and world socialism by military means because of the state of mutual deterrence in the nuclear age. Brezhnev stated this clearly in 1975:

Détente became possible because a new correlation of forces in the world arena has been established. Now the leaders of the bourgeois world can no longer seriously count on resolving the historic conflict between capitalism and socialism by force of arms. The senselessness and extreme danger of further increasing tension under conditions when both sides have at their disposal weapons of colossal destructive power are becoming ever more obvious.[43]

---

38. F. D. Kulakov, "Leninism Is the Great Creative Force in Communist Construction," *Pravda*, April 22, 1972. For other discussions in the 1970s, see Yu. Molchanov, "Peaceful Coexistence and Social Progress," *International Affairs* (Moscow), no. 12 (December 1976), especially p. 11; and A. Bovin, *Izvestiya*, September 11, 1973.

39. F. Ryzhenko, "Peaceful Coexistence and the Class Struggle," *Pravda*, August 22, 1973.

40. Brezhnev, "Report of the Central Committee of the CPSU to the XXIV Congress of the Communist Party of the Soviet Union, March 30, 1971," *O vneshnei politike*, p. 179.

41. Interviews with members of the Central Committee of the CPSU.

42. See A. Pumpyansky, "A Triumph of Realism," *Komsomol'skaya pravda* [Komsomol Truth], June 4, 1972; and many other Soviet articles at that time and subsequently.

43. Brezhnev, *Pravda*, June 14, 1975.

Soviet ideology, positing a continuing conflict between communism (socialism) and capitalism (imperialism), provides a natural basis for Soviet acceptance of competition along with cooperation as a part of détente and peaceful coexistence. "Détente took shape as a result of the dialectical interaction of two foreign policy courses of opposite class nature and ultimate class direction—the socialist and the bourgeois."[44] Accordingly, "cooperation and confrontation are most important facets of peaceful coexistence, as components of a single process. Their unity is of a dialectical character: they cannot be isolated from one another, nor can one of them be discarded and the other retained."[45] Acceptance of continuing conflict does not, however, include war between states. "It is vitally important to preserve peace in order to build the new society, socialism, and communism."[46] In addition, "world peace is determined to a decisive degree by the reality of peaceful coexistence between socialism and capitalism."[47] At the same time, in light of the military hostilities between nonaligned countries (for example, Iraq and Iran) and even between socialist countries (for example, China and Vietnam) in recent years, Soviet theoreticians have now come to advocate "extending the principle of peaceful coexistence to cover not only relations between socialist and capitalist countries, but also its operation on a wider scale."[48]

In short, détente, and peaceful coexistence, "does not and cannot mean forgoing the objective processes of historical development. It is not a safe conduct for corrupt regimes. . . . It does not eliminate the need for social transformations. But the people themselves in each country resolve this question."[49] There should be neither attempts to "export revolutions" nor "to export counterrevolution."[50]

After the signing of the détente agreements of 1972 and 1973 with the United States, at a time when Soviet leaders were especially sensitive to charges from the left, Brezhnev took the occasion of a global communist-led World Congress of Peace-Loving Forces to reaffirm that "revolution, the class

---

44. N. Lebedev, "The Dialectics of the Development of International Relations," *International Affairs*, no. 9 (September 1980), p. 109.

45. Ibid., p. 109.

46. Ibid., p. 111.

47. [Maj. Gen.] A. S. Milovidov and Ye. A. Zhdanov, "Social-Philosophical Problems of War and Peace," *Voprosy filosofii* [Questions of Philosophy], no. 10 (October 1980), p. 43.

48. Ibid., p. 43. The first indications that peaceful coexistence should extend to relations among states that do not have different social systems came in the early 1970s. The first instance I have noted was an article by Aleksandr Bovin, *Izvestiya*, September 11, 1973.

49. "Statement of the Soviet Government," *Pravda*, May 22, 1976.

50. Brezhnev, Speech of January 29, 1974, *O vneshnei politike*, p. 382. This long-standing Soviet view had been restated many times since the 1960s.

struggle, and liberation movements cannot be abolished by agreements. No power on earth is capable of reversing the inexorable process of the renovation of the life of society."[51]

In the mid-1970s, and especially in the period leading up to and following the Twenty-fifth Party Congress in 1976, Soviet theoreticians began to develop a concept of a "fundamental restructuring of international relations" to exclude war. In June 1974 Brezhnev commented in his Supreme Soviet election speech: "Evaluating the general correlation of forces in the world, we already several years ago reached the conclusion that there exists a real possibility to achieve a fundamental change in the international situation."[52] A year later, in 1975, on the eve of the Helsinki Conference on European security and the Vladivostok SALT accord with President Gerald R. Ford, Brezhnev went further. He declared:

In the past few years, conviction in the possibility, and moreover in the necessity, of peaceful coexistence was confirmed in the consciousness both of the broad popular masses and also in the ruling circles of the majority of countries. International détente has become possible because a new correlation of forces has been established in the world arena. . . . Norms of peaceful coexistence between states have already been consolidated in many binding official bilateral and multilateral documents, as well as in political declarations.[53]

Foreign Minister and Politburo member Andrei A. Gromyko stressed in 1981 that when the program of détente had been launched at the Twenty-fourth Party Congress ten years earlier, the party had first "perspicaciously" evaluated the international situation as providing "favorable opportunities for the restructuring of the entire system of international relations that had evolved in the postwar period as a result of the change in the correlation of forces in the world in favor of socialism."[54] And in 1973, Brezhnev and Gromyko had been saying that " 'détente is not a temporary phenomenon but the beginning of a fundamental restructuring of international relations.' "[55]

Soviet theoreticians and commentators have further elaborated on this point, stressing the role of détente, growing Western acceptance of peaceful coexistence, the attainment of strategic parity, and general world political developments; in sum, "the changing correlation of forces between the two

51. Brezhnev, Speech of October 26, 1973, ibid., p. 349. The speech was given just a few weeks after the overthrow and murder of President Salvador Allende in Chile; Brezhnev referred to that event just before the statement cited here.

52. Brezhnev, Speech of June 14, 1974, ibid., p. 397.

53. Brezhnev, Speech of June 13, 1975, ibid., p. 473.

54. A. Gromyko, "Leninist Foreign Policy in the Contemporary World," *Kommunist*, no. 1 (January 1981), p. 14.

55. See A. A. Gromyko, Speech to the UN General Assembly, *Pravda*, September 26, 1973, in which he cited Brezhnev as having stated that in a recent speech.

social systems in favor of socialism has been the decisive factor determining the acceleration of the fundamental restructuring of international relations."[56]

Soviet commentators have stressed the dynamic nature and role of détente, which has been central to this process of "restructuring." In Vladimir Petrovsky's words, "Détente is regarded by the Soviet Union not as a static condition, but as a dynamic process, in the course of which the restructuring of international relations on the principles of peaceful coexistence will be completed."[57]

Brezhnev and other Soviet leaders, as well as Soviet theoreticians, have stressed that the accomplishments of détente by the mid-1970s had not been easy and that they had not yet been made "irreversible." Indeed, "the dialectics of the breakup of the old structure of international relations and the creation of a new one is not simple, because it is a process involving efforts to overcome contradictions and resistance from opponents of détente and peaceful coexistence."[58]

An interesting elaboration of the Soviet conception of détente in the mid-1970s was the coining of the term "military détente," with reference to the application of détente to military affairs, principally in agreed "confidence-building" measures, crisis management, and arms control and arms limitation agreements. The expression was apparently first used by Brezhnev in his speech to the Twenty-fourth Party Congress in 1971.[59] It began to be used widely after the Helsinki Conference in 1975 to refer to measures aimed at reducing military confrontation in Europe. Both applications of the term, to European security and to broader arms control, are discussed in later chapters.[60] Here, however, it is important to note the relation of military détente to the Soviet conception of restructuring international relations. As one Soviet academic analyst put it, within détente as a whole, "Military détente is an indispensable

---

56. N. Lebedev, "The Struggle of the USSR for the Restructuring of International Relations," *Mezhdunarodnaya zhizn'* [International Life], no. 12 (December 1975), p. 7. Lebedev is head of the Moscow State Institute of International Relations.

57. V. F. Petrovsky, "The Struggle of the USSR for Détente in the Seventies," *Novaya i noveiy-shaya istoriya* [Modern and Contemporary History], no. 1 (January–February 1981), p. 3. Petrovsky is both an experienced diplomat and a leading scholar in the field of diplomatic history.

   In addition to the sources cited above on this discussion, see V. V. Kortunov, "The Relaxation of Tensions and the Struggle of Ideas in Contemporary International Relations," *Voprosy istorii KPSS* [Questions of History of the CPSU], no. 10 (October 1975), p. 16; and see D. Tomashevsky, "Toward a Radical Restructuring of International Relations," *Mirovaya ekonomika i mezhdunarodnye otnosheniya* [The World Economy and International Relations], no. 1 (January 1975), pp. 3–13 (hereafter MEiMO); and V. V. Kortunov, *Perestroika mezhdunarodnykh otnoshenii i ideologicheskaya bor'ba* [The Restructuring of International Relations and the Ideological Struggle] (Moscow: Znaniye, 1977). Kortunov is an official of the Central Committee.

58. Lebedev, *Mezhdunarodnaya zhizn'*, no. 12 (1975), p. 10.

59. Brezhnev, *O vneshnei politike*, p. 175.

60. See chapters 14 and 22.

condition and one of the most important means for restructuring international relations on the principles of peaceful coexistence."[61] While political détente was seen as primary and "decisive" and the first step, military détente was also said to be necessary.

Military détente, as political détente, rests on the new correlation of forces and, above all, on strategic parity between the United States and the Soviet Union: "From the standpoint of the possibilities and prospects for military détente, it is extremely important that imperialism has already been forced to take seriously into account the realities of the contemporary world, above all the fact of Soviet-American 'nuclear parity'—the condition which has developed of a dynamic equilibrium of the strategic nuclear missile power of the two states."[62] And on the basis of this military parity, political parity can lead to the consolidation of military as well as political détente in formally regulated relations, all in the framework of the restructuring of international relations. "New and important in principle is the fact that under the contemporary world correlation of forces a real possibility has appeared to use the traditional treaty form for gradual alterations of interstate military-political relations, bringing them into correspondence with the tasks of restructuring the whole system of international relations on a new basis."[63]

Following the Twenty-fifth Party Congress in 1976, Soviet political—and military—theoreticians began to elaborate a theory of states and types of peace (as well as war). Thus, in addition to distinguishing various categories of local wars and other forms of warfare, several categories of "levels of peace" with different characteristics began to be developed. Peace was identified as a dialectical combination of cooperation and conflict. The lowest level was the cold war, defined as the mere absence of military hostilities, a "negative peace." This level might include not only harsh political, ideological, and economic warfare, but also tensions that could erupt into armed conflict. Détente was the second level of peace, a "positive peace." Within détente, which includes many gradations and forms, were two sublevels: political détente and military détente. The former included the development of political, economic, scientific, and cultural ties and cooperation; the latter extended into arms control, especially disarmament. "Thus 'cold war,' or negative peace, is merely an absence of war not buttressed with positive social content. Political and military détente are stages of positive peace, based on the principles of peaceful coexistence, which are realized in the peaceful cooperation of states and in arms reductions."[64]

---

61. A. Nikonov, "Military Détente and the Restructuring of International Relations," *MEiMO*, no. 6 (June 1977), p. 28.

62. Ibid., p. 31.

63. Ibid., p. 33.

64. Milovidov and Zhdanov, *Voprosy filosofii*, no. 10 (1980), p. 46. This interesting article includes many useful bibliographic references to the burgeoning Soviet literature on the philosophical anatomy of war and peace.

In the Soviet conception, peace is not the only or ultimate objective. Soviet theoreticians have made clear that "unlike pacifists," Marxist-Leninists do not regard peace as an absolute goal and do not regard "any peace as progress." Lenin's adaptation of Clausewitz' thesis is reflected in the shrewd observation that "like war, peace is a continuation of policy."[65] The distinction is in the means: "The essence of peace presupposes the achievement of political objectives by non-armed means, that is, by economic, scientific, technical, diplomatic, cultural, and ideological means . . . by nonviolent means of conducting policy."[66] Foreign Minister Gromyko, in a major article on Soviet foreign policy in the authoritative theoretical journal of the Communist party, has laid out the ideological position for the Soviet political elite. He stated that "the fundamental underlying principles" of Soviet policy are: "proletarian internationalism and peaceful coexistence of states with differing social systems." As he explained further, "Proletarian internationalism as a fundamental principle of Soviet foreign policy means that this policy consistently upholds the basic interests of world socialism, the forces of the international communist and workers movement, and of the national-liberation movement. As for peaceful coexistence, it represents a specific form of the class struggle—peaceful competition, ruling out the use of military force, between the two counterposed social-economic systems—socialism and capitalism."[67] In short, it was clearly recognized that peace is "waged" under peaceful coexistence, notwithstanding a theoretical construct of an ascending structure of levels of peace with growing components of cooperation and disarmament.

In concluding this overview of the Soviet conception of détente it is instructive to note what the Soviets have indicated détente does *not* mean. The most clear and strong statements have been articulated in recent years as part of a critical retrospective analysis of the American interpretation of détente in the 1970s, or, as one important member of the party Central Committee staff calls it, "détente American-style."[68] Imperialists put "at the center of their conception of détente and peaceful coexistence the idea of the preservation of the status quo. One cannot agree with such an interpretation. The policy of peaceful coexistence has clearly drawn boundaries. Its sphere is relations among states."[69] Only in one crucially significant respect do the Soviets accept this approach: the absolute necessity of averting world nuclear war. "The policy of peaceful coexistence is designed to find a solution to the most acute political problem of our time—to avert a total nuclear missile clash. . . . It is possible and necessary to ban war as a means of 'clarifying relations' among

---

65. Ibid., p. 38.

66. Ibid., p. 44.

67. Gromyko, *Kommunist*, no. 1 (1981), p. 14.

68. V. Kortunov, "Disastrous Relapses into a Policy of Strength," *Kommunist*, no. 10 (July 1980), p. 102.

69. A. Bovin, "The Permanent Significance of Lenin's Ideas," *Kommunist*, no. 10 (July 1980), p. 79. Emphasis added.

states. And in this sense peaceful coexistence includes the requirement of the status quo. But it is impossible to 'ban' a civil war or national liberation war, to 'ban' revolution as a means of changing social and political systems."[70]

While Western observers have usually seen Soviet statements in support of national liberation and progressive revolutionary movements as reflecting an offensive thrust in Soviet foreign policy, Soviet leaders have in fact usually made such statements in a defensive context that related to internal controversies within the world communist movement and domestic Soviet politics. Controversy on this point became especially clear after the first major steps in détente with the United States in 1972.[71] Nor did the issue die. A consultant to the International Department of the Central Committee commented in *Pravda* in 1976 that the question of the impact of détente on the class struggle "often crops up in the international workers movement," including among anti-Soviet radicals whom he accused of "leftist fabrications to the effect that détente strengthens the positions of capitalism." Acknowledging that détente had "complicated" the global ideological struggle and given some new opportunities to opponents of socialism, he argued that on balance détente had been more favorable to the class and national liberation struggles.[72] In addition, it has been constantly stressed that peaceful coexistence and the prevention of war are of the highest priority for world socialism, benefiting the peoples of the world.

The Soviets have, especially in retrospect since the late 1970s, noted that capitalist leaders sometimes justified détente on the basis of its achievement of expanded relations "as a means of bringing about the gradual internal 'erosion' of socialism, as a means to 'dull vigilance' and for the ideological penetration of the socialist countries." And "the overall normalization of relations with the USSR was portrayed as a means of compelling our country to reduce or even to cease active assistance to the national liberation, antiimperialist and socialist movements in other countries." These views were depicted as inconsistencies in the *Western* approach to détente.[73]

The Soviets also object strongly to the concept of linkage, contending that steps in détente should not be tied to other matters. In particular, the Soviets are sensitive to any implication that they need détente more than the United States does, and they constantly affirm that the United States and the Soviet Union have an "equal interest" in détente and arms control. (American and Soviet use of linkage in practice is discussed later.)

---

70. Ibid. Emphasis added. See also Kortunov, *Kommunist*, no. 10 (1980), p. 102.

71. See the discussion in chapter 9.

72. Yu. Krasin, *Pravda*, September 24, 1976.

73. Yu. A. Zamoshkin, "Ideology in the United States: For and Against Détente," *SShA: Ekonomika, politika, ideologiya* [USA: Economics, Politics, Ideology], no. 4 (April 1982), p. 7. (Hereafter *SShA.*)

The Soviet conception of détente relies heavily on negotiation of specific issues, especially security matters. Thus at the Twenty-third Party Congress in 1966, the Soviet leaders stressed their aim "to resolve disputed international questions by means of negotiations and not by means of war."[74]

Finally, the Soviets claim to have initiated the policy of détente and to have been its champions against reluctant and opposing Western imperialist circles.[75] The Soviets place great weight on their relations with Western Europe and the European détente in East-West relations. But they also recognize (and during the 1970s came to stress) the special importance of Soviet relations with the United States. Not only are these relations "an important factor on which to a great extent the situation in the world as a whole depends," but they are also uniquely important with respect to "the degree of danger that a global conflict will arise,"[76] and the incalculable destruction that a world nuclear war would entail for everyone. Hence, "the creation of the optimal conditions for the contest between the two systems within the framework of peaceful coexistence and cooperation in order to prevent a global catastrophe and to end the arms race is inseparably linked with the nature of relations between the USSR and the USA."[77] While Soviet-American détente prevailed, the Soviets were at pains to assure others that the special significance of Soviet-American relations "does not signify, by any means, that the USSR and the USA have any special rights or advantages relative to other peoples." At the same time, however, they asserted that the two countries, "as the most powerful and influential powers of our times . . . bear a special responsibility for the preservation and consolidation of international peace and security."[78]

In the Soviet conception, détente and peaceful coexistence would serve "to make the world safe for historical change," so to speak, by depriving the imperialist powers, above all the United States, of resort to military force to curb the revolutionary social-economic-political transformations that would ultimately lead to world socialism and communism. The Soviet Union itself would serve the cause of revolutionary change not by military action, but by

---

74. "Resolution of the Twenty-third Congress of the CPSU on the Report of the Central Committee of the CPSU," April 8, 1966, *Materialy XXIII s'yezda KPSS* [Materials of the Twenty-third Congress of the CPSU] (Moscow: Politizdat, 1966), p. 157.

75. For example, see V. Zagladin, Radio Moscow, TV Studio 9, May 26, in Foreign Broadcast Information Service, *Daily Report: Soviet Union*, June 11, 1979, p. CC1. (Hereafter FBIS, *Soviet Union*.) He attributed the origination of détente to Brezhnev at the Twenty-third Party Congress in 1966. For Brezhnev's speech at the Congress, see *O vneshnei politike*, p. 40. See also A. Sovetov, "Leninist Foreign Policy in the World Today," *International Affairs*, no. 3 (March 1980), p. 6, typical of many other Soviet commentaries. Zagladin is first deputy chief of the International Department of the Central Committee.

76. V. F. Petrovsky, "The Role and Place of Soviet-American Relations in the Contemporary World," *Voprosy istorii* [Questions of History], no. 10 (October 1978), p. 91.

77. Ibid., p. 80. He also cites Brezhnev in this regard.

78. Ibid., p. 91.

balancing and serving to counter and deter America's use of its military power, and by pursuing its own economic and political development at home and the expansion of its political influence abroad. Peaceful coexistence among states would provide stability to the international system and to the historical process, but *not* to the status quo. As Brezhnev put it, the historically inevitable class struggle between the capitalist and socialist systems would be directed into ideological, economic, and political "channels that do not threaten wars, dangerous confrontations, or an uncontrolled arms race."[79]

Soviet belief that there is an underlying historical process and that the Soviet Union is riding the wave of the future does not mean they see their own role as passive. Soviet leaders are active and experienced political and diplomatic practitioners, and Soviet policy is geared to seize opportunities to advance Soviet interests and influence. Détente in no way superseded active competition in the world political arena, but it was based on a recognition of the need to limit competition to actions short of war with the imperialist powers in the nuclear age.

Declared Soviet policy has been very consistent. The Soviet Union has steadfastly supported détente and peaceful coexistence among states. It has also supported the progressive movement of history and revolutionary transformation of society. If relations between the Soviet Union and the United States became more tense, it was because the United States was attempting to interfere with the course of history in the third world and even in the socialist world. Soviet advocacy of peaceful coexistence is real and not a mere rationalization, much less a deception of the West. But it is also not a prescriptive constraint on Soviet policy action, which continues to be guided by calculations of relative cost, risk, and gain in any initiative or response. Moreover, *actual* Soviet policy has always contained a strong competitive element, along with the cooperative elements. That competitive element may increase, and even become confrontational, *if* required to meet competitive or confrontational challenges.

As noted in the discussion of American policy pronouncements, it is necessary to bear in mind the limits of public (and even internal) statements of policy as a guide to understanding actual patterns of action. Clearly, for anyone outside the Soviet milieu there are special problems in weighing Soviet pronouncements. Most Soviet statements cited here have been directed to the Soviet elite and establishment. They represent authoritative statements of what the Soviet leaders at least want their own constituents to believe is Soviet policy. But they are also a reflection of the mindset and framework of cognition and perception of the policymakers themselves. Those in the leadership may differ in internal deliberations about whether to accept a given agreement under negotiation, or whether and what kind of assistance to provide to a revolutionary movement abroad, but the terms of their private debates are set

---

79. L. I. Brezhnev, *Leninskom kursom* [On Lenin's Course] (Moscow: Politizdat, 1974), vol. 4, p. 81.

in the same mold as reports to the Central Committee or lead articles in *Pravda*.

Veiled reflections of real policy differences do appear in the Soviet media. Moreover, contrary to a widespread impression, there are sometimes significant differences in the weight to be given to various Soviet authors and publications. Some reflect specific institutional interests; others reflect political constituencies. Differences in viewpoint and schools of thought exist in the Soviet academic institutions and press. Analysts must familiarize themselves with these considerations, and must take into account the standing of the author, intended audience, and purposes of any Soviet statement. While this process enlarges opportunities for analysis, it also requires caution in using sources. For example, many commentators from various institutes of the Academy of Sciences dealing with international relations and Soviet-American relations are naturally among those contributing most to discussions relevant to the present study. The relationship of these institutes, of individual leading scholars, and of published academic analyses to the Soviet official and policy-making establishment is complex. As sources of publicly articulated Soviet policy, they are usually informed and authoritative. In presenting interpretations they may or may not be consonant with (or, indeed, may influence) official thinking. But such problems are part of the challenge for those of us who professionally study Soviet affairs. In this study Soviet sources have been extensively researched and used to illustrate in their own words the Soviet view (or in some cases diverging views). Statements about policy are, of course, only one source for analysis. But particularly for examining Soviet policy conceptions, they are a valuable source.[80]

In concluding this summary analysis of the Soviet conception of détente, it should be recalled that while the Soviet leaders have accepted a policy of détente throughout the 1970s and 1980s, various members of the Soviet leadership and various constituencies of the Soviet political system have not always agreed on some of the political issues relating to détente. A number of such disagreements arose during the period under review and are examined in this study. Moreover, the Soviet leaders have had to adapt to the change in American policy from the mid-1970s to the mid-1980s.

It should also be observed that the Soviet approach to détente has had both strengths and weaknesses, even apart from those aspects of the policy and strategy that have been more or less effective from the Soviet standpoint and more or less objectionable from an American standpoint. First, the Soviet view of the existing world order includes recognition that the world is in a state of flux, and they have therefore been prepared for change to a greater extent than the United States has, given the more static American vision of the status

---

80. In many cases, either in the text or in brief footnote notations, I have provided information on the standing or position of Soviet authors cited. It may be appropriate also to note that I have been using Soviet source materials in analyzing Soviet political and military affairs for thirty-five years.

quo. The Marxist-Leninist view of history may (as I believe) be basically flawed, and its projection of a particular pattern of world revolutionary change in error. But it does provide a flexible framework for accepting ebb and flow in the correlation of forces in the world. In many other respects, however, the Soviet leaders display little flexibility.

In retrospect, the Soviets were wrong in their evaluation that the United States was ready to accept the changed correlation of forces as they appeared to *Soviet* leaders in the early 1970s. While the Soviets have not directly acknowledged that error, they have had to recognize the fact of a changed American outlook and policy, a change that they ascribe to a victory for unreconciled foes of détente in the United States.

The Soviets have been reluctant to see that their own erroneous expectations about other aspects of détente also contributed to the deterioration of relations from the mid-1970s to the close of the decade. In particular, the Soviet leaders harbored illusions not only that the United States was ready to accept changes in the third world but, even more, that it would regard active Soviet support for "progressive" changes in the third world as compatible with Soviet-American détente.

The Soviet approach has also been based on an implicit double standard with respect to waging the ideological struggle under peaceful coexistence. That approach assumes that it is all right and consistent with détente for the Soviet Union to carry on such a struggle in the capitalist and third worlds, but that the same does not apply to the United States or others within the socialist world. The Soviet distinction between state and other activities is too contrived and too biased to Soviet advantage, given the disparities in the extent of state control in communist countries as compared with that in many others. The Soviet effort to distinguish the impact of such activities on *state relations* is more valid. But in the West state relations cannot be insulated from other activities. Moreover, waging a political and ideological struggle tends to undermine, if it does not contradict, declared desires for increasing trust and confidence, and ultimately even the ability to conduct a policy of détente. This observation is not meant to suggest that the Soviet Union alone has been engaging in political and ideological competition, only that there was an internal contradiction in the Soviet conception and expectation as to what could be done under détente.

In general, the Soviet leaders expected in the 1970s to achieve more clout in international affairs as a result of their increased relative power than they were able to obtain. As a result, they pursued policies that contributed to undercutting support for détente in the United States and that antagonized elements of world opinion not only in the West but in the third world. The Soviet intervention in Afghanistan is the clearest example, and one that also illustrates an inability to control events not only in terms of reactions elsewhere, but within Afghanistan itself.[81]

---

81. See chapter 26 for a detailed analysis of Soviet involvement and intervention in Afghanistan.

The Soviet belief that the United States had accepted military parity, and that the two sides could agree on what constituted parity and could succeed in controlling the arms race, also proved too optimistic, a subject addressed shortly.

Finally, while it is possible to take issue with the premises and aims of Soviet policy, as I do, it is harder to argue either that the Soviet policy has been inconsistent with *their* conception of détente, or that they have deluded the West about their understanding of the meaning of détente, or to speak of Soviet violation of détente—in the context of an interpretation that they never accepted and have openly and consistently rejected.

The real task is both to clarify and enlarge the areas of common interest on which cooperation can be built, and to identify and seek to manage the continuing competition in the large areas of diverging and conflicting interest which remain. This task was *not* sufficiently understood or pursued in the 1970s by the leaders on either side.

Parity and Détente

Détente in the 1970s was predicated on parity. The emergence, or at least the symbolic and prospective emergence, of strategic nuclear parity between the United States and the Soviet Union, and a presumptive rough overall military parity between the two alliances, contributed to a foundation on which the two superpowers believed they could achieve arms limitations and broader political cooperation in defined areas of mutual interest, notwithstanding their continuing status as adversaries. Strategic parity was implicitly acknowledged as the basis for the SALT process, analyzed in a succeeding chapter. Its role as a basis for the broader political relationships between the United States and the Soviet Union—and as a factor affecting Soviet political aims and actions—has, on the other hand, been too little appreciated.

Soviet acceptance and advocacy of military parity, and disavowal of military superiority, in the 1970s (and continuing under the more strained circumstances of the 1980s) have not been accorded the attention they deserve. To be sure, Soviet assertions that the levels of existing and programmed strategic forces are designed only to maintain parity with American forces must be judged on the merits of an objective evaluation of actual developments, rather than being accepted on faith. And such evaluation is no easy task, given the differences in the structures of the forces, differing political and geographic strategic situations, and uncertainties about future needs of the two sides. Moreover, differences in perspective affect judgments by both sides of their own requirements and of the objectives of the other side in developing its military forces, and significantly affect the very process of evaluation.[82] None-

---

82. See Raymond L. Garthoff, *Perspectives on the Strategic Balance* (Brookings Institution, 1983).

theless, while assertions of an aim of maintaining parity and not seeking superiority may not say much about capabilities, they do purport to express an intention in a way that establishes a limiting standard that both sides can accept. And they thereby provide a basis for agreement on a *principle* that can be used in the strategic arms limitation dialogue to support concrete constraints directed at preserving forces which both sides acknowledge as representing parity.

During the cold war period, many would have considered Soviet acceptance of the very principle of parity to be an achievement (although, of course, no substitute for concrete arms limitations). Yet when it occurred in the 1970s, this was virtually ignored. There have been no authoritative Soviet statements advocating superiority as a goal since the Twenty-fourth Party Congress in 1971, and to the contrary, since the beginning of 1977 everyone from Politburo members and marshals to hawkish political colonels have consistently and explicitly disavowed superiority.

This Soviet acceptance of parity and renunciation of superiority is of political significance both domestically and internationally. While such declaratory policy may appear merely to be propaganda, in fact it does make a difference. It is highly unlikely that Soviet military programs are justified internally in terms at variance with programmatic Communist party doctrine, which now incorporates détente and military parity as firm aims of Soviet policy. New military requirements have to be justified in terms consonant with parity. Moreover, a consistent public renunciation of superiority and acceptance of parity has to have an internal political effect.

Internationally, the Soviets cannot reasonably expect political benefits from a military superiority that they deny they have or aspire to. Regrettably, in past decades many in the United States have often alleged actual or imminent Soviet military superiority, based on bomber, missile, civil defense, and military spending gaps. It is now acknowledged that that superiority did not exist. Since the latter 1970s, the assertion of Soviet superiority has been made again, with much hue and cry. Undoubtedly the concern is often genuine. Frequently, however, those who consider increased American military programs necessary either to ensure parity or to reacquire superiority sound the alarm to gain support. It is true that Soviet strategic military power has increased enormously—but so has that of the United States.

Most would agree that during the 1970s the Soviet Union moved from nominal to real parity with American strategic nuclear power. As of the mid-1980s, although some would say that one or the other side has an edge, most acknowledge a general parity. In the United States, however, many voice great concern that this country will slide into inferiority, while in the Soviet Union similar concern is expressed over what is perceived to be an alleged American intention and active military program to upset the strategic balance in pursuit of superiority.

Part of the issue is that parity has a different significance to American and Soviet leaders. Even if there were no problems in defining or assuring strategic parity, and even assuming a readiness on both sides to accept parity, that state still holds radically different implications for the two sides.

For the leaders of the Soviet Union, parity with the leading imperialist power—and American acknowledgment of that status—was and is a tremendous achievement, an unprecedented advance over the inferiority which had characterized the entire two-thirds of a century of Soviet rule. Soviet leaders have assumed that attainment of parity in strategic power, and its recognition as one of the two global superpowers, confer a special status that should connote equality in rights for world behavior. From Moscow's standpoint, the United States has long enjoyed rights that the Soviet Union has not been able fully to exercise. A double standard has been applied that allows the United States—but not the Soviet Union—the right to ply the world's oceans and seas, to have military bases up to the very borders of the other power, and to intervene in order to support or to depose rulers of small- and medium-size countries (such as Iran in 1953, Guatemala in 1954, Lebanon in 1958, Brazil in 1964, the Dominican Republic in 1965, South Vietnam in 1955–75, Chile in 1973, and Grenada in 1983). In the past, America's overbearing power even meant that it could impose direct restraints on the Soviet Union, preventing an equal exercise of sovereign rights, to say nothing of precluding Soviet resort to comparable extralegal rights of intervention beyond its acknowledged sphere of influence in Eastern Europe. The most glaring, and to the Soviets painful, instance was the unilateral American action in 1962 that compelled the Soviets to withdraw their missiles from Cuba. The installation of the missiles in an allied country with its approval had been entirely in accordance with international law, and, moreover, it concorded with American practice. It is not surprising that at the earliest opportunity the Soviet Union sought—although without success—to test its budding position of parity to redefine less constrictively that restraint on Soviet weapons in Cuba (in 1970, as described later).

For the United States, parity undoubtedly has represented a situation of *less* advantage than in the preceding era of American superiority, an era that encompassed the entire third of a century since its assumption of a continuing active global role at the end of World War II. The United States had not sought its superiority and hegemonic role, nor, for that matter, did it really strive to retain it (to the chagrin of some). Nevertheless, it had become accustomed to its exercise and its fruits.

American acquiescence in the loss of superiority, a situation that evolved gradually during the period roughly through the 1970s, was conditioned principally on a recognition by the Johnson-Nixon-Ford administrations of the inevitable end to a historically ephemeral period of American nuclear supremacy. Short of the morally and practically unacceptable option of initiating a nuclear war, there was no way to prevent eventual Soviet acquisition of a strategic nuclear capability essentially matching (though not negating) the nuclear deterrent of the United States. *Mutual* deterrence was inevitable, although its timing and the nature of the strategic military relationship were to some degree dependent on American actions and military programs.

American acceptance of an implied parity in mutual deterrence even well in advance of the fact was politically remarkable. At the height of the cold war, the United States had proclaimed a doctrine of "massive retaliation," with the American deterrent to serve as a shield not only against Soviet attack on the United States and its allies, but initially against all manner of "communist encroachments" around the world. Yet even then, as early as December 1953, President Dwight D. Eisenhower also stated that the outcome of a nuclear war between the "two atomic colossi" would be the destruction of world civilization.[83] While American policy continued to be based on the existing balance of power with its American superiority, recognition of the unacceptability of nuclear war save as a last resort to a direct attack by the enemy on the United States or its allies, and recognition of the inevitable Soviet acquisition of a similar nuclear deterrent, grew through succeeding administrations.

During the mid- and late 1960s, the war in Vietnam largely absorbed American attention. The rapid growth of Soviet strategic power in the late 1960s and attainment of a parity of mutual deterrent power was, however, clearly anticipated and accepted by Secretary of Defense Robert S. McNamara[84]—and, perhaps with less clear recognition, by the Johnson administration and the nation as a whole. There were, to be sure, voices of protest at the time, and still more in later years, arguing that the United States should seek strenuously to retain (or, later, to regain) superiority and to contest Soviet attainment of parity. But they were muted by the general focus on Vietnam and other issues, and by wide acceptance of the idea of negotiated arms control, an approach that at least tacitly accepted parity.

Acceptance of the shift from American superiority to parity was bipartisan (as has been the current of dissent). President Nixon showed his acceptance at the very outset of his administration by discarding his rhetorical campaign call "to restore our objective of clear-cut military superiority"[85] and substituting as a goal strategic "sufficiency."[86] While ambiguity and some controversy over what would constitute "sufficiency" remained, the goal of superiority was never again raised, and the later record made clear that Nixon (and his successors through the 1970s) had accepted nuclear parity with the Soviet

---

83. "Address before the General Assembly of the United Nations on Peaceful Uses of Atomic Energy, December 8, 1953," *Public Papers of the Presidents: Dwight D. Eisenhower, 1953* (GPO, 1960), p. 817.

84. See Robert S. McNamara, *The Essence of Security: Reflections in Office* (Harper and Row, 1968), pp. 51–67.

85. Richard Nixon, CBS Television Address, "Defense Dialogue," October 24, 1968. During most of his campaign, however, Nixon had sought to avoid assertions concerning the strategic balance. See Whalen, *Catch the Falling Flag*, pp. 64–65, 72–74.

86. "The President's News Conference of January 27, 1969," *Presidential Documents*, vol. 5 (February 3, 1969), p. 178. Nixon expressed a preference for the term "sufficiency" over either "superiority" or "parity"; only some time later did he specifically endorse parity or equality. Nevertheless, the basic shift had been made on this early occasion.

Union.[87] This acceptance of parity was, moreover, indirectly related to the parallel decisions to seek a shift from an era of confrontation to an era of negotiation and, more specifically, to proceed with negotiations on SALT.

Nixon deserves considerable credit for his readiness to accept the idea of strategic parity as sufficient to meet American defense needs, and thus as a basis for negotiation with the Soviet Union. (This is particularly so given that less than a year and a half earlier, when Nixon had foreseen that "the Soviets may reach nuclear parity with the United States" in the decade of the 1970s, he had concluded that such a development could contribute to creating "a crisis of the first order").[88] His acceptance of parity reflected a certain maturity of judgment and recognition of the basically defensive orientation of American interests in the world. At the same time, it is probably fair to say that Nixon's acceptance of parity was also facilitated by a *lack* of understanding at the time of some of the political implications of this shift.[89] In addition, there was virtually no national public discussion of the issue in the United States.

President Nixon acknowledged the fundamental significance of parity when he discounted superiority because "there is a point in arms development at which each nation has the capacity to destroy the other. Beyond that point the most important consideration is not continued escalation of the number of arms but maintenance of the strategic equilibrium while making it clear to the adversary that a nuclear attack, even if successful, would be suicidal."[90] Kissinger also defined "strategic equality" as meaning that "whoever may be ahead in the damage they can inflict on the other, the damage to the other in a general nuclear war will be of a catastrophic nature."[91] And "each side has the capacity to destroy civilization as we know it."[92]

Soviet spokesmen and commentators have also defined parity as basically the mutual capability to destroy one another: "Parity does not mean

87. See Nixon, *RN*, p. 415; the discussion in Jerome H. Kahan, *Security in the Nuclear Age: Developing U.S. Strategic Arms Policy* (Brookings Institution, 1975), pp. 142–50; and the very useful analysis by I. F. Stone, "Nixon and the Arms Race: How Much Is 'Sufficiency'?" *New York Review of Books*, March 27, 1969, pp. 6–18.

88. Richard M. Nixon, "Asia after Viet Nam," *Foreign Affairs*, vol. 46 (October 1967), p. 122.

89. When Nixon praised the shift to parity in a talk with Brezhnev in 1973, Kissinger comments, "This was the only time in my association with him that his usual sure touch deserted him in talking to a Communist leader." Kissinger himself, writing years later, states that he believed strategic parity "was bound sooner or later to turn into a strategic nightmare for us, freeing the Soviet superiority in conventional forces for intervention in regional conflicts." Kissinger, *Years of Upheaval*, p. 1292.

90. Nixon, *RN*, p. 415.

91. "Secretary Kissinger's News Conference of December 23 [1975]," *State Bulletin*, vol. 74 (January 19, 1976), p. 70.

92. Secretary of State Henry Kissinger, "Détente with the Soviet Union: The Reality of Competition and the Imperative of Cooperation," Statement to the Senate Committee on Foreign Relations, September 19, *State Bulletin*, vol. 71 (October 14, 1974), p. 512.

absolute equality of available means. It means that we can mutually destroy each other with sufficient certainty."[93]

American acceptance of parity in strategic military power in the 1970s was genuine and was reflected in the SALT negotiations. *Political* parity has been another matter. Nor, for that matter, did the Soviet leaders really expect the leaders of the United States gratuitously to yield equality in political influence, alliances, economic power, or other sources and manifestations of national power. The Soviet leaders are not moved by altruism and do not expect American leaders to be. What they have sought was parity in terms of their *status* as a superpower—including equal application of rules of international behavior. This aspiration has not been overtly, or perhaps even consciously, rejected by the American side, but neither has it been granted or accepted in practice.

Soviet acceptance of strategic parity has not presented the same problem of conceding political parity, because the Soviet Union had not heretofore enjoyed advantages derived from predominant global military power. The Soviet leaders have shown no disposition whatsoever to relinquish any equality of status to the United States within the area of established Soviet hegemony. On the other hand, they appear to have accepted realistically a tacit area of American hegemony within which they too have shown restraint (in the NATO area and—despite American claims to the contrary—in the Western Hemisphere other than Cuba). In the third world as a whole, however, they seek parity of access, opportunity, and competition. In ideological terms, as was observed earlier (and will be discussed later in concrete cases), they have insisted upon the right to support national liberation movements and socialist states in the third world. The essence of the matter has not been, however, ideological commitment (genuine though that may be)—it is a question of power. And under conditions of global strategic parity, they have sought global parity in competing on local ground (and seas) without either side resorting to its nuclear power, or to any overt use of its military power except in very special cases.

The Soviet calculus of relative power is expressed in terms of the "correlation of forces" between any two competitors, including adversaries in international politics.[94] The forces being weighed in such an assessment of

---

93. [Col.] D. Proektor, interview in *La Stampa* (Rome), November 7, 1979; see also A. Bovin, Budapest Domestic Television Service, July 5, 1979, in FBIS, *Soviet Union*, July 10, 1979, p. AA1; and G. Trofimenko, *Nepszabadsag* (Budapest), September 24, 1980, in FBIS, *Soviet Union*, September 29, 1980, p. AA2.

94. For an extensive analysis of the Soviet concept of "the relation (or correlation) of forces," see Garthoff, *Soviet Military Policy*, pp. 77–97; and Michael J. Deane, "The Soviet Assessment of the 'Correlation of World Forces': Implications for American Foreign Policy," *Orbis*, vol. 20 (Fall 1976), pp. 625–36. For Soviet discussions, see G. Shakhnazarov, "On the Problem of the Correlation of Forces in the World," *Kommunist*, no. 3 (February 1974), pp. 77–89; Sh. Sanakoyev, "The World Today: Problem of the Correlation of Forces," *International Affairs*, no. 11 (November 1974), pp. 40–50; Georgi Shakhnazarov, "The Victory—The World Balance

power comprise the full range of tangible and intangible economic, military, political, diplomatic, and psychological elements Military power, which includes strategic nuclear offensive and defensive military forces, is but one element of this power—important, indeed essential, but not the determining element.[95] This attitude is an important divergence from the American tendency to stress a more direct (and abstract) comparison of military capabilities and even inventories of weapons. The Soviet approach not only gives greater attention to other aspects of power (especially psychological and diplomatic), but also views military power, and therefore relationships in military power, in a broader context that encompasses *all* forms of power at the disposal of a state, and with more attention to the potential political *utility* of military power.

The Soviets have always expressed optimism with respect to the overall correlation of forces between the Soviet Union and the United States and between the socialist camp and the imperialist camp (the more usual comparison). Since 1947 they have spoken regularly of a shift in this relation "to the advantage of socialism."[96] They have not, however, spoken of a shift to an absolute imbalance in favor of the socialist camp (although this is an interpretation that has, erroneously, often been made in the West). Indeed, it is not clear whether the Soviet leaders believe there is even now overall parity between the two camps, although they wish to cultivate that impression and claim parity. In any case, they see the relative improvement in the military position of the USSR as having created a rough strategic parity with the United States and in turn as an important element in the shift in the global relationship in a favorable direction. More concretely, they see this shift as having made possible not only the strategic arms limitations, but détente itself, in the 1970s.

Soviet political and military analysts date the attainment of strategic parity (or a strategic balance or equilibrium) between the Soviet Union and the United States to the end of the 1960s and beginning of the 1970s. The essence of this change was that now no longer was only the Soviet Union vulnerable: "By the beginning of the 1970s not only the fact of the absolute vulnerability of American territory, but also the inevitability of a crushing

of Strength—Peaceful Co-existence," *New Times* (Moscow), no. 19 (May 1975); pp. 4–6; and A. Sergiyev, "Leninism on the Correlation of Forces As a Factor of International Relations," *International Affairs*, no. 5 (May 1975), pp. 99–107.

95. For example, see O. Bykov, "Strengthening the Balance or Gambling on Superiority?" *MEiMO*, no. 11 (November 1981), pp. 19–31; Yuri Zhilin and Andrei Yermonsky, "Once More on the World Balance of Strength," *New Times*, no. 46 (November 1980), pp. 18–19; and Yu. Davydov and L. Berzin, "The Correlation of Forces in the International Arena and the Ideological Struggle," *Mezhdunarodnaya zhizn'*, no. 11 (November 1983), p. 20.

96. Thus, for example, Lebedev attributed the change in the correlation of forces "to the advantage of socialism" to two main developments—the creation of the socialist system of states after World War II, and the collapse of the old colonial empires—and not to increasing Soviet military power. See Lebedev, *Mezhdunarodnaya zhizn'*, no. 12 (December 1975), pp. 6–7.

retaliatory strike if the United States delivered a nuclear missile strike against the USSR, had become completely evident to everyone in the American ruling class."[97]

Particularly since the late 1970s, Soviet analysts have admitted that, in terms of concrete measures of the balance, parity was in some respects and in some degree nominal in the late 1960s and early 1970s: the United States still had a margin of superiority, despite the clear basis for mutual deterrence and equality in some quantitative indexes. They say this in terms of a retrospective recognition that some *American* leaders considered they still had this margin. Thus, the Nixon administration in 1972, even while publicly acknowledging parity, "still continued to believe that the United States was militarily superior to the Soviet Union to some degree."[98] But this situation was transient. "Whatever the perceptions of the American political leaders and strategists at the beginning of the 1970s, by the end of the decade they had to realize and officially acknowledge that the strategic arms of the two sides were equivalent not only in quantitative but also in qualitative respects."[99] Sometimes the situation is stated in terms that "the military-strategic capabilities of the USSR and the U.S. are approximately the same."[100]

In addition to strategic parity between the United States and the Soviet Union, the Soviets also ascribe a general parity between the military power of NATO and the Warsaw Pact. The general Soviet position has been that parity has existed throughout the 1970s, although with growing American efforts in the latter years of the decade and in the 1980s to upset it in a quest for superiority.[101]

---

97. For example, see A. Arbatov, "A Strategy of Nuclear Recklessness," *Kommunist*, no. 6 (April 1981), p. 103; G. A. Trofimenko, *SShA: politika, voina, ideologiya* [U.S. Politics, War, Ideology] (Moscow: Nauka, 1976), pp. 271–77; G. I. Mirsky, "International Observers Roundtable," Radio Moscow, August 5, in FBIS, *Soviet Union*, August 6, 1979, p. CC2; V. Teplov, "To Uphold the Policy of Detente," *International Affairs*, no. 5 (May 1980), p. 103; G. A. Trofimenko, "U.S. Foreign Policy in the Seventies: Words and Deeds," *SShA*, no. 12 (December 1976), pp. 15, 19; Yu. Davydov, "The U.S. and the Conference on European Security and Cooperation," *SShA*, no. 10 (October 1975), p. 6; and Maj. Gen. M. Cherednichenko, "Military Strategy and Military Technology," *Voyennaya mysl'* [Military Thought], no. 4 (April 1973), pp. 41–42. Some later commentaries say that parity was attained "in the 1970s." See S. Menshikov, "Militarism and World Politics Today," *International Affairs*, no. 2 (February 1984), p. 17. And some concede that "real parity" was not achieved until *late* in the 1970s. See G.A. Trofimenko, "The Military Strategy of the United States—Weapon of an Aggressive Policy," *SShA*, no. 1 (January 1985), p. 12.

98. G. A. Trofimenko, "Washington's Strategic Forays," *SShA*, no. 12 (December 1980), p. 53.

99. Ibid.

100. A. A. Platonov, "A Major Achievement in the Area of Arms Limitation," *SShA*, no. 9 (September 1979), pp. 14–15. "A. A. Platonov" is a pseudonym for the former head of the Soviet SALT delegation, Deputy Foreign Minister Vladimir S. Semenov.

101. See Aleksei Arbatov, *Voyenno-strategicheskii paritet i politika SShA* [Military-Strategic Parity and U.S. Policy] (Moscow: Politizdat, 1984), for the most thorough and documented presentation.

Parity in the strategic balance has thus been seen as a major development contributing to a favorable trend in the shift of the overall correlation of forces, a point often noted by Soviet political leaders.[102] The overall significance of the Soviet attainment of parity was well expressed at the important plenum of the Communist Party Central Committee that reevaluated détente following the Carter administration's scuttling of American-Soviet cooperation after Afghanistan. The plenum report declared: "The military strategic balance which has been achieved between the world of socialism and the world of capitalism is a gain of fundamental historic significance. It serves as a factor containing [or, deterring] the aggressive strivings of imperialism, which accords with the vital interests of all peoples. Calculations on destabilizing this balance are doomed to failure."[103]

In terms of international politics, the significance of attaining parity was reflected in Foreign Minister Gromyko's words to the Twenty-fourth Party Congress in 1971: "Today there is no question of any importance which can be decided without the Soviet Union or in opposition to it."[104] Parity is also depicted as stabilizing international security: "The political significance of a stable strategic balance is indisputable; it is the guarantee not only of the security of the two sides, but of international security as a whole."[105] And "the existing military-strategic parity undoubtedly exerts a stabilizing effect on the international situation."[106] Hence the Soviet conclusion that "in the interests

---

102. For example, see Politburo members N. V. Podgorny, *Izvestiya*, February 13, 1975; and M. A. Suslov, *Pravda*, April 23, 1975. See also G. Arbatov, "The Power of Realistic Policy: On the Results of the High-Level Soviet-U.S. Talks," *Izvestiya*, June 22, 1972; and [Col.] L. Semeyko, "The [U.S.] Course toward Military Superiority," *Krasnaya zvezda* [Red Star], March 24, 1979.

103. *Materialy plenuma tsentral'nogo komiteta KPSS, 23 iyuniya 1980 g.* [Materials of the Plenum of the Central Committee of the CPSU, June 23, 1980] (Moscow, 1980), p. 13. The Russian word *sderzhivayushchyi* can be translated either as "containing" or "deterring," and is in fact used in translating both American terms as well as applying to both in original Soviet usage.

104. A. Gromyko, in *XXIV s'yezd kommunisticheskoi partii sovetskogo soyuza, 30 marta–9 aprelya 1971 goda: stenograficheskiy otchet* [XXIV Congress of the Communist Party of the Soviet Union, March 30–April 9, 1971: Stenographic Account] (Moscow: Politizdat, 1971), vol. 1, p. 482.

    Too much should not, however, be read into this statement. Some in the United States have interpreted it as foreshadowing an activist global policy based on a presumption of a new military advantage. Yet the Soviet leaders have said much the same thing ever since World War II. Compare, for example, Foreign Minister Vyacheslav M. Molotov's statement of February 6, 1946: "The USSR has now become one of the most authoritative world powers. Today important problems in international relations cannot be settled without the participation of the Soviet Union or without heeding the voice of our Motherland." V. M. Molotov, *Voprosy vneshnei politiki* [Questions of Foreign Policy] (Moscow: OGIZ, 1948), pp. 24–25.

105. Semeyko, *Krasnaya zvezda*, March 24, 1979.

106. A. Platonov [V. Semenov], "The Military Balance and the Preservation of Peace," *Mezhdunarodnaya zhizn'*, no. 1 (January 1982), p. 50; and see Bykov, *MEiMO*, no. 11 (1981), p. 19; and Petrovsky, *Novaya i noveishaya istoriya*, no. 1 (1981), p. 10.

of maintaining international security neither side should take measures to change it [the existing approximate strategic balance between East and West] in its favor."[107] The problem comes, of course, in the differing perceptions that each side has of the actions of the other seeking to change the balance in its favor.

In the Soviet view, attainment of strategic parity with the United States "has become a distinguishing feature of the new stage of international relations."[108] Parity thus provided the foundation for détente[109] and specifically for military détente and strategic arms limitation talks.[110]

From the Soviet standpoint, while the objective fact of parity is of fundamental importance, American *recognition* and implied acceptance of it is also a matter of key significance. The emergence of strategic parity was "an objective process of change in the correlation of forces in the world arena (which, of course, is the main thing), and also the recognition of this real fact by bourgeois political leaders and theorists."[111] Academician Georgy A. Arbatov stressed in 1972 that "the correlation of forces is not some abstract formula but perceptible reality which *compels* the imperialist powers to adjust to the new situation."[112] As another Soviet analyst observed, "The official recognition of strategic parity between the U.S. and the USSR by President R. Nixon, a recognition that the U.S. could not change that equilibrium—at least in the

107. V. Shestov, "Struggle for Disarmament: Achievements, Difficulties and Prospects," *International Affairs*, no. 2 (February 1981), p. 99. "V. Shestov" is the pseudonym of V. V. Shustov, a leading Soviet diplomat specializing in disarmament.

108. A. Arbatov, *Bezopasnost' v yadernyi vek i politika Vashingtona* [Security in the Nuclear Age and Washington's Policy] (Moscow: Politizdat, 1980), p. 213.

109. Of many such statements, see, for example, V. Petrovsky, "Dogmas of Confrontation (On American Concepts of 'Global Conflict')," *MEiMO*, no. 2 (February 1980), p. 25; O. Bykov, "The Main Problem for Humanity," *MEiMO*, no. 3 (March 1980), p. 6; Bykov, *MEiMO*, no. 11 (1981), p. 19; and A. Voronov, "The Chimera of Military Superiority," *International Affairs*, no. 2 (February 1980), p. 21.

110. For example, Arbatov, *Voyenno-strategicheskii paritet*, p. 3, states that strategic parity is "the *only* possible basis for agreements constraining the arms race and the main bulwark of a policy of preventing thermonuclear war." Emphasis added. See also the references cited in note 109; L. Brezhnev, *Pravda*, May 4, 1978; V. Zhurkin, "SALT-II: An Important Contribution to Strengthening Peace," *MEiMO*, no. 8 (August 1979), p. 7; [Col.] Ye. Rybkin and S. Kortunov, "Military Parity as a Factor for Security," *Mezhdunarodnaya zhizn'*, no. 7 (July 1982), p. 59; [Lt. Gen. Ret.] M. A. Mil'shtein, "At a Dangerous Crossroads (Concerning Certain Trends in Washington's Current Military Policy)," *SShA*, no. 10 (October 1978), p. 5; and A. Bovin, Radio Moscow Domestic Service, "The SALT II Treaty—An Important Step in Curbing the Arms Race," June 19, in FBIS, *Soviet Union*, June 20, 1979, pp. AA6–7.

111. Literally, the last two nouns would be translated "politicians" and "ideologues," but in both cases such literalness would obscure the intended meaning. Platonov, *SShA*, no. 9 (1979), p. 15.

112. G. A. Arbatov, "An Event of World Significance," *SShA*, no. 8 (August 1972), p. 9. Emphasis added.

1970s—had an enormous influence on the foreign policy thinking of the ruling circles of the United States and on the alignment of forces in Washington."[113] Other Soviet observers have stressed that American recognition of parity in the early 1970s—even if not always reconciliation to its continued acceptance in the future—was based on the "objective reality" of "the formation of an over-all equilibrium in the strategic balance between the USSR and the U.S." That recognition was not granted as a "gift to the Soviet Union."[114] Finally, not only was emerging parity the necessary foundation for SALT, but "the official U.S. recognition of parity with the USSR is the very essence of the Soviet-American agreements on limiting strategic arms (SALT I and SALT II), signed in 1972 and 1979."[115]

It may be asked how, or whether, acceptance of strategic parity with the United States (and between the camp of socialism and the camp of capital-ism) could be ideologically permissible to Marxist-Leninists. It may be further questioned whether the Soviet leaders have, in fact, accepted a state of parity and are willing to continue it.

Soviet leaders and spokesmen have been clear on both points. So-viet military leaders, in confidential publications not openly available, made plain as early as 1969 that a nuclear balance had developed between the Soviet Union and the United States involving parity in the capacity for devastating retaliation and therefore mutual deterrence.[116] This state of nuclear balance or equilibrium, or strategic parity, between the two superpowers and between the NATO and Warsaw Pact alliances has been authoritatively acknowledged on numerous occasions by Brezhnev, Andropov, Chernenko, and other Politburo leaders, military leaders, and other spokesmen and commentators throughout the 1970s and 1980s. Since the beginning of 1977, it has been supplemented by reiterations that the Soviet Union wants to preserve the balance and will not seek military superiority—nor concede such superiority to the other side. The most authoritative statement was in the General Secretary's Report of the Central Committee to the Twenty-sixth Party Congress in February 1981: "The military strategic balance prevailing between the USSR and the U.S., and between the Warsaw Pact and NATO, objectively serves to safeguard

---

113. A. A. Kokoshin, "Internal Reasons for the Turn in Foreign Policy," *SShA*, no. 7 (July 1980), p. 3.

114. G. A. Arbatov, "Strategic Parity and the Policy of the Carter Administration," *SShA*, no. 11 (November 1980), p. 30.

115. G. A. Trofimenko, "The Principal Postulates of American Foreign Policy and the Fate of Détente," *SShA*, no. 7 (July 1981), pp. 8–9.

116. See, in particular, General of the Army S. P. Ivanov, "Soviet Military Doctrine and Strategy," *Voyennaya mysl'*, no. 5 (May 1969), p. 47; and Maj. Gen. V. I. Zemskov, "Wars of the Contemporary Era," *Voyennaya mysl'*, no. 5 (May 1969), p. 57. See also the extended discus-sion of this general subject in Raymond L. Garthoff, "Mutual Deterrence, Parity and Strate-gic Arms Limitation in Soviet Policy," in Derek Leebaert, ed., *Soviet Military Thinking* (London: George Allen and Unwin, 1981), pp. 92–124.

world peace. We have not sought, nor are we now seeking, military superiority over the other side. This is not our policy. But neither will we permit such a superiority over us to be established."[117] On other occasions Brezhnev specifically declared: "We do not want to upset the approximate balance of military power that now exists . . . between the USSR and the U.S."[118] And, "the Soviet Union for its part considers that approximate equality and parity are sufficient for defense needs. It is not our aim to seek military superiority. We understand that this very concept loses meaning today in the face of the enormous arsenals of nuclear weapons and delivery means already accumulated."[119] And Konstantin Chernenko, shortly before succeeding Andropov, restated that the "balance of military forces which had come into being in the international arena" along with the general correlation of social-political forces, made the avoidance of war and peaceful coexistence possible.[120]

Soviet theoreticians reconcile their ideological expectations of a continuous progressive shift in the correlation of forces in the world with acceptance of continuing strategic military parity by arguing that there is no contradiction in the maintenance of "military-strategic parity" while "the overall balance of strength in the world continues to change in favor of peace and socialism."[121] Thus Soviet writers argue strongly against the idea that stabilizing strategic parity means stabilizing the correlation of forces in the political (and class) struggle in the world. Peaceful coexistence based on strategic parity "does not and cannot mean some kind of status quo between socialism and capitalism."[122] Further, "when we speak in Party documents about changes in the correlation of forces and that it will continue to change in favor of the forces of peace, democracy and socialism, we are talking about the relation of social-political, class forces. As for the military component of the correlation of forces in the international arena, the Soviet position on their significance is clear and unambiguous." Along with renunciation of any aim of superiority, this statement added that the aim of Soviet policy is "the consolidation and preservation of the balance, parity, of the two counterposed military forces."[123]

117. L. I. Brezhnev, "Report of the Central Committee of the C.P.S.U. to the XXVI Congress of the Communist Party of the Soviet Union and the Immediate Tasks of the Party in Domestic and Foreign Policy," *Pravda*, February 24, 1981. The word translated as "balance," *ravnovesie*, could equally be rendered as "equilibrium."

118. L. I. Brezhnev, "The Great October Revolution and the Progress of Mankind," *Pravda*, November 3, 1977.

119. Brezhnev, *Pravda*, May 4, 1978.

120. Chernenko, *Izbrannye rechi i stat'i*, p. 637.

121. Zhilin and Yermonsky, *New Times*, no. 46 (1980), p. 19.

122. Shakhnazarov, *Kommunist*, no. 3 (1974), p. 88; and see Zhilin and Yermonsky, *New Times*, no. 46 (1980), p. 19.

123. V. K. Vadimov, *Chto kroetsya za mifom o 'sovetskoi voyennoi ugroze'* [What Is Left Out in the Myth of the 'Soviet Military Threat'] (Moscow: Znaniye, 1980), p. 27.

Soviet commentators have gone on to say that even if the socialist bloc had military superiority, "the nature of socialism is alien to any gamble on victory at the cost of the death of millions of people and the destruction of material achievements in the flames of war."[124] Or, as Brezhnev put it to the Party Congress in 1981, using straightforward, nonideological terms, "to count on victory in a nuclear war is dangerous madness."[125] Brezhnev's colleagues and later successors, Yury V. Andropov and Konstantin U. Chernenko, made simi lar statements in major leadership pronouncements.[126]

The Soviet position is that the official acknowledgment of parity by both sides refers not only to the existing parity of the 1970s to date, but also to the future. "With respect to the global correlation of forces between the strongest powers of the two military-political blocs, that is the Soviet Union and the United States, as has been officially recognized by both sides an approximate parity, that is a balance of strategic forces, has developed *and will be preserved.*"[127] Often cited is the official U.S.-USSR communiqué issued at the close of the Vienna summit meeting in 1979, which included a specific commitment by both sides that each "is not striving and will not strive for military superiority."[128] To sum up the Soviet position, "The Soviet Union proceeds from the assumption that there exists today an approximate military-strategic balance between East and West and that in the interests of maintaining international security neither side should take measures to change it in its favor. That is an important prerequisite for maintaining relations of peaceful coexistence."[129]

Beginning in 1977, however, and with increasing momentum in the early 1980s, Soviet leaders and commentators have argued that the United States has refused to reconcile itself to parity and has again embarked on a pursuit of strategic superiority.[130] Throughout the 1970s they warned that

---

124. Shakhnazarov, *Kommunist*, no. 3 (1974), p. 88.

125. Brezhnev, *Pravda*, February 24, 1981.

126. See Yu. V. Andropov, *Pravda*, April 23, 1982; and K. U. Chernenko, *Pravda*, April 23, 1981. These statements were made in speeches on behalf of the leadership on the anniversary of Vladimir I. Lenin's birth. Both later repeated this view after succeeding Brezhnev in the leadership.

127. Brezhnev, *Pravda*, May 4, 1978. Emphasis added.

128. "Joint U.S.-U.S.S.R. Communique, Vienna, June 18," *Vienna Summit, June 15–18, 1979*, Department of State, Selected Documents, no. 13 (GPO, 1979), pp. 6–7.

129. Shestov, *International Affairs*, no. 2 (1981), p. 99.

130. For example, see A. Arbatov, "The Military-Strategic Balance and the Policy of the Reagan Administration," *MEiMO*, no. 10 (October 1984), pp. 3–14; Trofimenko, *SShA*, no. 7 (1981), p. 11; Shestov, *International Affairs*, no. 2 (1981), p. 98; A. Nikonov and R. Faramazyan, "A Dangerous Policy of Fueling International Tension," *MEiMO*, no. 2 (February 1981), p. 49;

"militaristic circles" continued to seek superiority and wished to upset the strategic balance; in the latter years of the decade they ascribed that aim specifically to the U.S. leadership. In 1978 Brezhnev referred to those in the West (clearly the ruling circles) who "do not wish to reconcile themselves to the approximate parity which has developed between the armed forces of the sides and want to attain superiority."[131] As a sophisticated Soviet analyst of American affairs put it in 1980, chauvinistic hard-line anticommunists in the United States during the latter half of the 1970s succeeded in placing much of the blame for American foreign policy setbacks not on "the unrealistic policy of the fifties and sixties," which he argues was their real source, but instead on détente and "the recognition by Washington of parity with the USSR in strategic arms."[132] Others have charged that those who mount campaigns against the alleged Soviet military threat do so because "in fact, they fear not dreamed up dangers of 'Soviet superiority,' but precisely equality and parity, counting on gaining military superiority for themselves through new efforts in the arms race."[133]

Soviet reaction to the plans of the Reagan administration in 1981 for a military buildup included the argument that the "approximate parity between the Soviet Union and the United States" is not only well-known, but "is, moreover, laid down in international treaties and agreements," so that "if the United States is now developing the arms race, it is doing so not to restore parity, but, on the contrary, to break it and achieve superiority."[134]

The sharply diverging American and Soviet evaluations of the strategic balance, and the impact of these divergences on détente as the 1970s

---

G. Arbatov and V. Falin, "Studio Nine," Moscow Domestic Television, March 2, in FBIS, *Soviet Union*, March 4, 1980, pp. A2–A3; S. Kondrashov, "Capitulation to 'Hawks,' " *Izvestiya*, January 11, 1980; Kondrashov, "International Observers Roundtable," Radio Moscow Domestic Service, January 20, in FBIS, *Soviet Union*, January 21, 1980, p. CC7; and A. Bovin, "The Sowing Wind . . .," *Izvestiya*, January 16, 1980.

131. Brezhnev, *Pravda*, May 4, 1978.

132. G. Trofimenko, "A Policy with No Future (On the So-Called Carter Doctrine)," *MEiMO*, no. 3 (March 1980), p. 20.

133. V. Nekrasov, "An Absurd but Dangerous Myth," *Kommunist*, no. 12 (August 1979), p. 97.

134. Gennady Shishkin, TASS chief foreign news editor, on "International Observers Roundtable," Radio Moscow Domestic Service, February 1, in FBIS, *Soviet Union*, February 2, 1981, p. CC3.

Soviet writers specifically charge that under the Carter administration, "while officially standing for the preservation to a substantial degree of a balance with the Soviet Union in the strategic sphere, the American leadership in reality was gambling on gaining strategic advantages relative to the Soviet Union," and while allegedly seeking only to assure or to restore parity was seeking military superiority. See G. A. Trofimenko, *Voyennaya doktrina SShA* [U.S. Military Doctrine] (Moscow: Znaniye, 1982), p. 33; and [Col.] D. Proektor, "Socialism and International Security," *Kommunist*, no. 7 (May 1977), p. 118. The Reagan administration is seen as pursuing superiority more openly.

unfolded, are discussed later.[135] The Soviet view has been consistent: strategic military parity is essential to assure Soviet security and to support Soviet claims to political parity. While Soviet military advantages beyond parity would be welcomed, the leadership fears that the United States is more likely to attain such advantages. Accordingly, strategic parity should be buttressed by military détente and strategic arms limitations that would curb opportunities for either side to gain advantages. In the Soviet view, strategic parity in a general sense would be very difficult for either side to upset. At the same time, parity has not yet been firmly established, and the United States might be able to gain significant advantages on the margin. Hence the Soviet Union must continue to pursue military programs to prevent the success of intensified efforts by the United States since the late 1970s to regain a degree of superiority, especially since continuing Soviet efforts to reach strategic arms limitations have met with setbacks, including, notably, the U.S. failure to ratify the SALT II Treaty signed in 1979.

The Soviet pursuit of "equal security" as well as parity means that their view of what constitutes "equal" strategic arms limitations goes beyond the prevailing American view. Soviet political (and especially military) leaders consider it essential to look not only at American military power counterposed to their own, but also at other opposing military capabilities, above all of America's allies. This view does not mean the Soviets seek absolute security, as is sometimes argued in the United States. But it does mean at the extreme that the Soviets measure their strategic military requirements against the combined forces of the United States, Britain, France, and even China.[136] In practice, however, the Soviets have shown they will settle for less so long as there is a level of sufficiency to meet their overall requirements, and so long as the forces of the allies of the United States are not a loophole through which the West can gain strategically significant advantages.

In a broader sense equal security is one of the key aspects of parity that makes it a foundation for détente. A secure deterrent for each side, an assumed capability to retaliate effectively to any attack by the other side, provides a fundamental strategic sufficiency and a real measure of equal security. While the military requirements seen by each side are not reducible to this one element, it does remain the fundamental bedrock to the arms—and arms control—policies of both sides.

Détente may also be seen as related to, and reflecting, a reduced threat. More precisely, the degree of tension or reduction of tension correlates with perceptions of threat. A state of parity and mutual deterrence facilitates political readiness (by leaders and publics) to improve political relationships and to support détente.

---

135. In particular, see chapter 22.

136. For example, see "The Tasks of Strategic Arms Limitation: Problems and Prospects," *Pravda*, February 11, 1978.

Thus the Soviet Union and the United States, at least through the 1970s, saw parity as a sufficient basis for meeting national security requirements, and hence as providing a foundation for détente, and more specifically for strategic arms limitation. Remaining problems in measuring parity of forces, and especially security, however, make difficult the task of reaching agreements that both sides see as mutually advantageous. Each side has been suspicious that the other is seeking military advantages and a degree of superiority. Nevertheless, the joint acceptance in the 1970s of parity as a standard for both sides, even if difficult to measure, was an important advance and provided a conceptual basis for possible agreements under favorable political circumstances.

In the latter half of the 1970s and first half of the 1980s, however, both Moscow and Washington grew increasingly suspicious that the other side was attempting to upset parity, and the perceptions that a prospective adverse imbalance in the strategic relationship was forming grew. Perceptions of an increased threat reduced support for military and political détente. Thus the relationship between parity and détente was also demonstrated by the later negative correlation, as well as by the direct and indirect indications of a positive correlation in the early 1970s as parity was acknowledged and détente prospered.

3 Confrontation to Détente: The Road to the Summit, 1969-72

ONE HAZARD of historical and political analysis is a tendency retrospectively to invest the course of developments and policymaking that lead to some historical event with an inevitability, purposefulness, and pattern more coherent than existed. A caveat with respect to this tendency certainly applies to understanding the rise and fall of détente in American-Soviet relations in the 1970s. It also should be borne in mind when looking at the path to the first Nixon-Brezhnev summit meeting in 1972. In reviewing what led to that important event, it is necessary to keep in mind that in 1969, indeed, at any point up to the summit meeting itself, there was great uncertainty and some reservations on both sides. Each saw a summit meeting and the launching of a new stage of relations as a possibility, even a likelihood; early on it became a goal of both. On the other hand, the leaders of each country were also pursuing other goals, to which they often gave priority. This fact, together with unforeseeable vagaries of history beyond the control of either side, meant that there were many possible outcomes to the interplay of events between 1969 and 1972, and made the actual outcome but one of many that might have been.

First Steps, 1969

The first point to note again as we begin this historical review is that the conception of détente developed by President Nixon and his national security adviser, Henry Kissinger, over the period from 1969 to 1972 was by no means fully developed at the outset. Rather, it evolved gradually as part of the process of improving relations, for the most part as the rationale for a political strategy, rather than constituting a source or basis for that strategy.

The dominant foreign policy preoccupation of Nixon and Kissinger in 1969, and indeed for the entire period through 1972, was not a détente summit meeting with Moscow, but finding an honorable exit from Vietnam. Improvement of relations with the Soviet Union, and a possible parallel rapprochement with China, were at that time seen as much as means to that end as they were ends in themselves. To a large extent it was only after the fact that they assumed the more logical pattern provided by subsequent rationalization in terms of a theory of détente. It is true that Nixon in a general way, and Kissinger more subtly and intellectually, conceptualized policy and sought to structure it much more carefully in a strategy of policy actions than had their predecessors (or successors). This process of conceptualization itself had an impact on policy, but it also represented rationalization as much as forward policy planning. This was especially true of American policy toward the Soviet Union and the development of détente from 1969 to 1972.

Not only was Vietnam the overriding foreign policy preoccupation but, especially for Nixon, it was also critically intertwined with domestic political considerations. This latter fact had a powerful effect on American policy toward the Soviet Union. Nixon was unable to disengage from Vietnam until the very end of his first administration. As a result, he sought to use a policy of détente (not yet called that) to support before the American voting public a claim of achievement in pursuit of peace offsetting his reluctant but stubborn continuation of the Vietnam War.

As noted, Nixon and Kissinger also believed from the outset that linkage offered the best prospect for leverage on Soviet behavior in pursuit of American objectives. For linkage to succeed, Nixon and Kissinger saw a need to marshal the resources required to manage that strategy. That meant gearing up political relations around the world, as well as controlling the workings of the U.S. government itself.

On the basis of their previous experience and psychological makeup, both men were predisposed to be suspicious and distrustful of governmental bureaucracy. Although it may seem odd, both men believed the bureaucracy of even their own administration was not to be trusted. Nor could it be counted on to manipulate policy in the manner they both conceived as essential for geopolitical maneuvering. Over time they progressively denied the bureaucracy the opportunity to participate in policymaking, and later even in policy implementation in widening spheres. Eventually, operating on these assumptions about the bureaucracy made them self-fulfilling prophecies. Nixon's choice of William P. Rogers as secretary of state was, to be blunt, predicated on an ability to use him as a front man, rather than as a partner or even participant in foreign policy–making.[1]

---

1. See Henry Kissinger, *White House Years* (Boston, Mass.: Little, Brown, 1979), pp. 26–32. As Kissinger comments, "Nixon considered Rogers's unfamiliarity with the subject [of foreign affairs] an asset because it guaranteed that policy direction would remain in the White House. . . . Few Secretaries of State can have been selected because of their President's confidence in their ignorance of foreign policy." Ibid., p. 26.

Kissinger had learned from past exposure to Washington, especially six unhappy months he spent in 1961 as a consultant to President John F. Kennedy's White House, the importance and locus of the levers of power. He moved quickly and successfully to capitalize on the key one—access to Nixon—gaining the president's confidence, and the opportunity to demonstrate his own ability to deliver what Nixon wanted.

One of the fascinating incidental, but not inconsequential, aspects of the development of American policy and relations with the Soviet Union (and of foreign policy as a whole) was the gradual rise in Kissinger's influence from 1969 on. It is usually assumed in retrospect that he had a preeminent role from the outset, but in fact his position in 1969 and 1970, and even 1971 and 1972, was not as secure or his power as complete as it later became. Kissinger's rise within the White House, his gradual displacement of Secretary of State Rogers, and the extension of his authority into economic affairs and defense, developed unevenly over time.[2] All of this in turn affected the development of American policy toward the Soviet Union on the road to détente.

On the international front, the new administration wished to demonstrate the importance of relations with its European allies. Nixon therefore gave first priority to an eight-day visit to Western Europe, beginning with a stop in Brussels, headquarters of both the North Atlantic Treaty Organization (NATO) and the European Community (EC). He departed for Europe on February 23, barely a month after his inauguration.

The Soviet leaders took the first initiatives in Soviet-American relations. They had indicated, publicly and privately, their readiness to begin the planned strategic arms limitation talks (SALT). At a reception on February 14, 1969, Soviet Ambassador Anatoly F. Dobrynin had taken Kissinger aside and, after making his acquaintance, requested an early meeting with the president, which was arranged for February 17. At that time Dobrynin broached the idea of a summit meeting, to which Nixon replied that such meetings required careful preparation. Dobrynin affirmed Soviet readiness to negotiate on a wide range of issues, although he was not receptive to linkage. It was a good beginning, but only a beginning. It showed Soviet interest in negotiating. But it remained to be determined whether and in what areas agreement could be reached.[3]

---

2. Nixon's view of the Kissinger-Rogers relationship is of interest. He notes Kissinger's concern over Secretary Rogers' "access to the Oval Office," and recounts that "Rogers felt that Kissinger was Machiavellian, deceitful, egotistical, arrogant, and insulting. Kissinger felt that Rogers was vain, uninformed, unable to keep a secret, and hopelessly dominated by the State Department bureaucracy. . . . Kissinger suggested repeatedly that he might have to resign unless Rogers was restrained or replaced." Nixon says he turned often to Chief of Staff H. R. Haldeman, and later John Mitchell, to serve as buffers between Rogers and Kissinger, and between them and himself. See Richard Nixon, *RN: The Memoirs of Richard Nixon* (Grosset and Dunlap, 1978), p. 433.

3. Kissinger, *White House Years*, pp. 112–14, 138–44.

Nixon used the occasion of Dobrynin's visit to signal that he wished serious exchanges to be conducted through Kissinger, not through the Department of State. At Nixon's request his White House chief of staff, H. R. Haldeman, kept Secretary Rogers from attending the meeting with Dobrynin, and although the director of Soviet affairs at the Department of State, Malcolm Toon, was present for the formal meeting, Nixon told Dobrynin privately that matters of special interest and sensitivity should be taken up with Kissinger.[4]

Nixon occasionally met with Dobrynin subsequently (next on October 20, 1969, when the Soviet Union agreed to the date for opening the SALT negotiations). But most meetings were between Dobrynin and Kissinger.[5] Nixon also initiated personal correspondence with Prime Minister Aleksei N. Kosygin in March 1969, along the lines of his conversation with Dobrynin. Kosygin's reply was noncommittal, but challenged much more directly than had Dobrynin the idea of linkage.[6]

Throughout 1969 and 1970 the Soviet Union continued to express an interest in improving relations. In March 1969 Dobrynin proposed opening consulates-general in San Francisco and Leningrad. For the first time since World War II, the May Day celebration in Moscow did not include a military parade, suggesting a less militant outlook. Even in his speech to the international conference of communist parties on June 9, Brezhnev reaffirmed a policy of peaceful coexistence with all the capitalist states, and specifically included the United States.[7] Then, in a major speech to the Supreme Soviet on July 10, Foreign Minister Andrei A. Gromyko called for closer Soviet-American relations. Gromyko specifically responded positively to Nixon's call for an era of negotiations to replace confrontation, saying that if the United States seriously was prepared to move in that direction, "we for our part are ready."[8] But it was not until 1971 that real movement began.

In retrospect, it is clear that the Soviet leadership sought improved relations with the United States in 1969, despite some internal reservations and differences over the issue in Moscow, in view of the direct Soviet military

---

4. Ibid., pp. 138–41.

5. Ibid., pp. 146, 523–25.

6. Ibid., p. 144. Although Nixon's letter was sent on March 26, Kosygin did not reply until May 27. The delay probably reflected some uncertainty in Moscow over use of this medium of diplomatic exchange.

7. L. I. Brezhnev, *O vneshnei politike KPSS i sovetskogo gosudarstva: Rechi i stat'i* [On the Foreign Policy of the CPSU and the Soviet Government: Speeches and Articles], 3d ed. (Moscow: Politizdat, 1978), p. 85.

8. A. A. Gromyko, *Vo imya torzhestva leninskoi vneshnei politiki: Izbrannye rechi i stat'i* [In Celebration of Leninist Foreign Policy: Selected Speeches and Articles] (Moscow: Politizdat, 1978), pp. 164–65.

confrontation with China, the still unsettled situation in Eastern Europe, the challenge from what would soon be known as Eurocommunists within the communist movement, and internal Soviet economic difficulties.

The deterioration of Soviet relations with China was marked by a series of armed clashes along the border, beginning in March and continuing through the summer of 1969.[9]

In Eastern Europe, Alexander Dubček was not finally removed from all his posts until October 1969, and the situation in Czechoslovakia remained uneasy, notwithstanding Soviet military occupation since August 1968. In fact, the Soviets were concerned over Eastern Europe as a whole. For this reason, they were particularly suspicious and unhappy about a decision by President Nixon to visit Romania in August while traveling around the globe.[10] They showed their dissatisfaction by delaying a favorable response to belated American offers to begin SALT.

The reverberations of the Soviet occupation of Czechoslovakia and the end to the liberal communist regime of Dubcek were the principal factors in stirring dissension in the world communist movement. That dissension manifested itself at the long-delayed conference of seventy-four communist parties in Moscow in June 1969.[11]

On the American side, while Nixon and Kissinger were certainly interested in developing a closer relationship with the Soviet Union, they were in no hurry. In fact, they were quite irritated at what they regarded as over-eager readiness by some elements in the U.S. government, as well as public opinion leaders, to respond quickly to Soviet indications of readiness to proceed with arms limitations and trade talks, without gearing such moves into the strategy of linkage that they were seeking to establish.[12]

Meanwhile, movement to disengage from Vietnam,[13] and to engage with China,[14] was slow in 1969 and 1970. Nixon and Kissinger did not want to press ahead in developing relations with the Soviet Union without parallel movement with China and leverage gained through linkage of those developments.

Nixon and Kissinger also wished to organize and secure better control over overall American defense and global political-military policies before

---

9. See chapter 6.

10. President Nicolae Ceauşescu had taken the initiative with an invitation immediately after President Nixon entered office. Both Nixon and Kissinger decided a visit during the president's August trip would be a useful way to test Soviet reactions, despite a recommendation against it by Ambassador Llewellyn E. Thompson, the leading expert on Soviet affairs.

11. See chapter 4.

12. Kissinger, *White House Years*, pp. 130–38. He describes the pressures and White House irritation.

13. See chapter 7.

14. See chapter 6.

acting on the proposed SALT negotiations, the principal pending item on the agenda of U.S.-Soviet relations. Hence, SALT was delayed until after the sharp debate and close vote over deployment of an antiballistic missile (ABM) system and approval of the 1969 defense program.[15]

The new administration also wished to temper its support of arms control with other political considerations to a greater extent than it believed its predecessors had done. Thus the Non-Proliferation Treaty, signed in 1968 after years of negotiation with the Soviet Union (and among the Western powers), was left in abeyance by the outgoing administration at Nixon's request. His decision was to proceed with its ratification, and on February 5, 1969, he formally requested the advice and consent of the Senate. What was not publicly known was that the day before that action Nixon had issued secret instructions *not* to press the allies to ratify—a distinct change from the Johnson administration.[16] This shift in priorities between arms control and general considerations of political alliance was indicative of the approach of the new administration.

Following his visit to Europe in February–March, Nixon made a second major trip, this time to a number of countries in East and South Asia (and en route home, to Romania) in July–August. Early during this trip, on a stopover at Guam, Nixon got carried away in a background briefing to the press corps and described his new approach to meeting the defense needs of the third world before it had been fully developed within the administration. While reaffirming American commitments and assurance of the nuclear deterrent shield to its allies and other key states, "In cases involving other types of aggression . . . we shall look to the nation directly threatened to assume the primary responsibility of providing the manpower for its defense."[17] Clearly the intention was to avoid any more Vietnams, but without disclaiming American interests, commitments, and support for friends.

The Nixon Doctrine, as the new policy was soon termed,[18] was not just rhetorical—although it marked a less far-reaching change than appeared at first glance.[19] In accordance with the new doctrine, the United States sought to build regional surrogate powers, such as Iran. In fact, Iran was one of the countries Nixon had had in mind, based on an internal study on the Persian Gulf situation, and when the shah, Mohammed Reza Pahlevi, visited Washing-

---

15. On SALT and related issues, see chapter 5.

16. The secret decision was set down in National Security Decision Memorandum (NSDM)-6 on February 4, 1969. It was first disclosed in Seymour M. Hersh, *The Price of Power: Kissinger in the Nixon White House* (Summit, 1983), p. 148.

17. Cited in Kissinger, *White House Years*, p. 225; and see pp. 220–23 on the background to the Nixon Doctrine.

18. As Kissinger notes, Nixon exerted some effort to get his name used to identify the new policy instead of calling it the "Guam Doctrine," as the press initially termed it. Ibid., p. 224.

19. For a Soviet view, see G. A. Arbatov and others, *'Doktrina Niksona'* ["The Nixon Doctrine"] (Moscow: Nauka, 1972).

ton in October 1969, Nixon made clear his policy decision to make Iran "one of the strongest" regional powers.[20]

The year 1969 was—Vietnam aside—unusually peaceful. No regional crises erupted involving the United States and the Soviet Union. The unsettled Middle Eastern scene, in particular the simmering Arab-Israeli conflict, remained not only a potential but indeed a probable source of future crises. But in 1969 Nixon and Kissinger preferred to leave that situation to one side as much as possible, and consequently were prepared to leave it to the State Department.[21]

There was one exception to the general absence of crises in 1969. In April the Democratic People's Republic of Korea (North Korea) had, in one of the erratic cases of gratuitous violence in which it indulges, shot down an unarmed American EC-121 reconnaissance plane about ninety miles from its coast. The administration's machinery for crisis management was not well in gear, and the military resources were simply not in place for an immediate retaliatory air strike, as Nixon—and Kissinger—favored.[22] Secretary of Defense Melvin R. Laird, Secretary of State Rogers, CIA Director Richard C. Helms, and the Joint Chiefs of Staff all opposed a military strike. According to one account, Kissinger decided on a tough line in part because he perceived it to be Nixon's preference and wanted to establish his own credentials as a hawk on such matters.[23] Nixon says Kissinger was concerned about Soviet, Chinese, and North Vietnamese assessments of U.S. mettle. In his memoir Kissinger refers only to his concern over the reaction of friendly Asian nations in judging the new administration's decisiveness. In any event, the United States did not respond except by reinstituting reconnaissance patrols, with protection. But, as Kissinger stresses, the United States "learned so many lessons for even grimmer crises that lay ahead."[24] The Soviet Union, incidentally, did not support the North Korean action and even helped the United States look for survivors.[25]

The years 1970 and 1971, by contrast, provided a less tranquil background for the continued wary movement toward limited rapprochement between the United States and the Soviet Union. In a few cases the actions of

---

20. Curiously, Kissinger makes no reference to the attention lavished on Iran in 1969. See Tad Szulc, *The Illusion of Peace: Foreign Policy in the Nixon Years* (Viking, 1978), pp. 167–68.

21. Kissinger, *White House Years*, pp. 341–79.

22. Kissinger stresses this point in his account; see *White House Years*, pp. 313–21; and Nixon, *RN*, pp. 382–85.

23. See Szulc, *The Illusion of Peace*, p. 85.

24. Kissinger, *White House Years*, p. 312.

25. The Soviet assistance, and indeed the Soviet position on the whole incident, is ignored in all the American memoirs and other accounts of the period.

   The Chinese, seeking to curry North Korean favor, strongly criticized the Soviet Union for "rendering services to U.S. imperialists." *Xinhua* (New China News Agency), April 22, in Foreign Broadcast Information Service, *People's Republic of China*, April 22, 1969, p. A1.

the two powers themselves created or transformed tense situations, but in most cases local and regional tensions, which in some instances became crises, were to break out and enmesh the two powers.

Testing Parity: The Cienfuegos Submarine Base

An event in the autumn of 1970 caused a muffled confrontation of wills between the leaders in Washington and Moscow: the Cienfuegos naval base incident.[26] While resolved quickly by quiet diplomacy, it represented a significant development because it marked a Soviet test of the relationship of the two powers in the dawning age of strategic parity.

The incident was precipitated by Soviet construction of a nuclear submarine base in Cienfuegos Bay on the southern coast of Cuba. The Soviets clearly intended to use the base to support their expanding naval presence on the world's oceans. This Soviet probe was particularly significant in view of the background of Soviet-U.S.-Cuban relations in the early 1960s. Cuba had been the source of unusual neuralgia to the United States ever since Fidel Castro took power. The resounding American defeat at the Bay of Pigs in 1961 was only partly offset by success in the Cuban missile crisis of 1962.[27]

From the American perspective, the Cuban missile crisis involved the surreptitious Soviet deployment of SS-4 medium- and SS-5 intermediate-range strategic missiles in Cuba, just ninety miles from U.S. shores. The Soviet Union had acted despite clear public warnings against doing so by President Kennedy, and in the face of its own denials and assurances. The United States successfully compelled the withdrawal of the missiles and restored the political and military status quo ante. It deterred a provocative Soviet deployment which would have altered the balance of strategic military power (that is, diluted American predominance). And the United States had reasserted the Monroe Doctrine and rebuffed a Soviet political as well as military encroachment on its vital interests in its own backyard. The outcome was regarded as an outstanding American victory in the cold war.

The Soviet leaders, from their standpoint, had been under no obligation to obey unilateral American injunctions against deploying weapons on

---

26. For a fuller account on which this discussion draws, see Raymond L. Garthoff, "Handling the Cienfuegos Crisis," *International Security*, vol. 8 (Summer 1983), pp. 46–66.

27. President Nixon had a special sensitivity, and hostility, to Cuba, dating from Castro's rise to power, on which President Kennedy had capitalized in his narrow defeat of Nixon in the 1960 election. One of Nixon's first acts in office in 1969 was to direct the Central Intelligence Agency (CIA) to intensify its covert operations against Cuba—just as the CIA was winding down those operations there and through the exile groups based in Miami. See Hersh, *The Price of Power*, p. 251; and Szulc, *The Illusion of Peace*, p. 175. Although Szulc attributes the pressure to Kissinger, in fact he was acting at Nixon's insistent behest. This has been independently confirmed to me by knowledgeable officials.

the territory of a Soviet ally—precisely as the United States itself had done in a number of states immediately around the Soviet Union—or to inform the American leaders of their intention to do so. The Soviets were doing nothing illegal or improper under international law. The United States had nonetheless chosen to use its superior military power to compel Soviet withdrawal of the missiles, humiliating the USSR (despite some face-saving elements, such as the equivocal American promise not to invade Cuba and an informal secret statement of intent to withdraw American intermediate-range ballistic missiles from Turkey). The American action had been an offensive use of military power—compellence, not deterrence—and spurred Soviet resolve to acquire countervailing strategic military power. The outcome of the Cuban missile crisis had been a rankling Soviet defeat in the cold war, and the Soviet leaders had been left with a bitter memory of that defeat and a continuing imposed restraint.

Hence, in 1970, apart from the intrinsic significance of a base for Soviet missile-carrying submarines—which would have provided certain measurable advantages to the Soviet Union and corresponding disadvantages to the United States—the establishment of the base would also have marked a symbolic repeal of the limits the United States had imposed on Soviet freedom of action. The Soviet leaders believed the USSR was acquiring strategic parity and wanted that new status recognized. One way would be to circumscribe the limitations forced upon them in 1962 restricting their military presence in Cuba. They sought to erase that legacy of American superiority and cold war, an imposed constraint not in keeping with parity with the United States as a global power, the status to which they aspired.

The mini-crisis of 1970 over Cienfuegos arose in September and was resolved by October.[28] On September 16, a U-2 reconnaissance plane photographed construction of a naval facility at Cayo Alcatraz in the Bay of Cienfuegos that included barracks and an adjoining soccer field. Analysts at the CIA, believing that soccer was little known in Cuba and knowing that it was a favorite Russian sport, concluded that the recreational area was probably being prepared for repeated use by Russian seamen.[29] Other features of the construction site suggested a submarine base. Moreover, a Soviet flotilla including a submarine tanker, an oceangoing tug, and a ship carrying two special purpose barges recognized as a type used to support nuclear-powered submarines had

28. The fullest account of this episode is given by Kissinger, *White House Years*, pp. 632–52. For background on the episode, see also Nixon, *RN*, pp. 485–90; and *Soviet Naval Activities in Cuba*, Hearings before the Subcommittee on Inter-American Affairs of the House Committee on Foreign Affairs, 91 Cong. 2 sess. (Washington, D.C.: Government Printing Office, 1971).

29. Incidentally, Kissinger claims personal credit for the shrewd insight about the soccer field ("In my eyes . . . as an old soccer fan"), and evidently did so at the time. In fact, it was an insight by a CIA analyst reported to Kissinger. Moreover, it was based on an incorrect premise—the Cubans had a long tradition of soccer, and its popularity was increasing. See Kissinger, *White House Years*, p. 638; and H. R. Haldeman, with Joseph DiMona, *The Ends of Power* (Times Books, 1978), pp. 85–86.

arrived at Cienfuegos just a week earlier, on September 9. The U-2 mission had in fact been prompted both by the arrival of the flotilla and by observation in an August reconnaissance flight of the then still unidentified early construction.

President Nixon wanted to make a strong response, but he also wanted to wait until after he had made a European visit scheduled for September 27 to October 5. The Pentagon favored a strong diplomatic action to evict the Soviets from the Cuban base; the State Department favored diplomatic clarification of the matter.

Kissinger objected to the delay, but after a National Security Council (NSC) meeting on September 23, the president decided to wait until after his trip.[30] Then on September 25 a leak led the Pentagon to brief the press on the details of the construction site and the naval visit—a briefing it made by mistake. Subsequently that same day Kissinger entered the picture with a background briefing to the press by a "White House source." He recalled President Kennedy's statement of November 1962 which outlined the understanding that the Soviet Union would not station offensive weapons in Cuba. Kissinger warned: "The Soviet Union can be under no doubt that we would view the establishment of a strategic base in the Caribbean with the utmost seriousness."[31] The next day Ambassador Dobrynin saw Kissinger and was reported to be "ashen" from shock when Kissinger spelled out the full basis for, and extent of, American concern.[32] Then Nixon and Kissinger departed for Europe.

By the time the president and Kissinger returned to Washington in early October, Dobrynin was waiting to tell them (on October 6) that there would be no Soviet naval base in Cuba. He reaffirmed and made more explicit the understanding that Soviet offensive weapons would not be stationed in Cuba.[33] The "crisis" was resolved.

The Soviet attempt to lessen the constraints imposed in 1962 had not succeeded, but there had been no public confrontation and no public backing down.

Several aspects of the incident deserve attention. First, there had been two interesting and instructive precursor actions by the Soviets. One involved a pattern of naval visits to Cuba. There had been a visit by Soviet

---

30. Kissinger, *White House Years*, pp. 637–44, provides considerable detail on these deliberations within the U.S. government.

31. Ibid., p. 646, and see pp. 644–46.

32. Ibid., pp. 646–47.

   Haig, standing in for Kissinger, held a follow-up meeting with Dobrynin in early October, to which he gives greatly inflated significance in his memoir, misrepresenting the occasion as though it had been the first and key meeting with Dobrynin. See Alexander M. Haig, Jr., *Caveat: Realism, Reagan, and Foreign Policy* (Macmillan, 1984), p. 100. Kissinger and Nixon do not even mention the Haig meeting.

33. Ibid., pp. 649–50.

naval ships to Cuba in July 1969, and a second in May 1970. Interestingly, both cases immediately followed entry into the Black Sea by U S naval ships asserting American rights to sail those waters, as had been done annually for years. The pattern was thus one of clear movement toward parity in naval practices. In addition, relations between Castro and the Soviet leadership had but recently been repaired after several years of strain (in fact, there had been strains ever since the Cuban missile crisis). On April 22 Castro had publicly declared his readiness to establish closer military ties with the Soviet Union. In addition, the USSR had been gradually upgrading the composition of the Soviet flotillas. The first one had included two old diesel torpedo-attack submarines (F-class), while the one in May had included a nuclear-powered cruise missile–launching submarine (E-II class). The one in September prudently did not include a submarine, only the support ships. Thus a gradual progression was being established.

The second precursor event was of an entirely different nature. On August 4, before the United States had any idea of a possible Soviet submarine base in Cuba, Soviet Chargé d'Affaires Yuly M. Vorontsov, in Dobrynin's absence, had called on Kissinger. In a mood of satisfaction at improving Soviet-American relations, he unexpectedly raised the question of reaffirming the Kennedy-Khrushchev understanding of 1962 with respect to Cuba. Kissinger reviewed the 1962 record and advised the president that an understanding had "never formally [been] buttoned down" in 1962. "It emerged that there was no formal understanding in the sense of an agreement, either oral or in writing." Nixon and Kissinger decided, without consulting others (including the secretaries of state and defense), that it would be useful to tie Moscow down by using the opportunity the Soviets had unaccountably proffered to "reaffirm" and activate the spongy 1962 understanding. So Kissinger assured Vorontsov on August 7 that the United States regarded the understanding as in effect, and "noted with satisfaction" that the Soviet Union also regarded it as "still in full force."[34]

---

34. Kissinger, *White House Years*, pp. 632–35. The first time even key senior officials in the U.S. government who had been involved in the Cienfuegos incident knew of the August 1970 exchange of assurances was this revelation by Kissinger in his memoir nine years later. The reason for the Soviet initiative in raising the 1962 Cuban understanding in August was perplexing. Kissinger, writing later in his memoir, still found it "hard to imagine" why the Soviets had raised the matter in view of their own actions then under way to test and weaken the constraint. One possibility was that the Soviet leaders sought to reassure the United States that the submarine base was not a step toward the placing of land-based missiles again in Cuba, in the hope that the United States would then acquiesce to the submarine base.

Kissinger had, as it turned out, jumped to a conclusion with respect to Vorontsov's message. "What he had come to convey," states Kissinger, "was his government's desire to reaffirm the Kennedy-Khrushchev understanding of 1962 with respect to Cuba." This way of putting the matter suggests Soviet readiness to reaffirm their acceptance of the constraints entailed. Fortunately, Kissinger accompanies his own interpretation with a verbatim quotation from Vorontsov's demarche: "We would like to stress that in the Cuban question we proceed as before from the understanding on this question reached in the past and we expect that the American

In fact, after the 1962 crisis had ended, the United States had never issued any public or official statement of commitment not to invade Cuba, since the requirements of the highly conditional statement of President Kennedy of November 20, 1962—which called for international inspection to verify the absence of offensive arms—had not been met. This studied silence on commitments had been a considered position maintained throughout the Kennedy and Johnson administrations.[35]

The 1962 understanding was thus actually not consummated until August 7, 1970, when for the first time American leaders unequivocally accepted the mutual commitments. Even then, it was done in a private exchange between the White House and the Soviet leadership without the knowledge even of the rest of the U.S. government. The Soviets not only affirmed the understanding in a note delivered by Vorontsov, but publicly reaffirmed it in an authorized TASS statement on October 13 which declared that the Soviet Union was not doing and would not do anything that would "contradict the understanding" reached in 1962. On November 13, 1970, the United States publicly confirmed the understanding. A State Department spokesman noted that on the basis of President Kennedy's statement of November 20, 1962, and the TASS statement of October 13, 1970, "we are confident that there is an understanding by the two Governments of the respective positions on the limits of their actions with regard to Cuba." Both governments preferred to gloss over the past uncertainties and differences and to attribute the basic understanding actually reached in 1970 to their predecessors in 1962. This history explains why after September 1970, the administration wished to date the American commitment to 1962 and stated that the 1970 understanding merely "reaffirmed," "clarified," and "amplified" the 1962 understanding to cover Soviet submarine missile systems.[36]

---

side will also strictly adhere to this understanding." Ibid., p. 632. It would certainly appear that the main purpose of the Soviets was to elicit an *American* reaffirmation of the understanding, rather than to stress their own desire to reaffirm it, although of course their reaffirmation was also entailed.

A senior Soviet official directly involved in the matter at the time informed me years later that the Soviet Union had raised the matter because of Cuban concern over a possible American attack. While Soviet intelligence did not confirm that possibility, Moscow still concluded it should elicit American reaffirmation of the understanding. It could then reassure Castro that it had taken the matter up with the Americans and that there would be no American intervention. The Soviets had a strong incentive to avoid precipitating a new crisis centered on Cuba. Only two years earlier Castro had agreed to return to the Soviet fold, and then because of Soviet economic pressures, and the Soviets did not wish again to arouse Cuban fears at being endangered by their rapprochement with the United States.

35. For a more detailed account of the 1962 crisis with attention to the unsettled nature of the commitments in its resolution and with close examination of the discussions at that time relating to submarine basing, see Garthoff, *International Security*, vol. 8 (1983), pp. 50–55.

36. Kissinger, *White House Years*, pp. 632–35. Nixon and Kissinger described the 1970 developments as acting to "reaffirm our understanding [of 1962] and amplify it to make clear that the

The outcome of the various statements was that the United States got a greater degree of Soviet commitment against permanent basing of missile submarines in Cuba, while the Soviet Union finally got American commitment to the 1962 understanding and a pledge not to invade Cuba.

The White House handling of the Cienfuegos crisis was indicative of the growing tendency by Nixon and Kissinger to effect a tight White House hold over policy and its implementation, a practice which came to affect many aspects of détente diplomacy.[37] Not only was the exchange of assurances with the Soviet government in August decided by Nixon and Kissinger alone, but they never even informed other senior figures in the U.S. government afterwards. Thus, for example, when Nixon saw Gromyko on October 22 and wanted to raise the matter of assurances one more time—and Gromyko, expecting this, *had* assurances to give him—Nixon did not do so because Secretary of State Rogers was with him and had not been informed of the state of play. Dobrynin gave the assurances to Kissinger the next day, and informed him that the Soviet government was "making the exchanges from August onward part of the understanding of 1962."[38]

The tight hold the White House maintained is revealed by other incidents. The Washington Special Action Group (WSAG) had been convened to deal with the mini-crisis on September 19, following the analysis of the U-2 photographs taken September 16. On September 23 the NSC met, as did the WSAG again on September 24. But while diverging views over the validity of the 1962 understanding arose in those discussions, Kissinger did *not*

---

agreement included activities related to sea-based systems." Richard M. Nixon, *U.S. Foreign Policy for the 1970's: Building for Peace*, Report to the Congress, vol. 2 (GPO, 1971), p. 160.

37. There is also considerable evidence that in maneuvering *within* the White House, Kissinger chose to stress the element of confrontation in order to establish his own position in dealing with such crises and to increase Nixon's dependence on him, and that he actually circumvented Nixon's own desire and intentionally leaked the story to the press. See Hersh, *The Price of Power*, p. 254. Kissinger himself described in some detail how dissatisfied he was with Nixon's decision to postpone a confrontation with the Soviets until after his trip to Europe and the midterm election, although Kissinger did not indicate he was responsible for the leak. See Kissinger, *White House Years*, pp. 642–47.

38. See Kissinger, *White House Years*, p. 650. Kissinger notes that Dobrynin described Gromyko's surprise and perplexity that Nixon had failed to follow through on the subject, and stated that Gromyko suspected some sinister reason, perhaps a surprise American initiative. Internal American bureaucratic-political actions can and do affect international political perceptions, as in this instance, and can affect the decisions and actions of others.

Kissinger had given Dobrynin a draft of the assurance on October 9. In his memoir Nixon claims authorship, stressing his use of the personal pronoun. On the other hand, Kissinger goes out of his way to state that he and his Joint Chiefs of Staff liaison officer drafted it, but that, "in order to emphasize our [American] determination, we headed it 'President's Note.'" Kissinger's account rings true, and Nixon probably did not recall the details when writing his memoir and finding a "President's Note" in his files. Nixon, *RN*, pp. 488–89; and Kissinger, *White House Years*, p. 650.

disclose the very material fact that in August he and Dobrynin had "reaffirmed" the 1962 understanding.[39]

In September, Chief of Naval Operations Admiral Elmo R. Zumwalt, Jr., did see Kissinger's aide-mémoire stating that "nuclear submarines would not be permitted to use Cuba as an operating base," but only *after* it had been given to Dobrynin, and then only surreptitiously via Captain Rembrandt C. Robinson, the Joint Chiefs of Staff liaison officer with Kissinger's NSC staff. Thus the Pentagon and the State Department had no opportunity to observe that the statement failed to define such critical questions as what would constitute an "operating base" and whether "nuclear submarine" meant nuclear-powered or with nuclear missiles or both, all important questions that would later be tested in practice. To some extent these issues were addressed in the October exchanges.[40]

A final meeting of the WSAG to discuss "Courses of Action in Cienfuegos" was held October 6, shortly after Dobrynin's meeting with Kissinger, although scheduled earlier. By this time, the matter had essentially been settled, and Kissinger shifted the action back to his own staff in working out the final language of the assurances (the aforementioned "President's Note").

The merits of the decision aside, a procedure that excludes key members of an administration from participation in and even knowledge of policymaking is not conducive to political discipline or practical effectiveness in policy implementation.

Subsequently, most of the Soviet support ships left Cienfuegos on October 10, although they visited another Cuban port and returned to Cienfuegos in November before finally departing in early January 1971, following further vigorous U.S. protests. In February another tender and a nuclear-pow-

---

39. Kissinger relates the discussions in these sessions, but fails to note that the White House did not divulge the August exchanges to the rest of the government. Kissinger, *White House Years*, pp. 639–43.

40. Elmo R. Zumwalt, Jr., Admiral, USN (Retired), *On Watch: A Memoir* (Quadrangle, 1976), pp. 310–13. When Zumwalt asked why usual channels were not used, Captain Robinson explained that it was in order to exclude Secretary Rogers and the Department of State.

   Kissinger, in his memoir, which was published after Admiral Zumwalt's memoir with its sharp criticism on this score, makes an exception to his usual style and pointedly acknowledges Robinson's assistance in drafting the October assurances. But he entirely glosses over the failure to consult with others on the August exchanges. Zumwalt, in turn, had stressed the negative effects that the absence of expert participation in August had had, but did not mention the October exchanges.

   The confusion over "nuclear submarines" was perpetuated in later official and unofficial understandings by an inaccurate and unintentionally misleading remark by President Nixon. In a television interview on January 4, 1971, he stated that the understanding covered "nuclear submarines" serviced in or from Cuba. Cited by Kissinger, *White House Years*, p. 651. This statement was given as authoritative and contributed to a confused and confusing series of official statements during the SALT II Senate hearings. *The SALT II Treaty*, Hearings before the Senate Committee on Foreign Relations, 96 Cong. 1 sess. (GPO, 1979), pt. 1, pp. 357–60, 408–10, and pt. 3, pp. 227–29.

ered but not missile-launching attack submarine (N-class) arrived, only to leave after a week and further protests.[41] Occasional visits were made in the years following, but never by a nuclear-powered ballistic missile–launching submarine, and a Soviet submarine base was not established.

Parity thus did not extend to including a Soviet ability to decide on its own or with an ally what its military presence was to be, at least in an area governed by an understanding with the United States.

World Developments

Other developments and occurrences in the world had mixed, and sometimes negative, effects on the development of U.S.-Soviet relations. Several call for at least noting here. In the Near East, an Egyptian-Israeli war of attrition along the Suez Canal in 1970–71 led to unprecedented extensive and direct Soviet military involvement in Egypt's air defense. Close Soviet ties with Syria prompted American concern during a short-lived Syrian invasion of Jordan in September 1970, as the Jordanians were suppressing a bid for power by the Palestine Liberation Organization (PLO). In 1971 Pakistani-Indian hostilities arising from the secession of Bangladesh from Pakistan precipitated American-Soviet tension in South Asia. Of particular concern to the Soviet Union, although not involving the United States, was a successful political action by workers in Poland that forced the party first secretary, Wladyslaw Gomulka, out of power in December 1970. That situation probably raised questions in the minds of some Soviet leaders about the risks that East-West détente in Europe posed to the communist bloc. And of course the war in Vietnam continued and was spreading to Cambodia.

Despite this unpropitious global environment, for the most part these developments—not connected by time, geography, or politics—tended to dissipate at two critical junctures, one, the spring of 1971, the time of the Soviet Twenty-fifth Party Congress, the second, the spring of 1972, the time of the summit meeting. Moreover, there were growing contacts between the Soviets and the Americans during these two years in which these and other issues were addressed. The two sides talked not only about the Cienfuegos naval base controversy, but also the Egyptian-Israeli war of attrition, the Jordanian-Syrian crisis, and the Indo-Pakistani war.[42] In addition, they addressed the war in

---

41. Kissinger, *White House Years*, p. 651. See also Barry M. Blechman and Stephanie E. Levinson, "Soviet Submarine Visits to Cuba," *United States Naval Institute Proceedings*, vol. 101 (September 1975), pp. 31–39, for a generally accurate account of Soviet submarine visits from 1969 to 1975.

42. The American and Soviet roles in relation to the Indo-Pakistani War of 1971 are discussed in the context of triangular diplomacy vis-à-vis China in chapter 8. The two Near Eastern crises are briefly discussed in the text following.

Vietnam and SALT. These latter two issues were a major topic in confidential correspondence between President Nixon and Soviet leaders (until May 1971, Prime Minister Aleksei Kosygin, and thereafter General Secretary Leonid Brezhnev). These contacts were supplemented by discussions between Kissinger and Dobrynin in Washington and an unusual and important pre-summit meeting between Kissinger and Brezhnev in Moscow in April 1972. And finally general relations, the Vietnam issue, and SALT were dealt with at the summit meeting itself.

With respect to the external global events, the Egyptian-Israeli war of attrition in 1969–70 gave birth to an abortive attempt at developing a common U.S.-Soviet position aimed at resolving the conflict. The effort failed principally because neither the United States nor the Soviet Union could deliver its respective client.[43] Another reason was the failure of the United States to mesh the "Rogers Plan," advanced by Secretary of State Rogers in 1969, with the main lines of American policy, including that with the Soviet Union, which was in Kissinger's hands.[44] And there were other reasons. Relative to the future relationship between the United States and the Soviet Union, however, American leaders had learned that they should seek to deal directly with Egypt rather than through the Soviet Union, while the Soviet leaders learned that the United States would not or could not pressure Israel to reach or fulfill an agreement with the Soviet Union and Egypt. Further, the Soviet leaders saw they were right in their judgment that Kissinger, and not Rogers, was the key American foreign policy decisionmaker. The failure had not resulted from an inability of the United States and the Soviet Union to work together and even to reach agreement: they could not control the Near Eastern parties. The Soviet leaders had, in fact, placed considerable pressure on Egyptian President Gamal Abdel Nasser to negotiate along the lines of the Rogers Plan, but without success. When the attempt to implement a cooperative U.S.-Soviet initiative failed, both powers greatly increased the supply of arms to the regional enemies. In fact, the Soviet Union went far beyond its usual cautious approach and supplied large numbers of Soviet air defense combat personnel as well as weapons and equipment.[45]

---

43. See William B. Quandt, *Decade of Decisions: American Policy toward the Arab-Israeli Conflict, 1967–1976* (Berkeley, Calif.: University of California Press, 1977), pp. 72–110. See also Kissinger, *White House Years*, pp. 341–79, 558–93; and Nixon, *RN*, pp. 478–85.

44. In addition to the accounts cited immediately above, see Hersh, *The Price of Power*, pp. 213–33; and Szulc, *The Illusion of Peace*, pp. 89–102.

45. One study concludes that Kissinger missed an opportunity to defuse the Egyptian-Israeli conflict before the Soviet decision to commit Soviet air defenses to Egypt; see George W. Breslauer, "Soviet Policy in the Middle East, 1967–1972: Unalterable Antagonism or Collaborative Competition?" in Alexander L. George, ed., *Managing U.S.-Soviet Rivalry: Problems of Crisis Prevention* (Boulder, Colo.: Westview, 1983), pp. 73–99. It has been reported that Soviet reluctance to provide air defenses was overcome only by a threat from Nasser to resign in favor of someone who could deal with the United States to seek the return of the Sinai. See Nadav Safran, *Israel: The Embattled Ally* (Cambridge, Mass.: Harvard University Press, 1981), pp.

The Soviet leaders had warned of this outcome in a letter Prime Minister Kosygin sent to President Nixon on January 31, 1970 (the first such direct letter). It advised him that "if Israel continues its adventurism, continues to bomb the territory of the U.A.R. [Egypt] and other Arab states, the Soviet Union will be forced to see to it that the Arab states have means at their disposal with the help of which a due rebuff to the arrogant aggressor could be made."[46] The letter, together with similar messages to Prime Minister Harold Wilson of Great Britain and President Georges Pompidou of France, called on the four powers to "compel" Israel to cease its attacks and abide by the cease-fire, and to establish a peace based on "speediest" Israeli withdrawal from the occupied Arab territories in accordance with the UN resolutions. When Kissinger sent the letter in to Nixon (in later years he would have taken it in personally), he characterized it as "the first Soviet threat to the new Administration"—a clear exaggeration.[47] In the end, the Egyptian-Israeli confrontation was dampened without the benefit of American-Soviet collaboration, and indeed with heightened mutual suspicion.

436–37. For an account of the Soviet decision and implementation of the supply of air defense forces to Egypt, see Alvin Z. Rubinstein, "Air Support in the Arab East," in Stephen S. Kaplan, ed., *Diplomacy of Power: Soviet Armed Forces as a Political Instrument* (Brookings Institution, 1981), pp. 471–88; and Lawrence L. Whetten, *The Canal War: Four-Power Conflict in the Middle East* (Cambridge, Mass.: MIT Press, 1974). On Soviet differences of view and Soviet policy formulation, see Ilana Kass, *Soviet Involvement in the Middle East: Policy Formulation, 1966–1973* (Boulder, Colo.: Westview, 1978), pp. 155–65 and passim; Dina R. Spechler, *Domestic Influences on Soviet Foreign Policy* (Washington, D.C.: University Press of America, 1978); and Karen Dawisha, *Soviet Foreign Policy towards Egypt* (London: Macmillan, 1979).

46. Kissinger, *White House Years*, p. 525.

47. Ibid., p. 560. Indeed, Kissinger himself has now noted that the Kosygin letter was part of a diplomatic maneuver to justify Soviet military reinforcement for Egypt already decided upon, and not a threat: "The Kosygin letter was not a warning but a smokescreen." Ibid., p. 562. Nonetheless, in his memoir, Kissinger attempted to justify his characterization of the Kosygin letter as a threat. He blurred the unilateral Soviet decision, if necessary, to provide air defense weaponry with its call for four-power action to restore the cease-fire and then establish peace. The Soviets did not threaten unilateral action with respect to these broader aims. In fact, they may well have thought that their advance private statement to the Western powers of their contingent intention to provide defensive arms should prevent undue alarm, as well as offer a last chance to obviate that action by getting Israel to stop its attacks. Ibid., p. 560.

Kissinger may have found it necessary to acknowledge and attempt to justify his characterization of the message as a threat because Nixon, in his memoir, had referred to that description of it by Kissinger at the time. Nixon himself did not treat it as a threat, and says that his reply to Kosygin was "carefully low-keyed." Nixon, *RN*, p. 479. See also Quandt, *Decade of Decisions*, pp. 95–97.

Incidentally, Kissinger was almost apologetic about having had to share knowledge of the Kosygin letter with Secretary of State Rogers and Assistant Secretary Joseph Sisco: "Normally this would have made it part of the special Channel [Kissinger-Dobrynin, White House only]." *White House Years*, p. 560.

One incident during the maneuvering over the Rogers Plan and American efforts to establish a cease-fire merits noting here. The Americans had been attempting to get the Soviet Union to remove its air defense personnel which had been introduced in the spring. Kissinger on June 26 remarked at a background press briefing that "we are trying to *expel the Soviet military presence*, not so much the advisors, but the combat pilots and the combat personnel" in Egypt. This statement was leaked immediately and provoked a brief but intense storm of controversy in the United States. While such a public statement was indiscreet, Kissinger's aim was in fact realized later.[48]

No sooner was the Egyptian-Israeli confrontation temporarily contained than a new crisis erupted in Jordan. In September 1970 the PLO *fedayeen* posed a direct challenge to King Hussein's rule in Jordan, and he reacted sharply with military means. The United States strongly supported him, with a public threat from Nixon to oppose any Soviet intervention, and a buildup of the Sixth Fleet in the eastern Mediterranean. Syria then entered the fray, moving a tank column into Jordan. The United States and Israel were prepared to intervene on Jordan's behalf unless the Syrians withdrew, a threat the United States made very clear to Moscow. The Syrians withdrew. The Soviet Union refrained from intervening and evidently urged the Syrians to pull back, particularly after American determination was made clear.

The incident demonstrated the greater capacity of the United States to influence developments in the region. Kissinger and Nixon, however, greatly exaggerated the Soviet role in stimulating both the Syrian decision to advance and then to withdraw. In terms of successfully influencing events to reach a desired outcome, the United States had clearly won. But it was by no means clear that the whole confrontation was a Soviet-American contest, as the Soviet Union was only marginally and indirectly involved.[49] Nevertheless, because Nixon and Kissinger erroneously believed there had been a U.S.-Soviet confrontation, they were left with an exaggerated view of American ability to "manage" Soviet policy in third world crises.

While no further eruptions in the Middle East in the months following brought direct American or Soviet involvement, in July 1971 there was

---

48. See Kissinger, *White House Years*, pp. 579–80. Kissinger can be forgiven for crowing in his memoir, "Three years later we made this prediction come true" (p. 580). For a vivid account of the incident, see Marvin Kalb and Bernard Kalb, *Kissinger* (Dell, 1974), pp. 222–24; and Hersh, *The Price of Power*, p. 228.

49. See Quandt, *Decade of Decisions*, pp. 110–27; Kissinger, *White House Years*, pp. 594–631, 930; and Hersh, *The Price of Power*, pp. 234–49.

Hersh presents a fascinating, detailed account based on interviews with a number of the American officials involved. He shows that Nixon and Kissinger inadvertently prompted a skewing of information that overstressed the Soviet role. Moreover, the United States became dependent on reports from a panicked Jordanian monarch and the Israeli Mossad (Intelligence Service) that exaggerated the Syrian threat. In the latter case, the intent may have been to gain American support for Israeli intervention. Although not providing demonstrable proof, Hersh's account is convincing. Hersh, *The Price of Power*, especially pp. 243–46.

a communist coup in Sudan. It was quickly overturned with Egyptian and Libyan assistance (Libya at the time wanted to prevent a tightening of a potential Soviet noose around Egypt). It is not known whether the Soviet leaders had been aware of and had supported the local communist bid for power. In any event, after it failed, President Ja'afar Mohammed al-Nimeiry of the Sudan virtually cut off relations with the Soviet Union and expelled Soviet military advisers.

Important new developments did begin to take place in the Middle East during 1971 and 1972. The arena of action shifted to diplomatic moves by both the United States and the Soviet Union and by the countries of the region, particularly Egypt under President Anwar al-Sadat. While the developments are discussed later, it is worth noting here that on two occasions in this period the Soviet leaders proposed remarkably far-reaching diplomatic collaboration with the United States. Only with the publication of Kissinger's memoir in 1979 did it become known that in September 1971 and again in April 1972 the Soviet leaders proposed joint Soviet-American sponsorship of a comprehensive settlement of the Arab-Israeli conflict, including joint guarantees of the 1967 Israeli-Arab borders, agreement on an embargo on further arms sales to countries in the area, and withdrawal of Soviet military advisers and forces from the area (then principally Egypt) and of American military personnel (from Iran). (This last provision was modified in April to allow limited, equal numbers of Soviet and American personnel to remain.)[50] Kissinger disparages the significance of the Soviet offer, evidently seeking to justify the fact that he and Nixon did not seriously pursue these proposals. Instead, in December 1971 Nixon and Kissinger decided, with Prime Minister Golda Meir of Israel, to abandon the attempt to reach agreement on a comprehensive settlement, and to conduct indirect Arab-Israeli talks through American good offices, overtly through the Department of State, but really through the Kissinger back channel.[51] Kissinger was, in fact, already deeply and secretly involved in working to draw Egypt into similar talks.[52] In the meantime, he did not want a settlement.

Trade and Linkage

From the outset, it was clear to both sides that economic ties, particularly American normalization and facilitation of increased trade, would be a natural and important element in the improvement of relations that was expected to attend a relaxation of political tensions. While both sides had a stake in expanded economic ties, the Soviets had more to gain, while the United States was in the position of being able to exercise some leverage.

---

50. Kissinger, *White House Years*, pp. 1288, 1292.

51. Ibid., p. 1289.

52. See Hersh, *The Price of Power*, pp. 402–14, for a revealing account.

The Soviet leaders were acutely aware of the imbalance in needs and leverage and naturally sought to downplay it, insisting that both sides had an equal interest in trade. As Academician Georgy Arbatov put it, the Soviet Union does not want economic "assistance" from the United States, only normalization and development of "mutually advantageous" trade.[53]

In fact, the question of increasing reliance on trade with the United States (and the West in general) became a political issue debated within the Soviet leadership. All Soviet leaders wanted an end to American discriminatory restrictions, and all favored some degree of increased commerce. But differences arose in the late 1960s and early 1970s over both the political costs of seeking trade and the economic and political risks of greater economic dependence on the West. Autarky had long been Soviet policy and practice, and institutional interests had developed that could be threatened by drastic change. While autarky had in part been born of necessity, it also nourished a certain self-reliance and security that economic interdependence did not. Moreover, some in the party apparatus preferred for ideological reasons to limit relations with the West. Brezhnev had thrown his support to increased economic ties with the West at the Central Committee plenum in December 1969. Then the Twenty-fourth Party Congress in March–April 1971 marked a major advance for those seeking economic modernization tied to increased trade with the West and détente. But not until 1973, after removing two opponents in the Politburo, did Brezhnev himself explicitly repudiate autarky as an element in Soviet economic planning, and state that Soviet economic policy "proceeds from the premise" of growing economic relations and cooperation with the West.[54]

Beginning in December 1969, and especially during the years 1971–72, as the foundations of Soviet-American détente were being laid, Brezhnev personally accepted and pushed more vigorously than any other top leader the policy of maximizing East-West trade. Indeed, the lack of enthusiasm of a number of his Politburo colleagues is clearly, if indirectly, on the record, and there are indications of even greater reservations on the part of many members of the Central Committee and officials in the economic bureaucracy.[55] Expansion of trade with the West also had strong constituencies,

53. G. Arbatov, "Soviet-American Relations in a New Stage," *Pravda*, July 22, 1973. Arbatov was smarting from attempts by the U.S. Congress in 1973 to tie normalization of trade to other political concessions by the Soviet Union, as discussed later in this study (see chapters 9, 10, and 13).

54. "L. I. Brezhnev's Speech on West German Television," *Pravda*, May 22, 1973.

55. See Peter M. E. Volten, *Brezhnev's Peace Program: A Study of Soviet Domestic Political Process and Power* (Boulder, Colo.: Westview, 1982), pp. 107–32, 161–65, for an interesting, if sometimes overstated, discussion. See also Erik P. Hoffmann and Robbin F. Laird, *The Politics of Economic Modernization in the Soviet Union* (Ithaca, N.Y.: Cornell University Press, 1982), pp. 74–175; Hoffmann and Laird, *"The Scientific-Technological Revolution" and Soviet Foreign Policy* (Pergamon, 1982), pp. 74–116; Bruce Parrott, *Politics and Technology in the Soviet Union* (Cambridge, Mass.: MIT Press, 1983), pp. 232–55; Connie M. Friesen, *The Political Economy of East-West Trade* (Praeger, 1976), pp. 49–53; Rensselaer W. Lee, *Soviet*

both in the economic bureaucracy and among those favoring political détente. Their views acquired further support as a consequence of Brezhnev's strong advocacy. But trade was still a political issue, and those who opposed it argued that economic ties could have disadvantageous internal economic, ideological, and political consequences even if successful, and in addition would lead to Western efforts to exploit the perceived Soviet economic need for objectionable political ends. Finally, the West could not be depended upon, and the Soviet Union should not provide it with undesirable future leverage. Brezhnev and others countered these objections by contending that trade could provide invaluable assistance to Soviet economic development and would contribute to the relaxation of political tensions.[56]

Brezhnev and his colleagues thus developed a political stake in the success of the economic dimension of détente, as well in the anticipated economic benefits. They probably had exaggerated expectations of the extent to which capitalist businessmen were eager for their trade and profits[57]—and certainly held an exaggerated view of the influence that capitalist business leaders had on policymaking in the United States. They were therefore inclined to discount the extent to which American leaders would hold up profitable economic ties in an attempt to extract political concessions.

American policymakers in turn, especially Kissinger and some senators, also exaggerated the degree of the Soviet need for American trade and especially the extent to which the United States could exploit their need to influence other aspects of Soviet policy. From the outset Nixon and Kissinger saw relaxation of trade restrictions and expansion of trade as a major carrot to influence Soviet foreign policy, as well as a major strand in the network of relationships they hoped to weave into a pattern of interdependence.[58]

Perceptions of Western Technology (Washington, D.C.: Mathtech, 1978), p. xiv; Thomas N. Bjorkman and Thomas J. Zamostny, "Soviet Politics and Strategy toward the West: Three Cases," *World Politics,* vol. 36 (January 1984), pp. 191–97; and Aron Katsenelinboigen, "Conflicting Trends in Soviet Economics in the Post-Stalin Era," *Russian Review,* vol. 35 (October 1976), pp. 373–99.

For the case that Brezhnev himself made a decisive shift in favor of increasing reliance on trade with the West at the December 1969 Central Committee plenum, see Parrott, *Politics and Technology,* pp. 239–41. Most of the other accounts deal with the period after 1971, when Brezhnev's leadership and advocacy were evident.

56. See Philip Hanson, *Trade and Technology in Soviet-Western Relations* (Columbia University Press, 1981), pp. 96–97, for a speculative inference as to another Soviet consideration. Hanson suggests that the Soviet leaders saw as one lesson of the 1968 Czech experience the hazards of political pressures arising from internal economic reform and that it was therefore preferable to use Western imports. There had not, however, been extensive economic reforms in Czechoslovakia, and this conjecture is doubtful.

57. A senior Soviet official with competence in the area told me that in 1972 the Soviets expected that trade with the United States would reach $10 billion by the end of the decade.

58. On this latter objective, as Kissinger later argued: "Over time, trade and investment may leaven the autarkic tendencies of the Soviet system, invite gradual association of the Soviet

There is no indication that Nixon and Kissinger and their associates understood that the expansion of trade was a political issue in Moscow. They took it for granted that the Soviet interest was strong, and that Brezhnev's emphatic support made it so. Better understanding of the complex Soviet political process might have led to earlier recognition of the limits on the leverage that could be gained from playing the trade card, and the risks of seeking too much. Nevertheless, the ultimate collapse of the principal elements of the trade arrangements that were negotiated did not stem from a failure by the Nixon-Ford-Kissinger administrations. Rather, it was caused by congressional efforts to establish a linkage to internal Soviet policies, a strategy pushed primarily for domestic American political reasons.

Nixon (and Kissinger), too, had a strategy of linkage: "the expansion of economic relations with improved political relations." They explained the strategy publicly as based on the consideration that "without some reasonable certainty that political relations would be stable and free from periodic turbulence, both sides would be reluctant to enter into long-term commercial relations. Nor would the Congress support an expanding economic relationship while our basic relations with the Soviet Union were antagonistic."[59] This presumption was partly true; these points were among the considerations. But there is little evidence that the business community was reluctant to enter into long-term relations, on the one hand, nor that U.S.-Soviet relations would cease to be antagonistic once détente had been launched, on the other.

In his memoir Kissinger is much more frank about his and Nixon's calculations. He writes: "Our strategy was to use trade concessions as a political instrument, withholding them when Soviet conduct was adventurous and granting them in measured doses when the Soviets behaved cooperatively. In general, we favored projects that required enough time to complete for us to have continued leverage on Soviet conduct."[60]

Initially President Nixon had adopted a very restrictive trade control policy. The 1949 Export Control Act came up for renewal early in his first term, and hearings were held from April through July of 1969. Many leading liberals, and conservative business interests as well, argued for removing "remnants of the cold war" from this basic trade legislation. Within the Nixon administration, the State and Commerce Departments also favored substantial trade liberalization.

---

economy with the world economy, and foster a degree of interdependence that adds an element of stability to the political equation." Kissinger, "Détente with the Soviet Union: The Reality of Competition and the Imperative of Cooperation," testimony before the Senate Committee on Foreign Relations, September 19, 1974, *Department of State Bulletin*, vol. 71 (October 14, 1974), p. 512.

59. Richard M. Nixon, *U.S. Foreign Policy for the 1970's: Shaping a Durable Peace*, Report to the Congress, vol. 4 (GPO, 1973), p. 33; and see pp. 34–35.

60. Kissinger, *White House Years*, p. 840.

Nixon and Kissinger, on the other hand, saw normalization of trade relations with the Soviet Union as a card they could play; as Kissinger later put it, "expanding trade without a political quid pro quo was a gift; there was very little the Soviet Union could do for us economically. It did not seem to me unreasonable to require Soviet restraint in such trouble spots as the Middle East, Berlin, and Southeast Asia in return."[61]

Early in his term Nixon experimented with leverage: he flatly told Ambassador Dobrynin the United States would expand trade in exchange for Soviet help in resolving the Vietnam conflict. He was rebuffed. He then decided that since he was taking a relatively soft stance on Vietnam (Vietnamization of the war), he would shore up his standing with his conservative constituency by taking a hard line on East-West trade. And he did. In fact, his decision in May 1969 was harder than Kissinger had recommended. This was the point at which Nixon decided, in the wake of the Soviet rebuff on helping America out of Vietnam, to hold back improvement of trade relations for a more general political quid pro quo.[62]

The Export Administration Act of 1969 declared U.S. policy to favor expansion of trade with the Soviet Union, but it left most implementation to the discretion of the executive branch, thus allowing for the policy of leverage through linkage. It is more than ironic—and for détente it was tragic—that in 1969 Nixon ignored the opportunity to get presidential discretion to grant most-favored-nation (MFN) status to the Soviet Union and countries of Eastern Europe. (Kissinger later rued this oversight, but did not appreciate it at that time.)[63]

Thus American policy was framed to use the trade dimension of détente to serve political purposes. One task, which was clearly recognized (especially after the early failure on Vietnam), was the manner and selection of foreign policy issues for effective linkage. Another, not sufficiently appreciated at the time, was determining how to control linkage once unleashed. The Nixon and Ford administrations would later find that, as Kissinger puts it, "Many of those who had castigated us for seeking to link trade to Soviet *foreign* policy began to criticize us for not linking it more aggressively to Soviet *domestic* policy."[64] The more immediate problem, though, was to start the process of stepping up trade relations, and to make clear to the Soviet leaders the price for particular steps in trade normalization and expansion.

Kissinger indicates that the main Soviet effort in seeking a relaxation of trade as part of the general development of détente came in September 1971, when Gromyko met with Nixon and tied down the basic agreement

---

61. Ibid., pp. 152–53.

62. Ibid., pp. 153–54. Kissinger sought to maintain some future flexibility in the way he phrased Nixon's NSC directive.

63. Ibid., p. 155.

64. Ibid., p. 155. Emphasis in original. See also the bitter comment by Nixon, *RN*, pp. 875–76.

to proceed to an early summit meeting.[65] But there are a number of indications that high-level negotiations, and linkages, had been under way much earlier in 1971. Thus, for example, Kissinger confirms that only after a May 1971 agreement on a new course for SALT did the White House approve a major American sale of machinery for the giant Kama truck factory.[66] Most tantalizing of all, in view of developments a year later, in June Nixon quietly rescinded the order President Kennedy had been forced to levy in 1963 requiring that 50 percent of all American grain sold to the Soviet Union move in U.S. ships.

Neither the official documents that have been released nor the memoirs of either Nixon or Kissinger disclose that the agreement on SALT reached in early May and publicly announced on May 20, 1971, had been privately linked to an American agreement on major grain sales to the Soviet Union and on the provision of credits for those sales. This agreement in turn required extensive negotiation with American labor unions, especially the maritime unions and the International Longshoremen's Association (ILA), during the summer and fall of 1971. The negotiations involved major concessions and commitments by the administration on wide-ranging matters, including the selection of an assistant secretary of labor and an agreement to have more American merchant ships constructed. Initially Kissinger was involved directly, including in talks in June with Jay Lovestone of the AFL-CIO and Thomas W. Gleason of the ILA, but the task was soon passed to someone more suitable—Charles Colson.[67]

The first clear official sign of steps to develop American-Soviet trade was a visit to Moscow in November 1971 of a delegation headed by Secretary of Commerce Maurice Stans. Parallel with this move came a series of deals announced in November: a $136 million sale of grain, two contracts for $125 million for mining and oil drilling equipment, and the $500 million series of contracts for equipment for the projected Kama truck plant. In December Soviet Minister of Agriculture Vladimir Matskevich came to Washington for talks on grain sales with Secretary of Agriculture Earl Butz.[68]

65. Ibid., pp. 838, 1133.

66. Ibid., p. 840.

67. For the investigative reporting detailing these very interesting and previously unknown relationships among détente, SALT, grain sales, and a number of internal domestic matters in the United States (including the birth of the alliance between Richard Nixon and the ILA), see Hersh, *The Price of Power,* pp. 334–35, 343–48.

68. In early July 1972 Kissinger told newsmen that high-level talks on grain sales had begun at a meeting of Minister Matskevich and President Nixon on December 9, 1971. This claim, not repeated in Kissinger's or Nixon's later memoirs, was made at a time when Nixon wished credit for such an initiative. In fact, the claim was misleading for two reasons. First, high-level exchanges on grain sales had begun at least by May, related to the SALT breakthrough of May 20, 1971. Second, the real reason for arranging for Matskevich to meet Nixon was unrelated to the purpose of his official mission; it was to afford Nixon a means to warn the Soviet leadership that if the Soviet-supported Indian victory over East Bengal (Bangladesh) became a major move against the heart of Pakistan, "the United States would not stand by" and that "all

A formal American governmental decision to move ahead in developing U.S.-Soviet economic and trade relations was made early in 1972. It was marked by the issuance of National Security Decision Memorandum (NSDM) 151 on February 14, 1972, over the joint signature of Kissinger and Peter G. Peterson, chairman of the Council on International Economic Policy (CIEP), and cited a decision by the president.[69] The NSDM directed the Department of State to develop recommendations for a U.S. position on a lend-lease debt settlement with the Soviet Union within two weeks. It also authorized the Department of Agriculture to take the lead in developing a position and scenario for handling grain sales to the USSR, again to be provided within two weeks. Moreover, the Departments of Agriculture and State were to explore with the Soviet Union the timing and modalities of opening negotiations. The recommendations were specifically to include the "US opening a CCC [Commodity Credit Corporation of the U.S. Department of Agriculture] credit line and a Soviet commitment to draw on it."[70] Nominally, the NSDM was in response to a report by a Council on International Economic Policy Ad Hoc Group on U.S.-Soviet trading relationships. But in fact, the NSDM provided a means of moving back channel White House negotiations into more normal channels in order to implement key decisions and commitments already made.

Negotiations proceeded in 1972 toward opening up commerce between the United States and the Soviet Union. Although full agreement had not been reached by the time of the summit conference, the prospect was clearly in sight, with virtual agreement on some important matters, such as credits for grain purchases.

Toward a Meeting at the Summit

The private high-level contacts provided both sides an opportunity to sound out the prospects for détente, as well as to deal with specific acute current issues, and were used for those purposes. Brezhnev employed the contacts in deciding to press his détente policy at the Twenty-fourth Party Con-

---

progress in US-Soviet relations was being threatened by the war on the subcontinent." Kissinger, *White House Years*, p. 904. The Indo-Pakistani War and its impact on U.S.-Soviet relations are discussed in chapter 8.

69. National Security Decision Memorandum–151 (initially published by error as 150), Council on International Economic Policy Decision Memorandum–6, "Next Steps with Respect to U.S.-Soviet Trading Relationships," February 14, 1972 (declassified March 9, 1977). The NSDM was based on a National Security Study Memorandum (NSSM) commissioned by Kissinger on January 17, 1972, calling for a review of "the pros and cons" of granting MFN status. The NSSM outlined in hypothetical terms the deal actually being negotiated in the back channel, including the trade-off of a lend-lease settlement for MFN status.

70. Ibid., p. 1.

gréss in the spring of 1971. Nixon and Kissinger used them as invaluable resources in developing their strategy for détente—and in doing so secretly,
without having to involve the formal governmental bureaucracy, which they
both disdained. As will be seen, both the SALT and Vietnam negotiations
were in part conducted in this secret way, with parallel open formal and back
channel negotiations. Finally, the development of bilateral relations was handled largely through this same mechanism of control.[71] While many individual
economic, scientific, and other projects were of necessity negotiated separately
by parts of the government apparatus, core negotiations and the orchestration
of the many separate parts was held closely in the White House.

Nixon and Kissinger had first broached the possibility of a summit
meeting with Prime Minister Kosygin in several meetings with Dobrynin in
mid-1970, and had even suggested a tentative agenda. The Soviet leaders were,
however, very reluctant to agree to one after the American incursion into
Cambodia. Throughout the summer Nixon continued to want a summit, to be
held in 1970, but the prospect receded.[72] By September a number of developments made a summit meeting in the near term less attractive to both sides:
Salvador Allende was elected in Chile and the Syrians moved into Jordan, as
discussed above. Moreover, the issue of the Cienfuegos submarine base had
arisen. Washington saw all three as involving Soviet challenges.

Thus, when Foreign Minister Gromyko met with the president on
October 22, 1970, he suggested, and only vaguely, a summit meeting for the
late summer of 1971, a signal that there was no strong Soviet interest in an
early meeting. In January 1971 Ambassador Dobrynin finally indicated a readiness to discuss a summit meeting, but only when Kissinger showed a readiness
to discuss the ongoing negotiations over Berlin. As Kissinger notes, he had been
linking American readiness to move on the Berlin negotiations to Soviet movement on SALT. Now Dobrynin was in turn linking a summit to progress on
Berlin.[73] Similar intricate maneuvering marked subsequent discussions of a pos-

---

71. Among other consequences of Nixon and Kissinger's practice of keeping a tight hold on policymaking and implementation was a further decline in the role of the American ambassador in
Moscow, then Jacob Beam. The Soviet preference for dealing through its ambassador in Washington was reinforced by the White House desire to do the same. This also meant cutting out
the Department of State in Washington. The increasingly reduced role of the American
ambassador in Moscow was dramatically underscored in April 1972. Kissinger and his aides
arrived in Moscow on Air Force One (accompanied by Ambassador Dobrynin) and spent four
days in talks with Brezhnev and other Soviet leaders—without Ambassador Beam even being
aware of their presence. See Kissinger's lamely apologetic comment that Beam "deserved
better than this apparent vote of no confidence that *our strange system of government* imposed on him." Emphasis added. Kissinger, *White House Years*, p. 1153.

72. See Hersh, *The Price of Power*, p. 211.

73. Kissinger, *White House Years*, p. 833. Dobrynin had first vaguely suggested to Kissinger, on
September 25, 1970, a possible summit meeting in the late summer of 1971. This was followed
by Gromyko's suggestion to the president in October. I have been advised by a knowledgeable

sible summit, until agreement was finally reached in September 1971 for a meeting in the latter half of May 1972 in Moscow, a decision publicly announced on October 12.[71]

Meanwhile, in mid-July 1971 President Nixon announced he would be visiting China, throwing a new element into the bargaining. The Soviet side began pressing with alacrity for a Moscow meeting before the president's visit to Beijing. Thus the United States, which had initially been the *demandeur* or supplicant for a summit, had reversed roles with the introduction of the China factor.

Two other aspects of the dialogue over a possible summit meeting deserve attention. In August 1971, as the United States moved to respond to the new Soviet interest in a meeting, on Kissinger's advice Nixon for the first time wrote to Brezhnev rather than to Kosygin. This move was prompted by Dobrynin's having stressed to Kissinger the general secretary's new role in foreign policy as evidenced at the Twenty-fourth Party Congress that spring.[75] (In this letter, Nixon also assured Brezhnev that American normalization of relations with China was not directed against the Soviet Union.)

The second interesting aspect of the dialogue on a summit meeting was that it had been conducted by the White House for over a year without ever informing Secretary of State Rogers or anyone else in the government. Accordingly, upon his arrival at the White House on September 29, 1971, Foreign Minister Gromyko was spirited in lest he say something in Rogers' presence before he could be warned. As Kissinger puts it in his memoir, this odd procedure was "vital" because "no one in our bureaucracy as yet knew that a summit had been agreed to." Kissinger described Nixon as returning, "beaming, from the private meeting to tell his Secretary of State that he and Gromyko had just settled plans for the Moscow summit, creating the impression that Gromyko had brought the invitation. . . . Gromyko played his part in some bafflement but with the poker face and aplomb that had seen him through decades of the infinitely more lethal Kremlin politics."[76]

At this time the Soviet side suggested that Kissinger make a secret advance trip to Moscow to prepare the way for the summit meeting—just as he had done in Beijing. Nixon decided against this (although, owing to later circumstances, the trip did occur), not for reasons of high policy, but because he

---

Soviet official that the timing of these early soundings from September 1970 through January 1971 was intended to permit a summit meeting, if agreed upon in time, to be announced so that it could be played up at the forthcoming party congress in March–April 1971.

74. Ibid., pp. 833–38.

75. Ibid., p. 837.

76. Ibid., p. 838. Kissinger relates this story with more than a little sangfroid if not downright satisfaction.

could not see how to arrange it "and keep on terms with Rogers." As Kissinger has observed, "Nixon had kept Rogers from visiting Moscow for nearly three years, partly because he wanted to be the first senior American to go there."[77]

As the summit meeting neared, the political problem of greatest importance remained the failure to reach a settlement in Vietnam. Other pending negotiations had been successfully concluded (such as the quadripartite agreement on Berlin in September 1971), were in train (SALT, although it still had a few important unresolved problems), or had passed from the scene (the Indo-Pakistani War of late 1971). Some of these other problems had involved—or, rather, had been linked to—the summit prospects. For example, in December 1971 Kissinger had hinted—both in a private conversation with the Soviet chargé d'affaires, and then in an inspired press leak—that the Moscow summit meeting might be called off if the Soviets did not prevail on India to end the war with Pakistan.[78]

The heightened tensions of the Vietnam War in 1972 posed serious problems for both sides. The Nixon administration was increasingly anxious to effect a settlement as its fourth—and the election—year rolled on, while the Soviet leaders became increasingly uncomfortable over public rapprochement with the United States at the very time that country was intensifying its military pressures on the USSR's North Vietnamese ally. Moreover, Nixon and Kissinger had placed high hopes on linkage to gain Soviet assistance in effecting a settlement. On March 30, in the midst of the difficult American–North Vietnamese negotiations, the North Vietnamese launched a major offensive. On April 12, in the course of ongoing discussions of the Vietnam issue between Kissinger and Dobrynin, the latter again proposed that Kissinger visit Moscow to discuss both Vietnam and the summit conference preparations. Nixon had mixed feelings about the idea (and, for that matter, about the summit at that juncture). Further, as Kissinger tells it, "Not the least of Nixon's concerns was how he would explain to Rogers yet another secret mission by his security adviser, this time to Moscow."[79] Nixon had turned down Rogers' own request to visit Moscow to prepare for the summit meeting. Finally Nixon resolved the problem by a ruse. He would go to Camp David while Kissinger was in Moscow and then inform Rogers that the trip was in response to a sudden invitation from Brezhnev for Kissinger to discuss Vietnam.[80]

---

77. Ibid., p. 839.

78. Ibid., pp. 900–01; and John Osborne, *The Fourth Year of the Nixon Watch* (Liverwright, 1973), p. 66.

79. Kissinger, *White House Years*, p. 1120.

80. Ibid., pp. 1120, 1123. I can attest that, soon after the event, when it transpired that Kissinger had also negotiated in Moscow on SALT, Secretary Rogers was highly indignant because he believed, on the basis of what he had been told by Nixon, that Kissinger was empowered to discuss only Vietnam.

Kissinger's Moscow Pre-Summit Meeting

So Kissinger went to Moscow for four days (April 20–24, 1972). The visit was of considerable importance in several respects. Whatever the effects on the later outcome of the American–North Vietnamese negotiations, it was an important link in the chain of American-Soviet exchanges on that subject. The visit also included important discussions on outstanding SALT issues. Finally, it played a significant part in developing a "charter" for détente that was adopted at the summit.

The summit preparations had begun in earnest in January 1972, when Dobrynin returned from a stay in Moscow bearing a letter from Brezhnev outlining a possible extensive agenda for the summit meeting. (This initiative, which came on January 21, immediately preceded Nixon's trip to Beijing in early February.) Dobrynin also gingerly raised with Kissinger the question of a possible declaration of principles in addition to a traditional communiqué. Kissinger and Nixon considered this to be a reasonable proposal and felt it would be better to attempt to make use of such a statement of principles than to balk, although they stalled for a time. On February 7, when Dobrynin again raised the matter, Kissinger agreed to look at a Soviet draft, but Dobrynin dodged that suggestion until March 9. At that time, he suggested using the recent (October 30, 1971) French-Soviet "Principles of Cooperation" as a basis. On March 17 Kissinger provided a draft communiqué, including principles, similar to the one issued with the Chinese in February. The draft, prepared by Kissinger's staff and with Nixon's approval, called for mutual restraint, noninterference in the affairs of other states, and renunciation of pressures for unilateral advantage. Nothing further was heard of the matter until Kissinger's visit to Moscow in April.[81]

Dobrynin also advised Kissinger in early February that the Soviet Union was ready to reopen talks to settle American lend-lease claims (for nonmilitary goods delivered during World War II). This fact was disclosed publicly, although its relationship to the expanding network of interrelated moves involving a number of areas of economic relations in the context of advancing toward a summit was not. In April a Soviet delegation quietly arrived in Washington for talks on the lend-lease issue.

Meanwhile in Washington, oblivious to all that was already going on, on March 14 Secretary of State Rogers sent a memorandum to the president saying that he planned to "take personal charge" of the summit preparations. Nixon did not discuss the matter with Rogers personally, but instructed Haldeman to request that *any* State Department contact with Dobrynin be cleared in advance. Then on March 17 Nixon dropped in on a Kissinger-Dobrynin tête-à-tête to inform Dobrynin that Kissinger was in charge of all major

---

81. Ibid., pp. 1126–27, 1131–32.

summit preparations (other than technical matters, such as the wording of exchange agreements and the like). The State Department was left to shuffle its own preparatory papers, making no real input.[82]

It should be noted that President Nixon by this time had considerable reservations about the Soviet role in helping reach a Vietnam settlement. Accordingly he had instructed Kissinger to discuss summit preparations and SALT only if and when a satisfactory position had been reached on Vietnam. In his memoir Kissinger offers a belabored, but on the whole convincing, case as to why he did not follow these instructions. Instead, after exacting the most he could on Vietnam, he went on to work out some important SALT solutions (which he had launched earlier with Dobrynin and was pursuing without the president even being aware of the fact). Moreover, he worked out not only the summit agenda, but also the text of what was to become the basic principles of American-Soviet détente.[83]

On April 22, following the discussions of Vietnam and SALT, Brezhnev presented a new draft declaration of principles, an elaboration of the draft provided by Kissinger on March 17. He invited Kissinger to amend— "improve"—it, and that evening Kissinger and his aide Helmut Sonnenfeldt did so. The very next day Kissinger and Gromyko agreed on a draft. Kissinger describes it as emphasizing restraint and calming conflicts, and as renouncing "any claim for special privileges in any part of the world (which we, at least, interpreted as a repudiation of the Brezhnev Doctrine for Eastern Europe)."[84] He does not refer back to the president's instructions "to emphasize the need for a single standard; we could not accept the proposition that the Soviet Union had the right to support liberation movements all over the world while insisting on the Brezhnev Doctrine inside the satellite orbit."[85] In his final reporting cable to the president (couched in terms to justify his having overstepped his instructions), Kissinger declared that he had reached "agreement on a declaration of principles to be published at the summit which includes most of our proposals and indeed involves a specific renunciation of the Brezhnev doctrine."[86] The principles, as will be seen, did not in fact include any renunciation of the Brezhnev Doctrine, much less a "specific" or explicit commitment, but only the most general language which perhaps "we, at least" (to use Kissinger's own strained expression) could interpret as making the doctrine inoperative. Kissinger made no reference to Nixon's instruction that he not

---

82. Ibid., p. 1128.

83. Ibid., pp. 1135–37, 1148, 1154–64; and see Nixon, *RN*, p. 592. Incidentally, Nixon devotes only a single page to Kissinger's April 1972 Moscow visit, in contrast to Kissinger's forty pages. The mission was highly important, and it is clear that Nixon did not recognize—or wish to acknowledge—its significance even when he wrote his memoir several years later.

84. Kissinger, *White House Years*, pp. 1150–51.

85. Ibid., p. 1136.

86. Cited verbatim from the reporting cable, ibid., p. 1153.

accept a text that allowed the Soviets to support liberation movements. Nixon, who did not follow such matters closely, never brought the matter up again. Indeed, there is nothing in the record to suggest that the proposed declaration of basic principles was discussed further with the president (who does not even mention it in his own brief comments on Kissinger's negotiations in Moscow). Nor were they discussed with "the bureaucracy," that is, the relevant cabinet officers and departments. Kissinger recounts how, en route to Moscow for the summit meeting, Nixon was "still concerned about how to surface the declaration of 'Basic Principles of US-Soviet Relations' " because Rogers still had not been told about it. Again, as in the earlier charade with Gromyko at the White House, Nixon "asked Brezhnev's help to introduce the document in a manner compatible with our bureaucratic necessities." Brezhnev later "took his cue" and proposed that Gromyko and Kissinger work on SALT and "might also give some thought to general principles that should govern relations between our two countries," while Rogers and Gromyko would discuss European security.[87] Finally, while working with Assistant Secretary of State for European Affairs Martin Hillenbrand on the communiqué, "in the waning hours of the summit, Gromyko surfaced without explanation the 'Basic Principles of US-Soviet Relations' agreed to in April." Hillenbrand was "too wise to make an issue of it. And so we navigated a summit for once without a White House–State confrontation."[88]

Other aspects of the American preparations for the summit meeting, including Kissinger's April trip, are addressed in the later discussions of SALT diplomacy and of triangular diplomacy and the Vietnam negotiations.[89] Such dissenting political voices as there were—and there were some skeptics— generally expressed concern or dissatisfaction only after the event. Indeed, little was known in advance except that a SALT agreement was expected.

Soviet Political Developments

On the Soviet side, there *was* significant disagreement over proceeding with the summit meeting after the United States in April escalated mili-

---

87. Ibid., pp. 1205, 1209, 1213.

88. Ibid., p. 1250. The avoidance of friction was purchased at some cost. State Department officials were only informed about a number of issues too late in the process to affect the outcome in the communiqué; the basic principles had been agreed to in April; and the final SALT provisions had been agreed to with the benefit of assistance and advice only from Kissinger's staff, as the SALT delegation had been held in Helsinki. To cite but one example from the communiqué: the Quadripartite Agreement on Berlin concluded in September 1971 is referred to as "relating to the Western Sectors of Berlin"—contrary to the United Kingdom, French, West German—and prior U.S.—position that the agreement applied to *all* sectors of Berlin. This was not a mere editorial detail. The other Western powers were appalled.

89. On SALT, see chapter 5; on triangular diplomacy and Vietnam, see chapters 6 and 7.

tary operations in Vietnam by mining Haiphong in response to the North
Vietnamese offensive. Politburo member Pyotr Ye. Shelest, possibly supported
in part by some other members, directly challenged the idea of proceeding with
the summit. According to one account, he said that Nixon would not be welcome in the Ukraine, and "I will not shake the hand that has been bloodied in
Vietnam." Brezhnev then turned to the other Ukrainian member of the Politburo, Vladimir Shcherbitsky, and asked if he agreed. He did not. Brezhnev
reportedly then commented to Shelest, "You see, Comrade, you can speak for
yourself, but you cannot speak for all Ukrainians."[90] According to some reports, Shelest carried his disagreement to the special Central Committee plenary meeting held on May 19 in final preparation for the summit.[91] Brezhnev
prevailed easily and Shelest was downgraded to the relatively lower position of
a deputy prime minister (one of a dozen) on the eve of the summit, May 21.
Then, on May 25, it was announced that he had been removed as Ukrainian
first secretary (a position in which, incidentally, Shcherbitsky replaced him).[92]
So it was Shcherbitsky who received President Nixon on his visit to Kiev.

90. See Hedrick Smith, "Soviet Sees Politics Behind Arms Pact," *New York Times*, June 9, 1972;
    and Jack Anderson, "Afghan Invasion: A Kremlin Mystery," *Washington Post*, January 29,
    1980. They cite classified intelligence reports detailing the Shelest story, including the remarks
    cited above. Shelest did participate in some protocol and social events at the summit meeting,
    along with other members of the Politburo, specifically President Nixon's dinner and the
    SALT signing. I was present and am sure Shelest shook Nixon's hand in a reception at the
    Kremlin just before the signing of the SALT agreements. I recall shaking hands with Shelest
    along with the other Politburo members there. But there were signs of unease, and Shelest
    refrained from joining in a toast to the SALT Treaty until Aleksandr N. Shelepin talked him
    into it.

91. The very holding of this special Central Committee plenum reflected Brezhnev's caution and
    the need to justify the position taken and to consolidate support. A regular plenum in Novem-
    ber 1971 had also addressed foreign policy issues, including the treaty with West Germany,
    which had also been debated within the Soviet leadership.

    Arkady Shevchenko, a former senior Soviet diplomat who defected in 1978, was at that time
    serving as an aide to Gromyko in Moscow and helped prepare Brezhnev's presentation to the
    Central Committee. Shevchenko, who did not attend the Central Committee meeting, does
    not report a clash at the meeting itself, but his account does make clear the divided views
    within the leadership. Shevchenko describes the initial uncertainty among Gromyko's deputies
    over what the decision of the leadership about the summit meeting would be following the
    mining of Haiphong. See Arkady N. Shevchenko, *Breaking with Moscow* (Alfred A. Knopf,
    1985), pp. 211–14.

92. Shelest was removed from the Politburo on April 27, 1973, shortly before Brezhnev's trips to
    Bonn and to Washington for the second summit meeting. Another reason for Shelest's ouster
    was his failure to curb Ukrainian nationalism effectively. A clear tip-off of his fall appeared in
    a sharply critical review of a book on the Ukraine he had published three years earlier, saying
    "there isn't even mention given to the cooperation and mutual assistance of the fraternal
    nations . . . of the united Soviet state." See "About the Serious Shortcomings and Errors of a
    Certain Book," *Kommunist Ukrainy* [Communist of the Ukraine], no. 4 (April 1973), pp.
    77–82. Shelest had instead accented that "the Ukrainian Soviet Socialist Republic has become
    one of the most highly developed countries in the world." Pyotr Shelest, *Ukraino nasha
    Radyans'ka* [Our Soviet Ukraine] (Kiev: Vydaunytstvo Politychnoyi Literatury Ukrainy,
    1970), p. 74.

One can well understand why the Soviet leadership was disturbed over the effect at that particular juncture of the reception of the American president and use of the summit meeting to unveil a virtual flood of cooperative Soviet-American endeavors, as well as the general launching of détente. Not only the Vietnamese but other Soviet allies and clients might conclude that their alignment with the Soviet Union might result in their interests being given short shrift if they conflicted with the common interests of the two superpowers.

At the same time, Brezhnev and most of his colleagues were prepared to accept the risks and costs of such reactions rather than jeopardize the long-sought recognition of parity and compact of equality with the most powerful country on earth. Moreover, other critical Soviet interests were at stake. The Soviets needed to counterbalance the establishment of American ties with China. President Nixon's visit to China in February, if not offset by a visit to the Soviet Union, could lead to a Sino-American alignment, with Moscow losing leverage with both in the ensuing triangular relationship. Another was détente in Europe. While progressing, it was still in a delicate formative stage, and the Soviet leaders had recognized for some time that a general European security agreement could be reached only if the United States participated. More immediately, West German ratification of the treaties with the USSR and Poland was pending—and uncertain. At Kissinger's April mini-summit meeting Brezhnev and Gromyko asked for American assistance with the impending ratification vote in the West German Bundestag. Kissinger replied that Hanoi's new military offensive made it difficult for the United States to be of use, thus linking both European security and Vietnam with the summit meeting, in the hope of using movement on the first for leverage on the second. Later in Washington, on May 9, just one day after the announcement of the American escalation in Vietnam, Kissinger was able to inform Ambassador Dobrynin that the Bundestag *would* ratify the Eastern treaties.[93] It was to do so on the very day that Brezhnev informed the Central Committee plenum in Moscow of the decision to proceed with the summit meeting, overriding Shelest's opposition. Another factor was the anticipated benefits of expanded trade with the United States and other advantages of détente, which would be delayed or sacrificed if the scheduled summit were canceled.[94] Indeed, such an action could prejudice relations during the expected four-and-a-half years spanning a renewed Nixon administration.

In addition to differences among the Soviet leaders over particular policy issues, the period from 1969 to 1973 marked Brezhnev's continuing struggle to gain dominance within the leadership. Differences over policy were

93. Kissinger, *White House Years*, pp. 1150, 1192.

94. As noted earlier in this chapter, there was continuing debate in the Soviet Union over the economic aspects of détente, with some Soviet leaders in favor but others concerned about increased economic interdependence with the capitalist West. For Brezhnev and others in the leadership, though not all, postponement of or prejudice to developing these ties would have been a real sacrifice.

ineluctably related to personal and factional differences within the leadership. And Brezhnev was developing a strong vested interest in the success of his policy of détente with the West, including the United States.[95]

The Soviet leadership was concerned about its vulnerability in the eyes of radical elements in the third world to charges (which the Chinese would certainly delight in trumpeting) that the Soviet Union was selling out to the United States for its own selfish interests. An official spokesman, writing in *Pravda* under a pseudonym, rebuffed unnamed opponents of the Soviet-American summit, commenting: "The dialogue took place despite the complexity of the international situation and in the sometimes direct opposition of those who like to warm their hands by fanning the fires of hostility and tension."[96] That this statement was principally directed against China, and was a defense of the Soviet position vis-à-vis North Vietnam, North Korea, Cuba, Egypt, and other Soviet clients, was clear from the context. The passage went on to identify "the fires of hostility and tension" as "between other states." Credit—and responsibility—for the achievements of the summit meeting were given to the Politburo and the Central Committee, which, it was stressed, "are conducting a foreign policy based not on mere ad hoc considerations or whims, but on the profound and fundamental interests of the Soviet people and world socialism and the interests of peace and progress for mankind." The defensiveness of the Soviet leaders was especially clear in the ensuing passage: "Negotiations which are conducted on the basis of positions of principle and involve reasonable tactical compromises fully in keeping with these positions are not a sign of weakness or softness, but an obligation for all who are guided in their actions by the real interests of peace and socialism rather than by 'revolutionary' phrasemongering."[97]

This argument in *Pravda* was directed not only at foreign communist or radical elements that might criticize the Soviet leaders' decision, but also at domestic doubts about the summit meeting and any residual opposition to détente as a whole. Even after the Twenty-fourth Party Congress in April 1971 and the Central Committee plenum of November 1971, some Politburo members and others still had reservations, as Shelest's case shows. Vadim Zagladin, a rising party official involved with international affairs, argued the point at some length, in effect adumbrating the *Pravda* article. In this context he cited the May 1972 Central Committee plenum's resolution that "the principled, consistent foreign policy of the USSR is responsive to the vital interests of the Soviet Union, world socialism, the national liberation movement, and it organically links decisions on immediate current tasks with a long-term perspec-

---

95. See Harry Gelman, *The Brezhnev Politburo and the Decline of Detente* (Ithaca, N.Y.: Cornell University Press, 1984), pp. 126–30, 156–60.

96. Yu. Chernov, *Pravda*, June 14, 1972. "Yu. Chernov" is a pseudonym used by the official spokesman of the Ministry of Foreign Affairs, Yury N. Chernyakov.

97. Ibid. Emphasis added.

tive and the aims of the struggle for peace, freedom, and the security of nations, social progress and socialism."[98] Zagladin also seemed to contrast favorably the decision of Brezhnev's Politburo to go forward with the summit meeting with Nikita Khrushchev's impulsive and abrupt cancellation of the Paris summit and planned visit of President Dwight D. Eisenhower to Moscow after the American U-2 reconnaissance plane was shot down over the Soviet Union on May Day, 1960. Elaborating on the *Pravda* article, Zagladin noted that "experience" had shown that ad hoc reactions, "self-limitation" to current considerations, and failure to take into account long-term perspectives "never brings advantage" and is "close to subjective improvization," a charge that had been levied against Khrushchev.[99] Arbatov also referred to "aggravations" in Soviet-American relations which "could have made these talks impossible" and noted that some forces (which he did not identify) had tried to shift the main line of Soviet foreign policy.[100]

The official Soviet *History of the Foreign Policy of the USSR*, edited by Politburo members Gromyko and Boris N. Ponomarev, stated that the decision to proceed with the summit conference in May 1972 "was not simple or easy for the Soviet leadership, because at that moment there occurred a sharp turn in U.S. military operations in Vietnam. However, the taking of such a decision was dictated by a broad, far-sighted approach to the question, by a calculation of the long-term interests of the Soviet people" and, it continues, "of its allies and friends, including the people of Vietnam. The question was one of reducing the threat of a new world war."[101] The retrospective evaluation further noted that "life has shown that the decision taken was correct," citing a number of reasons including a general boost to détente and

---

98. Cited by V. Zagladin, "Principle and Consistency," *Novoye vremya* [New Times], no. 22 (May 26, 1972), p. 5. Zagladin is now first deputy chief of the International Department of the Central Committee.

    Shevchenko, the former Soviet diplomat, reports having been called by Zagladin prior to the summit meeting to protest on Ponomarev's behalf the fact that the draft Basic Principles agreement did not make clear continuing Soviet support for the national liberation struggle. Gromyko obtained Brezhnev's decision, and the matter was not raised in the Politburo meeting that approved the Basic Principles. Shevchenko, *Breaking with Moscow*, pp. 205–07. It was thus fitting that Zagladin, on the basis of the discussion in the Central Committee meeting, should make this point publicly at the time of the summit.

99. Ibid.

100. Georgy A. Arbatov on Moscow Television, June 8, 1972 (as cited in Hedrick Smith, *New York Times*, June 9, 1972).

101. A. A. Gromyko and B. N. Ponomarev, eds., *Istoriya vneshnei politiki SSSR, 1917–1980* [History of the Foreign Policy of the USSR, 1917–1980] (Moscow: Nauka, 1981), vol. 2, 4th ed., p. 493. The *History* also states that the proposal for the summit meeting came from the U.S. side, and that Soviet agreement was given only after the United States had met "requisite preconditions" set down by the Soviet leaders: the Berlin agreement, signing of the agreement banning bacteriological weapons, and constructive negotiation on SALT. Ibid., p. 492.

international security, justification of peaceful coexistence, "a tremendous growth in the authority and influence" of the Soviet Union, a deterrent effect on the more belligerent capitalist circles, and creation of "more favorable conditions for political resolution of international conflicts, including the war in Vietnam."[102] The Soviet leaders thus justified their decision to go ahead with the summit to themselves and to political critics on the left abroad and at home.

The White House considered it a very serious possibility, if not probability, that the Soviets would not hold the scheduled summit meeting because of the American escalation in Vietnam. President Nixon in particular was so concerned the Soviets would cancel it that he seriously considered preemptively canceling it himself.

On May 2 Kissinger returned from a disappointing secret meeting in Paris with Le Duc Tho that indicated no movement toward a settlement by the North Vietnamese. Indeed, the Vietnamese stand was interpreted as meaning that they considered victory in sight without having to meet American terms. As a result, Nixon (and Kissinger and most close advisers except Secretary of Defense Melvin R. Laird and Secretary Rogers) believed a strong American military escalation was needed. As Kissinger recounts in some detail, this factor fueled Nixon's strong inclination to cancel the summit meeting himself rather than be humiliated by a Soviet cancellation.

After an exchange of letters with Brezhnev, which only hinted at the American conclusion that the Soviets might cancel the summit meeting, the president finally decided to go ahead and leave it to the Soviet leaders to cancel if they decided to do so. Kissinger credits John B. Connally with being most persuasive in arguing that the onus should be on the Soviets to cancel. It is typical that Nixon sought advice on a possible cancellation only from Kissinger, Connally, Haldeman, and Haig—not Rogers or others. It is fortunate that he widened the group to include Connally, or it is probable he would have canceled the meeting. It is also interesting that Haldeman and Nixon both state that it was *Kissinger* who recommended postponing the summit and that only after Haldeman objected did Nixon suggest they both consult with Connally. All accounts concur that Connally's support for Haldeman's position led Nixon to change his stand—and persuaded Kissinger, too.[103]

There was never any indication from the Soviet side that it might cancel the summit meeting. Kissinger says that after he notified Dobrynin in advance of the president's speech of May 8 on the mining and bombing, the ambassador was "gloomy about the reaction in Moscow." Nevertheless, two days later when Dobrynin presented the official Soviet reaction, and in further

---

102. Ibid.

103. See Kissinger, *White House Years*, pp. 1176–89; Haldeman, *The Ends of Power*, pp. 228–30; and Nixon, *RN*, pp. 600–03, 607. Kissinger and Haldeman omit reference to Haig as a participant, probably because he was junior and perhaps he was silent. Nixon includes him.

discussions the next day, it became clear that the summit meeting remained as scheduled.[104]

Indeed, Soviet determination to proceed with the summit meeting despite the bombing of Hanoi and Haiphong showed how serious their interest in détente was and what a high priority it had. Conversely, Nixon and his administration showed they were ready, if necessary, to sacrifice détente in order to wage the geopolitical competition by pressing ahead with military means in seeking a solution in Vietnam. While this indication of priorities was little recognized in the West, it must not have passed unnoticed in Moscow.

Preparation for the summit included meetings between Kissinger and Dobrynin on twelve of the sixteen days from May 3 through 18, interspersed with efforts to resume negotiations with the North Vietnamese. And in separate parallel secret talks, plans were also being made with the Chinese for a further visit by Kissinger to Beijing in June, right after Moscow.

By mid-1972 several main strands of policy—and of events—had come together to create the necessary critical mass to launch American-Soviet détente. They were: European détente, with the Berlin settlement sought by the West and the treaties with West Germany sought by the Soviet Union (and Poland); a Sino-American rapprochement, sought by the United States (as well as by China), which the Soviet Union could not prevent but wished to counterbalance; a SALT agreement (although with some residual difficulties resolved only at the summit meeting itself); an incomplete but progressive meeting of the minds on expanded trade, sought principally by the Soviets; hope for Vietnam, in that, though the issue was still unsettled, at least both the Soviets and Chinese had demonstrated an unwillingness to permit solidarity with North Vietnam to override their own interests in rapprochement with the United States; and internal political support for détente high on both sides.

---

104. Kissinger, *White House Years*, pp. 1188–94; Nixon, *RN*, p. 607. Kissinger does not mention that, in contrast to the negative expectations of the White House after the bombing, the Soviet experts at the State Department correctly predicted the Soviet leaders would not cancel the summit.

Years later, in his memoir (not in the volume dealing with the 1972 summit), Kissinger was to look back with greater geopolitical sangfroid and remark: "Nixon's 1972 summit in Moscow took place under nearly ideal circumstances. Two weeks before, Nixon had ordered the resumption of bombing of North Vietnam and the mining of its harbors. When Moscow maintained its invitation nevertheless, the Kremlin showed that it would subordinate some of the concerns of its friends to Soviet-American relations. We in turn had demonstrated that we were fully prepared to risk détente for what we considered vital interests." Henry Kissinger, *Years of Upheaval* (Boston, Mass.: Little, Brown, 1982), p. 287.

4   Europe Moves to Détente, 1966–72

A NUMBER of events in 1966 prompt selection of that date as the starting point for a review of the movement to détente in Europe, which preceded, then overlapped, and finally outlasted the efforts to improve American-Soviet relations. Initiatives were made that year by President Charles de Gaulle, who sought an independent role for France in bridging East-West estrangement. They were also made by successive governments in the Federal Republic of Germany (West Germany), which gradually abandoned its line of political aloofness for one of contact with the East, though maintaining an ultimate aim of German reunification. And in 1966 President Lyndon B. Johnson, in a speech drafted by Zbigniew Brzezinski, an academic expert of East European origin serving a tour with the Policy Planning Council of the Department of State, called for fostering a greater degree of independence in the communist countries of eastern and central Europe through "peaceful engagement."[1] At the Twenty-third Party Congress in March 1966, General Secretary Leonid I. Brezhnev combined slashing attacks on the United States and West Germany with a call for "achieving European security" on the basis of the territorial status quo.[2] This theme assumed more concrete form and was advanced more vigorously at succeeding meetings of the Warsaw Pact leaders. In a series of formal declarations beginning at Bucharest in July 1966, they ex-

---

1. The term *peaceful engagement* was first used in an article by Zbigniew Brzezinski and William E. Griffith, "Peaceful Engagement in Eastern Europe," *Foreign Affairs*, vol. 39 (July 1961), pp. 642–54. It was first introduced as a political theme in a speech by Johnson in October 1966. In an earlier speech, in May 1964, Johnson had advanced the same idea in terms of "building bridges" between East and West. See Lyndon Baines Johnson, *The Vantage Point: Perspectives of the Presidency, 1963–1969* (Holt, Rinehart and Winston, 1971), pp. 471–75.

2. L. I. Brezhnev, "Report of the Central Committee of the CPSU to the XXIII Congress of the Communist Party of the Soviet Union, March 29, 1966," in *O vneshnei politike KPSS i sovetskogo gosudarstva: Rechi i stat'i* [On the Foreign Policy of the CPSU and the Soviet Government: Speeches and Articles], 3d ed. (Moscow: Politzdat, 1978), pp. 42–44.

pressed their desire to proceed on the basis of a "relaxation of tension," or détente. Finally, in 1966 the North Atlantic Treaty Organization (NATO) allies commissioned a study of the future tasks of the alliance. The ensuing Harmel Report called specifically for a policy of détente to complement continuing efforts in defense.

De Gaulle's Détente

De Gaulle's initiatives broke the ice and facilitated moves by others to thaw the frozen state of confrontation between West and East in Europe. De Gaulle visited Moscow with some fanfare in June 1966 and edged toward recognition of the fact of two German states. That same spring and summer French Foreign Minister Couve de Murville visited Warsaw, Prague, Bucharest, Budapest, and Sofia. France also stepped up cultural exchanges with Eastern Europe. De Gaulle himself visited the two countries with the strongest traditional and cultural ties to France—Poland and Romania—in 1967 and 1968 and sought to play up their historical associations. President Nicolae Ceaușescu in Romania, already launched on a path of limited independence, welcomed this attention. In Poland, First Secretary Władysław Gomulka prudently and pointedly recalled the failure of the Polish-French alliance before World War II to save either country and stressed the Polish alliance with the Soviet Union and the Warsaw Pact as the cornerstone of Polish policy and guarantor of its security. Both Romania and Poland stated that recognition of the German Democratic Republic (East Germany) was necessary before there could be real détente in Europe. De Gaulle also planned to visit Czechoslovakia, Hungary, and Bulgaria, but these plans were not realized before he resigned the presidency in April 1969.

De Gaulle was not only moving to the East, he was also moving from the West, so to speak. Parallel with his movement toward détente with the East, in 1966 he loosened his ties with the Western alliance, withdrawing from the integrated NATO military organization and forcing NATO to move its headquarters and other facilities from France. On his visits in Eastern Europe de Gaulle constantly referred to the problem of a divided Germany, and the generally unsettled state of political affairs between East and West, as "a European question," to be settled by European nations, not including the United States or the two alliances, NATO and the Warsaw Pact.

Under President Georges Pompidou, France continued its policy of Eastern détente, but with reduced effect. France also moderated its relationship toward NATO and the United States. In 1970 Pompidou visited Moscow, while Brezhnev visited France the following year. French-Soviet agreements to consult in times of tension (October 13, 1970) and on general principles of cooperation (October 30, 1971) were concluded, and on the latter occasion France supported convening a European security conference. Détente was even a French word. Still, de Gaulle's ambitions notwithstanding, France was never in a position to bring about a general East-West détente.

West Germany's Ostpolitik

West Germany, on the other hand, occupied a key position. Chancellor Konrad Adenauer had taken a rigid position that in effect made reunification of Germany a precondition of détente. Under Adenauer's successor, Ludwig Erhard, there had been abortive attempts to initiate a more active *Ostpolitik* (Eastern Policy), while continuing not to recognize East Germany. In March 1966 West Germany sent to all governments, including the Eastern European communist ones (though not, of course, East Germany), a "Peace Note." It offered to exchange declarations not to use force in settling international disputes. The overture was rejected. Chancellor Kurt Kiesinger, who took office in December 1966, further modified West Germany's policy. During the succeeding three years of his Christian Democratic incumbency and that of the Christian Democratic–Social Democratic Grand Coalition under Chancellor Willy Brandt, a cautious *Ostpolitik* was begun, and the "Hallstein Doctrine" policy of nonrecognition of any government that recognized East Germany was finally abandoned.

In January 1967 Romania defied Moscow and established relations with West Germany. Several other Eastern European countries (Bulgaria and Hungary, in particular) also showed an interest, but the Soviet leaders quickly convened a Warsaw Pact meeting in early February in Warsaw and obtained a pledge from all the others not to recognize West Germany until it recognized East Germany.

The accession to power of Willy Brandt as chancellor in October 1969, supported by a new coalition of his Social Democratic and the Free Democratic parties, initiated a new active German *Ostpolitik* based on recognizing East Germany and the territorial changes effected after World War II. Brandt also sought to allay any genuine Soviet and Eastern European concerns. On November 18, 1969, West Germany signed the Nuclear Non-Proliferation Treaty. On January 14, 1970, Brandt offered to negotiate a nonaggression pact with East Germany—but without extending diplomatic recognition. Negotiations included a meeting between Brandt and East German Prime Minister Willi Stoph in Erfurt in East Germany in March 1970. But East Germany (and the Warsaw Pact, less Romania) remained adamant on full recognition.

In its active pursuit of *Ostpolitik* beginning in late 1969, West Germany's strategy was first to negotiate directly with the Soviet Union itself, then to settle the Oder-Neisse border with Poland, and finally to negotiate with East Germany. The quadripartite negotiations on Berlin would proceed in parallel. Thus, while Brandt established early contact with East Germany to show his readiness to accept that state, he still wanted to reach agreement with the Soviet Union first. Brandt and Foreign Minister Andrei A. Gromyko met a number of times personally in the summer of 1970. On August 12, 1970, Brandt and Prime Minister Aleksei N. Kosygin signed a Non-Aggression Pact in Moscow. It both included a reciprocal agreement not to use force against each other, and implicitly acknowledged geopolitical realities. On December 7 a treaty was concluded with Poland recognizing the postwar Oder-Neisse border.[3]

Further progress in realizing *Ostpolitik* and movement toward eventual reciprocal recognition of the two Germanies, and also toward agreement in the quadripartite negotiations under way on Berlin, came only after Walter Ulbricht resigned in May 1971 as party chief in East Germany and was succeeded by Erich Honecker. Ulbricht, sometimes called "the last Stalinist," had been most reluctant to accept any movement from the status quo—even one that Soviet leaders believed to be in Soviet and East German interests. Eventually the Soviet leaders persuaded Ulbricht to bow out. While the approaches of the two German states differed, and continue to differ, it did prove possible to accommodate both the East German idea of a demarcation (*Abgrenzung*) between the two German states, and Brandt's idea of "two states within one German nation." Finally, on December 22, 1972, the two Germanies signed a treaty entailing reciprocal recognition.[4]

Kissinger reveals in his memoir that Nixon and he were suspicious and "worried" by Brandt's *Ostpolitik*. They were moved to develop an American détente with the Soviet Union in part to preclude a West German–led European détente with the Soviet Union from excluding the United States and thus splitting the Western alliance.[5] Kissinger also claims, unconvincingly, credit for salvaging Brandt's *Ostpolitik* through his own back channel to Soviet Ambassador Anatoly Dobrynin.[6]

---

3. The West German treaties with the USSR and Poland were not ratified until May 19, 1972—a timing that coincided with the first Nixon-Brezhnev summit; see chapter 3.

4. On the German *Ostpolitik* of the latter 1960s and early 1970s, see William E. Griffith, *The Ostpolitik of the Federal Republic of Germany* (Cambridge, Mass.: MIT Press, 1978); Lawrence L. Whetten, *Germany's Ostpolitik: Relations between the Federal Republic and the Warsaw Pact Countries* (London: Oxford University Press, 1971); Angela Stent, *From Embargo to Ostpolitik: The Political Economy of West German–Soviet Relations, 1955–1980* (Cambridge University Press, 1981); Josef Korbel, *Detente in Europe: Real or Imaginary?* (Princeton, N.J.: Princeton University Press, 1972); and Andrew Gyorgy, "Ostpolitik and Eastern Europe," in Charles Gati, ed., *The International Politics of Eastern Europe* (Praeger, 1976), pp. 154–72.

5. See Henry Kissinger, *White House Years* (Boston, Mass.: Little, Brown, 1979), pp. 408–12, 423–24, 529–34, 789–99; and Kissinger, *Years of Upheaval* (Little, Brown, 1982), pp. 143–48, 154–59, 731. For additional light on Kissinger's antipathy to Brandt, see Seymour M. Hersh, *The Price of Power: Kissinger in the Nixon White House* (Summit, 1983), pp. 416–18.

6. Kissinger, *Years of Upheaval*, p. 156.

The developments in West Germany's *Ostpolitik* (and Soviet *Westpolitik*) were evolving against the background of other events and developments affecting East-West relations in Europe.

NATO and the Warsaw Pact

The North Atlantic Treaty, signed in 1949 at the depth of the cold war, and NATO constitute an alliance for military defense. The durability of the alliance bears witness to the fact that it has also reflected broader common interests of its members. But defense and deterrence against possible Soviet military attack remains its fundamental raison d'être.

As noted, in December 1966, at the initiative of Belgian Foreign Minister Pierre Harmel, a study group was commissioned to prepare a report on "The Future Tasks of the Alliance." The Harmel Report, as it was called, was approved by the member governments on December 14, 1967. It explicitly recognized that in the time since the alliance had come into being, "the international situation has changed significantly and the political tasks of the Alliance have assumed a new dimension." The first task of the alliance remained "to deter aggression and other forms of pressure and to defend the territory of member countries if aggression should occur." But the second task, articulated for the first time, was "to pursue the search for progress towards a more stable relationship in which the underlying political issues can be solved." The objective of working "to further a détente in East-West relations" was explicitly affirmed, as was the conclusion that under existing circumstances "military security and a policy of détente are not contradictory but complementary." This position was reaffirmed in subsequent NATO communiqués and declarations, which came to use the term "twin pillars" of defense and détente. It should, however, be noted that there was still some caution with respect to the need to achieve not merely better relations, but also a settlement of real differences. Again to cite the December 1967 alliance charter for détente, "The relaxation of tensions is not the final goal but is part of a long-term process to promote better relations and to foster a European settlement. The ultimate political purpose of the Alliance is to achieve a just and lasting peaceful order in Europe accompanied by appropriate security guarantees."[7]

The adoption of the Harmel Report led to the first NATO studies of mutual force reductions in Europe during 1968–70. In June 1968, while these studies were getting under way, NATO held its semiannual ministerial meeting in Reykjavik, Iceland. It affirmed the readiness of the members of the alliance to "explore with other interested states specific and practical steps in the arms control field" and declared that "a process leading to mutual force

---

7. "The Future Tasks of the Alliance: Report of the Council," in *NATO Final Communiqués, 1949–1970* (Brussels: NATO, 1971), pp. 188–92.

reductions should be initiated."[8] This was the first step in launching the process that in the 1970s became the negotiations on mutual and balanced force reductions (MBFR). Some allied officials were uneasy about this initiative, since the implications of force reductions were not yet clear. Soon after the Reykjavik appeal, the Soviet Union and some of its Warsaw Pact allies intervened in Czechoslovakia, and movement toward détente and European security arrangements was suspended.

During this period the Warsaw Pact was very active with a number of political and security initiatives. The pact had been founded in 1955 in response to the admission of West Germany into NATO and to provide a multilateral framework for Soviet military deployments in Eastern Europe, especially after the Austrian State Treaty of 1955 and withdrawal of Soviet (and Western) troops from that country. In the 1960s the Warsaw Pact assumed a more active role both as an integrated military alliance and as a political alliance of European communist states aligned with the Soviet Union.

The Warsaw Pact's Political Consultative Committee, meeting at the levels of heads of government and party in Bucharest in July 1966, issued a formal Declaration on Strengthening Peace and Security in Europe. The Bucharest declaration went beyond earlier appeals for East-West nonaggression agreements and called for convening a "conference on questions of European security and cooperation." The conference was to be "European," implicitly but clearly excluding the United States.[9] While "relaxation of tension" was mentioned, the main thrust was on such political action as the dissolution of the two alliances, stabilization of the political status quo in Eastern Europe (including recognition of the two Germanies), and withdrawal of American military power from Western Europe. The declaration attacked the United States (and West Germany) as instigators of international tension and military confrontation in Europe. The United States was also accused of seeking "to make Western Europe an instrument of U.S. global policy," including involvement in "adventures" in Asia. The Asian issue was also contained in a separate declaration at Bucharest on American aggression in Vietnam, designed to rally the pact in support of North Vietnam.[10]

The Bucharest declaration initiated a concerted Soviet campaign for a conference on European security that lasted until the conference was held in 1973-75.

There was a second major initiative in support of a European security conference, launched from a slightly different forum—the Conference of European Communist and Workers' Parties, held in Karlovy Vary (Karlsbad),

---

8. "Mutual and Balanced Force Reductions," in *NATO Final Communiqués*, pp. 198-99. I was then serving as counselor in the U.S. Mission to NATO and represented the United States in preparing these studies.

9. For the Russian text of the Bucharest declaration, see *Pravda*, July 9, 1966; and in English, see Robin Alison Remington, *The Warsaw Pact: Case Studies in Communist Conflict Resolution* (Cambridge, Mass.: MIT Press, 1971), pp. 209-21.

10. *Pravda*, July 8, 1966.

Czechoslovakia, in April 1967. This conference, which included nonruling communist parties from Western Europe (but not representatives from Yugoslavia or Romania, which chose not to participate), was more ideological. Nevertheless, the message and proposals in a proclamation issued by the conference were essentially the same. The Karlovy Vary statement sought to stimulate sentiment in Western Europe for the expiration of NATO in 1969 at the conclusion of its original twenty-year term. The proclamation also attacked President Johnson's bridge-building as subversive. At the same time, it did express "readiness to support any initiatives or proposals pursuing the purpose of achieving a détente and strengthening the security of the peoples of our continent."[11]

The next meeting of the Warsaw Pact Political Consultative Committee, held in Sofia in March 1968, did *not* repeat the call for a European security conference. Instead, it concentrated on the specific themes of nuclear nonproliferation, with West Germany particularly in mind, and American aggression in Vietnam (themes included in both the Bucharest and Karlovy Vary statements).[12]

The trend of political liberalization in Czechoslovakia probably influenced the pause in the first half of 1968 in Soviet advocacy of a conference on European security. It certainly influenced the later positions of *both* alliances. So did other developments within the Soviet-led Eastern alliance. One occurred at the Sofia Warsaw Pact meeting: Romania declined to sign the Proclamation on Nuclear Non-Proliferation—the first time a formal pact statement was issued with less than unanimous endorsement by the active members. Even more significant was a decision *not* taken at the Sofia meeting. It later became known that the Soviet Union had attempted to make changes strengthening the Warsaw Pact military command. Again, Romania refused to agree.[13] Without tracing through the developments in Czechoslovakia and the Warsaw Pact that led to military intervention by the Soviet Union in Czechoslovakia in August 1968, it should be noted that the entire focus of the pact was on its serious internal fissures. These bolstered the fears of Western influence in the East and dampened interest in initiatives to increase East-West contact at a time of Eastern vulnerability.

---

11. *Pravda*, April 27, 1967. One change that was introduced quietly is worth noting. While the Bucharest declaration had called for "the withdrawal of all forces from foreign territories to within their own national borders," the Karlovy Vary proclamation proposed "the withdrawal of foreign troops from the territory of European states." While both statements would involve American withdrawal, the latter formulation would permit Soviet troops to remain in Eastern Europe.

12. See *Pravda*, March 9, 1968, for the communiqué that highlighted these two themes, and two separate proclamations, one on nuclear nonproliferation, the other a "Declaration on the Threat to Peace Created as a Consequence of the Widening of the American Aggression in Vietnam."

13. See Remington, *The Warsaw Pact*, pp. 94–112, for the incident and later actions by the Warsaw Pact leading to the intervention in Czechoslovakia, less participation by Romania. For earlier Romanian-Soviet frictions, see pp. 56–93.

In turn the intervention in Czechoslovakia seriously dampened Western enthusiasm for détente, at least for a time. But it did not lead to any concerted Western curtailment of the largely unofficial, or at least nonpolitical, moves in greater East-West trade and cultural interchange that had quietly but steadily been developing throughout the 1960s. The most dramatic effect of the intervention in Czechoslovakia was the cancellation of the planned summit meeting in Leningrad between President Johnson and Prime Minister Kosygin, at which the SALT negotiations were to be launched. That summit was to have been announced on the day following the intervention.

In the spring of 1969 the Soviet Union and the Warsaw Pact, more desirous than ever to nail down the status quo in Eastern Europe, resumed their campaign for a European security conference. Pact leaders meeting in Budapest in March 1969 adopted an "Appeal from [the] Members of the Warsaw Pact to All European Countries," again excluding the United States and calling for a meeting to include representatives of "all interested European states." While recognition of the status quo was now almost a precondition of the conference, no longer did the pact call for dissolution of the two alliances. From this point on only Romania called from time to time for dissolution of the two pacts. But at this same meeting agreement was reached to reorganize the Warsaw Pact military command, the original Soviet plan having been modified to take into account objections by Romania (and apparently by some others).

The Budapest appeal, while it modified a few particulars of earlier statements, was more notable for the points of continuity and the resumption of the 1966–67 campaign. Further, the criticism of West Germany and the United States was less pronounced, in part, evidently, to maintain a consensus that included Romania. There was a stronger emphasis on détente, peaceful coexistence, and peace.[14]

In an independent move, in May 1969 Finland also proposed a conference on European security and cooperation, thus later earning the honor, as a neutral country, of hosting the conference. Presumably the Finnish government saw an opportunity to serve its own interests through a move that Moscow would appreciate but that would not offend the Western powers.

Subsequent Warsaw Pact meetings in Prague (October 1969) and Moscow (December 1969) reaffirmed the same line. A significant new element was introduced at the June 1970 meeting in Budapest: a readiness to accept the participation of the United States and Canada was expressed.[15] The Soviet decision to include the United States amounted to recognition that this step was necessary if East-West détente was to progress. It also showed that East-

---

14. For the text, see *Pravda*, March 18, 1969. For a good analysis of the Budapest appeal and this phase of intra–Warsaw Pact relations, see also Remington, *The Warsaw Pact*, pp. 113–33.

15. For the texts, see *Pravda*, November 1, 1969; December 5, 1969; and June 27, 1970. The 1970 conference issued a memorandum and commissioned Hungary to deliver it "to all interested states," including the United States and Canada. The text also explicitly invited U.S. and Canadian participation.

West détente was a higher-priority interest than continued use of the issue to try to divide the Western alliance by excluding the United States. The other evolving aspect of the Warsaw Pact's position on East-West détente was the gradual pressure on East Germany not to insist on all its aims in such a way as to prevent the multilateral diplomatic process from getting under way,[16] or to hamstring conclusion of the parallel bilateral West German–Soviet negotiations that eventually led to the first breakthrough, the FRG-USSR Agreement signed August 12, 1970.[17]

Appeals for a European security conference and a relaxation of tension between East and West continued: at Berlin (December 1970), Bucharest (February 1971), Warsaw (December 1971), and Prague (January 1972).[18] From that time on the action shifted mainly to diplomatic negotiation.

After Czechoslovakia NATO had become even more wary in its approach to multilateral East-West political negotiations. NATO ministerial meetings in 1969 and 1970 continued to favor relaxation of tensions and détente and to express support for bilateral (essentially, West German) negotiations and for the negotiations on Berlin, once initiated. In December 1969, at the Brussels meeting, NATO noted the renewed appeals of the Warsaw Pact for a European security conference and issued a cautious Declaration of the North Atlantic Council on European Security that stressed the necessity for "careful advance preparation" and "prospects of concrete results." It also reaffirmed and adumbrated the Reykjavik proposal for mutual and balanced force reductions.[19] Meeting in Rome in May 1970 the alliance made its position on security talks much more specific, in effect tying multilateral talks to progress in the German and Berlin negotiations then under way. The proposal for MBFR was again advanced, this time in a special declaration delivered to Warsaw Pact members by the Italian government (a technique the Warsaw Pact used a month later with its Budapest appeal for European security talks).[20]

Thus from 1966 through 1970 the Warsaw Pact steadily pushed for a conference on European security, while from 1968 through 1970 NATO pressed for talks on mutual and balanced force reductions. But each was very wary of the other's proposals. In 1971 and 1972, although still wary, both alliances moved toward reciprocal acceptance of these proposals, facilitated greatly by the agreements reached in 1970–71 as a result of the *Ostpolitik* of West Germany and the Berlin negotiations.

---

16. See Remington, *The Warsaw Pact*, pp. 134–64.

17. See *Pravda*, August 13, 1970.

18. For the text, see *Pravda*, December 4, 1970; February 20, 1971; December 3, 1971; and January 27, 1972.

19. "Declaration of the North Atlantic Council," in *NATO Final Communiqués*, pp. 215–18. Coincidentally this declaration followed by just one day the Warsaw Pact's Moscow communiqué.

20. "Declaration on Mutual and Balanced Force Reductions," in ibid., pp. 223–24.

It should be noted that one of the principal reasons NATO advocated the talks on MBFR was to help ensure continued American deployment of very large forces in Europe. Ever since 1966 Senator Mike Mansfield of Montana had periodically been introducing a sense of the Senate resolution calling for a substantial reduction in American forces in Europe. For a variety of reasons, including rising anti-Vietnam and antimilitary sentiment in the United States, but also stemming from views that the Western alliance was inflexible and was not attempting to reduce the risk of military confrontation in Europe, public and Senate support for Mansfield's position grew. NATO advocacy of mutual troop reductions was intended to combat this development both by displaying NATO's readiness to agree to reductions and by making it possible to argue that unilateral reductions would undercut the incentive for the Soviet Union and the Warsaw Pact to agree to reciprocal reductions.[21]

On May 14, 1971, there was an unexpected development: Brezhnev undercut Mansfield just when it appeared likely the senator would succeed. At the Twenty-fourth Party Congress in March 1971 Brezhnev had strongly reaffirmed the idea of a European security conference. He also included a statement (which did not receive much notice at the time) that the Soviet Union supported "a reduction of armed forces and armaments in areas where the military confrontation is especially dangerous, above all in Central Europe."[22] Two months later and just five days before a vote that seemed likely to pass Mansfield's resolution, Brezhnev stated in a speech that there was considerable interest in force reductions in central Europe and suggested that those questioning the Soviet attitude toward these reductions were like people who try to judge a wine without tasting it. He challenged: "You have to muster the resolve to try the proposal you are interested in by tasting it. Translated into diplomatic language this means to start negotiations."[23] In the congressional debate on Mansfield's resolution, which contained a mandate to cut the approximately 300,000 American servicemen in Europe to 150,000, the administration and other opponents used Brezhnev's statements to good effect, bolstering their argument that the United States should not unilaterally reduce its forces when there appeared to be an opportunity to negotiate reciprocal reductions. The resolution lost, 36 to 61.

It seems clear the Soviet leaders were concerned over the unpredictable consequences of a sudden massive American military withdrawal. Such a move could prompt fears and possibly a turn to militarization in Western Europe, especially West Germany. It could lead to a change in policy in West Germany and the United States about nuclear weapons for Germany. While it

---

21. Kissinger makes very clear that this was the only reason for U.S. interest in MBFR. Kissinger, *White House Years*, pp. 399–402, 947–48.

22. Brezhnev, *O vneshnei politike*, p. 181.

23. The wine-tasting analogy presumably occurred to Brezhnev because he was speaking in Tbilisi, Georgia, a wine-growing center in the Soviet Union. L. I. Brezhnev, *Pravda*, May 15, 1971.

might lead some Western Europeans to be more ready to negotiate on Warsaw Pact terms, it could lead others not to negotiate at all. In any event it seems clear the Soviet action was deliberate, and it was followed by additional indications of a readiness to negotiate.[24]

The NATO ministers, meeting in Lisbon in June 1971, decided to select a representative to explore the prospects for force reduction talks with the Soviets and in October designated NATO Secretary General Manlio Brosio. While Soviet spokesmen continued to speak in favor of force reductions, they ignored Brosio. One reason was an objection to a bloc-to-bloc approach.[25] Clearly the Soviet leaders wanted to move ahead on a European security conference, about which the West still had reservations, and implicitly tied the two together. The agreement on Berlin in September had removed one reservation, but others remained. The NATO ministerial communiqué in December 1971 affirmed NATO's readiness to move ahead with a security conference as well as MBFR, but the content of a European security conference was still very unclear and had many pitfalls.[26] For its part the Warsaw Pact, meeting in Prague in January 1972, endorsed both, but with reservations. At the summit meeting in May 1972 Nixon and Brezhnev finally agreed to proceed on both. Had that meeting not occurred then, it is still likely that agreement to proceed

24. Not everyone considers Brezhnev's action to have been deliberate. Kissinger, most notably, argues, "Nothing illustrates better the inflexibility of the Soviets' cumbersome policymaking machinery than their decision to stick to their game plan even when confronted with the Mansfield windfall. It should be pondered by those who see every Soviet maneuver as part of a well-considered design." Kissinger, *White House Years*, p. 947.

I agree with Kissinger's general point, but not in this instance. The Tbilisi speech was not a foreign policy address, and the comment on force reductions had been deliberately inserted. Kissinger errs in stating that Brezhnev was expressing "a long-standing Soviet policy," and also that "the Soviets as quickly dropped it." Ibid., pp. 946, 948. Soon thereafter Aleksei Kosygin, Andrei P. Kirilenko, Nikolai V. Podgorny, and Kyril T. Mazurov—four other Politburo members—cited Brezhnev's Tbilisi speech as a basis for negotiations, and on June 11 Brezhnev himself clarified favorably a point of key interest to the West, stating that the Soviet Union was ready to discuss reductions of both foreign and indigenous troops. Brezhnev, *Pravda*, June 11, 1971. Kissinger appreciated the impact Brezhnev's statement had in preventing the serious blow that the Mansfield Resolution would have been to U.S. and NATO policy. This understanding has led him to interpret the Soviet policy decision as though it were the fruit of, as he puts it, "the carefully calibrated measures of the Administration toward the Soviet Union." Hence his improbable conclusion that "our willingness to discuss détente had lured Brezhnev into an initiative about mutual force reductions that saved our whole European defense structure from Congressional savaging." Ibid., p. 949.

25. I recall a Soviet diplomat saying at the time that the Soviet Union and the countries of the Warsaw Pact were not a "dark continent" in need of a Western "explorer"—the countries concerned would have to negotiate and should therefore discuss the matter through normal diplomatic channels.

26. Kissinger indicates U.S. policy considerations in agreeing, reluctantly, to move toward a CSCE in this period (Kissinger, *White House Years*, pp. 412–16, 424) and in 1972, when he and Nixon held to a strategy not only of linking CSCE with MBFR, but linking movement on both to Soviet assistance on a settlement in Vietnam (ibid., pp. 1128, 1249–50).

with both the MBFR and a conference on security and cooperation in Europe (CSCE) would have ensued.

A multilateral preparatory conference on the CSCE opened in Helsinki on November 22, 1972, and on January 31, 1973, similar exploratory talks on MBFR began in Vienna.[27]

The Berlin Agreement

Parallel with the bilateral *Ostpolitik* of West Germany and the maneuverings of NATO and the Warsaw Pact leading toward détente, and specifically toward the CSCE and MBFR negotiations, quadripartite talks among the four World War II powers occupying Berlin began on March 26, 1970. They concluded with an agreement on September 3, 1971.

Berlin had been the flash point for crisis in 1948 (it led to the Berlin Airlift of 1948–49), in 1958–59 (when Khrushchev issued an ultimatum for a separate peace treaty, which proved to be a bluff), and in 1961 (it resulted in a series of military demonstrations on both sides and to the Berlin Wall). Both the West and East wished to defuse the Berlin situation, although, of course, on their own terms to the maximum extent possible. Clearly, by 1970–71 *Ostpolitik* made an attempt more promising than theretofore. So did the tentative moves toward European security measures of one kind or another. And agreement on Berlin would greatly facilitate the possibility of an American-Soviet détente. Indeed, the agreement did contribute to the *Ostpolitik*, to the first Soviet-American summit meeting, to NATO readiness to move toward a CSCE, and to the Warsaw Pact's readiness to join MBFR talks.

The Berlin issue existed because the four wartime allies against Nazi Germany had established a quadripartite occupation rule over Berlin in 1945. Later, as the three Western occupation zones of Germany merged to become the Federal Republic of Germany, and the Soviet zone became the German Democratic Republic, the Western zones in Berlin merged as West Berlin, while the Soviet zone in East Berlin was merged into East Germany. The Western powers refused to recognize the merger of East Berlin, however, and insisted on retaining their secondary occupation authority as it extended to all Berlin.

The issues in the Berlin problem were highly complex, but the basic ones were clear. From 1948 to 1962 the Soviet Union sought to expel the Western presence from the city, which amounted to a Western enclave more than one hundred miles deep in communist East Germany. Throughout the 1960s and 1970s the USSR continued to seek preferably to end or at the least to constrict to a minimum the ties between West Berlin and West Germany. On the other hand the Western powers were determined to maintain their

---

27. See chapter 14.

presence in and access to Berlin, as well as the free political system of the Western sector. There was one divergence between the American, British, and French position on the one hand, and the West German on the other. The presence of the former three nations was justified by virtue of the postwar occupation regime. As such, they could not recognize West German authority in West Berlin, since it would have meant conceding their own. Therefore they never supported the integration of West Berlin into West Germany.

The constitution of the Federal Republic of Germany designated Berlin as the capital of "Germany" and gave West Berlin the status of a "federal district" that could send delegates (nonvoting) to the Bundestag in Bonn. While the other Western powers did not formally approve this status, they did acquiesce in it. The Soviet Union continues to object. East Berlin is the official capital of the German Democratic Republic and elects representatives to its parliament (also, however, nonvoting). As noted, the Western powers still claim and symbolically exercise occupation rights over East as well as West Berlin. Since August 1961 the notorious Berlin Wall has effectively divided the city, with East German control over access to and from East Berlin, except for token patrols of the Western powers.

In the period under study here, the initial event of significance was a Soviet diplomatic protest in December 1968, repeated over the next few months, about a planned meeting of the West German Bundestag in West Berlin in March 1969 to elect the president of the Federal Republic. To emphasize its objection, East Germany began some minor harassment of civilian traffic from West Germany to West Berlin (a technique used often before).

Soviet efforts to persuade the new Nixon administration to get West Germany to cancel its plans for the (from the Soviet standpoint, provocative) Bundestag presidential election session in West Berlin coincided with Nixon's February trip to Western Europe, his first as president. One stop was to be West Berlin. Nixon not only refused to press the West Germans as the Soviets wanted, but made a stirring reaffirmation of American commitment to defend "the people of free Berlin"—skirting the legal issue, but taking a clear political stand. The election in March took place without incident.

At the time of this minor confrontation Ambassador Anatoly F. Dobrynin told Kissinger that there were "political possibilities" to negotiate regular access to Berlin. Nixon followed up with a letter to Prime Minister Aleksei Kosygin on March 26, offering to discuss Berlin. Kosygin's reply was that the Soviet Union had no objections to such a discussion, but he made no further overture. Not wishing to pursue a bilateral effort, Nixon and Kissinger likewise did nothing further. On July 10 Gromyko publicly expressed Soviet readiness to "exchange views as to how complications concerning West Berlin can be avoided," and Brandt, then foreign minister in Chancellor Kurt Georg Kiesinger's coalition government, urged the West to accept Gromyko's offer. But the matter dragged on as the West consulted, the Soviets delayed their response, and the election in West Germany produced a change of government.

In the face of the new Brandt government's *Ostpolitik*, on September 24 the Soviet Union proposed talks on Berlin. On December 16, 1969, the allies responded positively. Talks on Berlin, conducted through the three Western ambassadors to West Germany and the Soviet ambassador to East Germany, began on March 26, 1970.[28]

The talks proceeded slowly until the West German–Soviet agreement in August 1970. The Germans had made clear that their ratification would not occur until a Berlin agreement had been reached, while the Soviets sought to use West German interest in the bilateral *Ostpolitik* as leverage on Berlin. After August 1970 the leverage shifted. (There was, in addition, a parallel question of reciprocal leverage and negotiation between Washington and Bonn that Kissinger describes well in his memoir.) At the same time, in early 1971 Kissinger and Nixon sought to use the Soviet interest in a Berlin agreement and European détente to advance American positions in SALT.

Kissinger makes clear in his memoir that much of the critical negotiation was conducted by him in Washington (using the Bahr channel to Brandt, as well), and that the White House could count on Ambassador Kenneth Rush in Bonn—the "ex officio" negotiator, as Kissinger puts it—not to involve the Department of State in the real negotiations.[29]

As with the *Ostpolitik*, Ulbricht's replacement by Honecker in May 1971 greatly facilitated reaching an agreement on Berlin. In fact, the timing fits so clearly with an intense period of negotiation on Berlin that Ulbricht's

---

28. See Kissinger, *White House Years*, pp. 405–12, 531–32, for a capsule review of these developments and in particular for an account of the Nixon administration's thinking and actions.

   In describing the initial contacts with the Brandt government, which occurred during a visit to the White House by Brandt's chief adviser, Egon Bahr, in October 1969, Kissinger notes that Secretary Rogers objected to the White House negotiations "on the not unreasonable ground that negotiations should be conducted in the State Department. Rogers and I, dealing with each other like two sovereign entities, finally made a compact": Kissinger would receive Bahr, but would not negotiate with him, and Assistant Secretary of State for European Affairs Martin Hillenbrand would be present. Kissinger further describes what he himself characterizes as "a not insignificant deviation from my compact with Rogers in that Bahr, after leaving the White House by the front door, reentered it through the basement for a private talk with me, primarily to establish a channel by which we could stay in touch outside the formal procedures. . . . my contact with Egon Bahr became a White House backchannel by which Nixon [and Kissinger] could manage diplomacy bypassing the State Department." Ibid., p. 411.

29. Rush was a political appointee beholden to Nixon. For Kissinger's enlightening account of how the White House used the Berlin negotiations to rein in *Ostpolitik*, as well as to seek, by linkage, to maneuver Soviet positions on SALT and other issues of interest to the United States, see ibid., pp. 531–32, 799–810, 821–33.

   A special communications channel to Rush and Bahr that excluded the Department of State was arranged through the U.S. Navy by Alexander M. Haig, Jr., and the Joint Chiefs of Staff liaison officer with the National Security Council. This officer was later found to be clandestinely slipping materials to the chairman of the Joint Chiefs of Staff, and also to Admiral Elmo R. Zumwalt, Jr., subsequently an outspoken critic of Kissinger and his secretiveness. Ibid., p. 810.

recalcitrance on that matter may well have been the factor precipitating his departure.

The negotiations were finally concluded primarily through confidential American (White House)–Soviet negotiations, then funneled through the four-power ambassadorial forum.[30] The "Quadripartite Agreement on Berlin" was signed on September 3, 1971. While both sides made concessions, each had met its principal objectives. For the first time there was a legal basis agreed upon for civilian access to West Berlin from West Germany. The West German presence in the city was curtailed, but not eliminated; there would be no more presidential elections by the Bundestag at the old Reichstag building in Berlin, but consular, cultural, and economic ties with West Germany were recognized. The Soviet Union guaranteed Western access; it could no longer permit or instigate East Germany to impose curbs and then wash its hands of the matter. For its part, the Soviet Union gained Western acceptance of de facto East German control of East Berlin, and the agreement precluded any attempt to incorporate West Berlin as an integral part of West Germany.[31] But the Soviet Union had to acknowledge continuation of the responsibilities of the four powers over the whole of Berlin.

---

30. Ibid., pp. 831–32. As the Berlin negotiation was concluding, Kissinger describes it thus: "Somehow we had to see to it that our own State Department did not complicate matters." And when the State Department finally saw the draft, experienced experts did, without challenging policy positions, point out many shortcomings of substance. Kissinger comments that "Rush received instructions through State Department channels asking him to rephrase paragraphs already settled in *private* negotiations." (Emphasis added.) And as Kissinger notes, "For the third time in three months a negotiation was being completed in which the regular bureaucracy had not participated, indeed, was unaware of its existence." In an attempted defense Kissinger comments, "There is no agreement that cannot be picked to death by professionals not involved in negotiating it," but he glosses over real and significant flaws.

The basic problem arose from Nixon and Kissinger's modus operandi. As Kissinger states, "We were in a serious quandary. We had to convince the nearly paranoid Soviets that the delay was not significant, yet the State Department could scarcely be told that it had no right to review an agreement of such importance. We could not guarantee that some bureaucratic nitpicker might not force us to reopen issues settled already twice with the Soviets." (The ability to "force" Nixon and Kissinger must be questioned—unless the bureaucrats had a real case.) "As usual Haldeman was assigned the task of fixing things. Brandt—at my suggestion— weighed in with a strong letter to Nixon endorsing the agreement as a 'major achievement'; this would be useful with Rogers. Nixon had a genius for thinking up explanations for a fait accompli." Further, "The final act of the play was a Presidential invitation to Rush to San Clemente" to get him away from Rogers in Washington. There Rush announced to a press conference that "he had completed a final review with the President and that the agreement was a 'major triumph for the foreign policy of President Nixon.' That ended our internal bickering." Ibid., p. 832. On Kissinger's persistent lack of awareness and sensitivity to the Berlin issue, recall also the incident cited in note 88, chapter 3.

31. Nixon and Kissinger also went through an elaborate deception of the Department of State in maintaining an adamant stand against granting the Soviet Union the right to a consulate-general in West Berlin—after having conceded this demand to the Soviet side long before. This story is well told in Hersh, *The Price of Power*, pp. 418–22.

The Berlin agreement facilitated East-West détente in Europe in a number of ways. First, it removed a perennial tinderbox for crises. Second, it greatly facilitated further progress for the *Ostpolitik* of West Germany, as well as the move toward general acceptance of East Germany by the West and the rest of the world. Third, it contributed to a favorable climate for European security measures (such as CSCE and MBFR). Finally, it contributed to the emerging American-Soviet détente.[32]

Eastern Europe and East-West Détente

When the Soviet Union activated a policy of European détente beginning in 1966, its leaders were acutely aware of the double-edged nature of this development with respect to Eastern Europe. On the one hand they wished to formalize Western acceptance of the status quo in central and eastern Europe, both as a curb against possible future German ambitions for reunification and to ensure (and to demonstrate to the people of the communist states in the region) that the Western powers would not try to change the territorial frontiers or the socialist systems of the Warsaw Pact states. On the other hand détente involved normalization of relations, with greatly increased cultural and personal contacts and economic ties, all of which exposed the peoples of Eastern Europe to aspects of Western life that would be attractive and potentially troublesome for internal discipline.

Notwithstanding these latter concerns, even before the political maneuverings on European security discussed above started, much less were resolved, the Soviet Union and its Warsaw Pact associates permitted growing cultural and economic ties. Political détente accompanied, and to a large extent followed, expansion of trade, tourism, and other contacts.

The percentage increase in European East-West trade during the 1960s was phenomenal, although in terms of the Western economies it remained generally small. Most Eastern European and Soviet trade continued to be among the members of the Council on Mutual Economic Assistance (CMEA, also called CEMA or COMECON). CMEA had been established in 1949, first as an Eastern economic counterpart to the Marshall Plan and later as a complement to the Warsaw Pact. Eventually it was broadened to include some other socialist countries not in the pact, such as Cuba and Vietnam. During the 1960s the CMEA countries gradually and reluctantly accepted the

---

32. By design, the final protocol of the Berlin agreement, and the West German treaties with Poland and the USSR, went into effect on the same day, June 3, 1972. This was just a few days after the first Nixon-Brezhnev summit meeting, at which it had been agreed to proceed in parallel with the CSCE and MBFR. West and East Germany signed their treaty involving reciprocal recognition on December 22, 1972, less than six months later.

fact of the European Economic Community as a Western entity in its own right, although trade continued to be handled on a country-to-country basis. West Germany was the most powerful economic force in the expanding East-West trade, although most countries of Western Europe became significantly engaged (as did even some smaller ones such as Finland, but also Austria and others, which developed proportionately substantial shares of trade with the East). The one notable exception among the Western powers was the United States.

The important West German political *Ostpolitik* and the moves by both alliances (including the United States, although not in a leading role) moved Europe toward political détente in the 1966–72 period. But these moves also followed, or at most accompanied, the growth of East-West economic and cultural ties in Europe.

Détente in Europe, in short, developed naturally, involving countries and peoples more than political acts and institutions. It emerged on a much more solid basis than the later, more dramatic rise of U.S.-Soviet détente precisely because it involved the interests of peoples rather than just the sometimes fickle political interests of leaders. East-West détente in Europe also had a more solid basis because the countries and governments of Europe (Western and Eastern) treated one another as countries, whereas the United States and the Soviet Union tended to treat them as affiliates of themselves or of their superpower adversary. The one apparent (and partial) exception supports this conclusion: de Gaulle did not succeed in establishing France as an alternate European power center, and France's role in détente became that of one of a number of Western European countries. West Germany, on the other hand, developed the greatest weight. This was so because it bent over backward not to assert a political role (other than to accommodate the status quo on its frontiers with respect to East Germany), and it let its economic trade and tourism find their natural—and substantial—place. With respect to the United States, its largely abortive proclamations about stimulating peaceful engagement and bridge-building in the mid-1960s looked suspiciously like contrived attempts to curtail Soviet political influence in Eastern Europe and to introduce American influence as a counter.

As to the role of *Ostpolitik* and of NATO and the Warsaw Pact relative to more regulated political and security relationships, the movement that led ultimately to multilateral CSCE and MBFR negotiations was gradual. It is difficult in some cases to determine which implicit (or occasionally diplomatically explicit) linkages among the various steps toward East-West détente in Europe constituted the quid pro quo for other steps. Nonetheless, it is clear that the whole complex of moves from their troubled beginnings in the latter half of the 1960s to the more rapid developments of the first half of the 1970s were intertwined. The *Ostpolitik* of West Germany required the Berlin agreement; the Non-Proliferation Treaty both required *Ostpolitik* and made its further development possible. The CSCE presupposed the *Ostpolitik* and was tied to beginning the MBFR talks. The developing economic and political relations were mutually supporting and in turn encouraged the turn to a quest for arms control and confidence-building measures. The overall result was the creation of a substantial network of shared interests among the countries of Eastern and Western Europe.

It is important to look at the development of détente and its impact on Eastern Europe from the perspective of the Soviet leaders as well. From the standpoint of the West the Czechoslovak crisis in East-West relations arose when the Soviet-led Warsaw Pact armies occupied the country in August 1968 and, during 1968–69, ousted the popular Dubček government. From the Soviet standpoint, however, the Czechoslovak crisis had arisen when a reformist movement outside and within the Czechoslovak Communist party and the government departed from the Soviet–Warsaw Pact guidelines on internal political control. Still, the crisis slowed the NATO–Warsaw Pact political maneuverings only briefly, although it did derail the start of U.S.-Soviet strategic arms limitation negotiations for a critical year. The other important effect the events in Czechoslovakia of 1968 had on East-West détente was to influence Soviet judgments about the ideological-political vulnerability of Eastern Europe.[33]

Other developments in Eastern Europe were also troubling the Soviet leadership. In particular, the attempts to stem the deepening economic slide in Poland led to resistance by workers, casualties, and the replacement of Gomułka by Edward Gierek in December 1970. On the other hand the relatively successful New Economic Mechanism introduced in Hungary in 1968 involved economic reforms without disturbing political discipline; the program, reaffirmed in 1970, continued throughout the 1970s.

The Soviet leaders sought to increase the role and scope of activity of the Council on Mutual Economic Assistance, particularly in 1970–71. It did so both to curb internal economic developments in Eastern European countries that tended to reduce Eastern economic cooperation and to make less necessary a turn to the West. A ten-year Comprehensive Economic Plan was worked out and agreed to in 1971. But there was no escaping the fact that the economic resources of CMEA—even including those of the Soviet Union— were simply inadequate to meet the economic needs of the member countries. These countries had to turn to the West as well and put their internal economic systems in better shape. Hungary did well on both counts, Poland most poorly, as was to become all too evident in the explosion there a decade later.

On the political-ideological front, the Soviet Union faced increasing fractiousness and fragmentation in the world communist movement—already

---

33. It can only be speculated whether a more fully developed détente might have had a sufficiently favorable impact on Soviet tolerance and might have reduced Soviet concerns in the late 1960s sufficiently to have averted direct intervention. All in all it seems to me unlikely. On the other hand, Roy Medvedev, a leading Soviet dissident historian, has expressed that opinion: "I'm quite sure that if the same changes had been made in Czechoslovakia in 1972–73, say, instead of 1968, there wouldn't have been any invasion." Roy Medvedev, *On Soviet Dissent: Interviews with Piero Ostellino* (Columbia University Press, 1980), p. 73.

rent in the early and mid-1960s by the Sino-Soviet ideological polemics and political struggle. A long-delayed Conference of Communist and Workers' Parties (seventy-five of them) was finally held in Moscow in June 1969. In contrast to the one held a decade earlier, several countries did not attend: Yugoslavia on the right, and China, North Korea, North Vietnam, and Albania on the left. Among those attending, several, including Romania and the leaders of a number of nonruling parties, were highly critical of the occupation of Czechoslovakia and of other aspects of Soviet leadership. Nonetheless the Soviet Union worked to repair the damage and to build a somewhat wider consensus by moderating its demands.[34] A later discussion deals with the important Eurocommunist challenge that developed in the mid-1970s in communist parties in Western Europe, despite these Soviet efforts.[35] On the other hand Soviet-Cuban and Soviet-Vietnamese relations were considerably improved in 1970–71 (mainly through increased economic, and in the case of Vietnam military, assistance). By the time of the Twenty-fourth Party Congress in Moscow in March–April 1971, all the ruling communist parties except China and Albania sent delegations.

The problems within the world communist movement in the late 1960s and early 1970s marked a period of transition from the Soviet-Chinese duel of the 1960s to what was to become an East-West duel *within* the communist movement in Europe in the 1970s.[36] But the principal Soviet concern at this time and later was the impact of détente on the communist parties and countries of Eastern Europe. As détente picked up momentum in Europe (and later as American-Soviet détente developed) the Soviet leaders sought to counter the subversive threats of Western political and popular culture. These were occurring because of rather than despite the relaxation in relations between the states of Western and Eastern Europe. Not only was this ideological struggle not diminishing under détente, as constantly noted, it was intensifying. Warnings had been sounded by the pre-détente Twenty-third Party Congress in 1966 and continued to be sounded through the Twenty-fourth Party Congress in 1971 that launched détente, and later as well. The concerns appeared in a steady stream of authoritative Soviet pronouncements and commentary. Initially they concerned the struggle within the capitalist world, including the national liberation movement. After Czechoslovakia, however,

---

34. See *Mezhdunarodnoye soveshchaniye kommunisticheskikh i rabochikh partiy: Dokumenty i materialy, Moskva, 5–17 iyunya 1969 g.* [The International Conference of Communist and Workers' Parties: Documents and Materials, Moscow, June 5–17, 1969] (Moscow: Politizdat, 1969); and Jeffrey Simon, *Ruling Communist Parties and Détente: A Documentary History* (Washington, D.C.: American Enterprise Institute, 1975), pp. 88–109.

35. See chapter 14.

36. In terms of broad priorities, the 1969 Conference of Communist Parties also concluded a phase in which the Soviet leadership had been focusing intensely on the struggle in the world communist movement. After late 1969 Brezhnev in particular turned his attention increasingly to East-West relations and détente.

more attention was devoted to a defensive strengthening of the unity of the socialist commonwealth.

Brezhnev did state at the Twenty-fourth Party Congress that "the Czechoslovakian events" (as Soviet commentary refers to both the pre- and postintervention phases) bore witness to the continued presence of "internal anti-communist forces" that "can under certain circumstances be activated and even pass over to direct counterrevolutionary actions counting on external support on the part of imperialism, which in turn is always ready to join with such forces."[37] But he did not go so far as some Soviet commentators who linked Eastern vulnerability and possible Western intervention directly to détente itself. In the words of one commentator in 1972, "The ideologists of anti-communism do not conceal their hopes that in conditions of a détente . . . the ideological staunchness of socialist states will be weakened and opportunities will arise for the ideological penetration of socialist countries with the object of undermining them from within."[38]

As noted, the Soviet leaders were suspicious and displeased by President Nixon's visits to Bucharest in 1969, Belgrade in 1970, and Warsaw in 1972. Continued American political attention to Eastern Europe was evidenced by Secretary of State Rogers' visits to Romania, Hungary, and Yugoslavia in July 1972, soon after the first summit and Nixon's visit to Poland. Rogers assured the Romanians that improvement of American-Soviet relations would not be at the expense of any other country, in effect reaffirming American support for greater Romanian independence in international relations. Rogers also stated in a publicly reported toast in Bucharest that the United States and Romania "share a basic conviction that all countries, whatever their size or their location and whether they are in the same or in different social systems, are equally sovereign and equally independent and have an equal right to run their own affairs free of outside interference. My visit here underlines the devotion of the United States to that basic principle."[39] And so it did. While not directly related, two months later Romania applied for membership in the International Monetary Fund and the World Bank.

American policy toward the countries of Eastern Europe under détente became more clearly defined in the mid-1970s, as will be noted later. But as early as 1970, in his first annual report to the Congress on *U.S. Foreign Policy for the 1970's*, written under Kissinger's guidance, President Nixon articulated American policy in a manner designed to meet two aims. He intended to allay Soviet suspicions that the United States would seek to increase tension in Eastern Europe. At the same time he sought to show support for the

37. Brezhnev, "Report of the Central Committee of the CPSU to the XXIV Congress of CPSU," March 30, 1971, *O vneshnei politike*, p. 164.

38. V. Kudinov and V. Pletnikov, "Ideological Confrontation of the Two Systems," *International Affairs* (Moscow), no. 12 (December 1972), p. 64.

39. "Secretary's Toast at Luncheon Hosted by President Ceausescu, Bucharest, July 6," *Department of State Bulletin*, vol. 67 (August 7, 1972), p. 169.

independence of the countries in the area and to reject the Brezhnev Doctrine. Nixon stated:

We are aware that the Soviet Union sees its own security as directly affected by developments in this region. . . . It is not the intention of the United States to undermine the legitimate security interests of the Soviet Union. . . . Our pursuit of negotiation and détente is meant to reduce existing tensions, not to stir up new ones. By the same token, the United States views the countries of Eastern Europe as sovereign, not as parts of a monolith. And we can accept no doctrine that abridges their right to seek reciprocal improvement of relations with us or others.[40]

Soviet commentary continued to exhort vigilance within and socialist solidarity among the USSR and the communist countries of Eastern Europe. Only since the deterioration and disappearance of the U.S.-Soviet détente have Soviet commentators openly attributed retroactively to the United States the motive of attempting to use détente to weaken the socialist community. Thus, for example, a discussion in late 1980 cited an article that had appeared in the American journal *Foreign Affairs* in 1973 as stating that "peaceful engagement" in East-West relations "will almost imperceptibly chip away at . . . the edges of the Communist doctrinal edifice." The Soviet commentator stated that "under the cover of détente the West planned to sow dissension among the socialist community countries" (and also to "undermine their influence in the world").[41] The attempt was of course said to have failed. As another article indicated, "Despite the hopes of imperialist reaction, détente has led neither to a 'softening' of the socialist system in the USSR, nor to the 'disintegration' of the socialist community. On the contrary, the 1970s were marked by a further strengthening of the world socialist system."[42]

While Soviet ideological preconceptions sustain a long-term optimistic view of the future of the socialist community under Soviet leadership, their political suspicions no doubt yield less optimistic short-term concerns that they rarely voice openly. Soviet charges of Western machinations in Poland in 1980–82, for example, served in part to explain away an embarrassing, severe failure to instill a socialist consciousness after more than a third of a century of communist rule (not to mention the economic and political failure). In part, they also served as an advance justification in case direct Soviet intervention were ever necessary. But they also revealed undoubtedly genuine Soviet concern over the impact of the wide contacts of all kinds, as well as the direct economic ties in particular, that resulted from East-West détente in Europe.

---

40. Richard M. Nixon, *U.S. Foreign Policy for the 1970's: A New Strategy for Peace*, Report to the Congress, vol. 1 (Washington, D.C.: Government Printing Office, 1970), pp. 138–39.

41. L. Vidyasova, "Anti-Communism—The Core of Imperialist Foreign Policy," *International Affairs*, no. 12 (December 1980), p. 70, citing *Foreign Affairs*, vol. 51 (July 1973), p. 721. Not mentioned is that the author of the article in *Foreign Affairs*, titled "U.S. Foreign Policy: The Search for Focus," was Zbigniew Brzezinski.

42. V. Kortunov, "Disastrous Relapses into a Policy of Strength," *Kommunist* [The Communist], no. 10 (July 1980), p. 102. The author is an important official on the Central Committee staff.

5 · Opening an Era of Negotiation: SALT I, 1969-72

IF PRESIDENT NIXON had been looking for a subject with which to open his proclaimed "era of negotiation" with the Soviet Union, the Strategic Arms Limitation Talks (SALT) were the obvious, even ideal, candidate. Arms control, especially of strategic nuclear weapons, offered promise for ameliorating a problem of great importance. It also commanded public support. In addition, while SALT had been proposed by the preceding Johnson administration, negotiations had not yet begun, and any agreement would be the unalloyed achievement of the new administration. Moreover, the Soviet leadership had signaled, both publicly and privately, its readiness promptly to enter into SALT. The terms of the negotiation would of course be set and managed by the administration itself.

Eventually the SALT negotiations did become first the pilot ship of negotiation, and later the flagship of détente, as well as the crowning achievement of Nixon's first term.

SALT and Détente, 1969

Initially, Nixon and Kissinger, his national security adviser, shied away from an early commitment to SALT, delaying its beginning for reasons of political strategy and tactics. While evidently expecting from the outset that eventually there would be SALT negotiations, neither Nixon nor Kissinger put much stock in arms control, and both had modest expectations for an agreement, or for what an agreement could do to limit the strategic arms competition. Instead, both saw SALT as a political enterprise, with potential domestic and international gains if it were carefully controlled. Moreover, the clear Soviet interest, even eagerness, to enter negotiations was interpreted as a sign that the Soviet Union wanted SALT—at least negotiations, and probably an agreement—more than the United States did. That meant potential leverage in getting Soviet concessions in other areas, perhaps a satisfactory American disengagement from the Vietnam War.

SALT was one potential instrument in a strategy of détente, as it later came to be called, that would govern American relations with the Soviet Union. That strategy had to be developed before the proper role of SALT could be determined. Therefore, no decision was to be made for some time. The first study on SALT was not even commissioned until March 13 in National Security Study Memorandum 28 (NSSM 28), twenty-eighth in priority.[1]

In addition, the president and his close advisers wished to determine their military requirements and program before deciding on arms limitations. This approach was reasonable: the reverse could have ended up unwisely constraining or unnecessarily embarrassing the administration, should it have to change either the defense program or the arms control position to bring them into line. The real choice was either to decide on national security requirements and gear both defense and arms control programs to those requirements, or to decide on defense preferences first and then tailor the arms control to fit. Given the low value placed on arms control by Nixon, Kissinger, and Secretary of Defense Melvin Laird, the decision was to decide first on the defense program.

Finally, the new Nixon administration wished to consider its arms control choices or options. The outgoing Johnson administration had prepared a SALT position and proposal the previous August. Then, at the last minute before public announcement of a summit meeting in Leningrad in September, at which SALT would be launched, the Soviet-led Warsaw Pact occupation of Czechoslovakia occurred, and the plans for a summit and SALT were aborted. The Soviet action in Czechoslovakia required a decent interval before such a meeting could take place. That necessity, combined with the outcome of the November 1968 election, spelled the end of the Johnson administration's hopes to launch SALT. It was quite appropriate for the new administration to want to study the issues, and to use that review as well as its decisions on political strategy and on defense programs as a basis for fashioning its SALT position.

Underlying all these questions of policy relating to general foreign political strategy, defense programs, and arms control was an equally important matter of politics. Typically, bureaucratic maneuvering and staking out of turf or responsibility occurs among the major institutions of government after a general change in command. In this instance that situation was intensified. The president himself launched a more than usually aggressive, though initially buffered, effort with and through Kissinger to establish internal channels for decisionmaking that were completely and directly under the control of the

---

1. NSSM 1 on Vietnam, NSSM 2 on the Middle East, and NSSM 3 on U.S. military posture were all commissioned on the very day following the inauguration, and their order indicated the highest priorities for national security studies.

White House. To anyone not familiar with the real workings of American government, this strategy may seem perplexing and odd—cannot a president simply state what he wants policy to be? As Jimmy Carter was later to discover to his surprise (and not just at the beginning of his term), he cannot. Richard Nixon had ample and direct earlier experience that reinforced his own proclivity to prefer a clandestine rather than an over-the-table approach to the exercise of power. This process not only led to parallel SALT negotiations with the Soviets through a White House back channel not made known to the official SALT negotiating delegation and executive departments, but also to serious errors in the negotiations that put a burden on the negotiating process and later on public and congressional confidence in the SALT agreements. Thus style and practice affected policy and diplomacy, sometimes purchasing near-term flexibility at a high long-term cost.

As the Nixon administration took office, the spokesman for the Soviet Foreign Ministry publicly declared on January 20 the readiness of the Soviet government to sit down at a conference table to discuss SALT—the "mutual limitation and subsequent reduction of offensive and defensive nuclear weapons"—as soon as the Nixon administration was ready to do so.[2] At his first press conference on January 27, 1969, President Nixon stated that he favored strategic arms talks, but raised the matter of "the context of those talks." He then adopted a familiar Nixonian pattern of speech, outlining two alternative courses of action, both of which he rejected. One called for arms talks regardless of political progress, the other held back from arms control until progress had been made on solving political problems. He than gave his own middle course—"to see to it that we have strategic arms talks in a way and at a time that will promote, if possible, progress on [resolving] outstanding political problems at the same time."[3] While casting this as a middle course between extremes, Nixon in fact was declaring a policy of linkage, of seeking Soviet concessions in other areas as the price for American participation in SALT. At the same time he kept the flexibility to decide, after probing, what if any gains could be attained from such linkage. On this and several other occasions the main area of linkage Nixon used as an example was the Middle East, although the one of greatest interest was Vietnam.[4]

The Soviet Union was very wary and sensitive to the new administration's vague linking or conditioning of SALT to progress (interpreted as Soviet concessions) on other issues. For one thing, this stance was a considerable change from the eagerness and persistence with which the Johnson admin-

---

2. L. N. Zamyatin and K. Y. Novikov, TASS, Radio Moscow, January 20, 1969, in Foreign Broadcast Information Service, *Daily Report: Soviet Union*, January 21, 1969, p. A8. (Hereafter FBIS, *Soviet Union.*) The formal TASS statement also appeared in *Pravda*, January 21, 1969.

3. "The President's News Conference of January 27, 1969," *Weekly Compilation of Presidential Documents*, vol. 5 (February 3, 1969), p. 177. See also Nixon's similar statement at his third press conference, "The President's News Conference of March 4, 1969," ibid., vol. 5 (March 10, 1969), p. 367. (Hereafter *Presidential Documents.*)

4. See chapter 7.

istration had pursued SALT for two years. For another, by mid-1968 the Soviet leadership had gone through some difficult decisions and internal debate before concluding that it would be desirable to pursue SALT.[5] Finally, not yet having attained strategic parity or American acceptance of parity, the Soviet Union saw the American tactic of linkage as looking suspiciously like an attempt to exert pressure from a position of strength.

Accordingly, in his first meeting with Secretary of State Rogers on February 13 Soviet Ambassador Dobrynin reaffirmed Soviet readiness to move forward on SALT, but expressed concern over American statements linking the subject to progress on other issues. When Dobrynin first met President Nixon four days later, while not acknowledging linkage, he attempted to preempt the matter by saying that the Soviet leadership was ready to move on a number of issues at the same time, including the SALT talks and the Middle East. Nixon remarked only that the United States was in the process of reviewing the whole strategic arms matter.

This was the American position for several months, as restated by Rogers, Kissinger, and others. The Soviets waited.

Nixon and Kissinger were both annoyed by what they regarded as the increasingly eager signs of positive interest in proceeding with SALT by members of the administration, in particular Secretary of State Rogers, Director of the Arms Control and Disarmament Agency Gerard C. Smith, and senior State Department diplomats such as Ambassador Llewellyn E. Thompson. Their interest was supported by public pressures fed by a range of commentators from academia and the media.[6] These officials were seen as bucking a clearly stated administration policy (privately affirmed to Rogers and others

---

5. Political controversy in the Soviet Union over the question of agreeing to SALT negotiations was indirectly but clearly expressed in the Soviet press in the years 1967–69, and over particular SALT issues in 1970–71. For example, when Foreign Minister Andrei A. Gromyko announced to the Supreme Soviet in June 1968 Soviet readiness to begin SALT, he lambasted unidentified "sorry theoreticians" "who try to persuade us that disarmament is an illusion." *Pravda*, June 4, 1968. A strong clue about at least one area of opposition was evident in an article by a Soviet military theoretician, Colonel Yevgeny Rybkin, three months later. He stated that "it is impossible to agree that disarmament can be realized by a quiet discussion of this acute and complex problem by representatives of the opposing social systems," and that hope of success in such talks was "an illusion"—the very charge Gromyko had castigated. Rybkin also more broadly attacked détente as a path to arms limitation and ridiculed "utopian 'tranquilization' of the class, political conflict in the international arena." Lt. Col. Ye. I. Rybkin, "A Critique of Bourgeois Conceptions of War and Peace," *Kommunist vooruzhennykh sil* [Communist of the Armed Forces], no. 18 (September 1968), p. 90. The military press also edited and deleted positive references to SALT from a number of statements by political figures, including another by Gromyko. See "Statement of A. A. Gromyko to the U.N. General Assembly," *Krasnaya zvezda* [Red Star], October 4, 1968. For a discussion of the internal controversy over SALT in the late 1960s and early 1970s, see Samuel B. Payne, Jr., *The Soviet Union and SALT* (Cambridge, Mass.: MIT Press, 1980), pp. 21–81.

6. In his memoir Kissinger dwells on this theme with many illustrations. See Henry Kissinger, *White House Years* (Boston, Mass.: Little, Brown, 1979), pp. 130–38. In his memoir Nixon makes virtually no reference to SALT in 1969, indeed, until he describes the summit meeting of 1972.

in a letter from the president on February 4). As Kissinger notes, while this pressure finally led Nixon to authorize Rogers on June 11 to inform the Soviets of U.S. readiness to begin SALT, the whole experience reinforced Nixon's tendency (supported by Kissinger) increasingly to move control and even the conduct of negotiations over to the White House. As Kissinger comments, "While his preference for secrecy would have inclined him in this direction anyway, the bureaucracy's indiscipline accelerated it."[7]

By June the administration had also completed its review of military policy and in particular had reached a position on an antiballistic missile (ABM) program, which the president announced on March 14. The ABM system became the foremost arms and security issue in public and congressional debate and was to dominate the administration's attention. On August 6 the Senate completed congressional authorization of the administration's ABM deployment program by a single vote—Vice President Spiro Agnew broke a tie.

The ABM debate of 1969 had a number of important consequences. First, it made President Nixon and his administration more fervent partisans of ABM deployment by virtue of the political contest in Congress. The debate also made it clear, however, that the longer term prospect for sustaining political support for ABM deployment was not good, and thus made the ABM system something Nixon was more ready to limit (and trade) in SALT. Finally, the intensity of the focus on the ABM issue gave it particular prominence in shaping a SALT position, both within the administration and in the public eye.

On March 14 Nixon announced his new ABM Safeguard deployment program. It modified the Sentinel program of Johnson-McNamara, designed to defend against China. Now the United States would concentrate on defense of intercontinental ballistic missile (ICBM) silos. Nixon declared that the program would be reviewed annually based on technical developments, "the threat," and "the diplomatic context including any talks on arms limitation."[8] He argued that the decision would not reduce Soviet interest or readiness to negotiate in SALT, and he reaffirmed American readiness to consider limitations on strategic defensive as well as offensive weapons.

When, on June 11, the United States did indicate to Dobrynin through Rogers that it was prepared to begin SALT at the end of July, it anticipated an early favorable response. Now, however, it was the Soviets' turn to delay. First, it had become clear that the United States was proceeding with both an ABM deployment program (confirmed by the Senate on August 6) and with the testing of multiple independently targetable reentry vehicles (MIRVs). Nixon was pursuing this strategy despite public calls by a number of senators and other opinion leaders for a temporary unilateral moratorium on

---

7. Ibid., p. 138.

8. "Ballistic Missile Defense System: Statement by the President Announcing His Decision on Deployment of the System," March 14, *Presidential Documents*, vol. 5 (March 14, 1969), p. 406.

testing MIRVs, an idea Nixon categorically rejected in a news conference on June 19. These decisions did not diminish Soviet interest in SALT; if anything, they may have reinforced the incentives to seek an agreement. But they may also have led Soviet leaders to reconsider their own position and to become more wary of the Nixon administration's intentions in the SALT negotiations. In particular, the form and extent of political linkage remained obscure.

Another political action by the United States had a negative impact in Moscow and may have prompted some negative Soviet linkage. Only two weeks or so after the American offer to open SALT, it was announced that President Nixon would visit Romania in August, a move that implied an active American effort to influence developments in Eastern Europe. August was the first anniversary of the Soviet-led occupation of Czechoslovakia. There was yet another factor. Since March the Soviet Union had been involved in a series of border clashes with China, initiated by the Chinese.[9] At the very least, the Sino-Soviet tension distracted the attention of the Soviet leadership.[10]

Both sides continued to express their interest in SALT, and on October 25 spokesmen in the two capitals announced that "negotiation on curbing the strategic armaments race," SALT, would open with "preliminary discussion of the questions involved" in Helsinki on November 17, 1969.[11] In a press conference following the White House announcement Secretary Rogers discussed the prospects for SALT. He stressed that the United States had not linked SALT to political activities elsewhere, that it had not laid down any conditions for the talks, but that perhaps the very fact of the talks, without becoming "euphoric" about it, "does tend to improve the atmosphere."[12]

Thus, following months of sparring and further consideration by both sides, and without parallel movement to resolve political issues, they launched the SALT negotiations in late 1969. SALT thus became the first effort to open "an era of negotiation."[13]

---

9. See chapter 6.

10. It also led First Deputy Foreign Minister Vasily V. Kuznetsov, who had earlier been selected to head the Soviet SALT delegation, to be reassigned to negotiate with the Chinese when talks with them finally opened in October.

11. "Strategic Arms Limitation Talks," October 25, *Presidential Documents*, vol. 5 (October 27, 1969), p. 1485.

12. "Secretary Rogers Discusses Forthcoming U.S.-U.S.S.R. Talks on Curbing Strategic Arms," October 25, *Department of State Bulletin*, vol. 61 (November 10, 1969), pp. 393–94. (Hereafter *State Bulletin*.)

13. The SALT I negotiations, which ran from November 1969 through May 1972, have been described in considerable detail in several studies. Of particular value are: the memoir of the head of the U.S. SALT delegation, Gerard Smith, *Doubletalk: The Story of the First Strategic Arms Limitation Talks* (Doubleday, 1980); John Newhouse, *Cold Dawn: The Story of SALT* (Holt, Rinehart and Winston, 1973); and Kissinger, *White House Years*, especially pp. 534–57, 802–23, 1128–50, 1216–46.

   I was the executive officer and senior Department of State adviser on the SALT delegation throughout SALT I and have drawn on my own knowledge of the negotiations.

The Negotiations

The preliminary SALT session in Helsinki met for five weeks, from November 17 through December 22, 1969. Neither side presented proposals, but there was a useful airing of issues and agreement on a work program. Most important, both sides demonstrated a serious and businesslike approach, and they agreed that as a result of the exchange "each side is able better to understand the views of the other with respect to the problems under consideration."[14] It was agreed to meet again in Vienna in April 1970, in accordance with a compromise that the sessions would be rotated between Helsinki and Vienna.

The success of the preliminary meetings was more important—and less assured—than the American side had realized. Members of the Soviet delegation indicated privately that the Soviet leadership had been quite tentative about its commitment to a continuing SALT negotiation until the American delegation had shown a serious interest in the initial exchanges. Acceptance of a full-fledged SALT negotiation was not only a Politburo decision, it was also approved by the Central Committee plenum in December 1969.[15]

The most notable feature of the Soviet position as set forth at the first SALT round was a strong endorsement of mutual deterrence and an expressed readiness to bolster deterrence through strategic arms limitations. In the very first substantive exchange the head of the Soviet delegation, Deputy Foreign Minister Vladimir S. Semenov, presented a statement cleared by the highest political and military leaders in Moscow. It expressed the following view:

Even in the event that one of the sides were the first to be subjected to attack, it would undoubtedly retain the ability to inflict a retaliatory strike of annihilating power. Thus, evidently, we all agree that war between our two countries would be disastrous for both sides. And it would be tantamount to suicide for the one who decided to start such a war.[16]

In concrete terms the Soviet side made clear its desire to limit ABM deployment to geographically and numerically low limits. Nor did it exclude a complete ban on ABMs. Surprisingly to the American side, the Soviets did not specifically raise the issue of a limitation on MIRVs.[17] Also signifi-

14. "United States and Soviet Union Conclude Preliminary Strategic Arms Limitation Talks: Text of Communique," December 22, *State Bulletin*, vol. 62 (January 12, 1970), p. 29.

15. Information from knowledgeable Soviet officials, who also stated that the Central Committee's approval had not been pro forma.

16. Quoted in Raymond L. Garthoff, "Mutual Deterrence and Strategic Arms Limitation in Soviet Policy," *International Security*, vol. 3 (Summer 1978), p. 126. (Two small errors in that text are corrected here.) See also the discussion by Smith, *Doubletalk*, pp. 84–87.

17. Kissinger correctly notes this fact, but incorrectly asserts that the Soviet delegation "showed no interest" and did not "respond when we brought it up." Kissinger, *White House Years*, p. 150. Under instructions the American delegation also did not raise the issue of MIRVs. In cautious

cant, but not immediately or fully appreciated, was Soviet insistence that for purposes of SALT strategic offensive arms should include all weapons capable of nuclear attack on the territories of the Soviet Union and the United States. This definition included American forward-based nuclear delivery aircraft in Europe and Asia and on aircraft carriers within striking range of the Soviet Union. This approach did not figure in the American conception, and to accept it would obviously be politically as well as militarily disadvantageous. Hence the Americans strongly objected.

The period from the end of the year until the resumption of the negotiations in mid-April 1970 involved intensive preparations, notwithstanding the already extensive studies conducted in 1969.[18]

The crucial issues in SALT I were limitations on ABM systems and MIRVs. At the time, however, there was great reluctance in some quarters to recognize that MIRV was the key issue in strategic offensive limitations. The United States had a clear advantage in their development and by early 1970 was on the verge of operational deployment. Rather than limit these American programs, both the ICBM and the submarine-launched ballistic missile (SLBM) systems, the whole American effort was placed on attempting to limit future Soviet *potential* MIRV capacity by cutting down the existing larger Soviet ICBM throw-weight, or payload capacity. The Joint Chiefs of Staff (JCS) as well as the Department of Defense (DOD) were above all protective of the imminent American deployments, and DOD took the lead in pressing for reductions in the greater number of larger land-based missiles in the Soviet force.

Others did not share this view. Ever since early 1969, the Arms Control and Disarmament Agency (ACDA) had taken a lead in seeking limitation of MIRVs, including a moratorium on tests pending SALT. (The MIRVs were rapidly approaching successful conclusion of tests paving the way for operational status.)[19] The Department of State supported this position. It was the inexorable pace of development of this new offensive missile technology,

---

informal discussions, however, Soviet delegates indicated interest and wondered why the American side had not brought the subject up. See Smith, *Doubletalk*, pp. 165–68.

18. The White House later described the work preparing for SALT as the construction of "building-blocks" that could then be fashioned into specific packages of proposals. See Richard M. Nixon, *U.S. Foreign Policy for the 1970's: A New Strategy for Peace*, Report to the Congress, February 18, 1970, vol. 1 (Washington, D.C.: Government Printing Office, 1970), pp. 142–46.

Preparatory work for SALT had, after some reshuffling, since July 1969 been concentrated in the hands of a Verification Panel chaired by Kissinger. The building-blocks approach did not really work, for reasons that will become apparent in this chapter.

19. An even broader proposal made by ACDA in 1969 for an overall freeze of strategic offensive and defensive forces by both sides was sidetracked and in effect rejected. See Smith, *Doubletalk*, pp. 160–61. A freeze of the strategic balance as it stood in 1969 would have been to the advantage of both sides, especially the United States.

rather than just eagerness for arms talks, that was impelling some to urge an earlier start to the SALT talks—a point Kissinger finesses in his retrospective account. The civilian and military leadership in the Pentagon was, however, adamant against limiting MIRVs.

As early as the spring of 1969 Kissinger (and probably Nixon) concluded that limiting MIRVs would be going too far with arms control, that to pursue limitations on both ABMs and MIRVs would lead to opposition from the Pentagon and the political right. Kissinger for one then decided to seek limitation only of ABMs, and not a limitation or ban on MIRVs.[20]

Public attention in 1969 focused above all on two questions: whether the United States should proceed with an ABM deployment, and when SALT would begin. By contrast, the occurrence that had the most significant consequences, development of MIRVs, received little public attention except from a small number of concerned experts, despite considerable support in Congress for a moratorium on MIRV testing.[21] Indeed, 1969 may have been the crucial time of decision, given how close a deployable MIRV system was to reality then. By 1970 the United States had MIRVs ready for deployment, while the Soviet Union had not even begun testing them.[22]

The critical time to establish the U.S. position on arms limitations and to advance a proposal came in the early spring of 1970. After several options had been developed along lines posed by Kissinger, President Nixon

---

20. I base this conclusion mainly on a discussion at that time with a close confidant of Kissinger. He stated that Kissinger had put the question to him just that way and that Kissinger had then given his own judgment to seek a limit on ABMs and not MIRVs. This choice was made not on analytical grounds, but on political grounds of "what the traffic would bear" and the Pentagon's strong stand in favor of MIRV. In his memoir Kissinger presents a vivid rhetorical defense for not taking early steps to limit both, although he does not acknowledge the real issues: "We were being pressed to take two momentous steps: first, to abandon our ABM without reciprocity; and second, to postpone our MIRV deployment as a unilateral gesture— in short, to forego both our missile defense and the means to defeat that already deployed by the Soviet Union. . . . What would be their incentive to negotiate limitations in an agreement? . . . To abandon ABM and MIRV together would thus not only have undercut the prospects for any SALT agreement but probably guaranteed Soviet strategic superiority for a decade. . . . Neither our ABM program nor MIRV testing created difficulties for SALT. On the contrary, they spurred it." Kissinger, *White House Years*, p. 212; and see pp. 210–12.

21. See Smith, *Doubletalk*, pp. 154–64; and Kissinger, *White House Years*, pp. 197–98, 211–12, 537–38, 541.

22. There was uncertainty about the status of Soviet MIRV development, and some American proponents of MIRVs went to considerable lengths to overstate and play upon those uncertainties and fears about possible Soviet MIRVs. Secretary of Defense Laird pushed the matter publicly, and Kissinger put unusually brazen pressure on Director of Central Intelligence Richard M. Helms and the intelligence community to alter a draft national intelligence estimate to support Laird's position that the Soviet SS-9 had a MIRV capability. The pressure was, however, ignored: although the paper was rewritten for clarity, the estimate was not changed. See *Foreign and Military Intelligence*, Final Report of the Senate Select Committee to Study Governmental Operations with Respect to Intelligence Activities, 94 Cong. 2 sess. (GPO, 1976), bk. 1, pp. 77–78.

approved the presentation of two alternative approaches to the Soviets. The arms control advocates (the Department of State and ACDA) basically favored the one that called either for limiting ABMs to the defense of Moscow and Washington (locations of the respective National Command Authorities, and hence referred to as an "NCA-level" limitation) or for banning ABM deployment altogether, freezing strategic offensive missiles at the existing American level of 1,710 ICBMs and SLBMs,[23] and banning deployment of MIRVs. The second alternative—favored by the Department of Defense (although not the JCS) called for the same approach to ABM, and for a reduction in the number of ICBMs and SLBMs from a base level of 1,710 to 1,000 by removing 100 missile launchers annually over a seven-year period; it did not call for limiting MIRVs. These alternatives appeared to represent a forthright and serious effort at arms control.

In fact, the U.S. proposals were loaded with other provisions that ensured their unacceptability, as Kissinger well understood and intended. (Presumably Nixon did too, although he was little involved personally and delegated much authority to Kissinger; he was also dependent on Kissinger for information and opinions on this subject.) The proposal to ban MIRVs was encumbered with an unnecessary demand for on-site inspection, while the proposal to reduce the ICBMs and SLBMs was couched in terms that would have heavily reduced the principal Soviet missile systems and not those of the United States.

In his memoir, Kissinger states that he himself favored another option, one that would have frozen the offensive levels and limited ABMs, but allowed MIRVs. He saw this alternative as "the most realistic and most consistent with our interests" because it would "arrest the Soviet offensive buildup, which was our most urgent concern," while giving the United States "the greatest flexibility for modernization" with its MIRV program. He comments that had this option been put forward as the preferred position, "all hell would have broken loose both in the Congress and in the bureaucracy. It would have been claimed that we had never even 'explored' a ban on ABM and MIRV." This proposal would also have met with a "tepid reception in the Pentagon."[24] Thus, while "convinced that the Soviets would never agree," Kissinger's recommendation, which was accepted by the president, was to offer the two more comprehensive approaches "as our opening positions. This would respond to Congressional and bureaucratic supporters of MIRV and ABM bans; it would give us the positive public posture of having favored comprehensive limitations." If the Soviets accepted either, it would have been, as intentionally crafted, lopsidedly to the advantage of the United States; by the same token, "if the Soviets rejected them, as I firmly expected, we could then put forward

---

23. Limitations on ICBMs and SLBMs were not keyed to numbers of missiles produced (which included those intended for testing and in the pipeline), but to numbers of deployed operational launchers for ICBMs and SLBMs.

24. Kissinger, *White House Years*, p. 543.

Option B [his preferred option] from a much stronger domestic and bureaucratic position."[25] In short, the opening positions of the United States, which called for a MIRV ban and for deep reductions, respectively, were not serious negotiating proposals.

Because of the central significance of these proposals to the whole course of SALT, it is necessary to look at this issue in more depth. The president's foreign policy report to the Congress in February 1970 described the SALT preparations as involving "the most intensive study of strategic arms problems ever made by this or any other government." It went on to explain that "too much depended on these talks, for our nation and all mankind, to rush into them partially prepared. . . . Discussions explored substantive issues rather than exchanging rigidly defined bureaucratic positions . . . we focused on comprehensive assessments of the issues and alternatives. . . . This presented me with clear choices . . . and clear rationales. . . . we plan to move in April in Vienna to more specific positions. We enter this next phase with a well-developed body of technical analysis and evaluations, which is being continuously expanded and improved by the Verification Panel and the NSC process."[26] In his memoir Kissinger repeats these panegyrics: "The result was the most comprehensive study of the strategic and verification implications of the control of weapons ever undertaken by our government and probably any government" and "our negotiating position would reflect not bureaucratic compromise but careful analysis of consequences and objectives."[27]

The reality was rather different. Kissinger, in describing the actual preparation of the negotiating positions in his memoir, is more candid. After a full National Security Council (NSC) meeting chaired by the president on March 25—three weeks before the negotiations were to resume and after five preparatory meetings of the Verification Panel—"there was no consensus; there was a babble of discordant voices." Nixon left the task of sorting out some options to Kissinger, who, without advising others that he had been delegated this task, on March 27 issued over President Nixon's name a directive "asking the agencies to reduce the chaos to four options for Presidential decision."[28] Even the existing machinery was too bulky. It was decided that a single person (I was designated) would be given the bare bones outline for the key elements of the four options (for example, "MIRV ban," "Safeguard-level ABM") and assigned the task of developing them (for example, what would a MIRV ban entail? How many ABM interceptors for the Safeguard level—

25. Ibid., p. 544.

26. Nixon, *U.S. Foreign Policy for the 1970's: A New Strategy for Peace*, pp. 143–47. See also the further praise for the system of SALT preparation in the next year's sequel, *U.S. Foreign Policy for the 1970's: Building for Peace*, Report to the Congress, vol. 2 (GPO, 1971), pp. 188–90.

27. Kissinger, *White House Years*, p. 149.

28. Ibid., p. 541. See also Smith, *Doubletalk*, pp. 116–18. The directive was National Security Decision Memorandum (NSDM)–49.

actually 879 were planned; I rounded it up to a limit of 1,000). I was made responsible for coordinating the positions of the agencies involved.[29] The four options were then reviewed at an NSC meeting on April 8 in a session described by Kissinger as "a Kabuki play." "All of this feinting and posturing was performed before a President bored to distraction. His glazed expression showed that he considered most of the arguments esoteric rubbish; he was trying to calculate the political impact and salability of the various options, of which only the broad outlines interested him."[30] So much for the "careful analysis of consequences and objectives" allegedly replacing "bureaucratic compromise" and providing "clear choices" for presidential decision.[31]

The alternative approach involving a ban on MIRVs as developed for NSC deliberation and presidential decision did *not* include on-site inspection to monitor compliance; Kissinger and Nixon added that requirement after the NSC meeting. The Department of Defense and the JCS had argued for on-site inspection as a verification requirement in a dissenting note, but the other agencies—the Central Intelligence Agency (CIA), the principal monitoring unit, as well as the Department of State and ACDA—were prepared to rely on verifying a ban on MIRV testing by American technical means (including satellites) as the mainstay for verifying a ban on MIRV deployment.[32] The Verification Panel and NSC meetings at which the various proposals were considered discussed on-site inspection either to overload the MIRV ban proposal so as to ensure its rejection by the Soviet Union (Defense representatives took this approach), because they wanted American MIRVs, or because giving the Soviet leaders some bitter medicine seemed tough and therefore a good stance. Technical analysis of verification requirements was not a consideration, as discussed below. Among those counseling on-site inspection at the NSC meeting were such "experts" as Vice President Agnew and Attorney General John N. Mitchell.

At the time of the NSC meeting and Nixon and Kissinger's decision on on-site inspection, *no* studies of what such an inspection would entail or could contribute to verification had been carried out. Only *after* the decision to demand it was an interagency study begun to determine the practical possibilities for such verification. Another reason was that it occurred belatedly to some that the United States itself might not want on-site Soviet inspection,

---

29. Smith, *Doubletalk*, pp. 118–19, notes that I was the person assigned this task. The discussion is based on my participation.

30. Kissinger, *White House Years*, p. 542.

31. "The happy task of distilling some recommendations out of this confusion fell on me," writes Kissinger. "I regret to admit that in doing so I was swayed by bureaucratic and political considerations more than in any other set of decisions in my period in office. . . . in the case of SALT, I knew that my recommendation would carry an unusual weight. Nixon simply would not learn the technical details well enough to choose meaningfully." Kissinger, *White House Years*, p. 543.

32. Kissinger is in error when he states that the MIRV ban option "presented at the NSC meeting" on April 8, 1970, had provided for on-site inspection; only the dissenting recommendation by Defense-JCS did so. Ibid., p. 541.

as it could result in the disclosure of secrets of U.S. weapons technology. The studies were completed two months later, as the United States was abandoning its proposal to ban MIRVs and to demand on-site inspection. They reflected the same continuing interagency divergences in opinion.[33]

The specific proposal to ban MIRVs that Kissinger formulated after the NSC meeting also included, to meet Pentagon preferences, on-site inspection to verify an ABM-corollary ban on upgrading surface-to-air missile (SAM) antiaircraft systems to attain ABM capability. This was done even though the very same ABM proposal in the other proposal options, including the proposal on missile reductions presented to the Soviets at that time, did not call for on-site inspection. (The argument was that under a MIRV ban, potential ABM capabilities of SAM systems could be strategically more significant. It was not very convincing.)

The MIRV ban proposal presented to the Soviet delegation in April was rejected immediately. One reason was the provision for on-site inspection, which the Soviets correctly understood was designed to make the proposal unacceptable. Another reason was that the United States was calling for a ban on MIRV testing and deployment—but not on MIRV production.[34] The Soviets also advanced a proposal on MIRVs, which called for a ban on their production and deployment, but not on testing (and with no on-site inspection).

From the American point of view the Soviet proposal was seriously deficient because a ban on developmental testing of MIRVs *was* the key to verifying Soviet compliance with the ban on deployment. Production of MIRVs was neither readily verifiable, nor adequate in the absence of a ban on testing. Finally, the United States had completed testing of a deployable MIRV and saw freezing that advantage as insurance against later abrogation of a ban on MIRVs.

From the Soviet standpoint the United States was attempting to buy intrusive on-site inspections that were politically unacceptable, even though it had earlier given assurances that in SALT it would rely to a maximum on national technical means of verification. Moreover, by banning flight-testing of MIRVs, the United States would deny the Soviet Union equal

---

33. See Smith, *Doubletalk*, pp. 171–73.

Kissinger, in a press conference after the signing of the SALT I agreements, admitted that "early in the negotiations we asked for onsite inspection," but that "once we analyzed the mechanism of onsite inspection we found . . . that the capability of cheating against onsite inspection is very great, and the national means of detection are more reliable for the kind of agreement we have made here." "News Conference of Dr. Kissinger, Moscow, May 27," *State Bulletin*, vol. 66 (June 26, 1972), pp. 878–79.

34. I was struck by the fact that my counterpart on the Soviet delegation, busily taking notes as Ambassador Smith introduced the U.S. proposal to ban MIRVs, simply put down his pen after the on-site inspection provision was read. Later he remarked privately, "We had been hoping you would make a serious MIRV proposal." The Soviets also saw the loophole of allowing MIRV production as a "booby-trap" and as a further indication that the United States was not serious about seeking a ban or limitation on MIRVs.

security, as that ban would freeze indefinitely an American advantage. Finally, by not banning production of MIRVs at a time when the United States was beginning production (while the Soviet Union was not in a position to do so), the American proposal would have left the United States with the option of producing and storing (merely not deploying) MIRV warheads in unlimited quantities.

The United States could not have given up its insistence that flight tests of MIRVs be banned, but it could at least have shown good faith and encouraged Soviet consideration of a ban on MIRVs by agreeing to add a ban on their production. The American delegation did request authority to propose such a ban on production, and without raising the politically sensitive question of on-site inspection, but the White House refused to authorize it. A ban on MIRVs or even a real negotiation on banning MIRVs was not desired. Exploration of such a ban ended at this time.[35]

Barring some unusual disclosure from Moscow, it may never be known whether a ban on MIRVs could have been agreed to if the United States had dropped on-site inspection and added a ban on production. The Soviets might still have considered the ability of the United States quickly to produce and deploy MIRVs in case of a later abrogation of the agreement as too great a risk. But that decision may never even have been posed in Moscow, and it was certainly never tested. Some senior Soviet officials involved with the issue believe Moscow would have agreed to a ban on MIRVs.[36] At the same time, while concerned over the U.S. lead in the development and deployment of MIRVs, some Soviet officials may have been relatively relaxed about not preventing MIRVs precisely for the reason that the United States should have been more interested in stopping them: in the long run the Soviet Union had the greater potential for MIRVs because of its larger ICBM throw-weight.

---

35. See Smith, *Doubletalk*, pp. 173–74.

Kissinger notes in his memoir that "everyone agreed that the Soviet proposal banning MIRV production but permitting MIRV testing was totally unacceptable," without even discussing the reverse hole in the American proposal or the American delegation's proposal to close both loopholes by adding both constraints. See Kissinger, *White House Years*, p. 546.

In briefing members of Congress in June 1972, Kissinger was even more disingenuous. In seeking to justify the administration's efforts to ban MIRVs, he misstated the Soviet position, alleging that the Soviets "refused a deployment ban as such. What they proposed was a production ban. . . . So, the Soviet counter-proposal for a production ban without a test ban was generally unacceptable to us and when we reached that stalemate, we could not proceed any further. This was the obstacle to proceeding on the MIRV's." "Question and Answer Session after a Briefing by Dr. Henry Kissinger," White House Press Release, June 15, 1972, p. 25. The question and answer exchange was not printed in the *Department of State Bulletin* or the *Weekly Compilation of Presidential Documents*.

36. I believe Moscow had not reached a final decision. Some members of the Soviet delegation and other officials concerned with SALT at the time and subsequently have indicated privately that the Soviet Union would have responded favorably to a balanced proposal on banning MIRVs, without on-site inspection but including a ban on testing as well as on production and deployment.

While it remains uncertain whether a vigorous American effort in 1970 to obtain a ban on MIRVs could have succeeded, it is very clear that no such effort was made. The Pentagon, and hence the White House, preferred to proceed with U.S. plans for major deployments of MIRVs rather than to limit Soviet deployment. It was, in retrospect (and to many at the time), a short-sighted judgment. While Kissinger in his memoir staunchly justifies and defends his actions at the time, in a moment of candor at a press briefing in 1974 he conceded: "I would say in retrospect that I wish I had thought through the implications of a MIRVed world more thoughtfully in 1969 and 1970 than I did."[37] Kissinger certainly received a great deal of informed advice on the issue in 1969 and 1970 from academic sources he courted at the time, as well as from the State Department and ACDA.[38] There were, however, contrary bureaucratic considerations, ranging from Kissinger's own staff through the entire government bureaucracy. And as noted earlier, Kissinger has admitted being swayed by such considerations.[39]

The second American proposal was presented soon after the one featuring a ban on MIRVs. Presented as of equal standing, it also called for freezing ICBM and SLBM launchers at the current American level of 1,710, and then reducing them by 100 each year for seven years. MIRVs were not limited, and there was no requirement for on-site inspection of the missile reductions—or for the identical NCA-level ABM limit as in the first alternative.

This U.S. approach to reductions, sponsored by a senior member of the U.S. delegation to the SALT talks, Paul H. Nitze, and by the Department of Defense, had serious flaws. First, it derived from an American definition of what should be regarded as strategic forces under SALT, omitting some American forces able to strike the Soviet Union; at the same time it included Soviet intermediate-range missiles that could not strike the United States. It singled out for reduction the one area of particular Soviet strength, land-based missile forces, and left other American forces either limited at existing levels (for example, heavy bombers) or completely unconstrained (for example, forward-based forces not regarded as strategic). Finally, the reductions proposal also called for a limit on Soviet "modern large ballistic missiles," in particular the SS-9 ICBM. Such missiles would be limited initially to 250 launchers (at the time the Soviet Union had 222 operational and 60 more under construction, for a projected total of 282). But the SS-9s would also be preferentially reduced over the seven-year period. While this approval would suit the United States very well, since the large SS-9 had a high MIRV potential, by the same token

---

37. "Transcript of Secretary Henry Kissinger's Background Press Briefing," December 3, 1974.

38. See Seymour M. Hersh, *The Price of Power: Kissinger in the Nixon White House* (Summit, 1983), pp. 147–56.

39. See note 31; also for a less sympathetic account than Kissinger's, see Hersh, *The Price of Power*, pp. 157–67.

the Soviets saw no reason to reduce it while the United States would be rapidly building its ICBM capability by the unconstrained addition of MIRVs (which it in fact began to do in June 1970). The United States could meet its obligations largely through reducing the number of its older B-52 bombers, which it was retiring in any case.

The Soviets, not surprisingly, also rejected the proposed approach to reductions out of hand in April 1970. This rejection has been cited by some commentators as evidence of Soviet rejection of any proposed reductions. But rejection of a proposal that would have had such a one-sided impact on Soviet capabilities was not an indication of opposition to balanced reductions.

After several months of negotiation it became clear to all that neither the MIRV ban nor the reduction proposals advanced by the American side in April provided a basis for possible agreement. Thereupon the United States introduced a new proposal in late July and early August. While retaining the ceiling of 1,710 ICBM and SLBM launchers, and a sublimit of 250 on large Soviet ICBMs, the proposal did not contain the MIRV ban (or on-site inspections), deep reductions, or the limits proposed earlier on Soviet non-intercontinental ballistic systems, intermediate- or medium-range missiles, and submarine-launched tactical cruise missiles. Nevertheless, the Soviet side continued to press for taking into account U.S. forward-based nuclear delivery systems within striking range of the Soviet Union. The American side continued to refuse to consider them as part of the U.S.-USSR strategic equation for political reasons relating both to military issues and the alliance. A stalemate developed on offensive arms limitations.

A quite different situation developed with respect to strategic defensive arms.[40] As noted earlier, the same ABM proposition was contained in both the overall American proposals of April 1970: limiting ABMs to defense of the National Command Authorities, Washington and Moscow. The decision to limit ABMs to the national capitals was, in two respects, rather surprising.[41] For one, it differed from the actual American ABM deployment program both in concept and in terms of congressional authorization and actual construction. For another, it was bound to appeal to the Soviet Union. It would

---

40. The following account of the SALT negotiation of ABM limitations is drawn in part from Raymond L. Garthoff, "Negotiating with the Russians: Some Lessons from SALT," *International Security*, vol. 1 (Spring 1977), pp. 10–13.

41. The options considered by the NSC included either NCA defense or zero ABM (that is, a complete ban on ABM deployment) as the defensive component of the approach banning MIRVs, and for the ICBM reductions approach, either of those options or the full Safeguard deployment (rounded up to a level of 1,000 ABM interceptors). Kissinger and Nixon's decision was to offer the NCA defense, because the Pentagon preferred at least a minimal deployment for operational experience. It was not, however, an issue on which advocates of an NCA defense felt strongly. The matter was not debated in the NSC meeting, and the choice was basically Kissinger's. He does not acknowledge that fact in his memoir; rather, in retrospect he is very critical of the decision to propose an NCA defense. See Kissinger, *White House Years*, p. 542; and Newhouse, *Cold Dawn*, pp. 182–85. Newhouse, however, erroneously assumed that both zero and NCA options were offered to the Soviet delegation in April.

permit retention of the ABM deployment to defend Moscow and thus relieve Soviet leaders of having to face the need to consider dismantling that system if the United States had pressed for a complete ban on ABM deployment.

In just one week the Soviet delegation, on instructions from Moscow, accepted the proposed NCA-level limitation on ABM deployment. While details of the numbers of interceptors and radars, the precise area of permitted deployment, and other points remained to be negotiated, by April 1970 the ABM element of SALT appeared to be well along toward resolution on the basis proposed by the United States: a minimal ABM system providing for defense of the NCA in Washington and Moscow.

The Soviets' quick acceptance of the NCA-level limitation was not unexpected to those who had correctly understood their position on the ABM limitation presented at Helsinki in late 1969. Some were disappointed because they wished to present the zero option as an alternative (which was planned, but only after the NCA level had been offered). Most advocates of a complete ban on ABMs realized that the Soviets would probably prefer to keep the Moscow deployment and, once given the choice of NCA, would not be interested in zero ABMs.[42]

Others, including Kissinger and probably the president (although he displayed a remarkable indifference), expected that the Soviet side would take the lead in proposing an ABM level higher than NCA. That move would place the onus on the Soviet Union and could then be used against congressional opponents of Safeguard. This was a massive miscalculation.[43]

It is clear that in opting for the NCA-level limitation the White House accepted a substantial shift from the strongly argued formal defense guidance adopted by the administration only a year earlier: that guidance included as one of four "criteria for strategic sufficiency," or objectives for American strategic force planning, "defending against damage from small attacks or accidental launches."[44] Inclusion of this objective was seen by advocates of nationwide ballistic missile defenses as an important victory. In accordance

---

42. See Newhouse, *Cold Dawn*, pp. 184–85.

43. The Soviet position was misjudged because of an awareness that the Soviet Union had begun to deploy ABMs and had earlier given strong rhetorical support for ballistic missile defense (BMD). Prime Minister Aleksei N. Kosygin had been reported as having said in 1967 that defensive systems should not be limited, and it was generally believed that the Soviets had hesitated over SALT because of a reluctance to limit their ABM systems. Those American leaders holding this view had not, however, availed themselves of later intelligence that made clear an important shift in Soviet thinking. For a comprehensive review of the changing Soviet view of both BMD and arms limitation in the 1960s and early 1970s, see Raymond L. Garthoff, "BMD and East-West Relations," in Ashton B. Carter and David N. Schwartz, eds., *Ballistic Missile Defense* (Brookings Institution, 1984), pp. 286–314.

44. The original decision and statement of the four criteria were secret, but public references were later made to them, and by 1971 they were publicly acknowledged by Secretary of Defense Laird in his statement on U.S. defense posture. See *Department of Defense Annual Report, Fiscal Year 1972*, March 9, 1971, p. 62.

with this decision, when President Nixon announced the Safeguard ABM decision in March 1969, he had described its objectives as including not only defense of land-based retaliatory forces, but also "defense of the American people against the kind of nuclear attack which Communist China is likely to be able to mount within the decade" and also "protection against the possibility of accidental attacks from any source."[45] These very references from the March statement were quoted again in the president's foreign policy report only days before the decision to propose the ABM limitations, an approach that meant abandoning even minimal nationwide protection of the American people from Chinese or accidental attack.[46] Nixon himself had said in his press conference on the Safeguard decision in March 1969 that he assumed "the Soviet Union would be just as reluctant as we would be to leave their country naked against a potential Chinese Communist threat."[47] Kissinger also has said he supported Safeguard because it seemed to him "highly irresponsible simply to ignore the possibility of an accidental attack or the prospect of nuclear capabilities in the hands of yet more countries. China was only the first." He opposed "turning our people into hostages by deliberate choice."[48] (Subsequently Kissinger also disclosed another then-secret reason the Nixon administration decided in early 1969 on the nationwide Safeguard ABM deployment: "providing a better base for rapid expansion against the Soviet Union.")[49]

In SALT planning as well, the basic guidance from the president for the first SALT session in Helsinki in November 1969 had specifically stated that "the President is committed to the area defense component of the Safeguard program."[50] Thus the United States entered SALT determined to have at least a minimal nationwide ABM defense.

Within a year the Nixon-Kissinger White House decided to ignore or override its own determination in defense policy of the necessary "criteria for strategic sufficiency." This decision was undoubtedly correct, and the pur-

45. "Statement by the President Announcing His Decision on Deployment of the [Ballistic Missile Defense] System, March 14, 1969," *Presidential Documents*, vol. 5 (March 17, 1969), p. 406.

46. Nixon, *U.S. Foreign Policy for the 1970's: A New Strategy for Peace*, p. 126.

47. "The President's News Conference of March 14, 1969," *Presidential Documents*, vol. 5 (March 17, 1969), p. 404. Nixon also stated that intelligence showed Soviet ABM radars to be directed against Chinese as well as American threats, and stressed historical Soviet emphasis on strategic defense.

48. Kissinger, *White House Years*, p. 208.

49. Ibid., p. 209. This had been precisely the Soviet suspicion.

50. This statement was made in NSDM-33 of November 12, 1969, providing the basic guidance for the SALT negotiations as the talks began. "Area defense" meant a defense of the continental United States. The term for a minimal nationwide defense used at the time was a "thin" nationwide defense; an approach to a heavier concentration of defenses was called a "thick" defense.

pose of the observation is not to criticize. Rather, it is to illustrate the hollowness of the claims of a "careful review" of strategic doctrine and the description of the criteria as "a significant intellectual advance" providing guidance and necessary "flexibility."[51] The reason for the sharp shift from building a nationwide ABM system in the spring of 1969 to advocacy of a limitation on ABM deployments to the national capitals in the spring of 1970 was clear: the U.S. Senate had shown it would not support a nationwide deployment, and prospects for completing even two or three sites to defend ICBM fields were very uncertain.

It has often been contended, under the Nixon administration and later, that congressional approval of an ABM deployment was necessary to get the Soviet government to agree to an ABM limitation. That argument is doubtful. Be that as it may, it is clear that only the prospect of Congress' withdrawing its support led the *American* government to agree to sharply constrained limitations on ABMs.

The United States advanced a new comprehensive SALT proposal in Vienna on August 4, 1970. As noted earlier, it replaced both the earlier proposal for a ban on MIRVs and the proposal for deep reductions in offensive arms limitations. It introduced a new ABM proposal: either NCA-level defense as proposed earlier, or zero ABM deployment, alternatives described as having equal status. The Soviet delegation was surprised by this move; the Soviet Union had already accepted the NCA limitation offered earlier—why now introduce an alternative?[52] In any case the Soviet side reaffirmed its choice of the NCA limitation.

Meanwhile, given the impasse on strategic offensive arms limitations, the Soviets hinted, as early as May 1970 at Vienna and in a proposal in June 1970 via the Dobrynin-Kissinger channel, that an initial step might be an agreement limiting ABMs alone (at the NCA level) or coupled with an agreement to reduce the risk of war through accident or miscalculation, while deferring the thorny offensive arms problem. (Measures to deal with the possibility of "accidental war" were also being discussed at SALT, and some elements of agreement seemed within easy reach, as discussed later.) Washington turned the idea down, but the proposal helped lead to the decision to table the new comprehensive offensive-defensive proposal of August 4.[53]

---

51. Nixon, *U.S. Foreign Policy for the 1970's: A New Strategy for Peace*, pp. 121–22.

52. The zero ABM alternative was not introduced with any expectation of Soviet acceptance, or indeed even desire for it. Kissinger has said why succinctly: "proposing a ban on ABM was the first step toward getting off the uncomfortable NCA position," and the new proposal of August 4 offered an opportunity to make this shift without yet withdrawing the NCA proposal. See Kissinger, *White House Years*, p. 549.

53. Kissinger reports Dobrynin's suggestion of June 25 without mentioning that a Soviet delegate had made the same suggestion to me on May 18, an approach that had promptly been re-

In December 1970 the Soviets formally proposed to decouple and conclude an ABM agreement as an initial step, and a draft ABM treaty was presented in March 1971. The United States, however, continued to insist on a single comprehensive agreement limiting strategic offensive arms as well as ABMs. Then in early May, Semenov and key members of his delegation began to hint in private talks about possibly coupling an ABM agreement with an "understanding" on certain limitations on ICBMs, including a sublimit on large ICBMs.

The U.S. delegation and government agencies considered this proposal to be a very interesting indication of a new shift in the Soviet position. Kissinger and Nixon, however, had a very different reaction: "a bizarre incident interrupted our efforts." Unknown to the American delegation or anyone outside the White House, Kissinger and Dobrynin had been secretly conducting negotiations on SALT for four months.

Kissinger and Nixon saw this sudden surfacing in the official SALT channel of central elements of their private negotiations as a circumvention of the presidential channel that raised "doubts about Soviet good faith." Above all, according to Kissinger, "Nixon was seized by the fear that Gerard Smith, rather than he, would get credit for the seemingly imminent breakthrough of linking offensive and defensive limitations." Kissinger states that he had earlier "reassured Nixon that such a breakthrough could occur in Vienna only if Moscow made a deliberate choice to bypass the Presidential Channel, not only on this issue but on all others." Now the Soviets appeared to Nixon and Kissinger to be doing just that. Accordingly Kissinger warned Dobrynin bluntly on May 11 that "sooner or later the President's tenacity and my control of the bureaucratic machinery would get matters to where we wanted them. The price, I told him, would be loss of confidence in the seriousness of a private, direct Channel. The President's anger at what he could only construe as a deliberate maneuver to deprive him of credit would be massive." Kissinger demanded a

---

ported to Washington. See Kissinger, *White House Years*, pp. 547–48; and Smith, *Doubletalk*, pp. 147–48.

During this period the Soviet side was trying to fathom the best means of authoritative but informal communication. President Nixon, it will be recalled, had himself informed Dobrynin in February 1969 that Kissinger was his chosen channel for serious confidential exchanges, but the SALT process with its permanent senior delegations was a possible exception. Moreover, there may well have been bureaucratic preferences and maneuvers on the Soviet side—not everyone in the Soviet Ministry of Foreign Affairs or other ministries represented in the SALT delegation, including Defense, may have wanted to channel communications only through Dobrynin. In any case, the Soviets occasionally probed and used alternate or parallel channels. In May 1970 Deputy Minister Semenov confirmed with Ambassador Smith an informal back channel in the SALT delegations (with me as the American representative). In June Dobrynin asked Under Secretary of State Elliot L. Richardson whether it would be better to deal through the SALT delegations or in Washington. For subsequent reverberations of this splintered approach, given the White House determination to monopolize serious negotiations, see the following pages.

reply to the latest proposals on the few remaining points within forty-eight hours. He received an answer within twenty-four. What the Soviet leadership had learned about Nixon, Kissinger, and the American administration was worth far more than quibbling over any details.[54]

The breakthrough announced by President Nixon on May 20, 1971, was a vague, brief announcement that the United States and the Soviet Union had agreed to seek to work out an ABM agreement and "certain measures with respect to the limitation of offensive strategic weapons."[55] In other words the United States accepted a separate ABM agreement, while the Soviet Union accepted the need to accompany it with some constraints on offensive weapons. Precisely what those offensive limitations would be (and, for that matter, the ABM limitations as well) remained to be determined. As became clear only later, in some important respects the resolution of the remaining issues on offensive limitations had been prejudiced by Kissinger's back channel negotiations.

In announcing the agreement, President Nixon described it as "a significant development in breaking the deadlock" in SALT and "a major step in breaking the stalemate." Even more attention should have been paid to his remark that "intensive negotiations, however, will be required to translate this understanding into a concrete agreement."[56] Unspoken but immediately evident was the fact that there would be no comprehensive or integral agreement.

The administration saw the May 20, 1971, agreement as a major achievement that could have been reached only through the special Kissinger-Dobrynin channel. This is highly unlikely.[57] Members of the Soviet delegation had been hinting at such a deal for months, and the only thing preventing the American delegation from exploring it was the rigid instruction from Washington to stand firm on the clearly nonnegotiable American proposal of the previous August. The White House viewed the achievement from several perspectives. One was a highlighting, albeit self-serving, of its own role, another a desire to depict (and see) the agreement as something only it could arrange. Ultimately it was more broadly related to the psychological motivations of Nixon and Kissinger. Kissinger himself, after noting some real (and some spurious) advantages to the agreement in terms of SALT itself, comments in a

---

54. See Kissinger, *White House Years*, pp. 817, 818, 814–15, 819; and see the discussion on pp. 802–23.

   The next stage in this drama was to disclose the secret negotiations of January to May to Secretary of State Rogers, Ambassador Smith, Secretary of Defense Laird, and the rest of the American government; see ibid., pp. 819, 822; and see Smith, *Doubletalk*, pp. 225–35.

55. "Strategic Arms Limitation Talks," May 20, *Presidential Documents*, vol. 7 (May 24, 1971), p. 783.

56. Ibid.

57. As a member of the SALT I delegation, I am virtually certain that a better agreement of the May 20 type could have been reached by negotiations between the delegations. See also the similar judgment of Ambassador Smith, in *Doubletalk*, pp. 233–35.

revealing passage of his memoir: "Within the government, furthermore, the May 20 agreement was a milestone in confirming White House dominance of foreign affairs. For the first two years White House control had been confined to the formulation of policy; now it extended to its execution." Kissinger sees it as a "chicken and egg" paradox whether "Nixon's suspicions of a lifetime or the distrust of him by a government staffed by the opposition for a decade" was the more responsible for the president's "endless guerrilla war to circumvent his own subordinates." But, writes Kissinger, "Nixon—assisted by me—found his own method of solving the problem."[58]

The White House also saw itself as increasingly under pressure from advocates of an agreement limited to ABM only.[59] In fact, what the Soviets had been proposing was not ABM only but ABM first. It is, however, true, as all concerned realized, that whatever leverage an American agreement on an ABM limitation had in obtaining more advantageous offensive limitations would be gone as soon as an ABM agreement was reached.

As has been learned only recently, the White House had unintentionally encouraged the Soviets from the start to conclude that a separate agreement on ABMs (or on ABMs in conjunction with an agreement against accidental war, or with "certain measures" to limit offensive forces) was attainable. Kissinger discloses in his memoir that as early as February and March 1970 Dobrynin had inquired whether the United States preferred a "limited" or a "comprehensive" agreement. He told Kissinger in March that the Soviet Union was prepared for either but saw advantages to a comprehensive approach. Kissinger notes with irony that Dobrynin reported this information "in a tone suggesting that I was being made privy to some important news." In fact the matter was far more important than he realized, an oversight that was still evident when he wrote his memoir. On April 9 Kissinger informed Dobrynin in advance that America would present at Vienna comprehensive alternative proposals on a ban of MIRVs and on reductions. At the same time he also stated that "if, however, the Soviets decided they were interested in a more limited agreement in the interim, we were prepared to explore it as well."[60]

This was a stunning invitation for the Soviets to counterpropose some limited agreement if they did not like the comprehensive approaches of the United States. Given that Kissinger recognized that the comprehensive U.S. proposals to ban MIRVs and reduce offensive missiles were clearly unacceptable to the Soviets, this invitation is all the more incomprehensible. Fi-

---

58. Kissinger, *White House Years*, p. 822.

59. See ibid., pp. 806, 812, 816; and Smith, *Doubletalk*, pp. 204–06.

60. Kissinger, *White House Years*, pp. 525, 544–45. Dobrynin received this preview on April 9 after having told Kissinger, "Moscow would consider it a sign of good faith if I [Kissinger] outlined our position before it was tabled at Vienna." Ibid., p. 526. Giving advance notice to the Soviet side through Dobrynin became a pattern. That approach was not necessarily disadvantageous, but concealing from the American delegation exchanges known to the Soviet delegation was.

nally, the Kissinger-Dobrynin exchanges in 1970 on the possibility of a limited type of agreement were an important element never disclosed to government agencies in Washington or to the delegation.[61] Knowledge by the Soviet leaders that the White House was receptive to a limited agreement seriously undercut American attempts from April 1970 to May 1971 to get comprehensive agreements and reduced any Soviet incentive to pursue them. In addition, as will become clear later, Kissinger's handling of the substantive issues related to the certain measures concerning strategic offensive arms seriously undercut the negotiation of the interim offensive agreement from May 1971 to May 1972. All in all the importance of the May 20 agreement and the back channel negotiations leading to it was great—but not for the reasons the White House touted at the time.

At the same time that Kissinger was showing casual disregard for the implications of the American indication of readiness to accept a limited agreement of almost any kind (Kissinger states, "I told him [Dobrynin] the main problem was to get concrete about *something*"),[62] the United States made two initial comprehensive proposals that Kissinger knew to be unacceptable. These two factors were a powerful signal to the Soviets that the United States did not really want a comprehensive agreement; it signaled American indifference, if not opposition, to any mutually advantageous comprehensive agreement. This casual action was actually one of the most important decisions in SALT—yet Kissinger made it alone, and evidently without being aware of its significance. Since the exchange was kept secret from the rest of the government, no one else could advise at the time or object later (or engage in "damage control"). In one sense Kissinger's action contravened, and certainly it undercut, the official U.S. government aim in SALT.

The situation stemmed from Kissinger and Nixon's lack of interest in SALT as arms control, and from their view of SALT as simply one key piece on the political chessboard. From that standpoint, the sole interest of the White House was getting concrete about something in SALT—an interest

---

61. The U.S. delegation did learn of the secret exchanges from private conversations with members of the Soviet delegation, which enjoyed greater trust from its government. As the delegation's point man in exploring negotiation positions with members of the Soviet delegation similarly assigned by its chief, I was told by them as early as May 18, 1970, of the exchange between Kissinger and Dobrynin, in which it was said that Kissinger and Dobrynin had agreed that a limited initial agreement would be possible, and that they (the Soviets) had the impression that an agreement on ABM systems alone would be in keeping with this approach. I was also told that it might be possible to have a limited agreement on ABM systems *and* some limitations on intercontinental offensive arms, in particular ICBMs, but not including MIRVs. Thus there was a clear indication a full year in advance of the Soviets' readiness to accept the "breakthrough" negotiated by Kissinger that was announced on May 20, 1971.

Similarly, in early May 1971 I learned of the separate high-level Dobrynin-Kissinger negotiations—including some aspects of the exchanges not disclosed by Kissinger even after the agreement was announced.

62. Kissinger, *White House Years*, p. 525. Emphasis added.

that waxed and waned over time. That attitude also led to the pursuit of agreements that were politically the most easy to reach in internal negotiations in Washington, rather than to the agreements that would be most effective in curbing the arms competition between the two powers. There is no indication that President Nixon was ever even informed of the Kissinger-Dobrynin exchanges on this point, and it is highly unlikely that he was, since Kissinger did not regard the matter as significant. But there is no reason to believe Nixon would not have approved—Kissinger's approach accurately reflected Nixon's own political interest and his lack of interest in arms control.

Although ABMs had been a central element in the May 20 agreement, the situation with respect to their limitation had become even more complex and confused as a result of the kaleidoscopic changes in the American position. In August 1970, it will be recalled, the U.S. delegation had introduced the alternative of zero ABMs, at which time the Soviets reaffirmed their acceptance of the American proposal for an NCA-level ABM limitation. The United States ignored that reaffirmation (as well as the draft Soviet ABM treaty providing NCA-level limitations, presented March 19). On March 26, 1971, the United States delegation on instructions advanced a new "third alternative," which again was said to have equal status with the other two. The new alternative called for *four* ABM sites for the United States for the defense of ICBMs, and a single ABM site for the Soviet Union for the defense of Moscow.[63]

---

63. Kissinger refers to "a Presidential decision on March 11 to go forward with the four-site 'Safeguard' system [in requests to the Congress] and to bring our SALT position into line with it. So powerful was the resistance of those favoring an ABM ban or NCA that this decision was not presented to the Soviets by our SALT delegation until after constant harassment from my office and a new formal instruction issued on April 22." Ibid., p. 813. This charge that the SALT delegation failed to carry out a presidential instruction for forty-two days is entirely untrue. NSDM-102, which was signed by President Nixon on March 11, decreed the third alternative, saying that initially it should be introduced in private to the head of the Soviet delegation. Further, the instruction—intended to provide guidance to the delegation for the next two-month session—did not say when the new alternative was to be introduced in the negotiation. The first meeting of the renewed talks was on March 15. At the second meeting, March 19, the Soviets put forward their draft NCA-level ABM treaty. On that same day the American delegation proposed to Washington that it present the four-to-one proposal. A "new formal instruction" was issued April 22; it was one in a series required because of gaps in the original guidance. For example, at first it was unclear if *either* side could choose four ICBM defense sites or one site for NCA defense, or whether the Soviet Union could have only its defense of Moscow while the United States could have four sites for ICBM defense. Not until May 8 did the delegation receive a directive from Kissinger clarifying the proposal: the United States could have four sites with 386 interceptor-launchers, the Soviet Union only one site at Moscow with 100 interceptor-launchers.

Smith's book, *Doubletalk*, written before Kissinger's was available, does not mention this matter because the alleged delay was not an issue until Kissinger's memoir conjured it up. I recently queried members of Kissinger's staff at the time. They recall only a concern of Kissinger's that the new proposal—so patently unequal and nonnegotiable—would leak before it was presented and be greeted by a storm of disapproval on the Hill, generating impatience on his part.

The Soviet delegation was astonished at this procedure and indignant at the proposal. They pointed out that the United States had earlier proposed an NCA limitation to which they had agreed, and then had offered two alternatives of equal status, one of which—the NCA level—the Soviets had accepted. Now the United States was proposing yet a third alternative. It was unacceptable, and the Soviets reaffirmed their choice of the NCA-level limitation.

Thus, during the second half of 1970 and the first half of 1971 it became increasingly clear that the United States was gradually disengaging from its own NCA proposal and was attempting to gain the right to salvage as much as possible of the Safeguard deployment for defense of Minuteman ICBMs, while authorization for expanding Safeguard deployment was proceeding slowly against considerable opposition in the Senate. The American delegation argued the merits of the ICBM defense on grounds of enhancing strategic survivability and stability, whereas the Soviets could—and did—simply play back American arguments of 1970 to support an NCA-level limitation.

When the delegations resumed work in Helsinki in July 1971 to translate the May 20 breakthrough into a real agreement, the United States proposed for each side a choice between one defense site to protect the NCA, or three sites to defend ICBM fields. The Soviets immediately rejected this proposal as essentially a modified replay of the unacceptable four-to-one proposal. And they saw it as a step back from the equal ABM limitation agreed upon and clearly implied in the May 20 approach. Meanwhile, participants on each side who were disturbed at the new trend toward allowing greater ABM deployment had come to reflect that if the United States was abandoning the earlier tentative consensus on an NCA level, a ban on ABMs deserved a fresh look.

On instructions, Ambassador Smith on July 13 privately queried Semenov about possible Soviet interest in an ABM ban. He made this probe at the same time the three-to-one proposal was formally being advanced. Semenov later replied, also on instructions, that the Soviet Union would be interested in hearing detailed considerations from the United States. At this point the White House lost its stomach for the idea, and Ambassador Smith was instructed to state that the United States did *not* consider a ban on ABMs appropriate for the initial SALT agreements being negotiated in accordance with the understanding of May 20. That ended discussion of a ban on ABMs.

It is regrettable that this unusual display of interest by the Soviets in a complete ban on ABMs in 1971 coincided with disbelief and lack of interest in the White House. As noted earlier, Nixon and Kissinger had initially assumed that the Soviet Union would want a thin nationwide deployment against China. When that dissolved, they recognized but overestimated Soviet interest in retaining the Moscow deployment. As Kissinger had stated publicly even earlier, "I doubt if the Soviet Union will give up the Moscow [ABM] system, and I doubt I would urge them to."[64] Undoubtedly the belief

---

64. Kissinger's interview in *Look*, August 12, 1969, cited by Newhouse, *Cold Dawn*, p. 165.

that the Soviet leaders would be loath to dismantle the Moscow deployment contributed to the White House's decision to propose NCA-level limitations. While never stated, it seems likely the decision in 1970 to propose an ABM limitation to which the Soviets might agree was related to Nixon's desire to have a summit meeting that year. When the Soviets accepted an NCA level and began suggesting an initial agreement limited to ABMs, Nixon was prepared to accept it.[65]

When the White House did authorize Ambassador Smith to parallel the formal charade of the three-to-one site option with a private probe on a complete ban on ABMs, Kissinger and Nixon were sure the Soviets would reject the idea. When, on instructions from Moscow, Semenov expressed interest, they hurriedly instructed Smith to drop the matter. Smith's original authorization had come from Kissinger in the president's name by a back channel, not through the usual NSDM instructions of the NSC machinery, and the agencies were not advised. The authorization was intended merely to assuage Smith's persistence. As a palliative to Smith when he was instructed to drop the idea, President Nixon personally sent him an instruction to impress on the Soviets that in the forthcoming SALT II negotiations the United States would "set as our goal a ban on ABMs." No such proposal was, however, ever considered in Washington or made in SALT II.[66]

Kissinger was sure the Soviets would turn down an ABM ban because he could not conceive of their giving up such an asset, especially when the United States had already signaled its readiness to accept a Soviet NCA defense. In addition, Dobrynin had indicated repeatedly that the Soviets preferred an NCA-level ABM. Another reason for Kissinger's attitude is that he simply could not bring himself to believe that the Soviet leaders would communicate any significant new position through its SALT delegation rather than through Dobrynin to him.[67] He maintained this belief despite several instances of that happening. Finally, an unusual misunderstanding in Vienna led Kissin-

---

65. Kissinger reports disapprovingly that "on July 11 [1970] Nixon specifically told me that he would pay this price to get to see the Soviet leaders." *White House Years*, p. 556. Ambassador Smith reports that Kissinger himself later wondered whether it had been a mistake not to have accepted the separate ABM treaty. Smith, *Doubletalk*, p. 226.

66. On the zero ABM authorization and discussion see Smith, *Doubletalk*, pp. 256–63, 485–86; and Newhouse, *Cold Dawn*, pp. 229–30.

   In fact, at the beginning of SALT II in November 1972 the American delegation was instructed *not* to reopen any issues related to the ABM Treaty. And as early as September 19, 1971, just a month after Nixon's personal instruction to Smith, the delegation was advised that Washington did not want any hortatory reference to a possible future ban on ABMs in the preamble of either the ABM Treaty or the Interim Agreement. Later Smith and Semenov did agree to refer in the preamble of both SALT I agreements to the role of those agreements in creating more favorable conditions for further negotiations on limiting "strategic arms"—but this careful formulation (allowing for further limitations on strategic defensive, as well as offensive, arms) was so subtle that the leeway it was intended to convey probably did not occur to anyone else before this disclosure of its origin.

67. See Newhouse, *Cold Dawn*, p. 229. Kissinger, curiously, makes no reference to the 1971 ABM ban proposal in his memoir.

ger and others to believe that various members of the American delegation were "hearing what they wanted to hear" from different Russians—either that Moscow was, or was not, interested in a complete ABM ban. In fact, what happened should have, if properly understood, actually reinforced the seriousness of the Soviet leadership's interest—although Washington got the opposite impression.[68]

As the White House was deciding to drop further exploration of an ABM ban, in August 1971, it did resolve another interagency stalemate in favor of seeking a ban on exotic future ballistic missile defense systems, such as those using lasers or charged particle beams. Owing to an extended bureaucratic battle over this issue and White House reluctance to resolve it, when the U.S. delegation set forth a draft ABM treaty on July 27, 1971, it included a blank article with an awkward note that an "appropriate provision" dealing with sea-based, land-mobile, and space-based systems would be put forth subsequently. This approach was taken even though, as early as July 2, a firm presidential instruction (NSDM 117) had called for a ban on exotic future technol-

---

68. This story has not been reported before. The initiative for consideration of a complete ban on ABMs in 1971 came from members of the *Soviet* delegation, who raised the possibility with me on July 9 and repeated it subsequently. For this reason, Ambassador Smith used a back channel communication to seek presidential authority to probe the Soviet position. Semenov confirmed to Smith on July 13 that his instructions permitted reacting to an American proposal, but that he needed to know more about U.S. views. Over the next two weeks, Semenov and several key members of his delegation confirmed the positive Soviet interest in a complete ABM ban. This led to a proposal by the American delegation (General Royal Allison of the JCS dissenting) to Washington requesting authority to spell out a concrete proposal. (Despite Nitze's concurrence, Secretary of Defense Laird and his deputy, David Packard, were opposed.)

While Washington was considering the matter, General Allison reported that in a luncheon discussion on August 2 his counterpart, General Konstantin Trusov, had stated that the Soviet Union did not intend to tear down its Moscow ABM system. Washington was informed promptly. General Allison and those who received the report of his conversation took that to mean the Soviets opposed an ABM ban that required a dismantling of the Moscow system. On the other hand, the Soviet delegation, including Semenov personally, strongly reaffirmed that the Soviet government had interest in "seriously exploring" a total ABM ban. Members of the Soviet delegation soon clarified what had occurred. The Soviet and American military interpreters confirmed that General Allison had reported General Trusov's words accurately: "We do not intend to dismantle the Moscow ABM system." But the *context* was different and therefore the meaning and significance. Trusov had been referring to the formal American ABM proposal then on the table: three ABM sites for the defense of ICBMs or one for the defense of the NCA. Trusov was saying that even if the Soviet Union had a nominal choice of three sites to defend ICBMs, it was not prepared to give up the Moscow defense. When Allison then asked if that meant the Soviets would not dismantle the Moscow system, Trusov said they did not "intend" to do so. He did not address the question of a reciprocal complete ABM ban at all—a subject then being handled exclusively by the two heads of the delegations. The explanation of what had happened was made known to Washington, but it was easier to dismiss the seemingly contradictory reports from Vienna—especially since that suited the White House's purposes. Part of this explanation has been recounted by Newhouse, who also reports the differing views in Washington, in *Cold Dawn*, pp. 228-31.

ogy systems, as well as on sea-based, land-mobile, and space-based ABM systems. Not until August 17 was authorization finally given to seek such a ban; six months later an agreement was finally reached that embodied it in a combination of articles and an interpretive statement. Initially the Soviet military—like its American counterpart—opposed the provision, and for the same reason: a general preference for leaving unfettered any military-technological modernization that was not being specifically limited. Finally, however, the Soviet side agreed and accepted the ban on deployment of future exotic ABM systems.

From August 1971, when the United States shifted from three to two American sites to one Soviet site, until April–May 1972, when two sites for each side were agreed to, it was clear (as indeed it had been much earlier to some of those involved) that the final outcome on the ABM deployment would be some equal combination of the right to one or two sites for each side.[69] The delegations finally worked out the final agreement on one site for NCA and one for ICBM defense for each side in April 1972 on a trip to Lapland, consequently termed the "Tundra talks."[70] The United States did

69. As early as May 1971 members of the Soviet delegation had discussed with me possible agreement on two sites for each side, although preferring one on each side.

Kissinger, according to some of his aides, had thought that a deal could probably be worked out with two U.S. sites for the defense of ICBMs to the one the Soviet Union had for Moscow. If the matter had been presented as a simple freeze, that outcome might have been possible. But since the ABM agreement was being prepared as a treaty of indefinite duration, equality of rights was a virtual necessity.

Subsequently Kissinger described the evolution of the ABM levels in a remarkably tendentious way. In his memoir, while he provides a very detailed account, he omits altogether the four-to-one and three-to-one proposals of March and July 1971. The only exception is the earlier noted reference to putting the U.S. position into line with the administration's request to the Congress for funding four Safeguard ABM sites—but without mentioning that the Soviet side was to be restricted to one site. Kissinger starts with the two-to-one proposal of August 1971 and describes the negotiations until two-to-two was agreed to in April 1972. Kissinger, *White House Years*, p. 1128.

This account was not Kissinger's first effort to bury the four-to-one and three-to-one proposals. On June 15, 1972, in briefing Congress on the ABM Treaty just signed, he omitted all the earlier history of NCA-level, zero ABM, four-to-one, and three-to-one options and stated: "Devising an equitable agreement on ABM's proved extremely difficult. . . . We proposed freezing deployments at levels operational or under construction; that is to say, two ICBM sites on our side and the Moscow defense on the other." "President Nixon and Dr. Kissinger Brief Members of Congress on Strategic Arms Limitation Agreements," June 15, *State Bulletin*, vol. 67 (July 10, 1972), pp. 44–45. And in the most remarkable case, in testifying before the Senate Committee on Foreign Relations in September 1974, Kissinger argued that the very SALT negotiation process itself was "conducive to further restraint." His example: "In the first round of SALT negotiations in 1970–72, both sides bitterly contested the number of ABM sites [to be] permitted by the agreement; two years later both sides gave up the right to build more than one site." Kissinger, "Détente with the Soviet Union: The Reality of Competition and the Imperative of Cooperation," September 19, *State Bulletin*, vol. 71 (October 14, 1974), p. 514.

70. See Smith, *Doubletalk*, pp. 364–69. Semenov had been called to Moscow (in connection with Kissinger's secret visit, although this was not known at the time). As Smith notes, in the absence of an appropriate counterpart for himself, I carried out a full exchange on the remain-

not at this time accept a Soviet proposal to defer the second site on each side (since the Soviets had only the NCA site and the United States could then complete only one of its two ICBM defense sites). But the proposals formed the basis for a later protocol, signed in 1974, that reduced the permitted deployment to one site for each side.[71]

By the time Nixon and Kissinger arrived in Moscow to conclude the SALT I negotiations, work on the ABM Treaty was completed, with one trivial exception. Even that point—that the two allowed ABM deployment sites be separated by no less than 1,300 kilometers, to reinforce constraints against internetting their radars—was agreed to in Helsinki and Moscow at the same time.[72] Thus, by the time of the summit, the ABM Treaty had been completed.

---

ing questions concerning an ABM treaty and reached an agreement, subject to approval. Advised by his delegation, Semenov chose in his talks in Moscow to treat the results of the Tundra talks as an authoritative American initiative, and this greatly facilitated their acceptance as the basis for confirming agreement on them during Kissinger's visit. Thus the U.S. delegation, unaware of Kissinger's trip, unintentionally preempted his wrapping up the ABM agreement (the Tundra talks took place on April 16; Kissinger arrived in Moscow on April 20).

In Moscow on April 22 during their talks on SALT, Brezhnev gave a note to Kissinger containing two main points related to ABM levels and SLBM limitations. One was the two-to-two ABM level (with all the various details as worked out in the Tundra talks, for example, 100 interceptor-launchers, a site deployment radius of 150 kilometers, and so on). Kissinger presents this all as Brezhnev's "new plan"; he gives no indication that he was aware that it had been worked out by the delegations. See Kissinger, *White House Years*, pp. 1148–49.

Kissinger also became confused in an exchange he had with Nixon by transworld secure telephone, in which Nixon claimed that Semenov had given Smith "exactly the same offer that you set forth in your message of April 22." Kissinger assumed Nixon was talking about the SLBM issue and argued vigorously that Semenov had told Smith only that Moscow was studying the issue. That was true for the SLBMs, but Semenov had also confirmed to Smith on April 22 the ABM deal that I had worked out in the Tundra talks and that Semenov had sold to Brezhnev. Kissinger was still not aware of this confusion over the two elements of the Brezhnev note when he later wrote his memoir. Kissinger, *White House Years*, p. 1162.

71. See Smith, *Doubletalk*, p. 388.

In his congressional briefing on June 15, 1972, Kissinger incorrectly stated, "The question of the deferral of the second site had been considered and had been rejected by both sides." "Question and Answer Session after a Briefing by Dr. Henry Kissinger," p. 13.

72. This small example illustrates the folly of conducting parallel negotiations and of having unprepared and inadequately staffed political leaders handle substantive summit negotiations. Both Nixon and Kissinger, innocent of many much more important aspects of the ABM Treaty, mention this unimportant provision in their memoirs, which loomed large to them only because of their personal involvement. Moreover, neither was able to describe the incident accurately. Nixon refers to it as "an important and controversial question." He states that after agreeing to the American proposal for a 1,500 kilometers distance, Brezhnev later "casually cut three hundred kilometers from the figure that had been agreed upon just a few hours earlier," saying the question "now appears to be cleared up. Twelve hundred kilometers is OK with us." Nixon replied "fifteen hundred" and records the exchange under the assumption that Brezhnev then agreed to accept 1,500 kilometers. Richard Nixon, *RN: The Memoirs of Richard Nixon* (Grosset and Dunlap, 1978), pp. 611–12.

Kissinger's account is, predictably, far more intricate, and at least he knows the outcome was agreement on the lower figure (1,300 kilometers, not the 1,200 recalled by Nixon). But Kissin-

There were several major issues in the strategic offensive arms negotiations that need to be traced from the May 20, 1971, agreement to the
concluding negotiations at the summit meeting. As a point of departure it is
useful to bear in mind that the principal issue as seen by Nixon and Kissinger

---

ger's account shows that his own confusion and incomprehension at the time and since were
also considerable. Kissinger recognizes that the question was "one of those trivial problems
that emerge as a residue in the last stages of any negotiation," but sonorously elaborates that
such questions are "generally as complex as they are unimportant because by then both sides
have exhausted their store of concessions." He states that the United States had proposed
1,500 kilometers and the Soviets had put forward 1,300 kilometers. "The difference was insub-
stantial; political leaders, it soon turned out, could make no contribution to resolving it; it
quite literally solved itself." *White House Years*, p. 1218. Three pages later Kissinger states in
a slightly different tone: "Brezhnev opened the meeting by accepting our proposed distance of
1,500 kilometers between ABM sites. Unfortunately, unknown to either leader the American
delegation in Helsinki had already settled for the Soviet proposal of 1,300 kilometers that
morning. Brezhnev had offered us a better deal than our negotiators had already accepted. It
made no difference; we were finally stuck with the version negotiated at Helsinki; the difference was marginal anyway." Ibid., pp. 1221–22. Yet again, in reference to negotiating the issue
with Gromyko, Kissinger says, "The difference of 200 kilometers on the distance between
ABM sites was not important; eventually I would yield on that, but not without establishing
some claim to reciprocity." Just two paragraphs later, with no indication of reciprocity in
concessions, Kissinger states, "I let the Soviets win one by confirming our delegation's acceptance of 1,300 kilometers as the distance between ABM sites." Ibid., p. 1235.

What actually happened was this. The United States had originally introduced the provision in terms that would locate the second Soviet ABM site in Asia, beyond the Urals. The
Soviets objected to such a reference, so the American delegation took a rounded functional
equivalent and proposed 1,500 kilometers from Moscow. While the Soviet side was still considering this proposal and wondering what the significance of that distance was, on May 23 the
American delegation decided (at General Allison's suggestion) to revise the proposal to 1,300
kilometers because that was the closest distance to the Urals, and given the deployment of
Soviet ICBM fields it made absolutely *no* difference. The difference thus was not "marginal"
or "not important," as Kissinger states, but nonexistent. Nor did the Soviet delegation ever
propose 1,300 kilometers or any other distance. There were no Soviet ICBM fields to defend
between 1,300 and 1,500 kilometers distance—so there was no substantive difference whatsoever in the two American proposals. Kissinger simply assumes that the greater distance must
have been "better" and that the Soviet side must have proposed the lower figure—both
incorrect assumptions. This issue was not "complex"—only the entanglement in Moscow was.
And it was not left for the summit meeting because the sides had both run out of concessions—no concessions were even involved. The only reason the question arose was because it
was a trivial last-minute detail not quite worked out when the Nixon-Kissinger party arrived in
Moscow on May 22—and because they had decided not to bring the American delegation, or
even anyone from it, to Moscow.

Kissinger gave yet another explanation at a later press conference, in which he said that the
1,500 kilometers limit had been accepted by the Soviets, but when a "working crew" looked
into it, "it turned out that 1,300 was a better figure for reasons that were too technical to go
into," so the *president* proposed 1,300 kilometers. (While as can be seen there is some truth to
part of this account, compare it with Nixon's or, for that matter, with Kissinger's later memoir
accounts.) Cited in Smith, *Doubletalk*, p. 422.

It still seems incredible that Nixon and Brezhnev, or Kissinger and Gromyko, should have
occupied themselves with such a nonissue. It is less surprising that, under the circumstances,
Nixon and Kissinger, at least, did not know what they were talking about.

was to assure some kind of linkage between an ABM agreement and limitations on strategic offensive arms. This tactic had a sound logical basis and made good sense in terms of bargaining leverage. Only the United States was then building an ABM system (the truncated Moscow system was essentially completed), and only the Soviet Union was then building new strategic offensive missile launchers, both ICBMs and SLBMs. Moreover, the large Soviet ICBMs were seen as by far the greatest threat, and the United States wanted to halt their buildup.

While getting the Soviets to agree to constrain their offensive buildup was the essence of the problem, the issue had two facets: one was coupling the ABM agreement with some offensive constraints, the other was the nature of the specific offensive limitations. Kissinger concentrated almost exclusively on the former, and the latter suffered as a result. And the Kissinger-Dobrynin negotiations of January to May 1971 were critical in establishing the basis for the negotiations by the delegations from May 1971 to May 1972.

The record of the Kissinger-Dobrynin exchanges has remained shrouded in secrecy and subject to confusion for a very good reason: Kissinger came to realize that he had not negotiated the substance of the offensive limitations advantageously, or even satisfactorily, and sought to conceal this fact. It was all the more important to do so as he had allowed no participation or sharing of responsibility for those negotiations with the rest of the government.

Kissinger reports that on February 4 Dobrynin confirmed an agreement in principle by the Politburo to couple an ABM agreement with "a freeze on deployments of offensive missiles," left, however, undefined. In reporting on a further discussion in mid-March, Kissinger refers to an agreement on a freeze on "strategic offensive weapons." He cites those words in quotation marks and then adds the words "both ICBMs and SLBMs" without quotation marks. This inclusion of SLBMs was Kissinger's own retroactive sleight of hand, theoretically an interpretation of the plural word "weapons" (although Kissinger did not include strategic bombers in such retroactive extrapolations). At that time, the Soviets agreed to modernization and replacement only by weapons of the same category—in other words, they agreed to freeze the level of modern large ICBMs (then SS-9s).[73]

In his peroration on the negotiation leading to the May 20 agreement Kissinger carries his own retroactive recasting of that agreement to the point of saying that it "implied" that the Soviets had "in effect accepted a freeze on new starts of strategic missiles; they had conceded a sublimit on heavy missiles; they had in effect dropped their claim that our aircraft based abroad be counted; and we had put them on notice that submarine-launched missiles would have to be limited or accounted for."[74] This wording is very

---

73. See Kissinger, *White House Years*, pp. 813–20; quotations from pp. 814, 815.

74. Ibid., p. 820.

slippery: the freeze on new starts applied only to ICBMs, as did the implied sublimit on heavy (large) missiles. Kissinger does make one differentiation when he says the Soviets had "in effect" accepted ICBM and large ICBM freezes, claiming only that he "put them on notice" that SLBMs would have to be "limited or accounted for." (The question might be asked how such vague and loose language could imply that something unnamed need be "limited or accounted for"—and what does accounted for mean?) The statement that they had "in effect dropped their claim" about American forward-based-system (FBS) aircraft is wrong. The Soviets explicitly continued to assert the claim; they did agree to defer it and omit any limitation on aircraft, strategic bombers and FBS, from the "certain measures" accompanying the ABM agreement.

The key problem was the SLBM launchers. And on this Kissinger does not reveal that the Soviet leaders had good reason, from the negotiating record, to interpret the vague term "strategic offensive arms" (sometimes translated as "weapons" or "armaments") as meaning only ICBMs of various classes, and *not* as including SLBMs. Ambassador Smith, who was allowed to read Kissinger's file on the talks after the May 20 agreement had been reached, has disclosed that Dobrynin had raised the question of SLBMs at the first meeting with Kissinger the previous January. He did so after Kissinger had proposed coupling an ABM agreement with a freeze on *ICBM* launchers. "Kissinger gave an equivocal answer that maybe the submarines would be covered but that this issue could be left for the detailed negotiations." This response was not good enough, and Dobrynin returned to the question in February: would SLBMs be included in the freeze or not? Kissinger replied that the United States would be "prepared to have it either way." Dobrynin quickly indicated that the Soviet Union preferred *not* to include SLBMs. And there the matter rested.[75]

Ambassador Smith has recalled how, when Kissinger finally told him on May 19 about the president's imminent announcement, "all through this conversation Kissinger referred to the offensive weapons part of the accord as an ICBM arrangement. He showed little concern that under this arrangement there probably was not going to be a freeze on SLBMs." Later, after being allowed to review the record in Kissinger's office, Smith again "pointed out to Kissinger that in effect he had agreed to exclude SLBMs." Becoming wary, Kissinger then said that "the record was ambiguous." Smith also reports that when he was later instructed by the president to press for including

---

75. Smith, *Doubletalk*, pp. 228–29. As Smith comments: "Here, in one sentence, the position which the United States had pressed for almost a year was changed. There is no evidence to indicate that this major change in SALT policy was ever considered in advance by anyone except Kissinger—and perhaps not even by him. It may well have been a random answer of a fatigued and overextended man who did not realize the immense significance of his words. It was to take a lot of effort and expenditure of bargaining power to redeem those words and restore the earlier U.S. position that SLBMs must be included in any SALT agreement. Dobrynin pocketed the offer diplomatically."

SLBMs in the freeze, "Kissinger's advice was to make a try for it but not to take much time and not to 'fall on my sword' over this issue."[76]

How could Kissinger have casually agreed to omit SLBMs? Members of Kissinger's staff, privy to his thinking at the time, have explained that Kissinger saw the whole matter in terms of pressure from hawks in the Pentagon and Congress over the Soviet ICBM buildup, especially the heavy SS-9 ICBMs. Therefore he focused on balancing the ABM agreement by stopping the ICBM buildup.[77] Kissinger was apparently unaware that the United States had neither programs nor capacities to resume construction and deployment of SLBM-carrying submarines during the period of the freeze, so that leaving SLBMs unlimited was of advantage only to the Soviet Union. But he had not studied the question or consulted with other parts of the government. Instead he had concentrated on what was required in terms of politics and on bargaining to get *some* offensive arms limitations to accompany the ABM agreement. He then focused on the ICBM buildup as the key offensive element, which it was. But he did so without realizing the extent of advantage to the Soviet Union in continuing its SLBM deployment. Nor did he foresee the negative effects that a continued increase in Soviet offensive arms levels would have on the American public's perceptions, nor the political-bureaucratic problems he would confront in Washington.

Kissinger also failed to take into account another spillover effect of his secret vest-pocket negotiation. When Semenov had begun in early May to disclose the deal to Smith, he and his delegation also clearly staked out the Soviet position in terms of offensive limitations embracing only ICBMs. Although the delegation reported that fact, the White House was not ready to disclose to its own delegation its parallel negotiations. Therefore it could not issue instructions directing or even permitting the delegation to question the absence of SLBMs (although that feature of the Soviet presentations was noted and reported).[78] Even *after* the May 20 announcement and Smith's

---

76. Nixon and Kissinger had not intended that Ambassador Smith and his delegation return to Washington for the White House announcement of a breakthrough. Semenov, however, forced their hand when he introduced the secret back channel dealings at the exchanges between the delegations in Vienna. While most of the U.S. delegation remained in Vienna, on May 10 Ambassador Smith, Nitze, General Allison, and I returned to Washington. Only on May 19 was Smith informed of the parallel negotiation and agreement. He and, separately, Nitze were allowed to "review the record," as Smith puts it, only in Kissinger's office. Kissinger states that he "showed Smith all the exchanges with the Soviets," but only "a summary" of his own conversations, although they constituted the most important part of the exchanges. It has been reported that the record shown to Smith and Nitze was hastily sanitized of possibly embarrassing information, although if so, not sufficiently to prevent disclosure of the damaging exchanges on SLBMs (and several other points discussed later). See Smith, *Doubletalk*, pp. 222–24; Kissinger, *White House Years*, pp. 818–19; and Hersh, *The Price of Power*, pp. 340–43. Hersh cites unidentified aides to Kissinger on the doctoring of the record.

77. Interviews with members of Kissinger's 1972 NSC staff involved with SALT.

78. Smith, *Doubletalk*, pp. 218–21, records that in his discussions with Semenov, the latter began to spell out the Soviet position based on the Kissinger-Dobrynin talks. Kissinger gives his

return to Vienna for the brief, concluding phase of that round of talks, the American delegation had no instructions or authority to discuss these matters.[79] Thus, by the time the two delegations returned to their capitals at the end of May to prepare for the continuing negotiations, the Soviet side had put on the record that the understanding excluded SLBMs, while the American side had not been able to reply.

As the American government began to prepare for the next round of negotiations, Kissinger decided it would be best not to disclose the extent of his own previous negotiations. Further, to the extent the official position of the United States now *differed* from what he had earlier said, the Soviets could bear the burden of changing it to conform with what he had earlier agreed to. Thus, when there was unanimous desire by U.S. agencies to seek inclusion of SLBMs, Kissinger, rather than disclose his earlier acceptance of their omission, was silent and let the position be established. This ploy put a heavy burden on those few, such as Ambassador Smith and Nitze, who knew of Kissinger's earlier agreement to exclude SLBMs. Kissinger expected that the Soviets would object strongly and that eventually the American bureaucracy would conclude that including the SLBMs was not necessary. Hence his advice to Smith to make a try to get them included, but not to "fall on his sword" over the matter.

Kissinger was dead wrong. The departments and agencies stood firm on the inclusion of SLBMs in the interim agreement on offensive arms. Ultimately, instead of persuading the rest of the American government that including them was not necessary and, owing to Soviet intransigence, not attainable, by the spring of 1972 Kissinger had to change the course of his back channel negotiations. At that point he decided to make the Soviet leaders an

version, and reaction, in *White House Years*, pp. 817–18. He describes Semenov's proposals as older ones that had been overtaken in his talks with Dobrynin by newer positions more to U.S. advantage. In fact, although Semenov was very careful and cautious, even more so than usual, key members of the Soviet delegation spelled out the Soviet position more fully in parallel talks with me. That position included: a freeze on any new ICBM construction (and an intriguing hint that even construction of new ICBM launchers under way might be halted); a sublimit on heavy (large) ICBMs; the exclusion of SLBMs; and separate offensive limitations, but to go into effect simultaneously. Other significant details were mentioned as well. Some of this discussion even went *beyond* the Kissinger-Dobrynin talks. These delegates also commented that the Soviet Union would have preferred a comprehensive offensive limitation, but one had proved unattainable because of the American positions on MIRVs and FBS. All this was reported to Washington by closely restricted cables.

79. See Smith, *Doubletalk*, pp. 244–46. The main issue at that point was whether the parallel negotiations on ABM limitations and talks on the "certain measures" on offensive arms would proceed at the same time, as the United States wished, or whether the ABM negotiations would proceed first, as the Soviet Union wished. The American delegation still had no instructions to respond to Soviet references to the offensive arms freeze as applying only to ICBMs. On May 25 two Soviet representatives told me that they were troubled that the American delegation "did not appear to be well informed on the nature of the interim offensive agreement under the May 20 approach."

offer they could not refuse—to accept a nominal constraint by formally including SLBM launchers, but at such a high level that in practice the Soviet Union would not actually have to constrain its SLBM buildup. Kissinger was inadvertently assisted in this sleight of hand by those who were levying the greatest pressure on the issue. By overstating the threat of an SLBM buildup, the Pentagon provided Kissinger the opportunity to use its inflated worst-case projections as the benchmark against which to measure a limitation of SLBMs at the level the Soviet Union was actually planning. This provided a basis for gaining Soviet acceptance.

The new breakthrough on SLBMs came in two stages, about a year after the original one that had set a new course toward an interim offensive constraint accompanying a separate ABM treaty. First was a remarkable working meeting between Kissinger and the Soviet leaders in April 1972. Second was Nixon's summit meeting a month later at which the SALT I accords were concluded. The summit was of secondary importance to the negotiations, although far more important symbolically.

Kissinger's visit to Moscow in April 1972 was a bold gamble. He had obtained Nixon's approval for the visit only to make a major pitch for movement on the stalled Vietnam peace talks. In this endeavor Kissinger made only limited progress. Nonetheless, in contravention of Nixon's instructions he also plunged into the SALT issues, making a remarkable deal on the SLBM issue. In addition, he also negotiated the basic charter of détente, embodied in the Basic Principles on Mutual Relations. (Other aspects of this visit will be discussed later.) [80]

Kissinger provides the most complete account of his visit, although it is carefully elaborated to suggest greater initiative by the Soviets and less by him, to conceal his own role. Thus he mentions Brezhnev's offering a new approach toward solving the issue of SLBMs by setting a limit of 950, as well as by accepting the principle of turning in older SLBMs or ICBMs to reach that number. The figure to be traded in was to be negotiated. Kissinger does note that this latter approach was based on a suggestion he had made to Dobrynin in March, using a formulation first proposed to the White House by Secretary Laird which required that any further SLBM buildup be compensated for by reducing older missiles. Kissinger contends that the limit of 950 on SLBMs would be "at least 200 less than our estimate of their capacity" within the five-year period of the interim agreement. [81]

What Kissinger does not say is that on March 9 *he* had proposed to Dobrynin a limit of 950 SLBMs (and a limit of 62 submarines), arguing that the Soviet Union was not planning to build more than that number of subma-

---

80. See chapter 9.

81. Kissinger, *White House Years*, p. 1149.

As a rule, throughout this discussion the term SLBMs is used for simplicity, although the negotiations concerned SLBM *launchers*, not missiles. In practice, the number of launchers equals the number of SLBM missiles deployed, but not those in inventory.

rines and missiles anyway.[82] In proposing compensation for a continued SLBM buildup by reducing older ICBM or SLBM launchers, Kissinger suggested as an illustration reducing the older SS-7 and SS-8 large ICBMs that the Soviets would probably be deactivating in any case owing to their obsolescence and vulnerability.[83] He did not refer to any comparable American buildup, knowing by this time that none was feasible within the next five years. And he justified the inclusion of SLBMs, which he himself had told Dobrynin in 1971 could be omitted, on the basis that the political situation within the U.S. government required it, as indeed was the case. Hence he was proposing an offer the Soviet leaders could not refuse and that would meet American demands for the inclusion of SLBMs. He made the terms palatable to the Soviets by permitting them to fulfill their planned programs.

Brezhnev's position on SLBMs included specific limitations on American systems and introduced the idea of taking account of the strategic submarine systems of Britain and France, America's allies, as well. Thus, while accepting Kissinger's plea that he and Nixon needed inclusion of SLBMs in order to gain approval of the SALT package, the Soviets did not rely on a freeze to hold the United States to the existing 41 submarines with 656 SLBM launchers. Rather, they proposed that number for the United States and a further overall total of 50 modern submarines with up to 800 SLBMs for the United States, Britain, and France. They also sought to justify the discrepancy between the Soviet and U.S.-Western levels by referring to American submarine forward bases. In practice this proposal would not have made a real difference in the five years covered by the Interim Agreement. But it would have established the precedent of taking into account the submarines and SLBMs of U.S. allies and of American ballistic-missile submarine forward-basing, and of providing compensation to the Soviet Union for the differential levels.[84] For

---

82. The origin of the numerical limits has become clear only gradually. The then-current U.S. national intelligence estimate projected eight possible Soviet strategic force mixes for 1977 in the absence of SALT constraints. Of these, the one positing the largest number of submarine systems estimated 62 submarines with 966 launchers. References to this possible source of the 950/62 levels have been made by Smith in *Doubletalk*, p. 372; and by Hersh in *The Price of Power*, p. 540, and see p. 534.

   In his memoir Kissinger comes close to acknowledging his authorship of 950/62. He states that Brezhnev's SLBM paper "in effect accepted" the formula "which I had put forward while 'thinking out loud' with Dobrynin in March. The Soviet Union *agreed* to a ceiling of 950 submarine-launched ballistic missiles." Kissinger, *White House Years*, p. 1149. Emphasis added. Ambassador Smith, who was later given a copy of the Brezhnev note, has stated that it specifically referred to the earlier exchanges in the Kissinger-Dobrynin channel. Smith, *Doubletalk*, p. 370. Hersh states that Kissinger later acknowledged to John Newhouse that he had supplied the SLBM and submarine numbers Brezhnev used. Hersh, *The Price of Power*, p. 540. Newhouse confirmed to me that Kissinger admitted that the numbers originated with him and were based on the high side of the national intelligence estimate of Soviet programs.

83. Kissinger is vague on this point, but it appears in an account for which Kissinger was the main source. See Henry Brandon, *The Retreat of American Power* (Doubleday, 1973), p. 315.

84. Kissinger does not mention this part of Brezhnev's SLBM proposal in his memoir. It is given in Smith, *Doubletalk*, pp. 370–71.

this reason, it became an issue in the negotiation. And there were many more concrete problems to be clarified and bargained before an SLBM limitation was finally reached in the hectic final days of the Moscow summit conference. Nevertheless, Kissinger won the first part of his gamble to get SLBMs included: the Soviets accepted his proposition that a formal SALT limitation be provided on SLBMs, though at a level not requiring the Soviets to curtail their modernization plans.[85]

Having sold the Soviet leaders on the inclusion of SLBMs on the grounds that it would *not* interfere with their continued SLBM buildup, Kissinger next faced the task of persuading agencies in Washington that this same limitation was a valuable arms control constraint advantageous to the United States.

Kissinger returned to Washington on April 24. His secret trip to Moscow was publicly disclosed on April 26; Ambassador Smith arrived in Washington that same day. Two Verification Panel meetings were held on April 28 and 29 and an NSC meeting on May 1. They were among the most stormy in all of SALT I.

The most important sale of Kissinger's Moscow deal went extremely well—Nixon was very pleased. As presented by Kissinger, Soviet acceptance of the inclusion of the SLBMs at a level of 950 launchers was a major concession. Nixon had not involved himself deeply in SALT issues, and he was even mollified that Kissinger had disregarded his instructions that there had to be progress toward a Vietnam solution before discussing SALT and the summit meeting. Nixon says as much in his memoir. He also states: "Brezhnev produced a SALT proposal that was considerably more favorable than we had expected, and as Kissinger reported, 'If the summit meeting takes place, you will be able to sign the most important arms control agreement ever concluded.' "[86] Kissinger evidently persuaded Nixon that the Soviet leaders had made a great concession by telling him that they would hold Soviet SLBMs to some 200 fewer than could be built without an agreement and would not limit any planned American SLBM program. And as Nixon knew, the SALT delegation had been trying for nearly a year, without success, to get Soviet agreement on the inclusion of SLBMs. Now Kissinger had got Brezhnev's acceptance.[87]

At that time the U.S. force of 41 nuclear-powered ballistic missile submarines with 656 SLBM launchers had been unchanged for five years and would remain unchanged for at least five more. Britain had four SSBNs, with no more planned; France had one operational, a second launched and nearly operational, and three others under construction or programmed over the coming five-year period, for a total of nine, as specified in the Brezhnev proposal.

85. Soviet production and deployment programs actually reached the 950/62 levels only shortly *after* the expiration of the five years of the Interim Agreement. Later the Soviets did deactivate older SSBNs (as well as the older ICBMs) so as to remain under the limits of the Interim Agreement when both parties decided to continue observing it informally. That, however, was not in the thinking of either side in 1972.

86. Nixon, *RN*, p. 592. Nixon is referring to the entire SALT I package, the ABM Treaty and the Interim Agreement, but it was the SLBM issue that was holding up overall agreement.

87. Neither Nixon nor Kissinger has described their discussion beyond the above-noted comment

Immediately after his return to Washington, Kissinger instructed two of his staff to prepare a study that would make the 950/62 limits look good by bracketing them with estimates presenting much higher possible Soviet buildups in the absence of SALT. The staff members got technical assistance from the CIA, but the desired result was reached only by assuming a stepped-up future Soviet effort.[88] The actual intelligence estimate, which had served in Moscow, was therefore superseded for purposes of the Washington SALT policy review by a specially prepared NSC paper that estimated not what the Soviets *would* do, but what they *could* do if they made a maximum effort. In his memoir Kissinger on several occasions refers to the 950 level as "at least 200 less than our estimate of their capacity to reach over that period," or "at nearly 200 below what Admiral Moorer estimated their *potential* program was." As for the sixty-two submarines, "our estimate was that their number *could* exceed eighty by 1978."[89]

---

by Nixon, but these were the arguments used with others and in his memoir. Unstated was the fact that the SALT delegation had not succeeded because it was, under instructions, seeking to get Soviet acceptance of a level of no more than 740 SLBM launchers—not 950.

There is no evidence that Nixon was ever aware that in 1971 Kissinger had given away inclusion of SLBMs. That move left the Soviet leaders every reason to believe that the new American call for their inclusion was nothing more than another charade in the formal negotiations. Indeed, there is reason to believe Nixon was unaware of the entire SLBM issue before the spring of 1972. When Nixon met with Gromyko in September 1971, he made the otherwise inexplicable observation that he had noted the continuing Soviet buildup in offensive launchers (meaning SLBMs), and did not object to that—in their place he would be doing the same thing. Needless to say, neither Nixon nor Kissinger chose to mention that gaffe. See Smith, *Doubletalk*, p. 327.

88. As a participant in the SALT process, I discussed the study with its author and others on the NSC staff at the time. It set up five strawman options for Soviet SSBN/SLBM construction, with 950/62 artfully placed as the next to lowest, 1,170/80 as the highest. (After the agreement had been signed, the official background guidance for senior executive branch officials testifying before Congress was to compare the 950 SLBM level of the agreement with a projected level of 1,050 without it.) Interestingly, these figures did *not* include the older G-class diesel submarines eventually excluded at the Moscow summit negotiations. For a published account of the preparation of this paper based on other interviews, see Hersh, *The Price of Power*, pp. 539–40. Kissinger, who in most cases deals with such matters in some detail, does not discuss the Washington SALT review following his April Moscow visit at all.

The NSC paper, issued on April 28 and closely held, was misleadingly titled "Possible Soviet Proposals to Include SLBMs in the Interim Offensive Freeze." Those apparently in the know understood that these were figures presumably already advanced by Brezhnev to Kissinger. But virtually no one then knew the real secret—that Kissinger himself had originated the 950/62 levels.

89. Kissinger, *White House Years*, pp. 1149, 1131, 1130. Emphasis added.

In his congressional briefing after the SALT agreements were signed, Kissinger stretched the numbers a little further—annual production of submarines went from eight to "at least eight to nine," or forty to forty-five over the five years of the agreement, in addition to the "something like 43 to 44 they now have." At the time the CIA's best estimate, later confirmed, was forty-two. Kissinger concluded by saying that without the agreement, instead of sixty-two "the Soviet Union *could* have built up to eighty or ninety submarines." "Question and Answer Session after a Briefing by Dr. Henry Kissinger," p. 15.

The tendency of the Pentagon to accent maximum threats played into Kissinger's hands. The chairman of the JCS, Admiral Thomas Moorer, had been briefed on the basis of the NSC paper. Accordingly he responded to leading questions by Kissinger at the Verification Panel meetings that the Soviet Union could build up to 1,050 SLBMs on 80 submarines without SALT. Therefore there was value in a 950/62 limit. Moorer also confirmed that the United States had no capability to build new ballistic-missile submarines during the next five years (without undesirably disrupting its current priority program of building nuclear attack submarines and prejudicing its Trident submarine plans). Ambassador Smith quotes Kissinger as having said before the Verification Panel meeting, "I'll deliver the Joint Chiefs and DOD. I worked on Moorer all week."[90] For insurance Kissinger had also made clear to Secretary of Defense Laird and Admiral Moorer that White House support for an accelerated Trident SSBN-SLBM program hinged on proceeding with this SALT SLBM limitation.[91]

Kissinger and Nixon faced objections from an unexpected quarter. Kissinger had dealt with the Pentagon neatly,[92] but to his and Nixon's surprise Secretary of State Rogers and Ambassador Smith objected to the high levels of SLBMs and submarines allowed, and to the makeshift partial arrangement for substituting new SLBMs for old missiles. Ambassador Smith relates in some detail how Kissinger expressed his astonishment and displeasure at the roles played by Smith and Secretary Rogers, both of whom wanted to press the Soviets for a better deal. Kissinger was greatly annoyed and concerned lest his deal with Brezhnev come unglued. Nixon was exasperated because, while he did not understand the details of the whole question, he remained suspicious that Smith and Rogers were upsetting the White House deal, which was needed for a successful summit meeting. When Smith learned at the NSC meeting on May 1 that a small but potentially very important change had been

---

90. Smith, *Doubletalk*, p. 374. See also Hersh, *The Price of Power*, pp. 540–41.

91. See Hersh, *The Price of Power*, pp. 535–37, 540–41; and Newhouse, *Cold Dawn*, pp. 246–47.

Although Kissinger does not discuss the April deliberations, he does pose the question as though the U.S. government "faced a major procurement decision that in turn would determine our SALT posture. . . . If we chose to build improved Poseidons, we would prefer to leave submarine-launched missiles out of the SALT freeze. . . . If on the other hand we chose to invest in the new Trident program, we would have to insist on the inclusion of SLBMs in SALT so as to freeze Soviet numbers while we used the five-year period to develop our new system." Kissinger, *White House Years*, p. 1130. In fact there was no issue or choice at all. One reason Kissinger poses the question is that he is attempting to cover his not having pressed for the inclusion of SLBMs in the spring of 1971. A second reason is that because of the SLBM deal Kissinger finally struck, he needed to underline the U.S. preference in 1972 for including SLBMs even at a high level for the Soviets.

92. Even so, as the final tense bargaining over submarines and SLBMs was under way in Moscow, General Alexander M. Haig, Jr., reported near mutiny by the restive JCS, especially when press leaks unleashed objections from the right, including those by such pro-defense people as Senators Barry Goldwater of Arizona and Henry M. Jackson of Washington. See Kissinger, *White House Years*, pp. 1232–33.

made in a proposed Nixon reply to Brezhnev—it eliminated a statement that the president did not agree "with certain considerations" in the Brezhnev paper given to Kissinger—he objected. President Nixon dismissed his objection with the comment "bullshit." The deal had clearly been sealed, and all the Washington deliberations were ex post facto posturing.[93] In his memoir Kissinger reflects this fact by his complete silence on the April 26–May 1 Washington studies and meetings, and in an inadvertent admission in his later account of the summit: "My April trip had *settled* that the Soviets would be permitted 950 SLBMs on sixty-two submarines."[94]

Without going into detail, it should be noted that the above discussion deals only with the first of a number of problems that arose in the negotiation by the delegation in Helsinki and the final Nixon-Kissinger negotiation in Moscow in May. The main issue concerned the American proposal for freezing the then *current* level of operational Soviet SLBMs and those under construction at 740, with a further buildup in SLBMs to 950, all of which were to be replacements (presumably for the 209 old SS-7 and SS-8 ICBM launchers). This approach preserved the concept of a freeze on ICBM launchers. The Soviets accepted the figure of 740, but *excluded* the approximately 100 SLBMs on older H-class nuclear and G-class diesel submarines. This issue was finally resolved at the summit by including the 30 SLBMs on the H-class submarines, but not the 60 older missiles on the G-class diesel submarines. (The 62 modern submarines, it was agreed, would not include these older units.) The bargaining involved a wide range of rationales, and the agreement served to blur the application of a freeze.[95]

---

93. For a detailed and revealing account of the discussions in Washington, including the NSC meeting, see Smith, *Doubletalk*, pp. 370–78.

94. Kissinger, *White House Years*, p. 1219. Emphasis added.

95. For the final stages of the negotiation on SLBMs, see Smith, *Doubletalk*, pp. 379–433; Kissinger, *White House Years*, pp. 1219–21, 1230–41; Hersh, *The Price of Power*, pp. 548–55; and Newhouse, *Cold Dawn*, pp. 253–55.

   Both the Soviet delegation in Helsinki and the negotiators in Moscow were adamant on not having to count (and thus retire for replacement) the 100 older SLBM launchers. They argued initially for 48 submarines as the baseline before replacement, implying 768 launchers. The Helsinki delegation said this number had not originated with the Soviets, implying that it was Kissinger's idea in April. The Soviet delegation stuck with 48 SSBNs (or, later, 740 SLBM launchers) as the baseline and offered several alternative rationales: stretching the definition of "under construction," compensation for British and French submarines, or compensation for American SSBN forward bases. At the very least the Soviet side considered its bargaining position strong because it had accepted the basic Kissinger 950/62 proposal as necessary for domestic American political-bureaucratic reasons. The final compromise was not militarily significant to either side, but it blurred the freeze concept and was so hastily done that several loose ends permitted opponents of SALT and détente to criticize the agreement later.

   Kissinger's presentation of the whole complex issue is breathtaking. On the one hand he was confidently managing and steering the discussions to a favorable conclusion, while on the other repeatedly claiming that "neither Brezhnev nor Nixon had mastered the technical issues." Kissinger, *White House Years*, p. 1220. He had not only supported Nixon's exclusion of the

There remained one other minor issue on SLBM replacement. In proposing that the Soviet Union retire—in effect, trade in—older ICBMs for additional SLBMs, the United States wanted to preserve equal rights under the agreement. Therefore it wanted the agreement to specify an American

---

SALT delegation, but had left his own technically knowledgeable staff in Washington. Thus, for example, when he acceded to the Soviet demand to exclude the G-class diesel submarines and their SLBMs, he was unaware that in 1970, after earlier attempting to exclude those same submarines, the Soviet SALT delegation had finally agreed to include them.

Kissinger repeatedly misstates positions taken by the American delegation. For example, he seeks to justify his own compromise by which the G-class submarines were excluded from a 740 SLBM baseline level at which the replacement of older missiles would be required by saying in a note that "the delegation in Helsinki was working on a different SLBM formula that would have reached much the same practical result by redefining the term 'under construction.'" Kissinger, *White House Years*, p. 1239. This claim is untrue. The delegations in Helsinki suspended work on a definition of "under construction" that was virtually agreed upon, one that would have precluded that result, in order to leave all options open to the negotiators in Moscow. But one of the *Soviet* proposals, to which the U.S. delegation made clear its firm opposition, would have resolved the issue by defining "under construction" to give the Soviets credit for 48 submarines, or 740 launchers, "operational and under construction," without including the G- or H-class submarines.

Another incident involved a warning by the American delegation that attempts to claim forty-eight modern Soviet SSBNs operational and under construction would cast doubt on the efficacy of national means of verification, since U.S. national means (U.S. intelligence) showed only forty-two or forty-three Soviet SSBN submarines. The Soviet delegation rapidly disavowed that approach; Semenov specifically stated that the Soviet proposal that was keyed to replacement after the forty-eighth submarine did *not* constitute a claim that the USSR had forty-eight modern submarines in operation and under construction (an admission Kissinger failed to use when this ploy was subsequently used successfully with him in Moscow). The entire Soviet approach implied that Kissinger in April had accepted an "offset" equivalent to forty-eight submarines. See Smith, *Doubletalk*, pp. 397–400.

Kissinger similarly states that Ambassador Smith's recommendation "offered no precise method for calculating the baseline." *White House Years*, p. 1230. That is untrue. Smith expressed a desire to continue pressing the American proposal to establish a baseline of 740 launchers comprising the existing 640 SLBMs on Y- and D-class submarines in operation and under construction, plus the 100 on G- and H-class submarines. It is difficult to see how anyone could have seen this as not offering a precise method for calculating the baseline.

Kissinger's own subsequent accounts have varied greatly. On the day the agreement was signed, he said that the U.S. estimate was in a general range of forty-one to forty-three submarines, while "the Soviet estimate of their program is slightly more exhaustive. They, of course, have the advantage that they know what it is precisely. (Laughter)." See "Press Conference of Dr. Henry A. Kissinger and Ambassador Gerard C. Smith, Spaso House," White House Press Release, May 26, 1972, p. 10. He said much the same thing the next day, specifically noting that the term "under construction" was in dispute, "first between our intelligence agencies, and second between us and the Soviets." Neither was true. When asked for a definition of "under construction," he replied, "Well, some of the more profound minds in the bureaucracy, which is not necessarily saying a great deal (laughter), have addressed this question," and went on to suggest that differences in definition "may account for the difference in our assessments of what the Soviets have under construction and what the Soviets tell us they have under construction." "News Conference of Dr. Kissinger in Moscow, May 27," *State Bulletin*, vol. 66 (June 26, 1972), pp. 872–73. By June 15, in his congressional briefing, Kissinger had

right to trade in its fifty-four old Titan ICBMs for SLBMs. The United States did not, in fact, plan to exercise that right, and in practical terms could not do so. The Soviets, however, pressed hard for the United States to give *assurances* that it would not exercise that right. Such assurances, however, would have been at odds with the purpose of establishing equal rights. At the summit conference, Nixon finally gave in to Soviet insistence and provided a written statement that the United States had no intention of exercising the right to trade in Titans for SLBMs. But to preserve the appearance of symmetry, this note was kept secret. When it finally became known in 1974, it caused a flurry of objections, especially because it undercut Nixon and Kissinger's solemn assurances to Congress in 1972 that there were no secret understandings.[96]

The other major issue left hanging after the May 1971 agreement, and to some degree prejudiced by it, was the constraints on modernization, specifically on reconciling permitted ICBM modernization with limits on more very large ICBMs. This issue was not settled until the May 1972 summit conference.

In Kissinger's negotiation of the May 20, 1971, agreement, it had been agreed that the "certain measures" involving a freeze on strategic offensive arms would not preclude modernization and replacement.[97] It had also been agreed that not only would the total number of ICBMs be "frozen," but

---

decided to say that "there is some difficulty in defining the term 'under construction'. . . . Therefore, this was a subject of some complicated negotiation to determine the level at which the trade-in [from 740 to 950] would start. . . ." "Question and Answer Session after a Briefing by Dr. Henry Kissinger," p. 16. That reason, of course, was neither the origin nor the explanation of the real difficulty in negotiating the baseline. But it was a plausible explanation for the public. In the official internal rationale paper issued by the White House as a guide to government officials in testifying and speaking on SALT, the "official" explanation was that "the number 740 was negotiated as a firm baseline which circumvents the difficulty in defining the construction process." See "SALT Rationale Paper: The Strategic Arms Limitation Agreements and National Security," Memorandum for the Secretary of State, Secretary of Defense, Director of ACDA, and Director of CIA, signed by Henry A. Kissinger, The White House, June 16, 1972, p. 12.

96. Kissinger attempts to pass this matter off in his memoir by commenting that "Nixon could tell Brezhnev painlessly that we would not exercise the option." Kissinger did not disclose that the assurance had been written, signed by Nixon, and was agreed to only after persistent Soviet demands. Kissinger, *White House Years*, p. 1221. See also Smith, *Doubletalk*, p. 428; and Hersh, *The Price of Power*, p. 553.

In his congressional briefing on June 15, 1972, Kissinger had replied to a question of Senator Jackson's by saying flatly—and untruthfully—"There are no secret understandings." A few minutes later, obfuscating the truth by making it seem like an afterthought, Kissinger slipped in, in response to a different question, an artful evasion: "There are, of course, in the discussions, general statements of intentions. For example, we have conveyed to the Soviets what I have also said here publicly on the record: that the option of converting the Titans into submarines, given our present construction program, was not something we would necessarily carry out. But we do not consider that as a secret agreement." "Question and Answer Session after a Briefing by Dr. Henry Kissinger," p. 21.

97. Smith, *Doubletalk*, p. 326.

that the number of modern large ICBMs (SS-9s) would also be frozen. Nevertheless, a host of subsidiary issues remained, and the resolution of some along lines favored by the United States had been prejudiced by Kissinger's agreeing, without qualification, to freedom of modernization and replacement.

Without reviewing the complex negotiation on this issue, one can say that by the time of the Moscow summit the situation was as follows: (1) agreement had been reached on a freeze banning the start of any additional ICBM silo launchers after July 1, 1972 (formalizing a de facto unilateral Soviet freeze on starting new silos adopted after May 20, 1971); (2) no existing ICBM silo launchers could be moved or replaced by new ones; (3) there would be no conversion of silos for small ICBMs to launchers for large (or heavy) ICBMs (thus freezing the number of large Soviet ICBM launchers at 308); (4) existing ICBM silo launchers still under construction could be completed; and (5) except as otherwise limited by the agreement, modernization and replacement of strategic missiles and launchers were permitted.

What remained unsettled were two related points: (1) most important, there was no definition of what were small and large (called light and heavy) ICBMs; and (2) there was no limit on increases in the size of silos undergoing modernization, a limit the United States sought in support of the ban on converting light to heavy ICBMs. At Helsinki the Soviets had argued that there was no difficulty in distinguishing light from heavy ICBMs. While the United States agreed there was no difficulty with respect to current ICBMs, it was concerned that future Soviet ICBMs might fall in between existing light ICBMs (such as the Soviet SS-11s) and heavy ICBMs (SS-9s) in size and volume. On the silo constraints, the Soviets argued this limit would impinge on the freedom to modernize and replace already accepted by the American side (ever since Kissinger's 1971 negotiations). After much discussion they were prepared to agree that there should be "no substantial (or significant) increase" in silo dimensions observable by national means of verification.

The American delegation had tried to tie down the key issue by seeking an agreement that *any* missile larger than the largest existing light ICBM (the SS-11, with about 70 cubic meters volume) would be classified as heavy. This was the optimum American position, since the United States itself was not planning any ICBMs larger than that, and it would provide the maximum constraint on Soviet missiles. It soon, however, became clear that Soviet objections indicated that the Soviet Union's new ICBMs with MIRVs, apart from the replacement for the SS-9 (the SS-18), would be larger than the SS-11 that they would replace.[98]

---

98. Indications for this conclusion, and the conclusion itself, were submitted to Washington by the delegation from Helsinki. For a review of the delegation's efforts, see ibid., pp. 325–26, 331–34, 353, 359–60, 338–91, 403–05. In one conversation a Soviet negotiator told me that the Soviet Union had two replacements for the SS-11 under development that had to be deployed because they would be the Soviet equivalent of the American Minuteman III with MIRVs. He finally indicated that the Soviet view of a light ICBM (and by implication the size of the new Soviet ICBMs) would not exceed halfway between the volume of the existing light and

Efforts to gain Soviet acceptance of the American definition of a heavy missile were thus bound to fail. The Soviet leaders would not, and could not realistically be expected to, give up their MIRV ICBM missiles already far along in development but lagging behind American MIRV development and deployment by five years.

On May 22, the day the presidential party arrived in Moscow, the delegation reported its conclusion that the Soviet side would not agree to the proposed definition of a heavy missile. The Soviet delegation did, however, agree on that same day to compromises on several remaining issues, including a compromise interpretive statement that "there would be no significant increase in the dimensions of land-based ICBM silo launchers" in the process of modernizing and replacing ICBMs. The U.S. delegation decided it was preferable not to define the term "significant increase" as 10 to 15 percent, a level its negotiator believed could be agreed upon.[99] It was well-recognized that such a compromise constraint (with or without the percentage limitation specified) would not affect the probably modest but essential modification that the new larger follow-on Soviet MIRV missiles would entail.[100]

---

heavy ICBMs. The SS-19, the larger of the two new Soviet ICBMs, has a volume of about 100 cubic meters. That is less than halfway between the SS-11, with 70 cubic meters, and the SS-9, with more than 200 cubic meters, and less than half the size of the heavy SS-9. It is, nonetheless, significantly larger than the SS-11 and has substantially more throw-weight. The American delegation, instructed to press for a limit of no more than a 70-cubic meter volume, could not explore alternative, higher definitions of a dividing line between light and heavy ICBMs. In SALT II, agreement was eventually reached defining the dividing line as no greater than the SS-19.

99. See Smith, *Doubletalk*, pp. 389–91, 404–05.

I was the negotiator for the American delegation, and in discussions between May 11 and 22 had elicited a Soviet proposal of 20 percent and then a range of 10 to 20 percent. I believed 10 to 15 percent was attainable. The delegation decided that it would be preferable to leave open the question of defining "significant increase," and on May 22 rejected the 10 to 20 percent proposal, making no counterproposal.

Kissinger is wrong when he states that the Soviet delegation had "refused to accept" a clarification of "significant increase" as meaning no more than 10 to 15 percent, when he states that the American delegation had proposed 10 to 15 percent, and when he states that the delegation proposed a unilateral statement defining "significant increase" at that level. In fact, the U.S. delegation never proposed 10 to 15 percent and the Soviet delegation never refused it, nor did the U.S. delegation ever propose or plan such a unilateral statement. The American delegation never offered to accept any increase above 10 percent. It suits Kissinger's purpose, however, to suggest that he obtained as a binding agreement a figure the American side desired but that the delegation could not obtain, and that the delegation was prepared to settle for a unilateral statement. Kissinger, *White House Years*, p. 1219.

100. Again, from the discussions at Helsinki it appeared likely that the new Soviet missiles would probably involve some deepening of the silos but little or no increase in diameter. The Soviets had suggested that perhaps national means could check on diameter but not depth. The comment hinted at a readiness to accept constraints on the former but not a ban on changes in the latter. The Soviet delegation had even floated a proposed compromise to

On Kissinger's instruction the delegation had prepared a fallback unilateral statement on the heavy missile issue. It read: "The United States would regard any ICBM having a volume significantly greater than that of the largest light ICBM now operational on either side [the Soviet SS-11] to be a heavy ICBM. The U.S. proceeds on the premise that the Soviet side will give due account to this U.S. understanding." No one on the American delegation believed the Soviets would consider as a real constraint "due account" to a unilateral American statement asserting something the Soviets had rejected. No one believed such a statement would have any effect on Soviet decisions with respect to missiles already under development—about which the United States had concrete intelligence, quite apart from the guarded hints of the Soviet delegation. Ambassador Smith had reported his assessment to Kissinger: "A unilateral statement by us may have some slight deterrent effect on any such new Soviet program, but I wouldn't put a very high estimate on the value of such deterrence."[101]

Kissinger and Nixon plunged into these issues in Moscow, and much confusion occurred on both sides.[102] At one point Brezhnev and Nixon

---

undertake "no substantial increase, observable with the aid of national technical means of verification, in the *external* dimensions of ICBM silos," thus constraining the diameter but not the depth. Indeed, the new family of replacement missiles (the SS-17 and SS-19 replacing the SS-11, and the SS-18 replacing the SS-9) involved deepening the silos, in some cases by about 10 to 15 percent, but little or no increase in their diameter. Information based on my participation in the negotiation.

101. Smith, *Doubletalk*, p. 400. Kissinger uncharitably, and incorrectly, attributes to the delegation the idea of a unilateral statement as a fallback. Kissinger, *White House Years*, p. 1231. The other information in this paragraph is drawn from my participation in the negotiation.

102. On the Moscow negotiations on this issue, see Kissinger, *White House Years*, pp. 1218–22, 1239; Smith, *Doubletalk*, pp. 410–17, 422–23, 430, 433; and, based largely on Kissinger and Smith but with some additional details, Hersh, *The Price of Power*, pp. 543–48.

Some aspects remain to be clarified. For example, Kissinger reports that Brezhnev "adopted a view . . . that there was no need to change the dimensions of Soviet silos and that the Soviets had no intention of increasing the *diameter* of their missiles; this *implied* that they would accept a freeze on silo dimensions as well as on missile volume." *White House Years*, p. 1220. Emphasis added. Kissinger is here reporting the same Moscow exchange that Smith says Kissinger characterized at the time as a Soviet assertion that it had no intention of increasing the *size* of its missiles. Moreover, Kissinger claimed the Soviets were prepared to drop the modifier "significant" from the interpretive statement on silo modification. Smith, *Doubletalk*, p. 413. Since this interpretation seemed to be at variance not only with the whole Soviet negotiating position, but also with the actual Soviet missile program (as the United States knew), it has been very puzzling. Kissinger's more recent account, while not presenting the precise record, strongly suggests that Brezhnev was saying that the Soviets were not planning to increase the diameter of their missiles in such a way as to require any change in the diameter or externally visible dimensions of their silo launchers. Brezhnev probably repeated the Soviet delegation's earlier proposal to drop the modifier "significant" (earlier the word was "substantial"), as it applied to diameter but not to depth. Kissinger and his aides failed to recognize this distinction or even to listen closely: "no change in diameter" does *not* imply no change in silo dimensions or in missile volume. What actually occurred was that the silos were deepened to allow for longer missiles with more fuel and the new MIRV warheads.

apparently nearly agreed on a ban on any significant increase of more than 10 to 15 percent in missile volume. This limit would have stopped the Minuteman III and SS–19 programs, thus leading to a partial MIRV ban.[103] Several days of frenzied negotiations ensued, with useful but awkward back channel communications (always incomplete and a few hours behind) between the White House party and the American delegation in Helsinki, between Brezhnev and Nixon, and more frequently between Kissinger and Gromyko and Deputy Prime Minister Leonid Smirnov, head of the Soviet Military-Industrial Commission.

The upshot of all this talk was twofold. The unilateral statement by the American delegation on heavy missiles was made, and a further clarification was added to the agreed interpretive statement on silo modifications specifying that a 10 to 15 percent increase would be a significant increase in silo dimensions. This constraint was one the delegation had considered and rejected, a decision that was reported to Washington several days earlier. Moreover, in the course of adding this more specific constraint a discrepancy in the translation led to the use of the term "dimensions" in describing the application of the 10 to 15 percent. This meant that what Kissinger had believed would limit the *size* of Soviet silos by 10 to 15 percent actually allowed a volumetric increase of 32 percent, since dimensions meant a possible increase of 15 percent in diameter *and* in depth.

Kissinger's memoir glosses over these matters in an odd way. First, in order to build up the achievements of the Moscow summit conference, he rails against a nonexistent proposal by the American delegation to make a unilateral statement that the American side considered significant to mean 10 to 15 percent, which he said the Soviet side had rejected. "To rest an agreement on a unilateral statement which the Soviets had rejected," Kissinger remarks, "seemed too risky to us at the White House; and therefore we placed the whole issue on the summit agenda." Accordingly, he writes, "I was determined to transform our delegation's nonbinding unilateral statement into a binding mutual definition," thus making the result at Moscow "an improvement."[104]

On the resolution of the far more important matter of defining a heavy missile, Kissinger notes—in a footnote—that the delegation tried to reach an agreed definition. When that proved impossible, it was authorized (on

Kissinger's too hasty assumptions and reaction threw the negotiation off track. And the delegation could not clarify the point because it had been given only Kissinger's own erroneous paraphrase of Brezhnev's proposal, rather than a text even as clear as the one he later gave in his memoir.

103. See Smith, *Doubletalk*, p. 415. Kissinger, either still unaware of the effect this constraint on *missile volume* would have had on Minuteman III or to obfuscate the issue, refers instead to an allegedly erroneous calculation by the JCS that a freeze on *silo size* would have precluded Minuteman III. Kissinger, *White House Years*, p. 1220.

104. Kissinger, *White House Years*, pp. 1219, 1235, 1239.

May 23) to issue the unilateral statement cited earlier. He does not note that this followed an attempt, and failure, in Moscow to get agreement on that matter. He also does not explain why, on this more important point than silo dimensions, it did not also seem "too risky" to the White House to "rest an agreement on a unilateral statement which the Soviets had rejected." Rather, he lamely comments in the footnote, "We overestimated the restraining effect of such a unilateral statement. (See my Congressional briefing of June 15, 1972)."[105]

What Kissinger is indirectly referring to is not a disjunction between estimates of one or another unilateral statement. Rather, it is a serious overstatement by himself in the cited congressional briefing on the agreement in response to a question by Senator Jackson. In defending the absence of a definition of heavy missiles Kissinger referred to the "safeguard that no missile larger than the heaviest light missile that now exists can be substituted." There was no such safeguard—only whatever effect the unilateral statement might have. Moreover, Kissinger went on to say that the combination of the unilateral statement with the agreed interpretation of no increase greater than 10 to 15 percent in silos "give[s] us an adequate safeguard against a substantial substitution of heavy missiles for light missiles."[106]

This unjustified overstatement was not based on "an overestimate of the restraining effect" of the unilateral American statement, but represented Kissinger's unsuccessful attempt to evade the issue. In fact, quite apart from indications by members of the Soviet SALT delegation, the United States had intelligence that a successor ICBM to the SS–11 would be larger. Additional intelligence confirmed this during the Moscow summit, when American receivers intercepted a radiotelephone conversation between Brezhnev and a senior military official confirming that the limit of 15 percent in silo dimensions would not preclude deployment of the new larger Soviet ICBMs.[107] Kissinger thus knew very well that the assurances he was providing to Congress in June 1972 were not valid.

This attempt to claim more of a constraint on future in-between-size Soviet ICBMs was to haunt SALT later, when the Soviets did introduce

---

105. Ibid., pp. 1219, 1239.

106. "Question and Answer Session after a Briefing by Dr. Henry Kissinger," p. 10.

107. Kissinger himself comments that when Brezhnev "seemed" (it was actually Kissinger and Nixon's misunderstanding) to be proposing no increase in missile volume, such a proposal was "incompatible with the weapons the Soviets were actually building" and "with projected programs." Kissinger, *White House Years,* pp. 1220–21. Smith notes that when he was advised of this reported Soviet position, he reminded Kissinger that "we already had intelligence indications that the Soviets planned to do just what they now were reported as saying they would not do." Smith, *Doubletalk,* p. 414. The leaked report that the United States had intercepted Brezhnev's limousine radiotelephone conversation about the Soviet missile increase was first disclosed by Jack Anderson; it is also reported by Hersh, *The Price of Power,* p. 547.

the SS-19. Many political figures and commentators termed this missile a Soviet violation of the SALT agreement; only a few correctly tied it to the White House's overstatements of June 1972. Indeed, the SS-19 has widely been considered evidence either of a Soviet failure to comply with the SALT agreement, or at the least of sharp Soviet practice in negotiating and interpreting the agreement. In fact, the Soviets were quite straightforward in declining to accept the tight restriction proposed by the United States because of their requirements for allowed modernization and replacement with MIRVs. The sharp negotiating practice was by Kissinger, but at the cost of a loss in American confidence in Soviet compliance and in SALT itself.[108]

Before the SALT I agreements themselves and their significance for détente are examined, one additional important strand to these issues taken up in SALT needs to be discussed briefly. It had both technical arms control and important international political aspects.

Earlier exchanges in 1968–69 before SALT formally began had identified both Soviet and American interest in improving crisis communication and avoiding possible miscalculations based on technical accidents, unauthorized or third-party use of nuclear weapons, and other ways in which war could occur by accident rather than by design. This subject was included as one of the points in the agreed work program adopted at the first Helsinki SALT session in December 1969.

These interrelated subjects were discussed at a number of plenary meetings of the SALT delegations in the spring and summer of 1970 and were dealt with in different ways. In 1970–71 a joint working group from the two delegations drafted what became an "Agreement on Measures to Reduce the Risk of Outbreak of Nuclear War Between the United States of America and the Union of Soviet Socialist Republics." It was initialed at SALT in August and formally signed and concluded by Secretary of State Rogers and Foreign Minister Gromyko in Washington on September 30, 1971. The agreement included various measures to guard against accidental or unauthorized use of nuclear weapons, to notify and consult in the event of any such occurrence, and

---

108. To cite but one example, seven years later columnists Rowland Evans and Robert Novak called the fact that the Interim Agreement "failed to pin down specific limits on the size of a replacement for the SS11" "the worst U.S. blooper in the 1972 SALT I treaty." They erroneously labeled this omission a "mistake, not discovered until long after ratification." "Trapped by Soviet duplicity three years later, Kissinger found himself lamely explaining away the sudden appearance of the big SS19. 'We obviously did not know in 1972 what missiles the Soviet Union would be testing in 1974,' Kissinger told a State Department press conference on Dec. 9, 1975."

Evans and Novak did not realize that Kissinger had deflected his own responsibility for obfuscating the whole issue in 1972 onto "Soviet duplicity" and "obvious" American innocence as to the next generation of Soviet missiles. See Evans and Novak, "The SS19 Loophole," *Washington Post*, July 27, 1979. This article appeared as the SALT II congressional debate was under way.

to consult and to act in situations involving unexplained nuclear incidents in ways to reduce possible misunderstandings.[109]

The second, more technical, subject was an upgrading of the "Hot Line"—U.S.-USSR Direct Communications Link—by switching to satellite communications systems. A special technical group handled this negotiation in the spring of 1971, and it, too, was signed by Rogers and Gromyko in September 1971.[110]

The third subject was highly political, and the United States decided against pursuing it except insofar as the technical aspects were covered by the other two agreements. This subject was possible joint American-Soviet action to deal with the problem of a "provocative attack" by a third nuclear power designed to provoke war between the United States and the Soviet Union (a concept referred to in some earlier American writings as a "catalytic attack"). For example, country X, possessing nuclear weapons and means of delivery, might fire nuclear missiles from submarines in the Pacific Ocean at targets in the United States, the Soviet Union, or both, calculating that the two powers would hold each other responsible. The Soviet delegation raised this possibility explicitly in its very first presentation in November 1969 and on many subsequent occasions. The Americans also alluded to it in several presentations. In all these instances the subject was the general threat of accidental or unintended war, with reference to possible accidental, unauthorized, or provocative third-party missile launches or attacks. In July 1970, however, Deputy Foreign Minister Semenov began to sound out American reaction to *joint* action by the two powers to *prevent* such possible third-party action.

Semenov's overtures on joint action to prevent provocative attack raised delicate and serious questions of condominium that concerned American relations with its allies and, above all, China—the clear focus of Soviet attention and a country with which the United States was secretly engaged in the preliminary stages of a rapprochement. It was, at the same time, an outgrowth of a legitimate Soviet concern (and conceivably an American one) and was germane to the discussion under way.

In mid-1970 the Soviet leaders were still testing the limits of potential Soviet-American détente and collaboration on security. They recognized full well the sensitivity of a collaborative stance against third-party (Chinese) provocative nuclear action—even though they evidently were not aware of the

---

109. See Smith, *Doubletalk*, pp. 98–99, 280–98, with the text of the "Accidents Agreement" on pp. 517–19; and Raymond L. Garthoff, "The Accident Measures Agreement," in John Borawski, ed., *Avoiding Nuclear War: Confidence-Building Measures for Crisis Stability* (forthcoming).

110. Smith, *Doubletalk*, pp. 292–98, with the text of the "Revised Hot Line Agreement" on pp. 521–23.

still very tentative and uncertain American-Chinese movement toward rapprochement and its role in American thinking. To the extent they suspected and feared such a rapprochement, however, they were all the more eager to head it off.

In mid-1970 the Soviet leaders were also still attempting to sort out the relative weight and alternative channels of communication and negotiation with the United States. The special Dobrynin-Kissinger channel had not yet developed into the principal route of diplomatic communication or become the forum for negotiation that evolved over the following year. Thus the Soviets used the Kissinger channel when tentatively exploring the summit meeting and exchanges on various issues, while using the SALT channel to sound out even very sensitive matters that were best identified with SALT from the standpoint of encouraging American receptivity. Hence the provocative attack issue was raised in Vienna rather than in Washington—only to fall afoul of a major misunderstanding.

The fact that the Soviet Union had raised the subject of collaboration to prevent or respond to an attempt at provocative attack was a closely kept secret during SALT I. Indeed, it became the subject of a special need-to-know clearance within the American government.[111] The subject was later disclosed to the NATO allies on a similar, very closely held, basis. In 1973, in his book on SALT I, John Newhouse broke the story of the provocative attack issue.[112] But it was not until Kissinger's memoir that details were first made known—in an account that also revealed a colossal misunderstanding by Kissinger himself that he was still not aware of years later when writing his memoir. Thus, in addition to illuminating this page in the development of American-Soviet relations, a clarification of the issue also provides a fascinating example of the failure of communication induced by mixing the Kissinger-Dobrynin and normal diplomatic channels, in this case the SALT negotiation.

On June 25, 1970, Dobrynin proposed to Kissinger an ABM treaty coupled with a scheme to reduce the danger of accidental war. After describing this proposal, Kissinger jumps to a startling conclusion: "Collusion against China was to be the real Soviet price for a summit. It surfaced again in the best spy-novel tradition. Semenov encountered Smith at the Vienna Opera and handed him an unsigned paper outlining the Soviet notion of an accidental-war agreement. If a nuclear 'provocation' were being 'prepared' by a third country, each country was to inform the other. If a provocative act took place, each party would be obliged to take retaliatory action against the offending country. The two parties were to hold regular consultations on these subjects."[113]

---

111. A special restrictive "POL" (for "Political") classification was established with a list of named authorizations. Even the earlier memoranda of conversations on the subject beginning June 2 were reclassified.

112. Newhouse, *Cold Dawn*, pp. 188–89. Newhouse received this information from members of Kissinger's staff with Kissinger's authorization.

113. Kissinger, *White House Years*, p. 554.

Dobrynin had in fact proposed an ABM agreement coupled with an accord on "reducing the danger of missile-nuclear war between the USSR and the US resulting from accidental or unsanctioned use of nuclear weapons."[114] In other words Dobrynin had proposed an ABM agreement coupled with an accidental war agreement along the lines being developed by the SALT delegations. This proposal was an attempt by the Soviet side to overcome American resistance to the idea of an ABM agreement alone as a first step. Their approach was to accompany the ABM treaty with a noncontroversial agreement on measures to avert accidental war, work on which was proceeding well in Vienna.

Why did Kissinger immediately jump to the conclusion the Soviets were pressing for a provocative attack agreement? He explains that this "became apparent when on June 30, out of the blue, Semenov at Vienna started expostulating on the dangers of accidental or unauthorized missile launches. And on July 2, Semenov said privately to one of our delegation that 'what we need to do is jointly take a stand that the two governments intend to act together to prevent the outbreak of war by accidental, unauthorized or provocative action from any quarter.' "[115]

Semenov on June 30 did indeed address the problem of accidental war. In fact, he made reference to "accidental, unauthorized or provocative attack" (inexplicably, Kissinger did not note it). But the discussion was not "out of the blue," nor was the reference to provocative attack "out of the blue." *Both* delegations had made such references since November 1969, and by coincidence on June 30 the U.S. delegation *also* referred to accidental or unauthorized use of nuclear weapons and to provocative attack by a third power. (The American delegation's statement had been cleared in Washington by all interested parties, including Kissinger's staff.)

The new element—joint action to prevent or retaliate against provocative attack by third parties—was in fact first raised by Semenov on July 2, as Kissinger notes, in a private talk with me. Semenov also informed me that he would raise the matter privately with Ambassador Smith on July 7 and in a plenary statement on July 10. Kissinger takes great umbrage at this Semenov-Garthoff talk: "This was a violation of the rules of our Channel, which was supposed to be limited to explorations on the Nixon-Brezhnev level—perhaps explicable by the Soviets' difficulty in fathoming an Executive Branch that practiced the separation of powers within itself."[116]

This brings the story back to the earlier-cited account by Kissinger of a Semenov Smith encounter at the opera at which, "in the best spy-novel tradition" "an unsigned paper outlining the Soviet notion of an accidental-war

---

114. Ibid., p. 547.

115. Ibid., p. 548.

116. Ibid.

agreement" was passed.[117] In fact, Semenov did not "encounter" Smith at the opera; Semenov and Smith, and their wives, went together to a Rostropovich concert. It was out of the ordinary to pass a paper on a politically sensitive subject on such an occasion, but the Soviets wanted an authoritative but deliberately informal procedure. As for the spy-novel tradition, as noted earlier, Semenov had discussed the entire subject in some detail with me five days before, and the decision to pass the paper at the opera was made jointly with me. Semenov had accepted my suggestion to pass the Soviet "considerations" on this subject to Smith informally on July 7, and he did. And then on July 10 he presented the Soviet proposal formally.

Semonov's proposals were not a "scheme to reduce the danger of 'accidental war' " or "the Soviet notion of an accidental-war agreement," as characterized by Kissinger. This was a new subject—and *not* the subject of Dobrynin's aide-mémoire of June 25. Believing that the Soviet leaders were attempting to link an ABM agreement and an anti-provocative-war agreement, Kissinger jumped to the conclusion that "collusion against China was to be the real Soviet price for a summit."[118] But this was neither the Soviet proposal nor the Soviet purpose. Far from attempting linkage in Kissinger's style, the Soviets were attempting to assuage U.S. reluctance to agree to an ABM agreement by itself as a first step. The Soviet move may in fact have represented an overture for an early summit—an important signal that Kissinger, attempting alone to weave several strands and instead tangling them, failed to appreciate. The cosmetic linkage was not adequate from the American standpoint (as Ambassador Smith also said when asked),[119] but it was an attempt on the Soviet side to advance, not slow down, agreement and a summit. This major error by Kissinger in confusing the accidental war and provocative attack proposals at the very least deprived the U.S. government of an indication that the Soviets were interested in moving toward an early summit—at just the time when President Nixon very strongly wanted to do that.[120]

The way in which the provocative attack subject was handled throughout made clear that Kissinger's interpretation was wrong. The probes on this subject in July 1970 were never related, in Vienna or in Washington, to the question of proceeding expeditiously toward a SALT agreement and a summit meeting. Kissinger's assumption was also belied by the fact that the Soviets promptly abandoned the anti-provocative-attack proposal, concluded the accident measures agreement as soon as the United States was prepared to do so (prior to but not delaying a summit), and proceeded to work toward an ABM agreement and summit.

---

117. Ibid., p. 554.

118. Ibid.

119. Ibid., p. 548; and Smith, *Doubletalk*, pp. 147–48.

120. Kissinger, *White House Years*, p. 556.

Kissinger immediately turned down the provocative attack approach, even before it was formally brought to the table. On July 9, on the basis of the Semenov-Garthoff and Semenov-Smith discussions of July 2 and 7, and the day *before* Semenov made the formal Soviet proposal at Vienna, Kissinger told Dobrynin that the Semenov overture was "unacceptable." A technical agreement providing for safeguards against accidental occurrences was one thing, and one that "we were ready to address jointly," but "political cooperation implying a major change in international alignments and clearly aimed against third countries was out of the question." Unquestionably, the Soviet proposal as advanced was open to possible misuses (for example, who would determine, and how, that a third country was preparing a provocative act?) and needed to be rejected. It is not, however, clear why Kissinger dismissed the entire subject out of hand. He did so, moreover, after consulting only with Nixon—he had no discussions with the secretaries of state and defense or others in the government. Kissinger writes that Nixon agreed "the accidental-war proposal" (again misconstrued) "had to be rejected and promptly," but he does not say why.[121]

Kissinger reports that Dobrynin feigned ignorance of Semenov's proposal and "quickly shifted the conversation to an ABM agreement. At this point I reminded him that we had been talking about a meeting at the highest level since April."[122]

Kissinger seems still not to understand that the Soviet ploy for a SALT linkage was an ABM treaty plus an accidental war agreement, and was intended to *facilitate* American agreement to an early summit meeting. It was not an ABM treaty plus a provocative attack agreement, intended to pressure the United States into a political concession as the price for a summit. This was a *Soviet* concession (albeit a minor one), not an attempt to press the United States. (There was another, quite different, relationship between the provocative attack proposal and ABM limitation, to which the discussion will return shortly, but it had nothing to do with maneuvering for a summit.)

The Soviet proposal of an ABM treaty plus an accident measures agreement was only the first bid in a negotiation already shifting to an ABM treaty plus certain limitations on Soviet offensive missiles. So the accident agreement continued to be negotiated in a normal way and was signed in September 1971 (after having been held up briefly by Kissinger until a summit in 1972 was agreed upon). The ABM agreement plus some offensive missile limitations approach was, as noted, decided upon on May 20, 1971. The Soviets carefully did *not* link the progress of the SALT negotiation to the politically touchy question of a provocative attack by a third country. Finally, the Soviet proposal, while politically sensitive and even potentially dangerous, was

---

121. Ibid., pp. 554–55.

122. Ibid., p. 555.

not a "blatant embodiment of condominium," still less a vehicle "to give the USSR a free hand against China."[123] Kissinger's misunderstanding of the relationship of the whole issue to the bargaining in SALT, and his cynical assumption that the Soviets could *only* have had a political design vis-à-vis China, rather than perhaps a genuine security concern, show the hazards of governmental decisionmaking by one man unadvised.

Kissinger's excessively manipulative approach thus led him to misconstrue the Soviet purpose, the nature of the proposal for an ABM agreement accompanied by an accident measures agreement, and the nature of the provocative attack proposal.

There was another curious and still unexplained aspect to this story. After flatly rejecting the idea of joint preventive or retaliatory action in his demarche to Dobrynin on July 9, Kissinger permitted the U.S. delegation and those few in the bureaucracy in Washington specially cleared for this subject to study the pros and cons of alternative ways of dealing with the Soviet proposal on provocative attack for another four months, before letting the rest of the U.S. government know that the American response was a flat rejection. Even then he did not make it known that Dobrynin had been so advised in July.[124] Not until early November did the White House issue instructions to turn down the provocative attack proposal when it was raised again. Only when that session of SALT was drawing to a close without the Soviets having raised the matter again (knowing that Kissinger had rejected it) did the White House respond to a recommendation by the delegation that it turn down the proposal without waiting. That was done on December 18.[125] The NATO allies were then advised on January 15, 1971, in a special restricted session of the North Atlantic Council, that the Soviets had advanced a proposal for collaborative action to prevent or respond to a third-country provocative attack and that the United States had rejected the idea.

One aspect of this issue requires further brief comment: the heretofore unnoted *substantive* relationship between the idea of collaborative Soviet-American political action to prevent a possible third-country provocative at-

---

123. Ibid., p. 554.

124. The SALT delegation had recommended on July 13 that for tactical reasons it would be preferable to leave the provocative attack proposal unanswered, while studying it further, and the Washington agencies agreed. This made it even more difficult for Kissinger, then or later, to acknowledge that as early as July 9, without consulting the departments and agencies, and even prior to having received the precise Soviet proposal, he had brusquely rejected it.

125. See Smith, *Doubletalk*, pp. 140–44. Smith describes the Semenov proposal and the issue as discussed in Vienna and gives the text of the American rejection. He does not describe the delegation and interdepartmental studies of the subject, handled chiefly by the Department of State, nor the North Atlantic Council meeting on the subject, described below on the basis of my own participation. Kissinger makes no further reference to the subject apart from acknowledging the Soviet proposals and his rejection of them in July 1970. Nor does he attempt to explain why, if the Soviet leaders were making a major attempt to pressure the United States, they failed to return to the subject.

tack and ABM limitation. Apart from Kissinger's misreading of a Soviet tactical tie or linkage with an ABM agreement, there was another respect in which the Soviets *did* see a connection between the two. This connection has been completely unnoted by Kissinger, Smith, and other observers. Yet there were explicit statements by Soviet negotiators suggesting a relationship between alternative political and military measures to deter a possible missile attack by the Chinese, and specifically that Soviet receptivity to a complete ABM ban might depend on a Soviet-American agreement to act jointly against a provocative attack by China. Most notably, in the first major Soviet SALT presentation on alternative possible ABM limitations on November 28, 1969, Semenov had specifically tied the possibility of a complete ABM ban to the necessity "to weigh the problems involved in providing a defense against possible unauthorized launches or provocations from third countries." By coincidence, at that same meeting the American delegation, while speaking against attempts to provide a ballistic missile defense for a nation's population, had (in accordance with its instructions) kept open all other possibilities, specifically noting a possible need for ABM deployments not only to protect ICBMs, but also to protect against possible accidental launches and third-country provocations. It specifically mentioned the People's Republic of China.[126]

The abrupt rejection of the Soviet approach on provocative attacks in July 1970 cut off further opportunities to clarify the Soviet position, just as the proposal in April 1970 of an NCA-level ABM limitation had cut off exploration of a possible ABM ban. When the United States began to abandon the agreed NCA approach to limiting ABMs and again raised the possibility of an ABM ban in 1971, Soviet negotiators again informally referred to the relation between a possible ban on ABMs and political reassurances against a provocative attack by a third country.

In assuming that the Soviet intent was to launch a spoiling action that would preclude an American-Chinese rapprochement and give the Soviet Union a free hand vis-à-vis China, and in acting precipitately on that premise, Kissinger failed to consider that the situation might instead, or in addition, have reflected Soviet defensive concerns. Moreover, the link between political reassurances against Chinese nuclear action and military reassurances as represented by the ABM defense of Moscow was logical and plausible. But Kissinger failed to see even that connection. This omission was another consequence of mistakenly construing a Soviet linkage of an ABM agreement with an anti-provocative-war agreement. Of course, even if the connection had been recognized, Kissinger might have responded the same way. Kissinger has admitted he was using the idea of a possible ABM ban only as a negotiating ploy, and the White House withdrew Smith's authority to pursue the subject as soon as the Soviet side unexpectedly showed positive interest. Regardless of whether the United States wanted an ABM ban, however, it still should have been interested in understanding the *Soviet* interests and purposes in advancing

---

126. The account in this paragraph is drawn from my participation in the negotiations.

positions in the negotiations, if only for tactical negotiating purposes. And it should have been interested for other reasons as well.

It is worth noting that apart from substantive considerations, and even apart from American negotiating tactics and strategy vis-à-vis the Soviet Union, Kissinger was keenly concerned with acquiring personal control of the SALT negotiations, indeed, of all negotiations with the Soviet Union. His resentment of initiatives by Semenov or any channel other than his own with Dobrynin clearly affected his judgment of the seriousness of any Soviet initiative. His attitude toward such initiatives was apparently also affected by his desire to discipline the Soviet leadership when it strayed from *the* channel.

In only one other instance did the Soviet side raise a political arms control issue in SALT. In December 1970 Semenov discussed privately with Smith (and Semenov's chief aides in parallel with me) the idea of a reciprocal obligation not to be the first to use nuclear weapons. Smith and I indicated that any American response would have to include the ability to meet a conventional attack on its allies by any means, including resort to nuclear weapons.[127] The no-first-use proposal was reported to Washington, where the decision was to reject it if formally advanced. In February 1971 I informed Yuly M. Vorontsov, Dobrynin's deputy, that this would be the American response if the subject were broached formally. In February the United States also advised its NATO allies. The idea was never raised again in SALT. As in the case of the provocative attack proposal, once a negative American reaction was encountered, the Soviet side made no effort to pursue the matter.

Apart from the direct exchanges in the SALT negotiating forum and other channels, both sides sought in various ways to signal their interests and preferences in order to underline their stated positions and to influence the position of the other side. In particular, in 1969, 1970, and 1971 the American leadership sought to obtain and use congressional approval for an expanded Safeguard deployment as leverage. The purpose was to demonstrate its ability and will to proceed with that deployment unless the Soviet side agreed not only to comparable limitations of its own ABM deployments (not to be expanded beyond Moscow), but also to limitations on offensive missile launchers—which the Soviet side was still building up, while the United States was not.

Much has been made of the value of the continuing ABM deployment program, and congressional support for it, in inducing the Soviets to agree to the SALT I ABM Treaty and the Interim Agreement on offensive arms. In a general sense the fact the United States had an ABM deployment program under way after September 1967 no doubt gave the Soviets an incentive to negotiate and reach an agreement. The Nixon administration's drive to gain authorization to build more sites in 1970 and 1971 added somewhat to the urgency. A decisive congressional rejection of ABM deployment would have reduced those incentives, although the Soviet leaders would not have taken

---

127. Smith, *Doubletalk*, pp. 190–91, notes the initial approach by Semenov.

even that action as providing lasting reassurance. But the incongruity of the American position on ABM limitation in 1970, and the clearly artificial nature of the American proposals in 1971, which were doctored to fit the ABM deployment program, raised Soviet suspicions and may have led them to be more cautious in SALT than they otherwise might have been. The signal was not all that clear.[128]

The main comparable Soviet signal was not recognized for a long time, then was not taken at face value by the White House, and was distorted and devalued by the Pentagon. It was, nonetheless, significant. At about the time the SALT talks began, the Soviet leaders initiated an unannounced unilateral freeze or moratorium on the construction of additional ICBM forces. This move was followed by the curtailment of some construction already under way during 1970. Intelligence analysts recognized the change, but policymakers who had a stake in keeping up the image of a relentless Soviet buildup acknowledged it only belatedly and partially. Then, in early 1971, as the talks stalemated, the resumption of construction of some eighty new launchers sent a different signal. This development was quickly reported. Following the May 1971 agreement the Soviet leaders unilaterally placed a complete freeze on any additional ICBM construction—a full year before the obligation in the Interim Agreement came into effect. But again there was great American caution in making public that there had even been any slowdown.[129]

In fact, during the whole course of the SALT I negotiation, work on a total of only eighty new Soviet ICBM launchers was begun—about equal to the number of older type launchers on which construction was abandoned in the summer of 1970. Allowing for some new construction starts earlier in 1970, the net increase was thus somewhere between zero and 80 additional ICBM launchers started during the two-and-a-half years of the SALT I negotiations, in contrast to the 250 to 350 ICBM launchers added in *each* of the preceding three years. But even this signal was not received clearly by the American government, and it was downplayed when it became publicly known.

---

128. Such signaling is subject to static, unintended messages originating in uncontrolled events. For example, while Nixon and Kissinger were pressing Congress to fund the third and fourth ABM sites in 1971, while planning on an agreement that would allow only two, a long-running local strike by construction workers in Montana led to very long delays in the construction of the second ABM site at Malmstrom Air Force Base during 1971–72. As a result construction there was only about 10 percent complete in May 1972 in contrast to 85 to 90 percent at Grand Forks, North Dakota. While this situation made it easier and cheaper to dismantle the second site, it is very unlikely that the Soviet leaders could conceive of a local labor strike holding up a high-priority national defense task. It is more likely that this action undercut the efforts to impress Moscow with U.S. determination to build four or more, or even two, sites.

129. The best account of these developments, although not accurate in every detail, is in Lawrence Freedman, *US Intelligence and the Soviet Strategic Threat* (Boulder, Colo.: Westview, 1977), pp. 153–59, 164–67. These signals and the basic data were first published in Raymond L. Garthoff, "SALT and the Soviet Military," *Problems of Communism*, vol. 24 (January–February 1975), pp. 30–31.

In concluding this review of the SALT I negotiations, it is useful to note a few points about the negotiating approaches of the two sides.[130]

The United States had taken the initiative in proposing SALT, but the administration that originated it did not survive to conduct the negotiations. The original American objective in 1966–67 had been crystal clear: to head off extensive ABM deployments of *both* sides so as to constrain the strategic arms race. That objective was readily attained in SALT I—indeed, was clearly attainable in November 1969 when SALT began. But between 1967 and 1969 and after, the American objectives grew. Increasing emphasis was placed on stopping the Soviet buildup in strategic offensive arms, especially the large and potentially counterforce ICBMs. That objective was also achieved, but at a time when it had been outstripped by both technology and American unwillingness to forgo its advantages in MIRVs. The more ambitious efforts to induce reductions in the Soviet arsenal of large missiles was doomed by the one-sided nature of the proposals advanced: the United States offered no comparable sacrifice in its own offensive programs.

The American initiative in starting SALT was one reason, but only one, for the Soviets' passive negotiating approach. The Soviet side in SALT I (and generally in other arms control negotiations, despite many public initiatives in advancing arms control proposals), has preferred to react to American proposals rather than advancing its own first. Some Americans have seen this as a disadvantage, as placing the burden of initiative on the United States. Others (including me) see it on balance as an advantage, as it permits the United States to stake out its preferred approach.

A principal feature—and shortcoming—of the American approach was its inconstancy. For example, the United States constantly shifted its position on ABM levels, showing not only inconsistency and instability, but unreliability. Both sides changed their positions at times, but only the United States went so far as to withdraw proposals once accepted by the other side, such as the NCA-level ABM limitation, or to drop an initiative when the other side unexpectedly expressed a positive interest, as in a complete ABM ban.

One reason for the inconstancy of American negotiating positions was the divergence in objectives within the U.S. government. Most of the key leaders were interested in arms control only secondarily. Kissinger always saw SALT not as a possible means to seek security through arms control, but as a device to gain political bargaining leverage through linkages. This attitude was based on his assumption that the Soviet leaders needed and wanted SALT agreements more than the United States did. Nixon shared this view to a large

---

130. A comprehensive analysis of American and Soviet negotiating techniques, tactics, and strategies in SALT would be very illuminating, but goes beyond the purposes of this study. None yet exists; the best synthesis, apart from the earlier cited sources on the SALT I negotiations, is in *Soviet Diplomacy and Negotiating Behavior: Emerging New Context for U.S. Diplomacy,* Committee Print, Special Studies Series on Foreign Affairs Issues, prepared by the Congressional Research Service, Library of Congress (GPO, 1979), pp. 443–511. See also Garthoff, *International Security,* vol. 1 (1977), pp. 3–24.

extent, but especially over time also came to see SALT as giving him a political high ground as a man of peace to offset his identification with the war in Vietnam. Eventually he saw the SALT agreements as the jewel in his summit crown. Secretary Rogers, Ambassador Smith, and others in the Department of State and ACDA did seek both effective arms control and improved political relations with the Soviet Union. In the Pentagon the JCS remained cautious and suspicious of arms control and preferred minimal constraints that left most options open. At the same time they supported a consistent and straightforward pursuit of limited arms control on an equal basis for the two sides. The technical offices in the Department of Defense, which represented that organization, had very little interest in or sympathy for arms control or for reaching agreements. They preferred to try out a constantly changing series of schemes designed to alter the strategic balance in favor of the United States. Some of their proposals were subtle, but most were embarrassingly obvious, showing no interest in negotiability and little expectation of or desire for agreement. With such a range of colliding aims and constant bureaucratic maneuvering in a shifting political context, it is no wonder the American stance on SALT was erratic.

The attempts by the Nixon administration to claim thorough and scientific preparation of SALT positions were belied by the obvious twists and changes in positions based on internal American political and bureaucratic considerations. One effect was to lead bureaucratic interests in the American government not to accept as final even presidential decisions on SALT positions and policy, as they knew they could often be circumvented or overturned when the next round of decisions was required.

This vacillation in establishing American SALT positions was compounded by the overlay of parallel negotiating channels, with the formal negotiating team not even apprised of the existence or actions of the White House channel.

The combination of self-imposed instability of objectives and positions and uncoordinated negotiations was unfortunate for several reasons. First, it weakened the ability of the United States to pursue a consistent and coherent negotiating strategy with the Soviet Union. While this situation sometimes meant that the Soviet Union could gain unexpected marginal advantages (as on the SLBM limits), it also meant that the Soviet side could not count on knowing which American positions and proposals were serious and firm and which were transient and changeable. That uncertainty led the Soviet side to test U.S. firmness even more than they would otherwise have done, sometimes to the detriment of *Soviet* attainment of its own objectives, as well as to the detriment of progress on mutually advantageous terms.

The Soviets' negotiating strategy was to lay the foundation for their positions in broad principles and then to establish tough initial negotiating positions from which to fall back as it was determined which American positions were firm. While this approach protected the Soviet side from premature or unnecessary concessions and compromises, it meant that serious Soviet concerns were sometimes dismissed by the American side because of the extreme (but often vague) form in which they were presented. Thus, for example, the Soviet concern over American FBS nuclear delivery systems represented, in my judgment, a serious Soviet concern and negotiating objective. Yet the Soviet side was never able to formulate specific negotiating proposals that the American side would see as serious. This observation does not mean that the FBS problem was easily soluble or perhaps soluble at all. It remained to plague the intermediate-range nuclear forces (INF) and START negotiations in 1981–83 and remains an important unresolved issue for the future. Nevertheless, the Soviet side's handling of its case was counterproductive to its own interest and purpose. Similarly, its reticence to provide more data and information on its own military forces reduced its ability to negotiate effectively—a lesson that appears, at least in part, to have been learned. In SALT II the Soviets were more forthcoming.

In some other cases the Soviet side was unduly reticent in identifying its concerns. In such key areas of Soviet weakness as MIRV development the Soviets were afraid to appear too eager and thus give the other side bargaining leverage. They also believed that if the United States showed a serious interest, they could then respond, and that if it did not, probably the United States was not prepared to limit MIRVs.

Finally, the initiative in proposing direct limitations on weaponry was reserved in Moscow to the Ministry of Defense and the General Staff, reporting to the Defense Council. The civilian agencies, principally the Ministry of Foreign Affairs and also the Central Committee staff, participated far more freely, and influentially, in developing Soviet responses to American proposals than in developing Soviet initiatives.

While the American approach was far more flexible—indeed, in some cases too pliable—it was moved more by internal maneuvering within the American government than by the desire to carry out a consistent strategy of negotiation. In other cases the United States was unable to compromise sufficiently to serve its own purposes. The dogged American efforts to gain reductions in the large Soviet ICBMs failed to do more than limit the total to 308. The reason is that while the United States was able to make clear its strong interest (indeed, probably to persuade the Soviets of the high value of *keeping* the SS-9 as a bargaining chip), it was never prepared to offer any reciprocal limitation of American offensive systems of concern to the Soviet Union. Too often the only aim became to fulfill White House National Security Decision Memoranda instructions (for example, limits on ICBM silo dimensions and a definition of heavy missiles that would constrain their size to that of the SS-11), rather than recognizing and facing the fact that the next generation of Soviet ICBMs with MIRVs was already long before decided on and would not be curtailed, especially when the United States was accepting *no* real limitation on its offensive forces in the interim freeze.

The negotiating approaches of the two sides reflected their differing political systems. The United States could act and react quickly and even change its objectives. But it could not do what the Soviets did in staking out stiff initial positions and then suddenly backing far off to a compromise—there were too many voices in the U.S. bureaucracy, the Congress, and the public (through uncontrolled press leaks) ready to jump on any substantial compromises as a sellout. Many Americans who would have liked to emulate the Russians in taking tough positions have failed to realize that the concomitant is a Soviet ability, when the positions of the two sides have been tested and established and areas of possible congruence scouted out, to make sweeping compromises. Too often in SALT (and more generally) when the Americans should have attempted to build bargaining room into their negotiating positions, advocates of a position would staunchly insist on maintaining it when the time was ripe to bargain it away.

When the United States did make a major fallback, it went too far. With the May 20, 1971, agreement it abandoned the attempt to negotiate a comprehensive strategic defensive (antiballistic missile) and offensive agreement. Nixon and Kissinger presented the May agreement to the rest of the American government as a fait accompli. This tactic was the way they chose out of the difficulty of having to decide on less extreme changes in position. But there were other alternatives between standing pat on an unacceptable proposal, as the American delegation was instructed to do from August 4, 1970, to May 20, 1971, and abandoning that approach altogether. Given that Nixon and Kissinger were unwilling to make the necessary difficult decisions on MIRV and FBS, something like the May 1971 change became necessary. But in choosing that option, they did not calculate the effects on future SALT negotiations on offensive limitations or on irretrievable opportunities for a comprehensive agreement; rather, they saw it as a salvage operation to meet a political need.

Kissinger has described the trade-off of Soviet offensive limitations for American ABM limitations in the May 1971 agreement as reflecting "the essential balance of incentives" that produced SALT I.[131] To the extent this is true it is an indictment of the Kissinger-Nixon approach to SALT. The balance of incentives should have involved offsetting strategically significant Soviet and American offensive limitations, including MIRV, with any marginal American advantage derivable from its stronger ABM system a secondary consideration. Instead, the result was an interim offensive agreement that limited the United States not at all, and the Soviet Union inconsequentially. It did not succeed in limiting both sides in a way that contributed to curbing the strategic arms race. Moreover, the United States was postponing serious efforts at offensive arms limitations at a time when it was launching a major new MIRV buildup that the Soviet Union was bound to match. One effect was seriously to prejudice future SALT efforts, dooming them to the marginal limitations eventually reached in SALT II seven years later. The limited value of that treaty reduced the support from advocates of arms limitation.

Kissinger, reflecting in his memoir the extensive self-praise found in the Nixon administration's annual presidential foreign policy reports and

---

131. Kissinger, *White House Years*, p. 208.

speeches at that time, presents an idealized account of the American negotiating strategy. It does not, however, stand up to the record, as many other passages in Kissinger's own account and those of Ambassador Smith and others demonstrate. In a more matter-of-fact offhand remark in his memoir on the later SALT II preparations, Kissinger refers back to the American "experience of SALT I, in which we had clarified our thinking as we went along."[132] That is a much more accurate description, although it still does not acknowledge the powerful impact of the internal political-bureaucratic considerations that dominated decisions such as the one not to seek a MIRV ban, but instead to present a proposal known to be unacceptable.

The parallel negotiations were carried to an absurd and counterproductive extreme in May 1972 when Ambassador Smith and the American SALT delegation were kept in Helsinki while Nixon and Kissinger grappled with unfamiliar issues.[133] One sentence from a private Kissinger back channel message to Smith at the height of those fractured negotiations shows this well: "You should understand that we are operating in a situation where we never know from hour to hour with whom we are meeting or what the topic will be. I will inform you as soon as we have something."[134] When they did "have something," the Soviets suddenly insisted that the agreements *must* be signed that very day, and Nixon and Kissinger acquiesced even though there was no time to prepare the final texts properly.[135]

And so the negotiations of SALT I were concluded on May 26, and the agreements were signed in the Kremlin shortly before midnight.[136]

The SALT I Agreements

The ABM Treaty represented a major arms control achievement that effectively limited ballistic missile defense to a strategically insignificant

---

132. Henry Kissinger, *Years of Upheaval* (Boston, Mass.: Little, Brown, 1982), p. 264.

133. Kissinger acknowledges in his memoir the error of keeping the delegations away from Moscow, but he still fails to recognize the extent to which their expertise and knowledge of the negotiating record could have helped produce a better result. He candidly states: "In retrospect it would have been better to have brought both delegations to Moscow and let them continue their work there in synchronization with the summit. Given Nixon's feelings about who should get credit, I doubt that he would have agreed if I had proposed it. We shall never know because I did not put forward the idea, not uninfluenced by vanity and the desire to control the final negotiation." Kissinger, *White House Years*, p. 1230.

134. Quoted by Smith, *Doubletalk*, p. 417.

135. Kissinger, *White House Years*, p. 1241. Earlier, when the negotiations were in their final stage, Gromyko and Kissinger had tentatively agreed to slip the signing for two days. Ibid., p. 1239.

136. A number of the ideas in the following section are drawn from Raymond L. Garthoff, "SALT I: An Evaluation," *World Politics*, vol. 31 (October 1978), pp. 1–25.

deployment. It contributed to containing one important area of arms competition by heading off a race in ballistic missile defense. It may also have restrained to some extent the continuing race in strategic offensive arms, though less than was hoped and less than it should have.

The "Interim Agreement on Certain Measures With Respect to Strategic Offensive Arms" was a much more limited accomplishment. It did place a loose cap on the numbers of strategic offensive missile launchers, and it led the Soviet Union to level off the number of ICBMs and to retire some older ICBM systems earlier than they would probably have done otherwise. But it did not limit MIRVs and a new race in multiplying missile warheads, and it did not limit qualitative missile improvements, including increased accuracy. It also did not limit aircraft or cruise missile systems. By limiting only ballistic missiles, it directed increased attention to them. The failure to limit the main developments impelling the strategic offensive arms competition in an interim agreement was, to be sure, only an interim failure. SALT II was intended to lead to a comprehensive strategic offensive arms agreement of indefinite duration to parallel the ABM Treaty.

The Interim Agreement was, however, a crucial failure. Both military-technological and later domestic U.S. and international political developments kept SALT II from success, and at least in retrospect it seems clear that a more serious effort should have been made in SALT I to deal with the complex of offensive arms issues, and above all with MIRV limitations. Both sides shared in this failure.

SALT I did show that strategic arms limitation agreements could be negotiated, notwithstanding the military, technical, security, political, and ideological differences between the two sides. It also contributed to a strategic dialogue to a limited degree, although not to the extent it could have. It did improve mutual understanding on at least some issues and for some time, although it did not dispel all suspicions or prevent later massive strategic misunderstandings.

The agreements to reduce the risks of accidental war and to upgrade the Washington-Moscow direct communications link contributed to crisis prevention and management. A Standing Consultative Commission was established that provides a forum for consultation on implementing procedures and questions on compliance, and potentially is available for other consultations. Acceptance and assurance of national means of verification, that is, of unilateral means of strategic reconnaissance such as observation space satellites, were buttressed by the formal obligation not to interfere with those means. This accomplishment was of major significance to arms control in assuring verification and was of political significance as well.

In retrospect, it is clear that the SALT I accords could have been greatly strengthened by the inclusion of a ban on antisatellite (ASAT) weapons. Neither side proposed a ban or even raised the matter. Yet agreement could probably have been reached at that time, heading off a later cycle of ASAT development by both sides. It would have contributed to a stronger ABM restraint, since ASATs have potential ABM capability. It might even have been used to press for a complete ABM ban, since the United States had an operational ASAT deployment at that time and the Soviets did not, while the Soviet Union had its operational ABM deployment at Moscow and the United States had none. Moreover, the United States was by then moving unilaterally to close down its deployed ASAT system.[137] The Soviet military, however, saw the American ASAT deployment as providing a serious capability that the Soviet Union must match.[138] But this window of opportunity for negotiating an ASAT ban was missed.[139]

Inclusion of a ban on antisatellite weapons in the ABM Treaty would have considerably strengthened ABM restraints, since ASAT systems inherently have potential antiballistic missile capabilities. But perhaps it could have meant even much more. A proposal to dismantle the existing operational American ASAT complex at Johnston Island (and the defunct one at Kwajalein) could have been tied to a proposal for Soviet dismantling of the operational ABM complex at Moscow—each side would dismantle its existing operational sites in a complete ABM-ASAT ban on deployment. As both an extension and reinforcement of such a deployment ban, a ban on testing of all ABM and ASAT systems could have been included. The operational American ASAT system in 1969–72 met the classic test of a "bargaining chip": something that appeared to the other side to be an unmatched asset and threat, while to the United States it was marginal and only maintained on a standby status. The United States had a position of strength from which to negotiate and a bargaining chip that it was prepared to cash in to reach reciprocal arms limits. Thus the American ASAT could have been used to induce Soviet agreement to an ASAT ban as part of the SALT I ABM Treaty. Since the Soviets saw the American operational and future capabilities as formidable and their own ASAT program not doing well in tests, they had substantial incentives to agree to a ban—but they believed they were in too weak a position to propose one. Responsible Soviet officials have recently told me they would have jumped at an ASAT ban in 1972. And the Soviet ASAT satellite-interception tests of 1968 through 1971 provided an incentive to the United States to agree to an ASAT ban before the Soviet Union developed a capability.

137. The United States had belatedly recognized the disadvantages to its own military posture of high-altitude near-space nuclear detonations and the high costs of continued maintenance of its Program 437 ASAT four-launcher complex at Johnston Island. In October 1970 the entire complex was placed on a standby status that required thirty days to reactivate operational interception capability. On April 1, 1975, the entire program was terminated.

138. Notwithstanding the actual state of the American ASAT program as noted above, the confidential Soviet General Staff organ *Military Thought* in April 1972 described the Thor system on Johnston Island (and an earlier American ASAT based on the Nike Zeus missile, Program 505, at Kwajalein Atoll, which had been deactivated as an operational system in 1967) as "existing, active operational systems," and noted American research and development on more advanced systems. See Major General M. Cherednichenko, "Scientific-Technical Progress and the Development of Armaments and Military Technology," *Voyennaya mysl'* [Military Thought], no. 4 (April 1972), pp. 35–36.

139. For later efforts at ASAT control, see chapter 22.

A complete ban on testing and deploying any ABM or ASAT systems would have been a powerful, mutually reinforcing, and verifiable arms control measure. Of course, an ABM, ASAT, *and MIRV* ban in 1969–72 would have made a major change in the whole strategic and arms control horizon.

In all, the recognition of the futility and risks of an unconstrained strategic arms race by the two powers, and the launching of a forum and basis for continuing strategic arms limitation measures, were substantial accomplishments. Strategic arms control also entered the national security planning process in both countries and brought their political leaderships into closer involvement in military security planning.

Particularly on the Soviet side, although also on the American side, the SALT I agreements both reflected and further contributed to the consolidation of acceptance of mutual deterrence and strategic parity. Concepts of parity, equal security, and strategic stability were accepted by both sides, although there were important and deep differences in perspective, evaluation, and application. These remained to be confronted in subsequent strategic arms negotiations, as well as in national security evaluations and decisions by each side.

Nixon and Kissinger accepted the general concepts of parity and sufficiency and sought to have SALT contribute to strategic stability. They were both, however, very skeptical of arms control as a means of establishing greater stability and relied much more on political strategies. They were also disinclined to foreclose American military options and were moved more by domestic political-bureaucratic pressures than by arms control considerations. Nonetheless, Nixon did state that a "major effect of the ABM treaty was to make permanent the concept of deterrence through 'mutual terror': by giving up missile defenses, each side was leaving its population and territory hostage to a strategic missile attack. Each side therefore had an ultimate interest in preventing a war that could only be mutually destructive."[140] Kissinger also on occasion embraced the doctrine of mutual deterrence, acknowledging that "perhaps the single most important component of our policy toward the Soviet Union is the effort to limit strategic weapons competition" in view of the unprecedented historic situation in which "each side has the capacity to destroy civilization as we know it." He went on to conclude that the SALT I agreements "represent a major contribution to strategic stability," as well as a significant step toward further arms limitations.[141]

Remarkably, in the Senate debates on the SALT I agreements, the basic arms control purposes and effects of the agreements, and the doctrinal question of mutual vulnerability implied by the ABM Treaty, were never really raised. The SALT I agreements of 1972 constituted a substantial step in

---

140. Nixon, *RN*, pp. 617–18.

141. Kissinger, "Detente with the Soviet Union: The Reality of Competition and the Imperative of Cooperation," Statement to the Senate Committee on Foreign Relations, September 19, *State Bulletin*, vol. 71 (October 14, 1974), pp. 512, 513.

strategic arms control, although an incomplete one owing to the weak constraints involved in the interim freeze on strategic offensive missiles and the unresolved differences on the whole complex of offensive systems. In addition, they contributed to a reduction of tensions and to the launching of a political détente between the United States and the Soviet Union.

SALT I and Détente, 1972

If the opening of the SALT I negotiations in 1969 represented a trial run or testing ground for "an era of negotiations," the SALT I agreements of 1972 were presented as the centerpiece of the summit meeting of the American and Soviet leaders that inaugurated détente between the two countries. The central symbolic political role of SALT had not been envisaged by Nixon and Kissinger in 1969, although during 1970 and 1971 SALT was increasingly seen as an important element in the strategy of détente they were fashioning. By 1972 success of SALT was also seen as an important political asset to President Nixon as he ran for reelection. It also benefited General Secretary Brezhnev, as he consolidated both his own power and the Soviet policy of détente. But although such transient (though not at the time unimportant) factors contributed to achieving the SALT and summit successes, far more important in the long run were the effects of SALT on the development of American-Soviet relations, and specifically on the development of the détente of the 1970s. As Kissinger stated in 1974 in one of his major articulations of American policy on détente, "When linked to such broad and unprecedented projects as SALT, detente takes on added meaning and opens prospects of a more stable peace. SALT agreements should be seen as steps in a [détente] process leading to progressively greater stability. It is in that light that SALT and related projects will be judged by history."[142]

SALT, and specifically the SALT I negotiations from 1969 to 1972 and the SALT I agreements, lent emphasis and gave substance to a trend of improving relations and using negotiation as a substitute for confrontation— precisely what was needed *because* of continuing competition. Within a few years this trend was to be reversed by other developments, discussed later in this study, but it is nevertheless significant as an indication of what can be done to mitigate continuing competition.

In the immediate run, notwithstanding the hyperbolic praise of the SALT agreements from Nixon and Kissinger at the time—which unduly inflated public expectations—their real expectations were much more modest and restrained. As Kissinger states, "SALT also gave us the opportunity to determine whether detente was a tactic or a new turn in Soviet policy."[143] It also served mundane aims of halting the Soviet buildup of ICBM launchers

---

142. Ibid., pp. 515–16, and the reference to détente as this process on p. 518.

143. Kissinger, *White House Years*, p. 1245.

without constraining the U.S. buildup of MIRVs. As noted earlier, while this situation was temporarily advantageous in military and political terms, it was disadvantageous in the longer run because it would not later constrain the *Soviet* buildup in MIRV systems in the latter half of the 1970s while SALT II dragged on.

The overselling of SALT began with comments by Nixon and Kissinger in Moscow, but more significant were the euphoric terms used by President Nixon in a dramatic address to a joint session of the Congress immediately upon his return to Washington. He began by stating:

Three-fifths of all the people alive in the world today have spent their whole lifetimes under the shadow of a nuclear war which could be touched off by the arms race among the great powers. Last Friday in Moscow we witnessed the beginning of the end of that era which began in 1945. We took the first step toward a new era of mutually agreed restraint and arms limitation between the two principal nuclear nations.

With this step we have enhanced the security of both nations. We have begun to check the wasteful and dangerous spiral of nuclear arms which has dominated relations between our two countries for a generation. We have begun to reduce the level of fear by reducing the causes of fear, for our two peoples and for all peoples in the world.[144]

Kissinger, in a special briefing to congressional leaders introduced by the president himself, stated the administration's strategy of détente and the role of SALT. He said that the president had from the outset "decided that the United States should work to create a set of circumstances which would offer the Soviet leaders an opportunity to move away from confrontation through carefully prepared negotiations" in SALT and "to create a vested interest in mutual restraint." Similarly he described the SALT policy process (in rather idealized terms) as part of a "broad design of what the President has been trying to achieve in this country's relations with the Soviet Union," claiming that "at each important turning point in the SALT negotiations we were guided not so much by the tactical solution that seemed most equitable or prudent, important as it was, but by an underlying philosophy and a specific perception of international reality." As a result of this approach, by the time of the SALT I agreements three years later it was said:

The SALT agreement does not stand alone, isolated and incongruous in the relationship of hostility, vulnerable at any moment to the shock of some sudden crisis. It stands, rather, linked organically to a chain of agreements and to a broad understanding about international conduct appropriate to the dangers of the nuclear age.

The agreements on the limitation of strategic arms is, thus, not merely a technical [arms control] accomplishment, although it is that in part, but it must be seen as a political event of some magnitude.[145]

---

144. "The President's Address to a Joint Session of the Congress at the Conclusion of His Trip to Austria, the Soviet Union, Iran, and Poland," June 1, *Presidential Documents*, vol. 8 (June 5, 1972), p. 977.

145. "President Nixon and Dr. Kissinger Brief Members of Congress on Strategic Arms Limitation Agreements," June 15, *State Bulletin*, vol. 67 (July 10, 1972), pp. 40, 42.

To be sure, not all American statements stressed the political achievement and the political promise of the SALT agreements. On the day the SALT agreements were signed, while Secretary of Defense Laird described them as "major first steps in limiting strategic arms competition," he also stressed that they were "made possible only by the United States' determination to negotiate from a position of strength. . . . Indeed, they were only possible because of U.S. strength." And he proceeded on this belligerent note to stress that "we still need to keep up our guard" and then announced a major new program of "modernization and improvement" of U.S. strategic forces, including "an acceleration of the Trident" submarine program.[146] While a little heavy-handed, Laird's stress on pushing ahead with a strategic arms buildup was fully supported by Nixon and Kissinger.

On the Soviet side, the SALT I agreements were widely praised as, in Brezhnev's words, "the first agreements in history concretely limiting the most modern and powerful weapons." Brezhnev also stressed the need to build on the agreements so as to convert the Interim Agreement into a permanent one, to place qualitative as well as quantitative limits on strategic arms, and to move from limitations to gradual reductions.[147]

The official Soviet Ministry of Foreign Affairs spokesman (writing in *Pravda* under a pseudonym) declared: "In the history of international relations it is difficult to find another example of such fruitful results achieved through negotiations."[148] The Soviets, too, saw SALT as the leading edge in moving toward an era of negotiation. They also saw it as tied to acceptance by the United States of peaceful coexistence. Another leading Soviet commentator described the SALT I agreements as one of the "practical results" of the acceptance of the principle of peaceful coexistence.[149]

The Soviets have thus seen SALT as both an important arms control process and, especially the SALT I ABM Treaty, as resulting in important arms control achievements. They have also stressed its importance in both Soviet-American political and security relationships. Thus, for example, the official *History of the Foreign Policy of the Soviet Union* discusses SALT not in the section on disarmament, but in the section on Soviet-American rela-

---

146. "Transcript of Secretary Laird's Interview by Newsman at Andrews AFB," Department of State Telegram, May 29, 1972, p. 2.

147. L. I. Brezhnev, *O vneshnei politike KPSS i sovetskogo gosudarstva: Rechi i stat'i* [On the Foreign Policy of the CPSU and the Soviet Government: Speeches and Articles], 3d ed. (Moscow: Politizdat, 1978), p. 259.

148. Yu. Chernov, "A Real Force in International Development," *Pravda*, June 15, 1972. "Yu. Chernov" is a pseudonym for Yury Chernyakov, the press spokesman for the Ministry of Foreign Affairs.

149. S. Beglov, "An Important Step in the Realization of the Peace Program," *Sovetskaya rossiya* [Soviet Russia], June 20, 1972.

tions.[150] Some Soviet observers have seen SALT as "the determining factor in Soviet-American relations."[151]

The Soviets have, especially since 1976, emphasized the need to advance détente further into the military sphere, in particular through arms control. The SALT I agreements have been praised as the first major achievements in military détente. Vladimir Petrovsky, for example, has described as "an act of great state wisdom" "the joint decision" of both the Soviet and American governments to "close the channel of an arms race" in ABM systems with its potential for "a dangerous destabilization of the international strategic situation." He refers to the SALT process as involving an important "mutual dialogue on strategic arms issues." Stressing the important place in Soviet-American relations of the problem of containing the arms race, he describes the SALT I agreements as "among the most important joint Soviet-American documents" and as "measures of military détente, concrete steps to reduce military confrontation." They "affect the very core of the military might of the two countries" and "establish the equal balance of the strategic forces of the USSR and the US." But they are also "acts of great political force, convincingly demonstrating that the USSR and the US not only must, but can, jointly undertake concrete measures to reduce the military threat."[152]

Of particular significance to the Soviet leaders was the implicit but strong endorsement of parity by the United States in SALT. As noted earlier,[153] the Soviets have seen parity as the foundation for SALT, and American acceptance of parity was a major result of the SALT agreements. One leading Soviet commentator has seen American recognition of parity with the Soviet Union as "the very essence" of the SALT agreements.[154]

While the American acceptance of parity implied by SALT meant American willingness to accept that its superiority was waning, Soviet deliberations on SALT also precipitated consideration of future prospects for the Soviet political and military relationship. It helped to crystallize a Soviet decision to accept parity for the foreseeable future and to seek through SALT to stabilize the strategic military balance. This also contributed to the Soviet decision to pursue a policy of détente.

---

150. See A. A. Gromyko and B. N. Ponomarev, eds., *Istoriya vneshnei politiki SSSR, 1917–1980* [History of the Foreign Policy of the USSR, 1917–1980], vol. 2, 4 ed. (Moscow: Nauka, 1981), pp. 494–95, 606. This discussion was similarly located in the earlier editions.

151. See A. Arbatov, *Bezopasnost' v yadernyi vek i politika Vashingtona* [Security in the Nuclear Age and Washington's Policy] (Moscow: Politizdat, 1980), p. 214.

152. V. F. Petrovsky, "The Role and Place of Soviet-American Relations in the Contemporary World," *Voprosy istorii* [Questions of History], no. 10 (October 1978), pp. 88, 89. Petrovsky is a senior official in the Ministry of Foreign Affairs.

153. See chapter 2.

154. G. A. Trofimenko, "The Principal Postulates of American Foreign Policy and the Fate of Détente," *SShA: Ekonomika, politika, ideologiya,* [USA: Economics, Politics, Ideology], no. 7 (July 1981), p. 8.

While the history of the Soviet decision to enter the SALT talks remains shrouded in secrecy, knowledgeable Soviet officials have privately indicated that the initial decision in 1967 was not to enter the talks at that time, but not to reject the American proposal for such talks. (There were also advocates for these alternatives—to begin talks in 1967, or to reject the idea.) In May 1968 the decision was made to proceed with SALT, although knowledgeable senior Soviet officials have commented that there were serious debates in the Politburo on the question of tying Soviet national security to agreements with the leading imperialist power. A later disputed issue was giving up defense of the Soviet land and people against a possible ballistic missile attack.[155] Even as late as the November–December 1969 preliminary SALT round, the question of future participation was open and was only approved by the Politburo and Central Committee in late December 1969. In 1971 and 1972 key Politburo decisions on SALT were often close, although after the Twenty-fifth Party Congress and Brezhnev's successful bid for a policy of détente toward the United States and his enhanced political power, much of the high-level SALT backup in Moscow apparently shifted to the Defense Council, already under his chairmanship. Even then, Brezhnev felt it necessary to defend his SALT policy publicly. Notably, in his election speech of June 11, 1971, he found it necessary to argue that despite capitalist hostility it was possible and prudent for the Soviet Union to negotiate on and agree to strategic arms limitations. "The struggle for disarmament," he said, "is a complex matter." But he stated that the Peace Program and disarmament proposals endorsed at the party congress were not "propaganda slogans, but slogans for action, reflecting political goals, which in our epoch are becoming more and more attainable." (That statement was followed, according to the official transcript, by "extended applause.") And while he described the negotiation of a strategic arms limitation as difficult, he guardedly said, "I would like to hope that the government of the United States will adopt a constructive approach."[156]

During the negotiations the American delegation learned to expect that major new Soviet moves would be keyed to the usual weekly (Thursday) Politburo meetings. SALT issues required at least four Politburo meetings during the week of the 1972 summit conference.[157] The continuing SALT process no doubt contributed to the rise of the national security clique represented by the addition of Defense Council members Defense Minister Marshal Andrei A. Grechko (and his successor Marshal Dmitry F. Ustinov), Foreign

---

155. Interviews in the early 1980s with two senior officials, both Central Committee members as well as government officials involved in SALT and Soviet-American relations.

156. Brezhnev, *O vneshnei politike*, pp. 193, 194.

   Kissinger notes that, in contrast to other political matters discussed at the 1972 summit meeting, Brezhnev as chairman of the Defense Council was able to discuss SALT with President Nixon without the participation of other members of the Politburo. Kissinger, *White House Years*, p. 1214.

157. Interviews with key Soviet officials.

Minister Gromyko, and KGB Chairman Yury V. Andropov to the Politburo in April 1973, and indirectly to the rise of Andropov, with the support of Gromyko and Ustinov, to succeed Brezhnev in November 1982.[158]

In addition to the impact of the SALT process and the SALT I agreements on American and Soviet internal thinking and political-bureaucratic arrangements, and on the development of the political détente between them, brief note should also be made of the wider impact of SALT in the world. In many countries in both Western and Eastern Europe and in politically aware circles in the third world, it was welcomed as a sign of reduced tension. The one notable exception was a cool, if not hostile, reaction from China—the principal country that saw its own security best served by Soviet-American tension.

The SALT process included continuing, close consultation by the United States with its allies, not only to reassure them of the course of this path-breaking negotiation about the arms on which their security also depended, but also to provide a useful forum and focus for a discussion of the evolving Soviet-American strategic relationship. Although not so designed or even consciously recognized at the time, SALT provided a cushion for allied acceptance of the transition from American superiority to strategic parity between the two superpowers. It allowed a balanced consideration quite different from the usual annual and ad hoc assessments of the Soviet and Warsaw Pact threat. Typically those assessments were couched in terms of an input into decisions about defense programming by the alliance, and inevitably they accented Soviet military strengths in that context so as to provide a supporting rationale that would mobilize opinion in favor of military improvements within the alliance.

Briefings for the North Atlantic Council had begun as early as March 1967, when the United States was first proposing SALT. During the period from January 1969 through June 1972 there were forty-five oral or written communications on SALT to the council in Brussels, including twenty-two visits by senior representatives of the American SALT delegation, who met with the council, and an additional six meetings with experts of the NATO countries that went into greater detail.[159]

---

158. For a useful discussion of Brezhnev's use of the Defense Council as a separate channel of decisionmaking and its change over time, see Harry Gelman, *The Brezhnev Politburo and the Decline of Detente* (Ithaca, N.Y.: Cornell University Press, 1984), pp. 63–69.

159. I participated in almost all these briefings, conducting eight of them, and can attest to their value and the appreciation of the allies. The frequent briefing and consultation continued with SALT II and later with the INF and START negotiations.

Mention should also be made of a relevant and useful NATO study. In 1967–68 the NATO Nuclear Planning Group, stimulated by the American ABM program, examined the question of possible ABM deployment by NATO. The consensus of that study, completed by April 1968, was not to deploy an ABM in Europe. Both that conclusion and the very fact of the joint study greatly facilitated support by the alliance for U.S. negotiation of the ABM Treaty.

The SALT experiment in launching an era of negotiation was thus quite successful. As viewed generally, and especially by the leaders in Washington and Moscow, it was a major substantive achievement in the central area of security and arms control that complemented a wide range of other accords that were reached at the time of the first American-Soviet summit meeting in 1972.

Before that event is discussed, another major geopolitical element affecting American-Soviet relations requires examination. If SALT was the main strand in bilateral negotiation, the development of triangular diplomacy among the United States, the Soviet Union, and the People's Republic of China was the main strand in global politics at the same juncture, 1969 to 1972. It was even more complex.

6 Establishing Triangular Diplomacy: China and American-Soviet Relations, 1969–72

IF THE PERIOD 1969 to 1972 saw a notable change in relations of the United States with the Soviet Union, it witnessed an even more remarkable transformation in American relations with China. With the USSR the United States had a fairly lengthy history of alternating good and bad relations. But it would not even officially admit the legitimate existence of the People's Republic of China (PRC), and for two decades the relationship had been one of unremitting isolation and confrontation. Now with the geopoliticization of American foreign policy under Nixon and his national security adviser, Kissinger, the United States saw advantages to bringing China into the global political arena and in establishing direct relations. As it happened, there was a conjunction of interests, as the Chinese leadership also decided both to end its self-isolation in the world community and to move to direct relations with the United States.

The relationships between the United States and the Soviet Union, and between China and the Soviet Union, played an important part in the development of Sino-U.S. political contact. Similarly, internal political developments—including the need to overcome long-standing orthodoxies of opposition—were involved in both countries, as well as calculations of geopolitical gain. Still, the circumstances and reasons of the two countries differed greatly, despite a common interest in containing Soviet power. While in retrospect it appears almost inevitable that both China and the United States would have seen the advantages of improved relations, politics is often moved more by factors other than logic, and there was nothing foreordained about Sino-American détente.

A number of specific developments in Chinese politics, American policymaking, and Soviet policy intersected from the latter part of 1968 through 1972 in leading to the establishment of a pattern of triangular diplomacy among the three powers. The threads of this development, some obvious, some quite obscure, must be woven together to understand what happened and why, and to appreciate the significance of these developments for the evolution of American-Soviet relations in the 1970s.

Sino-Soviet Relations

The most appropriate starting point is the long-worsening conflict between China and the Soviet Union. The best-known event in Sino-Soviet relations in this period, indeed in a span covering nearly the entire decade before and the one following, was the dramatic eruption of a series of armed clashes on the Sino-Soviet border from March to September 1969.[1] Although the dispute between the two countries had reached the level of conflict almost a decade earlier, in this instance the clashes awakened American awareness of the depth of the hostility between the two communist powers. This sharpened conflict also clearly reduced the ability of either country to devote its energies to countering American interests. Beyond that, to imaginative policy planners the conflict offered opportunities for increasing American political leverage with one or the other or, optimally, both. But that potential could not be realized while the United States had no contact with China.

An event a year before the border clashes really triggered not only the worsening of Sino-Soviet relations, but also the rethinking in Beijing (Peking) that led China to turn toward the United States. This event was the Soviet military occupation of Czechoslovakia in August 1968. The Chinese leaders were clearly concerned about the possibility that the Soviet leaders would seek to apply the so-called Brezhnev Doctrine—the right to intervene in another socialist state to preserve true socialism from alleged counterrevolutionary threats—to China. Their concern was, however, broader and not focused on an immediate threat to China. Rather, they feared further Soviet military intervention elsewhere in Eastern Europe. Immediately after the occupation of Czechoslovakia Zhou Enlai attended the annual National Day celebration at the Romanian embassy in Beijing on August 23 and pointedly assured Romania of China's support. Of particular interest was his calling the Soviet intervention in Czechoslovakia an act of "collusion" with the United States designed to divide the world. He reasoned that American acquiescence

---

1. The best comprehensive analysis of the border conflict in the context of the overall development of Sino-Soviet relations from late 1968 to 1972 is Richard Wich, *Sino-Soviet Crisis Politics: A Study of Political Change and Communication* (Cambridge, Mass.: Harvard University Press, 1980). As the subtitle indicates, this book is particularly keyed to analysis of the underlying significance of various statements and other signals the two countries were sending in their political interaction.

in this Soviet action meant that the Soviet Union must acquiesce in American control of South Vietnam.[2]

At the same time, the United States was issuing parallel veiled warnings against any further Soviet military intervention in Eastern Europe; of particular concern were Romania and Yugoslavia. These warnings foreshadowed the later recognition of common Chinese and American interests in curbing Soviet expansion.

Beyond the expressions of Chinese support for Romania, China signaled in another way its new policy toward Eastern Europe and the reform movement within the fragmenting world communist movement. Beginning the very day after the Soviet occupation of Czechoslovakia, Beijing ceased its time-honored polemical attacks on Yugoslavia.

Other communist parties, including those of Italy and France from the day of the Soviet occupation of Czechoslovakia, strongly denounced Moscow's action. The Chinese saw there a new basis for curtailing Soviet influence and expanding their own within the international communist movement. On September 2 Zhou Enlai again selected an appropriate occasion—the National Day of North Vietnam—to elaborate further the evolving Chinese policy. He asserted that a "socialist camp" no longer existed. He again argued that the Soviet intervention in Czechoslovakia, which North Vietnam had supported, meant that in return the United States would demand a higher price in Vietnam and that the Soviet Union would accede.[3]

After Czechoslovakia, the Chinese launched a new campaign of polemics against "social imperialism," as Soviet expansionism was now termed. No longer did they attack just ideological revisionism; instead, they also began to make common cause with Romania, Yugoslavia, and, in due course, the Eurocommunist revisionists whom they had previously reviled.

In China itself the "Great Proletarian Cultural Revolution" was still under way. On September 5, 1968, the last two provincial Revolutionary Committees were established, significantly in Xinjiang (Sinkiang) and Tibet.

---

2. For the text of Zhou Enlai's speech, see "Chinese Government and People Strongly Condemn Soviet Revisionist Clique's Armed Occupation of Czechoslovakia," *Peking Review*, vol. 11 (August 23, 1968), supplement, p. iv.

   Zhou Enlai more often referred to American-Soviet relations as a combination of "colluding" *and* "contending"; he and other moderates argued that the element of contention between the two superpowers gave China an opening to play them off against one another—if China took that opening. Others in the radical political faction, and in the military, still regarded the United States as the chief threat and therefore opposed the moderates' move to establish ties to the United States in order to gain leverage for triangular diplomatic maneuver. For the original and most complete exposition of this thesis, see Thomas R. Gottlieb, *Chinese Foreign Policy Factionalism and the Origin of the Strategic Triangle*, R-1902-NA, prepared for the Office of the Secretary of Defense (Santa Monica, Calif.: Rand Corp., 1977).

3. For the text of Zhou Enlai's speech, see "Premier Chou En-lai Makes Important Speech," *Peking Review*, vol. 11 (September 6, 1968), pp. 6–7.

The report from Xinjiang stressed its extremely important strategic position in the struggle against Soviet revisionism, U.S. imperialism, and Indian reactionaries.[4]

Some elements within the Chinese leadership concluded that it was time to reestablish (or at least to be seen to be reestablishing) minimum contact with the United States. This approach was not, however, unanimously favored in Beijing; in fact, some leaders opposed it. On November 25, 1968, the Chinese chargé d'affaires in Warsaw proposed to the American embassy a meeting on February 20, 1969. The Chinese made the offer public the next day.[5] Radio Beijing also referred, for the first time since China had initiated its international isolationism during the Cultural Revolution in 1965, to the Five Principles of Coexistence.[6] China was clearly signaling its return to the world stage.

The most significant Chinese move in response to the Soviet intervention in Czechoslovakia was also the most perplexing: an escalation of the border tension by precipitating a major armed clash on March 2, 1969.

The Sino-Soviet frontier had long been a source of dispute, and as relations between the two countries deteriorated sharply from 1959 to 1964, the border issue was magnified. Incidents had been occurring from time to time, especially on the Central Asian border. Although negotiations on the border issue had been undertaken, the Chinese had broken them off in 1964. This unsettled situation continued throughout the 1960s. Then during the first two months of 1969 there was an upsurge in incidents, as both sides patrolled the disputed areas more vigorously. One such place, called Damansky Island by the Russians and Zhenbao by the Chinese, was involved in eight incidents in the first two months of 1969—as many as in the whole of 1968. While not populated, this was one of the larger of the several hundred disputed islands, many of which had formed as the rivers that marked the border changed course after the original boundaries had been agreed to.

The Chinese of course blamed all the clashes on the USSR, and vice versa. On the basis of the fragmentary information available, however, it is impossible to know in most cases whether the Chinese or the Soviets were most responsible for any one of the many incidents that summer, which both sides said numbered in the hundreds. In this instance, though, careful studies have led Western scholars to conclude that the clash on March 2 resulted from a

4. Xinhua [New China News Agency; hereafter NCNA], Radio Urumchi, September 6, 1968, in Foreign Broadcast Information Service, *Daily Report: China*, September 9, 1968, p. E1. (Hereafter FBIS, *China*.)

5. For reasons discussed later, that meeting, although agreed upon, was not held. It would have been the 135th in a series of meetings begun in 1955 but suspended a few years earlier.

6. Xinhua [NCNA], Beijing Radio, November 26, 1968, in FBIS, *China*, November 26, 1968, p. A2; and "Statement by Spokesman of Information Department of Chinese Foreign Ministry," *Peking Review*, vol. 11 (November 29, 1968), pp. 30–31.

planned Chinese ambush. Thirty-one Russians, including the patrol commander, were killed. On March 15 there was another clash, this time evidently
precipitated by the Russians; it involved much larger forces, and both sides lost
larger numbers of men. During the following months literally hundreds of
incidents occurred at many places along the border, including especially serious
engagements on the Xinjiang-Kazakhstan border in August.[7]

The Chinese decision to raise the level of confrontation in March
may have reflected internal political calculations. The border clashes were certainly used to stir up widespread patriotic demonstrations in China (allegedly
400 million participated), and they certainly confirmed that Chinese policy was
on an anti-Soviet track. They may also have been intended to dissuade the
Soviet leaders from further intervention in Eastern Europe.[8] Moreover, the
initial clash preceded only by days a major meeting of world communist parties
in Moscow. The timing may also have been synchronized to coincide with a
visit to India by Marshal Andrei Grechko, the Soviet minister of defense.[9]

Following the March battles the Chinese began to stress a new
theme in their propaganda and polemics: the Soviet leaders were now termed
"the new tsars,"[10] a label that further stressed the Chinese claim that the
Soviet Union had become an aggressive expansionist state, rather than being
merely ideologically errant and domineering.

While the Soviets retaliated against the first Chinese military action forcefully, they did not use the opportunity to escalate military pressure
on China. On March 21, soon after the exchange of attacks at Damansky
Island/Zhenbao, Prime Minister Kosygin tried to reach the Chinese leaders by
telephone. The Chinese refused to make the connection, replying by memorandum that the Soviets should use normal diplomatic channels.[11] On March

---

7. There is a considerable literature analyzing the 1969 Sino-Soviet border conflict. A good summary analysis is Thomas W. Robinson, "The Sino-Soviet Border Conflict," in Stephen S. Kaplan, ed., *Diplomacy of Power: Soviet Armed Forces as a Political Instrument* (Brookings Institution, 1981), pp. 265–313. See also Wich, *Sino-Soviet Crisis Politics*, pp. 97–112, 163–92.

8. Whether this was the Chinese purpose or a coincidence, only a few weeks after the March 2
   clash, following riots in Prague, the Soviet leaders definitively removed Dubček from office and
   installed Gustav Husák as head of the party in Czechoslovakia. This was the culminating act in
   the recapture of the Czech party and government after the Soviet occupation.

9. Chinese army units in Tibet near the Indian border were also reported publicly to have demonstrated in protest over the clash.

10. On April 18 a documentary film entitled "Anti-China Atrocities of the New Tsars" began
    showing in Beijing. The term was by then used constantly in the Chinese press.

11. This astonishing episode became known when it was derisively disclosed by Marshal Lin Biao
    at the Ninth Party Congress on April 1, 1969. Nixon mentions in his memoir "an amusing
    story" that Zhou Enlai told him at the 1972 summit meeting: after the 1969 border clash,
    Kosygin tried to call first Mao and then Zhou, but the Chinese telephone operator allegedly
    told him: "You are a revisionist, and therefore I will not connect you." Zhou said this action
    had been "unauthorized." See Richard Nixon, *RN: The Memoirs of Richard Nixon* (Grosset

29, the Soviets proposed, without publicity, resumption of the 1964 talks on the border issue. During the Chinese Ninth Party Congress in April the Soviets again issued a nonpolemical note proposing a resumption of the border talks, and they temporarily called off the anti-Chinese polemics in their media. Finally, while they continued to fire on Chinese patrols on the disputed Damansky Island, they did not occupy it themselves.[12] Thus their stance was firm, but not escalatory.

The occupation of Czechoslovakia also provoked a storm of protest within the world communist movement to which the Soviet leaders had to respond. On October 18, 1968, they postponed the international conference of communist parties they had long been organizing.[13] A Preparatory Commission with representatives of six parties—including the Romanians and the Western European Eurocommunists, as they were soon to be called—had met on November 18–21, 1968, and agreed to hold the international conference the following May. At a second meeting of the Preparatory Commission that took place in Moscow on March 17 the Soviets sought to mobilize support against the Chinese, but it was clear the full conference would not adopt an anti-Chinese platform. The China issue—and the related issue of Soviet leadership in the communist movement—nonetheless dominated the preparations for the international conference. The March meeting had been expected to be the last before the full conference, but given the difficulty the Soviets had marshaling support, a third preparatory meeting was set for May, with the final conference put off until June.

Meanwhile, the Soviet ideological position was set forth in a series of key editorial articles in the party's theoretical journal, *Kommunist*. They stressed "proletarian internationalism," meaning discipline in support of the Soviet line.[14]

---

and Dunlap), p. 568. Even if initially unauthorized, the Chinese leaders decided to reply by written diplomatic memorandum rather than by telephone or direct wire.

12. See Wich, *Sino-Soviet Crisis Politics*, pp. 274–75.

13. The Soviets again began to move forward with preparations after Dubček was removed and Czechoslovakia had reluctantly accepted a treaty authorizing the stationing of Soviet troops in the country.

14. The key articles, all unsigned editorials based on authoritative Central Committee pronouncements, were: "Proletarian Internationalism—Banner of the International Communist Movement," *Kommunist* [The Communist], no. 12 (August 1968), pp. 24–30; "Under the Banner of Proletarian Internationalism," *Kommunist*, no. 18 (December 1968), pp. 3–7; "The Living Heritage of the Comintern," *Kommunist*, no. 4 (March 1969), pp. 3–10; and "Strengthen the International Unity of Communists," *Kommunist*, no. 7 (May 1969), pp. 3–11. Another key article, "The Communist Movement Has Entered a New Upsurge," *Kommunist*, no. 11 (July 1969), pp. 3–16, was signed by Brezhnev. Two other key unsigned articles specifically addressed the conflict with China: "The Situation in China and the Position of the Communist Party of China at the Present Stage," *Kommunist*, no. 4 (March 1969), pp. 86–103; and "The Policy of the Mao Zedong Group in the International Arena," *Kommunist*, no. 5 (March 1969), pp. 104–16.

Another important meeting occurred on March 17 in Budapest: a summit conference of the leaders of the Warsaw Pact. Here, too, the overriding Soviet concern with China, which was increasingly central in its attention, led the Soviet leaders to propose that the Eastern European countries offer demonstrative support for the Soviet Union by dispatching token forces to the Far East. President Nicolae Ceausescu of Romania openly and flatly declined, stressing that Warsaw Pact obligations were confined to Europe. Even more important, it was clear that most if not all the other Warsaw Pact countries of Eastern Europe also opposed the idea. The Soviet leaders had little choice but to abandon it.[15]

The Soviets were left on their own to oppose China. In March they surfaced Wang Ming, a former general secretary of the Chinese communist party in the 1930s, who had long been in obscure retirement and exile in the Soviet Union. While there were serious differences among the Chinese leaders in Beijing, none wanted Soviet sponsorship, and this ghost of the past carried no weight. Later in the summer, as the border conflict erupted anew in Central Asia, the Soviets took a more ominous step and began to publicize former Lt. General Zunun Taipov, an ethnic Uighur exile from Xinjiang and longtime resident of the Soviet Union, who had participated in Soviet-aided local nationalist uprisings against the central Chinese authorities in the mid- to late 1940s.

The Ninth Congress of the Communist Party of China, held in April 1969, was a key event in turning Chinese policy. The main thrust of international policy was a dual confrontation with both the Soviet Union and the United States. Lin Biao, Mao's designated successor, delivered the political report. Although wary of the idea of closer Chinese ties with the United States, he leveled heavier criticism at the Soviet Union. The authoritative Soviet *History of Diplomacy* (edited by Politburo members Andrei Gromyko and Boris Ponomarev) dates the turn in Chinese foreign policy to "a rapprochement with the imperialists against the Soviet Union" to the Ninth Congress (although the change was not sharply clear in authoritative doctrinal terms until the Tenth Congress in 1973).[16] It is ironic that during the preceding decade one of the principal Chinese criticisms of the Soviet Union was that its leaders were insufficiently bold—indeed, were soft—on American imperialism.

Also in April some Chinese diplomatic missions abroad circulated a new map that gave Chinese place names for various locations in the Soviet Union, including Vladivostok. This move prompted Soviet charges of "cartographic aggression."

At the international Conference of Communist Parties, held in Moscow in early June, the Soviets violated the concession that they had reluctantly made previously to the Romanians and Eurocommunists not to engage

---

15. Wich, *Sino-Soviet Crisis Politics*, pp. 123–40.

16. A. A. Gromyko and B. N. Ponomarev, eds., *Istoriya diplomatii* [History of Diplomacy], 2d ed. (Moscow: Politizdat, 1978), vol. 5, bk. 2, pp. 410, 414–16.

in anti-Chinese diatribes. Brezhnev pressed his attack on the Chinese Communist party as far as he could at the conference, an ideological-political arena for the international communist movement. He coupled this attack with a diplomatic initiative, attempting to generate support for an Asian collective security system. Although this idea was advanced in a speech titled "For the Strengthening of the Solidarity of Communists, for a New Upsurge of the Anti-Imperialist Struggle," as subsequent clarification made evident the initiative was directed against China.[17] The Soviet Union subsequently mounted a campaign in its bilateral diplomatic contacts with a wide range of Asian countries, but without much success.[18]

Although the Soviets could not enlist any anti-Chinese support, they still considered the conference a qualified success. It had at least taken place. Moreover, despite many signs that important segments of the international communist movement would not accept the discipline of Soviet-defined proletarian internationalism, the conference again showed the extent of Chinese isolation. On the other hand, a growing number of European communist parties were refusing to join in anti-Chinese statements, a significant point. In fact, from 1969 on Romania and Yugoslavia, together with Eurocommunists such as the parties in Italy and Spain, successfully opposed Soviet efforts to excommunicate the Chinese from the international communist movement.

In its bilateral dealings with China the USSR was much more amenable to negotiation on concrete issues. Apart from a series of complex signals of intent[19] and strong protests alleging Chinese responsibility for the series of border clashes, official Soviet statements were remarkably open on seeking negotiations.[20] On June 8 the Chinese did agree to meet at the technical level on navigation on the border rivers. These talks began on June 18 at Khabarovsk, but were temporarily broken off by the Soviets on July 13 after a border clash on the Amur River, and then were resumed and agreement reached on August 8—just before serious new clashes in Central Asia. Thus there were

17. L. I. Brezhnev, *O vneshnei politike KPSS i sovetskogo gosudarstva: Rechi i stat'i* [On the Foreign Policy of the CPSU and the Soviet Government: Speeches and Articles], 3d ed. (Moscow: Politizdat, 1978), p. 86.

18. The Soviets would even attempt to recruit pro-Chinese Pakistan into the collective security system. Prime Minister Kosygin raised the matter with President Agha Mohammed Yahya Khan when the latter visited Moscow in June 1970. When Yahya raised the subject of arms supply, the Soviets tied it to Pakistani participation in a collective security system. Yahya rejected the proposal and subsequently briefed Chinese Ambassador Zhang Tong on the exchange. See G. W. Choudhury, a knowledgeable former Pakistani diplomat, *Chinese Perceptions of the World* (Washington, D.C.: University Press of America, 1977), pp. 29–30.

19. See Wich, *Sino-Soviet Crisis Politics*, especially pp. 121, 274–76.

20. See, in particular, the statements of March 29 and June 13, texts of which are in *Vneshnyaya politika sovetskogo soyuza i mezhdunarodnye otnosheniya: Sbornik dokumentov, 1969 god* [The Foreign Policy of the Soviet Union and International Relations: A Collection of Documents, 1969] (Moscow: Mezhdunarodnye otnosheniya, 1970), pp. 72–80, 127–38.

intermittent contacts and ameliorations. On the whole, however, the border conflict dominated throughout the summer, and Sino-Soviet relations grew worse.

China, too, had been trying to gain the support of some countries in Eastern Europe, as noted. As early as August 1968 it had begun to reverse its policy toward Yugoslavia. This shift was significant because Yugoslavia had been the butt of Chinese surrogate attacks on Yugoslav—meaning Soviet—revisionism ever since the late 1950s. Beginning in 1969 relations between the two countries also began to develop. In January a Yugoslav trade delegation visited China, and in October ambassadors were exchanged for the first time in eleven years.

Chinese relations with Romania had for some time been close. In fact, Prime Minister Gheorghe Maurer of Romania had made a secret visit to Beijing in 1967. After the Soviet intervention in Czechoslovakia the ties rapidly grew closer. Having rejected Soviet proposals for token military support the year before, in July 1970 the Romanians even leaned the other way, sending Minister of Defense Ion Ionita at the head of a military delegation to China. The delegation was there two weeks, during which the Chinese praised Romanian "independence." By June 1971 Ceauşescu visited Beijing—the first visit by an Eastern European party chief since the open Sino-Soviet break at the beginning of the 1960s (except for the special case of anti-Soviet Albania's Enver Hoxha). Also in 1971 Santiago Carrillo, head of the Spanish Communist party, visited China. He brought a secret letter from the Communist party of Italy proposing a resumption of long-absent party relations. Establishing close ties with the Eurocommunists was, however, more than the divided Chinese party leadership could agree on until after the Maoist period ended late in the decade.

There were practical limitations to Chinese aid to Eastern European countries. As in 1968, in 1970–71, a time of heightened Soviet polemics with Yugoslavia and Romania, Zhou Enlai told a Yugoslav newsman in an interview, "we shall extend such support as we can," but noted "we are far from Europe and, as you know, one of our popular proverbs says: 'distant waters cannot quench a fire.' "[21] The Chinese did not want to encourage the Romanians or Yugoslavs to go so far as to prompt Soviet intervention, and they could offer nothing more than moral support.

The Soviets introduced an ominous new note into the situation in the late summer, following a major new flare-up of fighting on the Central Asian border between Xinjiang and Kazakhstan in mid-August. Responsibility is not clear. These particular clashes might well have been started by the Chinese to stress their claims in the area, or by the Soviets to show the Chinese they could not choose the areas of engagement. In any event, on August 28 *Pravda* hinted—by saying that a Sino-Soviet war resulting from Chinese adventurism would affect "the destiny of peoples"—that a war would become nu-

---

21. *Viesnik* [The Herald] (Belgrade), August 28, 1971.

clear.[22] This statement was but one element in a series of militarily related moves. In May, although not publicly identified until August, a new and more senior officer, Colonel General Vladimir F. Tolubko, had been named to head the Far Eastern Military District. There was speculation in the West that this appointment might have portended a Soviet threat to use nuclear missiles against China, since Tolubko had been serving as deputy commander of the Strategic Missile Forces. While some such signal may have been intended, it seems far more likely that the main reason for his selection was prior experience in the Far East. Early in 1970 Tolubko was promoted to four-star general of the army rank. In August, although, again, not publicly known until the November 7 parade, a new Central Asian Military District was formed out of part of the old Turkestan Military District, comprising all areas along the Sino-Soviet border from Afghanistan to Mongolia, and was placed under General of the Army Nikolai G. Lyashchenko.

The Soviet military forces in the Far East and Siberia had been doubled from about a dozen understrength divisions in 1961 to twenty-five by 1969. After the initial clashes in 1969, a major buildup began, reaching forty-five divisions by 1973. Similarly, the number of tactical combat aircraft increased from about 200 to 1,200 by 1973. There were other changes as well. In the late 1960s and early 1970s all fifty or so older SS-4 medium-range ballistic missiles (MRBMs) and SS-5 intermediate-range ballistic missiles (IRBMs) in the area were replaced by at least 120 SS-11 variable-range ballistic missiles (VRBMs) of intermediate or intercontinental range.

In retrospect it is clear that in 1969 the Soviets made a decision to build up their military forces in all categories in the Far East–Central Asian areas to a level that was relatively self-sustaining and thus permitted waging a two-front general war in Europe and Asia, if that contingency should arise. Thus just as the United States was discarding a two-war strategic planning framework to shape its forces, the Soviet Union was adopting one. Both cases reflected changing relations with China.

But the more immediately apparent and politically relevant development in the summer and fall of 1969 was the war of nerves the Soviets deliberately created by raising the possibility of a nuclear strike on China. The relatively subtle hint in the *Pravda* editorial on August 28 was driven home publicly by Victor Louis, a shadowy Soviet journalist affiliated with the KGB. In an article in the *London Evening News* on September 16, he mentioned the possibility of a Soviet nuclear strike on the Chinese nuclear weapons test site. The Soviets also began a campaign of informal comments along similar lines by Soviet diplomats (often KGB officers) to European and Asian diplomats. Kissinger recounts one such discussion by a Soviet diplomat with a mid-level State Department officer on August 18: the Soviet diplomat inquired as to the American reaction to a Soviet attack on Chinese nuclear facilities. Moreover, the Soviets also sent to the leadership of a number of communist parties in

---

22. Editorial, "Peking's Adventuristic Course," *Pravda*, August 28, 1969.

Europe and Asia confidential letters that seemed to justify a possible Soviet need for a preemptive strike against threatening nuclear bases in China.[23]

The United States countered that possibility by taking the unusual step of having Director of Central Intelligence Richard C. Helms give a background briefing to a group of diplomatic correspondents on August 27. In a further step, on September 5 Under Secretary of State Elliot L. Richardson commented publicly, in a more veiled but clear reference, that while the United States would not involve itself in Sino-Soviet relations, "we could not fail to be deeply concerned, however, with an escalation of this quarrel into a massive breach of international peace and security."[24]

Kissinger notes most of these developments but does not recount the discussion in mid-August that led him to take the matter seriously. The event was a meeting with Allen Whiting in San Clemente. Kissinger has told others that it decisively influenced his thinking on this subject. It was only then that he learned what had concerned his own intelligence evaluators: Soviet bomber units had been brought from the Western USSR to Siberia and Mongolia in June 1969 and had engaged in mock attacks against targets made to resemble nuclear facilities in Northwest China.[25]

It remains uncertain to this day whether the Soviet leaders were considering an attack (probably with conventional weapons) against Chinese nuclear facilities. It may be that there was at least a contingency plan, or the entire affair may have been an elaborate bluff. In any case the threat did have an impact on both Sino-Soviet and Sino-American relations, and ultimately on triangular diplomacy.

It should also be noted that later reports that the Soviet Union had approached the United States in 1969 about a possible joint attack on Chinese

---

23. See Henry Kissinger, *White House Years* (Boston, Mass.: Little, Brown 1979), pp. 183–85. Kissinger does not note that the unnamed Soviet embassy official concerned was a KGB officer.

   As evidence of the Soviet military rattling its sabers, Kissinger also cites (p. 184) articles he describes as commemorating "the thirtieth anniversary of the beginning of World War II," thus imputing an offensive twist. In fact, these articles were explicitly devoted to the twenty-fourth anniversary of the *end* of World War II. One purpose may well have been to remind the Chinese that the Soviets won a victory over the Japanese army in Manchuria in August 1945.

24. Ibid., p. 184.

25. See Marvin Kalb and Bernard Kalb, *Kissinger* (Dell, 1975), pp. 259–60; and Allen S. Whiting, "Sino-American Détente," *China Quarterly*, no. 82 (June 1980), p. 336. Kissinger was the source of the Kalbs' account.

   Secret war games ("situational analyses") involving Soviet strikes on China were conducted in Moscow in 1969, and one of the key considerations in them was the possible American reaction, according to a Soviet scholar, then at the Institute of the World Economy and International Relations, who had the opportunity to talk with three of the organizers and participants in these exercises. See Dimitri K. Simes, "Soviet Policy toward the United States," in Joseph S. Nye, Jr., ed., *The Making of America's Soviet Policy* (New Haven, Conn.: Yale University Press, 1984), p. 305. Simes emigrated to the United States in 1972.

facilities were unfounded.[26] The Soviets did, however, probe the U.S. attitude and reaction (and reactions of others). Some Chinese who opposed the Sino-American rapprochement, however, took the position that the United States and the Soviet Union had planned a joint "new military adventure" that threatened China with nuclear war.[27]

On September 3, during this phase of worsening Sino-Soviet relations with its whiff of possible war, Ho Chi Minh, the veteran communist leader in Vietnam, died. Zhou Enlai hurried down from Beijing to pay his respects, but stayed less than a day so as to leave before the Soviet delegation led by Prime Minister Kosygin arrived. Kosygin stayed for four days, during which time the Vietnamese, seeking to patch up the Sino-Soviet split so as to have more secure backing in the Vietnam War, made public a last testament of Ho, in which he appealed for communist unity. Kosygin was prepared to meet the Chinese, but they attempted to evade a meeting. Only after Kosygin actually left Vietnam and was on his way back to Moscow did the Chinese indicate they were willing to receive him. To their surprise Kosygin, en route home, did return to Beijing from Dushanbe, in Soviet Tadzhikistan, on September 11. Zhou Enlai met him at the airport for discussions. Despite this treatment, which was akin to keeping a neighbor on the back porch for a chat, and despite the fact that the talks were publicly characterized as "frank," meaning strong disagreement, the meeting did have a positive effect on relations.[28] An agreement was reached to exchange ambassadors (for some time

26. H. R. Haldeman was the principal source of a flurry of charges that the Soviets had approached the United States for a joint attack, as he claims in his memoir published in 1978. See H. R. Haldeman with Joseph DiMona, *The Ends of Power* (Times Books, 1978), pp. 89–93. His account is replete with other serious errors on this subject. Kissinger denied the charges, as did Secretary of State William P. Rogers, although his denial was less significant given his limited access to information. The Soviets denied them vociferously. See Hedrick Smith, "Haldeman Book Says Soviet Asked U.S. in '69 to Join Nuclear Attack on China: Ex-Aide Asserts Nixon Refused—Kissinger and Rogers Deny Account," *New York Times*, February 17, 1978; "Kremlin Reiterates Denial of Plan to Attack China," *Washington Post*, February 20, 1978; and Victor Zorza, "A Solution to Haldeman's Chinese Puzzle," *Washington Post*, February 22, 1978.

27. Speech at a mass meeting by Xie Fuzhi, political commissar of the Beijing Military District and newly named member of the Politburo, November 28, 1969. See "Peking Rally Warmly Celebrates Albanian Liberation Anniversary," NCNA English language press release, *Survey of the China Mainland Press*, American Consulate General Hong Kong, no. 4551 (December 5, 1969), p. 21.

28. Wich, *Sino-Soviet Crisis Politics*, pp. 199–200. In his memoir Kissinger shows a surprising unfamiliarity with the facts of the belated Chinese invitation and the significance of the meeting. According to his account he had not been briefed at the time and interpreted the event hastily, on the wing so to speak, to Nixon. He evidently has not reviewed the matter since, as he still suggests that it showed that "Sino-Soviet relations were approaching a crisis point." See Kissinger, *White House Years*, pp. 184–85.

While the Kosygin-Zhou airport meeting at the time helped to calm down the situation and led to some ameliorating steps, in due course it too became the source of still further friction and disagreement over what had been agreed at that time.

each had been represented only by a chargé d'affaires). Trade was also discussed. Finally, there was agreement in principle to resume the border negotiations suspended five years earlier.

After the Kosygin-Zhou meeting both sides toned down their polemics. More important, the border conflict subsided. On October 7 the Chinese announced that agreement had been reached to open negotiations on that conflict. To achieve it, both sides had compromised. The Soviets had given up their preference that the talks be technical, headed by border guard officials, and had agreed to political meetings at the deputy ministerial level. The Chinese set aside their demands for a prior overall settlement, troop withdrawals, recognition of the illegitimacy of the "unequal treaties" of the past, and acceptance of the usual principle for riverine border delimitation.

The Chinese announcement explicitly made clear that China would not be intimidated by threats of nuclear war, specifically referring to the rumored threats of strikes on nuclear facilities. "Should a handful of war maniacs dare to raid China's strategic sites in defiance of world condemnation, that will be war" and the 700 million Chinese people would deal with the aggression.[29] By giving this subject such prominent attention, the Chinese acknowledged that it was of serious concern and implied that the threat might indeed have influenced them to agree to the negotiations.

While fears of a Soviet attack on China subsided, it was a long time before they disappeared entirely. In February 1970, for reasons having nothing to do with any renewal of Soviet pressure or intelligence observations, Kissinger commissioned his staff to prepare contingency plans for possible Sino-Soviet hostilities.[30] As late as 1972 Brezhnev was still denying "absurd propositions" that the Soviet Union "intended to attack China," which he characterized as an "anti-Soviet" idea "dreamed up in Beijing."[31]

On October 27 Brezhnev appealed for "a positive, realistic approach" in the forthcoming negotiations, which he said should include "border and other questions." Finally, in referring to the Kosygin-Zhou meeting he broke a precedent of three years' standing by referring to "Comrade" Zhou Enlai, a fraternal communist form of address.[32] On the occasion of Soviet National Day on November 7 the Chinese reciprocated in their fashion by having Deputy Foreign Minister Qiao Guanhua, their negotiator for the border talks, attend the reception at the Soviet embassy in Beijing.

On October 20, 1969, First Deputy Minister of Foreign Affairs Vasily V. Kuznetsov and Qiao Guanhua met in Beijing. The talks were accompa-

---

29. "Statement of the Government of the People's Republic of China," *Peking Review*, vol. 12 (October 10, 1969), pp. 3–4.

30. Kissinger, *White House Years*, pp. 693–94; and Roger Morris, *Uncertain Greatness* (Harper and Row, 1977), p. 97. Morris was in charge of the contingency study.

31. Brezhnev, Speech in Budapest, November 30, 1972, *O vneshnei politike*, p. 247.

32. Brezhnev, Speech of October 27, 1969, *O vneshnei politike*, p. 96; also in *Pravda*, October 28, 1969.

nied by a notable decrease in polemics for the first two or three months (except for one strong attack by Zhou Enlai on November 23, probably required for internal political reasons). The talks were not conclusive, but the very fact that negotiation had replaced border fighting was significant. They continued intermittently for years. In August 1970 Deputy Foreign Minister Leonid Ilychev succccded Kuznetsov as the Soviet representative.

Neither side has publicly discussed these negotiations, which lasted into 1972. Some Western accounts have assumed they were but a shuffling of arguments. Soviet officials have privately said that the talks were more far-reaching than simply the border issue, although that remained their chief focus, and that they led to some agreements. For instance, prompted by the experience of Kosygin's failure on March 21, 1969, to establish direct contact by telephone with the Chinese leaders, the Soviet side proposed reestablishing such communications. The Chinese finally agreed, on a state-to-state (rather than party-to-party) basis, and a governmental hot line was restored in 1970.[33] In separate technical talks agreement was also reached in December 1970 on navigation of the border rivers. There was also the agreed-on exchange of ambassadors arranged by Kosygin and Zhou a year earlier; Soviet Ambassador Vasily S. Tolstikov arrived in Beijing on October 10, 1970, while his Chinese counterpart, Ambassador Li Xinguan, arrived in Moscow November 22. The order of arrival made clear that the Soviet side had been the most interested in upgrading its representation—and the long delay made clear that even agreed improvements moved very slowly.

Gradually Sino-Soviet trade picked up as well, although still on a limited basis: up to $290 million a year in 1972, compared with $2.1 billion in 1959, the last and peak year before the Sino-Soviet rift.

Both the Soviet Union and China continued to be suspicious and to attack various actions of the other. The Soviets continued to seek an Asian collective security system directed at isolating China, while the Chinese continued, after mid-1970, to call for a United Front against the Soviet Union. They each attacked steps of the other to improve relations with the United States, which country both also denounced regularly. For example, an authoritative Soviet commentary following the Chinese-American ambassadorial talks that had begun in January and February 1970 cited as a planned American maneuver a Western press story. The commentary implied that the Chinese could count on the United States in the event of a Sino-Soviet war, saying, "The imperialists' latest propaganda maneuver is aimed at thwarting the Soviet-Chinese negotiations."[34] The Chinese castigated the United States and the

---

33. Information from a knowledgeable Soviet official in an oral communication. The Moscow-Beijing hot line, unlike the Moscow-Washington telex, is a scrambler telephone permitting secure voice transmission.

34. I. Aleksandrov, "To the Advantage of Imperialism," *Pravda*, March 19, 1970. "I. Aleksandrov" is an established collective pseudonym for authoritative Central Committee commentaries.

Soviet Union alike. Shortly after the unveiling of the Nixon Doctrine at Guam and Brezhnev's call, at about the same time, for an Asian collective security system, the New China News Agency labeled Nixon and Brezhnev as being interchangeable—"the same merchandise is peddled under two different labels." [35]

Thus the precipitous plunge in Sino-Soviet relations that began after Czechoslovakia was arrested by October 1969, but within a context of continuing mistrust and hostility. Sino-Soviet relations ranged from not good to bad and back, but not to worst or better. The polemics were still there, but alternated with periods of a relative lessening of tension. For example, shortly after President Nixon's visit to Beijing in early 1972 (and with wary warnings of the need to see what it would mean in practice), Brezhnev sought to shore up the Soviet position in triangular diplomacy. He acceded to an earlier Chinese propaganda proposal to make peaceful coexistence between states the basis for Sino-Soviet relations, saying that if the Chinese were not ready for more, then the Soviets could agree to that. Brezhnev also offered "specific and constructive" proposals for nonaggression and a border settlement. [36] By then, however, the Chinese leaders did not believe they needed agreement with the Soviets on that basis. On October 1, 1972, the Chinese National Day, the Chinese issued an important and authoritative policy statement. In an unusual example of flexibility, dexterity, and economy it cited verbatim a portion of a statement by Mao first made on May 20, 1970—but the context of the quotation was changed so that what Mao had leveled as an attack on the United States in 1970 was now directed against the Soviet Union. [37]

The varying state of Sino-Soviet relations continued both to reflect, and in some cases to influence, Chinese and Soviet positions on other issues. It also affected other relationships, including Sino-American and Soviet-American ones.

Sino-American Relations

When in November 1968 the Chinese proposed resuming the desultory Sino-American ambassadorial talks the following February, the outgoing Johnson administration advised President-elect Nixon, who replied immedi-

---

35. Xinhua [NCNA], press release, August 5, in FBIS, *China*, August 6, 1969, p. A3.

36. Brezhnev, Speech of March 20, 1972, *O vneshnei politike*, p. 231.

37. Mao Zedong, "People of the World Unite and Defeat the U.S. Aggressors and All Their Running Dogs!" Xinhua [NCNA], "Strive for New Victories," May 20, in FBIS, *China*, May 20, 1970, pp. A1–2; and a joint editorial by *Renmin Ribao* [People's Daily], *Hongqi* [Red Flag], and *Jiefanjiun Bao* [Liberation Army Daily], October 1, in FBIS, *China*, October 2, 1972, pp. B1–5.

ately that the United States should agree to the proposed meeting.[38]

Nixon, with a long political history of being ardently anticommunist, and specifically anti–Communist China as well as anti-Soviet, was an improbable architect of rapprochement with those countries. At the same time he was better able to do this because of his tough reputation. Nixon had written an article published in *Foreign Affairs* in October 1967, before his successful political rebirth, in which he had spoken of "pulling China back into the world community" in "the long run." But he had also warned against "conceding to China a 'sphere of influence' " in Asia and argued for a major strengthening of noncommunist Asia before a "dialogue with mainland China can begin."[39] Again in 1968, just after his nomination as presidential candidate, Nixon argued: "We must not forget China. We must always seek opportunities to talk with her, as with the USSR. . . . We must not only watch for changes. We must seek to make changes."[40] General Vernon A. Walters, an old acquaintance from Nixon's vice presidential days, has reported that when President-elect Nixon invited him for a chat in January 1969, he told Walters that one thing he wanted to do was to establish contact with the Chinese.[41]

Kissinger indirectly admits his own relative unfamiliarity with Chinese affairs—"China had not figured extensively in my own writings."[42] Associates of Kissinger at that time have commented that initially he felt intellectually insecure on Chinese affairs and was skeptical of Nixon's idea of rapprochement. As noted, Nixon made his first decision on China policy—his recommendation that the Johnson administration accept the Chinese invitation to resume Sino-American ambassadorial talks in February—in November 1968, before he had selected Kissinger to serve in his administration. And it was Nixon who clearly established the basic thrust of American policy toward

---

38. Retired Ambassador Robert Murphy, serving as foreign policy liaison for the presidential transition, was the channel. Kissinger had not yet been selected and was not involved.

39. Richard M. Nixon, "Asia after Viet Nam," *Foreign Affairs*, vol. 46 (October 1967), pp. 122–23. In his memoir Nixon neglects to recall the major limiting conditions on an opening of any relations with China that he set forth in the 1967 article. See Richard Nixon, *RN: The Memoirs of Richard Nixon* (Grosset and Dunlap, 1978), p. 545.

40. Interview of Richard M. Nixon in "Nixon's View of World—From Informal Talks," *U.S. News and World Report* (September 16, 1968), p. 48.

41. Vernon A. Walters, *Silent Missions* (Doubleday, 1978), p. 525. Walters concedes the idea "seemed quite farfetched" to him at the time.

42. Kissinger, *White House Years*, p. 164. In his memoir Kissinger cites a passage he had written in 1961 about the possibility of a Sino-Soviet rift, citing himself as having written that *if* such a thing occurred, the United States should take advantage of it. Writing in 1979 he comments that "we know now that the rift had already occurred." In 1961 both the alert scholarly community and the intelligence and policy analysis community in the government were well aware, at a time Kissinger was not, that a serious rift had already occurred.

China. Only later did Kissinger become an enthusiastic convert.[43] China policy also was an area—like Soviet policy and Vietnam policy—that the president decided at the outset to retain as much as possible in his own hands (which, in practice, increasingly meant in Kissinger's); it would be managed directly from the White House.

Nixon clearly had contact with China in mind, but he was not at all certain how to bring it about and on what terms. Kissinger notes in his memoir some instances of Nixon's uncertainty and inconsistency in 1969.[44] At his first press conference on January 27 Nixon did refer, in reply to a question on his China policy, to the scheduled Warsaw ambassadorial meeting, saying that the United States "look[s] forward to that meeting" and "will be interested to see what the Chinese Communist representatives may have to say." But he then went on to say that the U.S. interest was to see "whether any changes of attitude on their part on major, substantive issues may have occurred. Until some changes occur on their side, however, I see no immediate prospect of any change in our policy."[45]

The Chinese, on the day after Nixon's inauguration, characterized Nixon as the newest "puppet" of the "monopoly bourgeois clique" to pursue "the vicious ambitions of U.S. imperialism to continue to carry out aggression and expansion in the world."[46] On February 18 they announced cancellation of the ambassadorial meeting scheduled for the 20th, following the defection of a Chinese diplomat to the United States.[47]

In his press conference on March 4 President Nixon again indicated his longer-term interest in improved relations with China, but shorter-term pessimism. "Looking further down the road," he said, "we could think in terms of a better understanding with Red China. But being very realistic, in view of Red China's breaking off the rather limited Warsaw talks that were planned, I

---

43. This change is indicated more clearly in the account by the Kalb brothers, written with Kissinger's assistance during the Nixon presidency, than in Kissinger's own memoir a decade later. See Kalb and Kalb, *Kissinger*, pp. 248–65. The Kalbs also note the role of Allen Whiting and others in assisting in Kissinger's study of China and Sino-Soviet relations in 1969–71, a point that Kissinger omits. See also Morris, *Uncertain Greatness*, pp. 202–08.

44. See Kissinger, *White House Years*, pp. 164–94, for his account of the "first steps toward China." Curiously, in his memoir Nixon skips over China policy in 1969–70 almost entirely; see Nixon, *RN*, pp. 544–47.

45. "The President's News Conference of January 27, 1969," *Weekly Compilation of Presidential Documents*, vol. 5 (February 3, 1969), p. 176. (Hereafter *Presidential Documents*.) He also stated that the United States would continue to oppose admission of "Communist China" to the United Nations ("it has not indicated any intent to abide by the principles of the U.N. Charter").

46. Cited by Kissinger, *White House Years*, p. 168.

47. Ibid., p. 169. Kissinger states that on February 6 the Chinese sent an unpublicized note of protest on the defection, which had occurred in the Netherlands.

do not think that we should hold out any great optimism for any break-throughs in that direction at this time."[48]

Although the prospects looked bleak, both sides were sending subtle signals. For example, the Chinese, in reporting on Nixon's first press conference, significantly made no reference whatsoever to his comments on the need for China to change its policy—a revealing contrast to their reaction to a similar statement by Japanese Prime Minister Eisaku Sato at about the same time.[49]

Unilateral actions provided other, even more important, signals. On February 1 Nixon asked Kissinger to plant in an East European channel the idea that the administration was "exploring possibilities of rapprochement with the Chinese." Kissinger did so and also decided to use the occasion to initiate a broad policy review on China. Accordingly, on February 5 he issued National Security Study Memorandum (NSSM)-14 requesting the interested agencies to examine the current status of U.S.-PRC relations, the nature of Chinese intentions and threat in Asia, the interaction of American and other countries' policies toward China, and alternative U.S. options or approaches toward China, with their costs and risks.[50] Other studies followed: NSSM-35 on March 28 on "Trade with Communist China" and, after the border clashes, NSSM-63 on July 3 on "Sino-Soviet Relations." The NSC Senior Review Group, chaired by Kissinger, first discussed the paper on China policy options on May 15.

The trade study included a specific request to reexamine the embargo on trade. The bureaucracy developed two alternative approaches, called informally the "fell swoop" approach, which envisaged a single sudden dramatic move and was favored by most China hands, and the "artichoke" approach of gradually peeling off restrictions layer by layer. Essentially for domestic political reasons the artichoke approach was adopted. On June 26 a National Security Decision Memorandum (NSDM) was issued directing that trade controls with China be modified. The first announcement of the removal of some trade controls, and a relaxation of some travel restrictions, was made on July 21.[51]

---

48. "The President's News Conference of March 4, 1969," *Presidential Documents*, vol. 5 (March 10, 1969), p. 362. Use of the term "Red China" followed the questioner's use of that term.

49. See Wich, *Sino-Soviet Crisis Politics*, p. 89. While American intelligence research analysts understood this signal at the time, it was not brought to the attention of Nixon and Kissinger, and Kissinger's detailed memoir shows him still unaware of it years later.

50. Kissinger, *White House Years*, pp. 169–70. In his memoir Kissinger does not identify the study as NSSM-14, but describes the content. See also Tad Szulc, *The Illusion of Peace: Foreign Policy in the Nixon Years* (Viking, 1978), p. 112; and Kalb and Kalb, *Kissinger*, pp. 252–53.

51. Kissinger, *White House Years*, pp. 178–79; and see Szulc, *The Illusion of Peace*, pp. 113–15.

On July 22, Nixon contrived to bring favorable references to the Chinese (and Russian) peoples into an off-the-cuff public talk with students on the occasion of the moon landing.[52]

Despite these positive steps there were contradictions in the administration's approach to China, as was manifest in the impromptu unveiling of the Nixon Doctrine at Guam on July 25. In overall terms the doctrine (or, more accurately, policy shift) envisaged a degree of American disengagement in Asia that should have appealed to the Chinese. That outcome, however, was not Nixon's foremost preoccupation at the time, as is clear from an accompanying jarring statement that China was "the greatest threat to the peace of the world," a comment not heard since Dean Rusk's retirement.[53]

Another source of contradiction was the need of the administration in its first months to establish its position and policy over a very wide range of issues. For example, a major preoccupation in the spring was the formulation of defense policy. In addition to its intrinsic importance, establishment of (and congressional support for) a defense program was seen as an essential step before engaging in strategic arms control talks (SALT) with the Soviets. The key defense issue, both in terms of domestic political debate and laying the groundwork before SALT, was the decision in March to proceed with the deployment of an antiballistic missile (ABM) system.

In announcing his decision on ABM deployment, modifying an earlier program of the Johnson administration, President Nixon maintained as an important element of his rationale the need to defend against a possible nuclear attack by China. To that he added a new idea of his own that implied a common American and Soviet interest in containing China. "I would imagine," said Nixon, "that the Soviet Union would be just as reluctant as we would be to leave their country naked against a potential Chinese Communist threat."[54] The next day, by coincidence, was the major Soviet counterthrust on the Ussuri border with China. The following day, March 16, the Chinese characterized the American ABM decision as "further evidence" of American "collusion with the Soviet revisionists to jointly maintain the nuclear threat and

---

52. "The President's Remarks to Students Completing a Year's Visit to the United States," July 22, *Presidential Documents*, vol. 5 (July 28, 1969), p. 1018. Nixon remarked on how sad it was that the Russian people and the Chinese people could not see the moon walk by astronauts Neil Armstrong and Gus Aldrin on television, and rambled on about how "I want the time to come when the Chinese people and the Russian people and all the peoples of this world can walk together and talk together."

53. The statement was made in a background briefing and no official text was released. The statement was, however, reported in the press.

54. "The President's News Conference of March 14, 1969," *Presidential Documents*, vol. 5 (March 17, 1969), p. 404.

nuclear blackmail against the people of the world, particularly against the Chinese people."[55]

Despite the contradictions, the Nixon administration made several diplomatic probes in 1969 seeking to establish contact with China. First was a request by Nixon to President Charles de Gaulle. When they met in Paris on March 1, according to Kissinger, it was de Gaulle who brought up the subject of China, but Nixon told him that he intended to begin "step-by-step contacts" and was determined to open a dialogue. A few weeks later when de Gaulle was in Washington for the funeral of former President Dwight D. Eisenhower, Nixon requested that he convey to the Chinese the American intention of improving relations with China and the spirit of the new American approach. The new French ambassador to Beijing, Etienne Manac'h, was instructed to pass Nixon's message along "at the highest level" and did so in early May.[56]

The second line of diplomatic contact was through Pakistan. On May 24, while in that country, Secretary of State Rogers discussed China at length with President Yahya Khan. He specifically inquired whether Pakistan as a longtime friend of both countries could help the United States quietly establish contact with China. Yahya Khan was quite receptive—such a rapprochement would be very much in Pakistan's interest—and agreed to do so.[57] On August 1, while on his world tour, President Nixon met with President Yahya Khan and stressed his personal interest in ending China's isolation. The Pakistani president was able to report that the Chinese had neither encouraged nor discouraged the initial sounding taken at Rogers' request, and they agreed to keep this channel to Beijing open.[58]

The next day, in Romania, President Nixon continued his efforts to open a channel to the Chinese. He asked President Ceauşescu to act as a channel of communication to the Chinese. Again, as in Pakistan, he also sounded a common note with both the Chinese and his hosts by expressing his opposition to any attempt to isolate China through an Asian collective security

---

55. Xinhua [NCNA], Radio Beijing, March 16, in FBIS, *China*, March 17, 1969, p. A1.

56. See Kalb and Kalb, *Kissinger*, pp. 254–55, for a well-informed account. In his memoir Kissinger, for whatever reason, omits this French connection except for a reference to Nixon's first conversation with de Gaulle on March 1, leaving the misimpression that that was the end of it. *White House Years*, p. 170.

57. Szulc, *The Illusion of Peace*, p. 116, describes this contact. Kissinger completely ignores it.

58. Ibid., p. 118; and see Kissinger, *White House Years*, pp. 180–81. Kissinger, having earlier chosen to omit reference to Rogers' role, is unable to mention that Yahya Khan reported on the results of his soundings. The fullest account of the Pakistani role as an intermediary between the United States and China has been provided by a knowledgeable former Pakistani diplomat: G. W. Choudhury, "Reflections on Sino-Pakistan Relations," *Pacific Community*, vol. 7 (January 1976), pp. 248–70; and Choudhury, *Chinese Perceptions of the World*, pp. 34–36.

system to contain China, as the Soviets were then urging. Ceaușescu promised to convey the American view and any Chinese response.

Both the Pakistani and Romanian probes were held in great secrecy, not only from the public but within the American government.[59] This secrecy within the U.S. government sometimes led to difficulties. Occasionally, it resulted in unintended steps that any outside observer would have assumed were part of a smoothly operating pattern. Thus Secretary Rogers' discussion with President Yahya Khan in May was part of a larger pattern of contacts, and a larger political design, of which he was unaware. On August 8 Rogers, traveling in Australia, decided on his own authority to send an open signal to the Chinese. He said that the United States realized that "mainland China will eventually play an important role" in Asia and that "Communist China obviously has long been too isolated from world affairs. This is one reason why we have been seeking to open up channels of communication." He noted the recent American liberalization of trade and travel restrictions. Finally, he said that the United States "look[s] forward to a time when we can enter into a useful dialogue and to a reduction of tensions. We would welcome a renewal of the talks with Communist China."[60] What the Chinese (and others) did not know was that Rogers had given this speech without the knowledge of the president or Kissinger and without having cleared the text. He was of course aware of the general idea of improving relations with both the Soviet Union and China. But he was unaware of the White House diplomacy through France, Pakistan, and Romania.[61]

The Rogers speech led Nixon and Kissinger to decide it was time to have a meeting of the NSC to establish a policy for the government as a whole—although without bringing others fully into the picture or into the management of policy and secret diplomacy by the White House. This meeting, held on August 14, was the first NSC meeting to address China policy, and

---

59. Nixon did attempt to send a signal to Beijing in a publicly reported toast to Ceaușescu: "Mr. President, your country pursues a policy of communication and contact with all nations—you have actively sought the reduction of international tensions. My country shares those objectives." To drive the point home he went on to address a seemingly new subject: "We are seeking ways of ensuring the security, progress, and independence of the nations of Asia, for, as recent history has shown, if there is no peace in Asia, there is no peace in the world." This was intended to suggest to China both the U.S. desire for contact and its intention to end the war in Vietnam. See "Exchange of Toasts between the President and President Ceausescu . . . ," *Presidential Documents*, vol. 5 (August 4, 1969), p. 1068.

60. "Address before the National Press Club, Canberra, Australia, August 8," *Department of State Bulletin*, vol. 61 (September 1, 1969), pp. 179, 180. (Hereafter *State Bulletin*.)

61. Szulc, *The Illusion of Peace*, pp. 115, 119. In his memoir Kissinger, while citing Rogers' address, does not reveal that it had not been cleared and was a surprise to the White House. He prefers to note it as a public indication of the American position, enabling him to say, "Thus by the end of August we had communicated with the Chinese by unilateral steps, intermediaries, and public declarations." *White House Years*, pp. 181–82. In fact, at the time he and Nixon were disturbed that their carefully orchestrated private approaches would be devalued by such a blunt public disclosure of American interest.

Kissinger states that most of those present were startled to hear Nixon expound the thesis that the Soviet Union was the more aggressive and that it would be against U.S. interests to let China be "smashed" in a Sino-Soviet war.[62]

On October 20, the same day the Sino-Soviet border talks resumed, Ambassador Dobrynin called on President Nixon to convey Soviet agreement on the opening of SALT arms limitation talks. He also formally warned against any attempt to profit from Sino-Soviet tensions. Nixon assured him that U.S. policy toward China was "not directed against the Soviet Union."[63]

Under Secretary of State Elliot L. Richardson also stated publicly that "we do not seek to exploit for our own advantage the hostility between the Soviet Union and the People's Republic [of China] . . . [but] to pursue a long-term course of progressively developing better relations with both."[64]

The next in the series of American signals was a decision to withdraw the U.S. patrol of the Taiwan Straits, a symbolic two-destroyer contingent. This decision was first disclosed to the Pakistanis, who were to communicate it confidentially to the Chinese, but to describe it as a gesture to remove an irritant and not as a change in the American commitment to the defense of Taiwan. Kissinger records that he also authorized a leak to Chinese officials in Hong Kong. The patrol was quietly discontinued in November.[65]

Beginning in November Chinese and American diplomats around the world initiated a number of direct contacts. Previously, Chinese diplomats would avoid even perfunctory contact; now, they occasionally took the initiative.

Nixon and Kissinger decided to approach the Chinese directly in Warsaw and so instructed Ambassador Walter J. Stoessel, Jr., in early Septem-

---

62. Kissinger, *White House Years*, p. 182.

63. Ibid., p. 187. Kissinger does not indicate why Nixon gave this assurance. Nixon explains that it was in response to a Soviet complaint that the United States was using Sino-Soviet relations at Soviet expense in its Vietnam policy—which, in fact, was the case. See Nixon, *RN*, pp. 405–06. It is also pertinent to note what Kissinger and Nixon thought about that assurance. In commenting on a *Soviet* assurance that a diplomatic step the USSR had taken (its treaty with India in August 1971) was not directed against the United States, Kissinger revealed his *own* view of the value of an assurance that a treaty was "not directed against" anyone: in his words, that formulation is "the conventional pacifier of diplomacy by which diplomats give a formal reassurance to those they wish to keep in suspense; it is an elegant way of suggesting that one has the capacity to do worse." Kissinger, *White House Years*, p. 874. While Kissinger's explanation sounds tough and knowing, professional diplomats ascribe much more significance to the specific circumstances surrounding any assurance. They do not use, nor do they assume others use, that kind of assurance solely for the purpose Kissinger arbitrarily assigns it.

64. Under Secretary Elliot L. Richardson, "The Foreign Policy of the Nixon Administration: Its Aims and Strategy," September 5, *State Bulletin*, vol. 61 (September 22, 1969), p. 260.

65. Kissinger, *White House Years*, pp. 186–87. Kissinger's account is apparently in error about the date of his authorizing the Hong Kong leak, November 26; the patrol was discontinued on November 7, and this fact quickly got out on its own.

ber. However, it seemed to him there were no good opportunities, and despite several reiterations of the instructions Stoessel did not succeed in making contact until, under intense pressure from Washington, he literally ran after the Chinese chargé on December 3 to tell him the United States was prepared for serious talks. The Chinese picked up the ball and two days later, on December 11, invited him to their embassy.[66]

Both sides used their public handling of this development to send further signals. On December 11 the Chinese announced the U.S. invitation to renew the Warsaw talks—and on the same day announced the departure (on a routine hiatus in the talks) of the Soviet border delegation for Moscow.[67] On January 8 the Chinese chargé d'affaires in Warsaw advised Stoessel of Beijing's agreement to a formal meeting on January 20.[68] That same day the United States announced the agreement to resume talks in Warsaw on the 20th. In so doing the Department of State spokesman referred officially for the first time to the "People's Republic of China."[69] The Soviets also engaged in signaling: *Pravda* and *Izvestiya* juxtaposed a TASS account of a Chinese "military psychosis" with the announcement of the Chinese-American agreement to reopen talks.[70]

The year 1970 thus opened with the resumption of direct American-Chinese contact. To the Soviets the United States stressed that it was not seeking to exploit Sino-Soviet tensions. Both Secretary of State Rogers and the Department of State spokesman explicitly stated this during the week before

---

66. Ibid., p. 188. Kissinger does not repeat in his memoir the suspicion and criticism of Ambassador Stoessel that he related to the Kalbs. See Kalb and Kalb, *Kissinger*, pp. 261–63. See also Szulc, *The Illusion of Peace*, pp. 121–23, and Bernard Gwertzman, "Diplomat's Fondest Memory: China Breakthrough," *New York Times*, September 24, 1982, for additional details.

67. Wich, *Sino-Soviet Crisis Politics*, p. 226.

68. Meanwhile, on December 23 the Pakistanis had reported the impression that Beijing was ready to resume the Warsaw talks without preconditions. See Kissinger, *White House Years*, p. 191. In December Romanian Deputy Foreign Minister Gheorghe Macovescu met with Nixon and also conveyed a message from the Chinese. Kissinger does not mention this visit, probably because he was not present.

69. "U.S. and Communist China to Resume Warsaw Meetings," January 8, *State Bulletin*, vol. 62 (January 26, 1970), p. 83. The editor of the *Department of State Bulletin* still used the familiar "Communist China" in writing his caption, but the text used the official designation. There had in fact been one previous unofficial reference by an American official—Under Secretary of State Richardson had referred to "the People's Republic" in addressing the annual meeting of the American Political Science Association on September 5, 1969. See "The Foreign Policy of the Nixon Administration: Its Aims and Strategy," *State Bulletin*, vol. 61 (September 22, 1969), p. 260. President Nixon first used the term at a reception for President Ceausescu on October 26, 1970. See "President Nixon Meets With President Ceausescu of Romania," *State Bulletin*, vol. 63 (November 23, 1970), p. 649.

70. See *Pravda* and *Izvestiya*, January 10, 1970.

the Warsaw meeting.[71] Even earlier, on December 22, Kissinger had privately reassured Ambassador Dobrynin that U.S. policy was not directed against the USSR.[72] But in a subsequent meeting with Dobrynin, on the very day of the Warsaw Sino-American talks, Kissinger was less positive, telling Dobrynin that his Soviet superiors would in any case not believe anything reassuring that Kissinger told him. Kissinger said further that if the Soviets were neuralgic over China, they should realize the United States was neuralgic over Vietnam. He also declined to tell Dobrynin what the talks covered.[73]

The Sino-American meeting on January 20 in Warsaw, which was followed by a second on February 20, went well. It visibly renewed a direct contact. Beyond that, the principal achievement of the resumption of bilateral meetings, according to Kissinger, was to set up the possibility of an alternative channel in the future: a high-level American emissary to China. Clearly such a level of exchange would be important, not only to achieve more authoritative dialogue, but also to permit close control of any talks by the White House.

Not everyone in the U.S. government viewed these events with favor. The Department of State vigorously objected both to the speed of movement toward a rapprochement without first resolving long-standing issues and to the proposed high-level emissary, especially when it became clear this person would not be a senior diplomat. Kissinger presents his side of this divergence in ways that make it seem as if petty concerns had moved the "bureaucracy" at the State Department. Kissinger does concede that at least some objections were raised because the professional diplomats "did not know what was passing in secret channels." He states that he "conceded [on] all State's pet projects—references to Taiwan" and the like, in exchange for the one key thing: his proposal to send a representative to Beijing.[74]

The Chinese, unaware in advance of this proposal for a high-level emissary, according to Kissinger, were also proposing that the talks continue either at the ambassadorial level "or through other channels acceptable to both sides." Kissinger comments that in the month between the first and second Warsaw meetings the White House "redoubled our search for less constrained channels."[75]

At this juncture, in fact preceding the second Warsaw meeting in February, Kissinger opened yet another diplomatic channel, this one through the Norwegian chargé d'affaires, later ambassador, in Beijing, Ole Aalgard. In

71. Robert McCloskey, Department of State spokesman, in a news briefing on January 14; and "Interview with William P. Rogers, Secretary of State," *U.S. News and World Report,* January 26, 1970, p. 30.

72. Kissinger, *White House Years,* pp. 192–93. See the comment in note 63 above.

73. Ibid., p. 524.

74. Ibid., pp. 684–92, and see pp. 189–90.

75. Ibid., pp. 687, 688.

his memoir Kissinger mentions this channel, although curiously he does not identify the mysterious chargé d'affaires of "a West European country." Aalgard, a friend of Henry Cabot Lodge, was recommended for his "claimed access" to the Chinese leadership. This channel was used less extensively than several established later, but it did continue.[76]

On the eve of the second Warsaw meeting Nixon and Kissinger had included in their first presidential foreign policy report explicit reference to a "desire for improved relations" with China. Also reiterated was that the United States was not seeking that improvement as "a tactical means of exploiting the clash between China and the Soviet Union," nor was it interested in "joining any condominium or hostile coalition of great powers against either of the large Communist countries," an assurance to China that there were limits to the budding prospect of an American-Soviet détente. The report also explicitly stated that the United States no longer considered Sino-Soviet military collaboration against the United States to be probable. On the other hand, it continued to justify the ABM program with the original rationale that "we cannot ignore the potential Chinese threat."[77]

Several days later the official Chinese news agency replied by blasting Nixon's "hypocrisy" in calling for better relations with China. It called the report "ridiculous" and "pitiable" and characterized it as a "paper tiger."[78] For his part Kissinger, who does not mention any public or private Chinese reaction to the report, nonetheless assumes that the conciliatory position of China at Warsaw two days after the report was published meant that its messages were "received and understood."[79] While this may be, China issued many contradictory signals over the next six months, reflecting what was later confirmed to have been a severe political struggle in the Chinese leadership.

The Warsaw meetings of January and February 1970 also laid the groundwork for a major American concession on Taiwan. On January 20 Ambassador Stoessel stated on instructions that "the limited United States military presence on Taiwan is not a threat to the security of your government, and it is our hope that as peace and stability in Asia grow, we can reduce these facilities on Taiwan that we now have." At the second meeting Stoessel went from the "hope" expressed in the first meeting to official intent: "It is my Government's intention to reduce those military facilities which we now have

76. Ibid., p. 688. See also Kalb and Kalb, *Kissinger*, pp. 270, 272, 286. The Kalbs identify Ambassador Aalgard as the channel; Kissinger was their source for this information.

77. Richard M. Nixon, *U.S. Foreign Policy for the 1970's: A New Strategy for Peace*, Report to the Congress (Washington, D.C.: Government Printing Office, 1970), pp. 142, 129, 125. This report was issued on February 18, 1970. The statement about not joining any hostile coalition was placed in the section on China to reassure the Chinese (p. 142).

78. Radio Beijing, in FBIS, *China*, March 2, 1970, pp. A3–4.

79. Kissinger, *White House Years*, p. 689.

on Taiwan as tensions in the area diminish."[80] The Chinese were later to succeed in getting a firm private commitment from the United States to withdraw all its military forces and facilities. These early unilateral American concessions were highly important, perhaps crucial, in the intra-Chinese struggle over foreign policy and domestic power in 1970.

At the February 20 meeting the Chinese also officially accepted the American proposal to send a presidential envoy to Beijing.

The scheduling of a third meeting in the spring was delayed, but a date of May 20 was finally agreed to. However, on May 1 the United States invaded Cambodia, escalating the war in Indochina. In protest the Chinese canceled the May meeting, ending the Warsaw channel. Kissinger saw this situation as regrettable on the one hand, but as providential on the other—it got rid of that channel and the involvement of the State Department.[81] In addition, by that time the other channels of communication Kissinger had been setting up had taken over.

Mao Zedong chose the very day of the canceled Sino-American talks to deliver a very sharp attack on the United States. The title of his statement was "People of the World Unite and Defeat the U.S. Aggressors and All Their Running Dogs!"[82] Nixon's immediate reaction was to order the navy to send every available ship to the Taiwan Straits: "I want them to know," he told Kissinger, "we are not playing this chicken game." Kissinger did not pass on the order to the Joint Chiefs of Staff (JCS) and persuaded Nixon that the Chinese bark was much worse than its bite.[83]

On June 27 the Chinese commemorated the twentieth anniversary of President Harry S Truman's decision to interpose the U.S. fleet between Taiwan and the mainland. It did so with a sharp attack that alleged, among other things, thirteen military intrusions since the Nixon administration entered office. One of the most disturbing signs was an apparent attempt on July 2 to intercept an American EC-130 flying a reconnaissance mission one hundred miles off the China coast. This act prompted Kissinger finally to realize that some elements in the Chinese power structure might be seeking to torpedo the possibility of a Sino-American rapprochement.[84]

---

80. Quoted from Ambassador Stoessel's reporting cables, cited by Seymour M. Hersh, *The Price of Power: Kissinger in the Nixon White House* (Summit, 1983), pp. 360–61. Kissinger carefully avoids all reference to this subject in his memoir.

81. Kissinger, *White House Years*, p. 693. The White House abandoned the Warsaw channel specifically in order to exclude the State Department. See Hersh, *The Price of Power*, pp. 360–62.

82. Radio Beijing, in FBIS, *China*, May 20, 1970, pp. A1–2. There was a spate of additional criticism, for example, "The New War Adventure of the Nixon Administration," Radio Beijing, in FBIS, *China*, May 5, 1970, pp. A2–3.

83. Kissinger, *White House Years*, pp. 695–96.

84. Ibid., p. 697.

On the other hand, Zhou Enlai had been reported to have told several diplomatic visitors that he wanted to improve relations with the United States. And on July 10 the Chinese released Bishop James Edward Walsh, an American missionary arrested in 1958 on trumped-up charges of espionage.

Kissinger was just beginning to realize that there was a serious internal struggle going on within the Chinese leadership. His and Nixon's failure to be more comprehending of Chinese politics in the period 1969–72 was making it much more difficult for those in the Chinese leadership, especially Zhou Enlai, to carry out a policy of rapprochement.[85] Nixon's statements in early 1969, as much as the defection of a Chinese diplomat to the United States, had led to cancellation of the desired February 1969 Warsaw meeting. The unusual secrecy of the American approach and the multiplicity of ill-coordinated probes made it even more difficult to still suspicions that the United States was engaging in a devious game. On the other hand, the Chinese leaders had also required secrecy, and it had permitted some useful probing.

The Central Committee held a critically important meeting in Lushan from August 23 to September 6, 1970, at which Zhou realized an important victory over Lin Biao and others opposed to an opening to the United States. Zhou's success was evident both in the purge of Zhen Boda, the Maoist ideologue of the radical Cultural Revolution, and in the subsequent greater freedom Zhou had to proceed. The general line of foreign policy shifted from the Ninth Party Congress line of dual confrontation with the United States and the Soviet Union toward recognition of the Soviet Union as the greater threat, although this policy was not explicitly declared until 1972 and was not made the formal party line until the Tenth Congress in 1973.

An authoritative Soviet source has disclosed that Mao Zedong and Zhou Enlai had conducted the preliminary secret Sino-American negotiations without informing other leaders, even Lin Biao. They did not reveal these exchanges and plans to receive a presidential envoy and to proceed toward rapprochement until the Lushan meeting, where the disclosure was a "bombshell."[86] While not confirmed, this report seems quite plausible.

Soon thereafter the Chinese sent a very clear and strong signal to the United States. On October 1 Edgar Snow, a leftist American who had been a friend of the Chinese communists and of Mao Zedong personally since the 1930s, was invited to join Mao on the reviewing stand at the Chinese National Day celebration. Nor was this all. Zhou Enlai received Snow for four hours on November 5, as did Mao himself on December 18. The Chinese were sure

---

85. On the general subject of Chinese objectives and internal Chinese political controversies, see James W. Garver, *China's Decision for Rapprochement with the United States, 1968–1971* (Boulder, Colo.: Westview, 1982). See also Robert Sutter, *Chinese Foreign Policy after the Cultural Revolution, 1966–1977* (Boulder, Colo.: Westview, 1978).

86. O. Borisov and M. Il'in, "The Maoist 'Cultural Revolution,'" *Voprosy istorii* [Questions of History], no. 12 (December 1973), pp. 79–80. "O. Borisov" is a pseudonym for Oleg Rakhmanin, a key Central Committee expert on China. "M. Il'in" is also believed to be a pseudonym.

these unprecedented honors for an American would be understood as confirmation of Mao's personal sponsorship of a Sino-American détente. While, as will be seen, the Chinese continued to communicate through both the Pakistani and Romanian channels, Snow had learned as early as his November talk with Zhou that withdrawal of the American military presence on Taiwan was the Chinese bottom-line quid pro quo for Sino American détente. And in December Mao, who mentioned to Snow having received "several urgent and authentically documented inquiries" from Nixon requesting a presidential visit, said he would be happy to receive him "either as a tourist or as President." Mao also mused over the American political process and commented that that probably meant a visit in early 1972, the election year. So Mao understood much about the American process, and about Nixon's political interests. Snow also later recounted that Mao had, however, expressed puzzlement over the signals he kept getting requesting the visit of an emissary "without the [American] State Department knowing about it."[87]

Incredibly, the United States did not understand the signal represented by the special status accorded Snow. Kissinger, in mocking self-deprecation and self-excuse, comments: "Unfortunately, they overestimated our subtlety, for what they conveyed was so oblique that our crude Occidental minds completely missed the point. . . . Excessive subtlety had produced a failure of communication."[88]

While missing the Chinese political upheavals and the "too subtle" Chinese signals,[89] the White House kept trying its own signaling. Further steps toward a loosening of trade restrictions were taken on December 19, 1969, and April 29 and August 26, 1970, as the United States peeled the trade artichoke. Attempts to develop new channels included bringing General Vernon Walters, Army attaché in Paris (and assistant to Kissinger in the secret Vietnamese peace negotiations since November 1969), to approach the Chinese military attaché in Paris. Both this attempt, made in June 1970, and another made in

---

87. The Chinese embargoed Snow from publishing the invitation to Nixon until after Kissinger's visit in July 1971, but assumed word would get to the president. As with Snow's presence on the reviewing stand, Mao again overestimated American coordination. A former intelligence analyst and White House consultant on China policy, Professor Allen Whiting, had volunteered, upon learning of Snow's meeting with Mao, to visit Snow in Switzerland and debrief him. Kissinger's NSC China adviser, John Holdridge, told him not to, since Snow was a leftist. Only some time later did the CIA learn from an undercover intermediary contact with Snow that Mao had expressed a willingness to receive Nixon. See Hersh, *The Price of Power*, pp. 364–67; Whiting, *China Quarterly*, no. 82 (1980), p. 338; and see Edgar Snow, "A Conversation with Mao Tse-tung," *Life*, April 30, 1971, pp. 46–48; and Edgar Snow, *The Long Revolution* (Bantam, 1972), p. 172. In his memoir Nixon incorrectly states that he knew of Mao's comment about readiness to receive him "within a few days after he made it." Nixon, *RN*, p. 547. Kissinger notes and explains this error in *White House Years*, p. 1487, note 6.

88. Kissinger, *White House Years*, pp. 698–99.

89. One reason for the failure in both respects was the administration's exclusion of policy and intelligence analysts from knowledge of what was going on in Sino-American relations.

September 1970 failed. (It does not seem to have occurred to Kissinger that a Chinese military attaché might well have been associated with Lin Biao's faction—but then he and Nixon seemed oblivious to such aspects of Chinese politics.)[90] In September Kissinger opened yet another diplomatic channel through his friend Jean Sainteny, former French delegate general in Hanoi.

On October 5 Nixon essayed a far from subtle signal in an interview published in *Time* magazine. He stated that China would inevitably assume a world role, and that "if there is anything I want to do before I die, it is to go to China."[91]

On October 25 and 26, with extraordinary coincidence and in rapid succession, the presidents of Pakistan and Romania visited Nixon in Washington. President Yahya Khan was about to go to Beijing, and Nixon asked him to convey that the United States believed a rapprochement with China to be "essential" and was prepared to send a high-level envoy such as Robert Murphy, Thomas Dewey, or Henry Kissinger. Nixon repeated the same general message to President Ceauşescu, but at the same time stressed U.S. desire to improve relations with both the Soviet Union and China.[92] As noted, Nixon used this occasion to refer publicly for the first time to the People's Republic of China.[93]

The Romanians later disclosed that Nixon told Ceauşescu he regarded Taiwan not as an international, but as an internal, problem to be resolved by the Chinese themselves in a peaceful way. That of course was Beijing's position. Although Kissinger has denied that report, it seems clear the United States signaled some give on Taiwan.[94]

In November Mao received Yahya Khan and Zhou received Romanian Deputy Premier Gheorghe Radulescu. On December 8 the Pakistani ambassador brought to Nixon a personal message from Zhou Enlai welcoming a special envoy from the president "to discuss the subject of the vacation of [withdrawal from] Chinese territories called Taiwan." In December the Chinese also replied through the French that they had received the U.S. request to establish a secure channel. And on January 11 the Romanians belatedly passed

90. Kissinger, *White House Years*, pp. 688, 696. Walters, *Silent Missions*, pp. 3–4, 525–26, states this approach was first tried in April 1970, but he mixes up other dates in his account of events between this probe in 1970 and another in 1971. Thus that date may be in error.

91. " 'I Did Not Want the Hot Words of TV' and Other Presidential Reflections in a Crisis Week," *Time*, October 5, 1970.

92. Kissinger, *White House Years*, p. 699. He added the reference to the Soviet Union in case the Soviets learned of the message from the Romanians.

93. Ibid. Kissinger notes this first use of the official name of China but fails to comment that while the press did not note this signal, Ambassador Dobrynin did. He called Kissinger that very night to inquire about the significance of the reference. Kissinger blandly denied that it meant anything. See Kalb and Kalb, *Kissinger*, p. 267.

94. Kalb and Kalb, *Kissinger*, pp. 267–68. The Kalbs were personally informed of this signal by Romanian officials; Kissinger's denial was probably pro forma.

along a message from Zhou Enlai and, surprisingly, Lin Biao not only confirming the earlier communications, but for the first time explicitly inviting President Nixon to visit Beijing, as he had Bucharest and Belgrade (underlining by this reference to Yugoslavia and Romania a counter-Soviet orientation).[95]

The American response to the Chinese leaders, sent through both the Pakistanis in December and the Romanians in January, was that the United States was prepared to discuss the whole range of international issues, including Taiwan.[96] No reference was made to a presidential visit.

On December 23 Ambassador Huang Zhen told Sainteny that the message from Kissinger the Frenchman had passed along in September had been received. The Chinese were evidently holding this French channel in reserve, and did use it later as well.[97]

The second annual presidential report on foreign policy, issued in February 1971, was again used to signal the Chinese. Released on February 25, it continued the new policy of referring to the People's Republic of China (although it referred to both "Communist China" and "Mainland China" as well). It also stated, "We are prepared to establish a dialogue with Peking [Beijing]." On the other hand, while these signals surfaced U.S. interest in rapprochement, the burden of responsibility for movement was placed on the Chinese (for example, "there could be new opportunities for the Peoples Republic of China to explore the path of normalization of its relations with its neighbors and with the world, including our own country"). Moreover, the American people were cautioned to be "realistic about the prospects. . . . so long as Peking continues to be adamant for hostility, there is little we can do by ourselves to improve the relationship." Still, "what we can do, we will."[98]

Steps to improve relations with China were set back in early 1971, as they had been the year before, by an escalatory American military initiative in Indochina. In May 1970 it had been the American "incursion" into Cambodia; in February 1971 it was the incursion of the American-supported South Vietnamese army into Laos. While Nixon and Kissinger were well aware this move would slow attempts to move toward rapprochement with China, they correctly estimated that it would delay this movement only briefly. On the other hand, there is no indication in Kissinger's and other memoirs indicating

---

95. Kissinger, *White House Years*, pp. 703–04.

96. Ibid., p. 704. Kissinger states that the reply through both channels was identical, but was to be transmitted in written form by the Pakistanis and orally by the Romanians, to show the slight U.S. preference for the former channel out of concern that the Soviets might be monitoring the latter.

97. Ibid., pp. 698, 703, 713. Sainteny had already served as an early unofficial channel to the North Vietnamese leaders, many of whom he knew personally. See ibid., pp. 258, 277–79.

98. Richard M. Nixon, *U.S. Foreign Policy for the 1970's: Building the Peace*, Report to the Congress (GPO, 1971), vol. 2, p. 109, and see pp. 105–09. This report was issued on February 25, 1971.

that the American leaders were aware of the increasingly tense relations developing between the Vietnamese and the Chinese and the additional complications the action in Laos posed. The failure of the South Vietnamese invasion and its withdrawal from Laos did, however, reassure both China and North Vietnam that the United States was not prepared to commit American troops to such offensive ventures. Moreover, the American troop withdrawals continued. On April 7 Nixon announced that an additional 100,000 Americans would be taken out of Vietnam between May and December 1971.

In March Kissinger convened first an NSC Senior Review Group interagency meeting on the NSSM studies of China policy issues commissioned in 1969 and 1970, and then an NSC meeting.[99] The members of the NSC, including Secretaries Rogers and Laird, were not, however, made privy to the extensive secret White House diplomacy with the Chinese leaders.

Meanwhile, the bureaucracy was permitted to proceed on the more limited visible track. The Under Secretaries Committee produced a list of possible substantive unilateral trade and other steps that went well beyond the cosmetic changes of 1969 and 1970. Kissinger favored a graduated series of steps, and divided the list into three parts. Nixon approved going ahead with the first set of measures, and on April 14 the United States announced it was lifting important aspects of the twenty-one-year embargo on American trade with China.[100]

By coincidence, the Chinese gave an even more important public signal that same day. On April 6 they had invited the American team to the Thirty-first World Table Tennis Championship match in Beijing, itself a signal. Then on April 14, Prime Minister Zhou Enlai received the team. Zhou used the occasion to state publicly that a new page had been opened in relations between the two peoples.[101] Zhou also opened China to visits by American newsmen. On April 30 Edgar Snow's article on his December interview with Mao appeared in _Life_ magazine.[102]

One other vignette of interest concerned a Chinese plan to hedge their bets by inviting Senators Edward M. Kennedy, Edmund R. Muskie, and George C. McGovern, along with news commentators James Reston, Walter Cronkite, and Walter Lippmann, to visit China. While the Chinese leaders were quite content to deal with Richard Nixon (as Mao had observed to Snow, "_at present_, the problems between China and the U.S.A. would have to be resolved with Nixon"), they did not want to hinge their investment in détente

99. Kissinger, _White House Years_, p. 705.

100. Kissinger called in the Soviet chargé, Yuly Vorontsov, the day before to inform and reassure him that the move had no anti-Soviet intent; he also had Ron Ziegler deny anti-Soviet intent in a White House press briefing on the fourteenth. _White House Years_, pp. 712–13.

101. "Premier Chou Meets Table Tennis Delegations of Canada, Colombia, England, Nigeria and United States," _Peking Review_, vol. 14 (April 23, 1971), pp. 4–5.

102. Snow, _Life_, April 30, 1971, pp. 27 ff.

with the United States on Nixon's political future—particularly when the contact and implied commitments had been so elaborately clandestine. When word of this invitation reached Nixon, and it did not come from the Chinese, he became very upset.[103] Nixon asked Kissinger to discourage the Chinese from doing anything that would benefit his political opponents and detract from his own anticipated triumph. Kissinger did so by asking the Pakistanis to pass along the importance of confining U.S.-Chinese contact to the established channel until an official link was securely established.[104]

Despite Nixon's efforts at strong control, the administration suffered from some indiscipline. For example, in April Vice-President Spiro T. Agnew told a group of reporters that he disagreed with the policy of normalizing relations with Peking and had argued against it at an NSC meeting.[105]

The most serious problems, however, were again caused by the extreme secrecy that Nixon and Kissinger imposed. On April 28, as one instance, the Department of State spokesman, in a statement cleared at the presumably informed policy level within the department, declared the American position on sovereignty over Taiwan to be "an unsettled question subject to future international resolution." Kissinger notes the incident and comments that this position had been rejected by both direct parties to the China dispute.[106] He does not, however, disclose the real reason for his concern—this position also contradicted a new position the White House had already taken in its secret exchanges with the Chinese.

Far more serious were public remarks by Secretary Rogers the very next day. Rogers, uninformed of the secret exchanges and the president's plans, discounted the just-published report of Mao's comments to Snow that China was ready to receive Nixon as not "a serious invitation." Moreover, he went on to describe China's policy as "expansionist" and "paranoiac" and commented that a Nixon visit might be possible "down the road a piece" *if* China joined the international community and complied with "the rules of international law." Finally, his statements contrasted with Nixon's and Kissinger's public (and, to the Soviets, private) assurances that U.S. efforts toward normalization of relations with China were not directed at the Soviet Union. Rogers stated that if these efforts to improve relations with China and the Soviet Union stimulated the conflict between those two countries, that was a "dividend" for the United States.[107]

---

103. See Whiting, *China Quarterly*, no. 82 (1980), p. 339.

104. Kissinger, *White House Years*, pp. 717–18. Kissinger does not mention the Chinese invitation to the other Americans. Rather, he raises the issue of Nixon's concern as though it were an idiosyncrasy.

105. Ibid., p. 713; and Nixon, *RN*, p. 549. Agnew's comment may be cited as an argument for Nixon and Kissinger's secrecy, although had Agnew been privy to Nixon's game plan he would probably not have made the comment.

106. Kissinger, *White House Years*, p. 720.

107. Ibid.

On May 9 Nixon and Kissinger sent their reply to Zhou via the Pakistanis, proposing a secret meeting of Kissinger and Zhou Enlai "on Chinese soil preferably at some location within convenient flying distance from Pakistan," after June 15. They envisaged an announcement soon after the meeting of the planned visit by President Nixon. Special emphasis was placed on secrecy.[108]

On June 2 Zhou accepted the arrangements as planned and subsequently set July 9 for the Kissinger visit. There still remained the problem in Washington of gearing the project in with the operations of the rest of the government without the visit becoming known. Nixon and Kissinger went to extremes. For example, the White House arranged for the American ambassador in Pakistan, Joseph Farland, a political appointee, to make a "private" trip back to California, deceiving the Department of State as to his purpose. In fact, he was to meet secretly with Kissinger. Farland was informed of Kissinger's trip and instructed not to let Secretary of State Rogers or any other American know. Communications were handled initially through a secret U.S. Navy channel and later through the CIA, all arranged by Kissinger.[109]

Kissinger had to arrange a cover trip to South Asia in order to get to Pakistan, whence he would secretly fly to China. Secretary Rogers and the State Department opposed the Kissinger trip, correctly seeing it, given the alleged purposes, as unnecessary and a bad precedent. Had they known the real reason for his going, they would have been even more upset, but at least the trip would have made sense.

There were other complications. Vice-President Agnew wanted to make a long-awaited trip to Taiwan to see Chiang Kai-shek. Independently, Secretary of Defense Laird wanted to inspect U.S. defense installations on Taiwan—a particularly sensitive matter on which Nixon and Kissinger were signaling the Chinese. Finally, just at that juncture the *New York Times* began to print the leaked Pentagon Papers on the war in Vietnam.[110]

---

108. Ibid., p. 724. The reference to some "convenient" location in China appears odd. Kissinger explains at length that Nixon had tried hard to arrange that Kissinger not precede him to Beijing—he thought, rightly, that it would steal some of the thunder of his own trip. It is also clear that Kissinger did not even halfheartedly comply with Nixon's repeated instructions on that point—which Nixon continued to reiterate right up to the time of Kissinger's departure for China. Ibid., p. 734.

109. Ibid., pp. 721–23. Kissinger muses in his memoir over his use of the back channel communications, but does not note his use of navy channels. Unbeknownst at the time, the latter led to the Joint Chiefs' learning of the plans for the secret China trip through a spy they had placed in Kissinger's own NSC operation.

110. Ibid., pp. 728–30; and see *New York Times*, June 13, 1971. Kissinger does not note that the Chinese might have seen the release of the Pentagon Papers, which were damaging to the previous administration, as a further signal of the intention of the present administration to get out of that war.

Kissinger recounts his visit to Beijing in July 1971 at great length and with evident pride and pleasure.[111] It succeeded admirably. Perhaps the most remarkable aspect of the Kissinger visit was the virtual thrall that Zhou Enlai cast over his visitor. Kissinger was charmed by both Zhou and Mao, and by the Chinese in general—in contrast to the Soviet leaders whom he was soon to meet.[112]

The principal issues were Taiwan and Vietnam, against the background of Sino-Soviet tension and American-Soviet maneuvering toward a détente. Kissinger was understandably secretive about the nature of the discussions on Taiwan and Vietnam, each of which involved very sensitive domestic and international political issues. While the full record is not yet available enough has become known to make clear that a substantive deal was made to withdraw American military forces from Taiwan and that some degree of Chinese support for American disengagement from Vietnam was elicited.[113]

Kissinger records that Nixon had urged him to keep in play a "possible move towards the Soviets" in order to exert leverage on the Chinese.[114] Direct discussion of the Soviet side of the triangle—obviously very significant in its impact—was appropriately minimal. While Zhou Enlai did make the standard Chinese attacks on Soviet (and to a lesser extent American) motives as superpowers, a category to which he said China did not aspire, there was one direct, practical discussion. Zhou proposed that Nixon visit the next summer, but tactfully added that he thought it more prudent that he meet the Soviets first. Kissinger countered by proposing that the summits take place in the order arranged—China first. Zhou, Kissinger reports, did not seem unhappy to learn that a Soviet summit had not yet been scheduled and that the United States was prepared to meet the Chinese first. He then offered the spring of 1972, to which Kissinger agreed.[115]

Kissinger does not disclose that he engaged in exceedingly frank discussions of the Soviet "threat" that both China and the United States faced. To some extent on his first visit in July 1971, and in greater detail on a second visit in October, Kissinger in fact provided ultrasensitive intelligence on

---

111. Kissinger, *White House Years*, pp. 733–84; Kissinger also treats in detail the developments in 1970–71 leading up to the trip, examined above, although with significant omissions. Ibid., pp. 684–732. Nixon, on the other hand, devotes only three short paragraphs to Kissinger's trip, and only a dozen pages to the entire background of China policy from 1969 until his own trip in 1972. Nixon, *RN*, pp. 544–58.

112. Kissinger, *White House Years*, especially pp. 742–47, 1058–74.

113. Hersh, *The Price of Power*, pp. 365–72, 375–76.

114. Kissinger, *White House Years*, p. 735.

115. Ibid., pp. 750–51. Zhou did not know for certain whether or when the Soviet summit meeting had been arranged and had probably proposed that the Chinese visit follow in order not to suggest something that might have to be rejected. The United States was thus left to indicate its preference, and the Chinese were pleased to be given priority.

Soviet military activities derived from communications intercepts and other sources. He even showed Zhou high-resolution satellite photographs, according to aides who assisted Kissinger in preparing for the two trips.[116] This material included intelligence on Soviet military forces and facilities along the Chinese border.[117] There is no indication the Chinese reciprocated.

Kissinger wanted to be sure that the Chinese appreciated the quality of American capabilities, and he also wanted to provide an earnest expression of the United States' intention to be a serious partner. It was, however, a major departure from the policy of evenhandedness in developing relations with the two major communist powers. Kissinger covers this unacknowledged intelligence disclosure in his memoir only by the disarming general statement that "I sometimes went so far as to let him [Zhou Enlai] see the internal studies that supported our conclusions."[118]

Kissinger also used the occasion of his first visit to China to make a gratuitous one-way promise to Zhou to "inform Peking in detail of any understanding affecting Chinese interests that we might consider with the Soviets."[119] This far-reaching commitment had not been discussed with or approved by anyone in the American leadership with the possible (but unlikely) exception of President Nixon. Indeed, it remained unknown to the secretary of state and others in government until the appearance of Kissinger's memoir years later.

It was also agreed that subsequent communications could be handled through the Chinese ambassador in Paris, Huang Zhen, and Major General Walters, the American defense attaché there.[120] This channel was used later that same month to arrange a secret meeting of Kissinger and Ambassador Huang on July 26. At that time Huang confirmed with Zhou that the Nixon trip would be preceded by another visit by Kissinger in October. Also on that occasion, General Walters reports, Kissinger again promised to "keep the Chinese informed of any talks we might have with other Socialist countries," meaning the Soviet Union, and said that that promise could be reported to Zhou Enlai. "This," notes Walters, "seemed to please and reassure the Chi-

---

116. See Hersh, *The Price of Power*, p. 376. I have been able independently to confirm this fact with intelligence officials who subsequently learned of the disclosures. Presumably President Nixon in some fashion approved them; it was not done through normal channels or cleared with Director of Central Intelligence Richard Helms.

117. In an apparently coincidental move, on July 28, 1971, the United States announced suspension of its previously unacknowledged aerial reconnaissance overflights (SR-71 aircraft and unmanned drones) over mainland China.

118. Kissinger, *White House Years*, p. 747. Kissinger was covered in another way: he (and later Nixon) had no American interpreters present for any of their private talks with the Chinese leaders—a practice they also used in the Soviet Union.

119. Kissinger, *White House Years*, p. 765.

120. Ibid., p. 753.

nese."[121] This promise went even further than Kissinger's earlier pledge to Zhou Enlai.

In his memoir Kissinger makes only a very brief and oblique reference to his meetings with Huang Zhen. He does note that he "took great pains to keep the Chinese informed of all our moves with Moscow *and of our assessment of Soviet intentions*"—indicating the broad way in which he interpreted his extraordinary promise to inform and consult with the Chinese on Soviet affairs. He notes discussions on the deteriorating South Asian subcontinent. By the context of his reference Kissinger hints that he presented the U.S. rejection of the Soviet proposal for a five-power disarmament conference as a favor to the Chinese. Indeed, he protests, perhaps too much, that "Peking, of course, was offered no veto over our policy or our actions." While this is literally true, he masks the fact that he leaned far to their side in order to curry Chinese favor.[122]

As Kissinger correctly observes, his surprise visit to Beijing and the announcement of the forthcoming Nixon summit visit stirred the Soviets into moving more rapidly toward some agreements leading to the May 1972 summit in Moscow. By September the Soviets reached agreements in the quadripartite negotiations on Berlin and concluded the Agreement on Measures to Reduce the Risk of Accidental Outbreak of Nuclear War, negotiated in the SALT talks. Gromyko visited Washington that month, ready to settle the Moscow summit meeting. Kissinger's second trip to Beijing was announced on October 5; on October 14, the Moscow summit was announced.

The new direct channel through General Walters in Paris was used to make arrangements for Kissinger's second visit. More importantly, it was also used for other messages that the United States did not wish to share with third parties. On October 2, in accordance with Kissinger's secret commitment to Ambassador Huang, Walters reported on the Nixon-Gromyko talks, and on October 9, five days in advance, the Chinese were advised of the forthcoming announcement of the U.S.-Soviet summit. On September 3 Walters had conveyed a message on the forthcoming U.S.-USSR Agreement on Measures to Reduce the Risk of Accidental Outbreak of Nuclear War, and on the fact that the United States and the Soviet Union were about to begin a negotiation on avoiding naval incidents at sea.[123] Later in November he relayed a request from the president for the release of Richard Fecteau and John Downey, two CIA officers captured in 1952 when the aircraft carrying them was shot down over China. Fecteau was released in December, having served almost all of his twenty-year sentence. Downey, imprisoned for life, was released in March 1973.

---

121. Walters, *Silent Missions*, p. 532.

122. Kissinger, *White House Years*, pp. 765–66, 768. Emphasis added.

123. Walters, *Silent Missions*, pp. 535, 538–39; and Kissinger, *White House Years*, p. 768. Walters omits reference to the agreement on measures to prevent accidental nuclear war, while Kissinger omits reference to the talks on incidents at sea.

In October and November 1972, as the perennial question of Chinese representation in the United Nations came up, the United States officially adopted a position favoring dual representation; it was ready to admit the People's Republic of China, but not to expel the Republic of China (Taiwan). That position lost, and the People's Republic of China was seated in place of Taiwan. This outcome resulted in considerable criticism in the United States, and Kissinger's presence in Beijing at that very time (so scheduled by the Chinese) was widely believed to have undercut the official U.S. stand on the issue in New York.

Subsequently it was agreed through the Paris channel that in an emergency the Chinese and American U.N. delegations could deal with one another. That channel, in fact, soon became the usual one. Kissinger and Ambassador Huang Hua had more than a dozen meetings in New York prior to the opening of liaison offices in Beijing and Washington in mid-1973.

The most significant development in this period involved the Chinese leadership. Lin Biao, the designated successor to Mao Zedong, had opposed the Chinese rapprochement with the United States. Although he had been overruled when the issue was joined at the Lushan Central Committee plenum in August 1970, he continued for the next year to oppose further steps, in particular the invitations to Kissinger and Nixon. Mao Zedong himself confirmed this internal struggle to Nixon in February 1972.[124]

In order to clarify the ideological basis for a rapprochement with the United States and to defend it against Lin Biao and other opponents, Mao and Zhou in August resurrected Mao's essay "On Policy," first formulated and published in 1940 to justify a policy of collaboration with the Kuomintang Chinese Nationalists of Chiang Kai-shek against the Japanese. The policy, designed for "an extremely complex struggle," called for a tactical united front with a less immediately dangerous adversary (the "secondary enemy") against a more dangerous "principal enemy."[125] This policy is not uniquely Chinese, but it has had a long tradition there; it was formerly termed "using barbarians to check barbarians." A similar, slightly more explicit, explanation had been given in a confidential internal Chinese document in mid-July, assuring its middle-level-cadre readers that Mao himself had invited Nixon, and that the offer represented "another tactic in the struggle against imperialism."[126] This new line provided a rationale for the suddenly revealed policy of rapprochement

---

124. Kissinger, *White House Years*, pp. 768, 1061.

125. See Wich, *Sino-Soviet Crisis Politics*, pp. 256–60. The article, titled "A Strong Weapon to Unite the People and Defeat the Enemy—Study 'On Policy,'" appeared in *Hongqi*, no. 9 (September 1971), and was also printed in *Renmin Ribao*, August 16, 1971, and broadcast by Radio Beijing that same day. See FBIS, *China*, August 18, 1971, pp. B1, B4, B6.

126. The document, dated July 21, 1971, is apparently authentic. See Chao Ch'un-shan, "The Change in Peiping's Foreign Policy as Viewed from the Line Adapted by the CCP," *East Asia Quarterly* (Taiwan), vol. 5 (October 1973).

with the United States. It did not, however, mean an end to opposition. In fact, dramatic events were to unfold in September.

At the time it was very unclear what had happened. On September 12 a Chinese military aircraft crashed in Mongolia (with no Mongolian or Soviet protest about an overflight). All the leaders of China then dropped out of sight for five days. All aircraft of the Chinese Air Force were grounded. On September 20 the annual National Day parade on October 1 was canceled. Gradually it became clear that Mao's designated successor, Lin Biao, vice chairman of the party Central Committee, deputy prime minister, and minister of defense, had been removed. The rumor that he had died trying to escape to the Soviet Union by air on September 12, 1971, was officially confirmed much later, in July 1972. Still later it was also reported that he had attempted to flee following an attempted coup d'état. Even later charges were made that he had planned to murder Mao, Zhou, and other leaders.

Most intriguing from the standpoint of the present inquiry were the reports circulating in China within a few months that Lin had planned to take with him to the Soviet Union secret recordings of the Zhou Enlai–Kissinger conversations of July 1971.[127] Later, in August, the Chinese press began to accuse the Soviet Union of collusion or instigation in Lin's plot. The Soviet press strongly rebutted these charges.

The outcome of the Lin Biao affair was helpful to the continuation of a Chinese-American rapprochement. With Lin's demise the ability of Mao and Zhou to continue their efforts to improve Sino-American relations was strengthened. There remained, however, the need for further diplomatic compromise on the issues of Vietnam and Taiwan. Kissinger's October trip considerably advanced negotiation of a solution, with both sides making partial compromises and restating their differences. Kissinger accepted Zhou's proposal that the communiqué at the Nixon summit meeting incorporate not only an agreed document, but also separate statements of the differing Chinese and American positions on other issues.[128]

On the eve of President Nixon's trip to China the third annual foreign policy report was issued. It included a long review of the development of U.S. policy toward China. The purpose, however, was not to signal to the Chinese, but to help prepare the American people for the rapprochement and to reassure them and others of the United States' continuing commitment to Taiwan.[129] It was again reaffirmed that "our policy is not aimed against Moscow." The report stated that the United States would not "use our opening to

---

127. See Lee Lescaze, "Lin Piao Attempt Seen to Give Russia Secrets," *Washington Post*, March 15, 1972.

128. Kissinger, *White House Years*, pp. 781–84.

129. Richard M. Nixon, *U.S. Foreign Policy for the 1970's: The Emerging Structure of Peace*, Report to the Congress (GPO, 1972), vol. 3, pp. 26–37. Issued on February 9, 1972.

Peking to exploit Sino-Soviet tensions . . . because it would be self-defeating and dangerous. . . . we will try to have better relations with both countries."[130]

On February 14 the United States further relaxed its trade controls on China. Trade was now allowed for all commodities that could be sold to the Soviet Union or Eastern Europe. This act ended the additional, more stringent limitations the United States had placed on trade with China, which went beyond the general Western restrictions on trade with communist countries. (The principal Western European countries, Japan, and the United States have for many years met in a Coordinating Committee for Multilateral Export Controls [COCOM] to set restraints on trade with the communist countries.)

The president's visit to China from February 21 to 28, 1972, was an important step in advancing American-Chinese relations, and hence triangular diplomacy. But it was far from the euphoric hyperbole Nixon used in his toast at the end of the visit: "This was the week that changed the world."[131] The Shanghai Communiqué issued at the close of the trip embodied a modus vivendi for Chinese-American relations that fell far short of full normalization of relations, but recognized that the two countries had common interests and that there was a need to communicate as well as to work to overcome gradually the remaining difficulties. Direct contacts began almost immediately in New York through the Chinese UN representative and Kissinger. A year later official liaison offices—embassies in all but name and protocol—were established in Washington and Beijing. For the next six and a half years, however, bilateral relations remained on a general plateau, until significant changes in American-Soviet relations led to new moves by both the United States and China. Nevertheless, in those intervening years triangular diplomacy did play a sometimes significant role.

The Chinese in 1972 were pleased that triangular diplomacy was being established, and that Nixon had chosen to visit Beijing *before* going to Moscow.[132] They were also pleased at American acceptance of a reference in the joint communiqué to opposing "hegemony"—the new code word for Soviet expansionism and domination.[133] There had been very little discussion of the Soviet Union at the summit, but little needed to be said.

In one unplanned and indirect way that has been overlooked the communiqué did have an impact on the launching of American-Soviet détente.

---

130. Ibid., pp. 35–36.

131. Nixon, *RN*, p. 580; on the trip see pp. 559–80; also Kissinger, *White House Years*, pp. 1049–96, for the most complete accounts; and Kalb and Kalb, *Kissinger*, pp. 303–23.

132. Ibid., pp. 567–68.

133. Kissinger, *White House Years*, p. 1075. Kissinger claims that it was the American side that first used the term, which later became standard Chinese rhetoric, p. 783. Nixon makes clear that, public pontifications aside, antihegemony *did* mean counter-Soviet. *RN*, p. 577.

At the request of the Chinese the United States agreed to include in the communiqué acceptance of the principle of "peaceful coexistence."[134] This precedent later made it difficult to oppose the much more meaningful inclusion of this principle in the agreement on Basic Principles of U.S.-Soviet Relations. According to several of Kissinger's close aides, this precedent in the Chinese communiqué influenced Kissinger to accept the Soviet formulation.[135]

The disposition of the difficult Taiwan issue that resulted from the visits was, in my judgment, wise. It was, however—as domestic opponents immediately suspected and charged—the result of prior secret understandings.[136] The flurry of criticism, which emanated not only from the right wing, was overcome, but it led some people to have suspicions about the secret diplomacy of Nixon and Kissinger, suspicions they were only too ready to apply, also with some justification, to the development of American relations with the Soviet Union.

One other point deserves mention. The United States committed itself to "the ultimate objective of the withdrawal of all U.S. forces and military installations from Taiwan." In the meantime, it was to "progressively reduce its forces and military installations on Taiwan as the tension in the area diminishes."[137] While these commitments involved a substantial American concession,[138] they also represented—as Kissinger intended—a substantial gain for American diplomacy: the Chinese now had a direct stake in helping see that "tensions in the area," above all the Vietnam War, be ended soon.

The final aspect of triangular diplomacy with respect to American-Chinese relations in the key year 1972 concerns the United States' handling of its relations with the Soviet Union. The way in which each member of the triangle treats its relations with a second in its contact with the third is an important aspect of the relationship. The United States often declared its evenhandedness in this respect. During the Nixon summit meeting in the Soviet Union Kissinger publicly declared that "our basic position with respect to

---

134. Kissinger, *White House Years*, p. 1492. Kissinger provides the entire text of the Shanghai Communiqué.

135. Interviews with close associates of Kissinger. See chapter 9.

136. In particular see Hersh, *The Price of Power*, pp. 490, 495–500.

137. Cited from Kissinger, *White House Years*, p. 1492.

138. There is considerable evidence that Nixon and Kissinger had gone beyond signaling hints to accepting what the Chinese regarded as a commitment to withdraw all American military forces and installations from Taiwan within a short period. See Hersh, *The Price of Power*, pp. 490, 495–500. As early as June 2, 1971, in the note inviting Kissinger to China, Zhou Enlai had stressed that "the first issue to be settled" was the concrete manner of effecting "the withdrawal of all the U.S. Armed Forces from Taiwan and Taiwan Straits area." Kissinger comments disingenuously that Zhou had "again framed the Taiwan problem in a manner most susceptible to solution: the withdrawal of US forces." Kissinger, *White House Years*, p. 727. What Kissinger neglects to point out is that that objective had already been the subject of negotiation and that it was "most susceptible to solution" only because the United States was prepared to accede.

both of these large Communist countries is that we will not discuss one of them in the capital of the other." [139]

Less than three weeks later, on June 16, the day after Kissinger made a major presentation to Congress on the SALT strategic arms agreements signed in Moscow, he departed for four days of talks in Beijing devoted principally to briefing the Chinese leaders on the Moscow summit meeting. [140] Kissinger was unsure whether he would be as warmly received in Beijing after the bombing of Hanoi and Haiphong, but found that he was. [141] On his first trip to China a year earlier Kissinger had broken new ground in American relations with a communist power in that he had provided sensitive intelligence on Soviet military developments of interest to the Chinese. On this visit he held a detailed discussion of the summit exchanges with the Soviet leaders and of their implications for American-Chinese developments. In both cases the nominally and officially evenhanded policy of the United States toward the two communist powers was in fact tilted toward the Chinese. It is an intriguing question whether even President Nixon realized the extent of the tilt.

Kissinger had, moreover, declined earlier to do the same for the Soviets. As he recounts in his memoir, "I had always opposed briefing Moscow on our conversations with the Chinese because it gave the Soviets too easy an opportunity to play their version back to Peking to stimulate Chinese fears of a Soviet-American condominium." [142] This double standard continued to be generally applied to U.S.-Soviet and U.S.-Chinese exchanges.

The Chinese, for their part, remained wary of their new tie with the United States, particularly given the continuing internal political conflict. A confidential Chinese internal document from 1973 justified the Nixon visit and Shanghai Communiqué in some detail. But it also showed that the removal of Lin Biao had not stilled Chinese doubts about the new policy of limited rapprochement with the United States. The document, issued by the army political department in Yunnan Province, labeled both U.S. imperialism and Soviet revisionism "arch enemies" and called for "resolutely combatting the hegemonism and power politics of the two superpowers." It flatly stated that "Soviet revisionism is our country's most threatening enemy." One reason was geo-

---

139. "News Conference of Dr. Kissinger, Kiev, May 29," *State Bulletin*, vol. 66 (June 26, 1972), pp. 890–91 (and from his news conference in Moscow the same day, see ibid., p. 888).

140. In his memoir Kissinger devotes but a single sentence to this visit, mentioning only that he briefed the Chinese leaders on the Moscow summit "to maintain momentum in our new relationship and to discomfit Hanoi." *White House Years*, p. 1304. He does not comment on how Moscow must have taken it.

141. As noted above, Kissinger omits from his memoir any comment on this trip, but he had disclosed to his friend Henry Brandon his uncertainty at the time as to the Chinese attitude. See Henry Brandon, *The Retreat of American Power* (Doubleday, 1973), p. 347.

142. Ibid., p. 524.

graphic propinquity, another that the Soviet Union was expanding, while American "aggressive power has been weakened." Hence the justification for using one enemy against another (without, however, allying with either), to "aggravate the contradictions between the United States and the Soviet Union," and frustrating Soviet desires to see a U.S.-China conflict.[143]

To justify dealing with Nixon, the document referred to the president, as Mao had, as the man who then had power. But it went on to say more explicitly that "Nixon is a man of transition, through whom we settle Sino-U.S. relations and get in touch with the people of the United States." After quoting the Shanghai Communiqué correctly on the delicate issue of "the ultimate objective" of "the withdrawal of all U.S. forces and installations from Taiwan," it said that prospects were much improved for negotiating a peaceful unification of the country "in the wake of the improvement in relations between China and the United States, *with the U.S. Army to be withdrawn from Taiwan.*"[144]

A Chinese official and former army general later remarked in a conversation with me that it was an old Chinese tradition to ally with a more distant enemy against a closer one, and all the more so when the closer one was seen as the more immediately dangerous. The official was too polite to mention the additional Chinese perception that Soviet power was growing and American power waning in East Asia. He did, however, hint at an additional factor—that as the United States moved further away militarily (by disengaging from Vietnam), it had been possible for the two countries to move closer politically.[145]

Soviet Reactions

The Soviet role in the formation of triangular diplomacy in the period 1969 to 1972 was essentially reactive. The détente with the United States and efforts to contain the deterioration of Sino-Soviet relations were an important part of the process. But the essential element was the establishment of Sino-American relations.

---

143. "The Great Victory of Chairman Mao's Revolutionary Diplomatic Line," Confidential Reference Material on Education on the Situation, no. 43, for Distribution to Companies and Above, April 4, 1973. See *Issues and Studies*, vol. 10 (June 1974), pp. 99–108, and (July 1974), pp. 94–105; and in both Chinese and English in *Chinese Communist Internal Politics and Foreign Policy* (Taipei: Institute of International Relations, 1974), pp. 130–40, 175–84. It is accepted as genuine by leading scholars; for example, see A. Doak Barnett, *China and the Major Powers in East Asia* (Brookings Institution, 1977), pp. 204, 383.

144. Ibid. Emphasis added.

145. From a conversation with me.

The substantial published commentary in the USSR generally criticized the Chinese for their rapprochement with the United States, claiming it to be an element in China's strategy of conflict with the Soviet Union. The Soviets were able, of course, to document this perception easily. They have cited Chinese writings identifying the Soviet Union as "the main enemy," and U.S.-Soviet rivalry is depicted as the basis for Chinese rapprochement with the United States in a "strategic maneuver."[146] Some Soviet accounts charged that China was seeking to maneuver itself into position to become a leading center in the rest of the world by playing upon concerns over the two superpowers, whether in conflict or seeking condominium over others.[147] Only occasionally were there comments that "despite the anti-Soviet designs of the Chinese leadership and the most reactionary *element* of the American ruling circles," the normalization and "improvement of American-Chinese relations could enable a clearing of the international climate."[148] The predominant reaction was, however, concern.

Soviet reaction to the Sino-American steps toward rapprochement was first articulated in a serious way when the Nixon visit was announced in July 1971. It took ten days for the Soviets to formulate their line of response.[149] From all indications, although the Soviet press had been criticizing Chinese attempts to curry favor with the United States since early 1969,[150] the secret visit by Kissinger in July and the announcement of the forthcoming Nixon visit stunned the Soviet leadership.

The key Soviet analysis of the significance for American policy and American-Soviet relations was given by the senior Soviet American affairs expert, Academician Georgy A. Arbatov. His analysis pointed out that America could have various interests in normalizing relations with China. Some were

---

146. For example, see D. V. Petrov, ed., *Mezhdunarodnye otnosheniya v aziatsko-tikhookeanskom regione* [International Relations in the Asian-Pacific Region], IMEMO (Moscow: Nauka, 1979), pp. 130, 136, and pp. 130–42; and V. A. Kremenyuk, V. P. Lukin, and V. S. Rudnev, eds., *Politika SShA v Azii* [U.S. Policy in Asia], Institute of the USA and Canada (Moscow: Nauka, 1977), pp. 225, 231, and 221–37.

147. N. Kapchenko, "Maoism's Foreign Policy Platform," *International Affairs*, no. 2 (February 1972), p. 37.

148. Ibid., p. 54.

149. I. Aleksandrov, "Concerning Peking's Contacts with Washington," *Pravda*, July 25, 1971. "I. Aleksandrov" is a pseudonym used for authoritative Central Committee commentaries.

150. For example, see the commentaries on Radio Moscow by B. Kuznetsov, "Peking Stretches Out a Hand to Washington," August 17, in FBIS, *Soviet Union*, August 18, 1969, pp. A2–3; and K. Osanin, "Duplicity Chinese Style," March 29, in FBIS, *Soviet Union*, April 1, 1969, pp. A9–10.

Later Soviet commentary has continued to stress Chinese initiative in encouraging a rapprochement with the United States in the period 1966–69, as well as thereafter. See G. F. Astafeyev and A. M. Dubinsky, eds., *Vneshnyaya politika i mezhdunarodnye otnosheniya kitaiskoi narodnoi respubliki, 1963–1973* [The Foreign Policy and International Relations of the People's Republic of China, 1963–73] (Moscow: Mysl', 1974), vol. 2, pp. 198–202, 248–55.

understandable and commendable—for example, as part of a general turn toward détente and an end to the cold war. Others were objectionable and harmful—motivated by hostility toward the Soviet Union. "So," he concluded, "the answer to the basic question connected with the President's visit to Peking and the changes in American-Chinese relations will be not in words, not in the diplomatic maneuvers of these countries, but in their deeds." And the Soviet Union would watch these developments "with close attention. For this is a matter of grave consequence for the Soviet people, for world socialism, for the entire international situation, for world peace."[151]

Soviet reaction to the Beijing summit was naturally negative but still restrained. The Soviets quickly fastened on the fact that Kosygin's talk with Zhou five months earlier had not only been relegated to an airport lounge, but had been described in the Chinese press as merely "frank," a long-standing euphemism used when there are serious differences. Not only had President Nixon been received royally and seen Mao personally, but the talks had been characterized as "frank *and serious*." As Kissinger observes, "The authentic Soviet response was diplomatic." The Soviets immediately moved more rapidly to schedule the Brezhnev-Nixon summit meeting and to reach a number of agreements.[152]

The Soviet press continued to be especially hostile toward China. Given the poor state of Sino-Soviet relations, as well as the Soviet desire to seek favor with North Vietnam and to improve relations with the United States, this attitude was to be expected.

In virtually all high-level contacts from the 1972 summit meeting on (and, less directly, through Ambassador Dobrynin from 1969 on), the Soviet leaders stressed their concern over China. They did so even when, as Kissinger observes, it could serve no useful purpose and could only alert the United States to the extent of Soviet concern.[153]

Kissinger's judgment neglects the possibility that the Soviet leaders truly believed the Chinese *were* a potential menace both to the United States and to the Soviet Union, and that the Americans might come to see that fact. The Soviet leaders, too, have security concerns.

The Soviets did in fact seek to deal with the United States as a partner in facing the contingency that the Chinese might seek to provoke a conflict between the Soviet Union and the United States. In the SALT negotiations, discussions took place from 1969 to 1971 on the subject of accidental outbreak of nuclear war (by technical malfunction, misconstrued intelligence indicators, unauthorized use of nuclear weapons, or a provocative act by a third party). In that context, in July 1970 the Soviets proposed agreeing on joint

---

151. Georgy A. Arbatov, "Questions Demanding an Answer in Practice," *Pravda*, August 10, 1971.

152. Kissinger, *White House Years*, pp. 766–67. Emphasis added.

153. See ibid., pp. 1145–46, 1226–27.

measures to forestall such a provocative action by a third party. They did not name China but implied clearly that it was the source of their concern.

The White House quickly turned down the idea, which Kissinger construed as designed to "shatter our hopeful China policy and imply a US-Soviet condominium." As noted in discussing the SALT negotiations, Kissinger was confused over an agreement on measures to avert accidental war and a political agreement to act against provocative nuclear attacks by third powers. The upshot was his wild misreading of the Soviet position: "Collusion against China was to be the real Soviet price for a summit" and "We were in effect being asked to give the USSR a free hand against China; it was a blatant embodiment of condominium."[154] Hence the proposal was rejected flatly, and probably not entirely to the Soviets' surprise. They certainly made no effort to make agreement on this subject the price of the summit or of progress on SALT.[155] Kissinger fails to comment on that fact, which contradicts his assumptions about the Soviet purpose.

Triangular Diplomacy and Other Powers

The emergence of the American-Chinese and American-Soviet sides of a triangular balance had its most immediate effect on American disengagement from the war in Vietnam, the subject of the following chapter. It also had a major and direct impact on at least the American handling of a regional crisis that erupted in the brief Indo-Pakistani War of December 1971.[156] It also had direct early effects on the foreign policies of the two Koreas and on the policy of Japan. While more remote geographically, it also had political effects on European affairs, in particular in Eastern Europe.

China was influenced strongly by the Soviet occupation of Czechoslovakia in turning to a more confrontational line toward the Soviet Union, including the initiation of border clashes, and in seeking at least exploratory contact with the United States. It is not clear whether consideration of their long Chinese flank may have influenced the Soviet leaders in deciding not to intervene in Romania or Yugoslavia in 1969. That it may have been a factor is suggested by an intriguing coincidence involving Soviet-sponsored pressure on the Federal Republic of Germany (West Germany). In February 1969 West

---

154. Ibid., pp. 548, 554–55. For a more informed discussion, see Smith, *Doubletalk*, pp. 139–44. For a discussion of the context of the SALT talks, see chapter 5 of this book.

155. A senior Soviet diplomat commented privately at the time that the fact that the Soviets had made this important proposal to the United States was, when viewed from a longer-term perspective, significant, regardless of the U.S. reaction. He stressed, perhaps defensively but not without believing it had a credible basis, that neither side needed such an agreement more than the other.

156. See chapter 8.

Germany was moving to hold its presidential election in West Berlin. At that time the German Democratic Republic (East Germany) began to harass civilian traffic on the autobahn to West Berlin. On March 3, however, the harassment stopped. March 3 was the day following the first Sino-Soviet border clash at Damansky/Zhenbao Island. On March 11, in a most unusual step, the Soviet ambassador in Bonn briefed Chancellor Kurt Kiesinger on the clash. Moreover, while of course not alluding to those developments, a Soviet political-military commentator drew a direct connection between the Chinese border actions and the West German election, alleging that "the Maoist armed clashes on the Soviet-Chinese frontier were synchronized by Peking with the election of the FRG president in West Berlin."[157] A few months later, as that issue receded and the prospects for West German–Soviet rapprochement grew after the election of Willy Brandt, the Chinese in turn accused Moscow of "collusion with West German militarism."[158] The Federal Republic of Germany also established relations with China in October 1972, its Eastern treaties with the Soviet Union in place.

In a more general way the evolving relationships among the United States, the Soviet Union, and China affected European affairs in many respects.

The impact on Japan was more immediate. The United States had not consulted or even informed the Japanese before its bombshell announcement after the event of the Kissinger mission and the planned visit by the president to Beijing. This "Nixon shokku" caused such serious initial reverberations that Gromyko rushed to Tokyo to see if the Soviets could gain influence. He was unsuccessful, however, for the same reason other Soviet overtures in the 1970s failed: Soviet intransigence over the northern territories, as the Japanese call the southern Kuril Islands and other small islands north of Japan that were incorporated into the Soviet Union after World War II. In sharp contrast, in July 1971 the United States offset the Nixon shock by announcing an agreement to return Okinawa and the Ryukyus to Japan, effective May 1972.

On September 1, 1972, Nixon met Japanese Prime Minister Kakuei Tanaka in Honolulu and expressed support for Tanaka's forthcoming visit to Beijing. There, on September 29 Zhou Enlai and Tanaka agreed to end the nominal state of war and to resume diplomatic relations.

The Chinese also effected a rapprochement with the Democratic People's Republic of Korea (North Korea) in the period from 1969 to 1971 in an effort to offset Soviet influence. For its part, North Korea wished to improve its ties with China as a balance to the Soviet Union. Like Vietnam, however, it also saw the movements of both the Soviet Union and China

---

157. Vasily Yefremov, "Self-Exposure of the Peking Adventurers," *Soviet Military Review*, no. 5 (May 1969), p. 55.

158. "A Dirty Deal," *Renmin Ribao*, December 22, in FBIS, *China*, December 22, 1969, p. A9; and "Soviet Government's Intensified Collusion with West German Militarism," *Peking Review*, vol. 12 (December 26, 1969), pp. 42–45.

toward better relations with the United States as reducing its leverage and further reducing any hope of obtaining backing for a military solution to the unification of Korea under its domination. The Republic of Korea (South Korea) also saw the American rapprochements with China and the Soviet Union as reducing U.S. interest in a confrontational stance. Accordingly, in secrecy even from their allies, North and South Korea exchanged secret visits by high emissaries (the chief of the South Korean CIA visited Pyongyang) in 1971–72. In surprise parallel announcements on July 4, 1972, they revealed their contact and desire to resolve their differences. Residual suspicions and conflicts soon overwhelmed this effort, but at least a precedent had been set, largely as a result of North and South Korean reactions to the emergence of triangular diplomacy.

Triangular Diplomacy in Perspective

Triangular diplomacy, that is, the calculated management of policy on mutual relations between and among the United States, the Soviet Union, and China, emerged during the period from late 1968 through 1972 because of the interplay of political developments at that time. It was not, and could not have been, designed and established by any one or two of these countries, or even by agreement among the three. It could only have emerged when mutual political relationships were ripe, including independence of action, interdependence of interactions, and a dynamic mix of competition and cooperation among the three states. At the same time it also required recognition of the potentialities and readiness of at least one of the three to act upon them, and a sufficient readiness by at least a second, in order for all three to have to become involved. There was in addition the complex web of relationships each had with other states, as the triangle interacted not only with one another but with others.

It is not entirely clear whether the United States or China should be assigned the major responsibility for setting the development of triangular diplomacy in motion. American policymakers, notably Nixon as its American progenitor, and Kissinger as its principal practitioner, understandably and properly credit their own initiatives,[159] while noting the Chinese contribution.

159. Nixon, and later Kissinger, certainly deserve credit for the American policy initiatives. On the other hand, in his memoir Kissinger claims that while many American experts on China in 1969 had favored an improvement in relations with Beijing, he cannot recall that anybody at the time had noted "the geopolitical opportunities for us with respect to the Soviet Union or the possibility that the Chinese might have an incentive to move toward us *without* American concessions because of *their* need for an American counterweight to the Soviet Union." *White House Years*, p. 165; emphasis in the original. Perhaps he cannot recall, or possibly he did not know, that many American experts on Chinese (and Soviet) affairs fully appreciated the possibilities at the time—many of them long before Kissinger did. Nor was the United

Chinese leaders have not spoken out so frankly (Zhou Enlai and Mao Zedong regrettably left no known memoirs, and Chinese records are less prone to leakage). Moreover, the Chinese do not publicly acknowledge a triangular system, although they understand it very well.[160] Probably the Chinese would see their own initiatives (and later concessions) as critical to the successful emergence of the system. Both views may be correct.

Soviet leaders also do not acknowledge a triangular system of diplomacy, except as a cynical Chinese (usually) or American design. In practice, however, they too, have been well aware of its reality. They could not be expected to acknowledge not only that their diplomacy had permitted the emergence of such a system, but that they were perforce coopted into it as the weakest side in the triangle. Yet that is what occurred from 1969 through 1972.

"Triangular diplomacy, to be effective," Kissinger has subsequently observed, "must rely on the natural incentives and propensities of the players. It must avoid the impression that one is 'using' either of the [other] contenders against the other; otherwise one becomes vulnerable to retaliation or blackmail. The hostility between China and the Soviet Union served our purposes best if we maintained closer relations with each side than they did with each other. The rest could be left to the dynamic of events."[161]

When Kissinger and Nixon as practitioners of triangular diplomacy most closely followed that advice, they were the most successful—as in influencing the North Vietnamese to accept a compromise agreement allowing American military disengagement from Vietnam.[162] When they tried too hard to manipulate events, as in the Indo-Pakistani War in 1971,[163] they were less successful, especially when the impacts on others are considered, as they should be.

It is as important to recognize the limits of triangular diplomacy as to see its potential. This, too, the Nixon-Kissinger team understood and acted upon. Again to cite Kissinger, "Sino-Soviet tensions followed their own logic;

States able to develop serious contact and, in due course, rapprochement with China without making important concessions (although Kissinger downplays this fact). It is true that many, perhaps most, China experts at that time underestimated the extent of China's desire for improved relations with the United States as a counterweight to the Soviet Union. Therefore they may have underestimated the United States' bargaining leverage. But the recognition of a geopolitical triangle was by no means Kissinger's discovery.

160. The one exception has been an article by Huan Xiang, "Viewing Wuhan's Development and Prospects from [the Perspective of] the International Political and Economic Situation," *Shijie jingji daobao* [World Economic Herald], Shanghai, July 9, 1984. Huan's acceptance of what he terms "great triangular relations" between China, the United States, and the Soviet Union as "what really determines the development of the world situation" has proved highly controversial in China. Ibid., p. 3.

161. Kissinger, *White House Years*, p. 712.

162. See chapter 7.

163. See chapter 8.

they were not created by us nor could they be manipulated by us directly. Each of the Communist antagonists was certain to be affected by our actions; each would seek to nudge us in the direction it favored; each would determine its relation to the other in part in terms of its assessment of our intentions and actions. But to seek to manipulate them was to make us their prisoner."[164]

American policymakers well understood that "in a triangular relationship it is undeniably advantageous for us to have better relations with each of the other two actors than they have with one another."[165] Perhaps the most important aspect of the American understanding of triangular diplomacy in these years was the corollary to that observation: "Our interests compel us to pursue our well-established policies of seeking improved relations with both the U.S.S.R. and China. Both courses are essential for maintaining a global equilibrium and shaping a more peaceful and positive international structure."[166] Finally, "We will make clear that we are not colluding with, or accommodating, one at the expense of the other."[167] Further, "Equilibrium was the name of the game. We did not seek to join China in a provocative confrontation with the Soviet Union."[168]

During the formative years of triangular diplomacy the Nixon-Kissinger administration skillfully used the parallel development of improving American relations with each of the other powers, while the relations of those two with one another remained bad, so that the United States had the greatest leverage in the triangular relationship.

---

164. Kissinger, *White House Years*, pp. 836–37.

165. Winston Lord, "The Triangular Relationship of the United States, the U.S.S.R., and the People's Republic of China," Congressional Statement, March 23, *State Bulletin*, vol. 74 (April 19, 1976), p. 517. This testimony (pp. 514–18) by the head of the Policy Planning Staff of the Department of State (and key China adviser and speech-writer for Henry Kissinger both in the White House and then in the State Department from 1969 to 1977) is an excellent brief statement of the American concept in the Nixon-Ford-Kissinger years.

166. Ibid.

167. Ibid.

168. Kissinger, *White House Years*, p. 764.

7 The Crucible for Triangular Diplomacy: Ending the War in Vietnam, 1969-72

WHILE PRESIDENT NIXON would probably have pursued an opening to China even if his principal foreign policy preoccupation from 1969 through 1972 had not been ending the war in Vietnam, that circumstance certainly contributed to the priority he assigned the task. The main interests China and the Soviet Union had in triangular diplomacy involved their conflict with one another and how relations with the United States could affect that relationship. In addition, the Vietnam hostilities raised particular interests and problems for both vis-à-vis North Vietnam and the United States.

The Nixon Administration's Expectations

President Nixon had high expectations of being able to end the war in Vietnam on honorable terms through Soviet pressure on North Vietnam. He made this point to a group of journalists as early as July 1968.[1] Kissinger, for his part, had written an article, "The Viet Nam Negotiations," that appeared in the January 1969 issue of *Foreign Affairs* and was widely taken to represent the approach of the new administration even though it had been written prior to Kissinger's selection to serve in the administration.[2] This arti-

---

1. A. James Reichley, *Conservatives in an Age of Change: The Nixon and Ford Administrations* (Brookings Institution, 1981), p. 107, and also pp. 116-21.

2. Henry A. Kissinger, "The Viet Nam Negotiations," *Foreign Affairs*, vol. 47 (January 1969), pp. 211-34. Because of its timeliness the article was actually released in December 1968. Kissinger had had some exposure to negotiations on the Vietnamese problem in the mid-1960s, which he discusses briefly in his memoir. See Henry Kissinger, *White House Years* (Boston, Mass.: Little, Brown, 1979), pp. 230-35.

cle called for seeking a solution through negotiation, but did not envisage a role for triangular diplomacy. Kissinger has subsequently admitted that at the time he had somewhat overly optimistic expectations about the Vietnam negotiations.[3] There is some controversy over the role Kissinger felt the Soviet Union could play. He claims not to have been very sanguine about enlisting Soviet aid in pressuring the North Vietnamese. On the other hand Nixon, who clearly had exaggerated expectations, has said that Kissinger was more optimistic than he about the prospects for success through private exchanges with the Russians.[4] Commentators close to Kissinger have stressed his early optimism in this respect in 1969.[5] Nixon's overoptimism in those early months is clear.[6] In his memoir Nixon himself states that in March 1969 he "confidently told the Cabinet that I expected the war to be over in a year."[7] Nixon expressed his optimism publicly on March 4, 1969, when he stated: "I believe the Soviet Union would like to use what influence it could appropriately to help bring the war to a conclusion." Well aware that any movement on this subject was most delicate politically for the Soviet leaders, he added: "What it can do, however, is something that only the Soviet Union would be able to answer to, and it would probably have to answer privately, not publicly."[8] It seems clear from the administration's record of diplomatic actions that it did indeed have high—in fact, excessive—expectations. Nixon exaggerated, at least initially, the extent of Soviet influence on the North Vietnamese, while Kissinger exaggerated the degree of American leverage on the Soviet leaders as well.[9]

The belief that the Soviets could influence the Vietnamese significantly was thus an important element in American policy toward the Soviet Union in 1969. Linkage was applied in the hope that Soviet interests in trade, arms control negotiations,[10] and détente in general would lead the USSR to help the United States extricate itself from Vietnam.

This initial effort was not successful, and from 1970 through 1972 the administration pursued a more sophisticated—and ultimately more suc-

---

3. Kissinger, *White House Years*, p. 262.

4. Richard Nixon, *RN: The Memoirs of Richard Nixon* (Grosset and Dunlap, 1978), p. 413.

5. See, in particular, Marvin Kalb and Bernard Kalb, *Kissinger* (Dell, 1974), pp. 142–72.

6. See Henry Brandon, *The Retreat of American Power* (Doubleday, 1973), p. 275. For Nixon's account, see *RN*, pp. 390–414.

7. Nixon, *RN*, p. 390.

8. "The President's News Conference of March 4, 1969," *Weekly Compilation of Presidential Documents*, vol. 5 (March 10, 1969), p. 365. (Hereafter *Presidential Documents*.)

9. Kissinger begs this question and assumes even in retrospect that if the United States had been able to apply the carrot and stick more forcefully, the Soviets could and would have done more. He writes: "The deepest reason for Soviet immobilism [on ending the Vietnam War] in 1969, however, was undoubtedly that conditions had not yet generated incentives and penalties of sufficient magnitude to impel decision." See Kissinger, *White House Years*, p. 160.

10. Kissinger gives a good example of Nixon's and his effort to use progress on SALT as a lever to move the Soviets to assist in resolving the Vietnam situation. Ibid., pp. 144–45.

cessful—approach. The focus was on negotiations and pressure vis-à-vis the North Vietnamese, supplemented by the development of relations with both the Soviet Union and China in such a way that each would find it in its own best interest to urge the Vietnamese to compromise.

The Nixon administration, to its credit, never believed that the Soviet Union or China was responsible for and in direct command or control of the North Vietnamese. Nixon and Kissinger did not believe, as leaders in the Johnson administration had, that the motive force in Vietnam and therefore the real enemy was Chinese aggression.[11] This clarity of perception permitted the administration to see—and to pursue—possibilities for triangular diplomacy that had not previously been adequately recognized at the policy level.[12]

Engaging Soviet Support

The Nixon administration made its first serious attempt to engage Soviet support for a compromise resolution of the Vietnam War in an important meeting between Kissinger and Ambassador Dobrynin on April 14, 1969, about two months after the February 17 meeting in which Nixon had told Dobrynin that Kissinger was his preferred channel for all matters of "special sensitivity."[13] Kissinger told Dobrynin that U.S.-Soviet relations were "at a crossroads." He noted that President Nixon was "prepared to make progress in US-Soviet relations on a broad front." (Nixon had personally added to Kissinger's outline of talking points for the meeting the need to extend more explicitly the prospect of economic cooperation.) But "the Vietnam war was a major obstacle," and the United States wanted Soviet assistance in negotiating its end.[14] He specifically proposed a special mission by Cyrus R. Vance to Moscow to discuss principles for SALT, but while there to meet secretly with an appropriate senior North Vietnamese representative to agree on a military and political settlement in Vietnam.

The United States also made clear an important counter point. If the American readiness to negotiate with Hanoi were not reciprocated, Kissin-

---

11. Kissinger is quite correct in asserting this claim. Ibid., p. 168.

12. It is not necessary to review here either the internal policy debates within the Nixon administration on Vietnam policy, nor the content or course of the Vietnam peace negotiations. A shelf of books has already been written on these subjects, including about one-third of Kissinger's first volume of memoirs covering the years 1969 through 1972. But the role that the United States ascribed to these negotiations in its relations with the Soviet Union, their impact on those relations, and finally their impact on triangular diplomacy as well are all relevant.

13. President Nixon, in his first meeting with Dobrynin on February 17, 1969, had raised the need to resolve the Vietnam problem but had not pressed the matter. Kissinger, *White House Years*, pp. 141–44.

14. Ibid., pp. 267–68.

ger hinted, the president would have to escalate the war sharply.[15] In such a case, American-Soviet relations would not advance as both sides wished. As Nixon later said in his memoir, in words almost certainly close to those used by Kissinger to Dobrynin, "a settlement in Vietnam was the key to everything."[16] Kissinger notes that in prior conversations with Dobrynin he too had "stressed that a fundamental improvement in U.S.-Soviet relations presupposed Soviet cooperation in settling the war." Moreover, to drive the point home, without making the linkage explicit, the United States "procrastinated on all the negotiations in which the Soviet Union was interested—the strategic arms limitation talks, the Middle East, and expanded economic relations."[17]

Although Kissinger and Nixon do not specifically relate it to this meeting, both acknowledge that Kissinger used with Dobrynin the good cop, tough cop technique. Kissinger cast himself as more reasonable and referred to Nixon as the tough hard-liner who could be restrained from violent and dangerous actions only if he, Kissinger, could show positive results from diplomacy and negotiation. Among close associates Nixon himself referred to this ploy as "the madman theory"—he, Nixon, could be a madman who needed to be restrained from excessive use of force.[18] And one early account that benefited from information supplied by Kissinger dates the use of this technique to Kissinger's key April meeting with Dobrynin on Vietnam.[19]

Dobrynin asked if the United States was making a Vietnam settlement a precondition for progress on the Middle East, economic relations, and strategic arms limitations. Kissinger avoided making a hard and fast linkage. But he said that while the United States was prepared to talk, progress would be more rapid if Vietnam were out of the way. And conversely, if there were no settlement, Nixon might take escalatory measures that would create a "complicated situation." Dobrynin protested that Moscow had only limited influence with the leaders in Hanoi, but promised to do what it could to forward the American negotiating proposals. He also said the Soviet leaders wished to continue negotiations for improved relations with the United States. Kissinger interpreted this as meaning the Soviets would "look away" if the United States escalated hostilities in Vietnam.[20]

---

15. For a highly critical exposé of the extent of both Nixon's and Kissinger's proclivity for using this alternative, see Seymour M. Hersh, *The Price of Power: Kissinger in the Nixon White House* (Summit, 1983), pp. 46–65, 118–35.

16. Nixon, *RN*, p. 391.

17. Kissinger, *White House Years*, pp. 266, 144.

18. See H. R. Haldeman, with Joseph DiMona, *The Ends of Power* (Times Books, 1978), p. 98; and Hersh, *The Price of Power*, p. 53.

19. Tad Szulc, *The Illusion of Peace: Foreign Policy in the Nixon Years* (Viking, 1978), p. 63. Szulc's account, otherwise correct, misdates the meeting as early May rather than mid-April. He knew only that it preceded Nixon's speech of May 14 on Vietnam.

20. See Kissinger, *White House Years*, pp. 266–68; Nixon, *RN*, p. 391; and Szulc, *The Illusion of Peace*, pp. 63–64.

At the April meeting Dobrynin sought to blunt American interest in escalating the war by remarking that China was trying to precipitate a clash between the Soviet Union and the United States. Escalation in Vietnam could only serve the interests of China—implying also a veiled threat of counterescalation. Kissinger replied that if that was the situation, the Soviet Union had a joint obligation with the United States to avoid complicating matters.[21] Kissinger also mentions an occasion, unidentified by time but evidently in 1969, at which Dobrynin tried to inhibit the United States from extending the bombing to include Hanoi and Haiphong, a practice stopped by President Lyndon B. Johnson in 1968. Dobrynin noted that if the bombing were escalated in that way, the Chinese military engineer battalions withdrawn earlier might be reintroduced into northern Vietnam, a move that would increase Chinese influence there. Kissinger merely replied "If you can live with it, we can," and Dobrynin dropped the subject.[22]

Kissinger discloses in his memoir that at the April 14 meeting he employed another technique, one he used often subsequently. He gave his talking points, with Nixon's own marginal notations and initials, to Dobrynin to read, authenticating the message (and the channel).[23]

The Soviets never did respond directly to the concrete proposals for a Vance mission forwarded on April 14 because they were reluctant to convey a negative response.[24]

In the absence of a Soviet reply Nixon turned to public diplomacy. In a major speech on Vietnam on May 14 he directed his proposals and appeal to North Vietnam; he did not mention the Soviet Union and China. Nixon did, however, comment that "if we are to move successfully from an era of confrontation to an era of negotiation, then we have to demonstrate—at the point at which confrontation is being tested—that confrontation with the United States is costly and unrewarding." He also argued that if the United States were to withdraw unilaterally and permit North Vietnam to succeed in the south by force, it would strengthen those in "the Communist world" who argue for a policy of confrontation with the United States and weaken those who argue against confrontation and for negotiation.[25]

---

21. Kissinger, *White House Years*, p. 268.

22. Ibid., p. 160.

23. Ibid., p. 268. Nixon also refers to this tactic and reproduces a page he had initialed for Kissinger to give Dobrynin. Nixon, *RN*, p. 391. It is *not*, however, the more detailed talking points that Kissinger summarizes and cites, with Nixon's marginal notations; evidently he had obtained Nixon's permission to hand over certain talking points, and then exercised his own discretion to provide others.

24. Kissinger says that Dobrynin later gave this explanation and that he surmises it was the real reason. Soviet officials have confirmed that interpretation to me. Kissinger, *White House Years*, pp. 268–69.

25. "Report on Vietnam: The President's Address to the Nation, May 14, 1969," *Presidential Documents*, vol. 5 (May 19, 1969), p. 694.

The United States continued to press forward in the formal Vietnam peace negotiations and, after August 4, 1969, in parallel secret talks between Kissinger and North Vietnamese Politburo member Le Duc Tho in Paris. Withdrawal of American troops and Vietnamization of the war, a term coined by Secretary of Defense Melvin Laird and adopted by Nixon, also got under way.

On September 27, during a meeting between Dobrynin and Kissinger, by planned coincidence Nixon telephoned Kissinger. The latter then said to Dobrynin that the president had just told him that Vietnam was the critical issue in U.S.-Soviet relations and that the next move was up to Hanoi.[26]

At a meeting on October 20, Dobrynin reported to the president that the Soviet Union was prepared to begin the SALT negotiations by mid-November. It was an offer Nixon could not refuse. He wished, however, to put some pressure on the Soviets over Vietnam. He therefore instructed Kissinger to tell Dobrynin that Nixon (the tough cop) was "out of control" on Vietnam. Kissinger, knowing that the president planned no major escalation, ignored the order.[27]

Nixon has recounted in some detail a revealing exchange with Dobrynin at the October 20 meeting. Dobrynin read a communication from his government that began by stating that Moscow was not satisfied with the present state of relations. It wanted the president to understand that "the method of solving the Vietnam question through the use of military force" not only had no prospect for success, but was "extremely dangerous." "If someone in the United States is tempted to make profit from Soviet-Chinese relations at the Soviet Union's expense, and there are some signs of that, then we would like to frankly warn in advance that such line of conduct, if pursued, can lead to a very grave miscalculation and is in no way consistent with the goal of better relations between the U.S. and the U.S.S.R."[28] The Soviet leaders were evidently very uncomfortable over the possibility of being whipsawed in triangular diplomacy. They may also have believed Nixon and Kissinger were deliberately overstating their view of Soviet influence over North Vietnam in an attempt to downplay the Soviet sacrifice in pressing Hanoi and hence to minimize Soviet claims for reciprocal favors.[29]

Nixon was equally tough in response. He also expressed disappointment over U.S.-Soviet relations but blamed most of the difficulties on Soviet intransigence. On China he reaffirmed that "anything we have done or are doing with respect to China is in no sense designed to embarrass the Soviet Union . . . [and] is not directed against the Soviet Union." On Vietnam, he

---

26. Nixon, *RN*, pp. 390–400; and Kissinger, *White House Years*, p. 304.

27. Kissinger justifies his action in ignoring this and other instructions of the president. Kissinger, *White House Years*, pp. 305–06.

28. Nixon, *RN*, p. 405.

29. This argument is advanced by Harry Gelman, *The Brezhnev Politburo and the Decline of Detente* (Ithaca, N.Y.: Cornell University Press, 1984), p. 109.

said "The only beneficiary of U.S.-Soviet disagreement over Vietnam is China" and now was the last opportunity to settle it. Nixon then questioned whether the Soviet Union really wanted the war in Vietnam to end. Finally, he commented, "You may think that you can break me. . . . You may believe that the American domestic situation is unmanageable [on Vietnam]. . . . I want you to understand that the Soviet Union is going to be stuck with me for the next three years and three months. . . . If the Soviet Union will not help us get peace, then we will have to pursue our own methods for bringing the war to an end." The president concluded by promising that if, on the other hand, "the Soviet Union found it possible to do something in Vietnam, and the Vietnam War ended, then we might do something dramatic to improve our relations. . . . But until then, I have to say that real progress will be very difficult." Dobrynin clarified that the president was not completely ruling out progress pending a Vietnam settlement.[30]

Kissinger mentions that during 1969 he made about ten different attempts in meetings with Dobrynin to enlist Soviet aid in ending the war in Vietnam. Dobrynin denied that the Soviets were interested in seeing the war continue but protested the limits of their influence on the North Vietnamese. At the time, and still today, Kissinger chose to interpret that line of response as being evasive rather than reflecting, even in part, the real limits of Soviet influence.[31]

In the first foreign policy report to the Congress, issued February 18, 1970, Nixon and Kissinger vented their disappointment with the failure of the Soviets to help reach a settlement: "To the detriment of the cause of peace, the Soviet leadership has failed to exert a helpful influence on the North Vietnamese. . . . This cannot but cloud the rest of our relationship with the Soviet Union."[32] In part this line was intended to put pressure on the Soviet leaders; in part the purpose was to explain the slow progress and lack of success in meeting the administration's early overly optimistic prognoses.

Seeking Chinese Support

The United States was also pursuing parallel efforts to get the Chinese to influence the North Vietnamese. In 1969 President Charles de Gaulle

---

30. Ibid., pp. 405–07. Nixon tells this account in even greater detail than cited here. He also mentions Kissinger's enthusiasm: "It was extraordinary! No president has ever laid it on the line to them like that." Nixon certainly had sounded like the tough cop. In his memoir Kissinger had lost his enthusiasm for the exchange and gave this whole episode just two sentences, omitting both Nixon's vehemence and Dobrynin's references to China. Kissinger, *White House Years,* p. 305.

31. Kissinger, *White House Years,* p. 144.

32. Richard M. Nixon, *U.S. Foreign Policy for the 1970's: A New Strategy for Peace,* Report to the Congress, vol. 1 (Washington, D.C.: Government Printing Office, 1970), p. 137.

charged Ambassador Etienne M. Manac'h with conveying a message from President Nixon to the Chinese leaders. The message made clear not only that the United States wished to improve relations with China, but also that Nixon "was going to withdraw from Vietnam come what may."[33] As Nixon continued to withdraw troops, the Chinese began to realize he meant what he said. In this way the basis was being laid to develop a Chinese interest in a Vietnam settlement.

The extremely limited and indirect nature of American contact with China from 1969 until mid-1971 meant that such efforts could only be indirect. Nonetheless, there were some signs of impact. Premier Zhou Enlai's message of February 22, 1970, to Nixon noted that "the possibility of expansion of the Vietnam war is seen as having lessened," while the danger of a war between China and the United States was "seen now as [only] a very remote possibility." Kissinger correctly understood these careful circumlocutions as meaning that the Chinese recognized the U.S. intention to withdraw and were signaling their own intention not to enter the war.[34]

In February 1971, when the United States directed and supported a South Vietnamese invasion of southern Laos, Nixon went out of his way in a news conference to state that "this action [in Laos] is not directed against Communist China."[35] The Chinese criticized the action strongly, but at the same time made clear they would do nothing more. Through an intermediary they signaled that they were only postponing talks with the United States. A month later Zhou Enlai even went to Hanoi to explain that the Chinese would not intervene over Laos and that they were convinced the United States was serious about withdrawing from Vietnam. Both the Soviets and the Vietnamese (as well as the Americans) saw the Chinese response to the invasion of Laos as much less vigorous than its response to the invasion of Cambodia a year before, when they were less sure of the American intention.

The Chinese did make a concentrated effort to persuade the Vietnamese to compromise. North Vietnamese Deputy Foreign Minister Nguyen Co Thach has revealed that in November 1971, when Prime Minister Pham Van Dong visited Beijing, Chairman Mao Zedong himself, in a tense meeting, urged the Vietnamese to accept a compromise. He also rejected a North Vietnamese request that China not receive Nixon in February.[36]

Thus, during 1971 the United States continued to pursue a dual track of Vietnamization and withdrawal of American troops on the one hand,

---

33. See Ross Terrill, *800,000,000: The Real China* (Boston, Mass.: Little, Brown, 1972), pp. 144–45. Terrill reports Ambassador Manac'h's account as told to him. Kissinger does not include this aspect of Nixon's message in his account.

34. Kissinger, *White House Years*, p. 689.

35. Cited in ibid., pp. 706–07.

36. See Hersh, *The Price of Power*, p. 442. Hersh later interviewed Nguyen Co Thach, who had been present with Pham Van Dong in Beijing.

and strong military efforts to prevent a North Vietnamese military victory on the other. The administration had come to realize that the key decisions were being made in Hanoi. While Soviet and Chinese assistance in moving Hanoi toward a compromise that would permit the United States to disengage without losing face remained an important part of the American strategy, it no longer had the central role hoped for in 1969. Instead, influencing Hanoi was seen to require military pressure. Usually this meant escalating American air strikes on North Vietnam. But in the spring of 1970 it had involved the American and South Vietnamese incursion into Cambodia, and in the spring of 1971 the South Vietnamese incursion into Laos. Even these more extreme actions did not derail moves toward détente with the Soviet Union or rapprochement with China. The escalation did, however, have other costly effects. As one astute columnist put it, "the Nixon Administration stepped up the war in Laos and Cambodia so that when the end came, Hanoi won not only South Vietnam but all of Indochina."[37]

1972: *Triangular Efforts*

At the beginning of 1972 President Nixon made a major speech on Vietnam that was designed to put pressure on North Vietnam by disclosing publicly much of the secret negotiations. The text was transmitted in advance to Moscow and Beijing. The Chinese replied (Zhou Enlai did so again soon after, at the Nixon summit) that they did not want to become "enmeshed" in the matter. The Soviets were even more reserved in disassociating themselves from the Vietnamese, although the United States was pressing Moscow harder, whether because it was held more responsible for the supply of weapons (as Kissinger asserts was the reason), or because it was considered more able to influence Hanoi.[38] Both Moscow and Beijing did, however, continue privately to urge the Vietnamese to compromise.[39]

During Nixon's visit to Beijing he stressed American determination to obtain a solution in Vietnam without capitulation and warned that a North Vietnamese offensive would meet a full military response. Zhou Enlai, while expressing sympathy and support for the Vietnamese position, also indicated an understanding of the American position. As Kissinger summed up: "We indeed understood each other; the war in Vietnam would not affect the im-

---

37. Flora Lewis, "Oil on the Fire," *New York Times*, April 29, 1983.

38. The speech was delivered January 25, 1972. Kissinger, *White House Years*, pp. 1102–05.

39. Hersh notes that the Albanians reported a sharp North Vietnamese snub to Zhou Enlai at a diplomatic reception in Beijing at that time and concluded that the Chinese had changed their policy of full support for North Vietnam. This contributed to the weakening of Albanian-Chinese relations. Hersh, *The Price of Power*, p. 502.

provement of our relations." Nixon and Kissinger concluded that the Chinese gave highest priority to improving their relations with the United States.[40]

On March 30, 1972, the North Vietnamese opened a major offensive across the demilitarized zone into South Vietnam. The United States met this challenge with a massive step-up in air attacks, including a large buildup in B-52 bombers in the theater. On April 3, Kissinger saw Dobrynin and, in his words, "accused the Soviet Union of complicity in Hanoi's attack." He sought to put the Soviets on notice that other matters would be affected: he pointedly declined Soviet suggestions that the United States urge West German ratification of the *Ostpolitik* treaties, facing a close vote in the Bundestag, because of the North Vietnamese offensive.[41]

On the same day Winston Lord, a close associate who had accompanied Kissinger to China on every trip, told Chinese United Nations Ambassador Huang Hua (the United States special direct contact with China) that the Chinese expression of support for the North Vietnamese was not helpful and "it could not be in the long-term interest of China for the United States to be humiliated in Indochina."[42]

The United States was, however, less demanding toward China than toward the Soviet Union. On April 18, as Kissinger was preparing to leave for Moscow, Nixon received a visiting Chinese Ping-Pong team in the White House, showing that rapprochement was on track despite the North Vietnamese offensive and the American bombing counteroffensive.

At this juncture Kissinger stepped up pressure on the Soviet Union by demonstratively slowing a number of ongoing negotiations.[43] The Soviets in turn proposed that Kissinger visit Moscow to discuss both the summit preparations and Vietnam—their first proposal for serious substantive discussions on Vietnam. Nixon was ambivalent, wishing to proceed with the summit meeting but wary over Vietnam. Finally he agreed, but instructed Kissinger not to discuss other matters unless there had been substantial progress on Vietnam. As Kissinger described it, "Nixon wanted to use the threat of canceling the summit to obtain Soviet cooperation in Vietnam." For his part, Kissinger "judged it wiser to shift the risks and the onus for cancellation to the Soviets and to use Moscow's eagerness for the summit as a device for separating Moscow from Hanoi." The upshot was that Kissinger disregarded Nixon's instructions.[44]

---

40. Kissinger, *White House Years*, p. 1087.

41. Ibid., p. 1114.

42. As Kissinger observes, this was a prescient observation. Ibid., pp. 1114–15.

43. Ibid. As part of this effort to influence Moscow Kissinger also wrote to Egon Bahr, West German Chancellor Willy Brandt's adviser, on April 8 that under the circumstances—the North Vietnamese offensive supported by Soviet-supplied arms—the United States doubted the value of détente. He calculated that Brandt and Bahr, with their *Ostpolitik* at stake, would press the Soviets. Ibid., p. 1117.

44. Ibid., pp. 1154–64; quotation p. 1154. Kissinger manipulated the situation to set up his Moscow visit and then disregarded Nixon's instructions. See also Hersh, *The Price of Power*, pp.

The Soviets reacted very mildly to an incident just a few days before Kissinger's visit that could have seriously influenced relations. The renewed American bombing damaged four Soviet ships in Haiphong harbor, with loss of life. The Soviets communicated a formal protest but did not make a major issue of the matter.[45]

Just before Kissinger's departure from Moscow, with the plans for the summit firmed up, Brezhnev told Kissinger that the United States was being challenged not by Moscow but by those opposed to the Soviet-American summit meeting—the North Vietnamese and the Chinese. Moscow was not behind the offensive, and Hanoi had been hoarding arms for two years. Brezhnev also assured Kissinger that he was committed to improving Soviet-American relations and was proceeding with the summit conference despite a formal North Vietnamese request to cancel it. He further promised to transmit American negotiating proposals to Hanoi.[46] Immediately after Kissinger's visit, Konstantin Katushev, the senior party official concerned with relations among the ruling parties of the communist states, was dispatched to Hanoi. The North Vietnamese did not, however, change their basic position, and the Soviets naturally declined to involve themselves directly in settling the issue.[47]

Just before the scheduled Nixon-Brezhnev summit, the situation in Vietnam led Nixon to escalate sharply the bombing attacks on North Vietnam. He chose to do so even if it were to result in the summit being canceled in retaliation. Not only was the summit not canceled,[48] it provided the occasion for the highest level American-Soviet exchange on Vietnam. Brezhnev offered to send one of the highest Soviet officials to Hanoi to urge a "negotiated settlement," that is, one involving North Vietnamese as well as American concessions. A month later Soviet President Nikolai V. Podgorny did go to Hanoi.[49]

Nixon and Kissinger have chosen not to discuss the details of the Soviet exchanges on Vietnam in their accounts, but other sources state that Kissinger outlined elements of concessions. They included a readiness to meet the North Vietnamese demand that any settlement include political as well as military elements, and to discuss the composition of an electoral commission of mixed membership. The purpose was to enlist Soviet aid in working on North

---

512–14. Nixon chose to downplay the whole matter. See Nixon, *RN*, pp. 591–92. For further discussion of Kissinger's April 1972 mission to Moscow, see chapter 3.

45. Kissinger, *White House Years*, p. 1122.

46. Ibid., p. 1151.

47. Ibid., p. 1182.

48. See chapter 9. The Soviet leaders undoubtedly resented Hanoi having put them on the spot by unleashing their offensive shortly prior to the Moscow summit meeting, in contrast to having held their fire before the earlier Beijing summit.

49. Kissinger, *White House Years*, pp. 1225–28, 1303; and Nixon, *RN*, pp. 613–14, 617.

Vietnam to reach a compromise, and this task required giving the Soviets some American concessions that Podgorny could take to Hanoi.[50]

The period from May to October 1972 saw further maneuvering by the United States and North Vietnam, with both trying to use their connections with the Soviet Union and China to influence the other, but both also relying on their own continuing military efforts. From May 9 to October 23 the United States (now with five attack aircraft carriers and over 200 B-52s in the theater) made 41,500 attack sorties on North Vietnam. The last American combat troops, on the other hand, were withdrawn on August 12.

By October both sides were pushing for an agreement before the American election. The North Vietnamese believed the possibility of an agreement before the election would be an incentive that could give them maximum bargaining leverage with Nixon. And again triangular diplomacy was brought more actively into play. During the crucial American–North Vietnamese negotiations during the fall and winter of 1972, both Moscow and Beijing urged the two sides (that is, North Vietnam) to deal. Throughout the developing American rapprochements with both the Soviet Union and China, the North Vietnamese had been suspicious that their interests would suffer. The aftermath of the Nixon summit meetings of February and May 1972 in Beijing and Moscow respectively bore out these suspicions increasingly. At the very least, neither the Soviet nor the Chinese leaders had been prepared to subordinate or sacrifice their own interests in improving relations with the United States to support socialist North Vietnam in a crucial struggle with the leading imperialist and interventionist power.

By August the official organ of the North Vietnamese Communist party chastised both the Soviet Union and China (not by name, but unmistakably) for "bogging down on the dark, muddy road of compromise" and "departing from the great, all-conquering revolutionary idea of the age." It complained of "terrible pressure" not only from the American bombing but also from "tendencies of compromise from outside."[51] The North Vietnamese blamed the United States for seeking a "balance of the great powers" to use "as a shield to give United States imperialism complete freedom of action in checking by use of force the national liberation movement, first of all in pushing back the patriotic struggle of the people of the Indochina peninsula." That was not all. "The American imperialists have applied a policy of reconciliation toward certain big powers in the hope of having a free hand," but, even worse, some communist countries have given preference to "peaceful coexistence over proletarian internationalism, serving their own immediate interests at the expense of the [world] revolutionary movement." The editorial concluded by affirming that "we Communists must persist in revolution and should not compromise."[52]

---

50. Hersh, *The Price of Power*, pp. 526–27.

51. See editorial, "Victory of the Revolutionary Course," *Nhan Dan*, August 17, 1972; and the editorial on August 19, 1972.

52. Ibid.

During the fall of 1972 the United States and North Vietnam moved toward agreement, leading Kissinger to make his famous pre-election statement that "peace is at hand."[53] That proved not to be the case. Some detailed investigative reporting has even suggested that Nixon sabotaged an agreement for electoral purposes.[54]

Ultimately, following Nixon's reelection and the heavy Christmas bombing of December 1972, the North Vietnamese (and, under American pressure, the South Vietnamese) did decide to compromise.[55] The North Vietnamese thus had to postpone their victory in South Vietnam for the decent interval upon which the United States insisted. Nor would they forget that both great communist powers had placed their own interests first in the triangular diplomacy of 1972.

Later, as Vietnamese relations with China deteriorated and Vietnamese-Soviet relations improved in the late 1970s, Vietnam remained silent on Soviet support for American efforts to reach a negotiated disengagement. On the other hand, they charged China with betrayal.[56] But apart from such retroactive manipulation of history, the limitations of both Chinese and Soviet support did seriously constrain Vietnamese policy toward the United States and serve American interests.[57]

Triangular diplomacy had been evolving throughout the four-year travail of the Nixon administration's quest for disengagement from Vietnam on honorable terms. It clearly played a part in leading to a negotiated settlement. It is difficult, however, to evaluate the relative importance of that factor as compared, for example, with the policy of unilateral American military pressure combined with American troop withdrawals. In the final analysis the North Vietnamese might on their own have concluded that the costs and risks of settling on the terms the United States was prepared to accept were preferable to continued conflict, irrespective of Soviet and Chinese prodding to compromise. It is even more difficult to evaluate the contribution of the fine-tuning of triangular diplomacy through numerous subtle and indirect signals (at least some of which were not recognized or interpreted correctly). But on the whole it is clear that triangular diplomacy became a fact and had some, possibly significant, bearing on the settlement of the Vietnam War.

The experience with triangular diplomacy in the Vietnam situation in turn contributed to the future of such diplomacy. Sino-Soviet differences

---

53. Kissinger, *White House Years*, p. 1395.

54. Hersh, *The Price of Power*, pp. 589–609.

55. For the context and motivations of the Christmas bombing and its aftermath, see Kissinger, *White House Years*, pp. 1406–70; and Hersh, *The Price of Power*, pp. 609–35.

56. See *Chinese Aggression against Vietnam: The Root of the Problem* (Hanoi: Foreign Language Publishing House, 1979); in particular see p. 33.

57. See John W. Garver, "Sino-Vietnamese Conflict and the Sino-American Rapprochement," *Political Science Quarterly*, vol. 96 (Fall 1981), pp. 447–64.

were exacerbated.[58] The end of the war removed one complicating factor in American relations with both Moscow and Beijing Even while the war raged on in 1971 and 1972, crucially important steps in both Sino-American rapprochement and Soviet-American détente were taken. As will be seen, in the late 1970s the relations of both China and the Soviet Union with Vietnam, and American lack of relations with that country, would again affect triangular diplomacy and American-Soviet relations.

---

58. It should be noted that the war in Vietnam had contributed to tensions in Sino-Soviet relations even before the United States or China sought a rapprochement and triangular diplomacy. It should also be noted that those in the U.S. government advising on Soviet, Chinese, and Sino-Soviet relations in the key period of the American decision to enter the war in Vietnam—1964–65—were, to my best recollection as a participant, unanimously wrong in believing that it would tend to bring the Soviet Union and China somewhat closer, some believed much closer, because of a need for both to compete in supporting North Vietnam. On the other hand, only a few experts—but some policymakers—believed such American involvement, including bombing, might lead either China or the Soviet Union to enter the war directly.

8   Triangular Diplomacy and Regional Conflict: The Indo-Pakistani War, 1971

THE BRIEF WAR between India and Pakistan in 1971 has been characterized by Kissinger as "perhaps the most complex issue of Nixon's first term."[1] If that is true, in substantial part the reason is that Kissinger and Nixon made it so. The war involved multiple and complex considerations, including several important ones stemming from triangular diplomacy, but Kissinger and Nixon magnified the inherent complexity—and adverse consequences—by fundamental errors in their reading of the situation and their responses.

The focus of this chapter is on the relationship between the Indo-Pakistani War and the development of triangular diplomacy and of American-Soviet relations. Triangular diplomacy contributed to the development of the crisis, strongly affected American policy throughout it, and in turn was influenced by perceptions stemming from it.

The principal and most readily available account of the entire Indo-Pakistani crisis and its relationship to American interests and to triangular diplomacy is Kissinger's memoir. Spanning seventy-six pages, this account provides a wealth of material, marshaled to buttress his thesis that an aggressive Indian policy backed by the Soviet Union threatened American interests, including the U.S. opening to China *and* the prospects for American-Soviet détente. In his judgment this challenge was met only by the far-seeing geopolitical comprehension, statesmanship, and courageous political stand of two beleaguered figures—Nixon and Kissinger—isolated even within the American government.[2]

---

1. Henry Kissinger, *White House Years* (Boston, Mass.: Little, Brown, 1979), p. 913.

2. Ibid., pp. 842–918. I am not the author of these vivid adjectives—they stud Kissinger's account. Nixon's memoir contains a much briefer, but also revealing, account. Richard Nixon, *RN: The Memoirs of Richard Nixon* (Grosset and Dunlap, 1978), pp. 525–31.

Fortunately there is also a balancing account from another informed participant involved in the U.S. government policymaking on this subject in 1971, one who had access to most of the same source materials Kissinger drew upon, and much more experienced in the regional issues—former Deputy Assistant Secretary of State Christopher Van Hollen.[3] Both accounts should be consulted, and both are used here, together with other sources.[4]

Eruption of the Indo-Pakistani Crisis

The roots of the Indo-Pakistani crisis go back to 1947, at the time India and Pakistan obtained independence from Great Britain. Pakistan, while uniting a large part of the Moslem population of the subcontinent, was strangely configured, being divided into two parts separated by a thousand miles, with India in between. Relations between India and Pakistan remained very poor, with bitter war in 1947–48, and war again erupting in 1965.

Over the years serious political problems developed between the politically dominant leaders of West Pakistan and virtually the entire population of East Pakistan—ninety-five million Bengalis. A free election in December 1970 had shown 98 percent of the people of East Pakistan in favor of autonomy. The central government in West Pakistan responded by imprisoning the leader of East Pakistan for treason and, on March 25, 1971, imposing martial law. Resistance ensued and was brutally suppressed. Thus in early 1971 the situation in East Pakistan was highly tense and unstable. Moreover, apart from Indian sympathies for the Bengali population of East Pakistan (and hostility toward West Pakistan), the situation was aggravated by masses of refugees fleeing to neighboring India. Conditions within East Pakistan, and relations between India and Pakistan, continued to deteriorate throughout the summer and fall.

As described by Kissinger, the leaders of the United States saw the situation in these terms: "We faced a dilemma. The United States could not condone a brutal military repression in which thousands of civilians were killed and from which millions fled to India for safety. . . . But Pakistan was our sole channel to China; once it was closed off it would take months to make alterna-

3. Christopher Van Hollen, "The Tilt Policy Revisited: Nixon-Kissinger Geopolitics and South Asia," *Asian Survey*, vol. 20 (April 1980), pp. 339–61. Van Hollen presents a counterthesis to Kissinger's, and a convincing rebuttal to many of Kissinger's contentions.

4. See, in particular, Robert Jackson, *South Asian Crisis: India, Pakistan, and Bangladesh, A Political and Historical Analysis of the 1971 War* (Praeger, 1975); David K. Hall, "The Laotian War of 1962 and the Indo-Pakistani War of 1971," in Barry M. Blechman and Stephen S. Kaplan, eds., *Force without War: U.S. Armed Forces as a Political Instrument* (Brookings Institution, 1978), pp. 135–221; Marvin Kalb and Bernard Kalb, *Kissinger* (Dell, 1975), pp. 294–301; and William J. Barnds, "India, Pakistan and American Realpolitik," *Christianity and Crisis*, vol. 32 (June 12, 1972), pp. 143–49.

tive arrangements. The issue hit Washington, moreover, in the midst of another of the cyclic upheavals over Vietnam."[5] In fact, Nixon and Kissinger's main consideration initially was the China connection within the framework of the emerging triangular diplomacy. On the more specific point, Kissinger does not adhere to the facts when he writes in attempted exculpation: "The issue burst upon us while Pakistan was our only channel to China; we had no other means of communication with Peking."[6] By his own account, at that time, March 25, 1971, the Chinese had been using two principal channels: the Pakistanis and the Romanians. In January 1971, it will be recalled, Kissinger had given both Pakistan and Romania the same message for transmittal to China, and he acknowledges that "the only difference was that the message [via the Romanians] was oral and not typed, indicating our *slight* preference for the Pakistani channel; we reasoned that Pakistan's position vis-à-vis China and the Soviet Union was less complicated than Romania's."[7] That is, it was believed to be more secure from the Soviets. Beyond those channels, Kissinger had also established French and Norwegian ones. Finally, in early March the Chinese had also opened a Japanese channel to the United States and in April turned to public signals as well—the famous Ping-Pong diplomacy.[8] Thus there was no fragile single Pakistani channel to China. Nor, for that matter, would China's interests in establishing contact with the United States, nor probably even those that led Pakistan to further this contact, have been affected by a different U.S. policy in the Bengal crisis.

Kissinger engages in transparent hyperbole when in his memoir he presents a straw man alternative: "A major American initiative of fundamental importance to the global balance of power could not have survived if we colluded with the Soviet Union in the public humiliation of China's friend—and our ally [Pakistan]."[9] What was the possible collusion with the Soviet Union? The unyielding position and reliance on force by the government of West Pakistan was, as Kissinger admits, not a viable course. The U.S. policy of blind support to the leaders of Pakistan, and failure to urge them to make timely concessions, did not prevent the independence of Bangladesh, nor—as Kissinger acknowledges—should that have been a U.S. goal.

Two important diplomatic events occurred during this period that undoubtedly were linked with each other and affected the evolving crisis in the subcontinent.

---

5. Kissinger, *White House Years*, p. 854.

6. Ibid., p. 913.

7. Ibid., p. 704. Emphasis added.

8. Ibid., pp. 708–10. Premier Zhou Enlai personally greeted an American Ping-Pong team that had been admitted to China, thereby signaling a desire to improve relations with the United States.

9. Ibid., p. 913.

In mid-July Kissinger made his secret visit to China via Pakistan. Immediately after the trip a direct American-Chinese channel was established through the U.S. and Chinese embassies in Paris, so Pakistan was no longer needed as a channel. Nevertheless, despite deprecating comments by Kissinger on permitting "fluctuating emotions" rather than a "sober perception of permanent national interest" to inform policy, Nixon and Kissinger themselves seem to have been influenced by sentimental considerations toward Pakistan (as well as by long-standing pro-Pakistani and anti-Indian biases they shared, as acknowledged, even if discounted, by Kissinger himself).[10]

During the summer and fall, West Pakistan was increasingly unable to prevent popular resistance, despite harsh repression. By November Indian military personnel were reported to have infiltrated the province in support of the indigenous resistance forces. Despite Paskistani claims at the time, however, there was no Indian offensive into East Pakistan in November.[11]

On December 3 the Pakistani air force attacked eight Indian airfields in the region around West Pakistan, and Pakistani armored forces thrust into the part of Kashmir administered by India. This action opened the Indo-Pakistani War of 1971.[12] After this Pakistani attack in the West, Indian troops quickly advanced into East Pakistan.

As early as July Nixon and Kissinger in secret policymaking sessions referred to the president's desire "to tilt toward Pakistan." This vivid metaphor, which later came to public attention in a spectacular leak, was used again in December during the Indo-Pakistani War.[13] Thus it has now been authoritatively disclosed that the policy of a tilt against India had in fact been adopted after the China connection was secure and before the outbreak of hostilities. It

---

10. Kissinger notes that he and Nixon were "profoundly grateful" for Pakistan's role in helping arrange U.S. contacts with China. In addition, he comments that Nixon disliked President Indira Gandhi and Indians more generally, while finding the Pakistani military chiefs "congenial." Ibid., pp. 914, 848–49.

11. In his memoir Kissinger, virtually alone among commentators on the subject, argues that the war began on November 22 by Indian attack in East Pakistan, basing that contention on a Pakistani radio claim of that date that had been refuted by events. Nonetheless, he persists with an impression that he states was formed at that time: "I had no doubt that we were now witnessing the beginning of an India-Pakistan war and that India had started it." Ibid., p. 885.

12. See, for example, the detailed account in Jackson, *South Asian Crisis*, pp. 106–23. The reasons for the move by Pakistan are less clear. It may have acted in the hope that, to forestall a wider war, the United Nations and the major powers would press India to accept a cease-fire on both fronts, permitting Pakistan to hold its ground in the East.

13. See Van Hollen, *Asian Survey*, vol. 20 (April 1980), p. 347; his account is based on notes of the Senior Review Group (SRG) meeting of July 31, 1971, a similar SRG meeting on July 23, and an NSC meeting on July 16. For the text of the leaked notes of the December 3, 1971, meeting, see Jackson, *South Asian Crisis*, pp. 213–14. Kissinger titles the chapter of his memoir devoted to this subject "The Tilt: The India-Pakistan Crisis of 1971." Kissinger, *White House Years*, pp. 842–918.

also was made before the second major external diplomatic development: the signature of a Soviet-Indian treaty.

The Soviet Angle

On August 9, 1971, Soviet Foreign Minister Andrei A. Gromyko and Indian Foreign Minister Swaran Singh signed in New Delhi a Treaty of Peace, Friendship and Cooperation between the two countries. This treaty, according to both Indian and Soviet officials, had been under consideration for about a year.[14] Clearly, however, both the Soviet Union and India saw value in concluding the treaty promptly after the announcement that Kissinger had visited Beijing and that President Nixon would be making a visit to China.[15] In his memoir Kissinger calls the treaty a "bombshell," although Washington, including the White House, did not regard it as such at the time.[16] Certainly the treaty provided Prime Minister Indira Gandhi a diplomatic triumph in the face of what seemed to be an emerging U.S.-China-Pakistan alignment, as well as reassurance against any military moves by China against India. Moreover, although Kissinger does not mention the fact in his account, he had just advised Ambassador L. K. Jha that India would not receive American support in case of Chinese intervention.[17]

While the treaty bolstered India's position in the growing dispute with Pakistan over East Bengal, it did not, as Kissinger implies, mean unequivocal Soviet support for India, or an end to Soviet efforts to encourage a political settlement.[18] In fact, although Kissinger does not refer to it, Secretary of State Rogers and Foreign Minister Gromyko discussed the issue on September 30 and agreed to counsel restraint both in New Delhi and Islamabad.[19]

---

14. The Soviet-Indian treaty was negotiated and signed in the same period as the Soviet treaties with Egypt and Iraq and reflected a more general Soviet policy of building bilateral relations with key third world partners on a more permanent basis, less dependent on volatile personalities and the fluctuations of local political developments. It also had a basis in Soviet-Indian relations apart from reaction to the evolution of Sino-American ties and triangular geopolitical relations. On this latter aspect, see Robert C. Horn, *Soviet-Indian Relations: Issues and Influence* (Praeger, 1982), pp. 49–76.

    For the text of the Treaty on Peace, Friendship and Cooperation Between the USSR and the Republic of India, see *Vneshnyaya politika Sovetskogo Soyuza, 1971 god* [Foreign Policy of the Soviet Union, 1971] (Moscow: Mezhdunarodnye otnosheniya, 1972), pp. 93–96.

15. See Jackson, *South Asian Crisis*, pp. 71–74.

16. Van Hollen, *Asian Survey*, vol. 20 (1980), p. 347.

17. Ibid., p. 348; and Seymour M. Hersh, *The Price of Power* (Summit, 1983), pp. 452–53.

18. See Jackson, *South Asian Crisis*, pp. 72, 83–87. See also William J. Barnds, "Moscow and South Asia," *Problems of Communism*, vol. 21 (May–June 1972), pp. 24–25.

19. Jackson, *South Asian Crisis*, p. 83.

Kissinger makes only one reference to the role that his trip to China and the emerging Sino-American rapprochement played in leading to the Soviet-Indian treaty. He suggests that the Soviets decided to retaliate by stirring up trouble and that they "deliberately opened the door to war on the subcontinent."[20] The treaty, he argues, whether intended to do so, "objectively increased the danger of war" by reassuring Indian military planners of continuing Soviet support in case of war—although there was no evidence to support that contention. In Kissinger's view, "The Soviet Union had seized a strategic opportunity. To demonstrate Chinese impotence and to humiliate a friend of both China and the United States proved too tempting. If China did nothing, it stood revealed as impotent; if China raised the ante, it risked Soviet reprisal. With the treaty, Moscow threw a lighted match into a powder keg."[21]

In describing the situation a few months later, without specific reference to the Soviet-Indian treaty, Kissinger argues that "the Soviet aim in the wake of our China initiative was to humiliate Peking and to demonstrate the futility of reliance on either China or the United States as an ally."[22] Elsewhere he broadens the Soviet purpose and design. Had the United States passively "acquiesced" in an Indian assault on Pakistan, it "would have sent a wrong signal to Moscow and unnerved all our Allies, China, and the forces for restraint in other volatile areas of the world. This was, indeed, why the Soviets had made the Indian assault on Pakistan possible in the first place."[23]

The underlying fallacy in Kissinger and Nixon's thinking throughout the crisis is that they persisted in assessing Soviet aims in terms of presumed Indian aims, and vice versa. Moreover, they attributed maximum offensive aims to both. Thus, in contrast to the assessments of the Department of State and the CIA, Kissinger and Nixon believed India's aim was to dismember Pakistan and end West Pakistan as an independent state. Both expressed this view repeatedly, and other participants describe it as an idée fixe of them both throughout the crisis. Similarly, they believed, contrary to evidence, that the Soviet Union must also want West Pakistan to be destroyed. They then interpreted developments in terms of those prejudgments.

Thus, when an important but ambiguous intelligence report was received in Washington soon after the war began, Kissinger and Nixon—alone among those privy to the intelligence and experienced in dealing with the region and the issues—immediately interpreted the report to mean that India was determined to destroy West Pakistan. As Kissinger describes it in his memoir the report said that apart from awaiting the liberation of Bangladesh (East Pakistan), Indira Gandhi would not accept a United Nations call for a cease-

20. Kissinger, *White House Years*, p. 767.

21. Ibid., p. 867.

22. Ibid., p. 876.

23. Ibid., pp. 913–14.

fire until "Indian forces would proceed with the 'liberation' of the southern part of Azad Kashmir—the Pakistani part of Kashmir—and continue fighting until the Pakistani army and air force were wiped out. In other words, *West Pakistan* was to be dismembered and rendered defenseless."[24] And Nixon writes in his memoir: "Through intelligence sources we learned that at a meeting of the Indian Cabinet Mrs. Gandhi had led a discussion of plans to expand the war on the western front and to invade West Pakistan."[25]

The intelligence did not say or mean what Nixon and Kissinger state. According to the actual text of notes of the intelligence briefing by Director of Central Intelligence Richard C. Helms, which is in the public domain, he actually reported the following: "before heeding a UN call for cease-fire, she [Indira Gandhi] intends to straighten out the southern border of Azad Kashmir. It is reported that prior to terminating present hostilities, Mrs. Gandhi intends to attempt to eliminate Pakistan's armor and air force capabilities."[26] It should be recalled that Pakistan had initiated hostilities with air attacks in the West. Within that context the report actually said three things. First, once Bangladesh was liberated, Gandhi *was* planning to accept a UN cease-fire. Second, before doing so, India intended to "straighten out the southern border of Azad Kashmir," presumably by moving beyond the previous cease-fire line there. This did not, however, mean that, as Kissinger put it, India was planning the "liberation" of southern Azad Kashmir or the "dismemberment" of West Pakistan. Third, Gandhi "intended" to "attempt to eliminate Pakistan's armor and air force capabilities," that is, to attempt in a retaliatory strike to knock out Pakistan's aircraft and tanks. Again, this did not necessarily mean that, as Kissinger would have it, India would "continue fighting until" successful in that attempt. Moreover, the attempt was to be aimed at "armor," not, as Kissinger inexplicably puts it, at the whole "Pakistani army." While attacking its armor would certainly put a dent in Pakistan's capability to attack again for a time, it would not render West Pakistan "defenseless."

The same tendentious interpretation that appears in Kissinger's memoir had, in briefer form, been included in the president's third annual foreign policy report to Congress, *U.S. Foreign Policy for the 1970's*, issued in 1972. It referred to "convincing evidence that India was seriously contemplat-

---

24. Ibid., p. 901. Emphasis in the original.

25. Nixon, *RN*, pp. 527–28.

26. The full text of the Washington Special Action Group (WSAG) meeting of December 8, including Helms's report, was printed in *New York Times*, January 15, 1972. The government subsequently acknowledged its authenticity. The precise original wording from the source had passed through several intermediaries—the CIA station, CIA headquarters, Helms, the White House and the WSAG, and the note taker. Kissinger acknowledges the report in *White House Years*, p. 901. The intelligence report had been received and was available to Kissinger and Nixon on December 7, the preceding day. For the text see Jackson, *South Asian Crisis*, pp. 224–28.

ing the seizure of Pakistan-held portions of Kashmir and the destruction of Pakistan's military forces in the West." The report concluded: "We could not ignore this evidence."[27]

Nixon and Kissinger based American policy virtually entirely on their own prior assumptions, which they saw as confirmed by their interpretation of the intelligence report, although in fact the interpretation had been derived from those erroneous assumptions. Moreover, this policy set in motion a course of confrontation not only with India, but with the Soviet Union as well.

Kissinger gave a background press conference, an unusual move for the still back room national security adviser, in which for the first time the United States charged India with responsibility for the war. He also publicly warned the Soviet Union that it had "an obligation to act as a force for restraint" and that "the attempt to achieve unilateral advantage sooner or later will lead to an escalation of tensions which must jeopardize the prospects of relaxation."[28] At the United Nations, Ambassador George Bush, on instructions, labeled India an aggressor.

A letter from President Nixon to General Secretary Brezhnev had been sent on December 6. This was prior to receipt of the crucial intelligence report.[29] Kissinger reports that even then he and Nixon had "decided that the best hope to keep India from smashing West Pakistan was to increase the risk for Moscow that events on the subcontinent might jeopardize its summit plans with the United States; in that case the Kremlin might urge restraint on India."[30] Before there was time for a reply, Soviet Chargé d'Affaires Yuly M. Vorontsov, in response to a conversation with Kissinger the day before, stated that the Soviet Union sought "a political solution in East Pakistan as a precondition for a cease-fire." Kissinger comments: "Clearly, Moscow wanted the war

---

27. Richard M. Nixon, *U.S. Foreign Policy for the 1970's: The Emerging Structure of Peace,* Report to the Congress, vol. 3 (Washington, D.C.: Government Printing Office, 1972), p. 147.

28. Kissinger, *White House Years,* p. 902. This background press briefing was given on December 7, before the WSAG meeting. It was printed in full in the *Congressional Record,* daily edition (December 9, 1971), p. 45734, by Senator Barry Goldwater of Arizona, to the unhappiness of the White House. The text is reprinted in Jackson, *South Asian Crisis,* pp. 207–09.

29. Kissinger, *White House Years,* p. 900. The United States had been in touch with the Soviets earlier on the developing crisis on the subcontinent, most authoritatively in a letter from President Nixon to Prime Minister Kosygin on November 26. Ibid., pp. 891–92. Neither the Kissinger nor the Nixon memoir explains the shift of addressees from Kosygin to Brezhnev. Nor was any explanation given to the Soviets. The Soviet leaders may have believed the United States was probing for differences among them, although more likely they saw the change as an escalation of concern. That reason was closer to the mark, although the Soviets almost certainly did not realize the real reason: the Department of State had drafted the November 26 message, and it was not privy to the fact that several months earlier the White House had shifted presidential-level communications from Prime Minister Kosygin to General Secretary Brezhnev.

30. Ibid., p. 900; and see p. 903.

to continue."[31] But he fails to note that the *only* precondition for a cease-fire was acceptance of the independence of Bangladesh—*not* an end to West Pakistan. And even Nixon and Kissinger had come to recognize the independence of Bangladesh was inevitable.

Brezhnev's reply came December 9. He proposed a cease-fire and resumption of negotiations with the leader of Bangladesh. Kissinger, while acknowledging a "hopeful side" to the message, was suspicious that it "might be a device to play for time" and, in accordance with his erroneous judgment on India's ambitions, comments that "we had to make sure that India would not use the interval to carry out its intention to destroy West Pakistan."[32]

By chance, Soviet Minister of Agriculture Vladimir Matskevich was visiting in Washington at the time. Kissinger had the idea of arranging for him to meet President Nixon in order that he convey to Brezhnev the seriousness the United States attached to the situation. Matskevich, to his surprise, was invited to the Oval Office to meet the president. "Bubbling with innocent goodwill," Matskevich conveyed "a personal greeting from Brezhnev, who was looking forward with anticipation to the Moscow summit." Kissinger reports that "Nixon replied that all progress in U.S.-Soviet relations was being threatened by the war on the subcontinent." Moreover, "if India moved forces against West Pakistan, the United States would not stand by."

Whether this blunt message reached Brezhnev is uncertain. Moreover, Nixon gives a strikingly different account of the meeting. He states that he asked Matskevich to convey his "seriousness in saying that it was incumbent upon the two of us as the leaders of the two nuclear superpowers *not* to allow our larger interests to become embroiled in the actions of our smaller friends." These are almost the very words Brezhnev might well have used in response.[33]

On December 10 another letter was sent to Brezhnev. Kissinger, keeping up the pressure, also read to Vorontsov a secret American aide-mémoire of November 5, 1962, in which the United States had promised assistance to Pakistan in case of Indian aggression. He warned Vorontsov that the United States would honor that pledge.[34]

Kissinger and Nixon both fretted over what more they could do to ensure that, as Kissinger put it to Nixon, "the Russians retain their respect for

---

31. Ibid., p. 901.

32. Ibid., p. 903.

33. Ibid., p. 904; and Nixon, *RN*, p. 528. Emphasis added. Nixon says he knew Matskevich was "a close friend of Brezhnev's" (which he did not know, but Kissinger had probably noted that Matskevich was the most senior Russian available and could convey a message directly to Brezhnev). Nixon evidently did not recall his own personal acquaintanceship with Matskevich, then a close friend of Khrushchev's, whom he had met when visiting Moscow as vice president in 1959. I accompanied Nixon on that trip and recall attending a luncheon for Nixon given by Matskevich, then, too, minister of agriculture.

34. Kissinger, *White House Years*, p. 905.

us. . . . We have to prevent India from attacking West Pakistan."[35] So, on December 10, they did something. They decided to send the U.S. Navy.

Kissinger relayed to Admiral Thomas Moorer, chairman of the JCS, a presidential order to send the aircraft carrier *Enterprise* and nine accompanying warships, with a complement of 2,000 combat-ready marines, from Vietnam to the Bay of Bengal. Thus was Task Force 74 created. There had been no NSC or other interagency meeting, or any discussion with the secretary of defense, the JCS, or the navy. (Needless to say, there would also have been no consultation with the secretary of state, even had he not been away at a NATO meeting.) The president is not constitutionally required to follow any particular procedure in exercising his authority as commander-in-chief of the armed forces. On the other hand, in the absence of any emergency or threat to the United States or its forces, some consultation at least within the executive branch is normally appropriate. One consequence was that the order creating and dispatching the task force did not even specify its mission.[36] Kissinger states that the move of the fleet (initially toward the Bay of Bengal, but holding east of the Strait of Malacca), was made "ostensibly for the evacuation of Americans, but in reality to give emphasis to our warnings against an attack on West Pakistan."[37] The task force was not given a clear mission because its purpose was simply to exist, to be there. Kissinger later explained to Secretary of Defense Laird that "our objective was to scare off an attack on West Pakistan," but did not disclose even to him that he really also had another objective: "we also wanted to have forces in place in case the Soviet Union pressured China."[38]

Later that same day, December 10, the Pakistani commander in East Pakistan offered a cease-fire. The State Department, Kissinger comments, was jubilant. Kissinger, however, was, in his own words, "disconcerted." "A separate cease-fire in the East would run counter to what had just been proposed to the Soviets. . . . it would magnify our principal worry by freeing the Indian army and air force for an all-out attack on West Pakistan." So the United States persuaded Pakistan not to offer the cease-fire. But Kissinger commented that "it was clear that this gave us only a brief breathing space. Within a short time the Pakistan army in the East would be destroyed. Indian

---

35. Ibid., p. 903.

36. Elmo R. Zumwalt, Jr., *On Watch: A Memoir* (Quadrangle, 1976), p. 367.

37. Kissinger, *White House Years*, p. 905. By this time there were only 47 Americans voluntarily remaining in Dacca, East Pakistan; the British had flown 114 out on December 12 and were prepared to evacuate the others. See Hall, *Force without War*, p. 193.

38. Kissinger, *White House Years*, p. 905. Emphasis added. Admiral Zumwalt, chief of naval operations, was not told even that; he later concluded that Nixon and Kissinger "probably" wanted to show China that the United States was a military power in the region and would respond, and that "maybe" the task force was useful in deterring an Indian attack on West Pakistan. See Zumwalt, *On Watch*, pp. 368–69.

troops would be freed for their planned assault on West Pakistan. We absolutely had to bring matters to a head."[39]

On December 11 Kissinger called in Vorontsov and delivered an ultimatum: the Soviet Union "had until noon on December 12 or we would proceed unilaterally." The United States must have assurances on West Pakistan. Vorontsov reported that Deputy Foreign Minister Kuznetsov had been sent to New Delhi "to arrange for a satisfactory outcome and to urge Indian restraint." As Kissinger recognized and told Nixon, that assertion was probably true. "But whether the Soviets were pressing for a cease-fire or egging on the Indians, our course had to be the same: we had to increase the pressure until we were assured by India that there would be a cease-fire and no annexation in the West."[40]

On December 12 Vorontsov called, one hour and fifty-five minutes before Kissinger's noon deadline. He advised that the Soviet reply was on the way and that its gist was an assurance that "India had no aggressive designs in the West." Kissinger, instead of being relieved, saw a dark purpose: the reply was "silent on the key point: its [India's] territorial aims in Kashmir. It was as compatible with a maneuver to gain time for a further fait accompli as with a genuine desire to settle."[41]

Vorontsov's call had come just as Nixon, Kissinger, and Alexander M. Haig, Jr., Kissinger's deputy, were meeting prior to Nixon and Kissinger's departure for a meeting in the Azores with President Georges Pompidou of France. They decided to use the emergency hot line to Moscow "to keep up the pressure"—the first time the Nixon administration had used the hot line. Nixon stressed that "time is of the essence" and that the Indian assurance lacked "concreteness."

At that point Nixon and Kissinger were informed that Huang Hua, the Chinese ambassador to the UN, with whom Kissinger had spoken earlier, wanted to see him with a message. There was no indication whatsoever of its content, the first from Beijing on the situation. As Kissinger admits, "We *assumed* that only a matter of gravity could induce them into such a departure [from always waiting until the United States requested a meeting]. We *guessed* that they were coming to the military assistance of Pakistan. . . . *If* so, we were on the verge of a showdown." "Nixon understood immediately,"

---

39. Kissinger, *White House Years*, pp. 905–06. For further details on the American role in dissuading President Agha Mohammed Yahya Khan from a cease-fire on December 10–11, see Jack Anderson, *The Anderson Papers* (Ballantine, 1973), pp. 278–84.

40. Kissinger, *White House Years*, p. 908. Kissinger did not specify what strong measures the United States would undertake unilaterally, beyond sending the fleet.

The American threat to act unilaterally was similar to the Soviet warning of October 24, 1973, in the Arab-Israeli October War, to which the United States replied with a full military alert, except that the American threat was an ultimatum not keyed to a prior U.S.-Soviet understanding.

41. Ibid., p. 909.

states Kissinger, "that if the Soviet Union succeeded in humiliating China, all prospects for world equilibrium would disappear. He decided—and I fully agreed—that if the Soviet Union threatened China we would not stand idly by."[42]

Accordingly, on December 12 they did something more: they sent the fleet into the theater of war. "To provide some military means to give effect to our strategy and to reinforce the message to Moscow, Nixon now advised the carrier task force to proceed through the Strait of Malacca and into the Bay of Bengal." The task force still had not been assigned a mission. Once again, "Nixon made this decision without informing either his Secretary of State or Secretary of Defense; it was not an ideal way to manage crises," Kissinger comments. But he muses, "It was symptomatic of the internal relationships of the Nixon Administration that neither the Secretary of State nor of Defense nor any other representative of their departments attended this crucial meeting, where, as it turned out, *the first decision to risk war in the triangular Soviet-Chinese-American relationship was taken.*"[43]

Having taken these steps, Kissinger notes, "It *now* became urgent to determine Soviet intentions and at the same time convince them that we meant business." So he called Vorontsov to inform him of the hot line message that had just been sent and the projected movement of the fleet, but also to reaffirm continued American readiness to cooperate along the lines of the president's letter, that is, a cease-fire in place on both fronts.[44]

At that point Nixon and Kissinger received the Chinese message and learned that China, too, simply wanted a standstill cease-fire. China had no intention of intervening. Hence there was no danger of the Soviet Union threatening China or of the United States being perceived as standing idly by. The fleet was now told to hold for twenty-four hours while the United States awaited the Soviet reply to the hot line message. At this point Kissinger comments that "amazingly, Pakistan, China, and—if Vorontsov could be believed—the Soviet Union, were now working in the same direction *under our aegis.*"[45]

The Soviet leaders, undoubtedly perplexed and probably suspicious over the American agitation, in effect repeated in their reply on the hot line on December 13 what Vorontsov had already said.[46] The next day Vorontsov

---

42. Ibid., pp. 909–10. Emphasis added.

43. Ibid. Emphasis added.

44. Ibid., p. 910. Emphasis added.

45. Ibid., p. 911. Emphasis added. The reference "under our aegis" presumes an American orchestration of triangular diplomacy extremely finely tuned. Other participants would have been astonished had they known of it.

46. Ibid., p. 911. The White House had replied on the hot line, too. As Kissinger notes, while it was a slower means of communication, *symbolically* it "conferred a sense of urgency." Ibid., p. 909.

brought a formal note reporting "firm assurances by the Indian leadership that India has no plans of seizing West Pakistani territory."

Kissinger states that he was still not sufficiently reassured as to Kashmir. At best this claim is disingenuous. As Nixon reports the same conversation, "Vorontsov said that the Soviets were prepared unconditionally to guarantee that there would be no Indian attack on West Pakistan *or on Kashmir*." Beyond that, neither the Indians, nor the Soviets as guarantors, were prepared to go. They would not agree to what *Kissinger* wanted, that India consider "Pakistani-held Kashmir as Pakistan territory."[47] Neither India nor Pakistan had ever, through decades of uneasy peace, been prepared to accept that the parts of Kashmir held and administered by the other were that other country's territory. The presence of the American fleet was certainly not going to lead the victorious Indians to capitulate on this long-standing dispute. That expectation was not reasonable, nor had it ever been directly advanced in the exchanges.

Kissinger adduces a second argument for not being satisfied with the assurance the Soviets had passed on: "Nor was anything heard from India." That contention, too, was disingenuous at best. India did give assurances on West Pakistan directly to the U.S. government, as well as through the Soviet intermediary the United States had chosen. India did not, of course, meet Kissinger's desire for capitulation on Kashmir. But both Indian Ambassador L. K. Jha in Washington and Foreign Minister Swaran Singh gave the United States assurances that India would not destroy West Pakistan. And on December 12 Prime Minister Gandhi in New Delhi denied in a public statement any territorial ambitions in West Pakistan.[48]

By this time the fleet had moved into the Bay of Bengal, attracting the attention of the media. Kissinger himself summarized the reaction: "Were we threatening India? Were we seeking to defend East Pakistan? Had we lost our minds?" Kissinger assures that the fleet's movement was based on "sober calculation."[49] (Meanwhile, the fleet also still did not know the answers to those questions.)[50] Kissinger explains the calculation: "We had some seventy-

---

Use of the direct communication link between heads of state designed for crisis management simply to underline a general diplomatic message should be sparing.

47. Nixon, *RN*, p. 530. Emphasis added. Kissinger, *White House Years*, pp. 911–12. It is not possible on the basis of available information to know whether, given this discrepancy, it is Nixon or Kissinger who is correctly reporting with respect to specific reference to Kashmir. In any case, Kissinger was seeking even more.

48. See Hall, *Force without War*, pp. 191–92; and Van Hollen, *Asian Survey*, vol. 20 (1980), p. 352. Kissinger, intent on justifying his mistaken position at the time, entirely omits reference to these public and private Indian assurances, nor does he mention a subsequent letter on December 15 from Prime Minister Gandhi to President Nixon that reaffirmed that India had no territorial ambitions in West Pakistan.

49. Kissinger, *White House Years*, pp. 911–12.

50. The White House finally approved a navy plan specifying a mission. It was, however, based on the navy's standing interest in countering the Soviet fleet and not on deterring Indian action in the West. See Hall, *Force without War*, p. 195.

two hours to bring the war to a conclusion before West Pakistan would be swept into the maelstrom. . . . We had to give the Soviets a warning that matters might get out of control on our side too. We had to be ready to back up the Chinese if at the last moment they came in after all. . . . Moscow was prepared to harass us; it was in our judgment not prepared to run military risks. Moving the carrier task force into the Bay of Bengal committed us to no final act, but it created *precisely the margin of uncertainty needed to force a decision by New Delhi and Moscow.*"[51]

Kissinger certainly intended to send a signal to India, the Soviet Union, and China by dispatching the fleet. But he failed to make clear what he was signaling.[52] The Indians studied the arrival of the U.S. fleet for the next few days *without* divining that it was meant to deter them from attacking West Pakistan. They considered various interpretations, but all seemed improbable. Finally they decided to ignore the fleet, except for destroying all ships in East Pakistani harbors by air strikes in order to prevent evacuation of the Pakistani army to the American fleet offshore for transfer to West Pakistan, in case that was its intended role.[53]

The Soviets did decide the fleet was probably designed to influence India not to carry the war into West Pakistan, but there is no indication their position was influenced by this action. The only effect of the U.S. naval movement was to lead the Soviets to counterbalance it by moving more Soviet naval ships into the area.[54]

---

51. Kissinger, *White House Years*, p. 912. Emphasis added.

   By this time a Soviet flotilla was gathering to accompany the U.S. fleet. It did so ostentatiously, but did not engage in harassment. The Soviets felt obliged to match the United States in impressing the Indians and Chinese. They may also have hoped to gain wider use of naval facilities in India by pointing out how situations could arise where those bases would be in the interest of India's security. In that objective they failed.

52. In one concrete, much more limited instance of an attempt at subtle signaling, on December 13 Kissinger sent Ambassador Gerard C. Smith, who was negotiating on SALT in Vienna, a message instructing that the American delegation should immediately adopt a cool and reserved attitude toward members of the Soviet delegation in view of the situation in South Asia. When Ambassador Smith mentioned to the head of the Soviet delegation that the situation in South Asia could have negative implications for Soviet-American relations and SALT, Kissinger was angry (although he attributed this reaction to the president). Kissinger then made clear that the idea was to show the American reaction by being chilly, but without mentioning South Asia. Smith expresses doubts about the usefulness of such signals. See Gerard Smith, *Doubletalk: The Story of the First Strategic Arms Limitations Talks* (Doubleday, 1980), pp. 341–42.

53. Hall, *Force without War*, pp. 192–94. The Indians were helped in reaching this conclusion by official U.S. background briefings of the press in Washington on an intentionally misleading "cover" story that the U.S. fleet might help evacuate the Pakistani forces from East Pakistan.

54. Ibid., pp. 198–201. The Soviet Union was monitoring the developing situation, both on the subcontinent and the American naval movements, by photographic reconnaissance satellites (Kosmos 463 and 464).

As for the Chinese, while they may have believed the fleet was sent for the purpose intended (of which the United States had informed them), their only reaction was a strong attack in the press following the crisis, leveled against both the American and Soviet naval concentrations in the area. The American fleet was correctly described as a "show of force to the Soviet Union and India," but this purpose was not applauded.[55]

The dispatch of the American fleet was counterproductive from a number of standpoints. The CIA's excellent intelligence source in New Delhi reported that Soviet Ambassador Pegov had reassured the Indians on December 13 that the Soviet Union did not believe the United States would intervene. Noting the presence of the Soviet fleet as well, he was also able to give a bold promise the Soviets knew would not be tested. He told the Indian leaders that "the Soviet Union will not allow the [U.S.] Seventh Fleet to intervene."[56]

The key participant *not* intended to be influenced by the American fleet apparently was the most impressed. Pakistani President Yahya Khan gave many indications to colleagues that he had real hopes of American military intervention. Apparently misunderstanding Kissinger's earlier urging not to accept a cease-fire in East Pakistan, and with hope buoyed by the approach of the American fleet, the limited purpose of which had *not* been explained to him, Yahya Khan extended the war and the attendant risks and tensions a few days longer. When the United States did not then come to Pakistan's aid, the net effect was disillusionment.[57]

On the way back to Washington from the Azores on December 14, Kissinger tried to impress the Soviet leaders again with the risks to the summit plans. In a background briefing for the press he said that "Soviet conduct on the subcontinent was not compatible with the mutual restraint required by genuine coexistence. If it continued, we would have to reevaluate our entire relationship, including the summit."[58] The press reported this last threat extensively and negatively, and identified Kissinger as the source.[59]

On December 16 the Pakistani commander in East Pakistan surrendered. On December 17 India proffered and Pakistan accepted an unconditional cease-fire in the West. There was no Indian attack on West Pakistan.

---

55. Cited in ibid., pp. 202–05.

56. Ibid., p. 201; and Jackson, *South Asian Crisis*, p. 231.

57. Hall, *Force without War*, pp. 209–10; see also Jackson, *South Asian Crisis*, pp. 141–42.

58. Kissinger, *White House Years*, p. 912.

59. This initiative by Kissinger greatly annoyed Nixon, who gave a higher priority to the summit. Nixon showed his displeasure by ignoring Kissinger to the point of not receiving him for several weeks, while, as Kissinger himself puts it, "letting me twist slowly, slowly in the wind, to use the literary contribution of a later period." Ibid., p. 918. For a fuller extract of the background briefing and an interesting account of how Kissinger intentionally stiffened it, see Kalb and Kalb, *Kissinger*, pp. 298–300.

Kissinger concludes: "There is no doubt in my mind that it was a reluctant decision [by India] resulting from Soviet pressure, which in turn grew out of American insistence, including the fleet movement and the willingness to risk the summit."[60] Kissinger is virtually alone in that self-justifying judgment. Even Nixon, whom Kissinger had persuaded of the dark designs of the Soviets and Indians, and of the threats to China and the future of triangular diplomacy, and whom Kissinger had also persuaded of the efficacy of his geopolitical maneuvers, saw the experience somewhat differently. He agreed that "by using diplomatic signals and behind-the-scenes pressure, we had been able to save West Pakistan from the imminent threat of Indian aggression and domination." But he diverged strikingly from Kissinger's stress on the need for a confrontation with the Soviet Union and for a U.S. decision not only to risk the summit and prospects for détente, but even "to risk war in the triangular Soviet-Chinese-American relationship." In contrast, Nixon concludes: "We had once again *avoided* a major confrontation with the Soviet Union" and he claims this to be a major achievement.[61] Evidently Nixon did not understand that Kissinger had been converting a regional conflict into one between the superpowers and had intentionally generated a confrontation, in the interests of establishing an equilibrium in the world balance of power through triangular diplomacy.

When all of Kissinger's frenetic crisis fever, histrionic signals, threats, attempted pressures, and the meanderings of the American fleet are set aside, the course of events actually unfolded in a way entirely consistent with the expressed positions taken by India, Pakistan, the Soviet Union, and China. By December 9—before the movement of the fleet, the hot line communication, or the misplaced alarm over a possible eruption in Sino-Soviet hostilities—*all* those participants had expressed support for a settlement along the lines finally agreed to: independence of Bangladesh, a return to the status quo in the West, and complete cessation of hostilities. In fact, India and the Soviet Union undoubtedly would have accepted this outcome at *any* time in the crisis, without the acrobatics of triangular diplomacy waged by a master geopolitician. It is only by substituting an unsupported presumption that the basis for India's recalcitrance on a cease-fire was a design to dismember West Pakistan for the clear and demonstrable Indian aim of securing independence for Bangladesh that Kissinger could have conducted the policy he did at the time or sought to justify it later. There is no indication, from the highly regarded secret intelligence source in India, or from any other source, that the Indian government agreed to the cease-fire in the West because of Soviet pressure. On the contrary, there are indications, beyond what the Soviets related at the time, that they were in fact counseling restraint and a negotiated outcome compatible with achievement of the Indian objective of an indepen-

---

60. Kissinger, *White House Years*, p. 913.

61. Nixon, *RN*, p. 530. Emphasis added. See also Kissinger, *White House Years*, p. 909.

dent Bangladesh. There is also no evidence that the Soviets had at any time pushed the Indians toward aggrandizement or military action.[62]

It must be questioned whether triangular diplomacy, or the strenuous American efforts to manipulate the course of events, had much to do with the outcome. Kissinger's account, if his dogged conviction that India was engaged in an almost relentless drive to destroy West Pakistan were accepted as sound, can be seen as involving India's acquiescing reluctantly to an American, and ultimately, under American pressure, to a Soviet insistence on sparing West Pakistan. It would then be possible to conclude that maneuver and pressure can, in some circumstances, help induce reluctant Soviet assistance in restraining or settling a regional conflict. And that is a lesson Kissinger and Nixon believed was to be drawn from the experience.

Kissinger also purports to have believed that he had frustrated a Soviet design to cripple triangular diplomacy. "In the growing India-Pakistan conflict the Soviet Union discovered an opportunity to humiliate China and to punish Pakistan for having served as intermediary."[63]

Kissinger and Nixon saw an even deeper dimension to the situation that related directly to future Soviet behavior in the world. Kissinger justifies the course he and Nixon pursued on the basis that "Moscow had seen a sufficiently strong reaction not to be tempted to test us in areas of more central concern."[64] The idea that the Soviets might have been favorably impressed by the U.S. actions (or that they saw them as a "strong reaction" to some Soviet challenge) is wholly dependent on acceptance of Kissinger's premise as to Soviet and Indian objectives in West Pakistan, objectives it is clear Moscow never held. But at the time, Kissinger (and Nixon, whom he persuaded) believed "we had to act in a manner that would give pause to potential Soviet adventures elsewhere, especially in the Middle East."[65]

How had the Soviets "tested" the United States, and what "adventures" was the U.S. policy inhibiting? "The naked recourse to force by a partner of the Soviet Union backed by Soviet arms and buttressed by Soviet

---

62. A CIA assessment argued that the Indian-Soviet treaty would help Prime Minister Gandhi maintain restraint and that that was what the Soviet leaders wished. Kissinger, determined to see Soviet instigation rather than restraint, dismisses this intelligence assessment as "fatuous." The CIA, in reaching its judgment, and the Department of State in agreeing with it, based their view on an evaluation of all sources of information, including the secret Indian intelligence source that Kissinger elsewhere esteems. Kissinger, *White House Years*, pp. 867, 901. See also Van Hollen, *Asian Survey*, vol. 20 (1980), pp. 347–51.

Seymour Hersh has stated that the Indian source was the veteran Indian politician Moraji Desai, then in the cabinet and later Indira Gandhi's successor as prime minister from 1977 to 1979. See Hersh, *The Price of Power*, p. 450.

63. Kissinger, *White House Years*, p. 767. The idea that the Soviet Union wished to "punish Pakistan for having served as an intermediary" between the United States and China is demonstrably not in keeping with Soviet policy toward Pakistan, discussed below.

64. Ibid., p. 918.

65. Ibid., p. 898; and see p. 903.

assurances threatened the very structure of international order," according to Kissinger, "just when our whole Middle East strategy depended on proving the inefficacy of such tactics and when America's weight as a factor in the world was already being undercut by our [internal] divisions over Indochina." Accordingly, "the assault on Pakistan was in our [his and Nixon's] view a most dangerous precedent for Soviet behavior, which had to be resisted if we were not to tempt escalating upheavals."[66] "We sought to prevent a demonstration that Soviet arms and diplomatic support were inevitably decisive in crises."[67]

Kissinger's views got some support from his staff experts on Soviet affairs, Helmut Sonnenfeldt and William G. Hyland. They had described the August Soviet-Indian treaty as opening up ominous possibilities, including a Soviet-Chinese struggle once removed: "Thus, the India-Pakistan conflict becomes a sort of Sino-Soviet clash by proxy." This analysis clearly appealed to Kissinger at the time (in citing it now, he terms it perceptive).[68] In actuality, Chinese and Indian involvement did not escalate as they had postulated it might. Instead, it was the United States that chose to escalate its involvement, both diplomatically and with maneuvers by its fleet intended to counter the presumed Soviet role on the Indian side. But the concept of proxies survived.

Three days after the cease-fire Nixon and Kissinger sent the Chinese an analysis containing "sobering conclusions." They included the judgment that "the governments of the People's Republic of China and the United States should not again find themselves in a position where hostile global aims can be furthered through the use of proxy countries."[69] Most significantly (and most tenuously) Kissinger cites in the context of seeking to establish the general toughness of the administration in countering Soviet aggrandizement the example of U.S. resistance to the proxy war by India.[70]

Whatever India's motives and aims, be they a benign and humanitarian interest in defending the people of East Bengal or vengeful and acquisitive designs on Pakistan, virtually no Western (or Pakistani) historian now, or political analyst at the time, would characterize India as having been a proxy for the Soviet Union. Nor would students of Soviet policy. The Soviet leaders undoubtedly wished to expand Soviet influence in the subcontinent. They had, since 1954, expended substantial effort to that end. They had, in particular, developed ties with India based on perceived congruent interests, including countering the American alliance with Pakistan. But they had also maintained and sought to develop ties with Pakistan. In 1966 Prime Minister Kosygin had successfully mediated the settlement of the Indo-Pakistani war of 1965, and in so doing had kept the confidence of Pakistan as well as India. And in 1971,

---

66. Ibid., p. 913.

67. Ibid., p. 886.

68. Ibid., p. 767.

69. Nixon, *RN*, pp. 530–31. Kissinger does not mention this communication

70. Kissinger, *White House Years*, p. 1255.

until the July 15 announcement of President Nixon's forthcoming visit to China, the Soviet Union had been remarkably evenhanded in its position toward India and Pakistan on the growing dispute.[71] Even then, and notwithstanding the Soviet-Indian treaty, as the crisis developed the Soviets continued to provide economic assistance to Pakistan, continued to refer to East Pakistan rather than to Bangladesh, as the Indians did, and for a long time called for a solution agreeable to "the entire people of Pakistan." To the unhappiness of the Indian government the Soviet leaders maintained this divergent position through high-level meetings in New Delhi and Moscow in September and October. At the same time, the continued supply of Soviet arms to India, in Soviet eyes, enhanced India's sense of security and strengthened Moscow's ability to influence and restrain New Delhi.[72]

There is one further aspect of the Soviet angle: Moscow's view of the *American* role in the crisis. In general, in their writings the Soviets have blamed the United States for not cooperating to resolve the war, as they acknowledge it had done in 1965. They cite as the reason Washington's concern over the growing tie with China.[73] While this evaluation may be self-serving, it is also on the mark. Kissinger would argue that he and Nixon were doing all they could to resolve the war in ways that served their view of the geopolitical balance of power. He, too, however, states that the U.S. position was established above all with an eye to its new relationship with China.

The Soviets have not given their assessment of the American efforts to manage triangular diplomacy in this crisis. It is difficult to believe they would have been impressed. India achieved its principal objective, the independence of East Pakistan, despite Chinese and American opposition. While that had not originally been a Soviet objective, the USSR came to accept it (as Kissinger indicates the United States also would have done). The unexpected harsh opposition by the United States turned India more toward the Soviet Union. And the Soviets were enabled by the movement of the U.S. fleet to demonstrate their ability to neutralize such a presence by matching it.

The China Factor

China had been closely associated with Pakistan ever since the 1962 Indian-Chinese hostilities. But there is no indication that China played an

71. See Jackson, *South Asian Crisis*, pp. 39–40, 69–71.

72. Cited in Van Hollen, *Asian Survey*, vol. 20 (1980), p. 348. This rationale for military assistance to a friend, but one that is not a satellite or proxy and that may resort to military action to serve its own perceived interests, is also held by American administrations, for example with respect to military assistance to Israel.

73. See A. A. Gromyko and others, *Istoriya diplomatii* [A History of Diplomacy], vol. 5, bk 2 (Moscow: Politizdat, 1979), pp. 456–68, in particular p. 458; and see L. Stepanov, "Current Problems of World Politics," *Mirovaya ekonomika i mezhdunarodnye otnosheniya* [The World Economy and International Relations], no. 4 (April 1972), p. 87.

active role in advising or assisting Pakistan. Neither Kissinger's nor any other account of the war indicates that either Pakistan or China shared with the United States any exchanges of view between themselves on the course of policy as the 1971 crisis developed.

On April 13 Chinese Prime Minister Zhou Enlai had written a letter to President Yahya Khan offering support for Pakistan, but also conveying that that support was limited, and indirectly counseling conciliation. The Chinese gave assurances that it would "firmly support" Pakistan in its "just struggle to safeguard state sovereignty and national independence," but conspicuously did not include support for its territorial integrity. Moreover, the Chinese advised that a return to normalcy was tied to "wise consultations"— broadly hinting that Yahya Khan needed to negotiate with the Bengalis of East Pakistan. Most intriguing was not only a comment on India's "gross interference in the internal affairs of Pakistan," but also a charge that "the Soviet Union *and the United States* are doing the same one after the other."[74]

As noted, Kissinger and Nixon's first thought with respect to China (and Pakistan) as the crisis loomed had been whether it would derail their grand plan for an opening to China and the construction of a strategic triangle as the basis for managing the balance of power. These concerns were almost certainly groundless. Short of open American support for India against Pakistan, nothing the United States might have done toward the Bengal situation would have affected the perceptions of national interests and power relations that were leading China toward rapprochement with the United States and that made Pakistan wish to do all it could to facilitate that development. Kissinger's trip and the plans for Nixon's trip were undertaken, after all, despite serious differences over U.S. actions in Vietnam, Taiwan, Chinese membership in the United Nations, and other issues. Even had the United States been less than fully supportive of Pakistan during the crisis, the original reasons for the rapprochement and Pakistan's support for it would have remained.

As the South Asian crisis deepened, the Chinese leadership was shaken by Minister of Defense Lin Biao's planned coup and attempted defection in September. It is interesting that, during Kissinger's visit in October, which involved twenty-five hours of discussion with Zhou Enlai on the world situation, there is no indication that either side raised the Indo-Pakistani situation. The first discussion apparently came on the occasion of Kissinger's initial secret meeting with Ambassador Huang Hua in New York on November 23. Kissinger provided a secret intelligence briefing on the military situation and they discussed plans for support of Pakistan in the Security Council.[75] Considering the important, in many ways central, role that the United States was according its China policy, and given the developing crisis on the subcontinent from March to December, it is extraordinary that the Chinese gave no signifi-

---

74. See the full text in Jackson, *South Asian Crisis*, p. 173. Emphasis added.

75. Kissinger, *White House Years*, p. 889.

cant indication of their views or interests to the United States at any time throughout that period. That fact alone should have told Kissinger something.

What the Chinese knew, and the American leaders should have known, was that there was really nothing they could or would attempt to do beyond giving moral and political suppport to Pakistan in the United Nations. And there is no indication the Chinese expected anything more from the United States.

The only Chinese geopolitical action was a modest effort to remind the Indians of the Chinese military presence and potential by initiating some military alert measures along the Chinese-Indian border in the period December 8–16, which they correctly assumed the Indians would monitor.[76]

There were two brief but significant moments of American-Chinese contact, important because of the failures in communication and the consequences of relying instead on Kissinger's insight. The first occurred in a meeting between Kissinger and Huang Hua on December 10. The second, referred to earlier, was when Huang indicated two days later that he had a message from Beijing.

When Kissinger met with Huang on December 10, he states it was obvious that Huang had no instructions. According to Kissinger, Huang "took a hard line." Despite all his experience (which by then included hearing Chinese, and many North Vietnamese, ideological statements for the record), Kissinger failed to recognize what was a ritual repetition of a hard public line in private discussion. He says that Huang stated that "East Pakistan would have been sacrificed to superior force" and that "we should not give up the principle of Indian withdrawal *prior* to negotiations." Huang also evinced concern over the precedent for dismembering other countries. Rather than recognizing that Huang was saying that China (and the United States) could do nothing to prevent the fall of East Pakistan and should therefore simply stand on principle for the record, Kissinger leapt beyond. He misread Huang's concern over

---

76. Hall, *Force without War*, pp. 205–06.

Some analysts have speculated that the buildup of Soviet forces on the northern borders of China played an important role in deterring Chinese intervention on Pakistan's behalf and that the Soviet Union must have realized this effect and counted upon it later in supporting Vietnam. See Harry Gelman, *The Soviet Far East Buildup and Soviet Risk-Taking against China*, R–2943–AF, prepared for the United States Air Force (Santa Monica, Calif.: Rand Corp., 1982), pp. 53–70. In a general sense, China was no doubt aware that if it attacked India, it would risk Soviet pressure and counterintervention in western or northern China. But the Chinese also appreciated the fundamental weakness of the Pakistani position in Bengal and would almost certainly not have been tempted to intervene by attacking India. They had not done so in the more significant Indo-Pakistani War of 1965, *before* the Soviet buildup on the Chinese border. Moreover, the internal divisions in China in the fall and winter of 1971 (during which, for example, the entire Chinese air force was grounded for weeks, and purges of Lin Biao's closest associates in the defense establishment were undertaken) made use of the Chinese army unusually risky. Both these considerations were probably much more significant than the Soviet border buildup in restraining any Chinese inclinations to intervene. Finally, the Soviet buildup did not prevent the Chinese from their military alert in December.

precedent to mean that China feared an attack by the Soviet Union, a fear that the United States had to allay by sudden commitments. Kissinger told Huang the United States "would not be indifferent to further Soviet moves" and "an attack on China especially would have grave consequences." He recounts that Huang also said that "China would never stop fighting as long as it had a rifle in its armory" and "it would surely increase its assistance to Pakistan." Even as Kissinger reports it, and only his account is available, this rhetoric was clearly not a signal of China's intention to involve itself militarily in the subcontinent. But, as Kissinger admits, "I took this—as it turned out, wrongly—to be an indication that China might intervene militarily even at this late stage."[77]

It was on this basis that Kissinger advised Nixon to order out the fleet and pursue a general policy of confrontation with the Soviet Union, including, in his words, "to risk war."

Kissinger did more in this conversation than misconstrue Chinese intentions. He also raised the stakes of the Indo-Pakistani War for Sino-American relations and triangular diplomacy. The Chinese had shown no concern whatsoever about American credibility or policy. If Kissinger's swollen fears over Chinese confidence in the United States had any basis, it was probably as a result of Kissinger's dramatically making it into such an issue. (This effect was reinforced by the Nixon-Kissinger letter of December 20, cited earlier.)

Nixon assessed the Chinese role more soberly. He notes that "the Chinese played a very cautious role in this period. . . . they would not take the risk of coming to the aid of Pakistan by attacking India, because they understandably feared that the Soviets might use this action as an excuse for attacking China. They consequently did nothing."[78]

The second instance in which Kissinger's insight was faulty was noted earlier: the panicky reaction to the news that the Chinese had a message to deliver, prompting hasty actions even before the message was received and read. As Kissinger observes, "The Chinese message was not what we [Kissinger and Nixon] expected. On the contrary, it accepted the UN procedure and the political solution." In a truly remarkable tour de force Kissinger interprets this to mean "Chou En-lai's [Zhou Enlai's] analysis was the same as ours."[79] Apparently Kissinger was unable to recognize that a need to accept the inevitable in East Pakistan had for some time been almost everyone's analysis except his own—even the Pakistanis had been ready to surrender on December 10, until he persuaded them not to do so.[80] He could only imagine identical analyses by the two master geopoliticians.

---

77. Kissinger, *White House Years*, pp. 906–07. All quotes of Huang's statements are Kissinger's reconstruction.

78. Nixon, *RN*, p. 530.

79. Kissinger, *White House Years*, p. 911.

80. Ibid., pp. 905–06; and Jackson, *South Asian Crisis*, pp. 141–42.

Kissinger also believed that his management of the crisis carried an important lesson for the Chinese. He included a veiled version of this lesson in the presidential foreign policy report: "Finally, it was our view that the war in South Asia was bound to have serious implications for the evolution of the policy of the People's Republic of China. That country's attitude toward the global system was certain to be profoundly influenced by its assessment of the principles by which this system was governed—whether force and threat ruled or whether restraint was the international standard."[81] This statement would appear to be a rather presumptuous reference to instilling respect for adherence to the UN Charter. Kissinger states what he really meant more succinctly and plainly in his memoir: "Peking [Beijing] had learned that we took seriously the requirements of the balance of power."[82] Whether the Chinese could have gained increased respect for the ability of the United States to manage that balance through triangular diplomacy or any other means by observing its performance in the Indo-Pakistani War is, however, doubtful.

Consequences and Implications

The Indo-Pakistani War of 1971 is significant to a study of American-Soviet relations not only because of the direct and indirect interrelation of the two powers in the crisis, but also because of the importance that the United States in particular attributed to triangular diplomacy in managing these relations.

Triangular diplomacy, still in its infancy, had a great deal to do with determining the U.S. position in the South Asian regional conflict. It had inconsequential effects on the Soviet and Chinese positions, which would have been essentially the same even in the absence of the new developments of 1969–71 in their relations with the United States. Pakistan was not really affected by the American diplomatic stance, while India became more alienated from the United States and somewhat closer to the Soviet Union. Similarly, neither Pakistan nor India would have acted differently in the absence of triangular diplomacy. The one exception relates to the Indian-Soviet treaty: it probably would not have been signed as early had it not been for the sudden and unexpected Sino-American move toward a rapprochement while the regional crisis was deepening.

Both the United States and the Soviet Union were supporting semi-allies: Pakistan and India were scarcely clients and definitely not proxies. The semi-ally of the United States, Pakistan, was the only one that could have

81. Nixon, *U.S. Foreign Policy for the 1970's: The Emerging Structure of Peace*, p. 149.

82. Kissinger, *White House Years*, p. 918.

defused the looming crisis by its own actions. At first the United States half-heartedly encouraged movement in that direction. But then, once war had broken out, for reasons of perceived triangular diplomatic effect, the United States stiffened Pakistan against withdrawal from East Pakistan and a quick end to the hostilities.

Although the unilateral U.S. maneuvers intended to serve triangular diplomacy had singularly little impact on the march of events in India and Pakistan, they did have a number of direct consequences on the future of triangular diplomacy (as well as other effects on American internal and foreign policy, and on the policies of several other states, principally India). Before those consequences are discussed, it is useful to review the errors of geopolitical judgment in the American attempt to manage triangular diplomacy in this crisis. One cause of these errors was that Kissinger and Nixon were virtually—sometimes literally—the only policymakers. And Nixon was almost wholly dependent on Kissinger's sometimes unique reading of the facts and their implications. Kissinger misread Soviet and Indian intentions, and Chinese expectations, the three key elements in the crisis. Timing was also a factor—the policymaking process (and crisis management in particular) under the Nixon administration was still in formation.[83] This crisis was one of the first in which the rest of the government was involved on one plane, while the real policy was made in the White House on another. This disjointed American policymaking also led to a famous leak of the notes on the Washington Special Action Group (WSAG) meetings, as well as other intelligence reports and the like.[84] Investigation of the leak in turn uncovered a secret spy operation of the JCS within Kissinger's NSC staff. One of the investigators of that incident was later involved in the White House "Plumbers" operation. And so on.

One consequence of this situation was increasing erosion of the public's confidence in the administration and its secret diplomacy, of Nixon and Kissinger's confidence in governmental bureaucracy, and of the bureaucracy's confidence in Kissinger and Nixon.

Triangular diplomacy as conducted by Nixon and Kissinger was not only indirectly affected by these domestic developments, but was itself directly responsible for them in several respects. First, one reason the bureaucracy could not be brought into policymaking on the South Asian problem until mid-July was its exclusion from the secret China policy. Later, the bureaucracy—the professional diplomats, intelligence estimators, military advisers, and even their cabinet chiefs—was not brought into the real policy decisions because Kissinger and Nixon rejected the assessments of those experts and did not want

---

83. For Kissinger's viewpoint, see ibid., pp. 864, 897.

84. The full texts of the minutes of the WSAG meetings of December 3, 4, 6, and 8, 1971 (actually detailed notes by a participating staff member) are reprinted in Jackson, *South Asian Crisis*, pp. 212–28.

to disclose their own. This fragmentation led to such fiascos as misinterpreting key intelligence reports and dispatching a naval task force for an ill-defined and ultimately counterproductive mission. Even the naval yeoman who was found stealing highly secret documents from Kissinger's briefcase, files, and classified trash container for the JCS was not prosecuted because, as an expert on this general subject has written: "He had traveled with Kissinger and others on a number of secret missions [including the Pakistan-China trip] and had had access to other top-secret information, which, if disclosed, could have jeopardized our negotiations with China and with North Vietnam."[85]

The tilt toward Pakistan and the failure to take into account the humanitarian element in international affairs alienated many in the United States and abroad.[86] (Some ten million refugees fled from East Pakistan to India, and thousands were massacred by West Pakistani troops before the Indians began to aid the indigenous resistance forces.)

The treatment of the strategic triangle as though it were the Trinity led to a grossly disproportionate emphasis on intended subtle signals to Soviet and Chinese leaders at the expense of the much louder and clearer negative signals to India and the world. In the minds of Kissinger and Nixon the publicized tilt toward Pakistan was but a corollary of the tilt toward China. The China tilt skewed the entire diplomacy of the United States toward South Asia, sacrificing real American interests and diplomatic leverage there not only during the crisis but for a long time thereafter. The impact naturally was greatest and most damaging in the case of American relations with India.[87]

India continued to base its policy on its own interests. It was convinced that the United States could no longer be counted on to view those interests without bias, and it therefore found Soviet understanding and support all the more welcome. At the same time the Indians were careful not to move too close to the Soviet Union. They declined to support Brezhnev's call for an Asian collective security system directed at China, effectively torpedoing that project. They continued to work toward a zone of peace in the Indian Ocean that would exclude both American *and Soviet* naval power.[88]

The American role in the 1971 crisis may have had one critical effect—it may have influenced India to develop nuclear weapons. At a time when China was developing and acquiring nuclear weapons, India could not count on the United States and did not want to become dependent on the

---

85. Nixon, *RN*, p. 532.

86. A Louis Harris poll found that two-to-one the American public disapproved of the Nixon administration's policy in the crisis, largely for humanitarian reasons. See Barnds, *Christianity and Crisis*, vol. 32 (1972), p. 143.

87. See, for example, Van Hollen, *Asian Survey*, vol. 20 (1980), pp. 359–60; Hall, *Force without War*, pp. 212–18; and Jackson, *South Asian Crisis*.

88. Hall, *Force without War*, p. 211.

Soviet Union. The deployment of the U.S. nuclear-armed aircraft carrier task force during the Indo-Pakistani War, with its implicit threat to India, was a factor in this decision.[89] Most of these negative consequences could have been seen—indeed they were seen—but that advice was ignored or spurned as inconsequential when weighed against what were visualized as the imperatives of triangular diplomacy.

Finally, American relations with the Soviet Union were affected in several important and little appreciated ways. First, there is no evidence to support (and much evidence to counter) the assumptions that were fundamental to Kissinger's purposes in attempting to manage Soviet policy in the crisis. Kissinger was sacrificing very palpable American interests and squandering American diplomatic leverage in South Asia to prevent a phantom Soviet desire for aggrandizement via an imagined Indian proxy. Kissinger denounced alleged Soviet responsibility for "recourse to force by a partner of the Soviet Union backed by Soviet arms and buttressed by Soviet assurances" that, he says, "threatened the very structure of the international order." These assumptions were wrong. Nor did Kissinger reflect on what the implication of such a code of conduct for détente would be for the United States. Should the United States, for example (paraphrasing Kissinger's formula to apply to the United States), be held directly responsible for "recourse to force by a partner of the United States backed by American arms and buttressed by American assurances" every time Israel resorts to armed action? Should the United States be held responsible for the Chinese attack on Vietnam in 1979, given that within the vortex of triangular diplomacy China was a partner of the United States, buttressed by American assurances (though not yet American arms)? Yet, Kissinger—and some successors—have continued to apply a standard of guilt by association to a variety of third world parties that he labeled proxies of the Soviet Union, with no better justification than that for India in 1971.

Finally, and perhaps most significant in the long run, was Kissinger's astonishing belief that he had succeeded in manipulating and controlling Indian, and above all *Soviet*, behavior in the 1971 South Asian war. Kissinger has cited this case (and the equally inapplicable case of the 1970 Syrian-Jordanian crisis) as instances of successful American taming of *Soviet* attempts at aggrandizement through proxies.[90] As noted earlier,[91] in the Syrian-Jordanian case as well as the Indo-Pakistani one, it was Syria and India respectively that made decisions, reinforced by Soviet advice which would have been the same *without* American geopolitical pressures managed from the White House. Yet Kissin-

---

89. See Van Hollen, *Asian Survey*, vol. 20 (1980), pp. 359–60. In debate in the Indian Parliament over the nuclear issue, proponents of an Indian nuclear capability repeatedly referred to the arrival of the American carrier in 1971 as a reason to attain such a capability.

90. For example, see Kissinger, *White House Years*, pp. 1255, 1143.

91. See chapter 3.

ger and Nixon believed they had found a way to manage perceived Soviet expansionist efforts in the third world. This unfounded belief, in turn, led to unjustified confidence that they could handle such regional challenges involving the Soviet Union in the future, especially under conditions of a détente that engaged broader Soviet interests with those of the United States. This illusion would eventually produce disillusion.

9 Détente Launched: The First Nixon-Brezhnev Summit, May 1972

THE SUMMIT MEETING in Moscow in May 1972 was a remarkable event. It reflected the desire of the leaders in both the United States and the Soviet Union to launch, for a number of shared and differing reasons, a relationship of détente. The American progenitors of the summit meeting regarded it as a great success, the result of a skillful combination of efforts to orchestrate Soviet policies through linkage. The summit was to be the base for future development of American-Soviet relations, it would reinforce America's position as the fulcrum in triangular diplomacy with the Soviet Union and China, and, especially for President Nixon, it was a symbol at home and abroad of his achievement in building a structure of peace.

The summit meeting was seen to have broad international political implications. While a peace settlement had not yet been reached in Vietnam, both the Soviet Union and China were making clear to Vietnam that their support would not extend to sacrificing their own interests and their readiness to develop ties with the United States. Similarly, it was believed that the Soviet interest in détente with the United States had served to restrain Soviet assistance to the Arabs. On a more global scale, a strategic arms limitation agreement had been reached that laid the basis for further reciprocal arms limitations. In Europe a Berlin accord had been reached, and the *Ostpolitik* of West Germany was now being wrapped in a broader context. European détente was now being complemented in American-Soviet détente, preventing a fissure from developing within the West. Finally, the policy of linkage was working. In preparing for the summit meeting an extensive array of bilateral agreements had been negotiated in advance. The intent was to have a dazzling parade of agreements to unveil at the summit. In all, ten documents were signed. The main ones were the Basic Principles of Mutual Relations and two SALT accords. In addition, there were agreements establishing a joint economic commission, as well as cooperative efforts in several areas—science and technology, medicine and public health, protection of the environment, collaboration in space exploration, and avoidance of naval incidents at sea. Each accord had its own merits, and some were potentially significant. Actual establishment of the economic commission was dependent on further agreements, but these were concluded in subsequent months. The accord on avoidance of incidents at sea between the two navies was the most substantive in actually helping to reduce tensions. The others, most dramatically the one that would eventually lead to a joint manned space rendezvous, were more significant symbolically. But taken together, as President Nixon said later, they "began the establishment of a pattern of interrelationships and cooperation in a number of different areas. This was the first stage of détente: to involve Soviet interests in ways that would increase their stake in international stability and the status quo."[1]

The Basic Principles of U.S.-Soviet Relations

The Basic Principles of Relations Between the United States of America and the Union of Soviet Socialist Republics, signed on the last day of the summit conference, May 29, represented a charter for détente. Interestingly, the United States and the Soviet Union saw the basic principles in very different lights. They were accorded far more significance by the Soviet leadership than by American leaders. In the West in general they were overshadowed by the greater attention accorded the SALT agreements signed three days earlier.

The first basic principle states that the United States and the Soviet Union "will proceed from the common determination that in the nuclear age there is no alternative to conducting their mutual relations on the basis of peaceful coexistence" and that despite differences in ideology, they will undertake to develop "normal relations based on the principles of sovereignty, equality, non-interference in internal affairs and mutual advantage."

The second principle states that "the USA and the USSR attach major importance to preventing the development of situations capable of causing a dangerous exacerbation of their relations. Therefore, they will do their utmost to avoid military confrontations and to prevent the outbreak of nuclear war. They will always exercise restraint in their mutual relations, and will be prepared to negotiate and settle differences by peaceful means." In addition, seeking "reciprocity, mutual accommodation and mutual benefit," "both sides recognize that efforts to obtain unilateral advantage at the expense of the other, directly or indirectly, are inconsistent with these objectives." Finally, "The prerequisites for maintaining and strengthening peaceful relations between the USA and the USSR are the recognition of the security interests of the Parties based on the principle of equality and the renunciation of the use or threat of force."

---

1. Richard Nixon, *RN: The Memoirs of Richard Nixon* (Grosset and Dunlap, 1978), p. 618.

The third principle records their recognition of a "special responsibility . . . to do everything in their power so that conflicts or situations will not arise which would serve to increase international tensions" and "to promote conditions in which all countries will live in peace and security and will not be subject to outside interference in their internal affairs."

These three are the most important principles. In another, the eleventh, the two powers "make no claim for themselves and would not recognize the claims of anyone else to any special rights or advantages in world affairs." They also state that "the development of U.S.-Soviet relations is not directed against third countries and their interests." The twelfth and final one states: "The basic principles set forth in this document do not affect any obligations with respect to other countries earlier assumed by the USA and the USSR."

The remaining principles cover general intentions to develop treaty relations; expand cultural, scientific, and other exchanges; work for arms limitations and disarmament; establish joint commissions; expand economic and commercial ties; and exchange views, including, "when necessary," summit meetings.[2]

The attitude of the United States toward the Basic Principles was made clear from the outset by the two key Americans involved, President Nixon and his national security adviser, Henry Kissinger. In his memoir Nixon gives the Basic Principles only two sentences, noting lackadaisically: "Finally, we signed a document containing twelve 'basic principles of mutual relations between the United States and the USSR,' which set forth a code of behavior" dealing with "the reduction of tension and conflict."[3] Nixon's lack of interest in the document was probably owing to his pragmatic bent, but also to the fact that he had played almost no part in its negotiation.[4] Because the text had been negotiated earlier and agreed to by Kissinger and the Soviet leaders, the subject was barely discussed at the summit itself.[5] Moreover, the document

---

2. "Text of the 'Basic Principles of Relations Between the United States of America and the Union of Soviet Socialist Republics,' May 29, 1972," *Weekly Compilation of Presidential Documents*, vol. 8 (June 5, 1972), pp. 943–44; and "Text of Basic Principles, May 29," *Department of State Bulletin*, vol. 66 (June 26, 1972), pp. 898–99. (Hereafter *Presidential Documents* and *State Bulletin*.)

3. Nixon, *RN*, p. 618. Nixon's main preoccupation relating to the document of the Basic Principles was to surface it at the summit meeting without a storm of protest from Secretary of State William P. Rogers, who knew nothing about its existence. See Henry Kissinger, *White House Years* (Boston, Mass.: Little, Brown, 1979), pp. 1205, 1209, 1213.

4. See the discussion in chapter 3.

5. Interviews with a member of Kissinger's staff present at the meetings in April and at the May summit conferences, and with a Soviet participant. In striking contrast to the several hours Kissinger and some of his staff, particularly Helmut Sonnenfeldt, devoted to working on the text of the Basic Principles, and to the absence of any review by others in the U.S. government, the Soviet leadership gave the text very careful consideration. Minister of Foreign Affairs Gromyko later commented that the principles had been "worked out as a result of tremendous efforts." See "The Thirty-sixth Session of the UN General Assembly: Address of A. A. Gro-

had received only minimal briefing and cursory review in the White House before the summit meeting. In fact, Nixon may well never have read the entire document, although it is only about 1,000 words. The content and text had been handled by Kissinger and two of his staff in Moscow, without reference to Washington, on the basis of very general guidance from the president that Kissinger had largely ignored.

For his part Kissinger acknowledged the limitations of the Basic Principles even before he left the Soviet Union. In two final news conferences, one before departing from Moscow, the second in Kiev, he said that the principles represented "an aspiration and an attitude" and that of course they would have to be implemented to make a substantive contribution: "If any of these principles is flouted, we will not be able to wave a piece of paper and insist that the illegality of the procedure will, in itself, prevent its being carried out." He stated that the United States "will attempt to implement these principles in the spirit in which they were promulgated," and that it had "no reason to suppose that this will not be done by the leaders of the Soviet Union." When asked if, had the document been signed earlier, the American mining of Haiphong would have been contrary to its spirit, he replied: "No set of principles can be used like a cookbook that can be applied to every situation. . . . So I think we are talking here about a general spirit which regulates the overall direction of the policy."[6] To justify the new principles he said, "We have not in the past attempted to lay down general rules of conduct ahead of the crisis by which the basic relationships of the countries could be defined." And in Kiev he used both the negative cookbook analogy he had coined in Moscow, and a road map analogy, which he later also included in the report of the president to the Congress upon his return.[7] Kissinger's public evaluation, made later in his memoir,[8] was that while "these principles were not a legal contract," they did establish "a standard of conduct by which to judge whether real progress was being made and in the name of which we could resist their violation."[9]

In his report to the Congress on the day of his return from Moscow, Nixon described the Basic Principles as being "like a road map. Now that the

---

myko," *Pravda*, September 23, 1981. This extensive and careful Soviet preparation has been confirmed to me by a Soviet participant.

6. "Moscow: Basic Principles and Joint Communiqué, News Conference of Dr. Henry A. Kissinger," May 29, *Presidential Documents*, vol. 8 (June 5, 1972), pp. 951–55.

7. "Kiev: United States–Soviet Agreements, News Conference of Dr. Henry A. Kissinger," May 29, *Presidential Documents*, vol. 8 (June 5, 1972), pp. 958–60.

8. Kissinger's personal evaluation, described by a close associate in an interview, was that the Basic Principles were "frosting on the cake" of détente, accepted simply because of the strong Soviet interest and because they seemed "harmless enough." As earlier noted, this was also Nixon's view.

9. Kissinger, *White House Years*, p. 1250.

map has been laid out, it is up to each country to follow it." He also said that as the principles were put into practice, "they can provide a solid framework for the future development of better American-Soviet relations."[10]

The administration's overall assessment is found in the fourth and last special foreign policy report of the Nixon administration to Congress, issued in May 1973 on the eve of the second summit meeting. The report, which reviewed the accomplishments of the administration's previous year, contained one of the few official (or unofficial) commentaries on the Basic Principles, expressed in Nixon's distinctive style of saying in an overly elaborate manner as much about what something is not as about what it is: "What we have agreed upon is not a vain attempt to bridge ideological differences, or a condominium of the two strongest powers, or a division of spheres of influence. What we have agreed upon are principles that acknowledge differences, but express a *code of conduct* which, if observed, can only contribute to mold peace and to an international system based on mutual respect and self-restraint. These principles are a guide for future action."[11]

These comments on the Basic Principles suggest that the administration was somewhat defensive about them, although its position was strictly appropriate. For the United States, the Basic Principles were seen as a logical and marginally useful general statement of aspirations about future conduct, not a set code or a solid *foundation* for détente.

In light of these attitudes, it is not surprising that the U.S. government gave the Basic Principles only minimal publicity. Although they were seen as a road map, they were not regarded as a cookbook with set recipes. There was, somewhat curiously, only relatively brief press or other attention to the Basic Principles in the United States. Moreover, there was *no* attention in the American media to the fact that Kissinger endorsed the concept of peaceful coexistence in the two press conferences on May 29 and subsequently. That acceptance of a long-standing Soviet term did, however, raise eyebrows among some Western diplomats and academic specialists.

The Soviet approach to the Basic Principles was very different. The idea had been theirs, based in part on earlier, similar agreements reached with other NATO countries, France and Turkey. In view of the leading role of the United States and the strong Soviet interest in a demonstration and codification of political parity with it, a document that established basic principles governing relations between the two superpowers was particularly desired. As an example of the importance attached to the principles, Brezhnev, in the very first meeting with Nixon, "avowed his dedication to a fundamental improve-

---

10. "The President's Address to a Joint Session of the Congress," June 1, *Presidential Documents*, vol. 8 (June 5, 1972), p. 979.

11. Richard M. Nixon, *U.S. Foreign Policy for the 1970's: Shaping a Durable Peace*, Report to the Congress, vol. 4 (Washington, D.C.: Government Printing Office, 1973), p. 37. Emphasis added.

ment in U.S.-Soviet relations" and said he considered the Basic Principles "even more important" than the SALT agreements.[12]

The approach the two sides took in preparing the Basic Principles is indicative of the relative importance accorded them. As noted, on the American side the decision to agree on those principles was made by only two men, Nixon and Kissinger, and only Kissinger negotiated the actual document. The Soviets, on the other hand, undertook the preparation of the Basic Principles much more seriously and carefully.[13]

The Ministry of Foreign Affairs, the body chiefly responsible, made multiple contributions, although there were differing views. All agreed that it would be most desirable to gain American endorsement of the keystone of the peace program launched at the Twenty-fourth Party Congress the previous spring (April 1971)—peaceful coexistence. Major responsibility for preparing for the conference was given to the relatively new Department for Planning Foreign Policy Measures (UPVM)[14] under Deputy Foreign Minister Anatoly Kovalev, who had been placed in charge of the department in July 1971. He had had responsibility for preparing for the visit of French President Georges Pompidou in October 1971, and Brezhnev and other leaders had been pleased with the outcome. UPVM prepared seven of the ten basic position papers for the summit meeting. The principal UPVM experts on the United States were Mikhail Smirnovsky, who headed the twelve-man USA Division within the department (one of its largest), and Vladimir Petrovsky. Also quite heavily involved was the USA Department (the American Desk) under Foreign Ministry Collegium member Georgy Kornienko. Owing to UPVM's sudden rise, the role of the USA Department was less central than would normally have been the case. UPVM argued that the United States might accept basic principles and specifically endorse peaceful coexistence, while the American Desk, too experienced with the Washington establishment, but unaccustomed to the Nixon-Kissinger modus operandi, was sure it would not.

Following the summit meeting and American acceptance of the Basic Principles and peaceful coexistence, half the members of the UPVM USA Division received special merit promotions, and the department won the right to coordinate preparation of the next American summit meeting as well as its centerpiece, an agreement on the prevention of nuclear war. (Later it was

---

12. Kissinger, *White House Years*, p. 1208.

13. The account that follows is based on interviews with a number of the Soviet participants.

14. UPVM (*Upravlenie po plannirovaniyu vneshno-politicheskykh meroprivatiy*) was named in deference to the Soviet conception that foreign (and other) *policy* was made at the level of the Politburo, whereas foreign policy *measures* were the appropriate province of a department in the Ministry of Foreign Affairs. UPVM had been established only in 1967. Its previous head, also a deputy foreign minister, Vladimir Semenov, had from late 1969 on been fully engaged as the principal Soviet SALT negotiator; hence the change in mid-1971.

also given the main role in backstopping the Conference on European Security and Cooperation, CSCE, and the negotiations on mutual balanced force reductions, MBFR.)

    If official American commentary described the Basic Principles as aspirations and a road map but not a cookbook, Soviet commentary was quite different. Brezhnev and other Soviet leaders, as well as media commentators, often referred to them as *first* among the very important achievements of the summit meeting (and, later, of all the summit meetings). The Politburo of the Central Committee of the Communist Party, the Presidium of the USSR Supreme Soviet, and the Council of Ministers issued a joint statement on June 1, 1972, on the summit meeting of Brezhnev, President Podgorny, and Prime Minister Kosygin with Nixon, giving the party and government's formal cachet of approval. Their statement ascribed "great international significance" to the Basic Principles and other agreements, saying that they "constitute a significant step in the development of Soviet-American relations, promoting the principle of peaceful coexistence of states with different social systems."[15] Brezhnev, in an address on the Fiftieth Anniversary of the Union of Soviet Socialist Republics, stated that it was "especially important" that both sides at the summit had shared the conviction that "no other foundation for these mutual relations was possible than peaceful coexistence. Precisely in this is the main meaning of the Soviet-American document."[16]

    There were a myriad of Soviet commentaries praising the Basic Principles and other agreements reached at the 1972 summit meeting. Perhaps the most effusive opened with the words, "It is difficult to find in world political history another instance of negotiations comparable to the Soviet-U.S. summit." It went on to describe the Basic Principles as a document in which "the most important and positive developments to date in Soviet-U.S. relations find concentrated expression."[17] Academician Georgy Arbatov described the Basic Principles as "a comprehensive and profoundly meaningful document"—at the same time, however, cautioning that "only actual practice will answer the question of how consistently these principles are implemented." But this, he noted, is true of "any international treaty" and "does not diminish in the slightest the significance of such treaties and documents since, on the one hand, they record and formalize changes which have clearly occurred in international relations,

---

15. "On the Results of the Soviet-American Talks," *Pravda*, June 2, 1972.

16. L. I. Brezhnev, "On the Fiftieth Anniversary of the U.S.S.R.," December 21, in *O vneshnei politike KPSS i sovetskogo gosudarstva: Rechi i stat'i* [On the Foreign Policy of the CPSU and the Soviet Government: Speeches and Articles], 3d ed. (Moscow: Politizdat, 1978), pp. 258–59.

17. Boris Dmitriev, "Working for World Peace: The Soviet-U.S. Talks," *New Times* (Moscow), no. 26 (June 1972), p. 4. "Boris Dmitriev" is a pseudonym for Soviet diplomat and scholar Boris Dmitriyevich Pyadyshev.

and on the other become a sort of platform for the struggle for new positive changes in relations among states."[18]

Soviet commentators ascribed the new "turn toward realism" by the leaders of the United States as reflecting "the force and effectiveness of Soviet foreign policy," as well as "the changed alignment of forces in the international arena as a result of the increasing might of the Soviet Union . . . and of the entire [world] socialist system as a decisive factor in contemporary international relations."[19] Further, "In this light the Basic Principles of Mutual Relations Between the USSR and USA adopted as a result of the Moscow summit talks acquire special significance. For fifty-five years the Soviet state has been tirelessly struggling to insure that the principles of peaceful coexistence between countries with different social systems were asserted and confirmed in international law. Now a document recording recognition of the principles of peaceful coexistence on the part of the leading country of capitalism has been added to the code of international law."[20] Many Soviet commentaries repeat this theme—that the Basic Principles agreement was "the first Soviet-US document to give international juridical form to relations between the two countries on the basis of peaceful coexistence."[21] In other words, "the Basic Principles are essentially a treaty defining the principles and prospects" for Soviet-American relations.[22]

Such judgments did not merely reflect the euphoria of the moment. For example, even in late 1978, when Soviet-American détente was deteriorating, a leading Soviet scholar and diplomat, Vladimir Petrovsky, described the Basic Principles as "a document of fundamental importance, which continues in full force at the present time." He identified its key provision as the acceptance of peaceful coexistence, and it became "the first joint Soviet-American juridical-legal document in which that principle found its official recognition by the United States"—a "great political achievement."[23] Petrovsky also stressed the "fundamental importance" of the "mutual pledge and goal" to do everything possible to avoid military confrontation.

---

18. G. Arbatov, "The Power of Realistic Policy: On the Results of the High-Level Soviet-U.S. Talks," *Izvestiya*, June 22, 1972.

19. S. Beglov, "An Important Step in the Realization of the Peace Program," *Sovetskaya Rossiya* [Soviet Russia], June 20, 1972.

20. Ibid.

21. Yu. Chernov, *Pravda*, June 15, 1972. "Yu. Chernov" is the pseudonym of the official spokesman of the Ministry of Foreign Affairs, Yury N. Chernyakov. See also, for example, Arbatov, *Izvestiya*, June 22, 1972; Mikhailov, *Pravda*, June 4, 1972; Dmitriev, *New Times*, no. 26 (1972), p. 4; and Ryzhenko, *Pravda*, August 22, 1973.

22. Dmitriev, *New Times*, no. 26 (1972), p. 4.

23. V. F. Petrovsky, "The Role and Place of Soviet-American Relations in the Contemporary World," *Voprosy istorii* [Questions of History], no. 10 (October 1978), p. 87. Petrovsky, it will be recalled, is a senior official in the Ministry of Foreign Affairs and was himself one of the authors of the inclusion of this principle in the Basic Principles.

In Russian eyes another highly important aspect of the summit meeting as a whole, and of the Basic Principles specifically, was U.S. recognition of the "critically important principle" of *equality* as a basis for the security interests of the two powers.[24] In Soviet discussions, this principle is usually termed "equal security," although that term goes beyond the actual text, which speaks of "recognition of the security interests of the Parties based on the principle of equality." Equality of treatment, while not unimportant, does not extend as far as equality of security. "The principle of equal security" was endorsed in the joint communiqué at the conclusion of the summit conference in connection with the continuing negotiations on limiting strategic arms, but not in the context of the Basic Principles.[25]

In a broader sense the thrust of the summit and its agreements was a reflection of a newly recognized parity between the United States and the Soviet Union. One of the many Soviet commentaries emphasizing this point, citing the *Washington Post*, stressed that "the Moscow summit signified recognition by the U.S. of the fact that the Soviet Union has achieved 'international, strategic and psychological parity with the United States.' "[26] This parity was, along with peaceful coexistence, the heart of détente from the Soviet standpoint. The formal report of the party and government leaders endorsing the results of the summit drew specific attention to "the principle of parity and equal security," linking these two elements of the Soviet position and identifying them as an accomplishment of the summit meeting.[27]

It would be easy to criticize and dismiss the significance of the Basic Principles with the benefit of hindsight and more than a decade of experience. The two countries have moved from high expectations created by the summit meeting to renewed confrontation. To do so, however, would be to overlook the value they may have had and may again have. Moreover, most criticism has been levied at alleged violations of the principles, rather than at the principles themselves. Indeed, almost the only references to them in the United States have been occasional allegations of Soviet violation of the code of conduct the principles embody. The Soviets have also criticized alleged American viola-

---

24. Ibid.

25. All quotations from the Basic Principles agreement are from the official U.S. text, cited in footnote 2 above; the Soviet texts in Russian and English do not differ. See "Text of the Joint United States–Soviet Communiqué," *Presidential Documents*, vol. 8 (June 5, 1972), pp. 945–51.

26. Dmitriev, *New Times*, no. 26 (1972), p. 4.

27. *Pravda*, June 2, 1972.

For another analysis of Soviet motivation and understanding of the Basic Principles that reaches essentially the same conclusions, see Coit D. Blacker, "The Kremlin and Détente: Soviet Conceptions, Hopes, and Expectations," in Alexander L. George, ed., *Managing U.S.-Soviet Rivalry: Problems of Crisis Prevention* (Boulder, Colo.: Westview, 1983), pp. 119–37.

tions. As will be seen, most of these charges on both sides stem from different understanding of the principles and of the situations to which they have been held *not* to have been applied. A more valid general criticism is that there was too little attempt at the time and since to understand the views of the other side and to seek to reconcile, or at least identify, differences in understanding. Very little attention has been paid to this question.[28]

It is extraordinary that the United States accepted the concept of peaceful coexistence, with its long and well-known history of interpretation by its Soviet authors, without at least putting its own interpretation on record at the summit meeting. I do not criticize American acceptance of the idea. Even the cold war was peaceful in the sense of an absence of war, and coexistence is desirable by any definition. Moreover, it would be foolish to seem to concede to the Soviet Union alone support for the continuation of a state of coexisting at peace, as that is also a vital American and world interest. But the failure even to identify differences in understanding not only permitted the Soviets to claim American acceptance of their concept, but, more seriously, also affected Soviet judgment of what the United States should and would find to be acceptable conduct by the USSR.

The Basic Principles also addressed in part the need for crisis prevention and management, a subject dealt with more directly at the second summit (and that is therefore discussed in the context of that meeting).

SALT

The main centerpiece of the summit in many respects was the conclusion of the SALT I agreements: the 1972 Anti-Ballistic Missile (ABM) Treaty, of indefinite duration, and an Interim Agreement providing certain offensive arms limitations for a five-year term while negotiations would continue to reach more comprehensive offensive arms limitations. The significance of the agreements in terms of the success of the summit meeting was great: while the Basic Principles provided a broad charter for détente and the batch of specialized agreements together added breadth to the efforts at cooperation, the SALT agreements marked a milestone in arms control. They represented a concrete step toward curbing the risks and costs of the arms race and symbolized an unprecedented initial step in reducing tensions and the risks of a nuclear war.

In their private evaluations Nixon and Kissinger were more reserved about the value of SALT than in their public praises. Nevertheless, they considered SALT I a considerable arms control—and political—achievement. In

---

28. The main exception in the American literature is the thoughtful discussion by Alexander L. George, "Crisis Prevention Reexamined," in George, ed., *Managing U.S.-Soviet Rivalry*, pp. 365–75.

addition, it was considered important as a sign of the administration's interest in peace, particularly welcome at a time when they had just authorized an escalation of the war in Vietnam and six months before the presidential election.

The Soviets recognized the role that strategic arms limitations, and the SALT I agreements in particular, could play in stabilizing mutual deterrence based on parity and in contributing to "military détente." In addition, they appreciated that the SALT process was playing a substantial role in the development of political détente between the Soviet Union and the United States in the formative years from 1969 to 1972.[29] Thus SALT was a central element in the accomplishment of the first summit in 1972, especially for the United States, which considered it the principal achievement. For the Soviet Union, SALT was of high importance, but the political agreement on Basic Principles was regarded as equally significant.

SALT dealt with the most sensitive and important military aspects of the relationship between the two greatest powers. Détente had not dispelled all suspicion and mistrust, and the leaders of both powers had to reassure concerned constituencies that along with détente and SALT, they would continue to meet the requirements for military deterrence and defense.

President Nixon, concerned about reservations on the part of conservatives and the military over arms control and détente, in his report to Congress immediately on his return from the summit coupled his advocacy of the SALT agreements with assurances that the United States would continue to take all necessary measures in its unilateral defense program to maintain its security and to protect its vital interests. He vowed that "no power on earth is stronger than the United States of America today. And none will be stronger than the United States of America in the future."[30] It was an artful and effective way of vigorously reassuring those who had qualms, yet was consistent with his acceptance of parity and a balance. Nor would it be contradicted if the Soviet leaders were to apply the same formula to their own defense status.

In fact, the Soviet leaders, especially the senior military men, did couple their strong endorsement of détente and SALT with reassurances that the Soviet Union would continue to do all that was necessary to maintain deterrence and the defense of the USSR. For example, General of the Army Viktor G. Kulikov, chief of the General Staff, in testifying in support of the SALT agreements at the ceremonial deliberations by the Supreme Soviet on ratification, stressed that the party and government "display constant concern for increasing the defense capability of the Soviet Union. The Soviet Armed Forces have at their disposal everything necessary to reliably defend the state interests of our Motherland."[31] And the acting foreign minister, Vasily Kuznet-

---

29. See chapter 5.

30. *Presidential Documents*, vol. 8 (1972), p. 978.

31. "In the Interests of Strengthening Peace and International Security," *Pravda*, August 24, 1972.

sov, when he presented the agreements formally, stated: "The understanding reached with the United States in the field of strategic arms limitation does not in any degree weaken the defense capability of the Soviet Union and the Warsaw Pact as a whole."[32]

In the Soviet Union the Ministry of Defense and General Staff had played a central role in determining the Soviet negotiating positions and an important role in the actual SALT negotiations. Owing to tight Soviet compartmentalization for security and the very limited advance discussion of SALT issues, many Soviet military officers were highly surprised by the announcement of these agreements reached with the chief imperialist adversary. Soviet military propaganda had to shift to a more subtle line justifying the opportunities for and desirability of such joint arms control, while also justifying continued vigilance and military preparedness.

One incident from the summit reflected a hazard of this type of diplomacy that Brezhnev probably had not anticipated. In response to the increasing difficulty the U.S. administration was having getting the Congress to approve new military programs that the administration was proposing to accompany ratification of SALT, President Nixon stated in a press conference on June 22: "Mr. Brezhnev made it absolutely clear to me that in those areas that were not controlled by our offensive agreement that they were going ahead with their programs. For us not to [do the same] would seriously jeopardize the security of the United States and jeopardize the cause of world peace, in my opinion."[33] The Soviets never offered a public rejoinder to this statement, but privately some have indicated with indignation that the Soviets had been "mouse-trapped." What apparently occurred was a passing discussion in which *both* Nixon and Brezhnev stated that they would abide by the agreements, but would of course go forward with military programs consistent with the agreed limitations.[34]

Cienfuegos: New Tests

The summit meeting was accompanied off-stage by a renewed Soviet reminder of its continuing sensitivity to the constraints on deployments in

---

32. Ibid.

33. "Transcript of the President's News Conference Emphasizing Domestic Matters," *New York Times*, June 23, 1972. Nixon also endorsed the bargaining chip strategy for military programs.

34. Based on interviews with American and Soviet participants in the summit discussions. Similarly, and also not in the memoirs of Nixon or Kissinger, on September 29, 1971, at an earlier meeting in the White House, Nixon had told Foreign Minister Gromyko that he did not criticize the Soviet Union for continuing to build up its offensive submarine-launched ballistic missiles—he said he would, too, in their shoes. Perhaps some day the tape of this conversation will be released.

Cuba, although on this occasion it did not press the issue in deference to American sensitivities. On May 1 a Soviet naval flotilla, including a G-II class diesel-powered ballistic missile submarine, arrived at Bahia de Nipe, a location far from Cienfuegos. This marked the first time a ballistic missile submarine had visited Cuba. It remained almost a week and then departed. The event was noted in the American press and prompted some speculation as to the conditions of the 1962 and 1970 understandings, but it did not become a public issue. Nor did it lead to a private confrontation.

This visit of a diesel-powered nuclear-missile submarine on the eve of the summit meeting clearly represented a test of the American reaction and of the limits of the 1970 understanding (with Kissinger's vague reference to "nuclear submarines"). It also related to two SALT issues still unresolved at the time—whether G-class diesel submarines should be counted as strategic systems under the SALT limitations, and whether the Soviet Union should get some compensation in its overall force levels for its lack of overseas submarine bases, in contrast to the U.S. Polaris and Poseidon forward bases. From the standpoint of the first of these issues, the visit of a G-class submarine was counterproductive to the Soviet interest, but from the standpoint of the second it could have been considered a helpful reminder that the Soviets did *not* have such a base. Should the United States reassert that such basing was not acceptable, the Soviets could use that position to support their claims for compensation. Whether for that or some other reason, Nixon and Kissinger did not bring the matter up at the summit. Nixon states in his memoir that "the Soviet leaders did not raise the subject of Cuba at all" and does not say that he did. Kissinger comments only that "Brezhnev volunteered a reaffirmation of the 'understanding' on Cuba in general and with regard to submarines in particular."[35] While Nixon did not discuss Cuba, one of Kissinger's staff at the meetings recalls that Kissinger complained that the Soviet Union was testing the constraints on submarine visits to Cuba; he believes Kissinger mentioned the very recent G-II visit. Brezhnev thus may not have volunteered the reaffirmation. In any case, there was little discussion and no confrontation.[36]

There had, however, been a powerful reaction of another kind to the Soviet submarine visit that did not go unnoticed in Moscow. Following the Cienfuegos confrontation of 1970 the United States had created a special squadron of destroyers and similar ships for surface surveillance of the general area. As on the occasion of an earlier visit by a Soviet flotilla in October 1971, in this instance the American surveillance patrol maintained close contact.

Another aspect of the developing détente must be mentioned at this juncture. Since October 1971 talks had been under way between the navies of the United States and the Soviet Union; the delegations were headed by Secretary (initially Under Secretary) of the Navy John W. Warner and Admi-

---

35. See Nixon, *RN*, p. 621; and Kissinger, *White House Years*, p. 1251.

36. Information from interviews.

ral of the Fleet Vladimir A. Kasatonov, first deputy commander-in-chief of the Soviet navy. Their final meetings were held on May 3–17, 1972, leading to an agreement on the Prevention of Incidents On and Over the High Seas. This was signed at the summit on May 25 by Secretary of the Navy Warner and the Soviet navy commander-in-chief, Admiral of the Fleet Sergei G. Gorshkov. During these negotiations American commanders at sea had been warned to avoid any incidents with Soviet naval ships that might jeopardize the negotiations.

As the Soviet flotilla left Nipe on May 6 (where the U.S. surveillance patrol had remained throughout its stay, just six miles off the harbor entrance), the G-II submarine submerged immediately outside the harbor entrance. The U.S. surveillance ships, aided by P-3 patrol aircraft based at Guantanamo Bay in Cuba, made sonar contact and forced the submarine to surface. Several times at night this sequence of events was repeated. The Soviets even fired flares to discourage the P-3 aircraft, and both Soviet and American ships engaged in high-speed maneuvers. The submarine was repeatedly forced to surface until the Soviet formation was well into the Atlantic.[37]

The Soviet leaders undoubtedly knew all about these events that had just preceded the summit meeting. But from all available evidence (including interviews with a number of American participants), it appears that neither Nixon nor Kissinger, the master controller of policy, knew anything about the entire incident even long after the event.

The Soviet leaders had also tested the 1962 and 1970 understandings in another way. Shortly before the Cienfuegos confrontation in 1970, but not involved with it, the Soviet Union had begun occasional flights of Tu-95D Bear turboprop reconnaissance aircraft from Murmansk to Cuba over the North Atlantic. Seven such flights (normally involving two Tu-95Ds) had occurred from April 1970 through 1972. Soon after the summit, in September 1972, a new pattern began. Some operational reconnaissance flights now began out of Havana, with return to Cuba, unlike the earlier flights that were limited to transit between the USSR and Cuba. Four such flights—from the USSR to Cuba, then operational flights over the high seas from Cuba, and later return to the USSR—occurred from September 1972 to April 1973. These flights all involved the naval reconnaissance version of the Bear, not the Long-Range Aviation bomber version.[38]

Secretary of Defense Laird wrote to Secretary of State Rogers in September 1972, after the first such reconnaissance mission along the East

---

37. This entire incident became known only when revealed in 1980 by the former commander of the U.S. surveillance force, Captain Leslie K. Fenlon, Jr., USN, Retired. See Fenlon, "The Umpteenth Cuban Confrontation," *U.S. Naval Institute Proceedings*, vol. 106 (July 1980), pp. 40–45.

38. The two aircraft types are visually distinguishable—the reconnaissance version has a large observation bubble and no bomb bay.

Coast, urging an immediate protest. He wrote again in January 1973, after his first letter was not acted upon. In fact, the action level at the State Department had found no basis for charging that the Soviets were violating the understandings of 1962 or 1970, so far as the latter were known. Only the White House knew the full content of the 1970 exchanges. Finally, a very senior officer of the State Department was orally instructed by Kissinger to sit on requests from Defense, and nothing was ever done. The Soviet reconnaissance Bears thus never became an issue between the United States and the Soviet Union.

The lack of American reaction *was* a response to Moscow. This is not to suggest it was the wrong response; indeed, there was no good basis for a challenge. But the matter was not handled by normal governmental procedures, and confidence in the system for handling such matters was eroded, particularly, in this case, at the Pentagon.[39]

Probably one reason Kissinger avoided normal channels involved another related experience. American concern over possible erosion of the 1970 understanding over submarines had arisen even before the May 1972 G-II submarine visit. For reasons that remain obscure, in January 1972 Kissinger formally requested in National Security Study Memorandum (NSSM)–144 an interagency study on "Soviet Naval Deployments in the Caribbean." The study was fully coordinated and submitted in March. It had, however, been seriously hampered and indeed vitiated by the refusal of the White House to provide access to the 1970 exchanges. The Interagency Political-Military Group (IPMG), a formal working group of the NSC, was not even provided for its top secret study the information Kissinger later put in his memoir. Accordingly, with great anger from the White House and despite some arm-twisting, the IPMG noted that it could not determine whether subsequent Soviet actions violated the 1970 understanding, since access to the exchange had been denied. The study was quietly shelved.[40]

In this instance, as in many others, Kissinger found that it was difficult to compartmentalize and manage the bureaucracy. Having excluded even the secretary of state from the knowledge of the key 1970 exchanges, he could not later disclose them. When the governmental system then balked, he was even more inclined to exclude it—as when he simply buried the Department of Defense concerns over the Bear reconnaissance flights, and when he vitiated the interagency study of the Soviet naval deployments in the Caribbean that he himself had requested. As time went on, more and more of the

39. This account is based on my direct involvement as deputy director of the Bureau of Politico-Military Affairs of the Department of State, 1970–73.

40. In this instance, I chaired the IPMG, and suffered General Haig's ire for persisting in requesting the record and then for noting in the report the denial to grant it. I had also been the principal Department of State staff officer in the 1970 Cienfuegos case and had been deeply involved in the 1962 Cuban missile crisis.

foreign policy of the United States was made, implemented, and often concealed from the remainder of the government by the Nixon-Kissinger White House.

Other Aspects of the Summit

In the months leading up to the summit meeting, the Soviet Union had continued to press its long-standing proposals for a conference on European security. One element in this campaign was the shift in 1970 to acceptance of the United States (and Canada) as participants. As movement toward a Soviet-American détente began to accompany the European détente, it became more advantageous to accept the United States in such a venture and less feasible to exclude it. On the other hand, the Western powers, especially the American administration, were still quite reserved toward the idea of the conference. At the same time, the United States and NATO were advocating negotiations on mutual and balanced force reductions (MBFR) in central Europe. At the summit meeting, the Berlin Agreement and the Eastern treaties of West Germany having been concluded, a general understanding was reached to proceed with both a European security conference and MBFR.

In his memoir Kissinger is rather diffident in his brief references to this subject. In the very first summit session Brezhnev stressed his interest in a conference on European security, to which President Nixon agreed "in principle," saying that only procedural obstacles remained. "This could mean anything" was Kissinger's later comment, a putdown of the president's acceptance in principle.[41] In neither of their memoirs do Kissinger or Nixon comment on the trade-off—the United States' acceptance of the European Security Conference in exchange for Soviet agreement to MBFR—but there was such an understanding. While not explicitly linking the two subjects, the joint communiqué noted the agreement to work toward both. Both countries also declared their readiness more generally "to make appropriate contributions to the positive trends on the European continent toward a genuine détente," a term not yet used to describe the bilateral American-Soviet relationship.[42]

Another subject of importance, especially to the Soviet side, was commercial and economic relations. While the summit did not result in any major economic agreements (apart from a decision to establish a U.S.-Soviet Joint Economic Commission), a great deal lay behind the general and bland language of the communiqué about creating "more favorable conditions" for

---

41. Kissinger, *White House Years*, p. 1208.

42. *Presidential Documents*, vol. 8 (1972), p. 949. The communiqué did condition consultation on the European security conference on the signing of the final Berlin Agreement protocol, which occurred June 3.

commerce based on "mutual benefit," with agreement on "the desirability of credit arrangements," and on working to conclude a trade agreement "in the near future," and concurrently to negotiate a lend-lease settlement.[43] While the summit meetings did not cover these matters at length, there had been hard bargaining during the private, high-level exchanges beforehand.

Perhaps one reason Nixon and Kissinger are reticent on this subject in their memoirs is that in this area the linkage and leverage were on the Soviet side (although the carrot incentive was on the U.S. side). Although the Soviets proceeded with the summit without formal agreements, there was in fact extensive informal agreement prior to the summit—such as on credits for large Soviet grain purchases, announced soon after the conference.

In a previous chapter it was noted that even in the Politburo there were reservations about Brezhnev's stress on developing trade with the United States. This divergence emerged in an unexpected way at the summit meeting. While Nixon was pressing a linkage between SALT and trade credits, Brezhnev and Kosygin insisted on the importance of trade in its own right. Suddenly, to the astonishment of Nixon and Kissinger, Podgorny, chairman of the Supreme Soviet Presidium, interceded to say that SALT was more important than commercial ties. He held this position through two rounds of an exchange with Brezhnev, during which Kosygin changed sides and supported Podgorny's position. Thus, despite the nature of the occasion, the fissure in the Politburo on this point emerged in this unusual incident.[44] Interestingly, at the first summit, although not at the later ones, the troika of Brezhnev, Kosygin, and Podgorny attended most sessions except those on SALT, where Brezhnev had special authority as chairman of the Defense Council.[45]

Soon after the summit another trade development raised questions of a different nature in the United States. In July and August 1972 six major American export companies in a series of unpublicized deals contracted with a Soviet importing agency to sell over 400 million bushels of wheat for about $700 million. In all, by the end of 1972 the Soviet Union had purchased over

43. Ibid., pp. 946–47.

44. Kissinger, *White House Years*, pp. 1213–16.

45. The political delicacy and balance were evident when the United States' reciprocal invitation for a summit meeting in Washington, in response to a discreet Soviet request, had to be addressed to all three Soviet leaders. Subsequently there was no indication that anyone but Brezhnev would come to Washington. Similarly, the third edition of the authoritative *History of Soviet Foreign Policy*, which went to press in January 1977, still referred to the 1972 summit as being conducted on the Soviet side by Brezhnev, Kosygin, and Podgorny. By the time of the fourth edition in 1981, however, Podgorny had fallen from power and Kosygin had died, and the sentence referring to the role of the troika at the summit meeting was deleted. See A. A. Gromyko and P. N. Ponomarev, eds., *Istoriya vneshnei politiki SSSR, 1917–1976* [History of the Foreign Policy of the USSR, 1917–1976], 3d ed. (Moscow: Nauka, 1977), p. 501; and Gromyko and Ponomarev, *Istoriya vneshnei politiki SSSR, 1917–1980* [History of the Foreign Policy of the USSR, 1917–1980], 4 ed. (Moscow: Nauka, 1981), p. 492.

$1 billion of American agricultural products. The U.S. Department of Agriculture facilitated the whole deal. The transaction followed immediately the signing by the United States of a credit agreement on July 8. Under it the Soviets committed to purchase not *less* than $200 million worth of American grain during the first year and $750 million over a three-year period; in return, they were granted $750 million in credits (no more than $500 million to be outstanding at one time) over the three-year period at commercial interest rates. The Soviets used nearly $400 million of these credits toward their 1972–73 grain purchases. Secretary of Agriculture Earl Butz had visited Moscow just a month before the summit. There the Soviets had skillfully played to his overriding desire to sell surplus American wheat by expressing interest in a three-year purchase agreement *if* credits were available. At the summit itself President Nixon had put in a plug for American grain sales, noting what a favorable impact it would have on American public opinion. According to Kissinger, the Soviet leaders had feigned only modest and equivocal interest. In late June, however, a Soviet deputy minister of agriculture came to Washington quietly, and Secretary of Agriculture Butz and Secretary of Commerce Peter G. Peterson negotiated the grain purchase and credit agreement. It was in this context that the Soviets quietly purchased nearly the entire U.S. surplus grain reserve. The prices were low, since the scale of purchase was not evident except to those interested only in its consummation and, until the end of August, benefiting from the official American subsidy payments to grain dealers.[46]

Initially there was a scramble to reap the political credit for the popular sales, with Secretary of Agriculture Butz scooping Kissinger (the latter was speaking for President Nixon at San Clemente). Then, as the scale of Soviet purchases became known (in part because of a critical speech by Democratic presidential candidate George S. McGovern on September 8), it suddenly became clear to all that the United States had been outmaneuvered by the shrewd "capitalist" commercial dealings of the Russians.

What followed was a scramble to avoid blame, first, for failing to realize and capitalize on the Soviet need for grain and, second, for not monitoring the situation and adjusting sooner to control the scope of the sales, the price rise, and the continued payment of unnecessary subsidies. The Soviets came in for more than their share of blame in American commentary. Nevertheless, as Kissinger later stated: "It was painful to realize that we had been outmaneuvered, even more difficult to admit that the methods which gained that edge were those of a sharp trader skillfully using our free market system.

---

46. See the good account by Joseph Albright, "Some Deal," *New York Times Magazine*, November 25, 1973, pp. 36ff.; and James Trager, *The Great Grain Robbery* (Ballantine, 1975). A postmortem on the transaction is summarized in considerable detail in two General Accounting Office (GAO) studies prepared for the Congress: *Russian Wheat Sales and Weaknesses in [the Department of] Agriculture's Management of Wheat Export Subsidy Programs*, B–176943 (Washington, D.C.: GAO, July 9, 1973); and *Exporters' Profits on Sales of U.S. Wheat to Russia*, B–176943 (GAO, February 12, 1974). On the summit discussion see Kissinger, *White House Years*, pp. 1269–70.

We had no one to blame but ourselves. . . . The Soviets beat us at our own game."[47]

One effect of the "great grain robbery," as it came to be called, was to dull the luster of the new American-Soviet détente, especially in the commercial field, whether such a reaction was justified or not. This episode alone did not seriously affect public support for détente. Nor did the United States have grounds for official complaint. If anything, the incident reminded some in the administration of the benefits of regulating commercial relations with the Soviet Union. In any case, negotiations on economic and commercial relations, set in train at the summit, soon followed.

In July, even before the grain sale episode, Secretary of Commerce Peterson had also visited Moscow to attend the first meeting of the U.S.-Soviet Joint Commercial Commission and to discuss settlement of the lend-lease debts, grant of most-favored-nation (MFN) status, credits, and establishment of commercial facilities in each other's capitals. The talks went very well and led to a draft basic agreement. Kissinger returned to Moscow in mid-September to review the whole range of bilateral relations and negotiated the main issue still outstanding: the dollar settlement on lend-lease.

Negotiations continued between Secretary of Commerce Peterson and Soviet Minister of Foreign Trade Nikolai Patolichev, leading to the signing on October 18, 1972, of a comprehensive trade agreement providing: U.S. grant of MFN status to the Soviet Union, provisions to prevent market disruption, reciprocal establishment of official commercial offices in Washington and Moscow, trade credits, and arbitration of commercial disputes. Total trade of at least $1.5 billion over three years was projected. On the same date a separate agreement recorded the terms for settling the outstanding lend-lease debt for civilian goods provided by the United States during the war—$722 million to be repaid over thirty years.[48] Four days earlier, on October 14, the two countries signed a Maritime Agreement providing for the opening of major U.S. and Soviet commercial ports and affording equal participation of U.S. and Soviet flagships in carrying cargoes between the two countries. In addition, a unilateral American presidential determination was made, as part of the overall deal, authorizing the Export-Import Bank to make its credit facilities available to the Soviet Union.

Apart from the fact that agreement had been reached by tying these three agreements and one unilateral action together, the lend-lease set-

---

47. Kissinger, *White House Years*, p. 1270; see also his discussion, pp. 1269–73. In one respect that Kissinger does not disclose he and the administration were particularly to blame. He writes as though the large Soviet demand for grain in 1972 came as a surprise. In fact, there is considerable evidence that Kissinger was aware of it in the spring. See Seymour M. Hersh, *The Price of Power: Kissinger in the Nixon White House* (Summit Books, 1983), pp. 531–34.

48. In his memoir Kissinger, presumably to enhance his reputation for shrewd bargaining, disclosed that this figure was $25 million above the minimum the United States was prepared to accept. *White House Years*, p. 1271.

tlement was explicitly conditioned on the granting of MFN. In turn, the grant of MFN was necessarily conditioned on congressional approval.

The achievement of these linked agreements from July through October of 1972 rounded out the economic elements of the complex of political, arms control, and other agreements reached in May. They represented the launching of the economic dimension of détente, as indicated but yet to be concluded at the time of the summit.

The role of these economic agreements in détente, and the web of interests foreseen by the American side, were alluded to in the next *International Economic Report of the President* to the Congress:

In a year of dramatic initiatives, President Nixon in 1972 helped move the world from an era of East-West confrontation into one of negotiation. In breaking the longstanding political and economic impasse between the United States and the Communist world, the President brought about a major reshaping of American foreign policy and advanced a giant step toward a lasting peace.

Such a peace must derive its stability from a web of mutual vested interests among nations, the many fields of human activity in which agreements could benefit all parties. . . . Increased economic interchange with the Communist world can both strengthen the fabric of international peace and provide tangible benefits to American workers and consumers.[49]

Nixon had waited until after the political agreements at the summit to conclude the economic agreements in the fall both for domestic political reasons and to improve the U.S. bargaining position. Nonetheless, there is reason to believe that the White House had become deeply involved in extensive hard bargaining with interested American constituencies (congressional, business, and above all labor) before the May summit, and that the Soviets were given assurances by that time that the economic package would soon be concluded. The story of these important domestic aspects of the road to the summit and the agreements recorded there and in the months following is conspicuously absent from the memoirs of Nixon and Kissinger.[50]

---

49. *International Economic Report of the President, March 1973* (GPO, 1973), p. 50. In passing, it might be noted that this report still spoke of "the Communist world" and "the Free World," language inherited from the cold war that was soon to fall out of usage for the balance of the 1970s. Incidentally, the drafters of this report in the governmental bureaucracy had spoken with prescience of a coming international energy crisis—a prediction assiduously excised at the political level in the White House before the draft became the president's report.

50. The president's foreign policy report in 1973, drafted under Kissinger's guidance, does record the administration's view that Congress would not "support an expanding economic relationship while our basic relations with the Soviet Union were antagonistic." With this and other considerations in mind, Kissinger and Nixon "linked the expansion of economic relations with improved political relations." Nixon, *U.S. Foreign Policy for the 1970's: Shaping a Durable Peace,* vol. 4, p. 33. See also pp. 33–35 for argumentation supporting the economic agreements. Kissinger disarmingly observes in his memoir that earlier grain deals had been blocked because "for a while our labor unions had prevented such sales by refusing to load Soviet ships and by requiring shipment in American bottoms." Indeed, those considerations had blocked grain

As a byproduct of the White House's close hold on virtually all negotiations with the Soviet Union, Congress was not involved in 1972 in the trade negotiations as it had been in 1962. This approach made it easier for some in Congress to raise new issues when the U.S.-USSR Trade Agreement and associated trade legislation came up for consideration, a factor that would become important in the wake of other developments.[51]

Another important interrelationship between domestic concerns in both countries and the weaving of a net of international economic relations developed rapidly. A Soviet "exit tax" for education levied on emigrants—designed to reimburse the state for having provided higher education—imposed in August 1972 drew heavy fire in the U.S. Senate and increased sentiment there for linking measures to facilitate trade, especially the granting of MFN, to increased Soviet emigration. Even before that tax Senator Henry M. Jackson of Washington had been preparing to demand Soviet relaxation of restrictions on Jewish emigration in an amendment to the first available legislation. Jackson first introduced his amendment on October 4, 1972, the very day the White House announced the forthcoming visit by Soviet Foreign Trade Minister Patolichev to Washington to sign the U.S.-USSR Trade Agreement.[52]

A similar amendment was introduced by Jackson in the Senate and Congressman Charles Vanik in the House in the Ninety-third Congress, in April 1973, to a general trade reform act in which the administration had included MFN for the USSR. This situation played into Jackson's hands. But in 1972 and 1973 the administration believed it could handle the issue through quiet diplomacy with the Soviet leaders, Congress, and the Jewish lobby, notwithstanding the fact that in October 1972 some seventy-two senators had cosponsored the Jackson amendment and that in April 1973 the Jackson-Vanik

---

deals since they were first attempted a decade earlier in the Kennedy administration. Kissinger says merely: "But those issues were resolved soon after the summit." Kissinger, *White House Years*, p. 1269. He does not, however, say what the administration did to secure acquiescence. It involved hard behind-the-scenes bargaining in Washington and substantial concessions not publicly disclosed until the well-documented exposé by Seymour Hersh. See Hersh, *The Price of Power*, pp. 334–35, 343–48.

51. See "United States–Soviet Commercial Relations: The Interplay of Economics, Technology Transfer and Diplomacy," in the House Committee on International Relations, *Science, Technology, and American Diplomacy*, vol. 1 (GPO, 1977), pp. 538–39. On U.S.-Soviet trade relations in 1970–72 more generally, see pp. 535–42.

52. For a fascinating and well-informed account and analysis of the history of the Jackson-Vanik amendment and the interrelation of domestic American politics and the key trade aspect of U.S.-Soviet détente in 1972–75, see Paula Stern, *Water's Edge: Domestic Politics and the Making of American Foreign Policy* (Westport, Conn.: Greenwood Press, 1979). For developments in 1972, highlights of which are noted above, see pp. 18–52, and for 1973, pp. 53–103. Representative Vanik had introduced a similar amendment to a House foreign assistance bill on September 22; it would have denied credits to any country that imposed an exit fee of more than $50. Although intended to be directed against the Soviet Union, it would have required cessation of U.S. credits for Israel as well. When this became known, it was quickly dropped in conference.

amendment had attracted a majority of both houses (including seventy-six senators).[53] President Nixon had made a critical decision on September 30, 1972. He made a deal with Senator Jackson not to use his influence to oppose the amendment (although he did not accept it), knowing that it would not be enacted that year, and in order to avoid a fight over the issue before the presidential election. Jackson knew that his approach would gain momentum and early commitment by many senators who would have stayed with the administration if urged to do so. He saw himself in a strong position to pursue the matter in 1973 and beyond—and *he* was looking to the presidential election of 1976.[54] Soviet moves quietly to waive the collection of the exit tax and openly to modify its application and to continue the flow of Jewish emigrants did not have the desired effect of causing the issue to fade away.

An important point brought out by these events very early in the development of détente is that there were domestic political considerations the administration did not control, and they portended serious later difficulties in managing the diplomacy of détente.[55]

Bilateral U.S.-Soviet cooperation developed gradually along the lines set in train at the summit. Political- and security-related cooperation also developed slowly and deliberately, with an emerging pattern of cooperation in some areas, despite recurring conflicts of interest in others. For example, the SALT II negotiations began in Geneva in November 1972, and the Standing Consultative Commission created to monitor the SALT agreements and assist in their implementation was formally established in December and met for the first time in May 1973. The initial meeting of the Joint Commission established under the agreement on the prevention of incidents at sea, chaired by admirals from the two navies, met in November 1972. Scientific and cultural exchanges began to increase in number and significance. For example, the new Joint Commission on Cooperation in Environmental Protection met in September and agreed to undertake some thirty-six projects in both countries.

Another aspect of the summit and the formal launching of American-Soviet détente was the *way* in which the process was managed on the American side. For one thing, the president had maneuvered to have the summit occur just about when it did—neither too early nor too close to the election. This timing led to stretching some negotiations and rushing others. While in most cases that made little difference, in some it did. In particular, attempts to manage the SALT negotiations were cut too fine. Some aspects of the negotiation were delayed for months, during which American negotiating

---

53. Ibid., pp. 18–81. Stern shows with impressively researched detail the fact that Jackson and a number of key Senate aides maneuvered the amendment ploy before approaching the Jewish lobby to join the effort. Ibid., pp. 18–39. For Kissinger's view, see *White House Years*, pp. 1271–73; and Henry Kissinger, *Years of Upheaval* (Boston, Mass.: Little, Brown, 1982), pp. 248–51.

54. Stern, *Water's Edge*, pp. 39–52.

55. See chapters 10, 12, 13.

credibility was devalued by holding to bankrupt positions on White House orders, followed by a rush to complete important issues that had been left too long unaddressed. This problem was compounded by Nixon's decision to hold the SALT delegations in Helsinki, while even the president himself, but mainly Kissinger and a few of his staff, negotiated details they often did not fully understand.

Kissinger defends as necessary the extraordinary procedures in the diplomacy of those years. In writing about the year 1971 leading up to the summit, he says of the achievements in SALT and in developing American relations with the Soviet Union and China:

All this was due in not inconsiderable degree to Nixon's insistence, with my help, on White House control of foreign policy. In 1971 we took over not simply the planning but also the execution of major initiatives. I have stated here that I do not consider the methods employed desirable in the abstract; certainly, they should not be regularly pursued. . . . No doubt Nixon went to extremes in trying to achieve dominance. There were many dedicated members of the agencies who would have been willing to help. . . . [Nixon's] approach was weird and its human cost unattractive, yet history must also record the fundamental fact that major successes were achieved that had proved unattainable by conventional procedures.[56]

The essence of the matter is to be found in that last sentence. *Was* that approach really necessary to achieve the results? From my own experience, particularly in SALT, and more generally over six administrations, and on the basis of a study of the record, I am not convinced that it was. I do not dispute the major successes in foreign policy in the Nixon-Kissinger years, and they indicate that successes could be reached with the methods used. That they "had proved unattainable by conventional procedures" was, however, not demonstrated. They occurred because of a particular conjunction of circumstances that had not prevailed, say, five years earlier. Moreover, the decline of détente and the subsequent problems and failures in sustaining a number of these major successes suggest that had they been attained through more conventional procedures and less sleight of hand, they might have had greater staying power.

Reverberations of the Détente Summit

The post-summit period saw a number of developments in the United States, the Soviet Union, and the world—some stemming from the summit, others arising independently—that affected the course of American-Soviet relations.

Even the president's return trip to the United States from Moscow had effects. A stop in Iran had been planned to cement (and signal) American

---

56. Kissinger, *White House Years*, pp. 840–41.

support for a strong regional power in that area on the Soviet border. It was also intended (although this was not self-evident) to demonstrate *to China* that the United States would continue to support a chain of countries aligned with the West and China. U.S. support for Pakistan six months earlier, even at a cost to the prestige of the United States and American relations with India, had likewise been undertaken partly to make clear to Moscow, but even more so to Beijing, that the United States would stand with its friends. Similarly, a stop in Warsaw was arranged partly so that President Nixon could relive his triumphal visit to Poland in 1959 as vice president, in part because it was an American election year, but most significantly in order to signal to the countries of Eastern Europe (and to Moscow and Beijing) that America would continue its active interest in them notwithstanding détente with the Soviet Union. It thus reinforced the message of the president's two earlier visits in 1969 to Romania and in 1970 to Yugoslavia.[57]

The summit or, more accurately, some of the surprises at the summit did generate concern on the part of a number of U.S. allies. Certainly there was widespread and strong support in Europe and the world generally for a relaxation of tensions in Soviet-American relations. Now European détente and American relations with the Soviet Union were coming into gear. Support for SALT, the principal concrete accomplishment of the first summit, was strong. At the same time there was also some uneasiness, particularly over certain aspects of the Basic Principles, which had not been discussed with the allies. Kissinger notes this development in a characteristically ironic way:

Suddenly, now that we had followed their advice [on détente], the Europeans revealed their schizophrenia. We heard that some Europeans complained about the "Basic Principles of US-Soviet Relations" because of the use of the phrase "peaceful coexistence"—an astonishing criticism considering that the similar declaration signed by France and in the German treaties went far beyond our formulations. There was disquiet that some of our principles of restraint preempted the European Security Conference—that is, that we had agreed to what our allies wanted to give away in their own name.[58]

There is some truth to Kissinger's complaint, but the very way he voices it helps explain why the Europeans were miffed. Incidentally, neither the French-Soviet declaration nor the German treaties contained the peaceful coexistence formulation, so the judgment that those documents went further is just that—a judgment. The claim seems justified in terms of the significance of the German treaties, but the comparison is not apropos; the French-Soviet declaration was similar in some respects to the U.S.-Soviet document and did precede it, but it would be hard to argue it went "far beyond." When the United States had last discussed possible American-Soviet endorsement of

---

57. Kissinger, also notes these three reasons. Ibid., p. 1265. I can attest to the importance to Nixon of the first one, since I accompanied him when as vice president he visited Poland and the Soviet Union in 1959.

58. Ibid., p. 1273.

joint "principles" with its allies, in January 1969, it had been in the context of SALT and a legacy of the outgoing administration. Moreover, the allies had voiced many concerns and objections before the new administration had dropped the entire matter for its own reasons. Nixon, on his first major diplomatic excursion and speaking to the North Atlantic Council in Brussels in February 1969, had assured the NATO allies that he would pursue the transition from confrontation to an era of negotiation "on the basis of full consultation and cooperation with our allies."[59] It would probably be unfair to say the United States violated this pledge, and no ally charged that it had done so. At the same time, the United States might have earned more solid support and gratitude if it had advised its allies *before* the Basic Principles agreement was signed and made public. Given that even the U.S. secretary of state had been kept in complete ignorance of the principles until the summit meeting, he and others had no opportunity even to advise such a move.

Thus there was some adverse allied reaction, although not serious objection. The flurry of concern did, however, lead Kissinger, who persuaded Nixon, to decide that "it was time to match our 1972 summits with Communist leaders with demonstrative reaffirmation of our Alliance commitments and a redefinition of Alliance purposes. Such was the origin of the Year of Europe that we undertook in 1973."[60] Unfortunately, when that idea was publicly unveiled, it too came as a diplomatic surprise, and the Europeans reacted coldly to the idea that they should be assigned a year by an American administration. That initiative, discussed later, eventually faded away.

In the United States attention was focused almost exclusively on the SALT agreements, which elicited wide support but also some vocal criticism. During the summer of 1972 the administration sought to reconcile its own different interests and to rally support for the SALT agreements. It sought to do so by coupling the case for SALT with appeals for increased military programs. The latter were desired by the Pentagon (and promised in return for its support on SALT), as well as by the White House (in part for future bargaining leverage), but were also intended to blunt criticism of SALT and détente as indications of a policy insufficiently active to protect American security interests.

Secretary of Defense Laird, in the course of his testimony, conditioned his support for the SALT agreements on congressional approval of new military programs. He was also reported to have said that the United States should prepare itself to negotiate with the Soviet Union "from a position of strength." Perhaps inadvertently, those words triggered a violent reaction by the Soviets, who associated them with the use of that term in the Truman administration to denote active containment, and thus with American use of its superior power in the hardest confrontations of the cold war. TASS stated

---

59. "Meeting with the NATO Council: The President's Remarks to Members of the Council in Brussels, February 24, 1969," *Presidential Documents*, vol. 5 (March 3, 1969), p. 312.

60. Kissinger, *White House Years*, pp. 1274–75.

that such an approach "contradicts the Basic Principles" with its "recognition of the security interests of the sides based on the principle of equality and the renunciation of the use of force or the threat to use it."[61] Clearly, suspicions remained on both sides that could lead people to construe or misconstrue statements and actions of the other side in ways that ran counter to a relaxation of tensions.

The Moscow summit meeting did have an impact on the Vietnam situation. The very fact that it took place while the United States was escalating its direct military action against North Vietnam, and was undertaking parallel moves toward establishing American-Chinese détente, undoubtedly contributed to Vietnamese readiness to bargain seriously with the United States for a settlement. The Soviets, for their part, did send President Podgorny to Hanoi on June 13 with at least an implied endorsement for consideration of the American terms offered in May and reiterated in Moscow at the summit meeting. Meanwhile, Kissinger visited Beijing in June. Triangular diplomacy was at work. The 1972 summit thus played a role, possibly an important one, in American disengagement from Vietnam, notwithstanding only limited Soviet leverage over decisions in Hanoi.[62]

Soviet involvement in the American-Vietnamese relationship, and more broadly Soviet pursuit of détente with the United States notwithstanding continued American military operations in Vietnam, had been a matter of concern in Moscow long before the acute issue of heightened hostilities arose on the eve of the summit. Indeed, early in 1967 Kosygin had commented in a confidential exchange with President Lyndon B. Johnson, in response to American proposals to initiate SALT talks, that American military involvement in Vietnam posed a problem. Only after President Johnson's turnaround on Vietnam in 1968 did the Soviets agree to begin the talks, and in exchanges that year on SALT they expressed their support for progress toward a peaceful settlement of the Vietnam problem.

In the aftermath of the summit meeting, even while the Soviet leaders and commentators praised its achievements highly, a certain defensiveness was evident vis-à-vis actual or potential criticism from the left at home and abroad. [63] Concern focused mainly, but not entirely, on vulnerability to charges of having let down the Vietnamese comrades. In a commentary in *Pravda* in which this concern was only thinly veiled, Academician Nikolai Inozemtsev justified improvement in Soviet-American interests as being in the interest of "all peace-loving forces." He claimed that "the overwhelming majority of Communist and Workers parties" and others supported it. ("Majority" does

61. TASS dispatch from Washington, Radio Moscow, June 22, in Foreign Broadcast Information Service, *Daily Report: Soviet Union*, June 22, 1972, p. H1.

62. See chapter 7. For Kissinger's account of these negotiations and associated maneuvers in triangular diplomacy and in American military pressure on the North Vietnamese—and ultimately on the South Vietnamese as well—see *White House Years*, pp. 1300–1476.

63. For a useful review, see Thomas N. Bjorkman and Thomas J. Zamostny, "Soviet Politics and Strategy toward the West: Three Cases," *World Politics*, vol. 36 (January 1984), pp. 207–10.

not mean all.) "But attempts are being made—although, to be sure only by a few—to replace common sense with unscrupulous speculation about some 'conspiracy between the two superpowers' and to the effect that the Soviet-American agreements are allegedly detrimental to some third countries." This charge he refuted.[64]

Apart from concern over Vietnam's reaction, the Soviet leadership was concerned that the Chinese might persuade others in the world communist movement that it had put Soviet interests above theirs in reaching these agreements, and more generally through moving into a new relationship with the United States. The Chinese did try to do so, but their efforts were less successful because of the developing Chinese-American relationship. As noted earlier, some in the Soviet Union itself had objections, usually based on their judgment as to the adverse impact of détente on the world communist movement and among "progressive" forces.

Concern over Soviet subordination of the interests of others to its interests *did* have an impact. Most notably, six weeks after the summit, Egyptian President Anwar al-Sadat expelled the approximately 20,000 Soviet military advisers and technicians in Egypt, as well as the Soviet reconnaissance aircraft based there, and sharply curtailed any Soviet use of military facilities in his country. His dissatisfaction with the Soviet Union had been growing for some time, and the Soviet-American summit was the last straw.[65]

Sadat's defection from Soviet tutelage was not a fortuitous occurrence. As Kissinger has since disclosed, between visits to Moscow in February and April 1972 Sadat had initiated secret communication with the United States.[66] Knowing of Sadat's dissatisfaction with the USSR, Nixon and Kissinger sought to play on it by keeping a cool distance from the Soviet Union on Mideast questions, including in the discussions and communiqué at the summit meeting. Sadat's main grievance was Soviet *restraint* in providing advanced weapons and especially diplomatic and military support. These he wanted in order to pursue a more vigorous Egyptian political—and, if necessary, military—offensive to dislodge the Israelis from Egyptian territory occupied in 1967. When he expelled the Soviet military presence from Egypt in July 1972, Sadat had decided that even though he had not yet received American assurance that the United States would be an alternative source of support, he would take his chances on improving relations with the West. Sadat had proposed a secret meeting of high-level representatives (Kissinger or CIA Director

---

64. N. N. Inozemtsev, "The Principled Nature and Effectiveness of Soviet Foreign Policy," *Pravda*, June 9, 1972.

65. See Anwar el-Sadat, *In Search of Identity: An Autobiography* (Harper and Row, 1978), pp. 228–31. Sadat gives a figure of 15,000 advisers, a total that was not up-to-date. As Sadat notes, the aborted communist coup d'état in neighboring Sudan in July 1971 also adversely affected his judgment of the reliability of the Soviet Union. Ibid., p. 226.

66. Kissinger, *White House Years*, p. 1276. See pp. 1276–1300 for a detailed account of the developments leading up to the Egyptian break with the Soviets in July 1972 and its immediate aftermath.

Richard C. Helms with Hafiz Ismail, Sadat's national security adviser), and the United States had agreed to a meeting to follow the summit.[67] At the summit meeting itself, Minister of Foreign Affairs Gromyko and Kissinger concluded some general working principles for a Palestinian-Arab-Israeli settlement. The United States expected that the vagueness of the principles, coupled with the fact that the Soviets were dealing with the United States on them, would raise additional doubts in Sadat's mind about his Soviet relationship. Indeed, Sadat said in his memoir that the Soviet-American summit communiqué was a "violent shock" to Egypt.[68]

Thus one of the first concrete results of the American-Soviet summit of 1972 proved costly to the Soviet Union and a diplomatic gain for the United States, and it came about as a result of Soviet restraint in the third world in the period of developing détente. Such a significant setback must have stirred further doubts in those Soviet circles with reservations about détente.

Another American action to curtail Soviet influence in the Middle East, taken literally on the morrow of the summit, was the initiation of covert military assistance to the Kurdish rebels in Iraq. This assistance was directed against a state that had just signed a treaty of friendship and cooperation with the Soviet Union only a month before. Within twenty-four hours of leaving the Soviet Union President Nixon, then in Tehran, had accepted a proposal from the shah of Iran, Mohammed Reza Pahlevi, to join in covert support of the Kurds. This decision had not been addressed by the interagency 40 Committee (which considers covert operations), the director of the CIA, or the secretary of state, nor was it even communicated to the secretary of state *after* the secret support began three months later, in August 1972.[69] Israel later joined in supporting the Kurds in order to tie the Iraqis down. (This use of the Kurds as proxies to serve Iranian, American, and Israeli interests continued until March 1975. At that time Iran and Iraq reached an agreement on terms favorable to Iran, in return for which Iran cut off aid to the Kurds, who were then overwhelmed.) While it is unclear whether Soviet intelligence learned of the American presidential decision in May 1972, or later, it seems highly likely that the USSR would have learned about it quite soon.

Another sign of increasingly active American efforts to expand its influence in the Middle East was the reestablishment of diplomatic relations between the United States and North Yemen in July 1972.

The United States had also been active in supporting its interests elsewhere in the world through covert operations. It later became known that

---

67. Ibid., pp. 1276, 1292–94.

68. Sadat also notes that the Soviets did not even brief him on the U.S.-USSR summit talks until five weeks later. Sadat, *In Search of Identity*, p. 229. See also William B. Quandt, *Decade of Decisions: American Policy toward the Arab-Israeli Conflict, 1967–76* (Berkeley, Calif.: University of California Press, 1977), pp. 150–53.

69. Tad Szulc, *The Illusion of Peace: Foreign Policy in the Nixon Years* (Viking, 1978), pp. 584–87. See also chapter 13.

in 1972 the United States had spent at least $10 million in covert funding to friendly political leaders in Italy. Less benignly, President Nixon had authorized active measures in Chile from 1971 to 1973, as he had in 1970, to bring about the removal of leftist Chilean President Salvador Allende.[70]

Despite these developments, Brezhnev and the Soviet leadership showed no signs of reconsidering their position. They did, however, exhibit some sensitivity to ideological and political justification of their policy of détente with the United States. Soviet reassurances to the world communist movement stressed both the benefits of détente to the development of the Soviet Union and other members of the "socialist commonwealth" (Soviet bloc), and the positive effect it would have on national liberation movements, progressive change, and peace-loving forces in the world. Such assurances undoubtedly represented genuine expectations, but they may also have been cast in more enthusiastic, and militant, terms than the Soviet leaders really believed. The most alarmist report concerns a reported statement by Brezhnev to a meeting of Eastern European leaders in Prague in February 1973. He is said to have described the course of détente pursued at the summit as tactical, an interim phase to be pursued while the Soviet Union and other socialist countries built up their economic and military strength over the following fifteen years or so.[71] This justification for détente was intended to reassure communist leaders in Eastern Europe, although it also reflected Soviet confidence in ultimate gains for world socialism resulting from an active policy of peaceful coexistence.

There were a number of other sometimes tangible indications of a tactical softening of Soviet behavior abroad. For example, to note one kind of covert action that could be observed and measured, after May 1972 until late 1976, when détente was faltering, there was a notable cessation of Soviet forgeries of alleged Western official documents used to support "disinformation" propaganda in Europe and the third world.[72]

Mention should also be made of the eruption again of Sino-Soviet hostilities in late 1972. While not necessarily directly related to the developing Soviet-American détente, the fact that several Soviet servicemen were killed in a new border clash on December 11, 1972, certainly reminded the Soviet lead-

---

70. Ibid., pp. 643–49. The Church committee hearings later made the American covert involvement in Chile well known. See *Covert Action in Chile, 1963–73*, Committee Print, Select Committee to Study Governmental Operations, 94 Cong. 1 sess. (GPO, 1975), pp. 26–39. See also Kissinger, *Years of Upheaval*, pp. 382–96; and Nathaniel Davis, "U.S. Covert Actions in Chile, 1971–73," *Foreign Service Journal*, vol. 55 (November 1978), pp. 10–14, 38–39, and vol. 55 (December 1978), pp. 11–13, 42.

71. See John W. Finney, "Brezhnev Said to Assure East Europe That Accords with West Are a Tactic," *New York Times*, September 17, 1973; and William Beecher, "Kissinger Scoffed at Report Brezhnev 'Used' Détente," *Washington Star*, February 11, 1977.

72. *Soviet Covert Action (The Forgery Offensive)*, Hearings before the House Subcommittee on Oversight of the Permanent Select Committee on Intelligence, 96 Cong. 2 sess. (GPO, 1980), pp. 65–66. This is a declassified CIA study.

ers of the value of East-West détente if East-East tension was building. At the summit meeting Brezhnev and the other Soviet leaders made almost embarrassingly clear their own suspicions and hostilities toward the Chinese. Brezhnev in particular hinted that both the United States and the Soviet Union should keep an eye on Chinese nuclear aspirations. Kissinger remarks that this concern "may well have been the Kremlin's deepest interest in détente."[73] In any case, the Soviets continued to raise the subject in the period leading to the second summit meeting.

Overall, despite these initial indications of opposition to détente from some quarters in both countries, and some initial Soviet setbacks internationally, both Brezhnev and Nixon counted the launching of détente between the two countries as a major success. This was true both for the foreign policies each was pursuing and in terms of a major achievement widely acclaimed and welcomed at home and widely around the world. Both sides saw the main task as consolidating and extending détente.

---

73. See Kissinger, *White House Years*, pp. 1226–27, 1251; and Nixon, *RN*, pp. 620–21.

10 Developing Détente: The Second Summit, June 1973

DÉTENTE had been launched with much fanfare at the first summit in Moscow, and subsequently both sides sought to develop and extend it. Renewed sponsorship at the highest level of additional agreements marked the second summit conference, held in Washington in June 1973. It was seen as the next step in an emerging institution of periodic summit meetings. The post-summit period in the latter half of 1972 flowed easily into a pre-summit phase in the first half of 1973.

Riding the Wave of Détente

In the United States, President Nixon was overwhelmingly re-elected over an opponent who also endorsed détente. At the same time, there were two disquieting developments in the election campaign and its aftermath, and although neither directly related to détente, together they came to have a very important adverse effect on it. Of greatest importance was the Watergate break-in and the attempted cover-up by Nixon and his aides. The other was an attempt by Nixon and this same coterie of aides to purge the executive branch and gain a more tightly controlled bureaucracy more directly responsive to presidential control. The executive branch plainly must serve the chief executive, but the always aloof and secretive Nixon (and in this sense also Kissinger) chafed under some real, but mainly imagined, lack of unquestioning loyalty by the disdained "bureaucracy," as they both were wont to term it. Indeed, the Watergate affair stemmed from and illustrates well the impulse to full power that drove the now reelected president. Rather than rely on the established executive agencies such as the FBI and CIA, as Nixon went beyond constitutional limits he turned to extralegal measures such as the infamous "Plumbers." Nixon's broader intentions and approach were clear from one astonishing

319

act: immediately after returning to the White House from his second inauguration he coldly demanded the resignation of his whole cabinet and White
House professional staff.[1] Most were kept on, but he had conducted this purge
in such a way that no one could consider himself immune and all sensed their
complete vulnerability. Many were vulnerable. The top ranks of both the interagency SALT delegation and the Arms Control and Disarmament Agency
(ACDA), for example, were decimated in January 1973 on the basis of a White
House hit list. Similar actions began in a number of departments, but in most
cases they were soon suspended as a result of the beginning waves of concern
over Watergate.[2]

Ultimately, by reducing public confidence in the authors of détente
and thus in détente itself, the effects of Watergate came to affect the ability of
the administration to conduct its détente strategy (this situation is discussed
later).[3] In the meantime, however, détente, SALT, and the agreement on a
settlement permitting American military disengagement from Vietnam were
widely popular, and American public support permitted and even encouraged
Nixon and Kissinger to proceed with the development of détente.

General Secretary Brezhnev was also riding high in the aftermath of
the summit. The Peace Program he had sponsored at the Twenty-fourth Party
Congress in 1971, calling for the first time for détente with the United States,
had succeeded beyond expectations. The United States had even endorsed
peaceful coexistence. In April 1973, in a move consolidating his position before
departing on visits to Bonn and Washington, Brezhnev succeeded in removing
his critics Pyotr Ye. Shelest and Gennady I. Voronov from the Politburo.[4] (In
ironic counterposition that illustrates the shifting fortunes of Brezhnev and
Nixon, the purge of Brezhnev's opponents occurred just three days before
Nixon was reluctantly forced to require the resignation of his chief lieutenants,
H. R. Haldeman and John D. Ehrlichman.)

The leaders of both countries wished to see further development of
détente at the Washington summit. The same broad objectives on the part of
each continued to support the desire to achieve and demonstrate continuing
improvement in relations between the two superpowers. Developments in the
European theater of détente and in the triangular diplomacy with China reinforced this decision.

---

1. See H. R. Haldeman with Joseph DiMona, *The Ends of Power* (Times Books, 1978), pp.
   167–68; and Henry Kissinger, *White House Years* (Boston, Mass.: Little Brown, 1979), pp.
   1406–08.

2. For a general discussion see Haldeman, *The Ends of Power*, pp. 168–88; see also A. James
   Reichley, *Conservatives in an Age of Change* (Brookings Institution, 1981), pp. 242–47.

3. See chapter 12.

4. At the same time, April 27, 1973, three senior leaders representing key institutions (and all in
   one way or another centrally involved with détente) were raised to full membership in the
   Politburo: Andrei A. Gromyko, minister of foreign affairs; Marshal Andrei A. Grechko, minister
   of defense; and Yury V. Andropov, chairman of the Committee of State Security (KGB).

Europe, Asia, and the World

The United States sought to tie Western Europe into the American design for a web of détente ties managed from the White House. Kissinger was the private author of a diplomatic initiative intended to serve this aim, as well as its public advocate. On April 23, 1973, in his first major public address—he was emerging from being the initially anonymous, and later open, background briefer into being an acknowledged national policy spokesman—Kissinger announced plans to develop "a new Atlantic Charter" and declared that 1973 would be "The Year of Europe." What he had in mind was moving Western Europe more into play, along with China, in global diplomacy under American aegis. Nixon, wholly absorbed in Watergate, looked upon the initiative as a way to distract attention from Watergate. He assigned the announcement to Kissinger, already being groomed to replace William P. Rogers as secretary of state.[5]

Kissinger, in his memoir, provides a lengthy, defensive explanation of the origins and purposes of the Year of Europe initiative.[6] Among the more arresting and revealing points is his explanation (naturally not made publicly at the time) that "we," meaning Nixon and himself, "sought to discourage the Europeans from unilateral initiatives to Moscow by demonstrating that in any competition for better relations with Moscow, America had the stronger hand."[7] While that explanation was not voiced at the time, it indicates why the Europeans were suspicious that the United States was in a sense treating Europe as another geopolitical piece on the chessboard rather than as an ally. Indeed, the Year of Europe initiative not only sought to place the Western European powers into geopolitical play, but also attempted to use linkage in

---

5. As a further sign of the secretive White House modus operandi, it might be noted that Secretary of State Rogers was in New York delivering another speech on the very same day, April 23. He was not even informed that Kissinger would be making this major address. No one but Nixon and Kissinger's personal NSC staff was aware of the speech, much less involved in its preparation. Kissinger notes, in partial explanation of the poor reception of his speech, that the usual advance notification of subject and briefings for the press had not been given because of the secrecy designed to exclude the State Department, or, as he puts it, "to reduce the bureaucratic backbiting between the White House and the State Department." See Henry Kissinger, *Years of Upheaval* (Boston, Mass.: Little, Brown, 1982), p. 101.

President Nixon himself had referred to 1973 as "the year of Europe" in January and February, but not under circumstances that made news. See "The President's News Conference of January 31, 1973," *Weekly Compilation of Presidential Documents*, vol. 9 (February 5, 1973), p. 107; and "The U.S. and Europe," *Department of State Bulletin*, vol. 9 (February 19, 1973), p. 153. (Hereafter *Presidential Documents* and *State Bulletin*.)

6. Kissinger, *Years of Upheaval*, pp. 128–62.

7. Ibid., p. 136. An example of the other edge of this blade is revealed in another of Kissinger's retrospective comments: "We were prepared to subordinate détente policy to the consensus of our allies. But not all our allies were ready for similar undertakings." Ibid., p. 731.

the relations between the United States and its allies. They were told, in effect, that to keep American troops in Europe for their security the allies should help the United States in its trade relations.

The attempt to deal this particular transatlantic bargain was unsuccessful, and was resented.[8] It came, moreover, just as Europe was in the throes of adjustment as a result of the expansion of the European Community from six to nine members, now including Great Britain.

The U.S. initiative did not meet with either the desired or expected success. What little effect it had was counterproductive. There had been inadequate consultation with the allies in Europe about a major initiative centrally concerning them.[9] In addition, they were unimpressed at being awarded a particular, limited time in the sun by the United States. As far as the larger allied powers were concerned, they already were a factor in world diplomacy. Nor did they wish to be placed in the same category as the Soviet Union and China, whose relations with the United States had dominated 1972. The Year of Europe initiative faded. In fact, American relations with its European allies during 1973 were more than usually strained.[10]

To some extent European concerns were aroused by the thought of other possible initiatives that might be sprung without consultation. On June 14, at the regular semiannual NATO ministerial meeting, Secretary of State Rogers found it necessary to assure the foreign ministers of the European allies that President Nixon would make no decisions or agreements with the Soviet Union detrimental to NATO interests.[11]

---

8. See Wilfrid L. Kohl, "The Nixon-Kissinger Foreign Policy System and U.S.-European Relations: Patterns of Policy Making," *World Politics*, vol. 28 (October 1975), pp. 15–18.

9. Kissinger discloses in his memoir that there had been closely held consultations at the level of heads of government with several principal allies before his speech, but he admits it was not sufficient. In one of his few acknowledgements of the limitations and disadvantages of secret back channel diplomacy among allies, Kissinger writes: "To attempt a major foreign policy initiative of this kind from the office of national security adviser was awkward. That was the way the President wanted it and with Secretary Rogers on the way out, I was certainly keen to try. We had achieved our successes in other areas without the State Department. But relations with Europe did not lend themselves to secret diplomacy followed by spectacular pronouncements. There were too many nations involved to permit the use of backchannels. North Atlantic diplomacy had well-established patterns for consultation that were guarded jealously, sometimes ferociously, by their bureaucracies. Had I been Secretary of State at the beginning, instead of national security adviser, I might well have been more sensitive to the need to engage allied foreign offices. But from the White House it was easier to deal with heads of government, and this antagonized the experts in the ministries whose goodwill was essential for the kind of detailed negotiations required by our initiative." Kissinger, *Years of Upheaval*, p. 729.

10. Ibid., pp. 162–94, 700–34, for a detailed and informative review, but one that is not dispassionate or unbiased.

11. Rogers no doubt believed this assurance, which he interjected in a departure from his prepared text. At that time neither he nor the allies knew that the Basic Principles agreement signed in Moscow a year before had actually been secretly negotiated beforehand—nor that a similar

Meanwhile, European détente did develop in 1973. A formal Conference on Security and Cooperation in Europe (CSCE) was decided on at a multilateral exploratory meeting that had begun in November 1972 in Helsinki. Exploratory talks on European mutual and balanced force reductions (MBFR) began in Geneva in January 1973, resulting in agreement to convene a formal continuing conference in Vienna in October.[12]

The mysterious unveiling and subsequent disappearance of the Year of Europe also aroused concern in some non-European countries that believed they, too, belonged on the agenda for that year. All in all, the initiative did not enhance the standing of American leadership among friends or boost its bargaining role with adversaries.

Elsewhere in the world, another development illustrating the tendency for the superpowers to become enmeshed in local conflicts involving their clients occurred in March 1973, when Iraqi military forces occupied territory in Kuwait to which Baghdad laid claim. This action followed by less than a year the signing of the Soviet-Iraq Treaty of Friendship. While the action was not in Soviet interests, the USSR supported Iraq and even dispatched a naval flotilla with Admiral of the Fleet Sergei Gorshkov, the Soviet navy chief, to visit Iraq during the confrontation. Iraq backed down when Great Britain supported Kuwait.

In February 1973 the White House also initiated a new secret diplomatic channel with Egyptian President Anwar al-Sadat, developing further the contacts initiated the previous year.[13]

In Asia, in September 1972 Chinese Prime Minister Zhou Enlai and Japanese Prime Minister Kakuei Tanaka agreed to end the state of war between their two countries and to resume diplomatic relations. The Sino-American rapprochement was now being accompanied by a Sino-Japanese rapprochement, contributing to Soviet concerns.

The most significant developments in Asia affecting American-Soviet relations were the signs of continuing American-Chinese rapprochement and a tangled triangular diplomatic maneuver involving Cambodia. In February 1973 Kissinger made his fifth visit to China. The principal concrete achievement was an agreement to establish official liaison offices—embassies in all but name and formal protocol—in Beijing and Washington. More significant were Kissinger's conversations with Zhou Enlai and Chairman Mao Zedong, and

---

surprise had been negotiated for the forthcoming summit. Nor did he know that this was to be his last NATO ministerial meeting. Most of the ministers were very cool to the Year of Europe initiative at the meeting, preferring to ignore it rather than debate it.

12. See chapter 14.

13. William B. Quandt, *Decade of Decisions: American Policy toward the Arab-Israeli Conflict, 1967–76* (Berkeley, Calif.: University of California Press, 1977), pp. 154–55.

Mao's stress on the need to contain Soviet hegemonic designs.[14] Soon after Kissinger's visit, the last three Americans imprisoned in China, one since 1950 (John T. Downey, a captured CIA officer), were released. Meanwhile, American-Chinese trade had risen from $5 million in 1970 to $900 million in 1973.

The latest chapter in the Cambodian affair, later termed by Kissinger "the lost opportunity," began with the fact that when the hostilities in Vietnam ended in January 1973 fighting in Cambodia continued. Since the overthrow of Cambodian leader Prince Norodom Sihanouk by Lon Nol in 1970, with at least some American encouragement, the situation had changed to the point where in 1973 the Soviet Union was supporting Lon Nol, the Chinese Sihanouk, and the Vietnamese the Cambodian communists, the Khmer Rouge. As Kissinger puts it, "Everybody's estimate of the Cambodians turned out to be wrong."[15] Be that as it may, Kissinger's interpretation is that the Chinese were counting on continued American bombing of Cambodia but that this subtle White House–Beijing scheme to bolster Sihanouk was undercut by the U.S. Congress, which cut off the bombing as of August 15, thus turning Cambodia over to the Soviet-allied Vietnamese. Kissinger even speculates that Zhou Enlai's fall from favor in China was caused by the failure of the Zhou-Kissinger diplomacy that resulted from the bombing halt. Kissinger is passionate in his criticism of the outcome as a resounding, even moral, defeat for the United States, but his argument is not convincing.[16] Cambodia in 1973 was another case, like the Indo-Pakistani War of 1971, in which American policy was contorted to fit an excessively intricate pattern of diplomacy conceived by Kissinger to permit a very subtle maneuver in triangular diplomacy— despite his later acknowledgment that "everyone" had estimated the situation incorrectly. It may also, as was the Indo-Pakistani War, be a case in which Kissinger's assumptions about the Chinese role were too clever by half.[17] The

---

14. See Kissinger, *Years of Upheaval*, pp. 44–71. In return for Mao's receiving Kissinger, President Nixon received the new Chinese liaison representative, Huang Zhen, on May 29 as soon as he arrived in Washington, although not required by protocol to do so.

15. Ibid., p. 343. Kissinger calls this section of his memoir "The Lost Opportunity," p. 339.

     By 1983, a decade later, the United States and China were supporting Sihanouk, Lon Nol's successor Son Sann, *and* the Khmer Rouge against a Vietnamese-puppet regime under Heng Samrin.

16. Ibid., pp. 339–69, for Kissinger's detailed presentation of his case. He does not, however, mention that although the victory of the Khmer Rouge might have been averted by continued American bombing, the burden of proof rests on demonstrating that outcome, and it seems much more likely that more bombing would at best only have delayed that victory. Nor does he note that the real turning point was the overthrow of Sihanouk by Lon Nol (with American encouragement) in 1970. Finally, the victory of the Khmer Rouge was no victory for Vietnam and the Soviet Union—the Khmer Rouge refused even to accept a Soviet ambassador, and in five years Vietnam, supported by the Soviet Union, was at war with the Khmer Rouge, which was being supported by China and soon by the United States as well.

17. See chapter 8 for the diplomacy of the Indo-Pakistani War.

Chinese view has not been disclosed beyond Kissinger's perception and rendition of it.

Expanding Bilateral Relations

Meanwhile, the bilateral SALT negotiations had made no real progress. SALT II, as it came to be called, began with a one-month session in November–December 1972. Then it began again, in a sense, with a new American delegation in a three-month session from March to June 1973. But the talks only revealed the wide gap between the very conservative initial positions adopted by both sides. The new Standing Consultative Commission established to help implement and monitor the SALT I agreements held its first session from May to July 1973.

Other American-Soviet bilateral ventures in cooperation set in train at the May 1972 summit were also under way, and additional areas were being mapped out for new agreements. The Joint Commission on Scientific and Technical Cooperation, for example, held its first meeting in March 1973.

Planning specifically for the Washington summit conference in June was sparked by a letter from Brezhnev to Nixon in February. Nixon has disclosed that it included Brezhnev's expectations concerning the signing of a treaty on nonuse of nuclear weapons, further progress on SALT, the signing of further trade and economic agreements, and accords in the fields of science, technology, health, and peaceful uses of nuclear energy. In addition, Brezhnev sought discussions on the situation in the Middle East, on relations between the two Germanies, and on European security and reciprocal force reductions in Europe. Some of these subjects (particularly nonuse of nuclear weapons or, as the American side preferred to put it, "further measures to prevent or to reduce the risks of war") were the subject of some correspondence and discussion through the special channel of Kissinger and Ambassador Dobrynin, while the technical cooperation areas were handled through the usual agencies on the two sides. There was, however, no real clarification of the agenda and prospects for concrete political and arms control agreements until Kissinger visited Moscow in early May.

Problems arose as well. Senator Jackson on March 15, 1973, introduced in the East-West Trade Relations Bill his amendment tying the grant of most-favored-nation (MFN) status for the Soviet Union to Jewish emigration. He had seventy-three cosponsors. Jackson did not even wait to learn the results of meetings in Moscow by Secretary of the Treasury George P. Shultz (accompanied by Kissinger's aide Helmut Sonnenfeldt) with Brezhnev, in which Shultz tried to explain the need for, and problem in gaining, congressional approval. Brezhnev told Shultz that the exit tax had been the consequence of a bureaucratic bungle in Moscow and that the Soviet Union was permitting Jewish emigration without collecting the tax. Immediately after the broader

Trade Reform Act of 1973 was introduced, on April 18 Jackson again, this time with seventy-six senators cosponsoring, introduced his amendment to that bill. That very day Nixon had advised a group of congressional leaders, including Jackson, that he had had a communication from the Soviet leadership that the Soviet exit tax had been suspended. Five days later Brezhnev himself assured seven visiting American senators, with whom he met for three hours, that the exit tax had been suspended.[18]

Kissinger has disclosed that as early as March 30 Dobrynin had informed the White House that the education tax on emigrants would be lifted. In response to a request that the White House be able to inform Congress (meaning a public disclosure), on April 10 Moscow authorized that step. Yet Nixon and Kissinger, still failing to appreciate fully Jackson's strategy and congressional interests, waited until a meeting with Nixon himself could be arranged on April 18—by which time the Trade Act, and Jackson's amendment, had been introduced. As Kissinger describes the scene, "Nixon expected to celebrate a great achievement" when he called the congressional leaders in and informed them that the Soviet leaders had withdrawn the exit education tax. Nixon believed the obstacle to granting MFN was now removed. So did Kissinger, who was so sure that he even informed Dobrynin that now "no outstanding issues stood in the way of implementing the US-Soviet trade agreement of 1972." Only after the April meeting, says Kissinger, did Nixon and he begin to understand that rather than wanting the best achievable arrangement, Jackson intended to keep the issue alive. Kissinger also argues that Nixon's initiative failed because Watergate had seriously weakened his clout. This was no doubt true, but it is unlikely it made the crucial difference.[19]

While these political maneuverings were taking place, trade was marching ahead. On March 20 the Export-Import Bank granted a loan of $202 million for Soviet purchase of industrial equipment, and on March 28 the Moscow offices of the unofficial U.S.-USSR Trade Council opened. This council included nearly 300 American firms in its membership. On April 12 a multibillion-dollar chemical-fertilizer barter arrangement was signed between Armand Hammer of Occidental Oil and Deputy Minister of Foreign Trade Nikolai Komarov. On June 8 Occidental signed a $10 billion twenty-five-year natural gas deal. And a new official U.S.-USSR Shipping Agreement was announced on June 5, increasing Soviet payments to American ships carrying grain to the Soviet Union.

An unusual competition had arisen between the expanding economic and commercial activity, on the one hand, and legislative efforts to restrict trade unless the Soviet Union made additional concessions on the other. In his memoir Nixon comments on the rare convergence of forces at

---

18. See Paula Stern, *Water's Edge: Domestic Politics and the Making of American Foreign Policy* (Westport, Conn.: Greenwood Press, 1979), pp. 65–69.

19. See Kissinger, *Years of Upheaval*, pp. 249–55, 979–98.

opposite ends of the political spectrum in a "curious coalition." "On the one side the liberals and the American Zionists had decided that now was the time to challenge the Soviet Union's highly restrictive emigration policies, particularly with respect to Soviet Jews. On the other side were the conservatives, who had traditionally opposed détente because it challenged their ideological opposition to contacts with Communist countries. My request in April 1973 for congressional authority to grant most-favored-nation trade status to the Soviet Union became the [negative] rallying point for both groups."[20]

Kissinger similarly notes that "conservatives who hated Communists and liberals who hated Nixon came together in a rare convergence."[21] While he overemphasizes the anti-Nixon sentiment, it is true that there was a growing uneasiness over détente as conducted by the Nixon-Kissinger team. Conservatives were hostile to agreements with the Soviet Union on ideological grounds. Liberals were concerned over a perceived amoral *Realpolitik* in American policy and at the same time saw sufficient progress away from the cold war that it seemed possible to indulge in criticism of internal Soviet practices.

At this point Kissinger went to Moscow—from May 6 to 9, 1973—to prepare for the forthcoming summit. He used the occasion to urge Brezhnev to help improve the prospects for congressional approval by giving the Soviet leader a hardship list of about 1,000 aspiring Jewish emigrants compiled by American Jewish leaders. For his part, Brezhnev agreed to look into those cases and indicated to Kissinger that the Soviet Union would keep up an annual level of Jewish emigration of about 36,000 to 40,000.[22]

The negotiations between Kissinger and Brezhnev and other Soviet leaders involved a general mutual reconnaissance of positions and exchanges of views on the political issues: the Middle East, CSCE, and MBFR. Kissinger also sought to reassure the Soviet leaders about the Nixon administration's ability domestically to carry its policies forward. Not only had the growing ramifications of Watergate raised questions, but so too had the cool congressional response to granting MFN to the Soviet Union, foreshadowed in late 1972 and specifically requested by the president in April, just a month before. But the two major subjects discussed were SALT and a possible agreement on reducing the risks of nuclear war.

The American SALT delegation had advanced a proposal in March for equal aggregates of ICBMs, SLBMs, and heavy bombers. This approach broadened the 1972 SALT Interim Agreement by including bombers and set equal ceilings. The proposal also would have imposed an equal ceiling on the

---

20. Richard Nixon, *RN: The Memoirs of Richard Nixon* (Grosset and Dunlap, 1978), p. 875, and see p. 876. Nixon does not note that his deal with Senator Jackson in the fall of 1972 had contributed to the commitment of many senators to the Jackson-Vanik amendment (see chapter 9).

21. Kissinger, *Years of Upheaval*, p. 983, and see pp. 979–85.

22. See Stern, *Water's Edge*, pp. 81–82.

number of ICBM launchers *and* an equal ceiling on ICBM throw-weight. MIRVs per se would not have been constrained.[23] This proposal was obviously not acceptable to the Soviet side, since it singled out the area of Soviet advantage (numbers and size of ICBMs) for equalization and would have required either no change on the Soviet side while permitting the United States to build up about 300 launchers for large ICBMs, or Soviet dismantling of its entire force of large ICBMs (and then some) while the United States curtailed nothing. But it also failed to elicit a Soviet counterproposal. From 1972 to 1974 the Soviet Union unwisely tried to gain bargaining leverage by proposing to perpetuate the unequal 1972 Interim Agreement freeze levels on ICBM and SLBM launchers.

In early May a new U.S. position was hastily decided upon, to be tried out before the summit meeting.[24] The new American SALT proposal would have set an overall equal aggregate of 2,350 ICBMs, SLBMs, and heavy bombers. The evidently nonnegotiable March proposal for equal numbers of ICBM launchers and equal ICBM throw-weight was discarded. Instead, a freeze on MIRV (and multiple reentry vehicles, or MRV) testing and deployment on land-based missiles was proposed, effective July 1, as at least an interim step while negotiations continued.

Regrettably this proposal was three years late. In the spring of 1970, as noted, the United States was just on the verge of deploying MIRVs. By May 1973 it not only had fully tested and developed them for its ICBMs and SLBMs but had been deploying them for over three years—while the Soviets had not yet deployed or even *tested* a MIRV.[25] So the new American proposal

---

23. This account of the SALT II negotiations in late 1972 and early 1973 is given in some detail here, since most published accounts deal only with SALT I or with SALT II in the Carter administration. There has been a gap with respect to the intervening Nixon-Ford period. The partial exceptions are Kissinger's informed but selective memoir, *Years of Upheaval*, pp. 256–74; and the memoir of Ambassador U. Alexis Johnson, the new head of the SALT delegation who served from February 1973 until the end of the Ford administration four years later. See U. Alexis Johnson with Jef Olivarius McAllister, *The Right Hand of Power* (Englewood Cliffs, N.J.: Prentice-Hall, 1984), pp. 582–91.

24. In fact, it was decided so hastily that only an incomplete proposal was approved (and issued in National Security Decision Memorandum [NSDM]–213 on May 3) before Kissinger's departure. Another NSDM (216 on May 7) was issued while he was in Moscow. This haste required the American delegation in Geneva, which was not fully informed, to withhold its presentation. It finally presented the position piecemeal on May 8, 11, and 15—after Kissinger had raised the new proposal in Moscow. One consequence of this sequence of events was that the Soviet side had no opportunity to consider the proposal in advance of the discussions with Kissinger.

25. The Soviet Union had begun testing an MRV warhead for the SS-9 in August 1968, the same month the United States began its MIRV testing. The USSR did not test a MIRV until July 1973. By the spring of 1973 it had become clear that the SS-9 MRV was *not* a MIRV or suitable for development into a MIRV, dispelling uncertainty and disproving the confident assertions of some American officials (including Secretary of Defense Laird) who in 1970–72 had contended it was a MIRV.

would have left the United States with fully developed MIRVs and 350 deployed Minuteman III ICBMs with 1,050 MIRV warheads while the Soviet Union would have had none.[26]

Kissinger recounts in his memoir the bureaucratic byplay in Washington and his own weakened ability to maneuver on SALT positions in this period. He notes that this revised, supposedly more moderate American position "neatly shut the Soviets out of MIRVing their ICBM force, which comprised 85 percent of their total throwweight, without significantly curtailing any program of our own." As he notes: "Not surprisingly, this proposal quickly disappeared into the limbo of one-sided proposals by which each side pleased its bureaucracy while it decided whether painful decisions were in fact necessary."[27] The Soviet leaders made clear to Kissinger in Moscow that these proposals were unacceptable, and at the summit meeting they were flatly rejected.[28]

The Soviet side had, in the spring of 1973, proposed a ban on testing and deployment of *all* new strategic systems during the period of the agreement, allowing only modernization of existing systems. While Kissinger and others saw this proposal as loaded in the Soviet favor and directed at the American Trident system, the United States was not interested in pursuing that radical a course by seeking to curb *both* Soviet and American modernization in equally stringent fashion.[29]

---

26. The proposals would also have banned intercontinental range cruise missiles and air-launched cruise missiles (ALCMs) with ranges exceeding 3,000 kilometers. All ground-launched cruise missiles (GLCMs) and submarine-launched cruise missiles (SLCMs) with ranges less than 5,000 kilometers, and ALCMs with ranges less than 3,000 kilometers, as well as medium-range ballistic missiles (MRBMs) and intermediate-range ballistic missiles (IRBMs) with ranges of less than 5,000 kilometers, would have been unconstrained. There was, however, also a general "noncircumvention" pledge that neither side would circumvent the provisions of the treaty through deploying other systems

27. Kissinger, *Years of Upheaval*, p. 271, and see pp. 262–71. See also Johnson, *The Right Hand of Power*, pp. 589–91. As Johnson notes, notwithstanding the lopsided advantage to the United States, the Pentagon preferred to keep its own forces unconstrained: "Defense and the Chiefs [JCS] were trying to end-run my instructions [from the president] calling for a MIRV freeze by not approving treaty language that stipulated such a freeze. The fact was the Chiefs did not want any SALT agreement that was negotiable." Ibid., p. 591.

28. Ibid., p. 271. Nixon, either (and probably) unaware what the proposals really meant or highly disingenuous, states in his memoir only this: "The Soviets were not yet ready to have limitations imposed on their own multiple warhead missile development, so he [Brezhnev] remained adamant against expanding the SALT agreements at this summit." Nixon, *RN*, p. 879. That single sentence had been, until Kissinger's memoir in 1982, the only published discussion of the nominal attempt to negotiate MIRV limitations in 1973.

29. Kissinger, *Years of Upheaval*, p. 270. Although Kissinger is being ironic, his comment that the Soviet "scheme did not invite much dispassionate analysis in our government" is also telling witness to the lack of interest in using the Soviet approach as a point of departure to press for severe but balanced constraints on both sides.

SALT thus remained at a stalemate. The principal agreement negotiated by Kissinger in May, and formally agreed to and signed at the summit,
was what became the Agreement on Prevention of Nuclear War (PNW), to
which the discussion will turn presently.

The Washington Summit

The press of Watergate was heavy by the time of the second summit. Just as Kissinger returned from Moscow, on May 10, only a little over a
month before Brezhnev was to arrive, a reshuffle placed General Alexander M.
Haig, Jr., in the position vacated by Haldeman on April 27, John B. Connally
temporarily took Ehrlichman's position, James R. Schlesinger replaced Elliott
L. Richardson at the Department of Defense, and William E. Colby succeeded Richard C. Helms at the CIA. On May 17 the Senate Watergate
hearings opened. John W. Dean, counsel to the president, was scheduled to
begin his testimony on June 18, the very day of Brezhnev's arrival in Washington; with great reluctance and under pressure from the Senate leadership, Senator Sam Ervin agreed to postpone Dean's appearance for a week, until after the
summit conference.

As will be recalled, in Moscow in May 1972 the Soviet side had
insisted that the invitation for a reciprocal visit be extended to President Podgorny and Prime Minister Kosygin, as well as to General Secretary Brezhnev,
but this was never followed through. Arrangements for Brezhnev's visit were
made through the usual Kissinger-Dobrynin channel. Brezhnev did, in his first
(and private) meeting with Nixon, state that he spoke for the entire Politburo
(thus underlining its recent purge). Nixon, in return, replied that "despite
domestic differences," he spoke for the majority of Americans. Nixon states
that Brezhnev nodded his head vigorously.[30] Both men were undoubtedly hoping that was true, Brezhnev especially in light of the developing relationship of
détente. Nixon later observed, with insight, the differences between Brezhnev's
demeanor and that of his predecessor, First Secretary Nikita S. Khrushchev, in
visiting the White House in 1959. Khrushchev had known he was speaking
from a position of weakness for which he compensated by taking an aggressive

---

30. Nixon, *RN*, p. 878. The only other person present was the Soviet interpreter Viktor Sukho-
    drev. This reliance on only a Soviet interpreter, in preference to having an American inter-
    preter present, continued a pernicious practice adopted by Kissinger in his Moscow meetings in
    April 1972 and May 1973, and by Nixon in May 1972. Kissinger and Nixon had also pursued
    this pattern at their meetings with the leaders of China in 1971 and early 1972. On this
    occasion Nixon met alone with Brezhnev and Sukhodrev for more than an hour without
    allowing Kissinger and Rogers in, as planned. Kissinger has now disclosed that Nixon never
    told him what was discussed. Kissinger requested a copy of Sukhodrev's record of the meeting,
    but the Soviet interpreter "never got around to providing it." Kissinger, *Years of Upheaval*,
    p. 291.

and boastful line. Brezhnev, speaking from a position nearer to parity, could afford to speak more quietly and openly.[31] Nixon does not comment that Brezhnev and his advisers may also have calculated that they had an advantage in that Nixon clearly needed a success.

The second Nixon-Brezhnev summit was held partly in Washington (and Camp David) and partly in San Clemente, California. Brezhnev was in the United States for the first time, and his visit included a trip across the country to the president's summer residence. He showed keen interest and enthusiasm in all aspects of the visit. The summit went well. Some long-standing differences were aired. One, for example, was the Middle East, although it received only four cryptic sentences in the joint communiqué. Here, however, as with other issues, far more lay beneath the surface.

In his memoir Nixon disclosed that at Brezhnev's initiative the Middle East received about three hours of discussion, with an emotional intensity almost comparable to the harsh exchanges over Vietnam that had marked the first summit conference. Nixon clearly misconstrued the significance of Brezhnev's warnings that, without at least some kind of informal agreement on principles, "he could not guarantee that war would not resume." Even in his memoir four years later Nixon interpreted this as an attempt by Brezhnev to "browbeat" him, although Nixon also noted that Brezhnev was of course aware that the United States was making slow but steady progress in reopening contacts with the Arab countries.[32]

Kissinger has added important information about this exchange on the Middle East. Brezhnev had, in his talks with Kissinger in May, "invoked the threat of war; he hinted at increasing difficulty in holding back his Arab allies." With President Nixon, Brezhnev was now not only again stressing the dangers of leaving the situation in the Middle East to fester, but also proposing that the Soviet Union and the United States agree then and there on a Middle East settlement. His proposal was based on complete Israeli withdrawal to the 1967 borders, with U.S. and Soviet guarantees to both sides. Many essential elements of any possible solution (especially for Israel) were, however, left for later local negotiation.[33] The proposal was not considered acceptable to the United States.

Even apart from the fact that the Soviet proposal was, not surprisingly, loaded in Arab favor, Nixon and Kissinger were in any case not prepared to negotiate on the Middle East at that time or in that fashion. They had, in fact, just turned aside a proposal by Secretary of State Rogers for a new American initiative.[34] As Kissinger remarks frankly, he and Nixon were "planning a major diplomatic initiative after Israel's elections in late October and were in

---

31. Nixon, *RN*, p. 879.

32. Ibid., pp. 884–86.

33. Kissinger, *Years of Upheaval*, pp. 296–98.

34. See Quandt, *Decade of Decisions*, pp. 158–59.

the meantime stalling."[35] Moreover, by that time Rogers would be gone. In short, unpersuaded of the urgency, despite Brezhnev's strenuous, almost frenetic, efforts, Nixon and Kissinger preferred to wait to manage the Middle East problem later. They failed to see what might occur.[36]

On Vietnam, the cardinal disputed issue in 1972, the communiqué was able to record that "the two sides expressed their deep satisfaction at the conclusion of the Agreement on Ending the War and Restoring Peace in Vietnam."[37]

Discussions on European security and MBFR were harmonious but not substantial, inasmuch as multilateral preparatory meetings had already reached agreement to proceed with a formal CSCE conference in Helsinki on July 3 and on an MBFR conference in Vienna on October 30, 1973.

More significant, but not mentioned in the communiqué, were the talks on China. Brezhnev gradually worked around in the course of several discussions to disclosing his real concern: that the United States was contemplating some secret military arrangement with China. Nixon sought to allay those concerns, but as he himself reports: "At the end of the meeting Brezhnev urged as diplomatically as his obviously strong feelings allowed that we not enter into any military agreements with China."[38] Kissinger adds interesting detail. He notes that Brezhnev clearly distinguished between the development of normal state-to-state relations between the United States and China, to which the Soviets did not object, and military arrangements, which would be quite another matter. Foreign Minister Gromyko later stressed this to Kissinger to make sure the message was received—he even said that a U.S.-China military agreement would lead to war because of Chinese aggressiveness. Brezhnev also proposed a secret exchange of views on China through the Dobrynin-Kissinger back channel.[39] The Soviets continued to try to obtain assurance that American-Soviet relations would continue to come before American-Chinese relations.[40]

With respect to bilateral relations the communiqué reported agreement "that the process of reshaping relations between the USA and the USSR on the basis of peaceful coexistence and equal security as set forth in the Basic Principles . . . is progressing in an encouraging manner. They emphasized the

---

35. Kissinger, *Years of Upheaval*, p. 296.

36. See chapter 11 for the sequel, the October 1973 war.

37. "General Secretary Brezhnev Visits the United States," *State Bulletin*, vol. 69 (July 23, 1973), p. 131.

38. Nixon, *RN*, p. 883.

39. Kissinger, *Years of Upheaval*, pp. 294–95, and see p. 233. Kissinger notes that he had made clear the United States had never had any military discussions with China—but neither he nor Nixon offered any assurances about the future.

40. Nixon, *RN*, p. 878.

great importance that each Side attaches to these Basic Principles."[41] The
Soviet view of this progressive development of détente was clearly spelled out
after the summit by Academician Georgy A. Arbatov: "The events of the
fourteen months since last year's Soviet-American summit meeting makes it
possible to say that an historically significant turn has become evident in relations between the USSR and the USA. Its essence is a transition from the 'cold
war' to relations of genuine peaceful coexistence, signifying not only the absence of war but also the easing of tension, the normalization of political
relations, the solution of emerging problems by negotiation, and the development of mutually advantageous cooperation in many spheres."[42]

As noted, one major new accord was unveiled, the Agreement on
the Prevention of Nuclear War. Agreement was also reached on new guidelines
or principles for the SALT negotiations. And a series of areas of bilateral
collaboration and cooperation was expanded or initiated.

Four new joint committees were added to those established the
year before, with agreements on exchanges of information and methodologies
in oceanography, transportation, agriculture, and peaceful uses of atomic energy (with the aim of developing new sources of energy). Other agreements
provided for expanding scientific, technical, educational, and cultural exchanges; expansion of passenger air service between the two countries; enlarge-
ment of commercial offices; and encouragement to establish a joint chamber of
commerce. (Another agreement provided for reciprocal income and other tax
exemptions for the increasing numbers of citizens working in the other country.) In all, ten new agreements or documents were signed. Most of the secondary ones were signed by cabinet officers, but Nixon and Brezhnev personally
signed the atomic energy agreement as well as the communiqué, the statement
on SALT negotiations, and, of course, the Prevention of Nuclear War agreement.

The statement on SALT, termed somewhat grandly "Basic Principles of Negotiations on Strategic Arms Limitation," really contained only one
new point: a pledge to make "serious efforts" to work out a "permanent agreement" on strategic offensive arms limitations by the end of 1974. Brezhnev
agreed only very reluctantly to setting a date, given the absence of any indication of how to bridge the wide differences in approach between the two sides.[43]
There was no real discussion of these differences at this summit meeting be-

41. U.S. Department of State, *The Washington Summit: General Secretary Brezhnev's Visit to
the United States, June 18–25, 1973*, Publication 8733 (Washington, D.C.: Government Printing Office, 1973), p. 49. Full texts of all the agreements, public addresses, and news conferences
are also included in *State Bulletin*, vol. 69 (1973), pp. 113–75.

42. G. Arbatov, "Soviet American Relations at a New Stage," *Pravda*, July 22, 1973.

43. Information from a participant. Neither Nixon nor Kissinger refers to Brezhnev's reluctance to
include the target date.

yond firm confirmation of the negative Soviet reaction to the proposals Kissinger had advanced in Moscow the month before.

The Prevention of Nuclear War Agreement

Partly owing to the absence of any other major political agreement, and partly by design on the Soviet side, the centerpiece of the summit was an Agreement Between the United States of America and the Union of Soviet Socialist Republics on the Prevention of Nuclear War, signed on June 22—the thirty-second anniversary of the German invasion of the Soviet Union in World War II (a date meaningful to the Soviet side,[44] but unnoticed on the American).

The Prevention of Nuclear War agreement, which is of indefinite duration, can be regarded either as profoundly important, or as frosting on the détente cake. The Soviets have regarded it as the former, American officials and commentators more as the latter. The significance of the agreement is, of course, almost entirely dependent on how it is regarded, interpreted, and applied, since it deals with actions in terms of purpose and intention.

In Article I the parties agree that "an objective of their policies is to remove the danger of nuclear war and of the use of nuclear weapons." Accordingly, "they will act in such a manner as to prevent the development of situations capable of causing a dangerous exacerbation of their relations, as to avoid military confrontations, and as to exclude the outbreak of nuclear war between them and between either of the Parties and other countries."

In Article II the parties agree "to proceed from the premise that each Party will refrain from the threat or use of force against the other Party, against the allies of the other Party and against other countries, in circumstances which may endanger international peace and security." Moreover, "they will be guided by these considerations in the formulation of their foreign policies and in their actions in the field of international relations."

In Article IV the parties further agree that if relations between themselves or between either of them and other countries "appear to involve the risk of a nuclear conflict," or if relations between other countries appear to involve the risk of nuclear war between them or either of them and other countries, the two powers "shall immediately enter into urgent consultations with each other and make every effort to avert this risk."

---

44. A. Artamonov, V. Matveyev, and N. Polyanov, "A Historic Day and a Historic Document," *Izvestiya*, June 24, 1973. These special correspondents covering the Brezhnev visit said: "Years and decades will pass . . . man will recall a portentous day in June 1973 . . . exactly thirty-two years after the beginning of the Great Fatherland War. It is a coincidence which is not devoid of profound symbolic meaning . . . The calendar page showing 22 June 1973 will remain in our memories as a synonym for the victory of realism over political recklessness."

The PNW agreement specifically states that nothing in it affects or impairs "the inherent right of individual or collective self-defense" under Article 51 or other provisions of the UN Charter, or the obligations of either party "toward its allies or other countries."[45]

Before discussing the PNW agreement further or reactions to it, it is useful to review its origins and negotiation. The Soviet side had proposed a pledge on "no first use of nuclear weapons" publicly and privately on many occasions in the 1960s, especially in the context of possible assurances to support the Nuclear Non-Proliferation Treaty. The United States and its allies had always rejected the proposal because it would deny use of a nuclear deterrent to a non-nuclear threat or attack. The Soviets raised the idea once tentatively and informally in SALT (in December 1970), but after being advised of a continuing negative American reaction, they never raised the subject again in that forum. As was seen, the idea of joint American-Soviet action to counter any possible "provocative" attempt by a third party to precipitate a war between the United States and the Soviet Union had also been raised in SALT. That, too, was rejected because of the possible implications of a joint Soviet-American stand against other parties (particularly China).[46]

In April 1972, when Kissinger was in Moscow preparing for the first summit, Brezhnev asked to see him alone and proposed a bilateral "understanding" between the two powers not to use nuclear weapons against one another, which he said would be a step of "immense significance." Kissinger turned the idea aside. In his memoir he comments that the Soviets, however, continued to pursue the idea and "we eventually agreed in June 1973 on a bland set of principles that had been systematically stripped of all implications harmful to our interests."[47] Such was Kissinger's frank judgment of the PNW agreement in his memoir published in 1979. This was the same agreement that he had described in 1973 as "a significant step toward the prevention of nuclear war" and potentially "a significant landmark in the relationships of the United States to the Soviet Union and in the relationships of the two great nuclear countries toward all other countries in the world."[48]

At the Moscow summit in May 1972 Brezhnev had again raised with Nixon the idea of an agreement on nonuse of nuclear weapons. Nixon provided a careful counterdraft, but deferred discussion of the whole matter to subsequent consideration through the Kissinger-Dobrynin channel.[49] Brezhnev "hinted that both countries might usefully keep an eye on the nuclear aspirations of Peking."[50]

---

45. *The Washington Summit*, p. 30.

46. See chapter 5.

47. Kissinger, *White House Years*, p. 1152, and *Years of Upheaval*, pp. 274–76.

48. *The Washington Summit*, p. 32.

49. Kissinger, *Years of Upheaval*, p. 276.

50. Kissinger, *White House Years*, p. 1251.

Dobrynin soon brought the subject up again with Kissinger, providing a new Soviet draft. Kissinger posed some pointed questions about its applicability to various possible wars. To his surprise the Soviets replied within some weeks—making clear that they indeed envisaged an American-Soviet pact ruling out use of nuclear weapons against each other even in a NATO–Warsaw Pact war in Europe (or any use in the Middle East or Asia). Kissinger immediately rejected these formulations as implying a Soviet-American condominium.[51] The subject was further discussed when Kissinger visited Moscow in September and when Gromyko visited Washington in October. Gromyko even tied the Brezhnev return summit visit to progress on this agreement. Then, as earlier noted in his letter of February 1973 to Nixon on the forthcoming summit, Brezhnev referred to his expectation of such an agreement.

Kissinger and Nixon were playing for time and seeking to wear down Soviet pressure for a commitment on the nonuse of nuclear weapons. From the start in the spring of 1972 they wished to keep the idea open to some degree because they believed even continued discussion would keep up Soviet interest in other things of greater interest to the United States. So they stretched out the discussion and negotiation. But by the spring of 1973, with the return summit planned, this tactic could no longer be continued. Accordingly, before Kissinger's May visit to Moscow, Nixon and Kissinger decided to enter into an agreement, but to shift the emphasis from nonuse of nuclear weapons to nonuse of force, with the risks of nuclear war not tied only to initial use of nuclear weapons.[52]

Nixon explains that he and Kissinger suspected that the main Soviet interest was its suspicion that the United States might conclude a military agreement with China—fears he termed "unfounded."[53] At Camp David in June 1973 Nixon assured Brezhnev that "we would never make any arrangement with either China or Japan that was inconsistent with the spirit of the Agreement for the Prevention of Nuclear War."[54]

In negotiating the text of the PNW agreement in Moscow in May 1973, Kissinger operated with great freedom, as he had in April 1972 when he negotiated the Basic Principles. He had only the most general instructions from Nixon, and no one else was involved in clearing positions. One result was an incident in the negotiations that involved an extraordinary diplomatic pirouette, even for Kissinger. Only after considerable discussion and still with reluctance, Brezhnev and Gromyko finally agreed to include a paragraph Kissinger had demanded on "non-intervention in other countries." Within an

51. Kissinger, *Years of Upheaval*, pp. 276–77.

52. Ibid., pp. 276–82.

53. Nixon, *RN*, pp. 880–81.

54. Ibid., p. 882. This promise by Nixon at least modifies the statement by Kissinger reported in footnote 39. There is no explanation for the inclusion of Japan in the statement.

hour Kissinger had had second thoughts on how such a provision would appear to world opinion and withdrew it. The Soviet leaders were highly perplexed."

Although there had been extensive exchanges during the period from July 1972 to May 1973, as noted, Nixon had left this matter entirely in Kissinger's hands. No other element of the U.S. government—including the secretaries of state and defense—were even apprised of the matter. There was, however, a unique—in fact, extraordinary—collaboration between Kissinger and his staff and Sir Thomas Brimelow, the leading British expert on Soviet affairs (and soon after British ambassador in Moscow). Uncharacteristically, Kissinger had asked his equivalent in London, Sir Burke Trend, for advice and that had led to Brimelow's participation. As Kissinger himself notes, "There was no other government which we would have dealt with so openly, exchanged ideas with so freely, or in effect [have] permitted to participate in our own deliberations." Kissinger credits Brimelow with most of the actual drafting. And it was a good job, even if under unorthodox circumstances. The crux of the Kissinger-Brimelow counterdraft was to remove from the Soviet draft anything that smacked of a priority to American-Soviet relations over American-allied relations and that singled out nonuse of nuclear weapons, as contrasted with nonuse of force or threat of force with any weapon.[56]

The Soviet preparation for the negotiation of the PNW agreement was very careful and thorough, but also closely held. During Kissinger's May meetings in Moscow, Brezhnev told him that only a few of his colleagues in the Politburo knew of the PNW project.[57] Assuming that to be true, it is an interesting indication of how the Soviet leadership worked at that time, soon after Gromyko, Andropov, and Grechko had been elevated to the Politburo. In any case the Soviet national security and foreign affairs bureaucracy was deeply involved, in contrast to the total exclusion of the Departments of State and Defense in the United States. The Department for Planning Foreign Policy Measures (UPVM), having reaped the rewards for its leading role in preparing the Basic Principles agreement for the 1972 summit, was given the principal assignment for this task. The PNW agreement was seen as expanding on the Basic Principles, above all in reducing still further the aura of acceptability of resort to military means, especially nuclear weapons.[58]

Both the Soviet Union, as the originator of the PNW agreement, and the United States saw it as an extension of the Basic Principles in develop-

---

55. Interview with a direct participant. Kissinger not surprisingly does not mention this episode in his memoir.

56. Kissinger, *Years of Upheaval*, pp. 278–84.

57. Ibid., p. 283.

58. Interviews with Soviet participants. See also the comment by V. Matveyev that "a great deal of painstaking work" went into preparing the PNW agreement, as well as the SALT agreements. V. Matveyev, "In the Interests of All Peoples," *Izvestiya*, August 7, 1973.

ing both the objective and the means of crisis prevention or crisis mitigation through urgent consultation. It was, however, precisely this element of superpower consultation about potential situations vitally involving third powers that raised concerns in various quarters over a possible emerging U.S.-USSR condominium. While the Soviets saw the chief significance of the PNW agreement as curbing American inclinations to resort to military force in critical situations around the world, Kissinger and Nixon, the only American leaders involved in the decision to conclude the agreement, saw it as an additional element in the web of incentives to Soviet observance of détente. But again, as with the Basic Principles, while Kissinger was an effective diplomatic negotiator, neither he nor the Soviet leaders used the occasion to engage in a real dialogue about the potential contingencies to which the agreement would apply. Each side saw an agreement that might be used to curb the other, but neither considered how the Basic Principles or the PNW agreement would constrain its *own* options and restrain its own behavior. Similarly, after the agreements were concluded, *neither* side engaged even unilaterally, much less together, in policy planning or contingency studies on the application of the principles.[59] Nor has this subject been given the attention it deserves in public commentary.[60]

The Basic Principles of 1972 and the PNW agreement of 1973 contributed to the launching and development of détente, but before long they also contributed to its failure. For these agreed documents on a code of conduct did not really reflect an agreed understanding or consensus on the *substance* of policy restraints. This discrepancy was bound to emerge and create strong feelings that the understandings were being violated and that détente was being betrayed.

Remembering allied dissatisfaction with the absence of consultation or even advance notice of the Basic Principles in 1972, Kissinger decided to consult in advance, although in his fashion—at only the highest levels and only with West Germany, Great Britain, and France—and confidentially to advise China. The U.S. diplomatic establishment was *not* made privy, even when the negotiation was concluded. Accordingly, as earlier noted, Secretary of State Rogers confidently informed the other NATO foreign ministers on May 14 that the United States would not sign anything detrimental to its allies. While a good case can be made that the PNW agreement was not detrimental

---

59. Interviews with Soviet and American policy planning and other officials.

60. There is one notable exception: Alexander L. George has studied crisis prevention and the efforts in this field begun in the Soviet-American détente of the 1970s, in particular in the Basic Principles and PNW agreement. See Alexander L. George, *Towards a Soviet-American Crisis Prevention Regime: History and Prospects*, ACIS Working Paper 28 (Los Angeles: University of California at Los Angeles, 1980); and Alexander L. George, ed., *Managing U.S.-Soviet Rivalry: Problems of Crisis Prevention* (Boulder, Colo.: Westview, 1983), especially chaps. 1, 2, 5, 15.

to the interests of the allies, it was clearly something in which they were keenly interested. Ambassador Donald H. Rumsfeld, then the U.S. permanent representative at the North Atlantic Council (NAC) in Brussels, informed the allies on June 21, the day before the PNW agreement was signed, of the bland forthcoming principles on further SALT negotiations, and stated flatly that it was "the only agreement on SALT which will be entered into" at the summit conference.[61] Again, while the PNW agreement was not strictly speaking a SALT agreement, the last discussion of the subject of nonuse of nuclear weapons had been in NATO consultations on SALT in 1971, when the United States had informed the council that it had rejected the Soviet probe of the subject in December 1970.[62]

On the morning of June 22, a few hours before signature, Secretary Rogers briefed the ambassadors of the NATO countries in Washington, while Ambassador Rumsfeld (with new last-minute instructions) briefed the NATO representatives in Brussels, and other senior State Department officials briefed the ambassadors of Japan, Australia, New Zealand, Israel, and Egypt. There were complaints from representatives of several NATO allies at the lack of advance notification, much less consultation. In fact, in a rather stormy NAC meeting in Brussels the British representative criticized what was in large part, though unbeknownst to him, a text drafted by his compatriot, Brimelow. The American delegation also had to call the permanent representative of West Germany out of the chamber to inform him that Chancellor Willy Brandt had been consulted in advance and had expressed no objection. All in all it was a situation of acute mutual embarrassment.[63] There were further grumblings when Kissinger responded to questions at a press conference that same day that the United States had "consulted several countries prior to the completion of this document" and also that "several NATO allies were closely consulted over an extended period." He declined to name the countries or to

---

61. From a participant at the NAC meeting.

62. The NAC discussion took place on February 24, 1971. There had also been an earlier consultation with the NAC on some draft objectives and principles for SALT, introduced on January 15, 1969, almost literally the last minute, by the outgoing Johnson administration. One of those principles was "to minimize the possible accidental appearance of conflict-fraught situations involving the use of strategic armaments" (originally it was a Soviet proposal, although *not* so identified to the allies). A number of them objected to that principle, as well as, in some cases, to the idea of any general, agreed-on, codified principles for SALT. That draft was not pursued further with the Soviets or the allies, but the consultation should have been known to Kissinger's staff and allied sensitivity on this subject taken into account. I participated in both presentations to the NAC.

63. Kissinger caustically notes the British and German NAC criticisms, although without mentioning the details I have noted here. Kissinger, *Years of Upheaval*, p. 286. He also charges that "for reasons of their own the leaders of Britain and West Germany had not kept their bureaucracies informed," when in fact *he* had stressed the need for the strictest secrecy in his discussion with those leaders. Ibid.

respond to a question about whether China had been consulted. As noted, the top leaders of the three major European NATO allies had been consulted (and the Chinese advised and reassured in advance).[64] Even those countries, however, except Britain, did not have much opportunity to advise and none to consent. Many others were chagrined that they had not been favored by inclusion in the select group consulted in advance. Negative allied reaction appeared at many levels and in varying contexts for months.

The most damaging commentary on the state of American consultation with its allies was the fact that when Brezhnev visited Paris on his way back to Moscow from the United States, he stressed to President Georges Pompidou that one of his main purposes in making the stop was to reassure France, and through it other European countries, that no agreements had been made between the USSR and the United States that would adversely affect other countries. And his comment was not rebuffed.[65]

Finally, a special meeting was arranged for the NATO Permanent Representatives to meet with Kissinger at San Clemente on June 30. In the face of hostile questioning he took a tactical offensive on the substance of the accord as a way of dealing with his defensiveness over allied criticism of the lack of consultation. He admitted there had been no real consultation on the PNW agreement but pointed out that there had been on SALT and other agreements. He described the PNW as "a very delicate negotiation" in which the United States had "turned around a Soviet proposal for a non-aggression pact" and had foiled Soviet efforts to single out nuclear weapons. He said it was "beneficial to the Alliance" and that it was "not in the Alliance interest to criticize it." Kissinger stressed that no distinction would be made in time of war between nuclear or other weapons on the basis of the agreement, which concerns restraint in peacetime, not strategy in war. Moreover, he said that Nixon and he had discussed the American understanding fully with Brezhnev and Gromyko. (Naturally he did not explain that virtually all the discussion had occurred during his visit to Moscow in May.) He acidly remarked that the United States had not been "beguiled by Soviet charms."[66]

Allied disgruntlement, while not deep, did persist and boiled up again at the December 1973 NATO ministerial meeting in Brussels, most directly in comments by French Foreign Minister Michel Jobert.[67] This occasion was, incidentally, Kissinger's debut at such meetings as secretary of state.

---

64. At the press conference Kissinger declined to answer the question whether he had discussed the PNW agreement with the head of the Chinese liaison office, whom he had seen a few days earlier. *The Washington Summit*, pp. 33–34. He had.

65. Communication from a participant at the meeting.

66. From the account of a participant. See also Flora Lewis, "Soviet Bid for Police Role with the U.S. Is Reported," *New York Times*, July 22, 1973; and Marilyn Berger, "Many U.S. Allies Worried by Recent Summit," *Washington Post*, July 14, 1973.

67. Marilyn Berger, "Kissinger in Clash at NATO," *Washington Post*, December 11, 1973; and Flora Lewis, "U.S.-French Clash Opens NATO Talks," *New York Times*, December 11, 1973.

The two focal points of allied concern, which subsequently faded, were discontent over yet another instance of surprise and lack of consultation in American dealings with the Soviet Union, and uncertainty over a possible American tendency to substitute its interest in negotiations with the Soviet Union for the priority accorded the alliance. Only the most extreme allied (and some neutral) critics really feared an American shift toward a condominium world order under the two superpowers.

Allied concern over the decoupling of nuclear weapons, through implied restraint on their use to meet a non-nuclear military threat, was stirred again when Brezhnev subsequently publicly interpreted the PNW agreement as meaning that "in effect, the United States assumed the obligation not to use nuclear weapons and force in general against the Soviet Union, its allies and other countries."[68] The United States reaffirmed its interpretation to its allies and to the Soviets, who clearly knew they were tilting the formulation they had used for the audience in Havana, although Soviet commentators continued on occasion to bend their interpretation.

Reaction in the United States was somewhat skeptical of the value of the accord, but generally neutral. The questioning mood was expressed in the heading of the main commentary in the *Washington Post*, "A-Pact: Policy Paper or Bold Venture?" Commentary elsewhere seemed to answer the question in the former direction—the *Philadelphia Inquirer*, for example, proclaimed: "Agreements Are Mostly Ballyhoo."[69] As the *Post* account concluded, and as Kissinger himself indicated, "Whether the agreement proves to be meaningful, or meaningless, depends not on the document itself, but what Washington and Moscow choose to do about it. It can be either another piece of international paper or a bold venture in international affairs."[70]

President Nixon characterized the PNW agreement not only as important in U.S.-Soviet bilateral relations, but also as "a landmark agreement for the whole world." Conceding that it depended on the will to carry forward its spirit, he stressed that the agreement took on "added meaning because of the personal relationship" that had been developed—a theme Nixon found useful to stress, given his own growing political vulnerability. He continued, in typical hyperbole, to state that "it means that we are dedicating ourselves to build a new era not only of peace between our two great countries but of building an era in which there can be peace for all the people of the world."[71]

---

68. L. I. Brezhnev, *O vneshnei politike KPSS i sovetskogo gosudarstva: Rechi i stat'i* [On the Foreign Policy of the CPSU and the Soviet Government: Speeches and Articles], 3d ed. (Moscow: Politizdat, 1978), p. 387. This statement was made at a general public meeting in Havana, Cuba, on January 29, 1974.

69. Murrey Marder, "A-Pact: Policy Paper or Bold Venture?" *Washington Post*, June 23, 1973; and James McCartney, "Agreements Are Mostly Ballyhoo," *Philadelphia Inquirer*, June 25, 1973.

70. Marder, *Washington Post*, June 23, 1973.

71. *The Washington Summit*, pp. 41–42. These statements were made in Nixon's public remarks on the occasion of Brezhnev's departure from San Clemente, June 24, 1973.

Brezhnev, too, described the PNW agreement as having "historic significance." He also praised the agreement to continue the SALT negotiations as meaning that "political détente is being backed up by military détente," and he endorsed the idea of the two countries working together to "win the peace."[72]

In the communiqué on the summit, Nixon and Brezhnev joined in stating that the PNW agreement "constitutes a historical landmark in Soviet-American relations and substantially strengthens the foundations of international security as a whole."[73]

In a series of three major press conferences during and after the summit meeting, Kissinger provided the administration's assessment and general line of interpretation of the various agreements and of the summit as a whole. He repeated his view of the year before that the first summit had produced a "roadmap" for "certain principles of conduct" and placed the PNW agreement in that context as well. It was the elaboration of control over nuclear weapons "in a political and diplomatic sense," with emphasis on the formalization of American-Soviet consultation. (These remarks, needless to say, did not sit well with some of the allies to whom the United States was stressing that nuclear weapons were not unduly singled out and that there would be no condominium of consultation and negotiation.) Kissinger had initiated use of the term "landmark" when he said on June 22 that the PNW agreement can be "a significant landmark" in bilateral relations between the two countries "and in the relationships of the two great nuclear countries toward all other countries of the world" (shades of condominium again). He further described the agreement as "a significant step toward the prevention of nuclear war and the prevention of military conflict." It constituted a formal obligation of the two powers "to practice restraint in their diplomacy" toward each other "and, equally important, toward all other countries" and to build a "permanent" peace; it "could make a landmark on the road toward the structure of peace of which the President has been speaking" since 1969. In answer to questions challenging the agreement, he added that "the purpose of this agreement is to legalize, to symbolize, and to bring about restraint on the part of the two nuclear superpowers in their international relationship" (again, condominium) and that "it cannot be approached from the point of view of a sharp lawyer pushing against the limits of every clause because if that is going to be the attitude, the agreement will not have any significance."[74]

---

72. Ibid., pp. 43–48. Brezhnev's remarks were made in a nationwide American TV and radio address broadcast on June 24, 1973.

73. Ibid., p. 50.

74. Ibid., pp. 31–33. These particular quotations are all from Kissinger's news conference of June 22 in Washington, immediately following signature and release of the PNW agreement. His other news conferences were on June 21, devoted mainly to the SALT negotiations, and June 25, at which he reviewed the accomplishments of the summit conference as a whole and the communiqué on the conference.

In his memoir a decade later Kissinger not only makes clear the marginal American interest in the PNW agreement at the time, but states that "in retrospect I doubt whether the result was worth the effort," because while the agreement itself was sound and "marginally useful . . . the result was too subtle; the negotiation too secret; the effort too protracted; the necessary explanation to allies and China too complex to have the desired impact."[75] Both at the time and now, Kissinger gives no consideration whatsoever to the effects of the PNW agreement on Soviet thinking, politics, and policy. While it would be naïve to take such an agreement at face value, a geopolitician's naïveté in dismissing a priori any possible political impact within the Soviet Union and on Soviet-American relations is remarkable.

It is clear from the presentations and explanations by Nixon and Kissinger that they, like Brezhnev, regarded the PNW agreement as essentially a political step rather than as a technical instrument for crisis prevention and management. For example, the only reference to the earlier 1971 agreement on measures to prevent accidental or unauthorized use of nuclear weapons appeared in the recitation of past accomplishments in the SALT negotiating principles (and one reference by Kissinger to that mention), an omission with respect to the content of the PNW agreement noted by some commentaries.[76]

The second summit amounted to the consolidation of a new phase in the building of a continuing relationship of détente between the two powers. This attitude was clearly signaled by Kissinger in his news conference after the summit. He commented that in 1972 "the fact of peaceful coexistence required special affirmation and the possibility of improving relations between the United States and the Soviet Union was thought deserving of special note, and this year we are speaking of a continuing relationship." He sought to offset any letdown from the lesser gains of the second meeting in comparison with the spectacular advance that marked the first one by noting that summit meetings were becoming "a regular part" of the American-Soviet relationship. "It is the strength of this relationship as it develops," he continued, "that the road is charted and that what we expect to see is a further evolution along a path which will be increasingly free of confrontation and which will become increasingly a part of a stable international system."[77]

The decision by Nixon and Kissinger to conclude the PNW agreement owed more to Soviet persistence, coupled with the absence of any other really new initiative, than to any enthusiasm over the accord itself or any effect it was likely to have on Soviet behavior. In terms of U.S. behavior, the only consideration—although a very active one—was that it not even appear to affect American commitments or means of meeting those commitments.

---

75. Kissinger, *Years of Upheaval,* pp. 285–86.

76. In particular, see the earlier cited article by McCartney, *Philadelphia Inquirer,* June 25, 1973.

77. *The Washington Summit,* comments from Kissinger's press conference, San Clemente, June 25, p. 53.

In response to a question at the press conference about concern over superpower condominium, Kissinger declared that "we have not agreed, and we shall not agree nor were we asked to agree, to anything that smacks of superpower condominium," but that "we believe that we have a common interest with the Soviet Union in promoting a peaceful order. We believe also that to the extent that a more peaceful conduct emerges . . . all nations bene-fit."[78]

On SALT, Kissinger stated with some exaggeration that "you can assume" that the two leaders had further "extensive discussions" on how to reach a permanent SALT agreement, and he stressed the "considerable hope" that such an agreement could be reached during 1974. There was really little more that could be said at the time.

Soviet Policy Achievements—and Problems

American interest in and attention to the summit and the PNW agreement rapidly receded. In the Soviet Union, however, the agreement re-mained the subject of frequent reference as a major achievement and of occa-sional detailed commentary. (In one important respect, as will be seen, it also precipitated a veiled internal debate over the impact of détente on military requirements.) In addition, paralleling the doubts and dissatisfactions ex-pressed to the United States by a number of allies and friends, a number of Soviet allies and friends also expressed uneasiness and indirect and private criticism to Moscow.

The divergence in the Soviet and American assessments of the PNW accord first emerged in the different treatment given it in initial com-ments at San Clemente immediately after signature. The Soviet press spokes-man, Leonid M. Zamyatin, issued an additional statement in Brezhnev's name on the first day after the signature "in view of the tremendous interest shown in the agreement." Citing Brezhnev, Zamyatin stated, "The crux of this agree-ment is to rule out the possibility of nuclear war between the United States and the Soviet Union. It also sets the aim of excluding an outbreak of nuclear war between either of the parties and other countries." He further said that "without doubt" it would have "a profound impact on the entire international situation."[79] The official Moscow TASS release of Zamyatin's statement two days later included those statements but went even further—the PNW agree-ment was described as "one of the most significant agreements in contempo-

---

78. Ibid., p. 56.

79. Quoted in the excellent reportage on this entire subject by Murrey Marder, "Brezhnev Extolls A-Pact," *Washington Post*, June 24, 1973.

rary international relations."[80] This praise was carried even further in an unsigned editorial in the Soviet academic journal on American affairs, which described the PNW agreement as "one of the most important documents in the history of international relations."[81]

In the United States there was little reference to the PNW agreement in the days and months following. In contrast, favorable Soviet references have continued. In the first year or so after the agreement was reached there were literally dozens of specific references by prominent Soviet leaders and in the political, military and popular press, with several major articles devoted entirely to it. Brezhnev himself went out of his way to praise the PNW agreement not only in domestic speeches but also, for example, in France, to the World Peace Congress, and more surprisingly to Vietnamese visitors in Moscow and to a Cuban audience in Havana. He described its significance as "enormous," "difficult to exaggerate," and a "major step in détente." In the Soviet Union the PNW agreement is usually ranked, together with the Basic Principles agreement of 1972 and the SALT I agreements (after the former and before the latter), as—to use Brezhnev's words to the Twenty-fifth Party Congress—"undoubtedly the most important" of the numerous Soviet-American accords.[82]

A joint statement of the party Politburo, the Supreme Soviet Presidium, and the Council of Ministers emphasized that the entire party and government leadership "entirely and completely approved the political and practical results of the visit, which has great fundamental significance and is an event of tremendous importance." The results were judged to constitute "convincing new proof of the strength and viability of the Leninist policy of peaceful coexistence" and the Peace Program adopted in 1971 by the Twenty-fourth Party Congress. The statement recalled that the Basic Principles agreed to at the 1972 summit marked "the beginning of a turn from distrust to détente." The "successful" new summit was said to have "laid a good foundation for the normal development of Soviet-American relations." The PNW agreement, of "permanent" (that is, indefinite) duration, was hailed as "an important step on the path to lessening and eventually to eliminating the threat of the outbreak of nuclear war and to creating a system of real guarantees of international security," and the "implementation in practice" of the Basic Principles and PNW agreements "will have truly historic importance for all mankind."[83] Thus

---

80. TASS, Radio Moscow, June 25, in Foreign Broadcast Information Service, *Daily Report: Soviet Union*, June 25, 1973, p. AA4. (Hereafter FBIS, *Soviet Union*.)

81. Editorial, "A New, Big Step Forward," *SShA: Ekonomika, politika, ideologiya* [USA: Economics, Politics, Ideology], no. 8 (August 1973), p. 3. (Hereafter *SShA*.)

82. Brezhnev, *O vneshnei politike*, p. 520, and see the references on pp. 284, 290, 294, 301, 305, 345, 387, 400. The listing of these three key agreements, in which the PNW follows the Basic Principles agreement and precedes SALT, was standard after 1973.

83. "On the Results of Comrade L. I. Brezhnev's Visit to the United States of America," *Pravda*, June 30, 1973.

the collective leadership, while fully endorsing the steps taken, was still somewhat cautious in predicting American fulfillment of the code of conduct and therefore the ultimate achievement of "historic" results. Indeed, this concern was made crystal clear in another passage referring to the entire developing Soviet-American détente relationship: "The consistent and steadfast fulfillment by both states of all the commitments they have assumed is the precondition for making Soviet-American relations a permanent factor of international peace, ensuring the irreversibility of the currently developing processes of détente."[84]

This theme of striving to make détente irreversible had been introduced in the Resolution of the April 1973 Central Committee plenum and was thereafter widely used by Soviet leaders and spokesmen until détente deteriorated sharply in the late 1970s.

While the Soviet leaders submerged any doubts or differences that may have existed among themselves over the commitment to developing a détente with the United States, there were signs that they recognized disquiet in the world communist movement and among other countries. Concern over the emerging American-Soviet détente arose both within the American-led alliance and in the Soviet camp. China and other countries, including some nonaligned ones, particularly those that sought to profit from American-Soviet competition, were troubled by what was happening. In some cases the expressions of concern, for example, over superpower condominium, probably were genuine. But in others they were disingenuous. Most of the disquiet originated in reaction to the overall development of Soviet-American détente. The PNW agreement, however, served as a particular focus or lightning rod attracting both genuine and pretended concern.

Soviet efforts to neutralize that dissatisfaction were aimed at the Chinese, who were clearly unhappy at the development of the U.S.-USSR détente, and at those who might be influenced by Chinese arguments. It was also aimed at Western, neutral, or other countries worried about condominium of the superpowers. The day the PNW agreement was signed TASS made the specific disclaimer that the accord was not directed against other countries or their interests.[85] While the Soviet press was filled with references to widespread approval and support for the Soviet-American agreements, a number of accounts also referred to negative reactions from various quarters. Some referred to sincere but misguided apprehensions, some to shocked and unhappy reactions of those (in NATO and China) who still supported the cold war. Many referred to "fabrications" about "alleged collusion between the two superpowers," often specifically referring in this context to the PNW agreement.[86] As

---

84. Ibid.

85. TASS, Radio Moscow, June 22, in FBIS, *Soviet Union*, June 22, 1973 pp. AA19–20.

86. For example, see M. Kudrin, "An Important Step toward Strengthening Peace," *Mezhdunarodnaya zhizn'* [International Life], no. 9 (September 1973), pp. 16–18; A. Bovin, "A Clear Position," *Izvestiya*, July 25, 1973; *Sovetskaya rossiya* [Soviet Russia], June 25, 1973;

late as the anniversary of the Bolshevik Revolution in November, Politburo member Andrei P. Kirilenko railed against "fabrications on superpower condominium."[87]

Nor was the matter limited to polemics in the press. Just as the United States privately received critical questions from a number of allies (and neutrals), so did the Soviet Union. Among those objecting were North Vietnam, not only at the idea of condominium, but at the call by the communiqué that *both* sides respect the peace settlement; Egypt again; and India.[88] Noted earlier was Brezhnev's reassurance to France.

On the other hand, the Soviets were guilty of a rare advance leak on the PNW agreement that could only have been an attempt to stir up concern on the part of China and Israel (in fact, both were very cool to the agreement). Victor Louis, a shadowy character serving as a widely known unofficial Soviet agent, supplied an article printed in the London *Evening News* (and in a Tel Aviv newspaper) on June 19, three days *before* the PNW agreement was signed and before the United States informed most of its allies and friends about it. His article stated: "Just now the signing of an agreement on the prevention of nuclear war would be a logical and crowning move in the new Soviet-American relations. If both sides would guarantee to curb a third country's use of nuclear arms, the world could really relax for the first time since the holocaust that ended World War Two."[89] Was Moscow trying to create doubts in Israel about U.S. security assurances? (Victor Louis was then in Tel Aviv, attending a meeting of the International Press Institute. At the time of the 1972 summit he had been in Taiwan. The Soviet Union does not of course have formal diplomatic relations with either Israel or Taiwan.)

For their part the Soviets, alert to such matters, have charged that the Chinese timed their fifteenth nuclear weapons test in June 1973 to coincide with the Soviet-American PNW agreement.[90]

V. Berezin, Radio Moscow, August 22, in FBIS, *Soviet Union*, August 22, 1973, pp. B2–3; and Yu. Zhukov and B. Strelnikov, "A Great Success," *Pravda*, June 24, 1973.

87. A. Kirilenko, "The Cause of October Lives in the Achievements of the Party and the People," *Pravda*, November 7, 1973.

88. See the informative account by Hedrick Smith, "Soviet Publicly Assures Its Allies That the New Accords with the U.S. Do Not Jeopardize Their Interests," *New York Times*, July 29, 1973.

89. Report from Victor Louis, "Brezhnev, Nixon Set to Sign World Peace Pact," *Evening News* (London), June 19, 1973; and Reuters dispatch from Tel Aviv of the same date.

90. See B. N. Zanegin, "On Some Aspects of American-Chinese Relations," *SShA*, no. 2 (February 1975), p. 41. Zanegin also noted that the sixteenth Chinese test coincided with the third Soviet-American summit a year later.

Soviet sensitivity to such subtle military demonstrations suggests that perhaps the Soviet ICBM tests spanning Soviet Asia immediately prior to Kissinger's visit to China in February 1973 may also have been more than coincidence.

Sensitive to criticisms that the improvement of relations with the United States at the second summit reflected or foreshadowed lessened Soviet support for national liberation and revolutionary progressive forces abroad, the Soviets reiterated their position that "a world without military cataclysms, and the consistent implementation of the Leninist principle of coexistence between states with different social systems—a principle which is the backbone of the agreement on preventing nuclear war—not only do not contradict the struggle of peoples for their national liberation, but on the contrary create more favorable conditions for it."[91] A leading Central Committee official intoned defensively in *Pravda* that "only those who are politically naïve can argue that we are witnessing some 'understanding between capitalism and socialism' at the cost of the Third World."[92] A number of accounts stressed that the Vietnam settlement with U.S. military withdrawal was a positive result of détente and "the most clear demonstration" of détente serving the struggle against imperialism.[93] The most adventuresome commentator went so far as to recall that President Nixon had met in Moscow with the Soviet leaders in May 1972 just after mining Haiphong and that throughout the nine days of the first summit meeting "occupied with talks about peaceful coexistence between the two great powers, Vietnamese patriots armed with Soviet weapons were shooting down American planes and fighting the American invaders on the ground. A paradox? No, but a striking illustration of how complex are the courses of world politics, how intricate the knots tied by the actual movement of world events. An illustration of how closely intertwined are the two basic lines of Soviet foreign policy—peaceful coexistence with the capitalist states, and fraternal assistance and support for the progressive, anti-imperialist forces." He argued that "the superficial mind" sees a contradiction and calls either for coexistence and no support for independence and social progress, or internationalism and no work toward cooperation between socialist and capitalist states.[94] But the Soviets deny the need for such a choice.

Turning to the substance of the accord, Soviet commentary on the PNW agreement stressed that "it is noteworthy that this most important So-

91. Kudrin, *Mezhdunarodnaya zhizn'*, no. 9 (1973), p. 15; and see D. Volsky, "Peaceful Coexistence and the Third World," *Soviet Military Review* (Moscow), no. 1 (January 1973), pp. 52–54; O. Mikhailov, "A Turn toward Cooperation," *Soviet Military Review*, no. 8 (August 1973), pp. 44–46; and A. Kiva, "Détente and the National Liberation Movement," *Soviet Military Review*, no. 7 (July 1974), pp. 49–51.

92. K. Brutents, "Relaxation of International Tensions and the Developing Countries," *Pravda*, August 30, 1973. Brutents is a deputy chief of the International Department of the Central Committee responsible for relations with third world countries.

93. F. Ryzhenko, "Peaceful Coexistence and the Class Struggle," *Pravda*, August 22, 1973; and V. Osipov, "Détente—Nothing Is Given," *Novoye vremya* [New Times], no. 7 (February 15, 1974), p. 8.

94. A. Bovin, "Internationalism and Co-Existence," *New Times* (Moscow), no. 30 (July 1973), p. 18.

viet-American agreement, which came into force upon signature, is concluded for an unlimited period" and therefore cannot be regarded as merely a "temporary accommodation."[95] It was also, according to another commentary, "irreversible."[96] Underlying the Soviet attributions of significance to the agreement is the view that, as with détente in general (as seen in the early and mid-1970s), the agreement consolidated "the actual state of affairs in relations between the Soviet Union and the United States on matters of war and peace" and was a "reflection of the contemporary correlation of forces on a broader plane between capitalism and socialism in the world arena."[97] In short, the Soviets saw the PNW agreement as representing an important American *political* recognition of Soviet attainment of military parity, *and* of the unsuitability of resorting to the threat or use of military power to serve the political objectives of capitalism.

Apart from believing that the American move to détente and agreement on such measures as SALT and the PNW agreement reflected a new objective relationship of relative power, the Soviets recognize that "the presence of the necessary political will for such steps [SALT and the PNW] was of great importance to their success."[98] While Soviet policy and political efforts are credited with attaining these successes, it was acknowledged that "the American side also has displayed an understanding . . . and joined efforts in order to secure the necessary change in Soviet-American relations."[99] The PNW agreement "bears witness to the extremely important changes in the views of American political and military leaders."[100] And the American attitude toward the Soviet Union was said (in 1973) to have taken "a radical turn toward improvement," contributing to the "historic shift in the relations between the USSR and the USA" marked by the second summit.[101] The American public opinion polls showed some shifts. On the eve of the first summit 60 percent of the public interviewed characterized relations as cold war. By the time of the second summit 66 percent believed relations had improved and 70 percent supported SALT and increased economic ties.[102] To be sure, Soviet

95. E. Baskakov, TASS, Radio Moscow, July 4, in FBIS, *Soviet Union*, July 5, 1973, p. AA1.

96. Valentin Zorin and Vitaly Kobysh, "Studio Nine," Moscow Television, January 31, in FBIS, *Soviet Union*, February 9, 1981, p. CC9.

97. Kudrin, *Mezhdunarodnaya zhizn'*, no. 9 (1973), p. 14.

98. V. Matveyev, "In the Interests of All Peoples," *Izvestiya*, August 7, 1973.

99. Editorial, *SShA*, no. 8 (1973), p. 4.

100. G. Trofimenko, "In a Pivotal Direction," *Mirovaya ekonomika i mezhdunarodnye otnosheniya* [The World Economy and International Relations], no. 2 (February 1975), p. 6.

101. A. Gromyko and A. Kokoshin, "US Foreign Policy Strategy for the 1970s," *International Affairs* (Moscow), no. 10 (October 1973), pp. 69–70.

102. Arbatov, *Pravda*, July 22, 1973, reports these data from the Gallup and Harris polls.

analysts also continued in the early and middle 1970s to warn that there was still resistance in the military-industrial complex and others opposed to détente in the United States, and that reverses could occur.[103]

One commentator, in noting the progress in developing a détente from mid-1971 to mid-1973, boldly recalled that the United States had escalated the Vietnamese hostilities by mining Haiphong less than two weeks before the planned summit in May 1972: "And one can quite understand those who felt that this new piece of adventurism blocked the way from Washington to Moscow. But feelings are one thing, politics another. The visit went through."[104] Adumbrating a theme first stated by Brezhnev in Washington, a Soviet political observer later characterized the first summit meeting as having laid "a good beginning for the normalization of relations," while the second "not only consolidated the progress that was accomplished last year, but was a mighty stimulus" for the future. "Whereas in 1972 the U.S. leaders expressed a readiness to formulate relations with the Soviet Union on the basis of the principle of peaceful coexistence and equal security, in 1973 the sides moved from the stage of approval of peaceful coexistence to the stage of transforming it into the general instrument of policy relative to one another and relative to the world." Moreover, "the signing of the Soviet-U.S. agreement, of indefinite duration on the prevention of nuclear war was *the most important step* on this path."[105]

The Soviets were interested above all in having the PNW agreement with the United States, as it was the other (and leading) superpower. They also wanted other countries to accept the same approach. The question of the accession of other countries to the PNW agreement had never been raised with the United States before its signature, and the stress on a bilateral relationship at the summit was natural. Almost immediately afterwards, however, the Soviets sought to get other countries to associate themselves with it. The first indication was in the joint party-government statement, in which the whole leadership endorsed the summit conference and the PNW agreement and expressed "the conviction that the readiness of other states to adhere to the principles of the renunciation of the use of force and of taking resolute steps to exclude the outbreak of nuclear war" would greatly contribute to international security.[106] This idea was picked up in a number of Soviet commentaries that summer and fall, usually with specific reference to the official statement. Gromyko included such an invitation to "endorse the principles" of

---

103. Ibid.

104. Bovin, *New Times*, no. 30 (July 1973), p. 18.

105. V. Korionov, "The Soviet Union and the United States on the Path of Détente," Radio Moscow Domestic Service, November 15, in FBIS, *Soviet Union*, November 15, 1973, p. B4. Emphasis added.

106. *Pravda*, June 30, 1973.

the PNW agreement in his speech to the UN General Assembly in September.[107]

Meanwhile, in August 1973 the Soviets made a private diplomatic approach to Great Britain proposing accession to the PNW agreement—without consulting or even advising the United States. This approach was turned aside by the British after consulting Washington. (The Soviets may also have made such a probe to France.) It was a curious and unusually awkward move for the Soviets to raise the question of accession with another country—and a close American ally at that—without having first discussed the matter with the United States.

The essence of the PNW agreement was that it extended the general policy of avoiding confrontations and the risks of war (also embodied in the Basic Principles) by including agreement to engage in urgent consultations to defuse political tensions *before* crises arose, as well as dealing with actual crises. In other words, it marked a further step toward developing a *crisis prevention* as well as a *crisis management* arrangement between the two nuclear superpowers. It thus built upon both the technical Agreement on Measures to Reduce the Risk of Outbreak of Nuclear War Between the United States of America and the Union of Soviet Socialist Republics, which had been signed on September 30, 1971, and the hot line direct communications link established in 1963 and modernized (with satellite communications) pursuant to another agreement that was also signed on September 30, 1971. It also built on the political Basic Principles signed in May 1972. The 1971 agreements were a spin-off from the SALT negotiations, designed to facilitate understanding and communications, particularly in the case of any accidental or unauthorized use or detonation of a nuclear weapon, so that the other side would not misinterpret the activity as an attack. The agreements were negotiated in SALT in 1970–71 and signed by Secretary of State Rogers and Foreign Minister Gromyko.[108]

Some Soviet commentaries have discussed, at least briefly, the arms control or crisis prevention role of the PNW agreement (although the general thrust of most discussions, as indicated earlier, has been on the political and policy significance). Academician Georgy Arbatov, noting that the prevention of nuclear war was "the most important area of congruent interests" of the two sides, held that the Basic Principles and PNW agreements reflected a realistic and far-reaching effort that went beyond a mere declaration of desire not to

---

107. "Speech of A. A. Gromyko," *Pravda*, September 26, 1973. One commentary went beyond the usual line to suggest, somewhat inaccurately, that the PNW agreement "in effect invites other countries to align themselves with its objectives"; see Kudrin, *Mezhdunarodnaya zhizn'*, no. 9 (1973), p. 13.

108. The texts of the agreements are in U.S. Arms Control and Disarmament Agency, *Arms Control and Disarmament Agreements* (GPO, 1980), pp. 28–33, 109–19. The White House held back from authorizing signature until the timing of the first summit meeting was agreed on in the fall of 1971, but decided not to hold up actual conclusion of the agreements during the eight months prior to the summit.

allow such a war. He argued, with much insight, the need for the development of three further conditions: "improvement of relations between the two countries and the growth of their mutual understanding and trust," "serious improvements in the international situation," and—pointing also to crisis prevention and management—"the prevention of new conflicts and crises and the creation of a mechanism that would make it possible in a timely way to resolve emerging problems through negotiation."[109]

Other Soviet commentators stressed "the urgent consultations which are provided for in the [PNW] agreement and are aimed at eliminating the risk of a nuclear conflict." Among these are technical military, as well as military-political, circumstances, especially "in the age of high-speed missiles." The Washington-Moscow direct communications link (DCL) has been provided for these contingencies "to insure technically the possibility of such consultations."[110]

With respect to prevention of political-military crises, one Soviet commentator cited with approval *Time* magazine's characterization of the PNW agreement as "a code of nuclear conduct."[111] Another linked the Basic Principles and PNW agreements together and characterized them as occupying "the central place in the chain of measures aimed at eliminating the threat of war from relations among states."[112]

The conclusion of the PNW agreement and the prominent attention given it in the Soviet Union posed a problem for the Soviet military establishment. There is no indication that the provisions of the agreement, or its purpose, or indeed its signature, were in any way opposed by the Soviet military. The PNW agreement was, however, concluded at a time when military theoreticians (and propagandists) were involved in a debate over the implications of détente. It was also a time when elements in the military establishment were concerned over maintaining the rationale for continued high outlays for their military programs. Some concern was expressed, unmistakably even though indirectly, that the widely praised PNW agreement could be taken to mean that the possibility of war was receding to an extent that would undercut the standard rationale for continuing a steady program to enhance military capabilities.

---

109. Arbatov, *Pravda*, July 22, 1973.

110. Matveyev, *Izvestiya*, August 7, 1973. See also Spartak Beglov, "Mr. Brezhnev's Visit," *New York Times*, June 29, 1973, a relatively early discussion stressing the need for urgent political-military consultation.

    The Direct Communications Link (DCL) is known more popularly in the United States as "the hot line" and in the Soviet Union as "the red line."

111. Kudrin, *Mezhdunarodnaya zhizn'*, no. 9 (1973), p. 15.

112. V. F. Petrovsky, "The Role and Place of Soviet-American Relations in the Contemporary World," *Voprosy istorii* [Questions of History], no. 10 (October 1978), p. 88. See also M. Kudrin, "Eliminate the Possibility of Nuclear War," *Soviet Military Review*, no. 2 (February 1974), pp. 55–56.

As early as the period following the first summit meeting, a political officer writing in the armed forces daily *Red Star* had cautioned any who might be inclined to believe that implementation of the principle of peaceful coexistence would "permit a slackening in our military preparedness." He said that would be "shortsighted politically" and not justified.[113] Two months following the second summit meeting, the chief of the propaganda department of *Red Star* again warned that some "military theorists and publicists" were returning to the question of the implication of nuclear weapons for the role of military power and that "many of them are linking their interpretation of this question with détente and the Soviet-American Agreement on the Prevention of Nuclear War." The author, Colonel I. Sidel'nikov, was careful to praise the PNW agreement as "a major act" and a "step of great importance." He also referred approvingly to the earlier Basic Principles. And he endorsed "the even more firm establishment of the principles of peaceful coexistence" as helping to "strengthen international security." "But," he continued, "it would be erroneous to believe that the danger of war has already been fully and finally removed." The PNW agreement "substantially decreases the possibility of such a war . . . but this agreement is not yet a ban on nuclear weapons." Moreover, it does not include the other nuclear powers. Accordingly, "as our military theorists consider, so long as this complicated problem remains unresolved, and the aggressive forces of imperialism and all kinds of adventurists [that is, China] are at work, there remains a requirement to be prepared to wage a war with any weapons."[114]

A number of articles in the Soviet press in 1973 and 1974 carried on a continuing debate over the implications of détente for defense requirements. These articles often, although not consistently, took a military versus civilian cast. None directly challenged either détente or defense, but various issues (including military theory, prospective threats of war, consequences of a nuclear war, and possible rechanneling of military expenditures to civilian uses) were addressed and indirectly, or sometimes even directly, "debated."[115] The

---

113. Colonel V. Khalipov, "Peaceful Coexistence and the Defense of Socialism," *Krasnaya zvezda* [Red Star], July 21, 1972.

114. Colonel I. Sidel'nikov, "Peaceful Coexistence and the Security of Nations," *Krasnaya zvezda*, August 14, 1973.

115. In addition to Colonel Sidel'nikov's article, others stressed military vigilance and preparedness. See Captain First Rank N. Shumikhin, "Socialism and International Relations," *Krasnaya zvezda*, September 13, 1973; Colonel Ye. Rybkin, "The Leninist Conception of Nuclear War and the Present Day," *Kommunist vooruzhennykh sil* [Communist of the Armed Forces], no. 20 (October 1973); Rear Admiral V. Shelyag, "Two World Outlooks—Two Views on War," *Krasnaya zvezda*, February 7, 1974; and Army General Ye. Maltsev, "Leninist Ideas on the Defense of Socialism," *Krasnaya zvezda*, February 14, 1974. For discussions where the main emphasis is on détente, see, for example, the various articles by Academician Georgy Arbatov, especially *Pravda*, July 22, 1973; "Types of Political Force," *Problemy mira i sotsializma* [Problems of Peace and Socialism], no. 2 (February 1974), and "New Frontiers

PNW agreement and peaceful coexistence theme were both directly involved, as in the key article cited above. The SALT agreements were rarely mentioned in this connection, except indirectly when arms limitations and reductions were sometimes noted, particularly by political leaders, as offering possibilities for reducing military outlays.[116] During the latter part of 1974 the debate subsided, and the military critics of excessive reliance on the PNW, and by implication détente, fell silent.[117]

In the period following the second summit, Brezhnev and his colleagues in the Politburo continued to stress détente. Ever since the April 1973 Central Committee plenum resolution, a call to make détente "irreversible" was sounded. In a toast in Washington in June Brezhnev had stated the Soviet desire to make the further development of Soviet-American relations irreversible.[118] He repeated this theme in twenty other speeches during 1973–74 alone, as did Kosygin, Podgorny, Suslov, Ponomarev—and Marshal Grechko, among others.

Finally, Brezhnev's position as head of the Politburo had been strengthened by the removal of Shelest and Voronov from the Politburo at the Central Committee plenum in April—the first removals for reasons other than death or infirmity since the ouster of Khrushchev nine years earlier. And after the next plenum, in December 1973, Brezhnev for the first time began to be referred to by the other Politburo members and in the press as "the head of the Politburo." Nevertheless, Brezhnev continued to lead by consensus, a collective leadership that was strengthened by the addition to the Politburo at the same time of Gromyko, Grechko, and Andropov. (Andropov had been a nonvoting candidate member.) Not since the days of V. M. Molotov, N. A. Bulganin, and L. P. Beria two decades earlier had the heads of these three institutions—the Ministry of Foreign Affairs, the Ministry of Defense, and the state security organization—all been members of the Politburo (or Presidium, as it was called in their day).

One external development had eased internal Soviet concern about the policy of détente with the United States. The agreement for a truce in

---

of Soviet-American Relations," *Izvestiya*, July 13, 1974; and by A. Bovin, *Izvestiya*, July 11, 1973 (evening edition only), and July 25, 1973. There were many others.

For another discussion, see Thomas N. Bjorkman and Thomas J. Zamostny, "Soviet Politics and Strategy toward the West: Three Cases," *World Politics*, vol. 36 (January 1984), pp. 199–202.

116. For example, see M. Kolosov, "A Major Contribution to Strengthening Security," *Pravda*, July 29, 1973. Prime Minister Kosygin, among others, made a less specific reference at that time to improved international security "liberating national resources for useful and creative aims." "In Honor of a Soviet Guest: Speech of A. N. Kosygin," *Izvestiya*, July 4, 1973.

117. In July 1974 Brezhnev himself strongly repudiated the idea that a nuclear war could be won. This contributed to ending the debate. See "Socialist Poland After Thirty Years: Speech of Comrade L. I. Brezhnev," *Pravda*, July 22, 1974. See also the further discussion in chapter 22.

118. *The Washington Summit*, p. 27.

Vietnam and American military disengagement had removed this issue, which had prompted opposition by Shelest and others in 1972.

The Central Committee plenums in April and December 1973 also saw further success for Brezhnev's policy of actively promoting increased trade with the advanced Western countries and linking this development to internal economic modernization. As was seen earlier, this policy had been—and remained—controversial in the Soviet Union. But soon after the April plenum, Brezhnev for the first time openly declared that Soviet economic plans were not based on autarky. And particularly on his visits to West Germany and the United States he stressed the importance of, and Soviet interest in, large-scale, long-term economic cooperation. This theme was further developed by the heads of a number of leading academic and theoretical institutions—including Nikolai Inozemtsev, director of the Institute of the World Economy and International Relations, and Georgy Arbatov, director of the Institute of USA and Canada studies—as well as by Deputy Ministers of Foreign Trade Vladimir Alkhimov and Nikolai Smelyakov, Viktor Spandaryan of USSR Gosplan, and *Pravda* commentator Yury Zhukov. But there clearly remained substantial resistance and widespread reservations.[119]

Growing Strains

Events in the world were soon to test in practice the crisis prevention measures adopted in the Basic Principles and the Prevention of Nuclear War agreements. Less than four months after the signature of the PNW agreement a new crisis was to develop in the Middle East that would test both accords.[120]

A test of a different kind was to involve the implications of the PNW agreement for unilateral military policy—something Kissinger had assured U.S. allies was not within the American understanding of the meaning of the accord. But the Soviet interpretation did lead its spokesmen to charge that U.S. policies for strategic nuclear targeting, as adopted first in the Schlesinger Doctrine of 1974 and later in Jimmy Carter's Presidential Directive (PD) 59 in 1980, were incompatible with at least the spirit of the PNW agreement. The same charge was not leveled against U.S.-NATO deployments of nuclear weapons or guidelines on contingent use of such weapons (as some of the allies had feared).[121]

---

119. For an excellent analysis see *Pressures for Change in Soviet Foreign Economic Policy*, FBIS Special Report, April 5, 1974 (confidential; declassified April 5, 1976).

120. See chapter 11.

121. In a specific criticism of the Schlesinger Doctrine, for example, Colonel V. Larionov said: "Discussion on regulating the methods of waging a nuclear war, however, in effect cannot help but cast a shadow on the understanding reached on its prevention." "Arms Limitation and Its Enemies," *Pravda*, April 7, 1974. Issuance of PD-59 in 1980 led Brezhnev himself to

The months following the second summit meeting saw several difficulties in American-Soviet bilateral relations emerge or grow, along with new
problems in the international arena, all of which strained the developing
American-Soviet détente. In addition, the internal political position of President Nixon continued to deteriorate.

In the Soviet Union activity by political dissidents increased, in
part stimulated by détente. The Soviet leaders, whether as a result of bureaucratic politics among themselves or as part of a generally shared judgment, do
seem to have concluded by the summer of 1973 that one price of an international relaxation of tensions was the need for a compensating repression of the
increasing internal dissidence emboldened by détente. While the administration in Washington did not make an issue in bilateral relations of Soviet efforts
to suppress the dissidence, the U.S. Congress and press did. On September 9
the nonofficial National Academy of Sciences threatened to end scientific cooperation with the Soviet Union if harassment of Academician Andrei Sakharov continued. On September 15 the Soviet government issued a statement
warning that "no one is allowed to violate the principles of our democracy," an
attempt to counter such Western protests and actions concerning its handling
of dissidents. Coincidentally just two days later the Senate approved a sense of
the Senate amendment to an appropriations bill in support of Soviet human
rights dissidents. On September 19 Brezhnev countered with a speech warning
the West not to attempt to exploit Soviet interest in improved international
relations by pressure for internal concessions, and Radio Moscow charged the
United States with interference in internal Soviet affairs.

On September 26 the House Ways and Means Committee adopted
the Jackson-Vanik amendment, with its requirement that Soviet restraints on
emigration be eased as a condition for granting MFN status. The next day
President Nixon asked the House to remove these restrictions. On September
28 Nixon received Gromyko and promised to do his best to get Congress to
grant MFN status to the Soviet Union. It was already clear, however, that the
prospect of his doing so was clouded—Nixon's clout was diminishing daily as
the Watergate investigation proceeded. Meanwhile, the Soviets did seek to
mitigate negative American reaction. On September 26 they announced ratification of two international covenants on human rights adopted by the UN
General Assembly in 1966, including a provision on free emigration. On October 1–3 Secretary of the Treasury Shultz attended the third plenary meeting of
the Soviet-American Trade Commission in Moscow, as that official forum of
bilateral cooperation continued. Shultz was told, however, that the Soviet government would make no more concessions on the emigration issue.[122]

House action on the Trade Reform Bill was expected on October
17 or 18, and it seemed likely the Jackson-Vanik amendment would be

---

say: "It is even difficult to imagine that it comes from the government of a country which has
signed an agreement with the Soviet Union on the prevention of nuclear war." *Pravda*,
August 30, 1980. See also the discussion in chapters 12 and 22.

122. Stern, *Water's Edge*, pp. 84–94.

adopted. The Ways and Means Committee had, however, failed on a tie vote to include one element of the amendment: the imposition of a ceiling on credits. It was not clear whether this restriction would or would not be included by the House as a whole. The administration's overall case had been weakened by Kissinger's absence from the committee hearings in September. Despite a promise to testify, he had been tied up with confirmation hearings on his nomination as secretary of state. But his presence probably would have made little difference.

The sequence of events was suddenly disrupted by the October War between Egypt, Syria, and Israel, and the Trade Reform Bill did not come before the House until December. Kissinger had been instrumental in getting the House action deferred. Then, in a dramatic if risky move, on October 25—at the height of the crisis—Kissinger suggested to some Jewish leaders that the entire section of the trade bill concerning U.S.-Soviet Trade (Title IV) be dropped completely, arguing that it would be contrary to Israel's interest to antagonize the Soviets at this point. A few days later the administration formally proposed dropping Title IV, a proposal that had no chance of being adopted. Kissinger even tried to get Israeli Prime Minister Golda Meir to intercede with the American Jewish leaders, but she declined and continued official Israeli neutrality on the Jackson-Vanik amendment. The Jewish leaders were divided; Jackson did a more effective rallying job (that included casting aspersions on Kissinger's handling of the October War) than did the administration.

Finally in early December the administration resolved a dispute between Kissinger, who at that point wanted to withdraw the whole Trade Reform Bill, and the administration's top trade officials, who wanted the multilateral trade authority it would grant. Nixon decided for the latter. The bill was voted on by the House on December 11, 1973, and passed overwhelmingly, with the entire Jackson-Vanik amendment on MFN linkage and credit restrictions incorporated. The next year would see the decisive battle in the Senate.[123]

On the world scene, the overthrow of King Mohammad Zahir in Afghanistan by Mohammad Daoud in July did not pose a problem for Soviet-American relations. The overthrow of President Salvador Allende of Chile by General Augusto Pinochet on September 11 did, however. It caused considerable concern in Moscow over American use of détente to expand its influence by supporting violent means against progressive socialist countries of the third world.[124] So, too, did the American diplomatic move, after the Arab-Israeli October War, to build its standing in the Arab countries at Soviet expense.[125]

---

123. Ibid., pp. 94–103.

124. See M. F. Kudachkin, "The Experience of the Struggle of the Communist Party of Chile for Unity among Leftist Forces and for Revolutionary Transformation," *Voprosy istorii KPSS* [Questions of History of the CPSU], no. 5 (May 1974), pp. 48–60. Mikhail Kudachkin is head of the Latin America Section of the International Department of the Central Committee of the CPSU.

125. See chapter 11.

The Soviet Union had placed a great deal of stock on the compatibility and contribution of East-West and U.S.-Soviet superpower détente to furthering progressive change in the third world. On the eve of the nonaligned summit meeting in Algiers in early September 1973, a leading Soviet journal of political commentary for both foreign and domestic circulation had stressed at length that "an unbiased examination of the international situation shows that the development of Soviet-US contacts has already had a salutory effect on the Third World. Transition from confrontation to stable peaceful co-existence makes it harder for the aggressive neo-colonial quarters to impose their diktat on the newly-emerged national states." The PNW agreement was specifically cited, with its pledge that the two parties "refrain from the threat or use of force" against other countries as well against one another. The article specifically mentioned the danger that would have been faced, in the absence of détente, by "the Popular Unity Government in Chile."[126] Then, less than a week later, the Popular Unity Government of Allende was overthrown.

If the success of the Allende government in making a peaceful transition to socialism had been a success of détente, then his fall was a failure of détente. Some critics of détente abroad, and perhaps in the Soviet Union as well, did argue that the coup against Allende showed a failure of détente, and some Soviet commentaries even acknowledged this charge, although rebutting it.[127] But the overthrow of Allende and the suspicion of American involvement (later confirmed in part)[128] were a serious blow to Soviet expectations.

Immediately after the summit meeting, on July 4, Washington announced another planned visit by Kissinger to Beijing (later postponed until November). Clearly the United States was using its growing rapprochement with China for leverage with the Soviet Union. When Kissinger did visit China in November, he discussed American-Soviet relations both with Zhou Enlai (already entering a period of political eclipse) and Mao Zedong, reassuring a suspicious Mao that there were no secret American-Soviet understandings or agreements.[129]

Increasingly Watergate dominated the scene in the United States. In August Judge John Sirica ruled against President Nixon on whether he had to supply key and incriminating tape recordings of conspirational conversations in the White House. From that time on Nixon became increasingly entangled in the tapes. It was also announced in August that Kissinger would replace Rogers as secretary of state, while remaining also as assistant to the president for national security affairs; he was sworn in in September. In November Con-

---

126. Dmitry Volsky, "Soviet-American Relations and the Third World," *New Times* (Moscow), no. 36 (September 1973), pp. 4–6.

127. Editorial, "Détente Benefits All Peoples," *New Times* (Moscow), no. 39 (September 1973), p. 1.

128. See *Covert Actions in Chile, 1963–1973*, Committee Print, Select Committee to Study Governmental Operations, 94 Cong. 1 sess. (GPO, 1975), p. 40.

129. Kissinger, *Years of Upheaval*, pp. 685, 690.

gress overrode a presidential veto on the War Powers Act, enacting a curtailment of the long, almost imperial domination of foreign policy by the executive branch.

Détente was developing and still dominant, but clouds were gathering on the horizon.

11 Détente and Competition: The October War, 1973

THE NIXON-BREZHNEV summit meeting in Washington in June 1973 marked the beginning of the second year of American-Soviet détente, a relationship that was flourishing. Yet in less than four months a local war in the Middle East was to lead to a higher degree of military alert and apparent confrontation between the two powers than at any time since the Cuban missile crisis over a decade earlier. How did this situation come to pass, and what did it mean for détente?

At first glance the October 1973 Arab-Israeli war appeared to affect American-Soviet relations as follows.[1] While neither power was directly involved, they were cast in opposition because the conflict between rival clients of theirs led them to provide support. Eventually this situation led in turn to a joint American-Soviet agreement to sponsor a cease-fire. When the cease-fire did not hold, there was a brief but dramatic flare-up of American-Soviet confrontation that seemed to threaten even the possibility of nuclear war. Once the cease-fire was firmly established, the superpower crisis dissolved, and the Arab-Israeli war ended.

Closer analysis raises aspects of the situation that modify this initial impression. It is necessary also to consider whether the superpowers had some responsibility for the generation of the conflict, particularly given their mutual commitment to seek to prevent crises from arising. The causes (and purposes) of the climactic confrontation also require careful consideration. Finally, rather than being merely an episode of regional strife that briefly engaged the two powers in a sharp but fleeting confrontation, in the United States the October War came to have a serious negative impact on the whole policy of détente with the Soviet Union.

---

1. Israeli, and many American, discussions refer to this conflict as the Yom Kippur War, while Arab accounts refer to it as the War of Ramadan, as it coincided with both holy days. It can most conveniently and impartially be referred to as the fourth Arab-Israeli war or, more simply, as the October War.

The Outbreak of the War

It is both necessary and instructive to examine those aspects of the outbreak and resolution of the Arab-Israeli war of 1973 that relate to and were affected by the détente in American-Soviet relations.

Important changes occurred in both Soviet-Egyptian and Egyptian American relations during the year and a half between the first Nixon-Brezhnev meeting in 1972 and the outbreak of the October War in 1973. As noted earlier, as a direct consequence of the establishment of the Soviet-American détente and the apparent subordination by the USSR of its interests in Egypt to that détente, Egyptian President Anwar al-Sadat decided that he could not rely upon Soviet assistance to meet his cardinal objective of recovering the Egyptian territory occupied by Israel since 1967. In July 1972 he therefore expelled the approximately 20,000 military advisers and limited independent Soviet military presence from Egypt.[2] That same month Sadat also reactivated a secret channel of communication with the White House that he had initiated in April.[3] Indeed, immediately *before* his decision to expel the Soviet military presence Sadat had received a back channel (or, as he described it, "under the table") message from the White House reminding him that the key to the Egyptian-Israeli impasse was in Washington, not Moscow.[4] From that time forward Sadat pursued both the Soviet and American connections. But primarily he relied on a unilateral path of preparing for a limited war with Israel as the only way to force a reopening of the issue of the occupation of the Egyptian Sinai.

Despite the Soviet expulsion, on August 29, 1972, Sadat wrote to the Soviet leaders that he would give them one more chance, until October, to prove their support and assist Egypt to recover its territory. This they did not do. Nevertheless, Sadat continued to pursue his dual diplomatic track. In Oc-

---

2. See the discussion in chapter 9. The most authoritative source is Sadat himself: Anwar el-Sadat, *In Search of Identity: An Autobiography* (Harper and Row, 1978), pp. 228–31. Sadat gives the figure of 15,000 advisers, but that was apparently not up-to-date; Heikal says the total was 21,000, which is probably more accurate. See Mohamed Heikal, *The Road to Ramadan* (Quadrangle, 1975), p. 175.

3. Henry Kissinger, *Years of Upheaval* (Boston, Mass.: Little, Brown, 1982), p. 205, and *White House Years* (Little, Brown, 1979), pp. 1292–1300.

4. Heikal, *Road to Ramadan*, pp. 174, 183.

Heikal also reports that Kissinger had told one of his staff that he did not understand Sadat. If Sadat had advised him in advance, he would have felt obligated "to give him something in exchange [for expelling the Soviet military advisers]. But now I've got it all for nothing." Heikal, *Road to Ramadan*, p. 184. Kissinger himself comments in his memoir that in 1972 he had had difficulty in "understanding why Sadat had not sought to negotiate their departure with us instead of giving it to us for nothing." Later he understood that Sadat needed to act boldly and quickly "to remove an encumbrance both to the war he was planning and to his projected move toward the United States." Kissinger, *Years of Upheaval*, p. 482.

tober 1972 the Egyptian prime minister, Aziz Sidqi, visited Moscow, while in Egypt the outspokenly anti-Soviet minister of war, General Muhammed Sadiq, was replaced (although not for his anti-Soviet reputation and inclination). The Soviets did respond at this juncture. While they refused to permit the Egyptians to purchase the advanced MiG-25 aircraft and electronic countermeasures equipment that they withdrew with their personnel, they did resume routine shipment of other arms. In December Sadat agreed to a five-year renewal of the agreement permitting the Soviet navy to use Egyptian facilities. Then, after General Ahmed Ismail Ali, the new minister of war, visited Moscow in February 1973, the Soviets began a substantial new supply of arms. For several months the Egyptians had no complaints.[5] After Egyptian military maneuvers and an Israeli mobilization in response to a perceived war threat in May, however, the Soviets declined to meet some Egyptian requests for arms, an action that led to public complaint by Sadat in July.[6]

While these events were occurring, Egypt continued to develop its secret contacts with the United States.[7] Hafiz Ismail, Sadat's national security adviser, after first visiting Moscow, in February 1973 went to Washington. But Sadat was not confident that, without a war, either the Soviet or the American diplomatic path would lead to Israeli withdrawal from the Sinai. Hence Sadat's main policy continued to be preparation for war to regain the occupied Egyptian territory, a theme he constantly reiterated publicly.

Sadat made his intentions so open that they came to be generally disbelieved. This was less true, however, of the Soviets. While not privy to Sadat's concrete plans (the precise date for the attack was made known to them less than two days in advance), the Soviet leaders were more inclined to believe him during 1973 than were the American or Israeli leaders. As a result they urged the Egyptians, both indirectly in public commentaries and directly in private talks, to turn away from the idea of war to negotiation. But they were not able to persuade Sadat that negotiations would be fruitful.

The last authoritative Soviet statement supporting Egypt's "right" not only to defend itself but also "to liberate its own lands" was made by Prime Minister Kosygin in an impromptu reply to a question at a press confer-

---

5. See Sadat, *In Search of Identity*, pp. 233–38. In an April interview Sadat publicly expressed satisfaction with the Soviet arms supply. "The Battle Is Now Inevitable," *Newsweek*, April 9, 1973, pp. 44–45, 49. The weapons supplied included some 175-mile-range SCUD ballistic missiles.

6. Anwar al-Sadat, Cairo Radio, July 23, in Foreign Broadcast Information Service, *Daily Report: Middle East and Africa*, July 24, 1973, pp. G21–22. (Hereafter FBIS, *Middle East.*)

7. As in many other instances the secrecy involved a lack of coordination about information within the U.S. government. The Department of State was not apprised of the secret White House–Egyptian contacts. In turn, according to Kissinger, it carried out some contacts on its own with the Egyptians that the White House did not know about. See Kissinger, *Years of Upheaval*, pp. 205–16, 223–27, for his detailed account of the State Department contacts. See also Heikal, *Road to Ramadan*, pp. 198–203.

ence in Stockholm on April 5, 1973.[8] Kosygin, however, also emphasized the Soviet view that a peaceful settlement was possible and preferable. From May 1973 on, Soviet commentary began to stress the need for the Arabs (including Egypt) to regain the Israeli-occupied territories by "peaceful means."[9] The Soviets also continued to emphasize the need for "unity" in pursuing a peaceful settlement, explicitly to prevent possible use of force by the *Israelis*, but with a strong implied criticism of *any* use of force to resolve the issue, meaning clearly an Arab resort to arms. General Secretary Brezhnev, in his sole relevant public comment during this period in a speech at Alma Ata on August 15, also referred only to peaceful settlement of such disputes.[10] Soviet commentaries made very clear their support for "realistic, responsible Arab politicians who prefer a political settlement" and warned against "pseudo-patriotic extremist slogans" and those who would "steer them [leading Arab countries] into adventurist courses."[11]

In addition to the published statements on the Soviet position and the attempts to influence Egypt and other Arab countries against going to war, the Soviet leaders sought directly to persuade Sadat (and probably President Hafez al-Asad in Syria) not to attack Israel. Sadat has disclosed that on four occasions before October 1973 Brezhnev warned him not to attack Israel.[12]

In addition, the Soviets, seeking to restore their relationship with Egypt but still wanting to cool Sadat's ardor for military action, had since early 1972 been paying more attention to Syria and other Arab countries, and to the Palestine Liberation Organization (PLO).[13] This effort was not effective in establishing a counterweight, however, and Syria joined Egypt in preparing for hostilities, while the other Arab countries supported the Egyptian position.

---

8. "A. N. Kosygin's Visit to Sweden," *Pravda*, April 7, 1973.

9. For example, see N. Kurdyumov, "Eradicating a Hotbed of Tension," *Pravda*, June 14, 1973; R. Petrov, "The Middle East Needs a Just and Lasting Peace," *New Times* (Moscow), no. 23 (June 1973), pp. 4–5; and many other press and radio references. Sadat later repeated that in communications with him the Soviet leaders had insisted on a peaceful resolution of the problem. See the interview with Anwar al-Sadat by 'Abd ar-Rahman ash-Sharqawi in *Rose al-Yusuf*, January 13, 1975, broadcast by Mena Radio, Cairo, January 12, in FBIS, *Middle East*, January 13, 1975, pp. D5–6.

10. "Speech of L. I. Brezhnev," Alma Ata, August 15, *Pravda*, August 16, 1973.

11. Dmitri Volsky, "New Opportunities and Old Obstacles," *New Times* (Moscow), no. 32 (August 1973), p. 15. The new opportunities were opportunities for peaceful settlement under détente.

12. Sadat, in interviews in *Al-Hawadith*, March 19, 1975, and *Al-Anwar*, June 27, 1975; cited by William B. Quandt, "Soviet Policy in the October Middle East War—I," *International Affairs* (London), vol. 53 (July 1977), p. 381. Later Sadat was less explicit but gave the same account of the Soviet position in his memoir, cited earlier.

13. See Galia Golan, *Yom Kippur and After: The Soviet Union and the Middle East Crisis* (Cambridge: Cambridge University Press, 1977), pp. 42–44, 56–63.

In April, Sadat and Asad met secretly in a remote town in the Egyptian desert and decided on a general war plan, with alternative target dates of May, August–September, or early October (probably October 6) 1973.[14] An operational war plan was also prepared. In May the Egyptian army carried out a major military maneuver, which the Soviet leaders (and the Israelis) took seriously.[15]

It was within this context that Kissinger arrived in Moscow in early May 1973 to prepare for the forthcoming Nixon-Brezhnev summit meeting. In a letter to Nixon in February Brezhnev had identified as his two priority subjects for consideration at the summit the proposed agreement on the prevention of nuclear war—and the Middle East.[16] The Soviets gave Kissinger a position paper that essentially reflected the Arab position, and they would not budge from it in their talks with him. Brezhnev did, however, indicate the increasing difficulty in restraining the Arab leaders and warned that there was danger of war. Kissinger does not refer in his memoir to the Egyptian war plan, nor to the Egyptian maneuvers, which took place while he was in Moscow. On his return, however, Kissinger directed the NSC staff to develop a contingency plan for Arab-Israeli hostilities.[17]

At the summit conference itself, Brezhnev time and again warned of the urgency of the problem and argued that the only way to head off an Arab-Israeli war was for the Soviet Union and the United States to agree on principles for a peaceful settlement of the conflict. Kissinger quotes him as having said, "I am categorically opposed to a resumption of the war. But without agreed principles . . . we cannot do this." Kissinger argues that the principles the Soviets prepared were not satisfactory, but also makes clear elsewhere that he and President Nixon simply did not *want* to negotiate the issue with the Soviet leaders. Rather, they wanted to do so with the Egyptians and Israelis. As Kissinger candidly comments in an aside in his memoir, "We were planning a major diplomatic initiative after Israel's elections in late October and were in the meantime stalling." He comments that Brezhnev "must have heard the same Egyptian threats as we had and may have shared our own estimate that such an attempt was bound to end in Arab defeat. He knew that our ally was militarily stronger and that we held the diplomatic keys to a settlement." After these repeated pleas by Brezhnev, Nixon deferred the whole

---

14. Sadat, *In Search of Identity*, p. 241.

15. The U.S. defense attaché in Cairo promptly acquired the Egyptian war plan, and it was passed to the Israelis. The plan did not, however, indicate the possible dates. Israel took seriously a large training maneuver by the Egyptian army in early May, and responded with an expensive and disruptive military mobilization. A number of sources have reported the American and hence Israeli acquisition of the war plan; the fullest account is in Tad Szulc, *The Illusion of Peace: Foreign Policy in the Nixon Years* (Viking, 1978), pp. 705–07.

16. Kissinger, *Years of Upheaval*, p. 280. This letter was dated February 21.

17. Information from a senior member of the NSC staff involved in the contingency study. In an interview, he stressed the May maneuvers and discounted the reported Egyptian war plan.

subject to Kissinger and Foreign Minister Gromyko, with a weak "I will agree [only] to principles which will bring a settlement. That will be our project this year. The Middle East is a most urgent place." Kissinger comments, "That was the end of it."[18]

Both Nixon and Kissinger evidently found the discussions difficult. What Brezhnev wanted so badly was for the United States to place pressure on Israel to withdraw from the occupied Arab territories. The key discussion occurred late at night in an informal two- to three-hour unscheduled session in Nixon's study at San Clemente, after Brezhnev had said he could not sleep and wanted to discuss the Middle East situation. Nixon has said that in emotional intensity the discussion almost rivaled the sharp confrontation over Vietnam in 1972. He comments, in an astonishing non sequitur of interpretation, "This testy midnight session was a reminder of the unchanging and unrelenting Communist motivations beneath the diplomatic veneer of détente." Nixon continues with the revealing comment that Brezhnev was aware of the "steady progress we had been making in reopening the lines of communication between Washington and the Arab capitals" and that "if America was able to contribute toward a peaceful settlement of Arab-Israeli differences, we would be striking a serious blow to the Soviet presence and prestige in the Middle East."[19] Kissinger, too, has described the Soviet plea as an outburst from Brezhnev, probably "as much from frustration as from conviction," and comments that Brezhnev wanted "to bulldoze us into solving his dilemmas without paying any price."[20] Most remarkably, Kissinger candidly states: "*We were not willing to pay for détente in the coin of our geopolitical position.*"[21]

In referring later to these Soviet warnings of the danger of the outbreak of war, Kissinger admits that "we dismissed this as psychological warfare because we did not see any rational military option that would not worsen the Soviet and Arab positions."[22] Whatever the Soviet leaders' motivations, Nixon and Kissinger, to judge from *their* memoirs, did not recognize that the great powers might have a transcendent responsibility to defuse a threatening situation.

Soviet efforts to warn the United States of the danger and the need for diplomatic action to head off the impending war continued. On September

18. Kissinger, *Years of Upheaval*, pp. 296–99.

19. Richard Nixon, *RN: The Memoirs of Richard Nixon* (Grosset and Dunlap, 1978), p. 885.

20. Kissinger, *Years of Upheaval*, p. 298. Kissinger was much too astute not to have realized that Brezhnev could not possibly have moved from the unacceptable initial pro-Arab position without at least some sign of American engagement on the issues. Yet he and Nixon intentionally averted any discussion of the real issues.

21. Ibid., p. 299. Emphasis added.

22. Ibid., p. 461. In his account of the later June 1974 Moscow summit meeting Nixon cites Brezhnev as having pointed out that his earlier predictions on the Middle East had come true, although the Soviets had not known then of the Arab plan to attack and in fact "had done everything they could to stop it . . . [but] 'We were unable to do so.'" Nixon, *RN*, p. 1031.

25 Gromyko, in his annual address to the UN General Assembly, warned: "The fires of war could break out at any time, and who could tell what consequences would ensue."[23] Three days later, when Gromyko visited Nixon at the White House, he "warned once again that it was dangerous to treat the Middle East as quiescent: 'We could all wake up one day and find there is a real conflagration in that area.' But the warning in fact lulled us."[24] At the time neither the Soviet[25] nor the American leaders knew that on that very day—the third anniversary of the death of former Egyptian President Gamal Abdel Nasser—Sadat had begun a ten-day countdown of final preparations for war.[26]

On October 3 Sadat called in Soviet Ambassador Vladimir Vinogradov and informed him that Egypt and Syria "have decided to start military operations against Israel so as to break the present deadlock." He added, "I would like the Soviet leaders to give me an urgent answer to this question: What will the Soviet attitude be?" Vinogradov asked when they "proposed to take that military action" and was told the date had not yet been fixed. It had, but Sadat and Asad had decided in advance not to disclose the date at this initial notification. Rather, on the next day, October 4, Asad in Damascus told Soviet Ambassador Nurriden Mukhitdinov that the attack would be launched on October 6.[27]

Also on October 4 Ambassador Vinogradov asked to see Sadat immediately, saying he had an "urgent message from the Soviet leadership." Sadat naturally expected to receive the Soviet reply to his query on the Soviet attitude, but the message dealt with a minor and tangential (although possibly significant) matter: the Soviet leaders requested permission for Soviet transport aircraft to land and evacuate the dependents of Soviet civilian experts in Egypt. Sadat says he was "practically dumbfounded." He said he had no objec-

---

23. See A. Gromyko, "Address to the Twenty-eighth Session of the UN General Assembly," *Pravda*, September 26, 1973.

24. Kissinger, *Years of Upheaval*, p. 463.

25. Several Western accounts have fed upon one another to give currency to an alleged letter (or, according to one report, a secret meeting in Bulgaria) on September 22 at which Sadat is said to have informed Brezhnev of his intention to attack on October 6. See Marvin Kalb and Bernard Kalb, *Kissinger* (Dell, 1974), p. 513; Szulc, *The Illusion of Peace*, p. 726; Walter Laqueur, *Confrontation: The Middle East and World Politics* (Quadrangle, 1974), p. 83; and Peter Allen, *The Yom Kippur War* (Charles Scribner's Sons, 1982), pp. 42–43. Sadat did meet with Soviet Ambassador Vladimir Vinogradov on September 22 and 24, but made no such communication to Brezhnev.

26. Sadat, *In Search of Identity*, p. 245. That same day Sadat gave a public speech in which he made no reference at all to the Soviet Union. *Pravda* reciprocated by criticizing unidentified attacks on the Soviet-Egyptian friendship that had been established by Nasser—an oblique criticism of Sadat.

27. Ibid., p. 246, corroborated by other accounts. Sadat comments that he and Asad had decided the latter should be the one to inform the Soviets of the exact date of the attack, forty-eight hours beforehand, "in view of my bad relations with the Soviet Union."

tion to the evacuation, but "where is their reply to my question?"[28] The Soviets made the same request for evacuation of Damascus.

On the night of October 4 and on October 5 the Soviets evacuated their civilian dependents from Egypt and Syria, even diverting some Soviet airliners to participate. Sadat recalls having thought at the time that it was "a bad omen" in that it reflected a Soviet assessment that the Arabs would lose and the lives of their people would be in jeopardy. The Soviets also withdrew their ships from the Alexandria and Port Said harbors on October 4 and 5 and held back another ship en route with supplies.[29]

Some Western observers, including Kissinger, have speculated as to whether the Soviet leaders in fact intended their conspicuous action in withdrawing their personnel to be a subtle "warning to us without betraying their allies."[30] This seems unlikely.[31] The move was probably a simple precautionary one. Nevertheless, it was certainly a signal of less than full support for (as well as a lack of confidence in) the Egyptians and Syrians. Both the Israeli and

---

28. Ibid., p. 247.

Sadat's account is, however, incomplete on this point. According to Heikal, Vinogradov also brought a Soviet response to Sadat's query: "the decision when to fight must be for Sadat alone to make" (that is, the Soviet Union would not share responsibility). Further, "the Soviet Union would give him the support of a friend"—a distinctly noncommittal indication that the Soviet Union would not be an ally in the enterprise. Heikal, *Road to Ramadan*, p. 34.

Heikal's account on this point, but Sadat's account generally, is supported by a reported discussion of the events by Ambassador Vinogradov, plausible but unconfirmed, printed in *as-Safir* (Beirut), April 16, 1974.

29. The Soviets also launched a standby reconnaissance satellite, Cosmos 596, on October 3 to enhance their intelligence on the Middle Eastern scene; it was brought back down on October 9. Additional Soviet reconnaissance satellites were 597, launched on October 6 (returned October 12); 598, launched on October 10 (returned October 16); 599, launched October 15 (returned October 28); 600, launched October 16 (returned October 23); 602, launched October 20 (returned October 29); and 603, launched October 27 (returned November 9). These were all sited so as to provide coverage of the area of Arab-Israeli hostilities.

Some commentators have speculated or assumed that the Soviets supplied Egypt with intelligence from these reconnaissance satellites. Sadat, however, complains in his memoir that "while the U.S. satellite hourly transmitted information to Israel, we received nothing at all from the Soviet satellite[s]." Sadat, *In Search of Identity*, p. 260. When Kosygin was in Cairo urging Egypt to agree to a cease-fire, he did provide aerial photographs to bolster his argument on the extent of Israeli penetration of the east bank, but the photographs were from MiG-25 aerial reconnaissance. See Heikal, *Road to Ramadan*, p. 235.

Sadat, incidentally, was in error in assuming that the United States was providing constant and full satellite intelligence information to Israel.

30. Kissinger, *Years of Upheaval*, p. 469. See also Quandt, *International Affairs*, vol. 53 (1977), pp. 385–86; and Alvin Z. Rubinstein, *Red Star on the Nile: The Soviet-Egyptian Influence Relationship since the June War* (Princeton, N.J.: Princeton University Press, 1977), pp. 260–61.

31. Soviet officials have never claimed having done it for this purpose. Some academic figures have argued, in conversation with Americans, that the United States was given warning of the impending hostilities by the Soviet evacuation, but in cases where the matter has been pursued no one has claimed that the Soviet action was designed to serve that purpose.

American intelligence services promptly noted the Soviet evacuation but discounted it as a sign of impending Arab hostilities. The most generally accepted theories in Tel Aviv and Washington were that it probably either represented Soviet fear of an Israeli attack or reflected a further worsening in Soviet-Arab relations.[32]

The Egyptian and Syrian attack on October 6 caught the Israelis by surprise, despite many indications it was coming. The Israelis received solid information from a secret source only a few hours before the attack, not enough time to mobilize or alert all forces.

Cooperation in Defusing Arab-Israeli Hostilities

The coming of the war posed the question of how the United States and the Soviet Union would react to this first serious conflict under the conditions of American-Soviet détente.[33]

The United States had established contact with the Soviets on the crisis just before the war began. Kissinger awakened Ambassador Dobrynin at 6:40 a.m., just one hour before the war started, in a last minute effort to avert what the Israelis had just informed him was imminent. He informed Moscow (and Cairo and Damascus) that Israel had assured the United States it would *not* initiate military action. The two powers remained in close contact throughout the war.

Overall, it can be said that the two powers cooperated in bringing about a cease-fire. Each, as would be expected, sought to maneuver events in such a way as to serve its own ends and, while seeking to expand its own influence, to reduce possibilities for the other to gain influence. There was, however, not only a shared objective of preventing the war from engulfing the

---

32. The American intelligence community concluded on October 5–6 that the evacuation probably reflected a worsening in Arab-Soviet relations. See William B. Quandt, *Decade of Decisions: American Policy toward the Arab-Israeli Conflict, 1967–76* (Berkeley, Calif.: University of California Press, 1977), pp. 167–70. Other Americans and Israelis believed that it more likely represented Soviet fear of a move by the Israeli military. For a retrospective dismissal of the latter idea see Kissinger, *Years of Upheaval*, p. 467.

33. There are many accounts of the October War. From the standpoint of this discussion the most important are Kissinger, *Years of Upheaval*, pp. 450–613; Quandt, *International Affairs*, vol. 53 (1977), pp. 377–89, and "Soviet Policy in the October Middle East War—II," ibid., vol. 53 (October 1977), pp. 587–603; Karen Dawisha, "Soviet Decision-Making in the Middle East: The 1973 October War and the 1980 Gulf War," *International Affairs* (London), vol. 57 (Winter 1980–81), pp. 43–59; Golan, *Yom Kippur and After*, pp. 74–128; Bruce D. Porter, *The USSR in Third World Conflicts: Soviet Arms and Diplomacy in Local Wars, 1945–1980* (Cambridge University Press, 1984), pp. 113–46; Robert O. Freedman, *Soviet Policy toward the Middle East since 1970* (Praeger, 1975), pp. 128–71; Rubinstein, *Red Star on the Nile*, pp. 248–87; and Paul Jabber and Roman Kolkowicz, "The Arab-Israeli Wars of 1967 and 1973," in Stephen S. Kaplan, ed., *Diplomacy of Power: Soviet Armed Forces as a Political Instrument* (Brookings Institution, 1981), pp. 438–63.

two powers, but also a desire to preserve the détente relationship. The apparent exception was a sharp confrontation marked by an exchange of messages and an American nuclear alert on October 24–25, discussed later.

On the first morning of the war, Kissinger told Dobrynin that the United States would strongly resist an empty appeal to the UN General Assembly—in which, predictably, the United States would stand virtually alone with Israel. Moscow, Kissinger urged, should not "destroy everything that it has taken us three years to build up."[34] And throughout the crisis the Soviet Union did not turn to the General Assembly and in fact discouraged the Arabs from doing so. Instead, the United States urged joint U.S.-Soviet action in the Security Council and sponsorship of a cease-fire. That is what ultimately occurred.

Over the period from October 6 to 20 the United States and the Soviet Union alternated between urging a prompt cease-fire and using delaying tactics to postpone one, depending on the tide of battle and estimates of the course of further hostilities. Initially the Soviet leaders, expecting a more rapid and decisive Israeli counteroffensive, offended Sadat by urging a cease-fire on the very first day of the war.[35] The United States, however, held back for some days, indeed until October 20, to permit the Israelis to advance. As Kissinger observes, the two powers in this phase "were, in fact, pursuing comparable strategies, each seeking to enable its friends to gain the upper hand on the battlefield."[36] Similarly, the two powers then began in parallel to resupply the two sides with arms and munitions (the Soviet Union from October 10 on, the United States from October 12 on). Both powers relied heavily on the effect of this show of support to their friends, as demonstrating that each would not permit the other to gain a decisive military advantage. Kissinger later characterized the period from October 13 to 20 as "the week of the airlift."[37] Both powers, however, used the leverage provided by their supply of

---

34. Kissinger, *Years of Upheaval*, p. 472.

35. See Sadat, *In Search of Identity*, pp. 252–54.

36. Kissinger, *Years of Upheaval*, p. 519.

37. Ibid., p. 537. He also notes that Nixon's attention during this period was absorbed by the growing Watergate crisis over the White House tapes.

There was an unseemly squabble involving bureaucratic maneuvers and press leaks over apparent efforts by Kissinger to hold back the airlift deliveries to Israel for several days in order to use the prospect of increasing supplies to influence the Israelis. Reportedly Kissinger secretly instructed Schlesinger to hold back, while telling the Israelis that only he, Kissinger, could help them with the supplies against the reluctance of Nixon and Schlesinger, but only if the Israelis accepted his advice. Kissinger denies the charge. Kissinger, *Years of Upheaval*, pp. 512–15. For an earlier Kissinger-inspired version of the events see Kalb and Kalb, *Kissinger*, pp. 525–40.

Nixon reaffirms his position and quotes Kissinger as having said that Schlesinger and Defense were causing the obstacles and delays. Nixon, *RN*, pp. 924–27. Thus after Nixon had decided to provide the arms requested by the Israelis, Kissinger is said to have ordered Schlesinger, in the name of the president, to stall in fulfilling the requests. At the same time he was

arms to press for a cease-fire when they believed the time was ripe.[38]

On October 16 Kosygin flew to Cairo to persuade Sadat personally of the need for a cease-fire in place, rather than demanding that Israel withdraw from the occupied territories. On October 18 Sadat agreed. By that time the Israelis had established a bridgehead on the west side of the canal, although the Egyptians remained in force in the Sinai.

By the evening of October 18, as soon as the Soviets had received Sadat's agreement to a cease-fire in place, Brezhnev sent an urgent message to the White House proposing a cease-fire. After informing Nixon, Kissinger, by his own account, stalled.[39] The next morning Brezhnev proposed that Kissinger go to Moscow for urgent consultations. Nixon and Kissinger decided to accept that proposal, but again delayed for most of a day. That night Kissinger attended a dinner given by the Chinese representative, Ambassador Huang Zhen, before a midnight departure for Moscow. He took along Ambassador Dobrynin.

Kissinger was dismayed to learn, en route, that Nixon had just sent a letter to Brezhnev giving Kissinger full authority for the negotiation. Kissinger did not want the Soviets to know this because it deprived him of a delaying tactic of saying he had to refer back to Washington for approval.[40] After Kissin-

---

telling Ambassador Simcha Dinitz that he was exerting every pressure on Schlesinger to move ahead. See Szulc, *The Illusion of Peace*, pp. 737–39; and Elmo R. Zumwalt, Jr., *On Watch: A Memoir* (Quadrangle, 1976), p. 433. Despite the supposed orders from Nixon via Kissinger, Schlesinger told Defense to be "overtly niggardly but covertly forthcoming" in meeting the Israeli requests. Zumwalt, *On Watch*, p. 434. Meanwhile, Kissinger was attempting to use the delays in the airlift to bargain not only with Israel, but also with American-Jewish organizations. He sought to get both to curtail their support for Senator Jackson's proposed amendment to the trade bill that would require a Soviet commitment on Jewish emigration from the Soviet Union. See Matti Golan, *The Secret Conversations of Henry Kissinger: Step-by-Step Diplomacy in the Middle East* (Quadrangle, 1976), pp. 45–61, a book initially blocked by Israeli censors because the author used secret Israeli documents. Nor does the intrigue stop there. Admiral Zumwalt has admitted that he privately told Senator Jackson at the time that the White House, not the Pentagon—meaning Kissinger, not Schlesinger—was responsible for holding up the supplies to Israel. Zumwalt, *On Watch*, p. 435.

38. On the American side the chief factor determining the amount of the arms supply was at least to match the size of the Soviet effort. Kissinger, *Years of Upheaval*, p. 531. On the Soviet side the main consideration was to satisfy the Egyptians and Syrians of the Soviets' earnest support and to prevent an Israeli (and American) military victory. On the calculations behind the arms supply by both sides, see Kissinger, *Years of Upheaval*, pp. 491–542; and Quandt, *International Affairs*, vol. 53 (October 1977), pp. 587–95.

39. Kissinger, *Years of Upheaval*, pp. 538–40.

40. Ibid., pp. 547–48. Kissinger observes: "History will not record that I resisted many grants of authority. This one I resented bitterly; it was a classic example of how 'full powers' can inhibit rather than enhance negotiating flexibility." Kissinger attempted to have the message stopped, but it was too late. While apparently the note had not yet been delivered to the Soviet embassy, it had been typed and signed. Moreover, Nixon had added a personal postscript in pen. As General Brent Scowcroft, deputy to Kissinger as national security adviser, who was in Washington, told Kissinger on the airplane, "This eliminated any flexibility I may otherwise have had for modification," that is, to change the text surreptitiously before signature.

ger's first discussions with the Soviet leaders the next day, he received another message from Nixon, to be conveyed orally to Brezhnev. It announced a remarkable change in the American approach. Nixon said he agreed with Brezhnev's view, as expressed at San Clemente in June, that the two leaders personally, representing the two great powers, "must step in, determine the proper course of action to a just settlement, and then bring the necessary pressure on our respective friends for a settlement which will at last bring peace to this troubled area." Kissinger was aghast. He immediately cabled his deputy, Scowcroft, telling him: "If I carry out the letter of the President's instructions it will totally wreck what little bargaining leverage I still have."[41] Kissinger decided, not for the first time while on a mission in Moscow, to ignore the president's instructions.[42]

By the day after Kissinger's arrival, October 21, after only a few hours of discussion, the Soviet leaders suddenly accepted the American proposal. Kissinger, used to tough bargaining, was amazed. Moreover, the Soviets wanted both countries to introduce it jointly in the Security Council immediately. Kissinger, wanting to delay, argued that he needed time (nine hours) for consultation. He also knew that, once adopted, the resolution would not mandate the actual cease-fire for twelve hours more. Brezhnev reluctantly accepted this delay.[43]

Kissinger flew to Israel from Moscow in order to secure Israeli acceptance—which was given, also reluctantly. He had, in fact, succeeded in giving the Israelis about twice the forty-eight hours he had promised them earlier, on October 18,[44] a fact Kissinger stressed to the Israelis.

Evidently he did more. By his own remarkably candid admission, Kissinger describes his reaction when he first learned, only some hours after the

---

41. Ibid., p. 551. Kissinger also phoned General Haig, the new White House chief of staff, to complain. Haig replied, "Will you get off my back? I have troubles of my own." Kissinger asked, "What troubles can you possibly have in Washington on a Saturday night?" Haig explained that the president had just fired Special Prosecutor Archibald Cox and that Attorney General Elliot L. Richardson and Deputy Attorney General William D. Ruckelshaus had resigned. It was the Watergate "Saturday night massacre." Ibid., p. 552.

42. Kissinger virtually admits to this action in his memoir. He states that he adhered to the earlier plan, approved before his departure, and he does not describe presentation of this new American position to Brezhnev. Nor does he indicate a Soviet reaction. Further, he discusses its putative effect on the Soviets in the conditional tense—it "would" lead to a morass, and so on. Ibid., p. 551. Although Kissinger does not admit directly that he decided to ignore the message, a member of his Moscow delegation confirmed to me that he did so. Because Kissinger reached an agreement on the cease-fire, and because of preoccupation with Watergate, Nixon did not inquire or find out what had happened. One serious student of the subject has erroneously assumed that because Nixon instructed Kissinger to deliver this message, it was done; see Alexander L. George, ed., *Managing U.S.-Soviet Rivalry: Problems of Crisis Prevention* (Boulder, Colo.: Westview, 1983), pp. 150–51.

43. Kissinger, *White House Years*, pp. 552–59.

44. Ibid., pp. 539, 544, 555.

cease-fire had gone into effect, that Israeli troops were again advancing: "I also had a sinking feeling that I might have emboldened them; in Israel, to gain their support, I had indicated that I would understand if there was a few hours 'slippage' in the cease-fire deadline while I was flying home."[45] In fact, while Kissinger's admission of this invitation to violate the cease-fire is remarkable, it understates what he actually did. Informed Israeli accounts make clear that Kissinger was even more explicit, commenting, for example, "Well, in Vietnam the cease-fire didn't go into effect at the exact time that was agreed on." Moreover, he intentionally scotched efforts to provide UN supervision for the cease-fire, knowing that the Israelis had been pressing for more time to destroy the Egyptian army.[46]

At 12:52 a.m. on October 22 the UN Security Council (China absent) adopted Resolution 338, jointly sponsored by the United States and the Soviet Union, mandating a cease-fire. The two powers, for all of their intense and continuing rivalry, had agreed on and successfully gained Egyptian and Israeli acceptance of a cease-fire.

American policy was being made almost exclusively by Kissinger. Except for Nixon's interjection on October 13 to press ahead on the airlift to Israel, and his attempt on October 20, foiled by Kissinger, to work out a comprehensive peace settlement in collaboration with the Soviet leaders, Nixon had been swamped by Watergate and other problems. Spiro T. Agnew was forced to resign as vice president on October 10, the Saturday night massacre occurred while Kissinger was in Moscow, and Nixon faced other daily crises.

Kissinger had a clear strategy. As he comments in his memoir, "From the outset, I was determined to use the war to start a peace process," thwarting the Arab attack (from designs against Israel itself, which it never had) so as to appear to have "repulsed an attack by Soviet weapons," while "trying to win Arab confidence so we could both emerge as mediator and demonstrate that the road to peace led through Washington," a process made possible by "restored self-respect on the Arab side and a new Israeli recognition of the need for diplomacy." Further, "We could begin our peace process with the Arabs on the proposition that we had stopped the Israeli advance and with the Israelis on the basis that we had been steadfastly at their side in the crisis."[47]

From the first days of the war Kissinger recognized that the Egyptians were the key to implementing his strategy. Moreover, the United States

---

45. Ibid., p. 569. Kissinger lamely tries to justify this invitation to cheat on the cease-fire by noting that because of a communication snarl-up, his message from Moscow to Tel Aviv via Washington had been delayed. But he recounts the precision of agreeing to the cease-fire for exactly 6:52 p.m. Israeli time, precisely twelve hours after the Security Council adopted the resolution.

46. See Golan, *The Secret Conversations of Henry Kissinger*, pp. 86–87.

47. Kissinger, *Years of Upheaval*, pp. 468, 470, 471, 476, 487.

was "the only government in contact with both sides. If we could preserve this position, we were likely to emerge in a central role in the peace process."[48] The Egyptians entered into direct, secret communication with the White House on the second day of the war and stressed throughout that they were determined to maintain that direct contact and that the Soviet Union could not speak for them.[49]

Thus for American diplomacy the key was to balance Israeli and Arab security in such a way that both would be beholden to the United States and that the Soviet Union would be rendered irrelevant to the peace process. At the same time, the United States sought to circumscribe Soviet assistance to the Arabs in ways that did not risk American-Soviet confrontation. It remained in constant communication with the Soviets, maneuvering to bring joint sponsorship of a cease-fire at a time and in a fashion that promoted American diplomatic leverage and minimized Soviet diplomatic relevance.

The Soviets, for their part, sought to keep (and if possible to rebuild) their influence with the Arab countries through a readiness to supply arms to prevent Israel from defeating the Arab armies. It is clear from all accounts that the Soviets were very cautious and reserved, seeking from the very first day of the war—to the annoyance and distrust of the Egyptians—to get a cease-fire.[50] Once it became clear the Israelis could not mount an immediate repulse and counteroffensive, the Soviets sought for the next week to defer a cease-fire, until Israeli advances began to threaten an Arab defeat. Then they again pressed the Arabs to accept a cease-fire. The Soviet objectives were modest: to retain and if possible recoup lost Arab confidence, and to bank on the possibility that the new collaborative relationship with the United States would allow the USSR to share in the peace process. But while the United States was quite prepared to reduce the Soviets' independent leverage by working together for a cease-fire at a time of its choosing, it was not prepared to share the diplomatic leverage that came with managing the peace process.

By the time of the cease-fire, as Kissinger exults, "we had achieved our fundamental objectives: We had created the conditions for a diplomatic breakthrough. We had vindicated the security of our friends. We had prevented a victory of Soviet arms. We had maintained a relationship with key Arab countries and laid the basis for a dominant role in postwar diplomacy."[51]

Then the crisis, apparently resolved, suddenly erupted anew.

---

48. Ibid., p. 487.

49. Ibid., pp. 481–82, 527.

50. See Sadat, *In Search of Identity*, pp. 252–65; Quandt, *International Affairs*, vol. 53 (1977), pp. 386–89; and Dawisha, *International Affairs*, vol. 57 (1980–81), pp. 51–52.

51. Kissinger, *Years of Upheaval*, p. 544.

The American-Soviet Confrontation

Only hours after the cease-fire went into effect it collapsed in a key sector. Whether, as the Israelis claimed and the Egyptians denied, some Egyptians first broke the truce remains undetermined. Essentially it is irrelevant. What is clear is that the Israelis either made up or took advantage of an Egyptian violation not just to prevent any Egyptian gain, but to mount an offensive of critical significance. The Egyptian Third Army Corps, some 25,000 men, was located on the southern sector of the eastern bank of the Suez Canal, with only a narrow overland link with Egypt proper. The Israeli army was advancing to cut it off completely. When the American ambassador, Kenneth Keating, raised the matter with Prime Minister Golda Meir, she admitted that the commanders of the Israeli army had pleaded with her not to accept a cease-fire until they could complete encirclement of the Third Army Corps. At the time, she and the cabinet had overruled them. Now, after the Egyptians allegedly broke the cease-fire, she had acceded to their request.

The Israeli case was, as Kissinger acidly notes, not credible.[52] The Egyptians, and the Soviets, protested to Washington immediately and vigorously. As noted, Kissinger admits that he had indicated in Tel Aviv that he would "understand"—that is, blink at—some "slippage" in Israeli conformity with the cease-fire and mentions the "sinking feeling" he had upon learning of the massive Israeli violation of the cease-fire; Kissinger observes "this new fighting was continuing far beyond the brief additional margin I had implied."[53]

The Soviet protests and urging that the United States get Israel to observe the cease-fire included an unprecedented note direct from Brezhnev to Kissinger. It was not even nominally addressed to Nixon.[54] The Soviets were in a desperate plight. Their credibility was on the line: with the Egyptians—with whom it was already low, but for whom they had just mounted a major arms resupply; with the Syrians, who had not yet accepted the cease-fire; and, indeed, with all the Arabs. The Soviets were not pursuing a forward diplomatic strategy, they were simply trying desperately to hold on.[55] And they were urging the United States to rein Israel in, calling only for a renewed Security Council cease-fire resolution.

---

52. Ibid., pp. 569, 571.

53. Ibid., p. 569.

54. The Soviet leaders were undoubtedly very suspicious about whether the United States, and specifically Kissinger, may not have been deceiving them in the cease-fire while quietly giving Israel a free hand. Soviet scholars have subsequently indicated that they were aware that that had happened. See Ye. M. Primakov, *Anatomiya blizhnevostochnogo konflikta* [The Anatomy of the Near East Conflict] (Moscow: Nauka, 1978), p. 173.

55. Kissinger, *Years of Upheaval*, p. 570. In addition to the highly unusual message from Brezhnev to Kissinger, the Soviet leader also sent two messages to Nixon within the span of a few hours. He used the hot line for the first time during the Nixon presidency. See Nixon, *RN*, p. 938.

Kissinger understood the Soviet plight, but it was of no concern to him as long as the Soviets did nothing more than wring their hands. On the other hand, Kissinger *was* deeply concerned about the situation for another reason: "If the United States held still while the Egyptian army was being destroyed after an American-sponsored cease-fire and a Secretary of State's visit to Israel, not even the most moderate Arab could cooperate with us any longer. We had to act quickly."[56]

Far from wishing Soviet intervention, Sadat even requested unilateral *American* action, if necessary, to enforce the cease-fire—an extraordinary proposal from the leader of a country with which the United States did not even have diplomatic relations and whose enemy had just been massively rearmed by the United States. Meanwhile, the Israelis were adamant against a cease-fire. Justifications based on alleged Egyptian violations were dropped: Israel did not *want* a cease-fire. Finally Meir acceded to American pressures to accept a new one, "urging" (not "demanding") return to the cease-fire line of the previous day, although with a more or less tacit understanding with Kissinger that it would be "difficult" to determine the actual line at the time the earlier short-lived cease-fire had taken place. By now, the Third Army Corps was cut off.[57]

Syria also accepted the new cease-fire, in accordance with UN Security Council Resolution 339 of October 23. By the next morning, however, the Egyptians reported new Israeli attacks. Again the Israelis claimed the Egyptians had attempted to break out of the encirclement, although implausibly in a direction *away* from Egypt. In any case the Israelis moved to occupy the Egyptian naval base at the city of Suez and were stopped only by heavy street fighting.[58]

Kissinger was increasingly alarmed not only at losing the confidence of Egypt and the other Arab states, but at possible Soviet intervention. Again Sadat pleaded with Nixon to intervene and enforce the cease-fire, if necessary "to intervene, even on the ground, to force Israel to comply with the cease-fire." Now the Soviets were publicly warning Israel of the "gravest consequences" if it did not stop its advance.[59] Kissinger told the Israelis that if Sadat asked the Soviets for troops to enforce the cease-fire, as he had the United States, "Israel would have outsmarted itself." Moreover, he said that Brezh-

---

56. Kissinger, *Years of Upheaval*, p. 571.

57. Ibid., pp. 571–75. The Israelis had picked up the idea of not knowing where the old cease-fire line was from an informal, cynical suggestion of Kissinger's: "How can anyone ever know where a line is or was in the desert?" Meir replied, "They will know where our present line is, all right." Kissinger comments, "Now I understood. Israel had cut the last supply route to the city of Suez." Ibid., p. 571.

58. Ibid., pp. 575–76.

59. "Statement of the Soviet Government in Connection with the Violation by Israel of the Resolution of the UN Security Council on a Ceasefire in the Near East," *Pravda*, October 24, 1973.

nev's own involvement made the issue even more dangerous and that "there were limits beyond which we could not go, with all our friendship for Israel, and one of them was to make the leader of another superpower look like an idiot."[60]

At midday on October 24 the Egyptians first privately and then publicly called on both the United States and the Soviet Union to send in forces to reinstate and ensure the cease-fire. Concern arose in Washington over how the Soviet leaders would react in their desperate predicament.

Early that evening Kissinger received a call from Dobrynin stating that the Soviet Union would support a resolution in the Security Council calling for the dispatch of Soviet and American troops to enforce the cease-fire. Kissinger said the United States would veto any such resolution. At 9:35 p.m. a crucial letter from Brezhnev arrived. It prompted an American response that escalated the American-Soviet divergence—essentially over the means to achieve a common objective—into a dramatic apparent military confrontation.[61]

Kissinger has provided the most complete and authoritative excerpts from Brezhnev's letter, including the precise text of the key paragraphs. The first of these was a proposal to "urgently dispatch to Egypt Soviet and American military contingents, to insure the implementation" of the Security Council cease-fire resolutions, "and also of our understanding with you on the guarantee of the implementation of the decisions of the Security Council."[62] The United States objected strongly to the idea of Soviet troops, for reasons Kissinger spells out very clearly: "We had not worked for years to reduce the Soviet military presence in Egypt only to cooperate in reintroducing it as the result of a UN resolution. Nor would we participate in a joint force with the Soviets, which would legitimize their role in the area."[63] In fact, Kissinger even goes so far as to say (at least in the safety of a retroactive statement) that "we were determined to resist by force if necessary the introduction of Soviet troops into the Middle East regardless of the pretext under which they arrived."[64]

---

60. Kissinger, *Years of Upheaval*, p. 576.

61. Ibid., pp. 579–84.

62. Ibid., p. 583. The omitted portion apparently includes Soviet criticism of the deliberate Israeli violation of the understanding reached between the USSR and the United States. See Zumwalt, *On Watch*, p. 445.

63. Kissinger, *Years of Upheaval*, p. 579.

64. Ibid., p. 580.

   There were contingency plans for the United States to introduce troops into the area, but their purpose would not have been to "resist by force introduction of Soviet troops," but to provide a matching demonstration and a quid pro quo for parallel withdrawals of Soviet and American troops once a cease-fire was agreed to. This information is from a senior NSC official involved in preparing the plans.

Kissinger also interprets the vague Soviet language on guaranteeing the implementation of the decisions of the Security Council as representing a proposal to send Soviet and American troops to "impose not just a cease-fire but a final settlement" and "the imposition of a comprehensive peace." There is no basis for this interpretation—unless it is to set up a straw man, "a US-Soviet condominium"—that Kissinger then claims credit for demolishing.[65] Clearly the United States could with its veto control whatever was to become "a decision of the Security Council." Kissinger seems too sensitive to charges of superpower condominium.

It was the element of the Brezhnev message beyond the proposal of joint action, which the United States was virtually bound to reject, that provoked alarm. Brezhnev had gone on to make a veiled threat of possible unilateral Soviet action if the United States refused to join with the USSR. He said: "I will say it straight that if you find it impossible to act jointly with us in this matter, we should be faced with the necessity urgently to consider the question of taking appropriate steps unilaterally." This message, Kissinger states, was "in effect an ultimatum. . . . It was one of the most serious challenges to an American President by a Soviet leader."[66] Kissinger quickly concluded not only that the United States must reject the Soviet proposal, but that "we would have to do so in a manner that shocked the Soviets into abandoning the unilateral move they were threatening—and, from all our information, planning. For we had tangible reasons to take the threat seriously."[67]

What were the tangible reasons? The most relevant intelligence concerned a cessation of the airlift of Soviet arms supplies on October 24. The reason may have been the cease-fire, but it may have been to concentrate and prepare the aircraft for the transport of Soviet troops. On October 10, as the war was unfolding, the Soviets had alerted their airborne troops command, which comprised seven small divisions totaling about 50,000 men.[68] The Soviet

---

65. Ibid., pp. 583–84.

66. Ibid., p. 583.

67. Ibid., p. 584.

68. The significance of this alert caused some confusion at the time and in retrospective accounts. First, American intelligence on October 10-11 identified the alert of three Soviet airborne divisions, but by October 11-12 confirmed that all seven had been placed on alert. Many accounts speak of an alert of seven airborne divisions as though that number were either arbitrary or, conversely, a calculated and calibrated force level to meet a given contingency, as contrasted with, say, six or ten airborne divisions. Ibid., p. 507; and Nixon, *RN*, p. 937. In fact, the Airborne Troops of the Soviet Army is a special resource of the high command, and alerting the seven operational divisions meant that the entire force was alerted. This explanation is not intended to disparage the significance of the Soviets' preparing themselves for the *possible* commitment of elements of that force under some contingencies, for example, if the United States accepted the proposal, but also possibly for unilateral deployment. Such a deployment might have been limited to the environs of Cairo and Damascus, or it might have taken place closer to the battle line.

naval force in the Mediterranean had gradually been augmented to reach eighty-five ships (by October 31 it reached ninety-six), including several landing ships presumably with naval infantry (marines) on board. There had also been reports of a Soviet merchant ship passing the Bosphorous on October 22 with radiating material (nuclear weapons?) on board.[69]

What had been an eventful day was followed by an even more eventful night and morning—what journalist Elizabeth Drew has called "Strangelove Day." Kissinger convened a meeting. According to contemporary White House statements it was an NSC meeting, although Kissinger acknowledges that "internal records" at the time termed it a Washington Special Action Group (WSAG) "meeting of principals"[70]—himself, Secretary of Defense Schlesinger, Director of Central Intelligence William E. Colby, Chairman of the JCS Admiral Thomas H. Moorer, White House Chief of Staff Haig, Deputy National Security Adviser Scowcroft, and Kissinger's NSC military assistant, Commander Jonathan T. Howe. Kissinger makes clear in his memoir that at no time did he discuss the crucial Brezhnev message with Nixon or even inform him of it. On Haig's recommendation Kissinger decided not to waken him—"Haig thought the President too distraught to participate in the preliminary discussion." It is still not clear whether Haig did discuss the matter with Nixon. Kissinger makes clear that Haig never told him he had done so and then carefully notes that "Nixon has written in his memoirs" that Haig did inform him and that he, Nixon, instructed that there should be a meeting and that "we needed action, even the shock of a military alert." It is unlikely that this conversation ever took place and specifically that Nixon approved in advance the idea of a military alert. Neither Kissinger nor Haig

---

Some accounts, which I have not been able to confirm, report a higher state of alert for one or a few airborne divisions on October 24. There was, in Washington at the time, unconfirmed intelligence indicating possible moves to send some airborne troops. A higher alert for one division would have represented a greater likelihood of use of that division. The first source to make this claim was David Binder, "An Implied Soviet Threat Spurred U.S. Forces' Alert," *New York Times*, November 21, 1973. One source reports that four airborne divisions were alerted on October 24 in addition to three on October 11, but in fact all seven were on alert by October 11. See Barry M. Blechman and Douglas M. Hart, "The Political Utility of Nuclear Weapons: The 1973 Middle East Crisis," *International Security*, vol. 7 (Summer 1982), p. 136.

69. Some subsequent accounts have played up the possible Soviet supply of nuclear weapons, perhaps for the Egyptian SCUD ballistic missiles, but this was never a serious possibility. It was not a principal consideration at the meeting at which an alert was decided upon. The most complete analysis and rejection of this possibility is by Yona Bandmann and Yishai Cordova, "The Soviet Nuclear Threat towards the Close of the Yom Kippur War," *Jerusalem Journal of International Relations*, vol. 5 (1980), pp. 94–110. These authors may, however, err in believing that the first report of a neutron-radiating cargo reached Washington only after the alert.

70. Kissinger, *Years of Upheaval*, pp. 586–87. Kissinger goes to great pains to protest the practical and legal irrelevance of the distinction—but also stresses that he chaired the meeting as presidential assistant and not as secretary of state.

ever said so in the meeting. This claim of Nixon's is particularly suspect because of his known prevarication on this very matter in statements at the time and subsequently, stimulated by the barrage of criticism from the press when his absence from this key meeting became known.[71] This claim led in turn to "informed" accounts in 1973–74 that related incorrect reports that Kissinger had immediately informed Nixon of the Brezhnev message and recommended an alert, and that "the President concurred and empowered Kissinger to take charge of the American response."[72] Nixon, and Kissinger, were very much on the defensive over the whole alert, as will be seen.

At the famous meeting (NSC, WSAG, or whatever) it was decided to issue a general DEFCON III military alert—Defense Condition 3, which is short of full readiness, but higher than a normal alert. The alert included the Strategic Air Command (SAC) and the North American Air Defense Command (NORAD)—thus involving American strategic nuclear forces—as well as other field commands in Europe and around the world. Other measures were also taken: the 82nd Airborne Division was placed on high alert, the sixty B-52s in Guam were returned to the continental United States to join the SAC alert, the carrier *Franklin Delano Roosevelt* and its squadron were moved from the western to eastern Mediterranean to join the *Independence*, and the carrier *John F. Kennedy* and its escorts were moved to the Mediterranean.

Only a few hours later the alert—which Kissinger had intended to be picked up promptly by Soviet intelligence and have an impact in the Kremlin—was headline news in the morning American newspapers. Kissinger was "shocked," as he notes in his memoir. "This unexpected publicity would inevi-

---

71. Nixon's claims to have actively participated—made in an attempt to cover up his absence—began at his own press conference on October 26, but he carries them further in his memoir. His description of his alleged conversation with Haig is also suspect because of other distortions in his account. For example, in the meeting that Nixon now admits not attending, Kissinger recounts how "an urgent message to Sadat in Nixon's name" was approved and dispatched immediately. Kissinger, *Years of Upheaval*, pp. 583, 592. For his part Nixon writes, "Late that night I sent Sadat" the message in question. Nixon, *RN*, p. 938. Nixon goes on to speak of a unanimous "recommendation" for the alert, which "we" flashed to American forces. He knew nothing about the alert until it appeared in the morning newspapers. Further, Nixon claims authorship of the letter to Brezhnev: "I sent a letter . . . directly to Brezhnev from me." Nixon, *RN*, p. 939. Kissinger correctly notes that the message was drafted in the meeting and "delivered to Dobrynin in Nixon's name" at 5:40 a.m., long before Nixon arose and in all probability before he even knew there was a message from Brezhnev. Kissinger recounts briefing Nixon about the Brezhnev letter, the response, the alert, and other American deployments only at 8:00 a.m. on October 25. He leaves some uncertainty by saying he "did not know what conversations Haig had had with Nixon in the early hours of the morning." Probably there were none, as Haig was *with* Kissinger when the latter briefed Nixon. Kissinger, *Years of Upheaval*, p. 593.

72. The Kalb brothers gave this particular account, since belied by Kissinger's memoir; they were beneficiaries of much White House backgrounding. See Kalb and Kalb, *Kissinger*, p. 554. Much of the remainder of their account of the U.S.-Soviet exchanges and even Kissinger-Dobrynin conversations *does* reflect valid inside information. See ibid., pp. 541–64.

tably turn the event into an issue of prestige with Moscow, unleashing popular passions at home and seriously complicating the prospects of Soviet retreat."[73]

The message to Brezhnev had said that "we could in no event accept unilateral action. . . . such action would produce incalculable consequences which would be in the interest of neither of our countries and which would end all we have striven so hard to achieve."[74] The American response then went on to propose an alternative to the dispatch of troop contingents: inclusion of Soviet and American observers with a UN truce supervisory force.

The alert did not resolve the situation.[75] It may have headed off a possible quick unilateral dispatch of a Soviet military contingent in response to Sadat's plan, and to that extent it contributed to preventing a much more difficult situation. But the alert (and the Brezhnev letter that prompted it) did not end the crisis. Rather, that was accomplished both by the United States' compelling Israel to accept a cease-fire and allow resupply of the Egyptian Third Army Corps, and by Sadat's actions. In response to American pleas Egypt substituted for its request for American and Soviet troops a request that the Security Council provide "an international force," which by UN precedent and practice would exclude U.S. and Soviet troops. This request effectively removed the earlier Egyptian request to which the Soviet leaders had proposed responding.

Brezhnev replied to the American communications within a few hours with a letter blandly ignoring the crisis of the night before and picking up the alternative proposed in the Nixon letter—dispatch of Soviet representatives to observe the implementation of the cease-fire—and by agreeing to act jointly with the United States in this endeavor. Kissinger comments: "The Soviets had backed off. The immediate danger was over." Meanwhile the Security Council had passed a third cease-fire resolution (Resolution 340) that same afternoon, "demanding" (no longer "urging") that the parties return to the positions of October 22 when the first cease-fire was called. Kissinger notes Israeli objection to the resolution, but does not comment further on American-Israeli relations during this critical period of October 24–25.[76]

---

73. Kissinger, *Years of Upheaval*, p. 591. Kissinger was also very unhappy, for the same reason, that in his press conference on October 26 Nixon played up the extent of a threat in his efforts to justify the action and persuade the public that the U.S. response had not been prompted by Watergate.

74. Ibid.

75. For analyses of the effectiveness of the October War alert as a political and military signal, see Joseph J. Kruzel, "Military Alerts and Diplomatic Signals," in Ellen P. Stern, ed., *The Limits of Military Intervention* (Beverly Hills, Calif.: Sage, 1977), pp. 90–95; and Blechman and Hart, *International Security*, vol. 7 (1982), pp. 132–56.

76. Kissinger, *Years of Upheaval*, pp. 591–99. Kissinger does say that he assured Ambassador Dinitz that "we had no intention of coercing Israel *in response to a Soviet threat,*" but he did not say the United States would not press hard once the threat was moot. Ibid., p. 590. Emphasis added.

The final phase of the crisis was played out from October 26 to 29. The American alert was lifted on October 26. The Soviets relaxed their much more limited alert measures, which did not include their strategic nuclear forces. The cease-fire was now effective. The Israelis did not, however, return to the October 22 line. The principal immediate problem therefore became resupply of the still isolated Third Army Corps, which the Israelis were very reluctant to permit. Kissinger does note some of the pressure the United States placed on Israel to permit the resupply, coupled with inducements in the form of promises to work for direct Israeli-Arab negotiations, as Israel wanted. The American goal was to preserve the Third Army Corps, Sadat, and the new U.S. position of potential leverage with the Arabs. But while quietly pressuring Israel to permit resupply of the Third Army and to enter negotiations, the United States did not demand that Israel return to the original cease-fire line.[77] The Soviets were effectively cut out of the action.

Late on October 26 Brezhnev, in a message again pressing the United States to stop the Israeli offensive and permit resupply of the Third Army Corps, for the first time discussed the American alert.[78] He stated that it had surprised him and noted that the Soviets had not responded, although the alert was an unprovoked action and did not promote a relaxation of international tensions and détente. The American reply the next day expressed U.S. commitment to the cease-fire and promised to press Israel to permit nonmilitary supplies to the Third Army. It also attempted to justify the American alert by quoting Brezhnev's letter of October 24. This explanation was also an attempt to discourage any new Soviet pressures.[79]

Finally, on October 27 first the Egyptians and then the Israelis agreed that military delegations from the two countries should meet and work

---

77. Ibid., pp. 601–05.

78. Brezhnev did not publicly refer to the alert in a speech that same day in Moscow or on any other occasion. The Soviet leaders did not wish to incite tension or raise any questions about relative Soviet and American roles in resolving the October War.

Heikal reports that the Soviet leaders were astonished by the American alert. Brezhnev told both President Houari Boumedienne of Algeria and President Hafez al-Asad of Syria that he thought it was a false alarm resulting from an American desire to overdramatize the crisis. Heikal, *Road to Ramadan*, p. 255.

TASS belatedly reported the American alert "in some areas, including Europe," and denied that the Soviet Union had given any grounds for concern that justified an alert. TASS, Radio Moscow, October 27, in FBIS, *Soviet Union*, October 29, 1973, p. B3. At least one commentator said that the alert was intended to frighten the Soviets but had been a waste of time. Yury Zhukov, Radio Moscow, October 29, 1973, in ibid., p. F6. Other Soviet commentaries picked up American commentary suggesting that domestic Watergate considerations had prompted the measure. See TASS, Radio Moscow, October 28, in ibid., pp. B3–4. While the U.S. action was exploited in propaganda addressed to audiences in Europe and Asia, the global, nuclear aspects of the alert were never disclosed.

79. Kissinger, *Years of Upheaval*, pp. 607–09. Kissinger does not refer to Brezhnev's admission of surprise over the alert; Nixon does note it. Nixon, *RN*, p. 942.

out the precise implementation of the cease-fire and that a convoy under UN auspices would supply food and water to the Third Army Corps. Still Israel delayed, first with respect to the Egyptian military delegation and then to the convoy. The new arrangements finally began on October 28–29. A letter from Brezhnev on October 29 and further conversations with Dobrynin and Gromyko on October 31 and November 1 marked continuing Soviet attempts to reinsert themselves into the action. But the action was in the United States: on October 28 Acting Foreign Minister Ismail Fahmy of Egypt and on October 31 Prime Minister Golda Meir of Israel visited Washington for talks on future steps. The Soviets were, after October 27, effectively out of the picture.[80]

The Soviet-American "confrontation" had ended, and the Arab-Israeli confrontation assumed a changed aspect, with direct negotiations replacing armed hostilities and with the United States the only outside power having the confidence of both and the resources and opportunities to influence them.

The prevailing American impression, boosted by Kissinger's detailed account of American-Soviet exchanges and the dramatic U.S. worldwide alert, is that a critical bilateral confrontation occurred, engendered by a clash of Soviet and American interests. Some stress the weakness of détente in preventing the confrontation, others the value of détente in contributing to its speedy and peaceful resolution.

There had been a brief and dramatic flare-up. But it was engendered not by a clash of American and Soviet objectives, but by an excessively dramatic maneuver by Kissinger for diplomatic leverage in the region. The United States and the Soviet Union shared fundamentally the same objectives in the so-called crisis of October 24–25. Moreover, while American-Soviet interaction *appeared* to be the critical element, the really crucial interaction was that between the United States and Israel. As outlined earlier, Kissinger's own statements confirm that the real American objective during the conflict as a whole was expansion of American diplomatic influence with the Arabs at the expense of the Soviet Union by preventing *either* a decisive Arab or Israeli victory, while placing the United States in the dominant position for postwar diplomacy and reducing to a minimum any Soviet role. In the phase ending with the cease-fires of October 22 and 23 the United States had essentially achieved this objective, and the Soviet Union had seen no alternative but to accept the situation. The new crisis of October 24–25 arose from the Israeli offensive that threatened the Egyptian Third Army Corps and therefore the whole foundation of the American diplomatic strategy.

The new crisis of October 24–25 also threatened Soviet as well as American credibility. *Both* the United States and the Soviet Union had to prevent an Israeli victory, especially after they had sponsored the cease-fire, and therefore both worked toward that common objective. The Soviet letter of October 24, while far from an ultimatum, did represent a real danger. The Soviets had spent over two decades cultivating the Arabs. Now they had sought

80. Kissinger, *Years of Upheaval*, pp. 608–24.

to use their détente with the United States to collaborate in ending the war. Rather than let all that collapse at Israeli hands, the Soviets would probably have provided forces if necessary, at least to defend Cairo and Damascus. But on October 24 Brezhnev was *appealing* to Nixon and Kissinger, not *challenging* them.

The Brezhnev letter represented, in effect, a sharing of the Soviet dilemma with the United States. It was in the first instance an overt plea to the United States to act together in defense and support of the *jointly* sponsored cease-fire. Far from representing a Soviet threat, it urged reinforcement of superpower collaboration as the preferred course of action. Recourse to limited, unilateral measures to meet its minimum requirements for credibility as a great power was specifically only a potential fallback. The Soviets had no reason to expect the American response would be a global nuclear alert. Nor, on the other hand, did they necessarily expect agreement on a dispatch of forces from the two countries—although increasingly they thought that might be necessary. What they did try to do was to reinforce the incentives for the *United States* to act in its own self-interest and in support of the joint efforts by compelling Israel to comply with the Security Council resolutions to which it had committed itself.

Kissinger, supported by Nixon to the extent of his then very limited participation, knew very well that for the American strategy to succeed—now a real prospect—it was absolutely necessary to stop Israel.[81] But for Kissinger the Brezhnev letter did not serve to reinforce readiness to act jointly with the Soviet Union in support of the earlier joint diplomatic action. Rather, it required new *American* initiatives that would stop Israel but *without* letting it appear that the Soviet Union was responsible for the pressure on Israel. (For reasons of domestic policy it was also necessary that the White House not seem to be responsible for compelling a halt to the Israeli advance, a consideration that further compounded the problem of the public handling of the matter.)

Kissinger had no interest whatsoever in supporting joint action, for a reason he freely acknowledges: it would have meant sanctioning a Soviet share in participation in the affairs of the region, while his objective was to exclude Soviet influence. He shows no sign that the United States, as coauthor of a joint U.S.-Soviet deal accepted by Israel, had a responsibility for seeing that Israel respected that solution. His indignation at Soviet attempts to impose a superpower condominium (which was indeed present in the Soviet approach) was not caused by moral shock at that idea. He correctly believed the

---

81. Recall again Kissinger's words: "If the United States held still while the Egyptian army was being destroyed after an American-sponsored cease-fire and a Secretary of State's visit to Israel, not even the most moderate Arab could cooperate with us any longer." Ibid., p. 571. Note that Kissinger's interest is exclusively the preservation of American diplomatic advantage, not support for joint superpower actions.

United States could do better for itself by shouldering the Soviets out of the action than by collaborating with them.

Kissinger saw a need on October 24-25 vigorously and urgently to blunt further Soviet consideration of the alternative of unilateral intervention in response to Sadat's request. (Later, after Sadat withdrew the request for U.S. and Soviet troops, Kissinger must have realized there was absolutely no possibility that the Soviets would intervene militarily "without the sanction of either the host country or the UN," even "against the will of the local government." Nevertheless, he gives resolute assurances that these phantom threats would have been firmly resisted.[82])

There was another, basic reason for the alert. Kissinger wanted to blunt criticism that the United States was not acting sufficiently forcefully. He wanted to show an American ability to face down the Soviets. He did not use the alert to shore up Nixon's faltering position, as many suspected at the time. Nixon himself attempted to do so after the event—in his news conference on October 26 and again in his memoir—by inflating both the Soviet threat and his own role in dealing with it in an attempt to portray himself as indispensable in the presidency.[83]

But above all Kissinger was applying his customary diplomatic jujitsu—using the Brezhnev ultimatum publicly as a foil to demonstrate American will and capability to face down any Soviet threat, while privately using it as leverage in pressing the Israelis into stopping their advance—and not because the Soviets wanted them to stop, but because the *United States* wanted them to. In this sense the most relevant comparison was not Nixon's farfetched reference to the Cuban missile crisis (the last time the United States had resorted to a worldwide alert), but the Christmas bombing of North Vietnam ten months earlier. In both cases the United States demonstratively, indeed excessively, slapped down the perceived opponent before the world, while at the same time stressing privately that although it would not permit an adversary to dictate to one of its protected associates—South Vietnam and Israel— it also would not permit that associate to deflect a course of action on which it was embarked that involved its own security interests as well as those of its protected associate. The alert was thus also a signal to Israel that the United States had broader interests at stake that it was determined to support.

Kissinger does not disclose fully the extent of his efforts to persuade Israel to accept the cease-fire and above all not to destroy the trapped Egyp-

---

82. Ibid., pp. 592-93.

83. See Nixon, *RN*, pp. 938-42; and "President Nixon's Press Conference of October 26," *Department of State Bulletin*, vol. 69 (November 12, 1973), pp. 581-84. (Hereafter *State Bulletin*.) Nixon even attempted to build himself up by saying Brezhnev understood the power not only of the United States, but also of this president, who had moved into Cambodia, bombed and mined North Vietnam on the eve of the first summit meeting, and bombed North Vietnam in December 1972. "President Nixon's Press Conference of October 26," p. 584. Kissinger also notes the incentive Nixon had to paint the crisis in the darkest possible tones. Kissinger, *Years of Upheaval*, p. 606.

tian army.[84] He notes that "we had to accomplish the goal while maintaining a public posture of close association" and if possible without "forcing us into open opposition." He admits having warned Ambassador Dinitz on October 26 that "there was a limit beyond which we could not be pushed" by Israeli efforts to stall and destroy the Third Army Corps. And Kissinger indicated that continued Israeli intransigence "would almost certainly result in *American* resupply of the Third Army, which the Defense Department was recommending."[85]

The Israelis expressed great anguish and insisted that while they were not persuaded, they would succumb to American pressure. Kissinger finally called in the Israeli ambassador and laid down the American demand, in Nixon's name, late in the evening of October 26. Kissinger comments, in justification of his stand, "My ultimate responsibility was as Secretary of State of the United States, not as psychiatrist to the government of Israel. With the utmost reluctance I decided that my duty was to force a showdown." He made clear that the United States could not permit the destruction of the Third Army, which Israel had surrounded after the cease-fire the United States had sponsored, that there must be nonmilitary supply for that army, and that there must be negotiation with the Egyptians. If not, the United States would join the other members of the Security Council in imposing those conditions. Kissinger admits he does not recall whether he checked with Nixon before making this crucial demarche to the Israelis "in Nixon's name." The Israelis gave in.[86]

Thus the October War ended without having disrupted the American-Soviet relationship, and indeed with a new and successful experience at reconciling a conflict directly affecting U.S.-Soviet competition in the third world. Moreover, in the key arena of Middle East diplomacy American leaders could boast: "We had emerged as the pivotal factor."[87]

There remain, however, questions about the obligations of the powers under détente in relation to the crisis, and also of the impact of the October War on Soviet and American views of détente.

Obligations of Détente and the October War

Some American observers, in October 1973 and subsequently, have charged that the Soviet Union failed in the crisis to meet its commitments

---

84. Kissinger notes dryly that "our shared interests did not embrace the elimination of the Third Army. . . . Israel had completed its entrapment well *after* a cease-fire (that we had negotiated) had gone into effect." *Years of Upheaval*, p. 602.

85. Ibid., p. 604, and see p. 603. For references to Israeli accounts of the U.S. pressure, see Quandt, *Decade of Decisions*, pp. 197–98.

86. Kissinger, *Years of Upheaval*, pp. 608–09. Nixon undoubtedly would have agreed, as Kissinger claims.

87. Ibid., p. 612.

under détente. Those who had always opposed détente with the Soviet Union were, in particular, quick to rush to that judgment. Senator Jackson, for example, accused the Soviets of violating détente and the American administration (in particular Kissinger) of being beguiled by it. Jackson was the first to leak the fact of the Brezhnev letter of October 24, which he publicly characterized as "brutal" and "threatening."[88] Even Melvin R. Laird, the counselor to the president, never more than lukewarm to détente, had complained publicly on October 16 that the Soviet Union was not doing all that it should to support détente.[89] Later Professor Richard Pipes, in a book attacking détente, claims that the Soviets "connived" with the Arabs to launch the surprise attack on Israel. He characterizes Brezhnev's letter of October 24 as an "ominous ultimatum." He concludes, "The Soviet Union violated the spirit and letter of these accords [the Basic Principles of 1972] almost at once."[90] A few months after the October War another tract against détente devoted to the war similarly asserts: "There is no doubt, on the basis of the evidence, that the Soviet Union violated both the letter and the spirit of the agreements signed at the Moscow and Washington Summit Meetings."[91]

In examining the détente obligations of the Soviet Union and the United States with respect to the October 1973 war, particular attention needs to be paid to the spirit and letter of the most relevant specific agreements. It should, however, also be borne in mind that the agreements are *political* documents, not binding beyond their interpretation by the parties themselves. The more legalistic a country's approach, the more minimalist or restrictive its interpretation of the documents. On the other hand, too broad an interpretation of their spirit can defeat their meaning too. It is, however, appropriate to consider the general responsibilities of détente, as well as concrete undertakings, so long as these are understood not as legal commitments, but as general objectives and even as requirements to sustain a relationship of détente.

The Basic Principles governing relations between the two powers signed at the summit in May 1972 included two provisions that might be

---

88. See ibid., pp. 531, 595. Kissinger notes that Jackson somehow learned of the letter. He was probably informed of it by Admiral Zumwalt, who was briefed by Admiral Moorer on the NSC/WSAG meeting and the letter. Zumwalt cites parts of the letter not made public and mentions his conversations with Jackson on the crisis. See Zumwalt, *On Watch*, pp. 435, 443–45.

89. Bernard Gwertzman, "Conflict over Soviet Ties Widens in Administration," *New York Times*, October 17, 1973.

90. Richard Pipes, *U.S.-Soviet Relations in the Era of Détente* (Boulder, Colo.: Westview, 1981), p. xiii.

91. Foy D. Kohler, Leon Goure, and Mose L. Harvey, *The Soviet Union and the October 1973 Middle East War: The Implications for Detente* (University of Miami Center for Advanced International Studies, 1974), p. 87. See also Stephen P. Gilbert, "United States Policy in the Middle East," in James E. Dornan, Jr., ed., *United States National Security Policy in the Decade Ahead* (Crane, Russak, 1978), pp. 162–65.

considered to apply to situations such as the October 1973 war. According to the second principle, "the USA and the USSR attach major importance to preventing the development of situations capable of causing a dangerous exacerbation of their relations. Therefore, they will do their utmost to avoid military confrontations and to prevent the outbreak of nuclear war. They will always exercise restraint in their mutual relations." And in the third principle, "the USA and the USSR have a special responsibility . . . to do everything in their power so that conflicts or situations will not arise which would serve to increase international tensions."

The Agreement on the Prevention of Nuclear War signed in June 1973, developing the crisis prevention provisions of the earlier accord, included a provision that the two powers "agree that they will act in such a manner as to prevent the development of situations capable of causing a dangerous exacerbation of their relations, as to avoid military confrontations, and as to exclude the outbreak of nuclear war." It also included an undertaking that "if relations between countries not parties to this Agreement appear to involve the risk of nuclear war. . . . [the two powers] shall immediately enter into urgent consultations with each other and make every effort to avert this risk."[92] In addition, it should be recalled that in the joint communiqués issued at the summit meetings of 1972 and 1973 the two powers had pledged to work for a settlement of the Middle Eastern problem.[93]

The first general obligation of the two powers under these détente agreements clearly was to consult, as well as to conduct their unilateral policies in such a way that at the very least they would not encourage, and preferably discourage or prevent, conflicts from arising. It is difficult to fault either side as having done anything that contravened that détente understanding, although both can be faulted more generally for not having worked harder to resolve the festering Arab-Israeli conflict. The Soviet Union did take the initiative in raising the problem repeatedly with the United States and in pointing to the danger of leaving it unresolved. The United States viewed the situation with greater equanimity, but that was its error.

Neither power had a very good record in meeting its "special responsibility . . . to do everything in their power so that conflicts or situations will not arise which would serve to increase international tensions." The Arab-Israeli conflict was long-standing and was bound to inflame new tensions unless and until the underlying grievances were dealt with. Neither of the powers was responsible for the origin of the conflict, nor did they control the adversaries; still, it would be difficult in terms of their general obligations to say that either did everything in its power to resolve the problem. It may be charged that the Soviet arms supply to the Arabs and the American arms supply to Israel, partic-

---

92. These agreements were discussed more fully in chapters 9 and 10. The quotations are from the official texts, cited in those chapters.

93. Here there is a legalistic distinction; in 1972 they agreed to work toward a "peaceful settlement in the Middle East," in 1973 merely toward a "settlement in the Middle East."

ularly in the absence of any movement toward resolving the problem, was not doing all that could and should have been done to defuse a dangerous situation. But it could also have been (and was) argued that arms supply was a restraining influence. The Soviet Union did withhold some requested arms—and thereby lost some influence. But both the United States and the Soviet Union also had other objectives in their arms supply and various unilateral actions that did not contribute to crisis prevention, even if those actions were not intended to incite conflict or prolong tension.

Both powers understood the situation and did not expect more than they got from the other. Early in the war, in a general philosophical address on October 8, Kissinger interjected a comment that "détente cannot survive irresponsibility in any area, including the Middle East."[94] But when asked about that statement a few days later, he clarified what he meant: "We also do not consider that Soviet actions as of now constitute the irresponsibility that on Monday evening I pointed out would threaten détente."[95]

Apart from general obligations to head off threats to peace, there is a question whether the Soviet Union was obligated to have consulted with the United States once it learned on October 3 that the Arab countries were going to attack, and particularly after it was advised on October 4 of the date of the attack. The United States did not know at that time whether and what the Soviet government had known in advance. On October 12, after it became known that the Soviet Union had evacuated its dependents before the attack, Kissinger was asked if the Soviets should have informed the United States in advance. He replied that if the Soviet Union had *encouraged* the attack—for which there was no evidence—it would be very serious. But if it had "learned of these attacks through its own intelligence or in some other manner and did not inform us, then this is a different problem. In an ideal world, one would expect closer consultation, but given the particular volatility of the Middle East, it would have been a heavy responsibility to make known certain advance information. Nevertheless," he continued, "we would like to stress that if either side in this relationship has certain knowledge of imminent military operations in any explosive part of the world, we would consider it consistent and indeed required—by the principles that have been signed between the United States and the Soviet Union—that an opportunity be given to both sides to calm the situation."[96]

Kissinger was on solid ground in distinguishing the real from the ideal world. Whatever the precise obligations under the Basic Principles, clearly the Soviet Union would not have told the United States when it was informed by an ally of a plan to launch an attack. Clearly the United States

94. "Moral Purposes and Policy Choices," Address by Secretary Kissinger to the Pacem in Terris Conference, October 8, *State Bulletin*, vol. 69 (October 29, 1973), p. 529.

95. "Secretary Kissinger's Press Conference of October 12," *State Bulletin*, vol. 69 (October 29, 1973), p. 535.

96. Ibid., p. 537.

would not have told the Soviet Union if it had known of an Israeli plan to attack an Arab country. While ideally either power should, in practice the political cost of underoutting an ally or friend is too great.[97]

Even the terms—the letter—of the two agreements do not support Kissinger's broader comment on a requirement to consult. The only specific requirement to inform and consult is in case relations between third parties "appear to involve the risk of nuclear war." This was not the case in October 1973. Moreover, while clearly a détente crisis prevention effort should extend as broadly as practicable, the United States and the Soviet Union were careful to include in both the Basic Principles and the Prevention of Nuclear War agreement explicit provisions *excluding* any commitment that contravened their obligations to allies. The Basic Principles "do not affect any obligations with respect to other countries earlier assumed" by the United States and the Soviet Union, and "nothing in this [Prevention of Nuclear War] Agreement shall affect or impair . . . obligations undertaken by either Party towards its allies or other countries in treaties, agreements, and other appropriate documents." The Soviet-Egyptian Treaty of Friendship and Cooperation had been signed May 21, 1971, and was in effect.

During the October War both powers sought—in addition to maneuvering for political advantage—to defuse the crisis and to end the war. Both adequately met the obligations of the agreements in this respect. The Soviet Union, in fact, wished to go further than the United States in pursuing a collaborative path in working toward a settlement. It saw UN Security Council Resolution 338 as the start of a joint endeavor, while the United States saw greater advantage in maneuvering itself into the pivotal role in Middle Eastern diplomacy.

Finally, as to the obligation "to avoid military confrontations" between themselves (contained in both agreements), it would be difficult to argue that the Soviet plan for a joint dispatch of troops or, if declined by the United States, possible unilateral action to help enforce an agreement jointly sponsored by the two powers, approved by the Security Council, and nominally accepted by the belligerents constituted a threat to instigate a military confrontation between the two powers. A unilateral dispatch of troops might not have been wise and might have raised tension and resulted in a possible confrontation—but it would not have been a violation of the agreements. The American global alert was probably, legalistically, more provocative in risking confrontation and was the only action by either side that raised the specter of nuclear war. But it, too, was not a violation of the agreements.

The one provision of the Basic Principles of 1972 most relevant to the role of both powers in the October War is one not previously noted because it does not specifically relate to crisis prevention: "Both sides recognize

---

97. Six years later, the United States interpreted its own obligations in a limited fashion when it failed to inform the Soviet Union or consult with it after being advised of Chinese plans to attack Vietnam.

that efforts to obtain unilateral advantage at the expense of the other, directly or indirectly, are inconsistent with these objectives." Clearly one of the principal aims of both the United States and the Soviet Union before, during, and after the October War was precisely "to obtain unilateral advantage at the expense of the other," directly and indirectly. In that respect, indeed, neither side has ever abided by the Basic Principles.

The governments of the United States and the Soviet Union did not accuse each other of violations of the principles of détente in 1973. To the contrary, leaders of both countries said that détente had contributed significantly to the peaceful resolution of the crisis. In his press conference on October 25, under intense pressure and in the shadow of the global military alert and apparent sudden American-Soviet confrontation, and in the face of suspicions that Watergate had prompted the alert, Kissinger presented a remarkably balanced review of the October War, American policy in the Middle East, American-Soviet relations, and the alert. While declining to disclose the nature of Soviet-American exchanges and effectively sidestepping Nixon's absence from the scene during the crucial hours, he sought to deflate the crisis. By the time of the press conference Kissinger knew that the Egyptian invitation for Soviet and American troops had been withdrawn and the possibility of a real crisis averted. But the impasse with Israel over the cease-fire had not yet been resolved.

When asked whether Soviet actions were threatening to exploit détente to U.S. detriment, Kissinger said the United States was not prepared to make that judgment. He noted that the United States and the Soviet Union "are at one and the same time adversaries and partners in the preservation of peace." He noted, quite correctly, that "as adversaries, we often find ourselves drawn into potential confrontations and each of us has friends that let themselves pursue objectives that may not be sought fully by either of us." When asked about the alert and the "brutal" note from Brezhnev, as Senator Jackson had termed it publicly, Kissinger declined to discuss the exchanges but said the alert was "precautionary," a step taken "because we thought there might be a possibility that matters might go beyond the limits. . . . But we are not yet prepared to say that they have gone beyond these limits [as specified in his speech of October 8]." Twice he stressed: "We do not consider ourselves in a confrontation with the Soviet Union" and "We are not talking of a missile-crisis-type situation." "As of now," he said, "the Soviet Union has not yet taken any irrevocable action. . . . We are not seeking an opportunity to confront the Soviet Union. We are not asking the Soviet Union to pull back from anything that it has done." Finally, "If the Soviet Union and we can work cooperatively, first toward establishing the cease-fire, and then toward promoting a durable settlement in the Middle East, then détente will have proved itself."[98]

---

98. "Secretary Kissinger's News Conference of October 25," *State Bulletin*, vol. 69 (November 12, 1973), pp. 589, 588, 592, 591, and in general 585–94.

President Nixon, in his news conference the following day, placed a very different emphasis on the crisis, in an attempt to depict himself as in charge and as indispensable. "A very significant and potentially explosive crisis developed. . . . It was a real crisis. It was the most difficult crisis we have had since the Cuban confrontation of 1962. But because we had our initiative with the Soviet Union, because I had a basis of communication with Mr. Brezhnev, we not only avoided a confrontation, but we moved a great step forward toward real peace in the Mideast. Now, as long as I can carry out that kind of responsibility, I am going to continue to do this job."[99]

Nixon praised the role of détente: "without détente, we might have had a major conflict in the Middle East. With détente, we avoided it." Moreover, as a result of the experience "we both now realize that we cannot allow our differences in the Mideast to jeopardize even greater interests that we have, for example, in continuing a détente in Europe, in continuing the negotiations which can lead to a limitation of nuclear arms . . . and in continuing in other ways that can contribute to the peace of the world."[100]

Even Secretary of Defense Schlesinger, not the foremost proponent of détente, said in a news conference that same day devoted mainly to the military alert, "I indicated that we were very far away from a confrontation. . . . I think that this whole episode indicates the limitations, in a sense, of détente, but it also indicates the strength of détente." The ability "to work out in collaboration with the Soviets the arrangement for two cease-fires is, I think, a tribute to the strength of détente—the communications that existed between the two so-called superpowers."[101]

In the final of these contemporary post-crisis commentaries, Kissinger on November 21 agreed that perhaps there had been something more of a confrontation than he had indicated on October 25 (this statement came in reply to a question about President Nixon's remarks on the gravity of the crisis). But he redefined what Nixon had been saying as meaning the gravity of the crisis "had it occurred." Kissinger stressed that détente did not mean that the United States and the Soviet Union always had parallel objectives—"détente is made necessary because as the two great nuclear superpowers we have a special responsibility to spare mankind the dangers of a nuclear holocaust." Moreover, "in this relationship, one will always have an element both of confidence and of competition" so that if and when a confrontation occurs, "it is important that enough confidence exists so that the confrontation is mitigated." He also stressed that "a confrontation occurred, really in the aftermath

99. "President Nixon's News Conference of October 26," *State Bulletin*, vol. 69 (November 12, 1973), pp. 581, 583, and see pp. 581–84.

100. Ibid., p. 583.

101. "Secretary of Defense Schlesinger's News Conference of October 26," *State Bulletin*, vol. 69 (November 19, 1973), p. 622. Somewhat obscurely he concluded, "I should underscore that detente refers to mutual relaxation of tension and that detente must be a two-way street, as in the close of this episode it turned out to be." Ibid.

of a settlement and as a result of actions which could not be fully controlled by either of the two sides. . . . But one also has to consider how rapidly the confrontation was ended and how quickly the two sides have attempted to move back and are now moving back to a policy of cooperation in settling the Middle East conflict." In short, détente "played a role in settling the crisis even though it had not yet been firm enough to prevent the crisis."[102]

Thus in its public stance at the time, and privately as well, the administration considered the October War as having tested détente, and that all in all détente had proven its mettle. The administration certainly did not believe that the Soviet Union had violated or abandoned détente by its actions.

The administration also never charged the Soviets, publicly or privately, with having acted contrary to the Basic Principles or Prevention of Nuclear War agreement. On two tense occasions it had warned the Soviets not to take actions that it said it would have regarded as incompatible with détente, but the USSR did not take those actions. On October 13, when the airlifts were under way and a tentative cease-fire had faded, Kissinger had warned Dobrynin, "We will not under any circumstances let détente be used for unilateral advantage" by a Soviet-sponsored Arab military victory.[103] And in "Nixon's" reply to Brezhnev on October 25 the United States made its only reference to the 1972 and 1973 agreements: "You must know, however, that we could in no event accept unilateral action. This would be in violation of our understandings, of the agreed Principles we signed in Moscow in 1972 and of Article II of the Agreement on Prevention of Nuclear War. As I stated above, such action would produce incalculable consequences which would be in the interest of neither of our countries and which would end all we have striven so hard to achieve."[104] The message went on to counsel: "Mr. General Secretary, in the spirit of our agreements this is the time for acting not unilaterally but in harmony and with cool heads."[105] Arriving a few hours after the sudden American global nuclear alert, this admonition to act with cool heads may have perplexed the Soviet leaders, but they continued to seek joint action, and the American side had no complaint.

In his memoir Kissinger remarks, "I do not believe that history will judge that *we* were the party being used. The war was contained, and the United States maneuvered successfully to reduce the Soviet role in the Middle East."[106] He also complains, understandably, about the currents of public dissatisfaction with détente during the October War; although his remarks are rather indiscreet, they are not inaccurate: "There was a growing debate over

---

102. "Secretary Kissinger's News Conference of November 21," *State Bulletin*, vol. 69 (December 10, 1973), pp. 704, 706, 707.

103. Kissinger, *Years of Upheaval*, p. 521.

104. Cited in Kissinger, ibid., p. 591.

105. Cited in Nixon, *RN*, p. 939.

106. Kissinger, *Years of Upheaval*, p. 507. Emphasis added.

détente, a mounting clamor that in some undefinable way we were being gulled by the Soviets. *The opposite was true, our policy to reduce and where possible to eliminate Soviet influence in the Middle East was in fact making progress under the cover of détente.*" Further, "*Détente was not a favor we did the Soviets. It was partly necessity; partly a tranquilizer for Moscow as we sought to draw the Middle East into closer relations with us at the Soviets' expense;* partly the moral imperative of the nuclear age."[107] So much for the basic principle of not seeking "to obtain unilateral advantage at the expense of the other [side], directly or indirectly."

Kissinger even extends his panegyric to the American nuclear alert as a tool of diplomacy beyond crisis resolution. He remarks that "the Soviets subsided as soon as we showed our teeth. We were thus able to use the crisis to shape events and reverse alliances in the Middle East in defiance of the pressures of our allies, the preferences of the Soviets, and the rhetoric of Arab radicals."[108]

The final summary statement by Kissinger, despite its character as an argumentative defense of the Nixon-Kissinger détente in the October War, also stands as a reasonable and balanced judgment of the role of détente in its initial trial in regional conflict. "Clearly," Kissinger writes, "détente had not prevented a crisis, as some of our critics with varying degrees of disingenuousness were claiming it should have—forgetting that détente defined not friendship but a strategy for a relationship between adversaries. After all, a principal purpose of our own Mideast policy was to reduce the role and influence of the Soviet Union, just as the Soviets sought to reduce ours. But I believe détente mitigated the succession of crises that differences in ideology and geopolitical interest had made nearly inevitable, and I believe we enhanced the national interest in the process."[109]

The Impact on Soviet Views of Détente

The October War, according to then Prime Minister Kosygin, was "a serious test of the policy of détente." He argued that had it not been for the development of détente in the preceding years, the crisis "would probably have assumed a far more dangerous nature."[110] Brezhnev repeated the same theme, specifically adding that if the war had broken out "at a time of general international tension and aggravated relations between the United States and the

---

107. Ibid., p. 594. Emphasis added.

108. Ibid., p. 980.

109. Ibid., p. 600.

110. "Speech of A. N. Kosygin," Minsk, November 14, *Sovetskaya Byelorossiya* [Soviet Belorussia], November 15, 1973.

Soviet Union, the conflict in the Near East might have assumed a scope endangering world peace."[111]

These statements by Soviet leaders (and echoed by many commentators) were made in the weeks immediately after the war. They marked a step beyond the strong continued endorsement of détente made during the war itself. For example, the slogans on the anniversary of the October Revolution (issued annually in the name of the Central Committee of the party) were published on October 14, 1973, when the outcome of the war was far from clear—indeed, just after both the Soviet Union and the United States had begun a major airlift of arms to the two sides. While calling on "the peoples of the world" to "demand the termination of the Israeli aggression," and sending "warm greetings"—nothing more—to "the Arab peoples waging a just struggle for the liberation of their lands," the slogans made no reference at all to the "imperialists" as supporting Israel. And the themes of support for détente and peaceful coexistence, including the new 1973 theme of making détente "irreversible," were undiluted.[112] On October 16, as Kosygin was arriving in Cairo to try to persuade Sadat to agree to a cease-fire, Aleksandr N. Shelepin, one of the Politburo members least devoted to détente, gave that policy his support in a speech to the World Federation of Trade Unions. He referred to the Peace Program adopted at the Twenty-fourth Party Congress two years earlier and praised the fact that "a shift has been achieved in the international situation away from confrontation, 'cold' war, and tension toward an improvement in the international atmosphere." He stressed that "the détente that has developed is not a temporary phenomenon, a mere episode, but the beginning of a radical restructuring of the international situation on the basis of peaceful coexistence." This formulation, to be sure, placed the emphasis on what détente would do to further peace, progress, and socialism, rather than on collaboration with the United States and other imperialists. And Shelepin referred to both the "support by reactionary imperialistic forces" for Israel, and the "still influential forces [in the West] which oppose détente and peaceful coexistence" and work against it.[113]

This divergence in emphasis on different *aspects* of détente characterized Soviet views thereafter. In addition to Shelepin, Politburo member Andrei P. Kirilenko, in the leadership's major speech on the anniversary of the revolution, vindicated and reaffirmed détente, but without stressing Soviet-American cooperation. Indeed he linked the recent Near Eastern crisis to

---

111. "Speech of L. I. Brezhnev," to the Indian Parliament, November 29, *Pravda*, November 30, 1973.

112. "CPSU Central Committee Slogans for the 56th Anniversary of the Great October Socialist Revolution," *Pravda*, October 14, 1973. With respect to Soviet support, the slogans on the Near East were in fact weaker than the year before.

113. "Speech of Comrade A. N. Shelepin," to the Eighth World Trade Union Congress, Varna, October 16, *Trud* [Labor], October 17, 1973. The *Pravda* version of his speech cut back on the criticism of imperialism, while preserving the praise of détente. TASS, "At the Trade Unions' Forum," *Pravda*, October 17, 1973.

"reactionary forces" and noted that the Soviets had "no illusions about imperialism."[114] Three other Politburo members, Mikhail A. Suslov, Nikolai V. Podgorny, and Yury V. Andropov, while all explicitly supporting détente in speeches in November and December, failed to follow Brezhnev and Kosygin in trumpeting détente as a major factor in the successful resolution of the October War.[115]

In several articles during and after the war Marshal Grechko, the minister of defense and since April 1973 a member of the Politburo, also emphasized the nefarious role of "the imperialists" in encouraging and supporting Israel.[116] Similarly, several other generals in their national day speeches in November said that the October War had shown the aggressive nature of imperialism and the continuing risks of war, despite détente.[117] This rhetoric is not, however, unusual; the purpose of such speeches is to raise morale by calling for vigilance. Shortly thereafter Marshal Grechko, in his first comment after the resolution of the conflict, said that détente had "prevented the dangerous eruption of the war in the Near East from assuming dimensions threatening general peace."[118] The Soviet military press also continued to support détente and cited the experience of the October War. Thus, for example, an article in *Red Star* reviewing the events of 1973 concluded, "Détente in our relations with the United States and other capitalist countries withstood a stern test and proved its strength and vitality during the alarming and dangerous October days in the Near East." The article also referred specifically to the joint initiative of the USSR and United States for a cease-fire as being a direct result of the détente relationship. "Détente," the article stated, "is not a fashionable word but a necessity in the nuclear age."[119]

The role of détente in the October War crisis was discussed at the Central Committee plenary meeting held in December. The October War had

114. A. Kirilenko, "Address on the 56th Anniversary of the October Revolution," *Pravda*, November 7, 1973.

115. M. Suslov, Radio Vilnius, November 28, in FBIS, *Soviet Union*, November 29, 1973, pp. R1–3; N. Podgorny, Radio Riga, December 26, in ibid., December 26, 1973, p. R3; and Yu. Andropov, Radio Tallin, December 27, 1973. None of these three speeches, all delivered in provincial capitals, was reprinted in the central press.

116. Marshal A. A. Grechko, "The Battle for the Caucasus [October 1943]," *Pravda*, October 8, 1973; Grechko, "On a Leninist Course of Construction and Peace," *Pravda*, November 8, 1973; and "Shoulder to Shoulder," *Krasnaya zvezda* [Red Star], October 18, 1983; and see the statement by Marshal I. I. Yakubovsky in *Sovetskaya Byelorossiya*, October 13, 1973, for a similar statement.

117. See General of the Army V. I. Petrov, Radio Khabarovsk, November 7, in FBIS, *Soviet Union*, November 8, 1973, pp. P4–6; Colonel General G. I. Salmanov, Radio Kiev, November 7, ibid., pp. P1–3; and Admiral of the Fleet N. I. Smirnov, Radio Vladivostok, November 7, ibid., pp. P3–4.

118. Marshal A. Grechko, *Komsomolets Tatarii* [Komsomol of Tatary], January 9, 1974.

119. Colonel A. Leont'yev, "Year of Great Changes," *Krasnaya zvezda*, December 31, 1973. This article was evidently intended to make clear to the Soviet military that détente had not been found wanting and remained a main line of Soviet policy.

involved a mix of competition, near confrontation, and collaboration with the United States. The principal concern at the plenum was to determine what the Soviet Union could do to salvage something from its long efforts to build influence in the Near East. The question of cooperation with the United States in the anticipated intensive diplomatic activity was one of the issues, not because of objections to that collaboration, but because of doubts that the United States would accede to such a Soviet role—a question over which the Soviet leaders harbored well-founded doubts and suspicions. (Additional policy courses the Soviet leaders decided they should pursue are discussed later in this chapter.)

Détente, as interpreted and practiced by Brezhnev since 1971, had relied heavily on building cooperation with the United States and on opening other paths that would assist "progressive" developments in the world to proceed without direct Soviet or American involvement. The whole course of American policy toward the Middle East since 1969, and especially efforts since 1972 to expel Soviet presence and influence, had raised serious questions that were brought to a head by the October War. The détente strategy also, as noted, had just suffered a serious blow in September 1973 when Chilean President Salvador Allende was overthrown and killed. The circumstances were different, but the operative question for Soviet policymakers was the same: is active détente with the United States serving broader Soviet aims?

Similarly, the rising congressional support for the Jackson-Vanik amendment to the trade bill raised doubts that most-favored-nation (MFN) status would be granted, despite renewed private assurances by Nixon and Kissinger that it would be. To help meet this threat to a main economic plank of the Soviet détente platform, the Soviets continued to permit emigration of Soviet Jews throughout the crisis and thereafter—despite explicit Arab (and Chinese) criticism that this policy aided Israel. Moreover, it was at the height of the October War (October 18) that coincidentally Nixon formally requested congressional approval of the trade legislation incorporating the extension of MFN to the Soviet Union.[120] In early November, after public Soviet support for the Arab embargo on oil sales to the United States, and while that issue remained alive, the United States did suspend consideration of MFN for the Soviet Union.

Brezhnev carried the day in the Soviet Union in affirming the continued value of his policy and strategy of détente and reliance on maximizing cooperation with the United States. Nevertheless, the October War had increased doubts in the collective judgment of the Soviet leaders—for some, of course, more than for others. Divergences within the leadership (and among various elements in the Soviet political establishment) continued to be expressed indirectly in the form of differences in emphasis and selection.[121]

---

120. Kissinger, in the same press conference on October 25 at which he sought to justify the global military alert, had argued against denying MFN to the Soviet Union.

121. For analyses of the treatment by the Soviet leadership and media of themes related to the

The main conclusion, however, remained that presented by Brezhnev on November 29 and on a number of later occasions. Many Soviet commentators have repeated it since 1973, even after renewed American-Soviet tensions in the late 1970s and early 1980s: "Thanks to the joint efforts of the USSR and the United States, which had become possible under the conditions of détente, a dangerous armed conflict in the Near East was successfully extinguished."[122] At the Vienna summit in 1979, in stressing the importance of Soviet-American détente, Brezhnev cited the joint effort in resolving the October War as an example of the USSR's "good experience of cooperation in international affairs."[123] In 1981 Gromyko also credited détente with having "successfully averted a serious threat to the peace" in the October War.[124]

Many of the Soviet evaluations have been very close to that of Kissinger cited earlier: while détente had not been sufficiently developed to prevent the outbreak of the conflict in October 1973, it had greatly facilitated American-Soviet cooperation in defusing the conflict and preventing its escalation.[125]

The Soviet policy of détente and cooperation with the United States did pose a problem for the Soviet leaders in their third world policy. Particularly after the Soviets (in response to the American alert) publicly denied having had any interest in military intervention in the area, they found many Arabs skeptical of Soviet protestations that détente with the United States was compatible with support for the progressive and national liberation struggle. The Chinese, the Libyans, and many other Arab commentators charged Soviet-American collusion and claimed that the Soviet priority was preserving détente with the United States. In rebuttal, most Soviet commentary tried indirectly to argue the Soviet case. One Soviet broadcast in Arabic on October 30 did, however, specifically acknowledge the charge, insisting that the "speedy and decisive support" given Egypt and Syria by the Soviet Union "dispelled and wiped out the myth" that "détente between the Soviet Union

---

October War, see Galia Golan, *Yom Kippur and After*, pp. 92–94, 109–12, 138–48, 160–68; Yaacov Roi, ed., *The Limits to Power: Soviet Policy in the Middle East* (St. Martin's Press, 1979); and Freedman, *Soviet Policy toward the Middle East Since 1970*.

122. V. F. Petrovsky, "The Struggle of the USSR for Détente in the 1970s," *Novaya i noveishaya istoriya* [Modern and Contemporary History], no. 1 (January–February 1981), p. 12; and see Petrovsky, "The Role and Place of Soviet-American Relations in the Contemporary World," *Voprosy istorii* [Questions of History], no. 10 (October 1978), p. 87. Vladimir F. Petrovsky is a senior official in the Ministry of Foreign Affairs.

123. "Speech of L. I. Brezhnev," *Pravda*, June 18, 1979.

124. A. Gromyko, "Leninist Foreign Policy in the Contemporary World," *Kommunist*, no. 1 (January 1981), p. 15. Gromyko does not, however, refer to the "joint efforts" of the two powers.

125. For example, see Vikenty Matveyev, "Détente and Conflicts," *New Times* (Moscow), no. 46 (November 1974), pp. 4–5.

and the United States and other Western capitalist countries can affect Soviet commitments to its friends and allies."[126]

All in all the Soviet leaders did not see American-Soviet competition for influence in the Middle East as incompatible with détente. They hoped the United States would place more reliance on joint efforts by the two powers, partly because they hoped to develop a relationship with the United States more generally, but also because they saw their own best opportunities for extending their influence in the region through sharing in the diplomacy in pursuit of a settlement. By the same token, however, they understood that Kissinger was seeking to minimize the Soviet role and leverage. Neither side had been prepared to forgo or foreclose other advantages for the sake of détente in the October War. But the experience of détente *had*, in their view, helped to regulate the American-Soviet competition at a time of potential danger. Moreover, in the first several months after the October War the Soviets did harbor hopes that they would be able to play a significant role along with the United States in the peace process.

The Soviet policy and strategy of détente with the United States and the West had, of course, much broader and more important aims and purposes to which the Soviet leaders continued to give high priority. But even in regional competition détente had proven useful in containing the risks of American-Soviet confrontation. The Soviet leaders turned to other complementary policy lines to meet further Soviet aims.

The Impact on World Politics

The October War, in addition to its impact on the Soviet and American evaluations of their détente relationship, had a number of further consequences that indirectly affected American-Soviet relations.

Both powers actively moved to seek advantage in the new round of diplomatic maneuvering. Soviet Deputy Foreign Minister Vasily V. Kuznetsov got to Cairo first—on October 30 (and then to Damascus November 3)—but he had nothing to offer but verbal support. Kissinger, arriving in Cairo on November 7, had in four days assured Egypt that Israel would observe a firm cease-fire, allow the resupply of the Third Army Corps and city of Suez, agree to a reciprocal return of prisoners of war, and lift its blockade of Egyptian ports. By mid-January the first Israeli-Egyptian disengagement agreement on the canal area had been reached, allowing Egypt to reopen the Suez Canal.[127]

---

126. "Myths That Have Been Dispelled," Radio Moscow, in Arabic to the Arab world, October 30, in FBIS, *Soviet Union*, October 31, 1973, pp. F3–4.

127. See Kissinger, *Years of Upheaval*, pp. 614–66, for the most complete and authoritative account. See also Quandt, *Decade of Decisions*, pp. 214–29.

Meanwhile, after a further round of visits by Kissinger to Cairo, Damascus, and Tel Aviv (and also Riyadh, Saudi Arabia), the formal conference agreed upon in the initial Israeli-Egyptian talks on November 11 was held in Geneva on December 21–22, with representatives of the United States and the Soviet Union as cochairmen. The two powers had cooperated in arranging the conference. In addition, the United States successfully pressed Israel into attendance, while the Soviets made considerable effort, at some cost, to gain Syria's attendance, although it was unsuccessful in doing so. But Syria was indirectly engaged. In addition the United States was now engaged bilaterally with Syria as well, not the case during the war. The Geneva conference was, however, the last-gasp effort to work out multilaterally a comprehensive settlement, and it never reconvened.[128]

What followed was, in effect, a resumption of American diplomatic soundings among the key Arab and Israeli parties in a series of excursions by Kissinger in what became aptly called "shuttle diplomacy." During this process in 1974 and 1975 Kissinger succeeded in arranging a number of further disengagements and partial Israeli withdrawals not only with Egypt (in January and March 1974 and September 1975), but also with Syria (in May 1974).[129]

On February 28, 1974, the United States and Egypt formally reestablished diplomatic relations. In June, in a last fling as president, Nixon made a tour of the Middle East, including Egypt, Jordan, Saudi Arabia, Syria, and Israel.[130] It was announced that United States–Syrian diplomatic relations were being restored. The United States also began to provide substantial economic aid to Egypt and Jordan, and a lesser amount to Syria (pursuant to an administration request submitted in April 1974). On March 18 the Arab oil embargo against the United States, imposed on October 20 at the height of the October War, was lifted.

Shuttle diplomacy had its successes and failures. It remains an open question whether it was the most productive course to have followed in seeking a settlement for the Arab-Israeli conflict. But from the American standpoint it clearly served two related purposes well: it secured for the United States the pivotal role in Middle East diplomacy, and it excluded the Soviet Union from the main arena of diplomatic action. This situation became clear to all by the spring of 1974.

---

128. For Kissinger's detailed account of the preparations for and conduct of the conference, see *Years of Upheaval*, pp. 747–98.

129. Ibid., pp. 799–853, 935–78, 1032–1110, for shuttle diplomacy through May 1974. See also Quandt, *Decade of Decisions*, pp. 224–81, for a briefer informed account of the entire course of the effort through 1975; and see Edward R. F. Sheehan, *The Arabs, Israelis, and Kissinger* (Reader's Digest Press, 1976).

130. Kissinger, *Years of Upheaval*, pp. 1123–43. Nixon regarded the tour as very successful; he was well-received, and the impression of normalcy in American conduct of international affairs was created. Little else, however, was accomplished.

The Soviet leaders accordingly began a major reassessment of their interests in the Middle East and of the best courses of action in pursuing them.[131] The Soviet leaders continued to press the United States to include them in the diplomatic activity, but to no avail.

The tenuous Soviet tie to Egypt had been greatly weakened by the purge of Ali Sabri and other pro-Soviet members of the Egyptian leadership as early as April–May 1971, and then by Sadat's frustration over Soviet unreadiness to lend full support to his efforts to force Israel into negotiations in 1971–73. That trend was furthered by growing secret Egyptian-American contacts in 1972–73 and direct relations after the October War. By April 1974 Sadat was receiving American arms and credits, was reorienting the Egyptian economy to the West, and was relying on the United States for diplomatic support. Sadat's expulsion of Soviet military advisers in July 1972 had been a major step, although it did not end Soviet naval access to Egyptian ports. By the spring of 1974 the Soviets reportedly refused Egyptian requests to defer payment on past arms deliveries and soon thereafter ended all arms supplies.[132] By March of 1976 Egypt canceled its 1971 treaty with the Soviet Union and unilaterally repudiated its arms debts.

With the sharp erosion of Soviet influence in Egypt, previously the centerpiece of Soviet efforts to build its role in the Near East, the Soviet leaders began in the spring of 1974 to attempt further development of their relations with Syria and Iraq and to establish new relationships with the PLO and Libya.

Syria was the priority target both because it represented the main Soviet investment and because of growing fears over American incursions through the shuttle diplomacy and disengagement negotiations. In April 1974, just as relations with Egypt were being cut back, the Soviets began to deliver the long-withheld MiG-23 fighters. They also agreed to defer repayment of Syria's billion dollar arms debt and received President Hafez al-Asad warmly in Moscow.[133]

Marshal Grechko visited Baghdad in March 1974 as part of the same process of building a broader net of Soviet ties in the area. MiG-23s followed. The Soviet Union also expressed support for Iraq in its campaign against the Kurds, who were being covertly supported by Iran, the United States, and Israel.

---

131. This assessment was mainly undertaken within the Ministry of Foreign Affairs and the Central Committee, but the relevant institutes of the Academy of Sciences were also brought in. For an analysis of the role of the institutes, see Oded Eran, "The Soviet Perception of Influence: The Case of the Middle East, 1973–76," in Roi, *The Limits of Power*, pp. 127–48.

132. Golan, *Yom Kippur and After*, pp. 206–13.

133. Ibid., pp. 213–19. The Soviets insisted on including in the communiqué on Asad's visit a defense of détente as meeting the interests of all states and as applicable in the Middle East, while still supporting the hard-line Arab positions favored by Asad. Ibid., p. 218. Interesting differences in emphasis among the Soviet leaders can be identified. Ibid., pp. 216–18.

In May a Soviet economic delegation visited Algeria, as did Marshal Grechko, and a Soviet naval squadron. Soviet military and economic assistance was increased not only to Syria, Iraq, and Algeria, but also to South Yemen, Somalia, Afghanistan, and Iran.[134]

Most striking was the move toward closer relations between the Soviet Union and Libya. In Paris, Libyan Prime Minister Abdul Salam Jalloud met briefly with President Podgorny on April 7 and was then invited for a ten-day state visit in Moscow in mid-May. An arms sale was arranged. There was a notable change in the commentary in the Soviet media on Libya, which went from critical polemic to favorable mention.[135]

Another significant new departure was increased Soviet support for the PLO, despite continuing Soviet support for a state of Israel within the pre-1967 borders and condemnation of PLO acts of terrorism. In August 1974, after a visit by PLO leader Yasir Arafat, the Soviet Union officially recognized the PLO.[136]

Thus one result of the exclusionary American diplomacy after the October War and loss of Soviet influence with Egypt was that the Soviet Union moved to build new ties with Libya and the PLO, as well as to reinforce its ties with Syria, Iraq, and Algeria. At the same time, in pursuing this broadened diplomatic effort in the Middle East and continuing their general policy of seeking to build ties with the third world, the Soviet leaders continued to argue the contribution détente between the great powers was making to global progressive revolutionary change.

Apart from its effects on American and Soviet thinking and actions and on the diplomacy and politics of the Middle East, the October War also had a considerable—and negative—impact on American–Western European relations. The American leaders and most European leaders were disappointed in some of their respective actions and attitudes while resenting others. Ironically, the disarray in the NATO alliance that existed during the October War and its aftermath buried the ill-starred Year of Europe envisaged by Kissinger.

As to American grievances, from the very start of the war the European countries had declined to join the United States in support of Israel. They even refused to allow the United States to use facilities to support the American airlift. The only exception was Portugal, which authorized use of the Lajes airfield in the Azore Islands, granted only after a very stiff American threat "to leave Portugal to its fate in a hostile world."[137] Two allies—not

---

134. Gus Ofer, "Economic Aspects of Soviet Involvement in the Middle East," in Roi, *The Limits of Power*, pp. 67–95.

135. Golan, *Yom Kippur and After*, pp. 199–200, 224–25, 241–42.

136. Ibid., pp. 232–40; and Galia Golan, *The Soviet Union and the Palestine Liberation Organization: An Uneasy Alliance* (Praeger, 1980). Various Soviet leaders expressed different degrees of support for the Palestinians, suggesting differing policy views among them.

137. Kissinger, *Years of Upheaval*, p. 520. The United States also rejected a Portuguese attempt to get arms aid for its colonial campaigns in Africa as a quid pro quo.

named by Kissinger, but identified by geography as Turkey and Greece—even refused to allow American overflights while acquiescing in Soviet ones.[138] The United States did fly some arms and military equipment to Israel from American stocks in West Germany, but had to fly circuitously around and through the Strait of Gibraltar in order to avoid overflying France, Britain, Spain, or Italy. After the Arab oil embargo (on October 20), noncooperation with the United States tightened. On October 25 the West German government made public what it had already communicated privately: no use could be made of West German territory to move arms from American depots to the Middle East. Spain, a bilateral ally that from the outset had refused to allow the United States to use its bases on Spanish soil, declared on October 25 that the U.S. alert did not apply to American bases in Spain. Britain would not even allow use of bases on Cyprus for American SR-71 reconnaissance aircraft located there to monitor the cease-fire or to support the U.S. airlift.[139]

On the diplomatic front Kissinger was very annoyed by a British change of heart and refusal to sponsor a cease-fire proposal on October 13 because its own soundings had indicated Arab objections.[140] Later Britain and France objected to an American idea for a UN emergency force that excluded the forces of the permanent members of the Security Council—this limitation was designed to rule out Soviet participation, but also precluded British and French, as well as Chinese and American, participation.[141]

More broadly, the allies declined to accept American urging that they curtail their economic and political relations with the Soviet Union as a means of pressure. Similarly they rejected American suggestions that they signal a slowdown in the preparations for the Conference on Security and Cooperation in Europe.[142] Instead, on October 26 (in reaction to the unilateral U.S. alert) the allies adopted a French suggestion and suspended work on the draft NATO declaration being prepared to meet the Year of Europe.

Finally, the allies did not accept the American strategy for Middle Eastern diplomacy, which they regarded as too gentle on Israel and too unresponsive to legitimate Arab interests. Although the Arab oil embargo reinforced this general West European view (to which the Netherlands was the only exception), it did not create it. Instead, the Europeans pursued their own policy in attempting to encourage a comprehensive settlement. Most jarring

---

138. Ibid., pp. 524, 709. The Soviets did not request permission.

139. Ibid., pp. 701, 713–14. Kissinger does not mention Cyprus directly, but that is what he is referring to. He also does not disclose that in retaliation he curtailed normal American intelligence sharing with Britain for a time. This information was obtained from informed American officials.

140. Ibid., pp. 509–11, 516–17.

141. Ibid., p. 713.

142. Ibid., pp. 710–11. Kissinger is not explicit on these American demands, but his text reflects them indirectly. They have been confirmed by other sources.

was a declaration by the European Community on November 6, while Kissinger was in Cairo, calling for Israeli withdrawal first to the October 22 cease-fire line, and then to the 1967 borders. Not only did this approach depart drastically from the American proposals and diplomatic strategy, but it was issued without advance consultation or even notification.[143]

American leaders were genuinely hurt and angered by the allied actions. Differences over policy toward the Arab-Israeli dispute were long-standing and well-known, and Kissinger did not expect real support. But he and other American leaders did not anticipate that the European allies would oppose U.S. positions and manifest that lack of support in such concrete terms and public opposition. After allied objections to the U.S. unilateral alert—about which the allies were not consulted, but only informed after the event—the United States began to express its dissatisfaction more frequently, both publicly and privately.

On October 25, after the West German government publicly announced that the United States could not move its arms from Germany to Israel, Washington sent an official note saying: "The USG[overnment] believes that for the West to display weakness and disunity in the face of a Soviet-supported military action against Israel could have disastrous consequences."[144] Kissinger admits this reaction was "bound to escalate tensions even further." But he excuses it as a reaction: he and presumably his colleagues in the leadership (he does not say that Nixon or anyone else cleared the note) were "infuriated by a sense of abandonment in a crisis, our nerves taut from several all-night vigils." And he notes the United States made similar complaints to the British and others. The State Department spokesman, Secretary of Defense Schlesinger, and President Nixon himself all publicly gave vent to the strong American annoyance with its allies.[145] Privately, and not very discreetly, Kissinger in particular displayed his anger. He was reported in the press to have said, "I don't care what happens to NATO, I'm so disgusted." While that remark was officially denied, other sources confirm that he made similar remarks on more than one occasion.[146]

In a letter from Nixon to West German Chancellor Willy Brandt on October 30 the United States laid out more fully the basis for its objections to the allied stand: "the Alliance cannot operate on a double standard in which U.S. relations with the USSR are separated from the policies that our Allies

---

143. Ibid., p. 718.

144. Cited by Kissinger, ibid., p. 714.

145. Ibid.

146. See David Binder, "Kissinger Said to Express Disgust at Allies' Position," *New York Times*, October 31, 1973; and Laqueur, *Confrontation*, p. 207. Heikal reports that he was present when Kissinger told a group in Cairo: "I don't care what happens to Western Europe. They can all go to hell as far as I am concerned. They are on their knees to us when they think they need us; but when they think they can do without us they behave completely irrationally." Heikal, *Road to Ramadan*, p. 255.

conduct toward the Soviet Union. By disassociating themselves from the US in the Middle East, our Allies may think they protect their immediate economic interests, but only at great long term cost. A differentiated détente in which the Allies hope to insulate their relations with the USSR can only divide the Alliance and ultimately produce disastrous consequences for Europe."[147]

Kissinger ties the allied reactions to a selfish drive to enjoy the fruits of independence and détente for themselves, while being unwilling to share the burden of defending Western security with the United States. And, as he puts it, "an Alliance for whose vitality partners are not prepared to curtail their freedom of action is on the way to disintegration."[148]

It is possible to sympathize with Kissinger's anger at the allied actions in weakening the American political position and in undercutting his grand diplomatic strategy. But even retrospectively Kissinger does not comprehend the basis for that stand. The European allies did not reject the principle that members of an alliance must be prepared to curtail their own freedom of action. They simply believed that it should apply to the United States as well. From their standpoint the United States was jeopardizing European security interests by supporting Israel, which had long flouted the UN Security Council (Resolution 242) by refusing to negotiate a peace settlement and relinquish the Arab lands it had occupied. That was what had led to the October War. Then the United States sought to drag them into support of Israel by airlifting arms there, an action that led to the Arab oil embargo that could have imperiled their interests for the sake of a course of action they regarded as unjust. To the allies the threat did not come from the Soviet Union, but from unwise actions by the United States, taken unilaterally and without consultation. The airlift had been bad enough. The U.S. military alert of its forces in Europe was too much. The United States had unilaterally, without consultation or even advance notification, directly placed the territories of the allies in a superpower confrontation where there had been none and when there was no Soviet threat to Europe.

The United States had used the alert to convert an Arab-Israeli conflict, into which the United States had plunged, into a matter of East-West confrontation. Then it had used that tension as an excuse to demand that Europe subordinate its own policies to a manipulative American diplomatic gamble over which they had no control and to which they had not even been privy, all in the name of alliance unity. The allies regarded all this as a perversion of the alliance. At the same time, the American strategy also engendered a threat to the European members. American diplomatic notes such as the two cited above were disingenuous. Where was the "Soviet-supported military action against Israel" on October 25, after the Soviet Union and Egypt had accepted a cease-fire and it was Israel that was continuing its advance? Was it

---

147. Cited by Kissinger, *Years of Upheaval,* p. 716.
148. Ibid.

the allies that were "disassociating themselves from the US in the Middle East"? Or was the United States disassociating itself from the alliance (and the true interests and purposes of the alliance) by its reckless commitment to Israel? At best, the United States was substituting a dubious American unilateral diplomatic strategy directed primarily against the Soviet Union in the Middle East for a policy of settlement of the Arab-Israeli dispute.[149]

The October War thus seriously exacerbated American-allied differences. It also threatened to undermine the alliance policy of détente toward the Soviet Union. Without attempting to reconcile the sharply divergent American and European perspectives on this point, it is clear that the latent underlying difference between the European East-West détente and the American conception of its détente strategy toward the Soviet Union surfaced in their respective reactions to the October War in a way that foreshadowed the emergence of a serious longer term divergence in the early 1980s.

The Impact on American Views of Détente

The most important consequence for détente of the events surrounding the October 1973 war was the negative impact of the experience on important elements of American opinion. Analytically and objectively the American-Soviet cooperation in defusing both the Israeli-Arab conflict, and their own involvement in a crisis confrontation, may be judged a successful application of crisis management under détente. This view certainly was not, however, the prevailing one in the United States at the time or since. Moreover, apart from the fact that long-standing opponents of détente such as Senator Jackson used the occasion to stir up doubts about détente and renewed suspicion of Soviet motives, an important new constituency began to shift toward opposition to détente.

Reflecting on the roles of the United States and the Soviet Union in enforcing compliance with the cease-fire mandated by the United Nations and accepted by both Egypt and Israel, many Israelis and dedicated American supporters of Israeli interests (who often tend to equate Israeli and American interests) began to realize that the Soviet-American détente *had* played a role. But they were uneasy over that role and what it could mean in the future. The apparent confrontation symbolized by the alert of U.S. strategic nuclear forces was perhaps less significant than the fact that the United States had pressed

---

149. The position of the allies has not been fully set forth in any single place. Kissinger's discussion is highly charged in defense of his own position, although it does describe some allied reactions, even if presented prejudicially. Kissinger, *Years of Upheaval*, pp. 707–22, 727–35. See also William C. Cromwell, "Europe and the Structure of Peace," *Orbis*, vol. 22 (Spring 1978), pp. 22–27, 31–32; and Laqueur, *Confrontation*, pp. 206–13.

Israel into doing precisely what the Soviet Union (as well as the United States) had wanted: to halt its advance short of complete encirclement of the Egyptian Third Army Corps east of Suez. In broader terms, the United States had pursued interests it shared with the other superpower rather than those it shared with Israel (as defined by Israel). A precedent seemed to have been established for superpower condominium in pressing Israel to accept decisions made by others on matters involving Israeli security interests. What if the United States and the Soviet Union some day reached agreement on political issues—such as trading Israeli-occupied Arab territory for peace between Israel and its Arab neighbors? Even many Israelis who favored such an outcome did not want it imposed by Soviet-American condominium. Thus they saw the convergence of American-Soviet interests and effective cooperation in imposing a cease-fire as a harbinger of greater future collaboration by the two superpowers in working toward a resolution of the Israeli-Arab-Palestinian problem. Of necessity a solution would involve pressures on Israel to compromise (as it would on the other parties to the dispute).

Many politically significant supporters of Israeli interests thus became disenchanted with the policy of détente with the Soviet Union. The lesson of October 1973 was not that U.S.-Soviet détente had *failed*, but that it had *succeeded*. This outcome could lead to a curtailment of Israel's jealously guarded freedom of action to determine unilaterally its own security requirements. While undoubtedly the United States would never sacrifice Israel's vital interests as it saw them, ultimate judgment on what constituted the best interests of Israel would increasingly be made in Washington rather than in Jerusalem. What was potentially at stake was not any particular political threat, but the unique and crucial support from the United States that Israel had been able to count on whenever a crunch came, no matter what the Israelis decided to do. A threat to that ace in their hand could, they feared, deprive Israel of its mastery of its own destiny. The Arabs had never had that advantage from any association with the Soviet Union, as the October War had demonstrated. But if in the future the Arabs could sometimes share the umbrella of American support, Israel's trump card would be gone.

American confrontation with the Soviet Union, or at least a relationship based more on competition than on détente, was seen as offering greater assurance of American support against those Arabs who, to secure their own interests against Israel, had no alternative but to seek Soviet support. Israel could again present itself to the United States as a valuable ally against Soviet encroachments in the Middle East, inasmuch as Israel's adversaries could be painted as Soviet supporters or surrogates. Under détente, there was too much danger that the Arab countries could seek support from the United States as well as the Soviet Union, since American and Soviet interests were no longer assumed to be always in conflict.

Many Americans who felt passionately about Israel's interests were also seasoned cold warriors who had, in any case, been uncomfortable to one or another degree about détente with the Soviet Union. Many were Jewish, particularly in the intellectual academic and opinion-making fields, for example, Norman Podhoretz, editor of *Commentary*; Irving Kristol, editor of *Policy Review*; Ben Wattenberg of the American Enterprise Institute and the Coalition for a Democratic Majority; Martin Peretz, editor of the *New Republic*; Eugene Rostow, soon to head the Committee on the Present Danger and later the Arms Control and Disarmament Agency in the Reagan administration; and Professor Richard Pipes, later head of "Team B" that argued for more ominous intelligence estimates of Soviet motives and still later Soviet affairs adviser in President Reagan's NSC staff. Many were neoconservatives, combining a liberal domestic political stance with a harder foreign policy line. Some were active in politics, for example, Senator Richard Stone of Florida, later to agitate on the Soviet-Cuban threat. Many others were not Jewish, for example, Senator Jackson, Senator Daniel Patrick Moynihan of New York, and AFL-CIO leaders George Meany and Lane Kirkland. Nor did all strong supporters of Israel turn against détente; for example, Senators Edward Kennedy of Massachusetts, Walter Mondale of Minnesota (later vice president), Jacob Javits of New York, and Abraham Ribicoff of Connecticut.

In the months and years after October 1973 there was an important swing in sentiment by a significant segment of the opinion leaders who gave particular weight to Israeli interests in opposing continuing development of close American-Soviet ties. This new attitude cut across the entire spectrum of relations, since Soviet-American détente in any realm tended to affect other areas: less support for SALT and American-Soviet security cooperation of any kind, and more support for unilateral American military programs; more suspicious assessments of Soviet intentions and capabilities; more critical objection to internal Soviet practices such as curbs on dissidents; and stronger support for tying the relaxation of trade restrictions to a Soviet quid pro quo such as explicit commitments on increased Jewish emigration. While these same issues would have arisen had the October War never occurred, a new negative attitude toward U.S.-Soviet collaboration was sparked in this constituency by American (as much as by Soviet) actions in ending the conflict.

There was yet another strain to the influential opposing American opinion, only partly overlapping that of the dedicated supporters of Israel. It was also not limited to anti-Soviet cold warriors. An American tradition has been reliance on the gun, juxtaposed, in most (but not all) of its national historical experience, against ideals that have constrained resort to violence in international relations. This sentiment for the use of power has occasionally emerged as chauvinistic pride in heroic American exploits of military valor. But in recent decades it has also inspired among some Americans a certain admiration (and sometimes envy) of Israeli military prowess. The image of David bravely standing up to Goliath was one source of this admiration. Another was a surrogate pride in Israeli military efficiency and successes—the 1956 and 1967 wars, the Entebbe raid, and so on—especially given the close American affinities and relations with Israel. In some sense Israel's victories made up for perceived American military failures—Vietnam, the Iranian hostage rescue, and so on.

American admiration for Israeli military proficiency, and for its political guts to use the gun, sometimes substitutes for the constraints the United States feels as a global power with many responsibilities, notwithstanding its great military power. Israel, on the other hand, sees no international responsibilities beyond serving its national security and survival; it has no real need for friends except the United States. Hence the perceived freedom, under the shadow of ultimate American support, to resort to military power to meet any perceived threat to its interests.

From this perspective, détente between the United States and the Soviet Union could mean American (and Soviet) pressure on Israel in some instances not to draw and fire the gun, as first became clear in October 1973. Not only some Israelis, but also some Americans rooting for the little gunslinger, have opposed what amounts to international gun control. Many of these same Americans chafed at the progress achieved in American-Soviet arms limitations in the 1970s. They wished to see the United States resort more to the gun—or at least to recover its reputation, and the fruits of that reputation, as the fastest and biggest gun in town. Détente and arms control marked a different path, one that these people never truly accepted. After October 1973 they increasingly gave voice to their opposition, although usually in terms of criticism of the Soviet role, rather than of the policy of détente and arms control per se.

Criticism of the Soviet role in the October 1973 war was but the first in a series of these indirect assaults on détente.

12 Détente Stalled: Watergate and the Third Summit, 1974

THE UNFOLDING domestic political crisis in the United States stemming from the White House cover-up of the Watergate break-in dominated American political life in the last year of the Nixon administration. It also, indirectly but unmistakably, dominated American-Soviet relations and stalled the development of détente in the first eight months of 1974.

American Politics and Policy

While it is unlikely that all the issues most active in relations between the two powers could have been resolved, the effects of Watergate ensured that none were. The Soviets were suspicious during 1973 and 1974 that the whole Watergate issue was a plot by American opponents of détente. While this belief was wildly off-base, it is true that an ultimate effect of Watergate was to prejudice progress on détente and to aid American opponents of that policy.

One important and pervasive effect of Watergate was that it almost totally absorbed the attention of President Nixon during the greater part of his last year in office. His final State of the Union message to the Congress on January 30, 1974, was hollow. The fifth in the innovative series of presidential reports on foreign policy was drafted but never issued. Secretary of State Kissinger had more responsibility than ever for the conduct of foreign policy, but often less leeway. In particular, Secretary of Defense Schlesinger stymied progress on SALT and in a number of other ways played a stronger role. Détente came under more sustained fire from its opponents, a larger and stronger coalition since the October 1973 Arab-Israeli war.[1] As Kissinger later ruminated,

---

1. See chapter 11.

"Watergate prevented the full fruition of the prospects then before us, not only in nurturing U.S.-Soviet relations but more generally in developing a new structure of international relations."[2]

On December 6, 1973, Gerald R. Ford was sworn in as vice president, following the resignation of Spiro T. Agnew. On February 6, 1974, the House of Representatives granted the Judiciary Committee the power to conduct an impeachment inquiry, and by May 9 the hearings had opened. Earlier, on March 1, H. R. Haldeman, John D. Ehrlichman, John N. Mitchell, and Charles C. Colson—all Nixon's principal White House aides at one time— were indicted. The investigation, spurred by new revelations, pressed forward to its climax with Nixon's resignation from the presidency on August 9, 1974.

The cancer seemed widespread. In January and February 1974 it became known publicly that Chairman of the JCS Admiral Thomas H. Moorer had in 1970–71 received very secret materials that had been surreptitiously purloined by a naval yeoman assigned to Kissinger's NSC staff. During his confirmation hearings Kissinger was queried on his role in an earlier White House order to the FBI to wiretap some of his own staff. He had neglected earlier to mention that he had listened to a taped interrogation of an admiral by one of the "Plumbers" (Nixon's special investigators).[3] This whole incident had other ugly aspects as well. First, it was the secrecy of the White House that had engendered those improper activities by another arm of the executive branch, an explanation that might give the rationale for, but does not justify, the action. Second, the offending yeoman and responsible naval officers were not court-martialed. Moorer himself had been named to another tour as chairman of the JCS in 1972, despite admissions of gross dereliction and strong hints of greater impropriety.[4] How could that have occurred? Had Moorer been blackmailed and tamed by the president into agreeing to support SALT in return for being permitted to remain unsullied and kept on in his position? The very fact that the question was being asked reflected the deteriorating confidence in the national leadership.

The repercussions of this wiretap controversy hit Kissinger at a sensitive time. Shortly before the Moscow summit meeting in June 1974 and just

---

2. Henry Kissinger, *White House Years* (Boston, Mass.: Little, Brown, 1979), p. 1254, with reference to the whole period after mid-1973.

3. See Marvin Kalb and Bernard Kalb, *Kissinger* (Dell, 1974), pp. 506–07.

4. See Jack Anderson, "Pentagon Spied out of Frustration," *Washington Post*, January 17, 1974; Michael Getler, "Moorer Got Kissinger Data, but Says He Disregarded It," *Washington Post*, January 19, 1974; Seymour M. Hersh, "Spying in the White House Said to Have Begun in 1970," *New York Times*, February 3, 1974; Hersh, "Moorer Concedes He Got Documents" and "Excerpts from Moorer Letter on Military Snooping and Kissinger Statement," *New York Times*, February 6, 1974; Hersh, *The Price of Power: Kissinger in the Nixon White House* (Summit Books, 1983), pp. 465–79; and Elmo R. Zumwalt, Jr., *On Watch: A Memoir* (Quadrangle, 1976), pp. 369–76.

after his return in triumph from the successful negotiations on disengagement in the Middle East, Kissinger was dismayed to be assailed at his first news conference on June 6 by a cross-examination on his role in the wiretapping. At a news conference in Salzburg, Austria, on June 11 he threatened to resign unless what he called innuendos on the wiretapping were cleared up. He even wrote to the Senate Committee on Foreign Relations asking to be cleared.[5] On July 12 Nixon finally wrote Senator William J. Fulbright that the responsibility for wiretapping the White House officials was entirely his, and the committee cleared Kissinger.

Also in June, Secretary of Defense Schlesinger seriously undermined the efforts by Nixon and Kissinger to work out a SALT agreement. On June 3, in a carefully planned maneuver, Schlesinger wrote a letter to Senator Jackson praising a SALT proposal the senator had advanced in April—thus disassociating himself from the official American position. This action greatly strengthened Jackson's hand and undercut Nixon and Kissinger. Nixon called Schlesinger on the carpet in the Oval Office on June 6 but was afraid to fire him.[6] To underscore his point and as insurance, Schlesinger also leaked a rumor to the press at that time that he had threatened to resign if he was not given a more important voice in such matters as SALT.[7] Schlesinger's actions effectively limited Nixon's SALT options at the forthcoming summit meeting.

On June 14 Paul H. Nitze, a hard-line former deputy secretary of defense and at the time the secretary of defense's representative on the SALT delegation, a post he had held since the talks began in 1969, resigned from the delegation. He did so, he said, because the position of the president was so weakened by the "depressing reality of the traumatic events now unfolding" that he could not take the necessary strong stand on SALT at the forthcoming summit meeting.[8]

It was clear that the strains and difficulties within the sinking Nixon administration were growing. At the same time the opposition to détente was being voiced more openly and loudly. Senator Jackson, who was aspiring to the presidency and who had consistently combined a liberal stand on many domestic issues with a hard-line anti-Soviet position, stepped up his campaign against SALT. He sought to capitalize on the weakened position of the beleaguered

---

5. See Henry Kissinger, *Years of Upheaval* (Boston, Mass.: Little, Brown, 1982), pp. 1111–23. See also Kalb and Kalb, *Kissinger*, pp. 615–17; and Tad Szulc, *The Illusion of Peace: Foreign Policy in the Nixon Years* (Viking, 1978), pp. 774–76.

6. For a good, if biased, account, see Kissinger, *Years of Upheaval*, pp. 1154–59.

7. See Thomas B. Ross, "Schlesinger Threatens to Resign," *New York Post*, June 21, 1974.

8. Michael Getler, "Nitze Quits SALT, Cites U.S. 'Events,'" *Washington Post*, June 15, 1974. Nitze has subsequently told me that he continues to believe there was a real risk that Nixon might have agreed to a very disadvantageous SALT agreement and that even the guidelines on SALT to which he did agree were unwise.

Nixon and of Kissinger as advocates of détente and SALT. On April 22 he had made a harshly critical speech on "Detente and SALT." That same day he also wrote to Secretary of Defense Schlesinger, bolstering opposition to SALT concessions within the administration. Jackson's charge that Nixon would sell out the country's national security interests at Moscow was rebutted by Kissinger on April 26, and later by events, but Jackson could always claim to have helped forestall unwise concessions in SALT.

Senator Jackson also continued to lead the attack against normalization of trade relations with the Soviet Union. He sought to link internal developments in that country, in particular Jewish emigration and the handling of political dissidents, to the granting of most-favored-nation (MFN) status for the Soviet Union. In December 1973 the House of Representatives passed the Jackson-Vanik amendment by a vote of 319 to 80 and defeated by a vote of 298 to 106 an administration attempt to remove the whole MFN issue from the trade bill. The arena of conflict then shifted to the Senate. From March to June 1974 Kissinger negotiated with both Senator Jackson and the Soviets. The more the Soviets gave—they agreed to increase Jewish emigration to at least 45,000 a year—the more Jackson demanded, to the discomfort of even other senators seeking a favorable outcome. Jackson, as Kissinger rightly observes, "wanted an issue, not a solution." Moreover, "Jackson and others in the anti-détente lobby were determined that Nixon should have no negotiating chips in Moscow."[9]

Jackson also broadened his assault on the development of American-Soviet trade and economic relations by including another restriction—both in the trade bill and in separate legislation on the Export-Import Bank—that established a flat limit of $300 million on all lending to the Soviet Union. As Kissinger concedes, "this time a preoccupied Administration was caught flat-footed."[10] Thus Jackson led a coalition hostile to détente that succeeded, on a number of fronts, in "erecting a series of legislative hurdles that gradually paralyzed our East-West policy."[11]

Other challenges to SALT and to détente were launched. Détente became an issue in the mainstream of American domestic politics.[12] For example, in the summer of 1974 the Committee for a Democratic Majority (CDM), a Democratic group including members of Congress (notably Jackson) and others in the media, labor, and academia who favored a more hard-line position in foreign relations and greater emphasis on defense, launched a campaign against détente. "The Quest for Detente," written by a CDM task force

---

9. Kissinger, *Years of Upheaval*, pp. 985–98.

10. Ibid., pp. 996–97.

11. Ibid., p. 985.

12. In his memoir Kissinger eloquently describes the decline in support for détente from disparate elements of the American political spectrum in 1973–74. Ibid., pp. 979–85.

chaired by Eugene V. Rostow, represented the first major head-on assault on the entire Nixon-Kissinger policy of détente.

On the other hand, in 1974 public opinion was still not disillusioned with Nixon and Kissinger's policy of détente, although questions were being raised. A Gallup poll in July 1974 showed that while only 26 percent of the population surveyed approved Nixon's conduct of the presidency, 54 percent approved his foreign policy.[13] Media coverage was mixed. For example, a survey of editorials in 110 newspapers around the country in April 1974 that had been written largely in response to reports of Kissinger's visit to Moscow and the announcement that Nixon would return to Moscow for a third summit meeting showed that while ten editorials favored the planned summit meeting, eight expressed caution and fourteen opposed it (the latter included the influential *Los Angeles Times, Baltimore Sun,* and *Philadelphia Bulletin*).[14] In this same survey eighteen editorials favored and only five opposed a buildup of U.S. military forces. Only five fully supported détente; seven saw it as a mixed blessing; and eight thought it bad. Twenty-five favored SALT II, thirty were cautionary, and only three opposed it. Thus, on the basis of this source, American opinion was beginning to be less sure of the benefits of détente but had not rejected it.

Nixon's weakened position also stirred political activity by others, not all of whom challenged détente. Senator Edward M. Kennedy, for one, opened his own dialogue with the Soviet leaders when he visited Moscow in May, where he was well-received.

International Developments

International developments also tended to distract attention from American-Soviet relations. The event of greatest significance was the successful American effort to assume a leading role in reducing tensions in the Middle East. This success, however, required that Kissinger spend most of his time on the difficult shuttle diplomacy, serving as a go-between in arranging disengagements between Israeli and Egyptian, and later Syrian, forces. A Geneva conference on the Middle East that included the Soviet Union as well as the United States met inconclusively on December 21, 1973. Other action, and what success there was, came through the unilateral American shuttle diplomacy. The first Israeli-Egyptian agreement on disengagement was signed January 18, 1974, while an agreement on Israeli-Syrian disengagement was signed May 31, as a

13. A. James Reichley, *Conservatives in an Age of Change: The Nixon and Ford Administrations* (Brookings Institution, 1981), p. 128.

14. From an unpublished survey by the U.S. Arms Control and Disarmament Agency, May 1974.

result of Kissinger's efforts. Finally, from June 12 to 18, just before his trip to Moscow, Nixon personally visited five key countries in the Middle East.[15]

The success of Kissinger's shuttle diplomacy was important for the United States not only in defusing Arab-Israeli tensions to a degree, but above all in building Arab confidence in the United States. It created room for maneuver in U.S. diplomacy, and not only resulted in the Soviet Union being shouldered out of the process, but greatly reduced its influence in the region. Most dramatically, Sadat not only turned still farther away from the USSR, but on April 18 announced that Egypt was ending its dependency on that country for arms and military assistance. The well-connected columnist Joseph Alsop responded by urging that the United States become the chief arms supplier of Egypt, and complete the "reversal of alliances" that Egyptian President Anwar al-Sadat had been seeking.[16]

Another result of the shuttle diplomacy was that on March 18 the Arab members of the Organization of Petroleum Exporting Countries (OPEC) lifted the oil embargo on the United States imposed during the October War.

In February Nixon and Kissinger had received Foreign Minister Gromyko in Washington, at which time they had agreed on the need to move toward a Middle East settlement. Kissinger then met with Gromyko several times in March and April, and on April 29 they agreed to work together for an Israeli-Syrian accord. But in reality the United States continued to work alone. The Soviets strongly resented the American efforts—and success—both in cutting the Soviet Union out of the main diplomatic action and in curtailing Soviet influence, and in building U.S. ties with the Arabs. Kissinger described a three-and-one-half-hour meeting with General Secretary Brezhnev on the subject during his visit to Moscow in late March as the "toughest and most unpleasant" he had ever experienced with the Soviet leaders.[17] Nixon received a less blunt but still clear expression of Soviet dissatisfaction with U.S. Middle East policy at the summit meeting in June.[18]

In another arena of the international political scene, Sino-Soviet relations again worsened. On November 11–14, 1973, Kissinger paid his second visit of the year to Beijing, reinforcing Sino-American ties. Kissinger hedged on the outcome of the Watergate crisis when he assured the Chinese leaders that improvement of American relations with China would continue "whatever happens in the future and whatever the Administration." The Chinese, in any case, pursued their own policy, which conflicted chiefly not with that of the United States but with that of its Russian neighbor. On January 19, 1974, the Chinese expelled several Soviet diplomats from Beijing for espionage and on

15. William B. Quandt, *Decade of Decisions: American Policy toward the Arab-Israeli Conflict, 1967–76* (Berkeley, Calif.: University of California Press, 1977), pp. 217–48.

16. Ibid., pp. 207–11, 238.

17. Ibid., pp. 236–37.

18. See Richard Nixon, *RN: The Memoirs of Richard Nixon* (Grosset and Dunlap, 1978), pp. 1031, 1033–34; and Kissinger, *Years of Upheaval*, p. 1165.

the same day seized the Paracel Islands in the South China Sea, which North Vietnam also claimed.

Brezhnev visited Cuba in January to help maintain Soviet-Cuban ties, in this way reaffirming an interest in a region in which the Soviet Union was notably inactive.

In December 1973 Romanian President Nicolae Ceauşescu had visited Washington, indicating that the United States had not dropped its interest in Eastern Europe. In April Secretary of Commerce Frederick B. Dent visited Romania and Bulgaria, as well as the Soviet Union.

The many interrelationships in East-West relations were also evidenced when, hardly in keeping with Soviet interests, Willy Brandt was forced to resign as chancellor of West Germany after it was discovered that his confidential secretary had been a spy for East Germany.

In April the death of former President Georges Pompidou provided an occasion for President Nixon to play a symbolic role by attending the funeral in Paris. There he met with President Podgorny, but their conversations were not substantial. Nevertheless, the trip permitted Nixon a brief escape from his latest troubles at home—charges by the Internal Revenue Service of fraudulent income tax reporting.

The most striking new international development in this period was the overthrow of the Marcelo Caetano government in Portugal by the Portuguese military in a coup on April 25 and the leftward drift of the military regime, especially following the replacement of General Antonio de Spinola by Vasco dos Santos Gonçalves on July 9. A year of uncertainty ensued. The new Portuguese government announced its intention to give independence to all the African colonies during 1975, a move that would bring to an end the last of the European colonial empires on that continent.

One international crisis that erupted in July, while it did not stem from or directly affect American-Soviet relations, was handled poorly by the distracted American leadership and had lingering adverse effects within the Western alliance for some time. On July 15 a coup d'état supported by the Greek junta was launched against Archbishop Makarios III, the president of Cyprus. Eventually it led to a Turkish invasion and de facto division of the country. By that time Nixon was wholly estranged from such policy matters. Kissinger's own role was ambiguous, and his efforts to deal with the situation were unsuccessful. Congress also insisted, over the objections of both the Nixon and Ford administrations, on suspending military assistance to Turkey. American interests were badly damaged by the whole affair. As one observer noted, "The Cyprus affair also marked the first major defeat for Kissinger"[19]—and for the new Ford administration. The Soviets were not involved.

In general the third world was relatively quiescent, but its importance was evidenced in new ways. The oil embargo and quadrupling of petroleum prices between mid-1973 and the end of 1974 showed a new element of

19. Szulc, *The Illusion of Peace*, p. 797, and see pp. 794–97.

potential power. India's explosion of a nuclear device on May 18 showed another.

Through it all there was Watergate, impinging on everything the American leaders did. Noted earlier was Kissinger's despair at being greeted on his return from a great success in the Middle East with sharp questions as to his role in the wiretapping. President Nixon was of course much more deeply embroiled. Three days after he returned from the Middle East, on June 19 the Judiciary Committee completed its hearings, and on June 24 issued four subpoenas for the critical tapes. The very next day Nixon departed for Moscow. Cynical observers in Washington, in gallows humor, wondered if he would ask for political asylum. Less than a month later, on July 24, the Supreme Court ruled unanimously against Nixon on the tapes, and the game was up. Impeachment proceedings began on July 27, and Nixon was only able to avoid the stigma of impeachment by accepting the slightly lesser stigma of resignation.

Nixon had persuaded himself up until almost the last minute that he could brazen it out. Thus during the spring and early summer he had tried to carry on as usual. He did not, however, have the clout to undertake initiatives that would antagonize potentially key support in his struggle to retain his office. His exercise of power was sharply constrained, part of the price of fighting for the presidency. Nowhere was this more evident than in the conduct of relations with the Soviet Union and the pursuit of SALT and détente.

Nixon proceeded with the third summit meeting in Moscow in June, seeking to exploit the momentum of détente—still a popular policy. But his ability to pursue new initiatives or even to persevere with established policies was greatly weakened. This weakness proved especially damaging to SALT. Two factors contributed to the stalemate over SALT, both of them in part the administration's own doing.

American Military Policy, SALT, and Preparations for the Summit

Continuing military programs in the Soviet Union provided ammunition to opponents of SALT and détente. Even as new claims of past American tendencies to underestimate Soviet military capabilities were being publicly sounded,[20] information (and misinformation) was being leaked and new *overestimates* of Soviet military advances were being purveyed.[21] Nor was it

---

20. See Albert Wohlstetter, "Is There a Strategic Arms Race?" *Foreign Policy*, no. 15 (Summer 1974), pp. 3–20; and Wohlstetter, "Rivals, but No 'Race,'" *Foreign Policy*, no. 16 (Fall 1974), pp. 48–81.

21. For example, see Joseph Alsop, "The New Missile Scoreboard," *Washington Post*, March 4, 1974.

only on the American side that suspicions and doubts as to the intentions of the other superpower were growing.

Largely as a consequence of the growing strength of Secretary of Defense Schlesinger, a new American doctrine on the use of nuclear weapons was developed in the latter half of 1973 and signed by President Nixon on January 17, 1974. The new "Policy for Planning the Employment of Nuclear Weapons" (National Security Decision Memorandum [NSDM]–242, prepared in response to National Security Study Memorandum [NSSM]–169), was top secret, but Schlesinger immediately made much of the substance public, and the concept became best known as the Schlesinger Doctrine on "selective targeting."[22] The principal purpose of the new doctrine was to strengthen deterrence, including "extended deterrence," or, in the words of the NSDM, "to deter nuclear attacks against the United States, its forces and its bases overseas" and to "deter attacks against U.S. allies and those other nations whose security is deemed important to U.S. interests." In addition, it was intended to inhibit political or military coercion of the United States and its allies.[23] The means to this end was the development of counterforce capabilities against hardened Soviet targets such as command and control centers and ICBM silos "for limited employment options which enable the United States to conduct selected nuclear operations." The intent was to show "[U.S.] determination to resist aggression," coupled with a "desire to exercise restraint." Limited nuclear war options, it was believed, would bolster deterrence and provide a useful means of reacting to actual limited aggression by the ability to control "the timing and pace of attack execution, in order to provide the enemy opportunities to reconsider his actions."[24]

To the Soviets this new American doctrine (and subsequent changes in military programs that increased counterforce capabilities, such as increased missile accuracies) spelled a greater capability to wage war and launch a first strike as well as to provide limited offensive nuclear war options. It was not hard for Soviet military and political analysts to accept the explanation that this policy was not a radical departure in American strategic thinking—for some time they had contended that the United States had always sought counterforce capabilities. But all the more, then, did they see the public pronouncement of this strategic doctrine as intended to signal the acceptability of limited nuclear warfare as an instrument of U.S. policy. As such it portended

---

22. For early accounts see Michael Getler, "U.S. Studies Re-Targeting of Missiles," *Washington Post*, January 11, 1974; John W. Finney, "U.S. Retargeting Some Missiles under New Strategic Concept," *New York Times*, January 11, 1974; Finney, "Debate over Change on Nuclear Strategy," ibid., January 22, 1974; and Finney, "Small Atomic Arms Are Urged for NATO," ibid., January 27, 1974.

23. Excerpts from the secret NSDM, including the portion cited here, were later made public by Jack Anderson, "Not-So-New Nuclear Strategy," *Washington Post*, October 12, 1980.

24. Ibid.

the possibility of dangerous American initiatives.[25] It was also seen as contrary to the path of strategic arms limitation, the SALT agreements, military-political détente, and, in particular, the Agreement on the Prevention of Nuclear War (PNW) signed only six months earlier.[26]

Certainly the new American nuclear doctrine reflected, at the least, a lack of confidence in détente, although it could be considered consistent with it on grounds of prudence. But it is clear that Schlesinger was skeptical of SALT and détente.[27]

The administration accompanied the new doctrine by a reversal of policy on the question of developing counterforce accuracies for strategic missiles. This change, announced at the same time, met a substantial challenge in the Senate, but that body finally supported the administration in June, just two weeks before the summit.[28]

The change in American doctrine and policy on developing counterforce capabilities had a particularly unfortunate effect on attempts to develop a strategic dialogue in SALT. In the course of the SALT I negotiations in 1971 the Soviet delegation had expressed concern over American programs to improve the accuracy of missiles to the extent that the United States would have counterforce capabilities against hard targets such as ICBM silos and command centers. The U.S. delegation, in accordance with authoritatively stated American policy (and with the knowledge and approval of Washington), vigorously argued that it was *not* American policy to seek such capabilities, that such an action would be destabilizing. A recent letter from President Nixon to Senator Edward W. Brooke of Massachusetts reaffirming that the United States did not intend to develop those counterforce accuracies was cited to the Soviet delegation. Now, three years later, the same president had

25. There was a multitude of Soviet commentary on the Schlesinger Doctrine to this effect. See, for example, [Lt. General Ret.] M. A. Mil'shtein and [Colonel Ret.] L. S. Semeyko, "The Problem of the Inadmissibility of a Nuclear Conflict (On New Approaches in the United States)," *SShA: Ekonomika, politika, ideologiya* [USA: Economics, Politics, Ideology], no. 11 (November 1974), pp. 3–12.

26. Ibid., pp. 11–12. On how this U.S. policy cast a shadow on the PNW agreement as well as on SALT, see also Colonel V. Larionov, "Arms Limitation and Its Enemies," *Pravda*, April 7, 1974.

27. It has been reported that Kissinger was caught by surprise by the issuance of NSDM-242. See James W. Canan, *The Superwarriors: The Fantastic World of Pentagon Superweapons* (Weybright and Talley, 1975), p. 151. Canan does not, however, offer any supporting evidence or source. General Brent Scowcroft, then the national security adviser, has told me he is sure the NSDM received the usual interdepartmental review, and recalls Kissinger's earlier support for broadening the president's military options. Remarkably, Kissinger makes no reference to the development of this doctrine in his memoir. Indeed, his discussion of American defense programs is couched almost exclusively in terms of impressions of the perceptions of Soviet leaders and other foreign and domestic observers. See Kissinger, *Years of Upheaval*, pp. 998–1006.

28. See John W. Finney, "Senate Endorses New Nixon Policy on Better ICBMs," *New York Times*, June 11, 1974. The vote was 48 to 37 and defeated a move to hold up approval pending further efforts to limit MIRVs in SALT.

reversed course and announced American programs to acquire the very capabilities previously denounced as destabilizing.[29]

The second development—or rather lack of development—that undercut a possible SALT II agreement at the forthcoming summit was high-level neglect of the SALT negotiations. In contrast to the active role taken by the SALT I delegation (in part the White House was reacting now against that very role), the SALT II delegation was kept on a very short leash. Moreover, Nixon's preoccupation with Watergate and Kissinger's with Middle East shuttle diplomacy not only permitted American defense policy to veer off in another direction, but also did not permit progress in SALT.[30]

The key question in SALT II that had unfortunately been finessed in SALT I was the limitation on MIRVs. The Soviet delegation as early as the first meeting of SALT II in December 1972 had urged that the subject be considered. It had, however, spoken in such an indirect and informal way that some members of the U.S. delegation were reluctant even to report the Soviet indication of interest.[31] By the fall of 1973 the Soviet side had advanced a draft treaty that proposed keeping the unequal levels for the missile launchers set by the Interim Agreement of 1972, together with unspecified limits on MIRVs. The American position, however, was keyed, as much for political as for military reasons, on equal numbers. A possible balancing of the differing force levels in pursuit of equal security, as the Soviet side was proposing, was not attractive. The United States made no new major proposals in the second half of 1973.[32] Finally, early in 1974 the White House turned seriously to the question. On February 19 it issued NSDM-245 setting forth the U.S. position calling for equal overall aggregates (2,350 ICBMs, SLBMs, and heavy bombers), *and* equal ICBM MIRV throw-weight.[33] Since Soviet ICBMs were much larger than American ones, this approach in effect meant the Soviets could place MIRVs on a much smaller portion of their ICBM force than could the United States. Moreover, since no limits were to be placed on the number of MIRV warheads, the United States could retain or even increase its large superiority in numbers of warheads.[34]

A real attempt to reach a new SALT accord was made belatedly by Kissinger on his advance trip to Moscow, a visit similar to those preceding the

---

29. See Raymond L. Garthoff, "SALT I: An Evaluation," *World Politics*, vol. 31 (October 1978), pp. 10–11.

30. Based on interviews with officials directly involved.

31. Based on my participation as the Department of State representative in the delegation.

32. See Kissinger, *Years of Upheaval*, pp. 1011–16. See also U. Alexis Johnson with Jef Olivarius McAllister, *The Right Hand of Power* (Englewood Cliffs, N.J.: Prentice-Hall, 1984), pp. 595–99.

33. Kissinger, *Years of Upheaval*, pp. 1016–18; and Johnson, *The Right Hand of Power*, pp. 599–600.

34. As observed earlier (chapter 5), a major cause of the failure to deal with MIRVs in SALT I was the American fixation on controlling throw-weight per se, rather than MIRVs. This new move was a belated half-step toward recognition of the real problem and its solution.

other summit meetings. As before, Kissinger conducted an important part of the real negotiations in his meetings with Brezhnev.[35] One important difference was that now he was secretary of state, his visit was public knowledge, and he was accompanied by representatives of the press. (On his first visit in April 1972, it will be recalled, not even the American ambassador in Moscow was informed until the end of the visit.) One consequence of his different status was that Kissinger held a press conference prior to the trip, in which he unwisely raised expectations by saying that the two sides were on the verge of a "conceptual breakthrough" in resolving the SALT impasse.[36]

One reason for Kissinger's optimism was an apparent agreement at an NSC meeting on March 21 on an approach that accepted unequal aggregates in the Soviet favor, to be offset by unequal levels of MIRVs in the U.S. favor.[37] Kissinger's optimism over SALT was also the result of his discussions with Ambassador Dobrynin, who had shown a high and positive interest. Again, in the tradition of the earlier trips, Dobrynin accompanied Kissinger to Moscow. This time he, too, came into contact with the press, to whom he also exuded optimism over the impending Moscow talks on SALT. This was not the first time, nor would it be the last, that Dobrynin and the Soviet embassy in Washington inadvertently gave a misleading signal on Soviet reactions to American SALT proposals. This, however, was the critical time for Kissinger.

By contrast, the considered Soviet reaction, Brezhnev soon made clear to Kissinger, was decidedly negative—the U.S. proposal singled out for limitation the one area of Soviet advantage, missile throw-weight, giving one-sided advantage to the Americans.[38] Accordingly the Soviet side counterproposed continuing until 1980 the unequal aggregates of the SALT I Interim Agreement and an equal limit of 1,000 missiles with MIRVs. After spirited discussion the Soviets proposed giving the United States a compensatory edge over the USSR in the form of the numbers of ICBM and SLBM missile

---

35. The record, including even Kissinger's memoir for the 1972, 1973, and 1974 pre-summit visits, as well as many other sources, does not convey the importance of these negotiations. During Kissinger's visit in March 1974, for example, Defense Minister Marshal Grechko was recalled to Moscow from Iraq for a Politburo meeting to consider new aspects of the SALT issue. See Victor Zorza, "A Victory for Soviet Hardliners," *Washington Post*, April 9, 1974. Yet in his memoir four years later Nixon refers to this critical Kissinger March parley with Brezhnev in a single sentence, describing it as merely "setting the agenda for Summit III." Nixon, *RN*, p. 1024.

36. "Secretary Kissinger's News Conference of March 21," *Department of State Bulletin*, vol. 70 (April 8, 1974), p. 353. (Hereafter *State Bulletin*.) See also Kissinger, *Years of Upheaval*, pp. 1020–21.

37. See Kissinger, *Years of Upheaval*, pp. 1018–20.

38. See Murrey Marder, "U.S., Soviet Fail to Progress on Arms Limitations," *Washington Post*, March 29, 1974; Marder, "U.S. Seen Misjudging Soviets: Moscow Found Unready for Early Nuclear Pact," *Washington Post*, March 31, 1974; and Joseph Kraft, "Letter from Moscow," *New Yorker*, July 29, 1974, pp. 68 ff.

launchers with MIRVs—1,100 to 1,000.[39] They also proposed reducing the number of antiballistic missile (ABM) deployment sites authorized under the ABM Treaty from two to one for each side.

Kissinger's earlier optimism (perhaps buoyed also by his forthcoming marriage) was sharply set back by the outcome of the March meetings—at which the Soviet leaders also berated him for excluding the Soviet Union from the Middle East peace process. At a news conference in London on his way back to Washington he sought to bridge the gap by a general comment that progress on SALT was being made. He also stressed the complexity of the issues. Reporters and commentators who had accompanied him to Moscow knew, however, and reported that there had been no conceptual breakthrough and that prospects for a SALT agreement at the forthcoming summit meeting were dim.

Discussions on SALT continued when Gromyko visited the White House on April 12 and when Kissinger met Gromyko in Geneva on April 28 and 29 and in Nicosia, Cyprus, on May 7. In Geneva, however, the Soviets rejected Kissinger's proposal of a differential in missile launchers armed with MIRVs of 1,000 for the United States to 850 for the Soviet Union, with an extension of the Interim Agreement aggregate levels to the year 1980.[40]

Early in the year the Soviets had also raised the issue of a nuclear test ban. Negotiations on a comprehensive test ban (CTB) had been under way for some time in the standing multilateral disarmament conference in Geneva. In February first Dobrynin and then Gromyko proposed that the two powers agree at the summit on a CTB, provided all the nuclear powers would accept it, a requirement that put China and France on the line. Nixon and Kissinger turned down the proposal. During Kissinger's Moscow talks in March, Brezhnev raised the alternative of a possible threshold test ban (TTB), which would preclude all underground tests above some limit, an approach that could surmount arguments over verification of small tests. He also did not raise the question of requiring acceptance by France and China. These discussions were promising, and although not conclusive, they led to new technical discussions in Geneva in April. Initially the idea was to set a limit based on seismic shock level, but that was replaced by the idea of setting a ceiling defined in terms of the yield of the explosion. Tentative agreement was reached on a limit of 150 kilotons.[41]

While details of these exchanges did not become known (they were not circulated to interested departments in Washington), opponents of the SALT II deal being considered provided Senator Jackson with information on the U.S. position. He launched a renewed strong attack in his speech of April

---

39. Kissinger, *Years of Upheaval*, pp. 1022–25.

40. Ibid., pp. 1026–27.

41. Ibid., pp. 1166–67.

22 mentioned earlier. Increasingly the administration was on the defensive. Still later, on June 21, just after the resignation of Nitze from the SALT negotiating team and just before the Moscow meeting, Jackson charged that in 1972 Kissinger had made a secret deal with the Soviet leaders that would permit them to exceed the Interim Agreement limits. Other leaked information formed the basis for a similar account in the *New York Times* the next day. Nitze had testified before Jackson's subcommittee on these matters the preceding day. In his memoir Admiral Zumwalt disclosed that he too had long been assisting Senator Jackson behind the scenes.[42]

The two questions at issue were minor. There was a theoretical loophole in the provision of the 1972 Interim Agreement (and a secret July 1972 clarification) under which the Soviets might have been able to build new diesel submarines for SLBM missiles or to upgrade SLBM missiles on existing diesel missile submarines. The second issue had arisen because the Soviets wanted an assurance that the United States would not exercise its right to dismantle its fifty-four old Titan ICBM missile launchers in exchange for building new SLBM launchers. As Kissinger was able to point out, a later agreement with the Soviets clarified and closed the submarine loophole. On the Titans, while an assurance had been given, in view of its shipbuilding program the United States could not in any event have built new missile-launching submarines to substitute for the Titans during the five-year period of the Interim Agreement.[43] But the first point did underscore the political disadvantages of the overly hasty summit negotiations by Kissinger and his aides and their failure to use additional expert staff assistance. The latter point on the Titans *did* involve a formal written assurance by President Nixon. While in itself the assurance did no harm to American security interests, it did make questionable the assurances given earlier to the Congress of no "secret deal."[44]

---

42. See Zumwalt, *On Watch*, pp. 427–30, 506.

43. The best overall account of the episode is in Leslie H. Gelb, "Washington Dateline: The Story of a Flap," *Foreign Policy*, no. 16 (Fall 1974), pp. 165–81. Gelb was author of the initial *New York Times* article, "2 Kissinger Deals Reported to Aid Russians on Arms," *New York Times*, June 22, 1974. See also Murrey Marder, "Jackson Claims Alteration in U.S.-Soviet Missile Pact," *Washington Post*, June 22, 1974; and Tad Szulc, "Covering SALT: Loopholes, Breakthroughs and Official Communiques," *Columbia Journalism Review* (September–October 1974), pp. 26–29. Kissinger felt obliged immediately to deny the thrust of the charges. See Marder, "Secret Accord Denied," *Washington Post*, June 23, 1974. Kissinger also devoted considerable attention to this issue in his press conferences of June 24 and 26, 1974. Kissinger's own account, while self-serving and glossing over some aspects, is basically correct. See Kissinger, *Years of Upheaval*, pp. 1143–51.

44. Kissinger's handling in his memoir of this aspect of the issue is especially slippery. Kissinger, *Years of Upheaval*, pp. 1147–48. His conclusion that "in other words, there was nothing 'secret' about this understanding" on the Titan missiles is simply not true. His argument is that "while the letter itself was secret, the intention was not," but that explanation confuses the difference between a current internal programming decision and an international commitment. Moreover, he (and Nixon) fails to note that the presidential letter of assurance was only reluctantly provided after Soviet insistence.

The explanations for these matters never quite caught up with the charges. Thus the charges did—as Senator Jackson and others responsible for the leaks intended—raise doubts about what the Watergate-beleaguered president might do at the forthcoming Moscow summit. Both SALT and détente were adversely affected by these flaws in the secretive Nixon-Kissinger modus operandi at the time of the first summit meeting. The enemies of détente won a round.

President Nixon provides in his memoir the fullest account of the general struggle at this juncture by the opponents of détente. He writes:

What was probably the most crucial and hardest fought battle of Summit III took place not in Moscow but in Washington, where the activities of the anti-détente forces reached almost fever pitch just as I was getting ready to leave for the Soviet Union. The liberals were now in full cry with what had become the currently fashionable outrage over Soviet repression of political dissidents and their restriction of Jewish emigration. The conservatives of both parties were still united in their determination either to limit trade with the Soviets or to ban it altogether. The military establishment and its many friends in Congress and the country were up in arms over the prospect that Summit III might actually succeed in producing a breakthrough on limiting offensive nuclear weapons or a limited nuclear test ban.

This convergence of anti-détente forces would have existed regardless of any domestic political problems. But Watergate had badly damaged my ability to defuse, or at least to circumvent, them as effectively as I otherwise might have been able to do. . . .

The U.S. military opposition to a new SALT agreement came to a head at the meeting of the National Security Council on the afternoon of June 20 when Secretary of Defense Schlesinger presented the Pentagon's proposal. It amounted to an unyielding hard line against any SALT agreement that did not ensure an overwhelming American advantage. It was a proposal that the Soviets were sure to reject out of hand.[45]

Nixon states that when he pointed out to the NSC that this proposal had no chance of being accepted by the Soviets, Schlesinger recalled (tongue in cheek) how impressed Khrushchev had been with Nixon's forensic ability in the so-called kitchen debate in Moscow in 1959. He suggested that Nixon could talk them into accepting it. Nixon writes that he recorded in his diary that night: "The NSC meeting was a real shocker insofar as the performance of the Chiefs [Joint Chiefs of Staff], and particularly of Schlesinger, was concerned." He states that the latter's comment that Nixon could talk the Soviet leaders into accepting such a deal "was really an insult to everybody's intelligence and particularly to mine." Nixon also noted, "Ford is on the kick that we ought to have a huge increase in the defense budget, and that that will give us a bargaining position with the Soviets." Nixon was convinced that approach would not work.[46]

45. Nixon, *RN*, pp. 1023–24.

46. Ibid., pp. 1024–25. See also Kissinger, *Years of Upheaval*, pp. 1157–59.

Schlesinger had also compounded the problem by providing optimistic background briefings on the prospects for a limitation on MIRVs at the summit meeting. At this same time Kissinger was backpedalling from his claim of a conceptual breakthrough and attempting to downplay expectations for an agreement.[47]

There had been signs of increasing Soviet disquiet over Nixon's status. As early as October 1973 Nixon had attempted to justify his firing of Archibald Cox as Watergate special prosecutor on the grounds that to keep him would make the president appear weak in the eyes of Brezhnev and other foreign leaders.[48] Now Watergate was having a *real* effect. On April 10 the *New York Times* commented in an editorial that it had been revealed that at Kissinger's March meeting the Soviet leaders had hesitated about reaching any agreements that required congressional approval, a perception that contributed to the failure to reach the expected conceptual breakthrough in SALT. "Watergate," intoned the *Times*, "after a considerable lag, now has begun to impinge increasingly on President Nixon's ability to conduct the nation's foreign policy."[49] Signs of Soviet unease were quite evident to me in conversations with Soviet officials in Moscow in April 1974. Further, Ambassador Walter J. Stoessel, Jr., reported from Moscow a comment by Brezhnev. The Soviet leader expressed admiration at the president for fighting back, but amazement that he could be challenged concerning, for example, his personal taxes.[50] When Gromyko saw the president on April 12, he told him that "on the human plane" he admired Nixon's standing up to "certain known difficulties." He also reassured the president that despite the increasing spate of anti-Soviet articles in the American press, the Soviet Union stood firmly in support of détente.[51]

The prospects for congressional approval of the U.S.-Soviet Trade Agreement of 1972 remained uncertain, and the legislative process was still sidetracked. The problem stemmed from the persistent efforts of many in Congress to play their own politics of linkage on the subject of internal Soviet control of dissidence and, in particular, the emigration of Soviet Jews. Nonetheless, at a meeting of the U.S.-USSR Trade and Economic Council in Washington on February 26, Secretary of the Treasury William E. Simon assured the USSR of the government's support for MFN status and Export-Import

47. See John W. Finney, "Schlesinger Sees Hope of Pact to Limit Warheads," *New York Times*, June 18, 1974; and Michael Getler, "Schlesinger Foresees Possible MIRV Curb," *Washington Post*, June 18, 1974. See also Richard J. Levine, "Major U.S.-Soviet Pact on Nuclear Arms Isn't Likely at Coming Moscow Summit," *Wall Street Journal*, June 18, 1974.

48. Elliot Richardson, *The Creative Balance: Government, Politics, and the Individual in America's Third Century* (Holt, Rinehart and Winston, 1976), p. 39.

49. Editorial, "The Watergate Summit," *New York Times*, April 10, 1974.

50. Nixon, *RN*, p. 1026.

51. Ibid. Nixon is in error in identifying the date of this meeting as April 11.

Bank credits whenever necessary to support U.S. exports. He also raised the projected level of trade with the USSR. On March 22 the Export Import Bank announced resumption of lending to the USSR (as well as to Poland, Yugoslavia, and Romania).

Dissidence in the Soviet Union and Soviet measures to deal with it continued. In February the government expelled Aleksandr I. Solzhenitsyn from the USSR. On the second day of the Moscow summit meeting itself Academician Andrei D. Sakharov went on a hunger strike. Soviet television technicians literally pulled the plug on an American TV broadcast that was trying to report on Sakharov's action (the Americans had been told that this reportage would not be allowed because they had been admitted expressly and only to cover the summit).[52] The Soviet Union did, however, seek to allay American objections, in particular by permitting larger numbers of Jews to emigrate and by continuing not to collect the exit tax.

Meanwhile the administration—its influence weakened by Watergate—continued to try to gain support for the trade arrangement it had negotiated. Also, on May 21, as a sweetener for the coming summit, the Export-Import Bank granted the Soviet Union a loan of $180 million for construction of a large fertilizer complex.

In the end Senator Jackson had the final word—again.[53] Just two days before the president left for Moscow, and while the flap over the alleged secret deals in SALT I that the senator had unleashed was still in the newspapers—indeed, the same day on which Kissinger held his press conference to lay the charge to rest—Jackson announced he was going to put forward new, but unspecified, conditions on any grant of MFN. This action, given his dominant position on the issue, effectively precluded a meaningful attempt by Nixon and Kissinger to work out a deal on the subject in Moscow.

The Third Summit

This summit conference was foredoomed to failure in making major new steps forward. Nonetheless, it did continue the pattern of summit meetings by the leaders of the United States and the Soviet Union, and it lent a little momentum to the stalled détente process. Despite one further effort a new SALT agreement could not be reached. But even if it had, it would surely have been the target of heavy fire in Washington no matter what the terms. Détente was, on balance, probably better served by the absence of a major centerpiece for the third summit.

---

52. Szulc, *The Illusion of Peace*, p. 791.

53. Kissinger, *Years of Upheaval*, pp. 985–98.

The meeting lasted from June 27 to July 3 and included an excursion to Yalta for part of the discussions. The Yalta, or Oreanda,[54] visit was the counterpart to Nixon's hosting Brezhnev at San Clemente in June 1973.

Both sides still harbored hopes for a SALT accord, but each was resigned to forgoing an agreement if the other stuck to previous positions. Both sides proposed levels of missile launchers with MIRVs slightly revised from those discussed in March and April, but neither was prepared to move far enough toward the other to reach agreement.[55] Kissinger pointed out that the levels proposed by the Soviets would be perceived in the United States as allowing them to catch up. The Soviets saw the American proposals as freezing indefinitely an American advantage. Nixon reports that as the impasse became clear Kissinger was concerned about going home empty-handed on SALT. But, in Nixon's words, "the Pentagon's last-minute about-face had made it impossible for us to engage in any flexible negotiating."[56] A SALT II agreement limiting MIRVs and strategic offensive arms remained beyond reach. All that could be agreed was to work toward a ten-year accord to cover the period until 1985.

Partly in order to maintain a semblance of momentum on SALT, agreement was reached on a formal protocol to the 1972 Anti-Ballistic Missile (ABM) Treaty that reduced from two to one the number of permitted ABM deployment sites. The Soviet side had been prepared in 1972 to agree not to exercise the right to deploy at the second sites allowed, but the United States had been unwilling to go along with this proposal. After the Congress in 1973 turned down the administration's proposal to deploy ABM defenses for the National Command Authorities in the nation's capital, the question of a second site for the United States became moot. Accordingly, after the Soviet side suggested in the March talks with Kissinger that both sides renounce the second sites, no one in Washington objected. Thus this further restriction of ABM deployment was signed in Moscow.[57]

Brezhnev and Prime Minister Kosygin surprised Nixon and Kissinger by again urging a comprehensive test ban (CTB). Kissinger had assumed that Soviet receptivity in the March and April talks to a threshold test ban (TTB) had settled the issue. Indeed, the Soviets did accept a TTB along the lines negotiated since late April by teams in Geneva, but only after determining that Nixon would not agree to a CTB. Nixon interpreted this attempt to revive a CTB as a sign that Brezhnev (and Kosygin, who unexpectedly became

---

54. To meet American sensitivities over the controversial repute of Yalta as a place for a U.S.-USSR summit meeting, because of President Roosevelt's meeting there with Stalin in 1945, the site was referred to at the time as Oreanda, the nearby area where the dacha was located.

55. Kissinger, *Years of Upheaval*, pp. 1169–71.

56. Nixon, *RN*, pp. 1031–32, 1035.

57. For the text, see "Agreements Signed at Moscow during President Nixon's Visit," *State Bulletin*, vol. 71 (July 29, 1974), pp. 216–17. See also Kissinger, *Years of Upheaval*, pp. 1165–66.

the active exponent of a CTB) were being "tough" and saw the Soviet pitch for a CTB as a "digression." Nixon countered by stating flatly that the TTB was "the only way we will get the support of the majority of our Congress. We cannot go to a total test ban."[58] Nixon did, however, express agreement with Kosygin on the value of a ban, and said he was "reaching the same goal by a different route."[59] After some further confused discussion, agreement was reached on a 150-kiloton TTB.[60]

The TTB Treaty was never ratified.[61] At the time of this writing a decade later it is still formally awaiting presidential submission for Senate advice and consent to ratification.

The nuclear test ban had become a major issue within the U.S. government by the spring of 1974, although it did not attract public attention in the way SALT did. The most complete account is by one of the chief internal opponents of a comprehensive or even a threshold ban, then Chief of Naval Operations Admiral Zumwalt. In his memoir Zumwalt describes in considerable detail the views and machinations of opponents of a test ban (and SALT) in the Pentagon and on the Hill. Part of the objection by the JCS was the failure by Kissinger to consult with them or to take their views into account, an omission that reinforced their objections on the substance of the issue.[62]

Admiral Zumwalt, a long-time ally of Senator Jackson and protégé of Nitze, had been very active in the pre-summit moves against SALT. During the summit meeting, on June 30, he retired and went public. Just hours before retiring he even gave a provocative "Meet the Press" television interview that he had virtually been ordered not to give. Because of the interview the White House, through Haig, instructed Secretary of Defense Schlesinger not to attend Zumwalt's retirement ceremony and not to present him with a medal, as

---

58. Nixon, *RN*, p. 1028. See also Kissinger, *Years of Upheaval*, pp. 1166–68.

59. Kissinger, *Years of Upheaval*, p. 1168.

60. Kissinger comments that "Kosygin was arguing against an agreement his own government was about to sign and Nixon accepted as an objective what he had turned down four months earlier. After creating total confusion for about an hour, the principals subsided and the subject was remanded to the foreign ministers." Ibid. Kissinger does not note that Kosygin may have been pressing the case for a CTB quite deliberately. Nor does he report that confusion was more widely shared. The evening before, when Kissinger had asked his staff for the TTB talking points and briefing book, it turned out there was none. Someone recalled that a 100-kiloton level would be a good round number and it was so agreed. The next day, after evading head-on rejection of a CTB, Nixon proposed a 100-kiloton TTB. Before the Soviets could respond, Kissinger corrected him to a 150-kiloton limit (having overnight called Washington to check and having learned that Secretary of Defense Schlesinger insisted on not going below a 150-kiloton level). The Soviets, bemused once again by the American negotiating acrobatics, agreed on the 150-kiloton-level TTB. Information from members of the American delegation.

61. For the text, see *State Bulletin*, vol. 71 (July 29, 1974), pp. 217–18.

62. See Zumwalt, *On Watch*, pp. 479–511, especially 495–97.

was customary on such an occasion. Schlesinger, however, ignored the order and both attended and presented the medal.[63] Such was the state of morale and discipline in the administration.

Agreement was also reached on a joint statement advocating measures "to overcome the dangers of the use of environmental modification techniques for military purposes." This accord encompassed, for example, weather modification measures.[64] In addition, several other accords were reached, including a Long-Term (ten-year) Agreement on Economic, Industrial, and Technical Cooperation, and further agreements in the fields of energy, housing construction, and artificial heart research and development. It was decided that consulates would be established in Kiev and New York.

In a private conversation with Brezhnev, Nixon urged that the Soviet leader "make some sort of gesture on Jewish emigration if only to pull the rug out from under Jackson." The president argued presciently that "if détente unravels in America, the hawks will take over, not the doves." Brezhnev produced some statistics to show they were doing so and at another point said that as far as he was concerned the Jews could all go.[65]

Of particular interest to President Nixon, Brezhnev accepted his proposal for an interim summit meeting in a third country late that same year to make another attempt to reach an agreement on SALT. Nixon also extended a by now routine invitation to Brezhnev to visit the United States in 1975, which he accepted. The plan for this meeting, but not the tentative interim one, was included in the communiqué.[66]

Again at this third summit meeting, Brezhnev raised in a private discussion with Nixon what the Soviet leadership regarded as a particularly serious and sensitive issue. He warned that China was a threat to peace and urged a nonaggression treaty between the Soviet Union and the United States to dissuade the Chinese from any attempts to embroil the two powers in conflict. This initiative was, as Kissinger notes, the last in a series of similar ones made since 1970.[67] Such a measure would, however, at the least reduce American ability to use its ties with China as leverage in triangular diplomacy. Indeed, it could be taken as American acceptance of Soviet military action against China (in defense, of course, whatever the actual circumstances).

Surprisingly, Nixon told Kissinger (within earshot of the Soviet interpreter) to pursue the idea in the back channel negotiations with Dobrynin,

---

63. Ibid., pp. 498, 507–10.

64. "Statement on Dangers of Military Use of Environmental Modification," State Bulletin, vol. 71 (July 29, 1974), p. 185.

65. Nixon, RN, pp. 1031, 1034.

66. State Bulletin, vol. 71 (July 29, 1974), pp. 185–90. For Nixon's proposal for a mini or interim summit meeting, see Nixon, RN, p. 1034.

67. Kissinger, Years of Upheaval, pp. 1173–74.

to be held in preparation for the planned interim summit. Kissinger was aghast. He told Scowcroft, his successor as national security adviser, that he would not carry out the order and would sooner resign. Later, on his own authority he simply told Dobrynin it was not a useful line to pursue. Nixon never returned to the idea.[68]

Nixon was not at his best at this summit. Observers reported that he seemed distraught and that his attention wandered in the meetings. He once cited incorrect figures in the SALT discussions and had to be corrected by Brezhnev. Watergate had taken its toll.[69]

Nixon's report to the nation speech on July 3, after his return, opened with the president wrapping himself in the American flag—it was the eve of the Fourth of July—and moved on to a reaffirmation of the quest for détente and a structure of peace. He again tied the agreements reached (modest as they were) to the "growing network of agreements" by which "we are creating new habits of cooperation and new patterns of consultation" with the Soviet Union and "a stable new base on which to build peace."[70]

The third summit, apart from further institutionalizing the process of détente and modestly sustaining its momentum, and despite the failure to reach another SALT agreement, did include several interesting new developments in the strategic dialogue between the two countries. During the meeting at Oreanda, Brezhnev briefed President Nixon and the American delegation on U.S. strategic forces and capabilities (including forward-based systems [FBS], as well as intercontinental forces), presenting an impressive array of American military capability as seen by the Soviets. Brezhnev was actively assisted by Colonel General Mikhail Kozlov, first deputy chief of the General Staff and chief of its Main Operations Directorate. Marshal Grechko also personally stressed to Kissinger the Soviet concern over American FBS and the apparent American drive for military superiority. On that same occasion, in an evident attempt to dissuade the United States from believing in the feasibility of gaining anything from an intensified arms race, a senior Soviet general even took the highly unusual step of advising an American counterpart that in its published evaluations the United States was *underestimating* the accuracy of Soviet ICBMs. He even provided specific information. The ploy probably backfired. While the American side was not persuaded by the Soviet presentation of the threat, some were impressed by the fact that the Soviets could see the threat in such terms. It was significant, too, that the Soviet political leaders

---

68. Ibid. Kissinger is very frank about his insubordination and comments merely that he doubts Nixon would have gone ahead with the idea. He also comments that "it was symptomatic of the disintegration of the Nixon Administration that this degree of suspicion could arise" between Nixon and himself on an issue they had worked together on for five-and-a-half years.

69. See Richard Valeriani, *Travels with Henry* (Boston, Mass.: Houghton Mifflin, 1979), pp. 141–42. See also Kissinger, *Years of Upheaval*, pp. 1164, 1170.

70. "Report to the Nation, July 3," *State Bulletin*, vol. 71 (July 29, 1974), pp. 191–95.

agreed to make such presentations and to let the Soviet military participate directly in the summit deliberations.[71]

Nixon's acerbic comments in his memoir on the positions taken by the American military (as well as by Secretary of Defense Schlesinger) were noted earlier. Following the summit, Kissinger offered a public comment, probably reflecting a sincere judgment on his part, that "*both* sides have to convince their military establishments of the benefits of [arms control] restraint, and that is not a thought that comes naturally to military people on either side."[72] It is not clear if his remark was directed more at the American or the Soviet military.[73]

Another sidelight on Soviet military participation in the SALT summit discussions has been disclosed unintentionally. In a news conference in December 1974 on "deep background"—not only not for attribution but also not for publication—Kissinger commented that he had colluded with Ambassador Dobrynin to slim down the attendance at some of the later meetings at the subsequent Vladivostok summit conference so as to cut out the Soviet generals there:

The meeting started with two generals sitting behind Brezhnev—and whenever we started getting concrete they started slipping little pieces of paper to him or butting into the conversation one way or the other. So, at the first break, Dobrynin came to me and asked whether we couldn't confine the meeting to three people on each side— which got rid of the two generals. So, after that, whenever numbers came up, we would explore the numbers, and then he would take about a forty-five minute break, either to consult the two generals, and, on at least two occasions, to consult Moscow.[74]

71. See Raymond L. Garthoff, "The Soviet Military and SALT," in Jiri Valenta and William C. Potter, eds., *Soviet Decisionmaking for National Security* (London: Allen and Unwin, 1984), p. 156; Kissinger, *Years of Upheaval*, p. 1171; Kraft, *New Yorker*, July 29, 1974, pp. 68, 70; and Michael Getler, "Soviets Reported Stepping up Flight Testing of New Missiles," *Washington Post*, July 27, 1974.

   Kissinger comments: "To be sure, Brezhnev did not give himself the worst of the analysis; at the same time, the argument was not preposterous; it was the classic worst-case scenario of military planning. . . . It is as unlikely to occur as it is necessary to prepare for it. The difficulty is how to negotiate restraints when two worst-case scenarios confront each other." Kissinger, *Years of Upheaval*, p. 1171.

72. "News Conference at Moscow, July 3," *State Bulletin*, vol. 71 (July 29, 1974), p. 210; and see Kissinger, *Years of Upheaval*, p. 1175. Emphasis added.

73. Schlesinger, at least, felt the point of the remarks sufficiently to make a defensive statement expressing his confidence in the devotion of the American military to arms control. He did so at a press conference within hours after Kissinger's remark, even before the presidential delegation left Moscow.

74. Secretary Kissinger delivered an off-the-record background press briefing to selected news correspondents on December 3, 1974. After later requests for its release, the transcript was provided on March 5, 1975, except for two excerpts that were said to be classified for security reasons. After lengthy judicial proceedings, on April 15, 1981, the Department of State released the two excerpts. The key part of one is cited here.

The differences of view within the Soviet Union will be discussed later. Briefly, the military did express caution and continued concern that those Soviet military programs not limited by SALT be assured, as well as that Soviet security interests be guarded in the SALT negotiations.

Soviet Politics and Policy

Whatever disquiet the Soviet leaders harbored over the clouded future of President Nixon—and of détente—they allowed no sign of it to enter public commentary. As had become customary, the Politburo of the Central Committee of the Communist Party, the Presidium of the Supreme Soviet of the USSR, and the Council of Ministers of the USSR issued a resolution of endorsement expressing full approval of Brezhnev's conduct of the meetings and praising the results of the summit conference as "a major new contribution to the improvement of Soviet-U.S. relations" and to peace and détente.[75] Academician Georgy A. Arbatov wrote the principal commentary, stating that "the process of the normalization and improvement of relations between the largest powers, on which peace throughout the world depends so much, is continuing successfully." He noted that this progress was so "despite the fact that this process is taking place under much less than ideal conditions, and that certain events (as was the case during the October War in 1973 in the Near East) can create certain difficulties." But he also gave due attention to the fact that "an acute clash has developed" around the summit meetings as part of "the ideological and political struggle now being waged around the question of détente, the shift from cold war to relations of peaceful coexistence."[76] He noted, as did other Soviet observers, the symbolic fact that Senator Jackson chose the very time of Nixon's meeting in Moscow to visit Beijing.

The Soviet leaders were deeply concerned over future American steadfastness in pursuing détente. They supported Nixon because he continued to endorse détente, but they were worried about the future of his presidency and the implications for détente of his decline (and later fall) from power. Accordingly, while Nixon peppered his toasts and speeches with references to the value of "the personal relations and the personal friendship that has been established by these [summit] meetings,"[77] the Soviets stressed both national and governmental ties and avoided linking themselves to Nixon's personal fate. This approach was particularly evident as Brezhnev included in his toasts references to Soviet relations with the Congress and the American peo-

---

75. "On the Results of the Third Soviet-American Summit Meeting," *Pravda*, July 6, 1974.

76. G. Arbatov, "New Frontiers of Soviet-American Relations," *Izvestiya*, July 13, 1974.

77. "Dinner Honoring Soviet Leaders, Spaso House, Moscow, July 2," Toast by President Nixon, *State Bulletin*, vol. 71 (July 29, 1974), p. 183.

ple.[78] But apart from a small flurry when the Soviets dropped one of Nixon's references to "personal relations" in published translations of the president's remarks, neither side made an issue of the difference in nuance.[79]

It is difficult to isolate the effect that Watergate had on the summit meeting from that of the shift to open opposition to détente in some political circles in the United States. While Nixon is hardly a disinterested party, there is considerable validity to the assessment he makes. While he underplays the further effect of Watergate in compounding other growing dissatisfactions, he is right to some degree when he writes in his memoir:

In my judgment my Watergate problems and the impeachment hearings did not play a major part at Summit III. Our intelligence beforehand—and my distinct impression while in the Soviet Union—was that Brezhnev had decided to go all out for détente and place all his chips on my survival and my ultimate ability to deliver on what I promised. It was the American domestic political fluctuations, most of which had preceded Watergate, that cast the greatest doubt on my reliability: the failure to produce MFN status and the agitation over Soviet Jews and emigration had made it difficult for Brezhnev to defend détente to his own conservatives. Similarly, the military establishments of both countries were bridling against the sudden reality of major and meaningful arms limitation and the real prospect of arms reduction if and as détente progressed. These problems would have existed regardless of Watergate.[80]

Whatever the assessment of the causes for the inability of the American side to move détente forward, it is clear that while the Soviets were unprepared to pick up the slack and do more than their share, they were interested in developing détente and arms control. Indeed, there is reason to believe that the Soviets had decisions pending in 1974 on several major military programs, and these were affected by their judgment about the solidity of détente and prospects for arms limitation. Most evident was the decision on how far to upgrade their ICBM force with MIRVs; whether and at what pace to develop an advanced ballistic missile launching submarine; whether to deploy a new intermediate-range missile; whether to develop a heavy bomber; and whether to develop a land-mobile ICBM. Already in 1974 the Soviets were beginning to become concerned over whether they could *maintain* the strategic parity they had not yet quite attained. The rising concern within the Soviet military that détente not curtail their programs while the United States moved forward with a new generation of weaponry based on more advanced technology should be seen in this context.

As noted, Soviet military (and political) leaders were concerned about the new turn in American military policy, expressed most sharply in the

---

78. See Brezhnev's toasts on June 27 and July 2, 1974, *State Bulletin*, vol. 71 (July 29, 1974), pp. 174, 183, 185.

79. See Kraft, *New Yorker*, July 29, 1974, pp. 72–73; and Kissinger, *Years of Upheaval*, pp. 1162–63.

80. Nixon, *RN*, p. 1036.

Schlesinger Doctrine in early 1974. A veiled debate arose among Soviet military and civilian commentators over the effects of détente on military requirements and the relative risks of the arms race versus possible underpreparedness. Fundamentally, the question was one of the extent of reliance to be placed on negotiated arms control, in preference to unilateral military preparedness. The subdued debate over the role of the PNW agreement of 1973 continued, now coupled with calls not only for vigilance, but also for military programs to offset new American programs.

These issues were the subject of differing judgments in a series of articles appearing from February to August 1974. While most of the discussions were by secondary figures, Marshal Grechko—virtually on the eve of the summit—was among those stressing the need to be prepared not only for the most likely course of events—détente—but also for "the most unexpected reversals, dangerous provocations and adventures on the part of the enemies of socialism and peace."[81] General of the Army A. Yepishev, too, warned against "conscious or unconscious underestimation of the military danger from imperialism."[82]

Some commentators in the West at the time concluded erroneously that Grechko was challenging Brezhnev.[83] While this view is incorrect, it is significant that various Soviet leaders chose to stress different themes and related nuances having policy implications. For example, Brezhnev did argue in a speech in June shortly before the summit meeting that "it is an immeasurably greater risk to continue to accumulate arms without restraint" than to risk an arms limitation.[84] Again in July Brezhnev criticized the age-old dictum that "if you want peace, be prepared for war." Instead, he said, "In our nuclear age, this formula conceals a special danger." Indeed, he went on to say that "in recent years such a mass of weapons has been accumulated as to make it

---

81. TASS, "Consolidate the Strength and Might of the Motherland: Meeting of Voters With A. A. Grechko," *Pravda*, June 5, 1974, and *Krasnaya zvezda* [Red Star], June 5, 1974. See also Grechko, "On Guard over Peace and Socialism," *Pravda*, February 23, 1974, and "V. I. Lenin and the Armed Forces of the Soviet State," *Kommunist*, no. 3 (February 1974), pp. 12–24.

82. General of the Army A. Yepishev, "The Unfading Light of a Great Feat," *Izvestiya*, May 9, 1974.

83. In particular, Victor Zorza and Joseph Alsop. See Zorza, "Kremlin Policy Struggle," *Washington Post*, February 26, 1974; Alsop, "The Grechko Factor," *Washington Post*, April 1, 1974; Zorza, "Grechko-Brezhnev Quarrel," *Washington Post*, April 2, 1974; Zorza, "A Victory for Soviet Hardliners," *Washington Post*, April 9, 1974; Zorza, "Moscow's Summit Debate," *Washington Post*, June 4, 1974; Zorza, "Kremlin Politics and Military Spending," *Washington Post*, July 2, 1974; Alsop, "The Power of Marshal Grechko," *Washington Post*, July 3, 1974; and Alsop, "The Soviet Refusal to Limit Strategic Arms," *Washington Post*, July 10, 1974.

84. L. I. Brezhnev, "Speech to Voters of the Bauman Electoral District of Moscow, June 14, 1974," *O vneshnei politike KPSS i sovetskogo gosudarstva: Rechi i stat'i* [On the Foreign Policy of the CPSU and the Soviet Government: Speeches and Articles], 3d ed. (Moscow: Politizdat, 1978), p. 402.

possible to destroy every living thing on earth several times over."[85] At the same time, in these same speeches and articles Grechko also strongly endorsed SALT and détente, while Brezhnev also reaffirmed the need for "unceasing attention to strengthening the defense capability of our socialist Motherland."[86] The differences in emphasis were significant as indications of the perceived need to balance the requirements for détente and defense, with members of the leadership stressing points of particular interest to themselves within that consensus. And this consensus clearly limited Brezhnev's flexibility in negotiation. It did not, however, challenge pursuit of détente or the process of negotiated arms limitation.

The earlier reluctance and reservations of a number of the Soviet leaders and members of the economic bureaucracy with respect to Brezhnev's détente policy of seeking to maximize East-West trade also came to the fore in 1973–74. Paradoxically, while the Soviet leaders, including Brezhnev, who favored increased trade were concerned by the growing indications that the weakened Nixon administration might not be able to secure congressional approval of MFN, others were increasingly doubtful that Moscow should seek increased economic ties,[87] despite the policy decision in 1971 to do so.

The routine joint endorsement of the summit meeting and its results by the leading party and governmental bodies reinforced the consensus for détente and arms limitation, to be pursued in a prudent manner. There was no overt challenge to détente and SALT such as was beginning to be heard, and felt, in Washington.

Later Soviet commentary was not encumbered by the need for diplomatic discretion and had the advantage of knowledge of subsequent developments. Unlike the unrelieved praise and optimism voiced in 1974, this later coverage presented a very different estimate of the ability of the failing Nixon administration to conduct a policy of détente in its last months. The following excerpts from two leading Soviet analysts of the American political system, taken together, sum up the Soviet interpretation of this period:

A political counteroffensive was also undertaken by the U.S. military-industrial complex, which saw a mounting threat to its own existence in the results of the détente policy and, in particular, in its prospects. This counteroffensive by the military-industrial complex and other rightist and reactionary forces, including Zionist circles, was launched at a time when the administration, which had done much to promote the policy of détente, was experiencing serious domestic political difficulties in connection with the Watergate affair. The Nixon administration fell victim to crisis phenomena that had been maturing for decades within the institution of the presidency, to its own

---

85. Brezhnev, "Speech to the Ceremonial Meeting of the Sejm of the Polish People's Republic on the Thirtieth Anniversary of the Rebirth of Poland, July 21, 1974," ibid., p. 417.

86. Ibid., p. 402.

87. See the discussion in chapter 3 and references in footnote 55 in that chapter. In particular, see Peter M. E. Volten, *Brezhnev's Peace Program: A Study of Soviet Domestic Political Process and Power* (Boulder, Colo.: Westview, 1982), pp. 111–23, 129–32.

abuses of power within the nation, and to the massive intrigues of its opponents. The diminishing authority of the president, the almost total preoccupation of Nixon and his closest advisers with the struggle for their own survival, the subsequent forced resignation of the chief of state and the transfer of power to Ford, who had little experience in international affairs, naturally affected progress in the policy of détente.[88]

And:

Great damage to détente was a serious side effect of Watergate. On the one hand, from the end of 1973 to the middle of 1974 the leadership of the Administration was practically paralyzed in the foreign policy sphere. In the process of losing the remnants of his authority and influence within the country, President Nixon was to an increasing degree incapable of carrying out further steps in the field of détente and arms limitation. The Watergate scandal also consumed more and more of the attention and energy of liberal circles in the United States, distracting them from problems of foreign policy and the arms race.[89]

Another long-term impact of Watergate was evidenced in the acid words of a Soviet commentator in addressing American interests in 1981 in establishing "rules of the game" for limiting nuclear warfare. He asked rhetorically upon what "gentleman's promises" an adversary of the United States could rely "if, as the history of recent years has shown, even the Americans themselves cannot rely upon the President's word of honor."[90]

Watergate and Détente

Attention to American-Soviet relations subsided in the United States soon after the summit (and in the absence of anything seen as a crisis). Almost everything was swallowed up by the inexorable denoucment of the Watergate drama. Both houses of Congress did hold hearings on détente (the House Committee on Foreign Affairs from May to July, and the Senate Committee on Foreign Relations from August to October, after Nixon's resignation). Their tone was one of malaise rather than debate, uneasiness but not yet disenchantment.

Over the long run Watergate was undoubtedly a serious blow to American-Soviet détente. While its effects on Soviet interest in détente were peripheral and ephemeral,[91] its direct and indirect effects on American politics

---

88. A. A. Kokoshin, "Domestic Causes of Changes in [U.S.] Foreign Policy," *SShA*, no. 7 (July 1980), p. 5.

89. A. Arbatov, *Bezopasnost' v yadernyi vek i politika Vashingtona* [Security in the Nuclear Age and the Policy of Washington] (Moscow: Politizdat, 1980), pp. 218–19.

90. Henry Trofimenko, "Counterforce: Illusion of a Panacea," *International Security*, vol. 5 (Spring 1981), p. 45.

91. In his memoir, which in general places very heavy weight on the destructive effect of Watergate, Kissinger focuses almost entirely on the impact in 1973–74; for his view on détente and

were very far-reaching. It is only over the longer run, and with the benefit of hindsight, that the full impact of Watergate in succeeding years can be appreciated.

In his final address to the nation, when he announced his resignation, Nixon argued that "the world is a safer place today" because of his efforts in détente. "This, more than anything," he said, "is what I hoped to achieve when I sought the presidency. This, more than anything, is what I hope will be my legacy to you, to our country, as I leave the presidency."[92]

When Gerald Ford succeeded to the presidency on August 9, 1974, his first interest was to effect as little change as possible in personnel and in policy, apart from banishing the reminders of Watergate as quickly as possible. The first major foreign policy pronouncement of the new administration was made by Secretary Kissinger to the Senate Foreign Relations Committee on September 19, 1974, in the course of its hearings on détente. Kissinger had carefully prepared this statement on U.S.-Soviet relations as a comprehensive elaboration of the American policy on détente. It served both to justify the policy pursued by the past administration and to launch the new administration on the same path. It included a strong renewed pitch for Congress to approve the trade accords negotiated with the Soviet Union in 1972 and not to tie such agreements to internal Soviet political developments such as human rights abuses. Instead, the statement linked bilateral détente to "responsible international behavior by the Soviet Union," which it said would be used as "the primary index of our relationship" and on which we would "insist."[93]

Kissinger argued that the "SALT agreements should be seen as steps in a process leading to progressively greater stability" and that "when linked to such broad and unprecedented projects as SALT, détente takes on added meaning and opens prospects for a more stable peace."[94] He stressed that détente itself is a process, not something to be achieved once and for all. Finally, he warned against placing too heavy demands on détente, particularly in terms of seeing it as an *American* device for changing the situation to its own advantage, that is, as a tool or weapon for changing Soviet behavior or positions. Détente had to remain of mutual advantage if it was to endure. In a prescient passage he warned: "The temptation to combine detente with increasing pressure on the Soviet Union will grow. Such an attitude would be disastrous. We would not accept it from Moscow; Moscow will not accept it

relations with the Soviet Union, see Kissinger, *Years of Upheaval,* especially pp. 122–27, 300, 1030–31, 1152–53, 1160–61.

92. Nixon, *RN,* p. 1083.

93. Statement by Secretary Kissinger, "Detente with the Soviet Union: The Reality of Competition and the Imperative of Cooperation," September 19, *State Bulletin,* vol. 71 (October 14, 1974), p. 518.

94. Ibid., pp. 515–16.

from us. We will finally wind up again with the cold war and fail to achieve either peace or any humane goal."[95]

It remained to be seen if the Ford administration could rescue détente from the doldrums and the increasing assaults from various quarters of domestic opposition. And, of course, much would depend on what both the United States and the Soviet Union did in the world at large and at home, as well as in their bilateral relations.

---

95. Ibid., p. 516.

13 The Ford Administration: New Efforts and New Obstacles, 1974–75

THE FORD ADMINISTRATION, the first in American history headed by a president who had never been elected to national office, inherited the Nixon administration's policy of détente with the Soviet Union. This policy was reaffirmed, in a fully elaborated official statement of its rationale, by Secretary of State Kissinger (also inherited from the Nixon administration) in his testimony to the Senate on September 19, 1974, cited earlier. President Gerald R. Ford himself strongly reaffirmed the policy in his first meeting with Foreign Minister Gromyko on September 20, 1974, at a summit meeting with General Secretary Brezhnev in November 1974, in his State of the World address on April 10, 1975, at a further encounter with Brezhnev at the Conference on Security and Cooperation in Europe (CSCE) meeting in Helsinki in July 1975, and at another meeting with Gromyko in September 1975. In 1974 and 1975 détente was both praised and pursued. As will be seen, however, a change would occur by early 1976 for a number of reasons.

The new president also moved to close out less pleasant aspects of Nixon's legacy. On September 8, 1974, he pardoned the former president for any criminal acts in office and sought to balance that act of compassion with another in a conditional amnesty for Vietnam War draft evaders on September 15. Neither fully succeeded in its purpose, however, with the pardon of Nixon meeting widespread public disapproval.

The third major legacy was the galloping economic recession that ran throughout 1974 and into 1975. This development dominated a gloomy State of the Union address on January 13, 1975, and much of the attention of the new administration was directed toward renewing public confidence through the WIN (Whip Inflation Now) program.

Despite general relief over the lancing of the Watergate wound and widespread public sympathy for the new president, regaining public confidence was not easy. While the recession commanded the greatest public attention,

438

the sphere of national security was marked in 1975 by unfolding scandals. It was revealed that the CIA was involved in domestic spying and foreign assassi nation schemes. This information was initially unveiled in the press, and was detailed and confirmed later in hearings by the Congress and in the report of a special Rockefeller commission of inquiry appointed by the president.[1]

The new president was generally regarded as an experienced politician, but one not versed in international and security affairs. He personally believed that his long congressional experience had provided more familiarity with international affairs than was generally acknowledged, but he recognized his lack of direct experience. Ford recalls in his memoir that on the day Nixon informed Ford of his intention to resign the next day, one of his first acts was to call Secretary of State Kissinger to tell him: "Henry, I need you. The country needs you. I want you to stay. I'll do everything I can to work with you." Kissinger agreed at once, commenting: "Sir, it is my job to get along with you and not yours to get along with me."[2] Ford also decided, in line with Kissinger's preference, to keep him as his national security adviser as well as secretary of state. Ford describes the "admiration and affection" he felt for Kissinger and states that he "respected his expertise in foreign policy" and the fact that he was "a total pragmatist who thought in terms of power and national interest instead of ideology." Kissinger, he felt, "had a global view of international relationships and tried to rearrange them in a way that would be beneficial to the United States."[3] When, the day before he was sworn in, Kissinger asked Ford whether he should press ahead with plans for a summit meeting with Brezhnev, the soon-to-be president replied: "Yes, of course." Ford explained in his memoir that "anything that would bring the arms race under control would be a plus for the entire world."[4]

In stunning contrast to Richard Nixon's secretive and vindictive action on the morrow of his second inauguration in January 1973, President

1. On January 4, 1975, President Ford announced establishment of a blue-ribbon Commission on CIA Activities within the United States. Headed by Vice President Nelson A. Rockefeller, it was to investigate the revelations in the press. See Seymour M. Hersh, "Huge C.I.A. Operation Reported in U.S. against Antiwar Forces, Other Dissidents in Nixon Years," *New York Times*, December 22, 1974. Ford acted one day after being briefed by CIA Director William E. Colby on the agency's own internal investigation, which had revealed a number of abuses and violations of the law. See Gerald R. Ford, *A Time to Heal: The Autobiography of Gerald R. Ford* (Harper and Row, 1979), pp. 229–30, and see 265–66, 325, 356. See also "Text of Report by Colby in Response to Charges of Domestic Spying by C.I.A.," *New York Times*, January 16, 1975. The Rockefeller commission reported its findings on June 10, 1975, while the Senate released a report on assassination plots on November 21, 1975. On February 17, 1976, Ford announced a number of reforms of intelligence practice. Several other intelligence activities were also disclosed publicly during 1975, including a largely unsuccessful attempt to raise a sunken Soviet missile-carrying submarine (only part was raised), revealed in March.

2. Ford, *A Time to Heal*, p. 30.

3. Ibid., p. 129.

4. Ibid., p. 33.

Ford called a meeting of the cabinet on his second day in office and stated that he did not want—indeed, would not accept—any resignations. The country needed stability and continuity.[5] Ford completed his team by bringing Rockefeller in as vice president, consolidating a moderate and centrist cast to his administration.

From the outset there were, however, seeds of friction and potential difficulty. Above all, there had been friction between the new president and Secretary of Defense Schlesinger in the past, and their relationship was not marked by the mutual respect that was essential.[6] During the first year of the new administration fissures relating to détente grew and became more evident and more damaging. While Ford strongly—at first even deferentially—accepted Kissinger's role, it was weakened by others, particularly Schlesinger. The secretary of defense strongly emphasized a growing Soviet military threat and advocated a much harder line in the SALT negotiations (to be addressed presently). He was also the first to raise concerns over possible strategic military aspects of Soviet activities in the third world, notably with respect to a Soviet naval missile storage facility at Berbera in Somalia, a situation he raised in June 1975. On that same occasion he also stressed Soviet buildup of a counterforce strategic missile capability.

The sudden fall of the anticommunist regimes in South Vietnam and Cambodia in April 1975 caused widespread American unease and self-doubt. The "decent interval" purchased by Nixon and Kissinger in January 1973 did not fully cushion the American public's opinion of the final failure of a decade of intense involvement in Indochina, or the impact on the new Ford-Kissinger administration. Recriminations were exchanged. Although Congress had declined to supply more military assistance to South Vietnam in the final failing weeks, further aid would not have prevented or even delayed the collapse. No one charged the Ford administration with the defeat, but the president could not entirely escape the consequences of the event, coming as it did only months after he took office. Above all, there was no escaping the American unease over whether it had done too much or too little in trying to stem a communist advance.

The *Mayaguez* incident in May, in which local communist (Khmer Rouge) forces in Kampuchea (Cambodia) seized a U.S. merchant ship, was scarcely a reassuring model of crisis management.[7] Forty-one lives were lost to rescue thirty-nine who, as it turned out, had already been released. Nevertheless, the attack boosted morale in the administration and the nation. The United States had shown it would not be pushed around, even by fate. It was

---

5. Ibid., p. 131.

6. See ibid., pp. 136, 320–24, for Ford's own account, attested to by others.

7. The best account of the handling of the *Mayaguez* incident is in Richard G. Head, Frisco W. Short, and Robert C. McFarlane, *Crisis Resolution: Presidential Decision Making in the Mayaguez and Korean Confrontations* (Boulder, Colo.: Westview, 1978), pp. 101–48. See also Roy Rowan, *The Four Days of Mayaguez* (Norton, 1975).

not afraid to use its military power to defend its injured interests—whether needed or not and albeit against one of the smallest of powers, one that was still establishing its own authority.[8]

In September 1975 two assassination attempts were made against President Ford within days of each other. These incidents boosted his popularity but awakened concern over the national leadership. In addition, the public opinion polls showed his performance rating dropping. Partly in response to those concerns, Ford rather suddenly carried out a major reshuffle of the national security leadership on November 2, 1975, about halfway through his foreshortened term of office. Ford reports that the first two men he advised of his decision, Kissinger and White House Chief of Staff Donald H. Rumsfeld, had both opposed the move, but he went ahead anyway. The Halloween Massacre, as it came to be called, did not still the concern.

Schlesinger was fired and replaced by Rumsfeld; CIA Director Colby was replaced by George Bush. Kissinger lost his second hat as national security adviser to his deputy, Lieutenant General Brent Scowcroft. And Rockefeller, who had earlier aspired to succeed Ford as president, was prevailed upon to announce he would not be Ford's running mate in the election. This sop to the right counterbalanced Schlesinger's ouster. Finally, Elliot L. Richardson was brought back to the cabinet as secretary of commerce, succeeding Rogers C. B. Morton.[9]

Schlesinger, in a parting shot, publicly endorsed a "détente without illusions" that was coupled with a strong defense. It was a scarcely veiled criticism of what he regarded as the Kissinger-Ford pursuit of a détente with illusions and insufficient attention to military programs. In an informal talk with journalists he was more blunt: "Henry [Kissinger] is always tough with everybody but the Russians,"[10] an unjustified judgment, but one that played to a growing concern. For his part, Scowcroft was supportive of détente and on friendly terms with Kissinger, and he proved a very able national security adviser to the president. Nonetheless, over time Kissinger's easy access to the president was reduced, weakening his position, as did the loss of his White House role intermediating the positions of other departments and agencies in the national security field. Paradoxically, even the removal of Schlesinger weakened Kissinger's position, in part because Ford thereafter felt it necessary to

---

8. Ford and, in particular, Kissinger, were determined to use force in the *Mayaguez* incident precisely to demonstrate that notwithstanding the fall of South Vietnam, the United States was ready to resort to military force when challenged.

9. Ford, *A Time to Heal*, pp. 319–31. Schlesinger was the only one to argue with Ford and attempt to get the decision reversed. Ibid., pp. 329–30. Ford recounts that he thought—rightly, as it turned out—that his troubles with Schlesinger would not end with his departure. Lieutenant General Daniel O. Graham, director of the Defense Intelligence Agency, in protest announced his intention to retire on the day that Schlesinger and Colby were dropped. He joined the ranks of the hard-line critics of détente.

10. Richard J. Whalen, "The Ford Shakeup: Politics vs. Policy," *Washington Post*, November 9, 1975.

make clear that he was not soft on meeting defense requirements, and also because Rumsfeld became an increasingly active advocate of defense over détente. Rumsfeld, long close to Ford and the president's own selection, had considerably greater access and influence than Schlesinger had had. Moreover, even before the shake-up, Kissinger's role had been weakened vis-à-vis Schlesinger and senatorial and other critics of SALT and détente. The reason was Nixon's purge of many strong advocates of the SALT talks, détente, and arms control at the start of his second administration. Their removal had deprived Kissinger of the fulcrum position he had held in 1970–72, when he could contrive to balance those on the right and left and steer a course from a central position.

Within a few months Ronald Reagan, former governor of California, was actively campaigning against Ford for the Republican presidential nomination, charging that Ford had fired Schlesinger because he was "afraid to tell the American people 'the truth about our military status,'" and that he deferred unduly to Kissinger as "the sole architect of our foreign policy."[11] The campaign by the opponents of détente included a direct assault by several members of the Nixon administration, notably former Secretary of Defense Laird in a piece in the widely circulated *Reader's Digest* and by a hard-line former assistant secretary of defense, G. Warren Nutter, in a booklet published by the American Enterprise Institute called *Kissinger's Grand Design*, with a foreword by Laird.[12]

Public opinion was also unsettled by a series of developments in 1975 beginning with the fall of South Vietnam and Cambodia in April and continuing with the leftward movement in Portugal, the advance of Soviet- and Cuban-supported forces in Angola, and agitation over human rights in the Soviet Union itself. All these situations added to a growing disquiet over SALT and the global military balance, as Americans came to see them as related to the policy of détente.[13]

SALT and the Vladivostok Accord

President Ford received Gromyko on September 20, 1974, in his first direct high-level contact. In Ford's words, Gromyko "hinted that his col-

---

11. See Ford, *A Time to Heal*, p. 346.

12. See Melvin R. Laird, "Is *This* Detente?" *Reader's Digest* (July 1975); and G. Warren Nutter, *Kissinger's Grand Design*, Foreign Affairs Study 27 (Washington, D.C.: American Enterprise Institute, 1975).

13. The significance of the developments in Portugal and a related trend toward Eurocommunism in several West European countries is discussed in chapter 14, developments in Angola in chapter 15, and the relation of détente and the issues of human rights and Jewish emigration from the Soviet Union later in this chapter.

leagues might be more 'responsive' to the Ford administration, just might be willing to make the sort of concessions that would enable us to agree on a new arms limitation pact."[14] With this hope Ford and Kissinger decided that after the latter's trip to the Middle East in October, he should go to Moscow. Although the SALT delegations were meeting in Geneva, their activity was limited to a general exploratory discussion of the principles for quantitative and qualitative limitations under a ten-year agreement, with neither side advancing concrete proposals.[15] Rather, in order to make the Kissinger consultations as fruitful as possible, a concrete proposal was sent to Moscow via the Kissinger-Dobrynin channel about a week in advance of his trip. It proposed equal overall levels of 2,200 launchers, of which 1,320 could have MIRVs. There was a further limit of 250 heavy systems (SS-9 missiles and heavy bombers). In addition, these large ICBMs could not have MIRVs; air-to-surface missiles with a range of more than 3,000 kilometers would also be banned; and there would be a limit on the pace of modernization to no more than 175 launchers each year. It was a complex proposal, tilted in U.S. favor, but a serious negotiating proposition. It was based on ideas discussed at several NSC meetings.[16]

Kissinger was in Moscow for four days, October 23–27. Ford notes in his memoir that he had expected the Soviets would hold to a hard line on SALT, especially because of the mounting difficulties the trade bill was facing in Congress. Accordingly he was "pleasantly surprised when Kissinger discerned a new moderation in the Soviet stand on SALT." Indeed, Kissinger's report was so encouraging that Ford authorized Kissinger, who had contacted the president from Moscow, to accept and arrange a special summit meeting with Brezhnev in the Far East in November if the progress on SALT warranted. (Ford was already scheduled to visit Japan and the Republic of Korea.) Before

---

14. Ford, *A Time to Heal*, pp. 183–84.

15. The delegations met in the fifth round of SALT II from September 18 to November 5, 1974, the first session since February–March and the Moscow summit meeting. The U.S. delegation was not authorized either to advance any proposals or to discuss any specific Soviet proposals that might be (but were not) advanced. Consequently only limited progress was made on secondary matters, mainly through modification of a few U.S. positions. See U. Alexis Johnson with Jef Olivarius McAllister, *The Right Hand of Power* (Englewood Cliffs, N.J.: Prentice-Hall, 1984), pp. 602–05.

16. Based on information from informed participants. This information goes beyond, and in part differs from, that given in Leslie H. Gelb, "Vladivostok Pact: How It Was Reached," *New York Times*, December 3, 1974, the only detailed press account.

The level of 1,320 launchers for missiles with MIRVs has raised curiosity, since it is clearly a selected number and yet did not accord precisely with U.S. or Soviet actual or planned forces. That number was chosen in order to give the United States some leeway in starting its planned Trident submarine program, but the specific number was reached by the simple formula of taking 60 percent of the proposed overall level of 2,200 launchers.

Kissinger's departure from Moscow it was announced that the president would meet Brezhnev at Vladivostok in late November.[17]

The talks went further toward identifying the final terms acceptable to the Soviet leaders than Kissinger reported at the time—giving him the advantage of knowing how to steer the preparations in Washington for the summit meeting. Brezhnev apparently indicated receptivity to either of two approaches: one would provide equal aggregates of strategic launchers and equal levels of launchers for missiles with MIRVs; the other would provide a differential that gave the Soviet Union a higher aggregate level and the United States a higher level of MIRVs. This was called the "offsetting asymmetries" approach. The two men discussed aggregate totals of 2,400 for the USSR and 2,200 for the United States, and MIRV levels of 1,100 or 1,200 for the USSR and 1,300 for the United States. Brezhnev was receptive. If agreement were reached on equal levels, Brezhnev would consider either an overall aggregate of 2,400 and the American-proposed level of MIRVs of 1,320, or the American-proposed aggregate of 2,200 and a lower level of 1,200 MIRVs. The Soviet Union would not agree to reduce the number (308) of its heavy ICBM launchers.[18] The Soviets did, however, indicate they would defer consideration of American forward-based nuclear systems and the British and French nuclear forces.

Schlesinger and the JCS, only partially informed about Kissinger's findings, urged Ford to hold out for equal numbers of launchers—which they

---

17. Ford, *A Time to Heal,* p. 200. For the published record of Kissinger's Moscow meetings see "Secretary Kissinger Visits the USSR, South Asia, Iran, Romania, Yugoslavia, and Italy," *Department of State Bulletin,* vol. 71 (November 25, 1974), pp. 701–04. (Hereafter *State Bulletin.*)

18. Information from interviews with informed participants; see also note 20.

The record, and the memories of participants, are inconsistent and confused on details of the exchanges of proposals on numbers. This is unsurprising since very few were involved in all the discussions with Kissinger in October and with Ford and Kissinger in November. Nonetheless, the figures cited represent the best collective consensus of several participants interviewed. Brezhnev was, however, prepared to reach the aggregate totals only by the end of the ten-year agreement, in 1985.

After Vladivostok, when there was widespread American criticism of the levels agreed upon as being too high, efforts were made to prevent public disclosure of the fact that the Soviet Union had been prepared to accept lower levels of missiles with MIRVs. President Ford had mistakenly told a group of senators that the MIRV limit agreed upon was 1,200, before the 1,320 figure was made public, but this was assumed to be a simple error on the number rather than the inadvertent disclosure of an alternative number that had been under negotiation. See John Herbers, "Arms Limit Said to Include 1,200 Vehicles for MIRVs," *New York Times,* November 27, 1974. And Kissinger had revealed American authorship of the 1,320 figure and admitted in a background off-the-record briefing for newsmen on December 3 that "we could have gotten a slightly lower MIRV figure," and later, "I'm not saying we couldn't have had a hundred less." But he did not make such disclosures on the open record, and subsequently the matter was forgotten. Quotations from the untitled transcript of the background briefing of December 3, 1974, released by the Department of State on March 5, 1975, pp. A-5 and C-1.

did not believe the Soviet side would accept—rather than accept a lower total level and compensating higher MIRV level for the United States. Kissinger, knowing (as they did not) that Brezhnev had already said he would accept equal numbers (and knowing the range of acceptable numbers), advised Ford to "hang tough" and hold out for equal numbers, pretending to "predict" they would come around.[19] A revised American proposal was sent to Moscow about a week before the meeting.

The Vladivostok summit conference took place on November 23 and 24 outside the city at a military sanatorium resort called Okeanskaya (Oceanic).[20] The discussions of SALT dominated the meeting and were essentially concluded on the first day. Agreement was reached on a framework for a ten-year agreement, including accord on an equal aggregate level (2,400 launchers and heavy bombers) and an equal sublimit for launchers of missiles with MIRVs (1,320).[21] Ford had opted for the equal levels principally because he believed this solution would find greatest public support, and for the higher level of MIRVs to meet the urgings of the JCS (some of whom were far from happy to find later that the Soviets had agreed to equal levels). Various non-controversial elements of the Interim Agreement of 1972 were to be carried over (for example, the ban on any additional ICBM silos and on converting any silos for light ICBMs into launchers for heavy ICBMs—although there was still no agreed definition for those categories). The Vladivostok agreement, however, was only the outline for a future treaty.

President Ford later described his reaction at the time as "euphoric" and commented that Brezhnev shared his enthusiasm. As he has noted in his memoir, at the time reaching an agreement seemed simple: "As soon as technicians had ironed out the few remaining problems, we would sign a SALT II accord."[22] Ford reaffirmed an invitation to Brezhnev to visit the United

---

19. Ford, *A Time to Heal,* p. 215. Ford does not indicate that he was aware of Kissinger's ploy.

20. The official documentation of the Vladivostok summit meeting is available in "The Visit to the Soviet Union," *State Bulletin,* vol. 71 (December 23, 1974), pp. 878–82, and the texts of the two related press conferences by Secretary of State Kissinger, ibid., pp. 893–905.

21. At Vladivostok, Brezhnev proposed a level of 2,500 (representing the actual Soviet level), and Ford proposed 2,100 (close to the actual level of operational American forces). With a little discussion, agreement was soon reached on 2,400, as informally agreed in October. Information from informed participants; see also Gelb, *New York Times,* December 3, 1974. Participants have indicated that in his October negotiation with Kissinger, Brezhnev coupled acceptance of a 2,400 equal aggregate to be reached by 1985 with an understanding that the United States would not raise its force level above the existing level of 2,200 during that period. It is not known whether Brezhnev dropped this demand at Vladivostok, or whether assurances or a statement of intent not to increase the U.S. level were privately given by Ford or Kissinger. Nixon, it will be recalled, had done this in a secret letter in the parallel case relating to the right of the United States under the SALT I Interim Agreement to build Trident submarines with SLBMs to replace old Titan ICBMs (see chapter 5).

22. Ford, *A Time to Heal,* p. 218.

States in 1975 (noted in the communiqué), and they planned the meeting for the spring, when the SALT II treaty was expected to be ready to sign.

The major elements of the Vladivostok agreement constituted a significant advance in SALT. Above all, the Soviet leaders had made a major concession—accepted with only the greatest reluctance by the Soviet military leaders—in agreeing to equal aggregate levels of ICBM launchers, SLBM launchers, and heavy bombers, with no compensation for or limitation on American forward-based nuclear delivery systems (FBS) capable of striking the Soviet Union. But some other aspects of the limitations had not yet been agreed to, and even the accepted numerical levels (2,400/1,320) were not included in the formal joint statement or initial press briefings. These points of contention (and some others not recognized then as being in contention) rapidly became real issues as the military "technicians" took strong positions on them.[23]

At the time the summit meeting was concluded it had been assumed that the few issues holding up formalization of the Vladivostok framework could be resolved in a few days, and all issues in a few months. A written aide-mémoire was to record in specific terms the actual accord. But the text of the aide-mémoire could not be agreed on until December 10, and by then at least one major new issue had arisen—over air-launched cruise missiles. This issue arose *after* the Vladivostok meeting as the language of the aide-mémoire was being negotiated. The Soviet draft aide-mémoire stated that when a bomber was equipped with air-to-surface missiles with a range greater than 600 kilometers, each missile would be counted as a delivery vehicle in the aggregate of 2,400. By contrast, the Americans wanted to specify air-to-surface "ballistic" missiles. The United States argued that the term air-to-surface missiles did not include air-to-surface *cruise* missiles, only *ballistic* missiles. The Soviets, on the other hand, insisted that the term included all types of missiles. Each side had a different recollection of what had been intended at the summit discussions.

In order finally to agree on an aide-mémoire, the absence of which was becoming embarrassing as the administration began briefing the Senate two weeks after the meeting, on December 10 the American side finally agreed to omit the word "ballistic," while arguing that that remained the intent. Kissinger sought to protect the American interpretation by putting it in writing in a note to Gromyko. But while well aware of the U.S. position, the Soviets felt they had won by getting American agreement to the more general term in the aide-mémoire itself. This concession may have been unwise, because the words "air-to-surface missiles" without the modifier "ballistic" certainly fa-

---

23. Although Brezhnev had Soviet military advisers, President Ford and Secretary Kissinger—with a total entourage of 140 Americans—had no military representatives present. (General Brent Scowcroft of the White House staff was not serving as a military representative.) While this omission probably did not affect the outcome, it did not help gain acceptance in the United States. For example, see Editorial, "Whose Triumph?" *Wall Street Journal*, December 2, 1974.

vored the Soviet position and probably encouraged them to believe the United States would come to accept their position.[24] But the secretary of defense and the JCS were adamant against banning long-range air-launched cruise missiles.[25] This issue was not finally resolved until 1977.

The second major issue to arise was whether the new Soviet bomber, code-named "Backfire" by NATO, was a theater system that should not be considered a "heavy bomber" or whether it was an intercontinental strategic bomber that should be. In this case the difference of views was known, at least on the American side, but Kissinger mistakenly believed that he could override the Pentagon's desire to insist on its inclusion. The decision was that the Backfire would not be considered a strategic intercontinental system. That choice would be one of the main objections raised by Lieutenant General Edward C. Rowny, at this time the JCS representative on the SALT delegation, and some other opponents of the SALT II treaty in 1979.

In the end the aide-mémoire referred simply to heavy bombers and made no attempt to define or to list types of aircraft in that category. Brezhnev had, however, made clear the Soviet position that the Backfire was not an intercontinental bomber, and Ford did not press the issue. Subsequently the secretary of defense and the JCS insisted that it be included in the limitations, and the U.S. SALT delegation was instructed to press for that position. Kissinger, however, had made known his views and the negotiating history in a background briefing for selected American reporters on December 3. Background briefings are not for quotation, attribution, or publication. But based on Kissinger's comments a number of American news sources stated that the Backfire would not be included—stimulating demands from others that it must be included.[26] Although the text of the background briefing was released a few months later, pursuant to a request under the Freedom of Information Act, two items were deleted and retroactively given a security classification, a highly unusual procedure. Not until 1981, after lengthy litigation and a successful challenge in court, were the two excerpts released. One concerned the Backfire. When asked whether Backfires would be included, Kissinger had said, "I would

---

24. Published accounts have assumed that divergences in interpretation and ambiguity of the phrase arose later. In fact, as described above, the problem became clear before the aide-mémoire was agreed on, although the divergence was not clearly understood or argued in the summit deliberations. The Soviets raised the idea of a limit of 600 kilometers on air-to-surface missiles in October and again at Vladivostok. The U.S. side did not raise any question about the formulation, assuming the discussion was about ballistic missiles throughout the Vladivostok meeting. Only after the summit meeting when the aide-mémoire was being drafted did the two sides come to realize that there was a clear difference of substance. There was no discussion of cruise missiles at the summit meeting.

25. Information from informed participants. The best available account, although not fully informed on this issue, is Thomas W. Wolfe, *The SALT Experience* (Cambridge, Mass.: Ballinger, 1979); see pp. 177–78 and assorted references for the cruise missile issue; on SALT in 1974–75 more generally, see pp. 155–217.

26. See, for example, Michael Getler, "Exclusions in Arms Pact Stir Controversy," *Washington Post*, December 4, 1974.

not expect them to." In response to a further question he said: "A lot of this is to be negotiated. From the legislative record of these negotiations one would exclude the Backfires." Asked if he meant the record at Vladivostok, he stated: "Well, October negotiations—Vladivostok negotiations, and what has been discussed at Geneva." Kissinger thus used a technique he favors—deftly slipping in delicate matters in a manner unlikely to be noticed. In this case he slipped in, in passing, his own October negotiations with Brezhnev where the heart of the Vladivostok agreement was really hammered out. "It would exclude the Backfires," concluded Kissinger. "Backfires would be in a completely different category."[27]

The substance of Kissinger's position had been known to a number of people in Washington, undoubtedly including the Soviet embassy, as well as opponents of SALT (and of Kissinger) in the Pentagon, who pressed the Backfire issue unremittingly regardless of the negotiating history. But this illumination of the record does place Soviet intransigence in a different light: Kissinger at least had in effect accepted the Soviet position. So, incidentally, did a later official American document that made clear the real increase in Soviet theater and naval capabilities provided by the deployment of the Backfire for those missions, in contrast to only a "potential" threat of the bomber for strategic intercontinental use.[28] The document said, in short, that the Backfire was not really an intercontinental bomber. No wonder the Soviets refused to consider it to be one in SALT.

In several respects the Backfire became the albatross of SALT II, just as the issue of including missile-launching submarines and their missiles in the interim strategic offensive weapons freeze dragged down the SALT I negotiations from May 1971 to May 1972. In both cases Kissinger established a position in his negotiations at the highest level in Moscow *without* the decision having been approved by the president and without review by the Pentagon and other interested Washington agencies. Indeed, he did so without any authorization. Moreover, Kissinger retained control over the only records of his negotiations, which he continued to conduct only through Soviet interpreters and accompanied only by members of his own trusted staff. In both cases, Kissinger later initially admitted in Washington to some people what he had done, but when the extent of opposition became clear, he blithely denied he had made any commitment. He then sought to maneuver the course of nego-

---

27. The basic transcript, with deletions, was released on March 5, 1975, by the Department of State. The withheld excerpts were finally released by the Department of State, April 15, 1981, in accordance with District Court Stipulation in Civil Action No. 75-0674, brought by Morton Halperin of the American Civil Liberties Union. On December 4, 1974, only one day after revealing to the press off the record that the Backfire would be excluded, after strong objections became known Kissinger blandly assured a group of senators that the Backfire was still open to negotiation. See Bernard Gwertzman, "Kissinger, after Senate Briefing, Calls Criticism of Arms Accord Surprising," *New York Times*, December 5, 1974.

28. U.S. Department of Defense, *Soviet Military Power* (Washington, D.C.: Government Printing Office, 1981), pp. 31, 47–48, 54.

tiation in such a way that he could finally square the outcome with his premature agreement. Meanwhile, the Soviet side felt it had made a deal and that if the peculiar American political decisionmaking process required deceptive maneuvers, it should not cost the Soviet Union any further concessions. Moreover, Kissinger's action gave the Soviet side considerable bargaining power with him in the continuing negotiations in which he played such an important role.

In both cases this process led to resentment directed at the *Soviets* (as well as at Kissinger to the extent his role was suspected). The result was a serious added burden on the SALT negotiations (and on the relationships between the negotiating teams, since the Soviet delegation was fully informed and the American one was not).

These conflicts hampered later attempts to negotiate a SALT II agreement based on the Vladivostok accord. They were not the only problem. In his press conference at Vladivostok Kissinger had referred to the accord as a "breakthrough," which it was. Both he and Ford also referred to it as capping the strategic arms competition, which was an exaggeration. By contrast, the general reaction in the United States was far less enthusiastic. Objections came from both sides: many advocates of arms control and disarmament—and some hard-liners like Senator Jackson—criticized the very high levels of arms retained, while other hard-line opponents were critical that the accord did not place greater limits on Soviet systems, especially the throw-weight and MIRV potential of large Soviet ICBMs. In addition, some critics raised doubts as to American ability to verify the limit on the numbers of missiles with MIRVs. Finally, during the initial days of maximum public exposure, the absence of important details such as the actual levels agreed on stimulated misinformation, speculation, doubts, and such comments as that of the *Wall Street Journal*: "Details of the agreement are being withheld, perhaps because they would interfere with the triumph."[29] Even more sympathetic commentators, such as Tom Wicker, were reserved about accepting the White House press secretary's announcement that President Ford "will return home in triumph." Conceding a possible breakthrough in SALT, Wicker commented, "Whether it will constitute a domestic political 'triumph' is another question."[30]

Nevertheless, on balance there was general support for the Vladivostok SALT accord. Secretary of Defense Schlesinger, JCS Chairman General Brown, and Senator John Stennis of Mississippi all supported it. The administration was confident it could rally further support. Kissinger did, however, consider it necessary to warn Congress that a failure to approve a SALT agreement based on the Vladivostok accord would pose "extremely serious" consequences for U.S.-Soviet relations. He stressed that if SALT faced the same uncertainties as the U.S.-Soviet trade agreement (then still hanging in the balance because of controversy over the trade bill in Congress), "the Soviet

---

29. Editorial, "A Triumph in a Poke," *Wall Street Journal*, November 26, 1974.

30. Tom Wicker, "Mr. Ford's Triumph," *New York Times*, November 26, 1974.

Union will only be able to conclude that a political détente with us faces domestic difficulties of an insuperable nature in the United States."[31]

In January and February 1975 both houses of Congress passed resolutions in support of the Vladivostok SALT accord, as there was no formal agreement for the Senate to approve or disapprove. It soon became clear that agreement on many matters was still to be reached. Public attention soon slacked off.

After Vladivostok the SALT delegations in Geneva wrestled to produce a SALT treaty based on the Vladivostok accord.[32] The United States stressed verification of the MIRV limitations, while the Soviet side saw no need for special verification measures; the United States again argued that the limit on air-to-surface missiles applied only to ballistic missiles, while the Soviets argued that it included cruise missiles; the United States claimed the Backfire was a heavy bomber and should be counted as such (notwithstanding the negotiating history that Kissinger had said showed it would be excluded). The Soviets raised a new point by arguing to include sea-launched cruise missiles with operational ranges over 600 kilometers as well as air-launched cruise missiles. Lack of progress led to reactivation of the White House back channel in May and to a series of discussions between Kissinger and Gromyko (in Geneva, July 10–11), Ford and Kissinger with Brezhnev and Gromyko (at Helsinki, July 30 and August 2), Gromyko with Ford and Kissinger (in Washington, September 18), and Kissinger and Gromyko (in New York, September 21–22).

The negotiations throughout 1975 can be summarized briefly. The delegations discussed a wide variety of combinations of limitations by number and range on various types of cruise missiles, the problem of how to treat the Backfire bomber (and in some proposals the U.S. FB-111 as well), and the possibility of combining all these systems in a single quota beyond the 2,400 level. Also discussed were possible means of verifying or "class-counting" as MIRV all missiles of a given class or type of ICBM when any missile of the class was tested and deployed with MIRV missiles, and of defining heavy ICBMs and allowable silo modifications. Both sides made concessions from time to time. The United States offered most of the suggestions, which covered a dazzling array of ingenious combinations. There was movement toward an agreement in July and August, but it was set back in September and Octo-

---

31. "Secretary Kissinger's News Conference of December 7," *State Bulletin*, vol. 71 (December 30, 1974), p. 919.

32. The aide-mémoire of December 10 called for the delegations to meet in Geneva "in January 1975," and they met on January 31. But the United States had not yet reached agreement even on instructions to the delegation, much less on all the substantive issues. Instructions were finally issued a week later, on February 6 in National Security Decision Memorandum (NSDM)–285, which set forth, inter alia, the positions described in this paragraph.

For a useful discussion of SALT developments during 1975 as seen by the chief of the U.S. delegation, see Johnson, *The Right Hand of Power*, pp. 605–16.

ber when Kissinger had to present radically new proposals that Ford had instructed him to work out with Schlesinger. The Soviet leaders rejected them as a step back.[33] It was at this juncture (although before receiving the definitive Soviet rejection of the September proposals) that Kissinger declared in a news conference that the new SALT agreement was about 90 percent complete. He also commented correctly: "I think in fairness one has to point out that most of the significant concessions over the last 18 months in the negotiations have been made by the Soviet Union."[34]

While the agreement was, in one sense, 90 percent complete as Kissinger suggested, in another sense the first anniversary of the Vladivostok accord found the two sides further apart than ever. New issues had arisen, while the old ones had not been resolved. Meanwhile, the planned summit meeting with Brezhnev in the United States had been postponed repeatedly: from the fall of 1974 to the spring of 1975, then to June, to September, and finally to 1976—where the matter eventually died.

One other aspect of SALT deserves mention. In the period leading up to Vladivostok a rash of charges was made in the United States that the Soviets had violated the SALT I agreement. Several conservative senators sent a letter to the president. As a result Kissinger decided to raise some questions concerning compliance with the Soviets at the next meeting of the Standing Consultative Commission (SCC) that had been established in accordance with the first SALT agreements at the end of 1972.[35] Accordingly, at the fifth session of the SCC (from January 28 to February 13, 1975) and at subsequent sessions

33. The U.S. proposals were also transmitted in a letter from Ford to Brezhnev. Brezhnev strongly rejected them in a reply on October 27, 1975. There is reason to believe that Kissinger at least may have recognized in advance that the Soviets would not accept these proposals, but that until they had conclusively rejected them Schlesinger would stymie other approaches that Kissinger hoped to pursue. The proposals emerged only after a stormy NSC meeting, following which Ford instructed Kissinger and Schlesinger to get together and agree on something to present. Hence, too, the presidential letter: Schlesinger could not claim that Kissinger had failed to present the proposal properly. Such was the mutual lack of confidence. The proposal would, among other things, have created a new ceiling (apart from the 2,400 aggregate) of 300 covering FB-111s and SLCMs of 600–2,000 kilometer range for the United States, and Backfires plus SLCMs of 600–2,000 kilometer range for the USSR. (The effect would have been to give the United States some 230 SLCMs, of which it had none, at no cost to other programs, while limiting Soviet Backfires to 300 with no SLCMs, or still fewer with any SLCMs.) For Ford's comments on his growing difficulty in working with Schlesinger, and Schlesinger's objections after the Helsinki discussions with Brezhnev, see Ford, *A Time to Heal*, pp. 320–24.

34. "Secretary Kissinger Interviewed on 'Meet the Press,'" October 12, *State Bulletin*, vol. 73 (November 10, 1975), p. 658. The comment on Soviet concessions was provoked by a leading question by Robert Keatley of the *Wall Street Journal* suggesting Soviet blame for the lack of progress.

35. See Clarence A. Robinson, Jr., "U.S. Seeks Meeting on SALT Violations," *Aviation Week and Space Technology* (November 25, 1974), pp. 18–19, for a generally well-informed account of the problem. It includes what was at the time a leak that the United States had decided to raise questions about compliance at the SCC.

the United States raised a number of questions on compliance—as did the Soviet Union. Among those raised by the United States was the Soviet use of covers over nuclear missile submarines fitting out after launch; among those raised by the Soviet Union was U.S. use of large covers over ICBM silos during modification, impeding verification of compliance with the limitations on silo modification.[36] Each side subsequently dropped or changed some practices to relieve the concern of the other, and it was officially concluded that no intentional violations had occurred.

The discussions in the SCC, conducted with diplomatic privacy, permitted useful clarification and reduced many official concerns. Soviet compliance with the SALT I agreements, however, remained a political issue in the United States. The aforementioned article by former Secretary of Defense Laird in the July 1975 issue of *Reader's Digest* gave particularly wide currency to charges of Soviet violations. These attacks contributed to the difficulty Ford and Kissinger had in dealing with Schlesinger's hard line on new SALT proposals. In December Senator Jackson mounted a major challenge to the administration on the question of Soviet violation or "circumvention" of the SALT agreements (despite assurances by Ford, Schlesinger, Rumsfeld, and Kissinger that there had been none).[37] In addition, by December Schlesinger had been fired. Even so, there were still serious differences within the administration over SALT, and the whole subject was now more politically heated than ever. Then a new obstacle arose that contributed to postponing Kissinger's planned trip to Moscow to negotiate on SALT: the indirect Soviet-American confrontation in Angola.[38]

The initial euphoria of Vladivostok, particularly on the Soviet side, was also soon dispelled by the collapse of the bilateral trade arrangements negotiated at the height of détente in 1972. The reason was U.S. legislation

---

36. Ibid. Not all the charges raised by one side were similarly paired with charges by the other.

   Incidentally, in a remarkable example of the bureaucracy's undercutting policy, despite a subsequent White House order to discontinue use of the 44-foot by 56-foot aluminum environmental protection shelters over the Minuteman ICBM silos, and despite further Soviet complaints, the covers were not removed until the matter was pursued more vigorously four years later by the next administration.

37. See, for example, articles by Senator Henry Jackson and Secretary Henry Kissinger, "The SALT Debate," *Washington Post*, December 28, 1975. At the time there were many articles dealing with the question, and on December 9 Kissinger had to devote most of a press conference to the issue. See "Secretary Kissinger's News Conference of December 9," *State Bulletin*, vol. 74 (January 5, 1975), pp. 1–10. To catch the full flavor of the attack, see Robert L. Bartley, "Kissinger and the SALT Talks," *Wall Street Journal*, December 19, 1975.

38. See Ford, *A Time to Heal*, p. 345. The Angola crisis is dealt with in chapter 15. Although Ford recalls the Angola situation as requiring postponement of Kissinger's trip, and it probably did contribute, a number of those intimately involved have stated that the main reason for deferring the trip was the disarray over SALT on the American side and inability to reach an agreed position to present to the Soviets.

that seriously undercut the deal the Nixon administration had negotiated and the Ford administration had attempted to carry out.

Trade and Politics: Linkage Run Rampant

President Ford inherited a doomed enterprise in the U.S.-Soviet Trade Agreement, signed in October 1972, but still lacking the essential implementing legislation by the U.S. Congress. This issue had developed from the early days of détente in 1972, and since then the gap between administration policy and congressional views had widened.[39] Clearly the weakened clout of the Nixon administration in 1973 and 1974 as the Watergate drama unfolded contributed to this gap, as did the administration's secretive conduct of policy. But the political machinations of Senator Jackson and others, combined with the conjunction of perceived interests of liberal pro-Jewish and pro–human rights groups on the one hand and conservative anti-Soviet, anti-détente constituencies on the other, also played a critical role. Domestic politics, as well as weakened confidence between the executive and Congress, came to dominate this major aspect of the foreign policy of American-Soviet détente.

The impingement of domestic political considerations on foreign relations was largely unintended by many of those involved. Senator Jackson favored increased political liberalization and Jewish emigration from the Soviet Union on their merits. But he also saw personal political advantage in championing these issues in as confrontational a manner as possible with respect both to the Soviet Union and to Kissinger and the détente policy of the Nixon and Ford administrations.

President Ford, himself so lately from Congress, sought at the outset of his administration to repair relations with the legislature. This was a major theme of his speech before Congress on August 12, 1974, only three days after assuming the presidency. On August 14 Ford met with Ambassador Dobrynin for the first time, and the parlous state of the trade legislation was the main topic of importance. On August 15 Ford invited Senators Jackson, Abraham A. Ribicoff of Connecticut, and Jacob K. Javits of New York to a breakfast meeting and promised to work with Moscow to gain their objectives, while trying to bring these key senators into a cooperative relationship. Jackson, as always, was the most difficult. On September 20 Ford met with him just before meeting for the first time with Foreign Minister Gromyko.[40]

---

39. See chapters 3, 9, 10.

40. Paula Stern, *Water's Edge: Domestic Politics and the Making of American Foreign Policy* (Westport, Conn.: Greenwood Press, 1979), pp. 145–50. The account of developments in this section draws heavily on Stern's excellent study. See also Joseph Albright, "The Pact of the Two Henrys," *New York Times Magazine*, January 5, 1975; and William Korey, "The Story of the Jackson Amendment, 1973–1975," *Midstream*, vol. 21 (March 1975), pp. 7–36.

The complicated triangular negotiations among the administration, Jackson and other senators, and the Soviets were directed toward meeting the substantive aims of the Jackson-Vanik amendment to the trade bill through Soviet assurances that would be acceptable to Congress in lieu of the amendment (or to justify its waiver). A target for Jewish emigration of 45,000 a year had emerged earlier (particularly after Kissinger's discussions with Gromyko in Cyprus in May, at which time this figure had been discussed). By September, however, Jackson had begun to agitate for 60,000: he had wanted to raise the demand to 75,000, but Javits and Ribicoff had balked. Instead they had agreed to try for 60,000 but to be prepared to fall back to 45,000. (The actual rate in 1973 was at an all-time peak of 35,000.) Negotiations involving Kissinger, Jackson, and Dobrynin had been proceeding, and it appeared that Dobrynin was prepared to accept a figure of 55,000 or 60,000.

At least as important an issue was the unresolved question of how Soviet assurances to the administration, and administration assurances to Congress, would be conveyed. A complicated exchange of three letters between Ford or Kissinger to Jackson, a return letter from him, and a third confirming Jackson's understanding were envisaged. But the administration wanted the text of its assurances to remain confidential, while Jackson wanted everything made public. The Soviets objected strongly to making anything that laid out their private "elucidations" in public, since as a matter of principle they would not officially make commitments. Kissinger discussed these issues with the three senators on September 19, and, as mentioned above, Jackson talked with President Ford on September 20. (In fact, Jackson and Gromyko passed in the hall in the White House, with further confusion developing when Jackson tried to joke that he was the devil in these talks, with gestures to indicate horns, a message the interpreter was unable to convey.)

A new element was added in September to the already complicated negotiations. The Senate passed the Stevenson amendment on September 19. It had originally been presented jointly by Jackson and Senator Adlai E. Stevenson III of Illinois in June for a different piece of legislation: the Export-Import Bank bill. It called, without reference to emigration, for a ceiling of $300 million over four years on new Export-Import (ExIm) Bank credit commitments to the Soviet Union and required that the president determine, for each transaction with communist nations over $40 million (later changed to $50 million), that it was in the national interest. Moreover, transactions with communist states would be limited to two years.

It was unclear whether the resolution of the elaborate negotiations over the Jackson-Vanik amendment to the trade bill would also apply to the Stevenson amendment to the ExIm bill. Ford assured Gromyko that the latter amendment would also be removed, although Stevenson was not party to the negotiations. In any event, Gromyko apparently accepted the general settlement of the issues, including a confidential exchange of letters, and President

Ford told him that he thought that on this basis the Congress would drop both the Jackson-Vanik and Stevenson amendments.[41]

Also on September 19, in the midst of these behind-the-scenes maneuverings, Secretary of State Kissinger delivered his major address on détente to the Senate Committee on Foreign Relations. In it he strongly defended the pursuit of normalized relations and increased trade with the Soviet Union and argued for the 1972 trade agreement and grant of most-favored-nation (MFN) status and credits. He decried attempts to introduce "issues regarding Soviet domestic political practices" as an "ex post facto form of linkage" that "casts doubt on our reliability as a negotiating partner" and transforms hoped-for results of policy into "preconditions for any policy at all." While recognizing "the depth and validity of the moral concerns expressed by those who oppose, or [would] put conditions on, expanded trade with the USSR," he argued that "a sense of proportion must be maintained about the leverage our economic relations give us with the USSR." Finally, he noted what had been achieved without direct linkage, including the great increase in Jewish emigration and the decision not to collect the exit tax.[42] But Kissinger understood that while he could present a good case, he would not be able to persuade most senators. Rather, he needed to deal privately with the key opinion leaders in the Senate on this issue, as he and the president had been doing.

During late September and early October the administration realized it had gone too far in the planned assurances—the third letter would commit the United States, and indirectly the Soviet Union, to whatever was in Jackson's letter, which clearly would exceed the administration's first letter, which in turn would exceed the actual assurance the Soviets were prepared to give. After a series of complicated maneuvers agreement was reached on a revised two-letter procedure (which Jackson accepted only under pressure from the Jewish lobby, which by this time correctly feared the senator was pressing too hard and that the whole arrangement would collapse).

On October 18 Jackson, Javits, and Vanik met with Ford and Kissinger in the White House to sign with fanfare the two letters that would resolve the trade-emigration issue. Jackson fully controlled the later meeting with the press, playing it to the hilt (Kissinger held no press conference on or off the record). Jackson referred to the agreement as a "historic understanding in the area of human rights" and implied that the Soviets had capitulated to

---

41. Stern, *Water's Edge*, pp. 148–56. The incident in the White House hallway is related on p. 155. President Ford reports that in his August 14 meeting Dobrynin told him that the Soviets would give an oral guarantee for emigration of 55,000 a year but not a written one that could be used by Senator Jackson. Ford, *A Time to Heal*, pp. 138–39. Ford found Senators Ribicoff and Javits prepared to accept an oral assurance, but Jackson was adamant against it. Ibid., p. 139. Ford mentions his discussion with Gromyko only briefly. Ibid., p. 183.

42. "Detente with the Soviet Union: The Reality of Competition and the Imperative of Cooperation," September 19, *State Bulletin*, vol. 71 (October 14, 1974), pp. 510–12, 518.

the campaign he had been waging. He even drew special attention to the shaky 60,000 figure as a "benchmark" for Soviet behavior and predicted that it would only be a baseline. Kissinger had sought to preserve flexibility by stating in the second letter that "the understandings in your [Jackson's] letter will be *among* the considerations to be applied by the President in exercising the authority" granted—leaving a large loophole for the administration (and the Soviet leaders). In answer to a question about the Stevenson-Jackson ceiling of $300 million credit in the Export-Import bill, Jackson said there was "no understanding."[43]

Jackson clearly was more concerned about his presidential ambition in the 1976 election than with the diplomatic consequences of publicity embarrassing to the Soviet leadership. He had earlier said he understood the necessity *not* to embarrass the Soviet Union and to let the Soviet leaders save face. But before the television cameras on the White House lawn he cast caution to the winds. Jackson's performance would end the whole deal.

October 18 marked the second anniversary of the conclusion of the original U.S.-Soviet Trade Agreement and associated accords. The Soviets had been paying installments on the Lend-Lease settlement, although they had been explicitly tied to a grant of MFN. Dobrynin and Gromyko had made clear at least some of the limits on what the Soviet leaders could accept in a public trumpeting of informal assurances. But others in Moscow had been skeptical of the whole attempt to build trade relationships with the United States, while still others were ideologically as well as politically opposed to negotiating on this subject. Now the Soviet leadership as a whole concluded it could not cave in to the ever-growing demands not only of the U.S. government, but of uncontrolled opponents who openly opposed détente and improved relations with the Soviet Union. The Soviets had contributed to resolving the issue by building up Jewish emigration from a trickle in 1970 to 35,000 in 1973. It was another matter entirely for Senator Jackson to say publicly, at the White House, that the Soviet leaders had made "a complete turn around" to accommodate his demands and to pronounce his own success at what "so many said . . . could never be accomplished."[44] Moreover, the administration could still use the law for leverage in the future, as the MFN grant was only under a waiver of the law for an eighteen-month trial period. Finally, there was the threat of a severe credit limitation: $300 million over the next four years would be much *less* than the $469 million extended by the ExIm Bank in the preceding fifteen months.

There were other irritants. On October 5 the U.S. government had blocked all grain trade with the Soviet Union, canceling about $500 million in contracts already signed with American grain dealers. This action had been taken as a stopgap measure to prevent another disruption of the U.S. grain

43. Stern, *Water's Edge*, pp. 156–65.

44. Ibid., pp. 163–64.

market as had occurred in 1972. Immediate negotiations led to authorization of sales of $400 million on October 19, after the Soviet Union gave assurances it would buy no more grain through the summer of 1975.

On October 15, even preceding Jackson's claim of victory at the White House, Brezhnev had found it necessary in advance of the forthcoming exchange of letters to reaffirm to domestic and foreign audiences alike that the Soviet Union would not simply roll over to meet American demands. He complained of attempts to tie "utterly irrelevant and unacceptable conditions" to trade with the Soviet Union and said that "it is high time that there should be a clear understanding" that an end be put to levying "demands on questions totally unconnected with the area of trade and economics" between the two countries.[45] After October 18 other Soviet spokesmen lashed out, although indirectly, at such "remnants of the cold war." Presumably there were official representations through Ambassador Dobrynin as well, although this has not been made known.

The administration attempted to retrieve the deal. President Ford instructed the White House press secretary on October 21 to issue a clarification which pointed out that the Kissinger letter contained no specific number on emigration and that "all of the assurances we have received from the Soviet Union" were in the Kissinger letter. He also drew attention to the loophole that in later review these assurances would be *among* the considerations taken into account. Responding the same day, Jackson escalated his claims. He dug in on the 60,000 and claimed that the Soviets were now "committed" by the assurances in Kissinger's letter to a "transition from their present restrictive policy" to a "future liberalized policy."[46]

It was in this context that Kissinger departed for Moscow to discuss SALT and to scout out the possibilities for a summit meeting. In these discussions, which were reviewed earlier in terms of SALT, the trade issue—or, more precisely, the problem of the U.S. administration's trade bill in the Senate—was also raised. Brezhnev was, in Kissinger's words, "livid," and he repeatedly "raged" at Senator Jackson's crowing over Soviet capitulation and stretching the general "assurances" reported by Kissinger into a "guarantee" of 60,000 or more Jewish emigrants annually.[47] Kissinger lamely (and disingenuously) told Brezhnev that he, too, had not expected the texts of the letters to be released. To make matters worse, Kissinger had discussed with Dobrynin the text of his own letter, but not the text of Jackson's letter, which went much further and introduced the specific numerical quota. While Kissinger was still in Moscow, Gromyko gave him a letter objecting to the "distorted picture of our position" conveyed in the letters and the "attempts" being made to ascribe to the Soviet

---

45. Ibid., p. 165.

46. Ibid., p. 166.

47. See "Last Tangle in Moscow," *Newsweek* (December 30, 1974), p. 27, and other newspaper accounts at the time. For their part the Soviets had never used the term "assurances," speaking instead of "elucidations" and "clarifications" of their *existing* policy and practice.

Union "some assurances and almost obligations" on emigration, even citing figures involving an increase. Gromyko was quite clear: "We resolutely reject such an interpretation" and "We believe it important that in this entire matter, considering its principled significance, no ambiguities should remain as regards the position of the Soviet Union."[48]

Kissinger now attempted a very deep finesse. He did not tell anyone except his own immediate staff about the letter from Gromyko. Clearly he hoped that the Soviet rejection of Jackson's interpretation could be "for the record" in Moscow but conveniently and silently buried in Washington. Undoubtedly he also hoped that the forthcoming Vladivostok summit meeting and promise of a SALT agreement would lead the Soviets to contain their anger and accept a *fait accompli* if the Senate did not agitate further on the matter. For that reason, too, he did not meet with the Senate, as requested, in mid-November to testify on the trade bill, preferring to wait until after Vladivostok, when Congress would be in a hurry to conclude its business before the Christmas recess.

When Kissinger finally testified on December 3, he was as always a master of ambiguity. He covered his position on the substance of the emigration assurances—he denied any Soviet commitment on numbers and stated that "if I were to assert here that a formal agreement on emigration from the USSR exists between our governments, that statement would immediately be repudiated by the Soviet government." While on its face that statement would, under most circumstances, have caused great concern, in the context of the October exchange of letters the Senate took it as a diplomatic way of saying that the agreement was not "formal," was not "between governments," and would be repudiated publicly if so asserted, but that nonetheless it *in fact* existed as an informal agreement. And Kissinger did convey a misleading impression when he reaffirmed, under questioning, that the "assurances," undefined, had been given by Brezhnev and Gromyko, as well as by Dobrynin.[49]

Accordingly, it was generally assumed in Washington that the Soviet MFN and linked emigration issue had been settled. Senator Jackson and the major Jewish lobbies now supported the trade bill, with the Jackson-Vanik amendment and an associated eighteen-month waiver, based on the assurances in the exchange of letters. The AFL-CIO continued to oppose the bill on other grounds (its principal provisions gave the president authority to reduce constraints in multilateral trade negotiations), but the split in the usual alliance of these two groups assured passage. The Jackson–administration–Jewish lobby forces together succeeded in cloture, choking off any debate on the floor.

Yet another issue arose on the day of the vote. Senator Harry F. Byrd, Jr., of Virginia, at Senator Jackson's behest, introduced yet another

---

48. Text released by the embassy of the USSR in Washington, D.C., December 18, 1974. I have used the word "reject" rather than "decline" as rendered in that text as a better translation of the word *otkazatsya* in the context used.

49. Stern, *Water's Edge*, pp. 173–74.

amendment that placed an overall ceiling of $300 million on all loans provided by agencies of the U.S. government. This meant that not only the ExIm Bank, but the Commodity Credit Corporation (CCC), which provided short-term credits for grain purchases, would be severely constrained from providing credit to the Soviet Union. The Byrd amendment was thus far more restrictive than the Stevenson amendment to the ExIm bill.

The Senate passed the trade bill, with the Jackson-Vanik amendment and its eighteen-month waiver provision, and with the Byrd amendment, ominously on Friday the 13th of December, by a lopsided vote of 77 to 4.

On December 18 three important developments occurred. The House-Senate conference committee began its deliberations on the trade bill. The conference committee on the Export-Import Bank bill met and agreed on that legislation, which included the $300 million credit limit on ExIm loans to the Soviet Union over a four-year period. And Moscow (and the Soviet embassy in Washington) released the still secret text of the October 26 letter from Gromyko to Kissinger, a rare Soviet display of diplomatic correspondence.[50]

Moscow had not been prepared to take the chances Kissinger was. It did not want to defer explanation that its assurances were *not* what the Senate had assumed. Nor was it prepared, alternatively, to assume much more far-reaching commitments than it had ever indicated it would accept, alleged commitments made by stretching Kissinger's ambiguities and adding Jackson's unilateral interpretations to them. The release of the October 26 letter was accompanied by a TASS commentary stating that the Soviet Union would "flatly reject as unacceptable any attempts . . . to interfere in internal affairs that are entirely the concern of the Soviet state and no one else." The Soviet actions were intended above all to avoid committing the Soviet Union by silence, but were also a last-ditch effort to influence the deliberations of the conference committee, since the administration was failing to clarify the situation or to prevent the new overall credit limit of $300 million.

The administration sought to deflate the significance of the letter Kissinger had concealed, pointing out that it had never said the Soviets had given assurances of 60,000 emigrants a year. Senator Jackson equivocated, attempting publicly to argue that the Soviet protests were intended only for Soviet domestic consumption and reaffirming his interpretation of the Soviet "commitments," while seeking to limit the damage by a tactic of pushing the legislation through (under fire from his usual ally, George Meany of the AFL-CIO). On December 19 the conference committee, and on December 20 both Houses, approved the trade bill.[51] (The Export-Import Act was signed the following day, but the even more restrictive loan ceiling was already enacted under the Trade Reform Act because of the Byrd amendment.)

---

50. Ibid., pp. 179, 184–87.

51. Ibid., pp. 179–87.

The administration now had no recourse but to try itself to limit the damage. On January 3, given the need for the bill's overall world trade and tariff provisions, President Ford signed the Trade Reform Act into law. He said, in signing it, "I must express my reservations about the wisdom of legislative language that can only be seen as objectionable and discriminating by other sovereign states."[52] He did not comment on the tortured charade of letters exchanged between Kissinger and Jackson purporting to express Soviet commitments, or on Kissinger's suppression of Gromyko's letter of October 26. Kissinger himself apparently still harbored some hope that the Soviet leaders would swallow hard and accept the act. Finally, technically the administration still had the option of interpreting assurances from the Soviet Union and exercising the eighteen-month waiver of the Jackson-Vanik amendment. But the legislative history made this politically infeasible unless the administration could produce assurances that supported the October 18 exchange. Moscow could not agree to that.

On December 18 Dobrynin had signaled that the Soviet Union would not accept the conditions for MFN in the legislation and that if they became law, the 1972 U.S.-USSR Trade Agreement would be voided. After diplomatic exchanges on the matter the Soviet government officially made its position known in a communication on January 10, 1975, and on January 14, Kissinger issued a statement to which the Soviets had agreed that the 1972 Trade Agreement could not be brought into effect "at this time."[53]

The heart of the official American-Soviet trade component of détente had collapsed. In practice, however, trade continued and in some aspects even flourished: the separate agreements on grain sales, the maritime agreement, and the joint trade council still moved forward. But the agreement settling the Lend-Lease debt was voided. MFN not only was not granted, but now bore the new albatross of restrictions on Soviet emigration. And credit was cut back sharply from what had been available and extended in the previous two years. The situation had refired the suspicions and hostilities of opponents of détente in the United States, with many senators feeling they had been taken for a ride by the Soviets or Kissinger or both. Linkage, or at least the excesses in its exercise, should have been called into question, but the usual reaction of those who had been burned was to blame other parties. The Soviet government, with considerable justification, considered itself the victim of double-dealing or incompetence by the American administration. The Soviet leaders learned something about American politics, and learned even more about the limits of American diplomacy.

---

52. Cited in ibid., p. 188, and see p. 189. Later Kissinger privately told a group of Jewish leaders, "No country could allow its domestic regulations to be dictated as we were pushing the Soviets to do." Cited by [Senator] Charles McC. Mathias, Jr., "Ethnic Groups and Foreign Policy," *Foreign Affairs*, vol. 59 (Summer 1981), p. 996, quoting a memorandum of the meeting on June 15, 1975.

53. Stern, *Water's Edge*, pp. 188–90.

The Soviet Union paid the third installment, due July 1, 1975, of the agreed $48 million down payment under the Lend-Lease settlement (having paid the other installments on October 18, 1972, and July 1, 1973). They have not paid the remainder of the $722 million settlement, due to be paid in annual installments *after* grant of MFN. The July 1975 payment did fulfill their obligations under the 1972 settlement and left open resuscitation of the debt settlement and resumption of payments later if MFN is extended.[54]

Some commentators have suggested that it was the Stevenson amendment to the Export-Import Act placing a ceiling on ExIm credits that really led to the Soviet rejection.[55] Certainly the congressionally controlled ceilings on credits (not only in the four-year Export-Import Act, but even more in the more stringent Byrd amendment to the Trade Reform Act itself) were a heavy blow to Soviet expectations. So, too, was the inexplicably weak effort by the administration to oppose them. It seems Kissinger failed to recognize their significance at the time. But the handling of the trade bill–emigration linkage and the denial of MFN, which was of considerable political as well as some economic significance, was almost certainly enough to have produced the Soviet reaction. The credit curbs, while they were economically even more important, only assured the negative Soviet response.

All parties involved in the failure to impose a linkage between trade normalization and emigration of Soviet Jews lost except one—Senator Jackson. The administration suffered a major defeat not only because of its inept handling of the issue, but because of its failure to achieve both what it had committed the United States to in the Trade Agreement with the Soviet Union and the leverage it had anticipated this carrot would have on influencing Soviet foreign policy. Kissinger no longer seemed the superdiplomat; indeed, his handling of the Gromyko letter in particular raised serious doubts in many quarters about his reliability as a negotiating partner. Ford himself suffered an embarrassing setback. The Soviet Jews (and the American Jewish lobby)—and the many in Congress really moved by human rights—saw Jewish emigration from the Soviet Union drop from 35,000 in 1973 to 21,000 in 1974 and 13,000 in 1975.

The Soviet Union failed to get the expected—and promised—liberalization of trade terms. To the contrary, new obstacles such as the cutback in credits were raised to the normalization of trade and general political relations

---

54. In his memoir President Ford, after reporting the outcome of the Trade Reform Act and noting the Soviet cancellation of the 1972 Trade Agreement, stated that the Soviets also "reneged" on their Lend-Lease settlement. This is entirely incorrect. Ford, *A Time to Heal*, p. 225.

55. See Harry Gelman, *The Brezhnev Politburo and the Decline of Detente* (Ithaca, N.Y.: Cornell University Press, 1984), pp. 148–51 and associated notes. Gelman, however, ignores completely the Byrd amendment and the Jackson public press conference. For other examples, see Daniel Yergin, "Politics and Soviet-American Trade: The Three Questions," *Foreign Affairs*, vol. 55 (April 1977), pp. 531–32; and Marshall I. Goldman, *Detente and Dollars: Doing Business with the Soviets* (Basic Books, 1975), pp. 68–69.

that would have been achieved by the removal of the discriminatory denial of MFN status. Moreover, the attempt through quiet diplomacy to meet American domestic political needs (which is the way the Soviets saw their concessions on emigration) had been publicly trumpeted in the worst possible way, exposing and enlarging on what the Soviets had been prepared to accept, and claiming the result to be Soviet capitulation. That situation was (as will be discussed presently) politically embarrassing and damaging to Brezhnev personally.

Senator Jackson, too, suffered some losses. He probably believed, right to the end, that the Soviet leaders would buckle under and acquiesce in his harder terms and that he would get credit for outnegotiating Kissinger, Nixon, and Ford. The failure to impose those terms denied him that. By supporting the Trade Reform bill once his amendment and terms had been accepted, Jackson took on a politically bruising fight with his old ally George Meany of the AFL-CIO. And the defection of Jackson and others meant a defeat for labor, too, which had opposed the bill because it encouraged export of American technology and—in their judgment—jobs. The AFL-CIO had therefore supported the Jackson amendment only so long as it weakened support for the trade bill—not once it was accepted. Jackson also had been counting on the expiration of the waiver to his amendment in eighteen months— that is, at the peak of his planned bid for the presidency in 1976.

Nevertheless, Jackson alone also gained from the outcome. First, he demonstrated his ability to outmaneuver a wide range of opponents, including Kissinger. And he had plenty of ammunition to fire at both Kissinger and the Ford administration, and at the Soviet Union, for the failure. He had shown his stalwart support for the Jewish lobby and his championing of human rights. Above all, he had dealt a heavy blow to American-Soviet détente, a central goal in his whole political program and one that he may well have valued even more than those he did not obtain.[56]

The Soviets made their displeasure actively known. Dobrynin had been recalled to Moscow for consultations on December 16, a diplomatic sign of coolness. On January 30 the Soviets demonstratively canceled some planned American wheat purchases (although by July they were again buying). On February 17 they announced a $2 billion five-year agreement with Great Britain to purchase technology using British credits. Within a few months the Soviet Union had received $10 billion in Western credits. As a result of the continuing upsurge in Soviet-Western trade with others, the United States dropped among Western trade partners of the Soviet Union.

On April 10 President Ford came out in his State of the World address not only with a ringing endorsement of détente, but with a specific plea to Congress to reverse its trade restrictions. But Congress never did so. On the

---

56. Once again, see Stern, *Water's Edge*, not only for a thoroughly researched, detailed, and balanced account, but also for a well-informed and shrewd analysis of the interests and motivations of Senator Jackson and others involved in this episode.

very next day Brezhnev told visiting Secretary of the Treasury William E. Simon that the Soviet Union remained foursquare for détente and for developing trade relations, but not on a basis that permitted American intervention in internal Soviet affairs.

The most important development in American-Soviet trade in the year following the end of the trade agreement was the conclusion on October 20, 1975, of a new long-term grain agreement providing more predictable regulation of this important commerce. It stipulated a minimum Soviet purchase of 6 million tons of American wheat and corn annually for the next five years, with additional purchases under agreed conditions or by bilateral agreement. It also included an American commitment not to exercise discretionary authority to impose an embargo on the 6-million-ton floor purchase.[57] This agreement effectively ended domestic opposition in the United States to the grain trade, which had been based on fear of inflationary effects such as those that occurred after the so-called "great grain robbery" of 1972. (These objections had found expression in a boycott of grain shipments to the Soviet Union by longshoremen in the Gulf ports and in a "voluntary" U.S. moratorium on grain sales from August to October 1975.)

Gradually the direct consequences of the great trade-emigration fiasco of 1974 were absorbed, and the development of trade—and of détente—continued. But it was not without lasting scars in both countries.

Soviet Politics and Doubts about Détente

The Soviet leadership had difficulty comprehending the fall of Richard Nixon and remained suspicious that it was largely the result of machinations by opponents of détente. They were, however, reassured by Ford's retention of Kissinger and the reaffirmation of détente by both men.

By the time of Kissinger's visit to Moscow in October 1974, the Soviet leaders were reassured that the new administration would continue the policy of détente. But they were troubled by the lack of progress on SALT, the clouded prospects for the trade legislation, and the continuing American efforts to freeze the Soviet Union out of a Middle East settlement and in general to circumscribe the Soviet role in the world.

Kissinger was hardly surprised at Soviet complaints over American efforts to shoulder it out of Middle East diplomacy—the United States was doing so successfully. When Gromyko visited the White House in September, he had reiterated this complaint and urged resumption of the Geneva confer-

---

57. The United States also attempted, unsuccessfully, to tie in a Soviet commitment to sell petroleum to the United States, in order to strengthen American bargaining leverage with OPEC producers. (This information came from participants in the negotiation.)

ence. But as Ford himself recounts frankly in his memoir, he wanted the Soviets to "keep out" of the Middle East, and he and Kissinger simply said they would keep the Soviets "informed," even though that response made Gromyko "very upset."[58] Kissinger in October, and Ford at Vladivostok in December 1974 and again in Helsinki in July 1975, reaffirmed that the Geneva conference (and Soviet participation as cochairman) would have its role, but said that it was not yet time. Kissinger's shuttle diplomacy was, meanwhile, in full gear. While the Rabat Conference of Arab States on October 28, 1974, gave the PLO full responsibility to represent the Palestinians, and Yasir Arafat thus could address the UN General Assembly on November 13, only the United States was able to defuse a new Israeli-Syrian crisis in mid-November.

The Soviets, despite setbacks, by no means gave up the game. On October 15 Brezhnev announced he would visit Cairo in January. But on December 30 the Egyptians postponed Brezhnev's visit indefinitely.

While Soviet concern over the trade legislation—well-advised, as it turned out—was strong, there was little Kissinger and Ford could do in October and November but reassure them. (Ford says that all he could say to the Soviet leaders about dealing with Congress was that "my fingers are crossed.")[59] The reassurances proved overoptimistic.

SALT was another matter: the Soviet leaders made major concessions to reach agreement, as noted. What needs to be stressed here is that the Soviet military leaders regarded as unjustified militarily the Soviet concession in agreeing to equal levels of strategic forces without allowance for U.S. FBS. While they accepted the decision to do so for broader political objectives, they were not happy with the decision. This attitude was heightened by what they saw as a series of American attempts in the months and years following to gain still greater unbalanced concessions, and to take advantage of the loophole to build up forward-based intermediate-range forces. Soviet writers have subsequently said that equal numerical levels were accepted, even though from their view this yielded *less* than equal security to the Soviet Union owing to geopolitical conditions. They did so to meet the 1972 congressional amendment in SALT I ratification requiring equal levels of intercontinental forces in follow-on agreements. In other words, the decision was justified in Moscow as a political concession to the United States necessary to reach agreement.[60] Soviet

---

58. Ford, *A Time to Heal*, p. 183. Ford states: "Even before I became President, Kissinger had achieved significant success in easing the Soviets out of the Middle East. I thought . . . their only aim was to promote instability, so I wanted to keep them out. Gromyko, of course, complained about this. . . . But Kissinger and I decided that we could accomplish more unilaterally. . . . 'We will keep you informed,' we'd say. That made him very upset."

59. Ibid., p. 217.

60. See G. A. Trofimenko, "Lessons of Peaceful Coexistence," *Voprosy istorii* [Questions of History], no. 11 (November 1983), p. 23.

commentators have alluded to the "major political decision" involved.[61] Soviet generals have also referred to this major concession,[62] and there have been many other indications of particular reluctance by the Soviet military to make this move. Indeed, as noted, at one point in the Vladivostok SALT deliberations the delegations were reduced to the top political leaders in a move designed to exclude the senior Soviet military advisers.[63] There have been indications of political reservations as well. For example, when the Carter administration later made an unsuccessful attempt in March 1977 to bypass the Vladivostok SALT framework, Gromyko's senior deputy, Georgy Kornienko, privately told ACDA Director Paul Warnke, "You shouldn't have disregarded the fact that Brezhnev had to spill political blood to get the Vladivostok accords."[64] Brezhnev, however, needed the Vladivostok accord on SALT as a balance against the falling Soviet expectations on trade. He could counter domestic political criticisms on the latter issue if he could point to substantial progress on security through arms control.

The standard joint statement by the Politburo of the Communist Party, the Presidium of the Supreme Soviet, and the Council of Ministers following the Vladivostok summit meeting gave full approval to Brezhnev's decisions and to "the important political results" of the conference. It also stressed the reaffirmation by the two states "to implement strictly and fully the mutual commitments established in the documents signed in 1972–74" as "the main prerequisite for further progress along the path of development of Soviet-American relations."[65] Clearly some doubted whether the United States had been implementing those commitments strictly and fully.

The December 1974 Central Committee plenum dealt primarily with economic matters. The collapse of the major plank in the economic platform of détente created a dilemma for Brezhnev and his colleagues. While it was always possible to blame the United States for what had happened, especially in this case, Brezhnev not only had banked heavily on Soviet-American

61. See A. Arbatov, *Bezopasnost' v yadernyi vek i politika Vashingtona* [Security in the Nuclear Age and the Policy of Washington] (Moscow: Politizdat, 1980), p. 222, citing also Gromyko, *Pravda*, April 1, 1977. I have been struck by the strong emphasis on this particular issue, and on the Soviet concession, in conversations with a number of Soviet political and military officials.

62. For example, see the account of statements by General of the Army Sergei F. Akhromeyev, then first deputy chief of the General Staff, in Senate Delegation Report, *SALT Discussions in the Soviet Union, August 25–30, 1979*, Report to the Senate Committee on Foreign Relations, 96 Cong. 1 sess. (GPO, 1979), pp. 7, 9.

63. Kissinger revealed this ploy in the background briefing on December 3, 1974, cited in note 27. See discussion in chapter 12.

64. Cited by Strobe Talbott, *Endgame: The Inside Story of SALT II* (Harper and Row, 1979), p. 73. Paul Warnke has confirmed it to me.

65. "On the Results of the Meeting between L. I. Brezhnev, General Secretary of the CC of the CPSU, and U.S. President G. Ford," *Pravda*, November 29, 1974.

détente in the past, but continued to do so. This placed limits on the extent to which it was in his interests to stress American unreliability and inconstancy, to say nothing of hostility. If the United States would not honor a fairly balanced trade agreement the president had signed, what guarantee could there be for a new SALT agreement or any other agreement? In addition, Brezhnev had gone rather far in making concessions on a sensitive matter that all Soviet leaders regarded as domestic policy. When, shortly before the plenum, President Podgorny publicly protested that "questions of sovereignty and of our internal affairs have never been and will never be a matter for political bargaining,"[66] he seemed to be saying these internal issues never *should* have been made a matter for bargaining—which, although unacknowledged publicly, they had.

Brezhnev's publication of the October 26 letter on December 18, immediately following the meeting of the Central Committee and while the Supreme Soviet was in session, was undoubtedly prompted by internal political imperatives as well as foreign diplomatic ones.[67] Some analysts have interpreted the December 1974 plenum as a defeat for Brezhnev's policy of détente.[68] That claim goes too far, but it is clear he was on the defensive at the time. He also was apparently ill. In any case he was absent from public view for some weeks, suffering from either medical or political ill health.

At the next semiannual Central Committee meeting in April 1975, Aleksandr N. Shelepin, a reputed hard-liner on détente, was ousted from the Politburo. He may have presumed too much about Brezhnev's vulnerability over the difficulties with Soviet-American détente. Interestingly, Gromyko gave the report on foreign policy developments at the plenum instead of Brezhnev. That report was also the first on foreign policy to a plenum since April 1973 and proved to be the last until June 1980.

Although politically Brezhnev weathered the collapse of the 1972 agreement on trade normalization, the failure of the Nixon and Ford administrations to deliver what they had promised was a serious blow to détente. Not only was the economic plank of the overall détente arrangement of greater importance to the Soviet side, but this failure placed in question the ability (and to some the seriousness) of its American partner to carry through. As one leading Soviet analyst later put it, "The nonfulfillment by the American side of its part of the comprehensive understanding [on trade conditions] reached at the 1972 Soviet-American summit meeting was the first unexpected development for the Soviet side, the first U.S. blow to détente."[69]

---

66. "Speech of Comrade N. V. Podgorny," *Izvestiya* and *Sovet Tozhikistoni*, November 30, 1974.

67. While perhaps overstating the case, Victor Zorza, "Brezhnev and the Emigration Issue," *Washington Post*, December 27, 1974, describes well the general climate of the Central Committee meeting and Brezhnev's defensive position.

68. Peter M. E. Volten, *Brezhnev's Peace Program: A Study of Soviet Domestic Political Process and Power* (Boulder, Colo.: Westview, 1983), pp. 129–32, makes this case, but without marshaling sufficient evidence to be convincing.

69. Trofimenko, *Voprosy istorii*, no. 11 (1983), p. 22.

The increasing militance of some Americans (including the successive secretaries of defense, Schlesinger and Rumsfeld, as well as opposition voices) caused uneasiness in Moscow. It also prompted some differences in assessment, to judge by public signs. Most notably, Minister of Defense Marshal Grechko, on May 29, 1975, while endorsing détente, warned about "forces of reaction and aggression" in the United States that oppose détente and that "have not abandoned their plans to resolve the conflict between capitalism and socialism by force of arms."[70] Only two weeks later Brezhnev, on the other hand, declared that the correlation of forces in the world arena was now such that "the leaders of the bourgeois world cannot seriously plan to resolve the historic conflict between capitalism and socialism by force of arms."[71] While one man spoke of bourgeois "leaders," and the other of unspecified "forces of reaction and aggression," the difference in emphasis between the two Soviet leaders was striking. Marshal Grechko had never been enthusiastic about the military component of détente and especially distrusted Western motives. As opponents of détente in the United States began to speak out, so did those in the Soviet Union who had reservations.

Meanwhile, apart from the problem of Jewish emigration and the attempts to reconcile American demands and Soviet objections to U.S. interference in Soviet decisions, other internal affairs were affected by détente and in turn had some impact outside the country. For example, in September the Soviet security police broke up a nonconformist art exhibit in an especially heavy-handed way, but then reversed itself and let the exhibit reopen. In December, just after the plenum, domestic travel restrictions within the USSR were relaxed. But the Soviets could not control all the ramifications of détente. In October 1975, for example, Andrei D. Sakharov was awarded the Nobel Peace Prize for his efforts, an honor not appreciated by the Soviet authorities.

Decisions at the December 1975 Central Committee plenum reflected some of the longer term effects of the troubles in Soviet-American détente. The change in economic priorities at the Twenty-fourth Party Congress in 1971, which gave priority to consumer goods over heavy industry, had been an unprecedented and important political as well as economic occurrence. It was more than coincidence that this same Party Congress had highlighted détente and peaceful coexistence as part of a Peace Program (although the internal economic program stood on its own). It was also no coincidence that Brezhnev emerged as foremost among the Soviet leaders in foreign as well as internal affairs at that same Congress. Now, after four years of failure to meet the revised priorities in investment, the Central Committee in effect dropped the effort (although the plan was not formally abandoned). The need to increase imports of technology from the West remained and was recognized, with an increase of about one-third in foreign trade projected. But the United

---

70. Marshal A. A. Grechko, "Speech to the Armywide Conference of Excellent-Rated Personnel in Combat and Political Training," May 29, *Krasnaya zvezda*, May 30, 1975.

71. "Speech of Comrade L. I. Brezhnev," *Pravda*, June 14, 1975.

States had proven not to be the major partner in this effort, as the Soviet leadership had assumed and sought.

Bilateral Relations in Troubled Times

The first year or so of the Ford administration saw an inconsistent pattern of ups and downs in American-Soviet relations. The Vladivostok summit in November 1974 and associated SALT accord seemed to both leaderships, at least initially, to be an important success. The CSCE multilateral summit in Helsinki in July 1975 seemed a great success for détente in Europe,[72] and in the bilateral talks there Ford and Brezhnev reaffirmed détente and agreed to renew their efforts to reach the elusive SALT accord seemingly grasped at Vladivostok. On July 17, 1975, the historic linkup in space of the American Apollo and Soviet Soyuz spacecraft seemed to symbolize growing collaboration between the two powers extending even out of this world.

But there were several severe shocks, as well as growing difficulties and mutual suspicions, the full seriousness of which would only become apparent later. A major issue on the Soviet side—and also for the Nixon-Ford-Kissinger administrations—was the congressional insistence on applying its own linkage between bilateral trade normalization and internal Soviet political liberalization. While that effort failed in its objective (though not in the anti-détente aim of some of the driving spirits of the opposition, such as Senator Jackson), it seriously reduced both Soviet incentives for further developing détente and American leverage in détente diplomacy.

The Soviets did take some steps in an effort to improve relations. For example, despite reservations from some leaders, a decision was made in 1974 to cease jamming Voice of America broadcasts—a concession to détente not reversed until 1980.

The Vladivostok accord on SALT became mired down because of several factors. One was the genuine difficulty in reconciling different strategic programs and, still more, differing strategic perceptions of the two sides. Compounding these difficulties was that, on the American side, many people were increasingly suspicious and resentful of Kissinger's vest-pocket negotiating style, while Kissinger and Ford (as Nixon had before him) saw a need for secretive and even sleight-of-hand negotiation in order to circumvent bureaucratic spoilers in the Pentagon who did not wish to see agreement, or at least not unless the terms were lopsidedly in favor of the United States. On the Soviet side, to the military the Vladivostok deal represented a major (and reluctant) concession on their part, but the American reaction had been simply to pocket that gain and then to press for more.

---

72. See chapter 14.

Events elsewhere in the world continued to affect American-Soviet relations. From the American perspective the first major Soviet challenge to its interests, aside from the ambiguous case of the October 1973 war, came late in 1975, when the Soviets and Cubans provided military support to the side they favored in the civil war that had erupted in Angola soon after independence.[73] From the Soviet standpoint the United States had been acting contrary to Soviet interests and to the Soviet interpretation of détente, and continued to do so. The Soviets' complaints continued to focus primarily on two key areas: the Middle East, and China and East Asia.

The constant high-level diplomatic demarches and private complaints of Brezhnev, Gromyko, and others over the U.S. policy of squeezing the Soviet Union out of the Middle East have been noted. This strategy was represented in the American support, if not (as the Soviets suspected) instigation, of Egyptian President Sadat's reversal of alliances. Stimulated directly by the first Soviet-American summit, and aggravated by the skillful American assumption of a unilateral peacemaking role after the Arab-Israeli October 1973 war, American engagement with Egypt increased and rapidly supplanted Soviet influence. This process reached its climax just after the period under review here when, on March 15, 1976, Sadat unilaterally abrogated the Treaty of Friendship and Cooperation between Egypt and the Soviet Union.

While turning Egypt from the Soviet Union to the United States was the principal element in the American Middle East strategy of driving back Soviet influence, it was not the only one. As noted, disengagement talks also prompted renewal of diplomatic relations between the United States and Syria in June 1974. Moreover, Nixon's visit to Tehran literally on the morrow of his first summit meeting in Moscow in 1972 marked a demonstrative turn to Iran as a regional partner. Together with Iran (and Israel) the United States also covertly aided the Kurdish rebellion of Mullah Mustafa al-Barzani and his Pesh Merga in Iraq from 1972 until the Algiers Accord of March 6, 1975, between Iran and Iraq. As one key element in this temporary settlement of the Iraqi-Iranian confrontation, the United States and Iran ceased covert military support of the Kurds.[74] The agreement between Iraq and Iran helped stabilize the area, encouraged Iraq to move to a more nonaligned position, reduced

---

73. See chapter 15.

74. The American decision in 1972 to join Iran in providing covert military assistance to the Kurds was prompted by a demand by the shah of Iran, as part of the arrangement under which he agreed to serve as a regional power supporting American interests. See chapter 9; see also William Safire, "Mr. Ford's Secret Sellout," *New York Times*, February 5, 1976; and Safire, "Son of 'Secret Sellout,'" *New York Times*, February 12, 1976. The fullest account is given in the Pike Report of the House Select Committee Investigating Intelligence Activities; it was never officially released, but was leaked and printed by the *Village Voice* (New York), February 16, 1976. Kissinger, referred to in the Pike Report as a "high U.S. official," had replied icily to criticism of the action in letting down the Kurds after having supported them: "Covert action should not be confused with missionary work." Aaron Latham, "Introduction to the Pike Papers," ibid., p. 85.

Iraqi need for Soviet military assistance and political support, and increased American opportunities to reestablish influence in Iraq.

The American strategy to reduce Soviet influence in the Middle East and to expand its own was in part a case of vigorously prosecuting the geopolitical competition between the two powers. It also reflected Kissinger's judgment that the Soviet Union was either unable or unwilling to pressure the Arabs toward a compromise with Israel. Rather, it kept urging the United States to press Israel to compromise—for which efforts the Soviet Union would seek credit with the Arabs. This seemed to be the lesson from American efforts to work with the Soviet Union on the Rogers Plan in the period 1969–72. For his part Kissinger recognized a need for Israeli, as well as Arab, compromise, but wanted the United States to gain whatever credit with the Arabs he could for getting Israel to move. And he wanted to be able to orchestrate the Arab and Israeli compromises in order to keep leverage with both. In addition, after 1972 Kissinger had learned that it was possible to deal with Sadat directly rather than through Moscow. Thus after Kissinger became secretary of state and assumed control over American policy and diplomacy in the Middle East in 1973, he pressed the American advantage and cut the Soviet Union out.

The Soviet Union was also active in the early and mid-1970s, especially with Syria and the PLO and with arms supplies to Iraq (although these were cut back after the 1975 Algiers Accord with Iran). But its position was greatly reduced from that prior to the beginning of détente, and some in Moscow saw a connection.

At virtually every meeting of Brezhnev and Gromyko with Nixon, Ford, and Kissinger from 1972 on, the Soviet leaders attempted to engage the United States in discussion of the Middle East and to press for greater Soviet participation in the peacemaking process. Ford delineates the Soviet approaches and American response very well in his memoir. Describing his meeting with Brezhnev and Gromyko at Helsinki in July 1975, Ford writes: "Once again, as they had the first time we met, the Soviets led off with a verbal attack against us. 'We don't like the way you're handling the situation in the Middle East,' Gromyko said. 'We understood that you were going to include us in the peace process and that our two countries would work together. Here you are, going off on a tangent. That is contrary to the spirit of détente, and it's upsetting us.' We responded in kind. Once these obligatory opening statements were out of the way, we got down to business."[75] To the Soviet leaders, this complaint was not merely a preliminary and conventional sparring gambit—it *was* about important business. But there was very little the Soviets could do about the tough American policy of exclusion except complain and hope that the Americans would at least see that it was a matter of real concern to them. Ford's account suggests he scarcely understood that. Kissinger well understood why the Soviets were unhappy, but took their concern as only a welcome confirmation of success.

75. Ford, *A Time to Heal*, p. 303.

There was one other thing the Soviet leaders could do. They could conclude that they had learned how the United States interpreted the provision in the Basic Principles that "efforts to obtain unilateral advantage at the expense of the other, directly or indirectly, are inconsistent with these objectives." And they could thus expect reciprocity when *they* found opportunities elsewhere to increase their influence and to reduce that of the United States.

In another key area, China was also beginning to resume an active diplomatic role. In November 1974 Brezhnev rejected sharply a Chinese proposal for a nonaggression pact conditioned on Soviet military withdrawal from the disputed border areas. There was a steady exchange of polemical attacks. For example, in August 1975 *Kommunist* called for "smashing Maoism, a danger to all countries,"[76] accompanied a few days later by a renewed Soviet call for an Asian collective security arrangement. In December 1975 the Chinese did return a Soviet helicopter crew whose craft had strayed into Chinese territory twenty months earlier, but the polemics did not subside.

In April 1974, when President Nixon had visited Paris on the occasion of former French President Georges Pompidou's funeral and met briefly with President Podgorny, the Soviet leader had stressed the threat of war from China's policies and suggested that the United States and the Soviet Union compel China to join in the arms limitation process.[77] Nixon was not responsive.

The Chinese continued to attack the Soviets sharply but were by no means inhibited in criticizing the United States as well. For example, the Chinese foreign minister declaimed strongly against both the Soviet Union and the United States in his address to the UN General Assembly in September 1975. In October the Chinese also criticized covert American support to Tibetan emigrés. But these criticisms of the United States were intended to influence negotiations between the two countries, not to substitute for them. By this time the Chinese, especially since the eclipse of Premier Zhou Enlai, felt they had been used by Nixon and Kissinger, as the United States was continuing to improve relations with the Soviet Union without moving to meet Chinese interests.[78] Nonetheless, in October Kissinger visited China in preparation for a visit by President Ford on December 1–5.[79] While these visits did not lead to any major new initiatives, they did continue the gradual process of rapprochement.

---

76. Editorial, "The Maoist Regime at a New Stage," *Kommunist*, no. 12 (August 1975), p. 122.

77. Henry Kissinger, *Years of Upheaval* (Boston, Mass.: Little, Brown, 1982), p. 1173.

78. The Chinese also resented Ford's meeting with Brezhnev in Vladivostok, in territory to which China laid historical claim. The Soviets presumably selected Vladivostok with this purpose in mind; the American leaders did not recognize the symbolic slap at China. See Gelman, *The Brezhnev Politburo*, p. 122.

79. President Ford's account of these visits is very sparse. Ford, *A Time to Heal*, pp. 335–37. Kissinger's memoir on this period will probably be more informative.

China also received a Japanese delegation sent in January 1975 to discuss a possible peace treaty. (The Japanese sent a similar mission to Moscow for the same purpose at the same time.) Throughout the year the Soviets repeatedly warned the Japanese against an antihegemony clause insisted upon by China: the clause did not mention the Soviet Union, but Moscow felt keenly that it was an anti-Soviet provision. On the other hand the Soviets adamantly refused to consider Japan's claim to the northern islands above Hokkaido. Then, as the prospects for a Japanese-Soviet treaty waned, those for a Japanese-Chinese treaty waxed.

China also moved toward closer relations with Western Europe. In September 1975 it established formal diplomatic ties with the European Community. Soviet alarm mounted as it became known late in 1975 that China was negotiating the purchase of fighter aircraft and other arms from both Britain and France. In December Britain, with American acquiescence, sold Spey jet engines to China. All in all, notwithstanding the CSCE and some encouraging prospects in Europe, Soviet interests in the world were not faring well, and the United States seemed—especially to Moscow—to be partly engineering and largely profiting from Soviet ill fortune.

SALT, despite its travails, loomed larger as the centerpiece of détente and as a common interest and prospective contribution to the security of both parties, especially as trade prospects dimmed and other diplomatic cooperation faltered. This judgment was reached in Moscow in particular. It also reflected the thinking of the Ford-Kissinger administration, but it was a thin reed in the American political context. As the next year was to show, the American consensus in support of détente was seriously weakening.

14 European Security and European Insecurities, 1973–76

THE MID-1970s saw a flowering of détente in Europe, exemplified above all by the convening of a European security conference and agreement in 1975 on a Final Act on European Security and Cooperation. MBFR was also launched. And *Ostpolitik* was rounded out.[1] As the 1970s unfolded, it became clear that *Ostpolitik* and European détente had greatly diminished long-standing Soviet fears of German revanche. Finally, East-West détente in Europe was now paralleled by American-Soviet détente.

There remained important differences and possibilities for serious friction. From the Soviet standpoint in particular, the growth of Eurocommunism, a more moderate European variant of the Soviet communist system, posed a new challenge to the legitimacy of Soviet leadership and hegemony in the communist states of Eastern Europe. From the standpoint of the United States, the emergence of greater communist standing in several countries in southern and western Europe raised concern over the strength of the Western alliance. Noted in earlier chapters were instances of friction between the United States and its European allies on other matters, some of them related to American-Soviet détente.

Détente and the European Security Conference (CSCE)

Multilateral preparatory talks on the Conference on Security and Cooperation in Europe (CSCE) began in November 1972 in Helsinki. By the next June sufficient common basis had been established, despite disparate in-

---

1. The Bundestag of West Germany ratified its treaty with East Germany on May 11, 1973. East Germany was rapidly recognized by most countries, and both German states were admitted to the United Nations on September 18, 1973. Between June 1973 and April 1974 West Germany negotiated treaties with Czechoslovakia, Hungary, and Bulgaria establishing diplomatic relations and settling differences. The basic framework of the *Ostpolitik* was just completed by the

473

terests and priorities, to enable a meeting of foreign ministers formally to open the CSCE, which met July 3–7, 1973, in Helsinki. At that time the agenda that had been worked out in the preparatory talks was adopted. It was also agreed that decisions would be reached by consensus, with each of the thirty-five participating states (all the European states except Albania and including the Vatican, as well as Canada and the United States) having veto power. The working phase of the conference extended from September 1973 to July 1975. The finale was a summit-level meeting of the thirty-five participants in Helsinki from July 30 to August 1, 1975.

The CSCE negotiations involved not only determining areas of common interest but, through give and take, reaching compromises on issues of difference. In this respect it was a complicated negotiation and led even such powers as the United States and, still more, the Soviet Union to accept some provisions they did not want. The many proposals of the participants were tossed into three "baskets." While the final agreement does not use that somewhat inelegant term, even official discussions of the CSCE have continued to use Baskets I, II, and III when referring to the three main parts of the Final Act, as the agreement was called.[2]

Basket I, "Security in Europe," resulted in a "Declaration on Principles Guiding Relations between Participating States." It consisted of ten principles on interstate relations: respect for sovereignty and sovereign equality, nonresort to the threat or use of force, inviolability of frontiers, territorial integrity, peaceful settlement of disputes, nonintervention in internal affairs, respect for human rights and fundamental freedoms, equal rights and self-determination of peoples, cooperation among states, and fulfillment of international obligations. Agreement was also reached on a "Document on Confidence-Building Measures and Certain Aspects of Security and Disarmament," which provides for advance notification of large military exercises and other similar measures to increase mutual confidence. (A separate and peripheral declaration encouraging security and cooperation in the Mediterranean was agreed on at the insistence of Malta.)

Basket II covers "Cooperation in the Field of Economics, of Science and Technology and of the Environment." It includes provisions concerning commerce, industrial cooperation, science and technology, the environment, transportation, promotion of tourism, and migrant labor.

Basket III, "Cooperation in Humanitarian and Other Fields," covers contacts among peoples, dissemination of information, and cultural and educational exchange. In addition to encouraging freer movement of people,

---

time Chancellor Willy Brandt had to leave office in May 1974. The United States recognized East Germany somewhat later—on September 4, 1974.

2. U.S. Department of State, *Conference on Security and Co-operation in Europe, Final Act,* Helsinki, 1975, Publication 8826 (Washington, D.C.: Department of State, 1975).

For an informed account of the CSCE negotiations, see John J. Maresca, *To Helsinki: The Conference on Security and Cooperation in Europe, 1973–1975* (Durham, N.C.: Duke University Press, 1985).

ideas, and information, it contains provisions on facilitating family reunification and visits, binational marriages, access to published and broadcast information, journalism, and various forms of cultural and educational cooperation.

Lastly, the Final Act also provided for continuation of the CSCE process and called for a first follow-up meeting to take place in Belgrade in the latter half of 1977.

Broadly speaking, the Soviets had three principal interests in the CSCE: to gain general acceptance of the territorial and political status quo in central and eastern Europe, enlarging on the bilateral West German agreements with the Soviet Union, Poland, and East Germany; to support reduction of interstate barriers to increased economic relations; and to further the general process of East-West détente. The Soviet Union was reluctant and unhappy about the need to include provisions concerning *internal* human rights and *personal* rights with respect to the transnational movement of people and information. While not averse to platitudinous (and even in their terms sincere) advocacy of human rights, it was highly suspicious of Western pressure on these subjects. In any case it strongly opposed giving up even the appearance and certainly the substance of full national control within the Soviet Union and other communist states of Eastern Europe. At least initially the Soviets were also reluctant about the arms control type of confidence-building measures (CBMs) that provided for advance notice of military exercises, exchanges of observers at field maneuvers, and the like.[3]

The Soviet leaders had from the outset been well aware of the risks, as well as the opportunities, in East-West détente, as discussed earlier. At the CSCE they were probably surprised and clearly unhappy at the strength of Western (and neutral country) solidarity and persistence in pushing the issues of human rights and freedom of movement of people and of information and ideas. They could not easily object in principle (many of these rights are accorded in the Soviet Constitution), and they did not want to object so sharply as to contradict their support for détente. In the end the Soviets reluctantly acceded to much of Basket III (and some provisions in Baskets I and II) because they found it necessary to do so in order to reach agreement. Of course, by that time the Soviet Union also had a substantial stake in the success of what had, even if in somewhat different circumstances and design, been a long-standing Soviet and Warsaw Pact initiative. Furthermore, they believed the carefully couched language of the agreement would protect their interests and freedom of action in any instance of political controversy over its application.

It should also be noted in passing that in addition to having had to accept the United States as a full-fledged participant, the Soviet leaders also had to take into account the interests of a wide range of states—including

---

3. All four of the confidence-building or arms control measures stemmed from proposals by NATO members, drawn from earlier NATO studies, although the alliance had never adopted them as guidance for NATO members at the CSCE. Indeed, as noted later, the United States was initially cool to the idea of CBMs.

those of Eastern Europe. In particular, from the very outset Romania adopted some positions at variance with those of the Soviet Union, notably in pressing for arms control CBMs.

On the Western side, the NATO countries maintained an effective informal caucus. In addition, the Helsinki conference marked the first time the enlarged European Community used a caucus to coordinate positions at a multilateral negotiation.

American reservations about the CSCE generally pertained less to specific elements in the package and more to broader concerns about East-West détente, a formal if indirect acceptance of the political status quo in Eastern Europe, and the possibility that the conciliation might produce a euphoria that would reduce support for military programs in NATO countries. There was, additionally, some concern for a time over whether the modest military CBMs would undercut the parallel MBFR process then under way, sponsored by the United States and NATO. This concern, however, moderated as it became clear that the CBMs in the CSCE would be modest and as second thoughts began to arise over whether the outcome of the MBFR would be to Western advantage.

The United States and many other Western participants increasingly saw the Basket III provisions on human rights and movement of information as areas that could be turned to advantage vis-à-vis the USSR and Eastern European communist countries. Further, the Basket I principles could be used against the Brezhnev Doctrine on permissible socialist interaction, while the Basket II provisions calling for more economic information in order to facilitate trade could help reduce the secrecy of the communist states in that area.

Ultimately each party naturally concluded the balance of advantages was in its favor. This attitude was not inherently contradictory, since many aspects of the agreement did reflect common interests and each party attached varying weight to the provisions it favored or disliked. Moreover, expectations about the future may have differed. In any event, future developments would affect greatly the application and implementation of the agreement. Commentary in both East and West (especially the United States) noted that the Final Act was but a step in the process of détente, with much dependent on future implementation.

The general European reaction—West, East, and in between—to the CSCE Final Act was quite positive. Apart from the drama of the conference and Europe's having a place in the sun (as Kissinger had earlier tried less successfully to promote with his Year of Europe), the feeling was widespread that a real relaxation of tensions was occurring in the East-West confrontation in Europe, a shift that was welcomed. There were, to be sure, cynical commentators as well as those carried away by euphoria. But the general reaction was that at least a hopeful and helpful step had been taken.[4]

---

4. A useful analysis of European perspectives on détente as it developed in the early and mid-1970s, while it does not report European reactions to the Final Act, is found in Gregory A. Flynn, "The Content of European Détente," *Orbis*, vol. 20 (Summer 1976), pp. 401–16.

The Soviet leaders monitored the deliberations of the CSCE closely as they proceeded from 1973 to 1975. The April 1973 plenum of the Central Committee, at which a number of changes in economic policy were effected and two members of the Politburo were removed, also discussed the CSCE. The Central Committee endorsed proceeding with the conference but also noted the need for heightened vigilance and no relaxation of party controls in both the Soviet Union and the communist states of Eastern Europe, in view of the dangers of "ideological subversion" under conditions of greater contact stimulated by détente.[5] On the eve of the final phase of negotiations on the CSCE the Central Committee plenum meeting in April 1975 again heard a report by Foreign Minister Gromyko on the CSCE.[6] (These two plenums were the only ones from 1973 to 1980 known to have dealt with foreign policy matters.) Finally, following the CSCE summit meeting at which the Final Act was signed, as is usual in such cases the Politburo of the Communist Party, the Presidium of the Supreme Soviet, and the Council of Ministers jointly expressed the leadership's "positive evaluation" of the Final Act.[7]

At the Twenty-fifth Party Congress, meeting in February 1976, General Secretary Brezhnev praised the achievements of the CSCE. Noting that the work of the conference had lasted for two years, and "the political preparation" for ten, he commented that "the results achieved are worth the efforts expended." (Perhaps he was assuring some who had suggested that the efforts—and compromises—had been excessive.) The results Brezhnev stressed were: "confirmation of the inviolability of borders" (mentioned first and separately); the "code of principles of interstate mutual relations"—which, he said, "in letter and in spirit answered the requirements of peaceful coexistence"; and the establishment of "favorable conditions for preserving and consolidating peace on the whole continent." He also noted in general terms the provisions for "peaceful cooperation in the fields of economic affairs, science and technology, culture and information, and in the development of contacts among people" and, finally, the military CBMs.[8] While clearly applauding the CSCE, Brezhnev also noted that there remained "complications in our relations with a number of capitalist states of Europe," based on the unwillingness of "influential circles in these states really to cast aside the psychology of the 'cold war'

5. "On the International Activity of the Central Committee of the CPSU in Implementing the Decisions of the XXIV Party Congress. Resolution of the Plenary Session of the CC CPSU Adopted April 27, 1973," *Pravda*, April 28, 1973.

6. "On the International Situation and the Foreign Policy of the Soviet Union," *Pravda*, April 17, 1975. The text of Gromyko's speech was not published either at the time or in subsequent compilations.

7. "On the Results of the Conference on Security and Cooperation in Europe," *Pravda*, August 7, 1975.

8. XXV s'yezd kommunisticheskoi partii sovetskogo soyuza, 24 fevralya–5 marta 1976 goda: stenograficheskii otchet [Twenty-fifth Congress of the Communist Party of the Soviet Union, February 24–March 5, 1976: Stenographic Account], vol. 1 (Moscow: Politizdat, 1976), pp. 41–42.

and consistently to conduct a policy of mutually advantageous collaboration and non-intervention in the internal affairs of other countries." Some, he said, even want to use the Final Act as "a cover for interference in the internal affairs of the countries of socialism, for anti-Communist and anti-Soviet demagogy in the style of the 'cold war.' "[9]

Subsequent Soviet commentary on the CSCE—and there has been a great deal—has continued to stress the positive accomplishments of the conference and Final Act in settling the European problem and establishing a "European code of peaceful coexistence," and to praise greater economic ties. It has also emphasized the unfinished business of realizing military détente (through MBFR and other arms control measures) and has noted the "subversive activities" by those opposing or perverting the Final Act through "interference in internal affairs" of the socialist countries.[10]

After 1975 Soviet commentators have frequently cited the Final Act as the highlight of European détente. Initially it was coupled with the fundamental documents of the Soviet-American détente (the Basic Principles of 1972 and the Prevention of Nuclear War agreement of 1973) as laying the foundation for détente and peace. By 1980, after the American-Soviet détente had collapsed, some commentaries reviewing the 1970s as "the decade of détente" cited the Helsinki accord as "the high point" of the decade and omitted the Soviet-American agreements.[11]

The reaction to the Final Act in the United States was startlingly different from that in the Soviet Union and Western Europe. The CSCE had, until President Ford's trip to Helsinki, been unknown to most Americans, in contrast to the widespread interest and general public support in Western Europe. The growing disenchantment with détente and politicking in the upcoming presidential election in 1976 led to criticism of the CSCE and of President Ford's journey to Helsinki to sign it. The *Wall Street Journal* urged Ford not to go, and even the *New York Times* called his trip "misguided and empty." Senator Jackson, known to be a candidate for the Democratic nomination, and Ronald Reagan, who was campaigning but had not yet announced as a candidate challenging Ford for the Republican nomination, opposed the CSCE Final Act. Reagan even said, "I think all Americans should be against it." There was also an outcry from a small but vocal number of ethnic Americans of eastern European descent. Finally, as Ford states in his memoir, some members of his own staff were defensive about the CSCE, and rather than vigorously supporting it, attempted to excuse it; some intimated to the press

---

9. Ibid., pp. 42, 43.

10. For a good example see S. Vladimirov and L. Teplov, *Kursom khels'inksykh dogovoronnostei* [The Path of the Helsinki Accords] (Moscow: Mezhdunarodnoye otnosheniya, 1980), from which most of these typical illustrative quotations are taken.

11. For example, even the preeminent expert on American affairs used precisely this formulation; see G. Arbatov, Interview on Radio Moscow, July 4, in Foreign Broadcast Information Service, *Daily Report: Soviet Union*, July 8, 1980, p. A1. (Hereafter FBIS, *Soviet Union*.)

that it was "another Kissinger deal that was forced down the President's throat."[12]

On the other hand, attention to the CSCE faded soon after President Ford's return from Helsinki, although rumblings of dissatisfaction continued to be heard. Both supporters of détente, and those who opposed it but still saw the possibility of using the CSCE process to prod the Soviet Union and its Eastern European allies on human rights and other issues, joined in Congress the next year in passing legislation establishing a Commission on Security and Cooperation in Europe. Signed by President Ford on June 3, 1976, the law established the commission as a mixed body, with six members from each house of Congress and one each from the Departments of State, Defense, and Commerce. The commission's mandate was to monitor the actions of CSCE participants on "compliance with or violation of" the articles of the Final Act. In practice, as later official reports acknowledged, it concentrated on compliance by the Soviet Union and its Warsaw Pact allies.[13] The commission also functioned both as a congressional committee, holding hearings and submitting reports, and as a participant in official government-to-government consultations on the CSCE and in the official CSCE follow-on conferences.

Mutual and Balanced Force Reductions (MBFR)

The CSCE was termed a conference on security in Europe, and in one sense that wording is appropriate. The Soviet Union has always argued that the basic security problems are political rather than military. While the United States and NATO have agreed that there is an important political dimension to security, as long as an adversarial relationship exists, there is also an important *military* dimension.

In the late 1960s and 1970s the West tended to approach European security (albeit gingerly) from the standpoint of military security. This has been the official (though only partial) rationale for NATO sponsorship of MBFR.[14] As seen earlier, Western interest in MBFR originally stemmed

---

12. All the points noted in this paragraph, and the quotations, are given by Gerald R. Ford, *A Time to Heal: The Autobiography of Gerald R. Ford* (Harper and Row, 1979), pp. 300–02.

13. *Implementation of the Final Act of the Conference on Security and Cooperation in Europe: Findings and Recommendations Five Years after Helsinki,* Report submitted to the Congress by the Commission on Security and Cooperation in Europe, 96 Cong. 2 sess. (Washington, D.C.: Government Printing Office, 1980), pp. 1, 2.

14. The term MBFR (mutual and balanced force reductions) is used for convenience and brevity; it is the standard term in the West. It should, however, be noted that the Soviet Union and its allies strongly object to the term because of the Western view of what constitutes "balanced" reductions. The official title of the MBFR conference is Conference on the Mutual Reduction of Forces and Armaments and Associated Measures in Central Europe (MURFAAMCE).

mainly from a belief that negotiating *mutual* reductions was the best way to stem a growing tide of American political opinion favoring *unilateral* reductions of the American military presence in Europe.[15] There was also, however, some real Western interest in reducing tensions in Europe by controlling and reducing the prospects of military confrontation in central Europe.

Initial Soviet coolness toward MBFR was based not only on a recognition that the real purpose in the West was to shore up the American military presence, but even more on suspicions about other possible goals: to provide a rationale for building up Western European (especially West German) military forces; to counter the call by the Warsaw Pact for a European security conference with an alternative grounded in more limited military considerations of security; and to gain access to Eastern Europe to collect military intelligence and carry out political subversion.[16] Only after the CSCE was launched in 1973 did the Soviets conclude that MBFR might in fact serve their interests by contributing to military détente in Europe, supplementing the CSCE and SALT. The Soviets saw military détente as the application of détente in the military sphere, in particular what in the West is termed arms control, including confidence-building measures, and arms limitation and reduction. While also applied to SALT and other arms control and disarmament proposals and negotiations, and to military dialogue and even unilateral military doctrine, the Soviets have most frequently used military détente in referring to Europe, and specifically to MBFR and CSCE confidence-building measures. After the Helsinki Final Act, military détente in Europe became a major theme, one that Brezhnev stressed at the Twenty-fifth Party Congress in February 1976, when he said, "Political détente needs strengthening by military détente."[17]

Paradoxically, just as the CSCE, so long sought by the Warsaw Pact, would become a mixed blessing from the Soviet point of view, many in the West, despite initial advocacy and even insistence by NATO on MBFR, would become disenchanted with it. But this change in attitude came gradually.

While the home of the CSCE was Helsinki, the base for MBFR has been Vienna. A preparatory phase opened on January 31, 1973, and contin-

---

Incidentally, in January 1973 the neutral Austrian hosts were very embarrassed by their use, in all innocence, of official placards that read MBFR. The Eastern participants were very displeased and objected, and the Austrians quickly removed the offending signs.

15. See chapter 4.

16. For an example of Soviet reference to the last of these concerns—identifying intelligence collection as an aim of President Lyndon B. Johnson's bridge-building approach—see L. Vidyasova, "NATO on the Eve of 1969," *International Affairs* (Moscow), no. 10 (October 1968), p. 19.

17. Brezhnev, in *XXV s'yezd Kommunisticheskoi partii*, p. 47.

ued until June 23. Formal negotiations began on October 30, 1973, and have run (with recesses) ever since.[18]

The first issue in MBFR involved the area of reductions and limitations. Both sides focused on central Europe, but with a question whether Hungary (and Soviet troops in Hungary) were to be included in the area to which reductions would apply. Hungary (and the Soviet Union and Warsaw Pact members) insisted it could not be included unless Italy were included on the NATO side. This issue was in effect settled at the preparatory talks when the Western participants agreed reluctantly, and "reserving the right" to reopen the matter, that Hungary not be a regular participant, but only an observer (together with a number of other countries not included in the area to which reductions would apply). There was some grumbling within the NATO group when the United States eventually moved to yield on this matter, but it was accepted.[19]

Another issue at the outset was whether to seek proportional reductions or asymmetrical reductions to a common ceiling. The Western side argued for the latter.[20] A third was whether all forces would be included, or only

18. In both cases the beginning of the preparatory talks on the last day of January and of the formal negotiations on the last day of October amounted to last-minute fulfillment of commitments the Soviets had reluctantly made to Nixon at the May 1972 and June 1973 summit conferences, respectively, that the talks would open no later than January and October 1973. The October meeting date, incidentally, coincided with the Soviet-American crisis over the Israeli-Egyptian cease-fire.

For a useful account of the MBFR negotiations from their origins to 1980, see [Colonel] John G. Keliher, *The Negotiations on Mutual and Balanced Force Reductions: The Search for Arms Control in Central Europe* (Pergamon, 1980).

19. The decision was probably the correct one on the merits of the case, although the matter was not susceptible to definitive judgment. There was considerable evidence that the Soviet Southern Group of Forces, four ground divisions and small air force units, located in Hungary, is oriented for contingent use in wartime toward the south rather than the west. The matter had, however, occasioned controversy in Washington (with the Department of Defense wishing to include Hungary and the Soviet forces there in order to get the maximum number of Warsaw Pact forces included for reduction), as well as later among the NATO members (most wanting to include it for the same reason). Some suspected the United States had already conceded this point to the Soviets in the Kissinger-Dobrynin talks leading to the agreement to proceed on MBFR. While that suspicion has not yet been publicly documented, it is well-taken. (I chaired the interagency MBFR Working Group under the Verification Panel in Washington during the period in early 1973 when the American position was being decided and the MBFR preparatory talks were held.)

20. A tangential aspect of this issue may be of interest. Earlier MBFR studies for the North Atlantic Council in Brussels in 1968–69 had been predicated on proportional reductions. Those studies, which were secret and never publicly disclosed, were not accepted by the alliance as a basis for later NATO negotiating positions. They had been, however, among documents passed by a spy in the NATO staff, a Turk named Imre, to an Eastern European intelligence service and hence were undoubtedly available to Moscow. The question arises whether the studies misled the Soviets into expecting NATO to accept proportional reduc-

ground forces (omitting air forces and nuclear arms); the Western position was ground forces only. A fourth issue was the West's proposal for two separate phases of negotiation and implementation, with the first stage covering only Soviet and American forces. This approach conflicted with the Pact insistence on including both stationed and indigenous national forces from the outset, with three stages of increasing reductions. A fifth issue, although initially without specifics, was a desire by the West to try to equalize the impact of geographic disparity; that is, American troops had to be withdrawn across the Atlantic, while Soviet troops would need to move only the relatively short distance to the Soviet Union. Finally, the Western side proposed unspecified additional "stabilizing measures, verification measures, and noncircumvention provisions." Other questions soon arose: would manpower reductions have to be undertaken by whole units, or could it be accomplished by thinning out units that remained; would American, Soviet, and other stationed forces to be withdrawn have to be demobilized or merely removed from the reduction area; and would the equipment of units withdrawn from the area also have to be withdrawn?

The initial Soviet proposal called for an overall 17 percent reduction over a three-year period. The U.S. one called for withdrawal of 29,000 American troops (not necessarily in units) and a four-division Soviet tank army with 68,000 troops and 1,700 tanks. In December 1975 the West made its first major shift by proposing to include some air and nuclear forces as well, although not in the overall troop calculation, and to withdraw 1,000 nuclear munitions.

The Soviets soon (February 1976) modified their proposal to seek a first-phase reduction of Soviet and American troops only, tied to a second phase that would reduce national forces (which would in the meantime be frozen at a ceiling set at existing levels). The Soviets would also withdraw some aircraft and missiles to match (although not precisely) those proposed earlier by the American side, and both sides would remove a few hundred tanks. They also called for disbanding the Soviet and American forces withdrawn.

In June 1976 the Warsaw Pact addressed another major issue that had arisen—the absence of an agreed-on data base. The Western side had provided not only figures for its own forces, but also its estimates of the levels of Eastern forces.[21] The Eastern side did not provide its own figures until June 1976, and then they did not accord with Western estimates, being lower by

---

tions. The Soviets could never use the illicitly obtained studies in the negotiations to support their position. (I was a participant in the preparation of the studies, and later in assessing the damage done by the compromise of these and other materials passed by the spy.)

21. In the spring of 1973, just as NATO was deciding to seek a "common ceiling" for the two alliances, U.S. (and then NATO) intelligence estimates of Soviet and Warsaw Pact troop strength in the central region were raised by 85,000 men in a reassessment of available data—increasing the gap between the two sides from 35,000 to 120,000. Information from informed senior American participants in MBFR.

some 157,000 ground forces, or 175,000 ground and air forces combined. While some differences in functions, and possible variant approaches in determining the correct figures, are to be expected, this substantial discrepancy caused a serious problem.

In general terms, these are the major issues that arose in the first four years of MBFR, from 1973 through 1976.[22] (A later chapter addresses developments from 1977 through 1980.)[23]

The problems have proved more complex, and the approaches of each side more conservative and responsive to its interests, than is required to reach agreement. Once undertaken, the MBFR negotiations assumed a ponderous and technically complex nature, and political incentives were not sufficient to lead to resolution of the issues. They did, however, provide a symmetry in military détente to the bilateral strategic SALT negotiations, and they marked a continuing effort toward mitigating the arms confrontation between the two military blocs in Europe.[24]

The United States and the Soviet Union did not enter into behind-the-scenes bilateral negotiations on MBFR issues. They did exchange general comments at several high-level bilateral meetings, but once the talks were launched in 1973, they remained in the multilateral channel.[25]

Western Europe, Eurocommunism, and Détente

Along with the political institutionalization of European détente in the mid-1970s, a number of matters arose that caused disquiet and concern in Europe, and even more in the United States and the Soviet Union.

The relationship between the United States and Western Europe has been grounded in a firm political and military alliance based on deeply rooted common traditions and continuing shared interests. It has been, nonetheless, subject to recurring friction and occasional tension, stemming partly from economic crosscurrents and competition, partly from divergent assess-

---

22. See Keliher, *The Negotiations on MBFR*, pp. 34–73.

23. See chapter 22.

24. There remained, however, a potential gap between SALT and MBFR, as neither covered intermediate-range nuclear delivery systems in Europe. This gap became very important by the late 1970s. See chapter 25.

25. One occasion when MBFR was raised peripherally occurred during Kissinger's important discussions of SALT in Moscow in January 1976. Brezhnev informed him that the Soviet Union would reject the then-recent Western proposal, but would respond with a counterproposal that included nuclear delivery systems and would also make a concession on the Western preference for initial reductions in only American and Soviet forces. His remarks foreshadowed the positions advanced in Vienna a month later. But they did not negotiate these points or other MBFR issues.

ments of threats and interests in Europe and elsewhere in the world, and partly from divergences over priorities and means of meeting shared goals. Rarely do differences within the family, so to speak, perceptibly affect American-Soviet relations or the East-West relationship as a whole. But some aspects of U.S.–Western European relations over the 1970s did have some impact.

President Nixon had demonstratively visited Western Europe (with his first stop at Brussels, headquarters of the North Atlantic Council and the European Community) within a month of his inauguration in 1969. Early in 1970 Prime Minister Harold Wilson of Great Britain, President Georges Pompidou of France, and Chancellor Willy Brandt of West Germany all visited Nixon and discussed general policy. Political approaches had been satisfactorily coordinated, but economic conflicts had arisen. Economic friction escalated during 1970 and 1971, and by the end of 1971 another round of bilateral Western summit meetings had become necessary to deal urgently with economic problems. While not the cause of these difficulties, the lack of an integrated economic-political strategy in Washington did not help—especially when, in August 1971, Nixon suddenly announced a series of new economic policies, including a 10 percent surcharge on all imports and suspension of the convertibility of the dollar. He announced these policies without any advance consultation with or even notification to the Western European (and Japanese) allies. As Kissinger (not an architect of economic policy) later put it cynically, "Nixon's unilateral decisions of August 15, 1971, had their desired effect. Allied cohesion had been strained but not broken."[26]

As noted earlier, Kissinger did initiate the Year of Europe in 1973 in an effort to improve relations generally, and specifically to relate European economic commitments to American defense commitments.[27] It proved a fiasco. Later, the impact and responses of the two sides to the Arab oil embargo in 1973–74 stirred further economic (and political) frictions in the Western alliance.

On matters more directly stemming from American-Soviet relations, occasionally European-American frictions arose over some U.S. moves relating to political détente with the Soviet Union. An example was the surprise ex post facto unveiling of the Prevention of Nuclear War agreement in June 1973. These détente moves were combined, on the other hand, with confrontational acts against the Soviet Union (the strategic forces alert in October 1973). Some moves in European détente similarly caused misgivings in Washington. On the whole, however, coordination among the United States and its Western European allies on political relations between West and East was good. Despite internal differences in economic interests within the West, at the summit meetings at Rambouillet in 1975 and Puerto Rico in 1976 the

---

26. See Henry Kissinger, *White House Years* (Boston, Mass.: Little, Brown, 1979), p. 962; see also pp. 380–87, 416–29, 949–67.

27. See chapter 10.

Western powers still were able not only to coordinate their general economic policies and institutions better, but also to coordinate their policy on economic credits toward the Eastern European countries and the Soviet Union, thus at least mitigating this source of conflict. Practice did remain different, with the United States remaining much more restrictive than Western Europe.

Surprisingly, the major cause of concern over the course of East-West relations that arose in Washington in the mid-1970s stemmed not from Soviet action, or developments in Eastern Europe, or even from American-allied relations, but from certain internal political developments in Western Europe.

On April 25, 1974, the leadership of the Portuguese armed forces deposed the government of Marcello Caetano that had succeeded the late dictator, Antonio de Oliveira Salazar. The new government seemed to have a rightist bent. But by mid-July the conservative head of state, General Antonio de Spinola, was replaced by a leftist group headed by Colonel Vasco dos Santos Gonçalves, and it included communists in the government. Also in July the Cypriot National Guard under Greek officers overthrew the government of Archbishop Makarios III, an event that was followed in rapid succession by a Turkish invasion of Cyprus and the fall of the right-wing junta in Athens. Within a very short time a de facto partition of Cyprus had occurred, and although the moderate Constantine Karamanlis had returned to power in Greece, political stability did not return to Cyprus. Meanwhile, Portugal began to dissolve the remnants of its empire, granting independence to Guinea-Bissau in August and recognizing a provisional government in Mozambique in September pending complete independence nine months later. (Though unrelated, it was also in September that Emperor Haile Selassie was deposed in Ethiopia.) Portugal also made clear its intention to grant independence to Angola, although its transition to independence in 1975–76 was difficult. Most important, Portugal itself continued in 1974 and 1975 to move to the left. Then in November 1975 Generalissimo Francisco Franco of Spain died, raising concern over the stability of the successor government in that country. And in Italy, in June 1975 the Communist party received a strong 33.4 percent of the vote in local, provincial, and regional elections, and in June 1976 got 33.8 percent in the national elections.

Thus the political situation in southern Europe was becoming more fluid, with a general turn to the left. One reason the principal communist parties in the region were gaining popularity and political strength was that they were adopting a more independent and moderate course. Despite that trend the overall move to the left raised substantial alarm among some Western political leaders, especially in the United States, and above all Kissinger.

Kissinger's concern was first sparked by the leftward trend in Portugal from September 1974 to September 1975, but he did not voice it until after the failure of a right-wing coup in March 1975, when he expressed "disquiet" over the risk to democracy. Prior to (and following) the May NATO ministerial meeting both he and President Ford expressed alarm over the effect on

NATO should a communist-dominated government come to power in Portugal. During most of 1975 Kissinger was pessimistic about the prospects for preventing a communist takeover within Portugal. Indeed, he was so pessimistic that he believed little could be done and tended instead to prepare to write off Portugal as a member of NATO and concentrated on isolating it. Fortunately a number of Western European governments (and even more, socialist parties in Western Europe) did not share this attitude and aided the dominant socialist party in Portugal. Frank Carlucci, the American ambassador, also kept insisting that the battle for Portugal was by no means lost.[28]

Kissinger correctly recognized that the causes of the Portuguese revolution and uncertain political course from 1974 to 1976 were internal. Opponents of détente in the United States, however, seized upon the leftward trend in Portugal as a sign of Moscow's hand and as a demonstration of the failure of the U.S. policy of détente with the Soviet Union. Kissinger, correctly stressing the internal causes of the political developments in Portugal, replied that "détente cannot be used as a means of asking the Soviet Union to take care of all of our problems on our side of the line,"[29] although he also said that any Soviet interference in Portugal would be considered inconsistent with détente—and with the CSCE. President Ford, however, in his one important comment on the subject, did link the Portuguese shift to the left to Soviet attitudes toward détente: "We are now carefully watching some serious situations for indications of the Soviet attitude toward détente and cooperation in European security. The situation in Portugal is one of them."[30]

In fact, the Soviet Union had covertly provided financial support to the Portuguese Communist party, although in all other respects it was careful not to interfere in Portugal. The Soviet ambassador in Lisbon stressed to Ambassador Carlucci that the Soviet Union would not seek to subvert Portugal, and was reported to have told Prime Minister Gonçalves that the Soviet Union

---

28. In later speeches (from September to December 1975) Kissinger stated that he and the U.S. government consistently sought to do *more* than the Europeans. The record does not, however, bear out this claim. Especially in the critical period from March through August 1975 Kissinger seemed to consider Portugal doomed to become communist. For a detailed and generally well-informed account see Tad Szulc, "Lisbon and Washington: Behind the Portuguese Revolution," *Foreign Policy*, no. 21 (Winter 1975–76), pp. 3–62.

29. "Secretary Kissinger's News Conference at Helsinki July 30 and 31," *Department of State Bulletin*, vol. 73 (September 1, 1975), p. 316; and see statements on June 23, ibid. (July 7, 1975), p. 18; July 25, ibid. (August 11, 1975), p. 202; and August 14, ibid. (September 15, 1975), pp. 393, 397, 399. (Hereafter *State Bulletin*.)

30. This statement appears in a major speech, "America's Strength and Progress toward Freedom and Peace," in which President Ford sought to gain support for détente, specifically from a critical segment of the political constituency: the address was delivered to the 57th National Convention of the American Legion, August 19, *State Bulletin*, vol. 73 (September 15, 1975), p. 412. This speech coincided with Kissinger's strongest warnings against Soviet interference, and came only shortly before the turning of the political tide in Portugal with the ouster of Prime Minister Gonçalves on August 29. Kissinger, "American Unity and the National Interest," ibid., p. 393.

had no interest in creating a confrontation with the United States over Portugal.[31]

The situation in Portugal soon turned against the communists. Prime Minister Gonçalves was forced out on August 29, and on November 25-26, 1975, a leftist coup attempt was crushed. By February 1976 the five principal political parties in Portugal and the armed forces reached a compact on democratic procedures. The Socialists handily won the elections in April 1976, and a moderate, General Antonio Ramalho Eanes, was elected president in June 1976.

Portugal was, however, only one element—even if for a time a dramatic one—in the changing political scene. From the outset Kissinger had seen it in this light, as he made clear in a statement in April 1975. He said, "The problem in Portugal, too, is very serious, because it could be taken as a test case for possible evolutions in other countries, and not only if the Communists take over." The "major problem" in the Western alliance, he continued, one that was overtaking U.S.-Western European differences, was "the domestic evolution in many European countries."[32]

It may be of interest to counterpose here a comment by Brezhnev on Portugal. The Soviet leaders were buoyed by the turn to the left in Portugal and the participation in the government of the Communist party of Portugal, one which followed Moscow's line. They saw the movement toward possible communist rule as a vindication of the possibility of peaceful transition to socialism under East-West détente. Brezhnev even contrasted this optimistic prospect with the recent defeat of the other principal case on which they had staked much hope—Salvador Allende's Chile. "Not the events in Chile," said Brezhnev, "but the events in Portugal lie in the general line of social development. The ultimate victory of the forces of democracy and progress is inevitable. (Applause)."[33] And the later failure of the far left, including the Communist party, in Portugal raised new questions (even if not asked publicly) in the Soviet Union.

Kissinger was also concerned about the other developments in western and southern Europe noted earlier, and about the development of Eurocommunism in the mid-1970s. Neither Kissinger nor Brezhnev was pleased when Georges Marchais of the French Communist party (PCF) joined Enrico Berlinguer of the Italian Communist party (PCI) in a joint statement in Rome in November 1975 that not only supported a "democratic path to socialism," but also opposed "all foreign intervention"—that is, Soviet or American inter-

31. See Szulc, *Foreign Policy*, no. 21 (Winter 1975-76), pp. 9, 44.

32. "Secretary Kissinger Interviewed for *L'Express* of France," April 12, *State Bulletin*, vol. 72 (May 12, 1975), p. 612.

33. L. I. Brezhnev, "Speech to Voters of the Bauman Electoral District of Moscow," June 14, 1974, in *O vneshnei politike KPSS i sovetskogo gosudarstva: Rechi i stat'i* [On the Foreign Policy of the CPSU and the Soviet Government: Speeches and Articles], 3d ed. (Moscow: Politizdat, 1978), pp. 403-04.

ference. On January 7, 1976, the Aldo Moro government fell after leaks in the press that the U.S. Central Intelligence Agency had spent six million dollars to support anticommunist candidates in the Italian elections. In April Kissinger publicly warned against the possibility of the PCI participating in a coalition government in Italy.[34] In July Brezhnev attacked the United States, Great Britain, France, and West Germany for influencing the Italian parties not to include the PCI in a government coalition by threatening to curtail financial ties.[35]

Kissinger's overall views, as expressed in a private and secret presentation in December 1975 to a meeting of American ambassadors assigned to European capitals, were leaked to the press in April 1976 and reluctantly confirmed.[36] He argued forcefully that if communist parties came to power in Western Europe, the NATO alliance as now constituted "could not survive" and "the foundation of our Atlantic security would therefore be eroded." Kissinger cited Portugal and Italy as situations that, while "not the result of detente or of Soviet policy," posed political problems for the United States and the West. He noted, "We cannot encourage dialogue with Communist parties within NATO nations," regardless of the existence of "fruitful relations" with Titoist Yugoslavia and "parallel policies" with Communist China. "The extent to which such a party [communist] follows the Moscow line is unimportant. Even if Portugal had followed the Italian model, we would still have been opposed. . . . the impact of an Italian Communist Party that seemed to be governing effectively would be devastating—on France, and on NATO, too." The accession to power of communist parties in Western Europe inevitably would create "a shocking change in the established patterns of American policy," Kissinger concluded.[37]

Kissinger's strictures on the perils of communist rule or even participation in the governments of NATO countries were backed by action in many ways. Contact by American embassies with local communist party members was strictly limited and controlled, a constraint that limited diplomatic reporting. The United States sought to prevent the legalization of the Communist party of Spain. Potential American interest in reducing Moscow's influence in the fragmented world communist movement, and in seeing a spread to Eastern Europe of the more liberal Eurocommunist influences, were subordinated to opposition to Eurocommunism. It was feared that Eurocommunism would make Western communist parties more palatable and attractive to the publics

34. "Secretary Kissinger Interviewed at Annual Meeting of the American Society of Newspaper Editors," April 12, *State Bulletin*, vol. 74 (May 3, 1976), pp. 567–69.

35. *Pravda*, July 30, 1976.

36. David Binder, "Kissinger Sees NATO End If Europeans Elect Reds" and "Summary of Kissinger Speech to U.S. Ambassadors," *New York Times*, April 7, 1976. The summary article presents the official text as distributed to embassies by the Department of State.

37. Ibid.; all quotations are from the official summary.

of Western countries. The United States gave a higher priority to the defensive purposes of protecting the Western alliance and American influence in it than to offensive interests in weakening Soviet influence in the East.

Eastern Europe, Eurocommunism, and Détente

While American concerns came to be focused on Western Europe, Soviet concerns were directed above all at Eastern Europe. There were signs of differing views within the Soviet leadership, some of whom evidently believed that Soviet pursuit of détente must take more account of the risks in Eastern Europe.

The European communist movement, West and East, from the late 1960s on was profoundly affected by two developments. One was the Soviet-led military intervention and suppression in 1968–69 of the liberal communist regime in Czechoslovakia led by Alexander Dubček and concomitant justification of that move by the Brezhnev Doctrine. The other was the movement toward détente in Europe. More generally, there was a Soviet attempt to tighten ideological orthodoxy and discipline *internally*—within the USSR, the socialist commonwealth in Eastern Europe, and the communist movement— precisely because of the parallel relaxation of political tensions *externally* through European détente. The inherent contradiction in the conduct of these two policies (there is no logical contradiction in the aim, in terms of Soviet interests) stems from the fact that the Western European communist parties are *Western*, as well as communist, while the Eastern European communist states are *European*, as well as communist, and represent states as well as parties. Moreover, the Western European and Eastern European communists interacted in many ways.[38]

Ideological, political, and geopolitical elements were involved in the skein of complex relationships, as is also true today. For example, in 1974 the Soviet ambassador in Paris ostentatiously paid a last minute preelection call on Giscard d'Estaing, clearly signaling Soviet support for him against the candidate of the left, François Mitterrand, although the latter was supported by the French Communist party. And the Italian Communist party not only criticized many aspects of Soviet internal and foreign policy, but opened its publications to Eastern European (and even Soviet) dissidents. The Spanish Communist party (PCE), legalized in 1977, soon formally discarded Leninism

38. See Vernon V. Aspaturian, Jiri Valenta, and David P. Burke, eds., *Eurocommunism between East and West* (Bloomington, Ind.: Indiana University, 1980), for a number of perceptive and informative discussions. See also Jiri Valenta, "Eurocommunism and Eastern Europe," *Problems of Communism*, vol. 27 (March–April 1978), pp. 41–54; and Richard Lowenthal, "Moscow and the 'Eurocommunists,'" ibid., (July–August 1978), pp. 38–49.

to become "Marxist and democratic." Soviet denunciation of the PCE did more to boost its standing in European leftist political circles (it remains weak in Spain) than to curb or punish it, as had been intended.

Eurocommunism was the term coined in 1975–76 to denote the new current of Western European communism that stressed independence of action for each party and embodied varying degrees of democratic and pluralistic tendencies. The term began to gain wide currency after publication of a book called *Eurocommunism and the State*, written by Santiago Carrillo, head of the Communist party of Spain, and published early in 1977.[39] The phenomenon, however, had been growing in the early and mid-1970s. A number of Western communist parties (including the PCI and the PCE) had forthrightly condemned the Soviet occupation of Czechoslovakia in 1968. Others (the PCF, initially) had criticized but also excused it, while still others (for example, the Communist party of Austria) split or expelled those who attacked the Soviet role. The open criticism of this action and the desire by these Western communist parties to distance themselves politically from the Soviet Union led to increased willingness to criticize other aspects of Soviet interparty, foreign, and even internal policies.[40]

Of particular relevance here is that, although the United States perceived Eurocommunism as threatening its interests in Western Europe, during the decade beginning in 1968 the Soviet Union came to see the United States as threatening its interests in Eastern Europe. In both cases East-West détente compounded the problem.

One consequence for détente was an odd congruence of American and Soviet positions in some cases: both opposed the legalization of the Communist party of Spain in 1976–77; both feared the rising influence of the Communist party of Italy in 1976; and both preferred center-right governments in France. These examples of congruence suggest that, conflicting American and Soviet interests notwithstanding, there was common ground. The United States may have preferred (although it would not have openly articulated the view) that the Western communist parties be (and be seen to be) aligned with the Soviet Union, while the Soviet Union may similarly have preferred to deal with capitalist Western European governments rather than hybrid or Eurocommunist ones. Most fundamentally, both Washington and Moscow may have preferred not to destabilize the East-West political equilibrium—they may not have wanted to see an independent pan-Europe based on local nationalism arise between them.

---

39. Santiago Carrillo, *'Eurocomunismo' y Estado* ["Eurocommunism" and the State] (Barcelona: Editorial Critica, 1977). Available in English as *Eurocommunism and the State* (Westport, Conn.: Lawrence Hill, 1978).

40. For a good, concise review, see Joan Barth Urban, "The West European Communist Challenge to Soviet Foreign Policy," in Roger E. Kanet, ed., *Soviet Foreign Policy in the 1980s* (Praeger, 1982), pp. 175–83.

During the preparations for the CSCE the Soviet leaders attempted to get a common platform supported by Western and Eastern European communist parties and were prepared to compromise on their preferred positions on some issues to gain a consensus. A series of meetings were held in 1974 (in Warsaw and Budapest) and 1975 (two in East Berlin). However, an undesired result was an alignment of Yugoslavia and Romania with the PCI and PCE on many issues. And by late 1975 the PCF came to embrace Eurocommunism.

Brezhnev had warned against "independent" "so-called 'Marxists,' " guilty of revisionism and nationalism, as early as the Twenty-fourth Party Congress in March 1971.[41] While the term Eurocommunism had not yet been coined, he described the concept well. Although he refrained then from criticizing any of the already independent-minded parties, he did name individuals expelled from some of them (such as Roger Garaudy in France and Ernst Fischer in Austria) who were guilty of holding views virtually the same (or even more moderate) than those of some of the Western European parties (for example, condemning the Soviet move into Czechoslovakia).

At the time of the Twenty-fifth Party Congress in February 1976 Brezhnev again tried to avoid a confrontation. He referred back to the 1969 conference of communist parties of the world and emphasized the need for "strengthening the unity of the whole movement." But he was acutely aware of the widening fissures among the European parties, to say nothing of the splits within the "world communist movement," even as he claimed that "many parties" were calling for a new world conference. He noted, without comment, that the European communist parties were preparing for their conference. He lashed out at "revisionism" on the left and right,[42] but did not attack Eurocommunism directly.

Brezhnev strongly endorsed the policy of détente, and in the context of détente in Europe he noted the need, notwithstanding the Helsinki Final Act (which was depicted as a great achievement for the foreign policy of the socialist states), "to wage a persistent struggle in order to make détente irreversible."[43] At the same time, the Soviet leaders were shocked by the strong independent and revisionist statements at the party congress by leaders of the communist parties of Italy, France, Britain, Sweden, and Austria, in addition to Nicolae Ceauşescu of Romania and Stane Dolanc of Yugoslavia.[44]

Because of the views expressed at the congress the Soviet leaders decided it was time to take off their gloves, as it were. Two weeks later Politburo member and senior ideologist Mikhail A. Suslov attacked Eurocommu-

---

41. Brezhnev, *O vneshnei politike*, p. 172.

42. Ibid., pp. 530–31.

43. Ibid., p. 519.

44. See chapter 16 for further discussion.

nists as "enemies of Marxism" and used a term used often thereafter to denote orthodox Moscow-aligned ideology—"real socialism"—as distinguished from sham socialisms.[45]

A European communist conference was held in East Berlin in June 1976, and it too led to a growing split in which the more orthodox, usually hard-line parties in the East and West aligned themselves against the more independent parties of Eastern and Western Europe. The split made agreement on a platform that could be used to instill greater discipline in the future impossible. Indeed, even to convene the conference the Soviet leaders had had to make far-reaching concessions, as reflected in the fact that the final statement from the conference recognized the right of each party to determine its own affairs.[46] Brezhnev was restrained in his own address.[47]

Again, the Soviet leaders were reduced to issuing unilateral statements of their position and to having trusted friends speak for them. Most notably, Communist party chief Todor Zhivkov of Bulgaria published an article in the Soviet-line international communist journal *Problems of Peace and Socialism* in December 1976 that denounced Eurocommunism as "anti-Sovietism" and as "subversion against proletarian internationalism."[48] As noted, in Suslov's speech of March 1976 the Soviet leaders and the orthodox Eastern European parties increasingly spoke of real socialism, a shorthand term that signified ideological and political alignment with the Communist party of the Soviet Union.

---

45. M. A. Suslov, "The Foremost Frontiers of Progress," *Pravda*, March 18, 1976. Suslov and his associate Boris Ponomarev had used the term "real socialism" before on two or three occasions in late 1974 and 1975. After 1976 it gained wider currency, for example, at a major international conclave of communist party ideologists and propaganda chiefs from seventy-three parties, held in Sofia, Bulgaria, in December 1978 (Ponomarev was the principal Soviet delegate).

46. The Soviet leaders had attempted to arrange a conference of all European communist parties to precede their own Twenty-fifth Party Congress but had not been able to do so. When the conference finally met, it brought together thirty-one European communist and workers' parties, which were all of them except the self-isolated parties of Albania and Iceland. The cost from the standpoint of the Soviet sponsors, however, was a free airing of highly critical and discordant positions. The statement and censored accounts of the proceedings were printed in *Pravda*, June 30 and July 1, 1976. By prior agreement the host East Germans had to print the full texts of all the statements, and did so in *Neues Deutschland* [The New Germany] (East Germany), June 30 and July 1, 1976.

47. Brezhnev, *O vneshnei politike*, pp. 540–50.

48. T. Zhivkov, "Year of Peace, Year of Struggle," *Problemy mira i sotsializma* [Problems of Peace and Socialism], no. 12 (December 1976), pp. 3–9. For the English-language version of the journal, see T. Zhivkov, "Year of Peace, Year of Struggle," *World Marxist Review*, vol. 19 (December 1976), pp. 3–9. The PCI replied sharply (see *L'Unita*, December 6, 1976), and the fractionation of views was evident when even Hungarian party chief Janos Kadar replied to a request by Western newsmen for comment on Zhivkov's article: "I do not share this view. The parties in the West act within specific conditions and this should be taken into consideration." Paul Hoffman, "Kadar Says Eurocommunism Is Not a New Anti-Sovietism," *International Herald Tribune* (Paris), December 9, 1976.

After 1977 the Soviet leaders began to deal with Eurocommunism in a different way. Instead of accepting the concept of an alternative Eurocommunist ideology, they have sought to deal with each party separately and to address individual issues as they arise. At the same time, to rally the parties the Soviets have pushed slogan concepts that are more difficult to challenge, such as real socialism. And Eurocommunism has in fact declined as a unifying or overarching mantle for the disparate Western parties, although the sharply differing approaches, criticisms, and conflicts have by no means diminished.

While peripheral to the immediate subject, it is necessary to note that the Soviet leaders themselves differed on how tactically to react to the growing challenge of Eurocommunism in the Western communist parties and to those parties' ties and potential influence on the parties ruling the Eastern European socialist states. (In the late 1960s there had been similar differences over how to react to the situation in Czechoslovakia in 1967–68 as well as to dissent within the Western parties.) In 1975 there were already diverging lines on nascent Eurocommunism in different Soviet commentaries. There has been no indication of firmly committed factions fighting over the issue, but evidently—and not surprisingly—it did become a political issue in the deliberations of the leadership and probably affected views on related matters concerning the application of the Soviet policy of détente to many East-West issues.[49]

Nor has the influence of Eurocommunism been limited to ideological and political maneuvering within the communist movement in the West and among communist leaders in the East. During the latter half of the 1970s the Western Eurocommunist parties increasingly commented on internal affairs in the communist countries of Eastern Europe and the Soviet Union itself. These parties even provided a forum for dissidents in the communist countries, raising a new and serious security problem for the leaders of these states.

The emergence of political dissidents in the Soviet Union and Eastern Europe who claim rights based on the Helsinki Final Act has posed a particularly serious problem for leaders in Eastern Europe and the Soviet Union. The Final Act provided a new basis for complaints by dissidents themselves, but more important it provided a basis (even if a contested one) for the expression of foreign interest. The Western countries, most strongly the United States, have used this opportunity in campaigns for human rights since the CSCE; this was especially true during the Carter administration. These actions posed a problem for the Soviet leaders. But they have used other provisos in the Final Act relating to noninterference in internal affairs to denounce attempted intervention by the imperialist powers, as discussed later.

The role of fraternal communist parties in the West in championing the rights of dissidents in countries of the Eastern bloc presents a different challenge. As early as the 1960s some Western communists, and even commu-

---

49. For a useful discussion, see Jiri Valenta, "Eurocommunism and the USSR," in Aspaturian, ed., *Eurocommunism between East and West*, pp. 108–21.

nist parties, spoke out against such events as the Soviet trial of Andrei Sinyav-sky and Yuly Daniel (protested in 1966 by the PCI and the PCF). The Prague Spring of 1968 in Czechoslovakia was a major factor in crystallizing Eurocom-munism, as many Western communist parties had welcomed Dubček's efforts to create "socialism with a human face." A coalition of seventeen Western European communist parties attempted to head off Soviet intervention in Czechoslovakia by actively lobbying against it. After the Soviets intervened, many Western communists and communist parties protested the Soviet inter-vention, and sought to mitigate later Czechoslovak efforts to suppress Dub-ček's reforms and the dissidents. The PCI in particular opened its publications to former Dubček reformers in exile or to writings smuggled out of the country (including those of Josef Smrkovsky, chairman of the National Assembly under Dubček, and Jiri Hajek, former foreign minister). A number of Eurocommu-nist parties lent material as well as moral support to the signers of Charter 77, the major Czechoslovak dissident challenge. It was signed by 242 leading intel-lectual figures and former political leaders, who demanded rights based on the Final Act. Hajek, a leading Charter 77 signatory, later confirmed the impor-tance of Eurocommunist support in the internal bargaining between Czecho-slovak dissidents and the authorities. (The hard-line Czechoslovak leader Vasil Bilák, in turn, served as a leading pro-Soviet opponent of Eurocommunism.) The PCI and other Western parties also supported Polish, East German, and Soviet dissidents (Roy Medvedev was among the latter) and published their writings. In 1976 Eurocommunist support for dissidence in Eastern Europe led the PCI to express concern over the measures in Poland to suppress the work-ers' disturbance of that summer. The PCI published an article in response to an open letter sent to it by the leading Polish dissident-activist, Jacek Kuron. These examples by no means exhaust the range of Western communist sup-port for dissidents.[50]

Thus détente, and especially the CSCE Final Act, encouraged dis-sidence both within Eastern Europe and the Soviet Union itself.[51] As in the Soviet Union, the leading dissidents in Eastern Europe came together to moni-tor compliance with the Final Act and to criticize shortcomings, and based their demands for civil rights on the Final Act. Most notable was the aforemen-tioned Charter 77 in Czechoslovakia.

The Soviet leaders had, of course, been wary of growing Western influence in Eastern Europe and the Soviet Union incident to the whole range

---

50. The examples cited above, and others, are to be found in Valenta, *Problems of Communism* (March–April 1978), pp. 41–54; and Eric Willenz, "Eurocommunist Perceptions of Eastern Europe: Ally or Advocacy?" in Aspaturian, ed., *Eurocommunism between East and West*, pp. 254–70, and see other chapters in that volume. Interestingly, Western European communists have avoided criticism of the suppression of human rights in Romania and Yugoslavia, evi-dently considering that independence from Soviet domination makes potholes on the "sepa-rate roads to communism" less in need of repair.

51. See chapter 16.

of widening contacts—economic, cultural, tourism, and others—under détente. The dissension in turn led to greater efforts to suppress or at least contain it— and in turn to further strains in Soviet relations with the Western powers, especially the United States.

With respect to the aims of American policy, the suspicion that such moves as President Nixon's visits to Romania, Poland, and Yugoslavia in 1969–72 caused in the Soviet Union was noted earlier. President Ford continued this practice by visiting Romania and Yugoslavia directly following the Helsinki CSCE summit in 1975. The United States also further normalized its relations with countries of Eastern Europe not only by recognizing East Germany in September 1974, but by seeking to settle outstanding claims (Hungary, March 1973; Czechoslovakia, July 1974, but not ratified by the U.S. Senate) and by reaching consular, cultural exchange, economic, and other agreements. Most-favored-nation trading status was granted to Romania in July 1975 and Hungary in July 1978, Poland and Yugoslavia already having it.

The principal Soviet concerns, however, were with longer-range American aims with respect to Eastern Europe. An address by Department of State Counselor Helmut Sonnenfeldt at the same conference of U.S. ambassadors to which Kissinger spoke was also leaked. It heightened Soviet suspicion, but in part because of widespread misinterpretation of Sonnenfeldt's remarks. He spoke specifically on American policy toward Eastern Europe, and his comments were promptly dubbed (initially by critics) the Sonnenfeldt Doctrine. The United States, he said, should "strive for an evolution that makes the relationship between the Eastern Europeans and the Soviet Union an organic one." This formulation was obscure, subject to the initial misinterpretation it swiftly earned that the United States endorsed and supported Soviet hegemony in Eastern Europe. In fact, he also said that the existing relationship was "unnatural" and that "our policy must be a policy of responding to the clearly visible aspirations in Eastern Europe for a more autonomous existence within the context of a strong Soviet geopolitical influence."[52]

While a far cry from public statements of American preference in the 1950s or even the 1960s, it was essentially a restatement of the position that underlay all American policy since the late 1950s under all administrations, with or without détente with the Soviet Union. (It had also been made to a conference of American ambassadors and was not intended for publication.)

It is sometimes suggested that the Nixon administration subordinated policy toward Eastern Europe to policy toward the Soviet Union. In the sense that American policy toward Eastern Europe was of lesser importance that observation was correct (it was also true under the preceding and subsequent administrations). But American policy toward Eastern Europe under Nixon's policy of détente was not fashioned to fit American-Soviet détente in

---

52. See "State Dept. Summary of Remarks by Sonnenfeldt," and David Binder, "A Modified Soviet Bloc Is Avowed as U.S. Policy," both in *New York Times*, April 6, 1976.

some way different from what it would otherwise have been and entailing greater sacrifice of Eastern European interests.

Improved terms for trade and economic relations were seen as the principal incentive the U.S. government could provide the countries of Eastern Europe. In 1973 the Nixon administration established internal policy guidelines that related economic incentives to desired conduct by the countries of Eastern Europe, seeking not only improved resolution of bilateral issues (for example, settlement of the claims of American citizens holding prewar government bonds as a prerequisite for consideration of possible MFN status and Export-Import Bank loans), but also "satisfactory" political conduct on international issues in which the United States had particular interest.[53] The connection between American policy and the relations of those countries with the Soviet Union was left implicit. The guidance did, however, establish a rank order for the Eastern European Warsaw Pact members, specifying a relative priority among them for commercial, cultural, and scientific agreements: those countries that were believed to hew to the Soviet foreign political line and internal political model most closely were at the bottom of the list.

Some aspects of Soviet-American relations have also impinged fairly directly on U.S. relations with Eastern Europe. For example, the congressional refusal to support the Nixon administration's trade relations policy in 1973–74, while directed against the Soviet Union, affected trade relations with Eastern European countries as well. If the negotiated agreement with the Soviet Union had passed without the crippling amendments, MFN would undoubtedly have been extended to the countries of Eastern Europe as well as to the Soviet Union.

The brouhaha over the Sonnenfeldt Doctrine in the spring of 1976 was followed by a notorious misstatement by President Ford during an election debate with Democratic presidential candidate Jimmy Carter on October 6. In discussing and defending the decision to sign the CSCE Final Act the year before, Ford responded to a newsman's comment about U.S. acceptance of Soviet domination in Eastern Europe. He said that the Final Act had not involved any agreement to such domination, but then went further and also said, "There is no Soviet domination of Eastern Europe." Referring to his own visits to Poland, Yugoslavia, and Romania he commented not only that "the United States does not concede that those countries are under the domination of the Soviet Union," but that he did not believe "the Poles consider themselves dominated by the Soviet Union." Carter challenged the point about actual Soviet domination. While the whole incident worked to Ford's disad-

---

53. These policy guidelines were laid down in a National Security Decision Memorandum, NSDM-212, on May 2, 1973, the text of which remains classified. See also an address by Deputy Secretary of State Kenneth Rush, "U.S. Policy toward Eastern Europe: Affirmative Steps," *State Bulletin*, vol. 68 (April 30, 1973), pp. 533–38.

vantage in the election campaign and confused the public understanding, it did not affect American policy.[54]

American interest in Eastern Europe and the U.S. approach to the countries in Eastern Europe has been predominantly influenced by considerations of the Soviet relationship to the area and to particular countries. The United States does not accept Soviet hegemony in Eastern Europe as a political right. At the same time, it does accept it as the prevailing political condition.

Both American and Soviet commentators sought to relate the Sonnenfeldt Doctrine to a "spheres of influence" division of American and Soviet hegemony in Western and Eastern Europe. The U.S. administration vigorously objected to this interpretation (as it did after the Ford statement). Soviet commentary took two different lines. Some commentators accepted the administration's explanations and blamed American opponents of détente for the leak and misinterpretation—"patently striving to cast a shadow over the process of normalization of relations between the United States and the Soviet Union, to sow mistrust and suspicion toward the policy of détente."[55] Other Soviet commentators characterized the Sonnenfeldt Doctrine as reflecting an official American attempt to enlist the Soviet Union in a trade of an Eastern European sphere of influence for the Soviet Union in exchange for an American sphere in Western Europe, Africa, and Latin America—an approach the Soviet Union flatly rejected.[56]

In fact, from the aftermath of the Hungarian revolution in 1956 through the 1960s the United States had abandoned even rhetorical policies of a "rollback" of communism and "liberation" and had established relations with the countries of Eastern Europe on the basis of the prevailing political situation. During the détente of the 1970s it developed these relations on a more normal basis. Paradoxically, by striving for less it achieved more in terms of actual American involvement and influence in the area.

Neither the United States nor the Soviet Union was prepared to articulate, or even fully to accept, a policy of dividing Europe into spheres of predominant superpower interest. But they recognized the political reality of a balance of power between the two counterposed alliances, and of the predominant power of the United States and the Soviet Union within them. The United States accepted the status quo in Eastern Europe in the mid-1970s, albeit as a base for peaceful change. At the same time, it opposed vigorously even some forms of peaceful change in Western Europe, as exhibited by the

---

54. See Ford, *A Time to Heal*, pp. 422–25.

55. V. M. Berezhkov, "The Fuss about the 'Sonnenfeldt Doctrine,' " *SShA: Ekonomika, politika, ideologiya* [The USA: Economics, Politics, Ideology], no. 8 (August 1976), p. 66.

56. See, for example, Henry Trofimenko, writing in the American journal *Foreign Affairs*, "The Third World and the U.S.-Soviet Competition: A Soviet View," vol. 59 (Summer 1981), p. 1028.

offensive against Eurocommunism and the possibility that communist parties might accede to power by parliamentary means in Portugal and possibly other countries in southern and western Europe. Implicitly, while it cautiously supported the possibility of change in Eastern Europe, the United States seemed to accept a predominant Soviet interest in its sphere, while forcefully reasserting the predominant American interest in Western Europe.

For its part the Soviet Union sought to strengthen the economic, political, and military relationships binding the Eastern European communist countries so that there would be an organic unity that would withstand the greater contact and interdependence between states of Eastern Europe and the West.[57] The efforts to integrate economic planning and build the network of Eastern economic ties beginning with the Council for Mutual Economic Assistance (CMEA) Comprehensive Plan of 1971 were described earlier. Beginning in 1972 Brezhnev held annual bilateral summit meetings with each of the Eastern European communist leaders in the Crimea, a practice that became a regular form of consultation. Similarly, the Warsaw Pact also developed more regular annual consultations at the foreign minister level, as well as occasional multilateral summit meetings. The military element of the alliance was adapted to the new system of consultation and coordination by regular meetings of the defense ministers; this came about after Romania had balked (and several other countries had been unenthusiastic) at earlier Soviet proposals for greater integration.

In addition to attempting to counter the inroads of Eurocommunism, the Soviet leaders also turned to high-level bilateral contacts in an effort to come to terms with centrifugal tendencies. Most notably, Brezhnev visited both Josip Broz Tito in Yugoslavia and Nicolae Ceauşescu in Romania in November 1976.

While ideological-political challenges were prominent, probably most basic was the economic one. Poland in the 1970s joined Romania (from the 1960s) and Yugoslavia (from the 1950s) in reorienting its trade more to the West than to the East, although that commerce was based on overextended

---

57. See Adam Bromke and Derry Novak, eds., *The Communist States in the Era of Detente, 1971–77* (Ontario: Mosaic Press, 1978); Charles Gati, ed., *The International Politics of Eastern Europe* (Praeger, 1976); Jan F. Triska and Paul M. Cocks, eds., *Political Development in Eastern Europe* (Praeger, 1977); Ronald H. Linden, ed., *The Foreign Policies of Eastern Europe: New Approaches* (Praeger, 1980); the chapter by R. Remington, "Moscow, Washington, and Eastern Europe," in William E. Griffith, ed., *The Soviet Empire: Expansion and Detente* (Lexington, Mass.: Lexington Books, 1976); Morris Bornstein, Zvi Gitelman, and William Zimmerman, eds., *East-West Relations and the Future of Eastern Europe* (London: Allen and Unwin, 1981); Andrzej Korbonski, "Detente, East-West Trade, and the Future of Economic Integration in Eastern Europe," *World Politics*, vol. 28 (July 1976), pp. 568–89; J. F. Brown, "Detente and Soviet Policy in Eastern Europe," *Survey*, vol. 20 (Spring–Summer 1974), pp. 46–58; Adam Bromke, "The CSCE and Eastern Europe," *The World Today*, vol. 29 (May 1973), pp. 196–206; and Adam B. Ulam, "The Destiny of Eastern Europe," *Problems of Communism*, vol. 23 (January–February 1974), pp. 1–12.

credit that proved by 1980–81 not to be viable. The warning signs of this economic overdependence had come earlier, including in particular the distur bances of 1976—at the very time an anonymous Polish communist leader was quoted as telling a Western newsman that "we Polish Communists have an ambition to play an important part in Europe, creating a mode of socialism acceptable to everyone, including our comrades in both directions."[58]

The Soviet Union tried in its own economic relations with Eastern Europe to help those countries adjust to new conditions. After absorbing the first impact of the energy crunch of the mid-1970s, in 1975 the Soviet Union began indexing its CMEA fuel transfer price to an average of world market prices over the preceding five years—a procedure that cushioned the shock to the countries of Eastern Europe but did not obviate their gradual adjustment. By the late 1970s the Soviet Union considered it necessary to decline to meet future increases in energy demand from Eastern Europe even on this basis.

Although little appreciated in the United States except by the few specialists on Eastern European economic affairs, the Soviet Union spent an estimated $80 billion subsidizing its Eastern European communist allies in the decade of the 1970s. During this same period, Eastern European indebtedness to the West increased nearly eightfold (from $9.3 billion in 1971 to $68.7 billion by 1979, of which over $20 billion was owed by Poland).[59]

The basic Soviet dilemma, which became increasingly clear in the mid-1970s, was that the Soviet Union and CMEA simply did not—and do not—have the economic resources needed to ensure economic progress and viability. On the other hand, turning to the West dilutes ties within the Eastern bloc and may create dependence on or preference for Western ties. (In addition, it may substitute, for a time, for needed internal economic reforms, stimulating both economic imbalance and political instability, as graphically demonstrated at the end of the decade in Poland.) The Soviet and Eastern European leaderships shared most of these concerns. While some differences do arise, both have a strong stake in assuring the continued viability of their countries as an end in itself, as a visible indication of their progress, and as the foundation for their political stability.

The other important consequence of détente for Eastern Europe and for East-West relations has been the diminished perception of a potential external threat. Noted earlier was the reduced fear that the Soviets and Eastern Europeans had of West Germany. More generally, détente loosened the cement of the Eastern alliance system insofar as it had been bolstered not only by Soviet power but also by a perceived latent Western threat, an especially important consideration in Poland and East Germany.

---

58. Cited by Malcolm W. Browne, "Poland Favors Linkage to Reds of East and West," *New York Times*, August 10, 1976.

59. See *East European Economic Assessment: Part 2—Regional Assessments*, a compendium of papers submitted to the Joint Economic Committee, 97 Cong. 1 sess. (GPO, 1981), p. 57.

It has not been the purpose of this discussion to analyze in detail Soviet–Eastern European relations, even in relation to U.S. interests.[60] It is, however, necessary to take into consideration this aspect of the development of East-West détente in Europe, and of the American-Soviet détente of the mid-1970s.

East-West détente in Europe in the 1970s developed across the board. Not only were the *Ostpolitik* agreements at the beginning of the 1970s significant in international politics, they also affected the daily lives of millions of people. The expansion of East-West trade directly affected the livelihoods of many Europeans, and affected them all indirectly. (The role of foreign trade and of East-West trade in particular in the economies of the Western European countries is much greater than for the United States.) Further, in 1977 6.8 million West Germans visited East Germany, while 1.3 million East Germans visited West Germany. By the end of 1976 over 60,000 East Germans had been permitted to emigrate to West Germany, and thousands of other ethnic Germans were being permitted to emigrate from the USSR. More widely, millions of Western European tourists visit Eastern Europe each year; less well-known is that by the mid-1970s more than one million tourists from Poland, Czechoslovakia, and Hungary visited the West (and all but a relative handful returned). The Iron Curtain was, at the least, not what it had been, despite the persistence of significant political differences. Significantly, comparatively few Americans visit Eastern Europe or vice versa.

Détente not only developed more widely in Europe than in the United States, but it also became much more of an organic process. The American-Soviet détente did not develop this characteristic, and the failure to grow deeper roots made it vulnerable later to currents of renewed confrontation.

Perhaps the most important aspect of East-West détente in Europe was that it contributed to the revival of a conception of Europe rather than the distinction between Western and Eastern Europe. This created certain ideological-political problems as it affected the communist movement (problems for both the Soviet Union and, as perceived, for the United States as well). Such developments as the CSCE certainly did not create the feeling of Europe as an entity, but they did contribute to it. Similarly, the absence of this feeling in the United States contributed to the largely indifferent and sometimes hostile American reaction to the CSCE Final Act, in notable contrast to the enthusiasm in Europe. Countries of Western and Eastern Europe again saw, and dealt with, one another in the first instance as countries sharing the geography and history of a great continent, even if also as members of adversarial alliances. The Soviet Union, too, as a European power, shared a certain perspective with the other countries of the continent. In contrast the United

---

60. See Raymond L. Garthoff, "Eastern Europe in the Context of U.S.-Soviet Relations," in Sarah Meiklejohn Terry, ed., *Soviet Policy in Eastern Europe* (New Haven: Yale University Press, 1984), pp. 315–48.

States, even during its phase of détente, saw Europe principally as a theater of U.S.-Soviet political engagement—of preeminent importance, but still one of several global theaters of economic, political, and military involvement. As American-Soviet détente declined, the American estrangement from the East-West détente in Europe, and to some degree from Europe itself, grew, although it did not become evident until the end of the decade.

15 Competition in the Third World: Angola, 1975–76

CHARACTERISTICALLY, the first real test of restraint in American-Soviet competition in the third world under détente was initiated by events neither planned nor foreseen by either superpower. Competition throughout the first half of the 1970s continued to be keen. The October War in the Near East had posed only a pseudoconfrontation, although the impact of the crisis created a real trial for détente. The first direct clash of competing American and Soviet drives for influence was their support of conflicting sides in an armed internal struggle for power in Angola in 1975–76. Angola became a test for American-Soviet détente because it involved a conflict of interests of the two sides, but more significantly because it exposed their divergent conceptions of détente.

Developments in Angola

The event that triggered the Angolan crisis was the Portuguese revolution which erupted in April 1974. Portugal's colonies in Africa (together with East Timor and Macao in East Asia) represented virtually the last of the European overseas colonial empires. After April 1974 independence for these colonies was no longer in question. Rather, in Angola the immediate issue was which of the contending factions would gain power. (By contrast, the unified, indigenous anticolonial movements in each of the other African colonies— Guinea-Bissau, Cape Verde, São Tome, and Mozambique—succeeded to power peacefully and easily during 1974–75.) A broader issue—the one of interest here—was not even clear at the outset, although the seeds of trouble were there: would one of the global powers see its interests damaged by the victory of a local contender supported by the other power? What would it portend for the nature of the competititon of the superpowers in the future? The stakes were not Angola itself, or even the influence the other side would gain from a

502

victory of the faction it favored. Rather the issue *became* the rules of competition under détente, a matter that was in no one's mind until much later.

In the aftermath of the Portuguese revolution those groups aspiring to control in Angola and outside powers with an interest in the outcome began to maneuver. The three main contending indigenous groups were the Popular Movement for the Liberation of Angola (MPLA), the Front for the National Liberation of Angola (FNLA), and the National Union for the Total Independence of Angola (UNITA). Each had a main tribal connection and its own ideological inclination, and within each were additional rivalries among individual leaders and cliques that played a strong part as well. Each also had its own, sometimes fluctuating, support from outside powers.[1]

At the time of the change in the Portuguese government the MPLA, headed by Agostinho Neto, was the most westernized of the three movements, with a European (Marxist-Leninist) ideology. Because of an internal power struggle, it had recently been cut off from earlier modest Soviet support. One faction, under Daniel Chipenda, that broke off from the MPLA briefly received some Soviet as well as Chinese support before gravitating into

---

1. There is substantial literature on the Angolan situation of 1975–76. Of particular value here is the major study by Arthur Jay Klinghoffer, *The Angolan War: A Study in Soviet Policy in the Third World* (Boulder, Colo.: Westview, 1980). Another basic work is John A. Marcum, *The Angolan Revolution*, vol. 2: *Exile Politics and Guerrilla Warfare (1962–1976)* (Cambridge, Mass.: MIT Press, 1978), pp. 241–81. Also very useful is Charles K. Ebinger, *Foreign Intervention in Civil War: The Politics and Diplomacy of the Angolan Conflict* (Boulder, Colo.: Westview, 1984); and Bruce D. Porter, *The USSR in Third World Conflicts: Soviet Arms and Diplomacy in Local Wars, 1945–1980* (Cambridge University Press, 1984), pp. 147–81. See also Suzanne Jolicoeur Katsikas, *The Arc of Socialist Revolutions: Angola to Afghanistan* (Cambridge, Mass.: Schenkman, 1982), pp. 55–84. Jiri Valenta has written several useful articles, of which the most complete and documented is Jiri Valenta, "Soviet Decision-Making on the Intervention in Angola," in David E. Albright, ed., *Communism in Africa* (Bloomington, Ind.: Indiana University Press, 1980), pp. 93–117. That same volume contains several other relevant chapters, in particular Edward Gonzalez, "Cuba, the Soviet Union, and Africa," pp. 145–67; and George T. Yu, "Sino-Soviet Rivalry in Africa," pp. 168–88. Particularly useful on American policy is Gerald Bender, "Kissinger in Angola: Anatomy of Failure," in René Lemarchand, ed., *American Policy in Southern Africa: The Stakes and the Stance*, 2d ed. (Washington, D.C.: University Press of America, 1981), pp. 63–143; Bender has contributed several other useful articles on the subject. Colin Legum has written several articles; see in particular his chapter on "Angola and the Horn of Africa," in Stephen S. Kaplan, ed., *Diplomacy of Power: Soviet Armed Forces as a Political Instrument* (Brookings Institution, 1981), pp. 573–605. Finally, *Angola*, Hearings before the Subcommittee on African Affairs of the Senate Committee on Foreign Relations on U.S. Involvement in the Civil War in Angola, January 9, February 3, 4, and 6, 1976 , 94 Cong. 2 sess. (Washington, D.C.: Government Printing Office, 1976), is a very useful source. (Hereafter *Angola*, Hearings.) Two accounts by official American participants are of particular note: Nathaniel Davis, "The Angola Decision of 1975: A Personal Memoir," *Foreign Affairs*, vol. 57 (Fall 1978), pp. 109–24 (Ambassador Davis resigned as assistant secretary of state for African affairs because of U.S. policy in Angola); and the informative account of the disillusioned chief of the CIA Angola Task Force in 1975–76, John Stockwell, *In Search of Enemies: A CIA Story* (W. W. Norton, 1978). Other studies and sources dealing with particular aspects of the Angolan situation, such as the Cuban role, are cited later.

the FNLA. Cuba had been, and remained throughout, the principal support of the MPLA. It also received some financial and other assistance from Algeria, from a number of Western European governments and socialist parties, and from the Communist party of Portugal. Its greatest domestic support was among the educated, the mulattos, and Portuguese-speaking Angolans. Its principal base for operations into the country was in the leftist People's Republic of the Congo (Congo-Brazzaville) just north of Angola.

The FNLA, headed by Holden Roberto, had long been receiving a subvention from the CIA, although in recent years a modest one. Roberto was married to the sister-in-law of President Mobutu Sése Sékó of Zaire (originally installed in that office a decade earlier by the CIA), and he and the FNLA were highly dependent on Zaire, where their base of operations was located. In addition, the FNLA received material support from Algeria, Morocco, Tunisia, India, China, and Romania (as well as the Ford Foundation and the AFL-CIO). The FNLA had by far the largest military contingent of the three groups. Its chief support within Angola was the Bakongo tribe along the border with Zaire.

UNITA, headed by Jonas Savimbi, had broken off from the FNLA. It had the largest active base in Angola, concentrated in the south, and drew support mainly from the Ovimbundu tribe there. It cooperated closely with the Namibian nationalist Southwest African People's Organization (SWAPO), which also operated from southern Angola but into Namibia. It was the most antiwestern or nativist faction, sometimes even racist, in its local appeals, especially against the cosmopolitan MPLA. It had the least outside ties or support, and that came mainly from China.

The Organization of African Unity (OAU) and some Western church groups such as the World Council of Churches had provided modest support to all three groups.

The new Portuguese government ceased all offensive military actions against the Angolan opposition in May 1974 and arranged cease-fire agreements with UNITA in June and with the MPLA and FNLA in October. All three movements opened offices in Luanda, the capital of Angola, in November 1974. They also began to scramble for power. The FNLA and the MPLA sent forces into Angola from Zaire and the Congo, respectively. The FNLA in particular made an attempt to seize power in Luanda in November,[2] while the MPLA drove out a smaller rival in Cabinda that same month.[3] There

---

2. See Klinghoffer, *The Angolan War*, p. 15; and see footnote 19, pp. 159–60, where several sources are cited, including the eyewitness account of a Swedish correspondent, Per Wästberg, who also reports that General Vernon A. Walters, the Portuguese-speaking deputy director of the CIA, was in Luanda and was involved. See also Per Wästberg, in *Dagens Nyheter* (Stockholm), March 11, 1975. The FNLA may not, of course, have been entirely to blame for the eruption of fighting in Luanda.

3. See Marcum, *The Angolan Revolution*, pp. 253–54. The defeated group was the Front for the Liberation of the Enclave of Cabinda (FLEC), a secessionist group representing the geographi-

was considerable bloodletting. Eventually the members of the OAU (especially President Jomo Kenyatta of Kenya) succeeded in getting Neto, Roberto, and Savimbi to meet in Kenya in early January 1975. At an ongoing meeting in Alvor, Portugal, on January 15 they agreed to tripartite collaboration with the Portuguese in a transitional government, to be formed at once. It was also to take over power from Portugal on November 11, 1975. The Alvor accord was the high point of efforts to achieve a peaceful and cooperative succession to independence.[4]

With respect to the outside powers during this period, the Portuguese in Angola were one element. While a massive return to Portugal of white colonists, many born in Angola, soon began (bringing with them to Portugal a right-wing political activism), the attitudes of the governing Portuguese military officials in Angola were of some significance. Their views were mixed, although on the whole the lame duck Portuguese administration in 1974 and much of 1975 reflected the leftist inclination of the Portuguese government at home and favored the MPLA. Nonetheless, they supported the Alvor accord. After September 1975, again reflecting the change in Portugal itself, the Portuguese government was less favorable to the left. In addition, many individual Portuguese directly aided each of the three Angolan movements during 1975; in particular, a number of former Portuguese secret police and colonial officials joined up with the FNLA.

All the outside powers bestirred themselves after the Portuguese revolution and end of the colonial war, as the contest for power in independent Angola grew. The first to move actively were the Chinese, who, beginning in June 1974, sent a substantial quantity of arms and 120 military advisers to the FNLA in Zaire.[5] In July the CIA began to increase covert funding to the FNLA.[6] By October–November the Soviet Union resumed funding and pro-

---

cally separate oil-rich exclave of Cabinda. Sympathetic Portuguese troops aided the MPLA, but most Portuguese officials and forces remained aloof.

While Congo-Brazzaville supported the MPLA and served as the conduit for Soviet and Cuban arms and military assistance to the MPLA during this period, its president, Marien Ngoubai, also supported one faction of the FLEC in the hopes of securing Congolese influence in Cabinda. This Congolese-MPLA conflict of interest remained through the summer of 1975 and even led to some restraint on the Soviet supply of arms to the MPLA through Congo-Brazzaville. See Klinghoffer, *The Angolan War*, p. 58; and Charles K. Ebinger, "External Intervention in Internal War: The Politics and Diplomacy of the Angolan Civil War," *Orbis*, vol. 20 (Fall 1976), p. 689.

4. Klinghoffer, *The Angolan War*, pp. 14–15.

5. Marcum, *The Angolan Revolution*, pp. 245–46. Neto had visited Beijing in December 1973 and obtained Chinese agreement to provide arms and military instructors even before the Portuguese revolution; see Valenta, in *Communism in Africa*, p. 98. The Department of State confirmed these crucial early Chinese actions; see *Angola*, Hearings, pp. 184–85.

6. Stockwell, *In Search of Enemies*, pp. 66–67.

vided a limited quantity of small arms to the MPLA.[7] By the time of the Alvor accord in January 1975, all three powers had increased their support. In addition, Romania and Libya began to supply arms to the FNLA.[8]

In January 1975, at the time of the Alvor accord, the general military strength of the competing forces totaled roughly 10,000–20,000 for the FNLA, 6,000–8,000 for the MPLA, 2,000–3,000 for UNITA, and 2,000–3,000 for Chipenda (soon to affiliate with the FNLA). Potential support within Angola was more difficult to judge.[9]

Just one week after the Alvor accord, the American secret intelligence and covert operations committee (then called the 40 Committee) met and decided to provide $300,000 to the FNLA.[10] While not enough to affect the situation in material terms, it was a sign of continuing support by the United States *after* the Alvor accord. This funding in turn encouraged the Soviets to maintain their support for the MPLA, although they would probably have done so in any case.

More important, it encouraged Roberto to make a bid for power despite the Alvor accord. In February and March 1975 the FNLA moved in force into Angola from Zaire and opened a military campaign against the MPLA. A motorized column of 500 men arrived in Luanda from Zaire. They openly attacked the MPLA headquarters in Luanda and killed fifty to sixty people at an MPLA training camp at Caxito. In April the FNLA broadened its

---

7. The principal source on Soviet support in the latter part of 1974 is a rather vague assertion to that effect by the Department of State in a response supplied to the Senate after a hearing on Angola; it did, however, establish that some direct supplies had arrived by November. The State Department also asserted that the supply of Soviet arms began in August, but did so on the basis of inference—assuming that $6 million worth of arms openly shipped to Dar es Salaam to the OAU "for African liberation movements" in August presumably had gone to the MPLA. *Angola*, Hearings, p. 184. The OAU was, in fact, supporting all three factions in Angola as well as other national liberation movements elsewhere. If some of those arms reached the MPLA, they were from the OAU. The slanted State Department version of the Soviet arms supply presented after the hearings has been picked up by others; for example, see Marcum, *The Angolan Revolution*, p. 253. Klinghoffer, *The Angolan War*, p. 17, more correctly dates initial Soviet arms supply to October 1974. And the chief of the CIA Angolan Task Force in 1975–76 notes, "Only in March 1975 did the Soviet Union begin significant arms shipments to the MPLA." Stockwell, *In Search of Enemies*, p. 68.

8. See Marcum, *The Angolan Revolution*, p. 246.

9. Klinghoffer, *The Angolan War*, pp. 15–16, and Marcum, *The Angolan Revolution*, p. 257, cite various estimates. The military contingents of the three groups had their own designations—FAPLA for the MPLA, ELNA for the FNLA, and FALA for UNITA.

10. Davis, *Foreign Affairs*, vol. 57 (1978), p. 110; and Stockwell, *In Search of Enemies*, p. 67. The earlier July 1974 subvention was made from CIA funds, without 40 Committee authorization. The original source of the information on the 40 Committee action, later confirmed, was Seymour M. Hersh, "Early Angola Aid by U.S. Reported," *New York Times*, December 19, 1975.

attacks on the MPLA.[11] The FNLA did not succeed in defeating the MPLA militarily, but its attempt to seize power was probably the principal blow in upsetting the delicate attempt to get the three groups to share power and compete politically.

By March, and continuing over the next several months, Soviet arms for the MPLA began to arrive in quantity both via Congo-Brazzaville and to a lesser extent directly to Angola with passive Portuguese acquiescence. Clearly these arms, most of which arrived by ship, had been dispatched much earlier. The Soviet decision to send them presumably preceded the American funding in January 1975, although it probably followed the military efforts of the FNLA in November.[12] Further Soviet increases in arms supplies to the MPLA during the summer of 1975 were, however, influenced by the active bid for power by the FNLA, supported by the Chinese and Americans, beginning in March. Thus, while the limited Soviet assistance in 1974 and early 1975 had been granted after the Chinese and American support for the FNLA in the summer of 1974, the further step-up in assistance in 1975 was probably designed to assist the MPLA to stay in the game. As Kissinger later testified, the administration interpreted the Soviet arms supply to the MPLA from 1974 through much of 1975 as "merely part of an effort to strengthen that group so it could compete militarily with the much stronger FNLA."[13]

By April 1975 another element entered the picture. The MPLA recruited the 3,000–6,000-man Kantangese irregular force that had been in Angola ever since it fled Zaire in 1964. The Portuguese had maintained this force and used it against the Angolan nationalist guerrillas. The Katangese joined forces with the MPLA because of their strong opposition to Mobutu and hence to his Angolan clients, the FNLA.[14] They were committed to combat after the introduction of regular Zairian troops into Angola in July.

Another, much more significant development occurred in May 1975. Following the March battles Neto turned to Havana, sending an emissary at the beginning of April. By early summer some 230 Cuban military advisers had joined the MPLA.[15] Later in the summer after the July battles,

---

11. See Marcum, *The Angolan Revolution*, pp. 257–59; Valenta, in *Communism in Africa*, p. 101; and Klinghoffer, *The Angolan War*, p. 17.

   The FNLA had just been augmented by Chipenda's adherence, following MPLA attacks on his dissident forces in February. This adherence gave the FNLA its first foothold in the south-central part of Angola. See Marcum, *The Angolan Revolution*, p. 258.

12. See Marcum, *The Angolan Revolution*, p. 259; and Klinghoffer, *The Angolan War*, p. 17. The March fighting, however, may well have prompted some hundred tons of Soviet arms flown in by chartered civil aircraft in April.

13. Kissinger, in *Angola*, Hearings, p. 52.

14. Marcum, *The Angolan Revolution*, p. 259.

15. Ibid., p. 273; and see Valenta, in *Communism in Africa*, pp. 100–01.

the MPLA reportedly turned to the Soviet Union for support in the form of military advisers and specialists, but the Soviets advised them to call again on Cuba.[16] The Soviet leaders were sympathetic but unwilling to involve themselves so directly.

Throughout this turbulent period in the first half of 1975, the so-called transitional government in Luanda continued to exist, though not to function very effectively, in the shadow of a diminishing Portuguese administration. In mid-June a number of African leaders persuaded Neto and Roberto to meet again in Kenya, where they negotiated a new agreement, the Nakuru accord. The transitional government even came up with a draft constitution in late June and created the first company of a new unified Angolan national army.[17] The accord was, however, weak from the start.

On July 9 heavy fighting broke out and spread rapidly. By mid-July the MPLA had expelled the FNLA and UNITA from Luanda. The FNLA, reinforced with some regular Zairian troops, scored a few successes (most notably the seizure of Caxito after a small battle, under the leadership of a former Portuguese counterinsurgency lieutenant colonel). But the MPLA scored unexpectedly well and soon had the FNLA on the run in the north and UNITA limited to the south.[18] The balance of military power was suddenly and rapidly shifting from the FNLA to the MPLA, despite the fact that the FNLA and UNITA had begun collaborating. It was at this juncture that the external powers again considered the situation.

Kissinger later testified that in July Zaire and Zambia "turned to the United States for assistance in preventing the Soviet Union and Cuba from imposing a solution in Angola, becoming a dominant influence in south-central Africa, and threatening the stability of the area."[19] Given that the presence of Cuban advisers was only confirmed in July, this concern over the Cuban and Soviet role was mainly anticipatory. Mobutu and Kaunda were concerned over a leftist regime supported by the Soviets coming to power on their borders. As will be seen, American concern had a broader foundation. But in any case Soviet support and a Cuban role were evident, and the MPLA was forging ahead.

In late May an interagency NSC Task Force on Angola was set up under the assistant secretary of state for African affairs, Ambassador Nathaniel

16. See Marcum, *The Angolan Revolution*, p. 443, footnote 257; William J. Durch, "The Cuban Military in Africa and the Middle East: From Algeria to Angola," *Studies in Comparative Communism*, vol. 11 (Spring–Summer 1978), p. 64; and Christopher Stevens, "The Soviet Union and Angola," *African Affairs*, vol. 75 (April 1976), pp. 143–45.

17. Marcum, *The Angolan Revolution*, p. 260.

18. Ibid., pp. 260–63. The MPLA also strengthened its position in Cabinda in June and July against renewed stirrings by the FLEC.

19. "Implications of Angola for Future U.S. Foreign Policy," Statement by Secretary of State Kissinger, January 29, *Department of State Bulletin*, vol. 74 (February 16, 1976), p. 177. (Hereafter *State Bulletin*.)

Davis. This task force made its report on June 13.[20] The principal thrust was that the United States should work with all powers involved, including the Soviet Union, to support OAU and Portuguese efforts already under way, and should seek to rechannel factional competition toward a political solution, relying heavily on the African states to contribute to that end. Efforts should also be made to prevent a great power confrontation. The risks of overcommitment of U.S. prestige in a doubtful course was one strong reason why the task force recommended against covert military intervention.[21] In essence, the task force was suggesting diplomatic efforts to encourage a political settlement among the three contending Angolan factions, and it opposed direct or indirect military intervention.

Prior to an upcoming NSC meeting and before the report was circulated, Kissinger directed that the recommendation of the task force be made but one of three options—the others being no involvement, and substantial military intervention—in order to provide more leeway in forming some other compromise solution.[22]

On June 27 the NSC itself met and discussed the situation in Angola. By early July Kissinger decided to shelve the NSC channel and return to the 40 Committee. It had not met on Angola since a January meeting that authorized the modest funding for the FNLA (but not UNITA). This time the CIA was assigned to write an options paper for a meeting of the committee on July 14; in effect it was being invited to draft a proposal for covert action. By this time, it will be recalled, the situation in Angola was deteriorating rapidly (from the standpoint of FNLA and UNITA).

Ambassador Davis wrote a strong critique of the CIA proposal for covert action on grounds of risks, costs, improbability of success, and negative consequences of the attempt—and its likely disclosure. He also questioned the premises of the plan, such as the argument that further arming the FNLA and UNITA would "discourage further resort to arms and civil war." And he stressed the absence at the time of an "irrevocable commitment of U.S. power and prestige in Angola" and warned that the proposed course would tend to establish that commitment. The CIA paper itself noted that the Soviet Union "can escalate the level of their aid more readily than we." Davis argued that even "if we are to have a test of strength with the Soviets," which he did not believe necessary, "we should find a more advantageous place."[23]

On July 14 the 40 Committee met—without Ambassador Davis being invited. Kissinger asked the CIA to provide a revised covert action plan within forty-eight hours, and on July 17 the 40 Committee again met to con-

---

20. Not to be confused with the separate internal CIA Angola Task Force, or similar groups within the Departments of State and Defense, in 1975–76.

21. Davis, *Foreign Affairs*, vol. 57 (1978), pp. 111–13.

22. Ibid. Davis has provided a valuable account of his own perspective.

23. Ibid., pp. 113–16.

sider it. It was approved by President Ford on July 18, and he authorized the disbursement of $6 million on July 18, another $8 million on July 27, $11 million in August, and $7 million in November. In addition, arms nominally valued at $16 million were provided pursuant to the July 18 decision. By July 29 weapons were being flown from the United States to Zaire for the FNLA.[24] Ambassador Davis, his recommendations rejected, resigned as assistant secretary of state for African affairs after only four months in the post.[25]

Also in mid-July the Chinese authorized Zaire to release to the FNLA large stocks of arms supplied earlier by China to Zaire.[26] The Chinese also sent a shipment of arms for UNITA to Dar es Salaam, but they were not permitted to transship through Tanzania for Zambia.[27] By this time the North Korean military instructors with the Zairian army were also training FNLA troops.[28] That faction also received a shipment of arms from Romania in August.[29] In mid-July, encouraged by the signs of new American support, Mobutu committed several units of his own Zairian paracommandos to combat in An-

---

24. Ibid., pp. 116–17; and Stockwell, *In Search of Enemies*, p. 55. Each of these accounts has a few errors or uncertainties relating to dates and other such details; the precise details given here are based on these and other sources. The $32 million authorized from July to November did not include the additional arms and military equipment, alleged to be worth $16 million. Because the arms and military equipment had been declared surplus, they were greatly undervalued. The House Select Committee on Intelligence estimated the real value of the military ordnance as at least double the nominal $16 million. See Bender, in Lemarchand, *American Policy in Southern Africa*, p. 87; and Klinghoffer, *The Angolan War*, p. 83. For discussions of the way the CIA disbursed the funds (under a program code-named IA FEATURE) see Stockwell, *In Search of Enemies*, pp. 206–12, 263–68, and many other passages; and Stephen R. Weissman, "CIA Covert Action in Zaire and Angola: Patterns and Consequences," *Political Science Quarterly*, vol. 94 (Summer 1979), pp. 283–84.

25. Davis, *Foreign Affairs*, vol. 57 (1978), pp. 117–19. The reason for his resignation, and the first, and well-informed, account of the action of the 40 Committee, surfaced publicly some six months later; see Seymour M. Hersh, "Angola-Aid Issue Opening Rifts in State Department," *New York Times*, December 14, 1975.

   Ambassador Davis's predecessor, Ambassador Donald Easum, had served only nine months, from March to December 1974, before Kissinger fired him for taking too favorable a stance toward the countries of Black Africa and for fostering peaceful change in southern Africa. Easum had voiced these views and on a tour of Africa had succeeded in arranging to be the first foreign diplomat to visit the new transitional FRELIMO government in Mozambique. Within forty-eight hours of Easum's return to Washington he was sacked. Davis, who had had little African experience and had served as ambassador to Chile at the time of the coup against Allende, had questioned his own selection for the post, but Kissinger had insisted.

26. Ebinger, *Orbis*, vol. 20 (1976), p. 689, based on interviews with officials of Zaire at the time.

27. Marcum, *The Angolan Revolution*, p. 265. The MPLA had close ties with the Mozambican FRELIMO, which influenced President Nyerere.

28. See Klinghoffer, *The Angolan War*, pp. 107–08.

29. Stockwell, *In Search of Enemies*, p. 67. Romania had in fact given material support to all three groups.

gola, marking the first introduction of third-country combat troops into the civil war in Angola.[30] In July South Africa began to supply arms and advice to UNITA and the FNLA (Chipenda faction).[31]

As these new infusions of outside aid for the FNLA and UNITA were being undertaken, by late July the MPLA had succeeded in securing control over twelve of the sixteen provinces of Angola.

By September the tide began to turn again. UNITA had in effect declared war on the MPLA and formed an alliance with the FNLA, dashing MPLA and Soviet hopes that a deal could still be struck with UNITA to isolate the FNLA.[32] In early August South Africa had begun to mount incursions of its own regular forces into southern Angola.[33] In mid-September Mobutu escalated Zairian intervention by committing two additional paracommando battalions. Eventually a mixed force of about 1,500 Zairian and FNLA troops, reinforced by Portuguese Angolans, began a slow advance on Luanda from the north.[34] All parties, with an eye to the approaching date for independence, November 11, were seeking maximum gain by positioning themselves to seek recognition as the government of Angola.

As a result of the push by the FNLA and UNITA and their outside supporters, the MPLA drive began to falter. At about this time, however, Havana was reaching a key decision about intervention, presumably in consultation with Moscow. By late September or early October it sent several hundred additional Cuban military specialists and advisers by air, along with the first 700 Cuban troops. No large-scale Cuban intervention was, however, anticipated by the United States—nor, perhaps, had it yet been planned.[35]

In October a critically important new development occurred. On October 23 the South Africans escalated their intervention by mounting a

---

30. Davis, *Foreign Affairs*, vol. 57 (1978), p. 121.

   A professional Soviet military analysis of local wars attributed the escalation of the Angolan war to include foreign intervention to this introduction of Zairian troops, regarded as Western proxies ("detachments of imperialist mercenaries"). See Major General V. Larionov, "Certain Questions of the Military Art from the Experience of Local Wars," *Voyenno-istoricheskii zhurnal* [The Military Historical Journal], no. 4 (April 1984), p. 48.

31. The new and growing tie between UNITA and the South Africans in August led to a break between UNITA and SWAPO; SWAPO then turned to the MPLA and sought Soviet support. See Klinghoffer, *The Angolan War*, p. 44; and Marcum, *The Angolan Revolution*, p. 277.

32. See Valenta, in *Communism in Africa*, p. 104.

33. Klinghoffer, *The Angolan War*, pp. 44–46, 50–51.

34. Stockwell, *In Search of Enemies*, p. 163.

35. Robin Hallett, "The South African Intervention in Angola, 1975–76," *African Affairs*, vol. 77 (July 1978), p. 355; and Durch, *Studies in Comparative Communism*, vol. 11 (1978), pp. 64–67. As to the American expectation, the chief of the CIA Angola Task Force met disbelief and silence when he suggested to the interagency Working Group in September that rather than just these few hundred, they should think in terms of 10,000–15,000 Cuban troops. But there was no intelligence to this effect. See Stockwell, *In Search of Enemies*, p. 170.

major thrust toward Luanda itself ("Operation Zulu"). About 2,000–3,000 South African regular troops (a contingent later doubled), accompanied by several thousand UNITA and FNLA (Chipenda) troops and a group of white Angolan and European mercenaries, moved north. By mid-November this force was at Novo Redondo, 500 miles north of the border and not much more than 100 miles from Luanda. The FNLA remained, although stymied, north of Luanda. The MPLA was reduced to control of Luanda and only three of the sixteen provinces, including the exclave of Cabinda.[36]

On November 7 Cuba began a major expansion of its direct military assistance to the MPLA, with a large-scale infusion of Cuban troops ("Operation Carlota").[37]

Initially the dispatch of the Cuban expeditionary force was handled entirely by Cuban aircraft and ships. After the United States successfully pressed Barbados and other countries not to allow Cuban transfer flights, in November–December the Soviet Union provided Cuba with longer range IL-62 aircraft, and in January began direct airlift of Cuban troops.[38] In addition, beginning November 13, after Angolan independence, a small number of Soviet military advisers arrived.[39]

On November 11, the day of independence, and prior to the large-scale Cuban military intervention, the MPLA, backed by Cuban artillerymen and Soviet-supplied 122 millimeter multiple rocket launchers of World War II fame, had defeated the FNLA-Zairian-Portuguese Angolan forces north of Luanda, with devastating effects on their morale.[40]

---

36. In early November Mobutu had made a second attempt to seize Cabinda, invading with a mixed FNLA-FLEC-Zairian force of about 3,000, with direct CIA arms support, but the MPLA, backed by Cuban advisers, defeated the attempt. Stockwell, *In Search of Enemies*, pp. 162–68, describes the attempt and the CIA support. Marcum, *The Angolan Revolution*, p. 274, suggests it was a diversionary move by Zaire to aid the FNLA attack against Luanda, but it is far more likely that Mobutu saw this as his last chance to seize Cabinda before the independence of Angola.

37. The most complete and apparently informed account of the Cuban initiative and actions to support the MPLA, by a sympathetic Colombian communist, is Gabriel García Márquez, "Operation Carlota: Cuba's Role in Angolan Victory," *Venceremos* [We Will Triumph], vol. 4 (February 1977), pp. 1–8 (cited by Klinghoffer, *The Angolan War*, pp. 110–35). A brief account is available in "Colombian Author Writes on Cuba's Angola Intervention," *Washington Post*, January 10, 1977. His account is, however, not reliable.

38. See Durch, *Studies in Comparative Communism*, vol. 11 (1978), pp. 65–69.

39. Ibid., p. 68. Various newspaper accounts and other sources noted here reported the earlier presence of Soviet advisers, but in fact the Soviets were scrupulous about not introducing their own military advisers until Angola was juridically independent. Many of the reports stemmed directly from a CIA disinformation campaign. See Stockwell, *In Search of Enemies*, p. 194; he cites as one specific early example David Ottoway, "Angola Group Claims Capture of 20 Russians, 35 Cubans," *Washington Post*, November 22, 1975, which alleged the presence and even capture of Soviet military advisers in September.

40. This battle is graphically described, on the basis of accounts by eyewitness CIA observers, by Stockwell, *In Search of Enemies*, pp. 213–15. The Zairian big guns—two North Korean 130

From the latter half of November to early January 1976 the MPLA, with growing Cuban military support in the field, pursued the retreating FNLA-Zairian troops in the north and stopped the South African advance in the south. By this time Cuban troops were arriving in substantial numbers. By the end of December they numbered about 7,000, by the end of January an estimated 10,000–12,000.[41]

American attempts through the CIA to recruit European mercenaries were quite ineffective.[42] The most significant consequence was later embarrassment and additional friction when several captured mercenaries, including an American, were executed.

By the end of February the MPLA had defeated its enemies and controlled all the important centers. The only remaining serious resistance came from UNITA guerrillas in the bush in the south and southeast. By March the war was over.[43]

Arguments have been advanced pro and con whether the South African advance into Angola in October prompted the Cuban military intervention. It seems quite likely that the earlier, more limited military intrusions by South Africa that began in early August, and its material support to UNITA and FNLA beginning in mid-July, were among the factors leading the MPLA to turn to Cuba for more extensive assistance. Cuba must, however, have made its initial decision to provide combat troops prior to the South African invasion on October 23.[44] The later decision to send substantial additional troops in November and subsequently probably was influenced by South Africa's deep incursion. In general the Cuban decisions on increasing military support to the MPLA were probably incremental and not made in terms of a single overall program. That support went from a few hundred advisers in the summer, and elements of Fidel Castro's "special reserve" armored division in September–October, to large combat units from November on.[45]

---

millimeter artillery pieces—misfired and blew up. The only reason the MPLA victory was not more effective was that the MPLA troops failed to follow through with a more audacious and rapid advance.

41. Davis, *Foreign Affairs*, vol. 57 (1978), p. 122.

42. Stockwell, *In Search of Enemies*, pp. 182–85, 220–26.

43. The general outline of these developments is well-known and widely recorded. An interesting brief military account of the Angolan civil war is included in a Soviet text on local wars by the Academy of the General Staff; see General of the Army I. Ye. Shavrov, ed., *Lokal'nye voiny: istoriya i sovremennost'* [Local Wars: History and Contemporary Times] (Moscow: Voyenizdat, 1981), pp. 193–200. American and Chinese support for the FNLA and UNITA, and South African and Zairian intervention, are noted. Soviet support is acknowledged, but the Cuban role is reduced to a single sentence about the participation of "Cuban volunteers." Ibid., p. 197.

44. See Valenta, in *Communism in Africa*, p. 111.

45. See Durch, *Studies in Comparative Communism*, vol. 11 (1978), pp. 64–69.

The Cuban military role in Angola has been interpreted by some, including Washington at the time, as a surrogate or "proxy" role on behalf of the Soviet Union. Cuba contends that its decision to aid the MPLA was entirely its own. Certainly the Cubans had maintained closer and more consistent support for the MPLA than had the Soviet Union. Most students of the Angolan war have concluded that Cuba acted on its own, but as an ally of the Soviet Union and in consultation with it. There is no evidence that the Soviet leaders applied any pressure on Cuba, and there are many indications, apart from the claims of Castro and other Cuban officials, of Cuban initiative. The Soviets clearly decided at least to support the Cuban assistance; what is unknown, but doubtful, is that they urged it.[46]

The question of whether the major Cuban military intervention was a reaction to South African military intervention is more difficult to answer. It is, however, not as important an issue as those who blame South Africa and exculpate Cuba, and those who insist the Cuban intervention came first, both contend. Both countries had been involved in less direct ways long before. It is probably more useful to see the major Cuban and South African escalations as roughly coincidental in time, but independent in execution. The political effect, however, was clear: in the eyes of most Africans the South African intervention excused the Soviet-supported move by Cuba. It was also seriously damaging politically to the FNLA and UNITA movements supported by the United States and China.

China extricated itself relatively early, washing its hands of the entire affair. As early as June the Chinese informed the FNLA that they would terminate financial support and that their military instructors would remain only until independence day, November 11.[47] The Chinese had been disillusioned by the very poor showing of the FNLA in Angola. In September Chinese Foreign Minister Qiao Guanhua was publicly cited as saying that the Chinese had ceased to send arms once a date for independence had been set. On October 27 all Chinese military advisers were openly withdrawn from Zaire. The Chinese also ceased to support UNITA. The first phase of this Chinese disengagement was based on a recognition that the FNLA was ineffective and on a desire not to be too closely linked with impending defeat. But the sharper break, marked by the ostentatious withdrawal of the advisers, was based on a determination not to be associated with the side collaborating with

---

46. See ibid., pp. 34–74, for an extensive review; William M. LeoGrande, *Cuba's Policy in Africa, 1959–1980* (Berkeley, Calif.: University of California Press, 1980), pp. 15–22; Abraham F. Lowenthal, "Cuba's African Adventure," *International Security*, vol. 2 (Summer 1977), pp. 3–10; Jorge I. Dominguez, "Cuban Foreign Policy," *Foreign Affairs*, vol. 57 (Fall 1978), pp. 96–98; Legum, in Kaplan, *Diplomacy of Power*, pp. 578–79; Klinghoffer, *The Angolan War*, pp. 109–20; Marcum, *The Angolan Revolution*, pp. 272–74; Katsikas, *Arc of Socialist Revolutions*, pp. 76–77, 81–82; and Valenta, in *Communism in Africa*, pp. 110–12.

47. Bender, in Lemarchand, *American Policy in Southern Africa*, p. 107; and Klinghoffer, *The Angolan War*, p. 105. This decision was reported to Washington at the time from American intelligence in Zaire.

South Africa.[48] The Chinese believed their credibility with other Africans would be compromised by any association with South Africa and that the loss of influence in Angola (also probably unavoidable) was far less important. Moreover, the FNLA was losing not because of any shortages of arms and support—which in any case the United States was supplying by midsummer— but because it was incompetent. When by late summer, the earlier Chinese efforts to aid UNITA had been stymied, UNITA had turned to South Africa for support (as had Chipenda's FNLA-affiliated group in the south). Later, it became clear that no Chinese (or American) military move was going to counter the Soviet-supported Cuban military intervention, while a South African connection was unacceptable no matter how effective. In short, despite their long-standing involvement, the Chinese cut their losses and disengaged even before the large direct Cuban intervention.

The United States reacted quite differently. Actively engaged in support of the FNLA and UNITA in an attempt to head off success by the Soviet-supported MPLA, the United States behind the scenes welcomed the South African intervention.[49] The massive escalation of Cuban participation with the support of the Soviet Union increased the stakes greatly, from Washington's perspective, and intensified its interest in defeating the Soviet-supported forces.

By November the administration had exhausted CIA and other available funds, and it had to turn to Congress. It made a request for an additional $28 million, to supplement the approximately $32 million already spent. Initially the matter was raised with great secrecy, but it quickly leaked to the press. By December there was a strong movement in Congress to oppose the administration's request for further covert support, and ultimately it banned any further American covert aid for Angola. The Senate passed this ban on December 19, 1975, by a vote of 54 to 22, while the House of Representatives passed its version by 323 to 99 on January 27, 1976. On February 9 President Ford reluctantly signed the legislation into law rather than have his veto overridden. The United States was no longer in a position to influence the situation in Angola by nominally covert action.[50]

---

48. See Marcum, *The Angolan Revolution*, pp. 264–65; Klinghoffer, *The Angolan War*, pp. 105, 107; and Valenta, in *Communism in Africa*, p. 103.

49. This fact was denied or obscured by official American statements at the time and thereafter (for example, see Kissinger, in *Angola*, Hearings, p. 53, and Schaufele, in ibid., p. 176), but it has subsequently been brought out in unofficial accounts by well-informed participants and scholars. See, for example, Klinghoffer, *The Angolan War*, pp. 45, 53–54; and Stockwell, *In Search of Enemies*, pp. 185–90.

50. See Bender, in Lemarchand, *American Policy in Southern Africa*, pp. 96–104. This legislation did not, however, prevent some continued support through funds and arms in the pipeline. Stockwell reports that some $5 million was still in hand and that as late as January the White House was trying to transfer other CIA funds for this purpose. On February 11, after the law was in effect, the CIA offered Savimbi of UNITA another $1 million, and on February 18 Kissinger cabled the American chargé in Zaire to promise continued American support to

Secretary of State Kissinger, President Ford, and others argued that the congressional action tied the hands of the United States and permitted the Soviet- and Cuban-supported MPLA to win.[51] It is, however, highly unlikely that congressional approval of the administration's request for an additional $28 million for Angola would have made any difference in the outcome, although it might have delayed it. Money and arms could not have stopped the Cubans. The congressionally mandated cutoff of further American support did, however, have some effects. For one, the South Africans soon decided to pull out their forces.[52] For another, it probably encouraged the Cubans to continue to help the MPLA. From December 9 to 25 the Soviets had suspended their support for the movement of additional arms and Cuban troops to Angola.[53] Resumption of Soviet air transport of Cubans just a few days after the Senate action does suggest that the Soviets no longer saw any need for restraint. (It was also in mid-December that the story of earlier American covert action in Angola leaked dramatically in the American press.)

In restrospect, the United States would have been better advised to have emulated the Chinese in disengaging from a lost cause.

On November 11 the rival factions had made separate declarations of independence and had formed rival governments—the MPLA in Luanda, and the FNLA and UNITA in Huambo. Most countries—including some African ones—had held back from recognizing either at that time. Because of the South African intervention in October–November, however, Nigeria, Ghana, Tanzania, the Sudan, and a number of other African states soon recognized the People's Republic of Angola (PRA) proclaimed by the MPLA.[54] The rival FNLA-UNITA government was never really organized and dissolved in a new short-lived internecine war in which the FNLA (Chipenda faction) in the south was defeated by UNITA and disintegrated. In early January the OAU, meeting at Addis Ababa, split evenly—twenty-two countries voting to recog-

---

UNITA, even though he knew it would not be possible to provide it. Stockwell, *In Search of Enemies*, pp. 233–35. Stockwell also recounts the messy process of disengaging from commitments to mercenaries, with pay-offs to avoid public scandal. Ibid., pp. 240–54.

51. President Ford strongly criticized Congress, saying that it "has unfortunately tied our hands" and permitted the MPLA victory. For example, see "President Ford's News Conference of December 20," *State Bulletin*, vol. 74 (January 19, 1976), pp. 77–78; and "The President's Remarks and a Question and Answer Session in the East Room," February 25, *Weekly Compilation of Presidential Documents*, vol. 12 (March 1, 1976), p. 288. (Hereafter *Presidential Documents*.) See also *State Bulletin*, vol. 74 (February 16, 1976), pp. 175–76; "Secretary Kissinger's News Conference of February 12," ibid. (March 8, 1976), p. 289; and Gerald R. Ford, *A Time to Heal: The Autobiography of Gerald R. Ford* (Harper and Row, 1979), pp. 358–59.

52. Stockwell, *In Search of Enemies*, p. 232.

53. See the statement in Senate hearings by Assistant Secretary of State for African Affairs William E. Schaufele, Jr., "The African Dimension of the Angolan Conflict," February 6, *State Bulletin*, vol. 74 (March 1, 1976), p. 280.

54. Marcum, *The Angolan Revolution*, p. 272.

nize the People's Republic of Angola, twenty-two favoring efforts to continue to work for a government of national unity. Not one African state advocated recognition of the FNLA-UNITA government or either component. Within six weeks, forty-one of the forty-six members of the OAU had granted the PRA recognition, and on February 11, 1976, the OAU recognized and accepted it into membership.[55] Portugal followed suit with recognition on February 22.

Remnants of the FNLA continued to exist for a time within Angola. Savimbi's UNITA managed to maintain a more successful and continuing guerrilla movement in the bush in south-central Angola. In February 1976 President Neto met Mobutu, and they signed an accord under which both countries agreed not to support opponents of the other, although this undertaking was not fully observed.[56] In late March the PRA and South Africa reached an agreement, following which the last South African troops in southern Angola withdrew.

Soviet relations with the PRA developed on a broad basis, leading to a twenty-year Treaty of Friendship signed on October 8, 1976, and ratified early the next year. Cuban relations with the PRA also developed well. In the spring agreement was reached on a gradual reduction of the Cuban troops in Angola from the 17,000 present by March, and reductions began in late May. About a year later, however, they ceased, and there was even an augmentation in 1977–78 to about 19,000, following an internal crisis within the MPLA leadership and external threats from South Africa and Zaire.[57]

The United States continued to give the PRA a very cold shoulder. In June 1976 the United States vetoed Angola's application for membership in the United Nations, although in a later vote in November it abstained. (The principal reason for the difference was that on the earlier occasion President Ford was unwilling, in the midst of a preconvention contest with Ronald Reagan, to appear soft on the Soviet-Cuban-Angolan connection. After the convention and the election more attention was given to the serious disadvantages of antagonizing broad African sentiment on the issue.)

One other development in the aftermath of the Angolan war is significant. As noted earlier, there were severe factional strains within the MPLA before the war, and these strains reemerged. Neto had the advantage of having led the party to victory, but he came under criticism from two directions. On the one hand there was an ultraleftist element that opposed the close connection with the Soviet Union and Cuba. It was responsible for a series of

---

55. Klinghoffer, *The Angolan War*, pp. 64–65. The United States worked, diplomatically and covertly, at Addis Ababa to prevent recognition of the PRA.

56. Ibid., p. 142.

57. Ibid., pp. 131–35.

   South Africa soon began incursions, sometimes deep into Angola, to attack SWAPO camps. On the Zairian border there were occasional crossings in both directions that escalated in March 1977 into a short-lived invasion of the Shaba province of Zaire by the Katangese. The Shaba invasion is discussed in chapter 19.

strikes and demonstrations, but this movement was effectively suppressed.[58] The other opposition was more difficult to deal with. It favored populist, antiwhite black power against the educated, multiracial elements in the party that supported Neto and encouraged white Angolans to remain or return. The leader of this faction, Nito Alves, also favored a more pro-Soviet and anti-Western line than that pursued by Neto. For example, the Neto government continued to honor the Gulf Oil Corporation operations in Cabinda. (Throughout the war Gulf had maintained excellent relations with the MPLA and had been protected by it against the Front for the Liberation of the Enclave of Cabinda (FLEC). Until the U.S. Department of State compelled Gulf to cease payments in December 1975, it had continued paying royalties to the MPLA. It resumed them after the war.) Alves wanted to nationalize the Gulf Oil installations, and he wanted closer ties to the Soviet Union.

Neto did not take Alves with him when he visited the Soviet Union in October 1976, and when he returned, he removed Alves as minister of the interior. In May 1977 Alves was expelled from the MPLA for creating a faction. That faction then made an armed bid for power. Despite the racist stand of Alves and his followers, they were joined by white Angolan-Portuguese communists (some of whom had returned to Angola after the unsuccessful communist insurrection in Portugal in November 1975). The coup succeeded in killing seven of the thirty-three members of the party Central Committee and many other officials, but was ultimately suppressed.[59]

The opposition and coup attempt by Alves was notable, but even more remarkable was the Soviet role. It is clear that the Soviets would have been happy to see Alves gain power, and there is reason to conclude that Alves believed he had Soviet support, as he was in close and constant contact with Soviet officials and intelligence officers in Luanda.[60] Students of Angolan affairs have tended to conclude that the Soviet Union knew of the Alves plot and failed to alert Neto, but avoided any incriminating connivance or support. While consistent with the known facts, that conclusion goes beyond them; the truth is simply not known. The Soviet reaction to the affair was cautious. The Soviets never criticized Alves, even after belatedly (four days later) congratulating Neto on suppressing the "anti-government action."[61]

The Cuban role stood in marked contrast. Castro had always expressed strong support for Neto. The Cuban press had reported the expulsion of Alves before the coup attempt and attacked him by name as the leader of

---

58. Ibid., p. 127. Ironically it included the Angolan Communist Organization.

59. Ibid., pp. 127–29. See also Gerald J. Bender, "Angola, The Cubans, and American Anxieties," *Foreign Policy*, no. 31 (Summer 1978), pp. 23–26; and LeoGrande, *Cuba's Policy in Africa*, p. 25.

60. A Soviet diplomat in Luanda had been expelled in the summer of 1976 reportedly for plotting with Alves, who was still minister of the interior at that time. See Bender, *Foreign Policy*, no. 31 (Summer 1978), pp. 25–26.

61. Klinghoffer, *The Angolan War*, pp. 28–31.

the rebellion after the coup. But Cuba did much more than just voice its support (which was personally carried by Raúl Castro on a visit soon after), Cuban troops directly participated in suppressing the pro-Soviet Alves forces, playing an important and possibly crucial role.[62]

The Alves affair cemented Angolan-Cuban relations, but led Neto to be cool in relations with the Soviet Union. If the Soviet leaders had had, as was often surmised in the United States, any designs on establishing military bases in Angola, or supplanting the United States' oil and other Western economic interests in the country, they were disappointed.[63] Since then Angolan policy has been based on a general political alignment with the Soviet Union and reliance on the continued presence of Cuban troops to prevent major external attack, but has also included encouragement for diplomatic and trade ties with the West. All major Western powers except the United States, as well as China, established diplomatic ties, and all including the United States developed economic relations. This policy continued under President José Eduardo dos Santos, who succeeded Neto when he died in 1979.

The American Perspective

It is not easy to recapture the perspective of a time that preceded a later intense experience. Thus it is difficult in retrospect to recall the extent of the lack of American interest in developments in Angola before mid-1975.[64] Kissinger and the administration were much more concerned over possible communist inroads in Portugal (and southern Europe as a whole) during most of 1974 and 1975 (as well as, of course, over many other problems in the world). It was not until the large-scale Cuban military intervention in November and December of 1975, supported by the Soviet Union, that the administration raised the question of the possible incompatibility of such actions with détente.

---

62. This action is well-established and has been indirectly confirmed by Neto and the Cubans. See ibid., p. 131.

63. In an interview with the *New York Times* Angolan Prime Minister Lobo do Nascimento made a point of denying that the Soviet Union had requested, or that the PRA would grant, military bases in Angola. This statement, and others by Neto, were intended not only to reassure the United States, but also to head off possible Soviet requests. See Michael T. Kaufman, "Angolan Leftist Charges U.S. with Economic War," *New York Times*, February 1, 1976. Later, Soviet naval reconnaissance aircraft were permitted to use the airport at Luanda from time to time, and naval ships have made port calls, as in other countries, but no Soviet naval or other military bases have been established.

64. One interesting and relevant indicator is that the CIA station in Luanda and even the station in Lisbon had both been closed in an economy drive shortly before the 1974 Portuguese revolution and eruption of civil war in Angola.

There was another reason that the United States had not seen, or posed, the situation in Angola in terms of a possible impact on its relations with the Soviet Union. The United States had, until July 1975, believed its "protégé," the FNLA, would win in Angola. Doubts and concern followed the clashes in March and the influx of Soviet arms after that time. By June and July the NSC and 40 Committee had decided to provide the extensive covert military assistance discussed earlier. Initially it was expected that this counter to the Soviet arms supply would assure a continuing favorable balance for the FNLA. Although later administration statements imply that the American objective throughout had merely been to assure shared participation by all contending Angolan groups, that position really was a fallback that arose only after the MPLA forged ahead in the summer of 1975. After that point sharing power would have meant bringing in the FNLA and UNITA; earlier it was believed they could assume power without having to cut in the MPLA.

Thus for the period from the spring of 1974 to the summer of 1975 the United States considered competition with the Soviet Union in Angola normal behavior under détente. It was only when the American-backed FNLA slipped from a position of superior strength (insofar as it could be measured, at that time, in terms of numbers of men under arms), and the possibility grew that the Soviet-backed, leftist MPLA might gain power, that the United States saw the competition with the Soviet Union as objectionable.

The United States had first sought to bolster the FNLA by the initial $300,000 grant immediately after the Alvor accord calling for joint participation in government. The American client, the FNLA, opened hostilities in March, and the first external intervention with foreign troops occurred when regular Zairian army forces entered Angola in July in support of the FNLA. Washington regarded these actions as appropriate competition.

The second reason for the relative American lack of concern until the latter half of 1975 was low stakes. Direct American economic or strategic interests were minimal. As Kissinger stated in November 1975, "The United States has no national interest in Angola."[65] Nor, for that matter, did the United States even object especially to the MPLA; as Kissinger frequently commented later, the United States would not have involved itself in a purely internal struggle in Angola—it did not oppose the coming to power of the similarly leftist FRELIMO in Mozambique.[66] To be sure, FRELIMO had received more support from China than from the Soviet Union and was not regarded as being as beholden to the Soviets. But until the mutual escalation of support in 1975 the Soviet Union was not actively aiding the MPLA (whose leaders, indeed, resented the earlier Soviet cutoff of assistance). In testimony in December 1975, Director of Central Intelligence William E. Colby stated that

---

65. "Questions and Answers Following the Secretary's Pittsburgh Address," November 11, *State Bulletin*, vol. 73 (December 1, 1975), p. 768.

66. "Secretary Kissinger's News Conference at San Francisco February 3," *State Bulletin*, vol. 74 (February 23, 1976), p. 219, and see p. 213.

there was little difference among the contending Angolan groups—all were "independents" and leftists. When asked why, in that case, the United States (and the Chinese) favored the side it did, he replied: "Because the Soviets are backing the MPLA is the simplest answer."[67]

The American stake in the Angolan situation was not *threatened* by the Soviet-Cuban involvement on the other side, it was *created* by it. Kissinger's first comment on the Angolan civil war and first veiled criticism of the Soviet and Cuban role came in a speech on September 23, 1975, when he remarked, "Events in Angola have taken a distressing turn, with widespread violence. We are most alarmed at the interference of extracontinental powers who do not wish Africa well and whose involvement is inconsistent with the promise of true independence."[68] By November 10 he referred specifically to both the Soviet Union and Cuba as the "extracontinental powers" providing arms and, in the Cuban case, advisers as well. At this time Kissinger also first voiced the idea that the United States regarded this outside interference as "a serious matter" and "as far as the Soviet Union is concerned, not compatible with the spirit of relaxation of tensions."[69] Two weeks later he was saying that the United States "cannot ignore" the Soviet involvement and supply of arms and "cannot be indifferent while an outside power embarks upon an interventionist policy—so distant from its homeland and so removed from traditional Russian interests."[70] When asked what his comments really meant, he explained that "it is difficult to reconcile this [Soviet involvement] with the principles of coexistence that were signed in 1972, and this would have to be taken into account by our policy if it continues."[71] Kissinger also warned that "continuation of an interventionist policy must inevitably threaten other relationships" between the two powers.[72] President Ford, agreeing with Kissinger the next day, said the Soviet actions were "not helpful in the continuation of

---

67. Cited by Bender, in Lemarchand, ed., *American Policy in Southern Africa*, p. 105. The CIA Director of African Affairs, James Potts, said the same thing to Senator Gene Tunney of California. Ibid.

 Incidentally, by mid-1975 Gulf Oil Corporation had concluded not only that the MPLA would win the civil war, but also that it was the only contender that could provide a stable government in Angola. Many congressmen were swayed by Gulf's open support for the MPLA and opposition to U.S. support for the other rival factions. See ibid., p. 140.

68. "The United States and Africa: Strengthening the Relationship," September 23, *State Bulletin*, vol. 73 (October 13, 1975), p. 574.

69. "Secretary Kissinger's News Conference of November 10," *State Bulletin*, vol. 73 (December 1, 1975), p. 777. See also "Secretary Kissinger's News Conference of December 23," ibid., vol. 74 (January 19, 1976), p. 69.

70. "Building an Enduring Foreign Policy," November 24, *State Bulletin*, vol. 73 (December 15, 1975), p. 843, and see p. 844 on the Cuban role. Kissinger repeated this theme to a NATO meeting on December 12; and "Secretary Kissinger's News Conference after North Atlantic Council Meeting," ibid., vol. 74 (January 12, 1976), p. 54.

71. "Secretary Kissinger's News Conference at Detroit on November 25," *State Bulletin*, vol. 73 (December 15, 1975), p. 860.

72. *State Bulletin*, vol. 73 (1975), p. 843.

détente," and on later occasions he said they were "not constructive from the point of view of détente" and were "inconsistent with the aims and objectives of détente."[73]

It is clear from these statements that beginning in the latter part of 1975 the administration was publicly arguing that the Soviet Union and Cuba were "outside," "extracontinental," "distant" powers without "traditional interests" in Angola and had no business interfering there by supplying military assistance. On the other hand, although just becoming publicly known, the United States had been covertly supplying military assistance—and thus fit those very descriptions. The argument that Soviet actions could be considered incompatible with détente and threatening to American-Soviet relations more generally was intended to give Moscow pause, but hardly reflected an application of rules of the game for competition under détente to which the United States itself had subscribed.

Beginning only in late October the United States raised the matter directly with the Soviet Union. Kissinger brought the situation in Angola up with Dobrynin three times in late October and November, President Ford once in December. Rather remarkably, these representations had an effect: from December 9 to 25 the Soviet Union suspended its delivery of arms by air to the MPLA (although the Cubans continued their assistance).[74]

Why did the United States not raise the question of external involvement with the Soviets before late October 1975? The reason is that both countries were engaged in precisely the same kind of covert arms supply and military training, and the U.S. leadership believed until late 1975 that the side it was backing would win. Moreover, from the spring of 1975 on, the United States had been assisting Zaire in its intervention and had at least not objected to South African intervention from August 1975 on. It was the escalation from Cuban advisers to Cuban troops in October and November (though still only in limited numbers at the time) that raised American concerns. It was then the United States began privately and publicly to warn the Soviet leaders against further support.

In December, just after Congress refused to permit further covert American support to the Angolan opponents of the MPLA, Kissinger first made comments at a press conference that directly addressed the overall relationship with the Soviet Union: "As far as our relations with the Soviet Union are concerned, we consider the [Soviet] actions in Angola incompatible with a relaxation of tensions, and they are certain to affect our relationship unless a diplomatic solution is found."[75]

---

73. "President Ford's News Conference of November 26," *State Bulletin*, vol. 73 (December 22, 1975), p. 895; and "President Ford Interviewed for NBC Television," ibid., vol. 74 (January 26, 1976), pp. 103, 100.

74. Kissinger, in *Angola*, Hearings, p. 52. Dobrynin also called on December 9 to reply to the earlier representations.

75. "Secretary Kissinger's Press Conference of December 23," *State Bulletin*, vol. 74 (January 19, 1976), p. 69.

That warning, curiously, was made nearly two weeks *after* the Soviet Union had ceased to airlift Cuban troops. Clearly it was prompted not by any new Soviet action but by awareness that Congress would not permit further American covert intervention to match or trump the Soviet and Cuban actions. Two days later the Soviets resumed their air transport of Cubans.

In January 1976 Kissinger renewed public pressure on the Soviet Union. He said, "The essence of the U.S.-Soviet relationship, if it is to proceed toward a genuine easing of tensions, is that neither side will seek to obtain unilateral advantages vis-a-vis the other, that restraint will govern our respective policies."[76] That note rang hollow after well over a year of covert military assistance by *both* sides in competing efforts to gain advantage at the expense of the other. It could scarcely have been expected to impress the Soviet leaders.

Kissinger and Ford wanted to restrain the Soviet-Cuban involvement, but by January 1976 they were not able to escalate or even threaten counteractions in Angola. So they had to look elsewhere. They had in effect two possible sticks—a cutoff of grain sales or holding back on SALT, both of which represented palpable Soviet interests. Both, however, were also *American* interests, too important to sacrifice in an attempt to restrain Soviet involvement in Angola.

American leverage in trade had, as noted, been drastically undercut by the Jackson-Vanik amendment that had sought to compel the Soviet leaders publicly to accept American conditions on emigration practices. Grain remained the major and growing item of trade. A new long-term trade agreement on grain supply had just been signed, and President Ford was not going to court the certain strong objections of the farm interests in an election year by upsetting that arrangement and their expectations. In a major speech to the American Farm Bureau Federation on January 5 President Ford assured his audience (and the Soviets) that his administration would not cut off grain over Angola. "The linkage of grain" to diplomacy, he said, would mean hardship to the American farmer and "a serious increase in tensions between the world's two superpowers," and would have "no effect whatsoever in Angola."[77] Kissinger sounded the same theme, arguing that "economic measures take too much time to affect a fast-moving situation like Angola."[78]

The other potential lever was SALT. But as Kissinger repeatedly stated in December and January, that was no solution. In his words, "As for the Strategic Arms Limitation Talks, we have never considered these to be a favor which we grant to the Soviet Union to be turned on and off according to the ebb and flow of our relations. The fact is that limiting the growth of nuclear

---

76. "Secretary Kissinger's News Conference of January 14," *State Bulletin*, vol. 74 (February 2, 1976), p. 125.

77. "President Ford Addresses American Farm Bureau Federation, January 5," *State Bulletin*, vol. 74 (January 26, 1976), p. 99.

78. For example, *State Bulletin*, vol. 74 (February 16, 1976), p. 180.

arsenals is an overriding global problem that must be dealt with urgently for our own sake and for the sake of world peace."[79] Kissinger did, however, warn the Soviets of an adverse impact on SALT, as well as détente, if there were no restraint: "Still, we have made clear that a continuation of actions like those in Angola must threaten the entire web of Soviet-U.S. relations. In this sense, both [SALT] negotiations and the overall relationship are in long-term jeopardy unless restraint is exercised."[80]

While attempting to place some pressure on the Soviet leaders without sacrificing major détente programs, the administration also found it necessary to defend détente against its critics. They were delighted to seize upon Soviet "lack of restraint," and the administration's admission of it, as a basis for attacking détente itself. Kissinger acknowledged this concern in a background briefing for the press off the record.[81]

Kissinger's real concern was not Angola at all. He maintained throughout that the United States had no real (much less vital) interests in Angola and was not even greatly concerned over the accession to power of a "Marxist," "pro-Soviet" group. What *did* trouble him was that the MPLA was winning against increasingly obvious U.S. efforts to prevent that outcome and, above all, *with* Soviet and Cuban "proxy" military aid.

In his testimony to the Senate on January 29 Kissinger stressed: "The United States must make it clear that Angola sets no precedent; this type of action will not be tolerated elsewhere."[82] He did not make the mistake of the succeeding administration and label as "unacceptable" existing situations that the United States could not control. But he did say: "Angola, we have stressed since November, is a pattern of behavior that the United States will not accept—that if continued it will have serious consequences for any possibility of easing of relations with the Soviet Union. . . . This is a pattern which, as one looks at other parts of the world, would have the gravest consequences for peace and stability."[83]

Kissinger was deeply concerned over the precedent and pattern because it involved Soviet initiative, use of military means, use of a proxy, and prospective success. But Kissinger was equally concerned because it represented

---

79. Ibid.

80. Ibid. See also *State Bulletin*, vol. 74 (February 2, 1976), pp. 126, 127; and ibid. (January 19, 1976), p. 72.

81. For example, see Murrey Marder, "Kissinger Fears Angola Uproar Can Hurt Detente," *Washington Post*, December 18, 1975; and Robert Keatley, "Kissinger Said to Fear That Angola Issue Could Hurt Long-Term Future of Detente," *Wall Street Journal*, January 21, 1976.

82. *State Bulletin*, vol. 74 (February 16, 1976), p. 182. This testimony was given just a week after Kissinger's return from Moscow to discuss SALT and other issues and as the MPLA was winning in Angola.

83. "Secretary Kissinger's News Conference of February 12," *State Bulletin*, vol. 74 (March 8, 1976), pp. 288, 289. See also "Questions and Answers Following the Secretary's Address at Laramie," February 4, ibid. (March 1, 1976), p. 260.

a failure of American counteraction. In his words, "Angola represents the first time that the Soviets have moved militarily at long distance to impose a regime of their choice, *It is [also] the first time that the United States has failed to respond to Soviet military moves outside the immediate Soviet orbit.*"[84]

While undoubtedly Kissinger was disturbed by the Soviet action in Angola and the fact that the USSR might be encouraged by its success, his greatest concern was the American failure. Again disdaining American interests in Angola itself, including strategic ones, Kissinger anguished publicly that "*the question is whether America still maintains the resolve to act responsibly as a great power*—prepared to face a challenge when it arises."[85] In part, of course, this concern was linked directly to the precedent set in Soviet behavior; the Soviet leaders could be encouraged by the lack of resolute American action. But his concern went even deeper, to a concept Kissinger identified as "global stability," that he rested entirely on American readiness to act and on perceptions by others (not only in Moscow) of that readiness. "If the United States is seen to emasculate itself in the face of massive, unprecedented Soviet and Cuban intervention,[86] what will be the perception of leaders around the world as they make decisions concerning their future security? . . . The failure of the United States to respond effectively will be regarded in many parts of the world as an indication of our future [lack of] determination to counter similar Communist interventions."[87]

In a major speech in March 1976, with Angola "lost," Kissinger gave vent to his frustrations in a statement he would never have made in his usual cool *Realpolitik* manner. Kissinger stated at various points that the détente process "requires reciprocity"; that "it cannot survive a constant attempt to seek unilateral advantage"; and that "if adventurism is allowed to succeed in local crises, an ominous precedent of wider consequence is set." Finally, "It [détente] cannot, specifically, survive any more Angolas."[88]

---

84. "The Permanent Challenge of Peace: U.S. Policy toward the Soviet Union," February 3, *State Bulletin*, vol. 74 (February 23, 1976), p. 209. Emphasis added. See also ibid. (February 2, 1976), p. 128.

85. *State Bulletin*, vol. 74 (February 16, 1976), p. 175. Emphasis added.

86. While American concerns were focused mainly on the Soviet Union and global geopolitics, there was also specific concern over possible repetition of the Cuban involvement. Kissinger strongly opposed this possibility in a statement in March that "the United States will not accept any further Cuban military adventures, that the United States will not accept the introduction of Cuban military forces in other parts of the world." "Secretary Kissinger Interviewed by Sigma Delta Chi Panel at Atlanta," *State Bulletin*, vol. 74 (March 29, 1976), p. 386.

87. *State Bulletin*, vol. 74 (February 16, 1976), pp. 175, 179.

88. "America's Permanent Interests: Address by Secretary of State Kissinger," March 11, *State Bulletin*, vol. 74 (April 5, 1976), p. 428. Kissinger used not the word détente, but various circumlocutions on "easing confrontation," "negotiating," "cooperative relations," "coexistence," and "this process." Just ten days earlier President Ford had decided to abandon the term détente for the election campaign.

While it may be said that history offers some support for Kissinger's dire judgment on the effect of "more Angolas," his purpose was to place maximum pressure on deterring the Soviet Union from further moves of that nature. He did not, however, give due regard to the impact those statements would have on Americans. Some would take them too literally, and others would use them later as a basis for challenging other considerations that Kissinger had set forth so eloquently on many other occasions. Such statements tended to curtail the very flexibility for future decisionmaking that Kissinger himself insisted upon.

The American perspective on the Angolan civil war was framed with little attention to the local political situation within Angola or even the broader African context. Initially covert assistance to the FNLA from mid-1974 to October 1975 was provided, not because of comparable Soviet assistance, but because the American leadership (that is, Kissinger) believed the FNLA would win. Later the objective was scaled down to one of offsetting Soviet aid to the MPLA, and finally to seeking participation for the FNLA and UNITA with the MPLA in a coalition government. But in reality this nominal purpose was secondary to the growing American stake in preventing, if possible, a perceived victory for a Soviet client provided with Soviet arms, and eventually also aided by a Cuban military expeditionary force. After Soviet support increased (and especially as further matching American support was precluded by Congress), the American administration began to stress the incompatibility of the Soviet pursuit of unilateral advantage in Angola with détente. The primary intent was to dissuade the Soviet leaders from future similar involvements.

Kissinger and Ford regarded the Soviet Union as taking advantage of the situation and became angry at Congress for not allowing the administration at least to counter and offset the Soviet-Cuban escalation of intervention on behalf of the MPLA. But Kissinger at least understood that the Soviet leaders were doing what the United States had done in this and other cases— they were pursuing competition in a third world area where they had local advantages. Kissinger was greatly concerned over the outcome because he wished to rein in Soviet use of a new technique—use of Cuban proxy forces in a situation in which Soviet or American forces could not be used. His charges of incompatibility with détente were intended to signal to the Soviet leaders the risks of endangering détente they were running. He certainly did not regard geopolitical competition as incompatible with détente, and under his guidance the United States, too, had been seeking unilateral advantages in Angola and elsewhere.

The Soviet Perspective

The coup d'état in Lisbon in April 1974, and the advent of a new Portuguese government intent upon divesting itself of its colonial empire, caught the Soviet leaders by surprise. Only weeks earlier they had finally in exasperation cut off financial support for the fragmented MPLA in Angola. Not until the late summer or early fall did the Soviets resume that assistance— and then after American resumption of support to the FNLA in July and, more importantly, after China had begun, in June, to ship arms and in addition to send military advisers to support the FNLA.[89] (Secretary General Cunhal of the Portuguese Communist party also reportedly had recommended that the Soviet leaders resume aid to Neto and the MPLA.)[90] Moscow was, throughout 1974, giving greater attention to the evolving situation in Portugal itself, but some Soviet commentaries suggested that parallel radicalization in Portugal and Angola could be reciprocally reinforcing.[91]

The main element in Soviet decisionmaking in the initial phase in 1974 probably was concern over Chinese gains at Soviet expense in Angola as well as Mozambique, and in other African countries more generally. The Soviet leaders were very much concerned that they not appear less able and willing than China to aid national liberation movements. Moreover, they feared that predominant Chinese influence both in Mozambique and Angola would prejudice their chances to influence all southern Africa in the future. And in Angola, Neto reportedly was already suspicious that the Soviet cutoff of assistance had been the result of a Soviet-American deal at the Washington summit meeting in which Angola had been placed in the American sphere as a consequence of the budding Soviet-American détente.[92] The Chinese factor in Soviet calculations has been noted by most students of the Angolan civil war.[93] It was, however, not given due weight in American policy consideration at the time or in most public discussions.

The important reactive element in the Soviet approach to the Angolan situation in 1974–75—that is, the fact that it was a response to external events—has not been given due weight in most American discussion, particularly in the public commentary in late 1975 and 1976 and subsequently. That commentary assumed that Soviet involvement was an offensive thrust, although perhaps opportunistic rather than part of a broad design. Clearly the

---

89. Valenta, in *Communism in Africa*, pp. 98–99, and see the earlier discussion in this chapter.

90. Ebinger, *Orbis*, vol. 20 (1976), p. 688, based on an interview with Secretary General Alvaro Cunhal of the Portuguese Communist party in Lisbon, November 9, 1974.

91. For example, Y. Gavrilov, "An Important Victory in the Struggle against Colonialism," *International Affairs* (Moscow), no. 10 (October 1974), p. 98.

92. Klinghoffer, *The Angolan War*, p. 21 (citing the Swedish journalist Per Wästberg, *Dagens Nyheter*, March 11, 1975). Wästberg's reporting suggests that he had good Angolan contacts, and his report probably reflects a rumor given some credence by Neto's faction, although there is no confirmation that this was Neto's view. The rumor was without foundation, but that is immaterial.

93. For example, see Klinghoffer, *The Angolan War*, pp. 101–08; Marcum, *The Angolan Revolution*, pp. 264–65; Valenta, in *Communism in Africa*, pp. 96–98, 103–04; Colin Legum, "The Soviet Union, China and the West in Southern Africa," *Foreign Affairs*, vol. 54 (July 1976), pp. 745–62; and Davis, *Foreign Affairs*, vol. 57 (1978), p. 120.

Soviets wanted to extend their influence in Africa, and Angola was seen as offering an opportunity that the Soviets took.

Soviet policy toward the evolving Angolan situation was both active and reactive. Soviet decisions to support the MPLA in its bid for power, not unlike parallel American decisions, were also made piecemeal in response to a changing situation. The increasingly active role of the two powers (and of the Soviet ally, Cuba) became an ever more important element during 1975.

Americans focused on the Soviet role and what they perceived to be an ominous new element of a Cuban proxy. For their part the Soviets saw not only both the Chinese and Americans as competing for influence with rival Angolan groups, but also what they believed to be an ominous new element— Sino-American collaboration in the competition in the third world. The Soviets had been suspicious of the development of Chinese-American ties ever since 1971, and it was easy for them to assume that it was more than coincidence that both China and the United States were supporting the FNLA and UNITA. Soviet analysts had been predicting and seeing signs of Chinese-American collaboration in the third world for some time, but there had been no clear evidence. By August and September of 1975 Soviet commentators began to express conviction and concern over that collaboration in Angola, including the coordination of covert assistance. Soviet media gave considerable play to a story in the *New York Times* in September that reported American-Chinese cooperation in covert aid to the FNLA and UNITA.[94] Dr. Vasily Solodovnikov, director of the Institute on African Affairs of the USSR Academy of Sciences, charged in November that the Chinese leaders had "entered into a conspiracy with the United States" in their opposition to the MPLA.[95] A later Soviet academic analysis attributed responsibility for the Angolan civil war to machinations of the U.S. CIA "with the participation of the Maoists and the Republic of South Africa."[96]

---

94. The article was by Leslie H. Gelb, "U.S., Soviet, China Reported Aiding Portugal, Angola," *New York Times*, September 25, 1975. TASS picked it up on September 26, and various Soviet commentaries followed. The article was generally correct in its reportage, *except* for overstating the nature of Sino-American collaboration.

95. "Maoists 'Conspire' with US in Angola," TASS, Radio Moscow, in Foreign Broadcast Information Service, *Daily Report: Soviet Union* (November 19, 1975), p. H3. See Valenta, in *Communism in Africa*, pp. 103–04, for a number of other references to similar Soviet articles.

   In mid-1976 Solodovnikov was named ambassador to Zambia, as part of a Soviet bid to counter Chinese influence in the region.

96. V. V. Zhurkin, "New Tendencies in the American Policy of 'Crisis Reaction,'" in G. A. Trofimenko, ed., *Sovremennye vneshno-politicheskie kontseptsii SShA* [Contemporary U.S. Foreign Policy Conceptions] (Moscow: Nauka, 1979), p. 175. Dr. Zhurkin is a deputy director of the Institute of USA and Canada.

   For further discussion of Soviet commentary on the Angolan civil war, see Bruce D. Porter, *The USSR in Third World Conflicts: Soviet Arms and Diplomacy in Local Wars, 1945–1980* (Cambridge University Press, 1984), pp. 152–59.

Although the American and Chinese actions in Angola were for a time parallel, that was not because of coordinated planning. In 1974 China supported the Chipenda faction of the MPLA and UNITA, as well as the FNLA, while the United States then supported only the FNLA. In June–October 1975 the Chinese ended their direct support as the FNLA was losing and especially after South Africa became more actively involved. The Chinese also promptly recognized the PRA when the MPLA won. Although these discrepancies with the American position could have been the result of an agreed and subtle division of labor between the two countries, they were not.

In December 1975 Kissinger twice stated in news conferences that while the United States and China had "parallel views," and even policies, in Angola, the American decisions and actions were not "coordinated" with the Chinese.[97] While he might have said this for ulterior reasons, this assertion rings true and accords with the known facts. Kissinger visited China in late October and accompanied President Ford there in early December 1975. Angola was discussed, but without coordinating the policies of the two countries, which were in fact diverging at that time. In public Senate testimony in late January Kissinger declined to respond to questions on the Chinese role in Angola, except to say that "their role there is more complicated than appears from the public press" (which had recently reported the Chinese withdrawal of military advisers from the FNLA in Zaire).[98]

The United States and China both opposed increased Soviet influence in Angola and the region and Soviet support of Cuban forces in this effort. But in other respects their interests diverged or conflicted. China, after all, had long been helping the Angolan and Mozambican national liberation movements, while the United States had been supporting Portugal until April 1974. The Chinese had begun to disengage from direct support of the FNLA in the summer of 1975 in part because the FNLA was increasingly identified as a CIA puppet, and the Tanzanians and Mozambicans had reproached the Chinese for aiding the imperialist-supported FNLA against the progressive Marxist MPLA. The South African involvement only sealed and accelerated the Chinese decision to draw away. In 1975 China and the United States were on opposing sides in the Rhodesian-Zimbabwe struggle. Moreover, the Chinese (and North Koreans) were already entrenched in Zaire and thus in a position to aid the FNLA. The rationale for their presence in Zaire was not collabora-

---

97. "Secretary Kissinger's News Conference at Peking December 4," *State Bulletin*, vol. 73 (December 29, 1975), p. 928; and *State Bulletin*, vol. 74 (January 19, 1976), p. 76.

98. Kissinger, in *Angola*, Hearings, p. 49. Kissinger's wary restraint ("all I am prepared to say in a public session") has been taken by some to reflect possible covert U.S.-Chinese cooperation. See, for example, Klinghoffer, *The Angolan War*, p. 104. In all likelihood what Kissinger did not want to disclose was the *differences* in the Chinese and administration views of the proper strategy to pursue in opposing Soviet influence, particularly because it raised questions as to whether U.S. policy was on the right track.

tion with the United States, but to the contrary Mobutu's desire to reduce Zaire's dependence on the United States, and he considered China a far safer alternative than the Soviet Union.[99]

Nonetheless, the Soviets were concerned over what they suspected was a developing Sino-American collusion—and, in any case, they were competing for influence with both. The Chinese rival was probably a more prominent Soviet consideration in 1974, and the United States increasingly in the latter half of 1975.

The Soviet Union's interests in Angola were not limited to advancing its own influence in that country and the region in competition with China and the United States. For two decades the Soviet leaders had harbored expectations and ambitions, largely unrealized, of extending their own influence as colonialism collapsed. Détente was a new element in the competition with the United States over Angola in 1975. Détente and peaceful coexistence with the United States did not, however, as the Soviets frequently stated, mean any lessening of the global "class struggle" or of Soviet support for progressive historical change. This point, it will be recalled, had been authoritatively voiced at the Twenty-fourth Party Congress in 1971, which outlined the Soviet policy of détente, and reiterated in conjunction with the Soviet-American summit meetings in 1972 and 1973.

As the Soviet leaders saw the situation in 1974–75, under détente the United States had been competing successfully in the Middle East, notably in turning Egypt from a Soviet ally into an anti-Soviet American ally, and in excluding the Soviet Union from the Arab-Israeli peace diplomacy after the October War. In addition, the American rapprochement with China posed new threats. Moreover, on its side the Soviet Union, at some cost to its revolutionary credentials (including constant Chinese sniping that the Soviet Union was collaborating with the United States at the expense of third world revolutionary forces), had been stressing the peaceful path of transition to socialism and the contribution of détente to facilitating this transition.

And what had happened? In September 1973 Salvador Allende of Chile, the prime recent example of peaceful transition to socialism, was violently overthrown—with covert American assistance. Then the second promising peaceful transition to socialism, Portugal, was aborted with the ouster of Prime Minister Vasco dos Santos Gonçalves on August 29, 1975—with covert Western (European) assistance.

Some analysts have speculated that some of the Soviet leaders may have favored a more active Soviet role in Portugal and been overruled, but were then able to obtain a decision to conduct a more active (but still cautious) Soviet role in Angola.[100] A former Soviet official has said that Politburo mem-

99. For indications of the sensitivity of Zaire and the FNLA to the separate Chinese and American roles, see Stockwell, *In Search of Enemies,* pp. 43–44, 64.

100. See Ebinger, *Orbis,* vol. 20 (Fall 1976), p. 688.

ber Aleksandr N. Shelepin had supported sending Soviet "volunteers" to back the leftist Gonçalves government in Portugal and to take a more active role in Angola, but that Brezhnev and the Politburo decided not to intervene in Portugal and only to support the Cubans in Angola.[101] This report is not confirmed, but Shelepin evidently did favor a tougher line generally, and he was soon thereafter removed from the Politburo. Others have suggested that prominent members of the International Department of the party Central Committee may have been led by their personal acquaintance and support of MPLA leaders to favor Soviet support.[102] While this may have been a contributing factor, it cannot have been decisive because there are too many other cases where similar association and moral support have not led to active Soviet involvement with its friends (for example, Joshua Nkomo and his Zimbabwe African Political Union [ZAPU] in Zimbabwe). Politburo member Nikolai V. Podgorny had been assigned particular responsibility in the Politburo for African affairs and had reportedly argued for a more active Soviet role in Angola. He is said to have been given the responsibility for the negotiations with the Cubans concerning their involvement in Angola.[103]

Whatever the specific alignments and arguments within the Soviet leadership over Soviet policy and action in Angola, it is clear that the leaders believed the course they undertook was fully consonant with détente and the tacit rules of competition as practiced by the United States. There is no reason to assume that Brezhnev and the majority of the Politburo were not determined to pursue Soviet interests as they saw them, and before November 11, 1975, this meant prudent support for the MPLA and thereafter for the PRA government. It is also highly likely that Brezhnev did not want to appear intimidated or weak in standing up for Soviet interests, either to U.S. leaders or to critics within the Soviet leadership.

As the Soviet leaders made their decisions on Angola in 1975, they were also preparing for the Twenty-fifth Party Congress in early 1976. At the Congress, Brezhnev addressed, indirectly, American charges that the Soviet actions in Angola were inconsistent with détente when he said: "Some bourgeois figures express surprise and raise a storm over the solidarity of Soviet communists, the Soviet people, with the struggle of other peoples and progress. That is either naive or, more likely, deliberate confusion. It is crystal clear that

---

101. Boris Rabbot, "Détente: The Struggle within the Kremlin," *Washington Post*, July 10, 1977. Rabbot was an adviser to Central Committee member Aleksandr Rumyantsev. Rabbot's report had not been available to Ebinger at the time he speculated on a trade-off decision in Moscow on Portugal and Angola.

102. Harry Gelman, *The Brezhnev Politburo and the Decline of Detente* (Ithaca, N.Y.: Cornell University Press, 1984), p. 49.

103. Boris Rabbot, "One View on Why Podgorny Was Ousted," *Christian Science Monitor*, June 13, 1977, p. 27. Rabbot's account cannot be confirmed, but Podgorny is known to have played an active role in African affairs.

détente and peaceful coexistence concern interstate relations" and that "détente does not and cannot in the slightest abolish or change the laws of the class struggle."[104]

Brezhnev reaffirmed that "our Party gives support and will continue to give support to peoples fighting for their liberation."[105] On the whole, however, Brezhnev's report to this Congress did not emphasize the national liberation struggle as strongly as the several preceding Congresses had.

With respect to Angola, Brezhnev made no specific reference to the Soviet role or to that of any other country, although he referred to "foreign intervention" against Angola as soon as it became independent by "imperialism" (the United States) and "the South African racists" and "their accomplices" (a term then in vogue referring to the Chinese), as well as to the assistance rendered to Angola in defense of its independence by "progressive forces in the whole world."[106]

The outcome in Angola, from the Soviet standpoint, helped to reassure that East-West détente was not an endorsement of the status quo in the world. A Soviet scholar and diplomat in November 1975 noted that détente was a misleading term for most Americans because they tended to equate it with the preservation of the status quo. He rejected any attempt by the United States to link détente with Angola and the national liberation movement, claiming that that amounted to an unjustified use of détente to attempt to make the Soviet Union renounce support for revolutionary and national liberation movements.[107] Another leading Soviet historian, writing several years later, in referring back to Angola in 1975, called the situation "a period of intensive development of the process of détente in Soviet-American relations" and an attempt by some in the United States to distort that policy. "Someone in the United States decided that, in view of the great interest of the Soviet Union in détente, one could attempt to coerce it to refrain from giving active assistance to the Angolan people fighting for independence. *But that was for our country a matter of principle*, it concerned *the strategic direction of the policy of the USSR* inspired by international goals. And the pretensions of the American side were, of course, deflected."[108]

---

104. L. I. Brezhnev, in *XXV s'yezd kommunisticheskoi partii sovetskogo soyuza, 24 fevralya-5 marta 1976 goda: Stenograficheskii otchet* [Twenty-fifth Congress of the Communist Party of the Soviet Union, February 24–March 5, 1976: Stenographic Account], vol. 1 (Moscow: Politizdat, 1976), p. 57.

105. Ibid., p. 36.

106. Ibid., p. 35.

107. B. Pyadyshev, "Opponents of Détente from Miami," *Za rubezhom* [Abroad], no. 45 (November 12, 1975).

108. A. O. Chubaryan, "The Foreign Policy of the USSR between the 25th and 26th Congress of the CPSU," *Istoriya SSSR* [History of the USSR], no. 3 (May–June 1981), p. 28. Emphasis added.

Thus the Soviet view remained, in the words of Politburo member Andrei P. Kirilenko (in a speech in Angola two years later): "Détente, warding off the threat of nuclear war for mankind and responsive to the most profound aspirations of all peoples, is also creating favorable conditions for the struggle for national liberation and social progress."[109]

Angola and Détente

Neither the Soviet Union nor the United States ignited the Angolan civil war. Neither wished to become entangled in it, still less to have it become an issue with an adverse impact on American-Soviet détente. It was not intended or seen, at least for a long time, as a test of strength of the two powers nor of the limits of competition under détente.

The competition between the United States and the Soviet Union for influence (and the corresponding Soviet competition with China) nonetheless led to escalating involvements that eventually expanded into a conflict over interpretation of the rules for superpower competition under détente. How deep the divergences in understanding were is somewhat less clear. Certainly the leaders on both sides had, despite the agreed Basic Principles of 1972, conducted themselves so as to gain advantages at the expense of the other in global competition, and each expected its rival to do likewise.

The Soviet leaders also felt a political need to establish their credentials in support of the newly independent People's Republic of Angola. When Angola became independent, they moved to more overt assistance, although still largely through support for their ally, Cuba, rather than by crossing the line from providing advisers and arms to a combat presence. The American leaders, above all Kissinger, saw a need to establish effective limits on the Soviet ability to play a geopolitical role by curbing an extension of Soviet pretensions that went well beyond traditional Russian spheres of interest.

Could the two powers have muted their conflicting interests by earlier consultation and agreement? The question cannot be answered easily. Probably they could have, but the uncontrolled actions of third parties added to the difficulty in practice and might have aborted any attempt. In 1974 the Soviets were responding initially to Chinese actions. Then in 1975 both sides escalated their involvement. The Alvor accord in January 1975 marked the high point of efforts by the OAU and other outside powers to induce the three rival Angolan groups to share power. One leading Soviet party official later stated that there had been a "mutual understanding" between the American and Soviet sides to support the Angolan coalition, and that the coalition gave way when one of the factions (the FNLA) began fighting—soon after receiving

---

109. "Speech of Comrade A. P. Kirilenko," *Pravda*, December 6, 1977. The speech was given in Luanda on December 5 at the First Congress of the MPLA.

covert CIA aid, a reference to the initial January 1975 action authorized by the 40 Committee.[110] It must, however, have been about the same time that the Soviet Union increased its assistance to the MPLA. Each side may well have been seeking to bolster its favorite group without necessarily abandoning the idea of a political coalition. It was, however, the American-supported FNLA, then by all estimates the largest and best armed of the three groups, that overconfidently first tried in March 1975 to gain power for itself by resort to arms.

Another Soviet official has said, "We were prepared to negotiate also on Angola. We could have talked about how the situation there could have been settled other than through civil war. But when it started the Americans did not want to talk to us."[111] It is not clear from this statement whether the Soviets had attempted to discuss the situation in Angola and were rebuffed, or simply that they were passively awaiting an American approach that never came. At this writing the record is still very incomplete.

According to Secretary Kissinger, in testimony in January 1976, the United States did not raise Angola with the Soviets until late October 1975.[112] His explanation is revealing in several ways. First, he said that initially the United States believed the Soviets were only seeking to bring the MPLA up to the level of "the then much stronger FNLA. It wasn't until much later that the Soviet arms deliveries to the MPLA seemed to do more than achieve parity with the FNLA." Then, "Once the Soviets had committed resources on that scale, there would have been no point in our raising the issue with them until we had shown by our actions the seriousness with which we viewed the situation."[113] In other words, the issue for Kissinger was never one of the rules of competition. And at no time in the internal deliberations in 1975 over the escalation of American covert involvement was "reciprocal restraint" or the question of compatibility of Soviet (or American) actions with détente raised. Not until later, in late 1975 and in 1976, did Kissinger raise the question of compatibility of Soviet behavior with détente, and then only in an attempt to influence the Soviet leaders to unilateral restraint, as the United States ran out of resources and options for further escalation. Crisis prevention was also not a factor in American deliberations.

From the standpoint of the Ford administration, as Ford and Kissinger have said repeatedly, the destabilizing factor was not a failure of détente or of Soviet performance under détente, but the refusal of the U.S. Congress to let the executive branch wage détente by withholding the stick of further

---

110. The official was Valentin Falin, then deputy director of the international information department of the Central Committee; see Don Oberdorfer, "Soviets Seek Closer Ties with U.S.," *Washington Post*, November 5, 1978.

111. Georgy Arbatov, interview with Frithof Meyer, editor, *Der Spiegel*, March 23, 1981, pp. 133–34.

112. Kissinger, in *Angola*, Hearings, p. 52.

113. Ibid.

American covert military escalation. It may be questioned whether that was the best interpretation of the role that détente could have played, but it was the administration's position. It may also be questioned whether it was a realistic and practical judgment once large-scale Cuban military forces had been committed. But as late as mid-February 1976, when asked what he believed should have been done, Kissinger replied: "We stated our preferences in December [when an additional $28 million in covert assistance funding had been requested], when the situation, in our judgment, was manageable and negotiable. It did not get out of hand until our domestic divisions deprived us of diplomatic leverage."[114]

The American leadership, as well as the public, had been jarred by the fall of South Vietnam in April 1975. The *Mayaguez* incident a month later had been seized upon to show that the United States was still ready and able to bomb someone when American interests had been infringed. Angola was seen as a challenge, but also as an opportunity. The administration wanted to best the Soviets in competition. And until mid-1975 it was confident it could do so in Angola. From then on its objective was scaled down to preventing a Soviet gain through the victory of a Soviet-backed group.

Ultimately, the most important aspect of the entire Angola episode from the standpoint of the American leaders was concern over setting a precedent that might encourage bolder and more active Soviet efforts to extend its influence, including further use of Cuban forces as a surrogate.

The principal Soviet concern was to avoid vulnerability to charges of inaction in support to a progressive, Marxist national liberation movement and fledgling socialist state. This concern complemented more concrete Soviet interests in expanding its own influence and in blocking the expansion of Chinese and American influence. The Chinese were the more feared because they competed for the same groups the Soviet leaders saw as the wave of the future. Therefore in their propaganda the Soviets stressed Chinese association with the imperialist United States and the association of both with racist South Africa. And the Chinese, to avoid that association, withdrew from the competition.[115]

The Soviet leaders were no doubt pleased with the outcome in Angola, including the successful Soviet-Cuban military collaboration, although they may have been disappointed in the less than effusive friendship of the new PRA government (and the renewed suspicions of Neto and his dominant group in the MPLA after the Alves affair). On the other hand, they were disturbed by what they regarded as the use of détente by the American leaders as a club in attempting to prevent Soviet support for the MPLA and PRA.

The Soviet leaders had not seen their own and Cuba's escalating involvement in Angola as anything other than a normal response to the opportunity to assist the MPLA against weak Western- and South African–sup-

114. *State Bulletin*, vol. 74 (March 8, 1976), p. 289.

115. The Chinese sought to regain some standing by promptly recognizing the PRA when the MPLA had won, as did Romania and North Korea.

ported factions that had ditched the Alvor accord and made an unwise bid for power. Although the scale of Cuban involvement grew beyond initial expectations, it is quite likely that the Soviet leaders failed to see how that would affect American policy. Rather, the attempt by the United States, after aiding one side in Angola, to prevent Soviet and Cuban aid to the other by threatening an adverse effect on détente between the United States and the Soviet Union was not given credence. Moreover, the Soviet leaders were not prepared to relinquish the right to aid friendly progressive movements in the name of détente; they saw no real relationship between the two and therefore no question of priorities or choice. Nor was the Soviet role seen as any departure from the standard of third world competition practiced by the United States, including in Angola. The Soviet decisions on Angolan involvement were therefore made on the basis of localized cost, risk, and gain—and on that basis the outcome justified the course taken.

The Angola affair had a negative impact on the general American image of Soviet behavior under détente. Political opponents of détente (and of the Ford administration) exploited the Soviet-Cuban military intervention. This reaction was diluted and offset to some degree by disclosures of covert American intervention, which elicited wide disapproval, and by concern over what was regarded as an unwise interest by the administration in deeper involvement. The negative impact on American-Soviet relations was, however, sustained to some extent by the administration's own vague assertions that the Soviet actions were incompatible with détente. Moreover, the administration (which coincidentally defensively dropped use of the term détente on March 1) decided, as a punitive measure against the Soviet Union over Angola, to defer its planned campaign to remove the trade restraints imposed by the Jackson-Vanik amendment and to postpone several cabinet-level visits to the Soviet Union.[116]

The case of Angola pointed up the underlying differences in the Soviet and American conceptions of détente, although not clearly. Both sides emerged from the rivalry in Angola without showing any signs that such competition under détente was other than what they had expected. And while it led the Soviets to repeat their position on aid to liberation movements and especially to newly liberated states,[117] and led the United States to make ominous comments on "no more Angolas," it did not lead to any attempt to

---

116. See chapter 16.

117. For example, the authoritative report by General Secretary Brezhnev to the Twenty-fifth Party Congress in February 1976 mentioned Angola *only* in the section referring to third world liberated *countries*, not in the section on the world revolutionary process and national liberation movements (although the latter section did mention the setbacks in Chile and Portugal at the state level). Moreover, he pointedly made no reference to the Soviet role in assisting Angola. Instead he referred generally to help from "progressive forces in the whole world"—hardly a clarion call for a more active Soviet role. See Brezhnev, *XXV s'yezd*, pp. 35, 36, 51–58. These distinctions were not, to judge from the record, brought to the attention of the American leaders. Nor have I seen them noted in any other analysis.

clarify, much less to strengthen, the obviously weak restraints provided by the Basic Principles of 1972.

Clarification of the relationship between détente in American-Soviet relations and continuing superpower competition in the third world thus remained an important, unsettled item on the geopolitical agenda.[118]

118. See chapter 19.

16   Détente on the Defensive, 1976

THE YEAR 1976 marked a turning point in American-Soviet relations, although not a conclusive one. The gap in American and Soviet understanding of the code of conduct they had subscribed to in the Basic Principles of 1972 had been growing under the impact of developments around the world. From the American viewpoint, particular issues were Soviet behavior in Angola and earlier in the October 1973 war, and concern over a possible gain for communism in southwestern Europe. From the Soviet standpoint, they were the American policy of excluding the Soviet Union from the Middle East, the attempt to use détente to intervene in Soviet domestic affairs, and the collapse of American economic normalization and facilitation of trade between the two countries.

Early in the year the leadership in Moscow reassessed the policy of détente. Despite a number of setbacks to the Soviet position it reendorsed that policy. In Washington, despite a desire on the part of the Ford-Kissinger leadership to pursue détente, a growing domestic political vulnerability led to a decision to shelve détente (and SALT) until after the election that year. The election campaign itself challenged détente directly, and the outcome—President Gerald R. Ford lost to Democratic candidate Jimmy Carter—left in question what policy the untried president, new to international affairs, and leading a party split between pro- and antidétente wings, would follow.

The American Political Context

In his memoir the first thing former President Ford notes about his last year in office is that in January 1976 the public opinion polls were unfavorable: 46 percent of the American public polled disapproved of his performance, only 39 percent approved. While domestic issues were important, he attributed much of the dissatisfaction to the growing attack on détente by the
538

coalition of conservatives in both parties and liberal "neoconservative" Democrats. This factor was to have considerable impact on his policies in the election year. He notes, correctly, that much of the dissatisfaction with détente was directed at Secretary of State Kissinger, whose relations with Congress had deteriorated, as they had with key constituencies such as the American Jewish community because Kissinger had leaned on Israel in the Middle East peace negotiations following the October 1973 war.[1] He does not add that, with Nixon gone, Kissinger had become the principal target of many others who had long been opponents of détente with the Soviet Union. Indeed, early in January Kissinger submitted a draft letter of resignation, but (as Kissinger had expected) Ford rejected it.[2]

As the election year began, the coalition against détente now included some former members of the Nixon and Ford administrations—James R. Schlesinger, his onetime deputy David Packard, Paul H. Nitze, Daniel Patrick Moynihan (who resigned on February 2 as U.S. representative to the United Nations), Admiral Elmo R. Zumwalt, Jr., and others. Senator Jackson intensified his opposition to SALT and improved relations with the Soviet Union as part of his platform in a bid for the presidential nomination. Ronald Reagan mounted a strong campaign for the Republican nomination on an antidétente platform. The well-known Russian émigré Aleksandr Solzhenitsyn attacked détente. Early in 1976 the National Strategy Information Council, a right-wing antidétente lobby, opened a Washington office and began to support a group that organized in March 1976, although it waited until one week after the election to announce formally and publicly the rebirth of a new Committee on the Present Danger. It was led by a distinguished bipartisan group of "cold warriors," many of whom had served in the cabinets of various presidents, including Eugene V. Rostow, Paul Nitze, Charls E. Walker, Clare Booth Luce, C. Douglas Dillon, J. Lane Kirkland of the AFL-CIO, Norman Podhoretz, editor of *Commentary*, David Packard, Dean Rusk, Admiral Zumwalt, Richard V. Allen, Henry H. Fowler, and others. Its principal efforts were directed toward defeating SALT II and building American military power for confrontation with the Soviet Union.[3]

---

1. Gerald R. Ford, *A Time to Heal: The Autobiography of Gerald R. Ford* (Harper and Row, 1979), pp. 347, 353–59.

2. Ibid., p. 354. Ford comments that he was "shocked" by Kissinger's offer to resign and says that "the country needed him—*I* needed him—to implement our foreign policy at this difficult time."

3. A predecesssor Committee on the Present Danger had been created in 1950 to mobilize public support for an American arms buildup and vigorous prosecution of the cold war, at that time with tacit support from the U.S. government. It closed in 1952. See Samuel F. Wells, Jr., "Sounding the Tocsin: NSC-68 and the Soviet Threat," *International Security*, vol. 4 (Fall 1979), pp. 141–51, for a discussion of both committees. A number of the members of the new committee had been associated with the neoconservative Committee for a Democratic Majority, which had begun to oppose American détente with the Soviet Union after the October 1973 war (it included in addition to Podhoretz and Rostow, Max M. Kampelman, who was to

Thus as the year began President Ford was concerned about the domestic vulnerability of his administration to a rising antidétente tide. Moreover, it was at this time that the Soviet Union and Cuba were succeeding in their effort to support the Popular Movement for the Liberation of Angola (MPLA) in its bid for power in Angola, while the Senate had barred further covert American support to the other contenders. Nonetheless, Ford decided to authorize Kissinger to make one more attempt ("our last chance," as Ford later put it) to negotiate a SALT agreement, to salvage the principal foreign policy achievement of the Ford administration, the Vladivostok accord, and to provide a basis for defending the policy of détente.[4]

A Renewed Drive for SALT II Fails

Kissinger flew to Moscow for negotiations on SALT, which ran from January 20 to 23, 1976. (A planned visit by Kissinger to Moscow in December had had to be postponed because of difficulties in Washington in working out an American position.) Kissinger and Ambassador Dobrynin collaborated on the scenario. Both sides wanted to press on to an agreement on SALT, if possible, to justify a summit meeting in the late spring or early summer in Washington, resuming the pattern broken in 1975. Ford and Kissinger (and General Secretary Brezhnev) were all eager to advance the process, well aware that later in an American election year the task would be even more difficult, if not impossible. Further, the Soviet Party Congress was convening in February, and Brezhnev hoped to be able to point to some new steps forward on SALT and on détente with the United States in general, such as announcement of a forthcoming summit meeting.

As before, the American decision on a SALT position stimulated strong controversy in Washington. Ford refers to the "rebuff" of the Pentagon: "Opposition came from Secretary of Defense Don Rumsfeld and the Joint Chiefs of Staff, and I recognized that they held the trump card. The Senate would have to ratify the new accord. If Rumsfeld or the Joint Chiefs testified against it, there was no way that the Senate would ever go along with it."[5] After several hard-fought NSC meetings President Ford authorized Kissinger to take two compromise proposals to Moscow. In addition, for the first time in all the high-level SALT meetings a senior civilian representative of the Pentagon accompanied Kissinger to Moscow.

---

become the official American "prosecutor" of Soviet human rights abuses in the Carter and Reagan administrations).

4. Ford, *A Time to Heal,* p. 353.

5. Ibid., p. 357.

The exchanges in January (and a follow-on high-level exchange of correspondence in February and March) marked the last real SALT negotiation in the Nixon-Ford-Kissinger era. The complexity of the issues within just the framework of the Vladivostok accord is evident from even a brief summary of these exchanges.[6]

Kissinger presented first the proposal most favored by the Pentagon (even though he and Ford correctly believed it to be nonnegotiable).[7] Only heavy bombers (to be counted in the 2,400 aggregate ceiling) would be allowed to carry air-launched cruise missiles (ALCMs) with ranges of 600–2,500 kilometers, and such ALCM carriers would also be counted in the 1,320 limit for MIRV carriers (and thus be an alternative to having all 1,320 as ICBMs and SLBMs with MIRVs). Sea-launched cruise missiles (SLCMs) on submarines would be limited to a 600-kilometer range. Apart from those limitations, all permitted cruise missiles—ALCMs on heavy bombers, SLCMs on surface ships, and land-launched cruise missiles (LLCMs, as they were then called, or after 1977, ground-launched cruise-missiles, or GLCMs)—would be limited to 2,500 kilometers. All Soviet Backfire bombers produced *after* October 1977 would be counted as heavy bombers under the 2,400 aggregate ceiling (this compromise solution, even if somewhat contrived, would mean that those bombers produced before October 1977, about 120, would not be counted, while all those produced subsequently would be). It would be further agreed that the long-standing failure to define heavy missiles would be remedied by using throw-weight as the basis, with the existing Soviet SS-19 ICBM as the largest allowed. That is, any larger ICBM would be a heavy missile and would thus be held to the existing Soviet SALT I interim freeze level of 308. This accord would mark a step forward in agreeing on a concrete limit, although it was a considerable concession from the previous American position, which had called for using the smaller SS-11 missile as the dividing line. Similarly the increase in ICBM silo launchers (ambiguously limited in 1972 to a 10–15 percent increase in silo "dimensions") would be limited to a concrete 35 percent increase in silo volume. This, too, would be a step forward in explicit limitation, but again represented an American concession.

Brezhnev and his advisers made the modest concession on their part in agreeing to the proposed heavy ICBM missile and ICBM silo limitations. But they were disappointed and dissatisfied with both the inclusion of the

6. *Ibid.*, pp. 357–58, gives the bare bones of the two American proposals and some account of Soviet views. The account provided here is based on information from well-informed participants. While there was substantial partially informed press reportage at the time, there is no comprehensive account of this phase of the SALT negotiations.

7. Kissinger had given the U.S. proposal to Dobrynin on January 14. As Dobrynin preceded him to Moscow, the Soviet leaders had had a chance to consider this proposal before Kissinger's arrival. It is not known if Kissinger also scouted out some possible fallback alternatives or modifications with Dobrynin. Kissinger's talk with Dobrynin, and the latter's departure for Moscow, came before the final NSC meeting of January 19.

Backfire bomber and the large leeway left with respect to American strategic cruise missiles. They accepted the proposed limitations on ALCMs and SLCMs on submarines, but rejected the permissive limits on SLCMs on surface ships (a relatively new American interest) and on LLCMs (on which the Soviets had been lax a few years earlier, not anticipating the American technological advance in this area). Brezhnev urged a 600-kilometer limitation on those systems, as well as on SLCMs on submarines. The Soviet side was also adamant on not including its Backfire medium-range bomber. The Soviets did, however, agree to provide "assurances" that the bomber would not be given intercontinental capabilities, declaring that the operational range (radius) would be limited to 2,200 kilometers. For good measure they also proposed that because of the much greater capabilities of the American B-1 bomber as compared to the existing heavy bombers on both sides, each B-1 be counted as *three* units under the 2,400 ceiling.

Kissinger then advanced the second American proposal, authorized by Ford despite objections by the Pentagon. The overall aggregate ceiling would be reduced from 2,400 to 2,300 by October 1980 (that is, three years after the expiration of the Interim Agreement limitations and entry into force of the Vladivostok ceiling of 2,400). Backfire would be limited to 275 for a five-year period and not counted in the 2,400 aggregate. SLCMs of 600–2,500 kilometers on surface ships would be limited to no more than 10 launchers each on up to 25 ships. Less emphasis was placed on the LLCM, although the proposed limitation was maintained.

The Soviet side showed more interest in this approach, although it was still adamant against inclusion of Backfire. It also still opposed any SLCMs on surface ships, or LLCMs, with ranges greater than 600 kilometers, but there was now agreement on ALCMs and SLCMs on submarines, which had heretofore been the principal American interests. Most encouraging, Brezhnev agreed to the reduction in the overall ceiling to 2,300, or perhaps even lower, by 1980, if the tighter SLCM and LLCM cruise missile limitations were accepted.

Kissinger returned from Moscow much encouraged at the "considerable progress" toward agreement on SALT. Again, former President Ford recounts: "Agreement, it seemed, was very near. But when Henry returned to Washington, Rumsfeld and the Joint Chiefs had growing reservations."[8] Indeed, Rumsfeld and General George Brown, chairman of the JCS, had been very concerned at the rapid movement and enthusiastic tenor of Kissinger's reports from Moscow. They had even contacted President Ford from Hamburg, Germany, where they were attending a NATO meeting, to urge that no agreement be reached until the terms could be thoroughly evaluated by the NSC. At a meeting of the NSC on January 21 while Kissinger was still in Moscow, Acting Secretary of Defense William D. Clements and Admiral Holloway, representing the JCS, joined by Fred Iklé, the director of the Arms Control and Disarmament Agency (ACDA), all expressed serious reservations

8. Ford, *A Time to Heal,* pp. 357–58.

about the Moscow negotiations. Subsequently Iklé requested a private meeting with the president (which would never have occurred if Kissinger were in town) at which he argued against the agreement shaping up in the Moscow talks. While Ford was not convinced by the arguments of the opposition, he was impressed with the potential political liability: several leaders at the Pentagon had made scarcely veiled threats of not being able to support a SALT treaty along the lines Kissinger and Brezhnev were negotiating, which went beyond the earlier approved position.[9]

After Kissinger's return, following several acrimonious meetings in Washington and despite Kissinger's serious doubts, Ford agreed to try a new interim approach that would set limits for only the three years to January 1979 on the troublesome cruise missile and Backfire issues, as follows: ALCM limitations as already agreed; flight-testing of SLCMs and LLCMs limited to 2,500 kilometers and deployment limited to 600 kilometers; deferral of the Backfire issue, except for interim acceptance of Soviet assurances that it would not increase its strategic capabilities or its rate of production; and a decrease in the 2,400 level after January 1979, when the cruise missile and Backfire issues would be settled on a long-term basis (for which negotiations would be continuing). These proposals were advanced through Dobrynin (who met with Kissinger on February 13 and with President Ford on February 16) and by letter from Ford to Brezhnev. A month later, on March 17, Brezhnev replied. He flatly rejected the attempt to defer the remaining issues in this way and angrily described the proposals as "a step back" from the second January proposal. Kissinger hoped that Ford would reconsider, but as Ford recounts, "Reluctantly, I concluded we would not be able to achieve a SALT agreement in 1976."[10] When Kissinger returned from Moscow in January, he had expected to make one more trip to Moscow in early March to complete the negotiation. Now that prospect had disappeared, and the negotiation lapsed.[11]

9. For example, the second proposal Kissinger had advanced—with Ford's authorization—allowed 275 Backfires over a five-year period. This level did not amount to a real constraint over the current production rate. The NSC option would have placed a much more significant limit on the Backfire—250 over a *ten*-year period. Incidentally, Schlesinger (unlike the JCS) had admitted the previous September in an NSC meeting that the Backfire was *not* of major strategic significance. Now Rumsfeld and Clement were supporting the JCS. For a well-informed report see Leslie H. Gelb, "Another U.S. Compromise Position Is Reported Reached on Strategic Arms," *New York Times*, February 17, 1976. Iklé was the most concerned about limitations on cruise missiles.

10. Ford, *A Time to Heal*, p. 358.

11. Kissinger attempted to persuade Ford to try again on SALT after he had won the Republican nomination and Jackson had lost the Democratic one, but Ford was not persuaded. Ford recounts in his memoir that after losing the election he pondered a number of what-if alternatives, including "What if we had been able to achieve a SALT II accord with the Soviets?" He does not, however, conclude that he made a critically wrong judgment under the circumstances prevailing at the time. See Ford, *A Time to Heal*, p. 437.

A last-gasp attempt to resurrect the SALT negotiations was made by Foreign Minister Gromyko when he was in the United States in September on his annual visit for the opening of the UN General Assembly. On September 29 he met with Kissinger in New York and on October 1 with President Ford and Kissinger in Washington. Gromyko attempted to resume the negotiations where they had lapsed near agreement at the end of Kissinger's January visit. Ford and Kissinger, however, were frozen into a position in which they could only raise again a variant of their February proposal, which Gromyko again rejected. September, in a close election contest, was no time to activate a smoldering controversy.

The SALT delegations in Geneva continued throughout the year to work on a draft treaty text (with divergences indicated in alternatives enclosed in brackets), on definitions and rules for counting systems, and on verification, but without any real attempt to deal with the basic issues concerning cruise missile limitations and the Backfire bomber.[12]

Thus, in effect SALT was shelved in March and April 1976 for the balance of the election campaign. As it turned out, that meant it was shelved for the duration of the Ford-Kissinger era of détente and SALT.

U.S. Politics and Foreign Policy: "Détente" Banished

The failure to reach a SALT agreement that could be presented as a positive political achievement, and fear that it would instead be a political liability in the election campaign, meant more than shelving the quest for a SALT II treaty. Although Kissinger did not concede it at the time, in retrospect it is clear it also marked the end of the summitry that had been part of the Nixon-Ford-Kissinger administrations.

While there were many facets to the political struggle in the United States during 1976, foreign policy was a significant one. SALT was a prominent issue, especially early in the year when an agreement was being actively pursued and was widely expected by foes as well as advocates. In January Nitze contributed a critique of the strategic basis for SALT in an

---

12. For Kissinger, there was special irony in the collapse of SALT II on the twin shoals of cruise missiles and the Backfire. He had been responsible for pushing cruise missiles in 1973, when the military was not interested in the systems, as a bargaining chip to aid the negotiations. Instead, they swamped them. See John W. Finney, "Cruise Missiles Provoke Conflict within the [U.S.] Military As Well As with Soviets," *New York Times*, January 21, 1976. The Backfire, as stated earlier, was a particularly difficult issue because Kissinger had told the Soviets it would *not* be included and then had told the American military and Congress it could be (see chapter 11).

The chief of the U.S. delegation has described the work of the delegation and the impact of the internecine struggle in Washington on the negotiations. See U. Alexis Johnson with Jef Olivarius McAllister, *The Right Hand of Power* (Englewood Cliffs, N.J.: Prentice-Hall, 1984), pp. 616–20.

influential article in *Foreign Affairs*.[13] Admiral Zumwalt, a close associate of both Nitze and Senator Jackson, and himself now a candidate for the Senate, slashed at the SALT II negotiations and Soviet compliance with SALT I. He also decried strongly Kissinger's practice of controlling dissemination of intelligence information, as well as manipulating SALT and other decisionmaking. Zumwalt also published a memoir covering his service as chief of naval operations from 1970 to 1974, in which he conveyed the same message.[14] The threat that Senator Jackson would hold SALT hearings on any agreement—with hostile witnesses such as Nitze, Schlesinger, and Zumwalt, and at best tepid support from current leaders in the Pentagon—was a daunting prospect to Ford. Moreover, Secretary of Defense Rumsfeld in his annual report ("Posture Statement") in February stressed the rising Soviet threat, as he did in a number of other speeches. Coincidentally, the CIA raised its estimates of Soviet military costs (based on new data and analysis, not on a spurt of new Soviet spending),[15] while the Congressional Research Service issued the first of a series of alarmist reports on the military balance.

Occasional developments that might have supported specific SALT solutions on the other hand, were received with more than a grain of salt. Most notably, a professional technical study of the capabilities of the Soviet Backfire bomber, prepared by experts at McDonnell-Douglas for the CIA and based on an exhaustive study of all intelligence, concluded that the range of the Backfire bomber was, indeed, about 3,400–3,500 nautical miles. This range was almost exactly what Brezhnev had contended to Kissinger in January and meant it was a medium rather than heavy bomber. Other experts in the Pentagon, however, continued to argue that the range was much greater—up to 6,000 nautical miles. It was darkly suggested that the CIA, then under a politician, George A. Bush, had "leaned" the study to support the administration's preferences. It was even charged (without adducing a source or proof) that Kissinger had

---

13. Paul H. Nitze, "Assuring Strategic Stability in an Era of Detente," *Foreign Affairs*, vol. 54 (January 1976), pp. 207–32.

14. See Clarence A. Robinson, Jr., "SALT 'Hold' Said to Hit Cabinet," *Aviation Week and Space Technology*, vol. 104 (January 5, 1976), pp. 12–14, citing Zumwalt and Ray S. Cline, former director of the bureau of intelligence and research in the Department of State, on Kissinger's pernicious control of intelligence. For the text of the main Zumwalt charges see "Zumwalt Disputes Policy on SALT," ibid. (January 19, 1976), pp. 46–50 (many less detailed accounts appeared in the popular press). See also Seymour M. Hersh, *The Price of Power: Kissinger in the Nixon White House* (Summit, 1983), pp. 207–08, 264.

15. The new CIA estimates, disclosed in May 1976, did not indicate any new increase in Soviet military spending and did not affect estimates of the size and capabilities of the Soviet armed forces. Rather, they showed that the share of economic resources devoted to defense had been higher than previously believed and that the economic burden on the Soviet Union was greater than theretofore realized. None of this meant a greater threat to the United States. These distinctions were, however, lost on the public, and the message seemed to be that the Russians were doing more on defense—with the implication that the United States should also do more.

directed the CIA to obtain that result.[16] Passions ran high, and few cared to heed Kissinger's advice that "no service is done to the nation by those who portray an exaggerated specter of Soviet power and of American weakness."[17] One reason was that Kissinger had been guilty of controlling the dissemination of intelligence in an unprecedented manner, of cutting key officials out of SALT (and many other) policymaking decisions, and of other practices that compounded the indiscipline, leaks, and other actions he in turn believed made those practices necessary.

Even apart from the controversies over the terms of a SALT agreement and the state of the strategic balance, the administration (and Kissinger above all) had been on the defensive over even the continuing pursuit of a SALT agreement because of the Angolan situation. On January 14, the day Kissinger announced at a press conference that he was going to Moscow, he had taken a very stiff position on the Soviet role in Angola, saying, "The United States considers such actions incompatible with a genuine relaxation of tensions." While acknowledging that there was a question whether, in such circumstances, "it is consistent with our policy to go to Moscow and to negotiate on SALT," he argued that the importance of SALT and the consequences of a failure justified, indeed required, the effort.[18]

As Kissinger arrived in Moscow, there was an unfortunate contretemps with Brezhnev, in the presence of American newsmen, in which Kissinger insisted Angola would be discussed, while Brezhnev and Gromyko said *they* at least would not discuss it. This conflict undercut Kissinger's hope, about which he was probably not optimistic, to appear to link progress with SALT on

---

16. As an illustration, see George F. Will, "Reckless Concessions," *Newsweek,* August 23, 1976, p. 84. "But suddenly the CIA under George Bush (former GOP chairman) has produced a report, based on partial data, that says Backfires have only about half the range previously thought. This report is politically convenient if the Administration wants to rationalize a concession." No evidence has ever been advanced to support charges that Bush or Kissinger exerted any improper influence on the evaluation. Prepared by aviation industry experts for the CIA, it was of necessity based—as were differing Pentagon estimates—on "partial data," given that there was no Backfire to test. The conclusion was, as noted, that the aircraft had about half the range that *some* Pentagon experts (not all, and not all CIA experts) had "previously thought." If the new study represented a new and more accurate evaluation on which to base a different U.S. position on the issue, and contributed to an equitable resolution of the issue, it would not be a concession to the Soviets. Thus while a SALT agreement would have been "politically convenient," there would have been no sacrifice of American security interests to political convenience, as implied. See also Rowland Evans and Robert Novak, "SALT II Strategy," *Washington Post,* August 9, 1976. For the charge against Kissinger see "Washington Roundup: Henry's Slant," *Aviation Week and Space Technology,* vol. 105 (September 13, 1976), p. 13.

17. "America's Permanent Interests," Address by Secretary Kissinger, March 11, *Department of State Bulletin,* vol. 74 (April 5, 1976), p. 427. (Hereafter *State Bulletin.*)

18. "Secretary Kissinger's News Conference of January 14," *State Bulletin,* vol. 74 (February 2, 1976), p. 125.

some amelioration of the impasse over Angola.[19] In the private talks Kissinger was well aware that he and Ford wanted a SALT agreement fully as much as Brezhnev did and was acutely aware of the limited U.S. leverage given the congressional ban on further support for the opponents of the MPLA. Kissinger argued to Brezhnev and Gromyko that the impact of the Soviet and Cuban action in the United States, even if it did not lead to American counteraction in Angola, was seriously affecting the American perception of Soviet policy and was thus harming the overall relationship. It could have an impact on trade relations and other aspects of bilateral relations and on détente as a whole. The Soviet leaders, however, continued to object to discussing Angola. The most they would say was that the Soviet and Cuban action was limited, had been requested by the legitimate and widely recognized government of Angola, and was necessitated by South African and "other" intervention from without.[20]

The Soviet side also had a complaint to lodge. Gromyko again objected to the continued American exclusion of the Soviet Union from the Middle East peace process and blockage of a Geneva conference. Kissinger continued the stalling operation that had characterized American policy toward Soviet involvement for the previous two years, despite lip service on such occasions to bringing the Soviet Union in "at the right time." Kissinger maintained this position even after Gromyko offered a substantial concession: that a renewed multilateral Geneva peace conference could resume initially without participation by the PLO. This concession only led Kissinger to conclude that the Soviets were being hurt by the successful U.S. policy of exclusion. In addition, the administration certainly did not want to stir up the Middle East pot at that point in international and domestic political developments. (On March 15, scarcely two months later, President Anwar al-Sadat of Egypt completed his reversal of alignments by unilaterally abrogating the Treaty of Friendship and Cooperation with the Soviet Union.) Domestically the administration did not want to rock the boat with any new Israeli-Arab peace steps, especially with Senator Jackson looking for issues.

In February and March Reagan began to step up his attacks on what he termed the "Ford-Kissinger" foreign policy, not only challenging the Panama Canal treaty negotiation and SALT, but also claiming that the United States had been permitted to slide into second place in the world and that the Soviet Union was taking advantage of détente at the expense of American prestige and security. Kissinger wanted Ford to rebut Reagan head-on, but Ford's domestic political advisers such as Rogers C. B. Morton and Richard B. Cheney disagreed.[21]

---

19. See Murrey Marder and Peter Osnos, "Aim of Kissinger Talks: Swap SALT for Angola," *Washington Post*, January 22, 1976.

20. Based on information from participants.

21. Ford, *A Time to Heal*, pp. 373–74.

In January 1976 President Ford had defended the policy of détente, replying in response to a question: "I think it would be very unwise for a President—me or anyone else—to abandon detente. I think detente is in the best interest of this country. It is in the best interest of world stability, world peace."[22] But under the press of Reagan's challenge he soon retreated, and by March he decided to jettison the very word "détente." Symbolically, in the heartland city of Peoria he said, "We are going to forget the use of the word detente. . . . What happens in the negotiations . . . are the things that are of consequence."[23] Instead he began to campaign vigorously for a policy of "peace through strength." On May 5 the Senate passed a compromise resolution reaffirming the substance of détente and endorsing SALT, but eschewing the word détente and calling for a position of military strength. These steps represented ambiguous attempts to disengage from a growing popular unease that détente had meant a weakening of American strength.

Kissinger, meanwhile, had been attempting to do the same thing in a more subtle way by redefining détente as *containment* of the Soviet Union rather than as building a *constructive* partnership. By contrast, in his first major statement in the Ford administration in 1974 (and the most complete elaboration of the American détente policy ever) Kissinger had defined détente as "the search for a more *constructive relationship* with the Soviet Union."[24] By mid-1975 he had shifted emphasis to say, "We consider détente a means to regulate a *competitive relationship*."[25] Finally, in February 1976, after Angola, Kissinger was defensively asserting: "The policies pursued by this Administration have been designed *to prevent Soviet expansion. . . . to contain Soviet power*."[26]

Apart from the defensive posture on détente adopted by the Ford administration in the early months of 1976 for domestic political reasons, Ford and Kissinger also wished to signal the Soviet leaders their determination, while pursuing détente, not to accede to what they regarded as excessively

---

22. "NBC News Interview," January 3, *Weekly Compilation of Presidential Documents*, vol. 12 (January 12, 1976), p. 22. (Hereafter *Presidential Documents*.)

23. "The President's Remarks and a Question and Answer Session," Peoria, Ill., March 5, *Presidential Documents*, vol. 12 (March 15, 1976), p. 350.

24. "Détente with the Soviet Union: The Reality of Competition and the Imperative of Cooperation," Statement by Secretary Kissinger, September 19, *State Bulletin*, vol. 71 (October 14, 1974), p. 505. Emphasis added.

25. "The Moral Foundations of Foreign Policy," Address by Secretary Kissinger, July 15, *State Bulletin*, vol. 73 (August 4, 1975), p. 166. Emphasis added.

26. "The Permanent Challenge of Peace: U.S. Policy toward the Soviet Union," Address by Secretary Kissinger, February 3, *State Bulletin*, vol. 74 (February 23, 1976), p. 204. Emphasis added.

assertive Soviet actions, especially the support, with Cuba, of the MPLA in Angola.[27]

In one sense these domestic and foreign strategies reinforced one another in contributing to a harder American stance toward the Soviet Union. But, as noted in examining the statements made by Kissinger on the Angola situation, in addition to whatever effect they might have had on deterring future Soviet action, they also gave powerful ammunition to American opponents of détente, who were unprepared to maneuver with the course of events as Kissinger had done. The attempts by Ford and Kissinger to discipline Soviet behavior undercut their rationale and public support for a policy of cooperation and competition.

Thus the Ford-Kissinger team indulged in very strong rhetoric intended to deter the Soviets and to avoid vulnerability to domestic charges of softness toward the Soviet Union. They took advantage of adversity, so to speak, to convert shortcomings into assets in waging the two-front confrontation with the Soviet leaders and domestic critics and rivals. In a reversal of his stand the preceding year Kissinger informed a congressional committee in testimony on January 30 that the executive branch would not seek relaxation of the Jackson-Vanik trade restrictions and ban on granting most-favored-nation (MFN) status to the Soviet Union as long as the Soviets remained involved in Angola. In his prepared statements he did, however, reject the idea of linking SALT to Angola, because SALT was not "a favor which we grant to the Soviet Union to be turned on and off according to the ebb and flow of our relations. The fact is that limiting the growth of nuclear arsenals is an overriding global problem that must be dealt with urgently for our own sake and for the sake of world peace." At the same time, he did argue that "a continuation of actions like those in Angola must threaten the entire web of Soviet-U.S. relations."[28] Such distinctions and modulations of policy, no matter how sound, are difficult to explain in a way that commands public support, particularly during an election contest in which the whole policy of détente was under heavy fire.

On March 15 the administration announced that meetings of the three cabinet-level joint U.S.-Soviet commissions on trade, housing, and energy set up in 1972 would be postponed as a signal of American displeasure over Soviet activities in Angola. In April the United States protested harassment of some American diplomats in the Soviet Union. In May and June the United States protested microwaves beamed at the American embassy in Moscow for unknown reasons, because of the possibility of a health hazard for the embassy staff. The deterioration in U.S.-Soviet bilateral relations also led Vice Pres-

27. See chapter 15 for a more detailed discussion of the Angolan situation and its impact on American-Soviet relations.

28. "Implications of Angola for Future U.S. Foreign Policy," Statement by Secretary Kissinger, January 29, *State Bulletin*, vol. 74 (February 16, 1976), p. 180.

ident Nelson A. Rockefeller, in a speech delivered in May in West Germany, to accuse the Soviet Union of seeking to establish a new world empire.

On the Soviet side, in May TASS disclosed and complained about U.S. refusal to grant visas to a trade union delegation scheduled to visit the United States, the result of opposition by the AFL-CIO. At an international meeting of communist party leaders in East Berlin a little over a month later, Brezhnev reaffirmed Soviet dedication to détente and complained that the United States was delaying SALT for political reasons. By mid-October, with the American election campaign at a high pitch, *Pravda* blasted campaign rhetoric on the Soviet Union and Eastern Europe by both Ford and Carter. But ten days later, just before the election, Brezhnev reaffirmed Soviet readiness to improve Soviet-American relations with any American administration prepared to do so.

Despite such negative developments and the negative impact of election rhetoric, there were some positive developments in bilateral relations. On May 28 the agreement on Peaceful Nuclear Explosions (PNE) was signed, complementing the Threshold Test Ban (TTB) treaty of 1974. The Ford administration did not seek Senate advice and consent on the TTB signed at Nixon's last summit, nor the companion PNE agreement, owing to anticipated opposition by conservatives. (At the last minute, the White House even delayed the signing of the PNE agreement—from May 12 to May 28—a panic reaction to Ford's loss of the Nebraska primary to Reagan.) On July 19 a U.S.-Soviet Shipping Agreement was concluded; it raised American charges to Soviet shippers to the world rate. As noted, Gromyko met with Kissinger and Ford in September–October to discuss SALT, although no progress was made toward agreement. More general discussions of bilateral relations were not acrimonious, but were unproductive. Détente remained on hold pending the American election.

Developments on the economic front were also mixed. American-Soviet trade remained fairly strong—in fact, owing to heavy grain purchases it set a new record. In January 1976, President Ford had publicly committed the administration not to embargo grain sales to the Soviet Union in retaliation for Soviet actions in Angola and had praised the Long-Term Agreement on grain sales reached the previous fall.[29] While some high-technology sales were not permitted, in October the Department of State announced it would allow the sale of Cyber-172 computers to the Soviet Union (and to China).

When the unofficial U.S.-Soviet Trade and Economic Council met in Moscow toward the end of the year (it had met in Washington at the end of the preceding year), the American cochairman joined in urging a repeal of the restrictions in the U.S. trade law on MFN and credits for the USSR. The American delegation was advised that over the two years since the Jackson-Vanik, Byrd, and Stevenson restrictions were imposed, nearly $2 billion in

---

29. "President Ford Addresses American Farm Bureau Federation," January 5, *State Bulletin,* vol. 74 (January 26, 1976), pp. 97–99.

trade deals had been lost by U.S. companies as a direct consequence of the financing restrictions. The administration did not, however, wish to press for MFN, especially after Angola, and this aspect of bilateral relations, as all others, awaited a new administration.

The legacy of the bitter political conflicts of 1976 over SALT and détente did not subside with the election, nor did continued concern over the continuing Soviet military buildup. Late in the year leaks began to appear in the press of more ominous intelligence findings by a "Team B" panel of experts. Team B had been established by Director of Central Intelligence Bush to conduct an outside review to check whether official CIA and other intelligence community estimates of Soviet strategic capabilities and intentions were too optimistic. Set up in June 1976, Team B made its report in December. Since its purpose (and composition—it included Professor Richard E. Pipes as chairman, Paul Nitze, and retired General Daniel O. Graham) had been to develop a less optimistic view, it is not surprising it came up with more ominous results.[30] The net result was to contribute to a general popular impression that the United States had been complacent over a buildup of Soviet military capabilities, and in judging Soviet intentions, under détente.

The Ford administration itself added to the growing concern in its last pronouncements. On December 26, 1976, as the Team B story surfaced, CIA Director Bush confirmed that the latest national intelligence estimate included worrisome signs on Soviet strategic objectives.[31] Secretary Rumsfeld's final annual report to Congress on January 17, 1977, again stressed a growing Soviet military threat.[32]

In his last State of the Union address to Congress, on January 12, 1977, President Ford still came out strongly for an early SALT agreement based on the Vladivostok accord, which he believed was "well within reach this year." He confidently reaffirmed: "We are maintaining stability in the strategic nuclear balance and pushing back the spectre of nuclear war."[33] But in discussing future defense needs he also said: "The United States can never tolerate a shift in [the] strategic balance against us, *or even a situation where the American people or our allies believe the balance is shifting against us.* The United States would risk the most serious political consequences if the world came to

---

30. The principal article on this issue is David Binder, "New CIA Estimate Finds Soviet Seeks Superiority in Arms," *New York Times*, December 26, 1976, although a number of others followed in many newspapers. See also, for the best general review of the Team B experiment, *The National Intelligence Estimates A-B Team Episode Concerning Soviet Strategic Capability and Objectives*, Report of the Subcommittee on Collection, Production, and Quality of the Senate Select Committee on Intelligence, 95 Cong. 2 sess. (Washington, D.C.: Government Printing Office, 1978).

31. Binder, *New York Times*, December 26, 1976.

32. *Department of Defense Annual Report, Fiscal Year 1978*, January 17, 1977, pp. 8-11, 17-18.

33. "State of the Union," The President's Address Delivered before a Joint Session of the Congress, January 12, *Presidential Documents*, vol. 13 (January 20, 1977), p. 32.

believe that our adversaries have a decisive margin of superiority." And while reaffirming a "rough equilibrium" and a "balance" in strategic nuclear forces, he also stressed a "steady, constant" Soviet buildup and the need to maintain American defense efforts.[34]

Soviet Politics and Foreign Policy: Reaffirmation of Détente

Congresses of the Communist party of the Soviet Union, held in recent decades at five-year intervals, provide an opportunity for Soviet leaders to take stock of the developing situation (internal and external, and economic, social, political, and military), to review the general line of policy and strategy, and to reaffirm or revise it. The Twenty-fifth Party Congress, meeting from February 24 to March 5, 1976, provided an occasion to review the four years of Soviet-American détente and the policy underlying it adopted at the preceding Congress in 1971. The Party Congress can also be an occasion to make changes in the leadership (or, more accurately, to announce and ratify such changes), and it elects a new Central Committee.

The public statements of the Soviet leaders at the Twenty-fifth Party Congress were, typically, full of confidence and the many successes of Soviet foreign policy, for the Congress is also a rallying time. Brezhnev and others strongly reaffirmed détente as the general line and recited a litany of summit meetings, agreements, and other achievements of détente with the United States and other Western powers. Moreover, there was a specific reaffirmation of support for the decisions of the May 1972 and April 1973 Central Committee plenary meetings on foreign policy; and the 1972 summit meeting was specifically endorsed, notwithstanding the war in Vietnam, as were the foreign economic policy decisions of April 1973.[35] Nonetheless, there were also indications of continuing difficulties, including in particular a reference to the role of "influential forces" in the United States opposing détente.[36]

Of particular interest to the West, in the wake of the active Soviet and Cuban role in Angola, was Brezhnev's reaffirmation of Soviet support for national liberation movements and of the consistency of that stand with détente. The tone was, however, clearly more one of defense against charges from the left that the Soviet policy of détente was being conducted at the sacrifice of support for revolutionary processes than it was one of defiance of the West.

34. Ibid., p. 37. Emphasis added.

35. L. I. Brezhnev, in *XXV s'yezd kommunisticheskoi partii sovetskogo soyuza, 24 fev.–5 marta 1976 goda: Stenograficheskii otchet* [Twenty-fifth Congress of the Communist Party of the Soviet Union, February 24–March 5, 1976: Stenographic Account], vol. 1 (Moscow: Politizdat, 1976), p. 91.

36. Ibid., pp. 43–44.

"Détente," said Brezhnev, "does not in the least abolish, nor can it abolish or change, the laws of the class struggle. No one can expect that under conditions of détente communists will make peace with capitalist exploitation or that the monopolists will become supporters of revolution. . . . We do not conceal," he continued, "that we see in détente a path to the creation of more favorable conditions for peaceful socialist and communist construction."[37]

While the fruits of détente were praised, the tenor of the formal report by Brezhnev and of other speeches was more subdued than was the case in Brezhnev's speeches in the period 1972 through 1974. For example, soon after the second summit meeting in 1973 Brezhnev had commented on the instructions of the Central Committee to the Politburo "to strive to insure that the favorable changes now being felt more and more in the international situation would become irreversible."[38] In other words, as Brezhnev put it in January 1974, "the task is to make irreversible the achievements in the field of détente."[39] Now, at the Twenty-fifth Party Congress in February 1976 Brezhnev commented that "in order to make détente irreversible, a persistent struggle will still have to be waged"—and he made even that statement only in the context of détente in Europe.[40] With respect to Soviet-American relations, he recalled the summit meetings with Presidents Nixon and Ford and noted the principal agreements: the Basic Principles, the Prevention of Nuclear War, and collectively the strategic arms limitations. As to the future, he predicted conditionally: "There is also a good prospect for relations with the United States in the future—to the extent that they continue to be based on a realistic foundation." In this context he noted the existence of "influential forces in the United States not interested either in improving relations with the USSR or in international détente as a whole." And he recalled "the attempts at interference in our internal affairs in connection with the discriminatory measures taken by the United States in the field of trade." That, he said, is "not a language in which one can talk with the Soviet Union. Now, I think, that is clear to all." At this point the Congress applauded.[41]

As the Soviet leaders were surveying the fruits of their general détente policy with the West, and in particular with the United States, in the period of intensive preparation for the Congress in late 1975 and early 1976, they must have come up with a very mixed evaluation. There are no indications that there were serious splits among the leaders, or of opposition to the

---

37. Ibid., p. 57.

38. L. I. Brezhnev, *O vneshnei politike KPSS i sovetskogo gosudarstva: Rechi i stat'i* [On the Foreign Policy of the CPSU and the Soviet Government: Speeches and Articles], 3d ed. (Moscow: Politizdat, 1978), p. 301.

39. Ibid., p. 387.

40. Brezhnev, *XXV s'yezd*, p. 43.

41. Ibid., p. 44.

general line of détente, or of any alternative approaches. But individually and collectively they saw, along with some substantial gains, other shortcomings and losses.

Most discouraging must have been the difficulty in seeking to translate acknowledged strategic parity with the United States into effective political parity, even though achieving that goal was regarded as a long-term process and not one that would occur easily or quickly. Moreover, in contrast to the SALT I agreements, which represented a solid achievement of mutual advantage, even a major Soviet concession at Vladivostok had failed to result in a SALT II agreement—and American backpedaling on the very eve of the Congress suggested it would take still more time before a second SALT agreement could be reached. Meanwhile Soviet consolidation of strategic parity with the United States was still incomplete and uncertain.

Détente in Europe had probably met, if not indeed exceeded, Soviet expectations at the time of the Twenty-third (1966) and Twenty-fourth (1971) Congresses. The Helsinki Final Act had crowned with success a decade of efforts to consolidate the postwar order in Europe. Now, however, détente with Western Europe was generating some unexpected problems in Eastern Europe, in the communist parties of Western Europe, and in the Soviet Union itself in the form of dissidence.

High among the international concerns at the Congress was the question of relations with the Eurocommunists. Not only did the differences that had emerged call for Soviet commentary, but the presence of fraternal delegates from various communist parties posed the issue directly. China of course was not represented—and was directly criticized by Brezhnev, although he also made the standard statement of interest in improving relations. Nicolae Ceauşescu of Romania and Stane Dolanc, representing Tito's Yugoslavia, reasserted the equality of all communist parties—jarring to the Soviets, who preferred to be acknowledged as the leading and authoritative voice of "proletarian internationalism." But this divergence was scarcely new. What was new and uncomfortable to the Soviet leadership was the revelation that emerged out of the speeches from the Congress rostrum to the Soviet party and public: that the gap between the Soviet Union and the most important Western European communist parties was deep and widening. One after another the heads of the parties of Italy, France, Britain, Sweden, and Austria (or heads of delegations, in those cases where party chiefs such as Josip Tito of Yugoslavia and Georges Marchais of the French Communist party chose not even to attend) not only demanded "equality and respect for the autonomy of each party," but posed various heretical ideas such as "dialogue with the Christian popular forces" (Italy), "domestic socialism" and "human rights" (France), and "personal freedom" and even a "plurality of political parties" (Britain). Brezhnev and Mikhail A. Suslov attempted to hold the line against such departures from real socialism, but this impact of détente within the communist movement, unanticipated at the previous Party Congress, could not be fully contained at this one.[42]

Elsewhere in the world, developments were uneven. The expulsion of the United States from Vietnam and the victory of North Vietnam had been an achievement, but not an unmitigated one. Vietnam was showing signs of independence, while communist Cambodia would not even accept a Soviet ambassador. And the United States was no longer materially and morally drained by its involvement in Indochina.

Despite détente the United States had effectively cut the Soviet Union out of the Middle East peace process and was making inroads into traditional Soviet influence with the Arabs, especially the key country of Egypt.[43] (There were to be other reverses in the Middle East and Africa. Soon after the Congress relations with Syria became strained as Syria moved in Lebanon against the PLO and the Lebanese left, leading the Soviets to suspend arms shipments and to criticize Syria openly. And the South Yemeni-supported rebellion in Dhofar collapsed after the "American proxies" Iran and Pakistan aided Oman.)

On the positive side of the ledger, the Soviets had obtained use of a naval facility in Somalia. Most important, the Portuguese revolution had speeded the end of decolonization, and the Soviet-supported MPLA emerged victorious in Angola just before the Congress—although with an adverse impact on Soviet-American détente.

With the possible exception of Soviet influence in Angola, it was hard to point to a single concrete geopolitical gain for the Soviet Union from détente with the West, and certainly nothing to match such losses as Egypt.

The Soviet leaders weigh success, in calculating "the correlation of forces in the world arena," in terms of power. But they also look at trends in terms of their ideological expectations. In light of this, the shift of the colonial system from imperialist rule to independence had proven much less of a shift toward Soviet real socialism than was anticipated. There was another problem. Ever since the mid-1950s the Soviet leaders had been placing particular stress on "the peaceful transition to socialism." Now, under conditions of international détente a most promising case had arisen in Chile, with the victory of Salvador Allende in free elections—a victory that was, however, crushed by local counterrevolutionary forces actively if covertly supported by the United States. Nonetheless, while disquieted, the Soviet leaders continued to proclaim that détente was compatible with, and indeed was the best means to aid, the

---

42. Ibid., p. 55. See the useful account by Jan F. Triska, "Foreign Policy: Communist States and Parties," in Alexander Dallin, ed., *The Twenty-Fifth Congress of the CPSU: Assessment and Context* (Stanford, Calif.: Hoover Institution, 1977), pp. 95–99; and the discussion in chapter 12.

43. At the time of the Party Congress the Soviet leaders clearly did not anticipate that Egypt would abrogate the treaty with the Soviet Union just two weeks later—to the contrary, the treaty was mentioned among the achievements since the preceding Congress.

progressive and national liberation struggle. Angola thus helped make up for Chile and Portugal, if not for Egypt.

In economic relations, trade with the West had developed and grown considerably. Overall, this was a substantial benefit of détente.[44] The sabotage of the trade agreement with the United States by anti-Soviet and antidétente forces had curtailed anticipated political as well as economic benefits, and this unexpected blow raised questions about the reliability of America as a détente "partner." But serious grain shortages in 1972 and 1975 had been surmounted thanks to substantial American supplies, and Soviet-U.S. trade overall was still rising despite the lack of MFN and credit.

Despite these international concerns, the major problem facing the Soviet Union, and the major focus of the Party Congress, was the faltering Soviet economic system. The economic goals of the Ninth Five-Year Plan established by the Twenty-fourth Party Congress had not been met, especially the increase in consumer goods. The whole system was becoming more sluggish and less productive. Higher expectations from trade with the West had perhaps made the situation a little worse, but they did not represent the basic problem—and the Soviet leaders well understood this. Moreover, there were widespread reservations within the Soviet leadership and political establishment about too much dependence on trade with the West. While détente with the West was neither the problem, nor the solution, to these fundamental problems with the Soviet economic system, there was an important interrelationship.

The economic difficulties did lead Kosygin and some other leaders to take issue with Brezhnev on economic policy.[45] Similarly, the serious reverse encountered in efforts to expand greatly trade relations with the United States contributed to placing Brezhnev on the defensive and to raising again some questions about the benefits of détente to the Soviet Union.

There were some changes in the Soviet leadership at the Party Congress, but they were not related to foreign policy differences. The only notable demotion was the removal of Dmitry S. Polyansky from the Politburo. Party Secretary Dmitry F. Ustinov, overseeing the defense industry, and Leningrad party chief Grigory V. Romanov were raised to full membership in the Politburo. Of particular relevance to relations with the United States, Georgy A. Arbatov, head of the Institute of USA and Canada Studies, was promoted to candidate membership in the Central Committee. Soon after the Congress, on April 26, Marshal Andrei A. Grechko, minister of defense and member of the Politburo, died. Three days later he was succeeded by Ustinov, the first civilian defense minister in two decades, although he had had many years of intimate association with military matters as a top administrator in the defense

---

44. Brezhnev called for stimulating export-oriented industries and developing new mechanisms for economic cooperation with the capitalist countries. Brezhnev, *XXV s'yezd*, pp. 81–82.

45. See George W. Breslauer, *Khrushchev and Brezhnev as Leaders: Authority in Soviet Politics* (London: Allen and Unwin, 1982), pp. 220–29.

industry. He would soon also be named—shortly after Brezhnev—a marshal of the Soviet Union. Another change soon after was the replacement of Marshal Viktor G. Kulikov by Marshal Nikolai V, Ogarkov as first deputy minister of defense and chief of the general staff.

While only indirectly related to Soviet-American détente, the assignment of Ustinov as minister of defense and the death of Grechko and elevation of Ogarkov placed in key positions men better able to consider such questions as strategic arms limitations in a broad context. Grechko had not opposed détente or SALT, but he had been concerned over the impact that both would have on perceptions of the imperialist threat and the need for vigilance, points that serve as justification for defense programs and for maintaining military morale. While Ustinov and Ogarkov shared these same concerns, they were better able to reconcile SALT and defense requirements and to consider modifications in military doctrine.

Authoritative Soviet restatements of détente continued throughout 1976. Ford's decision to cease using the word détente was not attacked, but was explained in the same terms Ford himself had used—avoidance of a "foreign" word. Even Ford's "peace through strength" formulation was interpreted as consistent with a policy of relaxation of tension. At the UN General Assembly in September Gromyko reaffirmed détente. Brezhnev did likewise in a speech on October 25 to the plenum of the Central Committee of the Party, just before the American election: he restated Soviet support for détente and for improving Soviet-American relations with whatever American administration was elected. He also noted that SALT had been stalled since March by the American election—and despaired that such an important enterprise should languish for such a reason.[46]

As the Soviet leaders reviewed the results of their détente policy, they also could not fail to consider the effects within the Soviet Union. To underline the point, five leading Soviet dissidents (including Andrei Sakharov and Andrei Amalrik) appealed in an Open Letter to the Presidium of the Party Congress for an amnesty for all political prisoners in the Soviet Union. There were also reports of a hunger strike by eighty political prisoners during the Congress. These actions followed some conciliatory moves by the government in January, such as easing the rules and fees for emigration and, in accordance with the Helsinki Declaration, easing travel restrictions on foreign correspondents in the USSR. The dissident Leonid Plyushch (whose release had been urged by the French Communist party) was allowed to go into exile in France. But the dissidents saw these as mere palliatives. Nor were they intimidated by stiff measures against linking dissidence with Western contacts, such as the arrest in April of Andrei Tverdokhlebov, the Moscow branch secretary of Amnesty International.

On May 12 nine leading dissidents (including Yury Orlov, Aleksandr Ginzburg, former General Pyotr Grigorenko, Elena Sakharova, and

---

46. Brezhnev, *O vneshnei politike*, pp. 573–74.

Anatoly Shcharansky) formed the Helsinki Monitoring Group in Moscow to follow compliance with the human rights provisions of the Helsinki Final Act. On July 22 this group charged the Soviet government with noncompliance. In November a Ukrainian Helsinki Monitoring Group was formed in Kiev (several others followed in other parts of the country over the next year). Meanwhile, in July Sakharov and twenty-three other dissidents sent an Open Letter to the USSR Academy of Sciences protesting violations of the human and professional rights of Soviet scholars.

The Soviet authorities tried a mixed response. They exiled Andrei Amalrik abroad in July, Vladimir Bukovsky in December (the latter in an exchange for the imprisoned Chilean communist leader Luis Corvalan). Some internal practices were ameliorated, some arrests were made. In the end the Soviet authorities were unable to stem the application of the Helsinki Final Act within the Soviet Union itself without greater use of force than they wished to exert.

In June 1976 the U.S. Congress also entered the picture by establishing a Commission on Security and Cooperation in Europe, comprising representatives from both the Congress and the executive departments, to monitor compliance by the signatories of the Final Act. This development only portended at the time what would later become a more serious irritant to American-Soviet relations, as the United States assigned more attention and weight to human rights.

As the course of Soviet-American relations became dependent on the American election, the Soviet leaders had to be content with a long holding period. The changeover to a new administration, the first Democratic administration since the Soviet-American détente was launched, created new uncertainties and concern in Moscow. Notwithstanding a widely prevalent American perception that Republican administrations are more conservative and therefore tough in relations with the Soviet Union, experience had led the Soviet leaders to be much more fearful of Democratic administrations: the Truman, Kennedy, and Johnson presidencies involved major confrontations in the cold war—the Cuban missile and Berlin crises, Vietnam, and periods of major American military buildups—while the Eisenhower, Nixon, and Ford administrations had been much more associated with détente. Moreover, the new president-elect had been ambiguous in his campaign, alternately endorsing and challenging détente. As will be seen, the Soviet leaders planned a major effort to reestablish détente with the new administration.

The worsening climate of détente also led to activities that had been suppressed or curtailed in the heyday of détente. Criticism of the United States and of the growing role of American "enemies of détente" began to appear in the Soviet press. The military press began to place more stress on vigilance and the rising American military threat. And the restraints on Soviet covert activities abroad began to be set aside. For example, in 1976 the KGB resumed covert forgeries of alleged American documents, after a cessation imposed in 1972. Undoubtedly this was a Politburo-level decision, and no doubt it had been far easier to obtain in view of American activities of this nature. Even those in the Politburo, conceivably including Brezhnev, who may have been reluctant to resume such practices were led to approve them after learn ing that the CIA had participated in assisting General Augusto Pinochet's military intelligence in forging documents alleging posthumously, in an attempt to justify the coup, that Allende had intended to behead the Chilean military commanders.[47] A cycle of practices inconsistent with the spirit of détente thus began to develop in the deteriorating climate of the latter 1970s.

China and U.S.-Soviet Détente

China had begun in 1975 to play a more active role in world diplomacy, a trend that continued. As the year began, despite a severe warning by Gromyko, on January 13, 1976, Prime Minister Takeo Miki of Japan announced that his country would sign a peace treaty with China containing an antihegemony clause to which the Soviet Union had strongly objected. The Japanese-Soviet peace treaty negotiations, by contrast, lapsed over the adamant Soviet refusal to negotiate the matter of the disputed northern islands. Relations between China and Europe were also being developed, and in April India sent an ambassador to Beijing for the first time in fifteen years. In April, fast on the heels of the Egyptian abrogation of its treaty with the Soviet Union, Egypt and China developed a number of measures of cooperation, including the mutual supply of Soviet-designed weapons to one another, on an unabashedly anti-Soviet platform. In May India and China's ally, Pakistan, resumed diplomatic relations. China was emerging on the world scene.

In contrast, China's approach to the Soviet Union was acrimonious. In March China attacked Soviet intervention in Angola and southern Africa in general. In April it accused the Soviet Union of trying to undermine NATO— thus implicitly defending NATO. On April 29 an explosion occurred at the gates of the Soviet embassy in Beijing. Also in April the Soviet Union accused China of stepping up military activity along its southern borders with Indochina.

The visit to China by President Ford in December 1975 was followed by visits by former President Nixon in February 1976 and former Secretary of Defense Schlesinger in September. Meanwhile, in April Schlesinger had publicly disclosed that the U.S. government had once considered the possibility of providing military assistance to China.

In China itself the death of Zhou Enlai in January opened up an intense leadership struggle. By April Deng Xiaoping had lost to Hua Guofeng.

---

47. See Tad Szulc, *The Illusion of Peace: Foreign Policy in the Nixon Years* (Viking, 1978), pp. 724–25.

The international repercussions of this development were not yet clear when Mao Zedong himself died on September 9.

Mao's death was a potential turning point toward which the Soviet leaders had long looked. Some, at least, nourished hopes of a radical improvement in Sino-Soviet relations, and as a whole they expected at least some improvement in relations and sought to encourage whatever tendencies there were among the Chinese leaders to move in that direction. (The expectations of Soviet experts on China were much less sanguine than those of many top leaders.) The Soviets immediately cut off the anti-Chinese polemics in the press, and on October 1, Chinese National Day, *Pravda* called for improvement in Sino-Soviet relations, reiterating that the Soviet Union had no territorial or other grievances against China. (They did not, of course, concede that China might have any valid grievances against the USSR.)[48]

But even before the *Pravda* article, the Chinese journal *Hong Chi* had, on September 26, resumed a clearly anti-Soviet line and also characterized the Soviet Union as a "paper tiger." On October 5 the Chinese representative in the UN General Assembly attacked the Soviet Union as "the most dangerous source of war today."[49]

Hua succeeded Mao as chairman of the Communist party of China on October 7, and it was soon revealed that the notorious "Gang of Four" had been arrested. Later, Deng would make a comeback. But an anti-Soviet line continued through all these changes in leadership.

After the Chinese rebuff of the Soviet overtures for improved relations, Moscow turned to a harder line. On October 14 the unofficial Soviet publicist Victor Louis published an article in Paris threatening that unless China adopted a more conciliatory policy toward the USSR within a month, it would force some unspecified but ominous "irreversible decision" by the Soviet leaders.[50] Brezhnev himself told the Central Committee plenum on October 25 that while the Soviet policy of seeking improved relations with China was "unswerving," "complicated internal political processes" were taking place in China and that it was "still difficult to tell" what the future Chinese line would be. The Chinese line of the previous decade and a half, he said, was in any case "fundamentally discredited in the whole world."[51] On November 6 the Politburo speaker at the anniversary of the Bolshevik Revolution, Fyodor D. Kulakov, refrained from the usual anti-China remarks, and for the first time in a decade the Chinese ambassador did not walk out of the ceremony. Only days

48. *Pravda*, October 1, 1976.

49. See Chih Feng, "Mao Tsetung Thought Will Forever Guide Us in Our Advance," *Hong Chi* [Red Flag], no. 10 (1976), in Foreign Broadcast Information Service, *Daily Report: China*, September 27, 1976, p. AA3; and Xinhua [NCNA], in FBIS, *China*, October 6, 1976, p. A3.

50. Victor Louis, "Moscow Is Waiting for a Gesture from Peking," *France-Soir* (Paris), October 14, in Foreign Broadcast Information Service, *Daily Report: Soviet Union*, October 15, 1976, p. C1.

51. Brezhnev, *O vneshnei politike*, p. 570.

later, however, on November 15 in Beijing, Vice Premier Li Xiannian dismissed as untrue Soviet reports of a relaxation of Sino-Soviet relations, and the Soviet ambassador walked out.[52] Nonetheless, on November 27 the Soviet negotiator, Leonid Ilychev, returned to Beijing to resume talks on border normalization after an interruption of a year and a half.

The United States had no plan to change its relationship with China, although some critics of détente with the Soviet Union, such as Senator Jackson and Schlesinger, advocated détente with China and alignment against the Soviet Union. Schlesinger was cordially received by Hua on his visit to China in late September. At about this time the Soviets escalated their indirect verbal threats through such devices as the Victor Louis article. Schlesinger, in an interview on October 10 after his return from China, said that a Soviet attack on China would be much more costly to the Soviet Union than any gain. And a few days later Secretary of State Kissinger commented that because of China's role in the world equilibrium, the United States would consider it "a grave matter" if China were "threatened by an outside power."[53] On a later occasion (with specific reference to Victor Louis's threat) he said that "an attempt to upset the world equilibrium by a massive attack on China would not be taken lightly by the United States."[54] Kissinger specifically disavowed, however, Schlesinger's earlier suggestions of possible arms sales to China, stating, "We have never had any discussions with China about the sale of arms" and "we have never had any defense discussions with China. I don't foresee any."[55] The United States wished China to be an actor in pentagonal diplomacy among the powers, along with Western Europe, Japan, and the two superpowers, but did not wish to align with either the Soviet Union or China against the other.

In accordance with the policy of diplomatic balancing, on October 29 the United States with studied evenhandedness simultaneously announced approval of the sale of the Cyber-172 computer systems to both China and the Soviet Union.

The year ended with China turning inward to stabilize a new internal leadership, having reestablished itself on the world scene, with Sino-American relations coasting short of full normalization, and with Sino-Soviet relations remaining hostile. The Soviet Union, nonetheless, was hoping that

---

52. See Xinhau [NCNA], in FBIS, *China*, November 16, 1976, p. A15.

53. "Secretary Kissinger's News Conference at Harvard, October 15," *State Bulletin*, vol. 75 (November 8, 1976), p. 579.

54. "Secretary Kissinger Interviewed on 'Face the Nation,'" October 24, *State Bulletin*, vol. 75 (November 15, 1976), pp. 608–09.

55. *State Bulletin*, vol. 75 (November 6, 1976), p. 579. Kissinger's disavowal of any discussions *with China* about arms sales did not, of course, refute Schlesinger's claim that the idea had been considered by the Ford administration.

internal political developments in China would provide an opening for improved relations, despite the disappointing rebuff after Mao's death. It remained unclear whether China and the United States would be prepared to take the next large step in normalizing their relations: during the American election campaign both candidates had again pledged support to Taiwan. The actual policy line of the incoming Carter administration was not clear. These uncertainties for the future marked the Chinese role in American-Soviet relations at the end of the first half decade of détente between the two powers.

17   The Carter
Administration, 1977

THE ADVENT of the new administration of President Jimmy Carter marked the first real transition in leadership since Nixon entered office in 1969, calling for an era of negotiations. Despite fluctuations in political influences and political line during the Nixon and Ford administrations, there had been substantial consistency to American foreign policy, in particular toward the Soviet Union, because of the central continuing role of Kissinger. Now, however, there was not only a change in political parties, but more important, a significant change in the cast of characters, beginning with the new president himself.

A New Administration and New Departures

President Carter's lack of national political experience had been an asset in the election campaign, but it was not so in office. His lack of experience and knowledge of the ways of Washington, as well as of world politics, contributed to a number of serious mistakes from the very outset. He had a quick intelligence and readiness to learn the facts. But his naïveté in both bureaucratic and global politics led to much vacillation and a checkered path for his ambitious and well-intended, but fragmented and inconsistent, foreign policy. Carter's own shortcomings were compounded by divisions among his advisers. Secretary of State Cyrus R. Vance and Secretary of Defense Harold Brown had the foreign and defense policy experience, and Assistant for National Security Affairs Zbigniew Brzezinski had policy-oriented conceptualization. They did not, however, share a common policy direction, and Carter failed to provide it. Indeed, especially at the outset, he often acted intuitively on his own, and even later he moved in different directions as events led him to turn to different advisers. The result was a policy that zigzagged.

Brzezinski had developed an important relationship with Carter as his mentor in international affairs when the former governor of Georgia became associated with the Trilateral Commission in the mid-1970s. Brzezinski was made a full member of the cabinet, and he chaired many important meetings in which Vance and Brown participated. This situation was unprecedented, even for Kissinger until after he became secretary of state as well as assistant to the president. Ironically, while an academic "statesman in waiting" at Columbia University in 1975, Brzezinski had written a celebrated article critiquing Kissinger's performance, in which he had called for more "architecture" and less "acrobatics" in American foreign policy. Unfortunately, the performance of the Carter administration more resembled acrobatics, while the architecture of the structure of peace erected in the Nixon years crumbled.

Carter's own initial conception of détente is hard to define. In the election campaign he had criticized Ford for not assuring sufficient reciprocity in détente, and he even said "the policy of *détente* has given up too much to the Russians and gotten too little in return," yet he also criticized Ford for abandoning the term.[1]

He was thus equivocal in his attitude toward détente during the election campaign. Early in his term he stated clearly, "Now, I believe in détente with the Soviet Union. To me, it means progress toward peace."[2] It is clear that Carter wanted to pursue a policy of continued relaxation of tension with the Soviet Union. What he failed to realize was that several of the other policies he decided to pursue were bound to *raise* tension with the Soviet Union.

Brzezinski had a particular and growing influence on President Carter's view of détente. The question of deciding on American relations with the Soviet Union was, however, complex. As Brzezinski states, "Of the many foreign policy debates within the Carter Administration, that over policy toward the Soviet Union was the most prolonged and intense." The common ground within the administration was a shared belief that détente involved both cooperation and competition; the difference arose over when and how it was appro-

---

1. The quotation is from "Playboy Interview: Jimmy Carter," *Playboy*, November 1976, p. 74, in which Carter gave the Helsinki agreement as an example of giving up too much. In another interview during the campaign he said the United States should be "tougher" in pursuing détente, and again gave the Helsinki conference as an example, even questioning whether the United States should have attended. "Head-to-Head on the Issues: Exclusive Interview with Governor Carter," *U.S. News and World Report*, September 13, 1976, p. 22. In another comment he explained that he wanted to "make détente broader and more reciprocal." See Robert Shogun, "Carter Seeks to Prove He's Not 'Fuzzy on Issues,'" *Los Angeles Times*, May 9, 1976. In his televised campaign debate with President Ford, Carter charged, "The Soviet Union knows what they want in détente, and they've been getting it. We have not known what we wanted, and we've been outtraded in almost every instance." "Transcript of Foreign Affairs Debate Between Ford and Carter," *New York Times*, October 7, 1976.

2. "The President's Address at Commencement Exercises at the University [of Notre Dame]," May 22, *Weekly Compilation of Presidential Documents*, vol. 13 (May 30, 1977), p. 777. (Hereafter *Presidential Documents.*)

priate to pursue cooperation, and when and how it was necessary to wage competition. Vance more often saw possibilities for the cooperative path; Brzezinski more often saw a need for competition. While Vance agreed with a general priority on competition, he also believed it was possible to regulate that competition and to build cooperation. His chief divergence with Brzezinski was over what Vance saw as Brzezinski's "concept of an overarching U.S.-Soviet 'geopolitical' struggle" dominating U.S. foreign policy.[3] Differences also arose over questions of linkage (Brzezinski sought to make détente more "comprehensive" by wider and tighter linkages) and of reciprocity (Brzezinski saw the Soviet Union as growing more assertive, a situation requiring that its assertiveness be either blunted or matched).[4] The differences in approach soon emerged and grew with each year.

Carter's first initiative toward the Soviet leaders was a letter to Brezhnev only six days after his inauguration. Carter stated that his goal was "to improve relations with the Soviet Union on the basis of reciprocity, mutual respect and benefit." He acknowledged Brezhnev's important statement in his speech at Tula on January 18 that the Soviet Union did not seek military superiority, and he assured the Soviets that the United States would not either. He also expressed hope that early progress in relations could be reached through a quick SALT accord, early agreement on a comprehensive nuclear test ban, and agreement on MBFR. And he expressed hope for an early summit meeting.[5]

Despite this approach, Carter did not put improvement of relations with the Soviet Union in the forefront of his foreign policy agenda. Under Brzezinski's influence, consonant with Carter's own experience with the prestigious unofficial international Trilateral Commission, and without objection from Vance, President Carter decided at the outset to reduce the profile and even the substance of American-Soviet relations. Instead the United States would devote greater attention to relations with both the other Western industrial powers (including Japan) and with the economically underdeveloped third world. This meant a new effort to build ties with the countries of Latin America (Jimmy and Rosalynn Carter's one foreign language was Spanish). Above all it called for resolution of the controversy over the Panama Canal—a domestically charged issue—to which he gave high priority. It also meant a new sympathy for the emerging countries of black Africa, a stand that also raised a domestic political issue. These problems at home were aggravated by the selection of the vocal Andrew Young as the American representative to the United Na-

---

3. Cyrus Vance, *Hard Choices: Critical Years in America's Foreign Policy* (Simon and Schuster, 1983), pp. 26–28.

4. Zbigniew Brzezinski, *Power and Principle: Memoirs of the National Security Adviser, 1977–1981* (Farrar, Straus, Giroux, 1983), p. 146, and see pp. 146–50.

5. Ibid., p. 151, and see pp. 151–55 for other early exchanges.

tions, although this appointment proved successful internationally. In short, the United States would no longer look at the world through the restricting prism of Soviet-American rivalry.

There was, however, one important exception. Disarmament and arms control were high among Carter's priorities, and pursuing these goals required continuing and even expanded American-Soviet collaboration. Carter wanted to press forward on SALT and to raise and pursue a wide range of other arms control and arms limitation projects with the Soviet Union. Four days after his inauguration Carter called for a halt to nuclear weapons testing, and in the first few months the administration proposed a number of new arms control talks.[6]

The course of action the new administration adopted on SALT was to move forward boldly, to achieve more than the Nixon-Ford-Kissinger approach. It led, when Secretary of State Vance visited Moscow in March, to a major new proposal calling for sharp reductions.

The idea of a bold new departure at that juncture, while well-intentioned, was unwise. It contradicted earlier signals to Moscow that the United States was ready to begin by consolidating the agreement "90 percent completed" by Ford and Kissinger in 1976. This problem was compounded by the fact that the proposal was raised suddenly and publicly. Finally, the substance of the proposal, while it might have been acceptable for normal bargaining purposes, was so fashioned to American advantage and Soviet disadvantage as to ensure a negative Soviet response. All these factors not only doomed the proposal to failure, but made the Carter approach a new obstacle in the path of American-Soviet relations.[7]

One outcome of the American attempt to strike out on a new path on SALT was adversely to affect Soviet judgment of the Carter administration, a fact that has not been sufficiently appreciated. Georgy Arbatov later observed, "The proposals which the American side made for the SALT II treaty in March 1977 were . . . decisive. The proposals were extremely one-sided and in fact amounted to a suggestion that the negotiations should start again from scratch. *This confirmed the impression in Moscow that Carter was not serious.*"[8]

The foreign policy outlook for the new administration was affected not only by the interests and aims of the president and his key advisers, but also by the limits and constraints imposed by domestic politics. As the Democratic candidate, Jimmy Carter had been supported by some who strongly favored détente with the Soviet Union, as well as by others who opposed it. Partisans of both views sought to influence the new administration. Carter had

---

6. See chapter 22.

7. See chapter 23.

8. Interview by Paul Brill with Georgy Arbatov, "Détente Is Not Dead," *De Volkskant* (Amsterdam), March 16, 1981, p. 5. Emphasis added.

intentionally consulted a wide spectrum of opinion (ranging from doves to hawks), probably more to gain broad support than to seek advice. The key men he selected for his administration caused hard-line conservatives such as Ben Wattenberg of the Committee for a Democratic Majority to complain about a studied omission of stalwart hard-line Democrats such as Paul H. Nitze, Eugene V. Rostow, Admiral Elmo R. Zumwalt, Jr., and Myer Rashish. When James R. Schlesinger was selected to head a new department of energy, they lamented that he had not been given a more direct national security role.[9] Carter's first choice for director of the CIA—the liberal Theodore Sorenson—had to be dropped when opposition mounted.

The key controversy arose when Carter selected Paul C. Warnke, an assistant secretary of defense in the Johnson administration, to be director of the Arms Control and Disarmament Agency (ACDA) and chief SALT negotiator. Although Warnke was eminently qualified, the fact that he was a stalwart advocate of arms control was enough to cause the right wing of the Democratic party to object. Led by Senator Jackson, conservatives of both parties in the Senate focused their opposition on Warnke's appointment as SALT negotiator. (In the hearings on the nomination they were supported by Warnke's one-time friend Paul Nitze.) On March 10 Warnke was confirmed after a bitter battle, but the vote was only 58 to 40. The opposition thus represented more than the one-third needed to block ratification of a SALT treaty.

Senator Jackson and others intended this action to signal that Carter needed to take their views seriously, and it had its effect. One reason the president decided at the outset to try for more far-reaching reductions under a SALT II treaty (to be levied mostly on large *Soviet* missiles), rather than pursuing the nearly completed Vladivostok approach, was to propitiate Jackson. But when that attempt failed and Carter returned to a less ambitious SALT II approach, rather than gaining credit with Jackson for having made a try, he was strongly criticized for retreating from his own proposals.[10]

Carter assumed he could maintain good relations with the Soviet Union, and enlist it in deeper arms reductions, even while launching his crusade against human rights violations and for democratic values. Using a formulation of Brzezinski's, Carter began characterizing American-Soviet relations—and détente—as a mix of "competition and cooperation."[11] This was a reasonable description of the actual state of détente, if not of its more idealized

---

9. See, for example, Rowland Evans and Robert Novak, "A Complaint from the Democratic Center," *Washington Post*, January 31, 1977.

10. See chapter 23.

11. "Remarks at the 31st Annual Meeting of the Southern Legislative Conference," July 21, *Presidential Documents*, vol. 13 (August 1, 1977), p. 1065; and see especially "Address at the Commencement Exercises," U.S. Naval Academy, June 7, ibid., vol. 14 (June 12, 1978), pp. 1052–53. See further the explanation by Brzezinski reported in Murrey Marder, " 'Cooperation, Competition' Seen in U.S.-Soviet Ties," *Washington Post*, October 19, 1977.

public conceptualization, throughout the 1970s. Initially, however, this description did not fully represent Carter's own conception of détente—until he had learned to his surprise that the Soviet leaders regarded as highly competitive, not to say offensive and provoking, the whole thrust of his human rights campaign (as well as of his new SALT approach).[12]

Carter did not wish to incite tension. In the same speech in which he had affirmed his support for détente, he stressed that "being confident of our own future, we are now free of that inordinate fear of communism which once led us to embrace any dictator who joined us in that fear. I'm glad that that's being changed."[13] But unlike his predecessors Nixon and Ford, and unlike Kissinger and probably Brzezinski as well, Carter failed to realize that the Soviet leaders would regard a major campaign challenging their internal political regime as inconsistent with détente.

The Carter administration launched its drive for human rights with a series of demonstrative gestures focused on the situation in the Soviet Union and Eastern Europe. The campaign happened to coincide with a series of events in several of those countries that made the issue unusually sensitive to them.[14] In fact, by a quirk of fate, the heightened official American expressions of concern over human rights in the Soviet Union coincided almost exactly with a conclusion by the Soviet leadership, arrived at in late 1976, that it must make a concerted effort to sever the growing ties between the increasingly bold and vocal dissidents and Western officials and representatives of the press. The dissidents, who were few in number, had very limited opportunities or access to facilities within the Soviet Union for circulating their protests. The Western connections not only produced publicity in the West, but also beamed it back into the Soviet Union.

The human rights emphasis emerged early in the Carter administration. In fact, in November 1976, while still president-elect, Carter sent a telegram of support to Soviet dissident Vladimir Slepak, and on December 22,

---

12. In a particularly frank admission to a group of editors in June 1977 President Carter conceded, "There has been a surprising, adverse reaction in the Soviet Union to our stand on human rights. . . . apparently that's provided a greater obstacle to other friendly pursuits of common goals, like in SALT, than I had anticipated." See "Interview with the President," June 24, *Presidential Documents*, vol. 13 (July 4, 1977), p. 922.

13. *Presidential Documents*, vol. 13 (May 30, 1977), p. 774. This speech was drafted in part by Brzezinski. See George Urban, "A Long Conversation with Dr. Zbigniew Brzezinski: The Perils of Foreign Policy," *Encounter*, vol. 16 (May 1981), p. 25.

14. In late 1976 there had been riots in Poland and lesser disturbances in Czechoslovakia and East Germany. Early in 1977, on January 7, some 242 dissident Czech intellectuals and former government officials issued a manifesto called Charter 77, demanding that the Helsinki accords and the United Nations Declaration on Human Rights be put into practice in Czechoslovakia. Soviet dissidents were planning a similar action, forestalled only by their arrest after they disregarded warnings. On January 8 a bomb exploded in the Moscow Metro. On March 8 a group of Soviet citizens of ethnic German origin demonstrated in Red Square, seeking to emigrate to West Germany. Their action raised concerns on the part of the Soviet leadership as to the wider consequences of a more lenient policy on Jewish emigration.

1976, Secretary of State–designate Vance received the exiled Soviet dissident Andrei Amalrik, who urged the new administration to do more to encourage democratization in the Soviet Union. Very soon after the inauguration, on January 26, the Department of State accused Czechoslovakia of violating human rights and harassing the signatories of Charter 77. The very next day it praised Soviet dissident Andrei Sakharov and warned that any attempts to intimidate him would "conflict with accepted international standards in the field of human rights." (The Moscow prosecutor had warned Sakharov on January 25 that if he continued his "slanderous and hostile activities," he would face criminal charges.) On February 7 the State Department expressed concern over the arrest four days earlier of Soviet dissident Aleksandr Ginzburg for currency violations (in connection with foreign contributions to a fund for imprisoned dissidents). On February 10 the State Department criticized the arrest of Yury Orlov, leader of the dissident Helsinki monitoring group. On February 17 Sakharov received a letter of support directly from President Carter. On March 1 President Carter and Vice President Walter F. Mondale received dissident exile Vladimir Bukovsky at the White House. Carter told him that the administration's commitment to human rights was "permanent." On March 17 the president, in his address to the UN General Assembly, reaffirmed his intention to continue to press for human rights around the world.

The human rights campaign was not directed exclusively at communist countries. As President Carter claimed, it included criticism and action against human rights violations elsewhere.[15] Nonetheless, the focus was principally on the Soviet Union and Eastern Europe; communist China, for example, was not similarly criticized.

One important reason for the administration's strong stand was the moral sense of Carter himself. Another was a reaction against what some members of the new administration and many others perceived to be an unbecoming, even amoral, reluctance on the part of the Nixon and Ford administrations to stand forthrightly against human rights violations in the Soviet Union. The stress on human rights was also in part a return to Wilsonian idealism after the realism of the Kissinger conception of détente.

It was also based in part on political calculation (as it turned out, miscalculation) that such a stance could attract neoconservatives, anti-Soviet partisans on the right, and idealists on the left, all without really affecting the substance of U.S.-Soviet relations.[16] This element of Carter's approach had been clear even before his election. On September 29, 1976, candidate Jimmy Carter had praised the Jackson-Vanik amendment as a human rights

---

15. American military assistance programs to Argentina, Uruguay, and Ethiopia were curtailed in February owing to human rights abuses.

16. This point is well made by John Lewis Gaddis, *Strategies of Containment: A Critical Appraisal of Postwar American National Security Policy* (Oxford University Press, 1982), pp. 347–48.

measure, and he had told Senator Jackson he would, if elected, "effectively implement" it.[17]

The new administration also activated broader, more assertive initiatives with respect to the Soviet Union and Eastern Europe. In March—four days before Secretary of State Vance arrived in Moscow with a new SALT proposal—President Carter requested substantial increases in funding to double the operations of Radio Free Europe and Radio Liberty, as well as to increase broadcasts to the USSR by the Voice of America by 25 percent. All three radio stations pressed the human rights issue. In Moscow the American embassy invited Soviet citizens to see a showing of the film *Dr. Zhivago*, which was banned in the Soviet Union. A number of private religious and other American groups increased the illegal import of religious and human rights writings into the Soviet Union (a practice begun a few years earlier, facilitated by loosened controls under détente). By the time of the preliminary meeting for the Conference on Security and Cooperation in Europe (CSCE) in Belgrade, it was clear that the United States would mount a diplomatic offensive on the human rights issue there as well. On August 5, the last day of the preliminary meeting, the U.S. Commission on the CSCE (an unusual mixed group of representatives from the executive branch and Congress, mandated by Congress to monitor the Helsinki Accord) issued an official report highly critical of the human rights performance of the Soviet Union and Eastern Europe. This report initiated a novel practice by the Carter administration that in effect involved "report cards" that graded the human rights performance of other countries. At the Belgrade meetings, beginning in November, the United States did indeed challenge strongly the Soviet Union and Eastern Europe over human rights abuses.

While criticism of human rights practices in the communist countries had considerable popular appeal in the West, there was also substantial disquiet in Western capitals over the apparently uncalculated assault on this issue by President Carter and his administration. In July both German Chancellor Helmut Schmidt and Canadian Prime Minister Pierre E. Trudeau warned Carter that a zealous campaign on the human rights issue threatened East-West détente.[18]

Within the administration Secretary of State Vance, while supporting the renewed emphasis on human rights, attempted not to single out Soviet shortcomings or to use the human rights campaign in a political offensive

---

17. See William W. Orbach, *The American Movement to Aid Soviet Jews* (Amherst: University of Massachusetts Press, 1979), p. 153.

   Only two weeks earlier Carter had said in an interview that he believed the Jackson-Vanik amendment to the trade act had been a "mistake," although he applauded the aim and stressed his commitment to work toward improving the human rights situation in the Soviet Union. See *U.S. News and World Report*, September 13, 1976, p. 22.

18. See International Institute for Strategic Studies, *Strategic Survey 1977* (London: IISS, 1978), p. 126.

against the Soviet Union. Further, as he puts it in his memoir, "My preference in dealing with human rights issues was to emphasize quiet diplomacy."[19] In his memoir Brzezinski defends the human rights initiatives, and specifically the letter from President Carter to Sakharov (which he had recommended be sent). He comments that to have failed to reply to the Russian dissident's letter would have invited comparison with Ford's decision not to meet with Aleksandr Solzhenitsyn, even though "one has to concede that this event did not help the relationship between the new Administration and the Soviet Union."[20]

The Soviets responded to the spread of dissidence with many arrests, usually after repeated warnings. Incitement from outside, including direct communications from the president of the United States, made the task more difficult—but also more necessary—in the eyes of the Soviet leaders.[21] By the summer and fall they began increasingly to exile dissidents abroad rather than to imprison them at home, although cases of the latter also occurred.

The internal Soviet efforts to contain and suppress dissidence spilled over more directly into Soviet-American relations. The heightened American attention to the human rights issue, coupled with increased dissident activity since the Helsinki Accord, had led, as noted, to expanding contacts between American newsmen (and embassy officers) and dissidents. On February 4 George Krimsky, a Russian-speaking Associated Press correspondent in Moscow who was active in covering the dissident movement, was arrested on trumped-up charges of espionage and expelled. This marked the first expulsion of an American newsman since 1970. There were a number of lesser instances of Soviet harassment of Western correspondents covering dissident activities. On June 11 Robert Toth of the *Los Angeles Times* was arrested and expelled on overblown charges of receiving state secrets (a paper on parapsychology) from a dissident Soviet scientist. Meanwhile, on March 25 a Belgian tourist was arrested and sentenced to five years' hard labor for distributing anti-Soviet tracts (apparently a valid case). On March 5 *Izvestiya* published an open letter by a former dissident, Dr. Sanya Lipavsky, a Jewish physician, who accused six leading Jewish dissidents of working for the CIA. On March 15 Anatoly Shcha-

---

19. Vance, *Hard Choices*, p. 46.

20. Brzezinski, *Power and Principle*, p. 156.

21. As noted earlier, the Soviet leaders had considered it necessary under détente to contain the influence of the widening contacts with the West. Nonetheless, on the whole, détente did contribute to the easing of repression. One eminent observer, the dissident Soviet historian Roy Medvedev, has argued that, overall, as a consequence of détente "the years between 1971 and 1976 were relatively easy on the dissidents." Then, in response to the Carter administration's stance, beginning in 1977 "the regime took a more rigid stand against dissenters." Roy Medvedev, *On Soviet Dissent* (Columbia University Press, 1980), p. 68.

Brzezinski suggests unconvincingly that "the Soviets stepped up sharply their suppression of human-rights activists" in 1977 "probably to drive home to Carter their sense of outrage, and to demonstrate our impotence." Brzezinski, *Power and Principle*, p. 156.

ransky—one of those named by Lipavsky—was arrested and accused of spying for the CIA. Aleksandr Ginzburg, another of those named, was arrested in February.

The charges of spying for the CIA were a new issue that directly tied the U.S. government not only to exhortations that stimulated dissidence, but also to espionage and, by implication, subversion. The picture was further clouded when President Carter personally declared that he was "completely convinced" that Shcharansky had never worked for the CIA, only to have it come out that Lipavsky, who had once shared quarters with Shcharansky, *had* been a CIA contact since 1975. Presumably Lipavsky had been a Soviet *agent provocateur* from the outset. Shcharansky also had supplied material to Toth that the Soviet authorities claimed to be classified security information (it related to the location of facilities where Jews seeking to emigrate had worked before being denied exit permits purportedly because of defense work and access to secret information).[22]

The Soviet leaders had attempted from the outset to persuade the new administration through quiet diplomatic representations that the campaign against internal Soviet affairs was inconsistent with détente and would have an adverse effect on Soviet-American relations. On January 25, the same day the State Department issued a statement supporting Sakharov, Ambassador Dobrynin called Vance to protest the action as unwarranted interference in internal Soviet affairs. President Carter later mentioned that when he met Dobrynin for the first time, the latter had brought up the subject.

Following other private expressions of concern, on February 20 TASS stated publicly that the vocal official U.S. support for Soviet dissidents would harm official Soviet-American relations. Vance responded that U.S. human rights policy would *not* damage bilateral relations. On February 26 *Pravda* contradicted him. After Bukovsky's widely publicized visit to the White House, Brezhnev himself stated in a speech on March 21 that "our adversaries would have liked to find some kind of forces against socialism in our countries. . . . Precisely for this reason a ballyhoo is being organized about the so-called 'dissidents,' a cry to the whole world about 'violations of human rights' in the countries of socialism."[23] At the same time he reaffirmed the aim of and need for détente. The following day President Carter told a group of congressmen, one of whom had expressed concern over the effect on détente, that his criticism of human rights violations would not jeopardize American-Soviet relations. Displaying the stubbornness and irritation he was feeling over the question, he said there was no need to be concerned "every time Brezhnev sneezes."

---

22. Further developments concerning espionage charges and activities in 1978 are discussed in chapter 18.

23. L. I. Brezhnev, "Speech to the XVI Congress of Trade Unions of the USSR," March 21, 1977, *O vneshnei politike KPSS i sovetskogo gosudarstva: Rechi i stat'i* [On the Foreign Policy of the CPSU and the Soviet Government: Speeches and Articles], 3d ed. (Moscow: Politizdat, 1978), p. 609.

Six days later, when Secretary of State Vance arrived in Moscow to present the new administration's SALT proposals, at their very first meeting Brezhnev objected to the continuing American "interference" in internal Soviet affairs over the human rights issue. Carter and Vance nonetheless continued to press the campaign in speeches and statements. On June 7 TASS accused President Carter of "absurd and wild concoctions" concerning human rights in the Soviet Union and again vowed this policy could harm Soviet-American relations.[24] Carter continued stubbornly to say it would not. In a news conference on July 12 he noted that the Soviet Union was "exaggerating" its differences with the United States over this issue and that he would continue to raise issues that might be controversial in American-Soviet relations. On July 21, in a major speech at Charleston, he said, "Part of the Soviet Union leaders' current attitude may be due to their apparent—and incorrect—belief that our concern for human rights is aimed specifically at them or is an attack on their vital interests."[25]

This divergence was the crux of the whole problem. President Carter believed his continued vocal agitation of the human rights issue *should* have no effect, as *he* was not (yet) linking it to other aspects of bilateral relations. But from the Soviet standpoint the United States had made a major and dangerous shift in its policy by giving great prominence and drive to a matter that, in their eyes, *was* "an attack on their vital interests." The Carter administration, if not consciously seeking to undermine the Soviet Union and Eastern Europe, nonetheless created the impression in the minds of the Soviet leaders that the United States would be satisfied only with a fundamental change in their system. They were also inclined to suspect nefarious motives, especially on the part of Brzezinski, rather than to credit naïveté on the part of Carter.

In short, the Carter administration did not intend human rights to be an important element in its policy for bilateral American-Soviet relations. But because of the sensitivity and significance of the question to the Soviet leadership, it was bound to become so. This misjudgment became especially important because of several other major miscalculations by the administration. The early cumulative effect of all these was to throw the main line of American-Soviet relations off balance.

Another consequence of the human rights campaign was to tie American relations with Eastern Europe even more closely to American-Soviet relations. U.S. policy toward Eastern Europe was a topic of some debate from

---

24. Yu. Kornilov, TASS, in Foreign Broadcast Information Service, *Daily Report: Soviet Union*, June 8, 1977, p. B2.

25. On July 9, 1977, President Carter was so riled by the Soviet objections that he resisted even meeting visiting Deputy Prime Minister Vladimir Kirillin, present in Washington to sign a five-year renewal of the U.S.-Soviet Agreement on Cooperation in Science and Technology, concluded at the first Moscow summit. Brzezinski persuaded him. For the quotation see *Presidential Documents*, vol. 13 (August 1, 1977), pp. 1067–68.

April to September 1977, with some in the Department of State arguing for a general increase of contacts in the area and improvement of ties based on bilateral relationships. While American policy did not evidence any great change, the internal policy guideline that emerged stressed a criterion of differentiation, under which the United States would reward Eastern European communist countries showing either greater independence from the Soviet Union or greater internal liberalization. This policy directive was formulated by Brzezinski and issued by the president in September 1977.[26]

In May Vice President Mondale visited Yugoslavia, and in September Yugoslav Vice President Edward Kardelj paid a return visit. A visit by Marshal Tito was envisaged the next spring. In October Secretary of Defense Brown visited Belgrade, and a modest increase in military sales was announced. Most significant, although in the pattern of his predecessors, President Carter himself visited Warsaw in late December.[27]

Despite the desire of the new administration not to place relations with the Soviet Union in the center of American foreign policy (except for SALT), bilateral relations were recognized as important. An argument, similar to that over human rights, developed over a summit meeting in the wake of the collapse of the overly ambitious Carter SALT proposals advanced in March. On April 13 Brzezinski first publicly advanced the idea that periodic U.S.-Soviet summit meetings would be useful, even if they produced no major agreements. Two days later President Carter said that he would welcome "a chance to meet with General Secretary Brezhnev on a continuing basis, annually at least," again without tying such meetings to major new agreements.[28] He hoped Brezhnev would come to the United States that year. He also said he saw no need to change the American SALT proposals (although he did not mean to relate the two matters as closely as the Soviets saw it). While this approach had merit, in light of the U.S. SALT proposals of March the Soviets saw it as reflecting an American desire to put off a SALT agreement.

---

26. Brzezinski stresses his own role in pressing for differentation; Brzezinski, *Power and Principle,* pp. 296–97. The policy review was begun with Policy Review Memorandum (PRM)–9 in April; the new policy was issued in Presidential Directive (PD)–21 in September 1977. The directive has not been made public.

For a discussion of PD-21 in the context of earlier U.S. policy, see Raymond L. Garthoff, "Eastern Europe in the Context of U.S.-Soviet Relations," in Sarah Meiklejohn Terry, ed., *Soviet Policy in Eastern Europe* (New Haven: Yale University Press, 1984), pp. 320–32.

27. Brzezinski notes that the State Department had cautioned against the visit as provocative to the Soviets and advised the president not to meet with Cardinal Stefan Wyszynski (Brzezinski and Rosalynn Carter called on the cardinal instead). The president also indicated a readiness to increase commodity credits to Poland, which was done the following year. See Brzezinski, *Power and Principle,* pp. 297–99.

28. "The President's News Conference of April 15, 1977," *Presidential Documents,* vol. 13 (April 18, 1977), p. 541.

On April 29 a Soviet spokesman officially declared that Brezhnev would not visit the United States in 1977 unless a SALT agreement were reached. On June 28 the White House spokesman stated that President Carter would like to meet with Brezhnev at a mutually acceptable time and place, possibly in 1977. Two days later Carter himself repeated this wish. In addition, on June 9 Carter wrote a personal letter to Brezhnev, not publicized, in which he proposed a summit for the purpose of keeping up a dialogue.[29] In response, when Ambassador Malcolm Toon presented his credentials to President Podgorny on July 5, he was given a letter for the president from Brezhnev in which the Soviet leader reiterated that a summit meeting was possible only if there was a SALT agreement. Thus the matter bogged down as a result of the SALT debacle and Soviet efforts to place pressure on the United States to reach an early SALT agreement.

In retrospect, the failure to hold a summit meeting in 1977, and the Soviet strategy of tying it to successful negotiation of a SALT accord, proved unfortunate. The vicissitudes of international politics and of the negotiations then led to a delay until mid-1979—too late in the Carter administration and after two-and-a-half years of mutual misunderstanding. An earlier summit would not have precluded or dispelled the problems that arose from 1977 into 1979, but it might have helped to mitigate them. As the Carter administration left office, Brzezinski remarked that one of its gravest mistakes had been the failure to hold more than just the one belated strategic discussion with Brezhnev.[30]

Initially, other more mundane aspects of American relations with the Soviet Union suffered from some neglect. The administration equivocated for a time before deciding to proceed with the selection by the outgoing administration of Ambassador Toon as envoy to the Soviet Union. Toon was a seasoned career diplomat with prior Moscow service—and a reputation as a hard-liner. Because of the administration's delay, the Senate did not confirm him until June.

On April 9 and 11 the United States seized two Soviet trawlers for fishing within the 200-mile restricted fishing zone, an action apparently not considered at the policy level. This was one of several instances of the bureaucracy's failing to inform policy-level officials and the White House about developments affecting American-Soviet relations. As a result, in July an Interagency Coordinating Committee on U.S.-Soviet Affairs was created to coordinate policy implementation. Despite that institutional step, and notwithstanding an internal presidential decision in August to link trade to other policy aims (PD-18), the White House and Department of State were surprised in September 1977 to learn from the press that the U.S. Department of Agriculture had

---

29. See Brzezinski, *Power and Principle*, p. 166.

30. Cited in James Reston, "Brezhnev: Let's Talk It Over," *New York Times*, February 25, 1981.

approved the purchase of fifteen million tons of grain by the Soviet Union, seven million tons above the agreed level. No consideration had been given to whether the United States wished to link that concession to other policy interests. (Subsequently, grain sales had to be cleared with the NSC staff.)

Developments around the World

Developments around the world, and American and Soviet policies and actions in other areas, also affected the overall development of American-Soviet relations. As noted, the new administration sought in general to reduce the prominence of American-Soviet relations and instead to enhance those with Latin America, Africa, and Asia outside the familiar context of East-West rivalry. Nevertheless, the element of competition with the Soviet Union remained and indeed was primary in some cases. The main thrust of the Carter administration's policy in 1977, however, was to look at local needs, opportunities, and problems on their own merits—and in terms of American national interests—rather than primarily in terms of a Soviet-American contest.

One seeming contradiction in Carter's foreign policy was his treatment of Cuba and Vietnam. On the one hand, he was pressing a human rights offensive against the Soviet Union and the Warsaw Pact countries of Eastern Europe (even if not with that intention). With respect to China, initially there was no active involvement, in large part because of the political struggle going on there. On the other hand, as part of its new emphasis on relations with other countries of the world the Carter administration sought to improve relations with two other communist countries—Cuba and Vietnam—with whom relations had long been strained.

As a demonstrative first step, on March 9, 1977, the United States lifted restrictions on travel by American citizens to Cuba, Vietnam, North Korea, and Cambodia (Kampuchea). The Ford administration's efforts in 1975 to improve relations with Cuba had been abandoned after the large-scale Cuban military role in supporting the Popular Movement for the Liberation of Angola in 1975–76. The new administration expressed hope that the Cubans would withdraw their troops from Angola, but in his confirmation hearings in January 1977 Vance specifically withdrew that as a precondition to improved relations and specific agreements as Kissinger had made it. During 1977 a considerable change in the climate of relations with Cuba occurred, marked by such developments as the conclusion of fishing and maritime agreements in April and the establishment in June of diplomatic interest sections in the two capitals.[31]

---

31. See *Toward Improved United States–Cuba Relations,* Committee Print, Report of a Special Mission to Cuba, February 10–15, 1977, 95 Cong. 1 sess. (Washington, D.C.: Government Printing Office, 1977) for a detailed account up to May 1977. See also Vance, *Hard Choices,* pp. 131–32.

In the fall of 1977, however, the Cubans concluded that the United States had adopted a new, tough posture toward them in order to help secure passage of the Panama Canal treaties by the Senate. They decided there was no serious prospect for improving relations with the United States. The trigger reportedly was a claim by Brzezinski in November 1977 that Cuba had dramatically built up its forces in Angola when in fact it had not.[32] Soon after, the Cubans sent large forces to Ethiopia, and the United States lost all interest in improving relations with Cuba.

With respect to Vietnam, Hanoi received an unofficial American group investigating Americans missing in action from the Vietnam War in March 1977. In May the two countries initiated talks in Paris on improving relations. Delays were caused by Vietnamese efforts to obtain economic assistance, which initially they were claiming as a right provided under the negotiations that led to the 1973 agreements. Later these efforts at conciliation were to flag.

One important priority of the new administration was settlement of the Panama Canal dispute. That required not only negotiation of two treaties, but, equally if not more difficult, advice and consent to ratification by the U.S. Senate. In September President Carter and President Omar Torrijos signed the treaties. This ultimately successful effort resolved a critical problem and enhanced American standing in Latin America. It also, however, began a long and debilitating internal political struggle in the Senate in 1977 and 1978, which in turn had a negative impact on SALT.[33] First, it slowed the SALT negotiation process by distracting the administration. Second, it led many conservative senators who finally supported the Panama Canal treaties to oppose the SALT II treaty in order to counterbalance their politically costly stand on the Panama Canal issue and regain the support of the conservative constituency that largely opposed both treaties. Senator Howard H. Baker of Tennessee was an outstanding example.

The administration also sought to take a more forthright position in opposing Rhodesia and South Africa and in supporting the countries of black Africa—a course that Kissinger undertook only belatedly and partially late in the Ford administration. Three events in Africa in 1977 were the focus

---

32. Wayne S. Smith, "Dateline Havana: Myopic Diplomacy," *Foreign Policy*, no. 48 (Fall 1982), pp. 171–72. Smith was director of the Office of Cuban Affairs, Department of State, at the time.

   In fact, Cuba had reduced its Angolan forces somewhat. Because the United States had considerably underestimated the number of Cuban troops in Angola in 1976, the corrected estimates made it appear there had been an increase. Another intelligence lapse and correction in 1979 concerning the Soviet military presence in Cuba were to have more serious consequences; see chapter 24.

33. The Senate finally gave its consent to ratification of the Panama Canal treaties on April 18, 1978.

of attention. All proved to be important precursors of greater problems to come in the next year, although the United States was not in the forefront of any at the time. First, Great Britain, actively supported by the United States,[34] made a major effort to negotiate a peaceful solution to the problem in Rhodesia (Zimbabwe). The Soviet Union, while providing moral support and minor material support to guerrilla opposition groups, and clearly favoring Joshua Nkomo's Zimbabwe African Political Union (ZAPU) over Robert Mugabe's Zimbabwe African National Union (ZANU), did not directly or indirectly involve itself or its allies in the conflict. Significant, though little noted, was the positive Soviet contribution to the ultimate success of the peaceful British solution: it did not veto the key UN Security Council resolution in October 1977 that provided the international basis of support for resolution of the conflict.

The second incident was an incursion by armed émigré marauders from Angola into the Shaba (Katanga) province of Zaire in March–April 1977. These forces had fled Zaire when Katanga was reincorporated in 1965. The MPLA in Angola had mobilized them and given them military training, assisted by the Cubans, during the Angolan civil war, after Zairian troops had intervened in Angola in 1975–76 in support of the National Front for the Liberation of Angola (FNLA). The Katangan incursion was repulsed with French, Moroccan, and Egyptian assistance (after the Zairian army made a very poor showing).[35] The United States expressed concern, but evinced little interest or real concern in the affair. As Secretary of State Vance commented in mid-1977: "The most effective policies in Africa are affirmative policies. . . . A negative, reactive American policy that seeks only to oppose Soviet or Cuban involvement in Africa would be both dangerous and futile. Our best course is to help resolve the problems which create opportunities for external intervention."[36]

The Soviet Union, on the other hand, was concerned about a possible Western-supported invasion of Angola, as it made known, along with its objections to the Western intervention in Zaire. On April 18 Brezhnev warned against further Western intervention. In May the National Union for the Total Independence of Angola (UNITA) guerrillas stepped up their activities against the Angolan regime.

---

34. Vance describes in considerable detail the American diplomatic efforts that contributed to a peaceful conclusion to the transition from Rhodesia to Zimbabwe. Vance, *Hard Choices*, pp. 256–72, 284–301.

35. See chapter 19.

36. "The United States and Africa: Building Positive Relations," Address by Secretary Vance, July 1, *Department of State Bulletin*, vol. 77 (August 8, 1977), p. 166. (Hereafter *State Bulletin*.) Vance also said specifically: "When such crises as the recent invasion of Zaire arise, we see no advantage in unilateral responses and emphasizing their East-West implications." Ibid., p. 169. This speech was the most authoritative overall statement of the new administration's policy on Africa.

The most volatile area, with developments consequential to American-Soviet relations, was the Horn of East Africa, particularly Ethiopia and Somalia. Events in the area got under way in 1977 and came to a climax in 1978. In February 1977 Lieutenant Colonel Mengistu Haile Mariam seized power in Ethiopia and turned that country's revolution toward a more radical and anti-American course. In April (soon after the United States had reduced its military assistance program because of human rights violations) Mengistu expelled the American military advisers and closed the U.S. communications/communications-intelligence station. Then in May he visited Moscow to seek military and other aid. (Also in May, and partly related to the change of course in neighboring Ethiopia, President Ja'afar Nimiery of the Sudan expelled Soviet military advisers from his country and denounced both the Soviets and the Mengistu regime.) Cuban President Fidel Castro, who was visiting a number of African countries at this time (March 1977), added Ethiopia to his itinerary (which also included Somalia, South Yemen and Libya). And President Podgorny visited Somalia in April in an attempt to patch up relations between that country and Ethiopia.

In June Somalia stepped up its incursions into the Ogaden region of Ethiopia and in July mounted an initially successful large-scale invasion. The Soviet Union, Cuba, and East Germany soon sent military advisers and arms, and Cuban combat troops followed. In November Somalia denounced its Treaty of Friendship with the Soviet Union, expelled all Soviet military advisers and other personnel, and broke diplomatic relations with Cuba.[37]

Another potentially explosive situation in Africa had arisen earlier: sporadic armed skirmishes had occurred on the Libyan-Egyptian border in June and July, before the situation settled down. Neither the Soviet Union nor the United States had been directly involved, but a Libyan-Egyptian war would have posed serious problems for American-Soviet relations.[38]

In the Middle East, the new administration wished to shift from Kissinger's shuttle diplomacy, which had stalled, to a comprehensive settlement. Vance had obtained Carter's agreement even before the inauguration to make a major new attempt to resolve the festering Arab-Israeli conflict and to accord the Soviet Union a role in the negotiations so that it would be less inclined to undermine U.S. efforts.[39] Less than a month after the inauguration Vance spent nearly a week visiting key capitals in the Near East as the first step in his shuttle diplomacy. A general consensus was reached soon after, and the president approved a course directed toward reaching a comprehensive settle-

---

37. External involvements in the Horn in 1977–78 are discussed in chapter 19.

38. The United States, in fact, counseled Sadat not to move against Libya. (Information from a senior U.S. government official involved in the decision at that time.) The Soviet role, if any, is not on the record, but it is highly likely that the Soviet Union would have counseled Qaddafi against becoming involved in a war with Egypt, given that Egypt enjoyed American support that the Soviet Union could not effectively neutralize or match.

39. Vance, *Hard Choices*, p. 164.

ment through reconvening the Geneva conference that had been bypassed under Kissinger's diplomatic strategy.[40]

President Carter soon stirred up controversy when he spoke out on the Arab-Israeli issue. On March 7 he told visiting Prime Minister Yitzhak Rabin of Israel that he favored "defensible borders" for Israel, perhaps unaware that that formulation could mean virtually no Israeli withdrawal from the occupied West Bank. There was a storm of Arab protest. Two days later Carter sought to compensate by calling on Israel, at a news conference, to withdraw to the 1967 borders with no more than "some minor adjustments." He also referred for the first time to a Palestinian "national homeland." This restatement of the traditional but not recently prominent American position drew Israeli ire without fully reassuring the Arabs. In May Carter, meeting with Syrian President Hafiz al-Asad (who only a month before had rejected a Soviet request for military base facilities), again spoke in favor of a "Palestinian homeland," further angering Israel. During the spring Carter also met with Egyptian President Anwar al-Sadat, King Hussein of Jordan, and Crown Prince Fahd of Saudi Arabia.[41]

The new American policy line of seeking a comprehensive settlement in the Middle East required a more active Soviet role. In May 1977, when they met at Geneva, Vance raised the subject with Gromyko. Meanwhile, in May Menachem Begin had become prime minister of Israel. He visited Washington in mid-July. In August Vance again visited the Middle East in an effort to elicit Arab and Israeli support for, or at least acquiescence in, resuming the long recessed Geneva conference. The reaction of the Israelis was decidedly negative, but they had no alternative. On August 29 Ambassador Dobrynin, in a meeting with Vance to review the situation, proposed a joint statement by Foreign Minister Gromyko and Secretary of State Vance when they met in September. Work proceeded on the statement. Under some pressure, on September 19 Foreign Minister Moshe Dayan, in a meeting with President Carter, agreed to accept a Geneva conference, subject to conditions that would preserve the Israeli position.[42]

The joint United States–Soviet statement was issued by Vance and Gromyko on October 1, 1977. It proposed guidelines and a procedure for Arab-Israeli negotiation of a comprehensive settlement, to be undertaken at a general conference to commence in Geneva no later than December 1, 1977.[43] It came as a surprise to almost everyone. Many pro-Israelis in the United States were highly critical.[44] So were others who objected that the United States was

---

40. Ibid., pp. 164–68.

41. Ibid., pp. 173–79.

42. Ibid., pp. 179–92.

43. "U.S., USSR Issue Statement on the Middle East," Joint U.S.-Soviet Statement, October 1, *State Bulletin*, vol. 77 (November 7, 1977), pp. 639–40.

44. Brzezinski cites the declaration as an example of a failure of diplomacy to take into account domestic concerns: "Insensitivity to domestic concerns could produce calamities, as was shown

bringing the Soviet Union back into the Middle Eastern peace process after Kissinger, Nixon, and Ford had labored so assiduously to exclude it. As early as his address to the UN General Assembly on October 4 President Carter was on the defensive, saying that the United States was not seeking to impose a settlement. Two days later he emphasized to Dayan that Israel did not need to agree to the wording of the U.S.-USSR statement.[45] Israel, which had reluctantly agreed in principle to a conference in September, agreed to the proposed procedures on October 11, but only after the United States acquiesced in a six-point working paper with interpretations that seriously diluted the mandate of the proposed conference. For example, the U.S.-Israeli paper stipulated that no party could participate without the unanimous agreement of the others— giving Israel a veto on participation by the PLO. (This point made more formal an assurance Kissinger had privately given Israel two years earlier.) By this time the question was less whether Israel would be prepared to work within the framework of the U.S.-USSR agreement, and more whether the United States itself would. The retreat of the Carter administration in the face of Israeli (and American pro-Israeli) objections raised serious questions whether the United States would hold to the October 1 agreement.[46]

The question was soon moot, derailed by an event unexpected by either the United States or the Soviet Union. President Sadat of Egypt had initially called the proposed new approach a "master stroke" because it would put pressure on the Syrians to be more accommodating. But, as Brzezinski notes, "he was then shaken by the manner in which the United States retreated when the statement came under attack both domestically and from Israel."[47] In October President Carter wrote Sadat appealing to him to make "a bold, statesmanlike move." Sadat understood Carter to be confessing in "despair" his own inability politically to move. Carter was therefore appealing to Sadat to break the stalemate.[48]

---

early in the Administration by the joint U.S.-Soviet statement on the Middle East which so outraged American friends of Israel." Brzezinski, *Power and Principle*, pp. 73, 108.

45. See Brzezinski, *Power and Principle*, pp. 108–10, for a revealing account of the U.S.-Israeli negotiations. See also Vance, *Hard Choices*, pp. 192–94.

46. As Brzezinski put it, "The United States had to back down," and "walked away from the statement," so that "within days the Administration appeared to be disassociating itself from the statement, thus finding itself tactically on the defensive." Brzezinski, *Power and Principle*, pp. 107, 175, 108.

Senior Soviet diplomats, including one with responsibility for this region, have told me they were convinced the American administration would not have held to the positions in the joint statement even if Sadat had not taken the initiative.

For a good account of the effect (and effectiveness) of Israeli influence, see Raymond Cohen, "Israel and the Soviet-American Statement of October 1, 1977: The Limits of Patron-Client Influence," *Orbis*, vol. 22 (Fall 1978), pp. 613–33.

47. Brzezinski, *Power and Principle*, p. 110; and see Vance, *Hard Choices*, p. 192.

48. Brzezinski, *Power and Principle*, p. 110.

Sadat did so very dramatically and effectively.[49] On November 19 he went to Israel, where he expressed a readiness to accept the state of Israel and to make peace with it. This initiative overcame even jaded Israeli suspicions sufficiently to lead to what eventually became the American-sponsored and -mediated Camp David settlement. But even in the fall of 1977, when the outcome of Sadat's initiative was not clear, it succeeded in overtaking the American-Soviet initiative and proposed course of action. On November 29 Gromyko publicly attacked the Sadat visit and privately informed the United States he would not attend the Cairo conference to which Sadat had invited the Soviet Union (and other Arab parties, which also declined). On December 25 Sadat and Begin began negotiations.

The Soviet leaders may have suspected American collusion in Sadat's move. Even if they did not, they bitterly held it against the United States that, once their presence was no longer essential (as it would have been in a general conference), the United States again froze them out of any participation.[50] Indeed, in 1980 after the complete breakdown in U.S.-Soviet cooperation under détente in the wake of the American reaction to the Soviet occupation of Afghanistan, a leading Soviet commentator stated that "the Carter administration has in practice unilaterally violated all the agreements reached with the Soviet Union," and went on to declare that "the *most striking example* of such reneging on commitments is the U.S. course on the Near East."[51]

The basis for the joint U.S.-Soviet statement of October 1, 1977, has long been unclear. Why, given the administration's rapid retreat and negative consequences for U.S.-Soviet relations, did it agree with the Soviet Union on the joint statement in the first place? Secretary of State Vance has made clear why he pursued the course he did from the outset of the new administration to Sadat's initiative, while Brzezinski has explained the most clearly why that course was abandoned. The Soviet side had taken the initiative in proposing a moderate draft to serve as a platform for reconvening the Geneva conference. Given the stalemate on the Arab-Israeli conflict the Department of State had seen the Soviet approach as constructive and offering promise. Brzezinski confesses in his memoir that he underestimated its domestic impact. Instead, "viewing it largely as a procedural preliminary to the convening of the conference, I forwarded it to the President with Vance's recommendation." In retrospect he believes it to have been a mistake (although he merely told the president that he believed it to have been a "tactical mistake" of timing).

---

49. Vance stresses that "no advance consultations took place" on Sadat's initiative; Sadat merely advised the United States the day before his trip. Vance states that "we were momentarily stunned by the decision." Vance, *Hard Choices*, p. 194.

50. "Answers of L. I. Brezhnev to Questions of a *Pravda* Correspondent," *Pravda*, December 24, 1977.

51. Sergei Losev, "Camp David, or 'Peace' American-Style," *Izvestiya*, February 5, 1980. Emphasis added.

Further, he stated that the administration should have been more cautious about moves involving Soviet reinvolvement in the Middle East.[52] American policy rapidly returned to seeking to exclude the Soviet Union from Middle Eastern affairs.[53]

There was still more action elsewhere in the Middle East and in South Asia. For one, President Ibrahim al-Hamdi of North Yemen was assassinated. In Pakistan, General Mohammed Zia ul-Haq seized power in July and canceled the elections planned for October. In India, Indira Gandhi lost the election in March and was replaced by a more pro-Western successor. In October, the military in Thailand ousted the neutralist civilian government.

All in all, during 1977 the third world experienced a number of changes of rule and alignment, mostly military and mostly away from the Soviet Union, with Ethiopia the principal exception. But there were no serious instances of American or Soviet involvement. The looming exception would be Ethiopia at year's end.

In the summer of 1977 China began emerging from its internal struggle with the rehabilitation of Deng Xiaoping in July as deputy chairman of the party and vice premier. In August the Eleventh Party Congress elected a new Politburo. Secretary of State Vance visited China later in August, although the trip did not lead to any change in American-Chinese relations. Neither side, at that point, had any initiative in mind. Carter did want to normalize relations but was giving higher priority to the Panama Canal treaties and to SALT. Both these initiatives were opposed by conservative forces, which would also oppose any change in relations with Taiwan that full normalization with China would require.[54]

American relations with Europe also continued on an inertial course, with one exception. The Carter administration believed that insufficient attention had been paid to NATO, in particular to strengthening NATO's conventional military capabilities. Early on—only three days after the inauguration—the new administration showed its strong interest in NATO by sending Vice President Mondale to visit the NATO Council in Brussels. It also made its concern about building up conventional forces clear at a NATO meeting in London in May (immediately following a Western economic summit meeting). At this point, at American urging the allies agreed on the aim of increasing their military expenditures by 3 percent annually in real terms. The United States also began a vigorous program to upgrade NATO's conventional military forces, including the U.S. reinforcement capability. A plan to develop a new enhanced radiation weapon (popularly termed the neutron bomb)

---

52. Brzezinski, *Power and Principle*, pp. 108, 113.

53. Vance devotes some sixty pages to the subsequent negotiations leading to the Camp David accord and Egyptian-Israeli peace treaty. He does so without any reference to Soviet reactions or absence from the process. Vance, *Hard Choices*, pp. 194–255.

54. American-Chinese relations in 1977 are discussed further in chapter 20.

caused considerable controversy, compounded by Carter's inept handling of the issue.[55]

The CSCE accord had mandated a review conference that began meeting in Belgrade in September 1977.[56] In preparing for that meeting the United States debated one important issue: whether to stress cooperation or compliance with the human rights provisions. Brzczinski readily obtained President Carter's approval for the second line. He also blocked the State Department's nominee for principal American delegate, instead getting Carter's agreement to name Arthur J. Goldberg, a politically known figure who could be counted on to push the human rights campaign. Moreover, Brzezinski obtained Carter's approval for a more vigorous role (and wherewithal) for Radio Free Europe, in Brzezinski's words, to "serve as an instrument for the deliberate encouragement of political change" in Eastern Europe.[57]

The Carter administration also promoted Hungary to a position of greater favor, so that it joined Poland and Romania (as well as Yugoslavia) as a recipient of most-favored-nation (MFN) trade status. The Crown of St. Stephen, a Hungarian national treasure and symbol of nationhood in the custody of the United States since 1945, was returned to Budapest by a delegation headed by Secretary of State Vance.[58]

As Carter's first year in office drew to a close, international developments had not affected the course of American-Soviet relations as much as the new administration's policies on human rights and SALT had. By year's end the Carter administration saw SALT back on track.[59] (Indeed, in October Carter overconfidently predicted an agreement "in a few weeks," amended on December 28 to "this [the coming] year.") Carter also observed that he expected Brezhnev would want to visit the United States once the negotiations on SALT, a comprehensive nuclear test ban, and arms limitations in the Indian Ocean had shown "substantial progress."[60] But he was no longer pressing the issue.

The Soviet Approach and Reaction

The Soviet leaders had been concerned about the advent of an unknown president and the departure of such a familiar (if not always loved) and key figure as Kissinger. While convinced that the basic reason for the American turn to détente was rooted in the changing correlation of forces in

---

55. See chapter 25.

56. See chapter 22.

57. Brzezinski, *Power and Principle*, p. 300.

58. Brzezinski notes that he was initially skeptical of the idea when the Department of State proposed returning the crown. Brzezinski, *Power and Principle*, p. 299.

59. See chapter 23.

60. "Conversation with the President," December 28, 1977, *Presidential Documents*, vol. 13 (January 2, 1978), pp. 1945–46.

the world arena, they also recognized that various American political figures could—and did—assess the situation differently. They were keenly aware that while there were sober realists (still, of course, adversaries), others might try to fight the changing world trends rather than accommodate them. Certainly the opposition of Ronald Reagan and others, and the fact that Ford had felt it necessary to bend in their direction in his campaign, were recent reminders.

Nor was the Democratic victory reassuring to the Soviet leaders. Contrary to prevailing American sentiment (Nixon's espousal of détente notwithstanding) that the Democratic party was on the whole more inclined to accommodation with the left in general and the communist powers in particular, the Soviet experience and view were quite different. Partial détente had come with Eisenhower, Nixon, and Ford, whereas the coldest years and hottest crises of the cold war had been under Truman and Kennedy. Moreover, the Democratic party included not only liberal realists like George C. McGovern and Hubert H. Humphrey, but also vocally anti-Soviet elements exemplified by Jackson and Nitze. And Jimmy Carter was an unknown.

The Soviet response in this situation was to make every effort to encourage the new administration to reaffirm détente. Soon after the election, on December 2, 1976, the president-elect's press spokesman Jody Powell disclosed that Brezhnev had pledged in a private communication that the Soviet Union would "go out of its way to avoid any crisis with the United States" and the new administration. On December 29 Brezhnev publicly (through a TASS release) welcomed a statement by the president-elect two days before in which Carter had expressed a desire to hold a summit meeting before September 1977 to conclude a new SALT agreement and discuss matters of common interest.[61] In December 1976 Brezhnev responded positively to the idea of a summit meeting, as the public and private signals from Carter were suggesting an early SALT agreement based on the Vladivostok framework. (This stance stood in marked contrast to the position Brezhnev would take a year later after the Carter administration had taken an unexpectedly different approach to SALT.) On the day after the inauguration President Podgorny, in sending his congratulations, expressed the hope that there could be "significant progress" in Soviet-American relations under the new administration.[62]

Even more significant was a major Soviet policy initiative to the new administration that Brezhnev unveiled in a speech in Tula on January 18, virtually on the eve of the inauguration. Brezhnev publicly articulated Soviet military policy and doctrine, explicitly renouncing the pursuit of military superiority or any capability beyond what was needed for deterrence. Further, he endorsed SALT and other arms limitations and reductions and described "what we mean by détente." "Détente," Brezhnev said, "is above all an overcoming of the 'cold war,' a transition to normal, equal relations between states. Détente is a readiness to resolve differences and conflicts not by force, not by

61. Don Oberdorfer and Morton Mintz, "Carter Sets Mideast SALT Bids," *Washington Post*, December 18, 1985.

62. N. V. Podgorny, "To His Excellency Jimmy Carter," *Pravda*, January 21, 1977.

threats and saber-rattling, but by peaceful means, at the negotiating table. Détente is a certain trust and ability to take into account the legitimate interests of one another."[63]

Brezhnev's Tula speech was a very important declaration. It had been carefully considered—and debated in the upper reaches of the leadership, with not everyone favoring such explicitness. It also reflected, in my judgment, a real desire by the Brezhnev leadership to level off Soviet defense programs and reduce the long-standing high level of defense expenditures, and to stabilize strategic parity. The leadership hoped that Brezhnev's speech would be studied by the new administration and taken as a signal to open a strategic dialogue. Alas, President Carter and his new administration, swamped in the business of getting on board and taking charge, paid the Tula initiative too little attention. They did not reject it; they simply failed to recognize its significance.[64]

A summit meeting in 1977 would have provided the opportunity to explore a political-military dialogue. The Carter administration, however, while wishing to have a summit in order to open a political dialogue, undertook its disastrous new departure on SALT in March. In response, the Soviet leaders, very unwisely as it turned out, decided to link any summit to SALT. The rationale was to exert leverage on the Americans to return to an early agreement based on the Vladivostok accord. This action defeated the Soviets' own purpose in seeking a summit meeting and dialogue in 1977. And, as will become clear, the situation changed drastically in 1978, with worsening relations, even though neither side wanted that outcome.

Another step of little prominence but some importance occurred in January 1977. General of the Army Nikolai V. Ogarkov was made a marshal of the Soviet Union and named chief of the General Staff and first deputy minister of defense, making him the senior professional military man.

Finally, Brezhnev took an important last step in consolidating his power in the spring. On May 24 Podgorny was removed from the Politburo, and on June 16 Brezhnev replaced him as president (chairman of the Presidium of the Supreme Soviet of the USSR). Almost certainly related to this change, on June 3 the draft of a new Constitution of the USSR, to replace the Stalin Constitution of 1936, was published. That draft, with some amendments, was adopted as the new constitution on October 7, 1977.[65] According to reports,

---

63. "The Outstanding Exploit of the Defenders of Tula: Speech of L. I. Brezhnev," *Pravda*, January 19, 1977; and see a more extended discussion in chapter 22.

64. The Tula pronouncements on political-military policy and détente are on the record. The information about the debates, decision, and desire for a dialogue are based on off-the-record interviews I held with leading officials of the Soviet Central Committee and other institutions. See also chapter 22.

65. There was at least one consideration of practical relevance. Article 119 made the Defense Council, headed by Brezhnev since 1964, responsible to the Presidium of the Supreme Soviet. If Podgorny had continued to head the Presidium, it would have made Brezhnev's position as chairman of the Defense Council nominally subordinate. Since 1977 the chairman of the Presidium of the Supreme Soviet is also chairman of the Defense Council, according to *Sovet-*

which are plausible but which have not been confirmed or disproved, Podgorny had objected to efforts to bolster détente—as well as to his replacement by Brezhnev.[66] In the fall of 1977 Brezhnev was also identified for the first time in an open publication as commander-in-chief of the Soviet armed forces.[67]

As the Soviet leadership sought to project its own strategy of détente and to engage the new administration, it sought to analyze the makeup of the new American leadership. Soviet embassy officers throughout the 1970s had sought to cultivate contacts, especially with members of Congress and congressional staffs, the government bureaucracy, the press, and other members of the American political elite. These efforts were redoubled with the turnover and realignments occasioned by the first real change in administration in the eight years since détente had begun. Soviet political analysts in the Central Committee, Foreign Ministry, and academic institutes concerned with foreign relations all concentrated on the reassessment.

Carter was little known (even to the American political elite). His entourage included familiar figures such as Vance, Brown, and, in particular, Brzezinski. The Soviets were strongly suspicious of Brzezinski, because of his émigré Polish origin and the tough political stance he had shown as a leading academic commentator over the years. Moreover, he was known to have inspired the bridge-building and peaceful engagement policies toward Eastern Europe that the Johnson administration had pursued and that the Soviets had considered hostile.[68]

---

skoye administrativnoye pravo [Soviet Administrative Law] (Moscow: Yuridicheskaya literatura, 1981), p. 375.

During the six months from late 1982 to May 1983, when there was no chairman of the Presidium until Yury Andropov succeeded Brezhnev in that position as well as general secretary of the party, Andropov was chairman of the Defense Council. His successor, Konstantin Chernenko, held all three offices. Mikhail Gorbachev undoubtedly heads the Defense Council.

66. See, in particular, the report of an émigré former Soviet party official, Boris Rabbot, "One View on Why Podgorny Was Ousted," *Christian Science Monitor*, June 13, 1977. Some Soviet officials have partially supported this general interpretation in interviews with me. They did not, however, support specific charges by Rabbot that Soviet policy in Africa was an issue between Podgorny and Brezhnev. See also the interesting discussion by Grey Hodnett, "The Pattern of Leadership Politics," in Seweryn Bialer, ed., *The Domestic Context of Soviet Foreign Policy* (Boulder, Colo.: Westview, 1981), p. 96.

67. The identification was made by a deputy head of the main political administration of the armed forces in a military journal; see Colonel General G. N. Sredin, "The Source of Strength and Might," *Voyennyi vestnik* [The Military Herald], no. 10 (October 1977), p. 10.

68. In 1964 I had been asked by a counselor in the Soviet embassy to introduce him to a Department of State policy official "other than the usual SOV [Office of Soviet Union Affairs] types" whom he knew well. I arranged a luncheon with a friend, a visiting professor then serving two years on the department's Policy Planning Council—Zbigniew Brzezinski. In 1980, while visiting Moscow, this Soviet diplomat, now a senior official in the Ministry of Foreign Affairs, recalled the occasion. One of his colleagues told me I had done the official no favor. Based on this personal acquaintance years earlier, the official had argued in 1977 that Brzezinski was more moderate than the prevailing view in Moscow held. By 1980 all were certain he had not been moderate. The Soviet diplomat is now a deputy foreign minister.

Later Soviet evaluations of Carter personally, and of his administration, were heavily colored by events that occurred subsequently. But during 1977 the predominant judgment shifted from uncertainty based on unfamiliarity to uncertainty based on an experience of inconstancy. Carter talked of disarmament but wanted NATO to build up its forces. While dropping the B-1 bomber, in 1977 he pushed forward with the neutron weapon (June), cruise missiles (July), a counterforce capability for the Minuteman III with the Mark 12A warhead (June), and plans for a global rapid deployment force (August). The SALT flip-flop was especially serious: the Soviets saw the U.S. proposals of March 1977 as sabotaging plans (and earlier assurances) for an early SALT II and launching of SALT III negotiations (which, contrary to prevailing American assumption, they really wanted). Finally, one of the few encouraging signs—the readiness to include the Soviet Union in working for an Arab-Israeli settlement—was quickly backpedaled by Washington almost immediately after the joint statement became public in October 1977. It was then abandoned entirely when Sadat proposed a different path.[69] As Marshall Shulman, special adviser to Vance on Soviet affairs, stated later when testifying before Congress, "From a Soviet point of view there is obviously a concern that the trend in the last few years has been toward the exclusion of the Soviet Union from effective action in the Middle East. . . . They bear this very resentfully and have spoken of it quite sharply many times. . . . It clearly is the situation that the Soviet position in the Middle East has deteriorated compared to what it was. That has been the outcome of diplomatic efforts on our part."[70]

All in all, as 1977 ended the Soviet leaders saw relations with the United States as uncertain. SALT was more or less back on track, although plagued by new issues, while new negotiations were under way on the Indian Ocean area, on curbing conventional arms transfers, on a comprehensive nuclear test ban, and on some other subjects. After briefly showing promise for a joint Soviet-American initiative, prospects for the Middle East were suddenly clouded, but by the same token still open to possible maneuver. The United States continued to advocate détente, and a wide range of joint activities launched in 1972–73 continued to develop. Trade was evolving without further American restraints.[71] The Soviet Union itself did, as Soviet leaders had in-

---

69. Military and most arms control issues are discussed further in chapter 22; SALT in chapter 23; and Near Eastern events as appropriate throughout this chapter.

70. *United States Policy and United States–Soviet Relations, 1979*, Hearing before the Subcommittee on Europe and the Middle East of the House Committee on Foreign Affairs, 96 Cong. 1 sess. (GPO, 1979), pp. 21–22.

71. There were a few exceptions at the margin, for example, in June the Department of Commerce denied an export license to sell a Cyber-76 computer to TASS in Moscow. But American restrictions, other than those legislated in December 1974, were not a major issue.

One other aspect of economic relations, of a very different kind, should be mentioned. In April 1977 the CIA made public an unclassified version of a study which concluded that before 1985 the Soviet Union would face a shortfall in domestic petroleum production relative to

formed Secretary of Commerce Juanita Kreps in June, cut back sharply their nonagricultural imports from the United States owing to the U.S. credit and trade restrictions (including the absence of MFN status). Imports of machinery and equipment were cut nearly by half in 1977, and still more in 1978–79, from the levels in 1975–76, and overall trade dropped by one-quarter despite large purchases of grain. This decline with the United States did not reflect a contraction of trading by the Soviets: they turned more to Western Europe and Japan, reversing their preference of the early to mid-1970s for dealing with the United States, since terms were now unfavorable for continuing that course.

Elsewhere, the Soviet Union saw a prospective gain in influence from Mengistu's accession to power in Ethiopia, especially in light of his turn toward the Soviet Union to meet the threat from Somalia. Responding to this move had required the sacrifice of Soviet political (and naval) gains in Somalia, as attempts to keep a foot in both camps failed. More broadly, however, local developments (which still probably stirred Soviet suspicion of American intrigue) had caused the Soviet Union to suffer setbacks. The Sudan expelled the Soviet presence and North Yemen veered toward the West. The Western powers and their African proxies had intervened in Zaire, while Zaire itself supported intrigues and a reactivation of Savimbi's UNITA rebellion against the Soviet- and Cuban-supported regime in Angola. That regime itself now regarded the Soviet Union with some suspicion in the aftermath of the failed coup attempt by Alves. India had moved to a more truly nonaligned course after Gandhi's defeat, and Pakistan more to the right and to the West under General Zia. Also disturbing were the moves by President Mohammad Daoud in Afghanistan toward a more nonaligned position and rapprochement with Pakistan, as well as less tolerance of domestic leftists, all encouraged and abetted by the shah of Iran. The only favorable development in the Middle East had been a resolution of the differences with Asad's Syria early in the year, with the two brought closer together by common opposition to Egypt and the United States. But Asad was also keeping a line open to the United States.

In Asia, the adjustments to the passing of Mao Zedong and Zhou Enlai in China had still not offered any promise of improved Sino-Soviet relations. Kampuchean raids on Vietnam led at the end of the year to a break in diplomatic relations and Vietnamese occupation of the "Parrot's Beak." The Soviet Union, which had no ties to the Pol Pot regime in Kampuchea, saw a

---

rising consumption. The shortfall would necessitate net imports of oil. While this prediction was not borne out by later events, the study may not have been in error, even if the projection was. By 1978 and thereafter it was evident that the Soviets were undertaking vigorous remedial actions to prevent the predicted shortfall. It is possible that the CIA report jarred the Soviet leaders into action to keep the prediction from coming true. See Central Intelligence Agency, *The International Energy Situation: Outlook to 1985*, ER77-10240U (CIA, 1977), p. 13; CIA, *Prospects for Soviet Oil Production*, ER77-10270 (CIA, 1977). See also *The Soviet Oil Situation: An Evaluation of CIA Analyses of Soviet Oil Production*, Staff Report of the Senate Select Committee on Intelligence, 95 Cong. 2 sess. (GPO, 1978).

possibility in the year ahead of developing closer ties with Vietnam (which had been evenhanded between China and the Soviet Union since 1975).

All in all, Soviet-American relations not only had not recovered from the doldrums of 1976, but had worsened under the Carter administration's human rights offensive. Although after an initial setback negotiations in SALT and other areas of military détente were under way and offered some promise, they were by no means assured. Both cooperation and competition with the United States were sluggish. The Soviet Union had not pressed an offensive, and despite the opportunity in Ethiopia, gains there were far from assured. In any case, they would not begin to equal the losses in Egypt, the Sudan, Somalia, and North Yemen. Nor did the Soviet leaders see other broad opportunities arising, or plan an offensive, in 1978.

18   A Turn toward Confrontation, 1978

THE ADVERSE EFFECTS of the failure of the American and Soviet leadership in 1977 to find a common wave length on which to communicate, exemplified and intensified by the failure to hold a summit meeting and reopen a high-level direct dialogue, became evident when real issues arose in 1978 and were not adequately resolved.

Cooperation or Competition?

The first major issue to arise in 1978 was superpower competition in a local conflict that erupted in the Horn of Africa. American leaders, favoring détente, saw it challenged by Soviet intervention in the Horn early that year. On January 12 President Carter expressed "concern about the Soviet Union's unwarranted involvement in Africa," especially the supply of arms, and expressed the "hope that we can induce the Soviets and the Cubans not to send either soldiers or weapons into that area."[1] But the United States did not provide either inducements or pressure to dissuade the Soviet Union from continuing to supply military advisers and arms and Cuba from supplying advisers and troops.

The Ethiopian and Cuban forces in early 1978 continued their successful drive to push the defeated Saudi army out of Ethiopia. By March 5 the last key center, Jijiga, had fallen, and on March 9 Carter announced that Somalia had agreed to withdraw its army completely from Ethiopia. He also expressed the expectation that after Ethiopian forces had reasserted control in that area, "withdrawal of the Soviet and Cuban military presence should be-

---

1. "The President's News Conference of January 12, 1978," *Weekly Compilation of Presidential Documents*, vol. 14 (January 16, 1978), pp. 56–57. (Hereafter *Presidential Documents*.)

gin."[2] Strong American representation to the Soviet Union (and a common Soviet and American interest) led the Soviets to warn Mengistu not to cross into Somalia itself, and the Ethiopians did not do so. Thus the superpowers succeeded in persuading the local warring parties to return to the territorial status quo ante and not to continue direct hostilities.

While the United States had favored the cessation of hostilities in the Horn and contributed to that outcome, another objective was not met. From the American perspective the Soviet Union, again aided by Cuba, had intervened successfully despite U.S. efforts. On March 1, 1978, Brzezinski had escalated administration complaints about Soviet and Cuban military assistance to Ethiopia by warning that Soviet activities in the Horn "would inevitably complicate SALT." This was the first time a Carter administration spokesman had linked SALT to other Soviet activities. *Pravda* replied the following day with a bitter attack that such linkage was an attempt at "crude blackmail."[3] Amid signs that Secretary of State Vance did not approve the Brzezinski statement, on March 2 President Carter himself clarified the administration's position by denying "any government policy that has a linkage between the Soviet involvement in [the] Ethiopia-Somalia dispute on the one hand and SALT or the comprehensive [nuclear] test ban negotiations on the other." He did, however, comment on the concern of the American people and the need for Congress to ratify any agreement. In that sense, he said, "the two are linked because of actions by the Soviets."[4]

While the American administration was expressing dissatisfaction with Soviet activities in the Horn of Africa,[5] the Soviet leadership was still trying to get its bearings on the basic Soviet-American bilateral relationship. On February 24 Brezhnev included in his speech to the Supreme Soviet several

---

2. "The President's News Conference of March 9, 1978," *Presidential Documents*, vol. 14 (March 13, 1978), p. 490. Carter emphasized the active American role by himself announcing the Somali decision, which had been conveyed to him the night before. It was followed by an American mission to Somalia March 18–23 to discuss arms requests. The talks did not result in an arms supply agreement because the Somalis refused to give up territorial claims to the Ogaden region or to forgo indirect intervention there through "irregulars." China followed the United States in sending a mission to Somalia in April, and signed an agreement on cooperation (presumably nonmilitary) on April 18. Flare-ups continued in May and June. On May 12 Lieutenant Colonel Mengistu Haile Mariam of Ethiopia threatened to invade Somalia if they continued, but the situation finally settled down.

3. Georgy Ratiani, "When a Sense of Responsibility Is Lost," *Pravda*, March 2, 1978.

4. "The President's News Conference of March 2, 1978," *Presidential Documents*, vol. 14 (March 6, 1978), p. 442.

   For Brzezinski's views, see Zbigniew Brzezinski, *Power and Principle: Memoirs of the National Security Adviser, 1977–1981* (Farrar, Straus, Giroux, 1983), pp. 185–86; for Vance's, see Cyrus Vance, *Hard Choices: Critical Years in America's Foreign Policy* (Simon and Schuster, 1983), pp. 87–91, 100–03.

5. The subject of Soviet and other involvement in the Horn of Africa in 1978 is dealt with in greater detail in chapter 19.

interesting comments on the state of relations with the United States. He stressed that the "foundation" of Soviet-American relations was grounded in the series of agreements reached at the summit meetings. He said that the path to further improvements in relations was open, but that in the United States (unidentified) "forces" not interested in good relations between the two countries, "nor in the relaxation of international tensions in general," were blocking that path "by all manner of obstacles." He implicitly criticized the American posture on SALT by stressing that the Soviet position was "consistent and definite." He urged rapid agreement on SALT and promised then to move to the next stage—which "would be a genuine turning point on the path to military détente." He also referred, among other things, to the "well known decisions of the American Congress" that created artificial difficulties to economic and scientific-technical cooperation.

Brezhnev was careful not to criticize the administration; rather he appealed to it. "In concluding, Comrades," he addressed his colleagues, "I would like to stress that we consider Soviet-American relations as an important element in the overall policy course of the Soviet Union, a course of strengthening peace, ending the arms race, and developing equal and mutually advantageous cooperation between our states."[6] While the American conception of détente was now defined as cooperation and competition, with an increasing stress on the latter, the declared Soviet definition remained cooperation—with criticism of those, unnamed, in and outside the American administration who favored competition and placed obstacles in the path of improved relations.

On March 3 President Carter commented on SALT in an interview, saying that "good and steady progress" was being made but that eventually a meeting of himself with President Brezhnev would probably be needed.[7] His next major statement on U.S.-Soviet relations came in an address at Wake Forest University on March 17, drafted by Brzezinski and his staff. Carter chose to stress the buildup in Soviet military power and his responsibility as commander-in-chief for strengthening U.S. military forces to meet security needs. Alluding to a recently completed "major reassessment of our national defense strategy," he was clearly emphasizing unilateral military programs. "We will match . . . any threatening power. . . . We will not allow any other nation to gain military superiority over us." Carter said that apart from the Soviet military buildup (which was reaching "functional equivalence in strategic forces with the United States"), "there also has been an ominous inclination on the part of the Soviet Union to use its military power—to intervene in local conflicts, with advisers, with equipment, and with full logistical support

---

6. L. I. Brezhnev, "Speech to the Session of the Presidium of the Supreme Soviet of the USSR," *Pravda*, February 25, 1978; and L. I. Brezhnev, *O vneshnei politike KPSS i sovetskogo gosudarstva: Rechi i stat'i* [On the Foreign Policy of the CPSU and the Soviet Government: Speeches and Articles], 3d ed. (Moscow: Politizdat, 1978), pp. 696–97.

7. "Interview with the President," March 3, *Presidential Documents*, vol. 14 (March 13, 1978), pp. 459–60.

and encouragement for mercenaries from other Communist countries, as we can observe today in Africa."

Although Carter reaffirmed American support for SALT and arms control, the tone was markedly different from that of a year earlier. Now he included all the qualifiers beloved by Senator Jackson and the JCS—"dependable, verifiable arms control agreements wherever possible"—and said, "Before I sign any SALT agreement on behalf of the United States, I will make sure that it preserves the strategic balance, that we can independently verify Soviet compliance, and that we will be at least as strong, relative to the Soviet Union, as we would be without any agreement." He also spoke of "significantly strengthening U.S. forces stationed in Western Europe" and of attention to defenses, to be addressed at the forthcoming NATO summit meeting, in view of what he described as an "excessive Soviet buildup" in Europe "beyond a level necessary for defense." The president was leaving the university, he noted in his speech, to fly by helicopter to the American nuclear-powered aircraft carrier *Nimitz.*

As for détente—a word never actually mentioned in the address—cooperation with the Soviet Union was possible to meet common goals. "But if they fail to demonstrate restraint in missile programs and other force levels or in the projection of Soviet or proxy forces into other lands and continents, then popular support in the United States for such cooperation with the Soviets will certainly erode."[8]

TASS promptly questioned whether the speech signaled a shift in American relations toward the Soviet Union and declared that "Soviet goals abroad" had been distorted as an excuse to escalate the arms race. On March

---

8. "Address at Wake Forest University," March 17, *Presidential Documents,* vol. 14 (March 27, 1978), pp. 529–35. The speech was followed by a background briefing by unnamed White House officials—not including Brzezinski—who stated that the speech was intended not only to warn the Russians, but also to reassure the American public on defense and to counter the criticism by hard-liners of SALT and the Panama Canal treaties. See, for example, Martin Tolchin, "U.S. Aides Say Warning to Soviet Also Aimed at Domestic Critics," *New York Times,* March 20, 1978. The "major reassessment" Carter referred to as "recently completed" was the Presidential Review Memorandum (PRM)–10 study, and Presidential Directive (PD)–18, issued eight months earlier; see chapter 22.

As noted, the speech was drafted in the NSC. Although Secretary of State Vance had had an opportunity to comment on a draft, he did not know what was in the final version until it was delivered and was not in a position to give a copy or even to describe its content and programs to Ambassador Dobrynin when they had lunch together on March 16. On the 17th, the day the speech was delivered, Dobrynin was en route to Moscow. Thus an opportunity was lost to clarify the message intended for the Soviet leadership. The incident also illustrated the shift from Kissinger's policy of regularly providing advance notice and explanation of such statements, which the Soviet leaders had come to expect.

Marshall D. Shulman, Vance's special assistant on Soviet affairs, did (without White House approval) advise the Soviet chargé d'affaires that the speech should be understood as designed primarily for domestic consumption and not as a sign of declining American interest in SALT or détente—an initiative that Brzezinski criticizes roundly in his memoir. See Brzezinski, *Power and Principle,* p. 189.

28 *Pravda* published a major article on Soviet-American relations by Academi-cian Georgy Arbatov that gave a more considered response. Arbatov noted that relations had been "sliding backward" and were "at a crossroads." He said the Carter administration was torn between those wishing to move ahead with détente and those opposed. He urged new efforts on SALT, which depended above all on a "political decision" accepting parity. Arbatov acknowledged that the "overall political atmosphere" had been adversely affected by the develop-ments in the Horn of Africa. But he denied Soviet responsibility and argued that Somalia would not have attacked in the first place unless it had been led to believe it could count on American support. He also charged that the ad-ministration's own rhetoric was responsible for worsening the atmosphere. Fi-nally, he argued that détente would not be possible if the two sides allowed "complicated circumstances" to keep them from working together to resolve the "main, decisive" problems in their relations.[9]

On April 7 Brezhnev himself reacted to Carter's speech. He avoided picking up the gauntlet directly; instead he again criticized unnamed "forces interested in the arms race and in charging an atmosphere of fear and hostility" and "sowing doubts as to the possibilities of practical measures in arms limita-tion and disarmament." (In introducing this passage he referred to such "forces both in the West, and in the East on our borders," although later he explicitly referred to such forces in the United States. The speech was made in Vladivos-tok, in the course of an unusual, long visit by Brezhnev and Defense Minister Ustinov to Siberia that followed shortly after China rejected the Soviet over-tures to improve relations.) Brezhnev used the occasion to recall the accord on SALT reached in Vladivostok with President Ford in November 1974. In this connection he was more direct in criticizing "the American government" for displaying "indecisiveness and inconsistency" and "glancing back at those cir-cles which from the very beginning have been against agreement and are doing everything to undermine it and free their hands for an uncontrolled arms race in nuclear-missile arms." He warned, in more prophetic words than he could have realized, that unless a SALT accord were concluded soon, it would mean a loss of all opportunity for agreement.[10]

SALT negotiations continued,[11] but they were bedeviled by Ameri-can objections to Soviet involvement in Africa. Secretary of State Vance raised the matter with Brezhnev and Gromyko in Moscow in April but was rebuffed. Following that visit, in a speech on April 25 Brezhnev referred to progress on SALT (and on banning nuclear testing), but also to "enemies of détente and disarmament in the countries of NATO," unnamed except that they included

---

9. Georgy Arbatov, "Soviet-American Relations: A Time for Crucial Decisions," *Pravda*, March 28, 1978.

10. Brezhnev, *O vneshnei politike*, pp. 699–701. Incidentally, Brezhnev paralleled Carter's naval trappings for the speech by delivering it on board the cruiser *Admiral Senyavin* in Vladivostok harbor.

11. See chapter 23.

"politicized generals and militant politicians." In particular he defended against the charge of Soviet intervention in the third world: "Imperialist propaganda, attempting to distort the conception and aims of the foreign policy of the Soviet Union, affirms that there is some kind of contradiction between the course of our foreign policy on détente and peaceful coexistence and our relations with countries liberated from colonialism. They attempt to accuse the Soviet Union and other socialist countries of interference in the affairs of new states. They even go so far as accusations of 'a policy of expansion' and 'raising tensions.' All that, of course, is a complete fabrication, having nothing in common with reality."[12] Nonetheless, Brezhnev strongly reaffirmed the need for détente and for arms limitation and reduction. He said détente was now "not a theory, a slogan or a good intention" but a reality. It now underlay relations in Europe and, "despite all of the current oscillations," Soviet-American relations as well.[13]

At this time not only was the situation in the Horn of Africa still volatile—Somalia was again sending irregular forces to infiltrate Ethiopia's Ogaden, while the Ethiopian army, this time without Cuban troops, was launching an offensive against the insurgents in Eritrea. But Chad was also in turmoil, the situation in Rhodesia was potentially explosive, and the Katangese in Angola had again launched an incursion into Zaire's Shaba province. This time they seized the city of Kolwezi. On May 18–20 French and Belgian paratroopers (brought in by American aircraft) rescued the civilian European hostages and drove the invaders back. Soviet spokesmen attacked the U.S.-supported Western European foreign intervention.[14]

When Gromyko visited the White House on May 27 to discuss SALT, on which some further progress was made, President Carter unwisely (and inaccurately) accused the Soviet Union of involvement in the Katangese invasion of Zaire. While this incident and its aftermath are discussed later,[15] here it is important to note that the administration spent several weeks attempting to support this stand (which Gromyko had promptly denied). The issue came to involve a domestic American dispute about the evidence supporting the president's position. That evidence concerned earlier Cuban training of the Katangans and did not prove Cuban (much less Soviet) instigation or support for the present invasion. The dispute ended with the president arguing not that the Soviets and Cubans had *launched* the invasion, but that Castro had not done enough to *prevent* it. Before leaving this incident it is also worth noting the marked contrast to the calm reaction of the administration to the first invasion of Shaba a year earlier.

---

12. Brezhnev, "Speech to the XVIII Congress of the All-Union Leninist Communist Union of Youth," April 25, 1978, *O vneshnei politike*, p. 705, and also see pp. 703–05 generally.

13. Ibid., pp. 702, 706.

14. See chapter 19.

15. Ibid.

The results were a worsening of relations with the Soviet Union at a delicate juncture, doubts in the United States about both Soviet conduct and the competence of the Carter administration, and increasing Soviet suspicion that the United States was intentionally turning toward confrontation in preference to détente.

Illustrative of the confusion evident during the dispute was Brzezinski's television interview on May 28 during the controversy over the Shaba affair. He replied to one question by affirming: "I can assure you that what the President said was right." But he then went on to say something entirely different—that the *Angolan* government must have *known* about it, which was far from meaning that even the Angolan government was responsible, to say nothing of the Cubans, or least of all the Soviets. Deftly shifting the argument from evidence of Soviet or Cuban involvement in the Katangan caper, Brzezinski made sweeping new accusations about Soviet behavior in general in the Middle East, Africa, and South Asia, and vis-à-vis China, as interventionist. "This pattern of behavior," he claimed, was not "compatible with what was once called the code of détente."[16] The press immediately picked up this charge as a sign that Brzezinski was putting the United States on a hard-line course with the Soviet Union.

In April the American press had begun to feature a number of articles about growing tensions between Brzezinski and Secretary of State Vance and the Department of State, often clearly stimulated by background interviews and conversations by administration officials with newsmen.[17] These tensions were indeed rising. They also reflected a change in policy direction already under way, whether consciously or not. President Carter, concerned over what he saw as a more assertive Soviet role in Africa, was increasingly inclined to endorse the harder-line policies favored by Brzezinski. Events in the world (and in domestic politics) were affecting the balance within the administration. And this shift in turn began to have major effects on some key foreign policy issues.

President Carter's Wake Forest speech of March 17, as earlier noted, placed a strong accent on defense preparedness. The NATO summit meeting on May 30–31 in Washington was the occasion not only for oratory, but also for launching a major new long-term defense program for the alliance.[18] From the Soviet standpoint the United States seemed to be holding back on SALT in order to give impetus to military programs. Some later Soviet

---

16. "Interview: National Security Adviser Brzezinski on 'Meet the Press,' " May 28, *Department of State Bulletin*, vol. 78 (July 1978), pp. 26–27. (Hereafter *State Bulletin*.) Note that Brzezinski's reference to a code of détente is in the past tense.

17. For example, see William Safire, "Reading Arbatov's Mind," *New York Times*, April 13, 1978; Richard Burt, "Tension Grows between Brzezinski and State Department," *New York Times*, April 17, 1978; Karen Elliott House and Kenneth Bacon, "Detente's Decline," *Wall Street Journal*, April 18, 1978; and "Tensions of State," *Newsweek*, April 24, 1978, p. 47.

18. See chapter 25.

accounts describe the May 1978 NATO summit decision as a critical turning point in torpedoing the Soviet-American détente of the 1970s.[19] While that sweeping judgment would be an exaggeration even in terms of depicting the overall Soviet view of the causes of the breakdown of détente, the 1978 NATO decision was an important negative development as far as the Soviet leaders were concerned.

The China Card I

A much more significant development was a new, parallel move by the United States to build a political-military encirclement of the Soviet Union. In May President Carter decided to play the China card.[20]

It is quite unlikely that Carter realized the far-reaching importance of his decision to authorize Brzezinski to undertake a major diplomatic mission to China in the spring of 1978. The deciding factor was the administration's perception of Soviet and Soviet-backed Cuban intervention in Africa, in particular in Ethiopia. The administration wanted to remind the Soviet leaders that it could bring pressure to bear by upgrading its ties with China and by shifting their nature toward strategic cooperation against the Soviet Union. The intent was to move the Soviet leaders toward more circumspect and docile competition around the world.

While all the senior members of the administration agreed to this general aim, there were very significant differences in approach and with respect to other objectives. Secretary of State Vance saw American-Chinese relations as a potential lever on Soviet behavior but believed triangular relations should be handled very carefully so as not to move the United States toward an alignment with China against the Soviet Union. That situation he saw as likely to lead the Soviet Union to respond with more rather than less assertive actions in the world, and ultimately to reduce American flexibility. Brzezinski, on the other hand, not only believed that the United States should show more vigor in competing with the Soviet Union by stimulating concern about its Chinese flank. He also thought there *should* be significant Sino-American alignment against the Soviet Union, and that this would enhance American leverage.

For his part Carter wanted somehow to demonstrate to the Soviet leaders that the United States could and would react forcefully to what he saw as destabilizing Soviet intervention in the third world, principally Africa, but also in such developments as the recent coup in Afghanistan that had brought

---

19. For example, see I. Kremer, "The Politics of Missed Opportunities," *Novoye vremya* [New Times], no. 7 (February 15, 1980), p. 6; and Yury Sherkovin, "A Different Mentality Needed," *New Times*, no. 17 (April 1981), p. 18.

20. For a full discussion of what is treated here only summarily, see chapter 20.

a pro-Soviet regime to power. After Vance won on the issue of linking SALT to Soviet-Cuban activities in the Horn, the United States had no other cards to play. So Carter decided demonstratively to remind the Soviets of the Sino-American connection. He also wanted to explore the possibilities for normalizing relations with China, which (with Vance's full agreement) he now wanted to accomplish in his first term.[21] The administration was thus in full agreement both on seeking to improve relations with China and on doing so at a time when it could also remind the Soviets that the United States, too, could compete geopolitically.

Carter also decided, probably without realizing the full significance of his action, to let Brzezinski carry the ball to Beijing. Vance was concerned about Brzezinski's ardent championship of developing the Sino-American relationship as a counter to American-Soviet relations and unsuccessfully opposed his making the trip. Carter assumed that since Brzezinski would be guided by agreed instructions, it would only be to the good if the Soviets were a little alarmed by the trip. Moreover, Vance had been to China—without notable success—and was at the time deeply involved in the SALT negotiations. As Carter wanted to send a senior emissary, he decided on Brzezinski.

The Brzezinski mission in May occurred at a critical juncture in Sino-Soviet relations. In March the Chinese had rejected Soviet overtures. At the same time Chinese-Vietnamese relations were rapidly deteriorating, and Soviet-Vietnamese relations were improving.[22] Brezhnev and Defense Minister Ustinov had personally visited the Soviet Far East in March on a tour stressing military defense against China. On May 9, just two weeks before Brzezinski was to arrive in Beijing, the border tensions led to a brief Soviet military intrusion across the Ussuri River into Manchuria.

Brzezinski played his opportunity in China to the hilt. He and his team of high-level NSC, State, and Defense officials went out of their way to give briefings on American strategic policy, on the possibilities for technological assistance, on aspects of the world situation, and on measures to counter Soviet policy and activities that were very much in tune with Chinese views. The talks included specific areas of collaboration in some situations, including Africa. Brzezinski added his own personal gestures such as comments about baiting "the polar bear" to the north, a remark made at the Great Wall. On another occasion, in Beijing, he said the Soviets supported "international marauders," referring to Soviet and Cuban actions in Africa.[23] Indeed, it was

---

21. Brzezinski had, in the spring of 1977, set the end of 1978 as a target for the full normalization of relations with China. See Brzezinski, *Power and Principle*, p. 53.

22. As early as January 8, 1978, after Vietnamese forays into Kampuchea in the border war developing between those two communist countries, Brzezinski described the conflict as "the first proxy war" between the Soviet Union and China. Brzezinski, Interview on CBS, January 8, 1978.

23. Fox Butterfield, "Brzezinski in China: The Stress Was on Common Concerns," *New York Times*, May 24, 1978.

sometimes difficult from the content to distinguish American from Chinese toasts. When Brzezinski returned, he told the *New York Times,* "The basic significance of the trip was to underline the long-term strategic nature of the United States relationship to China."[24]

Thus a card intended initially by Carter to retaliate for Soviet and Cuban actions in Africa was converted into a long-term strategic relationship binding the United States and China more closely. Moreover, the Chinese, recognizing Carter's desire to move toward normalization of relations, skillfully rewarded Brzezinski by doing so, breaking the stalemate that had prevailed since the Shanghai Communiqué in 1972. The Chinese wished to show that the Brzezinski line of a common strategic platform directed against the Soviet Union would pay off in normalizing relations, in contrast to the low-key effort to develop bilateral relations on their own merits that Secretary of State Vance had put forward without success during his visit in August 1977. The success of Brzezinski's mission also boosted his own standing in the president's eyes, and hence in the Washington power structure.

Choose: Confrontation or Cooperation

These several policy lines pursued by the United States—the challenges over intervention in Africa (reciprocally perceived), the NATO summit decision to boost military programs, and Brzezinski's trip to play the China card, as well as the changing balance within the Carter administration itself— all peaked before mid–1978.

In late May, soon after Brzezinski's return from China, Gromyko met with President Carter. Brzezinski comments that "the meeting did not go well," in part because the Soviet attitude was difficult but in part because Carter seemed (to Brzezinski) too eager for SALT.[25] In fact, as Vance notes in his memoir, Gromyko brought a major Soviet concession on SALT: agreement to freeze the number of warheads that could be deployed on various types of ICBMs. But Vance also notes that Carter and Gromyko had "acerbic exchanges" over Soviet and Cuban involvement in Africa and over human rights.[26]

Two days later Secretary of State Vance submitted a memorandum to the president formally requesting a review of relations with the Soviet Union and posing the issue of the "two differing views of the U.S.-Soviet

---

24. Bernard Gwertzman, "Brzezinski Gave Details to China on Arms Talks with Soviet Union," *New York Times,* May 28, 1978.

25. Brzezinski, *Power and Principle,* p. 319.

26. Vance, *Hard Choices,* pp. 102–03.

relationship." He did not specifically identify the one view as his own and the other as Brzezinski's, but that was scarcely necessary. Vance noted, "We have always recognized that the relationship between the U.S. and the Soviet Union has been a combination of cooperation and competition, with the competition not preventing either side from seeking agreements in our mutual benefit in such areas as SALT." He then posed the question as he saw it: "Now, however, we are coming to the point where there is a growing pressure on the part of some people to have us portray the competitive aspects of the relationship as taking clear precedence over the search for areas of cooperation." He also noted the increasingly public speculation in the press that the government was divided over policy and proposed that either he or the president give a broad speech on American relations with the Soviet Union.[27]

Vance had been strongly impressed by the implications of the growing deterioration in U.S.-Soviet relations and by the fact (as evidenced in the Gromyko meeting) that the Soviets also seemed to be increasingly disturbed by the trend. He believed that American display of hostility could lead to new hard-line Soviet actions to which the United States would feel compelled to respond. Vance revealed a number of reservations on his own part about the turn in American policy. Recognizing that the Soviet leaders saw the administration's human rights efforts as aimed at overthrowing their system, he warned the president that "there was a critical point beyond which our public pressure was causing the Soviets to crack down harder on Soviet dissidents." He warned against "trying to play off China against the Soviets." Instead, he argued, the United States should "accept the fact of competition with the Soviets, and we should not link Soviet behavior in the Third World to issues in which we had so fundamental an interest as SALT." He called for using U.S. influence to deter Soviet behavior in the third world and believed the United States "held most of the cards in the East-West competition." The United States should not exaggerate Soviet threats and should "project a sense of confidence and consistency" in its public statements. This private letter was Secretary of State Vance's major effort to prevent what he saw, correctly, as a turn in American policy.[28]

Brzezinski also urged that Carter make a speech on relations with the Soviet Union—but with different content. While Vance recommended lowering tensions, Brzezinski urged a tougher line, especially on global geopolitical competition, using other elements of bilateral relations as leverage through linkage.

As reports of the differences within the administration increased and uncertainty grew over whether the United States was on a path of détente

27. These passages are cited by Brzezinski, *Power and Principle*, pp. 319–20; Vance does not give the exact language in his own account.

28. Vance, *Hard Choices*, pp. 101–02.

or confrontation with the Soviet Union, Carter did make a major speech on American-Soviet relations. Presented at his alma mater, the U.S. Naval Academy in Annapolis, on June 7, the speech offered an odd mixture of détente and confrontation. Carter began by restating the familiar theme of his administration that the American-Soviet relationship was one of both competition and cooperation and that the United States wanted to expand cooperation but was strong and prepared to meet competition. Carter stated, "Détente between our two countries is central to world peace." At the same time he argued, "To be stable, to be supported by the American people, and to be a basis for widening the scope of cooperation, then détente must be broadly defined and truly reciprocal. Both nations must exercise restraint in troubled areas and in troubled times."[29]

As the speech continued, the tone grew increasingly combative. "Our long-term objectives must be to convince the Soviet Union of cooperation and of the costs of disruptive behavior [in the world]." But Carter also raised to the level of "our principal goal" the aim of helping to "shape a world which is more responsive to the desire of people everywhere for economic well-being, social justice, political self-determination, and basic human rights." This implied a strong American role with respect to Soviet internal affairs. And he went much further. He referred to Soviet "abuse of basic human rights in their own country, in violation of the agreement which was reached in Helsinki," which he said had "earned them the condemnation of people everywhere who love freedom." Moreover, "by their actions, they've demonstrated that the Soviet system cannot tolerate freely expressed ideas or notions of loyal opposition and the free movement of peoples." Apart from agitating aggressively on the issue of human rights within the Soviet Union, Carter also issued a very strong challenge to the whole Soviet system, internal and international. In an unprecedented statement he declared: "We want to increase our collaboration with the Soviet Union, *but* also with the emerging nations, with the nations of Eastern Europe, and with the People's Republic of China. We are particularly dedicated to genuine self-determination and majority rule in those areas of the world where these goals have not yet been attained."[30]

Finally came the punch line: "The Soviet Union can choose either confrontation or cooperation. The United States is adequately prepared to meet either choice."[31]

Carter may have meant to reaffirm that, while the United States preferred détente, the actions of the Soviet Union could require confrontation. But to the Soviet leaders (and to many Americans) the president seemed to be

---

29. "United States Naval Academy," President Carter's Address at Commencement Exercises, Annapolis, June 7, *Presidential Documents*, vol. 14 (June 12, 1978), p. 1053.

30. Ibid., pp. 1053–54. Emphasis added.

31. Ibid., p. 1057.

throwing down the gauntlet.[32] "President Challenges Soviet Leaders" was the banner headline of the *Washington Post* the next day.

The Annapolis speech was so disjunctive in its combined reaffirmation of détente and articulation of a confrontational strategy that the general reaction was perplexity. Many comments were made, not all in jest, that Carter must have stapled together two drafts prepared by Vance and Brzezinski. The *Washington Post* subtitled its lead story "Two Different Speeches"; the *New York Times*, "Carter on Soviet: An Ambiguous Message"; and the *Washington Star*, "Did Carter Leave Them All Baffled with Annapolis Speech?" The *New York Times* commented editorially: "The White House Lions and the State Department Beavers have struggled to a draw. If we heard him right in his address on the Russians yesterday, President Carter told the Lions to keep on roaring about Soviet behavior in Africa and he told the Beavers to keep on building a structure of arms control agreements. And he told the Russian leaders that he must govern a nation of both lions and beavers."[33] Clearly the speech was a confusing political signal.

Brzezinski has said that the Annapolis speech was written largely by the president himself, including the challenge to choose cooperation or confrontation, and that he and Vance then reviewed it jointly.[34] Vance notes that

32. President Carter made a change in the text of the speech as he delivered it, hardening one point of particular interest. According to the advance copies of the prepared text, Carter had planned to say: "I am convinced that the leaders of the Soviet Union want peace. I cannot believe that they could possibly want war." In the speech as delivered and officially reprinted, the first sentence substituted "the Soviet people" for "the leaders of the Soviet Union." Ibid., p. 1053. Did Carter harbor real doubts on that score, or did he not wish to give the Soviet leaders that much credit?

33. Murrey Marder, "President Challenges Soviet Leaders: Two Different Speeches," *Washington Post*, June 8, 1978; Bernard Gwertzman, "Carter on Soviet: An Ambiguous Message," *New York Times*, June 9, 1978; Mary McGrory, "Did Carter Leave Them All Baffled with Annapolis Speech?" *Washington Star*, June 12, 1978; and editorial, "From Linkage to Sausage," *New York Times*, June 8, 1978.

34. Brzezinski, *Power and Principle*, pp. 320–21. Brzezinski expresses surprise that Vance did not object to some of the tougher statements, including the challenge of choice. There was, however, no agreement over the terms of détente, which Brzezinski downplays. For example, the passage cited contained a bland statement that "détente must be broadly defined." This wording was the outcome of a serious disagreement over whether the United States should state that détente must be *comprehensive*, that is, linking all aspects of behavior and providing a foundation of political linkage, as Brzezinski wanted. Vance successfully argued against "comprehensive" and settled for the looser (and more obscure) phrase "must be broadly defined." (This information is from a participant in the discussions among the president, Vance, and Brzezinski.) Some of the compromises led to virtually incomprehensible language. For example, what should have been an important paragraph reads, in its entirety: "The word 'détente' can be simplistically defined as 'the easing of tension between nations.' The word is, in practice, however, further defined by experience, as those nations evolve new means by which they can live with each other in peace." *Presidential Documents*, vol. 14 (June 12, 1978), p. 1053. Sins of syntax aside, its meaning remains elusive. One of its authors could not later

Carter ended up "splitting the difference" between his and Brzezinski's drafts, so that "the end result was a stitched-together speech. Instead of combating the growing perception of an administration rent by internal divisions, the image of an inconsistent and uncertain government was underlined."[35] Yet the speech was, in a way, an accurate reflection of President Carter's own thinking at that stage. It reflected a personal desire for cooperation. But it clearly escalated the confrontational element, reflecting what President Carter and Brzezinski saw as a need to meet a mounting Soviet geopolitical challenge in the third world.

From the perspective of the Soviet leadership, the speech appeared to represent not a choice for them, but a choice for confrontation already made by Carter. Moreover, if détente was indeed a mix of cooperation and competition (as both sides had accepted in fact, if not always in rhetoric), why suddenly pose an either/or choice? The only reason would be to afford an excuse for abandoning détente and blaming the other side. *Pravda* charged that the speech posed impermissible demands on the Soviet Union, coupled with a warning that noncompliance with those demands would undermine détente. It also commented that "the basically aggressive 'hard line' of Brzezinski, widely known for his anticommunist bias, is getting the upper hand in the White House. This policy is fraught with a return to the cold war . . . with a transition to confrontation."[36]

A major Soviet statement on Soviet-American relations followed a few days later.[37] It explained that "an acute struggle has been going for quite a time now in the ruling circles of the United States over détente and relations with the Soviet Union." The U.S. government was accused of "whipping up the arms race" (including the NATO plan for long-term buildup), of adopting a dangerous anti-Soviet alignment with China, of turning to armed intervention in Africa, of deliberately slowing down negotiations on strategic arms limitations, and of "deliberately worsening bilateral relations with the USSR." Carter's Annapolis speech was specifically criticized. Noting that the speech had been designed to clarify U.S. policy, the Soviet statement argued that it

---

explain it to me. Incidentally, as an informed press commentary noted, the president's domestic political advisers, in particular Hamilton Jordan, were consulted separately and also had a hand in the drafting. See Martin Tolchin, "Political Aides Lent a Hand for Foreign Policy Talk," *New York Times*, June 8, 1978.

35. Vance, *Hard Choices*, p. 102.

36. Vladimir Bolshakov, "The Week Internationally," *Pravda*, June 11, 1978.

37. The Soviet response was very carefully considered. The Politburo itself met twice to discuss the matter, the first time two days after the speech. It approved the statement issued as an unsigned editorial article in *Pravda* on June 17. (This information is from an informed Soviet source.) TASS reported the American reactions in unusual detail, stressing that the piece had been received as "an important foreign policy statement." At the same time the article, while obviously authoritative, had no official status.

had failed to do so because it sought to reconcile the irreconcilable: support for détente and improved U.S.-Soviet relations, coupled with an attack on the Soviet Union. The article stated that it was "evidently not fortuitous" that in endorsing détente the president had failed to mention the agreement on Basic Principles of Mutual Relations of 1972 and the Agreement on Prevention of Nuclear War of 1973. It was "precisely in these documents" that the Soviet Union, as well as the United States, had both made a choice for détente.[38]

The sharply conflicting American and Soviet statements of June 1978 reflected the growing gap in understanding and even in communication between the two powers, as well as underlining the turn toward confrontation. Carter said "détente must be broadly defined and truly reciprocal"; the Soviet statement stressed "the mutual commitments" of détente set out in the agreements. Each criticized the other for destabilizing activities in Africa. Each saw the other as stimulating the arms race. Each spoke in favor of SALT but saw the position of the other as the obstacle. Each regarded its stance as defensive, and that of the other as offensive.

To the Soviet leaders Carter's statements about working with other communist nations to promote democracy looked like a direct challenge to work toward establishing pro-Western governments not only in the third world, but in Eastern Europe as well (which Carter also referred to as "a tightly controlled bloc"). The speech also reflected the shift toward a higher priority on U.S. relations with China. The first *Pravda* article earlier cited commented: "Not only has the American president permitted intolerable attacks on the social system in the USSR, he has demanded freedom of action for imperialist agents in the socialist countries."[39] The later *Pravda* statement, which had referred to a "deliberate worsening of bilateral relations," noted "unilateral American restrictions" being placed on ties and contacts between the two countries, and interference in internal affairs. It stressed the effect of these actions was to erode "the still very modest foundation of mutual confidence which was created through so much labor, effort and patience, and which is so necessary for strengthening peace, ending the arms race, and furthering détente. Particularly disastrous for mutual confidence are attempts to interfere in the internal affairs of the other side. And such attempts have now been elevated in the United States to the level of state policy." Confidence was expressed in "the monolithic unity of Soviet society" against "malignant propaganda from abroad, and subversive actions of Western special services." Even so, "such actions engender ever new doubts as to the real intentions of the leaders of the United States and certain nations allied to it, poison the atmosphere, and complicate cooperation."[40]

---

38. Editorial, "On the Present Policy of the U.S. Government," *Pravda*, June 17, 1978.

39. Bolshakov, *Pravda*, June 11, 1978.

40. Editorial, *Pravda*, June 17, 1978.

President Carter was not only holding fast to the emphasis on human rights that he had championed from the outset, but was also pressing the issue virtually as a precondition to détente. At least, so it seemed to the Soviet leaders, and not without some foundation. This policy of linkage of détente to Soviet internal developments, as noted, marked a sharp departure from the Nixon-Ford administrations and a rejection of Vance's advice.

Carter also reiterated, in harder terms, the compromise formulation of a linkage of SALT with other problems in foreign relations. While disclaiming any "desire" to tie SALT to such things as actions and disputes over intervention in Africa, he noted that public opinion in the United States is "an integral factor in the shaping and implementation of foreign policy" and such "threats to peace will complicate the quest for a successful [SALT] agreement. This is not," he said, "a matter of our preference but a simple recognition of fact."[41]

While to a degree that observation was valid, the Carter administration itself failed to recognize that to the extent it linked SALT and détente with Soviet intervention in the Horn of Africa, it not only opened up greater opportunities to opponents of SALT, but also increased the risk that others would seek to link détente to other aspects of Soviet behavior.

The Soviet response raised for the first time a counterlinkage. Without tying it to actions so far taken, the Soviet statement sharply warned of the consequences of further American-Chinese collusion directed against the Soviet Union: American "alignment with China on an anti-Soviet foundation would rule out the possibility of cooperation with the Soviet Union in reducing the danger of nuclear war and, of course, of limiting arms."

In concluding, the Soviet statement stressed that "the present course of the United States is fraught with serious dangers . . . for the entire course of development of international relations." But it reaffirmed détente as an imperative for peace: "We are not accepting the invitation to join a funeral for détente and for the hopes of millions of people for a peaceful future."[42]

Secretary of State Vance, with President Carter's agreement, sought to cool the sharpening confrontation. On June 19 he testified before the House Committee on International Relations in response to a letter of alarm from fourteen of its members over the deterioration of American-Soviet relations. In a measured statement (which he later said he had written and personally shown to the president for approval) Vance restated that détente is a "two-way street." But rather than having the edge that that observation has when made by opponents of détente, Vance's statement restored some balance: the future of relations would depend on what both Americans and Soviets did. The United States would continue to strive for détente and arms control. While President Carter had flung down the gauntlet of a single, stark choice by the

41. *Presidential Documents*, vol. 14 (June 12, 1978), p. 1057.

42. Editorial, *Pravda*, June 17, 1978.

Soviet Union, Vance stressed the range of issues and aspects of bilateral relations. He said, "As the relationship between our two nations continues to evolve, *both sides will continuously be making choices between an emphasis on the divergent elements* of our relationship and an emphasis on the cooperative ones."[43] Thus both countries faced choices, over time, on various issues, and Vance cast even the choices in terms of varying emphases *within* a mixed relationship of competition and cooperation—that is, détente.

Two days later the official spokesman of the Department of State issued a very brief and judicious official view of the June 17 *Pravda* statement. He said it had been given careful attention and that while there were points of disagreement, "we do not think it would serve a useful purpose to precipitate another round of rhetorical exchanges."[44] The challenge to choose confrontation or cooperation was not going to be pressed, at least at that time.

Vance's testimony had cooled the burgeoning polemic with the Soviets, but commentary was again filled with speculation about the apparent shifts within the administration. After his combative May 28 "Meet the Press" interview Brzezinski had been asked to avoid public statements for a while, so he had not personally been in the forefront. But the Brzezinski tone of the Carter speech (even if also Carter's own), followed by the notably differing statements by Vance, led to comments such as that in the title of a Joseph Kraft column, "Vance 1, Brzezinski 0 (Halftime)."[45]

Another aspect of the situation was the growing tendency of the Soviet press to attack Brzezinski as the devil behind the recent hardening of anti-Soviet positions (at the same time implicitly not criticizing Vance and often implying the vacillation—or irrelevance—of the president). *Pravda* had said on May 30 that Brzezinski "stands before the world as an enemy of détente."[46] Many other commentaries seized on his openly anti-Soviet remarks in China and judged (correctly) his role in playing the China card. The reference to Brzezinski's "aggressive hard line" in the June 11 *Pravda* article was noted.

On June 23, while visiting Fort Worth, Texas, President Carter was asked about the apparent differing views of Vance and Brzezinski and about

---

43. "Elements of U.S. Policy toward the Soviet Union," Statement by Secretary of State Vance, June 19, *State Bulletin*, vol. 78 (August 1978), p. 15. Emphasis added.

44. Hodding Carter, *Transcript of Press Briefing*, June 21, 1978.

45. Joseph Kraft, "Vance 1, Brzezinski 0 (Halftime)," *Los Angeles Times* (and many other newspapers); the same article was titled "Vance's Role" in the *Washington Post*, June 22, 1978. On the other hand, and in fact more accurate as to the trend, *Time* magazine displayed two photographs, the first showing Secretary of State Vance checking his watch while standing next to but apart from President Carter and National Security Adviser Brzezinski, the second showing him walking away, as Carter and Brzezinski earnestly continued their conversation. Commented *Time*: "The scene was only symbolic, but it was Brzezinski who had the President's ear last week." "Rapping for Carter's Ear," *Time*, June 12, 1978, p. 18.

46. Vitaly Korionov, "With a Sore Head," *Pravda*, May 30, 1978. Korionov is associated with Soviet hard-line commentary.

the U.S. attitude toward the Soviet Union. Stung by various reports that he was not in charge, Carter stressed that he made the final decisions and objected that some people look for a scapegoat and attack others. He specifically repudiated the Soviet attacks on Brzezinski "when I'm the one who shapes the policy after getting advice from him and others." He said there was "overwhelming cooperation and compatibility" among Vance, Brzezinski, Brown, and others who advised him and that American foreign policy was shaped "in complete harmony." As to U.S. policy toward the Soviet Union, it was "stable." He emphasized cooperation and expressed determination to achieve a SALT agreement, but also said that the United States was determined to remain strong and that "we're not going to let the Soviet Union push us around."[47]

On this uneasy note the debate over détente and its relation to competition in the third world (and with third powers such as China) tapered off,[48] as other issues in American-Soviet relations arose.

World Developments

On June 20 Yugoslav President Josip Tito warned of a growing danger of war as a result of what he saw as a "breakdown of détente." He had visited the United States in March (and was to visit the Soviet Union in May 1979). Tito accused both superpowers of interference in Africa and other regions of the third world. On July 25 he again issued a similar warning at a conference in Belgrade of foreign ministers from nonaligned countries, urging them to be wary of foreign intervention in Africa. He also criticized unnamed countries (clearly meaning primarily the Soviet Union and Cuba) for attempting to tilt the nonaligned movement toward either of the blocs.

In Europe, détente was business as usual. Brezhnev was well received on a visit to Bonn in May, at which a twenty-five-year economic agreement was signed. In June Turkey (despite clear American disapproval) signed an agreement establishing "principles of friendly cooperation" between the two countries (Turkish-American relations remained strained over Cyprus). The CSCE follow-on conference in Belgrade finally expired in March, with no agreement except to convene again in Madrid in 1980. In June the Warsaw Pact countries put on the table a new, more forthcoming position at the MBFR talks in Vienna.[49]

---

47. "Remarks and a Question-and-Answer Session," June 23, *Presidential Documents*, vol. 14 (July 3, 1978), pp. 1159–60.

48. On June 25 Brezhnev returned to the attack, this time over American policy toward China. See "The Immortal Victory of Minsk!: Speech of Comrade L. I. Brezhnev," *Pravda*, June 26, 1978.

49. See chapter 22.

In the Middle East, Egyptian-Israeli talks were stymied. In March, after fighting erupted in Lebanon, Israeli forces occupied the southern third of the country, not to withdraw until June. The major development in the region, however, was a dramatic turn in the two Yemens in June. President Ahmed al-Ghashmi of North Yemen was assassinated by a bomb brought by an unwitting emissary of President Salem Rubayi Ali of South Yemen—who, in turn, was deposed and executed two days later by a more radical faction led by Abd al-Fattah Isma'il, who had evidently been responsible for getting rid of both presidents. North Yemen remained neutralist; South Yemen moved toward closer alignment with the Soviet Union.[50]

Soviet relations with China continued to move toward sharper confrontation, while relations with Vietnam moved toward closer alignment. Worsening Vietnamese-Chinese relations was the key element in both cases. In June Vietnam became a full member of the Council for Mutual Economic Assistance (CMEA), while in June and July China cut off all economic assistance to it. (In July China also cut off all aid to Albania—which, however, turned down bids from the Soviet Union and several other countries of Eastern Europe to improve their still strained and minimal relations.) Most significant, on August 12 Japan and China signed a treaty of peace and friendship. That same day Moscow denounced the action as an accord aimed at expanding Chinese influence in Asia. The Soviets saw the move as directly related to the American action in playing the China card—and, indeed, the United States *had* encouraged Japan to take that step.[51]

Overlapping these developments in American-Soviet competition and other world events were new strains in aspects of American-Soviet relations that related more directly to actual and perceived interventions by both countries (but chiefly Soviet perceptions of American interference) in the internal affairs of the other.

Disputes on Internal Affairs and Détente

In his speech at Annapolis in June President Carter had not only challenged the Soviet leaders to choose confrontation or cooperation, but indirectly challenged their whole political system. In addition to charging violation of the Helsinki agreement, he also decried the Soviet Union's unwillingness to tolerate free speech, dissidence, and the unfettered movement of people.[52] While his comments were an unexceptional restatement of the American

---

50. See chapter 19 for this and subsequent developments in the Yemens.

51. See chapter 20.

52. *Presidential Documents*, vol. 14 (June 12, 1978), p. 1054.

view, in the context of the Carter administration's human rights campaign and the challenge to choose they posed a question: did Carter mean that the United States intended that the Soviets must change their system or permit internal developments that would do so?

The Soviet leaders harbored precisely that suspicion. In their June 17 response to Carter's speech they stated: "Attempts to interfere in the internal affairs of the other side are particularly disastrous for mutual confidence. And such attempts have never been raised in the United States to the level of state policy. Seemingly nice sounding motives are being chosen for them: 'human rights,' 'humanism,' 'defense of freedom.' But in fact we have here the very same designs to undermine the socialist system that our people have been compelled to counter in one or another form ever since 1917."[53]

Soviet actions to curb dissidence by arrests and trials had led to unofficial American protests and boycotts by American intellectuals. On May 19 a large number of the members of the Committee of Concerned Scientists, including fifteen Nobel Prize winners, expressed concern over the sentencing of Yury Orlov to seven years imprisonment and five years internal exile. The next day an American delegation from the National Academy of Sciences canceled participation in a scientific symposium in Moscow in protest, and on June 2 another delegation of fifteen high-energy physicists canceled a planned trip. On June 21 Soviet Jewish activists Vladimir Slepak and Ida Nudel were sentenced to five and four years internal exile, respectively. The U.S. government promptly condemned the sentence. On July 13 Aleksandr Ginzburg was convicted of anti-Soviet agitation and sentenced to eight years hard labor, while the next day Anatoly Shcharansky was convicted of treason, espionage, and anti-Soviet activities, although he was sentenced to only thirteen years. On July 14 Anatoly N. Filatov was sentenced to death for espionage.

As early as May 30 the U.S. government retaliated for the Orlov case by letting it be known that the scheduled October visit to Moscow by Secretary of Health, Education, and Welfare (HEW) Joseph A. Califano, Jr., would not take place. On July 7 a visit by the deputy head of the Environmental Protection Agency was canceled. When on July 8 the forthcoming Ginzburg and Shcharansky trials were announced, Secretary of State Vance condemned that decision, warned that the trials would harm the climate of American-Soviet relations, and canceled two more planned visits by official U.S. delegations to the Soviet Union. On July 24 another visit by an official delegation was dropped. The next day the White House confirmed that in the future each planned visit would be reviewed case-by-case, but in general high-level official visits to the Soviet Union were being deferred in protest over Soviet violations of human rights.[54]

---

53. Editorial, *Pravda*, June 17, 1978.

54. This policy was not applied to SALT and other arms control meetings, although this exception was not mentioned at the time.

Beyond agreeing on deferring high-level visits, the administration was sharply divided over the proper response. The issue was posed in early July over the question of American retaliation to Soviet internal repression of political dissidents by imposing constraints on trade, specifically on technology transfer. Supporting that response were Brzezinski, Secretary of Defense Brown, and domestic affairs and public affairs advisers Hamilton Jordan, Stuart Eizenstat, Gerald Rafshoon, Jody Powell, and Robert J. Lipshutz. Opposed were Secretary of State Vance, his under secretary for economic affairs, Richard N. Cooper, and Secretary of the Treasury W. Michael Blumenthal.

The advocates of retaliation won.[55] On July 18 the U.S. government denied an export license for a Sperry Univac computer (intended for TASS for use at the 1980 Olympics), and new licensing requirements were imposed for the export of equipment for oil and gas exploration and production. On July 31 Deputy Foreign Minister Anatoly Kovalev condemned U.S. attempts to use trade "as an instrument for political pressures on the Soviet Union" and criticized the cancellation of official bilateral contacts.

The advocates of trade with the Soviet Union continued to press their case. On August 10 Secretary of Commerce Kreps approved a pending application by Dresser Industries to sell a drill bit factory and an electron-beam welder valued at $145 million, on which the president had deferred decision in July. This action was taken with the approval of the Department of State but without White House concurrence or knowledge. Carter was reported to be furious but did not want to provoke Kreps to resign. In November Secretaries Vance, Kreps, and Blumenthal again proposed a broad review of U.S.-Soviet trade policy designed to lift the restrictions. President Carter rejected the request for an NSC review.[56]

The Senate had also voted, on July 26, to reimpose the visa restrictions on visits by foreign communists that had been removed the year before in conformity with the Helsinki Accord on the free movement of peoples. The purpose was retaliation (plus the strong AFL-CIO objection to the removal of the restrictions in the first place), although this action seemed to signal that if the Soviets could violate the Helsinki Accord, then the United States could too.

In this atmosphere of superheated focus on Soviet human rights violations the administration found that it could not entirely control the question of linkage, or at least the spillover effects. On July 14, the day of the Shcharansky sentence and the day after Ginzburg's, George Meany of the AFL-CIO denounced those trials and urged suspension of the SALT negotiations. While not going that far, Senator Robert C. Byrd of West Virginia commented that he saw no chance for ratification of SALT in the prevailing

---

55. Brzezinski, *Power and Principle*, pp. 322–23.

56. Ibid., pp. 324–25.

atmosphere. On July 10 Secretary of State Vance had specifically rejected the idea of holding up SALT over the issue of dissidents in the Soviet Union.

Several other developments directly complicating bilateral relations also occurred at this time. On June 1 audio-surveillance bugs were found in the U.S. embassy in Moscow.[57] On June 12 the Soviet police arrested an executive of International Harvester, F. Jay Crawford, for alleged currency violations; he was released to the custody of the American ambassador on June 26, pending a later trial. Coincident with his release, two Soviet employees of the United Nations, arrested on charges of espionage in New York two days before Crawford's arrest, were turned over to the custody of Ambassador Dobrynin. (On September 7 Crawford was convicted but was given a suspended sentence and released.) On June 27 two American reporters, Harold Pipes of the *Baltimore Sun* and Craig Whitney of the *New York Times*, were ordered to face slander charges, with the trial scheduled for July 5. On June 29 the State Department warned the Soviet government to "reflect very carefully" on the broader implications of this matter.

Meanwhile, in a move equally unwanted by the Soviet authorities and the American embassy, a group of seven Soviet members of a Pentacostal religious sect rushed into the embassy chancery and sought asylum; they were to remain there for five years.

The conviction and sentencing of Shcharansky, and on the same day in another court Anatoly Filatov, on charges of espionage for an unnamed "foreign power" caused particular concern. As noted, Shcharansky had been publicly accused by a former dissident colleague, Dr. Sanya Lipavsky, of working for the CIA. Since the accuser was himself both a KGB *agent provocateur* and in fact *had* been working for the CIA, the case was especially complicated.[58] Filatov was a diplomat with the Ministry of Foreign Affairs who was convicted of having been recruited by the CIA while working in a foreign country (Algeria) in 1974 and of having engaged in espionage for the United States until his arrest in 1977. In addition, on June 13, 1978, an article in *Izvestiya* surfaced the fact that nearly a year earlier, on July 15, 1977, Vice Consul Martha Peterson of the American embassy had been caught red-handed planting a cache for a Soviet agent (in the form of a fake rock) that contained cameras, gold, money, poison ampules, and instructions. The article did not identify the intended recipient (Filatov), but did note that the decla-

---

57. While a protest was made, the United States did not publicly exploit this clear case of Soviet electronic espionage because the Soviet Union had found similar American devices in several Soviet embassies in third countries. It was considered that no useful purpose would be served by a rancorous public exchange showing that *both* sides were guilty of such activities.

58. In an *Izvestiya* article and a public press conference on May 6 Lipavsky had also accused the recently convicted Ginzburg, Slepak, and Nudel of "working for the CIA," but they had not been tried or convicted on that charge. *Izvestiya*, March 5, 1977. He did not name Filatov, who was not a dissident.

ration of Peterson as persona non grata had not been made public at the time at the request of the American ambassador. It was now being made public only because the United States had continued such activities *and was raising a* ruckus over alleged Soviet espionage in the United States, a reference to the case of the two Soviet UN employees. The Soviet article closed by saying, "Who profits from a new round of anti-Soviet hysteria? Not the cause of détente and not those who think realistically and who know that confrontation is politically disastrous."[59]

The American action over which the Soviets were retaliating was the arrest on May 20 of Valdik Enger and Rudolf Chernyayev, two Soviet officials employed by the United Nations and not possessing diplomatic immunity. On October 30 they were each sentenced to fifty-year prison terms. The Department of State and the CIA had objected to their arrest and trial, with attendant publicity, arguing that such cases should continue to be handled by quiet expulsion.[60] But the White House supported the Department of Justice. In fact, the clamor over the arrest broke an unwritten rule of some standing and led directly to the Soviet retaliation of unveiling the Peterson case, as well as the arrest of Crawford.[61]

The United States protested the convictions of Shcharansky and Ginzburg but was publicly silent on Filatov.[62]

Earlier in the year there had been a spectacular defection: a senior Soviet official serving as under secretary for political and security affairs in the

---

59. Yulian Semenov, "Who Stands to Benefit?" *Izvestiya*, June 13, 1978. See also an unsigned article, "Damaging the Interests of Détente," *Izvestiya*, June 16, 1978, that commented further on the affair. It may be of interest that the government newspaper, rather than the party daily *Pravda*, was used in this case, as it was earlier to report the accusations by Lipavsky. Perhaps the reason was a desire to reflect the interstate nature of the problem.

60. For example, on January 19, 1978, the United States had quietly expelled two Soviet trade mission officials in retaliation for the quiet Soviet expulsion of a U.S. embassy officer in active contact with dissidents in Moscow.

In April 1979 Enger and Chernyayev were traded to Moscow for five imprisoned dissidents, including Ginzburg, the latter arriving in New York on the same Soviet aircraft that then took Enger and Chernyayev to the Soviet Union.

61. See John M. Goshko, "Administration Divided on Spy Arrests," *Washington Post*, August 29, 1978, for an informed account of the division within the administration, the decision, and the consequences.

62. The United States was also silent on Filatov at the official level. For example, the embassy protested to the Soviet Foreign Ministry the arrests of Shcharansky and Ginzburg, but not Filatov. In the Brzezinski-Dobrynin negotiations on the exchanges of Ginzburg and certain other prisoners, however, the United States requested commutation of the death sentence for Filatov, and this was promised. Carter and Brzezinski have disclosed this confidential negotiation in their memoirs, although without naming Filatov as the spy who was spared. See Jimmy Carter, *Keeping Faith: Memoirs of a President* (Bantam Books, 1982), p. 147; and Brzezinski, *Power and Principle*, p. 338.

United Nations, Arkady N. Shevchenko. He had been providing information to the United States for several years before seeking asylum on April 10 rather than returning to the Soviet Union.[63] This case, while undoubtedly embarrassing to the Soviet Union, did not impinge on Soviet-American relations.

In August a former low-level but well-placed CIA employee, William Kampiles, was indicted (and later convicted) for selling very sensitive documents on American intelligence collection satellites to the Soviet Union.

One other aspect of the world of espionage and political intrigue requires note. As the Filatov-Peterson case was becoming public knowledge, several leaks of information, and mixed speculation and misinformation, in the American press raised the specter of incompetence or worse within the American government. The details were not always consistent, nor ever officially clarified, but charges were made that an American spy in Moscow (usually identified with Filatov and with a cover name variously given as "Trigon" or "Trianon") had been caught because of loose talk by Brzezinski's NSC deputy, David Aaron. This charge was denied and never substantiated. Then it was leaked that a spy (sometimes identified as Filatov, and Trigon or Trianon) had passed over a cable that reported on a conversation between Kissinger and Dobrynin disparaging Brzezinski and the administration. (Kissinger confirmed that he had met Dobrynin but denied the reported comments.) Other stories tied Trianon to earlier cases of conflicting views by various CIA and FBI agents on suspected double agents going back to the 1960s. Finally, the alleged Trianon cable on Kissinger was related to the actual dismissal from the CIA of David Sullivan, an analyst whose interpretations of Soviet activities had been received by his superiors with skepticism. As a result he had provided very sensitive, highly classified documents to members of Senator Jackson's staff. After he was fired for this action, he was hired by the conservative Senator Gordon Humphrey of New Hampshire until Senator Humphrey found he himself had been used to raise the Trianon-Aaron story and also dismissed Sullivan.[64] Nonetheless, Sullivan continued to work for a series of other hardline conservative senators. This kind of speculation, charges, denials, and the like did not instill confidence in American-Soviet détente.

---

63. Shevchenko later published a memoir disclosing his spying and his decision to defect. Arkady N. Shevchenko, *Breaking with Moscow* (Alfred A. Knopf, 1985).

64. The first Trianon story appeared in "A CIA Spy in the Kremlin," *Newsweek*, July 21, 1980, pp. 69–70; a fairly comprehensive review of the Trianon-Aaron case is to be found in Philip Taubman, "Capital's Rumor Mill: The Death of an Agent and the Talk It Started," *New York Times*, September 23, 1980; and for the Trianon-Sullivan story, see Daniel Schorr, "The Trigon Caper," *New Republic*, October 4, 1980, pp. 18–20. The confusion over details was compounded when the Soviets later disclosed that another Russian named Aleksandr Nilov, who had been recruited by the CIA in Algeria in the mid-1970s, had been arrested and tried in 1977–78. His code name was "Tigr" (tiger). See Captain First Rank M. Korenevsky, "At Your Service—Tiger," *Krasnaya zvezda* [Red Star], June 22, 1980. That there were two Russian agents for the CIA is clear, as is the fact that they were caught. Little else has been reliably confirmed publicly.

An Amelioration of Relations

By August the Soviet authorities shifted their policy to allow the emigration of dissidents rather than arresting and imprisoning them, although a few such cases continued to occur. A number of dissident intellectuals were permitted to emigrate in the last five months of the year (several after a quiet request by Senator Edward M. Kennedy of Massachusetts, who visited Moscow in early September). Meanwhile, as early as June it had become known that the Soviet authorities were permitting greater Jewish emigration than at any time since 1973–74. By the end of the year some 30,000 had been allowed to depart, nearly double the average for the four preceding years.

Internal dissidence, and its stimulation by détente, remained a problem for the Soviet leadership. Efforts to crack down on the more outspoken dissidents were one element of the Soviet response. More significant, if less dramatic and of less interest in the West, was a broader effort to shape up the internal programs of indoctrination and to rekindle ideological interest. The problem of dissidence was discussed at the plenum of the Central Committee in November 1978, and renewed study led to a Central Committee Resolution in April 1979, "On the Further Improvement of Ideological and Political Educational Work."[65]

The administration responded to the improved human rights situation by approving some of the oil-drilling equipment initially denied (in August). This decision was made in time for Secretary of Commerce Kreps to announce it during a visit she and Secretary of the Treasury Blumenthal made to Moscow December 4–7. This trip also marked the end of the boycott by the Carter administration on high-level (non-arms-control) contacts imposed in the summer. Brezhnev personally met Kreps and Blumenthal and assured them that if the United States was prepared to rectify the situation in bilateral relations, the Soviet Union would be a reliable trading partner.

In 1978 U.S.-USSR trade reached a new high, totaling some $2.8 billion, even without most-favored-nation (MFN) status. That figure compared, however, with $5.6 billion in West German–Soviet trade the same year.[66]

American-Soviet relations generally were improving in the early fall of the year. The status was described broadly by Shulman, Vance's adviser on

---

65. The November 1978 Central Committee discussion has not been published; my information is from a knowledgeable Soviet source. The April 26, 1979 decree has been published; see *Spravochnik partiinogo rabotnika*, vypusk dvadtsaty, 1980 [Party Worker's Handbook, no. 20, 1980] (Moscow: Politizdat, 1980), pp. 319–31.

66. Jack Brougher, "1979–82: The United States Uses Trade to Penalize Soviet Aggression and Seeks to Reorder Western Policy," in U.S. Joint Economic Committee, *Soviet Economy in the 1980's: Problems and Prospects*, 97 Cong. 2 sess. (GPO, 1983), pt. 2, p. 424.

Soviet affairs, in testimony before the House Committee on International Relations on September 26. Without understating the general and then current problems between the two countries, he analyzed the reasons both the United States and the Soviet Union had for containing and reducing tension. He noted that the perceptions of the two sides differed (an important point rarely even acknowledged in official statements), giving a number of trenchant examples. Noting that any excessive and "euphoric expectations from the period of détente as it appeared to exist six years ago" had by then dissipated, he avoided use of the term détente to describe the current relationship, but reaffirmed the need for the two sides to restrain political and military competition and to seek to build cooperation on the basis of a realistic assessment of the situation.[67]

During much of the summer and early fall the administration, and the president personally, were heavily engaged in the negotiations between Egyptian President Sadat and Israeli Prime Minister Begin. From September 6 to 17 they met at Camp David, where the famous accord was reached. The achievement was much resented by the Soviet Union inasmuch as the United States had successfully excluded it from the process. The Soviets subsequently sought, with only limited success, to curry favor with the widely dissatisfied Arabs, most of whom realized that if Israel were ever to move on the Palestinian issue, the United States and not the Soviet Union would have to be centrally involved.

Further progress on SALT was made at meetings of Gromyko, Vance, and Carter at the end of September, and by Vance and Brezhnev in Moscow in October. There was, however, no breakthrough. At the end of October Warnke resigned, although not because of any development in the negotiations. Also in October the Committee on the Present Danger proposed an eight-point comprehensive defense buildup, while continuing strongly to oppose SALT.

Negotiations on a comprehensive nuclear test ban (CTB) had been a priority objective of President Carter from the very beginning of his term. The negotiations met, however, with increasing opposition within the U.S. government, with Schlesinger, Brzezinski, and the JCS opposing a CTB. Accordingly, by mid-1978 Carter had abandoned his initial intention to press for that accord before a SALT agreement. By September 1978 he had virtually gutted the negotiation by reversing the U.S. position so that now the United States would define a "comprehensive" nuclear test ban to *permit* small nuclear tests ("experiments"). This radical change in the U.S. position was only one in a series in the CTB negotiations, but it was a critical one and left the negotiations foundering.[68] One consequence of the failure of the CTB negotia-

67. Marshall D. Shulman, "Europe: An Overview of U.S.-Soviet Relations," Statement before the Subcommittee on Europe and the Middle East of the House Committee on International Relations, September 26, *State Bulletin*, vol. 78 (November 1978), pp. 28–33.

68. For further discussion of the CTB negotiations under the Carter administration, see chapter 22.

tions was to enhance the importance of SALT as the one key step in arms control still being seriously pursued.

President Carter's failure to attend the UN Special Session on Disarmament in May had also been regarded as a downplaying of arms control by the administration and as part of the same harder-line shift of mid-1978 on China and on human rights.[69]

In mid-November a delegation of twelve American senators from both parties, headed by Abraham A. Ribicoff of Connecticut and Henry L. Bellmon of Oklahoma, visited Moscow to discuss American-Soviet relations and arms control. They were well-received and at their request were able to meet with Central Committee officials and senior Soviet generals for extended and frank discussions. They also met with Prime Minister Kosygin for a revealing if acrimonious exchange in which Kosygin bristled at the idea that the Democratic-led Senate must be convinced of the merits of a SALT agreement. Kosygin (and Politburo member Grigory Romanov, also present) said that they knew the role of the Senate in the American political system—but in a way that clearly demonstrated they did not. As a result of the flare-up and debacle of the meeting with Kosygin, a previously unplanned meeting with Brezhnev himself was held on November 18. Such meetings can be useful—not so much to increase the area of agreement as to improve to some degree mutual understanding of the bases for nonagreement.[70]

While the Senate delegation was in Moscow, on November 15 the American press reported on the basis of leaked information that Secretary of Defense Brown had sent a secret memorandum to the president on October 23 warning of a dangerous new situation that had arisen—the Soviets were supplying MiG-23 fighter-bombers to Cuba. Indeed, crated MiG-23s had begun to arrive in Cuba in late April, and there had been a brief reference to this in a press item on October 30.[71] Brown had sent the secret memorandum, as reported. Ironically, however, its purpose had been to alert the president to the potential domestic *political* sensitivity of the arrival of more advanced aircraft,

69. This judgment was widely held in the West and in the Soviet Union. A Soviet commentator, for example, noted that from May 16 to 26 the Voice of America, the BBC, and the West German Deutsche Welle broadcast 319 items on the trial of dissident activist Yury Orlov, while carrying only 84 items on the UN Special Session on Disarmament then being held. Yakov Kachan, Radio Minsk, June 6, 1978.

70. I have been given a full account of these meetings and have talked with several of the participants on both sides. It should be noted that there are dangers, as well as advantages, from such encounters. Sometimes *mis*understandings are generated or perpetuated, in addition to improved understanding of areas of agreement and difference, but with the added disadvantage of being thought to have been confirmed firsthand. Nonetheless, on the whole such meetings do improve understanding on both sides. For one published account accenting the negative, see Robert G. Kaiser, "Soviet Talks Shook Visiting Senators," *Washington Post*, December 24, 1978.

71. The original little-noted article was an Associated Press release by Fred Hoffman, October 30, 1978; the celebrated leak was an article by Rowland Evans and Robert Novak, "Cuba's Mig-23s," *Washington Post*, November 15, 1978.

not to argue that the military significance was great or that the action was improper.

A considerable brouhaha developed in the press during the last two weeks in November. Within the administration, Brzezinski in particular saw the provision of more advanced aircraft as provocative, even if not directly contravening previous understandings.[72] Vance discussed the matter with Dobrynin in four meetings (plus another between Gromyko and Ambassador Malcolm Toon in Moscow) in November. As a result of these actions the Soviets gave assurances that the MiG-23s provided were not capable of nuclear attack. At the same time, however, they restated their intention to modernize the Cuban air force with conventional aircraft.[73] Finally, in a press conference on November 30 President Carter said that the Soviet authorities had provided assurances against any violation of the 1962 understanding settling the Cuban missile crisis and that the United States had no evidence of any nuclear weapons in Cuba. Concern rapidly abated, but the incident showed the underlying tension in U.S.-Soviet relations.[74]

Developments in a number of places elsewhere in the world remained uneasy, but subcritical. The Soviet Union sought to shore up its positions of influence in three key areas by concluding treaties of friendship with Vietnam (November 3), Ethiopia (November 20), and Afghanistan (December 5). Within the Warsaw Pact, however, Romania in November successfully objected to Soviet proposals for closer integration of the alliance and for increased defense expenditures. Moreover, the United States demonstratively reacted by arranging a previously unscheduled visit to Romania by Secretary of the Treasury Blumenthal in early December.

Efforts to resolve the transitions to independence of Namibia and Zimbabwe continued, without participation—or interference—by the Soviet Union and its allies. Similarly, although the revolution in Nicaragua was gaining momentum, the Soviets did not involve themselves (and Cuban assistance was on a scale well below that from several noncommunist Latin American and Western European countries). Late in the year the revolution in Iran was

---

72. Brzezinski's NSC staff carefully researched not only the White House and Department of State records on the 1962 and 1970 understandings, but also the files in the John F. Kennedy Memorial Library.

    Brzezinski tried to stir up interest in a more forceful American reaction to the MiGs in Cuba, notwithstanding the lack of a basis for diplomatic protest, but Vance was opposed and Brown did not wish to raise the issue. See Brzezinski, *Power and Principle*, p. 346.

73. Vance, *Hard Choices*, pp. 132–33.

74. "The President's News Conference of November 30, 1978," *Presidential Documents*, vol. 14 (December 4, 1978), p. 2101; and Department of State, "Questions and Answers" (released to the press), January 17, 1979.

    For a detailed review of the background and 1962 understanding, see Raymond L. Garthoff, "American Reaction to Soviet Aircraft in Cuba, 1962 and 1978," *Political Science Quarterly*, vol. 95 (Fall 1980), pp. 427–39.

rapidly moving toward a climax, again without Soviet intervention (in contrast to more active, if not effective, American efforts to channel the transition).

In the Soviet Union itself Brezhnev further consolidated his position in November with the election to full membership on the Politburo of his close associate Konstantin Chernenko and removal of Kyril Mazurov.

Subsequent Soviet commentary has claimed that "Soviet diplomacy took active measures directed at overcoming the difficulties which had arisen in relations with the United States."[75] Specifically, it has been stressed that in the last nine months of the year there were six meetings between Foreign Minister Gromyko and Secretary of State Vance. While this record was offered to exculpate the Soviet Union from responsibility for the deterioration in relations, in fact both sides were trying to reinvigorate détente.

In December resolution of the few remaining SALT issues was so far advanced that even before Vance and Gromyko met in Geneva from December 21 to 23 the two sides were discussing a possible summit meeting in Washington in mid-January at which the SALT II Treaty would be signed.[76] Thus both SALT II, and the long-sought first summit meeting of Presidents Carter and Brezhnev, were on the threshold of consummation.

The China Card II

Suddenly, on December 15 President Carter and Party Chairman Hua Guofeng in Beijing announced in a joint statement that full normalization and establishment of diplomatic relations would take place as of January 1, 1979, and that Vice Premier Deng Xiaoping would visit Washington in late January for what was in effect a mini-summit meeting.

The Soviet Union was taken aback. Sino-American normalization was expected, but not so imminently. In view of the China card being played since that spring, this major new step in rapprochement looked more ominous. Above all, Brezhnev did not intend to agree to a summit meeting that would appear as second to one by the Chinese. To make matters worse, as the final SALT issues were being resolved in Geneva and plans were being discussed for a possible summit early in 1979 despite the China surprise, the United States suddenly (on December 22) toughened its position on a key issue relating to verification (encryption of telemetry on missile tests)—and, moreover, through an open-line instruction from Brzezinski to Vance.[77] The Soviets saw this as deliberate pressure.

---

75. A. A. Gromyko and B. N. Ponomarev, eds., *Istoriya vneshnei politiki SSSR, 1917–1980* [History of the Foreign Policy of the USSR, 1917–1980], vol. 2 (Moscow: Nauka, 1981), p. 606.

76. See chapter 23.

77. Ibid.

The Soviet Union delayed to assess the new situation. Meanwhile, four days after announcing establishment of full relations with China, President Carter said in a television interview that he had just received a personal message from President Brezhnev "very positive in tone" and that "I can say without any doubt that our new relationship with China will not put any additional obstacles in the way of a successful SALT agreement and also will not endanger our good relationships with the Soviet Union." He noted the imminent Vance-Gromyko talks on SALT, and assuming they were successful, "we will extend immediately again an invitation to President Brezhnev to come here during the middle part of January."[78] Carter's eagerness to dispel the doubts being expressed in the United States as to the impact of again playing the China card at that juncture led him to distort the Soviet reaction, perhaps even to himself as well as to the world.[79] Two days later TASS rebutted the president by reporting that the message from Brezhnev had, while acknowledging that normalization of relations between the United States and China was "natural" and occasioned no objection, also expressed Soviet concern about the direction U.S.-Chinese relations might take and objected to an anti-Soviet antihegemony clause in the American-Chinese joint statement.[80] (Soviet reaction was hardly improved when that same day, December 20, Yugoslavia and Romania both welcomed the American-Chinese action.)

In addition to the unfortunate timing of the change in instructions to Vance in the SALT negotiations, in December the United States also again turned down a Soviet suggestion to resume the suspended negotiations on arms limitations in the Indian Ocean. In effect the United States (after a bitter internal dispute between Brzezinski and the Department of State that spilled over into the press) drew back from serious negotiations on controlling conventional arms transfers.[81] While not related, the conjunction of this series of developments adverse to bilateral arms negotiation (including the earlier reversal on a CTB) helped fuel Soviet suspicions.

---

78. "Diplomatic Relations between the United States and the People's Republic of China," Interview with Walter Cronkite of CBS, December 19, *Presidential Documents*, vol. 14 (December 25, 1978), p. 2276.

79. Even in his memoir several years later, Carter stubbornly (and erroneously) describes the situation as follows: "Then Brezhnev reversed some of these private assurances through the Soviet news media." But he now recognizes: "The Soviets soon made it clear to us that they would not consider any summit meeting" until after Deng's visit. Carter, *Keeping Faith*, p. 234.

   Vance stresses the harm that came from "announcing normalization [with China] on the eve of a critical SALT meeting and the backgrounding which accompanied it." See Vance, *Hard Choices*, pp. 109–13.

80. TASS, Radio Moscow, December 20, in Foreign Broadcast Information Service, *Daily Report: Soviet Union*, December 21, 1978, p. DD1.

81. See chapter 22.

Thus, as the year ended, the United States had suddenly reversed its priorities to give precedence to strengthening ties with China over an early summit and SALT agreement with the Soviet Union (even though President Carter may have believed he could have both). Playing the China card twice in the year posed, for both sides, a new dimension that exacerbated their adversarial relationship. Competition in the third world had caused friction again— above all the American objection to Soviet support for Ethiopia, and the Soviet objection to U.S. exclusion of the Soviet Union from the Arab-Israeli negotiations. But most important was the general erosion of expectations both that cooperation could be developed and that competition could be reduced. Détente in American-Soviet relations rested more than ever on SALT—and, if not yet fully appreciated by either leadership, on the closely related question of the political viability of détente in the United States. The American president had posed the overriding issue in midyear— détente or confrontation. He did so on the basis of Soviet actions that growing numbers in the United States saw as not in keeping with détente, but also after taking American actions that the Soviet leaders saw as not in keeping with détente. While détente remained the proclaimed aim and policy of both sides, there had been a turn toward confrontation as a result of the cumulative impact of actions by both countries.

19 Competition in the Third World: Africa and the Middle East, 1977–79

FOLLOWING the victory of the Soviet- and Cuban-supported Popular Movement for the Liberation of Angola (MPLA) in Angola in early 1976, there was a year of relative respite in third world turmoil and great power involvement. Kissinger made a fairly sharp turn in American policy toward Africa, marked by an extensive personal visit to six countries on the continent in late April and early May 1976. His trip was not without its embarrassments, however, especially the decision by Nigeria not to receive him.

In Lusaka, Zambia, in April Kissinger made a major speech that set forth a new direction in policy,[1] superseding the decision early in Nixon's first term in 1969 to tilt toward and give priority to relations with the white and colonial regimes.[2] The essence of the new approach was to separate solution of the problems of Rhodesia and Namibia from the intrinsically much more difficult problem of the Republic of South Africa and to work for negotiated settlements involving peaceful transitions of power in the former. The new

---

1. "United States Policy on Southern Africa," Address by Secretary Kissinger, April 27, *Department of State Bulletin*, vol. 74 (May 31, 1976), pp. 672–79. (Hereafter *State Bulletin*.) Kissinger also spoke on North-South problems in Nairobi on May 6, and on aspects of African affairs in Monrovia, Liberia, on April 30, Dakar, Senegal, on May 1, and in press conferences elsewhere. See ibid., pp. 657–72, 679–710.

2. The Nixon administration's policy toward South Africa was later disclosed through accounts by participants and a leak of the key secret policy paper, National Security Study Memorandum (NSSM)-39 of August 15, 1969. See Mohamed A. El-Khawas and Barry Cohen, eds., *The Kissinger Study of Southern Africa, National Security Study Memorandum 39 (Secret)* (Westport, Conn.: Lawrence Hill, 1976), for the full text of the study and its appendixes, pp. 76–182. The directive that requested the NSSM-39 study had been dated April 10, 1969. Opponents called the 1969–76 policy of support for existing South African rule "the tar-baby option." See the interesting, critical account of the policy toward Rhodesia by Kissinger's quondam aide, Anthony Lake, *The "Tar Baby" Option: American Policy toward Southern Rhodesia* (Columbia University Press, 1976).

Ford-Kissinger policy line was promptly criticized by the Republican challenger, Ronald Reagan.[3]

The Soviet Union did not assume a forward or activist role in south-central Africa, nor did the Cubans provide a major or direct support to the Zimbabwean and Namibian national liberation guerrillas, as many in Washington had feared. Nevertheless, a year later a local crisis arose in the Angolan-Zairian border area that soon involved both superpowers.

Shaba I and II

In the spring of 1977, and again a year later, exiles invaded the mineral-rich southern province of Zaire, Shaba (formerly Katanga), two incursions that have come to be called Shaba I and Shaba II.

In late February 1976 President Mobutu Sése Sékó of Zaire had met with President Agostinho Neto of Angola in Brazzaville, Congo, as the MPLA was consolidating its victory. Mobutu promised to discontinue support for the Front for the National Liberation of Angola (FNLA), the National Union for the Total Independence of Angola (UNITA), and the Front for the Liberation of the Enclave of Cabinda (FLEC).[4] In practice, however, Zaire continued to give support to the FNLA, which continued to make forays from Zaire into Angola.[5] These activities began to increase in early 1977.[6] In addition, the Angolans believed that they had uncovered a plot in February 1977, involving Zaire, South Africa, France, and Western mercenaries, to invade their country late that year.[7] Whether well-founded or not, this suspicion and the continuing violation of Mobutu's pledge not to permit émigré raiders to operate from Zairian territory led the Angolans to decide on a punitive response in kind.

The means of retaliation were the thousands of armed gendarmes and civilians who had fled to Angola in 1964–65 when the Congo (later Zaire) reestablished control over Katanga after the fall of Moise Tshombe. For many years a Katangan armed group was permitted to operate as a local ally of the

---

3. See "Ford Gives Support to More African Aid," *Washington Star*, May 26, 1976.

4. For discussion of these Angolan armed opposition groups and the Angolan civil war of 1975–76, see chapter 15.

5. Arthur Jay Klinghoffer, *The Angolan War: A Study in Soviet Policy in the Third World* (Boulder, Colo.: Westview, 1980), pp. 59, 133.

6. William M. LeoGrande, *Cuba's Policy in Africa, 1959–1980* (Berkeley, Calif.: Institute of International Studies, 1980), pp. 23, 25.

7. Gerald J. Bender, "Angola, the Cubans, and American Anxieties," *Foreign Policy*, no. 31 (Summer 1978), p. 14.

Portuguese authorities. In 1974 the Katangans switched allegiance to the MPLA and in 1975–76 were trained along with MPLA troops by the Cubans. The Katangan armed militia, numbering about 5,000 men, fought against the Zairian and FNLA troops who entered Angola in 1975. The MPLA also gave them considerable autonomy over the part of northeastern Angola where they had settled and had farms and even diamond mines.

The Katangans' long-standing antipathy to Zaire had been sharpened by the fighting in 1975 and early 1976 and by later clashes with people crossing the border. The Katangan force—now known as the Congolese National Liberation Front (FLNC)—now attacked from Angola.[8] Whether the initiative came from the Katangans or the Angolan government is not established, but the Angolans were at least believed to have permitted the Katangans to invade their old homeland, now called Shaba province.[9]

The FLNC invasion, Shaba I, came on March 14, 1977. The 2,000 Katangans were reportedly well-received by the local population. The incursion posed a threat to Mobutu's rule even beyond Shaba province. When the Zairian army proved completely ineffective, Belgium and France took the lead in organizing support for Zaire, and Morocco sent 1,500 troops that were flown in by the French. Within a month the Katangans had retreated back into Angola, accompanied by some 50,000 to 70,000 Zairian refugees fleeing Shaba. The situation returned to normal.[10]

The American reaction was very restrained. On Secretary of State Vance's recommendation President Carter sought to "deal with the Shaba invasion as an African—not an East-West—problem," and Vance met quietly with congressional leaders and gained their agreement to that approach.[11] Although the United States supported Mobutu with some nonlethal military equipment and spare parts, his request for American tanks was turned down. Carter went out of his way to avoid escalating the local conflict and to stand apart. He remarked on March 24, 1977, that the United States, while a "friend" of the Mobutu government, had "no outstanding commitments in Zaire."[12] He acknowledged exchanging information with the Belgians and

8. See LeoGrande, *Cuba's Policy in Africa*, pp. 23–25.

9. The FLNC leader later claimed that he had acted because of a threat by Angola to disarm his force, so the Angolans may not have approved the action. See *Jeune Afrique* [Young Africa], June 10, 1977.

10. See Peter Mangold, "Shaba I and Shaba II," *Survival*, vol. 21 (May–June 1979), pp. 107–10. See also LeoGrande, *Cuba's Policy in Africa*, p. 24; and Bender, *Foreign Policy*, no. 31 (1978), pp. 14–15. The estimate of Zairian refugees cited above is Mangold's; Bender estimates 200,000 to 250,000. The exact number is not known but was very large.

11. See Cyrus Vance, *Hard Choices: Critical Years in America's Foreign Policy* (Simon and Schuster, 1983), pp. 70–71.

12. "The President's News Conference of March 24, 1977," *Weekly Compilation of Presidential Documents*, vol. 13 (March 28, 1977), p. 443. (Hereafter *Presidential Documents*.)

French and later said that the United States did not "disapprove" or "interfere in" the French, Moroccan, and Egyptian decisions to provide assistance.[13]

Mobutu had immediately charged that the Katangan invaders were accompanied and advised by Cubans and blamed Angola and Cuba for staging the invasion. He did this both to explain away the Katangan success and Zairian failure and to gain Western support. In fact there was never any evidence of a Cuban role other than the earlier training of the Katangans, as President Carter himself acknowledged.[14] Kissinger, in his first public speech after leaving office, tried to stir up support for a greater show of American resolve, but to little effect.[15] The matter did not become an issue in American-Soviet (or even American-Cuban) relations and soon faded away.

A period of improvement in Angolan-Zairian relations followed in 1977 after Shaba I. Soon, however, hostile incursions resumed and then intensified, both by the Katangans into Zaire (December 1977) and then by Angolan émigrés from Zaire into Angola. The FLEC again became active in Cabinda, while Zaire began to aid UNITA in the south of Angola. In March 1978 the FNLA attacked Kaianda, a border town in Angola, and in April it was reported that Angolan towns were strafed by Mirage jets from Zaire.[16] Then on May 6 South African aircraft, presumably attacking suspected Namibian guerrillas, bombed deep in southern Angola.

Given this situation, the Angolans apparently decided to unleash the Katangans again. (They may also have been hoping to get rid of them: friction had arisen over such issues as FLNC opposition to Angolan efforts to move from the border area some of the large number of refugees who had voluntarily fled Shaba with the retreating FLNC in 1977, as well as over Angolan unhappiness with the FLNC's recruitment of new soldiers from among the refugees.)[17]

A little over a year after Shaba I, on May 11, 1978, the Katangan FLNC again invaded, this time even more successfully, occupying the major city of Kolwezi.[18] Once more the weak regime in Zaire was badly shaken. But this episode, called Shaba II, would become more than a replay of the first one.

The 4,000-man FLNC invading force, by capturing Kolwezi and some of its European population, posed a clear threat not only to Mobutu but

13. Ibid., and "Interview with European Newspaper Journalists," April 25, *Presidential Documents*, vol. 13 (May 9, 1977), p. 645.

14. "The President's News Conference of April 22, 1977," *Presidential Documents*, vol. 13 (April 25, 1977), p. 593.

15. "Kissinger Urges U.S. and Soviet to End Rhetoric: Says Strong Statement on Zaire Is Needed," *New York Times*, April 6, 1977.

16. Bender, *Foreign Policy*, no. 31 (1978), pp. 13–16.

17. Neil Matheson, *The 'Rules of the Game' of Superpower Military Intervention in the Third World, 1975–1980* (Washington, D.C.: University Press of America, 1982), pp. 27–28; and see Bender, *Foreign Policy*, no. 31 (1978), p. 15.

18. Mangold, *Survival*, vol. 21 (1979), pp. 111–12.

to Western economic investment and interests in Shaba and the whole of Zaire.[19] Again Belgium and France (to some degree in competition) mounted a direct counterintervention on May 18, and this time they had direct support from the United States. American C-141 military transport planes carried their paratroopers to Kolwezi (and later, in June, carried Moroccan, Senegalese, and other African troops to replace them). In all, nearly 2,500 Belgian and French troops and a little more than 2,500 African troops took part in an operation that lasted about two months.[20] (The United States also had placed units of its 82d Airborne Division on alert, but the need did not arise to call upon them.) The Katangans were forced to withdraw into Angola.

Once more Mobutu accused the Cubans of responsibility for the invasion. As before, there was no evidence of any Cuban role. This time, however, although the facts were the same as the year before, the American reaction was markedly different. On May 25, 1978, President Carter claimed that in addition to the government of Angola, Cuba also shared "a burden and a responsibility" for the Shaba II invasion. He stated: "We believe that Cuba had known of the Katangan plans to invade and obviously did nothing to restrain them from crossing the border. We also know that the Cubans have played a key role in training and equipping the Katangans who attacked."[21] He did not make reference to a Soviet role, nor was there even circumstantial evidence of any.[22]

Just two days later, on May 27, Foreign Minister Gromyko visited the White House. On this occasion President Carter lashed out at Soviet and Cuban activities in Africa and accused the Soviet Union of involvement in the

---

19. Matheson, *The 'Rules of the Game,'* pp. 74–75, 92–93, 106–07.

20. Ibid., p. 13; Mangold, *Survival,* vol. 21 (1979), p. 112; LeoGrande, *Cuba's Policy in Africa,* p. 26; and W. Scott Thompson, "The African-American Nexus in Soviet Strategy," in David E. Albright, ed., *Communism in Africa* (Bloomington, Ind.: Indiana University Press, 1980), pp. 204–06.

   Vance has made known that the Belgians planned to keep a battalion in Zaire and requested American participation in a Western security force. Carter strongly objected, believing any remaining international force should be African. "The French, with our support, then took the lead in assembling an African security force to protect Zaire." Vance, *Hard Choices,* p. 90.

21. "The President's News Conference of May 25, 1978," *Presidential Documents,* vol. 14 (May 29, 1978), p. 971.

22. President Carter and other senior American officials did not refer to any East German role in training or directing the Shaba II invasion, as reported by Colin Legum, "East Germans Set Up Zaire Attack," *The Observer* (London), May 21, 1978. This allegation, based largely on Legum's accounts, has been repeated and elaborated on by others, notably Lieutenant Commander Shannon R. Butler and Jiri Valenta, "East Germany in the Third World," *U.S. Naval Institute Proceedings,* vol. 107 (September 1981), pp. 60–61; and cited by John M. Starrels, *East Germany: Marxist Mission in Africa* (Washington, D.C.: Heritage Foundation, 1981), pp. 26–27. Legum reports an extensive East German assignment in 1976 to destabilize Zaire, leading to the planning of the Shaba invasions. There has been no corroboration of this report.

Katangan invasion of Shaba. Gromyko defended Soviet actions in Africa, including assistance to Ethiopia after it had been attacked, but denied any role in the Shaba affair. While no official account of the May 27 White House meeting has been published, unofficial but well-informed accounts report that Carter was indignant at Gromyko's denial. As Gromyko left the White House, he replied to reporters' questions that the matter had been raised and that the president's information on Soviet involvement was incorrect, a diplomatic response. Secretary of State Vance, departing at the same time, defensively (and, as it turned out, unwisely) countered that the president had been "fully and accurately informed."[23] Many Americans expressed skepticism, and the issue rapidly became whether the administration knew what was going on.

The very next day, May 28, National Security Adviser Brzezinski gave a (then still rare) public interview on NBC television, scheduled because he had just returned from China. The first question he was asked was what he could say about "the evidence," since President Carter had made charges, Gromyko had said the president had "bad information," and, by then, Castro too was denying Cuban involvement. Brzezinski replied: "First of all, I can assure you that what the President said was right. The invasion of Katanga or Shaba from Angola could not have taken place without the full knowledge of the Angolan Government. It could not have taken place without the invading parties having been armed and trained by the Cubans . . . and we have sufficient evidence to be quite confident in our conclusion that Cuba shares the political and the moral responsibility for the invasion." Brzezinski did not even mention the Soviet Union. When pressed further on whether the evidence was "clear and specific that the Cubans were directly involved in the invasion of Zaire," he made a distinction between "direct involvement" and "responsibility." He conceded the Cubans were not involved in "direct participation," in "command and control," or indeed in "presence on the ground." Rather, "we believe that the evidence we have sustains the proposition—more than that, sustains the conclusion that the Cuban Government and in some measure the Soviet Government bear the responsibility for this transgression . . . which is not conducive to international stability nor to international accommodation."[24] He offered no evidence to support the conclusion on "some measure" of Soviet responsibility.

Two days later, on May 30, *Pravda* replied to Brzezinski's telecast. The charges of Soviet involvement were flatly denied: "The Soviet Union did not participate in the events in Zaire. There has never been a Soviet citizen in

---

23. Persons present at the White House meeting have verified this account. One described Carter's reaction as reflecting a feeling that Gromyko was lying to him—reminiscent of Gromyko's deception of President John F. Kennedy during the Cuban missile crisis. For one account of the meeting see "A New Cold War?" *Newsweek*, June 12, 1978, p. 10.

24. "Interview: National Security Adviser on 'Meet the Press,'" May 28, *State Bulletin*, vol. 78 (July 1978), p. 26.

that country with arms in hand. . . . Nor are there Cuban soldiers or military specialists in Zaire."[25]

In remarks on May 30 to the NATO summit meeting, President Carter himself again, but more generally, criticized "the activities of the Soviet Union and Cuba in Africa." On June 2 he briefed still skeptical congressional leaders on the intelligence evidence that Cuba had trained and equipped the Katangans.[26] Shortly thereafter Castro himself told two visiting American congressmen that he had tried to block the impending invasion when he learned of it (a fact that Cuba had earlier communicated privately to the senior American diplomat in Havana, after Carter's first public statement on May 25). Following Castro's statement, Carter laid out his final argument in a press conference on June 14: the Cubans had 20,000 troops in Angola, including 4,000 in the region from which the Katangans had moved, and were "deeply involved" in the Angolan government and transportation system. Moreover, "there's no doubt about the fact that Cuba has been involved in the training of Katangan people who did invade. We have firm proof of this fact. And the knowledge that Cuba had of the impending invasion has been admitted by Castro himself. . . . The fact is that Castro could have done much more, had he genuinely wanted to stop the invasion. He could have interceded with the Katangans themselves. He could certainly have imposed Cuban troops near the border, because they are spread throughout Angola, to impede the invasion. . . . He could have notified the world at large that an invasion designed to cross and to disturb an international border was in prospect. And he did not do any of these things. . . . So, there is no doubt in my mind that just on the basis of these facts alone, my statement is true."[27]

After that the issue died down, but a local flare-up had been turned into an East-West issue.[28] The United States accused the Soviets and their

25. Vitaly Korionov, "With a Sore Head," *Pravda*, May 30, 1978.

26. Skepticism was also reported in the State Department and the CIA, as well as in the committees on foreign affairs of both Houses of Congress. See LeoGrande, *Cuba's Policy in Africa*, p. 26. Secretary of Defense Harold Brown limited himself to saying that there was no evidence of Cubans in Shaba. Bernard Weinraub, "Brown Describes Sources on Link of Cuba to Zaire," *New York Times*, June 5, 1978. For press accounts laying out the intelligence basis for the administration's case, see "White House Cites CIA Material on a Cuban Role in Zaire Invasion," *New York Times*, June 16, 1978; and Richard Burt, "Lesson of Shaba: Carter Risked Serious 'Credibility Gap,'" *New York Times*, July 11, 1978.

27. "The President's News Conference of June 14, 1978," *Presidential Documents*, vol. 14 (June 19, 1978), pp. 1092–93. Carter acknowledged that the Cubans had informed the American diplomat that Castro had tried unsuccessfully to reach President Neto of Angola to urge him to prevent the Katangan invasion.

Ironically, several of the points advanced in this homily on what Castro could have done "had he genuinely wanted to" could be used to indict Carter himself for failing to take any steps to prevent the Chinese invasion of Vietnam nine months later, after having been advised of their intention and having observed the preparations.

28. By the time Carter and Brzezinski wrote their memoirs several years later, Brzezinski gave Shaba II only a few sentences and Carter even less (neither even mentioned Shaba I). Carter

Cuban allies (whom it termed "proxies") of another intervention, while the Soviet Union accused the United States, France, and Belgium of "intervention" in Zaire because of moving in troops and countering the Katangan invasion. The United States had opened with the president charging *Soviet* involvement in an invasion of Shaba, for which there was no evidence. Soon thereafter Brzezinski had to admit directly, and the president implicitly, that not even the Cubans had participated in or, on the basis of any evidence, stimulated the invasion. Brzezinski did charge Cuban and "in some measure" Soviet "responsibility" despite no direct involvement or participation. Finally, Carter charged that Castro had not done enough to *stop* the invasion, for example, by interposing his own forces. No party disputed the earlier Cuban training of the Katangans. But surely the United States would not want itself to be asked to accept responsibility for the actions of all armed groups it had once assisted with training. All in all the American performance was not an inspiring diplomatic venture. By confronting Gromyko over an issue that had only very weak support, Carter condemned his administration to several weeks of efforts to focus attention on other matters that did not sustain the original charge.

The Chinese had also attacked the Soviet (and Cuban) role in both Shaba I and II. At least symbolically the United States and China seemed to be working together. Secretary Vance had met with Foreign Minister Huang Hua in New York on June 2, immediately preceding a visit by Huang to Zaire, where he blamed the Soviet Union and its "agents" (the Cubans) for the invasion.[29]

In Zaire Mobutu gradually reestablished control with the help of the Moroccan and Senegalese troops (the last of the French departed in mid-June).[30] On July 29 Neto and Mobutu met again and agreed to reestablish relations and to prevent future border crossings by dissident exiles. This time

---

has selective recall, erroneously saying only that "the Cubans aided Katangan rebels in an invasion of Zaire." Jimmy Carter, *Keeping Faith: Memoirs of a President* (Bantam, 1982), p. 222. Brzezinski describes the American action in supporting the French as "an important step showing our determination" and noted that he believed at the time that it would "convey a useful lesson to the Chinese." He is also careful in qualifying the role he still imputes to Cuba, and there is no mention of any Soviet responsibility: "We in fact took this action in response to major unrest in Zaire, apparently fomented with some Angolan and probably Cuban assistance." Zbigniew Brzezinski, *Power and Principle: Memoirs of the National Security Adviser, 1977–1981* (Farrar, Straus, Giroux, 1983), p. 209. Vance, by contrast, reviews both Shaba I and II and admits that despite the arguments that he, too, made at the time, the basis for U.S. claims of Cuban support for the Shaba II invasion was based on "some ambiguous and, as it turned out, not very good intelligence to this effect." Vance, *Hard Choices*, p. 90.

29. George T. Yu, "Sino-Soviet Rivalry in Africa," in Albright, ed., *Communism in Africa*, p. 186.

30. The United States supported proposals to build a "pan-African force" to help maintain order in Zaire (in particular against undisciplined elements of the Zairian army). Contingents from several African countries participated, but no formal force was ever established.

Mobutu decided the game was too risky and he disbanded the FNLA and ordered its leader, Holden Roberto, out of the country. (Roberto went to France, when no African country would admit him.) The Angolans, with some difficulty (and with Cuban assistance), disarmed the returning Katangans and relocated them in Angola, and the FLNC faded away.[31]

Why had the Carter administration reacted so differently to Shaba II than it had to Shaba I? And why did it overreact in accusing the Cubans and even the Soviets of involvement and responsibility? The reason was a new policy of militancy and confrontation with Moscow that was vividly spelled out in the president's speech at the U.S. Naval Academy in Annapolis on June 5. The cause of this heightened sensitivity to Cuban and Soviet activities in Africa, and of the determination to demonstrate firm resolve, was an important development in the Horn of Africa that had taken place in the year between the two Shabas.

The Horn of Africa

Several seemingly disparate events relating to the Horn of Africa occurred in February 1977. In retrospect, the conjunction of these developments would soon precipitate another regional war and crisis in which the superpowers became involved, further exacerbating relations between them.

The first development was that on February 3 Lieutenant Colonel Mengistu Haile Mariam emerged as the new leader of Ethiopia after a struggle within the ruling Dergue (Provisional Military Administrative Committee). Ever since Emperor Haile Selassie was forced to abdicate in September 1974, the Dergue had been following an erratic but leftward course. Conflicts over policy and power had climaxed that day in a dramatic shootout in which the previous leader, Brigadier General Teferi Bante, who had led the more moderate faction, was killed.

The second development was the beginning of a series of armed incursions from Somalia into the Ogaden desert province in the south of Ethiopia, an area ethnically Somali. The incidents reflected the growing restlessness

---

31. See Matheson, *The 'Rules of the Game,'* p. 28; and Gerald J. Bender, "Angola: Left, Right and Wrong," *Foreign Policy*, no. 43 (Summer 1981), p. 57.

The United States did not cease its interest in destabilizing the Angolan government. On May 1, 1978, CIA Director Stansfield Turner and David Aaron, Brzezinski's deputy, consulted with Senator Dick Clark of Iowa (author of the law prohibiting the United States from sending military aid to Angola) to sound out his reaction to channeling assistance to Jonas Savimbi's UNITA through a third country. Clark said the scheme would violate the law and he would oppose it. The idea was apparently not pursued further. See "Countering the Communists: Zaire's Crisis Raises the Issue of Soviet-Cuban Influence," *Time*, June 5, 1978, pp. 26–28; former Senator Clark also confirmed the incident to me.

of the Soviet-armed Somali government of General Mohamed Siad Barre, with its irredentist claim on the territory.

Third was an initiative by the then new Carter administration. On February 24 it singled out Ethiopia as one of a few select countries to be excoriated for human rights abuses, for which it was to be deprived of further military grant aid.

Fourth was President Castro's quick congratulations to Colonel Mengistu, followed by the arrival of a senior Cuban military leader, General Arnaldo Ochoa Sanchez, on February 20, followed shortly by a brief unannounced visit by Castro himself in early March.

In March and April 1977 there was an intensification of international efforts to deal with the threatening Somali-Ethiopian clash, but in some cases the efforts resulted only in new friction among those involved. Castro, perhaps on his own initiative, although probably after consulting with the Soviets, made his quick visit to Ethiopia, as mentioned. He also visited Somalia (where the Cubans, along with the Soviets, had been providing military advisers for several years). Then he held a secret and sudden summit meeting with both General Siad and Colonel Mengistu in Aden in March. Castro urged the Marxist rivals to submerge their nationalistic differences in a regional federation of progressive Marxist nations, combining not only Ethiopia and Somalia, but also the People's Democratic Republic of Yemen (South Yemen), an "autonomous" Ogaden, an "autonomous" Eritrea, and Djibouti.[32] The greatest sacrifices appeared to fall on Ethiopia, the biggest country, and with a population several times larger than that of all the others combined, as its rebellious Eritrea and restive Ogaden provinces would become autonomous. It was, however, Siad who objected, posing an unacceptable prior condition of independence for the Ogaden.

Castro's imaginative but unrealistic attempt to reconcile deeply held nationalist feelings in a broader, consolidated ideological union was unsuccessful. Others followed with different attempts aimed at a more modest reconciliation. President Podgorny, who had oversight responsibilities for African affairs in the Politburo,[33] combined a trip to Tanzania, Zambia, and Mozam-

---

32. Castro revealed his proposed federation in a speech a year later, on March 18, 1978, *Granma*, March 19, 1978. Its substance, however, had already been leaked, especially by the unhappy Somalis. For further discussion see Bruce D. Porter, *The USSR in Third World Conflicts: Soviet Arms and Diplomacy in Local Wars, 1945–1980* (Cambridge University Press, 1984), p. 195. For the Cuban role, see LeoGrande, *Cuba's Policy in Africa*, pp. 35–51, especially p. 38; and William J. Durch, "The Cuban Military in Africa and the Middle East: From Algeria to Angola," *Studies in Comparative Communism*, vol. 11 (Spring–Summer 1978), pp. 73–74.

   France had already announced that Djibouti would become independent in June. Castro, however, did not consult that future country, located in the center of the proposed federation and ethnically comprising Ethiopian Afars and Somali Issas, nor was it present.

33. Soon thereafter Podgorny was ousted from the Politburo, although for other reasons. He had reportedly wanted, however, to take a more active Soviet role in southern Africa than Brezh-

bique relating to the situation in Rhodesia with some shuttle diplomacy between Somalia and Ethiopia, but to no avail. Mengistu then flew to Moscow in May for a state visit and to conclude a major arms assistance agreement.[34] While Mengistu was greeted in Moscow as a "genuine revolutionary leader," this accolade also reflected the Soviet judgment that he was not yet a real socialist.[35]

Ethiopian-American relations, by contrast, continued to deteriorate. On April 23, 1977, after having been confidentially informed of American plans to close several military installations, Mengistu publicly took the initiative and demanded that the United States close them and withdraw its personnel. Five days later the United States announced a halt to pending arms deliveries and canceled the remaining $100 million credits for arms sales.[36]

Somalia was also the target of increased external attention. As early as the fall of 1975 both Iran and Saudi Arabia began efforts to woo Somalia away from alignment with the Soviet Union. By 1977 the Saudis had offered to help meet the Somali interest in a reliable alternative source of arms by offering to pay for its arms. Reportedly this offer was repeated in May in Washington by Saudi Crown Prince Fahd but was not taken up by the United States.[37] Egypt and the Sudan also sought to reduce Soviet influence in the region.[38]

In March 1977, just as Castro and Podgorny were trying to bring Somalia into a socialist federation, another conference was held in Taiz, North Yemen, attended by heads of state of Somalia, South Yemen, the Yemen Arab Republic (North Yemen), and the Sudan. Sudanese President Ja'afar Mohammed al-Nimeiry took the lead in arranging the conference, along with President Ibrahim al-Hamdi of North Yemen, supported by Saudi Arabia and Egypt

---

nev and the Politburo believed wise. See Boris Rabbot, "One View on Why Podgorny Was Ousted," *Christian Science Monitor*, June 13, 1977.

The Soviets are reported to have first begun sounding out a possible agreement among Ethiopia, Somalia, and Eritrea in 1976. See Colin Legum, "Angola and the Horn of Africa," in Stephen S. Kaplan, ed., *Diplomacy of Power: Soviet Armed Forces as a Political Instrument* (Brookings Institution, 1981), p. 628.

34. Secret Ethiopian-Soviet talks on possible arms supply had begun in 1975, and an initial unpublicized agreement was reached in December 1976. The first deliveries were made in the spring of 1977. See Porter, *The USSR in Third World Conflicts*, pp. 192–96; and Legum, in Kaplan, ed., *Diplomacy of Power*, pp. 614–16.

35. On the general course of Soviet-Ethiopian (and Soviet-Somali) relations, see Marina Ottaway, *Soviet and American Influence in the Horn of Africa* (Praeger, 1982).

36. Steven David, "Realignment in the Horn: The Soviet Advantage," *International Security*, vol. 4 (Fall 1979), p. 75; and James E. Dougherty, *The Horn of Africa: A Map of Political-Strategic Conflict* (Cambridge, Mass.: Institute for Foreign Policy Analysis, 1982), p. 30.

37. Thompson, in Albright, ed., *Communism in Africa*, p. 200.

38. The Sudan had been the target of a Libyan- and Ethiopian-sponsored attempted coup in April 1976. Continuing concern over Soviet designs led the Sudan in May 1977 to expel the ninety remaining Soviet advisers, making complete the turn away from Moscow begun in 1971.

(although neither attended the meeting).[39] The Soviets were not pleased by Siad's attendance; the Somalis, in turn, wanted the Soviets to understand they might have alternatives and that Somali interests had to be met.

Soviet arms shipments to Ethiopia coincided with a step-up of operations in May in the Ogaden by Somali irregulars. The West Somalia Liberation Front, armed and supported by Somalia, began to field a force of at least 3,000 guerrillas in a campaign more sustained than the earlier raids. As the Soviet Union was still supplying arms to both sides in what was looming as a conflict between them, this situation caused serious problems for the Soviets in their efforts to cultivate the Ethiopians. The Soviets strongly urged the Somalis to desist.

The Eritrean rebels also began to step up their operations. In addition to the Islamic Eritrean Liberation Front (ELF), supported by Saudi Arabia, Egypt, and the Sudan, and the more radical Marxist Eritrean People's Liberation Front (EPLF), supported by Iraq, Syria, and Somalia, the conservative Eritrean Democratic Party (EDP) now fielded a new army introduced from the Sudan in June.

The initiation of Soviet arms shipments to Ethiopia, and the arrival there of a small number of Cuban military advisers in May, led Washington to reconsider its position. A possible Soviet lodgment in Ethiopia could, in its view, affect the overall security of the region adversely. Washington's new attitude in turn coincided with efforts by Somalia to seek U.S. arms.

It has now been disclosed that the initial Somali probes of American willingness to replace the Soviets as arms supplier in exchange for a reversal of Somali alliances began in early 1977 and were increased in May and June.[40]

At this juncture, President Carter gave an interview on June 10 in which he spoke somewhat ambiguously about his own "inclination" to "aggressively challenge, in a peaceful way, of course, the Soviet Union" in its own sphere.[41] He specifically mentioned Somalia. Asked in a press conference to clarify this reference, which seemed quite puzzling to the press representatives who were unaware of the private diplomatic probes, Carter explained, "We don't want to be in a position that once a country is not friendly to us and once they are completely within the influence of the Soviet Union, they should forever be in that status." He again mentioned Somalia (and, curiously, Ethiopia) as examples. While Carter's speech was vague, it seemed to the Somalis

---

39. See Dimitri K. Simes, "Imperial Globalism in the Making: Soviet Involvement in the Horn of Africa," *Washington Review*, special supplement (May 1978), p. 33.

The idea of a conservative Arab-dominated Red Sea group had been discussed at a private meeting of Egyptian, Saudi, and Sudanese leaders in Khartoum, Sudan, earlier in 1977. In June 1977, on a visit to South Yemen, Nimeiry tried to revive the idea but was rebuffed, and the initiative died.

40. Vance, *Hard Choices*, p. 73.

41. President Carter, "Interview with Magazine Publishers Association," June 10, *Presidential Documents*, vol. 13 (June 20, 1977), p. 866.

to signal that the United States wanted, in Carter's later words at another press conference, "to win the friendship of nations that in the past have not been close to us who may have been heavily influenced by or very closely friendly with the Soviet Union and who may still be."[42]

In mid-June the Somali ambassador met with President Carter to present an urgent new request for military assistance. Carter mentioned difficulties but said the United States would see if it could help through its allies. The Somalis interpreted this as a forthcoming response.[43]

The Somalis had been making very clear to their Saudi interlocutors what they needed to "win their friendship": an alternate source of arms. President Carter now seemed to be saying that the United States wanted to gain Somali friendship. And on July 1 Secretary of State Vance seemed explicitly to promise the quid pro quo. After noting the increase in Soviet arms and Cuban military personnel in Africa, he said, "All sides should be aware that when outside powers pour substantial quantities of arms and military personnel into Africa, it greatly enhances the danger that disputes will be resolved militarily. . . . This danger is particularly great in the Horn," where "the tensions among nations in the area present complex diplomatic challenges." Vance went on to say, "We seek friendship with all the governments of that region. . . . We will consider sympathetically appeals for assistance from states which are threatened by a buildup of foreign military equipment and advisers on their borders, in the Horn and elsewhere in Africa."[44] Under the circumstances the Somalis could hardly consider this language as anything other than an authoritative American statement of readiness to supply arms to them to meet the Soviet-Cuban buildup in Ethiopia.

An American agreement "in principle" to supply defensive arms to Somalia was made in early July and conveyed secretly to the Somalis in a coordinated response by the United States, Britain, and France (those countries also having been approached) on July 15.[45] On July 26 a Department of State spokesman disclosed that the United States (and Britain and France) were "in principle" prepared to provide arms to Somalia. This rather surprising statement led to a further public elucidation of American policy by the president and the secretary of state.

On July 28 President Carter commented publicly that while the United States did not want to compete with the Soviet Union in arms supply,

42. "President Carter's News Conference of June 13," *State Bulletin*, vol. 77 (July 4, 1977), p. 3.

43. The first disclosure of this meeting was by Secretary of State Vance in his memoir. See Vance, *Hard Choices*, p. 73.

44. Secretary Vance, "The United States and Africa: Building Positive Relations," Address to the NAACP in St. Louis, July 1, *State Bulletin*, vol. 77 (August 8, 1977), pp. 169–70.

45. This decision in early July was later disclosed publicly by Anthony Lake, director of the policy planning staff of the Department of State, in an official address, "Africa in a Global Perspective," October 27, *State Bulletin*, vol. 77 (December 12, 1977), p. 845. The July 15 approach was not made public at the time. See also Vance, *Hard Choices*, p. 73.

in the case of Somalia "we are trying to work not on a unilateral basis but in conjunction with other nations like the Saudis," rather than in bilateral competition with the Soviet Union.[46] Secretary Vance replied to a similar question the next day and also chose to bring up Somalia. He disclosed the Somali requests for economic and military assistance and said that "they indicated that they wished to have an alternate source of supply to meet their defensive needs." He went on to say that "insofar as military assistance is concerned, we have indicated that, in principle, we would be prepared to consider the furnishing of some military assistance for defensive arms . . . in conjunction with a number of other countries who have been approached."[47]

In addition to these public and diplomatic statements of the American position of readiness to aid the Somalis, there were further private communications that the Somalis took seriously, whether or not they were serious and authorized. In particular, in June Dr. Kevin Cahill, President Siad's personal physician and American friend, had reportedly been told by a Department of State official that the U.S. government was "not averse to further guerrilla pressure in the Ogaden" against Ethiopia. Whether this accurately represented what Cahill had been told, it did not reflect the real U.S. position. Yet it was the message conveyed. Moreover, Siad no doubt was inclined to see it that way, particularly since it supported what he wanted to hear and seemed to confirm more discreetly the lack of clear conditions in the official public statements that spoke vaguely only of "defensive weapons" and not of defensive circumstances.[48]

The timing of these American indications of readiness to supply arms to Somalia is of crucial significance. President Carter's statements of June 10 and 13, and his private reference in his meeting with the Somali ambassador in mid-June to help from U.S. allies, were reinforced by the impressions of American policy direction that the Saudis conveyed to the Somalis. One result was that in mid-June the Somalis escalated their support to the West Somalia Liberation Front by committing regular Somalian army troops (although without publicly acknowledging it at the time). The Somalian offensive in the Ogaden was already proceeding apace when Secretary Vance spoke publicly on July 1. By the time of the president's and secretary of state's further statements

---

46. "President Carter's News Conference of July 28," *State Bulletin*, vol. 77 (August 22, 1977), p. 222. Why the United States should have expected that acting in conjunction with regional allies would dispel Soviet concerns was not apparent.

47. "Secretary Vance's News Conference of July 29," *State Bulletin*, vol. 77 (August 22, 1977), p. 229.

48. Dr. Cahill repeated these statements to a correspondent; see Arnaud de Borchgrave, "Crossed Wires," *Newsweek*, September 26, 1977, pp. 42–43.

The Department of State official was Matthew Nimetz, then the counselor of the department, and a personal friend of Dr. Cahill. He does not recall having made the statement as quoted, but states that after checking with the appropriate senior department official he did reaffirm to Cahill to pass on to Siad the U.S. interest in improving relations with Somalia.

on July 28 and 29, the Somalis had "liberated" most of the Ogaden—and committed most of their army, up to 40,000 troops. At that point there could be no doubt that the Somalis had invaded Ethiopia in force and were detaching, liberating, or seizing (depending on the perspective) the Ogaden.

Meanwhile the Saudis, whose credentials as an intermediary able to speak for the United States had seemingly been validated by President Carter's own public comments on June 10 and July 28 that the United States was "working very closely with the Saudi Arabians" in "trying to improve relations with Somalia," had been assuring the Somalis of American support. They indicated that the price would be a complete break with the Soviet Union—a long-standing Saudi aim and clearly an American preference. Siad visited Saudi Arabia in July and reportedly was told that the United States would supply an arms package totaling $460 million, to be paid for by Saudi Arabia, if Somalia broke completely with the Soviet Union.[49]

In early August a Somali mission arrived in Washington to discuss its arms requirements. (An American mission to discuss arms supply was at the same time dispatched to the Sudan.) And in August, on a visit to Beijing, Secretary of State Vance discussed Somalia with the Chinese—who were already providing it with modest military assistance.[50]

In August the Soviet Union cut off all arms supply to Somalia while stepping up its supply to Ethiopia. Earlier, in July, the Soviet Union had tried unsuccessfully to pressure the Somalis to curtail their operations in the Ogaden by demonstratively withdrawing some of its military advisers and, for a time, cutting its arms supply. At the end of August Siad flew to Moscow in a last attempt to restore Soviet support for Somalia, which had existed since his seizure of power and installation of a Marxist regime in 1969.[51] Brezhnev did not receive him. Siad learned that while Moscow wanted to retain its close ties with Somalia, it also believed there was a major opportunity for socialism in Ethiopia and that it would not support Somalian efforts to gain the Ogaden. The Soviet press now referred openly to a Somali "invasion" of Ethiopian

---

49. Matheson, *The 'Rules of the Game,'* p. 91.

50. Sino-Soviet competition in the Horn had been under way since the early 1960s. It was resumed in 1970 by the Chinese after a lapse of a few years. In 1977 Chinese support for Somalia against the Ethiopians rose in direct correlation to the growth in Ethiopian-Soviet rapprochement.

   For discussions of the Chinese-Soviet factor, see George T. Yu, "Sino-Soviet Rivalry in Africa," in Albright, ed., *Communism in Africa*, pp. 183–87; and Lieutenant Commander L. G. Shelton, Jr., "The Sino-Soviet Split: The Horn of Africa, November 1977 to February 1979," *U.S. Naval War College Review*, vol. 32 (May–June 1979), pp. 78–87.

51. Other leftist military coups of "the class of '69" (a series of coups in 1969) had taken place in the Sudan, which had now also reversed alignment; South Yemen, which was still leaning toward the Soviet Union in 1977, but was also considering a balance of Chinese and Saudi ties; and Libya, which was independent but worked with the Soviet Union in some cases.

territory with regular troops.[52] As early as May the Somali defense minister, General Mohamed Ali Samatar, had gone to Moscow to seek assurance that the Soviet Union would not provide arms to Ethiopia. When the Soviets refused, President Siad had said that Somalia "would not be able to remain idle in the face of the danger of the Soviet Union's arming of Ethiopia" and would make "a historic decision."[53] Now, in August, that decision was at hand.

Then an unexpected development occurred. The United States suddenly announced that it would not supply arms to Somalia. It had "decided that providing arms at this time would add fuel to a fire we are interested in putting out."[54] American interest in detaching Somalia from the Soviet Union was now more than counterbalanced by reluctance to support a blatant invasion of one country by another—an invasion that had even led the Organization of African Unity (OAU) to support Ethiopia in the name of the legitimacy of the established territorial status quo. A later Department of State policy statement made clear that the American decision in early July was to "consider favorably requests by Somalia for arms that could be used *in defense* of Somalia's internationally recognized borders." By August, very belatedly, the United States recognized that Somalia was intent on using its arms to extend its borders to incorporate the Ogaden. Accordingly the new American position was that "a policy of restraint is the wisest course," specifically, "refusal to supply arms to either side."[55]

While ostensibly evenhanded, the decision dashed Somali expectations. Various unconfirmed reports, at least some of which originated in Mogadishu, the Somalian capital, claimed that the United States had made commitments of arms supply to the Somalis and that it was on this basis that they had attacked in the Ogaden in July.[56]

It seems unlikely that the United States made any firm commitments, and clearly it did not countenance a Somali invasion of the Ogaden. It is, however, very likely that Siad and his colleagues believed the United States was so intent on squeezing out Soviet influence and building its own relations with Somalia by supplying arms that it would have little choice but to go along, even if reluctantly, with the Somali action. Certainly they saw the continued high-level reaffirmations of a positive American interest in military assistance throughout the escalating conflict in July as readiness to provide support.

---

52. *Izvestiya*, August 16, 1977.

53. Legum, in Kaplan, ed., *Diplomacy of Power*, p. 616.

54. Department of State spokesman, September 1, 1977, cited in Matheson, *The 'Rules of the Game,'* p. 101. Emphasis added. The Somalis were first informed of this decision on August 4 by Assistant Secretary of State for African Affairs Richard Moose. See Vance, *Hard Choices*, p. 73.

55. *State Bulletin*, vol. 77 (December 12, 1977), p. 845.

56. See, in particular, de Borchgrave, *Newsweek*, September 26, 1977, pp. 42–43.

The reversal of the American position in August, made known publicly on September 1, not only was a blow to the Somalis but also upset U.S. allies and friends who had been urging the Somalis to change course—namely, Saudi Arabia, Sudan, Egypt, and Iran. The United States even refused Saudi Arabian and Iranian requests for permission to deliver old American arms in their own arsenals to Somalia. Both President Sadat of Egypt and President Nimeiry of the Sudan personally made representations to President Carter during visits to Washington.[57] Nonetheless, this new stand on arms for Somalia remained U.S. policy throughout the rest of 1977.

If American-Somali relations were changed by this turn of events, it was too late for Somalia to change its commitment to winning the Ogaden by arms, or to change the collision course of Somali-Soviet relations. The final blows for the Somali leaders were the continued Soviet arms supply to Ethiopia and the arrival of Cuban combat troops, both of which would change the outcome of the war.

Meanwhile, September–October proved to be dark days for Colonel Mengistu and the Dergue in Addis Ababa.[58] The Somali army had swept forward from July through September, driving the Ethiopians out of 90 percent of the Ogaden. In effect it seized all but two beleaguered bases at Harar and Dire Dawa. Their capture would have secured the Ogaden, but would also have posed a direct threat to Ethiopia—already beset by the long-standing campaign against the secessionist Arab Eritreans and four other serious internal civil wars with restive tribes or provinces.

The Soviet Union and Cuba, acting in closer concert than they had at the beginning of the civil war in Angola, were determined not to let their new ally be defeated.[59] Cuban military advisers and Soviet arms began to arrive during November, and at the end of that month the Soviets began a massive airlift of Cuban troops and Soviet tanks and other arms. It lasted for six weeks, supplemented by further supply by sea. The Soviet-Cuban military buildup from the end of November 1977 through February 1978 was impressive. Cuba sent between 12,000 and 17,000 troops, including three combat brigades, to Ethiopia from Cuba and Angola, while the Soviet Union sent up to $1 billion worth of arms.[60]

---

57. See Legum, in Kaplan, ed., *Diplomacy of Power*, p. 619.

58. Ibid., p. 620.

59. See Jiri Valenta, "Soviet-Cuban Intervention in the Horn of Africa: Impact and Lessons," *Journal of International Affairs*, vol. 34 (Fall–Winter 1980–81), pp. 361–64; and Porter, *The USSR in Third World Conflicts*, pp. 198–99.

60. For a useful review of the Soviet supply of arms and advisers see Porter, *The USSR in Third World Conflicts*, pp. 200–05.

On October 19 Anatoly Ratanov, the Soviet ambassador in Addis Ababa, publicly announced that the Soviet Union had stopped all arms supply to Somalia. See Simes, *Washington Review* (1978), p. 34.

By October the Somali forces had reached the end of their resources and were stalemated. During November the Ethiopians were able to hold on, while in December and January they built up their strength, buttressed by Cuban troops and advisers, as well as Soviet arms and tactical command advice.

When the presence of Cubans in combat (though then still in small numbers) was confirmed in mid-November, and with the supply of Soviet arms to Ethiopia continuing,[61] Siad reacted sharply. On November 13 he broke diplomatic relations with Cuba and expelled all Cuban advisers. That same day he also expelled all Soviet military advisers (there were 1,678 including dependents) and abrogated the Somali-Soviet Friendship Treaty of 1974. The Soviet Union of course lost use of the naval facility at Berbera.

This action removed any remaining restraint on the Soviets. About two weeks later they initiated the dispatch of large numbers of Cuban combat forces and the massive arms lift.[62] Thus the Somali decision may have had an important impact. But it is also true that at least some further Soviet and Cuban buildup had been planned in any case.

Soon after the Somali action the Soviets in effect took over planning for the Ethiopian and Cuban (and token South Yemeni) forces in an operation under General Vasily I. Petrov, the first deputy commander-in-chief of the ground forces of the Soviet army, supported by a staff including at least three other Soviet general officers (including General Grigory Barisov, formerly chief of the Soviet military advisory mission in Somalia).

The Somalis may have hoped that the shock of their action would lead to a Soviet reconsideration, and they did not go so far as to break diplomatic relations, as they did with Cuba. More important, they certainly hoped for and probably expected a change in policy by the United States.[63] The Saudis reportedly had earlier told them that the American price for military assistance would be a break with the Soviets; this had now occurred. But there was no change in the U.S. position as the Soviet-Cuban buildup proceeded through December and January.

The American allies in the region then attempted to aid Somalia, fearing that a Soviet-supported Ethiopian counteroffensive would threaten So-

---

61. See Valenta, *Journal of International Affairs*, vol. 34 (1980–81), p. 361.

62. Legum, in Kaplan, *Diplomacy of Power*, pp. 621–24, especially useful for details on the Soviet air- and sealift of military supplies.

In conjunction with the Cuban military support, Defense Minister Raúl Castro secretly visited Ethiopia in January 1978. See LeoGrande, *Cuba's Policy in Africa*, p. 39.

63. Vance has revealed that "in October, the Somalis informed us that in return for our cooperation and friendship, they would abrogate their treaty with the Soviets and end all military ties with Moscow." The American response was that it would be prepared to supply defensive arms if the Somalis withdrew from the Ogaden. Despite this conditional and limited response, immediately after cutting ties with the Soviet Union, the Somalis turned again to the United States with a new request for arms. See Vance, *Hard Choices*, p. 74.

malia itself. Iran, with Saudi support, publicly warned that it would intervene militarily to assist Somalia in the event of attack. The Saudis also cooperated with Iran and Pakistan in supplying Somalia with some military supplies, probably surreptitiously including American-made arms (which, had they formally asked, the United States would have denied permission to send).[64] In January President Sadat also privately raised with the United States the possibility of deploying Egyptian troops to Somalia, to which the White House agreed, although the step was never taken.[65]

The development of American views and positions during 1977 with respect to Somalia has been traced, as has the role of Arab and other Moslem anticommunist countries in the region in encouraging a closer and cooperative American-Somali relationship. The clash between American and Ethiopian positions and the sharp deterioration in relations in the spring of 1977 were noted. Thereafter, the United States in effect wrote off Ethiopia. It did, however, give some consideration to the views of other American friends either supporting Ethiopia, or at least not supporting Somalia and favoring the territorial status quo.

The general support within Africa for the principle of territorial integrity reinforced President Carter's own moral and legal objections to the Somali attack on Ethiopia to detach the Ogaden. Among many African countries the conflict in the Horn was of concern because of their stake in the principle of territorial integrity. This was especially true for the Sudan (both Arab and African) and Kenya. Somalia had earlier openly voiced territorial demands and aspirations to liberate not only the Ogaden from Ethiopia, and Djibouti, but also a large Somali-populated area in northeastern Kenya. Somalia had actively supported ethnic Somalian insurgents in Kenya at various times. Thus Kenya became a strong supporter of Ethiopia in defense of its own interests.[66]

Another supporter of the Ethiopian cause and opponent of both Somalia, a member of the Arab League, and the Arab independence movement in Eritrea was Israel. A long-standing Israeli tie to Ethiopia persisted through the changes in government in Addis Ababa, based on Israeli determination to prevent the Red Sea from becoming an "Arab lake." This aim led Israel to support Ethiopia against both the Eritrean separatists and Somalia. Although some of the more obvious signs of an Israeli role were curtailed in

---

64. See Shimshon Zelniker, *The Superpowers and the Horn of Africa* (Tel Aviv: Tel Aviv University, Center for Strategic Studies, 1982), p. 29.

65. Brzezinski, *Power and Principle*, p. 181. Brzezinski speculates that Sadat had hoped for American financial and logistical support and did not follow through when that was not volunteered. Without having been privy to the exchange, I would speculate that Sadat may have not acted because the conditions he envisaged—probably a direct threat to Somalia—never arose.

66. For a good review of general African, and in particular Kenyan, views, see Samuel M. Makinda, "Conflict and the Superpowers in the Horn of Africa," *Third World Quarterly*, vol. 4 (January 1982), pp. 93–103.

1976–77, after unwanted publicity to the tie, Israeli military counterinsurgency experts were still being sent to Ethiopia in 1977. More than one observer has noted the incongruity of Israeli military and other (including intelligence) assistance to Mengistu's Ethiopia not only while the Soviet and Cuban role was growing, but also while Colonel Qaddafi's Libya, South Yemen, and the PLO were all giving Mengistu strong support.[67]

Israeli sources have disclosed that during June and July 1977 the Dergue used its Israeli connection as a go-between with Washington, reportedly warning that U.S. action and offers of arms supply were encouraging Somali aggression—as indeed proved to be the case. They report that as late as September Mengistu appealed to the United States for aid, but to no avail.[68]

In September, after the successful Somali sweep across the Ogaden and while the Soviet Union was still attempting to straddle relations with both Ethiopia and Somalia, Colonel Mengistu made a remarkable public criticism of the Soviet Union for "complicity" in the Somali invasion after having assured him earlier that it would not do so.[69] He publicly hinted at a request for assistance from the United States by speaking of American arms still owing from earlier arrangements. There was no American response.[70]

In late January 1978 the Ethiopian counteroffensive began, supported by two Cuban combat brigades and advisers with a substantial superiority in aircraft, tanks, and other arms. The Somali army had no further reserves and was soon defeated. On January 17 the United States rejected yet another Somali request for arms. As the Somali army began to retreat and the Ethi-

---

67. See Legum, in Kaplan, ed., *Diplomacy of Power*, pp. 608, 619; and Michael A. Ledeen, "The Israeli Connection," *Washington Review*, special supplement (May 1978), pp. 46–49.

68. See Zelniker, *The Superpowers and the Horn of Africa*, p. 28.

   Vance, without going into specifics, notes in his memoir that in June "there was some evidence that Mengistu was unhappy with the Soviets and was still willing to maintain contact with us." Vance, *Hard Choices*, p. 73.

69. The precise basis for Mengistu's charges is not known. Evidently the Soviet leaders seriously underestimated Siad's determination to take the Ogaden, and believed that their own stern warnings to him not to do so, coupled with the unlikelihood of an American decision to underwrite a Somali attack across recognized borders, would deter him from an open attack. This expectation then led them to give assurances to Mengistu in May that they could not back up. Thus the Soviets may in a sense have been victims of the inexplicable American laxity in permitting Siad to gain an unwarranted impression that the United States would support his aggression.

70. David, *International Security*, vol. 4 (1979), p. 79.

   Mengistu may have had an ambivalent attitude toward the United States. Certainly as a radical leader in a revolutionary regime his early strong stand against the great power that had supported the old regime and still had military bases in the country was natural. He was, however, also a graduate of the U.S. Army Command and General Staff College. There is no indication on the record that the United States made any effort to contact Mengistu until a visit by Brzezinski's deputy, David Aaron, in February 1978 seeking Ethiopian commitment not to carry its successful counteroffensive into Somalia.

opians and Cubans to advance toward the Somali border, the key question became whether the victorious Ethiopian army would stop there or invade Somalia. The United States began making vigorous representations to forestall that occurrence.

Whether influenced by these public and private American expressions of concern, there were other political and military considerations that led the Soviets and Ethiopians to conclude it would be wise to stop at the border rather than pursue the broken Somali army. Opinion in Africa, which was supportive of Ethiopia in its own defense and in defense of the principle of territorial integrity, would largely turn against even a "counterinvading" country. And Arab opinion would be unnecessarily alienated (a consideration to the Soviet leaders, if not to Mengistu). Both the Soviet and Ethiopian leaders must have taken into account the still serious internal security situation in Ethiopia itself. Moreover, the Soviets may have hoped to recover their influence in Somalia if Siad were ousted in the absence of American support. Coincidentally, on April 9, 1978, an unsuccessful military coup was launched against Siad.[71]

The American representations marked a renewed U.S. role, one that at least was in line with events. The Ethiopians and Soviets gave assurances they would stop at the border, and they did so.[72]

On March 9 President Carter himself announced the Somali decision to withdraw from the Ogaden as though it were a concession to peace rather than a failure at war.[73] An American call for a withdrawal of the Soviet and Cuban military presence in Ethiopia fell on deaf ears. Nonetheless, at least the conflict had been contained. Moreover, Somalia was no longer allied with the Soviet Union, although now Ethiopia was.

In later years the Somalis would again support irregular guerrillas in the Ogaden, while eventually the Ethiopians found a Somali opposition group (led by a colonel who had participated in the abortive coup against Siad in April 1978) to carry guerrilla warfare into Somalia. Nevertheless, by mid-March 1978 the 1977–78 war in the Horn had ended.

---

71. Stephen T. Hosmer and Thomas W. Wolfe, *Soviet Policy and Practice toward Third World Conflicts* (Lexington, Mass.: Heath, 1983), p. 392, gives details; the authors' estimate is $850 million, rather than the $1 billion usually cited, for example, by Simes, *Washington Review*, vol. 1 (1978), p. 35, and Valenta, *Journal of International Affairs*, vol. 34 (1980–81), p. 363.

   There is no indication that the Soviets were involved in the attempted coup by dissatisfied Somali officers.

72. See Legum, in Kaplan, ed., *Diplomacy of Power*, pp. 624–65. Secretary of State Vance and President Carter personally announced the receipt of Soviet assurances in press conferences on February 10 and March 2. See "The Secretary: News Conference, February 10," *State Bulletin*, vol. 78 (March 1978), p. 16; and "News Conferences [of President Carter], February 17, March 2 and 9 (Excerpts)," ibid. (April 1978), pp. 20–21.

73. Ibid. (April 1978), p. 21.

With the Ethiopian victory in the Ogaden, attention shifted to Eritrea. While the Somalis had been pressing Ethiopia hard in the south in the summer and fall of 1977, the Eritrean opposition had succeeded by early 1978 in gaining control of 90 percent of the region—all of it, in fact, except a few main cities.[74] In late 1977 Lieutenant Colonel Atnafu Abate, the second-ranking member of the Dergue, returned from surveying the situation in Eritrea and recommended, as the Soviets and Cubans also were advising, a negotiated settlement with the Marxist EPLF (Eritrean Popular Liberation Front), the main Eritrean guerrilla separatist movement, providing antonomy to Eritrea. For this statesmanlike advice Mengistu promptly executed him as a CIA agent.[75]

The Soviets accommodated Mengistu's stand, and as the Ogaden campaign was being concluded they turned their attention to Eritrea. General Petrov and numerous Soviet military advisers assisted in launching a major Ethiopian offensive in Eritrea, which eventually recovered almost all the cities and much of the province, although it failed to eradicate the several Eritrean guerrilla movements.[76]

While the Soviets overcame their preference for a political solution with the Eritreans and actively assisted the Ethiopian offensive, the Cubans did not. For ten years the Cubans (together with a number of Arab countries) had aided the Eritreans by training guerrilla cadres in Cuba, and they were not prepared simply to reverse their position. To some extent Cuban assistance to the Ethiopian army elsewhere worked against the Eritreans. Some Cubans remained in Asmara, but they did not take an active role in fighting the Eritreans and publicly announced they would not do so. The South Yemeni, also assisting Ethiopia, similarly declined to fight the Eritreans.[77]

---

74. Legum, in Kaplan, ed., *Diplomacy of Power*, pp. 620, 625–26.

 In addition, in October 1977 the Sudan had succeeded in getting agreement at a meeting in Khartoum for a nominal merger, and at least improved cooperation, between the ELF and the EPLF—for a time.

75. LeoGrande, *Cuba's Policy in Africa*, p. 44.

76. Legum, in Kaplan, ed., *Diplomacy of Power*, pp. 626–27.

77. Ibid., p. 627; Valenta, *Journal of International Affairs*, vol. 34 (1980–81), p. 363; Marina and David Ottaway, *Ethiopia: Empire in Revolution* (Africana, 1978), pp. 149–71; LeoGrande, *Cuba's Policy in Africa*, pp. 42–45; and A. Y. Yodfat, "The Soviet Union and the Horn of Africa," *North East African Studies*, vol. 113 (1979–80). Some accounts, particularly those seeking to stress a Cuban "proxy" role, have recounted unverified reports of Cuban engagement in Eritrea. Perhaps some instances occurred, but the general picture was one of Cuba conspicuously staying aloof from the Soviet support to the Ethiopians in Eritrea.

 The South Yemeni had supported the Eritreans until May 1976, when the Soviets persuaded them to disengage. Like the Cubans they did not wish to take up arms directly against a former ally.

In the renewed phase of the Eritrean campaign throughout 1978 and continuing thereafter, not only the conservative Arab countries (notably Saudi Arabia, Egypt, and the Sudan), and of course Somalia, but also Syria and Iraq continued to support the Eritreans, while Israel, Libya, and the Soviet Union supported the Ethiopians, and the Cubans and South Yemeni stood uncomfortably apart although on Ethiopia's side.

During 1978 Soviet-Ethiopian and Cuban-Ethiopian ties continued to develop. By November 1978 Ethiopia signed a Treaty of Friendship and Cooperation with the Soviet Union, just a year and a week after the Somalian-Soviet treaty had been abrogated. Some friction remained in Soviet-Ethiopian relations, however, as the Soviets continued to favor a settlement with the Eritreans and, more important, as they continued to press Mengistu to establish a real communist party in Ethiopia.[78] (Just as the Soviets hoped to build an institutional base for relations that was not dependent on Mengistu, he remained suspicious of such a base, believing that it would be a constraint on and potential alternative to his autocratic rule. Nonetheless, on the tenth anniversary of the revolution, in September 1984, he did establish a communist Workers' Party of Ethiopia, under his own tight control.)

Soviet-Cuban collaboration in Ethiopia in 1977–78 was much more closely coordinated than in Angola in 1975–76, but the Cubans still maintained their own policy, most notably with respect to Eritrea. Moreover, in the spring of 1978 Cuba arranged for the secret return to Ethiopia (on a South Yemeni passport) of Negedu Gobezi, leader of the outlawed All-Ethiopian Socialist Movement (MEISON) defeated earlier by Mengistu. When the Cuban role was discovered, the Cuban ambassador to Ethiopia was expelled as persona non grata, and a cloud came over Cuban-Ethiopian relations. Several thousand Cuban troops left at about that same time, though some 12,000 remained.[79]

The Soviet-Cuban collaboration in Ethiopia had broader consequences. First, it established further grounds for Cuba to call upon the Soviet Union for military and economic assistance to compensate it for its sacrifice on behalf of the Soviet-led socialist commonwealth. It may also have led to greater Soviet readiness to countenance Cuban support for the emerging revolutionary movements in the Caribbean basin and Central America. Second, it further raised the Cuban profile in international affairs, although it probably

---

78. See Paul B. Henze, "Communism and Ethiopia," *Problems of Communism*, vol. 30 (May–June 1981), pp. 63–64.

   For a concise review of internal Ethiopian political developments from the fall of Emperor Haile Selassie through 1977, see Suzanne Jolicoeur Katsikas, *The Arc of Socialist Revolutions: Angola to Afghanistan* (Cambridge, Mass.: Schenkman, 1982), pp. 126–47.

79. LeoGrande, *Cuba's Policy in Africa*, pp. 44–46; and Henze, *Problems of Communism*, vol. 30 (1981), p. 58. This situation was thus, with roles reversed, parallel to the *Soviet* support for Alves' challenge to Neto in Angola in 1977, while *Cuba* continued to support Neto. It is highly unlikely that there was a calculated "division of labor" between Cuba and the Soviet Union in cultivating and encouraging alternative leaders.

cost Cuba some of the favor it had won in Africa for its aid to the MPLA in Angola.[80] It certainly prejudiced possibilities for improvement in Cuban-American relations and for lessened Cuban dependence on the Soviet Union. Finally, it contributed greatly to American suspicions and concerns over the role of the Soviet Union and its supportive Cuban "proxy" in the third world.

The basis for the Soviet decisions in the whole episode is fairly clear.[81] The Soviet leaders took the opportunity presented by the locally generated Somalian-Ethiopian conflict, and the move of a new radical Ethiopian government to break its ties with the United States, to establish a clear policy of Soviet support for the Mengistu regime and to demonstrate the practical effectiveness of that tie. The Soviets attempted, unsuccessfully, to keep their Somalian tie as well. They made a real effort to dissuade Siad from his attack on the Ogaden, seeing better prospects for developing relations with both countries if war could be avoided. When necessary, however, they chose Ethiopia. Undoubtedly they were influenced by its greater size, population, and potential importance. The decision on a high-profile Soviet-Cuban involvement was also facilitated by the widespread acceptance of the legitimacy of Ethiopia's defense of its recognized borders.

The American role in the unfolding of the war in the Horn of Africa was much more indirect, save for the critical part in the Somali decision to invade the Ogaden in July, which resulted from the belief that the United States was ready to supply arms and render support. While Siad might have escalated the intervention into the Ogaden in any case, the record seems to reflect caution until the supply of American arms seemed assured. At that time, the beginning of July, Siad committed the entire Somali army. In any event, the United States blundered badly in indicating a willingness to supply arms while Somalia was escalating its military intervention, and later reversing that stance and refusing to supply arms or even to permit common Middle Eastern friends to supply American arms. One observer has characterized this incident as "among the most glaring cases of bungled government decision-making in recent American diplomatic history."[82] The United States either should not have indicated any readiness to supply arms, or should have clearly conditioned any such promise on Somalia's refraining from intervention in the Ogaden.[83]

---

80. LeoGrande, *Cuba's Policy in Africa*, pp. 46–51.

81. For a useful analysis by an informed British diplomat, see Harry Brind, "Soviet Policy in the Horn of Africa," *International Affairs*, vol. 60 (Winter 1983–84), pp. 75–95.

82. Thompson, in Albright, ed., *Communism in Africa*, p. 200.

83. It is difficult to reconcile the extensively documented record of American actions and statements, public and private, with Secretary Vance's clear statement of policy as he recommended it and President Carter approved it in May–June 1977. In his memoir Vance states that "we approached our relations with Somalia with caution," recognizing from the outset the risks of a Somali invasion of the Ogaden, and of placing the United States on the wrong side of a territorial aggression and giving the Soviets and Cubans justification for involvement. Yet

The conjunction of American-Ethiopian estrangement and the American cutoff of arms supply to Ethiopia with the U.S. encouragement of Somalia (especially as misconstrued by General Siad) led Somalia to unleash its attack on Ethiopia. The result, as one astute observer has put it, was that "the Americans had provided the Russians with both motive and opportunity to effect their reversal of alliances."[84]

The American refusal to supply arms to Somalia was matched by its rejection of Mengistu's last plea in September. In essence, the U.S. policy in the latter months of 1977 was to stand apart from the conflict. It was only as the Soviet Union began to increase its support for Ethiopia in November and December, and especially in early 1978, that the United States became seriously concerned and began to make the matter an issue in American-Soviet relations.

The failure of the United States and the Soviet Union to engage in frank discussions on the unfolding crisis during 1977 was a repeat of the pattern with Angola in 1975, with variations. In the Horn the United States did not have a favored candidate to win the conflict, as in the case of Angola, while the Soviet Union had an interest in reconciling Somali and Ethiopian positions and in preventing an open conflict between them. It would therefore appear that a concerted American-Soviet effort to dissuade Somalia from attacking Ethiopia might well have succeeded. But neither the United States nor the Soviet Union was prepared to exercise a joint role of restraint. The Soviet Union was moving to displace American influence in Ethiopia with its own while trying to keep its ties with Somalia as well. For their part, the United States and its Arab friends were trying to turn Somalia from its Soviet alignment, and the United States was unwilling to accept Israel's advice to compete with the Soviet Union to regain the favor of Mengistu's Ethiopia.

The United States made no approach to the Soviet Union to seek joint action. In fact, it made no approach at all until well *after* the Somali invasion of the Ogaden, until after Somalia renounced its Soviet relationship, and, most important, until well after the Soviets had decided and moved to provide urgently needed arms and military advisers to Ethiopia to stem the Somali advance. It was only after the Soviet Union had made its decisions and taken actions that Brzezinski began to press President Carter to oppose the Soviet moves actively. Even then, as Brzezinski comments in his memoir, "throughout the late fall of 1977 and much of 1978 I was very much alone in the U.S. government in advocating a stronger response."[85] The first American action to counter the Soviet activity was to criticize it publicly in the United

---

the United States repeatedly encouraged the Somalis and at least let them believe in and act on a misperception of the American position. See Vance, *Hard Choices*, pp. 72–74.

84. See Coral Bell, "Virtue Unrewarded: Carter's Foreign Policy at Mid-term," *International Affairs* (London), vol. 54 (October 1978), pp. 564–65. Bell may, however, overstate the Soviet readiness to reverse alliances.

85. Brzezinski, *Power and Principle*, p. 179.

Nations on November 22, a step approved by Carter at Brzezinski's urging. Then, on December 14, at a dinner with Ambassador Dobrynin, Brzezinski threatened American action through other regional powers (Iran and Egypt supported by Saudi Arabia, although none was identified), saying that the United States would "stop restraining" its friends in the region if the Soviet Union persisted in supporting Ethiopia. It is clear that Brzezinski's main specific concern was to warn against the Ethiopians crossing from the Ogaden into Somalia in their counteroffensive. Dobrynin gave him assurances on this point (later repeated more formally).[86]

Brzezinski also inserted in a letter from Carter to Brezhnev, sent later in December, criticism of the Soviet actions in the Horn. He also did include, very belatedly, an expression of "hope that the United States and the Soviet Union could collaborate in making certain that regional African disputes do not escalate into major international conflicts . . . [and] to avoid becoming involved in regional conflicts either as direct protagonists or through proxies."[87]

In January Gromyko proposed a "joint U.S.-Soviet mediation effort," but Brzezinski dismissed this approach as "pointing to a condominium" and as tending to "legitimize the Soviet presence in the Horn."[88] (It should be recalled that this proposal followed soon after the abortive joint U.S.-Soviet initiative on the Middle East announced October 1, 1977—which the United States had promptly scuttled by backtracking after strong objections from Israel.) Brzezinski characterizes the Gromyko proposal for joint U.S.-Soviet mediation in the Horn as "the classic Soviet solution to regional disputes"—an unintended compliment, since joint diplomatic action by the United States and the Soviet Union would clearly have been preferable to direct or indirect unilateral or adversarial military interventions in such regional disputes. When President Carter met on January 25 with one of the Soviet leaders directly involved in such questions, Party Secretary and candidate Politburo member Boris Ponomarev, he took a confrontational approach. He forcefully warned that while the United States did not wish a confrontation, the Soviet actions

---

86. Ibid., pp. 179–80.

87. Cited in ibid., p. 180. Vance approved this text.

88. Gromyko's proposal was not disclosed publicly until Brzezinski's memoir was published. Ibid., pp. 180–81.

It is evident that any joint or even coordinated American-Soviet role would have ratified a Soviet role in the area. It could, however, also have been used to constrain that role and to exclude the superpowers from any direct military presence or conflict. The United States would have had to forgo unpromising efforts to exclude a Soviet role, but could have had an opportunity to channel what was bound to be a continuing Soviet involvement. Most intriguing, and evidently unnoted in Washington, was that the offer almost certainly meant that the Soviet leaders were prepared to accept for both Ethiopia and Somalia a status less than satellites and to forgo a Soviet military presence—if the United States was prepared to do the same.

were creating that risk in a region of sensitive importance to the United States.[89]

Brzezinski relates in his memoir that in November, with Carter's approval, he had begun background briefing the press in such a way as to inspire a spate of articles describing and criticizing the Soviet role and growing Soviet-Cuban military presence in Ethiopia "in an effort to make the Soviets more sensitive to the proposition that their conduct was not compatible with the notion of mutual restraint."[90]

From January through March 1978, as the Soviet and Cuban military role grew and enabled the successful Ethiopian-Cuban counteroffensive to regain the Ogaden, a serious divergence arose within the U.S. government over how to react. The different viewpoints came out clearly at a Special Coordinating Committee (SCC) meeting held February 21. Brzezinski pressed for stronger warnings to the Soviet Union and stronger countermoves in the region. He strongly urged a strategy of linkage, seeking to exert leverage on the Soviet leaders by warning of the adverse effect of their involvement in Ethiopia on other aspects of Soviet relations with the United States. He had been able to obtain President Carter's agreement to the limited warnings noted earlier. He wanted, however, to do much more. He states that he had sent the president a series of memoranda in which he urged that the United States find ways to make the war in the Horn "increasingly costly to the Soviets in its political and military dimensions" (January 11) and that "the Soviet leadership should be unambiguously but quietly advised of [the] potentially destructive impact on the U.S.-Soviet relationship of Soviet military involvement in Ethiopia" (January 18).[91]

Vance strongly opposed linkage of Soviet involvement in the Horn with other aspects of U.S.-Soviet relations, in particular SALT.[92] He opposed it as both ineffective in producing the desired results in the Horn, and as counterproductive to other American interests to the extent it did curtail other relationships of mutual interest. He and Secretary of Defense Brown also opposed Brzezinski on most other proposed countermeasures in the area, notably the dispatch of an American aircraft carrier task force. Brzezinski believed such a demonstrative naval deployment "would send a strong message to the Soviets and would provide more tangible backing for our strong words."[93] He also argued that what was at stake went far beyond the Horn itself: "To a great

---

89. Ibid., pp. 180–82. Brzezinski remarks that he was "very gratified" by Carter's stance. The occasion was a visit to the United States by a group of Soviet parliamentarians, headed by Ponomarev.

90. Ibid., p. 180.

91. Ibid., pp. 181, 184.

92. See Vance, *Hard Choices*, pp. 84–92. For Brzezinski's quite differing view, see Brzezinski, *Power and Principle*, pp. 185–89.

93. Brzezinski, *Power and Principle*, p. 182.

extent our credibility was under scrutiny by new, relatively skeptical allies in a region strategically important to us." In particular, he believed that "if Soviet-sponsored Cubans determined the outcome of an Ethiopian Somali conflict, there could be wider regional and international consequences . . . greater regional uncertainty and less confidence in the United States."[94] No doubt Kissinger would have agreed. Indeed, Brzezinski may have had in mind Kissinger's dispatch of the carrier task force to the Indian Ocean in 1971 at the time of the Indo-Pakistani War. But Kissinger was not involved, and Carter agreed with Vance and Brown against such an action. Vance and Brown argued that if an American carrier were deployed, and Somalia were then invaded by Soviet-supported Ethiopia, "it would be perceived as a defeat for the United States," and they did not want to engage in a "bluffing game."[95] The JCS, agreeing with Secretary of Defense Brown, also opposed deployment of a carrier task force.[96] No one else supported Brzezinski.

The SCC thus recommended against deploying a carrier to the area. It also decided that "there should be no direct linkage between Soviet and Cuban actions in the Horn and bilateral activities involving either country and the United States."[97] Brzezinski acceded to this consensus for tactical reasons—in order to avoid having an adverse decision registered if he pressed the issue. But he did not give up the question.

The consensus was also that general warnings should be made to the Soviets that their growing involvement, as Secretary of State Vance put it earlier in a news conference on February 10, "cannot help but have an effect upon the relationship between our countries. It affects the political atmosphere." He specifically noted that the United States would bear the Soviet actions in mind as it pursued the ongoing talks on arms limitation in the Indian Ocean—but also stressed that "we will continue with those talks."[98] Similarly,

---

94. Ibid., pp. 182–83.

95. Vance, *Hard Choices*, p. 87.

96. Brzezinski, *Power and Principle*, p. 183. Brzezinski, writing in his journal at the time, blamed "the Vietnam bug" for the position Vance, Brown, and the JCS took. This view does not credit their real concerns over what would in fact have been a bluff.

97. Ibid., p. 184. In his account of this same decision, Vance does not include the modifier "direct" before linkage and uses the more emphatic verb "there *would* be no linkage"; neither purports to be quoting verbatim the document containing the decision, but the difference in nuance clearly reflects their differing views. See Vance, *Hard Choices*, p. 87. Emphasis added.

98. "The Secretary: News Conference, February 10," *State Bulletin*, vol. 78 (March 1978), p. 15.

Despite Secretary Vance's determination to proceed with the Indian Ocean talks—one of the Carter administration's initiatives in attempting to extend détente to U.S.-Soviet relations in the third world—the United States discontinued its participation after February 1978. The incentive for American participation, from the standpoint of Brzezinski and Brown, ended when the Soviets were expelled from the naval base at Berbera, Somalia, in November 1977. In addition, the United States increasingly wished to expand its military presence in the area, especially after the conflict in the Horn and as other disturbances arose in the region, such as the fall of the shah of Iran.

on February 27 the Department of State released a brief comment on a speech by Brezhnev on February 25 on Soviet-American relations, stating that "it is evident that the character of our general relations also depends upon restraint and constructive efforts to help resolve local conflicts, such as in the Horn of Africa" and decrying "intervention" by continued shipments of arms and military personnel.[99] But Secretary Vance and the Department of State were describing linkage as a political fact of life, not as a strategy for applying leverage by deliberately curtailing other aspects of U.S.-Soviet relations.

Brzezinski, however, as noted, wanted to go further. And he did. On March 1 he arranged for Vice President Mondale to invite him to join one of Mondale's morning press briefings. In response to an anticipated question on linkage between Soviet assistance to Ethiopia and SALT, Brzezinski replied, "We are not imposing any linkages, but linkages may be imposed by unwarranted exploitation of local conflict for larger international purposes." He went on to note complications not only for the SALT negotiation, but also for eventual ratification of any agreement.[100] The press immediately headlined this statement as advocacy of a policy of linkage. Brzezinski protests that this report was overdrawn, as strictly speaking it was. It could, however, have been avoided if Brzezinski had replied to the question as Vance did the very next day: "There is no linkage between the SALT negotiations and the situation in Ethiopia."[101] President Carter, called upon to clarify the administration's stand, on the same day stated that the United States did not "initiate any government policy" of linkage between the Horn and SALT, but then went on to paraphrase Brzezinski.[102] Vance was very angry with Brzezinski and unhappy with the president's attempt to smooth over the difference. In his memoir he remarks, "We were shooting ourselves in the foot," correctly anticipating that stirring up public opinion in that fashion would complicate the ratification of SALT. He argues that "we were creating a perception that we were defeated when, in fact, we were achieving a successful outcome."[103]

The linkage war laid bare to the public the growing friction within the Carter administration between Brzezinski and Vance on relations with the Soviet Union. And the internal maneuvering had later reverberations. Brzezin-

99. "Department Statement," Press Release 95 of February 27, 1978, *State Bulletin*, vol. 78 (April 1978), p. 43. Brzezinski refers to this statement (erroneously dating it as February 25 and Brezhnev's speech as February 24) in *Power and Principle*, p. 184. Brezhnev had not referred in his speech to the situation in the Horn.

100. Brzezinski, *Power and Principle*, p. 185.

101. Cited in ibid.

102. "The President: News Conferences of February 17, March 2 and 9 (Excerpts)," *State Bulletin* vol. 78 (1978), pp. 20–21.

103. Vance, *Hard Choices*, p. 88. Not all would agree that a successful outcome had been achieved, but Vance's point about exaggerating Soviet success and American failure is well taken.

ski, as he makes very clear in his memoir, continued from March 1978 on to emphasize in his frequent memoranda and discussions with the president what he regarded as a Soviet strategy of "selective détente." By that he meant the Soviets were working constructively to consolidate parity in the arms control area, but were at the same time "unwilling to accommodate in ideological and political areas" and were "quite prepared to exploit Third World turbulence to maximize our difficulties and to promote its interests."[104] He believed that the Soviet pursuit of "a strategy of indirect expansionism" would breach containment of Soviet geopolitical advances. Finally, he concludes in retrospect that the Soviets became "emboldened" by the weak U.S. response in the Horn (and Angola before it). As they became emboldened, the United States overreacted, particularly with respect to a pseudo-crisis over a Soviet brigade in Cuba in the late summer of 1979,[105] and to Afghanistan.[106] While many would agree that the brigade fiasco derailed the ratification of SALT at a critical juncture, few would say that the episode resulted from Soviet "emboldenment." After all, the brigade had been in Cuba quietly long before the conflicts in Angola and the Horn. Nonetheless, Brzezinski sees a direct connection, which led him on a number of occasions to remark that "SALT lies buried in the sands of Ogaden."[107]

Brzezinski recognizes that "of course, our ability to assist the Somalis was not helped by the fact that they were the nominal aggressors in the Ogaden."[108] But to Vance and others this consideration was more than nominal, not only in moral terms but in hardheaded political terms, especially in Africa.

There were also significant differences in evaluation of the Soviet role in the Horn. The Soviet Union had played an active part and had used the circumstances (an Ethiopian revolution, American-Ethiopian estrangement, and a Somali invasion of Ethiopia) to serve its purposes by providing extensive military aid to the new Ethiopian ruler. The Soviet Union was clearly competing with the United States for influence in the region. But were the Soviet leaders guilty of reckless or unfair competition? Secretary of State Vance did not believe so, and in objective retrospect the record seems to support his judgment. The Soviets were acting not from altruism but in their own interests. Nonetheless, they were acting in accordance with the internationally accepted principle of assistance in collective defense of Ethiopia against an aggressor. For this same reason the OAU had supported Ethiopia, despite the distaste of many of its member governments for the regime of Colonel Mengistu. Beyond that, the Soviets did act in accordance with private American

104. Brzezinski, *Power and Principle*, p. 188, and see pp. 186–88.

105. See chapter 24.

106. See chapter 26.

107. Brzezinski, *Power and Principle*, p. 189.

108. Ibid., p. 178.

pleas for "Soviet cooperation and restraint in protecting Somalia from the consequences of its invasion of the Ogaden."[109] What was probably really bothering Brzezinski, and President Carter, was not so much that the Soviets were acting irresponsibly as that they were acting successfully. But they chose to see, and certainly to depict, the behavior as improper.

One consequence of the crisis in the Horn was a general toughening of President Carter's stance toward the Soviet Union, demonstrated in his speeches at Wake Forest University in March[110] and Annapolis in June 1978, both of which contributed to a general reciprocal hardening of relations in 1978.[111]

The most significant aspect of this trend deserves particular attention. Brzezinski sees as "one important beneficial outcome from these troublesome months" that the government began to consider more systematically "the advisability of developing strategic consultations with the Chinese in order to balance the Soviets." Brzezinski discloses in his memoir that as early as March 3 he recommended to the president that Carter send him to deal directly with the Chinese—something Brzezinski had been seeking to advance for some time (as early as November 1977 he had wrangled an invitation from the Chinese). His request would soon lead to a momentous visit.[112]

China had, incidentally, maintained modest but friendly relations with both Ethiopia and Somalia. As the Soviets developed a military support relationship with Ethiopia in 1977–78, China criticized Soviet meddling, but not the Ethiopians. After the expulsion of Soviet military advisers from Somalia, China and Somalia developed closer relations. China was not, however, a significant actor or factor in the diplomatic and military activity around the Horn.

With respect to the code of détente and third world conflicts, the absence of direct discussion and attempts to influence local parties in regions of conflict continued. These actions further established a pattern of American-Soviet maneuvering for respective advantage, with the United States issuing complaints and warnings when the situation became adverse, especially when it appeared that the Soviet Union would gain influence from having supported the other side. The conflict in the Horn, and Soviet-Cuban involvement, in Brzezinski's words, "represented a serious setback in our attempts to develop with the Soviets some rules of the game in dealing with turbulence in the Third World."[113] Yet the Soviet Union did propose joint Soviet-American

---

109. Vance, *Hard Choices*, p. 116.

110. Brzezinski, *Power and Principle*, pp. 188–89.

111. See chapter 18.

112. Brzezinski, *Power and Principle*, pp. 189, 190, 202–03; and see chapter 20.

113. Ibid., p. 178.

American hard-line analysts have been even more clear, and severe, in their judgment. "Soviet intervention in the Horn further illustrates the Soviet penchant to abrogate the

mediation, a proposal that was rejected (and only made known publicly five years later in Brzezinski's memoir). Moreover, the United States made no proposal for joint action or even discussion of the problem, and only called for restraint by the Soviets when they were winning.

The conflict in the Horn *did* represent a further setback to development of rules of the game of superpower geopolitical competition in the third world. The reason was that no attempt was made to do so, not that an effort was made and failed.

Flare-up in the Yemens

In the southwestern corner of the Arabian peninsula North and South Yemen coexist uneasily.[114] Apart from the remaining (though now much diminished) strategic importance of the harbor at Aden in South Yemen, the absence of oil or other resources of interest in world politics has contributed for the most part to keeping the area of relatively little contemporary interest except to its inhabitants and neighbors. Once known as "Arabia Felix," a land of agricultural wealth and homeland of the fabled Queen of Sheba, the region (in particular North Yemen) still sustains a considerably greater population than Saudi Arabia and all the other states of the peninsula combined. For that reason as well as location, the Yemens are of potential strategic significance.

---

interstate behavioral norms reflected in the detente agreements." Did it do so by aiding a sovereign state that had been invaded and requested Soviet assistance? Those holding such a view focus their objections at least equally on the United States: "once again unilateral American passivity allowed the Soviet Union to dominate the political orientation of an extremely strategic area." Did it do so by not shipping arms to Somalia? by not attacking Ethiopia? by not sending in American (or surrogate) armies? "Such American behavior can only justify any Soviet perceptions that under peaceful coexistence the West has been forced to accept increasingly limited foreign policy options because of the changing correlation of forces." Yet when the Soviets recognize that there are occasions justifying involvement and others not, they are credited with prudence (or at least opportunism) rather than weakness. Nonetheless, this is but a more extreme expression of a widely felt American uneasiness over perceived Soviet gains in the global geopolitical competition in the third world. The quotations above are from Keith Payne, "Are They Interested in Stability? The Soviet View of Intervention," *Comparative Strategy*, vol. 3 (1981), p. 16.

In striking contrast, Secretary Vance in his retrospective evaluation concludes that "in the face of adverse conditions, our policies in the Horn and in Shaba had been remarkably successful," although he acknowledges that "a large segment of Congress and the public saw confusion and weakness, not only regarding Africa, but more significantly, in our ability to manage our relations with the Soviet Union." Vance, *Hard Choices*, p. 92.

114. The best general historical account is Robin Bidwell, *The Two Yemens* (Singapore: Longman/Westview Press, 1983). See also J. E. Peterson, *Yemen: The Search for a Modern State* (Baltimore: Johns Hopkins University Press, 1982); and Katsikas, *Arc of Socialist Revolutions*, pp. 167–89.

During the 1960s the Yemens also became a battleground of competing regional, and even global, powers. Following the death of the ruler of North Yemen, Imam Ahmad, in 1962 President Nasser of the United Arab Republic (Egypt) supported a coup by Colonel Abdullah al-Sallal, who established a republican government. Civil war ensued. Eventually Nasser sent in a large Egyptian expeditionary force, but did not succeed in ending the continuing, drawn-out conflict with royalist tribes.[115]

By 1967 the Egyptians, smarting from their defeat in the war that year with Israel, began to withdraw from what had become a very costly and unsuccessful venture. As the Egyptians were disengaging, a coup in late 1967 overthrew Sallal. The Soviet Union, which had actively supported Egypt to this point, developed its own ties after 1967 and began providing military assistance to the new government.[116]

That same year South Yemen became independent, following the withdrawal of Great Britain. By 1969 it had become the first Marxist Arab regime and has had close, but varying, relations with the Soviet Union ever since. In addition, since the early 1970s Cuba and East Germany have been active in supporting the South Yemeni army and security forces, respectively. During 1977–78 South Yemen actively supported the Soviet-Cuban role in the Horn of Africa.

Relations between the two Yemeni states have been ambivalent but basically hostile. The ambivalence has led to periodic declarations of intent to unite, while the sharp rivalry between their leaders and the evolution of divergent political systems have also led to periodic eruptions of border hostilities and sponsorship of rival internal dissidents.

Assassinations have been staples of the political process, especially in North Yemen. On October 11, 1977, President Ibrahim Muhammed al-Hamdi and his brother, the chief of the security service, were murdered. The prime minister had been assassinated in London only six months earlier. These murders were the consequence of internal tribal and other political rivalries within the country,[117] not outside instigation.

Then on June 24, 1978, a bizarre development began to unfold. President Ahmad Hussein al-Ghashmi of North Yemen, Hamdi's successor, was killed by a bomb when an emissary from the president of South Yemen opened his booby-trapped briefcase in Ghashmi's office. It was unclear to the Yemeni and to others whether the assassination was a particularly brazen act

---

115. North Yemen has been rent politically by sociosectarian differences between the warring tribal sect of the north, the Zaidis, and the more settled agricultural Shafiis in the southwest.

116. A useful detailed account, with particular attention to the Soviet role, is Richard E. Bissell, "Soviet Use of Proxies in the Third World: The Case of Yemen," *Soviet Studies*, vol. 30 (January 1978), pp. 87–106. The article has one serious flaw: it treats Nasser as a Soviet proxy, rather than as an independent actor who welcomed Soviet support in the form of materiel in a venture undertaken for Egyptian and pan-Arab purposes.

117. Bidwell, *The Two Yemens*, pp. 274–76.

by South Yemeni President Salem Rubayi Ali or by some third party. For his part, President Rubayi knew *he* was not responsible. Moreover, he was suspicious that it had been part of a plot against him as well. Therefore two days later he apparently attempted to arrest his rival, party chief Abd al-Fattah Isma'il. The Cuban- and East German-trained security forces and army, however, supported Isma'il, and instead Rubayi was seized and executed. It is still a matter of conjecture whether Isma'il, or some other party, was responsible for killing the North Yemeni president.[118] Isma'il took over as ruler of South Yemen and increased ties with the Soviet Union.

The double assassination and execution of the two presidents was seen in Washington as weakening North Yemen and turning South Yemen closer to the Soviet Union. In fact, the feud between Isma'il and Rubayi had been primarily an internal political rivalry. Only secondarily was there an international political aspect: Rubayi was interested in balancing South Yemen between the Soviet Union and Saudi Arabia, with continuing but lessened dependence on the Soviet Union, while Isma'il was anti-Saudi (as well as a convinced Marxist) and was therefore less troubled by stronger Soviet and Cuban ties.[119] Rubayi also was more prepared to improve relations with North Yemen, which had closer Saudi Arabian ties. In addition, he had been prepared to accept closer Chinese ties and had begun to build a Chinese-trained militia as a counterweight to the Cuban-trained army and East German-trained security organs.[120] He had increased trade relations with Western Europe, and in October 1977 he had met with Secretary of State Vance when both were at the UN General Assembly, where they discussed resumption of long-broken diplomatic relations. Indeed, a senior official of the Department of State was literally en route to Aden in June 1978 when Rubayi was executed. This visit may even have been a factor leading Isma'il to act when he did, as well as to Rubayi's further turn toward Saudi Arabia and North Yemen.[121]

Rubayi had absorbed the small Communist party (and the Baathists) into a National Front in 1975. Finally, in March 1976 he had reestablished

---

118. Ibid., pp. 277–78. See also Katsikas, *Arc of Socialist Revolutions*, p. 187. The later official accounts that attribute the initiative to President Rubayi in moving against party chief Isma'il may be in error; Isma'il may have taken the initiative in a coup.

   Some commentators have suggested or assumed that the Soviet Union was responsible, but there is no corroborating information. For example, Lieutenant Commander Charles T. Creekman, Jr., "Sino-Soviet Competition in the Yemens," *Naval War College Review*, vol. 32 (July–August 1979), pp. 78–79, presumes the Soviets were responsible for switching briefcases, but without claiming to have evidence. It could as easily have been Isma'il, a scenario that seems much more likely, and there are other possibilities. See the reporting by Jean Gueyras, *Le Monde*, February 27, 1979, for a strong case that it was not the Soviets but local rivals.

119. Ibid., pp. 265–71, 296–99.

120. Creekman, *Naval War College Review*, vol. 32 (July–August 1979), pp. 77–79.

121. Bidwell, *The Two Yemens*, pp. 284–85.

diplomatic relations with Saudi Arabia and had ended the border skirmishes with it. Symbolically, in July Rubayi went to Saudi Arabia, while Isma'il went to Moscow. Perhaps leading to the assassination, in October 1976 Rubayi had lost a key position when he was compelled to give up the portfolio of minister of defense, which was assumed by a pro-Isma'il (and pro-Soviet) man, Ali Ahmad Nasir Antar. In early June, shortly before the fateful assassination, Ali Antar, who had been systematically removing officers loyal to Rubayi, visited Moscow. Isma'il had evidently been seeking assurance of Soviet support or at least acquiescence in his plan to remove Rubayi.[122] The Soviets probably assured Isma'il of their continued support, but stood apart from direct involvement in his plotting in case he failed.

Parallel with the Soviet Union's long and active involvement in South Yemen and efforts to build its influence in North Yemen as well were a complex web of local political rivalries, Saudi competition in North Yemen, and Chinese competition in South Yemen. It was precisely this interplay in the Arabian peninsula, rather than any Soviet offensive throughout this broad geopolitical region of crisis, that brought about the political assassinations in 1978. This interpretation became all the more clear when the pro-Soviet Isma'il was in turn ousted from power by the moderate Ali Nasir Muhammed al-Hassani. But before that event came an important development that brought both the United States and the Soviet Union into direct competition in the region.

As early as 1975 the United States had reached an agreement with Saudi Arabia to provide $138 million in arms over five years to modernize the North Yemeni army, but not to include modern tanks and jet aircraft. The program was channeled entirely through Saudi Arabia, which footed the bill. Jordan was to provide training for the Yemeni, and if necessary the United States itself would also provide training directly. This program proceeded, but the North Yemeni resented that the aid was all channeled through Saudi Arabia and did not include modern tanks and jets equivalent to those the Soviet Union was by that time supplying to South Yemen.[123] In the summer of 1978, after the double assassination, the Carter administration decided to act, and to do so demonstratively, to counter Soviet influence in South Yemen by improving American ties with North Yemen. In July a team from the U.S. Department of Defense visited first Riyadh, Saudi Arabia, and then Sanaa, the capital of North Yemen, to outline a new military aid program, with a greater direct American role. But the program fell far short of what the Yemeni wanted and had expected—which was a full and direct United States–North Yemeni bilateral relationship and program of military assistance, something

---

122. Ibid., pp. 269–71, 296–99.

123. "Prepared Statement of Lt. Col. John J. Ruszkiewicz," in *U.S. Interests in, and Policies toward, the Persian Gulf, 1980,* Hearings before the Subcommittee on Europe and the Middle East of the House Committee on Foreign Affairs, 96 Cong. 2 sess. (Washington, D.C.: Government Printing Office, 1980), pp. 103–07. Colonel Ruszkiewicz served as U.S. military attaché in North Yemen from April 1978 to January 1980.

that went far beyond what the American delegation was even empowered to discuss. As a result, the North Yemeni were sharply disappointed and balked at such things as the American desire to rush in some obsolescent World War II arms to parade "Made in USA" in the annual National Day parade. The Saudis, while accepting the U.S. proposals, also did not want a direct U.S.-Yemeni relationship that would cut them out.[124] Colonel Saleh, meanwhile, suppressed two attempted coups in September and October 1978.

On February 23, 1979, following a series of clashes on the North-South Yemeni border by insurgent forces on both sides, each armed by the other, President Ali Abdullah Saleh of North Yemen called in the American ambassador to state that South Yemen was attacking his country, with Soviet assistance, and asked what the United States proposed to do.[125]

Just at the time Washington heard this news, it also heard that the shah of Iran had been ousted. The United States concluded that the fall of North Yemen would endanger Saudi Arabia and, moreover, would contribute to an impression of American impotence.[126] Having just lost one of its regional pillars of strength—Iran—the United States had to assure the other—Saudi Arabia. Indeed, the administration saw the situation as posing a major new crisis in a Soviet-orchestrated campaign to extend its influence and control. Thus the administration in Washington believed it was facing a serious challenge, but also an opportunity, in this latest crisis.[127]

President Carter exercised his emergency authority to waive the normal thirty-day waiting period for congressional consideration of major arms sales and expedited the transfer of $390 million of arms (about half to replace Saudi stocks that were to be transferred rapidly to North Yemen, the other half to be shipped from the United States).[128] The Saudis quietly agreed to pay for this entire transfer. The arms included sixty-four M-60 tanks, twelve F-5E

---

124. Ibid., pp. 107–11. One small but telling sign of its dissatisfaction was that the Yemeni authorities presented the head of the visiting U.S. delegation from the Department of Defense upon his departure not with the customary coveted Yemeni dagger and scabbard, but with token bags of Yemeni coffee beans.

125. Ibid., p. 112.

126. Brzezinski in particular had for some time believed the Soviet leaders were attempting to undermine the Saudi government. See note 172 below. He was also greatly concerned about impressions of an American lack of power or will to use its power.

127. Politically, a successful decisive American action to counter a Soviet-supported thrust by South Yemen was seen as the chief positive dividend. In addition, as a Department of Defense official said to a colleague at the time: "President Carter has to take a stand somewhere in the region, and he can do it cheap in Yemen because Saudi Arabia is paying all the bills." Quoted by Ruszkiewicz, ibid., p. 108.

128. This was the first emergency waiver under the Arms Export Control Act, and there are strong indications that not only did the White House want to send military assistance quickly, it also welcomed the chance to use the waiver. See Christopher Van Hollen, "North Yemen: A Dangerous Pentagonal Game," *Washington Quarterly*, vol. 5 (Summer 1982), pp. 137, 140; and especially Ruszkiewicz, in *U.S. Interests in . . . the Persian Gulf, 1980*, pp. 117–18.

jet fighters, and armored personnel carriers. Some were airlifted in by giant C-5 transports. Since the North Yemeni were not trained in these weapons, additional Saudi and Jordanian advisers, and about seventy American military advisers, were also sent.[129] In addition, despite reluctance expressed by the Department of State, Brzezinski persuaded Carter to dispatch two AWACs aircraft to Saudi Arabia and to send the aircraft carrier *Constellation* toward the Gulf of Aden in a show of force.[130]

The American resolve to react was certainly demonstrated. Whether it was warranted is doubtful, for four reasons.

First, the fighting was much more limited than initially reported, and it is doubtful that South Yemen intended it to pose a real threat to North Yemen. A bitter controversy erupted even within the American embassy. Initially, none of the embassy's sources or own resources was able to confirm the claims of President Saleh. Later the CIA began to receive reports of serious fighting from its Yemeni sources and from Saudi sources, but the defense attaché was not able to obtain confirming information—and later disproved a number of the reported developments accepted earlier by the embassy and the CIA. It eventually became clear that the reports of fighting had been greatly exaggerated.[131] There was, however, uncertainty and real concern at the time.

Second, the very day the president signed the waiver (March 16) and long before the arms arrived in North Yemen (or the *Constellation* to the area), the Arab League had succeeded in arranging a cease-fire between the two countries. Moreover, President Saleh of North Yemen and President Isma'il of South Yemen on March 30 announced talks on unification of the two countries![132]

Third, there is no evidence that the Soviet Union was involved in the South Yemeni border skirmishes. In fact, the evidence (and logic of the political situation) suggests that the Soviet Union sought throughout to prevent a direct conflict between the two states in order not to drive North

---

129. See Christopher S. Wren, "In Yemen, the East and West Do Meet," *New York Times*, May 7, 1980; and Van Hollen, *Washington Quarterly*, vol. 5 (1982), p. 140.

130. See Brzezinski, *Power and Principle*, p. 447. Brzezinski felt vindicated because in this crisis, unlike the one in the Horn a year before, his proposal to send a carrier task force to the region was accepted.

131. See Ruszkiewicz, in *U.S. Interests in . . . the Persian Gulf, 1980*, pp. 112–17, 153. Ruszkiewicz was not a disinterested party in the dispute that developed within the U.S. intelligence community, but he presents a generally convincing case. See also Van Hollen, *Washington Quarterly*, vol. 5 (1982), p. 139.

   American reporting was hampered by the uncertain security that made travel unsafe, even apart from the reported conflict, by the fact that the border is unmarked in wild mountainous terrain, and by the absence of American diplomatic representation in South Yemen.

132. Van Hollen, *Washington Quarterly*, vol. 5 (1982), p. 140. The talks took place, but were desultory and did not lead to a merger.

Yemen closer to Saudi Arabia and the United States and in order to maintain influence with both countries.

Finally, and most disconcerting of all in Washington, the North Yemeni a few months later concluded a new arms deal with the Soviet Union that was twice the size of the American one. The American leaders were stunned by this unexpected development. Before the end of the year about 200 Soviet military advisers were in North Yemen. In all, some sixty jet aircraft and several hundred Soviet and Polish tanks were sent.

The American leaders had assumed that North Yemen, like Somalia, would break with the Soviet Union and turn to the United States. In part this serious error in judgment was a consequence of mistaken earlier U.S. intelligence and policy with respect to the seriousness of the South Yemeni threat and the need of North Yemen for American support. In fact, the North Yemeni had exaggerated and used the threat to get aid from the United States. The latter's persistence in dealing through Saudi Arabia and refusal to provide more modern arms (although the North Yemeni could not handle what was being provided) allowed North Yemen to cut a better deal (on credit) with the Soviets. It was in fact under no great threat from South Yemen, and it did fear the Saudis. For their part, the Saudis had considerably curtailed the supply of American arms after the cease-fire, not wishing North Yemen to become too strong and more independent of their influence. Now the North Yemeni were becoming stronger and less dependent on the Saudis, and because of Soviet arms (with which they were, in addition, more familiar). American and Soviet advisers both served in North Yemen, providing training on the new weapons being delivered.[133]

As noted, there was an unexpected development in South Yemen a year following the Yemeni war, when President Isma'il was ousted on April 20, 1980, by Prime Minister Hassani. Inasmuch as Isma'il was reputedly the more pro-Soviet and Hassani the more moderate, this change puzzled Washington, especially at the policy level where such events were usually looked at from an East-West standpoint.[134] In fact, local politics usually predominate, as in this case.[135] South Yemen continued to maintain its close relationship with the Soviet Union.

---

133. Wren, *New York Times*, May 7, 1980; and Edward Cody, "U.S., Saudi Concern Increasing at Soviet Arms Aid to N. Yemen," *Washington Post*, June 5, 1980. Both men were writing from North Yemen and provided a good review of these developments. See also Ruszkiewicz, in *U.S. Interests in . . . the Persian Gulf*, 1980, pp. 170–71, 173–74; and Van Hollen, *Washington Quarterly*, vol. 5 (1982), p. 140.

134. There were many analysts in Washington, especially those in intelligence, who were much more aware of the role of local political intrigues, but at the policy level the East-West aspect was salient.

135. The usual intrigues continued. Isma'il was given an honorary party title but stripped of all power. Hassani became president and secretary general of the party, as well as prime minister. Ali Antar, the defense minister, had supported Hassani in removing officers close to Isma'il in

So ended the ill-starred Yemeni crisis of 1979.[136] The United States had reacted quickly, too quickly, to what it perceived as a new step in a Soviet offensive along the arc of crisis.[137] The most valid basis for the American reaction was the perceived need to reassure the Saudis, who were greatly alarmed by the situation. But some in the administration went beyond eagerness to demonstrate a new tough and active general policy of military counterintervention. They saw a chance to gain a North Yemeni proxy to match the presumed Soviet use of a South Yemeni proxy in a surrogate contest.[138] Instead, the United States was used by the North Yemeni, and then left high and dry as they saw greater opportunities in balancing Soviet and Saudi influences. In looking into why plans had been dropped to investigate the intelligence failure, the American military attaché on the spot, who had been reporting all along that there was no good evidence of a major attack from the south, was told by the responsible officer in the Defense Intelligence Agency: "Let me put it this way. If Yemen had not happened at that particular time, it would have been invented."[139] In some respects it was.

1979–80, as he had those close to Rubayi earlier. Both Hassani and Antar favored improved relations with Saudi Arabia and the West, not as an alternative alignment, but as a partial counterbalance to avoid complete dependence on the Soviet Union. Hassani soon made clear his policy of continued close alignment with Moscow. But politics continued on their usual course, and in early 1981 Ali Antar was relieved of the defense post after he apparently began removing officers beholden to Hassani. See Bidwell, *The Two Yemens*, pp. 279–81, 324–29, 332.

Some interpreted the change in government as a Soviet-engineered jettisoning of the more radical Marxist Isma'il in order that the moderate Hassani could unite the two Yemens and bring both closer to Moscow. This thesis was, however, predicated on unification, which did not occur. See Amos Perlmutter, "The Yemen Strategy," *New Republic*, July 5–12, 1980, pp. 16–18.

136. Fighting continued intermittently between the North Yemeni government forces and the South Yemeni–supported National Democratic Front (NDF), an insurgent coalition formed in 1976 and much involved in the 1979 fighting. In mid-1982 the NDF was virtually shattered. See Mark N. Katz, "Sanaa and the Soviets," *Problems of Communism*, vol. 33 (January–February 1984), pp. 21–34.

137. President Carter, Secretary of State Vance, and National Security Adviser Brzezinski all chose not to discuss the American role in the Yemeni episode in their memoirs, except for Brzezinski's expression of satisfaction at having persuaded the president to send an aircraft carrier to the area.

138. President Saleh of North Yemen made clear his understanding of, and lack of appreciation for, this view. At the height of the crisis and American moves to aid his country he accused both the Soviet Union *and* the United States of playing a "superpower game" in the region. Dan Morgan, "U.S. Expedites N. Yemen Arms; Saudis Cautious," *Washington Post*, March 10, 1979. Saleh was playing his own game.

139. Cited by Ruszkiewicz, in *U.S. Interests in . . . the Persian Gulf*, 1980, p. 120.

The Arc of Crisis Moves East

The series of forceful, Soviet-supported seizures of power and agitations of the status quo beginning with Angola in 1975–76 seemed, in the eyes of American policymakers, to develop momentum in 1977–78. The Ethiopian crisis (even though it was directed toward restoration and defense of the status quo ante of Ethiopian territory) was especially wrenching, and appeared to be part of a pattern—one that even included the use of "proxy" Cuban armed forces. Shaba II, and in retrospect even Shaba I as well, were seen as only once or twice removed from Soviet machinations—with the Katangans a "proxy" for Angola and (from Washington's perspective) for Cuba, and therefore ultimately for the Soviet Union. In 1978–79 there was the disturbing series of assassinations, coups, and border clashes in the Yemens—with South Yemen the "proxy" for Soviet interests (and with a Cuban and East German presence in South Yemen as well). Then in October 1979 South Yemen formally signed a Treaty of Friendship and Cooperation with the Soviet Union.

And there was still more elsewhere. Southern Africa remained unsettled and in armed turmoil, especially Rhodesia, but also Namibia. Cuba still had a military presence in Angola. The Soviet bloc was indirectly aiding the National Patriotic Front, especially Joshua Nkomo's Zimbabwe African People's Union (ZAPU) in Rhodesia (Zimbabwe) and the South West African People's Organization (SWAPO) in forays into Namibia. These situations did not, however, as Washington had feared, lead to Soviet or Cuban intervention.

The status quo was also weakening in the whole northern tier of the Middle East (increasingly referred to as Southwest Asia) as well. Terrorism by both the left and right in Turkey was causing growing unrest in the late 1970s until the military took control in September 1980. (The Soviet bloc was correctly suspected of covertly aggravating the situation, but it did not cause or control the internal conflict.) In Afghanistan the army overthrew the nonaligned government of President Mohammad Daoud in April 1978 when he attempted to suppress the Marxist political opposition. An avowedly Marxist and more pro-Soviet regime came to power, and by December 1978 the government of the new Democratic Republic of Afghanistan had signed a Treaty of Friendship and Cooperation with the Soviet Union (as had Ethiopia in November). By the end of 1979 the internal struggle within Afghanistan led to a direct and large-scale Soviet military intervention. But even before that, throughout 1978–79, Afghanistan was regarded as an example of further Soviet penetration in the region.[140]

Iran had long been regarded as a bastion of pro-American power in the region. Especially since 1972, in accordance with the Nixon Doctrine, American leaders had seen the shah of Iran as a local paladin defending Ameri-

---

140. See chapter 26.

can interests. Suddenly, in late 1978 and the early weeks of 1979 this bastion collapsed.[141] It should be noted that the Soviet Union was as surprised as the United States by this development, nor did Soviet efforts to turn the situation to their advantage succeed. The new head of Iran, the Ayatollah Khomeini, after expelling American influence, was vigilant not to allow an influx of Soviet influence in its wake, and he first tamed and then destroyed the pro-Soviet Tudeh party.

The revolution in Iran in 1979 had, nonetheless, a significant impact on American-Soviet relations. In the first place, the United States saw this momentous development as offering opportunities for the Soviet Union to extend its influence both in Iran and in nearby countries previously sheltered by the shah's power. Even though Khomeini's Iran and the brand of Islamic fundamentalism it represented was anticommunist and anti-Soviet, it threatened to be subversive of existing rule—be it monarchies or republics, autocracies or democracies—in many countries in the Middle East. The Soviet Union and local communists might be able to take advantage of the resulting chaos.

The American leaders had another fear—that the Soviet leaders would seek by more direct action to take advantage not only of local unrest, but also of perceived American weakness in the region. Thus the concerns that had been developing since 1977 over an "arc of crisis"[142] running from Africa to Southeast Asia were greatly intensified not only by the collapse of Iran, but by American impotence to stem that development. Thus a loss of confidence on the part of the United States, and a fear that the Soviets would perceive that loss of confidence and act on it, led to American efforts to develop new positions of strength in the region. The feeling of impotence and fear that the Soviets would exploit the situation was to climax at the close of the period under review here, in the wake of Iran's seizure of the American embassy and its staff as hostages and the demoralizing, drawn-out efforts to free them. This crisis was compounded by the overt Soviet military intervention in Afghanistan. Ultimately these events led to the proclamation of the Carter Doctrine and the virtual abandonment by the United States of the policy of détente with the Soviet Union. These developments, examined in detail in subsequent chapters, were but the extension of the growing concerns, and more tentative responses, in the period from 1977 through 1979.

---

141. On American policy and the fall of the shah of Iran and rise of the Ayatollah Ruhollah Khomeini, which are not discussed here, see Michael Ledeen and William Lewis, *Debacle: The American Failure in Iran* (Knopf, 1981); William H. Sullivan, *Mission to Iran* (Norton, 1981) (Sullivan was U.S. ambassador in Tehran at the time); Fereydoun Hoveyda, *The Fall of the Shah* (Wyndham, 1979); Brzezinski, *Power and Principle*, pp. 354–98; Carter, *Keeping Faith*, pp. 434–58; and Vance, *Hard Choices*, pp. 314–48.

142. The term "arc of crisis" was coined by Brzezinski in an address to the Foreign Policy Association on December 20, 1978. See Bernard Gwertzman, "Brzezinski Says Soviet Arms Pact Will Not Weaken U.S.," *New York Times*, December 21, 1978, and "The Crescent of Crisis: Iran and a Region of Rising Instability," *Time*, January 15, 1979, p. 18.

Along with the disturbances in the internal situation in Turkey and the far more drastic upheaval in Iran, coupled with Soviet consolidation of its position in Afghanistan, the United States also faced deteriorating relations with Pakistan in 1978 and 1979. Internal sociopolitical factors in Pakistan led not to open unrest, but to greater repression. General Mohammed Zia ul-Haq effectively (at least for the time) controlled the internal opposition; early in 1979 he executed his predecessor, the last elected president, Ali Bhutto. Concern over this and more general violations of human rights were exacerbated by a growing American conviction that Pakistan was developing a nuclear weapon. In response, in April 1979 the United States cut off economic aid to Pakistan and in June refused to reschedule its debt (military aid had been suspended since the 1971 war). Thus the causes of American concern over Pakistan were very different from those in most other countries in the area. The United States continued to be the most influential external power, and these decisions were American. Nonetheless, the effect was a curtailment of American influence and the provocation of anti-Americanism. In November 1979, as the American embassy in Tehran was being seized, Pakistanis reacted to a report that the United States had been responsible for the seizure of the Grand Mosque in Mecca by burning the American embassy in Islamabad. The Pakistani authorities for their part provided only minimal assistance in rescuing the occupants. (On this same occasion Libyans also attacked and burned the American embassy in Tripoli.) The report alleging American involvement and responsibility for the events in Mecca was wholly unfounded, and no Moslem government gave it credence before it was quickly disproven. But the news flashes—including some from sources clandestinely controlled by the Soviets—had lit the anti-American tinder waiting for any stimulus.

And there was still Vietnam. Late in 1978 the Vietnamese, who had consolidated their control in South Vietnam and Laos since 1975, invaded and occupied Kampuchea (nominally in support of a new Kampuchean government) soon after they signed a Treaty of Friendship and Cooperation with the Soviet Union. Washington saw this incursion as activating an ominous new front that extended the arc of crisis from Africa all the way to Southeast Asia. As early as January 1978, soon after Vietnam joined the Soviet-led Council of Mutual Economic Assistance, Brzezinski had called the Vietnamese a "Soviet proxy." When Vietnam now moved into Kampuchea (which had itself aggressively contributed to the border clashes with Vietnam over disputed territory), the move was seen as *Soviet*-sponsored.[143] That move soon had other serious ramifications—China attacked Vietnam, in part in retaliation for the occupation of Kampuchea.[144] Later the Vietnamese became involved in incidents on the border of Thailand, where many Kampucheans had taken refuge, using that country as a sanctuary to train and mount forays into Kampuchea.

143. See chapter 20. Although the Soviets supported the Vietnamese, the initiative and interest were Vietnamese.

144. See chapter 21.

The notion that these actions stemmed from a coordinated Soviet offensive over a broad arc of crisis was almost certainly not valid, but it seemed plausible to some beleaguered decisionmakers in Washington. Not all adopted this view. Throughout this period of recurrent disturbances and local crises in Africa and Southwest and Southeast Asia, there were in fact widely differing views within the Carter administration. As noted, the developments in the Horn of Africa in late 1977 and early 1978 had pitted Brzezinski against Secretary of State Vance over both the interpretation of the Soviet role and the appropriate American reaction. As this divergence persisted, it affected American policy formulation. Initially President Carter had been more inclined to favor Vance's view, but the Soviet-Cuban role in Ethiopia troubled him, and the concatenation of events in 1978 and 1979 seemed to lend more and more weight to Brzezinski's continued importuning for a tougher American stance.

In July 1978 Carter received Presidential Review Memorandum (PRM)–36, an interagency study of the role of the Soviets and Cubans in Africa and ways for the United States to counter it. While not conclusively supporting Brzezinski's view, it tended to do so. In the latter part of 1978 Brzezinski increasingly pressed the president on the challenge in the arc of crisis. In February 1979, after the fall of the shah, he sent a memorandum to the president urging a "new security framework" in the Middle East–Persian Gulf region. By this time Secretary of Defense Brown had come to take a more active role in supporting Brzezinski, as did Secretary of Energy James R. Schlesinger, by virtue of the apparent threat to oil resources in the Middle East. Schlesinger, a veteran hard-liner who supported a military buildup and was a skeptic on détente, had been Kissinger's nemesis on SALT in the Ford administration.

In June 1979, according to Brzezinski, an important series of meetings was held on the subject of the American military presence in the region. Vance and his deputy Warren Christopher were pitted against Brzezinski, Brown, and Schlesinger.[145] By this time the talks on arms limitations in the Indian Ocean and conventional arms transfers with the Soviet Union had been jettisoned. Moreover, by the spring of 1979, the time of the Yemeni pseudo-crisis, Carter was prepared to send an aircraft carrier into the area, in contrast to his negative reaction a few months earlier when Brzezinski had urged that same action in response to events in the Horn.

In the midst of this turmoil came the summit meeting with Brezhnev in June 1979, at which the SALT II Treaty was concluded. In most other respects the summit did not succeed. It did not lead to improved understanding between the two sides of their differences over the global competition, much less to finding ways to bridge those differences.[146] Indeed, new issues soon arose.[147]

---

145. Brzezinski, *Power and Principle*, pp. 446–47.

146. See chapter 21.

147. See chapters 21, 24, 25.

The Iranian seizure of the American embassy and hostages galvanized the administration into action. In an NSC meeting on December 4, 1979, three weeks before the Soviet coup and occupation of Afghanistan, President Carter accepted Brzezinski's proposal to meet the threat in the arc of crisis by a major buildup in American military capabilities in the area. One element in his decision was to approach the governments of Oman, Somalia, and Kenya to gain continuing American access to naval and air facilities in those countries.[148] In addition, a sizable American fleet was to be concentrated in the Indian Ocean.

The Soviet occupation of Afghanistan in the final days of 1979 crystallized both the perceived threat and the American reaction, which was expressed in the Carter Doctrine. But both the perceived threat and direct American response (as well as the indirect response of gradually curtailing détente with the Soviet Union) had been developing for several years, with a focus on the arc of crisis in the Afro-Asian third world.[149]

It may be useful, as an example, to look at the continuation of the story of American military relations with Somalia. Following the Somali defeat in early 1978 by the Soviet—and Cuban—supported Ethiopians, the United States offered in June of that year to supply defensive arms if the Somalis would give assurances that they would not again attack the Ogaden. Nothing came of that offer. By 1980, however, the administration had a much more active interest and now offered military assistance—$40 million in military assistance for two years and $137 million over two years in economic and refugee assistance, all in exchange for the use of the naval facilities at Berbera[150] and a 15,000-foot airstrip on the Gulf of Aden. The modest economic aid did not prove an issue, but Congress agreed to only $20 million in military

---

148. Brzezinski, *Power and Principle*, p. 446.

149. Events in Central America—later to become a principal focus of American concern—were not attributed to Soviet design in 1978-79. The Sandinista-led insurrection in Nicaragua in early 1978 moved to victory in July 1979 without Soviet assistance and with relatively minor aid from Cuba, less than that received from Western European social democratic parties and democratic Central American countries. Not until April 1979 did the local Communist party join the Sandinista front. A Salvadoran coup in 1979, and later an insurrectionary movement in 1980 after the promised reform proved largely stillborn, also received no aid from Cuba until late 1979, and none from other members of the Soviet bloc until after May 1980, when token military assistance began. Thus appropriately, although somewhat surprisingly, the American administration did not see or complain of outside communist support for the Salvadoran insurgents until they launched an ill-considered major attack at the end of 1980— long after Afghanistan. Similarly, the Guatemalan insurgents were not politically unified and did not begin to receive assistance from Cuba until 1980. The incoming Reagan administration in 1981 chose to take a very different position on the Soviet and Cuban roles.

For the handling of the Sandinista revolution in Nicaragua by the Carter administration up to the fall of General Anastasio Somoza Debayle, see Richard R. Fagen, "Dateline Nicaragua: The End of the Affair," *Foreign Policy*, no. 36 (Fall 1979), pp. 178–91.

150. It was found that the naval facilities at Berbera, which had been perceived as so threatening when available to the Soviet navy, were in fact quite inadequate and required major dredging and construction for even austere use by the U.S. Navy.

assistance, and that was conditioned on "verified assurance" that no regular Somali army troops remained in the Ogaden or would enter it.[151] Negotiations with Kenya and Oman also led to agreements in 1980 on the use of military facilities in those countries.[152]

The Carter administration, in one of its last acts in office, left as a legacy to its successor a consolidated outline for a regional security framework, set forth in Presidential Directive (PD)-63 drawn up by Brzezinski and signed by President Carter in January 1981.[153] It also left the actual arrangements in place or under negotiation in the area from the Horn to the Gulf.

Divergent Perceptions on Intervention in the Third World

This discussion has focused on Soviet or Soviet-supported interventions in the latter 1970s, although related interventions and counterinterventions by the West in the third world have also been noted. In part this focus reflects the fact that the Soviet leaders were pursuing an active policy in the region. In part it also reflects the American perception that Soviet involvement in 1977–79 in the broad arc of crisis from Africa to Southeast Asia represented a wide-ranging and aggressive assault on the status quo. These Soviet actions were seen as a geopolitical challenge not only to American policy, but also to American conceptions of the détente relationship with the Soviet Union. That perception had a significant negative impact on détente. The crowning event that drove the final nail into the coffin of the bilateral détente of the 1970s was the direct Soviet military intervention in Afghanistan at the end of 1979.

The Soviet leaders' perceptions of the events of this period were quite different from those of the U.S. leaders. These differences in perspective and perceptions of the two sides are important to a better understanding of the reasons for the deterioration of relations in the 1970s, and to a more sound understanding in the future. Such an understanding does not necessarily eliminate differences or obviate conflicts. But recognizing the elements of validity of the contradictory perceptions of the two sides, which neither has really done, may lead to a modification of views and to a clarification of how the two adversaries can better deal with their competition.

---

151. The administration's testimony on written assurances from the Somali government was undercut by CIA testimony that elements of three Somali regular army battalions were at that very time in the Ogaden with the guerrillas. This revelation led to the one-year limit and the insistence on "verified assurances." See Dougherty, *The Horn of Africa*, pp. 58–62; and Zelniker, *The Superpowers and the Horn of Africa*, pp. 35–38.

152. Dougherty, *The Horn of Africa*, pp. 55–58; and Zelniker, *The Superpowers and the Horn of Africa*, pp. 36–37.

153. Brzezinski, *Power and Principle*, p. 469.

Many in the United States saw Angola, and even the October War of 1973, as being Soviet attempts to gain influence. While the United States had faced down the challenge in 1973, it did not succeed in doing so in Angola in 1975–76. And from 1977 on it seemed that the Soviet Union and its Cuban and Vietnamese "proxies" were ever more on the march, particularly in Ethiopia in 1977–78 and Indochina in 1978, in the Shaba incursions in 1977 and 1978, in the coups in South Yemen and Afghanistan in 1978, in the occupation of Kampuchea in 1978–79, and finally in the occupation of Afghanistan in December 1979.

Initiative has usually been ascribed to the Soviets, sometimes in terms of seizing opportunities, but sometimes as involving a more deliberate plan for geopolitical envelopment of the oil of the Persian Gulf, or as twin pincers in Southwest and Southeast Asia. While local events have sometimes been recognized as contributing to those opportunities, there was growing concern and unease in the late 1970s that the Soviet advance was being facilitated by increasing signs of weakness in American military power, resolve, or both.

In the Soviet view the United States had been aggressively pursuing policies under détente to reduce Soviet influence and to gain advantage for itself throughout the third world. It had, from the very outset of détente in 1972, worked to exclude the Soviet Union from the Middle East—a key area adjoining the Soviet Union itself. The Soviets noted with suspicion and foreboding the decision in Presidential Directive (PD)–18 as early as August 1977 to establish a greater rapid deployment capability for distant military intervention, even though the United States did not move actively on that stated policy until 1979. They noted that the United States had, especially after 1978, developed collaborative relations with China on an anti-Soviet basis. Even in the third world, particularly in the volatile arc of crisis, Moscow saw the United States or its allies and associates as having almost invariably taken the first steps in external intervention or involvement.

Thus Moscow's perception is that the United States (and the West generally) has been taking the initiative and aggressively seeking ways to stem the tide of indigenous progressive change and national liberation. (China, too, has been seen as taking a parallel road in some cases in pursuit of its own hegemonistic aims.) This point is important, as Moscow views normalcy, or the status quo, not as a static condition but as a flow of progressive historical change. While peaceful coexistence between established states characterizes détente, détente does not preclude revolutionary change within states; in fact, détente should abet it.

Thus to Moscow the United States had supported its NATO ally Portugal in attempts to suppress the national liberation movements in Angola and the other Portuguese colonies until 1974, and had assisted Rhodesia and South Africa in resisting majority rule (national liberation). After the revolution in Portugal, as Angola moved to independence, the United States, China, and Zaire supported Roberto's FNLA, and the West and South Africa supported Savimbi's UNITA. The support of both groups was regarded as intervention to ensure Angolan independence under local leaders subservient to Western (or Chinese) control. In response, the Soviets and Cubans had backed Neto's MPLA—although overtly only after Angola's independence, the collapse of the fragile tripartite pre-government in Luanda, and the introduction of Angolan forces from Zaire. Only after South Africa penetrated deep into Angola did Cuba introduce troops on a large scale. Both the Soviets and Cubans saw their actions as justified not only by historical processes but by political-military necessities stemming from *Western* initiatives. (In partial support of this interpretation, the absence of Western-supported or South African movements into Mozambique, and the parallel absence of the introduction of Soviet or Cuban forces into that country, might be noted.)

Ethiopia was a sovereign country with a recently radicalized government that was consolidating its power (and had universal diplomatic recognition). It was attacked by regular Somali military forces pursuing avowed irredentist claims on Ethiopian territory—after the United States encouraged Somalia in an effort to draw it away from its alliance with the Soviet Union by a promise of arms. The Soviet Union and Cuba supported the Ethiopian government with military supplies and troops to defend its own territory and stopped short of carrying the successful counteroffensive into Somalia itself.

In Southwest Asia there were the coups and crises in Afghanistan and the Yemens in 1978–79. From the Soviet perspective the American role was far more active and far less defensive and benign than the United States claimed. The United States had, particularly under the Nixon Doctrine, relied on its two regional paladins (or "proxies"), Iran and Saudi Arabia, in Southwest Asia.

The Soviet Union also perceived Saudi Arabia to be actively seeking to maximize its influence in both North and South Yemen at Soviet expense and that of its local allies. Moreover, in 1978, before Rubayi was overthrown, the South Yemeni were also turning to the Saudis and the Chinese as a counterweight. And in 1979, as earlier noted, a senior American diplomat was literally en route to South Yemen to discuss restoration of diplomatic ties when the intermittent border war was agitated and the U.S. initiative was aborted.

Saudi Arabia was seen to be serving American (as well as her own) interests in many other cases in Africa and the Middle East, for example, in supporting the Eritreans against Ethiopia, in helping to bring Somalia and the United States together, and in helping to turn the Sudan from the Soviet Union to the United States.

In the period preceding the Afghan coup of April 1978, President Daoud had been the subject of considerable attention by the shah of Iran, who persuaded him to mend his fences with Pakistan (allied with both China and the United States) over the disputed Pushtu territories and to turn against the domestic left. It was Daoud's arrest of the Afghan communist leaders that led their sympathizers in the Afghan army to depose him.[154]

---

154. See chapter 26.

The Soviet perception of responsibility for initiating the conflicts presented above differed from that of the United States, which saw only Soviet instigation and exploitation. Moreover, there is clearly substantial foundation for the Soviet perception.

The Soviets have a long list of other instances of American and other Western intervention, many of which are not presented in the American recitations because of the absence of Soviet involvement. One example, mentioned earlier, was how Iran and the United States used the Kurds in Iraq in a proxy intervention against an ally of the Soviet Union from 1972 to 1975. Similarly, proxy Iranian troops and British, Jordanian, and Pakistani advisers turned the tide in the defeat by Oman of the South Yemeni–based Popular Front for the Liberation of Oman (PFLO, formerly the PFLOAG) in Dhofar in 1973–75.[155]

Africa presented the largest number of coups, wars, and interventions. From 1975 on Morocco was engaged in hostilities with the Polisario, an indigenous West Saharan movement that has fought Morocco since that country (and, initially, Mauritania as well) occupied the territory in 1975 after the end of Spanish colonial rule. In 1976 the Polisario established the Sahrawi (Saharan) Arab Democratic Republic, which has been recognized by some sixty governments, including over half the African states (and, since 1984, by the OAU). For several years the United States was officially neutral, but in October 1979, in order to strengthen ties with Morocco and gain use of additional military facilities, it agreed to provide arms to Morocco for use against the Polisario. Then in 1980 Congress approved the sale of counterinsurgency weapons to Morocco. The Polisario has received its principal support from Algeria, but also from Libya and a number of other African states. It has received Soviet-made arms from these supporters, but not from the Soviet Union.

In January 1977 a mercenary force attacked Cotonu, Benin (formerly Dahomey), in an attempted coup against the leftist regime, but was defeated. The insurrection was widely reported to have had covert or unofficial French support. (A similar ill-fated Portuguese-led mercenary assault on Conakry, Guinea, in November 1970 had led to a show of Soviet support in the form of a naval visit, followed by a continuing naval patrol. This support contributed to an increase in Soviet influence in Guinea until the late 1970s.)[156]

---

155. See J. E. Peterson, *Oman in the Twentieth Century: Political Foundations of an Emerging State* (Barnes and Noble, 1978), pp. 188–93.

The Chinese had earlier supported the PFLOAG, but ceased doing so after the Sino-Iranian and Sino-American rapprochements in 1972–73. In the 1973–75 period Cuba and Libya, as well as Iraq, also supported the South Yemeni–PFLO effort against Oman, and the Soviet Union supported the effort only indirectly. On the other side, in addition to Iran, seconded British officers and Jordanian and Pakistani military specialists assisted the Omani, while the United States provided indirect support.

156. See Bradford Dismukes and James M. McConnell, eds., *Soviet Naval Diplomacy* (Pergamon Press, 1979), pp. 130–33.

The Zairian support for Angolan émigrés raiding Angola from 1976 into 1978 (raids that were responsible for triggering both the Shaba I and II invasions by the Katangan exiles), and continuing South African support for Savimbi's UNITA, were noted earlier. Similarly, South Africa was responsible for supporting the Mozambique National Resistance (MNR), which began in the spring of 1978 to mount raids into Mozambique.[157] South Africa itself repeatedly mounted military attacks against SWAPO Namibians and exiled oppositionist South Africans (and occasionally others) located in the adjoining sovereign states of Angola, Mozambique, Botswana, and Zambia. In 1977 the leftist President Marien Ngoubai of the People's Republic of the Congo (Brazzaville), bordering on Angola and Zaire, was assassinated but was succeeded by another Marxist military regime.

In 1979 a rash of antileftist coups occurred in Africa. A coup with French military support removed Emperor Jean Bédel Bokassa of the Central African Empire (subsequently again the Central African Republic). (Neighboring Chad was the scene of an alternating succession of Libyan- and French-supported regimes from 1977 to 1981.) Idi Amin Dada was thrown out of Uganda in 1979 by a Western-supported Tanzanian invasion, following an ill-advised incursion by Ugandans into Tanzania. And in the same year the leftist dictator Francisco Maçias Nguema was ousted in Equatorial Guinea, and leftist regimes in Guinea-Bissau and Ghana were overthrown.[158]

In Rhodesia, the agreement governing the transition to African rule in what became Zimbabwe was drawn up by the British and supported by the United States. It brought Robert Mugabe of ZANU to power in 1980. He had been supported mainly by the Chinese, in contrast to Nkomo of ZAPU, who received Soviet support. While hardly an "intervention," since Great Britain was in a sense the departing power and had dealt with all parties, from the Soviet standpoint the Western powers had engineered a solution bypassing their favored party, thus winning that round of competition. Nonetheless, the Soviet Union did not attempt to prevent the Western-arranged peaceful transition in Zimbabwe, and this restraint contributed to the favorable outcome. The United States was rewarded for its wisdom in not intervening directly in the Rhodesian conflict, which it would have been prone to do had it presumed that Rhodesia/Zimbabwe was a pawn in East-West competition.

The bloodiest intervention of all was little-noted—Indonesia's suppression of the Democratic Republic of East Timor, the former Portuguese

---

157. The MNR was established by the Rhodesian Intelligence Service in 1977. In 1978 it operated in collaboration with the South African authorities. After the Rhodesian internal settlement in 1979 the MNR passed to direct South African control. It then absorbed a smaller South African–supported Mozambique Resistance Movement. Under an agreement with Mozambique in 1984, South Africa undertook not to support the MNR any longer.

158. Additional actual and attempted coups have continued to occur since the period of this review, such as the suppression of a leftist coup in Gambia by the Senegalese, and an unsuccessful South African mercenary coup attempt in the Seychelles, both in 1981.

colony of East Timor, from 1975 to 1979 and after. A local left-wing movement, the Revolutionary Front for an Independent Timor (FRETILIN), had
been victorious in a three-month civil war that followed the departure of the
Portuguese. Its victory prompted Indonesia to invade in December 1975. Over
the next four years more people died than in any other war in the latter half of
the 1970s. The war was confined to Indonesia and East Timor and took place
without Western participation—or serious criticism. Indonesia, however, continued (after a brief interruption) to receive American military assistance, and
the United States abstained when the United Nations condemned the Indonesian invasion and annexation of East Timor. The Soviet Union and its allies
played no role, but strongly criticized the Indonesian action and Western support.

Earlier conflicts in Asia, from the Korean War to the Vietnam
War, had involved extensive American intervention and use of proxy forces. In
Korea the United States had the mantle of the United Nations and contingents of armed forces from a dozen countries. In Vietnam it brought in a larger
number of South Korean military forces than the Cubans had introduced in
Angola or Ethiopia, as well as Australian, New Zealand, and Philippine contingents. While the United States and these countries did not view these forces as
proxies, from the Soviet viewpoint they certainly were.

American allies, protégés, or protectorates continued to resort to
military interventions. Israel is the notable case, with its repeated operations in
Lebanon in the late 1970s and early 1980s (and other actions from Entebbe in
1976 to the bombing of the Iraqi reactor in 1981). There were also the examples in western and southern Africa cited earlier. Again, while the United
States and the countries involved did not regard these as proxy actions, from
the Soviet standpoint they were activities by local paladins serving the interests
of the imperialists.

Finally, the Soviets interpreted the overall pattern of these actions
to mean that the United States did not *in practice* see détente in the 1970s as
marking any radical departure from the tradition of direct, proxy, and allied
intervention of the 1950s and 1960s. What was new was the possibility that the
Soviet Union could play a somewhat more active (if still carefully selective)
role in countering, or emulating, such activities in the third world.[159] There
were ample precedents and parallels for its doing so. Even the introduction of
Cuban proxies into Africa in Angola (apart from its being, in important part,
an initiative of Castro's initially) followed an American precedent—it was the
United States that had brought its own Cuban proxies—anti-Castro Cuban

---

159. This brief recital of Western intervention also serves as a reminder of the very large number
of crises and political upheavals in which the Soviet Union has refrained from intervening. In
these cases it deemed such a move to be inappropriate because of insufficient local opportunity, excessive requirements for commitment of Soviet resources or prestige, high risks or
costs, or for other reasons.

mercenaries—into the Congo (Zaire) in 1964 to help Mobutu establish control.[160]

This quick review of the record as seen from the perspective of the Soviet leaders makes clear, on the basis of just the decade of the 1970s, the decade of détente, that while the Soviet leaders pursued their own interests vigorously, in doing so they were less influenced by Kissinger's (and later Brzezinski's) lectures on a code of conduct and reciprocal restraint than by U.S. actions as they perceived them.[161] To paraphrase another member of the Nixon administration, Attorney General John N. Mitchell, the Soviet leaders looked at what the United States did, not what it said.

This brief review also makes clear the great difference in Soviet and American perspectives. Each, of course, has a basis in reality, but perceived by each side through distorting filters of selectivity, emphasis, and preconception. While American attention focused on Cuban troops in Angola and Ethiopia, and Soviet use of naval facilities in Ethiopia and South Yemen, Soviet attention focused on French troops in Djibouti, the Central African Republic, Chad, Senegal, Gabon, and the Ivory Coast, and on American use of military facilities in Morocco, Kenya, Somalia, Oman, Bahrein, and Egypt. Both sets of facts are real, but neither is *the* facts.

As noted earlier, the American reaction to events in Southwest Asia such as the Iranian revolution has been to fear Soviet intervention, while the Soviet reaction has been to fear American intervention in this area adjoining the Soviet Union. Thus as the regime of the shah was falling, the Soviets warned that American military intervention in Iran would be a matter affecting its security interests.[162] Similarly, the Soviets were highly suspicious of the longer-term purposes of the American buildup of a major fleet in the Indian Ocean in 1979–80.

---

160. Victor Marchetti and John Marks, *The CIA and the Cult of Intelligence* (Knopf, 1974), pp. 31, 117; this information was confirmed by official sources.

161. This account has been limited to developments grounded in actual historical fact and presumably available to the Soviet leaders, even though perceived through the bias of preconceptions. Soviet propaganda includes many other examples of alleged American and other Western intervention, either distorted or imagined, some of which the Soviet leaders may also believe.

   For another analysis making this point, see Robert Legvold, "The Super Rivals: Conflict in the Third World," *Foreign Affairs*, vol. 57 (Spring 1979), pp. 755–78.

   For a conveniently available, articulate Soviet view of this general issue, prepared for an American readership, see Henry Trofimenko, "America, Russia and the Third World," *Foreign Affairs*, vol. 59 (Summer 1981), pp. 1021–40.

162. Brezhnev himself delivered a clear warning in November 1978, stating, "Any interference, especially military intervention, in the internal affairs of Iran—a state bordering on the Soviet Union—would be regarded by the USSR as a matter affecting the interests of its security." See "L. I. Brezhnev's Reply to the Question of a *Pravda* Correspondent," *Pravda*, November 19, 1978.

The Soviets see active and purposeful actions by the imperialists, especially the United States, and their minions, protectorates, and proxies, to maintain and where possible expand their sway in the third world. They see a Western propensity to use force, including military force, to prevent a natural, progressive, political and economic revolutionary advance of society. This picture contrasts with what they had expected to see in the 1970s—a lessening of American and in general Western resort to force. The reason was basically the overall change in the correlation of forces in the world, and also a more sober and realistic recognition of the changing structure of global power by American and Western leaders. The growth of Soviet military power and the approach to military parity with the United States were seen as elements affecting the global balance and the calculations of Western leaders, although not as the central factor. The changing economic structure (especially within the Western world and between the Western and third worlds) was seen as another important factor—one of particular importance in Marxist analysis. So, too, the American experience in Vietnam and more generally in the 1960s, as reflected in American changes in policy such as the Nixon Doctrine, led to expectations of a lessened—but by no means abandoned—dependence on military means to deal with political and economic challenges.

The American tendency has been to see new challenges as arising from situations either instigated or at least exploited by a Soviet Union feeling its oats as a new global power. The fear has been that Soviet military parity with the United States would lead the Soviets to be bolder in expanding their power and influence, although by means other than military. Détente, the United States believed, could give the Soviet leaders a stake in not upsetting the status quo and thus restrain its impulses to exploit expansionist opportunities. But then the course of events from Angola through Afghanistan was seen as a successful Soviet pursuit of expansion overriding any restraint from détente.

Both the American and Soviet leaders have also shared a tendency to exaggerate the clarity and purposefulness of the intent of the other to seek aggrandizement, and the degree of coherence, control, and consistency of policy and action. Each side has consistently overestimated the capabilities as well as the aggressive intentions of the other. Both sides have also tended to fail to see the extent to which their own actions were in fact aggrandizing (and still more the extent to which they could be so perceived, particularly, although not exclusively, by the adversary).

As a corollary, both sides have also frequently underestimated the extent to which third parties influence events. Third parties are not just arenas of Soviet-American conflict, nor merely pawns or proxies of the other side, nor just the stakes in bilateral global competition. While they are sometimes one or more of those things, they are also actors in their own right. For better or worse (both for their own interests, and for others) they often initiate or precipitate developments drawing in the great powers and sometimes forcing decisions on Moscow or Washington—decisions that the other capital often mis-perceives and misinterprets as being a devious offensive scheme.

The United States on the whole has tended even more than the Soviet Union to underrecognize the independent roles and initiatives of third world countries and third parties (although in some cases the Soviet leaders also have erred grossly). Paradoxically, the United States, with an ideology championing pluralism and pragmatism in the conduct of foreign relations, has tended in recent decades to view the world in excessively oversimplified terms—all other political realities are subordinated to a conflict between a "Free World" and a "Communist World," headed respectively by the United States and the Soviet Union. While this view had become attenuated by the 1970s and was partially submerged under détente, its rebirth by the early 1980s showed its deep roots. The lack of a comprehensive American worldview meant that superpower rivalry loomed as the overarching political reality, and it was then given an ideological rationale.

The Soviet leaders, on the other hand, while originally proceeding from a stereotyped ideological view that defined world politics in terms of two antagonistic classes, had learned from more than sixty-five years of experience that reality is far more complex. Without abandoning their central ideological worldview, they see a great variety of political entities, including friendly capitalist states and hostile communist ones, from the standpoint of Soviet interests.

Thus the Soviet leaders are only too ready to see interimperialist rivalries, especially in terms of competition for economic resources, that lead to diverging and conflicting policies within the West. The Soviets have learned as well that the third world has given birth to a variety of socialisms and political systems. The Soviet Union was, for example, keenly aware of and concerned over Chinese actions in Africa and in the arc of crisis, while the United States was scarcely aware of Chinese activities in Angola, Mozambique, the Horn, South Yemen, and other places, and failed to recognize Soviet-Chinese rivalry as a factor in a number of these situations, in some cases a factor affecting Soviet decisions.

Incredibly, even the most ideologically neutral and geopolitical or realistic American leaders, Nixon and Kissinger, saw the Syrian-Jordanian clash of 1970 and the Indo-Pakistani War of 1971 as Soviet proxy wars.[163] Later Kissinger conceded that the fall of South Vietnam in 1975, and the adverse (from the American standpoint) situation in Portugal in mid-1975, were not caused by Soviet machinations but by "internal dynamics." But even then he saw these situations as ultimately determined by Soviet and American actions, and faulted the United States for not having done more.[164] And Kissinger, in

---

163. Henry Kissinger, *The White House Years* (Boston, Mass.: Little, Brown, 1979), p. 1255.

164. "Secretary Kissinger Interviewed for U.S. News and World Report," *State Bulletin*, vol. 73 (July 7, 1975), pp. 17–18. He was critical of what he believed was insufficient action by the

defending détente as not being a one-way street, argued in mid-1975: "Some of the events that have happened in the world that have been against our interests have been caused by the Soviets; others have not. Some have been caused by our failure to take adequate unilateral actions—for those we have no one but ourselves to blame."[165] Even in acknowledging that "not all local wars and regional conflicts affect global stability or America's national interest," Kissinger argued that "if one superpower systematically exploits these conflicts for its own advantage and tips the scales decisively by its intervention, gradually the overall balance will be affected." Thus, "if adventurism is allowed to succeed in local crises, an ominous precedent of wider consequence is set."[166] That, as was seen, was the lesson of Angola to Kissinger—and to many Americans.[167] The Soviet Union was pushing because the United States was not standing fast. Kissinger, in his memoir, while highly critical of the self-defeating actions of Americans in undermining détente, nonetheless argues that "the fundamental assault on détente came from Moscow," referring to its actions and those of its proxies in Angola, Ethiopia, South Yemen, South Vietnam, Laos, Cambodia, and Afghanistan, and, in the early 1980s, by its pressures on Poland.[168]

Brzezinski, who was on the whole more attuned to the realities of third world political dynamics, nonetheless also subordinated this recognition to the rivalry of the superpowers. In a retrospective critique of the Carter administration's policy he saw a "failure to confront early enough the Soviet policy of combining detente on the Central European front with military expansion (first by proxy and then directly) in areas peripheral to our sensitive geopolitical interests." The United States should, in his view, have "responded more assertively through credible political-military reactions."[169] He notes the divided view on this question within the Carter administration, but believes that events in the 1977–80 period "tended to confirm my view of the U.S.-Soviet relationship" and led to his view predominating and to the policy pursued in the latter half of the Carter administration.[170] Yet even as late as November 1978, in a pessimistic mood, Brzezinski wrote in his private journal

---

United States in Portugal. He was, however, prematurely pessimistic: three months later the leftists were ousted from power in Portugal, without American action. On this same occasion he also candidly acknowledged that as for the Middle East, the Soviet leaders could well blame their reduced influence there on American actions.

165. Ibid., p. 17.

166. "America's Permanent Interests: Address by Secretary Kissinger," March 11, *State Bulletin*, vol. 74 (April 5, 1976), p. 428.

167. Ibid., p. 429; and see chapter 15.

168. Henry Kissinger, *Years of Upheaval* (Boston, Mass.: Little, Brown, 1983), p. 1030.

169. Brzezinski, *Power and Principle*, p. 517.

170. Ibid., p. 518.

that "the Soviets no longer take us seriously and are asserting themselves in Iran and South Yemen and southern Africa and Cuba."[171]

Geopolitical considerations certainly figure in Soviet and American decisionmaking on third world interventions, but it has been the dynamics of local situations rather than geopolitical ambitions that have been responsible for the agenda of crises. The Carter administration, and in particular Brzezinski, saw a pattern of Soviet initiative in Africa, then in surrounding Saudi Arabia,[172] and finally in a massive pincers in Southwest and Southeast Asia. In fact these actions were not part of a grand design but were several separate mosaics—the Vietnamese-Kampuchean-Chinese-Soviet parallelogram bore no intrinsic relationship to the separate courses of events in the Horn of Africa, the Yemens, the Middle East, and Afghanistan. Similarly, while the Soviets saw American interest from 1977 on in building a rapid deployment force for the Middle Eastern–Indian Ocean area, they failed to appreciate the extent to which their own actions (and some other developments, notably the collapse of the rule of the shah of Iran and the subsequent hostage crisis) contributed to the American decisions to build a permanent military presence in the area.

The purpose of this review of the different perspectives on superpower interventions in the third world is not to weigh and judge them, but to point out their pervasiveness, salience, and consequences. The review in some detail of the crises and conflicts in the Middle East in 1973 (chapter 11), Angola (chapter 15), and Zaire, the Horn of Africa, and the Yemens shows the misperceptions and, even more, distorted imbalance in the views of the events and of their significance by leaders in both Washington and Moscow. These divergent perceptions reflect in part conflicting ambitions and reciprocal fears, as well as different expectations based on differing worldviews and conceptions of détente.

In reviewing the differing perspectives on third world conflicts, and especially on superpower involvement in them, the emphasis has been on American views of *Soviet* intervention, and Soviet views of *American* and other Western intervention. These views are an important part of reality, one not given due weight on either side. The real situation is not, however, limited to reactive (or defensive) moves by the two sides, even allowing for self-convincing arguments that justify offensive thrusts as defensive or reactive actions.

The United States has sometimes seen itself as required, even destined, by its predominant power to restore the peace and defend the status quo. (Usually it describes this role as assuming a burden, although elsewhere in

---

171. Ibid., p. 520. This list of examples of successful Soviet "assertions" in 1977–78, including Iran and "southern Africa," is rather odd. The important point is that it reflects Brzezinski's way of seeing the situation.

172. Ibid., pp. 181, 196. Time and again in his memoir Brzezinski stresses his concern in early 1978 over what he describes as "Moscow's misuse of detente to improve the Soviet geopolitical and strategic position around Saudi Arabia," especially through its Cuban proxy in Ethiopia and South Yemen. Ibid., p. 203.

the world it is often seen to be a self-appointed role nominally as the world's policeman while really serving U.S. interests.) In practice the United States has, for whatever blend of motivations, and for what its leadership and people have almost always perceived as acting for defensive purposes, frequently turned to the threat or use of force.[173] And even apart from occasional resort to force, the United States has played a far more active, not merely reactive, role in world politics than most Americans realize.

On the other hand, the Soviet leaders, with the bias of their ideological beliefs and from the vantage point of their perspective, have overstated the extent of active and offensive U.S. initiative. They also see their experience with the United States as validating their ideologically conditioned expectations that the leaders of the imperialist powers will use any opportunity to exert leverage and pressure on them and others when circumstances allow. The Soviets are not merely projecting their own intentions, although they too seek to take advantage of opportunities to pursue their own interests. While the Soviets may, as noted, overestimate American offensive initiative, friends of America in the world also see it as playing a much more activist role than most Americans do, including most American leaders (with Nixon, Kissinger, and Brzezinski as notable exceptions to a significant degree).

Although both sides in practice rely principally on political and economic means to sustain and advance their own influence and curb that of the rival superpower, both are especially sensitive to the use of military instruments.[174] In the United States there has been a particularly unhelpful tendency to speak loosely about the salience of "the military dimension" or the prominent use of "the military instrument" in characterizing Soviet policy. In fact, the supply of arms is quite different from the use of arms. Differences in political circumstances are also important. Finally, it is important to recognize the distinctions among the purposes of using military instruments: to *influence* target countries, to *support* them, or to *coerce* them.[175] Arms sales and military training programs may serve the first or second or both of those purposes. Both the United States and the Soviet Union have used military instruments widely for these two purposes. Acquisition of military bases and facilities for use by the superpower rivals usually serves other strategic purposes of that power, but may also be used to support the host country.

---

173. For a useful overall survey, see Barry M. Blechman and Stephen S. Kaplan, eds., *Force without War: U.S. Armed Forces as a Political Instrument* (Brookings Institution, 1978).

174. This discussion has concentrated on the military and political-military activities of the two superpowers because they have been the most significant elements affecting Soviet-American relations. It should be borne in mind that both the United States and the Soviet Union are in active and widely varying political competition in bilateral relationships, United Nations activities, the diplomacy of the nonaligned movement, and other interactions. In economic relations, while there is also active competition, the United States and its friends and allies have vastly greater resources and opportunities.

175. I am indebted to my colleague Michael MccGwire for clarifying this important distinction.

Direct use by the superpowers of their own military forces to support other countries has been much more limited. The United States made massive commitments of American troops in the Korean War and the Vietnam War and provided military forces in a number of other cases, such as in Lebanon in 1958 and again (under different circumstances) in 1983. The Soviet Union has done so in providing air defenses to Egypt (1970–72) and Syria (1982–present) and supporting Cuban forces in defending Ethiopia from Somali attack (1977–78). All of these were, it will be noted, protective situations.

All the cases of direct coercive use of Soviet military power have occurred in its directly adjacent national security zone—Hungary (1956), Czechoslovakia (1968), and Afghanistan (December 1979–present). Each case was unquestionably perceived by the Soviet leaders as strategically defensive and protective against counterrevolutionary challenges, although objectively and analytically the actions were coercive. While the defensive nature of the Soviet action may not be accepted, the significance of the subjective perception of a defensive purpose should not be neglected in evaluating the Soviet propensity to use force and in predicting whether, where, and when the Soviet Union might do so again.

On the whole the United States has used its own military forces coercively more frequently: carrying the Korean War north of the thirty-eighth parallel (1950), occupying the Dominican Republic (1965), bombing North Vietnam (1964 and 1965–72), bombing and then invading Cambodia (1970), bombing Kampuchea in the *Mayaguez* incident (1975), setting up and shooting down Libyan fighters over the Gulf of Sidra (1981), and invading Grenada (1983). All these instances had declared defensive purposes and were perceived in Washington as defensive, but whatever the justification they, too, were coercive uses of military force.

Both powers also use their military power coercively through threats of use more frequently than actual use. For example, Soviet troop concentrations near Poland in 1980 and 1981 served to influence Polish behavior. Similarly, American military concentrations near Nicaragua from 1981 to the present (1985) have been intended to influence Nicaraguan behavior.

Both American and Soviet leaders have exaggerated the propensity of the other to resort to military force. The record actually shows discrimination and caution, particularly by the Soviet Union. For example, the Soviet-supported Cubans in Angola since 1976 have been held back to protect the regime in Luanda rather than sent out to repulse South African forays and even most assaults by UNITA guerrillas. The Soviets kept the Ethiopians from invading Somalia after defeating the Somali army and forcing its withdrawal from Ethiopia in 1978. Nor did the Soviets use their forces in Syria to prevent the Israeli defeats of Syrian forces in Lebanon. They have exercised restraint in not attacking the Afghan insurgents in their sanctuaries in Pakistan and Iran (beyond a few signals to remind of that capability). The question is not one of who was right or wrong in any given instance, or whether particular actions by either side were justified, or whether they were wise (a separate question). There *is* a record of use of force by both powers that helps illuminate the circumstances under which, and the ways in which, each uses or chooses not to use military force.

It may be useful in concluding this discussion to look more closely at Soviet policy on involvement in the third world as it was developing in the mid- and late 1970s, to supplement and to place in context the differing perspectives on intervention discussed above.

Soviet Policy on Third World Involvement

The Soviet Union, having less than the United States, is less satisfied with the status quo. More important, a central tenet of its ideology and worldview is that the world is undergoing a progressive revolutionary change. Nevertheless, in important ways the Soviet Union has become a status quo power, too. There was a basis for the Kissinger strategy of détente to help the Soviet Union build a stake in the existing international political and economic system that went beyond the bedrock of a shared Soviet and American, and truly world, stake in survival in the nuclear age. But especially with respect to the third world there was less of a basis. Moreover, apart from questions of Soviet national interests in the third world (to which the Soviet leaders naturally give particular attention), there also remains more of the ideological expectation of progressive change there in the relatively near term than realistic contemporary Soviet leaders apply to their expectations regarding the advanced capitalist West.

In general terms, the Soviet leaders have had no difficulty reconciling their pursuit of détente and peaceful coexistence with the capitalist states and the continuing class struggle in the world. The latter they see in any case as an objective phenomenon not subject to their own or anyone else's control. As noted, the Soviet leaders have had recurrent difficulty persuading some Marxist-Leninists and other progressive and national liberation movements that they have not been selling out the interests of those movements in building closer Soviet political, economic, and military (arms control) ties with the West. But that problem, too, has posed no great difficulty to Soviet ideologists and propagandists.

The broadest issue for the Soviets has been the obverse of the main American concern, and it stems from the latent discrepancy in expectations of the two sides of the impact of détente, noted earlier. The Soviet leaders saw the attainment of strategic parity as establishing a strategic standoff that would reduce the ability of the United States to resort to military means in efforts to stem the progressive drive of history. This outcome was demonstrated most notably in the failed effort in Vietnam. The first policy issue this belief posed for the Soviet leaders was whether, when, and how this changed strategic situation permitted (or, required) more active *Soviet* support and assistance to revolutionary change. In broadest terms the Soviet leaders can be taken at their word when they say they do not believe in or practice the export of revolution, but only oppose the export of counterrevolution (Western intervention against revolutionary change). To the extent that they believe their ideology—and the record of history and experience—revolution cannot be successfully exported, as it must have indigenous roots and a base. The Soviets know that launching a guerrilla movement, much less a successful one, will not succeed in virtually any Western and many third world countries.

The Soviet leaders do not, however, conceive of their own role as passive and do not preclude an active role when the correlation of forces makes that prudent. The Soviet role may be limited to verbal or moral support or may extend to economic assistance, political and diplomatic support, supply of arms, or to Soviet-supported socialist (for example, Cuban), or even direct Soviet military assistance of various kinds. Angola and Ethiopia are the outstanding examples.

On a practical basis, the question is posed in terms of possible Soviet support for specific national liberation and progressive revolutionary groups. The Soviet leaders consider several factors: opportunity, means, risks, estimated costs—and gains. Here, too, Soviet experience tempers and influences its ideological inclinations.

The Soviet Union takes as a core tenet of its policy and indeed its political system that its interests are identical and inseparable from the progressive tide of history. The Soviet Union is the base of the world communist and revolutionary movement and must above all be preserved. Thus it is led to believe that "what's good for the Soviet Union is good for the world revolution." While the Soviet leaders are jaded realists on one plane, the legitimacy of their entire system and their own rule, and their own ideological worldview, depend on the validity of their identification with the cause of mankind. To be sure, this identification is highly convenient: it means that whatever endangers the Soviet Union and its achievements, whatever risks nuclear war, or whatever reduces the power of the Soviet state, is anathema to the cause of history. No action threatening, or even adversely affecting, the interests of the Soviet Union can be justified. This ideological mindset justifies any policy that enhances the Soviet position. In particular, it powerfully reinforces and provides ideological sanction both for prudence and the avoidance of great risks and for the expansion of influence.

This way of seeing the world also justifies any action that contributes to enhancing the power of the Soviet state. Thus when the risks and costs *are* deemed acceptable, and when the prospects for serving Soviet interests are seen as sufficiently promising, the Soviet leaders are prepared to deal pragmatically with support not only to those with shared ideological sympathies, but also to others, including even local noncommunist regimes with anticommunist internal policies. The Soviet leaders do not approach such matters from a coldly cynical standpoint, but their judgments on what action is right are inseparable from their judgments on what is expedient. There are, of course, differences in judgment within the Soviet leadership with respect to particular situations.[176]

As the Soviet leaders moved toward détente and peaceful coexistence in Europe in the late 1960s, and with the United States in the early 1970s, they did not see any prospect for a wave of revolutionary action in the third world or still less of direct Soviet intervention there. Vietnam was a special case of an uncompleted national and communist revolution. Elsewhere in Asia, the Middle East, Africa, and Latin America the Soviets expected, through their activities as a great power rather than as the patron of revolution, to continue gradually to expand their own influence, but rarely to exert control. Economic means, including the special categories of arms sales and supply as well as selected trade incentives, were already a major instrument of Soviet policy and would be developed further. In fact, the Soviets used economic means to rein in Cuba, a quasi-independent communist ally that had stressed guerrilla action in the third world, in its advocacy and support for the armed path to socialism. This disciplining of Cuba became effective in 1968.[177]

China, which had openly challenged the Soviet Union in the world communist movement since 1960 and especially after 1963, then had withdrawn into the internal turmoil of the Great Proletarian Cultural Revolution in the late 1960s. While the Soviet Union would never again command leadership over a unified world communist movement, at least by 1969 it had restored a modicum of stabilization to a loose movement and had stemmed the fragmentation supported by China.

---

176. While differences in policy assessment and positions among Soviet leaders are not openly disclosed, they do occur. Moreover, there are differences of analysis among Soviet scholars and commentators that help identify and illuminate the differences in assessment and points of view relevant to the policy process. For a particularly keen analysis see Jerry F. Hough, *The Struggle for the Third World: Soviet Debates and American Options* (Brookings Institution, 1985).

177. The critical point at which Cuba's independence of view and position was effectively curtailed and brought under Soviet discipline was the aftermath of the Soviet occupation of Czechoslovakia. Castro had purged from the party and arrested a number of veteran Communist party leaders from pre-Castro times. He accused this microfaction of being loyal not to Cuba but to the Soviet Union. Castro had also been criticizing the Soviet ideological position on revolution in the third world as being insufficiently active. The Soviets responded by declining to provide a needed increase in oil exports to Cuba. Then Castro withheld support for the Soviet intervention in Czechoslovakia and seemed about to criticize that action. At that juncture the Soviets made clear that they would not tolerate Cuban defiance and could cut off economic aid. Castro, faced with economic collapse as the price for his more independent stance, reluctantly knuckled under. See Jorge I. Dominguez, *Cuba: Order and Revolution* (Harvard University Press, 1978), p. 162.

The détente line the Soviets championed in 1969, and especially after 1971, stressed not only progress, but peace and disarmament. This global approach, aimed at a broad constituency of public opinion, at peoples as well as at states, complemented and supported the policy of peaceful coexistence. While the Soviet leaders never excluded a violent path to revolutionary change, they continued in the 1970s as in the 1960s to stress a peaceful transition to socialism. National liberation was, however, still seen as requiring and justifying armed resistance in the relatively few remaining colonies, almost all in Africa. But Soviet sympathy was given primarily in moral rather than material terms to those opposing Portuguese, Spanish, Rhodesian, and South African rule.

In Latin America, in addition to curbing Cuban support for guerrilla warfare, the Soviet leaders used their influence with local communist parties to oppose resort to force. During most of the 1970s, for example, the Soviet Union and even local communist parties subject to its influence stood aloof from the incipient guerrilla struggles in Nicaragua, El Salvador, Guatemala, and Colombia. The small Communist party of El Salvador, for example, did not join the armed resistance until 1980. Only late in the struggle of the Sandinistas in Nicaragua did the Cubans begin to provide assistance, and even then the Soviets themselves held back. Instead they followed two other courses. In Chile they supported (and counseled restraint to) Salvador Allende in taking the parliamentary electoral path (1970–73). In Peru they sold arms to the left-leaning military rulers (from 1973 to 1977).

The change in Soviet policy to selective direct support of the MPLA in Angola and Mengistu in Ethiopia was traced earlier. In the case of Angola, after some hesitation the Soviets gave strong backing to an independent Cuban initiative to support the MPLA with military advisers. In Ethiopia the Soviets apparently requested Cuban assistance. While the evidence is largely circumstantial, it is possible that as a quid pro quo to Cuba for its military assistance in Ethiopia (and attempted diplomatic support in dealing with Somalia, and assistance in South Yemen), the Soviet leaders agreed to back a more active Cuban role in supporting the guerrillas in Nicaragua in 1979 and El Salvador in 1980.[178] Apart from meeting Cuban desires, the Soviets also were responding to the failure of Allende's attempt to maintain power by peaceful means, a turn away from the left by the Peruvian military, and the electoral defeat of Michael Manley in Jamaica in 1980. These events were seen as evidence of a lack of success for peaceful transition to socialism. In Europe, the defeat of the leftist military regime in Portugal in 1975, and the failure of

---

178. Another apparent quid pro quo payoff for the Cuban role in supporting the national liberation struggle abroad has been an increase in Soviet subsidization of the Cuban economy, mainly through purchases of Cuban sugar at inflated prices far above those on the world market. See Jan Vanous, "Soviet and Eastern European Foreign Trade in the 1970's: A Quantitative Assessment," in *East European Economic Assessment*, pt. 2: *Regional Assessments*, A Compendium of Papers Submitted to the Joint Economic Committee, 97 Cong. 1 sess. (GPO, 1981), p. 690.

the "opening to the left" in Italy, carried the same message. By contrast, the success of the MPLA in Angola backed by Soviet and direct Cuban aid, and of the Sandinistas in Nicaragua (and even the successful coup d'états by small leftist groups in Grenada in 1979 and Suriname in 1980 in the Caribbean), boosted the claims of advocates for armed revolutionary action.

Another lesson the Soviets learned in this period was that reliance on bourgeois (including leftist) military and other regimes was unwise because they proved very unstable. The vast wave of ousters or defections of Soviet-cultivated military and political leaders in Africa in the late 1960s and early 1970s, in some cases in countries to which large supplies of arms had been provided or other Soviet investments made, showed the unreliability of regimes not based on a local communist party. Hence the efforts, eventually successful, to persuade Mengistu in Ethiopia to create a local communist party. Thus, while leftist military coups had succeeded in Iraq, the Congo, Somalia, Libya, South Yemen, and Peru in 1968–69, subsequently the Iraqi regime purged the local communists, Peru turned back to the center, Libya remained unpredictable and very independent, and Somalia switched sides in 1977 (as Sadat and Nimeiry had done). Several other lesser military dictators in Africa who had turned to the Soviet Union, including Maçias Nguema in Equatorial Guinea and Idi Amin in Uganda, were ousted within the decade.

In analyzing the developing situation in the third world, Soviet scholars and party and government officials were not of one mind. Some stressed the variety and unpredictability of political developments and limited opportunities for Soviet influence on the political scene; others saw a greater field for Soviet action in helping to shape the course of events. Some placed primary reliance on political propaganda and diplomacy, others on economic and arms assistance, others on possible support for more active guerrilla and military operations.[179]

The most novel and politically significant of these approaches to the Soviet role in the third world, and in particular in regional conflicts, was the possibility of more direct Soviet military involvement. Pronouncements by the Soviet military have consistently stressed the fundamental missions of deterrence of an enemy attack and defense of the Soviet homeland (and of its allies)

---

179. For an interesting series of discussions of Soviet views and activities relating to the third world, see Robert H. Donaldson, ed., *The Soviet Union in the Third World: Successes and Failures* (Boulder, Colo.: Westview, 1981); *Soviet Policy and United States Response in the Third World*, Report prepared for the Committee on Foreign Affairs by the Congressional Research Service, Library of Congress (GPO, 1981), pp. 27–145; W. Raymond Duncan, *Soviet Policy in the Third World* (Pergamon, 1980); Porter, *The USSR in Third World Conflicts*; and the chapters by Rajon Menon, David Albright, Zalmay Khalilzad, and Robert Donaldson, in Roger E. Kanet, ed., *Soviet Foreign Policy in the 1980s* (Praeger, 1982), pp. 263–349. For contending Soviet views see Hough, *The Struggle for the Third World*; Elizabeth Kridl Valkenier, "The USSR, the Third World, and the Global Economy," *Problems of Communism*, vol. 28 (July–August 1979), pp. 17–32; and Hosmer and Wolfe, *Soviet Policy and Practice toward Third World Conflicts*, pp. 66–68.

if attacked. In addition, Admiral of the Fleet Sergei Gorshkov and other Soviet naval spokesmen in particular had begun, in the late 1960s and early 1970s, to refer to the Soviet navy's role in defending not only the Soviet Union, but Soviet "state interests."[180] There are indications that the chief military and political leaders nonetheless remained very cautious in identifying instances where state interests would justify military involvement. Later Minister of Defense Marshal Andrei Grechko and other military spokesmen began to suggest a still more far-reaching role for Soviet military power. In 1974 Grechko wrote, "At the contemporary stage, the historic role of the Soviet armed forces is not limited only to their function of defending our Fatherland and the other socialist countries. The Soviet state in its foreign policy actively and purposefully opposes the export of counterrevolution and the policy of oppression, and supports the national-liberation struggle, resolutely resisting imperialist aggression in whatever distant part of the globe it appears."[181] While that is an unprecedented (and rarely paralleled) statement in Soviet writings ascribing a role for the Soviet armed forces in supporting the national liberation movement, that role clearly is to deter and hold in check *Western* resort to military power in support of counterrevolution. As Grechko puts it, "By their combat might the socialist armies objectively hold back the reactionary forces of imperialism."[182] At *no* point have Soviet military or political spokesmen ascribed to the Soviet armed forces a role in promoting revolution, other than the more passive (which is not to say unimportant) one of making *Western* use of military power less likely.

An editorial article in the confidential Soviet general staff journal, *Military Thought*, at about the same time expanded on the ways in which the military power of the Soviet Union served as a "bulwark of peace and the security of peoples." It included a reference to "economic, political, moral and, when necessary, military assistance" of the Soviet Union and other countries of the socialist community "in support of the national liberation struggle of the peoples of Asia, Africa and Latin America."[183] This assistance was identified as that which they "have undertaken and are undertaking." This formulation clarified that the military assistance to which the editorial referred was not of a more direct nature. Nonetheless, this formulation clearly embraced the kind of assistance given in the next five years in Angola and Ethiopia, as well as the continuing supply of arms to many countries in peacetime. But the main point of the article was this: "Our country's international contribution to the world

---

180. For example, see Admiral of the Fleet S. Gorshkov, "The Development of the Soviet Navy," *Morskoi sbornik* [The Naval Journal], no. 2 (February 1967), p. 20.

181. Marshal A. A. Grechko, "The Leading Role of the CPSU in Building the Army of a Developed Socialist Society," *Voprosy istorii KPSS* [Questions of History of the CPSU], no. 5 (May 1974), p. 39.

182. Ibid.

183. "The Defensive Might of Socialism—A Bulwark of Peace and the Security of Peoples," *Voyennaya mysl'* [Military Thought], no. 2 (February 1974), p. 9.

revolutionary process has primarily proceeded along the line of the successful building of a socialist society and its reliable defense against imperialist attackers," both as an example to other countries entering on the socialist path and in "reliably restraining [or deterring] the aggressive aspirations of imperialist reaction, hamstringing its efforts to export counterrevolution, and facilitating the struggle of other peoples for social progress."[184] By the time another article on this theme appeared in *Military Thought* some three-and-a-half years later, notwithstanding Soviet support for Ethiopia in its war with Somalia, there was no longer any hint of a direct Soviet military role to support the national liberation movements beyond that indirectly related to defending the Soviet Union, which defense was obviously in the interests of all progressive peoples.[185] Another article in late 1977 made explicit the nature of "military assistance," defining the term to mean "supplying arms and equipment, training cadres, and the like."[186]

In developing Soviet military thinking, and presumably contingent military planning, increased attention has been given to local wars in the third world. Soviet military writings have expanded their treatment of local wars, although they have refrained from developing doctrine for a direct military role for the Soviet Union.[187] From such sources there seems to have been an interesting *decline* in Soviet optimism about third world military conflicts in the latter half of the 1970s, after an increase in the early years of the decade— a trend opposite to that of a growing Soviet interest as widely perceived in the West.[188]

Much attention has been devoted in the West to the development in the 1970s of Soviet military capabilities for projecting military power into the third world. Increased capabilities have been in evidence in the showing of the flag in naval presence in distant waters and in air- and sealifts of arms in several Soviet-supported interventions or supply of arms to allies or friends

---

184. Ibid., pp. 10, 6.

An earlier article had also stressed the example of Soviet experience, as well as training and the supply of arms, in supporting military defense by national liberation revolutions. See Lieutenant Colonel L. Kruglov, "Features of the Armed Defense of the National Liberation Revolution," *Voyennaya mysl'*, no. 1 (January 1973), p. 24.

185. Major General V. F. Samoilenko, "The Great October Socialist Revolution and the World Revolutionary Process," *Voyennaya mysl'*, no. 9 (September 1977), pp. 14–24, especially pp. 23–24.

186. Colonel General G. Sredin, "Great Historic Mission," *Kommunist vooruzhennykh sil* [Communist of the Armed Forces], no. 22 (November 1977), p. 54.

187. For an excellent detailed study see Mark N. Katz, *The Third World in Soviet Military Thought* (London: Croom Helm, 1982). See also General of the Army I. Ye. Shavrov, *Lokal'nye voiny: istoriya i sovremennost'* [Local Wars: History and the Present] (Moscow: Voyenizdat, 1981).

188. Ibid., pp. 95–157.

from October 1973 through 1978 (in Angola and Ethiopia Cuban troops were transported as well). And in August 1979 two regiments of the 106th Guards Airborne Division were flown from the Soviet Union to South Yemen and back in a test of capabilities.[189] This increased capability is significant for some purposes and in some areas. It should not, however, be overstated. In part, capabilities that may secondarily or even incidentally permit a greater projection of power in the third world may in fact have been acquired principally for other purposes. Thus, while measuring capabilities is important, there are limitations on the use of such data for inferring or predicting Soviet intentions.[190] Enhanced Soviet capabilities for projecting military force may thus enlarge the field of potential opportunities for Soviet action if the risks, costs, and gains warrant action in the eyes of the Soviet leaders, but they do not lower the threshold of risk those leaders are prepared to assume.

Military capabilities not only add to the resources the Soviets can use in conducting policy in the third world, but also contribute to Soviet interests and requirements—as they do in the United States. Thus in the 1970s the Soviet Union developed a particular interest in acquiring naval and naval air reconnaissance facilities that would extend its effective range and the sustainability of distant naval presence. The acquisition, and later loss, of the most extensive of these facilities (in Egypt and later Somalia) probably made the Soviet leaders more wary of counting on such arrangements, although South Yemen and Ethiopia have provided partial substitutes in the area of the Horn and the Indian Ocean. Other use of local facilities (with a lesser Soviet role) in Syria and Iraq also contribute. The common tendency among American commentators is to impute this Soviet presence to an interest in cutting Western lines of access to crucial resources such as petroleum. That interpretation, however, flies in the face of all indications of a much more modest purpose. The Soviet leaders do wish to reduce Western political influence in many areas, as well as to expand their own, but there is no evidence to support

---

189. Mark L. Urban, "The Strategic Role of Soviet Airborne Troops," *Jane's Defense Weekly* (July 14, 1984), p. 30. This was the same division reportedly alerted for possible commitment in October 1973; on the other hand, it was not employed in Afghanistan.

190. Note two examples. Soviet amphibious capabilities have been enhanced, and on occasion small contingents of such forces have appeared with the Soviet navy in distant areas. But on the basis of both deployments and training, the Soviets continue to give priority to the conventional roles of supplementing the main armed forces in the Northern European and Northeast Asian theaters. Similarly, the Soviet airborne troops, organized since 1946 into a separate Airborne Troops (VDV) command, have remained at seven small divisions, plus an eighth training division, for several decades. In 1982 the designation of the VDV was changed from a direct resource of the Minister of Defense, and most of the VDV divisions were assigned to specific traditional theaters. This change would not have been made if the primary, or even a principal, mission of these troops was deployment to distant places abroad. In case of need, the Soviet leadership obviously can deploy from one to all eight airborne divisions, and some or all amphibious units, to some distant location. But if that were the predominant expectation for the force as a whole, it would not make sense to have routine command and training for most of them subordinate to peripheral land theaters.

speculation that the Soviets are—uncharacteristically—ready to assume the global risks attendant to any regional use of their military presence directly against the Western powers. Indeed, as this review of recent history has shown, the Soviet leaders have been cautious even in indirect use of their own military resources or those of their allies, even where U.S. forces were not involved.

Cultivation of political influence has by no means always led to a grant of military facilities for Soviet use. Guinea, for example, in 1978 withdrew permission for Soviet use of Conakry as a base for long-range aerial maritime reconnaissance. Libya, Angola, and Mozambique have not granted bases, although Angola permits occasional use of naval facilities. Even Vietnam only reluctantly allowed regular Soviet use of Camranh Bay and the Danang airbase, and only since 1979, following the Chinese invasion of Vietnam and increased Vietnamese dependence on the Soviet Union.

Nonetheless, an expanded Soviet military presence does contribute to the Soviet ability to become a global power, and the acquisition or retention of military facilities has in some cases become an interest in its own right.

Soviet political doctrine has continued to deny a Soviet military role to stimulate or even support revolution in the third world, although some vagueness attends the possibility of a direct Soviet role, including military, in offering assistance against Western support for counterrevolution. In addition, as a number of third world countries have become Marxist, and in some cases even Marxist-Leninist (communist), the question is raised about Soviet support to such regimes against internal challenge (although the Soviet Union always attributes external imperialist support for counterrevolution, as in Afghanistan in 1978–79 and Poland in 1980–81). The so-called Brezhnev Doctrine asserts the responsibility of the socialist commonwealth (the Soviet-led bloc) to prevent the reversal of a socialist revolution. In practice, this doctrine has been applied only in Eastern Europe to wayward members of the Warsaw Pact—in Hungary in 1956, and in Czechoslovakia in 1968. Its shadow certainly fell over Poland in 1980–81. But even in Eastern Europe it was not applied in other cases—to Tito's Yugoslavia, or later to Albania, or to deviant Romania. Western commentaries suggesting that the Brezhnev Doctrine was applied in Afghanistan, thus constituting an extension of the doctrine beyond the Warsaw Pact, are incorrect. Afghanistan was, and is, not regarded as a member of the socialist commonwealth. On the other hand, the general disinclination to see a friendly government replaced by a hostile one, and to see Soviet influence removed and American or Chinese influence supplant it, could lead to Soviet intervention in cases where the Brezhnev Doctrine does not strictly apply. Afghanistan is the clearest case. But the most important consideration is a pragmatic evaluation of possibilities. The Soviet Union obviously was not in a position to aid Allende in Chile or the leftist leaders in Grenada. Although the Soviets did cite the December 1978 treaty with Afghanistan as a consideration in justifying their intervention there, they did not use the existence of such treaties in Egypt or Somalia to attempt to prevent those governments from expelling a Soviet military presence and denouncing the treaties.

Soviet decisions on the use of one or another diplomatic, economic, or military instrument of policy will continue to be made pragmatically and with prudence. But increasing Soviet ties with some third world countries do raise the stakes for Moscow and the possibility of Soviet assistance or intervention.

Soviet political stakes, including an ideological element in cases of fellow communist states, play a part, as do Soviet economic and in some cases military considerations. So, too, do Soviet capabilities (including capabilities to project military power) and the stakes in any given case. Western capabilities are also relevant. Least relevant, despite considerable attention in Western public discourse, is the global strategic nuclear balance. To anticipate the discussion in a later chapter, the most dramatic Soviet military intervention—that in Afghanistan in December 1979, where Soviet armed forces were used—was based on a number of considerations. There is no evidence, and considerable basis for doubt, that the strategic balance played any part whatsoever in that Soviet decision. Similarly, most Americans saw the Soviet intervention in Afghanistan as a continuation and escalation of a series of steps in an expansionist course that included Angola and Ethiopia. The Soviet leaders, however, saw it as a quite different case involving Soviet security interests in no way comparable to the unrelated earlier actions in Africa that stemmed from competitive involvements, required different evaluation of opportunities, and were situations in which Soviet military forces had not been committed.[191]

Soviet policy in the third world in the period 1975 through 1979 included somewhat more active measures than in most earlier periods, but did not represent a major difference. There was a belief on the part of the Soviet leaders that the changed world picture, with the shift in the overall correlation of forces and Western recognition of peaceful coexistence and détente, *should* facilitate transition toward socialism in the third world. This view contributed to a readiness to assist progressive and national liberation forces, especially when the Western imperialists continued to intervene against them. Particularly favorable conditions appeared in Angola after the departure of the Portuguese, when American, Chinese, and, in particular, South African support, turned African opinion overwhelmingly to the Soviet- and Cuban-supported MPLA. In Ethiopia, the Somali invasion threatened the postcolonial state borders that most African states had decided must be preserved, a situation that placed Ethiopia in the role of defender. This happened just as Ethiopia had turned from the United States to the Soviet Union for outside support. Such attractive circumstances for intervention occur rarely.

The Soviets have active offensive aims of expanding their influence, mixed with defensive aims of countering American and other imperialist intervention. While propagandists from one side or the other may focus only on the offensive or defensive rationales, analysis makes clear that both have played a role in Soviet decisions.

---

191. See chapter 26.

More broadly, both sides—and especially official and officially inspired views in the Soviet Union and the United States—have tended to downplay or ignore the initiatives of their own side, while attributing greater initiative and offensive purposes to the other. In fact, both sides actively seek to enhance their own influence, although neither side wants to acknowledge this fact openly (and, especially on the American side, not even to itself).

Neither the United States nor the Soviet Union has in fact applied the noble but unrealistically altruistic principles of the charter of détente, the Basic Principles of Mutual Relations of 1972. The United States was the first, eventually echoed by the Soviet Union, to charge the other side with violations by intervention in the third world in pursuit of unilateral advantage (and often also aimed at reducing the influence of the rival power). In many instances the charges may have been well-founded by objective standards, but the force of such charges is greatly diminished by the failure of each side to recognize its own parallel transgressions. Reciprocal restraint continues to be advanced, no longer as a common aim, but as an indictment of the other side. In fact, what exists *is* reciprocal—it's just not restraint.

20 The China Card, 1978

FOLLOWING the spectacular breakthrough in American-Chinese relations early in the decade, after 1973 American-Chinese relations evolved sluggishly. Then in 1978, as noted earlier, the United States played a China card. The changing nature of the geopolitical interaction among the three powers requires both a closer look and a broader view of their interrelationships.

From Triangular Diplomacy to Quasi Alliance

When Nixon and Kissinger effected the remarkable reversal in American policy toward China in 1971–72, the new rapprochement was predicated on further development of ties leading to full normalization of diplomatic relations. It was, however, not until January 1, 1979, that full normalization of relations was achieved. In the early 1970s the intervening international political context and the concrete basis on which reciprocal formal diplomatic recognition was finally accorded had not been envisaged. Formal normalization of relations marked a significant step forward in bilateral Sino-American relations, but it was almost incidental to a much more far-reaching transformation in their political relationship that occurred from May 1978 through 1980.

The American-Chinese rapprochement of 1971–72 had paralleled an American-Soviet rapprochement and was designed in important part, both by the American and Chinese leaders, to enhance the political leverage of each vis-à-vis the Soviet Union in a triangular diplomatic balance. The new U.S.-Chinese rapprochement of 1978–80 occurred in a different context—one of deterioration in American-Soviet relations. And it had a different purpose—alignment in confrontation against the Soviet Union. In 1971–72 the United States and China had repaired their previously very bad relations; in 1978–80 the two moved beyond just normalization to develop such intimate relations as the collaborative collection of military intelligence on Soviet targets by using American sensors stationed on Chinese soil, and coordination of covert arms

690

supply to anti-Soviet guerrillas in Afghanistan. In 1971–72 contacts had been reestablished that permitted both the United States and China greater diplomatic maneuverability; in 1978–80 their maneuvering was limited to a degree by commitment to a common anti-Soviet line (in practice, the limits meant much greater modification of and restrictions on U.S. than on Chinese maneuver). In short the basis of American rapprochement with China changed from one that *increased* U.S. diplomatic flexibility and political maneuverability in the early 1970s to one that *reduced* that flexibility in the later years of the decade. Earlier the American position supported a policy of influencing American-Soviet relations to American advantage by permitting a modulation of incentives and disincentives. Increasingly the U.S. position became commitment to a common anti-Soviet line that provided no incentives, while the disincentives were ones the United States could not fully control. The U.S. alignment with China against the Soviet Union threatened to overstep the fine line between deterring hostile Soviet action and provoking adverse Soviet countermoves that otherwise would not have been undertaken.

The United States based the new American-Chinese rapprochement on a desire to offset and punish Soviet moves in Africa, Afghanistan, and elsewhere. Whatever its effectiveness may have been in that respect (it was arguably not only unproductive, but counterproductive in terms of that objective), the rapprochement also produced other consequences that had not been considered adequately. Congruence in U.S. and Chinese policy was built only on a competitive, even confrontational, axis of U.S. relations with the Soviet Union. As such it tended to shift *American* policy away from an adjustable balance of competition and cooperation with the Soviet Union. Although this policy reflected a Soviet-American estrangement that was growing for other reasons, it also contributed to that process. Still worse, by building Sino-American relations on an anti-Soviet foundation, the United States prejudiced *future* opportunities for improving its relations with the Soviet Union by making that option possible only if the United States were to change its relations with China. Thus even if *Soviet* policy merited improvement in U.S.-Soviet relations in ways advantageous to American interests, that course could then only be pursued at the cost of relations with China—which the United States also wished to maintain and improve.

How did the United States come to shift from the intended role of fulcrum in a balance of power to alignment with China against the Soviet Union? As noted, a principal factor was the American perception of a growing Soviet geopolitical challenge along an arc of crisis from Africa to Southeast Asia, a perception based on a series of Soviet involvements beginning with Angola in 1975–76 through Afghanistan in 1979–80. In addition, the United States was uneasy over trends in the global military balance, which it perceived as being threatened by a Soviet buildup. Chinese interest in recruiting the United States into a united anti-Soviet front made the shift possible, indeed easy. The eagerness of the Chinese did lead some to be wary of too rapid recourse to this realignment, but it appealed to those who preferred a confrontational stance in American-Soviet relations.

The popular term applied to the American policy—"playing the China card"—may have been apt in describing the American policy motivation—but it should have drawn attention to a crucial shortcoming of the approach: China was—and is—not a card; it is one of the players. While the United States and China do share some security interests vis-à-vis the Soviet Union, their national interests and objectives are by no means identical or always congruent. The Chinese considered it in their interest to oppose American-Soviet détente and SALT and up to a point to exacerbate American-Soviet relations—since that not only posed threats and costs to the Soviet Union, but also drove the United States to curry Chinese favor. Moreover, to the extent the United States came to be regarded as a quasi ally of China, it shared responsibility for Chinese actions that it had no control over and that were directly contrary to American interests.

Finally, it needs to be noted that while the Soviet Union has been suspicious about American rapprochement with China from the outset, the Soviet assessment and reaction are affected by the nature of the American-Chinese relationship. While the Soviet leaders were naturally not happy to see the United States gain greater diplomatic leverage through triangular diplomacy from 1971 through 1977, they were considerably more concerned by the semi-alignment and quasi alliance with China in the period 1978 through 1980. Their concern had several causes. First, it was implicit that the United States was prepared to sacrifice existing and potential opportunities for improving relations with the Soviet Union in favor of closer ties with China. Second, the *basis* for this change was avowedly anti-Soviet. Third, China gained greater freedom for action against Soviet interests, even if not directly supported by the United States (for example, the Chinese invasion of Vietnam in February 1979). Fourth, the extent and consequences of military cooperation and American military assistance to China were a source of uncertainty. Finally, there were the implications for overall American policy toward the Soviet Union and the implied American commitment to a long-term policy of confrontation.[1]

Following the highly successful visit to China by President Nixon in 1972, liaison offices equivalent in function if not in protocol rank to embassies had been established in 1973 in Washington and Beijing, and American-Chinese relations were effectively conducted on a basis of de facto, though not de jure, recognition. Trade developed rapidly in the first few years, although it slackened in 1975-76. Political relations also slackened, chiefly as a consequence of the internal political troubles and changes in both countries. Nixon

---

1. I was particularly struck by the significance attached to the changed rationale and basis for the new American relationship with China in 1978-80 as expressed by Vadim Zagladin, first deputy chief of the International Department of the Central Committee, in a conversation in Moscow in October 1980.

was weakened in 1973–74 and then replaced by Ford, who in turn was challenged within his own party by those who opposed any change in the American relationship with Taiwan that full normalization of relations with China would require. In China, after 1974 Zhou Enlai was on the defensive against the Gang of Four, and only some time after the deaths of Zhou and Mao Zedong in 1976 was Deng Xiaoping, during 1977, able to secure the reins of power.

Thus the opportunity facing the Carter administration in 1977 was to develop what were then languishing ties with China. In China Deng soon moved to consolidate power and embark on a new course of internal economic and other modernization that required Western assistance.

Initially the Carter administration, while seeking to prevent American-Soviet relations from dominating its foreign relations as a whole, nonetheless gave priority to SALT and to placing its relationship with the Soviet Union on a new basis, ahead of any new move toward China. Nonetheless, in a plan for foreign policy over the four years of the administration that he prepared in the spring of 1977, Brzezinski made full normalization of relations with China one of ten priority objectives, with the aim of accomplishing that objective by 1979.[2] After the failure of the administration's SALT initiative in March 1977 and the growing dispute with Moscow over human rights, Brzezinski posed the alternative of turning toward China. President Carter, in his Notre Dame speech in May 1977, did invite an opening toward China and for the first time characterized American relations with China as "a central element of our global policy, and China as a key force for global peace."[3]

Coincidentally, at the same time the Soviet leadership showed signs of giving up its attempt to cultivate better relations with Mao's successors.[4] Nonetheless, in October 1977 the Soviet Union and China concluded an agreement on navigation in the channel at the confluence of the Ussuri and Amur rivers. And in November Foreign Minister Huang Hua attended the National Day reception at the Soviet embassy in Beijing, the first such high-level attendance in eleven years.

The Carter administration continued to give priority to the SALT negotiations with the Soviet Union. As noted, Secretary of State Vance made considerable progress in placing those negotiations back on track in talks with Foreign Minister Gromyko in July and September. And Carter continued to

---

2. From an interview with Brzezinski. See also "The Best National Security System: A Conversation with Zbigniew Brzezinski," *Washington Quarterly*, vol. 5 (Winter 1982), p. 79. Brzezinski ascribes to his own role in developing China policy "a preeminent or central role but certainly not an exclusive one."

3. President Carter, commencement address at the University of Notre Dame, May 22, *Weekly Compilation of Presidential Documents*, vol. 13 (May 30, 1977), p. 778. (Hereafter *Presidential Documents*.)

4. See I. Aleksandrov, "Peking: A Course toward Wrecking International Détente under the Guise of Anti-Sovietism," *Pravda*, May 14, 1977. "I. Aleksandrov" is a nom de plume used for authoritative party statements, particularly those on Chinese affairs.

call for détente with the Soviet Union, notably in a speech at Charleston in July.

Meanwhile, the new administration's policy study on relations with China, launched in April pursuant to Presidential Review Memorandum (PRM)–24, was completed in June. It recommended pursuing normalization and acceptance of the cardinal Chinese demand for an end to U.S. diplomatic relations with Taiwan. There was full agreement among Carter, Vance, and Brzezinski on this central point.[5]

President Carter decided to send Secretary of State Vance to China to pursue prospects for normalizing relations.[6] On August 22–25 Vance visited Beijing and sought to move the bilateral American-Chinese relationship forward. He was not, however, receptive to Chinese complaints of American appeasement of the Soviet Union or to denigration of the value of SALT. The Chinese clearly had hoped for something more than a reiteration of support for the Shanghai Communiqué of 1972, and the visit was not successful. An excessively upbeat White House comment on "progress" and the "success" of the visit even prompted an unusual authoritative comment from Deng Xiaoping himself that the exchanges had not been very successful.[7]

Deng was particularly disappointed because his turn toward the West was a contested issue in his broader struggle for power, at that juncture still not assured. The Eleventh Congress of the Chinese Communist Party, which had concluded on the very eve of Vance's visit, had strengthened Deng's position, but it was a coalition ruling group, and opposition to Deng and to his policy and programs remained.[8]

When Carter decided on the Vance trip in July, he reportedly told him: "Cy, lay it all out on the line."[9] In a supposedly off-the-record dinner with several newsmen in January 1981, just before leaving office, Carter is reported to have said that he sent Vance to China in 1977 to normalize relations but

---

5. Michel Oksenberg, "A Decade of Sino-American Relations," *Foreign Affairs*, vol. 61 (Fall 1982), pp. 181-83. Oksenberg was the chief China expert on the NSC staff from 1977 through 1980 and was directly involved in the negotiations leading to normalization. See also Cyrus Vance, *Hard Choices: Critical Years in America's Foreign Policy* (Simon and Schuster, 1983), pp. 75–79; and Zbigniew Brzezinski, *Power and Principle: Memoirs of the National Security Adviser, 1977–1981* (Farrar, Straus, Giroux, 1983), pp. 197–200.

6. See Vance, *Hard Choices*, pp. 78–79; and Brzezinski, *Power and Principle*, pp. 200–01.

7. For details on the trip see Vance, *Hard Choices*, pp. 79–83.

8. A vivid example of the ambivalent Chinese attitude toward the United States was expressed by Chairman Hua at the Party Congress, when he cited Lenin on the need in a united front to cooperate with a capitalist state like the United States even though it would be only a "temporary, vacillating, unstable, unreliable and conditional ally." Quoted by Parris Chang, " 'China Card' or 'American Card,' " *Asian Pacific Community*, no. 11 (Winter 1981), p. 127. See also Jonathan Pollack, *The Lessons of Coalition Politics: Sino-American Security Relations*, R-3133-AF (Santa Monica, Calif.: Rand Corp., 1984), pp. 27–29.

9. Oksenberg, *Foreign Affairs*, vol. 61 (Fall 1982), p. 182.

that the secretary of state had returned without accomplishing his mission.[10] Undoubtedly Carter, and Vance, were disappointed, but in his memoir Carter is more restrained when he describes the Vance mission as "exploratory" and the results as limited by political caution on China's part.[11] Further, unexpected difficulties in the Senate over the Panama Canal Treaty by the time of Vance's visit led the secretary to be somewhat cautious. They also caused Carter himself to put the whole subject on the back burner for a number of months after Vance's return.[12]

Underlying differences remained between Vance and Brzezinski over the relative priorities to be given to developing relations with the Soviet Union and China. The Chinese, and the Soviets, were well aware of the shifting balance between the two points of view within the Carter administration: on the one side Vance's evenhanded approach toward the Soviet Union and China, on the other Brzezinski's desire to move into a closer relationship with China coupled with a tougher position toward the Soviet Union.[13]

During 1977 the question of a possible American tilt toward China began to be associated with the question of developing a military security relationship and providing American military technology to China. In June the fact leaked that a special governmental policy study dealing with the subject was under way. The conclusion reached in PRM-24, urged by Secretary of State Vance, was that on balance it would not be desirable for the United States to provide military technology and arms to China. But the fact that the administration had raised the question, and that Brzezinski was known to favor a different conclusion, meant the issue remained near the surface.

In reality, ever since 1973 some elements in the defense establishment (including Secretary of Defense Schlesinger) and in the political opposition to détente (such as Senator Jackson) had become intrigued with the idea of building the Chinese military capability as a way to complicate and burden Soviet military planning. After Schlesinger had left office (and had visited China as a private citizen), he publicly referred, in a television commentary in April 1976, to the possibility of the United States providing weapons to China. In an article in October 1976 he urged an American quasi alliance with

---

10. "Over Dinner, Carter Cast Kissinger as 'Devious,' Reporter Says," *Washington Post*, October 18, 1982.

11. Jimmy Carter, *Keeping Faith: Memoirs of a President* (Bantam Books, 1982), pp. 190–91.

12. Oksenberg, *Foreign Affairs*, vol. 61 (1982), p. 182; Vance, *Hard Choices*, p. 83; Brzezinski, *Power and Principle*, pp. 201–02; and Carter, *Keeping Faith*, p. 192. During Vance's visit to China, Brzezinski reveals, Carter had second thoughts about what the Senate would accept and rather suddenly drew back from instructions based on his earlier decision.

13. To cite but one of many Soviet discussions, see B. N. Zanegin and V. P. Lukin, "Between a 'Triangle' and 'Quasi Alliance' (American-Chinese Relations at the Present Stage)," *SShA: ekonomika, politika, ideologiya* [USA: Economics, Politics, Ideology], no. 9 (September 1981), pp. 25–28. (Hereafter *SShA.*)

China.[14] The Ford administration had, however, carefully limited its actions to quietly approving the sale of jet engines by England (in December 1975) and releasing Cyber-172 advanced computers to *both* China and the USSR (in October 1976).

A Rand Corporation analyst, Michael Pillsbury, had first floated the idea of arms sales and a broad range of American military security relationships with China in a much-discussed article in *Foreign Policy* in the fall of 1975. Not known then was that Pillsbury had been conducting secret talks with Chinese officials (in particular, a Chinese general and two other military men representing China on the Military Committee of the United Nations).[15] Pillsbury's talks with the Chinese military representatives from 1973 through 1976 were highly unusual: he worked at Rand on security-classified research for the Departments of the Air Force and Defense, and his reports on his meetings in New York were circulated to a dozen or so top officials of the NSC, Department of Defense, and Department of State as secret documents. His article in *Foreign Policy* was based on a secret study (designated L–32) he had written in March 1974, based on Defense Department interest in a briefer memorandum he had written in the fall of 1973. Officials in the Department of Defense (in particular Andrew Marshall, director of net assessment, Department of Defense, and Morton Abramowitz, a Foreign Service officer serving as deputy assistant secretary of defense for East Asia and Pacific affairs) were very interested in the subject and undertook a number of internal studies in the Department of Defense, later presented to Secretary of Defense Schlesinger (in December 1974) and to an NSC Asian specialist and close associate of Kissinger's, Winston Lord (in early 1975). Thus in the mid- to late 1970s there was increasing interest in the Defense Department in military ties with China.[16] Moreover, as noted, the interest included sensitive secret quasi-official contacts, developed especially by the stridently anti-Soviet chief of Air Force Intelligence, Major General George Keegan.[17] All in all, the development of these

---

14. James R. Schlesinger, "Face the Nation," CBS TV, April 11, 1976; and "Inside China Now: Report on 23-Day Visit by James Schlesinger," *U.S. News and World Report*, October 18, 1976, pp. 40–42.

15. Pillsbury had first met the Chinese officers through the Chinese UN representative, later foreign minister, Huang Hua in 1972, when Pillsbury himself was serving as a UN civil servant. He continued and expanded the dialogue with them after joining the Rand Corporation in April 1973; that contact continued through 1976.

16. There was also some resistance to the idea, especially from professional military planners, who were much less inclined to see a communist foe of twenty-five years as a quasi ally whom the United States should aid with arms and cooperate with militarily.

17. General Keegan's office was first involved, along with the FBI, in clearing Pillsbury's contacts, since Pillsbury held security clearances under the Rand Corporation's Project Rand contract with the U.S. Air Force. Later Keegan directly supported the meetings. But his interest went much further. Indeed, on one occasion a civilian officer in Air Force Intelligence accompanied Pillsbury to meet the Chinese general and passed on an alarmist report attributed to a Soviet defector alleging Soviet designs on China, known as "the Samokhin paper." The Samokhin

ties and the idea of military collaboration with China are a fascinating story in bureaucratic politics on a number of levels.[18]

President Carter decided in the summer of 1977 to accept Secretary of State Vance's position (and the Department of State recommendation in PRM-24) not to play the China card by entering into a military security relationship with China, thus overriding Brzezinski's arguments. The reason was that Carter gave higher priority to maintaining détente with the Soviet Union and to pursuit of a SALT II agreement, and he believed with Vance that any such opening to China would damage the prospects for these objectives.

As shown earlier,[19] by the spring of 1978 Carter was, by contrast, inclined to take a much tougher stance toward the Soviet Union. In addition to growing public concern and criticism by the opposition, Carter and other leading members of his administration (to varying degrees and with differing recommendations on what action to take) also believed it necessary to do something to counter what was perceived as a growing Soviet readiness to advance its interests around the globe, especially but not only in Ethiopia. Moreover, SALT was going much more slowly than had been expected (especially by Carter himself, who had been overly optimistic in the fall and winter of 1977). Brzezinski urged linkage to counter Soviet and Cuban involvement in the Horn of Africa, and more generally in the Afro-Asian arc of crisis he saw developing. But there was little to link in American-Soviet relations. One possibility was SALT, but Vance persuaded Carter not to use it. Then, new circumstances in the spring of 1978 led Carter to decide to play the China card and to send Brzezinski to Beijing.[20]

---

paper was never declassified and released publicly. This special interest by U.S. Air Force Intelligence persisted. For example, when it sponsored a conference on Soviet military doctrine at Reston, Virginia, in September 1980, the only foreign representatives present were two military attachés from the Chinese embassy.

18. The investigative scholarship that turned up most of the details on the Pillsbury affair and related Defense Department studies was carried out by Banning Garrett, who has contributed perceptive analysis on this whole subject. See Banning Garrett, *The 'China Card' and Its Origins: U.S. Bureaucratic Politics and the Strategic Triangle* (Berkeley, Calif.: University of California, forthcoming); and Garrett, "The United States and the Great Power Triangle," in Gerald Segal, ed., *The China Factor: Peking and the Superpowers* (London: Croom Helm, 1981), pp. 76–102. Garrett acquired highly censored versions and at least verified the existence of a number of the Rand and Defense Department studies of 1973–76 through requests under the Freedom of Information Act. I have independently confirmed most of his points and have added others from interviews and conversations with a number of those involved, including Pillsbury.

19. See chapter 18.

20. In his memoir President Carter notes that Vance had opposed this move when it was first raised (in February), but that he later decided (in mid-March) to send Vance to Moscow to negotiate on SALT and Brzezinski to Beijing to improve relations with China. See Carter, *Keeping Faith*, pp. 193–94.

Brzezinski notes stiff opposition from Vance and the State Department, and his own sustained effort from late 1977 on to obtain Carter's agreement to his trip. To this end he sought

Before turning to that key development, it is useful to take note of what had been occurring in Chinese politics and Sino-Soviet relations. Deng Xiaoping, who had been formally rehabilitated only in July 1977, gradually strengthened his position. The Chinese leadership in 1978 reoriented priorities embodied in the "Four Modernizations" policy line, including highest priority on economic reform and revitalization. (Military modernization was included in fourth place.) As a concomitant, there was an increasingly explicit emphasis on turning toward the Western powers for assistance in economic and technological (and potentially military) modernization. Diplomatically there was a new stress on a "united international front" opposed to Soviet "hegemonism." This stance had been introduced at the Eleventh Party Congress in August 1977 and was carried further at the Fifth National People's Congress in March 1978.

The Soviet Union recognized the implications of China's turn to the West.[21] This turn was further evidenced in the conclusion in February of a $20 billion trade agreement with Japan. It was also underlined in another way: the Chinese rejected a secret Soviet proposal for new talks, made February 22, on the eve of the Fifth Congress. The Soviet proposal had called for high-level talks and for the two sides to base their relations on peaceful coexistence.[22]

Sino-Soviet relations had nevertheless shown some signs of modest improvement in late 1977. Agreement was reached in October on navigation in a disputed channel at the confluence of the Ussuri and Amur rivers, and in November the Chinese foreign minister attended the National Day reception at the Soviet embassy in Beijing for the first time in eleven years. But China's rejection of the Soviet proposal on March 9 and insistence on a partial military withdrawal all along the Sino-Soviet border reflected a renewed deterioration in relations.

At this time of growing Sino-Soviet tensions and a Chinese turn to the West Chairman Brezhnev and Defense Minister Ustinov made a well-publicized and unprecedented tour along the Sino-Soviet border from March 28 to April 9. On April 5 they watched field maneuvers near the site of the actual military clash in 1969. Also at about this time the Soviet Union began to deploy SS-20 intermediate-range ballistic missiles in the region near Lake Baikal and to station Backfire medium bombers in the Far East.[23] On the eve of

---

and eventually obtained support from both Vice President Mondale and Secretary of Defense Brown. See Brzezinski, *Power and Principle*, pp. 202–06. For Secretary Vance's views on the policy line and the Brzezinski trip see Vance, *Hard Choices*, pp. 114–16.

21. For example, see A. A. Gromyko and others, *Istoriya diplomatii* [History of Diplomacy] (Moscow: Politizdat, 1979), vol. 5, bk 2, p. 416.

22. Ibid., p. 431.

23. These deployments were not directed just at China: at about this time the Soviet Union also began to garrison the "northern territories," the islands north of Hokkaido claimed by Japan. Nonetheless, the general strengthening of forces in Siberia was directed principally at China, and even the moves directed at Japan followed its signing a peace treaty with China.

Brezhnev's Siberian trip, the Chinese on March 26 demonstratively made public their rejection of the confidential Soviet proposal. Finally, on May 9—just two weeks before Brzezinski's trip to Beijing (and after it had been announced)—an armed Soviet patrol crossed the Ussuri River into China, purportedly in hot pursuit of a fugitive. The Chinese did not, however, engage the patrol, and it was quickly withdrawn; three days later Moscow issued a statement of regret at the "unintended" intrusion.

Meanwhile, on May 9, in his annual article on the anniversary of the victory in Europe in World War II, Minister of Defense Marshal Ustinov stressed Chinese military aims and dangers. Soon thereafter, at the UN Special Session on Disarmament, Foreign Minister Huang Hua declared that the Soviet Union was "the most dangerous source of a new world war."[24]

One other strand of growing importance also affected the shifting scene, in particular by contributing to China's interest in closer Western and especially American ties. It was Vietnam and its changing relations, and relationships, with China, the USSR, and the United States. Vietnam had tried, from the time of its final victory in the south in April 1975 until 1977, to steer a course between the Soviet Union and China, seeking to avoid either excessive dependence on or unnecessary antagonism to either power. Strains with China nevertheless grew.

Another developing problem that affected Vietnamese relations with China adversely was Kampuchea (Cambodia). Vietnam harbored traditional designs of hegemony over Kampuchea, although it had not sought to press its position. Pol Pot and the Khmer Rouge leadership that had seized power in 1975 had from the outset taken an anti-Soviet position, refusing even to accept a Soviet ambassador. In fact, during 1975–76 the Khmer Rouge (mainly engaged in a brutal genocidal campaign to reconstitute the whole society) had aligned itself with China. Relations with Vietnam became strained. In 1975 Vietnam had refused to evacuate some areas of Kampuchea, and in 1977 the Khmer Rouge began to step up border incursions into Vietnam. Although Pol Pot was received by Vietnam in September 1977, the visit was not successful in mitigating (much less resolving) the differences. Late in 1977, following escalating Kampuchean border incursions, the Vietnamese thrust deep into Kampuchea, although they then withdrew. In December Kampuchea suspended all relations with Vietnam and ignored its call for talks.

In January 1978 China offered her good offices to negotiate with the Kampucheans on behalf of Vietnam, but the understandably suspicious Vietnamese declined. In February the Vietnamese offered a peace plan that included reciprocal military withdrawals from the border area, but Kampuchea refused to consider it. By this time China was sending substantial military supplies to Kampuchea, including long-range artillery. In March the Vietnamese nationalized the rice trade in the south and undertook other measures

---

24. Huang Hua, "Superpower Disarmament Fraud Exposed," May 28, *Peking Review*, vol. 22 (June 2, 1978), p. 13.

(including introduction of a new currency in May and restrictive replacement of identity cards). The chief burden of these measures fell on the ethnic Chinese commercial population of the south, and a major exodus to China began. On May 12 China announced plans to terminate twelve aid projects in Vietnam and to use the funds to assist the Chinese residents expelled from Vietnam. On May 24 (the day after Brzezinski's visit ended) Beijing accused Vietnam of expelling 70,000 ethnic Chinese. On May 30 it announced it was canceling fifty-one more aid projects in Vietnam. On June 16 China demanded the closing of the three Vietnamese consulates in China. On June 29 Vietnam suddenly joined the Soviet-bloc Council on Mutual Economic Assistance (CMEA).[25] On July 3 China formally cut off all economic assistance to Vietnam and withdrew all Chinese technical advisers.[26] On July 12, having absorbed a claimed 126,000 ethnic Chinese refugees, China closed its border with Vietnam. The Vietnamese-Kampuchean border was again inflamed by forays and counterforays by the two sides.

Early in the Carter administration, in May 1977, a series of American-Vietnamese meetings had begun in Paris, resuming a dialogue Kissinger had broken off in July 1973. The Vietnamese still expected some economic assistance from the United States and intended to reciprocate by being more forthcoming on resolving the American missing-in-action cases. There are indications that Vietnamese expectations about the readiness of the Carter administration to restore relations and provide economic aid were excessively high. In fact the Carter administration had planned a gesture of humanitarian economic assistance, but discarded the idea before it became publicly known after negative reactions in congressional soundings. As the Vietnamese continued formally to insist on some economic aid, the talks stymied. These developments all preceded the Vietnamese decision to join the CMEA and, in the judgment of some observers, contributed to it.[27]

---

25. The Soviet decision to admit Vietnam to the CMEA was undertaken in such haste that its other members were not even advised until they met in Bucharest on June 27, at which time they were faced with a virtual Soviet *fait accompli* in which they acquiesced. Information from senior officials of CMEA governments.

26. A few months later a senior Vietnamese minister of state, Nguyen Co Thach, confirmed to an American scholar that Vietnam would not have become a member of CMEA except for the Chinese actions. See Gareth Porter, "Vietnam's Soviet Alliance: A Challenge to U.S. Policy," *Indochina Issues*, no. 6 (May 1980), p. 3.

By interesting coincidence, the Chinese leaders faced another problem at about the same time and reached a parallel decision: on July 13 they cut off all assistance to Albania. While unrelated to developments in Indochina, or to Soviet-Albanian relations, the move was indirectly related to Sino-Soviet relations. Just a month later, from August 16 to 29, Hua Guofeng paid a visit to Romania and Yugoslavia, carrying Chinese competition with the Soviet Union into the Soviets' backyard, so to speak. This action paralleled what the Soviets were doing in relations with Vietnam.

27. See Vance, *Hard Choices*, p. 122; and Porter, *Indochina Issues*, no. 6 (1980), p. 2.

By 1978 Vietnam finally gave up its demands for American economic assistance, even though that aid had been promised under the 1973 Paris accord.[28] In September 1978 the United States again indicated (in private talks in New York between Assistant Secretary of State Richard Holbrooke and Minister of State Nguyen Co Thach) its desire to normalize relations but declined to set a timetable. This failure preceded the Vietnamese decision to proceed with the Treaty of Friendship with Moscow.[29] Moreover, as early as January 1978 Brzezinski had been calling Vietnam an "Asian Cuba" engaged as a proxy on Moscow's behalf.[30] Thus the United States was not prepared to seek accord with Vietnam. Finally, after the spring of 1978 the United States was influenced by a new consideration: to normalize relations with Vietnam would antagonize China, and the United States was staking its foreign policy strategy on the China card. On October 11 President Carter formally decided to defer any normalization of relations with Vietnam for this reason.[31]

Thus at the time President Carter decided to turn toward China in retaliation for Soviet activity in the third world, Sino-Soviet relations were again strained, Vietnam was turning sharply toward the Soviet Union and away from China, and China was supporting Kampuchea against Vietnam. It is also likely that at approximately this juncture Vietnam was deciding to move against Kampuchea, for which it needed Soviet backing, while China was beginning to conclude it might have to take drastic action against Vietnam, for which it needed American backing to deter Soviet retaliation in support of Vietnam. The United States, meanwhile, had indirectly helped this diplomatic realignment by choosing not to accept the Vietnamese offer to reestablish relations, giving the Vietnamese no alternative to the Soviet Union. The Soviet Union, wishing in any case to increase its influence in Vietnam (and preferably to gain air and naval facilities there), now considered that it needed Vietnam as an ally to distract China.

Brzezinski's China Policy

Whether President Carter fully realized it, in overriding Secretary of State Vance's objections and sending Brzezinski to Beijing he set in train the

---

28. See Paul Kattenburg, "Living with Hanoi," *Foreign Policy*, no. 53 (Winter 1983–84), p. 133.

29. Porter, *Indochina Issues*, no. 6 (1980), p. 4; and see Vance, *Hard Choices*, p. 122.

30. Interview of Brzezinski on CBS "Face the Nation," January 8, 1978; and see Bernard Gwertzman, "Indochina Conflict Seen as 'Proxy War,'" *New York Times*, January 9, 1978.

31. This decision to give priority to developing relations with China, and for that and other reasons not to seek improved relations with Vietnam, has been confirmed by several senior members of the Carter administration in interviews. The president's October 11 decision is disclosed in Oksenberg, *Foreign Affairs*, vol. 61 (1982), p. 186.

development of a rapprochement with China on an anti-Soviet basis. The president did intend the China card as a counter to Soviet and Cuban activities in Africa, but his action had much broader and deeper consequences. While the president intended to boost relations with China, and chose to do so at a time of strain in relations with the Soviet Union, it is very unlikely he realized he was giving priority to Chinese relations at a time and in a way that would contribute to American-Soviet estrangement.

Brzezinski has in recent years referred on several occasions to the United States' development of relations with China as one of the main achievements of the Carter administration and as one of his principal contributions to that administration.[32] When asked in a published interview, "Where do you see your own role most conspicuously represented in the successes of the Carter Administration?" he mentioned as the first of five personal contributions: "I played a not irrelevant part in achieving US-Chinese normalization and then in the expansion of that relationship (including the security dimension). This has wider geopolitical dimensions."[33]

Brzezinski has also disclosed that when he went to Beijing in May 1978, "I went with a secret Presidential instruction in my briefcase empowering me to start a new phase in the American-Chinese relationship. It authorised me to tell the Chinese (and I quote): *'The United States has made up its mind'*—because the Chinese had kept saying in their propaganda that we had been half-hearted and had not made up our minds."[34] While, as Brzezinski states, he had been "charged with the task of generating fresh momentum in the American-Chinese relationship," he also notes that—in contrast to Secretary of State Vance in August 1977—he was able to do so "because I [Brzezinski] took as my point of departure our common strategic interests" vis-à-vis the Soviet Union and used that as the basis for "heavily enlarging the scope of the whole relationship."[35]

At the time of Brzezinski's visit and in reporting publicly on it afterward, he stressed the element of advancing American-Chinese normalization and bilateral interests, and wide-ranging consultation in international affairs, noting also that the United States and China had "parallel interests."[36]

During the visit, with substantial publicity at the time, there were several more ebullient indications of a shared anti-Soviet strategic interest.

---

32. For example, Brzezinski, *Power and Principle,* p. 528.

33. George Urban, "A Long Conversation with Dr. Zbigniew Brzezinski: 'The Perils of Foreign Policy,'" *Encounter,* vol. 56 (May 1981), p. 28.

34. Ibid. The italicized sentence is the title of the chapter in Brzezinski's memoir on his China trip and policy. Brzezinski further discloses that he and his China expert, Oksenberg, drafted the president's instructions. See *Power and Principle,* p. 207. He provides the full text as an appendix.

35. Urban, *Encounter,* vol. 56 (1981), p. 28.

36. In particular, see "Interview: National Security Adviser Brzezinski on 'Meet the Press,'" May 28, *Department of State Bulletin,* vol. 78 (July 1978), pp. 26–28. (Hereafter *State Bulletin.*)

Brzezinski, for example, was reported by journalists as having engaged in a good-natured footrace with some of his hosts at the Great Wall of China, challenging that the "last one to the top fights the Russians in Ethiopia!" In turn the Chinese described him as "the polar bear tamer."[37] There is no doubt Brzezinski was able to establish much better political rapport with the Chinese than Vance had: their political positions were in fact much closer.[38] Further, as was seen, rising tensions in American-Soviet relations, and in Sino-Soviet relations (including over Vietnam and Kampuchea), raised the incentive for closer ties between the United States and China. Finally, the president had authorized acceptance of the three basic conditions China had set for normalization: termination of American diplomatic relations with Taiwan, withdrawal of all American military personnel and installations from Taiwan, and abrogation of the U.S.-Republic of China (Taiwan) security treaty.[39]

In his memoir President Carter describes the Brzezinski visit as having been "very successful." He comments, in a passage unwittingly confirming the success of the Chinese design to reward Brzezinski and further his influence to the detriment of Vance, "The leaders in Peking [Beijing] seemed to enjoy the strategic and philosophical discussions with Zbig, and let me know through him that they were . . . prepared to move forward."[40] The Chinese also characterized Brzezinski's visit as "positive" and "useful" and immediately complied with his request that they curb the stream of anti-American propaganda in the Chinese media.[41]

It has since been disclosed that the Chinese provided impetus for Brzezinski's mission. They had conveyed an invitation to him through two different channels, calculating on the compatibility of his and their positions and playing on White House–State Department rivalries, about which they had been well-trained by Kissinger. On the very day after the Senate approved the Panama Canal Treaties, removing that obstacle, the Chinese had been informed that Brzezinski accepted their invitation and would be in Beijing in May.[42]

In China Deng was able to use the new American policy as presented by Brzezinski as a weapon in his internal struggle for power. By the fall of 1978 Deng was urging a more pragmatic approach, and by late November he

---

37. See "Making Friends in Peking," *Time*, June 5, 1978, p. 19.

38. A former senior Pakistani diplomat has reported that when he visited Beijing in 1976, the Chinese were even then very interested in and favorably impressed by Brzezinski. See Golam W. Choudhury, *Chinese Perception of the World* (Washington, D.C.: University Press of America, 1977), pp. 41–42.

39. Brzezinski, *Power and Principle*, p. 208.

40. Carter, *Keeping Faith*, p. 196.

41. Ibid.

42. Oksenberg, *Foreign Affairs*, vol. 61 (1982), pp. 183–84; and see Brzezinski, *Power and Principle*, pp. 202–06.

had won, permitting him to move on to the next stage—normalization of Sino-American relations through a Chinese concession on the American relationship with Taiwan.

Although Vance had unsuccessfully opposed Brzezinski's trip, he did not oppose normalization of American-Chinese relations. What he feared—correctly—was that an initiative entrusted to Brzezinski would be seen in both Moscow and Beijing as signaling a tilt in the American position from one of being the balance in the triangle toward one of alignment with China and against the Soviet Union.[43] And there were other signs of acceptance of Brzezinski's position on the complementary subject of policy toward the Soviet Union.[44] For example, Vance had proposed that Gromyko visit the White House during Brzezinski's visit to China—an idea Brzezinski learned of in time to quash.[45]

The Brzezinski visit did much more than reactivate movement toward American-Chinese normalization of relations and warn the Soviet Union that the United States could move closer to China. Brzezinski also held a number of meetings with Chinese leaders in which he covered the world scene, with particular emphasis on parallel American and Chinese interests in countering Soviet activities in Africa, the Middle East, and South Asia. Discussions included the meaning of the recent coup in Afghanistan and how to counter it, and Eastern Europe, a subject of particular interest to Brzezinski and of renewed interest to the Chinese. Brzezinski urged the Chinese to oppose Soviet moves in Africa, for example, by using their influence with Mugabe in negotiations on Rhodesia-Zimbabwe and by advising Mozambique to deny sanctuary to the Rhodesian guerrillas. He also urged the Chinese to support Jonas Savimbi's UNITA in Angola, which the United States could not do owing to congressional constraints. Brzezinski also urged development of Chinese relations with Saudi Arabia and a discreet channel of communication with Israel. The Chinese in turn stressed the need to counter Soviet support for Vietnam, and the Vietnamese actions against the ethnic Chinese minority and pressures against Kampuchea.[46]

Brzezinski was accompanied by a high-powered delegation with representatives from the Departments of State and Defense, as well as the NSC. Brzezinski personally briefed the Chinese in depth on the SALT negotiations and the strategic situation, in an effort to disabuse them of the idea that the

---

43. The State Department, without White House authorization and to Brzezinski's annoyance, as a courtesy advised Ambassador Dobrynin before the public announcement on April 26 of Brzezinski's forthcoming trip to China.

44. See chapter 18.

45. Brzezinski, *Power and Principle*, p. 208.

46. Ibid., pp. 211–15. Brzezinski mentions some, but not all, of the specific points noted in this paragraph; all were confirmed to me by participants in the discussion.

United States was negotiating from (or toward) weakness.[47] This readiness to discuss confidential American negotiations with the Soviet Union was intended to demonstrate how forthcoming the United States was with the Chinese, but by that same token it rankled the Soviet leaders greatly.[48] It also illustrated the shift in policy from 1977 to 1978 (and from Vance to Brzezinski). Not only had Vance not been so forthcoming on his August visit, but President Carter had personally indicated the administration's pre–May 1978 position when he stated in a session with media representatives, "We exchange ideas with the Chinese on SALT. We try not to violate confidences. If the Soviets tell us something in a negotiating session that we consider to be of a confidential nature, we certainly don't tell the Chinese about it. But we tell them our basic position."[49] Brzezinski's return to greater intimacy and confidence in private disclosures to the Chinese leaders paralleled a feature of Kissinger's earlier exchanges.[50] In addition, Samuel Huntington, Brzezinski's NSC associate in preparing the major assessment of the strategic balance in 1977 (PRM-10), briefed Chinese officials on that study and on Presidential Directive (PD)–18 based upon it. These reports remained secret.

In addition to the unprecedentedly open consultation on sensitive security issues, experts in the delegation discussed a range of important subjects that would come to affect bilateral relations in the security field. Abramowitz, the deputy assistant secretary of defense who had earlier prepared the studies of possible arms assistance and other military cooperation with China, consulted with Chinese officials of the Ministry of Defense.[51] Benjamin Huberman, an associate director in the Office of Science and Technology Policy (OSTP) in the White House, discussed possible technological contacts and exchanges. One significant demonstrative step was taken as an earnest of U.S. readiness in this area. Brzezinski proffered an offer (which had been specifically approved by Secretary of State Vance and Secretary of Defense Brown, as well

---

47. This fact was reported at that time. For example, see Bernard Gwertzman, "Brzezinski Gave Details to China on Arms Talks with Soviet Union," *New York Times*, May 28, 1978. See also Brzezinski, *Power and Principle*, p. 211.

48. When he saw Vance on May 31, Gromyko strongly protested the U.S. briefing of the Chinese on SALT. See Vance, *Hard Choices*, p. 103.

49. "Interview with the President," April 15, *Presidential Documents*, vol. 13 (April 25, 1977), p. 554.

50. He also resumed another practice introduced by Kissinger: greater disclosure of policy and intelligence to the Chinese than to the Soviets, amounting to favoritism. To be sure, if the Chinese were to become a quasi ally, and the Soviets no longer to remain a partner in détente, that stance was appropriate. But such a change had not yet been made policy.

51. Pillsbury, author of some of the first such studies as well as an earlier advocate of such military ties, as noted earlier in this chapter, apparently by coincidence was also in Beijing at the time of the Brzezinski visit (as a private citizen). He saw Brzezinski, who had been his professor at Columbia University. The Chinese found this coincidence intriguing.

as by Carter, just a few days before the trip)[52] to sell China airborne geological scanning equipment; sale of such equipment to the Soviet Union had previously been denied owing to its strategic significance.

Brzezinski also discussed more sensitive matters in private sessions. One was the attitude of the United States toward possible sales of military equipment to China by America's European allies. Brzezinski indicated a new readiness on the part of the United States to be forthcoming with respect to sales of defensive arms by its allies. This shift undoubtedly contributed to Deng's ability to persuade his colleagues in the Chinese leadership to turn to the West, and to the subsequent dispatch of deputy prime ministers to France and Great Britain in October to discuss such purchases. The United States did not publicly disclose its new stand until November 3, when Secretary of State Vance (ironically, since he had been the least enthusiastic) announced it. While forcefully restating American policy not to sell arms to China, he indicated that the United States would not oppose Western European sales of defensive armaments to China: "This is a matter which each [nation] . . . must decide for itself."[53]

It is likely, although it has not been confirmed, that Brzezinski also discussed privately the common intelligence interests of the United States and China. There is reason to believe that the dialogue included disclosure of American intelligence on Soviet military developments of particular interest to China.[54]

Additional nonmilitary and nonintelligence technological cooperation was considered and a number of agreements reached during a visit in July by Frank Press, the president's science adviser. Press later described his team as "very likely the most senior delegation of U.S. government scientific officials ever taken abroad."[55] The discussions were fruitful, and in January 1979 President Carter and Vice Premier Deng Xiaoping signed a formal Agreement on Cooperation in Science and Technology, followed by thirteen additional later protocols.

---

52. This decision, made on May 16, was not passed on to the government agencies in Washington so as to preclude any leaks and permit Brzezinski to unveil it in Beijing.

53. "The Secretary: News Conference of November 3," *State Bulletin*, vol. 78 (December 1978), p. 19. A public statement of the U.S. position was necessary because on October 31 the French announced the sale of $700 million in antitank missiles to China. Also in November, and without public announcement, the administration approved a request by France to sell an American-designed nuclear reactor to China. See also Vance, *Hard Choices*, pp. 113–14.

54. It is possible that on this occasion the United States also first proposed sharing technical intelligence monitoring of military testing activities in the Soviet Union, although that subject may not have been raised until the Deng visit to Washington in January 1979. See chapter 21.

55. For an informative account see Frank Press, "Science and Technology in the White House, 1977 to 1980: Part 2," *Science*, January 16, 1981, pp. 249–50. A planned trip by Press to Moscow at about the same time was canceled in retaliation for Soviet actions against dissidents.

After Brzezinski returned, the president, in a meeting on June 20 with him, Vice President Mondale, Vance, Brown, and Hamilton Jordan, decided to move toward normalization of relations with China that year, after the fall congressional elections, and in tandem with movement toward a SALT II treaty with the Soviet Union.[56] A State Department analysis saw as a favorable time for normalization the period between the fall 1978 elections and the SALT II Senate debates and 1980 election campaign.[57]

During the period July to December Leonard Woodcock, head of the American liaison office in Beijing, set forth the U.S. position on normalization.[58] The United States also continued to signal its serious interest in other ways. For example, on June 30 a pending decision on sales of sixty F-4 fighter-bombers to Taiwan was decided against. On September 19 President Carter himself received Chai Zemin, head of the Chinese liaison office in Washington, and stressed the American position. On November 4 Woodcock submitted a draft communiqué and a target date of January 1, 1979, for reciprocal recognition. At this point the initiative essentially passed to the Chinese. The United States had made clear its minimum requirements on ties with Taiwan (the only really serious issue of difference) and had set a target date. The question was whether the Chinese could and would accept.

Deng Xiaoping was still waging his campaign against doctrinaire Maoism and against the remaining moderate Maoist faction in the leadership. Immediately following the announcement on November 3 of a Soviet-Vietnam treaty, Deng went to Thailand, Malaysia, Singapore, and Burma seeking support or at least understanding for a more forceful policy against Vietnam. But what he needed above all was the support of a Chinese-American agreement. By late November Deng had prevailed in Beijing on turning to a more pragmatic internal political line. Deng also saw the United States at a crucial crossroads—something he may have appreciated better than President Carter. The United States had flashed the China card in May; now it was on the table. At the same time the United States was in the throes of negotiating the final

---

56. On these negotiations see Carter, *Keeping Faith*, pp. 196–98; Vance, *Hard Choices*, pp. 113–19; Brzezinski, *Power and Principle*, pp. 223–33; and Oksenberg, *Foreign Affairs*, vol. 61 (1982), pp. 185–88. Two other channels were also opened: Brzezinski began to meet with the Chinese representative in Washington to discuss the world political context for the two countries' bilateral relationship; and Holbrooke at the Department of State became the lightning rod for such subjects as Chinese protests over American arms to Taiwan. Oksenberg, ibid., p. 186; and Brzezinski, ibid., pp. 203, 229.

57. In his memoir President Carter cites a diary entry on this meeting dated May 16—clearly an error, since Brzezinski departed for China after that date. Carter, *Keeping Faith*, p. 194. The NSC China expert, Michel Oksenberg, dates the meeting as June 20 and states that a tentative target date of December 15 was set for establishment of relations. Oksenberg, *Foreign Affairs*, vol. 61 (1982), p. 185. Brzezinski also cites the June 20 date and mentions a memorandum by Vance dated June 13 proposing a target date in mid-December for announcement of normalization. Brzezinski, *Power and Principle*, p. 223.

58. Oksenberg, *Foreign Affairs*, vol. 61 (1982), pp. 184–86.

issues in SALT and was planning a January summit meeting with Brezhnev contingent on the successful conclusion of these negotiations. This U.S.-Soviet summit meeting could still be derailed by prompt agreement on Sino-American normalization on January 1. An important meeting of the Central Committee in Beijing in mid-December, it was later learned, considered in addition to economic reforms three related subjects: party and governmental changes strengthening Deng's control, the question of Chinese military action against Vietnam, and relations with the United States. The American initiative was thus very timely in terms of Chinese political developments.[59]

On December 4 the Chinese gave Woodcock a counterdraft that accepted the proposed January 1 date. In Washington Carter and Brzezinski called in Ambassador Chai and told him that if the negotiations were satisfactorily concluded, the United States would invite "one of your top leaders." On December 13 Deng called in Woodcock and told him that he himself would accept the invitation to Washington and proposed that his visit follow normalization within one month—effectively placing an obstacle in the way of the planned January U.S.-Soviet summit and signing of SALT II, of which Ambassador Chai had been informed by Brzezinski.

Carter and Brzezinski personally worked on the communiqué in the final negotiation (Secretary of State Vance was in the Middle East, but returned for the announcement). On December 15 (December 16 in Beijing) the two governments issued the joint communiqué announcing both the establishment of diplomatic relations as of January 1, 1979, and the forthcoming visit by Deng.[60]

The Chinese had decided to compromise. They accepted the American position in order to forestall the Soviet-American summit (which was, indeed, put off, with SALT also delayed temporarily) and to consolidate Chinese-American relations and a new rapprochement, furthered by Deng's visit. Once the United States had advanced the January 1 date, Deng had been given a powerful incentive, and tool, for spoiling Soviet-American relations and for setting up the opportunity to "discipline" Vietnam for its alliance with the Soviet Union and increasing threat to Kampuchea.

Secretary of State Vance, while favoring normalization of ties with China, had opposed the Brzezinski trip and the stress on closer strategic ties with China. He had not expected that normalization would or could come so quickly or at such an inopportune time from the standpoint of maintaining a balance in American relations with the Soviet Union and China. When Vance was dispatched to the Near East by Carter, it had been agreed that if the Chinese accepted the American proposals, there would be no announcement before January 1, after Vance's crucial meeting with Gromyko in Geneva on SALT. In his absence, the date for the announcement was changed to Decem-

---

59. Carter has disclosed this later intelligence on the Central Committee meeting in his memoir. *Keeping Faith*, p. 198.

60. Ibid., pp. 197–99; and see Oksenberg, *Foreign Affairs*, vol. 61 (1982), pp. 187–88.

ber 15.[61] Vance had also not been involved in deciding on the invitation to
Deng in the final negotiations. He understood the negative impact on the
Soviet position, but still hoped for agreement on SALT and the expected early
Carter-Brezhnev summit meeting. Vance sought, and obtained, Carter's agreement to balance the U.S. rapprochement with China with further steps to
improve relations with the Soviet Union, including specifically the grant of
most-favored-nation (MFN) status.[62]

Brzezinski undoubtedly understood that the administration was
making a basic reversal of priorities between American relations with China
and the Soviet Union. He probably was convinced, correctly, that the prospects
for reaching the SALT agreement would not be permanently prejudiced and
that a U.S.-Soviet summit would only be postponed. But he understood that
the United States was signaling a closer relationship with China and a less close
one with the Soviet Union—a move he believed was appropriate.[63]

President Carter, however, seems not to have understood the implications of this shift. He badly wanted a major foreign policy success. SALT and
a Soviet summit meeting had seemed near, several times in fact, only to slip
away. The success at Camp David had earlier encouraged Carter to press for
normalization. But by the end of the year efforts to reach a Middle Eastern
summit had just collapsed. Success with China, and on U.S. terms, was now at
hand, and he seized the opportunity. He also believed, and publicly stated
even against clear evidence, that progress on both SALT and the anticipated
early Soviet summit meeting would not be affected.[64] Indeed, he evidently
hoped to be able to duplicate President Nixon's political gain in 1972 from his
two-pronged success of both a Chinese and Soviet summit meeting—failing to
recognize that his own approach no longer comprehended complementary
or even compatible policies toward the Soviet Union and China. He had
played the China card, and had won, but he had not measured accurately the
stakes or the sentiment of the other players. He also did not seem to realize
that he had also changed the balance of power on foreign policy within his own
administration.

---

61. Vance, *Hard Choices*, pp. 117–19.

62. Carter, *Keeping Faith*, p. 201. Carter presents the matter as though he and Vance happened
to agree on the dual approach, but it was Vance's strong argument to which Carter agreed. He
quotes from his diary entry for December 31, 1978, describing an "excellent" tête-à-tête at
Camp David with Vance, during which he says they had agreed that "the most significant
responsibility we have is to balance our new friendship with the PRC [China] and our continued improvement of relations with the Soviet Union."

63. Brzezinski took particular delight in personally informing Ambassador Dobrynin of the U.S.-
China announcement a few hours before it was made. He arranged that Dobrynin's arrival
would be covered by the press so that Dobrynin would be put on the spot. He reports with
evident satisfaction that Dobrynin was "absolutely stunned," that his face turned ashen and
"his jaw dropped." See Brzezinski, *Power and Principle*, p. 232.

64. See chapter 18.

The normalization of American-Chinese relations was undoubtedly in the U.S. interest and a positive achievement. It was, however, regrettable from the standpoint of the broader American interest in developing and maintaining better relations with both the Soviet Union and China that normalization was undertaken at a time and in a manner that had such negative effects on this broader interest.

Soviet Reactions

During the activation of American-Chinese relations in 1978 the Soviet leadership found itself unable to counter the adverse development. Warnings to the United States were less effective as the balance of influence within the administration shifted from Vance to Brzezinski. Demonstrative actions directed at China were even less effective. In addition, China was able to secure Japanese agreement to a peace treaty in August that embodied an antihegemony clause, signaling at the least that Japan gave a higher priority to its relations with China than to those with the Soviet Union. The Chinese also greatly improved relations with Western Europe and even began to challenge the Soviet Union in Eastern Europe, as exemplified by Chairman Hua Guofeng's visit to Romania and Yugoslavia in August.

These were several waves of Soviet expression of concern. In the first, following Brzezinski's China visit (and Carter's Annapolis speech), the focus was on persuading the U.S. leadership not to play the China card. In a relatively rare example of Soviet linkage, *Pravda*, in a major article on June 17 addressed to Washington, signaled clearly that progress on SALT would be endangered by pressing an anti-Soviet collaboration with China. More broadly, Soviet-American détente was said to be incompatible with an American alignment with China. The chief villain was seen at this time not as the United States, but as China. As *Pravda* warned: "Soviet-American confrontation, and still better war, is the cherished dream of Peking. Perhaps Washington will give thought to this matter coolly, without rashness."[65] It advised that while U.S. leaders might wish to exploit "the difficulties which have arisen in Sino-Soviet relations," they should not overlook the fact that "the Chinese leaders are playing a game of their own" in seeking to aggravate American-Soviet relations."[66]

During the rest of the year Soviet commentary continued to reflect a wary attitude as Soviet leaders sought to assess the situation. Earlier, in the

---

65. "On the Present Policy of the U.S. Government," *Pravda*, June 17, 1978. This same authoritative unsigned editorial strongly criticized Brzezinski by name, as well as obliquely charging him with seeking "alignment with China on an anti-Soviet basis."

66. Ibid. Brezhnev also attacked American "attempts to play a 'China card' against the USSR" and failure to evaluate correctly the Chinese line. Speech in Minsk, June 25, 1978, in L. I. Brezhnev, *Izbrannye proizvedeniya* [Selected Works], vol. 3 (Moscow: Politizdat, 1981), p. 327. See also "In the Central Committee of the CPSU," *Pravda*, August 27, 1978.

first months of the Carter administration, the Soviet leaders had suspected a possible American turn toward China, especially after leaks on PRM-24 and possible military assistance and other security ties. At the time they had threatened countermeasures.[67] Within a few months, however, they had been reassured by both private U.S. assurances and the absence of new moves during and after the Vance visit to China in August. Now they again saw vacillation and knew there were differences within the administration. Still, the conjunction of other rising difficulties in American-Soviet relations during 1978 caused continuing concern.

In a revealing interview for Western consumption, Academician Georgy Arbatov in November referred to the "temptation . . . to develop the improvement of relations with China in a way that would help increase leverage on the Soviet Union." He objected not to Western moves to improve relations with China, but to doing so on an anti-Soviet basis, commenting that that rationale "can affect our relations." Of the range of possible courses, the worst would be "for China to become some sort of military ally to the West, even an informal ally. Then the whole situation would look different to us. We would have to reanalyze our relationship with the West. If such an axis is built on an anti-Soviet basis then there is no place for détente."[68] The December announcement of the normalization of U.S.-Chinese relations raised Soviet concerns greatly, but it was not yet clear how far the United States would go in playing the China card.

In retrospect, Soviet accounts consider the May 1978 visit of Brzezinski as the critical turning point to a new stage of American-Chinese relations—and partially to a new, concomitant decline in American-Soviet relations. "That visit," in the later words of two leading Soviet specialists on Chinese-American relations, "signified a sharp zigzag in the policy of the Carter administration from a relatively considered and evenhanded 'triangular diplomacy' to a single-minded pro-Peking and anti-Soviet orientation."[69] Many Soviet commentators attribute the shift in this new phase to the personal influence of Brzezinski, while Secretary of State Vance is identified (correctly) as having wished to maintain a more evenhanded policy.[70] But Soviet analysts also stress that there was more involved than a Brzezinski factor in the fundamental U.S. shift away from détente, that they see involved in the change in American relations with both the Soviet Union and China.[71]

---

67. See Aleksandrov, *Pravda*, May 14, 1977.

68. Jonathan Power, "The New Voice of the Kremlin," *The Observer* (London), November 12, 1978, an interview with Georgy Arbatov.

69. Zanegin and Lukin, *SShA*, no. 9 (1981), p. 28. See also Aleksandr Bovin and Vladimir Lukin, "More Than Billiards but Less Than Chess: Ten Years of the 'Shanghai Communiqué,'" *Literaturnaya gazeta*, February 24, 1982.

70. For example, ibid., p. 27.

71. See S. K. Merkulov, *Amerikano-Kitaiskoye sblizheniye (vtoraya polovina 70–x godov)* [The American-Chinese Rapprochement in the Second Half of the Seventies] (Moscow: Nauka, 1980], pp. 19–22.

In discussing Soviet reactions, and especially analytical assessments, it is necessary to bear in mind that there are in the Soviet political establishment a multiplicity of views on many aspects of such questions. While all Soviet analysts see the American-Chinese rapprochement of the 1978–80 period as adverse to Soviet interests, they vary on such questions as the extent, consistency, and success of a close American-Chinese relationship—and on just what that relationship has been and may become. Some are more alarmist than others. Some see the United States as taking the lead, while others continue to describe dark Chinese designs and to question whether the American leaders are being taken in. Thus there are differences of some significance between commentators who came to see an American-Chinese military alliance and a broad attempt at encirclement of the Soviet Union, and those who continued to doubt the viability of the American-Chinese rapprochement.[72]

In considering Soviet reactions to the development of American-Chinese relations in the period from 1978 through 1980, it is necessary to take into account the record of that evolving relationship as seen from the Soviet perspective. Charges in 1979 of American-Chinese collaboration on intelligence, and in 1980 of military assistance to the Afghan resistance, at the time were largely ignored or indignantly rejected by most Americans, but later were determined to be well-founded. All the more, the Soviet concerns over American economic favoritism to and political alignment with China voiced in 1978 and later, largely discounted at the time in the West, proved prophetic.

Another aspect of the Soviet reaction, evident in 1978 and later, was the failure to recognize the extent to which American policy toward China was affected by *Soviet* actions. While the Soviets were well aware that the United States justified its turn toward China on the basis of Soviet actions in the Horn of Africa, a continuing Soviet military buildup, and later Afghanistan, they heavily discounted those actions as the real *causes* of the policy shift. Rather, they saw them as pretexts and arguments used by opponents of Soviet-American détente. The Vance-Brzezinski division was seen as symbolizing pro- and antidétente elements within the Carter administration (to say nothing of wider pro- and antidétente forces), which would be contending regardless of Soviet actions. Even within that frame of perception the Soviets should have recognized (and some did) some effect of their actions on the struggle between

72. An unusual "dialogue in print" illustrates the point. Aleksandr Bovin, a politically prominent commentator for *Izvestiya*, and Vladimir Lukin, an academic specialist in Chinese and Sino-American relations, collaborated on an article published in February 1982. Bovin kept stressing the "highly uneven" and unstable nature of the American-Chinese relationship, and even expressed doubt when Lukin referred to a "general tendency toward rapprochement." Bovin stressed Chinese designs and said: "Washington, for all its antipathy to the Soviet Union, is disinclined to swallow the Chinese bait with eyes closed." So he concluded that "U.S. policy will fluctuate somewhere between a 'triangle' and a 'quasi alliance.'" Lukin challenged that open judgment: "At present the pendulum is obviously closer to a 'quasi alliance.'" Bovin rejoined, "Possibly. The question is how long this 'at present' will last." Lukin had the last word: "It is nice to talk to an optimist." *Literaturnaya gazeta*, February 24, 1982.

pro- and antidétente forces in the United States. This factor was, however, even to the extent recognized, considered secondary to the Soviet calculation of its own interests; Soviet policy could not be subordinated to the vagaries of American political contests.

Soviet reaction to the sudden announcement of the normalization of U.S.-Chinese diplomatic relations in December 1978 was restrained. But as noted, it raised new concern (apart from consternation that the agreement undermined the still pending tentative Brezhnev-Carter summit meeting). Brezhnev commented publicly in terms that raised no objection to the normalization of relations, but noted that the Soviets would watch carefully to see on what basis it was carried out in practice. From that they would "draw corresponding conclusions for Soviet policy."[73] Soviet accounts, at least through 1979, continued to stress the Chinese role in pressing the Sino-American rapprochement, including by noting that "the establishment of diplomatic relations between the PRC and the U.S., although the result of the efforts of both sides toward a mutual rapprochement, was evidently connected above all with initiatives and concessions by Peking."[74] The chief question for the Soviet leaders, then, was how the United States would develop its ties with China.

The China Card in Play

American and Chinese initiatives converged, first in the Brzezinski visit to Beijing in May, and then in the agreement on diplomatic normalization in December 1978. This was, of course, only the beginning of a new phase of American-Chinese rapprochement. After the crucial political breakthrough of 1978, general normalization—with particular stress on economic cooperation—followed in 1979, while further strategic and military collaboration was launched in 1980.[75] These three years thus saw a movement from the triangular diplomacy of the earlier 1970s to American-Chinese quasi alliance by the end of the decade. This significant shift occurred against the background of (and further contributed to) a sharp deterioration in American-Soviet relations that ultimately moved from détente with mixed cooperation and competition to confrontation and containment.

That course of events remained, at the close of 1978, only one of several possible scenarios. At the same time Secretary of State Vance was firmly asserting, on behalf of the administration, that "it is our strong and unequivocal policy that we do not intend to, nor will we, sell military equip-

---

73. L. I. Brezhnev, "With a Victory of Labor," *Pravda*, December 23, 1978.

74. V. B. Vorontsov, *Kitai i SShA: 60–70-e gody* [China and the United States: The Sixties and Seventies] (Moscow: Nauka, 1979), p. 150.

75. See the discussion in chapter 21 on events in 1979 and chapter 27 on 1980.

ment—weapons—to either the People's Republic of China or to the Soviet Union."[76] This evenhandedness was explicitly extended to trade advantages such as MFN status.

During the first nine months of 1978 the State Department also continued its efforts to develop improved relations with Vietnam. In fact, normalization of relations was agreed to at a meeting between Assistant Secretary Holbrooke and Ministeı of State Nguyen Co Thach on September 29. But from September to November Brzezinski worked to persuade President Carter to drop that plan because it would be construed as anti-Chinese (and pro-Soviet). Carter finally decided against improving relations with Vietnam.[77]

Another development in Asia of great importance in its own right and in its impact on triangular diplomacy was the signing of a Treaty of Peace and Friendship between China and Japan on August 19.[78] The Soviet leaders considered this move, which they had sought unsuccessfully to prevent, to have been engineered by the United States as a further deal with the China card: it bolstered China's role at Soviet expense and enhanced American leverage. The Soviets attributed the Japanese decision to sign the treaty, with language against hegemony by any power that they correctly saw as directed at the Soviet Union, to urgings by Brzezinski, who had stopped in Tokyo in May on his way back from Beijing.[79] These Soviet suspicions were well-founded. Brzezinski has subsequently disclosed that not only did he urge Prime Minister Takeo Fukuda and Foreign Minister Sunao Sonoda to sign the treaty with the antihegemony clause, but he had done so on his own initiative without authorization (and knowing that the Department of State had been objecting to the antihegemony clause). Only after his return did President Carter give his approval to the *fait accompli.*[80]

Events in the world were, moreover, moving swiftly, and some would very soon affect U.S. relations with China and the Soviet Union in ways that could not then have been foreseen.

In addition to the U.S.-China announcement in mid-December of their intention to establish full diplomatic relations on January 1, the year 1978 ended with two other developments significant to relations among China and the two superpowers. The first was a significant but virtually invisible step indicative of the worsening in Sino-Soviet relations: on December 29 *Pravda*

---

76. "The Secretary: News Conference of November 3," *State Bulletin*, vol. 78 (December 1978), p. 19.

77. Brzezinski, *Power and Principle*, pp. 228–29; and Vance, *Hard Choices*, pp. 122–23.

78. See Robert E. Bedeski, *The Fragile Entente: The 1978 Japan-China Peace Treaty in a Global Context* (Boulder, Colo.: Westview, 1983), for a good overall study.

79. See Merkulov, *Amerikano-Kitaiskoye sblizheniye*, p. 22.

80. See Brzezinski, *Power and Principle*, p. 218. It is doubtful that Carter would have overridden State Department objections if the question had been posed before Brzezinki's meetings in Tokyo.

reported that the previous day Brezhnev had received and congratulated General of the Army Vasily I. Petrov on a new appointment. Not disclosed was that his post was a new theater command that involved the Far Eastern, Transbaikal, and Siberian military districts and the Pacific Ocean Fleet. This new Theater of Military Operations (TVD) command in the Far East was the first such consolidated regional command in that area since 1953 and the end of the Korean War.

Beginning in 1978 and continuing over the next several years, the Soviet Union also bolstered its military forces in the Far East. Mobile SS-20 intermediate-range ballistic missiles began to be deployed. The first decisions for this deployment program must have been made at least by 1975, but there was a later augmentation that appears to have been decided on in 1978–79. In 1978 Backfire medium bombers also began to be deployed in the Far East, although this would most likely have occurred in any event under modernization. On the other hand, a new development probably prompted by the closer Sino-American and Sino-Japanese ties was the deployment of a motorized rifle division and more advanced tactical fighter aircraft to the southern Kuril islands just north of Japan. This deployment also serves as an example of military security considerations being given precedence over political ones, inasmuch as the deployment stirred up considerable Japanese concern and resentment. (This was particularly true because the Japanese continue to claim these islands, which they term "the northern territories" of Japan.)

The worsening of Sino-Soviet relations thus contributed to an intensification of military as well as political confrontation between the two countries. In striking contrast, American-Chinese relations had in parallel led to a sharp reduction in contingent military as well as political counterposition. At the beginning of 1977 Secretary of Defense Donald Rumsfeld had still been speaking, in his annual report to Congress, of China as a potential threat to the United States and its allies: "We must take this [threat] into account in the design and deployment of U.S. strategic nuclear forces."[81] By February 1978 Secretary of Defense Harold Brown was speaking of Chinese capabilities not as a possible threat to the United States but as "a strategic counterweight to the Soviet Union."[82] And by the beginning of 1979 he was also able to say that "the long period of political confrontation between the United States and the PRC [People's Republic of China] has in fact ended," and the development of the Sino-Soviet conflict, "has drastically reduced the probability that the United States would become involved in an Asian war against either China alone or the Soviet Union and China together."[83] Nothing was said any longer

81. *Department of Defense Annual Report, Fiscal Year 1978* (GPO, 1977), Executive Summary, p. 13, and see text p. 29.

82. *Department of Defense Annual Report, Fiscal Year 1979* (GPO, 1978), p. 23.

83. *Department of Defense Annual Report, Fiscal Year 1980* (GPO, 1979), p. 52.

about a need to consider Chinese military capabilities in planning forces to meet American military requirements.

The second development at the close of 1978 was far more immediately ominous. The Vietnamese had some months earlier concluded that military elimination of the Pol Pot regime in Kampuchea was necessary to end its disruptive incursions and the growing threat it represented as a protégé of China in view of the worsening of Sino-Vietnamese relations. In addition, the Vietnamese had always aspired and intended to establish their own hegemony over all of Indochina, as they were doing in Laos. Accordingly, on December 25 the Vietnamese launched a major military assault on Kampuchea. By January 7 Phnom Penh had fallen, and most of the country was soon in Vietnamese hands. A Vietnamese-sponsored puppet government headed by a former minor Kampuchean official named Heng Samrin had been established only days before the attack and was installed in Phnom Penh. Remnants of the Pol Pot Khmer Rouge regime continued, however, to offer resistance in parts of the country, and the Vietnamese were soon tied down in a large-scale, continuing pacification campaign.

The Soviet role in the Vietnamese decision to invade Kampuchea is not known, but it is highly likely that the Soviet Union acquiesced only reluctantly. The Soviets must have been concerned over the Chinese reaction, particularly at a time of developing Sino-American ties (although the decision to attack had undoubtedly been made before the surprise U.S.-Chinese announcement) and at a critical time in Soviet-American negotiations. But they needed the Vietnamese and could not veto their decision or fail to back them.

Thus as 1979 began, playing the China card had brought triangular diplomacy back to the forefront of American-Soviet relations. It had done so at a time and in a way adversely affecting the long-delayed achievement of a SALT agreement and prospective efforts to improve bilateral relations at the summit.

21 The Vienna Summit amid Renewed Tensions, 1979

THE YEAR 1979 began with SALT—and an American-Soviet summit—in suspense as the Soviet leaders reassessed the situation after the sudden and unexpected American move toward further rapprochement with China. Brezhnev opened the year with a pronouncement in the American news magazine *Time*. He stated: "To be frank, on the whole over the last couple of years there have been few encouraging aspects of Soviet-American relations." When asked for his understanding of the word détente, Brezhnev replied that "a relaxation of tensions, or détente for short," means a state of international relations opposite to the "permanent tension" of the cold war. "Détente," he went on, "means a willingness to resolve differences and disputes not by force, but by peaceful means. . . . Détente means a certain degree of trust and ability to take into account each other's legitimate interests."[1]

Brezhnev's comment on the China card made clear the particular Soviet objection to what he saw as American readiness to "encourage in every way and stimulate" those in China who "openly have declared their hostility to the cause of détente, disarmament and stability in the world; those who lay claims to the territories of many countries and stage provocations against them; those who have proclaimed war inevitable and mounted active preparations for war. Is it really difficult," he continued, "to understand that this means playing with fire?"[2]

---

1. See "An Interview with Brezhnev," *Time*, January 22, 1979, pp. 16–19; and "Comrade L. I. Brezhnev's Replies to Questions of the American Magazine *Time*," *Kommunist*, no. 2 (January 1979), pp. 3–7. The quotations here are translations from the Soviet version, but there is no substantive discrepancy between the two versions.

2. *Kommunist*, no. 2 (1979), pp. 5–6.

China Plays the "American Card"

Brezhnev's interview did not make the year's first issue of *Time*; twenty-one pages of that issue were devoted to the magazine's "Man of the Year"—Deng Xiaoping, "Visionary of a New China."[3]

The Chinese had managed the timing of the Deng visit and establishment of full relations, and they exploited their opportunities to the full.[4] Just before leaving Beijing for the United States, Deng had also granted a *Time* interview. It was published on the very day of his first meeting with President Carter, January 29. Deng made very clear China's position: "We proceed from the establishment of a united front against hegemonism"—that is, a united front of China and the United States, and Japan and Western Europe, against the Soviet Union.[5] This statement was a far cry from that of President Carter less than two weeks earlier: "We never intend to use our improved relationships with China against the Soviet Union," a remark he made defensively in response to a query about his reaction to Brezhnev's concern as expressed in the *Time* interview.[6] President Carter seemed to believe that if he simply asserted that the United States did not *intend* to use its relationship with China "against the Soviet Union" that that disavowal should dispel any concern of Brezhnev's (or of anyone else, including American critics of too close alignment with China).

President Carter did intend—as he stated—to seek improved relations with both China and the Soviet Union. But he was not speaking on behalf of China (nor even, perhaps, of all his own advisers). Carter hoped and may have expected to be able to move forward in January with both the China initiative and the Deng visit, and a summit meeting with Brezhnev and the SALT treaty. But Deng and the Chinese knew very well that normalization of Chinese-American ties at that particular juncture would unsettle the Soviet leaders. At the least it would postpone and change the context for a Soviet-American summit and SALT.[7] A Carter-Brezhnev meeting following the Chinese-American rapprochement would not only be delayed, its impact would be changed and downgraded as a platform for renewed Soviet-American détente.

Deng was very explicit about Chinese aims in seeking to influence American attitudes: "If we really want to be able to place curbs on the polar

---

3. *Time*, January 1, 1979, pp. 12–41.

4. For a fuller account, see chapter 20.

5. "An Interview with Teng Hsiao-p'ing," *Time*, February 5, 1979, p. 34. Deng (Teng) was featured for the second time in five weeks on the magazine's cover.

6. "The President's News Conference of January 17, 1979," *Weekly Compilation of Presidential Documents*, vol. 15 (January 22, 1979), p. 57. (Hereafter *Presidential Documents*.)

7. See chapter 20.

bear, the only realistic thing for us is to unite." He also disparaged the SALT II agreement, the importance of which Carter was praising: "We have constantly said not that we are opposed to such agreements, but that they are of no use." And he specifically deprecated SALT (and by clear implication any American-Soviet agreements) as compared with improving Chinese-American relations: "One should not rely on such a thing [as SALT agreements]. In seeking world peace and world stability, such agreements are neither as significant nor as useful as the normalization of relations between China and the U.S."[8]

The close relationship between the position of Deng and that of National Security Adviser Brzezinski was underlined not only by their common use of such terms as curbing the Soviet "polar bear," but also by Deng's extraordinary acceptance of Brzezinski's personal invitation for dinner on his first evening in Washington, January 28, even before the state dinner at the White House as President Carter's guest the following day.[9] Also during the visit the president authorized Brzezinski "to initiate some special negotiations with the Chinese" on coordinating intelligence, which Brzezinski personally continued until agreement was reached by the end of the year.[10]

President Carter made clear in his memoir that the outline of U.S. policy he presented to Deng had been drafted by Brzezinski. It stressed American concern over the Soviet exploitation of an arc of instability from Africa to Southeast Asia and the Soviet buildup of military power, as well as the American intention to maintain a strong and active global role. Needless to say, a close congruence of views emerged, and Carter, in evaluating Deng's visit, concludes: "To me, everything went right, and the Chinese leader seemed equally pleased."[11]

On the eve of Deng's visit President Carter had reaffirmed that "we will be cautious in not trying to have an unbalanced relationship between [our relations with] China and the Soviet Union."[12] Nonetheless, and despite the earlier Soviet objections (including in Brezhnev's letter to the president), the United States seemed to back away from this stance in the joint communiqué

---

8. *Time*, February 5, 1979, p. 34.

9. See Zbigniew Brzezinski, *Power and Principle: Memoirs of the National Security Adviser, 1977–1981* (Farrar, Straus, Giroux, 1983), p. 405. A controversial guest on the latter occasion was former President Nixon, whom Deng had asked to see.

10. Ibid., p. 419. Brzezinski does not identify the topic of the secret "special negotiations." It is highly likely they concerned collaboration in establishing technical intelligence facilities in China for monitoring Soviet missile development, on which agreement was reached later in 1979.

11. Jimmy Carter, *Keeping Faith: Memoirs of a President* (Bantam Books, 1982), pp. 202–03.

12. "The President's News Conference of January 26, 1979," *Presidential Documents*, vol. 15 (January 29, 1979), p. 173.

at the conclusion of Deng's visit.[13] Issued February 1, it stated that the two countries "are opposed to efforts by any country or group of countries to establish hegemony or domination over others."[14] That very day Ambassador Dobrynin met with Secretary of State Vance to seek a clarification of American policy in light of the language in the communiqué. Vance reaffirmed that use of the term antihegemony was not intended by the United States to be directed against the Soviet Union. Undoubtedly the Soviet leaders took this explanation with a large grain of salt, given that the Chinese had long equated this phrase with an openly anti-Soviet line, based on a definition of hegemony as Soviet expansionism and domination.[15]

The reason for the Soviet concern was not the establishment of Chinese-American relations, nor even slaps in their direction, but uncertainty over the extent to which the United States would develop an anti-Soviet alignment with China. In this respect, as noted, the Soviet leaders were deeply suspicious of Brzezinski and his influence on Carter.[16] They were also concerned over the extent to which the Chinese could succeed in playing the American card. In addition to Dobrynin's expressions of concern to Vance, on February 9 Prime Minister Kosygin stressed to Frank Press, the president's science adviser, Soviet concern over the permissive American reaction to a number of anti-Soviet remarks Deng made during his visit in the United States.[17] One of Deng's public (as well as private) statements in the United

---

13. Privately, however, President Carter angrily rejected a proposal by Secretary of State Vance to repeat that assurance in his statement at the close of the Deng visit. See Brzezinski, *Power and Principle*, p. 408.

14. "Visit of Vice Premier Deng of China: Joint Press Communique, February 1, 1979," *Presidential Documents*, vol. 15 (February 5, 1979), p. 213.

15. Secretary of State Vance could not tell Dobrynin that he had argued strongly *not* to include the phrase. Not only had President Carter taken Brzezinski's advice to include it, their discussion had led to the *addition* of the words "or domination," supposedly to soften the standard Chinese phrase. It actually strengthened it. The Department of State had initially proposed that there be no formal communiqué in order to avoid such questions, but the White House decided otherwise. Inclusion of the sensitive phrase was not discussed with any senior advisers on Soviet affairs. See Brzezinski, *Power and Principle*, pp. 407–08.

16. Brzezinski's own memoir provides much to sustain those suspicions. To cite but one small example, Brzezinski discloses that he "took advantage" of a private briefing with President Carter at the beginning of the Deng visit to get the president's agreement to delete from his planned toasts and press comments assurances that the new American-Chinese relationship was not directed against others (meaning above all the Soviet Union). These assurances were ones that Vance's State Department had earlier prevailed on Carter to include. See Brzezinski, *Power and Principle*, p. 406.

17. Press was in Moscow on February 7 to sign a renewal of the U.S.-Soviet Agreement on Cooperation in Science and Technology originally concluded in May 1972. He had been scheduled to visit Moscow in the summer of 1978, but his trip was deferred as part of the policy of retaliation for Soviet arrests of dissidents. He had visited Beijing in July 1978 for meetings that led President Carter and Vice Premier Deng to sign a similar U.S.-China Agreement on Cooperation in Science and Technology on January 31, 1979.

States, neither endorsed nor disavowed by his American hosts, was a threat to teach a "lesson" to the Soviet-allied Vietnamese.

In fact, on February 17 China did invade Vietnam This action was in response to the Vietnamese invasion of Kampuchea in late December and to the deterioration in Chinese-Vietnamese relations in 1978 and the expulsion of many ethnic Chinese from Vietnam.[18] But of particular relevance to American-Soviet relations was that Deng had openly signaled China's intentions while visiting the United States and that China clearly believed its new closer relationship with the United States provided some protection against Soviet intervention in support of Vietnam.

China had played its American card. In retrospect it became clear that the Chinese had taken advantage of the opportunity given by the United States for timing the establishment of U.S.-China relations in order to upset Soviet-American plans for an early summit and SALT agreement. They had also built American expectations for and stake in a new relationship with China. Finally, they had also used this opportunity to shore up the position vis-à-vis the Soviet Union before invading the Soviet ally Vietnam. The Chinese met with success on each count.

On February 20 President Carter voiced the American response to the move by the Chinese military: "We will not get involved in conflict between Asian Communist nations. Our national interests are not directly threatened, although we are concerned, of course, at the wider implications." He also commented that normalization of relations with China "is already an accomplished fact and will not be reversed." Most surprising, and not pursued further, was his statement that "while our influence is limited, because our involvement is limited, we remain the one great power in all the world which can have direct and frank discussions with all the parties concerned. For this reason, we have a useful and important role to play in the restoration of stability."[19] The political line taken by the United States—from its first official comment on the day of the attack and later in UN debates—tied the question of the withdrawal of Chinese troops from Vietnam to the question of the withdrawal of Vietnamese troops from Kampuchea, in effect supporting the Chinese position.[20]

---

18. See chapter 20.

19. President Carter, "Remarks at a Special Convocation of the Georgia Institute of Technology," February 20, *Presidential Documents*, vol. 15 (February 26, 1979), p. 303. The last-cited comment by Carter presumably reflected his pride that the United States now had full relations with China; it ignored the absence of formal American relations or other direct access to Vietnam or Kampuchea.

20. This policy line was proposed by Brzezinski and accepted by Carter. See Brzezinski, *Power and Principle*, pp. 411–12. Brzezinski candidly comments: "I knew that such a proposal would be totally unacceptable to the Vietnamese and to the Soviets, and hence would *provide a partial diplomatic umbrella for the Chinese action* without associating the United States with it." Ibid., p. 411. Emphasis added.

In his memoir Carter reveals that not only had Deng publicly hinted at a military move against Vietnam while in the United States, he had privately even "outlined his tentative plans for China to make a punitive strike across its border into Vietnam." Carter (accompanied by Mondale, Vance, and Brzezinski) related that he "tried to discourage him." Then, "as it was growing quite late, I suggested to him that we continue the conversation the following morning." The next day Carter met alone with Deng (save for an interpreter) and both orally and in a personal handwritten note "summarized my reasons for discouraging a Chinese invasion of Vietnam." Deng again thanked Carter for his views but continued to describe the plans. Carter states that his "impression" was that "the decision had already been made. Vietnam would be punished."[21] Even with hindsight when writing his memoir, Carter still seems oblivious to the fact that the United States was seriously compromised by having had advance confidential information about the Chinese plans and by his advance acquiescence, given that he had done nothing more than share some arguments about adverse world political consequences aimed at "discouraging" a decision to attack he recognized had probably already been taken. Nor does he seem aware that, on a visit in which "everything went right," the United States had been used, to the detriment of its own interests.

Brzezinski makes clear in his memoir that he did not even try to dissuade the Chinese. On the contrary, in a separate private talk with Foreign Minister Huang Hua he "shared with him my concern that the Chinese might be forced to withdraw." Brzezinski remarks, "I hoped that my warning would *encourage* the Chinese to concentrate on a swift and decisive move."[22] He also characterized Deng's discussion of China's plans to attack Vietnam and calculations of Soviet reactions and Chinese countermoves as "the single most impressive demonstration of raw power politics that I encountered in my four years in the White House."[23]

After the Chinese attack the American position continued to reflect equanimity, if not satisfaction. On February 27, while Chinese troops were still advancing (although against stiff and effective resistance), Secretary of the Treasury W. Michael Blumenthal arrived in China for trade negotiations. On March 1 the American embassy in Beijing and the Chinese embassy in Washington officially opened. Not only was the United States proceeding without interruption to pursue relations with China, despite the invasion of

---

21. Carter, *Keeping Faith*, pp. 206, 208–09. Brzezinski says Deng had been even more clear that "China *must* still teach Vietnam a lesson" and "had weighed all the alternatives and decided to undertake the action, even if it involved a confrontation with the Soviet Union." Brzezinski, *Power and Principle*, p. 410. Emphasis added.

22. Brzezinski, *Power and Principle*, p. 410. Emphasis added.

23. Ibid., p. 25. Brzezinski makes this statement in admiration, remarking that against the background at that time of debate in the American administration over what to do about the deteriorating situation in Iran, "I secretly wished that Deng's appreciation of the uses of power would also rub off on some of the key U.S. decision makers."

Vietnam, it was even (as events revealed) moving rapidly to develop still further areas of collaboration.[24] Brzezinski acknowledges believing that "the Chinese action in some respects might prove beneficial to us," for example, "by demonstrating that an ally of the Soviet Union could be molested with relative impunity." As he concludes, "The new American-Chinese relationship had successfully weathered its baptism of fire."[25]

The United States did not consult with the Soviet Union about the impending Chinese attack in the days after Deng's private authoritative disclosures and pointed public remarks about military actions against Vietnam, even after American intelligence independently monitored the substantial buildup of Chinese forces on the Vietnamese border.[26] The American leadership did not consider that this situation called for consultation under either the 1972 Basic Principles accord or the 1973 Agreement on the Prevention of Nuclear War. This fact undoubtedly colored internal Soviet assessments of the American attitude toward the conflict—and of the American interpretation of the principles set forth in the bilateral agreements.

The United States did, however, send an unpublicized note to the Soviet government at the outset of the Chinese action, urging that it not take any action, including a military response, that could exacerbate the situation. The note stated that the United States was prepared to exercise similar restraint. Inasmuch as it was an ally of the Soviet Union that had just been attacked, that offer of parallel restraint was at best disingenuous.[27] The message, moreover, was sent on the hot line. The Soviet reply, its content described only as "strongly worded," did not alter Carter's determination to stay on the course previously adopted, one that Brzezinski admits, with understatement, was "a slight tilt in favor of the Chinese."[28]

An official "Statement of the Soviet Government in Connection with the Aggression of China against the Socialist Republic of Vietnam" was released February 18. It stated, "The Soviet Union will fulfill its obligation assumed under the Treaty of Friendship and Cooperation between the USSR and the SRV" (November 3, 1978) and "responsibility for the consequences of the continuation of Beijing's aggression against the Socialist Republic of Viet-

---

24. Secretary of State Vance had argued against going ahead with the Blumenthal visit at that time because of the Chinese invasion. President Carter, on Brzezinski's advice, decided to proceed with the visit and more generally to develop closer relations. Information from interviews with senior officials involved. See also Brzezinski, *Power and Principle*, pp. 413–14.

25. Ibid., p. 414.

26. Interviews with senior American officials.

27. The offer of parallel restraint was included at Brzezinski's suggestion. Some thought it seemed to convey a concession. As he confides in his memoir, Brzezinski, while arguing for that language at the time on grounds of reciprocity, believed that it subtly implied a parallel American willingness to respond militarily if the Soviet Union did so. See Brzezinski, *Power and Principle*, p. 412.

28. Ibid., p. 413.

nam will rest entirely on the present leadership of China."[29] Two days later TASS criticized the United States for not condemning the Chinese invasion.

Soviet commentary was highly critical of the U.S. reaction to the Chinese action. It was, however, by no means uniform. A February 19 commentary on Radio Moscow went so far as to state: "A number of facts prove that the aggression against Vietnam was planned and decided upon as early as when Brzezinski, U.S. presidential national security adviser, visited China [in May 1978]. Details were finalized when Deng Xiaoping visited Washington."[30] Yet on that same day another commentator on Radio Moscow reported, "The Americans are now energetically emphasizing that they tried in every way to talk their Chinese friends out of large-scale military actions," adding, "Well, probably that is the way that it was."[31] Nevertheless, the most usual line was that the United States had either connived with the Chinese or been "used" by them and then gave its tacit consent to the venture. For example, one commentary stated, "Nor can the fact that the war against Socialist Vietnam was practically prepared by Beijing with Washington's tacit consent fail to evoke anxiety." This commentary cited as evidence the *New York Times* reference to Deng's statements to American senators that Vietnam needed "to be given a bloody lesson."[32] But a later *Pravda* commentary concluded, "Even the United States is beginning to understand the cost of the policy of 'playing the China card.'"[33]

On February 24 Vance met with Dobrynin to caution against Soviet military involvement in the conflict and to warn against exploiting the situation to acquire military air or naval bases in Vietnam. Dobrynin naturally refused to rule out either possibility and made clear that many in Moscow believed the United States had encouraged China to attack.[34]

---

29. The statement was broadcast on Radio Moscow on February 18, and published in *Pravda*, February 19, 1979. Soviet references usually cite it as "published on February 19." See Foreign Broadcast Information Service, *Daily Report: Soviet Union*, February 19, 1979, p. L1. (Hereafter FBIS, *Soviet Union*.)

30. Glebov, Commentary, Radio Moscow, February 19, 1979, in FBIS, *Soviet Union*, February 23, 1979, p. L4. This commentary was broadcast in Mandarin to China and may have been designed to stir up *Chinese* concern over the American role. Glebov noted that Deng had dined with Brzezinski immediately after his arrival.

31. Aleksandr Bovin, "The Vietnamese People Will Be Able to Defend Their Independence," TASS, Radio Moscow, February 19, in FBIS, *Soviet Union*, February 21, 1979, p. L5. Bovin is a political observer for *Izvestiya* and an influential commentator who has staunchly supported Soviet-American détente.

32. Sergei Kulik, TASS, "Aggression Cannot Be Hidden by a Lie," Radio Moscow, February 20, in FBIS, *Soviet Union*, February 21, 1979, p. L6.

33. Vladimir Bol'shakov, "International Review," *Pravda*, March 11, 1979.

34. Cyrus Vance, *Hard Choices: Critical Years in America's Foreign Policy* (Simon and Schuster, 1983), pp. 121–22.

The speeches of the Soviet leaders in the Supreme Soviet election campaign in late February provided a chance to gauge the effect on Soviet thinking about relations with the United States. In addition to assailing the Chinese leaders for attacking Vietnam, a number of the Politburo members castigated them for deviating from Marxism-Leninism and becoming accomplices of, or acting in concert with, "reactionary forces" and "international imperialism." Some spoke of American "connivance." But the general line was directed mainly at the Chinese.[35]

Foreign Minister Gromyko, however, criticized American "playing—to put it mildly—the 'China card'" (the phrase between dashes was not in the published version but was a flourish in his actual delivery of the speech). He said, "If this is being done in order to pressure the Soviet Union, such attempts are futile and can only yield the opposite effect." His main point, however, was again to warn the United States of the dangers of *Chinese* exploitation of American support. And he commented, "The Chinese leaders are striving with particular eagerness to set the Soviet Union and the United States at loggerheads."[36] Gromyko was warning the United States both against playing the China card and against being used as the Chinese played the American card. That same day a Radio Moscow commentator carried the point even further: "One not unimportant result of the Vietnam adventure, according to the designs of the Chinese leadership, is meant to be the creation of complications for the process of détente in general, and for U.S.-Soviet relations in particular." He warned of an ultimate Chinese design to precipitate a war between the Soviet Union and the United States.[37]

In his speech, on March 2, Brezhnev was generally conciliatory with respect to relations with the United States. He made no reference to the United States in conjunction with the Chinese invasion of Vietnam nor to the China card. Instead he spoke of the near completion of a fair compromise on SALT and of looking forward to a summit meeting with President Carter, "I hope in the not distant future."[38]

---

35. Not long before *Pravda* reported that Beijing had sent secret instructions to its embassies abroad that described its policy as a "revolutionary compromise." That compromise was designed to obtain assistance from the imperialists in order to create "a proper political climate" so that in the long run China could deal more effectively with both "social imperialism" (the Soviet Union) and capitalism (the West). See V. Stepanov, "Instructions from Peking," *Pravda*, January 31, 1979.

36. A. A. Gromyko, "For the Further Prosperity of the Motherland and for World Peace," *Sovetskaya Byelorussiya* [Soviet Belorussia], Minsk, February 27, 1979; and live on Radio Minsk, February 26, in FBIS, *Soviet Union*, March 1, 1979, p. R3.

37. Aleksandr Petrov, Commentary, Radio Moscow, February 26, in FBIS, *Soviet Union*, February 27, 1979, p. C4. Petrov also criticized "Washington's tacit blessing of China's attack on Vietnam, and its rapprochement with Beijing, against the background of the present bloody aggression against socialist Vietnam, [which] cannot help the improvement of Soviet-U.S. relations."

38. Speech of L. I. Brezhnev, "For the Happiness of the Soviet People," *Pravda*, March 3, 1979.

In addition to vigorous diplomatic support for Vietnam, the Soviet Union canceled military leave and hinted at direct action if it proved necessary. Most significantly, in February–March the Soviet Union carried out military exercises in the area north of China in a major show of force that was readily picked up by Chinese (and American) intelligence, although not publicized. In these exercises the Soviets reportedly moved tanks firing blank rounds right up to the border, illuminated Chinese positions with floodlights, and flew tactical air sorties along, and in some cases over, the frontier.[39]

The Chinese withdrew from Vietnam in the first half of March. Then on April 3 China announced it would not renew its Treaty of Friendship with the Soviet Union, signed in 1950 and expiring in 1980. Another development in April 1979 caused a minor flurry of interest at the time but was generally dismissed. A group of American senators led by Senator Joseph R. Biden of Delaware visited Beijing, where it was told by Deng Xiaoping that China would be willing to provide intelligence collection facilities for the United States directed at the Soviet Union to help monitor a SALT agreement, so long as they were operated entirely by the Chinese. The American press reported this rather bizarre offer, as it was generally considered, and the Soviet media commented on it. Probably no one at the time realized it was an indiscreet reference by Deng to something Brzezinski had raised in 1978 that was in fact being negotiated in great secrecy at that very time and would soon be put into effect.[40]

The Arc of Crisis

While the developments in Sino-Vietnamese-Soviet-American relations were evolving in the first months of the year, other momentous developments were also occurring, especially in the Middle East.

In January the shah departed Iran, and in February the Ayatollah Khomeini returned and took power. While the Soviet Union was pleased to see the departure of a close American ally from the Middle Eastern scene, the unsettling effects of the advent of a fundamentalist religious and nationalist

---

39. The first detailed references to these exercises appeared in the press two years later following a visit by two American newsmen to the Chinese border area, where local citizens described what they had observed. See Michael Weisskopf and Howard Simons, "Armed Mongolian Herdsmen Ready to Defend Border Village," *Washington Post*, February 9, 1981.

   Vance records in his memoir a White House background briefing for the press about a Soviet military buildup, for which he asserts "we had no such evidence." Vance, *Hard Choices*, p. 122. This discrepancy is unexplained.

40. The original article was by Jay Mathews, "China Offers to Monitor SALT Data," *Washington Post*, April 20, 1979. Confirmation that this arrangement had become operational in 1980 was reported in Philip Taubman, "U.S. and Peking Join in Tracking Missiles in Soviet," *New York Times*, June 18, 1981.

regime posed problems and concerns for the Soviet Union as it did for the United States. The Soviet Union did not attempt to intervene in the situation, while American efforts to manage a transition evaporated rapidly.[41]

While Iran was in the turmoil of revolution, adjacent Afghanistan was beginning to feel the disruption of a growing revolt against the reforms and attempts by the Marxist regime of Nur Mohammad Taraki to centralize political control. On February 14 rebels seized the U.S. ambassador, Adolph Dubs, as a hostage. In the police effort to rush his captors on February 19 he was slain. The United States protested the role of Soviet advisers who had apparently been present and acquiesced when the police stormed the place where Dubs was being held.

New troubles also erupted in the south of the region. On February 24 forces from South Yemen crossed into North Yemen in support of dissident elements there. Border hostilities erupted between the two countries. On March 7, in response to a request for aid, the United States began a substantial airlift of arms (including twelve F-5E fighter-bombers, sixty M-60 tanks, and seventy military advisers) to assist the government of North Yemen. This action (and Soviet advice) may have helped induce South Yemen to agree to a cease-fire on March 17.

As a general sign of American interest and readiness to aid a non-communist country under attack, the U.S. response may have been effective. In particular, it was responsive to a Saudi Arabian request. And (at least initially) it was considered in Washington to demonstrate U.S. readiness to stand up to an attack by a country regarded in Washington as a Soviet proxy. But the entire venture was far from successful in its broader purposes. First, North Yemen had greatly magnified the attack in an attempt to get direct American military aid (rather than, as had been the case, getting aid channeled through Saudi Arabia). Second, there were too many independent "proxies" on *both* sides. The complexities were underlined when, to the consternation of Washington, the leaders of North Yemen turned to the Soviet Union for a massive military assistance program that soon involved up to 600 military advisers, dozens of aircraft, and hundreds of tanks. The United States was virtually left out. Somewhat later the pro-Soviet leader of South Yemen, who had earlier disposed of the presidents of *both* Yemens, was himself deposed by a more moderate, although still pro-Soviet, leader.[42]

Elsewhere along the arc of crisis, on April 6 the United States cut off military and economic assistance to Pakistan owing to that country's continuing construction of uranium enrichment facilities capable of producing

---

41. While the Soviet Union did not attempt to intervene, it did seek to position its own assets in the country, mainly the long discredited Tudeh communist party. In addition, an unofficial Soviet Persian-language radio station sought to incite anti-American sentiment, which the United States officially protested to Moscow on February 16.

42. A more complete account of events in North and South Yemen, including external interventions, is provided in chapter 19.

fissionable materials for nuclear weapons. In addition, although presumably coincidentally, only two days earlier General Mohammad Zia ul-Haq had hanged former President Zulfikar Ali Bhutto.

There had been relative calm in one center of tension in the region, or more accurately, the action was primarily diplomatic rather than military. Egypt and Israel had been trying, since the Camp David accord of September 1978, to reach concrete agreement on a peace treaty between the two countries and on interim autonomy for the Palestinians in the Israeli-occupied territories. They had failed to meet their December deadline. Finally, after further direct participation by President Carter in renewed Camp David meetings, on March 26 agreement was reached on a peace treaty—although not on Palestinian autonomy. Almost all other Arab states (except the Sudan, Oman, and Somalia) broke diplomatic relations with Egypt and suspended it from the Arab councils such as the Arab League, which departed Cairo. This action was a heavy blow to Egypt and to the United States. While the Soviet Union sought to build its own ties with the Arab states, it could do so only marginally.

Perhaps the most important event in terms of its long-term impact was not a geopolitical conflict, but an economic action (that obviously also had political and strategic implications). On June 28 OPEC, led by its Middle Eastern members, and reacting in part to the chaos in Iran, raised the base price of petroleum by 24 percent—on top of a 14.5 percent increase the previous December. This action aggravated the recession and other economic problems in the United States (including reducing the value of the dollar) and in Western Europe. Its longer-term impact in the non-oil-producing countries of the third world was even more severe.

The series of conflicts in the Horn of Africa, Iran, Southwest Asia, and Southeast Asia over the year or so from early 1978 into 1979 dramatically focused attention on this arc of crisis, to cite the term coined by Brzezinski. Before the year was out still more dramatic events would occur in both Iran and Afghanistan.

Several important developments elsewhere in the world in the first half of the year would also affect American and Soviet perceptions and relations. Castro opened the port of Mariel in Cuba from April to September, permitting (or in some cases compelling) 125,000 Cubans to leave for the United States. In Nicaragua, the Sandinista-led revolution, with some support by the United States at the end, overthrew the Somoza dynasty on July 19. Neither of these events involved American-Soviet confrontation. As the Sino-American-Soviet relationship again settled down and while the arc of crisis was in its own travail, efforts had continued to reach the long-elusive SALT II Treaty and American-Soviet summit meeting.

The Vienna Summit

Brezhnev and Carter both wanted to proceed with a summit meeting at which a SALT treaty would be signed. Carter had included in his State of the Union message to Congress in January 1979 the wish "to welcome President Brezhnev to our country in the near future," an endorsement of détente (although qualified as "genuinely reciprocal and broadly defined"), and a statement that a SALT II Treaty was "among our top priorities."[43] President Carter indicated this desire in a private message to Brezhnev in February, after the Deng visit. As noted, Brezhnev replied affirmatively in his election speech to the Supreme Soviet on March 2. Further private exchanges between the two presidents was accompanied by active diplomatic consultation. Secretary of State Vance and Ambassador Dobrynin met twenty-five times between the first of the year and May 9, when agreement on a SALT II Treaty was finally announced.

In retrospect it would appear that a combination of the sudden announcement in December of the normalization of American-Chinese relations and the tightening up of the negotiating positions by both sides interfered with what might have been a year-end agreement and January summit meeting. But from February to May there was a real desire on both sides to reach a SALT agreement, which both saw as the centerpiece for a summit. The final issues simply proved difficult to resolve.[44]

In the United States President Carter and his administration continued to stress the importance of SALT. Particularly in early April—although belatedly in the view of many supporters of SALT—the administration finally opened a strong public campaign. On April 4, in a talk to the Chicago Committee of the Council on Foreign Relations, Brzezinski, who supported SALT throughout despite his hard line on many issues concerning the Soviet Union, said that SALT was "essential," would enhance U.S. security, and would be "an historic achievement."[45] Secretary of Defense Brown addressed the Council on Foreign Relations in New York on the following day and made a similar strong statement on the contribution of SALT to the national defense.[46] President Carter made a major address on SALT on April 25,[47] and on May 9

---

43. "The State of the Union: Annual Message to the Congress, January 25, 1979," *Presidential Documents*, vol. 15 (January 29, 1979), p. 158. Carter was more restrained in the widely reported State of the Union Address to the Congress, in which he neither mentioned a summit invitation nor used the word détente. Although he strongly argued the benefits of SALT, he also placed the burden for achieving agreement on the Soviets: "If the Soviet Union continues to negotiate in good faith, a responsible SALT agreement will be reached." "The State of the Union: Address Delivered before a Joint Session of the Congress. January 23, 1979," ibid., p. 107.

44. Secretary of State Vance has expressed essentially this same judgment. See Vance, *Hard Choices*, pp. 112–13.

45. Brzezinski, "Arms Control: SALT II and the National Defense," April 4, *Department of State Bulletin*, vol. 79 (May 1979), pp. 48–51. (Hereafter *State Bulletin*.)

46. Secretary of Defense Harold Brown, "Arms Control: SALT II and the National Defense," April 5, *State Bulletin*, vol. 79 (May 1979), pp. 51–55.

47. President Carter, "Remarks at the Annual Convention of the American Newspaper Publishers Association," April 25, *Presidential Documents*, vol. 15 (April 30, 1979), pp. 693–99.

Secretary of State Vance and Secretary of Defense Brown jointly announced the successful conclusion of the negotiations.[48]

In January a private group calling itself "Americans for SALT" was established to lobby for the treaty. But the best organized and strongest lobbying groups were the opposition on the right. Of these the most impressive was the Committee on the Present Danger, although others were even more active. Under the aegis of the American Security Council, a Coalition for Peace through Strength disposing of a campaign budget of $10 million had, by the beginning of the year, lined up 175 senators and congressmen and 89 special interest groups, including the Reserve Officers Association, the American Federation of Small Businesses, and Americans for a Safe Israel, in an anti-SALT drive. The American Conservative Union, with a membership of one-third of a million, had produced a thirty-minute anti-SALT film already shown on 209 television stations around the country. All this had occurred before the contents of the treaty were publicly unveiled or even fully negotiated.

On April 27 Secretary of State Vance and Secretary of the Treasury Blumenthal met with Dobrynin to discuss U.S.-Soviet trade. They advised that the administration had been sounding out Congress and hoped that after the summit meeting the time might be propitious to lift the trade restrictions and gain acceptance of most-favored-nation (MFN) status for the Soviet Union. Congressman Charles Vanik of Ohio, cosponsor of the critical Jackson-Vanik amendment in 1974, had on January 5 publicly said in a newspaper interview that he might support the removal of legislative restrictions on trade with China, the Soviet Union, and communist countries of Eastern Europe. Senator Adlai E. Stevenson III of Illinois proposed legislation that would allow MFN status and credits to both China and the Soviet Union by permitting a simple presidential determination on emigration practices. It would also raise the Export-Import Bank credit limit for each country from $300 million to $2 billion. Senator Jackson, however, remained adamantly opposed to lifting the restrictions on MFN status and credits to the Soviet Union. The administration's hope that after a summit meeting Congress would support its declared policy of evenhandedness toward the Soviet Union and China, specifically with respect to MFN status and credits, was not met.[49]

---

48. "Arms Control: SALT II Treaty Concluded," *State Bulletin*, vol. 79 (June 1979); pp. 23–27.

49. Because the administration itself was seriously divided on this policy, it was not effective in Congress. Brzezinski admits in his memoir that he and Secretary of Defense Brown only "ostensibly" agreed on a policy of evenhandedness: he argues that a "mechanically evenhanded" treatment would have favored the Soviet Union, since it was stronger. A proposal by Vance and Blumenthal in March to go to Congress with a request for MFN status for both China and the Soviet Union was sidetracked by Brzezinski and Mondale (who was unhappy over the prospect of a fight with Senator Jackson). By the end of July President Carter for the first time decided to propose MFN status for China before the end of the year. As soon as Carter confirmed this decision in a breakfast meeting on August 3 (in preparation for Mondale's planned visit to China), Brzezinski immediately called in the Chinese ambassador to

On July 7 the United States signed a Trade Agreement with China that called for MFN status. The administration's formal policy continued to seek, after SALT ratification, approval for MFN status for both China and the Soviet Union, but it seemed increasingly likely that Congress would support MFN for the former but not for the latter.

As the Carter administration began to plan for the forthcoming summit meeting, the familiar divergence between the policy lines of Vance and Brzezinski toward the Soviet Union reappeared. Vance wanted to focus on SALT and on reaffirmation of the basic framework of détente in American-Soviet relations. Brzezinski wanted the president to engage in a broad dialogue on relations, with emphasis on the negative impact of the Soviet military buildup and of Soviet (and proxy) military activities in the third world, in particular the Indian Ocean area, on détente. Carter himself wanted to emulate Nixon by developing an array of concrete agreements covering a number of areas. (One of these areas, trade and economic relations, was ruled out despite urging by the State Department that Secretary of the Treasury Blumenthal and Secretary of Commerce Juanita Kreps be included in the delegation. Brzezinski was able to persuade Carter that this approach would create public expectations of a trade agreement that would be followed by disappointment when one did not ensue.) The result was a compromise eventually fashioned at the summit itself.[50]

Two events occurred in Washington shortly before the summit. First, on June 7 President Carter announced that the administration would proceed with production and deployment of the MX mobile ICBM system. He hoped by this action to persuade those at home who doubted that the United States would continue with strong military programs and to make more difficult (and therefore less likely) strong Soviet objection to that decision.[51] Second, on the eve of the president's departure for Vienna for the summit conference, Senator Jackson, addressing the neoconservative Coalition for a Democratic Majority, not only formally declared his opposition to the still unreleased SALT II Treaty, but accused the administration (and those of Nixon and Ford) of following a policy of "appeasement" of the Soviet Union. Secretary of State Vance rebutted the charge the next day, but it was a most inauspicious send-off for the president and for the administration's policy. The attempt by President Carter from the very start of his administration to hold a

inform him, "thereby sealing the matter" before there could be any reconsideration. See Brzezinski, *Power and Principle*, pp. 415–18.

50. See ibid., pp. 340–41.

51. Brzezinski, supported by Brown, was the prime mover in making the MX deployment decision at this time in order to help create "a proper strategic and geopolitical context" for the summit meeting. See Brzezinski, *Power and Principle*, pp. 331–38. Vance accepted as valid a military requirement for modernization and reduced vulnerability, and politically he hoped this action would reassure the JCS and members of Congress, thus strengthening support for the SALT treaty. See Vance, *Hard Choices*, p. 138.

door open to Senator Jackson and those of like mind, made at some cost, had failed utterly. In addition, Lieutenant General Edward L. Rowny, the JCS representative on the SALT II delegation since 1973, resigned and retired in order to oppose the treaty.

The Vienna summit was the first in nearly five years, since President Ford had gone to Vladivostok. By protocol, it should have taken place in the United States, but Carter acceded to Soviet requests citing Brezhnev's health.

President Carter was very excited about the summit meeting, which he had long wanted. He spoke with former Presidents Ford and Nixon and had a long talk with W. Averell Harriman, the wartime U.S. ambassador to Moscow, asking all for advice. The CIA showed him motion pictures of previous summit meetings.

Brezhnev was not in the best of health but managed. He was accompanied by three other Politburo members, not only Gromyko and Dmitry Ustinov, logically included as the foreign and defense ministers, but also his protégé, Konstantin Chernenko, newly elected to full membership in the Politburo. Marshal Ustinov and Marshal Nikolai Ogarkov, first deputy minister of defense and chief of the General Staff, had been included after Carter sent word that his delegation would include Secretary of Defense Brown and Chairman of the JCS General David Jones.

The centerpiece of the summit, and the only major item of concrete business, was the signature of the SALT II Treaty—seven years after the signing of SALT I. In addition, it gave the leaders on both sides a chance to exchange views and take a better measure of one another.

Brezhnev remarked at their first encounter, "God will not forgive us if we fail." Carter was so taken by this unexpected spontaneous reference to the Deity by the communist leader that he quickly jotted it down on his ever-ready yellow pad for later reference.[52] President Carter was determined (as he had told American newsmen before the summit meeting) to take a firm position against Soviet support for Cuban proxy troops in Africa and other destabilizing actions in the third world, and to the continuing overall and strategic nuclear Soviet military buildup. He did so, but this stance only prompted Brezhnev to reaffirm strongly Soviet support for national liberation movements and progressive forces in a changing world, which he said were the result not of Soviet initiatives but of objective historical processes. Indeed, in a toast on the second day of the summit Brezhnev decided to make this point publicly. He confirmed that the "Soviet people are in solidarity with the national liberation

---

52. Persons present have confirmed this. For contemporary reportage see "The SALT Summit," *Newsweek*, June 25, 1979, p. 26; and Terence Smith, "Brezhnev and Carter Begin Vienna Parley in Friendly Discord," *New York Times*, June 17, 1979. While such references to the Deity are not uncommon among Soviet communists of Brezhnev's generation, the official Soviet spokesman in Vienna, Leonid Zamyatin, sought to make the reference more orthodox by retroactively revising it to say Brezhnev had referred to "future generations" rather than "God."

struggle." And he strongly objected to attempts to portray historical processes in various countries or national struggles for independence or social progress as "Moscow's intrigues and plots." "Why then," he complained, "pin on the Soviet Union the responsibility for the objective course of history and, what is more, use this as a pretext for worsening our relations?"[53]

Jimmy Carter may not have been familiar with the Soviet view, but it was not new. Once both sides had stated their views and positions, no real dialogue ensued. The hopes of some American participants for a real clarification of the rules of competition under détente were not realized.[54] There was, on the other hand, ready agreement by Carter and Brezhnev on the dangers of miscalculation and the need for clearer understanding and communication to avert potential catastrophe. But there were no concrete proposals by either side on how to meet this commonly perceived danger.

President Carter, having in mind the brouhaha over the Soviet shipment of MiG-23 fighter-bombers to Cuba the year before, told Brezhnev that a Soviet buildup of arms in Cuba would adversely affect the relationship of the two countries. Brezhnev reaffirmed strict Soviet observance of the 1962 understanding. In retrospect this brief discussion assumed unanticipated significance when a scant three months later, with no Soviet buildup, Carter suddenly declared "unacceptable" the presence of a Soviet brigade in Cuba that had been there for years.[55]

Carter and Brezhnev also both referred to military programs of the other side as requiring like response by each. Beyond that no real dialogue developed on this issue either. Brezhnev referred to news reports of large increases in the American defense budget for the next year, and Carter replied that the Soviet Union had much larger increases than the United States did.[56]

---

53. President Brezhnev, Dinner Toast, June 16, 1979, in *The Vienna Summit*, Selected Documents no. 13, Department of State (Washington, D.C.: Government Printing Office, 1979), p. 3. It seems quite likely that Brezhnev sincerely believed various circles were using this issue as a pretext to worsen relations, rather than believing that it was a cause of genuine concern in the United States. There is no indication President Carter was able to allay this perception of Brezhnev's. His restatements of the American view seemed to the Soviet leaders to reinforce the image of the president as bending to currents hostile to détente, if indeed he did not to some degree share them. See also Carter, *Keeping Faith*, pp. 254–56.

54. For example, see Brzezinski, *Power and Principle*, p. 344; also interviews with senior Department of State participants. Secretary of State Vance does not address the matter in the brief account in his memoir.

The U.S. drafters did attempt, without Soviet acceptance, to include a statement on the need to develop further a code of conduct through regional arms discussions, notwithstanding the failure to do so in the conventional arms transfer (CAT) talks (discussed in chapter 22).

55. Interviews with senior members of the delegation. See chapter 24.

56. This exchange was disclosed by official spokemen and appeared widely in the press; for example, *Newsweek*, June 25, 1979, p. 26. Incidentally, Carter was in error in ascribing a larger *increase* in Soviet military spending; he meant that the Soviets had, by U.S. estimates, a continuing larger expenditure than did the United States.

Brezhnev expressed concern about the planned multiple basing arrangement for the MX. Marshal Ustinov, in his talks with Secretary of Defense Brown, was more emphatic in objecting to the proposed (but not yet official) multiple shelter deceptive basing arrangement for the MX missile system, which he contended would be inconsistent with SALT undertakings on verifiability. Brown assured him that any MX basing plan adopted by the United States would be consistent with the SALT II Treaty, but the question was not resolved. The treaty was signed despite this Soviet reservation, but because the matter was not dealt with adequately, it would come back as an issue later.[57]

The leading members of the Carter administration had agreed on the desirability of attempting to develop a direct dialogue between the military leaders of the two sides. With this aim explicitly in mind, Dobrynin had been told well in advance of the American intention to include Secretary of Defense Brown and JCS Chairman General Jones in the delegation, and of the U.S. hope that they could meet with their counterparts. In response, Marshals Ustinov and Ogarkov were present, and a meeting of the four was arranged. They did not, however, do more than get acquainted and exchange favorable comments on SALT and general views on mutual and balanced force reductions (MBFR). Although the United States had taken the initiative in arranging the meeting in order to stimulate a general strategic dialogue among military leaders, President Carter proposed to Brezhnev that the military men discuss MBFR issues. That was agreed, although the Soviet representatives had not understood that MBFR was to constitute the main agenda item. The American participants were not prepared to discuss wider strategic issues overlapping the subjects being discussed by the presidents. Nonetheless, before the meeting ended Ustinov did insist on expressing the Soviet objection to the reported U.S. plan for MX basing, as noted above.

There were some last minute difficulties with one aspect of the SALT agreement having to do with the form and specificity of Brezhnev's assurances that the Backfire bomber would not be given intercontinental strategic capabilities.[58] It escalated into a personal challenge between Presidents Carter and Brezhnev. In fact, there was no real issue, even though the exchanges at the time made it appear to some participants (including Carter) that the Soviet Union was testing U.S. (and the president's) determination.[59]

---

57. This and other references to the military talks are based on interviews with Brown, General Jones, and other sources, including Colonel General Nikolai Chervov, one of the two Soviet generals who accompanied Ustinov and Ogarkov.

58. The final language of the treaty and associated official statements had been agreed to only on June 14, the day before the summit began. See chapter 23.

59. See chapter 23. For an informed reconstruction of this episode see Martin Schram, "Vienna: Bomber Issue Gave Carter His Baptism in Summitry," *Washington Post*, June 24, 1979; and see Carter, *Keeping Faith*, p. 250. Vance did not see it as anything more than "some confusion over the acting out of the scenario Dobrynin and we had prearranged." Vance, *Hard Choices*, p. 139.

In 1982, when the subject of nuclear freezes had become an active political issue, Carter claimed to have proposed at the summit meeting a "freeze on the production and deployment of all nuclear weapons" that Brezhnev had turned down.[60] What Carter had said at Vienna was that the United States was prepared for a moratorium on production and deployment of any new missiles and launchers in the context of reductions, a comment that was addressed more broadly at the planned SALT III negotiations. He raised the subject briefly in a plenary meeting and then discussed it in somewhat more detail in a later private meeting at which only interpreters were present with the two leaders. In that private session Carter gave Brezhnev a xerox copy of some ideas he had jotted down on a yellow pad and discussed briefly with Vance, Brown, and Brzezinski. These ideas included "stopping the production of nuclear warheads and launchers." According to Carter's own memoir account, Brezhnev did not turn it down but agreed, subject to other nuclear countries being involved. Carter also proposed an annual 5 percent reduction from the SALT II force levels for each of five years, pending a SALT III agreement. This proposal Brezhnev did turn aside because he was not prepared to consider further reductions until other American nuclear delivery systems and those of America's allies were also dealt with. These new ideas had not been presented to the Soviet side beforehand, or even considered by the American arms control–national security bureaucracy.[61]

As to the European nuclear context, as noted above it was Brezhnev rather than Carter who raised it—Carter had not mentioned the plans for new long-range theater nuclear missiles then being considered in NATO. Brezhnev said that American forward-based nuclear systems (FBS) and all medium-range systems in Europe, British and French as well as American, must be discussed in SALT III. Carter tried to fob that issue off to the talks by the military leaders, but they did not discuss it in their meeting either.[62]

The main concrete achievement of the Vienna summit meeting was signature of the SALT II Treaty.[63] The principal overall achievement was the very occurrence of the summit, which gave the American and Soviet leaders the opportunity to talk personally. The principal drawback was that the conference came so late. Moreover, it was soon overwhelmed by other events. Indeed, the Vienna summit really interrupted only briefly the decline in détente and the deterioration in relations between the two powers.

The communiqué issued at the conclusion of the summit meeting,[64] and the toasts and other remarks of the two leaders, in some ways pro-

---

60. See John Vinocur, "Carter Discloses He Offered Freeze in Atomic Arms to Brezhnev in '79," *New York Times*, May 7, 1982.

61. Based on interviews with senior members of the delegation. See also Carter, *Keeping Faith*, pp. 246, 251–53, 255; and Vance, *Hard Choices*, p. 139.

62. Based on interviews with senior members of the delegation.

63. See chapter 23 for a discussion of the SALT II negotiation.

64. Diplomatic communiqués purporting to summarize and report on conferences reflect the actual proceedings only in part. Not only are some things suppressed or glossed over, but many—

vide more interesting indications of their concerns, aims, and aspirations than did their more formal exchanges. For example, a comparison of the communiqué of the Vienna Carter-Brezhnev summit meeting of 1979 with those issued after the four summits of 1972–74 reveals that it was the first to *fail* to refer specifically to "the principle of peaceful coexistence," first accepted by the United States in May 1972. While not discussed by Carter and Brezhnev, senior members of the two delegations argued the matter at some length. The Soviet side strongly wished to reaffirm it and argued that it was now part of the long-agreed policy of détente endorsed by both sides. (They also argued that its absence would raise undesirable questions—in fact, the absence went virtually unnoticed.) Brzezinski felt that Kissinger had erred in accepting this Soviet formulation in the first place and that there was no need to perpetuate the mistake. The Soviets did not wish to escalate the matter and risk rejection at the level of the presidents, and they reluctantly accepted its omission.[65]

For some time Carter had not been referring to détente itself. He used the word but once in his toasts and remarks at Vienna, and then it was in the context of détente in Europe.[66] On the other hand, the Carter administration in 1979 did not oppose détente, and in the communiqué "the sides expressed their support for the process of international détente." In addition, the communiqué referred to the SALT treaty as making "a substantial contribution to the prevention of nuclear war and the deepening of détente" and to the "deepening of mutual understanding between the sides on several issues [that

---

and sometimes important—statements in communiqués may never have been mentioned in the meetings of the principals. Moreover, the language of communiqués is often drafted and negotiated, and occasionally completed, before the meetings begin. The actual hammering out of language by their representatives does not merely record agreements, but is the forum that determines the areas of agreement. The communiqué on the Vienna meeting was mainly drafted in Washington beforehand by senior representatives of the Department of State and the Soviet embassy. The Soviet representatives consulted with Moscow for instructions and approval on a number of occasions during the preparation of the text.

65. Information from senior members of the U.S. delegation. The Basic Principles of Mutual Relations of 1972, which includes reference to peaceful coexistence, was, however, reaffirmed in the communiqué.

66. It was a most peculiar reference. In his dinner toast to President Brezhnev on June 17 Carter stated: "I hope, Mr. President, that detente, which has been growing in Europe because of *your* [sic] great work, can now encompass other regions of the world." *Presidential Documents,* vol. 15 (June 25, 1979), p. 1050. Emphasis added. Incidentally, in the selected documents on the summit published by the Department of State, *Vienna Summit,* and in the *State Bulletin,* the interjection "Mr. President" was omitted, presumably because it did not appear in the prepared text of this toast. *Vienna Summit,* p. 4; and *State Bulletin,* vol. 79 (July 1979), p. 53. This remarkable praise for the Soviet role, and for Brezhnev personally, in contributing to détente in Europe was intended to stand in contradiction to the implied criticism of less constructive Soviet activities in the third world. Carter went on to state: "I hope we can work together so that rules of restraint . . . can progressively be applied to other troubled regions of our planet."

is, not on all issues] as a result of the meeting." It was also said to contribute to "strengthening détente, international security and peace."[67]

The communiqué did note that the two presidents had "devoted particular attention to situations of tension that complicate the international situation and interfere with positive developments in other areas."[68] In fact the summit had not really addressed this issue, so critical to the viability of détente and bearing seeds of confrontation in the relationship between the two countries.

President Carter did, in a less combative and challenging way than he had at Annapolis a year earlier, refer again to a choice of alternative courses both countries faced: the path of restraint and cooperation, and the "road of competition and even confrontation." He also noted, as Brzezinski often did, the far greater likelihood of a continuing mix of both.[69]

Brezhnev, for his part, having experienced the whole development of relations over the decade (and, of course, for even longer) noted that in the early 1970s many areas of agreement had been reached—and "it was not easy to come to those agreements." He went on to note that "subsequently relations between our two countries began to develop unevenly. They went through a period of stagnation and even regressed somewhat from the charted course. This affected the entire world situation as well." He then expressed the view that the summit meeting could "become an important step in improving Soviet-American relations and ameliorating the international climate." He also commented that the two countries had gained "some quite good experience in cooperating in international affairs. Suffice it to mention, for example, our joint efforts to stamp out the hotbed of war in the Middle East in 1973," and he also mentioned cooperation in preparing for the Helsinki Conference on Security and Cooperation in Europe (CSCE).[70] Brezhnev further commented that the Soviet leaders were careful not to categorize the United States as an "enemy" or "adversary" and asked the same treatment from American leaders. There was no response.[71]

---

67. *Vienna Summit*, pp. 7–8. The Soviet leaders declined to include the preferred U.S. formulation of the aim of making détente "comprehensive and reciprocal," language meant to exclude selective détente or lack of reciprocal restraint, a formulation devised by Brzezinski and not favored by Vance.

68. Ibid., p. 8.

69. Ibid., p. 4. In his memoir, however, Carter comments that he concluded that there was "no reason to change our basic policy of 'cooperation when possible, competition when necessary.'" Carter, *Keeping Faith*, p. 261. A persistent issue in his administration was whether cooperation was possible in any particular area (as Vance usually believed) or whether competition required containment or confrontation in any particular situation (as Brzezinski usually believed was necessary).

70. *Vienna Summit*, pp. 3–4.

71. In his memoir Carter mentions Brezhnev's request but makes no comment as to a reply. *Keeping Faith*, p. 255. Other members of the delegation state that the subject was not addressed by the United States.

On the issue of military competition, the communiqué noted, "The two sides reaffirmed their deep conviction that special importance should be attached to the problems of the prevention of nuclear war and to curbing the competition in strategic arms." The SALT II Treaty was, of course, intended to make a major contribution to that aim. But even in his remarks at the ceremony on the signing of the treaty, Carter, on the defensive because of domestic opposition, felt obliged to note that the treaty "will not end the continuing need for military strength and for readiness," although in deference to the occasion he concluded by somewhat incongruously adding "on both sides."[72]

The American side did attempt to include in the communiqué a flat statement that no one could win a nuclear war, but the Soviet side (presumably Marshals Ustinov and Ogarkov in particular) did not wish to do so, and that wording was not included. It is of interest that later Brezhnev and other Soviet leaders did make such a statement and that two years later the Soviet side would undoubtedly have been prepared to include it. The Soviets did accept the statement in the communiqué that "both sides recognized that nuclear war would be a disaster for all mankind." Finally, they were willing to include another important statement that they might not have been willing to include at the time of the first summit: "Each [side] stated that it is not striving and will not strive for military superiority, since that can only result in dangerous instability, generating higher levels of armaments with no benefit to the security of either side."[73]

The communiqué also noted the continuing efforts to reach agreements on a comprehensive nuclear test ban, nuclear nonproliferation, MBFR, antisatellite arms limitations, limitations on transfers of conventional arms to other states, bans on chemical and radiological weapons, and arms limitations in the Indian Ocean area.[74]

One important subject discussed in the private session of the two presidents alone with interpreters, and not mentioned to the press, was the complex of issues relating to trade and emigration of Soviet Jews. The communiqué states only that "the two sides confirmed that economic and commercial relations represent an important element in the development of improved bilateral ties. Both sides stated their position in favor of strengthening these relations, and recognized the necessity of working toward the elimination of

---

72. *Vienna Summit*, p. 5. This statement thus awkwardly declared a real Soviet need for military strength and readiness against the United States, although undoubtedly Carter simply meant to be evenhanded and to recognize the Soviet perception of such a need, whether justified or not.

73. Ibid., p. 7. Also see chapter 22.

74. Many of these statements were initiatives of the Carter team in 1977, and all had been the subject of negotiations; see chapter 22. By June 1979 the United States had already abandoned efforts in several of these areas (for example, the Indian Ocean talks) or was having second thoughts on whether to pursue them (such as the antisatellite arms limitation).

obstacles to mutually beneficial trade and financial relations."[75] Carter writes in his memoir of "Brezhnev's special emphasis on the need for increased trade," but also of "the Soviets' absolute unwillingness to tie this subject to emigration policy or other human-rights issues."[76]

President Carter expressed his appreciation for the large increase in Jewish emigration (the number was higher than ever before, having reached nearly 30,000 in 1978 and rising to an all-time peak of 51,000 in 1979). He also stated his intention to seek a change in the trade legislation in order to be able to accord MFN status to the Soviet Union, believing that the improved climate after the summit meeting and SALT agreement would support such a shift in Congress. In addition, he reiterated the administration's stated policy of evenhandedness and balance in moving forward at the same time with MFN status for both China and the Soviet Union.

Carter raised the question of human rights practices, making a special—and unsuccessful—appeal for the release of Anatoly Shcharansky. Brezhnev explained that Shcharansky had been tried and convicted of espionage in a Soviet court of law, and he was bound to uphold the law of the land.[77] The communiqué did not address that subject; it did reaffirm "respect for sovereignty and non-intervention in each other's internal affairs."[78] (Brezhnev, in his remarks upon signing the SALT treaty, noted that by doing so, "we are helping to defend the most sacred right of any individual—the right to live.")[79]

The one subject of great concern to Brezhnev, to which he devoted 90 percent of his presentation in the private tête-à-tête meeting, was China and the nature of American relations with it. Brezhnev noted the territorial claims by China against most of its neighbors and stated—obviously with the recent Chinese attack on Vietnam very much in mind—that the Chinese "seem to want the United States to cover their political rear." He spoke approvingly of normal relations with China for the United States (and for the Soviet Union, too, if possible), but also remarked, "We would consider anything beyond the present line between China and the United States with grave concern, and Soviet-American relations would suffer." He stressed that the Soviets would not under any circumstances engage in an anti-U.S. adventure. President Car-

75. *Vienna Summit*, p. 8.

76. Carter, *Keeping Faith*, p. 260. He does not indicate an awareness of the history of these issues over the preceding seven years.

77. Ibid., p. 260. In preparation for the summit, the Soviet leader had agreed in April to exchange five leading dissidents for two imprisoned Soviet spies and to commute the death sentence of a convicted Russian spy for the United States. For background see the discussion in chapter 18. The five dissidents released were Valentyn Moroz, a leading Ukrainian nationalist; Georgy Vins, a leading Baptist; Aleksandr Ginzburg, a human rights activist; and Edvard Kuznetsov and Mark Dymshits, two Jews convicted of an attempted escape by hijacking. See Brzezinski, *Power and Principle*, pp. 338–39, for an account of the negotiation of their release.

78. *Vienna Summit*, p. 6.

79. Ibid., p. 5.

ter simply repeated what he had said on his own initiative in the larger session earlier—that improvements in American-Chinese relations would never be at the expense of American-Soviet relations and would be for the good of all.[80]

There were some human and personal touches in the summit encounters. President Carter, who was initially rather stiff and formal, loosened up in the course of the four days. By the third day he referred in a toast to "my new friend, President Brezhnev." Brezhnev once startled the Americans by jokingly commenting, "We think everyone is for detente and good relations except a few people such as—him," pointing suddenly and incongruously at Vance. Vance was discomfited. Everyone burst into laughter, and Brzezinski good-naturedly pointed his finger at himself, to which some of the Russians quickly assented.[81]

In his remarks on the occasion of the signing of the SALT II Treaty Brezhnev went out of his way to "specially mention the contributions [to the SALT treaty] made by Secretary Vance and Minister Gromyko, Secretary Brown and Minister Ustinov." For good measure he added, "President Carter and I have also had to do a good deal of work."[82] To the Americans, the references to Vance and Brown, while undoubtedly deserved, seemed to highlight the omission of Brzezinski. This effect may or may not have been intended. It is also possible that the absence of a direct counterpart to Brzezinski on the Soviet side is the explanation. In any case, whatever the implication in that respect, the chief purpose of Brezhnev's comment was probably to stress the role of Marshal Ustinov, the Soviet minister of defense, who was attending his first summit conference.

SALT, Détente, and Carter under Fire

President Carter returned to Washington and directly addressed a joint session of Congress on June 18, as President Nixon had done in May 1972 after his first summit and the signing of the SALT I agreements. Carter hoped to launch a renewed détente. But the more apt comparison would have been to Nixon's third summit meeting, rather than the first. As with Nixon in 1974, Carter was at the nadir of his political standing and was a wounded president, if not yet an actual lame duck. The summit may have boosted Carter's standing, but it also provided a focus for criticism and political attack.

---

80. Carter, *Keeping Faith*, pp. 258–59, 254–55.

81. Reported in the press at the time. *Newsweek*, June 25, 1979, p. 27. This incident has been confirmed in interviews with participants and is mentioned by Carter. *Keeping Faith*, p. 247.

82. *Vienna Summit*, p. 5. The chiefs of the respective SALT delegations, also present but of less than ministerial rank, were not specifically mentioned.

In mid-1979 public opinion polls showed President Carter with an approval rating of only 30 percent of the public, below even the lowest rating Nixon had received. On July 17, in a surprise move that echoed one of Nixon's unusual actions, Carter asked all the members of his Cabinet to submit their resignations. On the following day he purged three members responsible for important areas of domestic policy—Secretary of the Treasury Blumenthal, Secretary of Energy Schlesinger, and Secretary of Health, Education, and Welfare Joseph Califano. (A little over a month later, to Carter's regret, Ambassador Andrew Young was forced to resign his post at the United Nations after an unauthorized contact with a representative of the PLO.)

Carter was facing opposition from the right on a wide range of his foreign policy initiatives. The Panama Canal Treaties had barely squeaked through the year before, and in the summer of 1979 the implementing legislation for them gave the opposition another opportunity, including some who had very reluctantly supported the treaties and now had a chance closer to the elections to vote their negative preference. In mid-March a leftist group took power in tiny Grenada in the Caribbean and turned to Cuba for support. The extreme right blamed the administration for easing Anatasio Somoza Debayle out in Nicaragua in mid-July and also (with curious ambivalence) either for letting in the 125,000 refugees from Cuba or for not having helped others to leave Cuba. The administration's policy on Rhodesia was also under fire. And the downgrading of relations with Taiwan still rankled.

On Soviet relations, the mounting drumfire of opposition to SALT before the summit meeting has been noted. It culminated in Senator Jackson's charge of "appeasement" on SALT and on détente with the Soviet Union in general.

This was the context to which President Carter returned from Vienna, flushed with what he regarded as a triumph but facing what he knew to be a mixed reception. He wisely refrained from attempting to depict the summit and the SALT agreement as panaceas for American-Soviet relations. "Of course," he said, "SALT II will not end the competition between the United States and the Soviet Union . . . there will always be some degree of tension in the relationship between our two countries."[83] He did say that he believed the meeting, as a continuation of the earlier summit encounters over the years, had provided a useful contribution and that as a result "we've moved closer to a goal of stability and security in Soviet-American relationships." And he said that he and President Brezhnev had "developed a better sense of each other as leaders and as men."[84]

---

83. "President Carter's Address to Congress, June 18," *Vienna Summit*, p. 9.

84. Ibid., pp. 9, 11.

  The U.S. delegation also proposed for inclusion in the communiqué a commitment to annual summit meetings and semiannual meetings of foreign ministers, but the Soviets were not prepared to accept that proposal.

Carter, however, never mentioned détente. While saying that he and Brezhnev had "laid a foundation [at the summit] on which we can build a more stable relationship between our two countries," he described American policy as one in which "we will seek to broaden the areas of cooperation, and we will compete where and when we must." He also stressed that he had made clear to Brezhnev that "Cuban military activities in Africa, sponsored by or supported by the Soviet Union, and also the growing Cuban involvement in the problems of Central America and the Caribbean, can only have a negative impact on U.S.-Soviet relations."[85]

SALT dominated his report, as it had the summit. President Carter stressed the central importance of preventing war and the role of the SALT II Treaty in reducing that risk. He noted, as Kissinger had earlier, that "SALT II is not a favor we are doing for the Soviet Union," implying that it was therefore not a useful tool for leverage on other issues through linkage. While forcefully arguing the case for the contribution SALT II could make, he was also—from conviction and political expediency as well—careful to assure his audience (Congress and the American people) that in addition to SALT "we must have strong military forces, we must have strong alliances, we must have a strong national resolve. . . . We have that strength—and the strength of the United States is not diminishing, the strength of our great country is growing, and I thank God for it." And using the classic comparison for reconciling acknowledgment of parity with projecting an image of strength, "Militarily our power is second to none. I'm determined that it will remain so."[86]

Rather than serving as a rallying point for the administration, SALT II became a lightning rod that attracted attacks on the administration, on détente, and on SALT. While many, often technical, aspects of the agreement were challenged, the real issue was not the treaty (which withstood criticism on its own merits rather well), but the policy of détente and the priorities of the Carter administration, including its defense policy.

On June 29 the North Atlantic Council representatives gave formal NATO endorsement to SALT II. Some American opponents of the treaty had been arguing that Europe had serious but suppressed misgivings. With the official endorsement this argument was not effective.

On July 9 the Senate Committee on Foreign Relations opened extensive hearings that lasted until October 10. On November 9, by a vote of nine to six, the committee recommended Senate consent to ratification, and ten days later officially reported the treaty to the full Senate. There were a score of reservations, understandings, and statements, but no formal amendments. The Senate Intelligence Committee also considered the treaty and issued a guardedly favorable report on October 5. On the other hand, the notably more hawkish Senate Armed Services Committee held its own hear-

---

85. Ibid., p. 11.

86. Ibid., pp. 9, 11. See also the discussion in Brzezinski, *Power and Principle*, pp. 344–45.

ings, and on December 10 it issued a report recommending against ratification. The vote was ten to none (with seven abstentions). It stated that the treaty as it stood, without "major changes," was "not in the national security interests." This was a significant but not necessarily fatal blow to the prospects for approval. Opponents did plan to introduce a number of significant substantive amendments in the full Senate debate, many of which were readily conceded to be "killer amendments." That is, they would almost certainly have been unacceptable to the Soviets, thus killing the treaty. Indeed, faced with the prospect of such amendments virtually from the day of signature on, Gromyko had as early as June 25 objected strongly to any reopening of the delicately balanced compromise agreement.

The broader issues in the SALT debate included trust of the Russians, including but not limited to technical capabilities for verification (the Carter administration countered that verification was adequate and the agreement was not based on trust). Some opponents who had supported SALT I while serving in the Nixon administration (such as retired Admirals Moorer and Zumwalt) attacked the treaty on grounds of imbalance and allegedly insufficiently tough American negotiating, but also because of alleged failures by the United States, in contrast to the Soviet Union, to keep up its own defense efforts. Kissinger and General Haig supported the treaty but equivocally, and similarly conditioned their support on major increases in American military programs (and, explicitly in Kissinger's case, on more vigorous response to Soviet global activities). Others opposed the treaty regardless of the level of the U.S. military effort and, in some cases, regardless even of the treaty's terms—they saw it as a symbol of a policy of arms control and détente they did not like.[87]

While President Carter returned to face a long and difficult summer struggling to marshal support for SALT II, Brezhnev and his colleagues returned to Moscow to find the standard full approval by the Politburo, the Presidium of the Supreme Soviet, and the Council of Ministers, that reflected a consensus in support of—and assured collegial responsibility for—the proceedings and agreements reached at each summit. The approval specifically noted the endorsement by both sides of the aim of deepening détente and stressed the need to reinforce political détente with military détente.[88]

In November Brezhnev's position was further reinforced by the election to full membership in the Politburo of Nikolai Tikhonov, Kosygin's principal deputy (and later successor) as prime minister, and of Mikhail Gorba-

---

87. For discussion of the SALT II ratification debate see Vance, *Hard Choices*, pp. 349–58, 364–67; and Brzezinski, *Power and Principle*, pp. 344–53.

88. "In the Political Bureau of the Central Committee of the CPSU, the Presidium of the Supreme Soviet of the USSR, the Council of Ministers of the USSR on the Results of the Meeting of Leonid Brezhnev, General Secretary of the Central Committee of the CPSU, President of the Presidium of the Supreme Soviet of the USSR with President Jimmy Carter of the United States," *Pravda*, June 22, 1979.

chev, a young party chief interested in economic reform, as a candidate member of that body.

Soon after the summit meeting, and continuing in the months following, a number of irritants reappeared in American-Soviet relations. Only days after Carter's return from Vienna he proclaimed (as he was obliged to do by legislation adopted in 1959) "Captive Nations Week" for the week of July 15.[89] In August and September a rash of defections of half a dozen leading Soviet dancers and figure skaters on foreign tour drew attention to internal popular dissatisfaction in the Soviet Union (and led the Soviet leaders as a precaution to cancel a scheduled tour abroad of the Moscow Philharmonic Orchestra). While the United States was not responsible for the defections, one incident in particular caused strain on both sides. The American authorities prevented the departure of a Soviet Aeroflot airliner for three days until the wife of defecting Bolshoi dancer Aleksandr Godunov could be interviewed under circumstances that would allow a determination of whether she was departing of her own free will (as eventually she did). This incident caused great indignation in the Soviet Union.

Soviet sensitivities were heightened when, on August 1, on the fourth anniversary of the Helsinki CSCE Final Act, President Carter blasted the Soviet Union, Czechoslovakia, and East Germany for human rights restrictions "inconsistent with the pledges made at Helsinki."[90] Not in direct response, but with an eye to reducing future incidents, in the latter months of the year the Soviet leaders rounded up the remaining members of the dissident Helsinki monitoring group in the Soviet Union.

On July 26 the president signed into law the Export Control Act of 1979. It did not contain amendments raising the credit restrictions on loans to the Soviet Union or loosening the terms for granting it MFN status. But there remained hope for MFN status in the next year, and the administration continued to tell the Soviets that it would seek to have the restrictions removed.

On August 1 it was announced that the Soviet Union was authorized to buy an additional twenty million tons of wheat and corn over the next fourteen months (raised on October 3 to twenty-five million tons). This was not, however, a concession to the Soviet Union. Although the purchases were mostly scheduled for the next year, this increase helped make 1979 by far the best year ever in American-Soviet trade—the total turnover was $4.5 billion (of which $2.4 billion was in grain exports). That year the United States had a surplus of $2.7 billion in trade with the Soviet Union.[91]

---

89. "Captive Nations Week, 1979," *Presidential Documents*, vol. 15 (June 25, 1979), p. 1141.

90. "Statement on the Fourth Anniversary of the Signing of the Final Act in Helsinki, August 1, 1979," *Presidential Documents*, vol. 15 (August 6, 1979), p. 1352.

91. Jack Brougher, "1979–82: The United States Uses Trade to Penalize Soviet Aggression and Seeks to Reorder Western Policy," in U.S. Joint Economic Committee, *Soviet Economy in the 1980's: Problems and Prospects*, 97 Cong. 2 sess. (GPO, 1983), pt. 2, pp. 421–22.

With SALT II still in abeyance, although for the most part the committee hearings had had satisfactory outcomes, and with other aspects of bilateral relations rocking along with the usual irritants, a major new incident arose that was not initiated or intended by either side. Fate dealt a wild card. American-Soviet relations faced yet another Cuban crisis—the most recent in a series comprising the Bay of Pigs landing in 1961, the Cuban missile crisis of 1962, the Cienfuegos submarine base contretemps in 1970, the problem of Cuban proxy military activities in Angola and Ethiopia in 1976 and 1978, and the flurry over the MiG–23s in Cuba in 1978.

The new imbroglio concerned a belated discovery by American intelligence of the existence in Cuba—at least for a number of years, perhaps since 1962—of a Soviet ground force brigade of some 2,600 men and weapons. While on the face of it such a unit clearly posed no threat to the United States, and it was not in contravention of the previous understandings of 1962 and 1970, it created a domestic furor in the United States. It seriously affected adversely the tenuous efforts to reestablish détente with the Soviet Union and imperiled the SALT II Treaty being considered by the Senate.[92]

On the same day on which President Carter unilaterally settled the unilaterally generated issue of the Cuba brigade, October 1, President Brezhnev issued a warning against the proposal in NATO to create new long-range missile theater nuclear forces (TNF). On October 6 he expanded his warning and issued a proposal to negotiate, conditioned on NATO not making a decision to deploy new missiles. But both the warning and the offer were too vague and too late, and on December 12, 1979, NATO decided to deploy 572 new American medium- and intermediate-range missiles.[93] At the time NATO saw the decision as a successful political-military move by the alliance to meet a perceived political-military threat in Europe. In the Soviet Union, on the other hand, it was seen as an unjustified escalation by the West of the arms competition and as a circumvention of the SALT II limitations, since the American missiles in Europe could strike strategic military objectives in the Soviet Union, while Soviet missiles in Europe could not strike such targets in the United States. Thus the Soviet leaders saw it as another major instance of the United States' playing the NATO card and doing so just six months after the SALT II Treaty had been signed at the Vienna summit. Symbolically, and concretely as well, the United States was seen as circumventing détente to build a position of power in the geopolitical confrontation.[94]

Even earlier Moscow had interpreted other signs in this light. Not only had the MX missile decision been announced virtually on the eve of the Vienna summit, but on September 7, at the height of the brouhaha over the brigade, the United States had, without further consultation, announced its

---

92. See chapter 24 for further details on this episode.

93. See chapter 25 for more detail on the decision and its implications.

94. See chapter 22.

decision to deploy the MX in a deceptive basing multiple-launch-point mode—despite Defense Minister Ustinov's objection to Secretary of Defense Brown at Vienna on this very matter.

September also saw a new Presidential Directive (PD)–50 (leaked to the press) requiring that any proposal on arms control or arms limitation be consonant with defense planning. Precisely because arms control had always been considered in that context (whether always wisely was another question), and with full deliberation on its interrelation with military considerations, the directive seemed superfluous and its issuance suspicious. The press leak further implied that the president was putting the skids on any arms control measures. While that purpose was denied, one purpose of the directive had been to reassure skeptics that military considerations would be given due weight in any arms control decision and to bolster the impression of a tough stance. In practice, the directive had little effect, although it did signify that on such issues as the Comprehensive Test Ban the administration was leaning to the conservative side. The directive did not, however, succeed in persuading critics or opponents, who chose rather to see it as an admission that previously the administration had not given due weight to defense requirements. And it did disquiet the Soviet leaders, who saw it as another symptom of a trend in policy adverse to the rewarming of détente.

The administration had, by autumn, also announced plans for a considerable increase in military expenditures, in part to meet perceived needs but in important part also to gain support from those elements in the Senate that insisted on an increase as a quid pro quo for support of SALT.

The cumulative effect of these many new problems and frictions in American-Soviet relations in the last half of the year undid the hopes raised by the summit. As viewed from Moscow, while some of these issues arose independently, Washington had contrived others or had at least used them to worsen relations, rather than tackling the issues in a spirit of détente. This was especially true of the affair over the brigade in Cuba. The official Soviet diplomatic history concludes that Carter capitulated to opponents of détente and that "under the influence of these [antidétente] forces, in the conduct of its foreign policy, which combined 'cooperation' with 'competition,' the Carter administration in the second half of 1979 made a sharp turn to the latter."[95]

In October 1979, the North Atlantic Assembly, a formal body of parliamentarians of the NATO countries, issued a report on *Detente: Results and Prospects,* based on four years of study. While aware of the difficulties and shortcomings in practice, the assembly chose to "reaffirm strongly the basic détente policy advocated by the Harmel report and adopted by the Alliance" in 1967. It concluded that while "new efforts are necessary in order to

---

95. A. Gromyko and B. Ponomarev, eds., *Istoriya vneshnei politiki SSSR, 1917–1980* [History of the Foreign Policy of the USSR, 1917–1980], vol. 2 (Moscow: Nauka, 1981), p. 606.

strengthen and broaden détente," "a firm political consensus had emerged to pursue détente as an Alliance policy."[96]

Two other events late in the year drew attention once more to the arc of crisis in South Asia. On November 4, soon after the issue of the Cuba brigade had finally dissipated, the staff of the American embassy in Tehran, Iran, was taken hostage. The Ayatollah Khomeini proved unwilling to free them. Three weeks later, on November 20, a band of extremists briefly seized the mosque in Mecca. The United States had in no way been involved, but malicious false reports blaming it led mobs to burn the U.S. embassy in Islamabad, Pakistan, and caused lesser anti-American disturbances in Turkey and Bangladesh. These were followed on December 2 by the burning of the U.S. embassy in Tripoli, Libya.[97]

The second event was the Soviet intervention in and military occupation of Afghanistan in the last days of December 1979.[98] This event led rapidly to a sharp downturn in American relations with the Soviet Union and to a shift from the troubled efforts by the Carter administration to sustain the weakened détente developed earlier in the decade while meeting points of competition, to a policy in which confrontational containment succeeded détente as the dominant element.

American and Soviet Relations with China

American relations with China receded somewhat from the forefront of attention in the spring and early summer of 1979, mainly owing to the spurt of attention to the summit meeting of Presidents Carter and Brezhnev in Vienna and the SALT II agreement. The momentum of the development of relations over a wide span of interests, however, proceeded rapidly. This evolution in relations was paralleled by a modest revival of Sino-Soviet relations.

When the Chinese announced on April 3, 1979, that they would not renew the Sino-Soviet Treaty of Friendship, they cushioned that action somewhat by proposing talks on bilateral issues, without preconditions. The omission of their earlier demand for prior withdrawals of Soviet troops from the border areas marked the invitation as possibly serious, and on June 4 the

---

96. *Detente: Results and Prospects* (Brussels: The North Atlantic Assembly, 1979), p. 9.

97. It is not clear whether clandestine Soviet operatives had anything to do with the inflammatory rumors leading to the outbreaks of November 20. By coincidence or otherwise, apparently reflecting a judgment that things were getting out of hand, on November 20 Soviet Persian-language radio broadcasts changed their line and began to call for the release of the American hostages in Iran.

98. The background of this action, its purposes, and its consequences became so important to American-Soviet relations that they are discussed in detail in chapter 26.

Soviet government proposed low-level talks (at the level of the Chinese chargé d'affaires) in Moscow in July or August. On July 25, notwithstanding another incident on July 16 on the Kazakhstan-Xinjiang border, the Chinese agreed to the talks but proposed raising the level to deputy foreign minister. Preliminary talks began on September 27, and on October 17 formal talks between deputy foreign ministers were renewed. The Chinese suspended them after the Soviets occupied Afghanistan. Nevertheless, the period of the talks from April to the end of the year made it apparent that both sides saw advantages in restoring a modicum of contact to counterbalance the renewed (if short-lived) American-Soviet détente. Similarly, as the United States and China were agreeing on economic ties, in August the Soviets and Chinese signed a trade agreement for the coming year.

In a curiously revealing sidelight to Soviet attention to triangular diplomacy, a survey of Soviet publications discloses that during 1979 a total of 67 articles were published on Sino-Soviet relations, but an even more impressive total of 104 articles appeared on *Sino-American* relations.[99]

The normalization of relations between the United States and China opened a floodgate of contacts, visits, and agreements. It followed the substantial unofficial and semiofficial contact that had gone on since 1972. From February 1972 to January 1979 over a hundred members of the U.S. Congress had visited China. Now there were opportunities for doing more than merely satisfying curiosity. At the official level, a recital of only the Cabinet-level visits is impressive: Secretary of the Treasury Blumenthal (February 24–March 4) was the first to visit, for the opening of the embassy. He was followed by Deputy Secretary of Agriculture Dale Hathaway (March 15–24), Secretary of Commerce Juanita M. Kreps (May 4–15), NASA Administrator Robert A. Frosch (May 19–31), Postmaster General William F. L. Bolger (May 27–29), Special Trade Representative Robert S. Straus (May 26–June 2), and Secretary of Health, Education, and Welfare Joseph A. Califano (June 22–30)—all in the first half of the year. Numerous congressional groups, and still more congressmen representing their states in state delegations, poured into China. Governor Jay Hammond of Alaska arrived even before the embassy was opened, followed by many others (including especially, although far from exclusively, others from the American West). The U.S. Conference of Mayors sent a delegation in June, and on November 2 St. Louis and Nanjing became the first to sign an official agreement as "sister cities."

Substantive agreements were also reached quickly. Secretary of the Treasury Blumenthal initialed an accord settling mutual claims (China paid $80 million in private American claims, while the United States unblocked Chinese assets). This settlement was formally signed by Secretary of Commerce Kreps, who also initialed a trade agreement signed later, on July 7, by

---

99. The bibliographical compilation was made by the Institute of Far Eastern Studies in Moscow. For this information see Gilbert Rozman, "Moscow's China-watchers in the Post-Mao Era: The Response to a Changing China," *China Quarterly*, no. 94 (June 1983), p. 221.

Ambassador Leonard Woodcock. The three-year Trade Agreement provided MFN status and removed restrictive constraints on trade, subject to approval by the Congress.

Two months after the U.S.-Soviet summit meeting Vice President Mondale visited China. His trip was important as a return for the Deng visit and was made the occasion for advancing a number of areas of cooperation. Mondale promised the Trade Agreement would be submitted to Congress by November 1 and announced an Export-Import Bank trade credit of $2 billion over the next five years. He also noted that the administration had (two weeks earlier) made a formal certification that the People's Republic of China be considered a "friendly nation" so that it would be eligible for aid under the Foreign Assistance Act. In addition, agreements were concluded on cultural exchanges and on cooperation in hydroelectric power.

The most significant aspect of Vice President Mondale's trip, however, was the beginning of a further turn toward strategic collaboration with China. In a major speech at Beijing University he made two important statements. First, he not only stressed the existence of "parallel strategic interests," but said that "we are committed to joining with you to advance our many parallel strategic and bilateral interests." Second, he went on to align the United States in support of China (six months after the Chinese invasion of Vietnam) by saying, "Any nation which seeks to weaken or isolate you in world affairs assumes a stance counter to American interests."[100] Subsequently, in China and Hong Kong, the vice president sought to take the edge off some of the negative reaction to these statements by saying, "We do not have and do not contemplate a military relationship with the People's Republic of China."[101] But clearly he had intended to show the China card again.[102]

The vice president's denials of a contemplated military relationship with China were at least somewhat disingenuous. Not only had discussions on intelligence monitoring of tests of Soviet military weapons been under way, but Mondale had personally suggested that the U.S. government and Secretary of Defense Brown would be receptive to an invitation for Brown to visit China.[103]

---

100. "Vice President [Walter Mondale] Visit to East Asia," Speech at Beijing University, August 27, *State Bulletin*, vol. 79 (October 1979), p. 10.

101. Cited in William Safire, "Louder Than Words," *New York Times*, October 4, 1979.

102. Senior Department of State officials of that time have since complained that these key passages in the vice president's speech had been added after they had seen an earlier draft. That claim is apparently true. A very senior White House official has commented in rejoinder that in any event there was no need to clear it with the Department of State. Interviews.

103. From interviews with senior officials. Brzezinski writes that since 1978 he and Brown had favored some collaboration on defense with China and that the United States should move toward it step by step. Carter had approved a proposal by Mondale (suggested to him by Brzezinski) that on his own trip he suggest a visit to China by Brown. When Carter agreed, Brzezinski privately told the Chinese to expect the request. Vance learned of the proposal

The Mondale trip was very successful in advancing American-Chinese relations. It also undercut any possibility (which was probably slight in any case) of movement in the Sino-Soviet talks then just getting under way. From the Chinese standpoint, on the other hand, it may appear that the Chinese initiative in starting the Sino-Soviet talks helped lead the United States not to rebuild its Soviet connection after the Vienna summit, but instead to make the moves toward China associated with the Mondale visit.

Thus during the spring and summer of 1979 the United States moved from a nominally evenhanded balance in relations with the Soviet Union and China to a decided tilt toward China. Moreover, in the case of Brzezinski it was not a choice made more or less reluctantly, but one intended to work against the Soviet Union. In Brzezinski's own words, the ongoing geopolitical competition "contributed to my feeling that it would be wise gradually to increase the pressure on the Soviet Union's eastern flank."[104]

The imbroglio over the Soviet brigade in Cuba erupted while Vice President Mondale was in China. And it was literally on the occasion of resolving that issue in American-Soviet relations that on October 1 Secretary of Defense Brown's forthcoming visit to China was disclosed.[105] On October 4 the *New York Times* printed a revelation based on a leak from the Pentagon that was no doubt orchestrated as a follow-on to the White House's disclosure of the Brown trip. It stated that the Department of Defense had concluded that the United States should bolster China's military strength so that China could assist the West in case of war with the Soviet Union.[106] The Defense Department document, "Consolidated Guidance No. 8," was described publicly as a "staff study," but it was in fact a serious planning report, prepared the previous April and submitted to Secretary of Defense Brown in May. It surveyed a number of military, diplomatic, and intelligence steps, some already under way, others to follow soon.

The Department of State sought to hold the line by reaffirming the still operative national policy that the United States would not supply arms to China. Secretary of State Vance responded to the leak immediately by saying, "Let me state flatly and categorically that it's nothing more than a story. We

---

only after Mondale had made it, and in September he objected, but was overruled by the president. See Brzezinski, *Power and Principle*, pp. 419–23.

A much broader account of the bureaucratic problems in reaching decisions in U.S. policy toward China and in their implementation in the period 1977–80 is provided by Michel Oksenberg, then the expert on China on the NSC staff, in Richard H. Solomon, ed., *The China Factor* (Englewood Cliffs, N.J.: Prentice-Hall, 1981), pp. 55–66.

104. Brzezinski, *Power and Principle*, p. 420. Brzezinski calls this section of his memoir "Not a Balance but a Tilt."

105. See chapter 24.

106. See Richard Burt, "Study Urges U.S. Aid to Chinese Military," *New York Times*, October 4, 1979; and see Safire, *New York Times*, October 4, 1979.

have no intention of changing our policy. We are not going to sell arms to the Chinese."[107] Vance was speaking in good faith, and indeed Carter had not decided to sell arms. But the president himself had disclosed on an unattributed "background" basis to newsmen the forthcoming trip by Brown to China. He saw the China card as his best resort when he had to settle for accepting the presence of the Soviet brigade in Cuba.

On October 16, in congressional testimony, Vance's adviser on Soviet affairs, Marshall D. Shulman, commented that "neither we [the United States] nor the Soviet Union are satisfied with the current state of our relations."[108] He then noted that "perhaps the strongest source of concern to the U.S.S.R. remains whether the United States will enter into a military supply relationship with China."[109]

In 1977 Secretary of State Vance had successfully drawn the line against supply of arms and military equipment to China in arguing against Brzezinski (at the time when PRM-24 was prepared), in 1978 at the time of the Brzezinski visit to China, and again in 1979. He was not, however, able to prevail on the broader issue of military contact and collaboration on intelligence. The initial steps launched by Brzezinski in 1978 were carried further in 1979. The later (1981) disclosure that agreement was reached in 1979 to establish U.S. intelligence monitoring stations in China has been noted. As the year ended, a dispute flared between Vance on the one hand and Brzezinski and Brown on the other over how far Brown should go in authorizing the sale of militarily related technology to China and, more broadly, over how *far* to tilt toward China.[110]

American-Chinese collaboration in 1979 was also evident in the support given by the United States (and the Association of Southeast Asian Nations, ASEAN) in the UN General Assembly to the Chinese-supported Khmer Rouge under Pol Pot as the legitimate representative of Kampuchea, rather than backing the Soviet- and Vietnamese-supported Heng Samrin regime. This was an unpalatable choice between the discredited genocidal Khmer Rouge and the Vietnamese-puppet successor regimes. Still, rather than abstain (as many Western European countries did), the United States joined China in supporting the Khmer Rouge.

There were, at the same time, some signs of divergence in American and Chinese policies in the third world. The Chinese, for example, welcomed the Iranian revolution (although they had had good relations with the shah) and the Nicaraguan revolution. Further, while the Carter administration be-

---

107. Bernard Gwertzman, "Vance Affirms Ban on Arms for China," *New York Times*, October 5, 1979.

108. Marshall D. Shulman, "An Overview of U.S.-Soviet Relations," *State Bulletin*, vol. 79 (December 1979), p. 40.

109. Ibid., p. 42.

110. Brzezinski, *Power and Principle*, pp. 423–24.

came estranged from Pakistan over its pursuit of an independent nuclear capability and over objectionable human rights practices, the Chinese remained in close support of Pakistan.[111]

Shulman, in his testimony in October, also reiterated the official preference for granting MFN status to both China and the Soviet Union ("we continue to hope that circumstances will permit favorable action in the same general time frame for both China and the Soviet Union"). But he also signaled the decision to go ahead—as Vice President Mondale had privately promised in Beijing in August—with the request for China, without trying again at the same time for the Soviet Union ("we believe it would not be reasonable to delay the China agreement for reasons unrelated to U.S.-China relations").[112] Thus an attempt was made to square the long-standing policy, favored by the Department of State, of treating Soviet and Chinese relations in tandem in an evenhanded manner with the new policy of giving priority to U.S.-China relations, a policy increasingly being substituted by the White House. One week later, on October 23, President Carter formally submitted the U.S.-China Trade Agreement to the Congress, with the Jackson-Vanik waiver to provide MFN status.[113] It was approved by both houses and signed into law in January 1980.

On December 31 the U.S. Mutual Defense Treaty with Taiwan expired.

As Brzezinski later summarized the situation with respect to American policy toward the Soviet Union and China as it developed over the year, "What had started as an exercise in evenhandedness by 1980 became demonstrably a tilt, driven by stark strategic realities"—as those realities were interpreted by and for the White House.[114] This trend was to be confirmed and given further impetus by the Soviet occupation of Afghanistan in the last days of the year.

---

111. In a curious isolated instance the Carter administration did criticize China on human rights (on October 15) because of an incident involving the sentencing of a prominent Chinese dissident to fifteen years imprisonment. But no punitive action was taken.

112. Shulman, *State Bulletin*, vol. 79 (1979), p. 44.

113. "U.S.-China Trade Agreement," October 23, *State Bulletin*, vol. 79 (December 1979), pp. 33–35.

114. Brzezinski, *Power and Principle*, p. 425.

22 The Strategic Balance and Military Détente, 1977–80

IN THE DEVELOPMENTS that led to the decline in American-Soviet détente in the latter half of the 1970s, various aspects of the military relationship between the two powers, and more generally between the two alliances, played a substantial part. It is necessary to consider several interrelated aspects of actual changes affecting the East-West military balance, perceptions of those changes and of their meaning by the two sides, and attempts to deal with the problem through arms limitations and other military détente measures during the critical period 1977 through 1980.

The Soviet Concept of Military Détente

The Soviet term "military détente," referring to the application of détente to military affairs, has been discussed earlier in the context of the general Soviet conception of détente and in terms of confidence-building measures and arms control in Europe, especially in the Conference on Security and Cooperation in Europe (CSCE) and mutual and balanced force reductions (MBFR) negotiations.[1] It is also applied to SALT and other arms control measures.[2] Indeed, one Soviet analysis concluded that "from the very beginning *political détente was interwoven with military détente to such an extent that military détente was the key point in political détente*. That distinguish-

---

1. See chapters 2 and 14.

2. For example, Brezhnev first used the term in 1973 in referring to the SALT process; the occasion was the second U.S.-Soviet summit meeting. See L. I. Brezhnev, *O vneshnei politike KPSS i sovetskogo gosudarstva: Rechi i stat'i* [On the Foreign Policy of the CPSU and the Soviet Government: Speeches and Articles], 3d ed. (Moscow: Politizdat, 1978), p. 284. For other references by him to military détente in the context of disarmament see ibid., pp. 306, 467, 701, 710, 732.

ing feature of détente in Soviet-U.S. relations remains to the present [1978] when the SALT negotiations and their success largely determine political relations between the two powers."[3] The reason given for that judgment is revealing: while the Soviet Union is credited with seeking détente (as exemplified in the decisions of the Twenty-fourth Party Congress in 1971) because of a foreign policy that calls for the pursuit of peace, it is held that the United States was led to a "more realistic policy toward the Soviet Union," to détente, and to SALT only reluctantly because the changing correlation of forces required that it do so.[4]

Soviet writers consider that "military détente is a relatively new concept in the theory and practice of international relations."[5] It is said to aim at the reduction and eventual elimination of military confrontation. In Soviet parlance, "Military détente is dialectically related to political détente. . . . By analogy with the well-known formula regarding the relationship between war and policy, we could say that military détente is an extension of political détente with its own distinctive means. Political détente comes first, preparing the ground for the more complex positive measures in the military field. . . . And in turn each successful step in the military field necessarily strengthens the general process of détente."[6]

Military détente was thus sought by the Soviet side in relations with the United States in the continuing SALT negotiations and in other arms control areas, beginning with the first summit meetings. In Europe, as noted, the conclusion of the Helsinki Final Act in 1975 was seen as opening the way for military détente.

The central security underpinning of détente has been the mutual interest of the two powers in preventing nuclear war. Soviet analysts nonetheless argue that "while the process of international détente assumes, as an essential precondition, the prevention of nuclear war, it does not end there."[7] By the mid-1970s Soviet observers found satisfaction in the fact that SALT had established "a certain formal codification of the Soviet-American nuclear balance" in order to maintain military stability, but they recognized that the Soviet Union could not rest on that accomplishment.[8] At the time that the

---

3. N. M. Nikol'sky and A. V. Grishin, *Nauchno-tekhnicheskii progress i mezhdunarodnye otnosheniya* [Scientific-Technical Progress and International Relations] (Moscow: Mezhdunarodnye otnosheniya, 1978), pp. 88–89. Emphasis in the original.

4. Ibid., p. 88.

5. B. D. Pyadyshev, "Military Détente in Europe: Two Approaches," *SShA: Ekonomika, politika, ideologiya* [USA: Economics, Politics, Ideology], no. 11 (November 1980), p. 6. (Hereafter *SShA*.)

6. Ibid., pp. 6–7.

7. G. A. Trofimenko, "U.S. Foreign Policy in the Seventies: Words and Deeds," *SShA*, no. 12 (December 1976), p. 27.

8. Ibid.

Carter administration took office U.S.-Soviet détente was showing signs of growing strain, although it was still largely intact. At that juncture an astute Soviet observer argued that "only major new constructive steps in the sphere of military détente are really capable of preventing a gradual slide toward nuclear catastrophe."[9] In the Soviet view these steps, as will be seen, included but extended beyond negotiated arms limitations. But before turning to the more far-reaching implications of military détente, it is appropriate to turn to the agenda for bilateral arms control negotiations at the beginning of 1977.

Carter's Arms Control Agenda

While the United States had not developed a concept of military détente, it had actively advocated and been actively involved in a range of arms control and security issues from the very outset of détente. President Carter had inherited the unconsummated Vladivostok accord on SALT, "ninety percent completed" until stymied by the politics of the 1976 election campaign, and SALT remained a keystone of arms control and détente. There were also the signed, but not ratified, Threshold (Nuclear) Test Ban (TTB) treaty and the treaty on Peaceful Nuclear Explosions (PNE). The MBFR talks on arms limitation in central Europe were stalemated. Apart from this agenda of unfinished business, the new administration also wished to launch an array of additional new arms control negotiations.[10]

When Secretary of State Vance spent several days in Moscow in March 1977, he sought not only to reopen the SALT negotiations, but also to expand the general American-Soviet dialogue and to propose joint consideration of a wide range of security issues. SALT remained the key element, although the Soviets flatly rejected the new U.S. SALT proposals and strongly reaffirmed the need to continue SALT on the basis of the Vladivostok accord and the closest later negotiating positions of January 1976. The two sides raised a number of other subjects, and it was agreed to establish new joint working groups to consider eight other areas of military détente (although that term was not used). In addition, MBFR was discussed, although without new proposals or movement on either side.

The Carter administration had mentioned several of the eight new subjects in earlier communications through Ambassador Dobrynin and in a letter to Brezhnev. Carter himself referred to several of them publicly in a press conference just two days before Vance left for Moscow. Some, however, were based on Soviet proposals or were subjects advanced by both sides. The

---

9. Ibid., p. 27.

10. One arms control idea that the United States and the Soviet Union had agreed to at the July 1974 summit meeting was concluded with the signing in Geneva on May 18, 1977, of a multilateral convention banning the modification of the environment for military purposes.

working groups were not, strictly speaking, to be constituted as negotiating bodies, but as bilateral groups to study the issues. Several became serious negotiations; two of the groups never met.

The eight working groups were to consider: (1) a comprehensive nuclear test ban (both a Soviet and an American proposal); (2) antisatellite weapons (an American proposal); (3) demilitarization of the Indian Ocean (both an American and an earlier Soviet proposal); (4) prior notification of test firings of long-range missiles (an American proposal); (5) limitations on the sales and transfer of conventional arms (an American proposal); (6) a ban on radiological weapons (an American proposal, derived from a broader Soviet proposal to ban new weapons of mass destruction); (7) a ban on chemical weapons (a Soviet proposal, but also long on the common agenda); and (8) civil defense (an American proposal). In addition, it was agreed to discuss further the problem of nuclear proliferation. Renewed efforts were to be made in the MBFR negotiation on limiting military forces in central Europe. The United States rejected a Soviet proposal to discuss a treaty on the renunciation of the use of force and of nuclear weapons.

The working groups on radiological weapons and chemical weapons began meeting in Geneva in May. By July 1979 a draft convention banning radiological weapons had been agreed to and was submitted to the multilateral Committee on Disarmament.[11] The problem of chemical weapons was more difficult, but the group completed its work later that year, and the subject reverted to consideration by the Committee on Disarmament.

The talks on a comprehensive test ban (CTB) were given special priority by both sides.[12] President Carter had publicly called for a complete end to nuclear testing only four days after his inauguration and had urged a CTB in his first letter to Brezhnev two days later.[13] Opened in June, the CTB talks were held on a tripartite basis, including Britain. In November 1977 the Soviet side made a major concession when Brezhnev announced a moratorium on peaceful nuclear explosions (later clarified as a three-year moratorium, but with prospects for indefinite continuation). This subject had posed a serious obstacle, given long-standing Soviet interest in and experiments with the potential use of nuclear detonations for large earth-moving tasks such as rechanneling rivers, and American suspicions about possible use of peaceful explosions for surreptitious testing of nuclear weapons. The Soviets also accepted the proposal for a treaty of indefinite duration. At this same time the chief of the

---

11. See Victor L. Issraelyan and Charles C. Flowerree, *Radiological Weapons Control: A Soviet and US Perspective*, Occasional Paper 29 (Muscatine, Iowa: Stanley Foundation, 1982), especially pp. 10–11 on the joint working group. The authors chaired the Soviet and U.S. delegations.

12. The discussion below is based on accounts by informed American participants in the CTB decisionmaking and negotiations from 1977 through 1980, including Ambassador Warnke and Ambassador Herbert F. York, the successive chiefs of the U.S. delegation.

13. See Zbigniew Brzezinski, *Power and Principle: Memoirs of the National Security Adviser, 1977–1981* (Farrar, Straus, Giroux, 1983), p.152.

Soviet delegation, Igor D. Morokhov, told Warnke that the Soviet Union was prepared to accept the American provisions for verification through national seismic stations on the territory of the other side and even through on-site inspections on challenge.

Prospects for a CTB had appeared good because of a clear interest on both sides. The Soviet move in late 1977 seemed to bring agreement near. Strong objections were raised, however, from two quarters in the United States. First, the JCS and the weapons laboratories argued that a complete ban on testing, including reliability proof tests on standard weapons, would pose risks to national security. Second, many voices in the Department of Defense and Congress, and many of those most distrustful of the Soviet Union, stressed the risk of less than absolute verification of compliance. These issues were debated publicly as well as within the government.

The CTB negotiations took a turn for the worse, in fact two turns for the worse, in 1978. In May the United States backed away from its own proposal for a CTB of indefinite duration, after the Soviet Union had accepted it. Instead, the United States proposed that the test ban be limited to five years. The Soviet side, although becoming suspicious, agreed to the five years.

The U.S. proposal, while intended to mollify opponents of a complete ban, had been made without the concurrence or support of the Departments of Defense or Energy or the JCS. In a Special Coordinating Committee (SCC) meeting on June 15, Secretary of Energy Schlesinger arranged for President Carter to hear briefings from Dr. Harold Agnew, head of the Los Alamos National Laboratory, and Dr. Roger Batzel, head of the Lawrence Livermore National Laboratory. Their testimony that the United States needed to conduct further developmental and proof tests of nuclear weapons, and that it might not be possible to identify very small yield Soviet tests, combined with the opposition from Brzezinski, the JCS, and (less strongly) Secretary of Defense Brown, led Carter to reverse his decision on a total ban on testing.

Accordingly, in September 1978 the U.S. delegation proposed permitting small nuclear experiments and also further curtailing the duration of the agreement to three years. Moreover, the United States was not able to define clearly the borderline between permitted nuclear experiments and banned small nuclear tests. And it wished the treaty to require renegotiation and reratification after three years rather than, as the Soviets wished, to be subject merely to renewal and extension.

What had begun in early 1977 as a priority American drive for a permanent comprehensive ban on all testing of nuclear weapons had by the end of 1978 become, through a series of reversals of position, a guarded approach calling for a short-term noncomprehensive limitation.

Throughout 1979 the American position continued steadily to harden.[14] The United States continued to change its position and backtrack. It

---

14. Coincidentally, the British position on the number of unmanned seismic stations to be set up in Britain for verification also changed. The British government, to the surprise even of the

now demanded that seismographs located in the Soviet Union for verification must be manufactured in the United States.[15] The American position was also changed to insist on real-time satellite readings of reports from seismic stations. The Americans even raised new issues on the preamble to the draft treaty, which they had said in 1977 would pose no problem. New instructions in 1979 required the U.S. delegation to reject the hortatory language on disarmament goals of a kind the United States had accepted in earlier agreements (and to do so despite British, as well as Soviet, urging).

The American delegation also had, as authorized, invited a Soviet team to visit and observe a seismic station in the United States. When, after six months of deliberation, the Soviet side accepted the invitation, internal bureaucratic bickering over financing (from whose budget the $25,000 required would come) and the scientific exchange agreements (none specifically covered seismology) forced a four-month delay in the U.S. response. In late 1979, after long internal delays in Washington, the United States also proposed that an American seismic station be established at the Soviet reactor center at Obninsk. The Soviets accepted the proposal a few months later. But as a consequence of the new tightening up on technology transfer to the Soviet Union after Afghanistan, the United States could not provide the seismographs and the delegation was compelled to backtrack and say it needed to study the question further. Later in 1980 both delegations had instructions not to raise the matter unless the other did so first, and the station was never established. Thus the United States backed away from this step to further its own proposal for national seismic stations on the territory of the other side for verification after the Soviets had accepted it.

The CTB negotiations, a promising early initiative that Carter at first believed would be a relatively easy and attainable step on the road to agreement on SALT,[16] became not merely stalemated but another cause of

---

British delegation, balked at more than one or a few stations, given the small size of the country compared to the United States and the Soviet Union. The Soviets remained adamant on principle that each country have an equal number of stations. Ten was the number accepted by both the United States and the Soviet Union. The U.S. administration did seek, unsuccessfully, to persuade the British to change their position. At the Vienna summit meeting President Carter even proposed to Brezhnev going forward on a CTB without Britain if necessary. Jimmy Carter, *Keeping Faith: Memoirs of a President* (Bantam, 1982), pp. 249, 229. But by then the principal stumbling block had become the ever-hardening American position.

15. The American delegation had earlier specifically indicated that the instruments could be made anywhere, so long as they met precise performance criteria agreed on. When this change in position was made known, Ambassador Andronik Petrosyants, the long-standing chairman of the State Committee for Utilization of Atomic Energy of the USSR and then head of the Soviet delegation, took Ambassador York aside, drew himself up, and said indignantly, "You must realize that we are not a sixth-rate Arab country." Information provided by Ambassador York.

16. By September 1978 the U.S. retreat on CTB led Gromyko to agree to Carter's observation that SALT should be given priority over CTB. See Carter, *Keeping Faith*, p. 231.

Soviet suspicion over American intent. The JCS and Secretary of Energy Schlesinger had opposed a CTB, and Brzezinski, too, had harbored strong reservations about it from the start. In his memoir Brzezinski candidly discloses, "Actually, I had relatively little confidence that we would make any progress in MBFR and CTB, and throughout the Carter years I was not very interested in these subjects. I saw them as nonstarters, but out of deference to the President's zeal for them, I went through the motions of holding meetings, discussing options, and developing negotiating positions. . . . I saw CTB as a likely embarrassment to any efforts on our part to obtain SALT ratification. I feared that our legislative circuits would become overloaded if we tried to obtain both SALT and CTB, but I respected the President's deep moral concern over nuclear weapons and I did what I could." That is, he did so as long as the U.S. proposals, in his words, "would not jeopardize our ability to continue the minimum number of tests necessary for our weapons program."[17] Secretary of State Vance and ACDA Director Warnke, while strongly supporting a CTB, accepted the president's decision to give priority to SALT. And CTB followed its retrograde path to stalemate.

Ultimately it was the decline in détente that made the political weight of those opposed too strong for the president to override. The course as well as the outcome of the CTB negotiations in 1978–79 contributed greatly to broader growing Soviet suspicion as to American lack of interest in arms control and preference for arms competition.

The antisatellite (ASAT) arms control talks raised a new and very important aspect of the strategic situation. The subject was prompted in part by renewed Soviet tests of an antisatellite satellite interceptor and by a last minute initiative of the outgoing Ford administration to launch an American ASAT program.[18] After raising the matter in March 1977 and gaining Soviet agreement to negotiations, the United States found that it needed a year to establish its position on the subject, including working out an ASAT research and development program.[19] By that time, when the United States had launched an antisatellite development program of its own, the Soviets were

---

17. Brzezinski, *Power and Principle*, note, p. 172.

18. On one of the last days of his presidency, in mid-January 1977, President Ford signed National Security Decision Memorandum (NSDM)–345 directing the Department of Defense to develop an operational ASAT system. The NSDM also called for a study of ASAT arms control options, but did not tie the U.S. development of an ASAT system to an arms control initiative. This initiative, while coming at the very close of the Ford administration, stemmed from a study initiated by General Brent Scowcroft, national security adviser to Ford, in 1975. Kissinger and Scowcroft had supported Defense Department desires to develop an ASAT and believed the United States should "arm to parley" and develop that military capability before entering arms control talks. This information has been provided by senior officials involved.

   The Soviet Union had tested an ASAT system intermittently from 1967 to 1971 and again beginning in early 1976. The United States had deployed two different operational ASAT systems in 1963 and 1964 but had deactivated them both by 1975.

19. President Carter was eager to open ASAT arms control negotiations and proposed talks in a letter to Brezhnev in February 1977 (which he disclosed in a press briefing on March 9). An

deemed to have a marginal but operational capability, publicly disclosed by Secretary of Defense Brown in October 1977.[20] Accordingly, the first meeting with the Soviets did not take place until May–June 1978 in Helsinki, followed by two other meetings in Bern in January–February 1979 and in Vienna from April to June 1979. A fourth meeting expected in early 1980 was never held because the Carter administration decided, as part of its retaliation for the Soviet occupation of Afghanistan, not to continue the talks.[21] The ASAT talks had not succeeded—an American attempt to get an interim agreement on a short-term moratorium on testing for the June 1979 summit was not success-ful[22]—but the talks had shown promise and had resulted in a largely agreed joint draft text.[23] Moreover, the Soviet Union unilaterally suspended ASAT testing during the talks, from May 1978 until April 1980, and made serious contributions to the negotiations.[24]

---

official study on space policy, Policy Review Memorandum (PRM)–23 was not launched until late March 1977, and a formal overall position on space policy was not established until over a year later, in Presidential Directive (PD)–37 in May 1978. By September 1977, however, an interim decision on ASAT had been made, establishing a two-track approach confirming uni-lateral development of an ASAT capability along with opening in parallel talks with the Soviet Union on possible ASAT limitations.

20. Bernard Weinraub, "Brown Says Soviet Can Fell Satellites," *New York Times*, October 5, 1977.

     Brown's estimate was based on the extent of Soviet ASAT testing from 1968 through 1971 and again in 1976–77; it also followed two successful tests. It was followed, however, by four successive failures over the next three years. In fact, nine of the thirteen tests since 1976 failed. The Reagan administration has retroactively ascribed an operational capability to the Soviet Union since 1971, when its first test series ended.

     While the Soviets probably now have an operational capability, it is of very low reliability and effectiveness. For their part the Soviets claim not to have an operational system deployed, and there is no clear evidence that they do. The one possible sign that they do was an ASAT launch along with deployed strategic offensive missiles in a multiple launch demonstration in mid-1982, although that ASAT interception failed. Both the U.S. contention that the Soviets have an "operational capability," and the Soviet denial that they have an "operational sys-tem," may be true.

21. Even before Afghanistan a split had developed in Washington between those who wanted an ASAT agreement and those who did not. Some saw signs of real progress; others feared that very outcome. In addition, the administration was led to be more cautious on the ASAT talks as a consequence of the difficult Senate debate over ratification of SALT II in the summer and fall of 1979. The decision not to resume the negotiations was facilitated, more than caused, by the post-Afghanistan curtailment of collaborative activities across the board.

22. The United States wanted only a short-term moratorium until its own program was ready for flight-testing. The Soviet Union insisted on a long-term or indefinite moratorium.

23. Agreement was closest on an accord not to *use* antisatellite weapons against each other's satellites (short of war), but more far-reaching limitations including a complete ban on testing and deploying ASAT weapons were considered to be attainable at least by some of the princi-pal participants.

24. For a general review of the antisatellite arms control picture, see Donald L. Hafner, "Averting a Brobdingnagian Skeet Shoot: Arms Control Measures for Anti-Satellite Weapons," *International Security*, vol. 5 (Winter 1980–81), pp. 41–60.

The planned working groups on notification of test firings of long-range missiles and on civil defense never met. The former subject was dealt with in SALT; the latter was simply allowed to die with no American follow-through after discussions were originally proposed and accepted.

Talks on limiting the transfer of conventional arms (CAT) began in December 1977 and continued until December 1978, when they, too, collapsed after an apparent reversal in U.S. policy and an undisguised battle over policy in Washington. The American proposal for CAT talks reflected President Carter's strong personal belief that it was necessary, and possible, to reduce the conventional arms race in the third world. The negotiations with the Soviet Union paralleled a similar unilateral U.S. policy of restraint on arms transfers announced by President Carter in May 1977, but also weakened over time.[25]

The basic problem was to define regions of the world where the two powers might be prepared to relinquish or curb this instrument of diplomacy. The United States proposed Latin America and sub-Saharan Africa as regions to consider; the Soviet Union wished to consider West Asia (including Iran) and East Asia (including China and South Korea) as well. The talks foundered on the inability not only of the two sides to reach agreement, but even of the U.S. government internally to do so. In early 1978 President Carter accepted a Department of State recommendation to consider specific geographic regions because of a desire to use the talks to engage the Soviet side in discussions on restraint in the third world. CAT was specifically related to the 1972 Basic Principles. Carter accepted the State Department's approach in preference to an Arms Control and Disarmament Agency (ACDA) proposal to begin the talks on a more technical basis, with the two sides jointly preparing a list of weapons that should not be transferred owing to their particular qualities. Having opened the door to negotiation on political issues, the president then decided later that same year to pull back rather than permit even discussion of regions politically sensitive to the United States. A serious divergence between Leslie H. Gelb, the State Department official chairing the American delegation at the CAT talks, and Brzezinski in the White House, over this latter issue broke into public and contributed to Gelb's decision to leave the government, as well as led to the collapse of the talks in December 1978. Even without this internal conflict the CAT talks were probably doomed from the outset, given not only the unresolved political differences between the two powers, but also the plethora of regional conflicts involving other powers and the existence of other important suppliers of conventional arms. But the way they were handled led the United States to abandon an initiative of its own to which the Soviet Union had responded favorably and responsibly.[26]

25. A review of the policy on conventional arms transfer had been launched on January 26, 1977 (PRM-12), leading to a Presidential Determination on April 16 and a formal Presidential Directive (PD-13) on May 13, 1977.

26. See Barry M. Blechman, Janne E. Nolan, and Alan Platt, "Negotiated Limitations on Arms Transfers: First Steps toward Crisis Prevention?" in Alexander L. George, ed., *Managing U.S.-*

Finally, the Indian Ocean demilitarization talks, which had begun in June 1977, continued into early 1978, but with any prospect of success overtaken by events in the Horn of Africa and later in Iran, long before Afghanistan. Here again the American position had not been thoroughly considered before the subject was advanced, leading to delays and to an embarrassing American disengagement from its own proposal for complete demilitarization (again, this stance had initially been proposed publicly by President Carter early in his tenure).[27] The formal U.S. proposal, made in the talks in October 1977, called for neither side to increase the prevailing level of its naval deployments in the area, to change the general pattern of deployment, or to acquire new bases. The temptations for propaganda exploitation (especially by the Soviet side) were great, and the real political situation too volatile, for technical arms limitations to have had much chance. Each side also sought to limit the other while keeping its own freedom of action. Indeed, opposition to the idea of arms control in the Indian Ocean area had grown within the U.S. government to such an extent that in the fall of 1978, after the Ethiopian-Somali situation had settled down, when the Soviet Union moved to resume the talks the United States declined. The Soviet navy had lost its base in Berbera, Somalia, and the Soviet naval presence in the area had declined to its normal level, while the United States did not wish to constrain its own freedom of action, especially given the deteriorating situation in Iran. Even so, at the Vienna summit meeting in June 1979 Carter again agreed in the joint communiqué with Brezhnev to reconvene the Indian Ocean talks. But the United States did not follow through. Even before the taking of the American hostages in Iran, in his speech on October 1 on the Soviet brigade in Cuba, President Carter went out of his way to announce that "we have reinforced our naval presence in the Indian Ocean."[28] The talks were dead.[29]

The panoply of new ideas for arms limitation and military détente placed on the agenda in 1977 was thus largely dissipated by 1979. Those that still survived tended to be old subjects again reverting to deliberations in multilateral forums (such as the CTB and radiological and chemical weapons), or

---

Soviet Rivalry: Problems of Crisis Prevention (Boulder, Colo.: Westview, 1983), pp. 261–81; and in shorter form, Blechman, Nolan, and Platt, "Pushing Arms," *Foreign Policy*, no. 46 (Spring 1982), pp. 142–50; Michael D. Salomon, David J. Louscher, and Paul Y. Hammond, "Lessons of the Carter Approach to Restraining Arms Transfers," *Survival*, vol. 23 (September–October 1981), pp. 200–08; and Andrew J. Pierre, *The Global Politics of Arms Sales* (Princeton, N.J.: Princeton University Press, 1982), pp. 285–91. For Brzezinski's viewpoint on his clash with Gelb see Brzezinski, *Power and Principle*, p. 175.

27. A formal governmental review was not even begun until April (PRM-25, dated April 7, 1977), and no definitive position was reached before the negotiations began.

28. "[President Carter's] Address to the Nation on October 1, 1979," *Department of State Bulletin*, vol. 79 (November 1979), p. 8.

29. For a more detailed discussion of the Indian Ocean arms limitation talks by a strong advocate see William Stivers, "Doves, Hawks, and Détente," *Foreign Policy*, no. 45 (Winter 1981–82), pp. 126–44.

were too sensitive to the general decline in détente—and to a lessening American interest in arms control—during those years for agreement to be reached (CTB and ASAT). The most important of these, CTB, also could not survive the political opposition and exploitable doubts about verification in the United States. The most promising new measure of potential significance, ASAT, was still alive, but faced increasing opposition in Washington. And then after the Soviet occupation of Afghanistan it too was set aside.

One additional arms control initiative that was *not* raised deserves brief mention. In early 1978 Secretary of State Vance and ACDA Director Warnke proposed to the president an initiative for negotiations on a cutoff of the production of fissionable materials for nuclear weapons, to be presented to the United Nations Special Session on Disarmament. Brzezinski opposed the idea and resorted to a time-proven bureaucratic means to derail it. He forwarded the proposal to Secretary of Energy Schlesinger (since the Department of Energy has responsibility for nuclear weapons production). As he expected, Schlesinger submitted a blistering assault on the idea. Brzezinski comments, "With his aid, I was able to nip this in the bud."[30]

In the multilateral arena, another aspect of nuclear arms control—nuclear nonproliferation—fared differently, as the United States and the Soviet Union shared a common objective. Accordingly, at the meetings of those countries that constitute the Nuclear Suppliers Group in London in 1978 the two superpowers saw eye-to-eye and worked together. There, as in bilateral American efforts to curb the transfer of nuclear technology, the chief problems arose from U.S. differences with West Germany and France over guidelines on commercial sales to other countries of nuclear power technology with inherent potential for contributing to the development of weapons. Soviet-American collaboration in curbing nuclear proliferation also extended to effective quiet diplomacy. In August 1977 the Soviet Union privately advised the United States government of information in its possession indicating that the Republic of South Africa was preparing to test a nuclear weapon. The United States confirmed the information, and quietly made very strong representations to South Africa. As a result, the test was not conducted.[31]

CSCE and MBFR

Other multilateral negotiations on arms limitations and confidence-building measures that were focused on Europe and inherited from the mid-

---

30. Brzezinski, *Power and Principle*, pp. 316–17.

The idea of a cutoff of the production of fissionable materials had first been proposed by President Dwight D. Eisenhower and had been the subject of private bilateral American-Soviet talks early in the Johnson administration. With the large stockpiles of weapons in both countries in the late 1970s the possibility of agreement seemed greater.

31. Information based on interviews with knowledgeable U.S. officials.

1970s continued, but without major accomplishment. At intervals from September 1977 to March 1978 the first follow-up meeting of the CSCE was held in Belgrade. The Soviet and Eastern European objective was to reinforce the climate of détente and to support it by incremental measures, in particular, additional confidence-building measures (CBMs) in the area of arms control. The Warsaw Pact members referred to this process as building military détente to complement the political détente represented by the CSCE Final Act. Some neutral and Western countries also advocated and proposed additional CBMs. For reasons to be noted, there was not, however, full discussion or agreement on any such measures.

The Western emphasis at Belgrade was on implementation of the Basket III undertakings on cooperation in humanitarian and related fields. To be more specific, the West pursued an offensive aimed at the shortcomings of and noncompliance with these provisions in the practices of the Soviet Union and other East European communist states. A protracted and rancorous exchange ensued. The Western position, which the United States had advocated the most ardently at both the NATO preparatory discussions and at the Belgrade CSCE meeting, was shared and generally supported by most Western countries. There was, however, some official and wider popular dissatisfaction in Western Europe with the concentrated focus on confrontation with the Soviet Union over the human rights issue. When the Belgrade meeting finally expired, there was considerable concern that the entire CSCE process was being weighed down by renewed American-Soviet polemics. The hope was that the next CSCE follow-on meeting, in Madrid in 1980, would prove more constructive.

The Belgrade CSCE meeting clearly established as a fact, despite Soviet objection, that the internal practices of the signatory states with respect to human rights, humanitarian concerns such as facilitating family reunification, and the flow of information and ideas would be subject to continuing international review, debate, and controversy. As seen from the American point of view this outcome was an achievement of détente. From the Soviet point of view it was contrary to the spirit of détente and reflected hostile designs that stimulated tension rather than reducing it.

One proposal advanced by the Eastern side at Belgrade, foreshadowed by the declaration of the Warsaw Pact a year earlier at its meeting in November 1976, was a proposed mutual undertaking against first use of nuclear weapons. The West dismissed it speedily, although Soviet sources have indicated that it had in fact been considered seriously by the Soviet political and military leadership as a response to the U.S. Schlesinger Doctrine of limited nuclear options.[32]

---

32. The Warsaw Pact proposal had been made at Bucharest, November 26, 1976, in the form of a draft treaty. See *Pravda*, November 27, 1976.

See also the discussion later in this chapter of a subsequent unilateral Soviet initiative on this subject.

Additional proposals for cooperative European security measures were advanced in other forums. At the UN Special Session on Disarmament in the spring of 1978 a number of countries proposed CBMs for Europe. France, notably, proposed a Conference on Disarmament in Europe to discuss CBMs to be applied "from the Atlantic to the Urals." The French later also proposed such a conference in the CSCE framework.

Beginning with the Warsaw Pact Political Consultative Committee semiannual meeting of foreign ministers in November 1978, the Soviet Union and its Pact allies proposed a number of additional CBMs relating to limiting the size of maneuvers, to observers, and to prior notification of military movements that went beyond the measures agreed on at Helsinki in 1975.[33] They also reaffirmed support for mutual force reductions. These proposals (with variations) were reiterated in May and December 1979, and in 1980 and 1981. Beginning in May 1979 they advocated a special conference on "military détente and disarmament in Europe." In October 1979 Brezhnev repeated and elaborated on these proposals, presenting them as a "Program for Strengthening Peace and Security in Europe."[34] But by that time American-Soviet relations (with East-West political-military relations in tow) had deteriorated to such an extent that these proposals were simply ignored.

The most active, if not productive, discussion of military détente remained the MBFR negotiations in Vienna on force reductions in central Europe. It is clear that while both sides have sought to reach an MBFR agreement, each has sought one that would improve its own military position. The West has wanted a greater reduction in Eastern, especially Soviet, forces in order to gain a parity that it has not been prepared to establish through its own military programs. The Soviet Union, claiming that parity exists, has wanted to retain the existing balance at a lower level and to prevent any reduction in American or other Western forces from being offset by a future buildup of the West German army.

The first new move of significance in MBFR since 1976 occurred in June 1978, when the Soviet Union made an apparent major concession by accepting the long-standing Western position of reductions to a common ceiling of 700,000 ground forces and 900,000 combined ground and air force personnel on each side.[35] The Soviet proposal also called for reductions of ground

---

33. On September 15, 1977, the Soviet Union had accepted an invitation and sent military observers to a NATO military exercise for the first time in many years, implying greater readiness to participate in such exchanges.

34. "Speech of Comrade L. I. Brezhnev," *Pravda*, October 7, 1979.

35. The new Soviet proposal was made at the 172nd plenary session of the MBFR talks on June 8 and was described in "On Very Important Negotiations," *Pravda*, June 9, 1978. For an analysis of this proposal and subsequent developments at MBFR see John G. Keliher, *The Negotiations on Mutual and Balanced Force Reductions: The Search for Arms Control in Central Europe* (Pergamon, 1980), pp. 73–95, 116–28.

force personnel and for reductions and limitations of selective armaments. It also accepted the Western preference to limit first-stage reductions to the United States and the Soviet Union. While this Soviet move marked a major step toward possible agreement, in practice it did not bridge the gap owing to a continuing important difference over the data on numbers of military personnel. As earlier noted, when the Eastern side finally produced figures on its own force levels in 1976, they did not match the Western estimates, a discrepancy that remained after 1978 despite the agreement on the objective of reductions to equal force levels and on what those levels would be.

The next major move was a new Western proposal in December 1979, replacing its proposal of December 1975.[36] The new proposal did not include a nuclear weapons element.[37] Reductions were proposed for the first phase on the basis of 30,000 Soviet ground force personnel in three divisions and 13,000 American ground force personnel, of which two-thirds would be in units and one-third a thinning out.[38] The common ceilings in the second phase would mean further Soviet and American, as well as Eastern and Western European, reductions—all predicated on prior agreement on the data on the levels of Soviet and U.S. forces. The new proposals were less extreme in terms of a divergence between Soviet and American unit reductions, but were still not equitable from the Soviet point of view. And the difference over current forces remained. There were also differences over several other issues, such as whether individual national forces would be held below existing levels (thus limiting, for example, a possible buildup of the West German army to compensate for reductions in some other Western force). In addition, the West had proposed more elaborate associated measures for inspection and verification of limitations on residual force. For the first time the West also proposed that these associated measures apply in the territory of the USSR.[39]

It is difficult for an observer to judge to what extent the difference in the data of the two sides, which amounted to about 200,000 ground and air force personnel (mostly ground forces, and mostly Soviet and Polish armies) reflect real differences in judgment versus efforts by one or both sides to slant

36. A more modest modification of the 1973 and 1975 proposals had been made in April 1978; it would no longer have required Soviet withdrawal of a tank army in the first phase, but still called for withdrawal of five Soviet divisions with 68,000 men and 1,700 tanks. Keliher, *The Negotiations on MBFR*, p. 84. On the December 1979 proposal see ibid., especially pp. 85–95.

37. Concurrently with the new Western MBFR proposal, NATO had decided to deploy new intermediate-range missile systems, one of which—the Pershing II—was to replace the shorter-range Pershing IA missiles offered in the 1975 proposal. Also, the 1979 NATO decision included a unilateral reduction by NATO of 1,000 obsolete nuclear warheads, withdrawal of which had been another bargaining feature of the 1975 proposal.

38. Keliher, *The Negotiations on MBFR*, p. 86.

39. Ibid., pp. 129–43.

the figures. The Soviets have not directly challenged the figures on Western forces, but have argued that some elements in the Western estimates of Eastern forces should not be included because those personnel perform the functions of nonuniformed personnel in the West. That fact is true, but it also constitutes an implicit Soviet admission that not all its men in uniform are counted, and that fact opens a large question of definition and judgment. The West insists on counting all active duty men and women in uniform. Regrettably, the question of defining the forces to be counted was not addressed before the data on force levels were submitted, and a technical issue quickly became a political one.[40] The Soviet military establishment is probably adamant on this issue because of its perspective on what is equitable.

Other issues may be resolved through compromise. For example, Chancellor Schmidt of West Germany proposed (in a speech in November 1979) that without accepting separate national ceilings it might be agreed that the forces of no country on either side should constitute more than 50 percent of the total force on that side after reductions to the agreed common ceiling. This approach would allay Soviet concerns about the Bundeswehr, while also ensuring that the Soviet forces in Eastern Europe not be increased through reducing one or more Eastern European armies. Also in June 1979 the Eastern side modified its formulation, although without changing the intent, to avoid national ceilings as such by requiring at least some reductions by each country in reaching the common ceiling.[41]

In 1980 both sides adjusted their positions. In July the Eastern side in effect adopted Schmidt's suggestion that no participant have more than half the collective level for its alliance. It also expressed readiness to discuss special procedures to assure that forces withdrawn not be reintroduced. Also in July the Eastern side, noting a unilateral Soviet reduction of 20,000 men, replied to the West's proposal of December 1979 by calling for initial reductions of another 20,000 by the Soviet Union and 13,000 by the United States. The positions were now very close on this point. In October the West replied that the precise size of the phase one reductions could be agreed upon when the data base and associated measures had been agreed upon.[42]

As the MBFR negotiations plodded along, each side turned increasingly to unilateral steps. The United States included as part of a NATO decision on theater nuclear forces the removal from Europe, as noted, of 1,000 obsolescent nuclear munitions it had tried in the 1975 proposals to trade under MBFR. And in October 1979, along with proposals for separate theater nuclear

---

40. Ibid., pp. 119–28.

41. Ibid., pp. 94, 117–18.

42. For a good general analysis as well as an account of developments in 1980, see Linda P. Brady, "Negotiating European Security: Mutual and Balanced Force Reductions," *International Security Review*, vol. 6 (Summer 1981), pp. 189–208. See also John Borawski, "Mutual Force Reductions in Europe from a Soviet Perspective," *Orbis*, vol. 22 (Winter 1979), pp. 845–73.

force negotiations, Brezhnev announced the unilateral withdrawal of 20,000 Soviet military personnel from East Germany to the Soviet Union.[43]

Nonetheless, unilateral measures to assure security rather than negotiations to enhance military détente predominated in the late 1970s. As the CSCE moved from a search for "confidence-building" measures to confrontation over internal affairs, and MBFR was stymied by the lack of confidence in official data and measures to assure implementation (more than over the force reductions themselves), concern grew over the nuclear balance in the European theater.[44]

Détente and Military Doctrine

Military détente, in the Soviet conception, should extend beyond the kind of specific negotiated measures discussed above to include as well unilateral modification of strategic conceptions and military postures. Without necessarily accepting the Soviet concept of military détente, it is appropriate to consider whether and how military doctrine should reflect policies of détente.

In a general sense many might agree with Brezhnev's comment that "it is not possible to combine for a long time the development of international détente with a constant increase in the military potentials of states, the improvement and buildup of arms."[45] Although this and other Soviet calls for restraint in arms buildup are addressed to the West, the basic idea is that states should exercise restraint in their military programs, both unilaterally and through negotiated arms limitations. The idea is one often expressed in the United States—although usually addressed to the Soviet Union, or at least to both the Soviet Union and the United States. The differing perceptions of the global strategic balance and the military balance in Europe, in the context of associated SALT and theater nuclear forces (TNF) arms limitations in the late 1970s, are addressed further in this chapter and two succeeding ones.

Military détente has occasionally been discussed in Soviet writings in terms of its relationship to military policy, deterrence, and military doctrine. The most explicit and potentially significant commentary was the unusual reportage on a conference of leading Soviet civilian (and some military) specialists on the subject of American military-strategic conceptions, which took place

---

43. Brezhnev, *Pravda*, October 7, 1979. This reduction was made and included the withdrawal of one Soviet division (the Sixth Tank Division). The Soviets, however, made other personnel adjustments in military units so that the net reduction may not have been 20,000. Subsequent Soviet submissions of new data to the MBFR talks (in June 1980) gave figures on the level of forces as of January 1980 reflecting the reduction, so it did not help reduce the discrepancy in the estimates.

44. See chapter 25.

45. Brezhnev, Speech of May 8, 1975, *O vneshnei politike*, p. 472.

at about the time of the Twenty-fifth Party Congress early in 1976. The focus of the conference was not only on American political-military policy, but also on "a number of important problems of Soviet-U.S. relations connected with the future of détente."[46] In discussing American military-strategic concepts it was stressed in the conference that "at present, in distinction from the past, the working out of U.S. military-strategic concepts is taking place under conditions when Soviet-American negotiations on arms limitation are under way." It was also noted that the main and "decisive" new factor was "the further change in the correlation of forces in the world, including in the military-strategic sphere." This change in the military correlation of forces was said to have led the United States to adopt such variants of doctrine as "limited strategic nuclear war"—the Schlesinger Doctrine on selective nuclear targeting or retargeting—and the general doctrine of "realistic deterrence."[47] Particular concern was expressed over the "extremely dangerous" risk of escalation inherent in "the aspiration to bring strategic nuclear forces into a war in a theater of military operations."[48] Moreover, "the accent on more active use of nuclear military power (even if on a limited scale) is *extremely dangerous* not only from the standpoint of escalation of nuclear war, but also *that it occurs in a period of détente, and that cannot fail to affect the political situation.*"[49] Similarly, despite an American acknowledgment that now "the use of military force is permissible only when it concerns the vital interests of the United States," and notwithstanding the "indisputable vital interest" in survival that had led the United States into "readiness to move from the cold war and confrontation to negotiations and détente," the absence of any American definition or even clear criteria for determining vital interests "obviously is no accident, since the lack of clear criteria leads to indeterminacies which, in the view of the Pentagon, should facilitate a policy of pressure and blackmail in crisis situations."[50] Another leading analyst stressed that the doctrine of the limited use of strategic nuclear weapons "in principle increases the probability of nuclear war, and even its theoretical adoption can have far-reaching dangerous consequences," including "the tremendous harm it is bringing to bear

---

46. The conference was an enlarged session of the senior staff of the foreign policy section of the Scientific Council on Economic, Political and Ideological Problems of the United States, chaired by Georgy A. Arbatov, director of the Institute of the USA and Canada. It included analysts of the Institute of the World Economy and International Relations (IMEMO) and other institutions not specifically identified, including military ones. The account of the meeting was printed under the title, "On Some New Tendencies in the Development of American Military-Strategic Conceptions," in *SShA*, no. 4 (April 1976), pp. 122–27. The phrase quoted here is from p. 122.

47. [Lieutenant General, Retired] M. A. Mil'shtein, ibid., pp. 122–23.

48. [Colonel, Retired] L. S. Semeyko, ibid., p. 125.

49. Ibid. Emphasis added.

50. Yu. G. Strel'tsov, ibid., p. 126.

against détente and in resurrecting international tension."[51] Academician Arbatov, who chaired the conference, stated in his summation that Soviet analysts "often only associate military détente with the limitation and reduction of arms and armed forces. It is necessary, obviously, to look on this question more broadly. *The concept of 'military détente' must, evidently, be extended to military doctrine and military-strategic concepts*, which are a most important component of military policy, and one of the factors influencing the arms race, both quantitatively and qualitatively."[52]

Clearly, the main thrust of the conference was on understanding and "exposing the dangerous military-strategic theories being formulated by reactionary circles in the United States, theories calculated to wreck international détente and the positive development of Soviet-American relations."[53] And it was rather clear, although implicit, that one way in which these American military doctrines were seen to be dangerous to détente and the arms race was by provoking or giving ammunition to those in the Soviet Union most distrustful of political and military détente with the United States and most inclined to see a need for strengthening *Soviet* military power.

There was yet another, extremely significant, aspect of the conference deliberations, and in particular of Arbatov's injunction to extend military détente to cover military doctrine: he did not limit this proposal to *American* military strategy and concepts. Détente, and military détente, after all, affect the actions of both sides. A dialectical approach would—while by no means equating the approach to the military doctrines of the two sides—comprehend military doctrines and strategic concepts of both sides.

There is reason to believe that Arbatov's extension of military détente to cover military doctrine reflected deliberations by the Soviet leadership in the period leading up to the Twenty-fifth Party Congress.[54] What is indisputable, in any event, is that the Soviet leadership did in fact soon modify its own authoritative statements of military doctrine and military policy in keeping with détente. There had been clear indications of a shift in the period from 1969 to the Twenty-fourth Congress in 1971, but they had been less discernible because the main change was a cessation of calls by the top political and military leaders for military superiority, and gradual adoption of calls for military parity and equality, especially in the context of the SALT negotiations.[55]

---

51. V. V. Zhurkin, ibid., p. 126.

52. G. A. Arbatov, ibid., p. 127. Emphasis added.

53. Ibid.

54. I have been told by two senior Soviet officials that Arbatov's statement "reflected" or "was made with awareness of" the highest level ongoing discussions of military doctrine. It seems unlikely that Arbatov was proposing a new approach and likely that the brief published reference to his remarks was a small tip of a larger iceberg of debate over the issue.

55. The standard military discussions of doctrine, as distinct from pronouncements by top military leaders, continued occasionally in the early and mid-1970s routinely to call for military superi-

Now, however, a new positive military doctrine explicitly renouncing military superiority as an aim of Soviet policy was being advanced.

Brezhnev himself unveiled the new military doctrine in a speech at Tula discussed earlier, given on the eve of the installation of the new Carter administration. He disavowed any goal of military superiority aimed at a first strike and reaffirmed an aim of deterrence:

Of course, comrades, we are improving our defenses. It cannot be otherwise. We have never neglected and will never neglect the security of our country and the security of our allies. But the allegations that the Soviet Union is going beyond what is sufficient for defense, that it is striving for superiority in arms, with the aim of delivering a "first strike," are absurd and utterly unfounded. . . . Our efforts are aimed at preventing both first and second strikes and at preventing nuclear war altogether. . . . The Soviet Union's defense potential must be sufficient to deter anyone from disturbing our peaceful life. Not a course aimed at superiority in arms, but a course aimed at their reduction, at lessening military confrontation—that is our policy.[56]

The Soviet position was spelled out more fully by Arbatov in *Pravda* shortly after the Tula speech. He vigorously refuted arguments that the Soviet Union was seeking superiority and accurately described in some detail areas of the strategic balance in which the Soviet Union was leading—the overall number of ICBM and SLBM missile launchers, and strategic missile throw-weight—and those in which the United States was leading—numbers of strategic bombers and bomber throw-weight, numbers of missile warheads, forward submarine bases, "and much else." Thus, he noted, "while enjoying an approximate equality (parity) in general, the two countries have within this

---

ority. One of the last references of this kind was in an unsigned article on "Military-Technical Superiority," *Sovetskaya voyennaya entsiklopediya* [Soviet Military Encyclopedia] (released for publication on July 20, 1976), vol. 2 (Moscow: Voyenizdat, 1976). The article posed military-technical superiority as an aim of the Soviet armed forces. The volume containing an article on "Superiority over the Enemy" carefully referred only to military operations in the field and *not* to overall military posture. See vol. 6, released for publication on October 10, 1978. In a major signed article on "Military Strategy," Marshal N. V. Ogarkov, first deputy minister of defense and chief of the General Staff, expressed determination not to permit "the probable enemy" to acquire military-technical superiority, but continued by affirming that "Soviet military strategy . . . does not have as its own objective the attainment of military-technical superiority over other countries." *Sovetskaya voyennaya entsiklopediya* (released for publication on September 7, 1979), vol. 7 (Moscow: Voyenizdat, 1979), p. 564. Emphasis added.

The confidential General Staff organ *Military Thought* continued in the latter 1970s to contain occasional references to "victory" as a theoretical objective if war came: "The main, decisive fundamental task of military science is to work out theoretical conceptions of the character and strategic content of war that imperialist circles may unleash, and for achieving victory in which our country and its armed forces must be ready." Major General N. G. Popov and Colonel M. I. Galkin, "Basic and Applied Military Science Research," *Voyennaya mysl'* [Military Thought], no. 9 (signed to press August 26) (September 1977), p. 43.

56. L. I. Brezhnev, "Outstanding Exploit of the Defenders of Tula," *Pravda*, January 19, 1977.

parity considerable differences (asymmetries) in various components of their armed forces, connected with differences in geographic situations, the nature of possible threats to their security, technical characteristics of individual weapons systems, and even in traditions of military organization." The main thing, though, is "the existence of an approximate balance, that is, a parity in the correlation of forces about which the USSR and the United States came to agreement with the signing of the principle of equal rights to security."[57]

Public acceptance of parity began to be stressed in early 1977, even prior to Brezhnev's speech, in political and military journals. For example, TASS political correspondent Yury Kornilov noted that "there exists parity, equality of military might. It is precisely this principle, the principle of parity and the principle of equal security stemming from it, that is steadily and persistently upheld by the Soviet Union."[58]

Again on the occasion of the sixtieth anniversary of the Bolshevik Revolution, in November 1977, Brezhnev returned to this theme, stating:

The Soviet Union is effectively looking after its own defense, but it does not and will not seek military superiority over the other side. We do not want to upset the approximate balance of military power existing at present . . . between the USSR and the United States. But in return we insist that no one else should seek to upset it in his favor.[59]

This was a more far-reaching statement than Brezhnev's earlier one at Tula, in which he denied an aim of superiority "with the aim of a first strike." His later statement denied superiority as a current or future aim for *any* purpose, including deterrence.

Many subsequent authoritative statements by military and political leaders since 1977 have echoed these themes of Soviet acceptance of strategic parity, equal security, the nonpursuit of superiority, deterrence, and the inad-

---

57. G. Arbatov, "The Great Lie of the Opponents of Détente," *Pravda*, February 5, 1977. He repeated this view in a broadcast interview on Radio Moscow on February 12. See Foreign Broadcast Information Service, *Daily Report: Soviet Union*, February 14, 1977, p. B3. (Hereafter FBIS, *Soviet Union*.) The fact that Arbatov was chosen to write the key article of guidance in *Pravda* indicates at least the role of military détente, and his selection is especially intriguing given his earlier pitch on this subject.

58. Yury Kornilov, TASS commentary, Radio Moscow, January 12, in FBIS, *Soviet Union*, January, 13, 1977, p. B5. Interestingly, some of the earliest statements appeared in the armed forces newspaper *Krasnaya zvezda* [Red Star]: "Who Sets the Tone?" January 12, 1977; and Yu. Kornilov, "Myths and Facts," January 14, 1977. See also, in particular, Colonel Ye. Rybkin, "The Twenty-fifth Congress of the CPSU and the Problem of Peaceful Coexistence between Socialism and Capitalism," *Voyenno-istoricheskii zhurnal* [The Military-Historical Journal], no. 1 (signed to press December 17, 1976) (January 1977) pp. 5–8.

59. L. I. Brezhnev, "The Great October [Revolution] and the Progress of Mankind," *Pravda*, November 3, 1977.

missibility of nuclear war.[60] Marshal Nikolai Ogarkov, for example, specifically cited Brezhnev's statement from the Tula speech as Soviet doctrine.[61]

There has been much controversy in the West over the Soviet attitude toward the concept of mutual deterrence. It is indisputable that beginning in the late 1960s in the Soviet military theoretical journal *Military Thought* (which is not available for public circulation) there was acceptance of the *fact* and the continuing *prospect* of mutual deterrence. During the middle and late 1970s there was also increasing public acceptance of this concept by Soviet political and military leaders and commentators. Moreover, strong support was given to using strategic arms limitations to bolster parity and deterrence.[62]

In terms of military détente, Brezhnev and others have sometimes criticized the idea of resting security indefinitely on a strategic balance of mutual deterrence. For example, in his speech on the sixtieth anniversary of the Bolshevik Revolution Brezhnev, after renouncing an aim of superiority and stating that the Soviets "did not want to upset the approximate balance of military power that now exists," went on to state: "Needless to say, maintaining the existing balance is not an end in itself. We are in favor of starting a downward turn in the curve of the arms race and of gradually reducing the level of the military confrontation. We want to reduce substantially, and then to eliminate, the threat of nuclear war—the most formidable danger for mankind."[63]

An early argument along this line was made in 1974 by two retired military men, General Mil'shtein and Colonel Semeyko, with the Institute of the USA and Canada. They stressed the importance of SALT and other Soviet-American agreements of 1972 and the Prevention of Nuclear War agreement of 1973, which they said were made possible only by "proceeding from *mutual* recognition of the fact that nuclear war would have devastating conse-

---

60. To note but a few by military leaders, see [Marshal] V. Kulikov, "Sixty Years in Defense of the Achievements of October," *Partiinaya zhizn'* [Party Life], no. 3 (February 1978), p. 28; [Marshal] N. Ogarkov, "In Defense of the Interests of the Soviet Motherland," *Partiinaya zhizn'*, no. 4 (February 1979), p. 27; N. Ogarkov, "The Myth of the 'Soviet Military Threat' and Reality," *Pravda*, August 2, 1979; N. Ogarkov, "In Defense of Peaceful Labor," *Kommunist*, no. 10 (July 1981), pp. 88–89; Marshal D. Ustinov, "Military Détente—A Demand of the Times," *Pravda*, October 25, 1979; and Marshal D. F. Ustinov, "Against the Arms Race and the Threat of War," *Pravda*, July 25, 1981. See also the additional later references in footnote 77.

61. Ogarkov, *Pravda*, August 2, 1979.

62. For an analytical discussion with extensive references and citations of Soviet sources see Raymond L. Garthoff, "Mutual Deterrence, Parity and Strategic Arms Limitation in Soviet Policy," in Derek Leebaert, ed., *Soviet Military Thinking* (London: Allen and Unwin, 1981), pp. 92–124.

63. Brezhnev, *Pravda*, November 3, 1977.

quences for mankind."[64] They argued that "the concept of 'nuclear deterrence,' which presupposes the existence of enormous nuclear forces capable of 'assured destruction,' is not an ideal solution to the problem of peace and the prevention of nuclear conflict." They urged moving forward on the path of détente, arms limitation, disarmament, and peaceful coexistence.[65] Another Soviet analyst similarly noted that "in principle [ideally], the Soviet Union objects to the preservation of peace by means of a 'balance of terror.' Genuinely lasting and firm stability must be based on a different foundation—namely, the eradication of mutual terror, suspicion, and threats. Military détente, based on far-reaching measures in the areas of arms limitation and disarmament, is the path to its goal."[66]

Nonetheless, Soviet analysts consider that the American loss of nuclear superiority in the 1960s that led to strategic parity and a balance, and the American recognition of parity in the early 1970s, "indicates that certain progress has been made toward a realistic assessment of the correlation of forces in the world."[67] The reason for the more realistic Western acceptance of strategic parity was not only that the United States had lost its previous superiority, but that military superiority had lost its former meaning: "Military superiority previously was of tremendous political significance and military policy was frequently based precisely on this consideration. Now, in an era when potential adversaries have built up nuclear arsenals of fantastic size, sufficient to annihilate one another many times over, this superiority in terms of 'strength' loses its former meaning. It does not open the way to military victories and it does not supply additional assurance of security."[68]

Soviet analysts continue to object to the Western preoccupation with military power and the military balance. "The making absolute of military strength inherent in the foreign policy of imperialism certainly occupies a leading place among the reasons for the slowing down of military détente," wrote one Soviet commentator in 1976. He continued: "Western political and military theorists consider natural that the process of international détente should take place against a background of continuing growth of strength. The theory of 'the balance of power' and the associated concepts of a 'balance of terror,' 'mutual deterrence' and the like . . . follows logically from this philosophy."

---

64. [Lieutenant General] M. A. Mil'shtein and [Colonel] L. S. Semeyko, "The Problem of the Inadmissibility of a Nuclear Conflict (on New Approaches in the United States)," *SShA*, no. 11 (November 1974), p. 4. Emphasis added.

65. Ibid., p. 9, and pp. 10–12. See also [Colonel] D. Proektor, "Two Approaches to Military Policy," *Novoye vremya* [New Times], no. 48 (November 1978), pp. 4–5.

66. G. A. Trofimenko, "Washington's Strategic Forays," *SShA*, no. 12 (December 1980), p. 57.

67. A. Svetlov, "The Struggle of the Soviet Union for Military Détente," *Mezhdunarodnaya zhizn'* [International Affairs], no. 1 (January 1976), p. 88.

68. Professor [Colonel] D. Proektor, "Problems of War and Peace: Two Approaches," *Novoye vremya*, no. 48 (November 24, 1978), p. 4.

But he also notes, "Of course, at the present historical stage and given contemporary military technology it would be incorrect to underestimate in the slightest the balance of military forces which prevails between the Soviet Union and the United States, and between the Warsaw Pact and NATO, as a deterrent to the aggressive proclivities of imperialism."[69] Thus while "objecting in principle" to "the political doctrine prevailing in the West according to which only a balance of military forces guarantees international security," at the same time "they cannot fail to take account of it, and hence their efforts to maintain an approximate military balance with the states of another system sufficient to meet the danger that upsetting the balance could be used by imperialist reactionaries to the detriment of socialism."[70] Hence, "Our [Soviet] military policy, together with our [Warsaw Pact] allies, must maintain a 'balance of forces' with the NATO countries" because "we cannot fail to take account of the fact that the balance of military forces has become an important condition for international stability and a necessary basis for negotiations on détente and disarmament." But it remains an aim also "to go further and gradually to reduce the present high level of the military balance, without destroying the existing parity."[71]

In summing up the accomplishments of détente in the 1970s, a leading Soviet diplomat and analyst noted that while "military strategic parity between the USSR and the United States became a realistic condition for securing peace and security," in addition "in the process of détente—and this, perhaps, is the most important thing—a start has been made on the formation of a system of lasting peace, a peace based not on the balance of terror but on equal security and trust." And for the future the task is to "eliminate tendencies towards acquiring unilateral advantages at the expense of the security of the other side, and to renounce aims of military superiority." Finally, "security, both national and international, and forward movement in the sphere of military détente will depend on how consistently that will be realized."[72]

Thus the Soviet theory of military détente, developed in the middle to late 1970s, is said to be based on preserving strategic parity and mutual deterrence while striving to move through arms limitations and reductions to lower those levels, and ultimately to replace a balance of fear with mutual trust.

The important shift in declared Soviet political and military doctrine to explicit disavowal of a quest for superiority and to acceptance of

---

69. [Colonel] D. Proektor, "Military Détente—A Paramount Task," *Mezhdunarodnaya zhizn'*, no. 5 (May 1976), p. 56.

70. Dr. [Colonel] D. Proektor, "Socialism and International Security," *Kommunist*, no. 7 (May 1977), p. 113.

71. Proektor, *Novoye vremya*, no. 48 (1978), p. 5.

72. V. F. Petrovsky, "The Struggle of the USSR for Détente in the Seventies," *Novaya i noveishaya istoriya* [Modern and Contemporary History], no. 1 (January–February 1981), p. 10.

deterrence and defense as means to assure security and to avert a catastrophic nuclear war has been noted earlier.

In Soviet usage, military doctrine is broader than the usual application of the term in American parlance. In the Soviet Union military doctrine is said to have two aspects: a political one, dealing with overall military policy, and a military-technical one, dealing with the means of waging war. The latter more or less corresponds to the usual Western definition. The most authoritative current Soviet military source laying down the definition and content of Soviet military doctrine is found in the *Soviet Military Encyclopedia* in two entries, "Military Doctrine" and "Military Strategy," in volumes published in 1977 and 1979, respectively.[73] They do not differ greatly in substance from similar statements over the preceding decade and earlier, but they do clearly bear the mark of military détente.

As defined in the *Encyclopedia*, "Soviet military doctrine is the system of guiding principles and scientifically-founded views of the Communist Party of the Soviet Union and the Soviet government on the essence, character and means of waging war" and on "the preparation of the armed forces and the country to defeat an aggressor." Brezhnev is cited disavowing any aim of superiority, and the Soviet policy of peaceful coexistence and efforts to avert nuclear war is stressed. Deterrence is clearly implied, but the main emphasis is on defense of the Soviet Union and its allies.[74]

The article on "Military Strategy" appeared in 1979 and was signed by Marshal Ogarkov. It constitutes an important source of basic current published guidance on military doctrine for the Soviet military establishment. "Soviet strategy," he said, "is determined by the policy of the Communist Party of the Soviet Union and the Soviet government, which combines the struggle for peace with preparedness to give a decisive rebuff to aggression, and reliably to defend the independence and socialist achievements of the Soviet people and the peoples of other friendly socialist countries. Soviet military strategy, as Soviet military doctrine as a whole, has a deeply defensive orientation, and does not provide for any kind of preemptive strikes or premeditated attacks . . . it does not pursue military-technical superiority . . . But any potential aggressor must clearly understand that in case of a nuclear missile attack on the Soviet Union or other countries of the socialist commonwealth it will receive an

---

73. The eight volumes of *Sovetskaya voyennaya entsiklopediya* [Soviet Military Encyclopedia] appeared in the years 1976–79. The editorial commission was composed of more than a dozen of the senior professional military leaders and chief theoreticians and was headed, until his death, by Marshal Andrei N. Grechko, the defense minister, and subsequently by Marshal Nikolai V. Ogarkov, first deputy minister and chief of the General Staff. The Encyclopedia is an authoritative official publication of the Ministry of Defense. Unnumbered page preface, "From the Main Editorial Commission," *Sovetskaya voyennaya entsiklopediya*, vol. 1 (1976). It was published in an edition of 105,000.

74. "Military Doctrine," unsigned, ibid. (signed to press May 16, 1977), vol. 3 (1977), p. 229.

annihilating retaliatory strike."[75] The article also states that "Soviet military strategy is based on the possibility of preventing war in the contemporary era," and it endorsed the SALT agreements.[76] Many other major articles since 1977 by Marshal Ustinov, Marshal Ogarkov, Marshal Kulikov, and other Soviet military leaders and theoreticians, in leading Soviet military and political organs, have stressed these themes of deterrence, defense, retaliation, parity, nonpursuit of superiority, disavowal of a first strike of any kind, and advocacy of strategic arms limitations, peaceful coexistence, and détente in discussing Soviet military doctrine, strategy, and policy.[77]

The development and exposition of the views of the Soviet leadership on the consequences of nuclear war and expectations of victory proceeded in parallel. The question is a complex one because Marxist-Leninist ideological expectations of the ultimate victory of socialism in the world have made it difficult for Soviet leaders to cast doubt on that victory by admitting the catastrophic consequences for all of a world nuclear war.

Soviet political doctrine had begun a significant transformation soon after Stalin's death.[78] A policy seeking to prevent war and pursue a course of peaceful coexistence has been official doctrine since the Twenty-second Party Congress in 1961.[79] By 1967 Brezhnev stressed, on the occasion of the

---

75. Ogarkov, "Military Strategy," ibid., vol. 7 (1979), pp. 563–64.

76. Ibid., p. 564.

77. To note but a few that appeared after the Twenty-sixth Party Congress in 1981, see Marshal D. F. Ustinov, *Sluzhim rodine, delu kommunizma* [We Serve the Motherland, the Cause of Communism] (Moscow: Voyenizdat, 1982), pp. 50–51; Marshal N. V. Ogarkov, *Vsegda v gotovnosti k zashchite otechestva* [Always Prepared to Defend the Fatherland] (Moscow: Voyenizdat, 1982), pp. 49, 55–57; Marshal N. V. Ogarkov, "For the Sake of Peace and Progress," *Izvestiya*, May 9, 1982; N. Ogarkov, "On Guard Over Peaceful Labor," *Kommunist*, no. 10 (July 1981), pp. 80–91, and especially pp. 85–89; Marshal D. F. Ustinov, "Against the Arms Race and the Threat of War," *Pravda*, July 25, 1981; [Lieutenant General] P. Zhilin, "Lessons of the Past and Concerns of the Present," *Kommunist*, no. 7 (May 1981), pp. 73–74; and Marshal D. Ustinov, "Loyal to the Cause of the Party," *Pravda*, February 21, 1981.

78. Some members of Stalin's Politburo even began to advance such views before his death. See Raymond L. Garthoff, "The Death of Stalin and the Birth of Mutual Deterrence," *Survey*, vol. 25 (Spring 1980), pp. 10–16. The first key development was the repudiation of the previous doctrinal tenet of the inevitability of war, providing a doctrinal foundation for the later efforts aimed at the prevention of nuclear war. See N. S. Khrushchev, "Report of the Central Committee of the CPSU," *XX s'yezd kommunisticheskoi partii Sovetskogo Soyuza, 14–25 fevralya 1956 goda: Stenograficheskii otchet* [The Twentieth Congress of the Communist Party of the Soviet Union, February 14–25, 1956: Stenographic Record], vol. 1 (Moscow: Gospolitizdat, 1956), pp. 36–38.

79. See *XXII s'yezd kommunisticheskoi partii Sovetskogo Soyuza, 17–31 oktyabrya 1961 goda: Stenograficheskii otchet* [The Twenty-second Congress of the Communist Party of the Soviet Union, October 17–31, 1961: Stenographic Record], vol. 3 (Moscow: Gospolitizdat, 1962), pp. 231–73. See also the discussion in Raymond L. Garthoff, *Soviet Military Policy* (Praeger, 1966), pp. 65–97, 191–206.

fiftieth anniversary of the Bolshevik Revolution, that consistent dedication to the revolutionary aims of communism in the world, precisely because it *was* based on confidence in the socialist cause, meant that "for its victory there is no need for wars between states" and that "Marxist-Leninists have always understood that socialism is not introduced from one country into another with the aid of military force."[80]

Such declarations should not be dismissed as mere propaganda. While a Soviet decision to resort to arms on the basis of a perceived threat or calculated advantage cannot be precluded, it is highly important to note that the ideology does not require use of Soviet military power to advance socialism in the world.

The "Program of the Communist Party of the Soviet Union" adopted at the Twenty-second Congress in 1961, while denying a need for war or its inevitability, did state that the result of a new world war would be a defeat for imperialism: "In the event the imperialists dare to unleash a new world war, the peoples will no longer be able to tolerate a system which plunges them into devastating wars. They will sweep away imperialism and bury it."[81] It is this ideological article of faith that has been cited by many Soviet writers, including military men, in the 1960s and occasionally in the early 1970s in predicting "victory" over imperialism if the latter should start a global nuclear war. The last such statement by a prominent Soviet leader, already an anomaly at the time, was by Marshal Grechko at an army-wide conference in early 1973. He repeated that if the imperialists launched a world war, "victory will go to us—to the socialist social system."[82]

By the mid-1970s Brezhnev and other political leaders began to state unequivocally that nuclear war presented "a danger to all mankind." Brezhnev made such statements on four occasions from July 1974 to June 1977.[83] In each instance he also stressed the policy of détente, peaceful coexistence, and arms limitation.

At the Twenty-sixth Party Congress in February 1981 Brezhnev said that "to count on victory in a nuclear war is dangerous madness."[84] Brezhnev's close colleague in the Politburo (and eventual successor), Konstantin Chernenko, speaking on behalf of the leadership in the annual address on the

---

80. Brezhnev, Speech of November 3, 1967, *O vneshnei politike*, p. 74.

81. From the text of the program; see *XXII s'yezd*, p. 271.

82. "Address of the Minister of Defense Marshal of the Soviet Union A. A. Grechko," *Krasnaya zvezda*, March 28, 1973. Analyses of other statements by Soviet military writers in the late 1960s and early 1970s show this same ideological, rather than military, basis for stated expectations of victory. The last authoritative statement of military victory as a requirement of Soviet military doctrine and strategy was by General of the Army S. Ivanov, "Soviet Military Doctrine and Strategy," *Voyennaya mysl'*, no. 5 (May 1969), p. 50.

83. See Brezhnev speeches of July 21, 1974, *O vneshnei politike*, p. 417; June 29, 1976, p. 545; November 24, 1976, p. 597; and June 21, 1977, p. 651.

84. Brezhnev, *XXVI s'yezd*, p. 16.

anniversary of Lenin's birth, stressed that "any nuclear confrontation would bring mankind incalculable calamities. It must not be permitted." And he noted that the "monstrous destructive force of weaponry" posed "a threat to the whole of civilization, even to life in our world. Hence the indisputable conclusion. It is criminal to look upon nuclear war as a rational, almost legitimate continuation of policy."[85] A year later, on the same occasion, Party Secretary Yury Andropov—soon to be Brezhnev's successor—noted that "the most terrible threat, the threat of nuclear war, has come to hang over mankind." He added that "war would bring victory to no one."[86] At a crucial Central Committee plenary meeting in June 1983, General Secretary Andropov declared that "any attempt to resolve the historic conflict between these [two world social] systems by means of a military clash would be fatal for mankind."[87] Gromyko reiterated that "there can be no victors in a nuclear war."[88]

Following an off-the-cuff comment by President Reagan that "unlike us, the Soviet Union believes that a nuclear war is possible and they believe it is winnable," Brezhnev repeated his statement to the Party Congress that "to try to defeat each other in the arms race, and to count on victory in nuclear war—that is dangerous madness." He then went on to add that "to initiate a nuclear war in the hope of emerging victorious from it can only be the act of one who had decided to commit suicide. No matter what might the attacker possesses, no matter what means of unleashing nuclear war he chooses, he will not attain his aims. Retribution will ensue ineluctably."[89]

Many Soviet commentaries have reiterated this position. Indeed, some diligent scholars rediscovered a reported statement by Lenin in 1918 that "there will come a time when war will become so destructive that it will be altogether impossible."[90] Whether in fact this statement (recalled later by Nadezhda Krupskaya, Lenin's wife) should be taken as a sign of Lenin's prescience

85. K. U. Chernenko, "Inspired by Lenin, Acting in a Leninist Way," *Pravda*, April 23, 1981.

86. Yu. V. Andropov, "Leninism—The Inexhaustible Source of the Revolutionary Energy and Creativity of the Masses," *Pravda*, April 23, 1982.

87. "Speech of Comrade Yu. V. Andropov, General Secretary of the CPSU Central Committee to the Plenary Session of the Central Committee of the CPSU on June 15, 1983," *Pravda* and *Izvestiya*, June 16, 1983.

88. A. A. Gromyko, "On the International Situation and the Foreign Policy of the Soviet Union: Report to the Supreme Soviet of the USSR," June 16, *Pravda* and *Izvestiya*, June 17, 1983.

89. Most American reportage of Reagan's initial remarks made on October 16, 1981, focused on another comment concerning limited nuclear war. The official transcript on the point emphasized here, and Brezhnev's comments from *Pravda*, October 21, 1981, were printed in "Brezhnev and Reagan on Atom War," *New York Times*, October 21, 1981.

90. Cited by A. Bovin, "The Lasting Significance of Leninist Ideas," *Kommunist*, no. 10 (July 1980), p. 78; and A. O. Chubar'yan, "The Foreign Policy of the USSR between the XXV and XXVI Congresses of the CPSU," *Istoriya SSSR* [History of the USSR], no. 3 (May–June 1981), p. 33.

is not of particular interest. What is of interest is that the Soviet leaders chose to cite it now in the party's chief theoretical political journal.

Military doctrine at the military-technical level was being adjusted with greater difficulty. There was a sharp decline after 1972 in references to "victory," which previously had been routine in discussions of objectives in a war if war were to come. Many statements have continued to refer to Soviet ability to rebuff and defeat an aggressor's attack. In explicitly turning to "the military-technical aspect of Soviet military doctrine," the 1977 article in the *Soviet Military Encyclopedia* calls, "in case an aggressor attacks," for "the conduct of decisive military operations using all the military power of the country and its armed forces." The offensive is characterized as "the most decisive form of military operations," although defensive operations might be necessary in some sectors before turning to the offensive.[91] Similarly, after stressing that "the possibility of preventing war in the contemporary era lies at the base of Soviet military strategy," Marshal Ogarkov, in his key article, also recognizes the possibility of "the outbreak of war" and the need to prepare so as to deter, or if necessary to wage, such a war. He states that if "a nuclear war is initiated against the Soviet Union" and becomes a protracted one, "the Soviet Union and the fraternal socialist states will have definite advantages over the imperialist states, advantages stemming from the just objectives of the war and the advanced nature of their social and state systems. This creates for them objective potentialities for achieving victory."[92]

These authoritative pronouncements on military doctrine and strategy have reflected a more explicit conformity of the political or political-military side of military doctrine with·the Soviet foreign policy of détente than previously, although Soviet military as well as political writings have always asserted nonaggressive aims. The military-technical element of military doctrine has continued to stress decisive, offensive operations once Soviet military forces are engaged in a politically defensive war. It also displays a reluctance to preclude the possibility of victory.

Thus Soviet military doctrine was made more explicit, if not modified, to accord with military détente and peaceful coexistence. In its political, or war versus peace, policy dimension, military doctrine was thus moving *away* from questions of waging war to place greater stress on preventing war, although its military-technical or war-fighting component continued to emphasize preparedness to wage war decisively, and with a particular accent on offensive operations and on being prepared to wage all-out warfare if nuclear war should come.

In June 1982 Brezhnev announced as a major new unilateral Soviet initiative a pledge not to resort to first use of nuclear weapons: "The Union of

---

91. "Military Doctrine," *Sovetskaya voyennaya entsiklopediya*, vol. 3 (1977), p. 229.

92. Ogarkov, "Military Strategy," ibid., vol. 7 (1979), p. 564. Ogarkov goes on to note that the potentials for victory also require "for their realization the necessary timely and all-round preparation of the country and its armed forces."

Soviet Socialist Republics," he said, "is assuming the obligation not to be the first to use nuclear weapons." He explained that "in taking this decision, the Soviet Union proceeds from the indisputable and determining fact in the contemporary international situation that should a nuclear war start it could mean the destruction of world civilization, and, perhaps, the end of life itself on earth."[93] While this declaration was made to the UN Second Special Session on Disarmament, it appeared in *Pravda* the next day, and was later confirmed as declaratory Soviet military doctrine.[94]

Two weeks later Marshal Ustinov followed with an article in *Pravda* that admitted that questions had arisen as to the timeliness (if not the soundness) of the unilateral renunciation of first use of nuclear weapons. He described the Soviet initiative as "unprecedented," as "exceptional, extraordinary," and as "a history-making landmark in the struggle for the prevention of nuclear war." But in light of what he interpreted to be "the growing aggressiveness of the policy of the United States," he also stated that "it was no simple matter for the Soviet Union to make the unilateral commitment not to be the first to use nuclear weapons." In a remarkable admission he said that "quite naturally, the Soviet people . . . are asking whether the right moment has been chosen for such a step and whether by this unilateral commitment we

---

93. L. I. Brezhnev, "The Second Special Session of the UN General Assembly," *Pravda*, June 16, 1982 (a translation of the text appeared in the *New York Times*, June 16, 1982).

94. Contrary to the general impression, this tenet was not completely new for Soviet military doctrine. Six months earlier, the Ministry of Defense had published a booklet in which it was stated flatly: "At the foundation of Soviet military strategy is the principle that the Soviet Union will not be the first to use nuclear weapons." *Otkuda iskhodit ugroza miru* [Whence the Threat to Peace] (Moscow:Voyenizdat, Ministerstvo Oborony SSSR, 1982), p. 12, and in the 2d ed., also 1982, p. 13. This booklet was first published in January 1982 (it had been signed to press on December 11, 1981). It was a further step in making a formal international pledge. For the English version see *Whence the Threat to Peace* (Moscow: Military Publishing House, 1982), p. 12 and 2d ed., p. 13.

Soviet officials have privately indicated that the subject of no first use had in fact been considered at high levels since the mid-1970s. The subject had even been raised publicly in the 1960s. In 1970 it was broached in SALT but not pursued when the United States took a negative position (see chapter 5). Following further discussions in Moscow, a new series of initiatives began after the Twenty-fifth Party Congress in 1976. In November 1976 the party chiefs of the countries of the Warsaw Pact, meeting as the Political Consultative Committee of the Pact, formally proposed a draft treaty banning first use of nuclear weapons. (The text is in *Pravda*, November 28, 1976.) In his Tula speech in January 1977 Brezhnev noted Western rejection of this proposal but reaffirmed Soviet support for a mutual renunciation of first use of nuclear weapons. (*Pravda*, January 9, 1977.) Since 1978 there have been conditional public pledges not to use nuclear weapons except in "extraordinary circumstances, aggression by another nuclear power against our country or our allies" ("Speech of Comrade L. I. Brezhnev," *Pravda*, April 26, 1978), and not to use nuclear weapons against nonnuclear states that had renounced nuclear arms ("Statement of A. A. Gromyko," *Pravda*, May 27, 1978). In September 1981 the Soviet Union had proposed a draft resolution in the UN General Assembly condemning any nuclear first use doctrines. (*Pravda*, September 24, 1981.) By mid-1982 the Soviet leadership decided to go all the way in renouncing first use of nuclear weapons.

are not incurring excessive danger for our people, our Motherland, the cause of socialism and progress in the whole world."[95] It is highly unusual for Soviet leaders to pose even hypothetical questions as to the wisdom of their decisions, and least of all on a question of national life and death. There is reason to believe these questions arose particularly among some Soviet military men.

Ustinov stressed the Soviet "duty" to seek "an end to the madness of the arms race" despite Western opposition, in view of the fact that nuclear war would be "a blow to all, a universal catastrophe." He stated straightforwardly that "the Soviet Union does not place its stake on victory in a nuclear war. An understanding of the impossibility of gaining the upper hand in such a conflict is also an argument in favor of the refusal to use nuclear weapons first." He then quoted Brezhnev's statement cited above on "the destruction of world civilization and perhaps the end of life itself on earth" and commented that "there is no place for any other opinions and evaluations if one takes a realistic and responsible view of the situation and does not walk in the clouds or engage in political speculation. People should look the truth in the eyes and not let the essence of what is happening be obscured."[96]

Ustinov specifically also discussed "the military implications" of the new Soviet commitment on no first use, including the impact on "the strategy and tactics of the Soviet armed forces" and on combat readiness, armaments, and improvement of command, control, and communications. The implications of a change in the political level of military doctrine were thus tied to a number of concrete implications for the military-technical level of doctrine. Finally, Ustinov dealt at length with the point that an aggressor would know that "the advantages of a preemptive use of nuclear weapons would not lead it to victory," and that with contemporary arms and means of detection "the United States would not be able to deal a disarming strike to the socialist countries. The aggressor would not be able to evade an all-crushing retaliatory strike."[97]

An authoritative Soviet statement of its military doctrine intended to influence the Western perception of its political-military posture specifically notes that "Soviet military strategy is neither immutable nor permanent" but "changes with the changing world." It goes on to state, "Soviet military doctrine, which has always been based on the principle of retaliatory, that is defensive, action, under the new conditions of the 1970s and early 80s not only says nothing about the necessity of victory in nuclear war, but even more emphatically than before stresses preventing war, maintaining the military balance, and

---

95. Marshal D. F. Ustinov, "On Averting the Threat of Nuclear War," *Pravda*, July 12, 1982. Ustinov was identified specifically not only as minister of defense and by his rank, as was usual, but also as a member of the Politburo.

96. Ibid.

97. Ibid.

lowering the level of military confrontation by means of military détente."[98]
Another similar authoritative presentation directed primarily to the West, issued by the Ministry of Defense, similarly states, "Soviet military doctrine is of
a strictly defensive nature."[99]

In weighing these passages, it is pertinent to note that although
their purpose is to influence Western opinion, they also reflect the development of Soviet thinking on military détente as expressed in authoritative internal Soviet statements, for example, at the three party congresses from 1971
(when the first mention was made of military détente) through 1981. Moreover, in addition to reflecting statements of party and state policy and political
doctrine, as earlier noted they also reflect authoritative internal guidance on
military doctrine for the Soviet military establishment issued by senior Soviet
military leaders.

During this period of significant change in Soviet military doctrine
at the governing political level, there occurred in parallel an upgrading of the
military role of Brezhnev and of the political management of the Ministry of
Defense. Ustinov, a veteran manager of the Soviet political-military complex
and party leader recently raised to the Politburo, was named minister of defense in April 1976 to succeed Grechko when he died. This change both removed a conservative old-line military man with encrusted views and tightened
Politburo direction. Ustinov was the first civilian named to that post in two
decades. Both Brezhnev and Ustinov were soon thereafter named marshals of
the Soviet Union. In January 1977 the more sophisticated Marshal Ogarkov
replaced Marshal Kulikov as the senior first deputy minister and chief of the
General Staff. In the new Constitution of the USSR as published in draft in
June and adopted in October 1977, the Defense Council headed by Brezhnev
was given constitutional status as a state organ. Brezhnev also became "president," chairman of the Presidium of the Supreme Soviet of the USSR, in June
1977. And in October 1977 he was publicly identified for the first time as
supreme commander-in-chief of the armed forces of the USSR. The conjunction of these signs of the increasing personal role of Brezhnev and of the

---

98. *Ugroza Evrope* [The Threat to Europe] (Moscow: Progress Publishers, 1981), p. 10; and in the
English language version (Moscow: Progress Publishers, 1981), p. 11 (the translation differs
slightly). A sequel discussed Soviet military doctrine in similar terms; see *Kak ustranit' ugrozu
Evrope* [How to Avert the Threat to Europe] (Moscow: Progress Publishers, 1983), pp. 7–20;
and in the English language version (Moscow: Progress Publishers, 1983), pp. 9–22. Both
booklets were published jointly under the auspices of the authoritative but not official Soviet
Committee for European Security and Cooperation and the Scientific Research Council on
Peace and Disarmament of the Academy of Sciences.

99. *Otkuda iskhodit ugroza miru*, p. 12; and for the English translation, see *Whence the Threat to
Peace*, pp. 11–12. These and other similar statements appear in the revised second edition of
the same title that came out later the same year, and in the third edition in 1984.

political leadership in military matters with top-level political and military articulation of a modified military doctrine was not unplanned.

It should also be noted that during the late 1970s the civilian institutes of the Academy of Sciences gained increasing scope to contribute to discussion, and ultimately perhaps to influence policy, on questions of military détente. Not only did the SALT process and other arms control negotiations of the 1970s lead to greater involvement and publication by civilians, but civilian political-military expertise developed. One step in this process was the establishment on June 23, 1979, just five days after the SALT II Treaty was signed, of a new organization to coordinate the work of institutions in this field: the Scientific Research Council on Problems of Peace and Disarmament. Its chairman was Nikolai Inozemtsev, director of the Institute of the World Economy and International Relations. His five deputies (each heading a section of the council) were also leading academic officials: Georgy Arbatov, director of the Institute of the USA and Canada; Oleg Bykov, a deputy director of Inozemtsev's institute; Dzherman Gvishiani, deputy chairman of the State Committee on Science and Technology (and Premier Kosygin's son-in-law); Evgeny Primakov, director of the Institute of Oriental Studies; and Moisei Markov, a physicist and veteran disarmament expert. This council sponsored new coordinated research and public information activities directed at audiences both abroad and at home.[100] Apart from propaganda, the work of this council includes making available to Soviet researchers and the public a wider range of information on the military situation in the world, and even discussion of military doctrine (coordinated with the Ministry of Defense), as in the earlier cited volumes on *The Threat to Europe* and *How to Avert the Threat to Europe*. Such activities represent a growing, though still limited, erosion of the previous monopoly on information and commentary on military affairs held by the professional military establishment.

While Soviet military doctrine was being refined in this way as part of the Soviet pursuit of military détente in the latter 1970s (and since), American political-military doctrine was moving in the opposite direction. Under "realistic deterrence" in the early and mid-1970s there had been a greater stress on capabilities for *waging* nuclear war—from the selective targeting or retargeting of the Schlesinger Doctrine of 1974 to PD-59 of the Carter administration in 1980. In one sense this focus may be said to mark something of a move toward greater convergence of American with Soviet military-technical doctrine, with its assumption that war-waging capabilities provide enhanced deterrence and a fallback should deterrence fail. But at the political level of military doctrine, the American espousal of limited nuclear war was seen by the Soviet

---

100. TASS, "A Scientific Council for Research on Problems of Peace and Disarmament," *Pravda*, June 23, 1979.

   Inozemtsev died in 1983, and was succeeded as chairman by Pyotr N. Fedoseyev, a vice president of the Academy of Sciences.

side as a move toward *use* of nuclear military power. Moreover, the United States almost completely ignored the Soviet move toward military détente. Even when noticed it was usually dismissed as propaganda or attempted misinformation.

Thus, Soviet doctrinal development in the latter 1970s can be examined under the rubric of military détente. By contrast, the contemporaneous, diverging change in U.S. military doctrine is more appropriately considered in the context of the reactions of the two sides to their perceptions of the evolving strategic balance. There was an array of arms control and arms limitation proposals advanced by the Carter administration in pursuit of its version of military détente. Nonetheless, in practice the most significant aspect of the Carter administration's arms and arms control policy, if not intended or even recognized as such by Carter, was the turn away from attempts to limit the threat of nuclear war by bilateral discussion, negotiation, and agreement (as exemplified in the Measures to Avert War by Accident, the Basic Principles, and the Prevention of Nuclear War agreements of the early 1970s) toward greater reliance on unilateral measures to enhance the American capability to survive, mobilize, and manage a nuclear war as an underpinning for deterrence and for an active foreign policy.[101]

The Strategic Balance: The American Perspective

As the Carter administration entered office, it found the ink scarcely dry on the latest National Intelligence Estimate (NIE 11-3/8-76) on "Soviet Strategic Capabilities and Objectives," signed by outgoing Director of Central Intelligence George A. Bush on January 7. This was the NIE that had been prepared with the assistance of the hard-line consulting Team B. And Secretary of Defense Donald H. Rumsfeld's final annual report to the Congress was released January 17, 1977.[102] Both presented an ominous picture of a So-

---

101. In an apparent partial and belated awareness of the emergence of this disjunction between arms control and military planning, in the wake of the SALT II congressional hearings President Carter issued a guidance (PD-50) in September 1979 (prepared and recommended by Brzezinski) that called for all measures in the arms limitation field to be measured against the criteria of military security and political aims and effects, as well as against arms control considerations. But it did not go beyond this general exhortation, and most members of the national security and arms control community were perplexed by the directive, which they believed only restated criteria long understood. In an interview Brzezinski has explained that the ACDA needed reminding. The directive could also be cited to members of Congress as evidence of the administration's dedication to assuring the compatibility of SALT II and all arms control measures with military security.

102. See Murrey Marder, "Carter to Inherit Intense Dispute on Soviet Intentions," *Washington Post*, January 2, 1977; Henry S. Bradsher, "New Intelligence View: Soviets Push Buildup All across the Board," *Washington Star*, January 16, 1977; Drew Middleton, "American Security

viet drive for military superiority, although as a goal not yet achieved. The latter report also set out an American military program to assure maintenance of a favorable balance. Major General George J. Keegan, Jr., the head of air force intelligence, who had retired at the first of the year, began a vocal alarmist campaign. He claimed not only that the Soviets were out to get superiority but that they had already achieved it. In a highly unusual move to balance this exaggeration of the Soviet threat, General George S. Brown, chairman of the JCS, speaking formally on behalf of the JCS, declared that the Soviet Union had *not* attained military superiority over the United States—but that "the available evidence suggests the USSR is engaged in a program to achieve" such superiority.[103]

In his first press conference, on February 8, 1977, President Carter sought to reassure the American people by stating, "At the present time, my judgment is that we have superior nuclear capability." After noting the areas of American and Soviet relative advantage, he continued, "I think that we are roughly equivalent, even though I think we are superior, in that either the Soviet Union or we could destroy a major part of the other nation." He noted probable losses of 50 million to 100 million people.[104] On February 24 in testimony to Congress, Secretary of Defense Brown reaffirmed the existence of strategic parity.[105] The judgment was reaffirmed in the subsequent annual reports of the secretary of defense and on other occasions over the four years of the Carter administration. But concern over the future remained and was to increase.

Several interrelated problems posed themselves: first, *assessing* the strategic balance; second, determining a *conceptual* basis for establishing American forces and capabilities; third, designing and pursuing American *mili-*

and Expanding Soviet Military Strength," *New York Times*, January 21, 1977; John W. Finney, "Assessing Soviet Strength Is a Team Task," *New York Times*, February 6, 1977; and *Report of the Secretary of Defense Donald H. Rumsfeld to the Congress on the FY 1978 Budget*, Department of Defense, January 17, 1977, executive summary, pp. 8–27, and main text, pp. 24–35.

103. Cited from General Brown's statement, submitted with a letter to Senator William Proxmire of Wisconsin, dated January 28, 1977. For press accounts see David Binder, "Air Force's Ex-Intelligence Chief Fears Soviet Has Military Edge," *New York Times*, January 3, 1977; and George C. Wilson, "Soviet Arms Superiority Is Denied by Joint Chiefs," *Washington Post*, January 31, 1977. For later press commentary on the debate see William Greider, "U.S.-Russian Arms Debate at Crossroads," *Washington Post*, February 20, 1977; and George C. Wilson, "The New Nuclear Math: How Much Is Enough for Security?" *Washington Post*, February 22, 1977.

104. "The President's News Conference of February 8, 1977," *Weekly Compilation of Presidential Documents*, vol. 13 (February 14, 1977), p. 157.

105. See George C. Wilson, "Defense Chief Cites U.S., Soviet Balance," *Washington Post*, February 25, 1977; and see UPI, "Brown Says U.S. Strike Capability Equal to Soviets,' " *Washington Post*, March 7, 1977.

tary programs to support the concept and to maintain the balance; and, finally, determining the role for negotiated *strategic arms limitations* as a supplement to unilateral military programs. Different senior members of the Carter administration placed different emphases on these issues and reached differing positions on the proper combination of measures to resolve them. There had been differences in the Nixon-Ford administrations as well, as noted, particularly over the role of strategic arms limitations. But the issue heretofore had been a relatively straightforward one of combined internal Pentagon resistance and outside political challenge as the limiting factors in determining how far the White House and State Department leadership might be constrained in pursuing a clear line of policy. Under the new administration there was from the outset, although it was not initially so evident, a four-way split between the president, his national security adviser, the secretary of state, and the secretary of defense.

President Carter's personal inclination and hopes were very different from the policy that emerged and developed during his administration. As was reported at the time (by opponents to whom it was quickly leaked), even before he formally took office he requested a study by the Pentagon on the possibility of reverting to a "minimum deterrence" capability, perhaps limited to 200–250 submarine-launched ballistic missiles—not, of course, on a unilateral basis, but as the possible goal of a negotiated deep reduction of strategic forces by both the United States and the Soviet Union.[106] The idea was soon dropped, but it was indicative of Carter's own personal inclinations.

On his inauguration day President Carter approved a proposal by his national security affairs adviser, Brzezinski, for a comprehensive assessment of the Soviet-American global power relationship, including their relative military but also political and economic strengths. PRM-10, issued on February 18, 1977, was conducted under Brzezinski's guidance.[107] It was completed in June and was followed by a series of meetings of the cabinet-level Special Coordinating Committee chaired by Brzezinski and including Secretary of State Vance and Secretary of Defense Brown. In August President Carter signed PD-18. It reaffirmed as the American objective maintenance of "essential equivalence" in the strategic balance with the USSR. Strategic nuclear weapons employment doctrine was dealt with only tentatively, subject to further study (sharply differing views having been advanced). But PD-18 did reaffirm the Nixon administration's NSDM-242 (the Schlesinger Doctrine) pending "further guidance for structuring the U.S. strategic posture." It also reiterated a secure

---

106. The key leak was to Rowland Evans and Robert Novak, "Carter's 200 Missiles," *Washington Post*, February 12, 1977. See also Edward Walsh and George C. Wilson, "Carter to Get Study on A-Deterrence," *Washington Post*, January 28, 1977.

107. The PRM-10 study, launched on February 18, was prepared in two parts. One was a review of the U.S. force posture conducted in the Department of Defense, the other a comprehensive net assessment of military, economic, political-ideological, and diplomatic factors prepared by the NSC staff.

retaliatory capability as the bedrock of American strategic power and, more explicitly than heretofore, directed that a "secure reserve" of strategic forces be maintained for use if nuclear war became protracted. It further declared that U.S. strategic forces should be sufficiently strong not only to retaliate but also to ensure that a possible nuclear war would end on the most favorable terms possible for the United States.[108] All in all, PD-18 represented a fairly major step toward prescribing a war-waging capability for the purpose of reinforcing deterrence, which it did by providing a resort if deterrence should fail.

The further studies on nuclear targeting called for in PD-18 led to increased attention to American command, control, communications, and intelligence (C³I) and generally endorsed and continued the more flexible selective targeting policy developed under Schlesinger.

The second step in developing a new strategic doctrine and posture was PRM-32, begun in September 1977, which addressed civil defense in the strategic balance. It led to a number of presidential directives and decisions (PD-22 in October 1977, another decision in June 1978, and finally PD-41 in September 1978). The relatively modest proposals for civil defense preparations, exaggerated in the press accounts, were in any case not sustained in Congress, and the civil defense picture remained virtually unchanged. The eclipse of civil defense in unilateral planning was accompanied by quietly dropping the idea of bilateral discussions that the Soviet Union had agreed to when it had been proposed in March 1977.

PD-53, issued in November 1979, addressed the problem of C³I identified in the earlier PD-18 studies. It was directed at securing telecommunications *after* a nuclear war had begun, thus directly supporting a war-waging concept.[109]

PD-57, signed in March 1980, addressed requirements for economic mobilization—marking the first serious attention to this problem since 1961. Again, planning for mobilization was directed at advance steps to support a wartime mobilization "surge" and survivability in nuclear war.

PD-58, issued in June 1980, was aimed at protecting the continuity of government in wartime—in particular the survivability of the National Command Authorities (the president and his designated successors as commander-in-chief).

---

108. For an account of PRM-10, PD-18, and related developments on doctrine for strategic nuclear employment in 1977–78, see Desmond Ball, *Developments in U.S. Strategic Nuclear Policy under the Carter Administration*, ACIS Working Paper 21 (University of California–Los Angeles, Center for International and Security Affairs, February 1980), pp. 1–23. For initial press leaks see Robert G. Kaiser, "Disputed Memo Assesses U.S., Soviet Strength," *Washington Post*, July 6, 1977; and Charles Mohr, "Carter Orders Steps to Increase Ability to Meet War Threats: Secret Directive on Strategy," *New York Times*, August 26, 1977.

109. Incidentally, the upgrading of the Moscow-Washington Direct Communications Link (hot line) to a system of satellite communications, agreed upon in the early arms control phase of SALT I in 1971, became operational on January 16, 1978.

Finally, and most notoriously, there was PD-59, signed by the president on July 25, 1980. Its substance was promptly—and deliberately—leaked to the press (unlike PD 41, 53, 57, and 58). PD 59 set forth the basis for a "countervailing strategy" (Secretary of Defense Brown's term, which he had used earlier), which sought to integrate the acquisition of strategic forces and strategic nuclear employment doctrine on the basis of a war-fighting capability and concept.

In one sense PD-59 appears to have been an attempt to replicate what at least some of its authors believed to be the *Soviet* war-fighting strategic concept—on the assumption such a concept would better deter the Soviet Union as well as provide a recourse for waging "slow-motion" limited nuclear war if deterrence failed. In addition, by implication though not explicitly, it called for superiority in order to dominate the calculation of the consequences of escalation for purposes of deterring war and to dominate actual steps in escalation in "intra-war deterrence" in the event of a war.

PD-59 (as is true of the others) has not been declassified and released, so that commentary, and both American public and Soviet understanding of the underlying concepts, must rest on the public record.[110] In presenting these concepts to the public in background briefings and in public speeches (the main one being Secretary of Defense Brown's speech of August 20, 1980, to the Naval War College), the emphasis was placed on the evolution of policy from the prior American strategic doctrine and on the goal of elaborating a countervailing deterrent. The policy was directed in part at what the United States perceived to be Soviet *views* on the relationship of war-waging capabilities to deterrence. This aim was reasonable inasmuch as perceptions underlie deterrence (although this approach may have unintended negative effects if the U.S. perception of Soviet views is incorrect). But the underlying concept was also directed at threatening what the United States perceived to be vital Soviet *interests*—including the whole structure of political control in the Soviet Union. While that concept may also be conceived as a deterrent, the Soviet leaders were prone to see it as U.S. pursuit of a war-waging capability to support intimidation or even the initiation of war. The policy was, therefore, a very sharply double-edged sword—particularly when used to support the acquisition of counterforce capabilities.

Brzezinski and Brown had (through their staffs) collaborated on the preparation of the series of studies on strategic doctrine and policy, but their interests and views were not identical. Brown placed much more emphasis on developing concepts and forces to maintain a balance for countervailing *deter-*

---

110. See in particular *Nuclear War Strategy*, Hearing before the Senate Committee on Foreign Relations on Presidential Directive 59 (September 16, 1980), 96 Cong. 2 sess. (Washington D.C.: Government Printing Office, 1981). The hearing was top secret, but this declassified version of the report was issued on February 18, 1981.

rence, while Brzezinski placed more stress on a *war-fighting* concept and capability, albeit in support of deterrence and other foreign policy aims.[111] There was sufficient congruence to present agreed recommendations to the president, and Carter increasingly came to support these policies over the period from 1978 to 1980 as relations with the Soviet Union deteriorated and the prospects for military détente receded. But the differences remained. Meanwhile, Secretary of State Vance, and later his successor, Edmund S. Muskie, came to play less and less of a role in determining strategy. Their eclipse ultimately became embarrassingly clear when it was learned that Secretary Muskie had not even been informed of PD-59 before it was signed and its main lines leaked to the press.[112]

The final stage of this development of military policy was a further codification of the new strategic doctrine in PD-62, issued in January 1981 just days before the close of the Carter administration and not disclosed in the press. It had been advanced by Brzezinski and was a legacy to the succeeding administration.[113]

Paralleling the development of a war-waging strategic concept and its articulation as declared policy, the United States began to move toward acquiring a war-waging counterforce capability.

---

111. Interviews with Brzezinski, Brown, and others.

Brzezinski has, since leaving office, referred to his active role in the modernization of American military doctrine, from 1978 to 1980, including PD-59, which he has characterized as "moving us towards a war-fighting doctrine." See Zbigniew Brzezinski, "The Best National Security System," *Washington Quarterly*, vol. 5 (Winter 1982), p. 79; and see George Urban, "The Perils of Foreign Policy: A Long Conversation with Dr. Zbigniew Brzezinski," *Encounter*, vol. 56 (May 1981), p. 20.

Brown has subsequently stated that in addition to a doctrinal modification to enhance deterrence, "the Carter Administration attempted to use this modest refinement in US nuclear strategy as a response to charges that the USSR had achieved strategic nuclear superiority." He concludes that "to a degree, this backfired. It encouraged widespread though mistaken interpretations by the public and by some experts in the United States and Europe that PD-59 signified a major step toward a strategy and plan for fighting a limited nuclear war. Moreover, few hardliners were impressed. Thus the handling of PD-59, by trying to gain the support of conflicting constituencies, lost more than it gained." Moreover, although he does not mention Brzezinski by name, he adds: "Overstatements by some officials, in describing PD-59, of belief in the feasibility of fighting nuclear war helped to increase public fears that governments take the prospect of nuclear war lightly." See Harold Brown, "Domestic Consensus and Nuclear Deterrence," in *Defence and Consensus: The Domestic Aspects of Western Security*, pt. 2, Adelphi Paper 183 (London: International Institute for Strategic Studies, 1983), pp. 21–22.

112. Secretary of State Muskie had been provided with a briefing book but had not yet read it when the story leaked and he was asked about it by the press. Nonetheless, while he had not intentionally been kept ignorant of the decision, he had not been consulted on it prior to its adoption.

113. See Brzezinski, *Power and Principle*, p. 469.

The Carter administration had entered office with a campaign pledge to reduce the military budget and with a widespread expectation that less emphasis would be placed on military considerations in policy. The initial budget action called for a decrease in military spending as projected by the outgoing administration, but in absolute terms it was an increase over the previous Ford budget (although largely offset by inflation). But any question of military retrenchment was soon dropped.

One of President Carter's early decisions, announced on June 30, was not to produce the B-1 bomber but to rely instead on long-range air-launched cruise missiles (ALCMs), initially deployed on refurbished B-52 bombers. He also decided to close down the production line for the Minuteman III ICBM, no longer needed as the planned buildup to 550 was completed. But the most significant decision in 1977 provoked relatively little attention or debate—the decision to deploy the Mark-12A warhead with the NS-20 guidance system on 300 of the Minuteman III missiles. This system had been ordered into production by Secretary of Defense Rumsfeld just one week before he left office (as was development of the ALCM and SLCM cruise missiles just two days before the inauguration). In late May the decision on the Mk-12A warhead was confirmed by the Carter administration. While there was a flurry of comment, this action did not generate the same wide interest as canceling the B-1 had or as deploying some entirely new missile system would have. But it was highly significant: it marked a major step in acquiring counterforce capabilities against Soviet ICBM silos and other hardened targets.

During the years 1977–79 American programs for acquisition of strategic counterforce capabilities became more and more extensive and comprehensive. The MX ICBM, approved by President Carter just one week before the signature of the SALT II Treaty in June 1979, was the most significant in its potential, while the Trident II (D-5) submarine-launched ballistic missile (SLBM) planned for the 1990s would combine greater invulnerability with precision counterforce capability.

The American leaders and informed public generally viewed the ongoing Soviet deployment of the SS-17, SS-18, and SS-19 ICBMs with MIRVs as threatening to give the Soviet Union a degree of strategic superiority, owing to the potential vulnerability of the entire U.S. Minuteman (1,000) and Titan II (54) ICBM force. In the fall of 1977 Soviet tests of the SS-18 and SS-19 disclosed much-improved accuracy, which increased their counterforce capabilities. Particular attention was given to the SS-18, which began to be deployed in the mid-1970s as a replacement for the large SS-9, which did not have MIRVs. Some 210 of the 308 SS-18s under the SALT I limits could theoretically destroy nearly all of the 1,054 American ICBMs in a first strike (assuming these missiles were not launched while the Soviet attack was under way). The fact that under such a scenario the Soviet Union would be left with 1,000 ICBMs while the United States would have virtually none was judged an unacceptable risk. The possible Soviet incentive to launch a first strike posed a possible American dilemma. It could destroy Soviet cities with its large remaining

SLBM force, but might then suffer a Soviet retaliation that would destroy its own cities. Or it could forgo that response and in effect capitulate to whatever the Soviets did in Eurasia.

There are many serious questions about the likelihood and significance of such a scenario. Technical questions about operational performance cast doubt on the ability of the Soviet Union (or any country) to mount such an attack successfully—the fact that ICBMs have never been tested in operational polar vectors, the "fratricidal" destructive effects of the first exploding warheads on incoming warheads, coordination of firing different kinds of systems, uncontrollable electromagnetic and other effects, and other unknowns. Further, even if these technical difficulties could be overcome, a potential attacker could never be sure that the enemy's missile force would not be launched on warning of the massive incoming attack. Nor could he afford to discount either the likelihood or the effect of the launch of all surviving bomber, SLBM, and other forces capable of striking in retaliation. Success would be highly problematic and doubtful at best.

Nonetheless, for political as well as military reasons the Carter administration (and its predecessors and successor) have concluded that it is not prudent to discount conceivable Soviet political and military moves based on some calculation of gain from the possession of a capability that the United States does not also possess. This qualification is significant, because the American response in this situation has been to seek both to reduce the vulnerability of the land-based ICBM component of the traditional U.S. triad of land, air, and sea-based strategic forces, *and* to counter anticipated Soviet possession of a counterforce capability by attainment of an *American* counterforce capability. In terms of the scenario outlined earlier, this approach would mean that not only would the United States not lose its entire ICBM force, it would also retain a capability to retaliate against the withheld Soviet ICBM force rather than only against the Soviet polity, economy, and population. But while it is possible to argue that counterforce capabilities have a retaliatory role, there is no way to allay suspicions that their real purpose is a first-strike capability, as Americans should recognize from their own reaction to increasing Soviet capabilities.

American concern about the strategic balance has thus focused above all on the prospective vulnerability by the middle or even early 1980s of the U.S. ICBM force—up to 95 percent could be destroyed if the technical obstacles could be overcome to an irreducible minimum. And throughout the latter half of the 1970s the Soviet Union continued steadily to deploy a new generation of ICBMs with MIRV warheads and improved accuracy, as well as to deploy improved longer-range SLBMs, later also with MIRVs.

Contrary to the charges of some opponents of the SALT agreements, the United States did not underestimate the pace of Soviet deployment of MIRVs when it negotiated the SALT I agreements. Indeed, estimates in the early 1970s assumed earlier testing of MIRVs than occurred, although later projections of improvements in accuracy were underestimated. The prospect of vulnerability of U.S. ICBMs some time by the mid-1980s had been recognized throughout. The first Soviet ICBM MIRV test occurred in 1973, and deployment of ICBMs with MIRVs began only in 1975. By the end of the decade the Soviet Union was well on the way to completing the deployment of the SS-17, -18, and -19 ICBMs with MIRVs[114] and was proceeding apace with the SS-N-18, a SLBM with MIRVs, and the SS-20, an IRBM with MIRVs. Thus in the middle and late 1970s the Soviets proceeded steadily to convert about 150 ICBM launchers a year to new systems, a process they had virtually completed by the end of 1981. Meanwhile, the 209 launchers for the older large SS-7 and SS-8 ICBMs were dismantled, and by 1975 dismantling or conversion of older ballistic missile submarines began in order to remain within the SALT I SLBM (and associated SSBN submarine) limits.

Although fully anticipated, the continuing Soviet deployment of more modern ICBMs and the increasing numbers of warheads were often cited in American commentary as an ominous development, a "relentless" buildup. In fact, it was *less* than the parallel American buildup in MIRV warheads during the 1970s. The American lead in absolute numbers of strategic bombs and warheads actually widened between 1970 and 1980.

SALT was supposed to have provided assurance to both sides that the strategic arms competition would be limited. And it did. Both the United States and the Soviet Union could count with substantial assurance on the other side not exceeding the agreed limits—and despite the formal lapse of the SALT I Interim Agreement in 1977 and the nonratification of SALT II since 1979, those limits have been held to (except for the reductions the Soviets would have had to effect in older systems if SALT II had been ratified).

The perception of the American public of a relentless Soviet strategic buildup served, however, to undercut the value of this assurance. One important reason is that the agreed limitations did not prevent the growing buildup of a counterforce capability on both sides. While this fact had been known to specialists and leaders, it had not been sufficiently appreciated by Congress or the public. The result was that to some extent SALT (and détente), and to some extent the Soviet Union, were blamed for a growing Soviet strategic threat. (A parallel concern over continued Soviet military programs in less than intercontinental systems, not limited by SALT agreements, also arose in Europe; it is discussed in a later chapter.) In one sense those on both sides who were responsible for the SALT policy decisions that failed to resolve this impending problem may be held accountable for having done too little. But the general tendency in the United States was to dismiss the SALT military détente *process* as having failed—or, frequently, as having been manipulated

---

114. The deployment under way in accordance with the terms of SALT I was changed by at least 100 in terms of the number of ICBMs with MIRVs planned, in order to accommodate the SALT II ceiling of 820 ICBMs with MIRVs. Some 50 fewer SS-17s and 50 fewer SS-19s were deployed.

by the Soviet Union to its advantage. This charge permitted opponents of détente and of the incumbent administrations an opportunity to malign, at the same time, the policy of détente, the Soviet Union, and the American administrations that pursued détente, and also to call for additional military programs.

The Committee on the Present Danger, the American Security Council, and a number of other organizations advanced these arguments frequently and forcefully. Other attacks on SALT continued as well; for example, in the widely read *Reader's Digest* in December 1977, former Secretary of Defense Laird again charged that the Soviets were cheating on SALT and that there had been an official American cover-up.[115] Nonetheless, the SALT negotiations proceeded, and in November 1977 the first five-year review conference on the ABM Treaty was held without occasioning calls for reconsideration. American public opinion polls showed an uneasy ambivalence: continuing strong support for SALT, but also increasing concern over the strategic balance. The year 1977 marked, however, a turning point in the findings of public opinion polls: more people believed the United States was spending too little on defense than that it was spending too much, a reversal of the views prevailing since the disenchantment over Vietnam in the late 1960s.

During the late 1970s new emphasis was given to a perceived military spending gap as an indicator of the alleged relentless Soviet military buildup. In his final report to Congress in January 1977 Secretary of Defense Rumsfeld had referred to an annual rate of increase in Soviet military spending of 4–5 percent during the first half of the 1970s, but with higher growth in the latter years, so that "there appears to be an acceleration in the growth of Soviet defense outlays."[116]

Secretary of Defense Brown, in his first annual report to Congress in February 1978, also stated that "the present disparity in defense spending between the United States and the Soviet Union—and still more the trend—is disquieting as an index of both Soviet capabilities and Soviet intentions."[117] He expressed particular concern over military investment spending. A year later Brown said the annual Soviet rate of increase in rubles for its defense effort was 4–5 percent. While conceding that all such comparisons of spending were "crude," he backhandedly related them to Soviet intentions: "Although Soviet intentions cannot be surely assessed, there can be no doubt about the steady increase in the Soviet defense effort each year for more than 15

---

115. Melvin R. Laird, "Arms Control: The Russians Are Cheating!" *Reader's Digest* (December 1977), pp. 97–101. See also AP, "Laird Says Ford Did Not Disclose SALT Violations," *Washington Post*, November 23, 1977.

116. *Department of Defense Annual Report, Fiscal Year 1978* (GPO, 1977), p. 9 (for the chart with the percentages and acceleration). Rumsfeld included the words cited here in his unpublished "talking points" and in a short form of the report entitled *U.S. Defense Perspectives, Fiscal Year 1978*, p. 9.

117. *Department of Defense Annual Report, Fiscal Year 1979* (GPO, 1978), p. 20.

years."[118] In 1980 he again stressed Soviet military spending, especially on investment and procurement.[119]

In his valedictory report in January 1981 Brown again stressed that the trend in annual military spending (measurement of which he said was "much less susceptible to the methodological problems of comparing absolute levels of U.S. and Soviet spending in a given year") was "clear and dramatic. Soviet defense spending has increased steadily and significantly by an average of four to five percent a year. . . . This Soviet trend has continued, even as the rate of growth in Soviet GNP has declined."[120]

As will be discussed later, the Reagan administration gave even more prominence to Soviet military investment expenditure.

In short, during the entire period from 1977 into the early 1980s, considerable weight was placed on the trend in Soviet defense spending, especially for the procurement of weapons and other investment, as a reflection—and indicator—of a growing Soviet threat. In the SALT II debate in 1979 this issue was given particular prominence, as Kissinger and a number of other earlier supporters of SALT conditioned their support for ratification of the SALT II Treaty on a commitment to an increase in the rate of U.S. defense expenditures to deal with the spending gap and its consequences. Others charged that the relentless continued increase in Soviet military spending showed that the Soviet Union was taking advantage of détente.

In fact, these confident estimates of a steady acceleration in Soviet military spending were wrong. While Soviet defense spending continues to be estimated as having grown at a rate of some 4–5 percent a year during the first half of the 1970s, revised CIA (and NATO) estimates since 1983, based on new and better information, show only a 2 percent increase a year for the period since 1976. Moreover, investment and in particular procurement of military hardware has leveled off since 1976—there was virtually *no* increase in rate of growth. "New information indicates that the Soviets did not field weapons as rapidly after 1976 as before. Practically all major categories of Soviet weapons were affected—missiles, aircraft, and ships."[121]

While the reasons for this reduced rate of defense expenditures are not entirely known, the "extended nature" of "the slowdown in the growth of military procurement . . . goes far beyond normal dips in procurement cycles."

118. *Department of Defense Annual Report, Fiscal Year 1980* (GPO, 1979), p. 5.

119. *Department of Defense Annual Report, Fiscal Year 1981* (GPO, 1980), p. 3.

120. *Department of Defense Annual Report, Fiscal Year 1982* (GPO, 1981), p. 17. It should be acknowledged that Brown also introduced a number of clarifying caveats on the comparisons with American spending and on the limits on judgments as to capabilities.

121. See "CIA Briefing Paper Entitled 'USSR: Economic Trends, and Policy Developments,'" in *Allocation of Resources in the Soviet Union and China—1983*, Hearings before the Subcommittee on International Trade, Finance, and Security Economics of the Joint Economic Committee, 98 Cong. 1 sess. (GPO, 1984), pt. 9, p. 306.

Growth of Soviet GNP had slowed, so that the share of GNP devoted to defense has remained about the same, but the earlier estimated growth in that share has not occurred.[122] The trend of reduced investment and expenditures may not be owing to détente, but it surely does not contradict détente. So the "relentless Soviet buildup" to an important extent reflected an American error in estimating Soviet outlays, rather than being a "disquieting index of Soviet intentions." There were, to be sure, significant real improvements in Soviet— and Western—military capabilities, but the spending gap proved no more solid than the gaps—bombers, missiles, ABM, and civil defense—of preceding decades. Nonetheless, it had its impact on U.S. perceptions in the period from 1976 to 1983, and even since that time (inasmuch as the change in estimates, while publicly reported, did not receive wide attention).

Throughout the preceding two decades of cold war and cold peace, the United States had maintained a clear strategic nuclear superiority. In the latter half of the 1970s, as the Soviet Union was consolidating its strategic parity, new fears had arisen in the United States. Unfortunately, the actual Soviet attainment of parity in the latter 1970s was not in synchronization with the political acceptance of parity and the public impression of parity in the early 1970s. What the Soviets saw as finally closing a gap through weapons deployment programs fully consonant with both the terms of the SALT agreement and achievement of parity, many in the United States saw as Soviet gains and pursuit of advantages violating at least the spirit of SALT, if not its letter, and threatening to go beyond to Soviet superiority. The real inconsistency was the relationship between the American public's *expectations* derived from SALT and the Soviet deployments. The interim freeze of 1972 had established a level of forces deployment that included some construction under way that had not yet been completed. In addition, only the level of strategic missile launchers had been limited, and the Soviets were again behind in time in deploying MIRVs in their strategic missile force. If the Soviet strategic deployments had occurred more nearly at the time of American deployment, and both sides had agreed to accept parity and stop at the same *time*, not merely at the same *level*, the public perception would have been quite different.

The Strategic Balance: The Soviet Perspective

One aspect of the early and growing concern of the Soviet leaders over the course pursued by the Carter administration was the question of

---

122. Ibid., pp. 308–09. For a very useful analysis, see Richard F. Kaufman, "Causes of the Slowdown in Soviet Defense," *Soviet Economy*, vol. 1 (January–March 1985), pp. 9–41. CIA testimony in November 1984 confirmed that "the stagnation in the level of procurement lasted for at least 7 years—from 1977 to 1983." *Allocation of Resources in the Soviet Union and China—1984* (forthcoming).

American intentions with respect to the strategic relationship.[123] This concern manifested itself with respect to SALT, but also more basically with respect to rising suspicions that the United States was pursuing a counterforce capability and strategic superiority for political intimidation, if not for even more ominous purposes.

From the standpoint of the Soviet leaders and military planners, just as the Soviet Union was closing the gap in numbers of strategic launchers in the early 1970s, the United States launched a new arms race in the deployment of multiple warheads. The American lead in strategic warheads in fact widened in the mid-1970s (given that the Soviet Union was five years behind in deploying ICBMs with MIRVs, and seven years behind with SLBMs with MIRVs). As Secretary of Defense Rumsfeld disclosed in January 1977, the balance in warheads was then 8,500 to 4,000 in the U.S. favor (and remained at 9,200 to 6,000 by 1980). But far more important was the imbalance in counterforce capabilities.

The Soviet leaders saw the growth of their own counterforce capabilities against the ICBM component of U.S. strategic forces as reinforcing the restraining or deterrent effect of their military power on American policy. But given their picture of the strategic balance, even the attainment of effective counterforce capabilities against the U.S. ICBM force was not seen as being so impressive or destabilizing as the United States thought. Moreover, it was not accompanied by any comparable advances in Soviet capabilities to deal with the far greater American strategic forces in the form of submarine missiles and bombers. By no stretch of the imagination could it, even in conjunction with all other Soviet capabilities, have provided a disarming strike threatening the entire American second-strike deterrent. The Soviets see their enhanced strategic capability as providing further insurance, but no military option. To the contrary, Soviet military and political analyses note the mix of superiorities in various categories of weapons and capabilities on each side in an overall combined balance. Thus, while a theoretical ability to destroy 90 percent of U.S. ICBM silos alarms many Americans, the Soviet leaders understand full well that even if they could have confidence in achieving such an outcome, it would not amount to a "disarming" strike. Moreover, there is no evidence or even indication that the Soviet leaders have regarded their ICBM capability as providing a military advantage translatable into a political "option" for their own policy.

In addition to seeing less of an advantage on their own side, the Soviet leaders see much more of a threat from U.S. forces than do Americans (even leaving aside the forces of other countries). With the increasing vulnera-

---

123. For an excellent background analysis of Soviet views on U.S. political-military policy see William B. Husband, "Soviet Perceptions of U.S. 'Positions-of-Strength' Diplomacy in the 1970s," *World Politics*, vol. 31 (July 1979), pp. 495–517; and William D. Jackson, "Soviet Images of the U.S. as Nuclear Adversary, 1969–1979," *World Politics*, vol. 33 (July 1981), pp. 614–38.

bility of fixed land-based missile silos, even if the Soviet Union had an effective attack capability against them, it could threaten only a fraction of the American force: less than 25 percent of U.S. strategic warheads are located on the land-based ICBM force. By contrast, nearly 75 percent of Soviet strategic forces are in fixed ICBM silos.

U.S. concern that a window of vulnerability would occur by the early or mid 1980s was projected very often in the latter 1970s. In reality, that window referred to the potential vulnerability of only a relatively limited portion of U.S. strategic power. While some American commentators have noted the larger Soviet ICBM force and therefore potentially greater threat to the Soviet Union in the late 1980s (or whenever the United States acquired a force of MX or Trident II missiles), there has been virtually no attention to the *current* greater American capability to destroy a *larger* proportion of the Soviet strategic force. Thus, even if 90 percent of U.S. ICBMs could be destroyed by the Soviet SS-18 force (theoretically, by only 210 SS-18s with 2,100 warheads, if the highest projected accuracies were achieved), that loss would represent the destruction of only 1,960 warheads, or 18 percent of the U.S. strategic force. On the American side, with *no* MX or Trident II missiles and using only its 550 Minuteman IIIs with their 1,650 warheads, concentrating its fire on the 820 Soviet SS-17, SS-18, and SS-19 ICBMs with MIRVs, assuming all had a full complement of MIRVs, the United States could threaten to destroy some 4,300 warheads, comprising 39 percent of the Soviet strategic force.[124]

This capability is the significance of upgrading the Minuteman III with the Mk-12A warhead and NS-20 guidance system in the late 1970s.[125] That step marked a major advance in acquiring counterforce capabilities against Soviet ICBM silos and other hardened targets: 300 missiles could theoretically target 900 Soviet ICBMs (or 450, with cross-targeting)—and the Soviets had no assurance the deployment would be limited to 300. Yet this development received relatively little attention in the United States because it did not involve a major new system. By contrast, it received considerable attention

---

124. See Warner R. Schilling, "U.S. Strategic Nuclear Concepts in the 1970s: The Search for Sufficiently Equivalent Countervailing Parity," *International Security*, vol. 6 (Fall 1981), p. 72, for the calculation cited. See also, for a censored but still clear official acknowledgment of the high counterforce potential of the Mk-12A and NS-20 systems for the Minuteman, *Fiscal Year 1980 Arms Control Impact Statements* (GPO, 1979), p. 17.

In this illustration, two weapons are programmed to strike each of the Soviet SS-17, SS-18, and SS-19 ICBM with MIRV silos. Whether they could destroy virtually all those ICBMs would depend in particular on the accuracy achieved *and* on the hardness of the Soviet ICBM silos—a factor the United States, and to a lesser extent the Soviet Union as well, can only estimate. (The outcome also assumes, as in the parallel case of a strike on the U.S. Minuteman force, that the missiles targeted had not been fired on warning before the incoming attacking missiles had struck.)

125. The Minuteman III with the Mk-12A warhead is said to have ten times the lethal potential of its predecessor, with an accuracy (CEP) of 250 meters, half the miss radius of its predecessor, while its warhead of 335 kilotons is more than twice that of its predecessor.

in the Soviet Union, especially since it occurred in the context of the revision of U.S. military doctrine and of strategic concepts for nuclear employment marked by the progression over the second half of the 1970s from the Schlesinger Doctrine to PD-59.

It was also decided in 1977 to proceed with development of the Pershing II medium-range ballistic missile, an extended range (1,100 nautical miles or more) version of the existing U.S. Army long-range tactical theater support missile, and a ground-launched cruise missile (GLCM) of intermediate range (1,500 nautical miles). Decisions on deployment in Europe were not made by NATO until 1979, but Soviet analysts stress the decision of the U.S. government as early as 1972 to develop these systems, which possessed a high counterforce accuracy, and in 1977 to proceed with them. The first test flight in the Pershing II program occurred on November 18, 1977. The Pershing II deployed in West Germany in particular provides a significant first-strike capability against strategic targets in the USSR.[126] The NATO decision on the theater nuclear force and its ramifications are discussed later. The important point here is its relevance to Soviet views of U.S. intentions and programs, which were regarded as directed toward acquiring military superiority. Above all, the conjunction of the elaboration of declared U.S. doctrine as represented in the public discussion of PD-59 on waging protracted limited nuclear war, the NATO decision to deploy the Pershing II and GLCM, the U.S. decision on the MX, and finally the postponements and indefinite shelving of the SALT II Treaty, all in 1979–80, were regarded by Soviet analysts as confirming the connection between the elaboration of a dangerous doctrine and decisions to pursue an array of programs for threatening forces.

American reaffirmation of its acceptance of parity was increasingly discounted. U.S. "military policy is simply an endless buildup of power in order [allegedly] 'to assure parity.'"[127] The subsequent course of development of American strategic forces surveyed above was thus seen in the context of a retraction by the United States of acceptance of strategic parity, the very basis of détente. The United States was seen as seeking to regain some measure of strategic advantage.

---

126. Decisions on the Pershing II and GLCM systems are discussed at greater length in chapter 25 in the context of theater nuclear forces; the reason for referring to them here is the role they play in relation to decisions on strategic doctrine and force programming. The Pershing II could reach strategic targets in the Soviet Union, such as ICBM silos and even more critically strategic missile and other command and control centers, within 10 minutes. The accuracy and warhead yield would be sufficient to destroy those targets. Developments such as the reported provision of the W86 earth penetrator warhead for the Pershing missile is seen by the Soviets as confirming that role for the system. The Pershing II is expected to have an accuracy (CEP) of about 30 meters; the CEP of the Soviet SS-20 is estimated at 400–500 meters.

127. [Colonel] D. Proektor, "Socialism and International Security," *Kommunist*, no. 7 (May 1977), p. 118.

In the Soviet perception, moreover, the United States was not only building up its military power in the late 1970s, but justifying this buildup by a campaign alleging a mounting Soviet military threat. Pressed initially by unofficial groups such as the Committee on the Present Danger beginning in 1976, by 1978–80 this view was also being advanced less stridently—but more effectively—by the Carter administration itself. By 1980, after Afghanistan (from the Soviet viewpoint an irrelevant factor), the Carter defense budget rose by more than 10 percent in real terms over the preceding year (which had already involved an increase in the rate of growth). And this increase was justified in part by the false claims of a steady increase in the Soviet rate of military spending.

Having significantly cut back its military spending and having leveled off its expenditures for weapons and other military hardware since 1976, as earlier noted, the Soviet Union could only interpret the grossly overstated U.S. reiterations year after year of the size of Soviet military outlays as a deliberate and ominous development. The Soviet political and military leaders did not see continued American assertions of a relentless buildup in Soviet military spending and procurement as an error in intelligence assessment (which it was). Rather they saw it as a policy to justify a desired American buildup while putting the blame on the USSR.[128] This belief naturally fed broader suspicions of American motives, deepening suspicions that seemed to be confirmed by the course of American policy and action over these years.

The U.S. campaign on Soviet military spending had also been used in 1978 to get the countries of NATO to commit themselves to at least a 3 percent annual increase in defense spending. In 1979 it had contributed indirectly to obtaining NATO agreement to deploy new U.S. missiles in Europe. Finally, the campaign had also been accompanied by the drawn-out negotiation of SALT II, was then used to press for an increase in American military spending as a condition for ratification of SALT II, and persisted even after the failure to ratify SALT II. From the very beginning of the Carter administration, the Soviets had regarded the American SALT positions with suspicion. It is to the SALT negotiations that the discussion now turns.

---

128. The Soviet political, military, and intelligence establishments have a high degree of respect for the capabilities of American intelligence and are therefore predisposed not to believe that apparent or self-admitted errors in its intelligence information are genuine, especially when the consequences of the error are self-serving (or are perceived to be self-serving). The story of the American discovery of a Soviet combat brigade in Cuba is a good example (see chapter 24). In the case of Soviet defense spending, the convenience of the error and its contribution to a hostile U.S. purpose virtually ensured Soviet misreading of the American ability to know. This interpretation also blocked the possibility that the Soviets would reconsider whether their own tight secrecy on such matters might not be counterproductive—as it clearly was in this case.

23 Snatching Defeat from the Jaws of Victory: SALT II, 1977–79

EARLIER CHAPTERS traced the tortuous course of the SALT II negotiations from their beginning in November 1972, in the afterglow of the SALT I ABM Treaty and Interim Agreement on strategic offensive missiles signed at the first summit meeting, to their shelving during most of the presidential election year of 1976.

In a farewell interview, Secretary of State Kissinger replied to a question about what he would have liked to finish in office by answering "the SALT agreement." He placed the blame for failure to conclude an agreement on "partly the other side, partly the election and partly internal disputes within the Administration." While he did not say how the blame should be apportioned among the three, it was probably not accidental that two referred to the internal American side. He also expressed the belief that "a SALT agreement ought to be attainable" in 1977.[1]

Carter's New Approach

After a vigorous internal review of U.S. positions (which each new administration undertakes) and consideration of a number of conflicting ideas on the best course to pursue, President Carter decided to try for a more ambitious and far-reaching SALT II agreement than the one directly based on the Vladivostok accord and 90 percent agreed to when President Ford decided in March 1976 to suspend new efforts during the election year.

The internal review had been launched promptly: it was the subject of the second Presidential Review Memorandum (PRM)–2, issued on January 24, 1977, which called for an initial meeting of the newly constituted Special

---

1. "Excerpts from Interview with Kissinger: Eight Years in Washington Evaluated," *New York Times*, January 20, 1977.

Coordinating Committee (SCC), to be chaired by Zbigniew Brzezinski, the new national security adviser, only four days later (in fact, it first met February 3). There followed a crucial two months of maneuvering and decisionmaking on the American SALT position.[2]

The key decision was whether to seek an early SALT II agreement building on Kissinger's early 1976 Moscow negotiations based on the Vladivostok accord, and then proceed to negotiate a SALT III agreement involving reductions. President Carter had indicated his intention to proceed along this path even prior to his inauguration. On December 3, 1976, in an appearance before the Senate Committee on Foreign Relations, he had criticized Ford for not having moved decisively to reach a SALT II agreement based on the Vladivostok accord (he had voiced this same theme on the "Today" television program a few days earlier). Carter added that *after* agreeing on SALT II, which was 90 percent complete, he would start immediately to seek reductions.[3] This statement not only created a public expectation, but reinforced Soviet expectations that had already been formed on the basis of a private assurance conveyed by W. Averell Harriman to Brezhnev in September 1976 on the basis of explicit authorization by presidential candidate Carter.[4]

Brezhnev made very clear the Soviet position (and expectation) in a speech on the eve of the inauguration. He stressed Soviet readiness to go further with arms limitations and reductions, but "first it is necessary to consolidate what has already been achieved" on the basis of the Vladivostok accord. He warned that new approaches would "only further complicate and delay the solution to the problem."[5]

Immediately after assuming office, President Carter in his first press conference again reiterated his willingness to set aside contentious issues and go ahead with a "quick agreement."[6] Meanwhile, in his first personal communication to Brezhnev, on January 26, he had pledged a "rapid conclusion" of the SALT treaty. And in his first meeting with Ambassador Dobrynin, on February

2. Strobe Talbott, *Endgame: The Inside Story of SALT II* (Harper and Row, 1979), presents an excellent, detailed, and well-informed account of SALT II from 1977 through 1979, including the internal American deliberations as well as U.S.-Soviet negotiations. For the initial American considerations and decisions in early 1977 see pp. 38–78. The memoirs of Brzezinski and Vance are also very informative sources. Zbigniew Brzezinski, *Power and Principle: Memoirs of the National Security Adviser, 1977–1981* (Farrar, Straus, Giroux, 1983); and Cyrus Vance, *Hard Choices: Critical Years in America's Foreign Policy* (Simon and Schuster, 1983). See also Robert G. Kaiser and Murrey Marder, "In Pursuit of a SALT II Agreement: The Secretive Birth of Carter's New Plan for Arms Reductions," *Washington Post*, April 11, 1977.

3. See Bernard Gwertzman, "Carter, in Reaction to Brezhnev, Vows Arms Curb Action," *New York Times*, December 4, 1976.

4. Talbott, *Endgame*, p. 39.

5. "Outstanding Exploit of the Defenders of Tula: Speech of L. I. Brezhnev," *Pravda*, January 19, 1977.

6. "The President's News Conference of February 8, 1977," *Weekly Compilation of Presidential Documents*, vol. 13 (February 14, 1977), p. 158.

1, he again spoke of quick agreement on a simple SALT II, leaving other issues to later negotiation, and said that after the successful conclusion of SALT II he would like to move on to substantial reductions, even to cutting the number of missiles to "several hundred."[7] Carter sent a second letter to Brezhnev on February 8, drafted by Secretary of State Vance and by Brzezinski, in response to a letter of February 4 from Brezhnev. In his letter the Soviet leader had stressed the need for a quick SALT agreement based on the Vladivostok accord. Carter's reply left open the options of either a quick agreement or a more "comprehensive" one. Brezhnev responded on February 25, again making clear the Soviet position that any agreement on SALT had to be based on Vladivostok. A further exchange took place in early March (this time at U.S.— Brzezinski's—initiative, using the hot line, to exclude the foreign ministries), again making clear the Soviet position.[8]

This was the state of play between the two governments when the U.S. negotiating aims and position were established in several meetings in the second half of March. The SCC had met frequently in February and March, and the position being developed became increasingly complex and increasingly inclined toward pressing at once for reductions below the levels agreed to at Vladivostok. When the various studies and options reached a point for presidential decision, Carter opted for a course quite different from the one he had earlier announced: he decided to seek a much more complex agreement, involving new, substantially reduced levels of strategic forces, new levels for heavy ICBMs, new levels of MIRVs, new limits on missile testing, and a ban on new types of ICBMs.[9]

Why the change? President Carter himself was restless with the arguments for caution and continuity and wanted to move boldly forward. Hence when several, although not all, of his principal advisers urged a more far-reaching SALT limitation, he was responsive. Brzezinski in particular, his deputy David Aaron, and Secretary of Defense Harold Brown all wanted to move ahead. The idea of merely winding up Ford and Kissinger's unfinished business did not greatly appeal to Carter and Brzezinski, who were attracted to striking out on their own and achieving more. Brzezinski was also convinced that Kissinger had not stood up strongly enough to the Soviet leaders.

There were other considerations. President Carter had breakfast with Senator Jackson on February 4, and although their basic aims and expectations on SALT were far apart, both agreed on the desirability of pressing for substantial reductions in strategic forces. A few days later Jackson publicly commended Carter's approach on SALT "so far." On February 15 the senator submitted a very detailed, extensive briefing paper and proposal (before those of the government bureaucracy were ready), which urged Carter not to "unnec-

---

7. See Brzezinski, *Power and Principle*, pp. 151–52.

8. Ibid., pp. 153–56, 160–61.

9. See ibid., pp. 157–160; and Talbott, *Endgame*, pp. 43–58.

essarily assume the burden of past mistakes" by simply picking up where Ford and Kissinger had left off.[10] Carter also consulted with Paul H. Nitze of the Committee on the Present Danger, who urged deep cuts, especially in Soviet ICBM throw-weight as well as in overall levels of strategic forces. Clearly, if Carter could bring together the two wings of his own party—the hard-line Jackson neoconservatives and the pro-détente, pro-arms-control wing, he would help assure support for SALT and gain wider political advantages as well. The fight over the nomination of Paul C. Warnke as chief SALT negotiator had not been encouraging and showed Carter the strength of the conservative element, reinforcing the need to take its views into account. There was, however, too little consideration given to the political effects of later compromises and departures from the initial positions if, as should have been anticipated, they proved nonnegotiable.

Brown was led to favor a more far-reaching approach for other reasons. He supported SALT on general principle, but saw that a SALT II agreement along the lines of Vladivostok would do little to help meet what was widely perceived to be a major looming problem for the United States—the vulnerability of ICBM silos. So he favored an attempt to reduce overall levels, but especially the levels of ICBMs with MIRVs. By the time the comprehensive proposal was offered, however, he had come to the conclusion that even if accepted it would not have alleviated the vulnerability problem (owing to the hard-target kill capability not only of the Soviet SS-18 large ICBM force, but also of the SS-19 force).

Vance and some of his advisers had serious reservations about a new approach and believed the best course was to seek an early agreement based on Vladivostok. But they were unable to persuade President Carter not to try a more ambitious deep reductions approach. Vance and Warnke did succeed in getting Carter's agreement that a second approach also be offered—one called "Vladivostok minus," the basic Vladivostok approach but one that set aside for the time being the contentious Backfire and cruise missile issues. Carter agreed, as long as it was made clear that he preferred the new comprehensive approach.[11]

The new approach was decided on in an unusually secret meeting on March 19 limited to "principals," a meeting that most of those working on

---

10. Talbott, *Endgame*, pp. 52–54; and see Murrey Marder, "Carter's Views on Soviets Applauded by Jackson," *Washington Post*, February 10, 1977. Jackson also expressed particular pleasure at the strong early anti-Soviet human rights moves of the Carter administration.

11. See Vance, *Hard Choices*, pp. 47–52. Brzezinski, *Power and Principle*, p. 159, cites a memo by Vance dated March 18 suggesting that Vance's (and Warnke's) position was not as reluctant as Vance himself depicts it, but this document does not change the basic divergence in approach.

The offer of a second alternative clearly undercut any possible Soviet consideration of the less palatable comprehensive approach. As it was, even the second alternative was not acceptable, but the technique of offering a choice (as in SALT I in April 1970) was, while well-intentioned, not well-considered.

SALT did not even know about. And its decisions were similarly closely held. Even upon arrival in Moscow most of the delegation was still uninformed. Thus when Leslie Gelb, the director of the Bureau of Politico-Military Affairs at the Department of State and Vance's chief staff adviser on SALT, was dispatched to brief the NATO Council in Brussels a week before Vance's trip to Moscow, not knowing of the meeting he left the allies with the impression that the United States would be seeking a limited Vladivostok agreement. (Vance himself clarified the U.S. position to the NAC to some extent on his way to Moscow, but this shift merely caused confusion over the sudden change in the American approach.) Within the U.S. bureaucracy, most of those who usually advised on SALT were not involved or informed. Thus, for example, none of those who advised on *Soviet* positions and reactions was involved before the decision or even informed until the Vance trip, except one experienced NSC staff member (William Hyland) who had argued the new approach would be unwise. The CIA was asked for Soviet views on SALT, but since it was not informed of the American position, it was unable to estimate reactions to that position. Marshall D. Shulman, Vance's special assistant on Soviet affairs, was told only the day before departure.[12]

Ambassador Dobrynin was informed of the main lines of the new Carter proposal just a few days before Vance departed for Moscow, but not in time to obtain a considered Moscow reaction. Dobrynin himself immediately responded negatively.[13]

Meanwhile President Carter stated publicly the objectives of his planned comprehensive approach on SALT in his address to the UN General Assembly on March 17, in which he also highlighted the theme of human rights. In a news conference on March 24 he continued his public diplomacy by commenting on a number of the other subjects his secretary of state would be raising in Moscow. They included Jewish emigration and human rights issues, as well as most of the arms control measures noted earlier. Moreover, the discussion at the press conference seemed to imply linkage of the issues, and in any case signaled a readiness to pursue contentious issues such as human rights in the diplomatic relationship of the two countries.

On March 28 Secretary of State Vance unveiled the new American comprehensive SALT proposal to the Soviet leaders. It called for reducing the

---

12. Talbott, *Endgame,* pp. 58–65; and Brzezinski, *Power and Principle,* pp. 159–60. Talbott erroneously dates the key meeting with President Carter on March 12; Brzezinski states it was March 19.

13. See *Hard Choices,* pp. 52–53; and Talbott, *Endgame,* pp. 64–65.

The Soviet embassy in Washington, in the weeks leading up to the Vance trip, may have added to the confusion over signals. While advancing the strong Soviet preference for a rapid agreement based on Vladivostok, in the course of seeking to elicit as much information as they could about the evolving American position and various views, the embassy may have inadvertently encouraged those in Washington who sought a different approach by indicating Soviet interest in reductions.

overall equal aggregate of strategic systems from the level of 2,400 agreed to at Vladivostok to between 1,800 and 2,000, and the number of launchers for missiles with MIRVs from 1,320 to 1,100 or 1,200. Other new features included reducing the numbers of modern large ICBMs to 150; the number of launchers for ICBMs with MIRVs to 550; a ban on development, testing, and deployment of any new types of ICBM (including mobile); and a limitation to 6 ICBM test firings and 6 SLBM tests annually. All types of cruise missiles above a 2,500-kilometer range would be banned, but all below that range would be unlimited in number. Long-range air-launched cruise missiles (ALCMs) (600–2,500 kilometers in range) would be limited to heavy bombers. The Backfire would not be included in the aggregate if the Soviets provided solid assurances that they would not increase its strategic potential.

A number of the features of the proposal reflected creditable arms control purposes, in particular the much tighter constraints on ICBMs with MIRVs and on any future ICBM systems (including the restrictions on flight tests). The tighter restraints and sacrifices were, however, much heavier on the Soviet side. In addition, the Soviets regarded the Vladivostok accord signed by the American president and by Brezhnev as a binding commitment, notwithstanding the change in administrations. Further, they had come to believe that the new administration would follow through on its public and private statements of intention to reach a quick agreement on that basis, before turning to reductions and other constraints. Brezhnev personally had "spilled political blood" in agreeing to the major Soviet concessions involved in the Vladivostok agreement (as Gromyko's principal deputy put it to Warnke). Now the Americans were unilaterally reopening that agreement in ways that pocketed the earlier Soviet concessions (especially noninclusion of the U.S. forward-based systems, or FBS). And they even went on to cut sharply the Soviet side of that bargain (retention of the 308 modern large Soviet ICBM launchers).[14] For its part, all the United States would forgo was its future MX ICBM system, and it would not press again for including the Soviet Backfire bomber (which, it will be recalled, the Soviets had understood from Kissinger *not* to be included at Vladivostok).

In many other respects the Soviet side was being asked to reduce its forces disproportionately. The Soviet Union was to cut its first-line active forces by 400–600 units, while the United States would cut only 0–100 such units; it would cut back 400–500 planned ICBMs with MIRVs, the United States none; it would have to cut back its large ICBMs from 308 to 150, the United States none. The substantial reductions were *all* to come on the *Soviet* side. In addition, the United States could have unlimited numbers of land-, air-, and sea-launched cruise missiles up to the 2,500-kilometer range. The proposal did not even contain any indication of readiness by the United States to exercise restraint on FBS or on transfers of arms to other countries—and the cruise missile proposals were far more permissive than those proposed in 1975

---

14. Vance, *Hard Choices*, p. 52; and Talbott, *Endgame*, pp. 60–61.

and 1976. The fact that the proposal was loaded in favor of the United States might have been more understandable and even an effective initial negotiating position if the negotiations were starting from a clean slate, but they were not.

Brezhnev and his colleagues flatly rejected the proposal after two days of deliberation on how to respond (they had no doubts about *what* to respond). The Americans noted that the Soviets seemed generally "hurt" by the very fact that such a proposal was being advanced. The United States was seen as attempting to roll back several years of hard-bargained progress in SALT and was seeking greater advantages for itself and greater sacrifices from the Soviet Union than in the positions earlier agreed on. Brezhnev therefore stressed, and Foreign Minister Gromyko soon after reiterated publicly, that if the United States insisted on reopening the agreed issues, the Soviet Union would have to as well, in particular those concerning the FBS. Vance and some other Americans new to the negotiation initially believed this reintroduction of the matter of FBS to be simply a spoiler or threat from the Soviet side. In fact, it was a logical and, from the Soviet standpoint, necessary position if the basic Vladivostok accord was being jettisoned. Similarly, some American officials (not Vance) and outside commentators at the time and since, either willfully or through insufficient understanding, have interpreted the Soviet rejection of this package as a rejection of reductions in general, which it was not. The Soviets were, however, committed to Vladivostok first and then to negotiating reductions in SALT III.

Brezhnev also made clear in his response that the Soviets were proceeding on the assumption that in the current negotiations the United States would accept the need for at least a unilateral American assurance, if not a formal bilateral undertaking, that it would not expand and would eventually reduce its FBS and that it would not transfer strategic arms to allies or other third countries. These substantive points were virtually the only ones Brezhnev stressed as requirements, apart from firmly reasserting the need to proceed on the basis of the previous negotiations based on implementing the Vladivostok accord. The reason he did so was a growing suspicion on the part of the Soviet military establishment that the United States intended to circumvent the agreed level for intercontinental systems. From the Soviet point of view, even the agreed level resulted in *less* than parity with U.S. intercontinental strategic systems, since it included systems deployed by the Soviet Union against China, Britain, France, and the American FBS.

The Soviets saw the second U.S. proposal—to defer the disputed issues and proceed with an early agreement—also as a step back from the U.S. position of early 1976. Nor did they regard it as equitable. Although it would allow Backfire, it would also allow American land- and sea-based cruise missiles to run free—a potential massive reinforcement of the FBS. While the American proposal did include one new element that reversed the U.S. position of the preceding seven years, even that seemed as much a threat as a concession: mobile ICBMs would be allowed within the aggregate. The Soviets therefore promptly rejected the second U.S. proposal as well.

The Soviet reaction to the new administration's proposed SALT approach was bound to be negative, given the one-sided nature of the provisions. It was, in addition, compounded by the Soviet understanding and expectation that the United States was ready to consolidate the 1976 draft implementing the Vladivostok agreement before plunging into reductions, a course that in Soviet minds was virtually equated with a serious interest in pursuing the SALT process. The Soviets' disappointment and suspicions were intensified by the fact that the Carter administration publicly trumpeted its new approach.

Most of the American decisionmakers had anticipated a negative Soviet reaction—not only Vance and Warnke, but Brown and Brzezinski as well. Only Carter seems to have believed the proposal might be accepted. But the others expected a Soviet counterproposal, rather than just a flat rejection even of consideration of the new approach. Some also felt the proposal of a deferral would be an adequate cushion in case the Soviets refused to provide a counterproposal of their own. Those in the bureaucracy who could have predicted the Soviet reaction and the negative impact on the Soviet perception of U.S. interest in SALT and in détente had not been advised in advance of the American proposal. Nor were those who had warned of serious difficulties in attempting to launch a drastically new approach—and, indeed, the broader adverse consequences of doing so—listened to.[15]

Vance then overrode the advice of some of his associates and candidly informed the world from a press conference in Moscow just before his return to Washington on March 30 that "the Soviets told us that they had examined our two proposals and did not find either acceptable. They proposed nothing new on their side."[16] Kissinger was one among many who questioned the advisability of publicly announcing a failure in this way. It also was bound to prompt conflicting public justifications by the two sides.

Indeed, Vance's candor had two unexpected and undesirable effects. First, it was taken by the Soviets as a challenge and an attempt to portray them as rejecting a reasonable and far-reaching disarmament proposal. Second, it led President Carter to feel he must take the offensive to offset the failure of his initiative.

---

15. Brzezinski expected a counterproposal and negotiated middle outcome. *Power and Principle,* p. 160. Vance expected a Soviet counterproposal and admits he was "angered" at the firm and "vehement" Soviet rejection. *Hard Choices,* pp. 53–55. Carter says simply, "I was angry over the Soviet attitude, and disappointed because we would have to set back our timetable for an agreement." Carter also states that he had showed the draft proposal to Kissinger, who thought it "had a good chance to be accepted." Jimmy Carter, *Keeping Faith: Memoirs of a President* (Bantam Books, 1982), p. 219.

16. "News Conference, Moscow, March 30," *Department of State Bulletin,* vol. 76 (April 25, 1977), p. 400. (Hereafter *State Bulletin.*) The several news conferences and the communiqué concerning the Moscow meetings are on pp. 389–421. In his memoir Vance does not discuss his decision to announce the Soviet rejection.

Carter did not even wait for Vance's return and an opportunity to talk with him. On March 30 he hastily called a news conference, disclosed parts of the proposal, and attempted to justify the approach as "a fair, balanced, substantial reduction in the arms race"—which is probably what he believed. He announced the agreement to establish eight working groups on various arms control subjects (discussed in chapter 22), which had not been disclosed in the joint communiqué in Moscow, in order to show some progress. He was much on the defensive in replying to questions asking if his assertive human rights stance was responsible for the failure. In the question-and-answer exchange Carter admitted that he did not yet even know whether the Soviet leaders had given reasons for rejecting the U.S. approach, much less what the reasons were. But he defended the proposal, including the unjustified claim that the deeper reductions the United States had proposed "would affect both of us about the same." He even got into such muddy waters, on which he was ill-informed, as to whether Kissinger had agreed that Backfire should or should not be included in the Vladivostok ceilings. He said he intended "to continue strong negotiations to let the leaders of our country know what we are proposing. And I'm not in any hurry." He also said, "We would like to have the subject of verification opened up dramatically"—a point not raised by Vance and bound to stir Soviet suspicion. Finally, referring to the next planned meeting of Vance with Gromyko in May, he said, "Obviously, if we feel at the conclusion of next month's discussions that the Soviets are not acting in good faith with us and that an agreement is unlikely, then I would be forced to consider a much more deep commitment to the development and deployment of additional weapons."[17] To Moscow, that statement sounded like a not very subtle ultimatum.

The very next day, in response to Carter's press conference, Gromyko held one in Moscow. He noted that President Carter had made a statement without even waiting for the return of his secretary of state. He also denied that various rumors circulating in the United States about Soviet rejection of an alleged broad U.S. disarmament proposal were correct—and proceeded to lay out in considerable detail the American proposal and Soviet objections to it. He expressed the basic frustration and resentment of the Soviet leadership when he said, "One cannot talk about stability when a new leadership arrives and crosses out all that has been achieved before." He stressed the unacceptability of the limitation on strategic ballistic missiles while strategic cruise missiles were unconstrained. And he reiterated the importance of the FBS and the nontransfer of strategic weapons, noting that to reach the compromise agreement at Vladivostok the Soviet side had been prepared to set the FBS aside from the agreement, "but now we have a different view of this question in the light of the latest U.S. proposals. This is a matter of our security and the security of our allies." He closed by reaffirming

17. "President Carter Discusses Strategic Arms Limitation Proposals," March 30, *State Bulletin*, vol. 76 (April 25, 1977), pp. 409–14.

the agreement to meet Vance in Geneva in May and said, "I think we will have plenty to talk about."[18]

The next day, April 1, Brzezinski held a press conference, his first major appearance as a spokesman for the administration, again without awaiting the arrival of Secretary of State Vance. He provided an extensive and well-prepared exposition and defense of the U.S. proposal. There was, however, an edge to his exposition; he stressed that if the Soviets accepted the whole proposed package, the United States would be willing to give up the MX, which "could be extremely, extremely threatening" to the Soviet Union by the early 1980s, and thus to forgo "as a basic strategic option, the acquisition of first-strike capability against their land-based systems."[19] Unfortunately, that statement confirmed that if the Soviets did *not* capitulate to the one-sided American proposal, the United States would *not* be willing to forgo acquisition of a first-strike strategic capability with the MX and other systems. To Moscow, the import of the president's general threat of March 30 was made only too clear by Brzezinski's follow-up punch.

Meanwhile, on April 3 the Committee on the Present Danger issued a new warning on the Soviet military buildup and threat.

Within the administration there were mutual recriminations over the failure, especially between officials in the White House and the Department of State.[20] Brzezinski took the toughest position, holding the view that "the ball was in the Soviet court and we should sit tight and wait for a counterproposal," because, as he saw the situation, "the Soviets must have assumed that Carter's public commitment to SALT gave them bargaining leverage that could be exploited," and their reaction was designed "to put us under pressure."[21] There was, however, general agreement on the need to return to more conventional diplomacy and negotiation. Moreover, despite reluctance in some quarters, there was movement toward formulating a position closer to the earlier disdained Vladivostok/1976 one.

---

18. "Press Conference of A. A. Gromyko [March 31]," *Pravda*, April 1, 1977.

   Both Brzezinski and Vance refer to Gromyko's statement as a reply to Vance's departure statement, without noting its explicit references to President Carter's statement the same day. Vance, *Hard Choices*, p. 54; and Brzezinski, *Power and Principle*, p. 164.

19. "Presidential Assistant Brzezinski's News Conference of April 1," *State Bulletin*, vol. 76 (April 25, 1977), pp. 414–21; the cited passage on p. 421 was the closing comment of the press conference.

20. Talbott, *Endgame*, pp. 75–78.

21. Brzezinski, *Power and Principle*, p. 165. Brzezinski even comments (retrospectively) that the Soviet leaders were attempting to get Carter to accept a quick SALT agreement so that the United States would "accept detente as the major priority of American foreign policy, with its implied acceptance of Soviet proxy expansionism in Third World areas." This statement says much more about Brzezinski's fears than about Soviet aims or expectations.

Back to the Negotiating Table

Again in great secrecy, a somewhat reshuffled inner circle prepared a new proposal for May—with greater participation by State and ACDA and less by Defense. The heart of the new approach was a treaty to run until 1985, coupled with an interim three-year protocol that would limit certain systems (above all land- and sea-based cruise missiles) pending further negotiation in SALT III, and accompanied by an elaboration of principles for SALT III. Meanwhile, discussions with the Soviets included a series of meetings with Dobrynin, including one with President Carter, as well as meetings with Brzezinski and separately with Vance and Warnke.[22]

Throughout the following two years of negotiations until agreement was reached in May 1979, the Soviet aim remained the negotiation of a "consolidation" agreement before launching into more far-reaching limitations and reductions. The Soviets took some initiatives, but for the most part they slowly and grudgingly accommodated U.S. positions to the extent necessary to achieve compromise. While much less is known about internal Soviet decisionmaking on SALT, it is not difficult to see the basis for Soviet positions on the various issues. Each side continued to seek constraints on the other while keeping its own options open, but the negotiations led to more balanced outcomes. This progress, however, took time.

In meetings with Vance in Geneva in May, Gromyko accepted the three-tiered approach and agreed that for the life of the basic treaty there could be some modest reduction from the starting point of 2,400, and that under the protocol deployment of long-range land- and sea-based cruise missiles would be banned for three years (although testing would not be). But Gromyko rejected attempts to reduce heavy Soviet ICBMs (this time the proposal was to cut the number from 308 to 190 rather than 150) and to place a moratorium on arming large ICBMs with MIRVs. And he insisted that ALCMs be included in the ceiling on MIRVs, as agreed at Vladivostok.[23]

As has been shown, Kissinger had held his SALT II team, fielded in early 1973, to a much more limited role than the SALT I delegation had played. After May the Carter administration allowed the delegations in Geneva again to have a more active role in negotiating than they had had since 1972. Carter and Vance relied more on Warnke and his team, although Vance continued to play a very active and critically important role.

Despite continuing work on a joint draft text, when Vance again met Gromyko in September, most major issues remained. With the SALT I Interim Agreement freezing the levels of strategic ballistic missiles (ICBMs

22. Talbott, *Endgame*, pp. 78–85. See also Brzezinski, *Power and Principle*, pp. 166–67.

23. Talbott, *Endgame*, pp. 85–88; Vance, *Hard Choices*, pp. 56–57; and Brzezinski, *Power and Principle*, pp. 167–68.

and SLBMs) due to expire on October 3, 1977, there was a certain artificial urgency to reaching a new agreement. But that accomplishment was not yet in hand. In terms of the substantive issues, in addition to the perennial Backfire and cruise missile ones, the United States had belatedly come to realize that the real strategic problem was not the throw-weight of the heavy SS-9 and SS-18 ICBMs, or even the placement of MIRVs on the heavy missiles, but the potential for MIRVs on *all* fixed land-based ICBMs—especially the Soviet SS-19, as well as the SS-18. Accordingly, instead of concentrating U.S. efforts on reducing the number of heavy ICBMs, as had been done in March and May, the United States now emphasized limiting the number of all classes of ICBMs with MIRVs. While a somewhat more equitable, and therefore potentially more negotiable, position than the March proposal, the stress on ICBMs with MIRVs still posed a problem, given that the Soviet Union had not at that point even begun to deploy an SLBM with MIRVs, while the United States had placed most of its MIRVs at sea. No matter how analytically logical and justifiable as an arms control measure, a new ceiling on ICBMs with MIRVs— which was not part of the Vladivostok accord—was bound to strike Soviet military leaders as impinging unduly and disproportionately on their forces, and to strike Soviet political leaders as American pursuit of a one-sided advantage.

If U.S. enthusiasm for a limit on ICBMs with MIRVs was growing, the overall limit on MIRVs caused problems if the United States were to include ALCMs on heavy bombers. Especially after Carter opted in June to cancel production of the B-1 bomber and to rely instead on ALCMs, the enhanced importance of this system increased U.S. reluctance to limit the numbers of ALCMs in competition with ICBMs and SLBMs having MIRVs. In addition, the Defense Department became increasingly restive over the operational constraints of a limitation of 2,500 kilometers on the range for ALCMs.

As noted, Gromyko met with Vance in September in New York, following exchanges between Vance and Dobrynin. Gromyko reacted very negatively to proposals modifying (but continuing) the March approach, especially a new limit of 250 on heavy systems that combined heavy ICBMs and heavy bombers. This approach permitted the United States to retain its planned B-52 ALCM-carrying force, but obliged the Soviet Union to drop its entire heavy bomber force and fifty-eight heavy ICBMs, or even more of its large ICBMs if any heavy bombers were retained. Vance again proposed a subceiling on ICBMs with MIRVs, but this time at 800 rather than the 550 mentioned in March (and tailored to fit the U.S. force). As the negotiations proceeded and moved to Washington, where Gromyko also met with President Carter, Gromyko indicated a readiness to consider a subceiling of 820 ICBMs with MIRVs, but only if there were no new subceiling on heavy ICBMs and if ALCMs were counted in the MIRV ceiling as agreed at Vladivostok. The United States responded by devising yet another subceiling, this time on ICBMs *and* SLBMs with MIRVs; it would count ALCM-carrying bombers in the broad ceiling of 1,320 MIRVs agreed to at Vladivostok (a matter now of political, as well as military, significance to the Soviet side), but the total number of ICBMs and SLBM launchers with MIRVs would be limited to 1,200. The number of ICBM launchers with MIRVs would be limited to 820, as Gromyko had proposed.

After a few days' consideration in Moscow, on September 27 Gromyko accepted the four-level approach but with slightly higher levels. In Geneva in June the United States had proposed reducing the overall Vladivostok aggregate level of ICBMs, SLBMs, and heavy bombers from 2,400 to 2,160 (a 10 percent cut that was almost precisely equal to the existing U.S. level). The Soviet side insisted that the initial level be 2,400—the magic number from Vladivostok—but now agreed to lower the level during the period covered by the agreement to 2,250. The level of 1,320 combined ICBMs with MIRVs, SLBMs with MIRVs, and ALCMs remained. But now Gromyko also agreed to a new subceiling within that level, limiting the number of ICBMs and SLBMs with MIRVs to 1,250 (rather than the 1,200 proposed)—still a major concession by the Soviets, since it limited their MIRV programs, and they had no ALCM program to pick up the slack. And he confirmed a limit on ICBM launchers with MIRVs of 820. The limit on modern large ICBMs remained at the existing level (308 launchers in the Soviet Union, none in the United States).[24]

The final figures were not agreed to until much later (2,400 going to 2,250 for the aggregate total; 1,320 for MIRV and ALCM systems; 1,200 for missile launchers with MIRVs; and 820 ICBM launchers with MIRVs). But it was relatively easy to reach a compromise agreement on them. The key differences between the Vladivostok and initial Carter approaches had been resolved. SALT II was back on the track.[25]

There have been subsequent Soviet allusions to September–October 1977 as a crucial time of missed opportunity for agreement. Clearly the Soviet leaders hoped that the series of compromises advanced or accepted by Gromyko in September would break the logjam and lead to an early agreement.[26] While the progress in the fall of 1977 constituted a substantial step

24. Soviet acceptance of a limit of 820 launchers for ICBMs with MIRVs entailed a cutback of at least 100 in the number the Soviet Union would otherwise have deployed, belying the disparaging comment often voiced in the United States that the SALT II Treaty only sanctioned limits allowing as many missile launchers as the Soviets wanted to build. The Soviets had planned to convert an additional 50 SS-11 ICBM launchers to SS-17 launchers and another 50 to SS-19 launchers, which would have brought the total number of launchers for ICBMs with MIRVs (SS-17, -18, and -19) to 918.

25. For an excellent, detailed review of the May through September deliberations in Washington and Geneva see Talbott, *Endgame,* pp. 88–132. Vance, *Hard Choices,* pp. 56–61, and Brzezinski, *Power and Principle,* pp. 167–70, provide less detailed but more authoritative accounts (correcting a few specific errors, but confirming most of Talbott's review).

26. In particular see V. V. Kortunov, "The CPSU in the Struggle for Détente: Confrontation of the Two Tendencies in International Affairs," *Voprosy istorii KPSS* [Questions of History of

forward and put the negotiations back on the Vladivostok line, it did not lead to an early accord. The reason is that a number of the old disagreements remained, while new ones soon arose as well. Backfire and the limitations on cruise missiles in the protocol still posed considerable problems, although they appeared soluble. Among the issues coming to the fore were several concerning verification, a subject that became more sensitive owing to renewed charges by American opponents of SALT that the Soviets had violated the existing SALT I agreements. On October 3 the SALT I Interim Agreement formally expired, but both sides had agreed to de facto continued compliance.[27]

The changed administration proposals that had come close to agreement in September became publicly known through leaks to those who favored a hard line on SALT, such as Senator Jackson and Nitze. Nitze in turn made public most of the details of the negotiations provided on a strictly secret basis in administration testimony to Congress.[28] Not only had the attempt in March to bring the hard-liners on board collapsed, but after October 1977 they mounted a strong renewed campaign against the approach to the still in-complete SALT II agreement. Thus nearly two years before the final agree-ment and presentation by the administration of its case for the treaty, the opposition was carrying on a vocal campaign against it. As noted earlier, this new campaign against SALT included renewed charges of Soviet violations and noncompliance with SALT I, such as those by Melvin R. Laird in an article in *Reader's Digest* in December 1977. The administration responded by issuing a declassified report on the proceedings of the Standing Consultative Commis-sion set up in 1972 to monitor the SALT agreements and other data refuting the charges of Soviet noncompliance and an American cover-up. But the ad-ministration, and SALT, were nevertheless from that time on constantly on the defensive in the public perception.[29]

The lost time and reduced mutual confidence involved in the ill-starred attempt by Carter to put SALT II on a new path in 1977 was even

---

the CPSU], no. 10 (October 1980), p. 32. Kortunov is a senior official of the party Central Committee, concerned with international affairs.

27. There had never been any issue between the United States and the Soviet Union over infor-mal extension of the constraints mandated by the Interim Agreement. Secretary of State Vance had formally told Gromyko on September 10 of the U.S. intention to continue comply-ing with those constraints, and on September 24 the Soviets joined in a statement of their parallel intention. "A Joint Soviet-American Statement on the Questions of Limiting Strategic Arms," *Pravda*, September 25, 1977.

The Soviets had proposed an exchange of formal letters extending the Interim Agreement, but the United States turned that proposal down because it would have required congressional approval. It was feared that such a step would have precipitated a premature SALT debate. In later Senate hearings, the administration's explanation that a unilateral statement of intention did not require congressional action was accepted.

28. Susanna McBee, "SALT Critic Reveals Details of Talks," *Washington Post*, November 2, 1977.

29. Talbott, *Endgame*, pp. 133–45. See also Vance, *Hard Choices*, pp. 61–63.

more basically affected by the general decline in American-Soviet relations. By the time the negotiation of SALT II was back on track, the roadbed undergirding that track was being weakened and would soon be disrupted by new American-Soviet confrontations over other issues in the world, such as the conflict in the Horn of Africa and the U.S. turn toward China.

1978: *Doldrums and Linkages*

Progress toward a SALT agreement in 1978 was erratic. Not only were the remaining issues complex, but as seen, the uneven general course of American-Soviet relations also affected the pace of efforts on SALT adversely. The Soviet role in Ethiopia, already an issue in the fall of 1977, by early 1978 was especially disturbing to Washington.[30] Thus when Vance and Gromyko met in April in Moscow, there had not been much progress on the major issues. Nor did they succeed in making headway, although they did compromise on some prominent (if not really significant) differences, such as accepting the American figure of 1,200 missile launchers with MIRVs (within the 1,320 MIRV plus ALCM ceiling earlier agreed on) and the Soviet second-stage aggregate level of 2,250. (In fact, the Soviets offered a choice of 1,250 and 2,200, or 1,200 and 2,250. The United States decided to keep the overall level of MIRVs lower.)[31]

---

30. Brzezinski in particular was strongly inclined in 1978 to hold back on SALT until the Soviet Union was more responsive to American views "on what was and was not acceptable" in competition in the third world. In his memoir Brzezinski comments: "I felt strongly that we were making a fundamental mistake in concentrating so heavily on SALT, without engaging the Soviets in a broader strategic dialogue . . . I had profound reservations about both the tactics and the substance of Vance's, and to some extent also the President's, approach to the Soviets." Brzezinski, *Power and Principle*, p. 317.

31. See Talbott, *Endgame*, pp. 146–53; Vance, *Hard Choices*, pp. 99–100; and Brzezinski, *Power and Principle*, p. 326, for discussions of this period. None of these sources, however, includes reference to the Soviet readiness to accept either the 1,200/2,250 or 1,250/2,200 compromises. I ascertained them from other participants.

   As Vance notes in his memoir, "Ironically, the April Soviet acceptance of a reduction of the Vladivostok ceiling and the new ceiling on MIRVed missiles was characterized by SALT opponents as a U.S. compromise, which was nonsense. To reach 2,250, the Soviets would have to eliminate over 250 systems; we would not have to eliminate any American systems. The same was true of the 1,200 figure. . . . Despite such a favorable outcome, several Republican senators issued a statement on May 3 attacking the administration for 'a frightening pattern of giving up key U.S. weapons systems for nothing in return.' They claimed the emerging agreement represented a retreat from the March [1977] comprehensive proposal, and described as U.S. concessions what in fact were Soviet moves toward our own positions." *Hard Choices*, p. 100. There was, of course, movement by both sides, but Vance is essentially correct. This example illustrates the woeful domestic consequences of the March 1977 proposals.

When Vance and Gromyko met again in Geneva in July, the American side was upset by the announcement that the Soviet dissident Shcharansky would be tried, while the Soviets were increasingly disturbed by the U.S. moves toward China. In a meeting with Vance in May Gromyko protested in particular the fact (reported in the press) that on his visit to Beijing Brzezinski had briefed the Chinese in some detail on SALT. The two sides in May also traded accusations over the interventions in Africa.[32]

The July talks did lead to agreement on one important new limitation: each side would deploy no more than one new type of ICBM. In May 1977 the United States had replaced its March proposal for a limit on test firings of missiles with a proposal to ban testing of any new types of ICBMs for the three years of the protocol (the MX would not be ready for testing for at least three years). The Soviets sought an exception: the right to one single-warhead ICBM without MIRVs to replace old types. (The Soviet military program evidently was considered adequate as to the SS-17, -18, and -19 ICBMs with MIRVs, but in need of an improved solid-fueled replacement for its single-warhead SS-11.) In April 1978 the United States proposed a ban on any new ICBM systems during the three years of the protocol, and then one new ICBM system (with or without MIRVs) during the treaty period until 1985. In May Gromyko advanced the most far-reaching arms control variant (and described it as such): he proposed a ban on *any* new ICBM for the duration of the treaty. But the administration considered the MX essential. In July, while agreement was not actually reached, Gromyko indicated that if other questions were resolved satisfactorily, the Soviets could probably accept the main element of the earlier U.S. proposal: allowance of only one new type of ICBM, MIRV or non-MIRV, on each side during the treaty period.[33]

Vance also informed Gromyko in July that after the three-year protocol expired the United States would retain the option of deploying the MX (notwithstanding Soviet agreement as early as October 1977 not to deploy its mobile SS-16 ICBM). This statement was considered necessary to assuage those who feared that the three-year ban on deployment of mobile ICBMs in the protocol would prejudice the MX—including Senator Jackson, Paul Nitze, and General Edward Rowny (the JCS representative on the SALT II delegation). The main problem was the form of mobile deployment. The Defense

---

32. On these and other issues see chapter 18.

33. From the standpoint of arms control (and of Soviet readiness to embark on serious arms control) it is highly regrettable that the United States was not prepared in 1978 to accept the Soviet proposal for no new ICBM (or even the single-warhead missile proposal, which prefigured the later American interest in 1983 in a Midgetman missile to replace the systems with MIRVs). But Brzezinski reflects the position he and Brown had urged, and the administration had adopted, in his retrospective comment: "There is no doubt that the Soviet concession on the new types [of ICBM] issue at the July meeting was a major break. It had the effect of sanctioning a possible U.S. MX deployment while obtaining for the United States significant limitations on Soviet ICBM modernization." Brzezinski, *Power and Principle*, p. 326. See also Vance, *Hard Choices*, pp. 103–04.

Department increasingly was inclined toward some multiple protective silo system, involving rotating missiles among up to ten times as many silos or trench launch points. This concept posed serious problems of verification, and the Soviets accordingly objected strongly. The United States said it would only deploy a verifiable system, but the issue simmered unresolved.

With agreement in sight on limiting the number of ICBMs with MIRVs, attention gravitated to a newly recognized aspect of the problem: the number of MIRVs per missile. Critics such as Nitze outside, and the JCS inside, the government raised the issue. There was little doubt in Washington about the value of such a limitation, but it was very difficult to devise limits that would be verifiable (to say nothing of negotiable).

The United States pressed for limiting existing systems to the number of MIRVs already tested and developed: four on each SS-17, six on the SS-19, ten on the SS-18, three on the Minuteman II, and ten for the future U.S. MX. The Soviets sought to limit the MX to six, since it would not be a heavy ICBM. There was agreement on limiting SLBMs to fourteen warheads, the largest number tested on the American Poseidon C-3 missile. The Soviets also raised the issue of the number of MIRV-equivalent ALCMs per heavy bomber, while the United States initially opposed such a limit. These issues, raised at the July talks, were not resolved.

Cruise missile problems remained as well. One issue, raised by the United States at the insistence of the Department of Defense, concerned the definition of the range of a cruise missile: the United States wished to build in some flexibility for different kinds of flight profiles, while the Soviets preferred a simple maximum (fly-out) range. The American concern was focused principally on the ALCM, while the Soviets wanted above all to confine the range of ground-launched cruise missiles (GLCMs) and SLCMs to a 600-kilometer range, with anything above that banned for the three-year life of the protocol. There was another issue, too. The Pentagon now wished to exempt cruise missiles with conventional warheads and limit only those with nuclear warheads. President Carter overruled Vance and Warnke and sought Soviet agreement on this approach, although no one was able to devise an effective way of distinguishing cruise missiles with nuclear warheads from those carrying nonnuclear warheads. The Soviets pointed out this problem and objected strenuously.

A host of other issues remained or arose, such as whether to ban or limit encryption of telemetry from missile testing as a verification aid. While agreements were reached on various issues, new ones appeared. That pattern prevailed throughout most of 1978.[34]

By the fall of 1978 there was a growing feeling in the Carter administration that SALT must be pushed through to agreement soon or it would collapse. By the time Gromyko returned to the United States in September, the Camp David Egyptian-Israeli accord had been reached, and one of Pres-

---

34. Talbott, *Endgame*, pp. 154–202.

ident Carter's closest advisers was quoted as recalling that the president said he hoped to "convert the force for peace-making we've unleashed here into something that will finally give us SALT."[35] The September meetings, including another between Gromyko and Carter, yielded progress on several issues but did not mark a major step toward final agreement.[36] In October Vance again went to Moscow. And again there was some further agreement and hints of still more, but no decisive advance.[37]

Meanwhile, partly in preparation for an eventual struggle over ratification of SALT and partly owing to his personal preferences, Warnke in October left the administration. A retired general, George Seignious, succeeded him as head of the ACDA, while his deputy on the SALT delegation, Ralph Earle, took over at the Geneva negotiating table. The transparent ploy of selecting a general to head the disarmament agency (an idea of Brzezinski's) did nothing to mollify the opposition.

Some of the Soviet proposals in September and October presented difficult choices. For example, Gromyko offered to remove altogether the 2,500-kilometer limit on strategic ALCMs carried on heavy bombers (rather than accept the loose American proposals advanced in September to redefine and thus extend that limit). This concession was conditioned on American acceptance of a tight definition on the 600-kilometer limit for GLCMs and SLCMs, and on applying limits to all ALCMs, not merely those carrying nuclear weapons. The Soviets were able to argue for those two points on the basis of verifiability—usually an American argument. Finally, several of the key American advisers (Brzezinski and Vice President Mondale, accepting an argument long pressed by Vance and Warnke) persuaded Carter that the earlier U.S. position would pose risks to this country when the protocol expired, as the Soviets could put longer range ALCMs with nuclear warheads on the Backfire and claim they were only conventionally armed and had only a 600-kilometer effective range. The JCS, too, were prepared to agree. Meanwhile, agreement was near on a compromise on the numbers of ALCMs per bomber. In addition, most American policymakers had decided to accept Soviet assurances on the Backfire—and to retain the option of producing a similar American aircraft, an extended range, stretched version of the FB-111. The cruise missile and Backfire issues were nearing resolution.[38]

In agreeing on a Vance-Gromyko SALT meeting in Geneva just before Christmas 1978, Dobrynin had conveyed the encouraging prediction that the two sides might then be in a position to announce a date for a summit

---

35. Ibid., p. 205.

36. See Vance, *Hard Choices*, pp. 105–07; Brzezinski, *Power and Principle*, pp. 326–27; Carter, *Keeping Faith*, pp. 231–33; and Talbott, *Endgame*, p. 205.

37. See Vance, *Hard Choices*, pp. 107–09; Brzezinski, *Power and Principle*, p. 328; and Talbott, *Endgame*, pp. 217–21.

38. Talbott, *Endgame*, pp. 206–25; and Vance, *Hard Choices*, pp. 105–09.

meeting at which Carter and Brezhnev could sign the SALT II Treaty. Tentative plans began to be made in Washington and Moscow for a summit in mid-January 1979, and in early December plans for a SALT summit in Washington in the week of January 15 were leaked to the press.[39]

It was at this critical juncture, as noted earlier, that the United States and China suddenly announced plans for establishment of full relations and a January mini-summit visit by the Chinese leader Deng Xiaoping.

When Vance met Gromyko again in Geneva a week later, a number of new issues arose in SALT—issues that eventually were solved but that slowed the conclusion of the agreement. Some progress was made; the Soviet side did not simply stonewall. On December 22 Gromyko did introduce a new issue, remote-piloted drone vehicles (RPVs), which some interpreted as a stalling issue prompted by the China move. But despite the surfacing of new problems, an early agreement still seemed possible, given progress on other issues. On December 22 Vance and his delegation (which included General Seignious, Paul Warnke as a special adviser, and Ambassador Earle) requested authorization on two remaining issues that they believed would permit agreement and still make possible a mid-January 1979 summit.

Regrettably, precisely at this point doubts had arisen in Washington on one of these issues—encryption of missile test telemetry. The key meeting in Washington at which instructions for Vance were discussed was chaired by Brzezinski and included Secretary of Defense Brown and CIA Director Turner (much involved with this particular issue). After the meeting Brzezinski telephoned the president and Carter authorized instructing Vance as the group had agreed. A cable was dispatched.

Upon receipt of the instruction, Vance called Brzezinski and angrily objected and appealed. By the time Brzezinski reached Carter, reconfirmed the instructions, and called Vance the secretary of state was already at the Soviet mission for the day's meeting—leading to a highly unusual and undesirable situation in which Brzezinski (masking the precise subject) again told Vance that the president was firm on the issue. Gromyko then heard Vance, implementing the instructions, seem to harden the American position on encryption by objecting to a Soviet test of the previous July. He reciprocated by insisting on resolution of all remaining issues before announcement of a summit meeting. Overall agreement could not be reached at that point.

Meanwhile, the White House had already alerted the television networks to a possible major broadcast by the president. Thus the remainder of that day in Geneva, December 23, was spent working out a way to indicate that further progress had been made, but nothing more. Apart from the specific

---

39. Talbott, *Endgame*, pp. 225, 229; and see Vance, *Hard Choices*, p. 109.

These published memoir accounts gloss over the fact that there was in fact specific tentative agreement on a summit meeting in mid-January to sign a SALT II treaty. The Soviets were unhappy that this secret diplomatic agreement was leaked by the White House. Information from U.S. and Soviet officials.

issues, the United States had overestimated Soviet readiness to proceed with the conclusion of SALT and the long-delayed summit meeting. And the Soviet leaders saw an American effort to squeeze them on some specific SALT issues, but even more to play the China card in conjunction with a Soviet-American summit conference. And to that they would not accede.[40]

1979: Success—and Failure

As seen earlier, events in 1979 greatly complicated the conclusion of the SALT II negotiations and undermined later ratification of the treaty once signed. The announcement in December of the Sino-U.S. normalization had been jarring; the character and the consequence of Deng's visit to Washington were still more damaging.[41] In January the Soviet leaders were in no mood to consider SALT compromises given that Chinese troops had invaded their ally Vietnam, just as Deng had indicated while he was in Washington. On the American side, the overthrow of the shah of Iran not only caused new political uncertainties but also deprived the United States of technical intelligence collection stations in Iran that constituted an important national means of verification for SALT. But the general increase in tension between the United States and the Soviet Union, and reciprocal loss of confidence, posed the major obstacle to rapid movement on SALT.

Following a private demarche to Brezhnev from President Carter through Dobrynin in February, the Soviet leader struck a constructive pitch in a public speech at the beginning of March. He stated his expectation that SALT would "probably" be signed in an early meeting with President Carter. In addition to the negotiations in Geneva, there was correspondence between Carter and Brezhnev from February to April (especially over the sensitive te-

---

40. Talbott, *Endgame*, pp. 225–48; Vance, *Hard Choices*, pp. 110–12; Brzezinski, *Power and Principle*, pp. 329–30; and Carter, *Keeping Faith*, p. 234.

 Following the unexpected U.S.-China announcement of a visit by Deng Xiaoping to Washington just a week before the planned summit meeting with Brezhnev, and then a hardening of American positions on several remaining SALT issues, the Soviets saw themselves being unacceptably used, and balked.

41. The impact of the U.S. decision in December 1978 to establish full relations with China on Soviet negotiating tactics on SALT is a matter of some uncertainty and dispute. Vance, who was absorbed in the SALT negotiation, regards its "manner and timing" as the primary factor in "the sudden surge of Soviet inflexibility." Brzezinski, who had pressed for the Chinese connection and handled it with éclat, is naturally not so inclined. Brzezinski cites Dobrynin as having said that the stalemate in SALT at that juncture was caused by the issues and not by the China moves (Dobrynin probably said the cause was the *American* position on the issues, rather than the *Soviet* reaction to American relations with China). See Vance, *Hard Choices*, pp. 112–13; and Brzezinski, *Power and Principle*, pp. 330–31. See also the discussion in chapter 21.

lemetry encryption issue) and frequent meetings of Vance and Dobrynin. A number of highly technical issues had to be hammered out involving limits on missile testing procedures (including missile test release simulations for possible penetration aids), and the allowable number of MIRVs, which neither the Soviet nor the American military wished to limit. Not to do so would, however, make verification of the increasingly precise and complex limitations being negotiated more uncertain. And opponents of SALT seized upon data leaked to them to publicize these matters in a manner prejudicial to the agreement still under confidential negotiation.

Ironically, although the number of issues resolved was outpacing the new problems and the conclusion of the agreement was seemingly in view, each remaining issue assumed ever greater intensity, if not significance. Vance met with Dobrynin some twenty-five times between January 1 and May 7. The Carter-Brezhnev correspondence has been noted. And the delegations in Geneva were hard at work. Finally, Vance and Dobrynin on May 7 resolved the remaining substantive questions—including the removal of the environmental shelters obscuring the Minuteman III silos that President Ford had promised four years earlier. The final clean-up of remaining secondary issues—involving far more than merely polishing up the language of the treaty—was completed in early June. In fact, the final details were ironed out only on June 14, the very eve of the summit meeting.[42]

The signing of SALT II at the Vienna summit—and the painful debate over ratification during the remainder of 1979—have been discussed in detail earlier.[43] In retrospect it is clear that the Carter administration did not do an adequate job preparing the ground in the United States to ensure sufficient public and congressional support for the SALT II Treaty. Some of the difficulties were not foreseeable or were not of the administration's making. For example, an important part of the Republican establishment at the center apparently decided as early as 1977 that it would support Carter on the Panama Canal Treaties—but not on SALT.[44] At that point the substance of the SALT treaty was still very much open and hence was not at issue. The problem was that, for political reasons, these Republican leaders did not believe they could afford to support the Carter administration on both issues. An important part of their constituency regarded the Panama Canal Treaties as a giveaway and the arms limitations as being soft on the Russians.

The Carter administration was partly to blame, however, for holding back so long before mounting a strong public campaign in support of

---

42. Talbott, *Endgame*, pp. 249–78; Vance, *Hard Choices*, pp. 133–35; and an interview with Ralph Earle. For additional details of the final days see the informed account in "The SALT Summit," *Newsweek*, June 25, 1979, pp. 26–27.

43. See chapter 21. See also, for the flavor of the discussion of the SALT issues at the summit meeting, Carter, *Keeping Faith*, pp. 250–53, 255.

44. Among a number of political figures or observers who have reached this conclusion, one who had some direct experience is Jimmy Carter. *Keeping Faith*, pp. 224–25.

SALT.[45] The opposition was going strong, as noted, long before the administration really started its efforts. Carter admits that he began the campaign for the treaty only with his speech to the American Newspaper Publishers convention on April 25, 1979.[46] In some cases attempts to help backfired, notably a visit to Moscow by a group of senators led by Senator Abraham Ribicoff. Meetings with some Soviet officials became confrontational and, if anything, reduced readiness by some of the senators to support the treaty.[47]

It is appropriate to note here briefly several points. First, the SALT II Treaty was an advance over the more limited Vladivostok accord in a number of respects. For example, it limited the numbers of ICBMs, as well as the overall number of missiles with MIRVs and the multiple-warhead delivery systems including ALCM. Even more significant, it established limits on "fractionation," or the numbers of MIRVs per missile. The final treaty was clearly more advantageous to the United States, and to real arms control in the common interest, than the Vladivostok accord had been or the incomplete agreement of 1976. But the improvements beyond the simpler Vladivostok framework worked out with such great difficulty from 1977 to 1979 were purchased at an excessive price. That price was not the concessions on the substance of the agreement, but the time consumed in negotiations and the erosion both of the strategic value of the limitations and above all of public and political support for SALT in the United States. A less comprehensive agreement as pressed for by Kissinger in 1975–76 could have been ratified more readily, notwithstanding the opposition. Similarly, the Carter administration could have gained more than enough support in 1977. (Also lost were the possible advantages that might have come from improved political understanding through an early Carter-Brezhnev summit meeting.) But by 1979 both the course of political events in the world (and in turn in the United States) and developments affecting the strategic balance had outpaced the negotiations. The SALT II process became a case in which the operation was a success, but the patient unfortunately died.

A good argument could still be made in 1979, and was made by the administration, for the advantages of the treaty as compared with no treaty.

---

45. For a trenchant review see Alan Platt, "STARTing on SALT III," *Washington Quarterly*, vol. 5 (Spring 1982), pp. 17–24.

46. Carter, *Keeping Faith*, p. 239. He still does not seem to realize how late this was.

   The State Department had begun a public information program on SALT in 1978, but it was a far cry from the strident efforts of the American Security Council, the Committee on the Present Danger, and other anti-SALT lobbying organizations.

   It must be recognized that the administration was handicapped in its efforts before signature because of the continuing negotiation. The specifics of the treaty were classified, and the United States and the Soviet Union had agreed not to make them public. In addition, parts of the treaty draft remained unresolved and in flux.

47. Ibid., pp. 236–37.

But that was not enough. If the treaty was "fatally flawed," it was not owing to its terms (as opponents charged) but to its protracted travail and delayed conclusion. Despite lengthy hearings and an array of esoteric criticism of particular aspects of the agreement (for example, on Backfire, the constraints on cruise missiles in the protocol, the verifiability of various provisions), opponents of the treaty did not present a case against the treaty that was convincing to the Senate or the public at large. Rather, the treaty foundered on three other shoals. First was whether it was sufficient for or even *relevant* to strategic needs—it would not, in fact, prevent a Soviet capability threatening to the American ICBM force. Second was a concern over whether the SALT process was sapping the U.S. will to maintain the military programs necessary to ensure a military balance. Finally, there was a question whether SALT (and détente) was in keeping with the political actions of the Soviet Union, which were perceived as posing a general threat to U.S. interests. The Carter administration concluded (in my judgment correctly) that these considerations did not outweigh the advantages of ratification. But first the inflated and inflammatory Cuba brigade issue, then the psychologically emasculating Iranian hostage situation, and finally the Soviet occupation of Afghanistan made ratification first uncertain and eventually not possible for the Carter presidency.

The fact that the terms of the treaty were, at the least, not disadvantageous to the United States could be seen by their later continued tacit observance by the Reagan administration. This acceptance was based in major part on strong if quiet urging by the JCS that overrode the more negative ideological preferences of some civilians brought in by the new administration. What the opposition most opposed was the form of shared commitment and political coaction with the Soviet Union that ratification of the treaty implied. Indeed, if concerns over parity, and public perceptions of equality, had been a real issue, clearly ratification would have been desirable: to reach the agreed equal levels the Soviet Union would have had to dismantle some 250 operational units, the United States none. In practice, even the Reagan administration in its first term *decreased* the number of American strategic forces, owing to unilateral decisions on cost-effectiveness of some older systems such as the Titan II ICBMs and older model B-52s, and the long lead time for new programs such as the B-1B bomber, the MX ICBM, and the Trident II SLBM. That reduction did not entail any reduction in Soviet forces.

SALT also attracted the wrath of those in the United States who opposed various unilateral military retrenchments. The cancellation of the B-1 bomber by President Carter, and his decision not to produce and deploy neutron weapons, have often been cited as restraints the Soviet Union did not match. But these actions were not intended or advanced as initiatives conditioned on, or even undertaken in the expectation of, reciprocal actions by the other side. Some people criticized the administration for *not* using such planned unilateral restraints as bargaining chips to get a reciprocal Soviet concession.[48] Many others have cited them as unrequited steps to which the Soviet Union should have responded. If it was in the American interest not to produce those weapons, then it would probably have been a mistake to make the decisions on their production dependent on reciprocation. It was not the fault of SALT, of the administration, or of the other side that unilateral actions taken by the United States in its own interest, such as the decision not to produce the B-1 bomber, did not elicit concessions from the other side. They were not concessions by the American side. Overall, however, both the Soviet Union and the United States have shown much less unilateral restraint than would have been in their long-term common interest. This fact is one reason why negotiated mutual obligations to undertake specified reciprocal restraints are so important and necessary.

In retrospect, it is clear that the attempt by the Carter administration to launch an ambitious new SALT approach in March 1977 was fatefully unwise. Even though SALT II got back on track within a few months in 1977, and was concluded by mid-1979, the SALT negotiations as conducted by the Carter administration from the outset caused the Soviets to have serious doubts and suspicions about the American administration, weakened the support the Carter administration got for SALT at home, and caused delays that pushed SALT into the path of other political issues from Ethiopia to the brigade in Cuba and to Afghanistan.

The Soviet leaders contributed to the failure of SALT II by their stubborn attempts to negotiate the most favorable terms they could obtain without being aware of the weakening foundation for the whole negotiation in the United States. For example, their refusal to accept more than grudging minimal (and ambiguous) restraints on missile testing telemetry cost the Soviet Union far more in political terms than it was possibly worth in military-technical terms. This outcome of the telemetry issue also laid the foundation for later suspicions and charges of noncompliance. Dragging out the negotiations

---

48. Ideally, cancellation of the B-1 should, however, have been used to elicit some Soviet concession in SALT. But particularly in view of the divided views on the decision within the administration, this would have been a very difficult and risky matter. First, a contingent decision to forgo the B-1 would have leaked and raised further opposition from proponents of the system. Second, both proponents of the B-1 and opponents of SALT would have pressed for demanding stiff and perhaps inordinate concessions from the Soviet Union as a price for nonproduction of the bomber, reducing negotiability and complicating the negotiation. If the demands had proved too high, or the Soviets had refused to bargain, the administration would have had to reconsider its decision. Cancellation of the B-1 under those circumstances, without having got a quid pro quo Soviet concession, would have engendered further opposition (as well as exposed the earlier bargaining attempt as a bluff). Alternatively, pressures to produce the plane would have risen, and might have demanded acquiring a system earlier rejected on its merits. If the bomber were neither "traded" nor produced, the administration would have been on the defensive for both its defense policy and its SALT negotiation performance. And if the attempt to use the bomber for bargaining had seriously impeded progress on SALT, it would also have been criticized by proponents of SALT. The whole question was far more complex than it appears on the surface.

in 1978–79 in the face of perceived American attempts to gain advantages and then in response to the U.S. playing of the China card, however justified that course may have seemed in Moscow, in retrospect was responsible for a crucial delay. Indeed, notwithstanding the understandable Soviet objections to the original American proposals of March 1977, with the benefit of hindsight the Soviet leaders might have seen (and in private some Soviet analysts have done so) that their reaction to that new approach did not in the long run serve their own best interests.

The Soviet reaction to the U.S. failure to ratify the signed SALT II Treaty in 1979–80, apart from indignation and anger, led to a retroactive reappraisal of the Carter administration's policy and of broader American aims. Brezhnev himself, after Carter withdrew the doomed treaty from Senate consideration in the aftermath of Afghanistan, referred darkly to the failure of ratification, "not without the connivance of government circles in the United States."[49] A Central Committee official noted, not without logic, that it had been inconsistent for Carter to play up the Soviet threat and then expect ratification of the SALT treaty.[50] There were differing views in Moscow over the extent of deviousness or merely vacillation and inconsistency on the part of President Carter himself, and over the meaning of shifts of influence among key members of his administration. The longer-term Soviet reaction was to conclude that the deeper cause of the U.S. failure to support SALT in the twilight years of détente was not the vagaries of personalities in the American leadership or shifts caused by such ephemeral factors as American politics or American (and Soviet) positions on the issues. Rather, it was a deeper unreadiness by the ruling circles in America to accept strategic parity. U.S. arguments over whether SALT was balanced or gave advantages to the Soviet side were not regarded as serious. In the Soviet view, the American leadership ultimately rejected SALT *because* it codified and preserved parity, whereas the aim in the United States was military advantage and superiority.[51]

The Soviet leaders also drew conclusions about the American political system and process, as well as about a shift in American aims. These conclusions were equally unsettling not only for the future of arms limitation but for the prospect of improving relations. This position was spelled out clearly by Genrykh Trofimenko, a leading Soviet specialist on the United States: "The fate of the SALT II Treaty, as of a number of other American-Soviet agreements, raised a very serious question as to whether in general it was possible to reach agreements with the United States. And it is not just a question of the fact that every new American administration likes to break the chain of conti-

---

49. "Answers by L. I. Brezhnev to Questions by a Correspondent of 'Pravda,'" *Pravda*, January 13, 1980.

50. Valentin Falin, Studio Nine, Moscow Domestic Television, March 1, in FBIS, *Soviet Union*, March 14, 1980, pp. A1–2.

51. See G. Trofimenko, "Lessons of Peaceful Coexistence," *Voprosy istorii* [Questions of History], no. 11 (November 1983), pp. 20–21. See also the discussion in chapter 22.

nuity and begin negotiations from a clean slate. It's a problem even within one and the same administration."[52] He continued by citing as "the first unexpected development for the Soviet side, and the first American blow to détente," the failure of Congress to support the package of economic agreements with reciprocal concessions negotiated by the Nixon administration. Instead, the complex of economic agreements was undercut by the Jackson-Vanik amendment that tied the American side of the package to further concessions by the Soviets. "That turn of affairs demonstrated that the United States was not ready to fulfill the obligations that had been given with great fanfare by its leaders in reaching agreements at the highest level."

"Drawing the corresponding conclusions," Trofimenko states, "greater attention was given in the Soviet Union to the position of Congress. In particular, in working out the SALT II Treaty the Soviet side took into account Public Law 92-448 adopted by the Congress and signed by the U.S. President in 1972, entering into force on the American side with the SALT I agreement. Section III of that law states that Congress accepts the principle of equality between the United States and the USSR reflected in the ABM Treaty and 'urges and requests the President to seek a future treaty that, inter alia, would not limit the United States to levels of intercontinental strategic forces inferior to the limits provided for the Soviet Union.'" This provision for equal levels of intercontinental forces, he claims, "was intended to give the United States in a new future agreement not only equality, but certain advantages," given the geopolitical situation. "Nonetheless, in order to curb the arms race and stabilize the Soviet-American strategic balance, the USSR was ready to treat such a strictly numerical equality as real equality and equal security without demanding for itself any compensation warranted by geopolitical considerations." (This reference applies to the Soviet concession of equal levels of intercontinental forces without taking into account the American FBS and British and French nuclear forces. This concession had been made to President Ford at Vladivostok in late 1974 and was maintained throughout the SALT II negotiations under the Carter administration.)

"And so SALT II was signed and presented to the Senate for ratification." Then, as Trofimenko correctly notes, the Senate Armed Services Committee reported that "in our judgment the SALT II treaty presently before the Senate fails to meet the criteria laid down in 1972," citing the language of PL 92-448 but arguing that the legislative history supported an interpretation calling for "equal numbers of intercontinental strategic forces taking account of throw-weight," in other words, inequality in numbers in order to get equality in throw-weight. "Such a way of putting the issue," says Trofimenko, "was unexpected even to Soviet specialists on the United States ready to expect anything." He stresses the absence of any reference to throw-weight in PL 92-488. (The later committee interpretation is, in fact, weak. While Jackson and some

52. Trofimenko, *Voprosy istorii*, no. 11 (1983), p. 22.

others may have been thinking about throw-weight, such an amendment would almost certainly not have passed in 1972.)

Trofimenko's conclusion is worth noting. "How can one reach agreements with a country the President of which cannot reach agreement with the Congress, and when even the Congress in an officially adopted resolution says one thing and then demands something quite different? This question inevitably arises in implementing any new agreement which may be reached with the United States, and not only on matters of arms control, in the future."[53]

Overall, the experience of the SALT II negotiation in 1977–79, even more than before, demonstrated that while a shared interest in avoiding nuclear war provided a basis for détente, parity, and negotiated strategic arms limitations, SALT alone could not carry the full weight of détente when other aspects of the relationship were greatly weakened. Military détente did, indeed, depend upon political détente.

---

53. Ibid., pp. 22–24.

24 A Wild Card: The Soviet Brigade in Cuba, 1979

AT THE END of August and the beginning of September 1979, a development that should have involved no more than a mild flurry of interest became, because of mishandling by the Carter administration, a domestic tempest and an American-Soviet pseudocrisis of confidence that lasted for several weeks. It adversely affected the standing of the Carter administration. Most important, it further seriously damaged—perhaps critically—the fate of the SALT II Treaty, and further weakened the détente in American-Soviet relations.

What Happened?

The event that immediately precipitated the trouble was a dramatic announcement by Senator Frank Church of Idaho, chairman of the Senate Foreign Relations Committee, at a press conference on August 30. He had called it hastily at his home in Idaho, where he was seeking to mend political fences in his bid for reelection. He was at the time under fire from the American Conservative Action Coalition for being soft on defense and relations with Soviet Union. Church disclosed that American intelligence had confirmed the existence of a Soviet combat brigade of ground forces in Cuba, numbering some 2,300–3,000 men. He said the "buildup of Soviet ground-troops to brigade strength has not been reported until recently." Church stated further that he had been advised by Secretary of State Vance that the Soviet embassy had been asked for a full explanation but that no answer had been received. He was very firm on what needed to be done: "The United States," said the senator, "cannot permit the island to become a Russian military base 90 miles from our shores, nor can we allow Cuba to be used as a springboard for Russian military intervention in the Western Hemisphere." He called on the president to "draw the line on Russian penetration of this hemisphere" and to insist on "the immediate withdrawal of all Russian combat troops from Cuba."[1]

The next day Department of State spokesman Hodding Carter read a prepared statement saying that "we have recently confirmed the presence in Cuba of what appears to be a Soviet combat unit" and that "we estimate that it consists of some 2,000–3,000 men," apart from other Soviet military advisory and technical personnel in Cuba (an additional 1,500–2,000 personnel). He noted that ground forces "did not figure in our bilateral understandings [of 1962 and 1970]," but that "nonetheless, we are concerned about the presence of Soviet combat troops in Cuba." He also said that "elements of the unit appear to have been there since at least 1976." Finally, he stated that the United States had called in the Soviet chargé d'affaires on August 29 to express its concern and would continue discussions.[2]

If the State Department announcement had been the first release, there would have been many questions and a flurry of comments before they were answered, but probably not a serious political "flap." But the inflammatory rhetoric of Senator Church—a dove—put the administration off balance and on the defensive. The subject rapidly became a major item of speculation.

The impact of the whole affair was not reduced when, on September 5 at a press conference, Secretary of State Vance said that "we regard this as a very serious matter affecting our relations with the Soviet Union. The presence of this unit runs counter to long-held American policies." Vance disclosed that continuing intelligence analysis had led to the conclusion that "this unit," and not just "elements" of it, had been in Cuba "since at least the mid-1970's." He confirmed that it was not covered by the 1962 or 1970 understandings. But he repeated that the brigade was "a serious matter" and "of serious concern," and that while the United States still did not know if it constituted a "base," it hoped to clarify that. Most important, he stated: "I will not be satisfied with maintenance of the status quo."[3] Vance did not explain why, if the brigade had been there at least since the mid-1970s and did not contravene any bilateral understandings, the status quo should not be satisfactory, but instead constitute a serious concern "affecting our relations with the Soviet Union." Headlines cited Vance as having said the status quo was "unacceptable," although Vance had not used that word.[4]

On the same day the administration intensively briefed a number of members of Congress, but with two contradictory purposes: first, to justify its own intelligence findings and statements of concern; and second, to per-

1. "2,300-Man Soviet Unit Now in Cuba," *Washington Post*, August 31, 1979.

2. "Soviet Combat Troops in Cuba," Department Statement, August 31, *Department of State Bulletin*, vol. 79 (October 1979), p. 63. (Hereafter *State Bulletin*.)

3. "News Conference of September 5," *State Bulletin*, vol. 79 (October 1979), pp. 14–15.

4. For example, Don Oberdorfer, "Vance: Status Quo Unacceptable to U.S.," *Washington Post*, September 6, 1979.

suade them that the situation was in hand and should not be regarded as *too* alarming. The result was predictably confusing, and various members of Congress moved off in different directions. Publicly Senator Robert Byrd of West Virginia tried to calm the whole issue, and privately he expressed surprise that Vance had gone so far as to suggest the status quo was not acceptable. Senator Church, whose comments received the major press play, said there was "no likelihood whatever" that the Senate would approve SALT II as long as Soviet troops remained in Cuba. Previously a foe of SALT linkage, Church now seemed more concerned with justifying his own extreme early statement on the unacceptability of the presence of the Soviet troops than with anything else. A few days later, on September 9, he took the further step of temporarily postponing the SALT II hearings in order to ride the Cuba brigade issue—having converted it into his crisis, to establish a new image of being a tough liberal. Also on September 6, Senator Richard Stone, a liberal Democrat from Florida with a strong anti-Castro constituency, who ever since the October 1973 war had taken an increasingly anti-Soviet, antidétente stance, claimed that the brigade (to which he had drawn attention even before its presence had been officially confirmed) was of a gravity equal to the original Cuban missile crisis. By implication he was calling for the same kind of military-political confrontation with the Soviet Union. While his position was extreme, many commentators again called attention to the MiG-23 issue, and there was a general resurgence of American neuralgia over Castro's Cuba and the Cuban-Soviet tie. Senator Robert Dole of Kansas said he would introduce a resolution to the effect that the Senate would not consider the SALT II Treaty until the Soviet troops were out of Cuba. Byrd quickly countered by saying what had become obvious—that he would not bring the treaty to the floor until it could get a fair hearing, and that might require first resolving the controversy over Soviet troops in Cuba.

The situation was rapidly getting out of hand. As the *Washington Post* stated editorially on September 7, "The Administration has gotten itself into a nice mess over the Soviet combat brigade now reported to be in Cuba."[5] In this situation President Carter decided on September 7 to break the silence he had been keeping in the hope the issue could be contained. In brief remarks to newsmen Carter stated, "This is a time for firm diplomacy, not panic and not exaggeration." He called for the nation to respond "not only with firmness and strength but also with calm and a sense of proportion." He noted that the brigade had evidently been there for some time, "perhaps for quite a few years," and that "it is not an assault force. It does not have airlift or sea-going capabilities and does not have weapons capable of attacking the United States." And he noted that the United States did not yet know the purpose of the brigade. But then, incongruously, the president went on to place his administration further out on the shaky limb on which it had been put by Senator Church's original comment on unacceptability and demand for withdrawal,

5. Editorial, "The Soviet Brigade," *Washington Post*, September 7, 1979.

and by Secretary of State Vance's statement that he did not regard the status quo as satisfactory. Carter said, referring to Vance's statement but in terms hardly in keeping with his own account of the situation or call for "a sense of proportion"—or indeed with the purpose of his own intervention into the controversy—that "the presence of a Soviet combat brigade in Cuba" was "a very serious matter and that this status quo is not acceptable." In attempting to hew to Vance's position, Carter nailed it down further. Moreover, despite his wish to keep the brigade issue separate from SALT, in an attempt to justify the course the administration had slipped into he stated defensively: "We do have the right to insist that the Soviet Union respect our interests and our concerns. . . . Otherwise, relations between our two countries will inevitably be adversely affected."[6] That conclusion provided ample ammunition for opponents of SALT and détente.

That same day, but preceding the president's remarks, National Security Adviser Brzezinski had spoken to a group of editors from around the country visiting Washington. Following a tack of his own, he said that Castro was a "puppet" of the Soviet Union and a "paid" active "surrogate" for Soviet foreign policy aims. Nonetheless, Brzezinski argued, SALT was important on its own merits and should *not* be linked to such matters as the brigade or indeed to Soviet-Cuban activities around the world. But again, the main effect was to jab American neuralgia over the Soviet-Cuban relationship. Subsequently Brzezinski (who had not been aware the president would say the status quo of the brigade was "not acceptable" before the statement was made) attempted to take the damaging edge off of that statement and restore some diplomatic flexibility. He argued that the presence of the brigade was unacceptable in the same sense that the Berlin wall was unacceptable—that is, something the United States did not condone, but was in fact living with.[7] But this explanation could not compensate for the president's stark language escalating the crisis atmosphere just when it most needed to be placed in calmer perspective.

The predictable result of Carter's unwise and unsuccessful attempt to smooth matters was to excite them, and to give enemies of his administration, détente, and SALT even more of a target. If he was going to be tough, they could be tougher. Senator Jackson, for example, had promptly seized on the apparent floundering of American intelligence over confirmation of the presence of the brigade as an argument that U.S. SALT verification capabilities surely must be deficient. While the argument was specious, it sounded reasonable to many. Now, a few days after Carter's statement, Jackson raised the ante to demand not only removal of the brigade, but also of the MiG-23s

---

6. "Soviet Combat Troops in Cuba," President Carter's Remarks to the Press, September 7, *State Bulletin*, vol. 79 (October 1979), pp. 63–64.

7. Transcript of Question-and-Answer Session between Brzezinski and editors of non-Washington newspapers, September 7, 1979; and see Zbigniew Brzezinski, *Power and Principle: Memoirs of the National Security Adviser, 1977–1981* (Farrar, Straus, Giroux, 1983), p. 349.

provided to Cuba in 1978. Or, he threatened, there would be no SALT II.[8] Coming from someone who was ardently opposed to SALT II no matter what the Soviets did about Cuba, this threat was of little value. But it was indicative of the reaction of the sharks as they scented blood in the troubled Cuban waters, stirred up by the administration's own thrashing about.

Senator Church, having earlier raised the whole issue so dramatically with his demand for the withdrawal of the Soviet troops, again escalated beyond the president on September 9. He repeated the call for immediate withdrawal, saying that the whole of U.S.-Soviet relations was "at stake." And he postponed the SALT II hearings.

While U.S. congressional and public opinion remained active during the remainder of September, the main action shifted to an American-Soviet dialogue and finally back to a unilateral American resolution of the crisis. Before turning to the American-Soviet discussion, however, it is useful to examine briefly the tangled prehistory of the emergence of the controversy.[9]

Why Did It Happen?

In a way, the Carter administration's reaction to the brigade in 1979, in contrast to its relatively smooth handling of the MiG-23 issue a year before, paralleled its excited and self-damaging handling of the second Shaba incident in 1978, in contrast to its calm response to the first Shaba incursion in 1977. The administration seemed driven to replay its successes a second time as failures.[10] This pattern was certainly followed in the early evolution of the crisis in the American political scene from August 30 to September 10.

In March 1979, in the period leading up to the SALT agreement and the Vienna summit, Brzezinski signed a White House directive to Director of Central Intelligence Stansfield Turner to check the situation in Cuba by

---

8. "Jackson Insists Soviet Withdraw Planes in Cuba," *New York Times*, September 12, 1979.

9. The ensuing account is based in part on excellent contemporary investigative reportage by several *Washington Post* reporters, confirmed and supplemented by my own interviews with a number of the key administration officials involved, including Brzezinski, Brown, and several intelligence officials. The main press articles are: Don Oberdorfer, "Chapter 1: The 'Brigada': An Unwelcome Sighting in Cuba"; Martin Schram, "Chapter 2: Response: Avoiding a Crisis Tone"; Walter Pincus and George C. Wilson, "Chapter 3: Dilemma: Saving SALT II," *Washington Post*, September 9, 1979; and Don Oberdorfer, "Cuban Crisis Mishandled, Insiders and Outsiders Agree," *Washington Post*, October 16, 1979. See also Gloria Duffy, "Crisis Mangling and the Cuban Brigade," *International Security*, vol. 8 (Summer 1983), pp. 67–87. Finally, I was kindly given the opportunity to consult the unpublished account by David Newsom, "The Soviet Brigade in Cuba: A Study in Political Diplomacy," Institute for the Study of Diplomacy, School of Foreign Service, Georgetown University, Washington, D.C., August 1982.

10. One former government official, comparing this crisis with the original Cuban missile crisis of 1962, described the brigade affair as "history repeated as farce." Ray S. Cline, "History Repeated as Farce," *Washington Post*, October 15, 1979.

reanalyzing existing information and flying close-in SR-71 intelligence collection missions.[11] The purpose was to check carefully that there were no Soviet violations of the 1970 understanding on Cienfuegos and the 1978 understanding on the MiG 23s before the summit. If there was anything that needed to be taken up with Brezhnev, the White House wanted to know.

When reanalysis of all available information and the results of the new surveillance indicated a possible Soviet army brigade, it came as a surprise to almost everyone.[12]

One new development that had been known was that Cuba obtained its first submarine from the Soviet Union in February 1979. Moreover, work was being done on a second pier at Cienfuegos, probably for berthing a second submarine that was expected.[13] This information was confirmed, but nothing that warranted raising a specific issue at the summit. Accordingly, in Vienna, in addition to general objections to Soviet-Cuban military activities in Africa and a general expression of concern over the future of Cuban activities in Central America and the Caribbean, Carter simply stated to Brezhnev that a Soviet *buildup* in its military presence in Cuba would affect U.S.-Soviet relations adversely.[14]

At about the time of the summit meeting, in mid-June, the National Security Agency (NSA), which collects and analyzes communications intercepts, completed a reassessment of all information and concluded that there was at least a Soviet ground forces brigade headquarters in Cuba.[15]

The political sensitivity of the subject had already led to unauthorized leaks by the NSA to several interested people in Congress. Senator Stone

---

11. Aerial reconnaissance of Cuba had been discontinued on President Carter's orders in January 1977, as a sign to Castro of American readiness to improve relations. At Brzezinski's urging, President Carter reinstituted the reconnaissance in November 1978 to check on the MiG-23 aircraft. Close-in surveillance with the high-altitude SR-71 did not require direct overflight, but could permit lateral slant photographic and electronic coverage of the island.

12. Brzezinski requested the intelligence review at the urging of his military assistant, then Colonel William Odom, who had been concerned ever since inconclusive intelligence in the fall of 1978 suggested the presence of a brigade. Based on interviews, in particular with Brzezinski and Major General William Odom; see also Brzezinski, *Power and Principle*, pp. 346–47.

13. The submarine, and a second one delivered later in the year, were F-class diesel attack submarines of limited potential.

14. The communiqué refers only to "an exchange of views concerning developments in Africa" and not at all to Cuba. Information from knowledgeable members of the American delegation.

15. NSA had only one analyst, out of its staff of thousands, working on Cuba. A serious controversy erupted in the intelligence community, with NSA and Army Intelligence arguing the existence of the brigade, while all other agencies—the Defense Intelligence Agency, the CIA, State, Air Force, and Navy—did not accept that conclusion. What was known—that is, the facts that were not in dispute—was that in 1976 and 1978 intercepted communications contained references in Russian to a "brigade," and in 1978 photographs had been taken of Soviet army weapons and equipment at two camps near Los Palacios. It was not, however, at all clear that these arms were not for Cuban units.

By July 19 there was a compromise agreement in the intelligence community, after Turner pressed for one, that the headquarters for a Soviet brigade and some unit other than advisory

began asking questions in a closed meeting with the JCS on July 11, and on July 15 he went public with charges about Soviet military activities in Cuba. Some of the charges were unfounded, others were vague. But on July 17, at hearings held by the Senate Armed Forces Committee, a Senate staff aide gave Stone a tip about a "recent buildup of Soviet combat troops in Cuba, perhaps as much as a brigade." Stone asked Secretary of Defense Brown, CIA Director Turner, and Lieutenant General Eugene Tighe, director of the Defense Intelligence Agency, in a closed session at the hearings about this "buildup" of a brigade. In view of the uncertainties, at that point he got an equivocal response, following which he said he would make his concerns public. The committee leadership as well as the administration witnesses wished to set the public record straight as far as they were able, so Secretary of Defense Brown, joined by Admiral Turner and General Tighe, helped draft a statement on the spot that was issued by Senators Church and Jacob Javits of New York on behalf of the committee, with Senator Stone dissenting.[16] This public statement said that there was "no evidence of any substantial increase in the size of the Soviet military presence in Cuba over the past several years," and that apart from a military advisory group there for many years, "our intelligence does not warrant the conclusion that there are any other significant Soviet military forces in Cuba." John Carbaugh, aide to ultraconservative Senator Jesse Helms of North Carolina, on the same day leaked the story of a Soviet ground force brigade in Cuba to ABC News. On July 19 the CIA had worked out a compromise intelligence assessment that at least a brigade headquarters and structure were in Cuba. Turner was briefing Vance on that finding when ABC News inquired about the story; it was told that the "command structure" for a brigade had been confirmed but not a full brigade. But the next day, citing unidentified congressional sources, Ted Koppel of ABC News broadcast on TV that "a brigade of Soviet troops, possibly as many as 6,000 combat-ready men, has been moved into Cuba within recent weeks." He noted administration denials.[17] But still the story did not precipitate widespread interest.[18]

---

groups were present. The purpose of the unit remained unclear, as was its size. A heavy new effort to collect intelligence was mounted to resolve the uncertainties, given the political sensitivity of the whole matter.

Brzezinski states that when the first indications of a possible Soviet ground force unit in Cuba were received at the White House, he alerted President Carter on July 24 and again urged Turner to step up the intelligence collection. Brzezinski, *Power and Principle*, pp. 346–47.

16. One person present who did not dissent openly, but did not join in the consensus or drafting, was Vice Admiral Bobby Inman, director of the NSA, who believed there was a brigade in Cuba. Without suggesting in any way Inman's complicity in the leaks, knowledgeable sources have confirmed off the record that the leaks on the brigade came from inside NSA to sympathetic congressional staff members and through them to the press.

17. On these events see Oberdorfer, *Washington Post*, October 16, 1979.

18. Another story by William Beecher ("Cuba: What Is Russia Up To?" *Boston Globe* and *International Herald Tribune*, August 6, 1979) was remarkably well-informed on then current

On July 24 Senator Stone—now sure he had an issue—wrote a letter to the president inquiring about all aspects of the Soviet military presence in Cuba. On July 27 Secretary of State Vance replied on behalf of the president, in a letter cleared with Defense and the CIA as well as the White House, saying essentially the same thing as the Church-Javits statement of July 19 with respect to the ground forces. It also addressed the 1962 and 1970 understandings and occasional Soviet submarine visits to Cuba.[19]

The intensified intelligence effort soon paid off. Intercepted communications in August disclosed plans for a field exercise by the brigade, and on August 17 satellite photography revealed the men, weapons, and equipment of a unit of small brigade size engaged in field maneuvers on San Pedro beach. On August 20 the same military exercise area was vacated, and the men and equipment were seen at the two camps near Los Palacios. The National Foreign Assessment Center issued a coordinated intelligence finding, without dissent, on August 22 confirming, by collating all the different sources and kinds of intelligence, the presence of a "Soviet combat brigade" comprising 3 infantry and 1 armored battalions, 40 tanks, 60 armored personnel carriers, artillery, and about 2,600 men, under the command of a Soviet Army colonel. The unit had no observable connection with Cuban military forces. The word "combat" was used to characterize its weapons and equipment and to distinguish it from logistics or advisory units. That term was not intended to designate its purpose, which remained unknown.

As this new information became known on August 22, most of the top administration figures were out of town.[20] President Carter, who was informed about it the next day, was on a Mississippi cruise on the paddle wheeler *Delta Queen*. Brzezinski was with his family vacationing in Vermont. In Washington it was concluded that since the brigade was not a new development, only one newly recognized and confirmed, there was no urgency, and it was agreed to await the return of senior leaders after Labor Day before any decision was made on what to announce or do. On August 27 the *National Intelligence Daily*, the highly classified principal daily intelligence bulletin, carried an account confirming the Soviet brigade.[21]

On August 29 the journal *Aviation Week* queried the Defense and State Departments about reports of a Soviet combat brigade in Cuba and said it was running a story. The reporter had the information that had appeared in the *National Intelligence Daily* two days before. The Copley News Service also

---

intelligence assessments (including reference to "a Soviet Army brigade headquarters"). But this story, too, attracted little attention.

19. The text of Vance's letter of July 27 was later released. See "Soviet Combat Troops in Cuba," Secretary Vance's letter, July 27, *State Bulletin*, vol. 79 (October 1979), p. 63.

20. Brzezinski had, however, been aware on August 14 of the advance intelligence on the planned maneuvers and had briefed Carter and consulted with Vance and Brown. It was not a matter considered to require urgent attention. See Brzezinski, *Power and Principle*, p. 347.

21. See Oberdorfer, *Washington Post*, September 9 and October 16, 1979; and Schram, *Washington Post*, September 9, 1979.

made an inquiry. Neither was given any information or confirmation, and both decided they had no story and printed none. But this outcome was not known at the time in the government. That same day the deputies to the cabinet-level Special Coordinating Committee met to discuss the new intelligence. David Aaron, Brzezinski's deputy, objected to a State Department proposal that the matter be raised with the Soviets. When Brzezinski was informed by telephone, he asked Aaron to defer any action until after Labor Day, when the president, he, and Secretary of Defense Brown would be back in Washington.[22] Secretary of State Vance, however, decided to raise the matter with the Soviets.

Of greater immediate consequence was another decision of Vance's. At his request Under Secretary of State David D. Newsom called eight congressional leaders of both parties the next day and told them about the brigade.[23] Only one decided to do something—Senator Church. He was concerned personally because the information seemed to undercut the statement issued on July 19 under his and Senator Javits's names, and he did not want to appear to have been a gullible tool of an uninformed administration.

Church called Vance and tried unsuccessfully to call President Carter. According to Church, when advised that the administration did not plan to make an early announcement, he told Vance that he intended to make the information public and that Vance's only response was: "I know you'll use your best judgment in what you say."[24] Vance recalls that Church asked what would happen if he made a statement and that he told him "it would be harmful," but that Church was the only one who could make the decision. Vance incorrectly believed Church would not raise the matter publicly.[25]

The next event was Church's disclosure of the story, described earlier, coupled with his demand for "the immediate removal of all Russian combat units from Cuba."

Why did Senator Church, an experienced political figure with a long and serious interest in foreign relations and a sincere belief in détente and strong support for SALT, decide to take it upon himself to prejudge a major American foreign policy position with a demand for a Soviet withdrawal, without knowing whether this stance was reasonable or attainable? As noted, Church considered himself politically vulnerable and personally entangled as coauthor of the July 19 public statement. Beyond that, he recalled only too well having been burned as a junior senator in 1962 on the Cuban missile crisis.

---

22. See Brzezinski, *Power and Principle*, p. 347.

23. Secretary of State Vance has explained his reasons for these decisions in his memoir. See Cyrus Vance, *Hard Choices: Critical Years in America's Foreign Policy* (Simon and Schuster, 1983), pp. 358–61.

24. Schram, *Washington Post*, September 9, 1979; Senator Church was his source on Secretary Vance's reaction. In a later interview Church recalled that Vance had said, "We'll trust you to use your judgment on that, Senator," a still more permissive formulation.

25. Vance, *Hard Choices*, p. 361.

On that occasion Republican Senator Kenneth Keating of New York had been alleging the presence of Soviet missiles in Cuba before their presence was confirmed (indeed, well before there were any), just as Senator Stone had in this case. Under assurances from the Kennedy administration Church had denied the presence of missiles. With the sudden discovery of the missiles he had been left out on a limb. So now Church decided he would make the announcement and would take a strong stand to encourage a successful diplomatic solution. He also had in mind the fact that his political standing in conservative Idaho had dropped and that he was under heavy fire from the right wing. Still, it is difficult to fathom why he took the extreme position of calling for withdrawal of the brigade.[26] It surely placed the Carter administration in a very exposed position, although neither the president nor Vance showed skill in extricating the administration from that position.[27]

It is befitting the essentially internal American political process that generated the whole incident that it has been possible here to discuss the first two weeks or so of the crisis with almost no reference to American relations with the Soviet Union—except in terms of the consequences of the internal U.S. political dynamic.

The Soviet Position

On August 29, the day preceding the fateful call to Senator Church, Under Secretary Newsom had called in Soviet Chargé d'Affaires Vladilen Vasev and inquired directly about the Soviet brigade that appeared to be in Cuba, expressing U.S. concern.[28] On September 5, shortly after Vance's press

---

26. See Gloria Duffy, "Crisis Prevention in Cuba," in Alexander L. George, ed., *Managing U.S.-Soviet Rivalry: Problems of Crisis Prevention* (Boulder, Colo.: Westview, 1983), pp. 285–318, for a good general discussion of the subject, and in particular for a more detailed account from Senator Church's point of view, including his recollections of 1962, based on Duffy's interview with him.

27. In his memoir President Carter provides a very superficial, abbreviated account of the affair, criticizing Church's role and glossing over his own. Jimmy Carter, *Keeping Faith: Memoirs of a President* (Bantam Books, 1982), pp. 262–64. Church responded with a rebuttal: Frank Church, "Carter on the Sinking of SALT: That's Not the Way I Remember It," *Washington Post*, November 19, 1982.

28. There had been one earlier U.S. inquiry and expression of concern. On July 27, the same day Secretary of State Vance signed the letter to Senator Stone, at Vance's request his adviser on Soviet affairs, Marshall D. Shulman, had called in the Soviet chargé d'affaires, then Aleksandr Bessmertnykh. Referring to the still little noticed press references to Soviet combat troops in Cuba, Shulman noted that the United States would be very concerned if there were a Soviet "base" in Cuba. No doubt this concern was reported to Moscow. The thrust of the congressional release (and of Vance's letter) had, however, been on a reported "substantial buildup" that in fact had not occurred, and on a Soviet "base" that did not exist. The main reaction in Moscow must have been puzzlement, soon to give way to suspicion about the U.S. purpose in stirring up a crisis without cause.

comments, Vasev delivered the first Soviet response to Deputy Secretary Warren Christopher. He was disturbed by Vance's statement and wanted to know on what basis the United States was raising the matter and what the "legal basis" was for its objection. He then gave the official Soviet reply to the query of August 29. The Soviet government stated that its military personnel in Cuba were maintaining a training center. The Soviet note made no reference to a brigade and denied the presence of "organized Soviet combat units." It also said that Soviet military personnel and a training center had been in Cuba for seventeen years (that is, since 1962) and had not changed in number or function. The United States did not release this information.

After the president's comments on September 7 failed to dampen the rising clamor over the issue, Vance pressed hard for Ambassador Dobrynin to return to the United States. Vance believed the Soviet ambassador could help explain to the Soviet leaders the need for some gesture on their part to help restore the situation before it swamped the SALT treaty and generally poisoned American-Soviet relations. Dobrynin was then in Moscow where both his parents were dying. Finally, after Vance appealed personally to Foreign Minister Gromyko, the latter asked Dobrynin if he could return—but making clear he would not order him to do so. Dobrynin agreed to do so immediately, leaving just after his father died and before his mother died, and arriving in Washington on September 9.

Between September 10 and 27 Vance met with Dobrynin six times and with Gromyko in New York twice (September 24 and 27), and there was an exchange of messages between Carter (September 25) and Brezhnev (September 27). The administration first tried to obtain Soviet agreement to withdraw the brigade, then to reorganize it and reduce its combat capability. The Soviets indignantly refused. The most they would agree to, and even this was a reluctant concession to help the Carter administration, was a statement that the Soviet Union had no intention of changing the status of its military training center, thus implying it was not and would not become a combat unit. This statement was made in Brezhnev's letter of September 27.[29] Senator Byrd had by this point lost confidence in the administration's ability to handle the situation (and he wanted to emphasize to the Soviets the congressional concern and risks to SALT). Accordingly, with Vance's consent, he met with Dobrynin on September 23. (Dobrynin was in New York with Gromyko, but flew to Washington on a Sunday in order to meet with Byrd without public notice.)[30]

Meanwhile, on September 11 *Pravda* had publicly set forth the Soviet position, repeating and expanding on the points in the private note of September 5. The editorial stressed that, "as was obvious by their number and functions, the Soviet military personnel in Cuba did not and could not repre-

---

29. See Vance, *Hard Choices*, pp. 362–63.

30. Robert G. Kaiser, "To Save SALT, Sen. Byrd Huddled in Secret with Soviet," *Washington Post*, October 28, 1979.

sent any kind of threat to the United States, or to other states."[31] The statement had obviously been very carefully crafted, as Soviet official pronouncements always are. While seeming to deny the existence of a brigade there, it did not actually do so. It correctly noted the continuing presence for seventeen years of a training center and of military personnel for technical and other assistance, saying that "neither the number nor the functions of the indicated personnel have changed over all these years." It then went on to state, "All kinds of assertions of the *arrival* in Cuba of 'organized Soviet combat units' are groundless."[32] But the statement, and probably the parallel private statements to the United States, did not deny or confirm the presence of a brigade, whether for training or some other purpose—for example, to provide security for the large nearby Soviet installation for the collection of communications intelligence against possible attack by Cuban exiles, American commandos, or, for that matter, errant Cuban troops.[33] It may have been a direct or indirect descendant of one of the four such Soviet brigades or combat teams deployed to Cuba in 1962 to protect the four missile complexes built in September and October and dismantled and withdrawn in November of that year.

Whatever the precise function of the brigade, the Soviets were quite correct in saying that it had been there a long time. Dobrynin is reported to have told Vance that if American intelligence was so incompetent that it had failed to spot the personnel in seventeen years, or so slipshod that it had failed to inform the government leadership, that problem was not Moscow's affair. Dobrynin asked two questions at his first session with Vance: Is the Soviet military presence a threat to the United States? And does it violate the previous Soviet-American understandings about Soviet activities in Cuba? Vance had to reply no to both.[34]

President Carter's sudden strong objection to the continued presence of a Soviet brigade in Cuba that had been there for years was particularly resented in Moscow, given that scarcely three months earlier at Vienna Carter had specifically cautioned Brezhnev that any *further* Soviet military *buildup* in

---

31. Editorial, "Who Needed That and Why?" *Pravda*, September 11, 1979.

32. Ibid. Emphasis added. The denial of any assertions (or the implied claim) of the "arrival" of a brigade or other unit was correct. It may also be true that the number and functions of "the indicated personnel" had not changed over the years, although that is less clear.

33. *Time* magazine, in its September 17, 1979, issue, accompanied an article on "The Storm over Cuba" with a photograph showing ominous large electronic shields beyond some fences. The picture was captioned "A Soviet-Built Intelligence Station in Cuba." The station was described as an advanced electronic monitoring complex east of Havana, and the article noted that one of the two locations of the brigade was near the "Soviet-built and Soviet-run electronics information-gathering installation." It soon became known that the complex in question had originally been built by an American company, ITT, before Castro took power. There is, however, a large Soviet electronic intelligence collection facility.

34. Oberdorfer, *Washington Post*, October 16, 1979, and confirmed by other sources.

Cuba would adversely affect the U.S.-Soviet relationship. There had been no such buildup, and Carter's words certainly had implied acceptance of the status quo by objecting only to further increases.

The Soviet leaders were puzzled, suspicious, and angered by the whole affair. They had done nothing but were suddenly being pilloried and falsely accused, not only by well-known opponents of détente, but by some people they had regarded as "sober realists" prepared to work for better American-Soviet relations. They correctly saw the damage the whole affair was doing to the renewal of détente sparked by the Vienna summit, but could not fathom why the Carter administration seemed to be inflating the whole issue into a miniconfrontation. The Soviets deeply suspected the administration itself of having stirred up the whole affair for obscure reasons, and the whole matter did not bode well. [35]

I was then in government service and had occasion at the time to discuss the matter with several senior Soviet officials, including the chief "America-watcher," Academician Georgy Arbatov, and the recently returned ambassador to Cuba from 1972 to 1979, Nikita Tolubeyev. None of them could understand the situation. The optimists were prepared to believe that the administration had not intended or sought the issue, but that some elements within it (the suspicion usually centered on Brzezinski) were sabotaging détente. The pessimists believed that Carter himself was seeking a pretext to get out of the SALT treaty and to blame the Soviet Union for a turn toward confrontation that he desired. After Afghanistan this latter view, probably not dominant in 1979, became the usual retrospective Soviet interpretation for the brouhaha over the brigade. It was believed that Carter had subsequently found Afghanistan to be a more "successful" pretext for scuttling détente and SALT. For example, a noted Soviet commentator in 1981 remarked with respect to the repeated excuses for the American failure to agree on strategic arms limitations: "And when there were no excuses they were simply fabricated. A case in point was the noise over the so-called Soviet brigade in Cuba. Today, in Washington, it is no longer even mentioned. But as soon as Poland and Afghanistan can no longer serve as excuses, the Soviet brigade in Cuba will be ushered up again, or something similar will be invented." [36]

The Soviets accepted the sincerity of Secretary of State Vance and of Senator Byrd, for example, in calling attention to the risks to SALT. But this time Moscow was not willing to pull hot U.S. chestnuts out of the fire.

---

35. It would be fascinating to know contemporary Soviet intelligence assessments of the brigade affair. With many overt contacts in Washington (in congressional circles, among the press, and others), and no doubt covert efforts as well, the Soviets must have been aware of many of the "facts" of the changing American intelligence on the situation, as well as of the changing political scene in Washington. But the U.S. position presented a perplexing problem in evaluation because it did *not* correspond to a rational policy initiative or response, whatever the motivations.

36. Valentin Zorin, Radio Moscow, April 18, in Foreign Broadcast Information Service, *Daily Report: Soviet Union*, April 20, 1981, p. AA3. (Hereafter FBIS, *Soviet Union*.)

The Soviets underestimated the risks to SALT, and because they regarded the whole affair as a manipulation, they also believed the American administration could, if it wished, end the brigade crisis—and, if it wished, could get Senate approval for SALT. They simply could not believe the whole affair had been generated and sustained by a train of accidents such as an unexpected and belated intelligence discovery of the brigade at that particular juncture, and an unexpected and unwanted demand for withdrawal from a pro-administration senator whom the administration had advised of the new intelligence. The most damning question was why the administration in its *own* statements declared as "not acceptable" a status quo that was not threatening or the result of any Soviet initiative—and to do so at a time when these same American leaders professed not even to know what the status quo was. Some suspected Carter, in political trouble, wanted a cheap "victory." But the Soviet leaders were not prepared to offer their prestige or interests as sacrificial lambs for that purpose. The more suspicious Soviet leaders saw the U.S. administration as artificially stirring up a pseudocrisis in order to ask the Soviet Union to make further concessions, in this case on Soviet-Cuban relations, in order to save the SALT II Treaty, which in their view had itself involved sufficient Soviet concessions.

The Soviet leaders thus saw the artificial stimulation of an atmosphere of crisis coupled with unacceptable public demands for a unilateral Soviet retreat over a small, long-standing, and nonthreatening military presence in an allied country. Moreover, the United States in 1963 had acquiesced in a continuing Soviet ground force presence in Cuba as compatible with the 1962 understanding.[37] The resolute American action in the Cuban missile crisis in 1962 had been justified (although the Soviets would not concede it, they could understand it) by a sudden threatening action by the Soviets that changed the status quo. In 1979 the American leadership—in an era of acknowledged parity in which both sides had pledged to recognize each other's security interests based on the principle of equality—was demanding a one-sided Soviet retreat from a long-standing and nonthreatening status quo. Of course they would not—and politically should not have been expected to—accede.

As the talks on the brigade had been proceeding and the outcome had become clear, on September 25 Gromyko had referred in his address to the UN General Assembly to the "artificiality" and groundless nature of the "campaign" against the Soviet Union and Cuba.[38]

---

37. This fact was later publicly disclosed by McGeorge Bundy, President Kennedy's national security adviser. See McGeorge Bundy, "The Brigade's My Fault," *New York Times*, October 23, 1979.

38. "The 34th Session of the UN General Assembly: Speech of A. A. Gromyko," September 25, *Pravda*, September 26, 1979. Gromyko made his reference in the context of a more general criticism of those (unnamed) who opposed détente. In a colorful metaphor he said, "There are still people in the world today who make a wry face at the word détente, like a hungry cat in

On September 25 President Carter, breaking a silence during the negotiations, stated that "the thing that concerns us . . . is that it's a combat unit." He noted the Soviet denial of a combat status, but again, echoing Brzezinski, repeated that "it is a combat unit located in a country, in this hemisphere, in a country that is totally dependent on the Soviet Union." He argued that although the brigade posed "no threat to our Nation's security," because of "Cuba acting as a Soviet puppet, this does cause a great concern for us." He devoted some attention to this theme of Soviet-Cuban collusion and Soviet use of Cuba for third world mischief. Most important, he doggedly repeated his statement of September 7 that "the status quo is not acceptable to us." But aware by then that the Soviet Union was not going to withdraw the brigade, he described the American objective as "trying, through diplomacy, to get the Soviets to eliminate the combat nature of this unit." And "if we do not succeed," he said, "*we* will take appropriate action to change the status quo."[39] This was in fact the only option left open to him. And there was very little the United States could do.[40]

The End of the Affair and the Aftermath

The patient diplomatic efforts of Secretary of State Vance, Foreign Minister Gromyko, and Ambassador Dobrynin finally led the administration to decide on a unilateral statement by President Carter that was not challenged but not endorsed by the Soviet Union.

On October 1, in a major televised address to the nation on "peace and national security," President Carter brought to a conclusion the administration's month-long effort to resolve the problem first through unilateral declaration and then through diplomatic exchanges with the Soviet Union.[41]

---

a kitchen garden at the taste of a pickle." He also said, "The attitude toward détente is the best indicator of any country's political intentions."

39. President Carter, "Question-and-Answer Session at a Town Meeting with Residents of the Borough of Queens," September 25, *Weekly Compilation of Presidential Documents,* vol. 15 (October 1, 1979), pp. 1754–55. Emphasis added. (Hereafter *Presidential Documents.*)

40. For differing perspectives on the Carter administration's deliberations in reaching this conclusion, see Vance, *Hard Choices,* pp. 362–64; and Brzezinski, *Power and Principle,* pp. 349–52. Brzezinski was very critical of the outcome and states that it was the one time he seriously considered resigning.

41. In addition to internal deliberations, culminating in two NSC meetings on September 27 and 28 after the talks with Gromyko ended, Carter convoked a panel of distinguished emeritus statesmen who held meetings on September 28 and 29, including one with President Carter on the 29th. The group comprised former Secretaries of State Kissinger, Rogers, and Dean Rusk, along with Averell Harriman, Clark Clifford, James Schlesinger, Nicholas Katzenbach, Roswell Gilpatric, John J. McCloy, and others. The advice of the group was in line with Carter's determination to close out the affair and may have helped him avoid some ill-considered alternatives. While calling for this advice may have been politically helpful, it also seemed to

Again Carter repeated that "the presence of Soviet combat troops in Cuba is of serious concern to us." Again he explained in some detail the origin of a Soviet military presence in Cuba in 1962 and the evolution of the brigade and the belated US identification of it. He reported that the Soviet leaders had called the unit a "training center" and had stated that they would not change "its function or status." Carter commented, "We understand this to mean that they do not intend to enlarge the unit or to give it additional capabilities." In addition, he noted that the Soviets reaffirmed the 1962 and 1970 understandings. All this was done at "the highest level of the Soviet Government."[42]

These Soviet assurances against future actions were a very meager result given the intensity of the diplomatic effort. While it was probably all the United States could reasonably have expected, it was not commensurate with the high level of concern the administration had displayed and continued to assert.

Accordingly, President Carter outlined a number of additional, unilateral steps the United States was undertaking. These included increased intelligence capability and surveillance of Cuba (and worldwide), a promise to other countries in the Western hemisphere to respond to any request for assistance against any threat from Cuban forces or Soviet forces in Cuba, establishment of a permanent Caribbean joint task force with headquarters in Florida, an increase in military maneuvers in the region, and an increase in economic assistance to meet the needs of countries in the region. Finally, in a rather odd addition to the list (made as a result of Brzezinski's urging and against Vance's advice), Carter added reference to the United States' having reinforced its naval presence in the Indian Ocean. He also incongruously reaffirmed the need for and value of the SALT II accord.[43]

In accordance with the October 1 speech, on October 5 SR-71 reconnaissance flights surveilling Cuba were resumed. On October 17, 1,800 Marines under the direction of the new Caribbean Joint Task Force landed

---

blow up the significance of the crisis still more. The move evoked recollections of Lyndon Johnson's gathering such a group (indeed, in part the same men) to advise him to change course on the Vietnam War; this image was not one Carter should have wanted in a no-win confrontation produced largely by the inept handling of the affair by his own administration. The idea of convoking the panel originated with Lloyd Cutler, the special White House counsel managing the SALT ratification campaign, and with media expert Hedley Donovan. Vance concurred in it, Brzezinski opposed it. See Vance, *Hard Choices*, p. 363; and Brzezinski, *Power and Principle*, pp. 350, 352.

42. President Carter, "Address to the Nation on Soviet Combat Troops in Cuba and the Strategic Arms Limitation Treaty," October 1, *Presidential Documents*, vol. 15 (October 8, 1979), pp. 1803–04.

43. Ibid., pp. 1804–05. These measures, and somewhat more detailed information on their implementation, were spelled out in a classified Presidential Directive, PD-52, which has not been made public. Brzezinski reports that he and Secretary of Defense Brown were responsible for some "toughening" of the speech. Brzezinski, *Power and Principle*, p. 351.

on the beach of the U.S. base at Guantánamo Bay in Cuba in a demonstrative exercise.

President Carter's speech was generally accepted as a resolution of the artificial brigade crisis, although public and congressional reaction was mixed. Most commentary focused on what exactly had occurred rather than on the future. The administration, especially Secretary of State Vance, continued to look for some helpful action by the Soviet Union, but in vain.[44]

The Soviet reaction to the brigade issue as it arose was discussed earlier. Even those most inclined to seek explanations in terms of American political processes were nonplussed. Later, Soviet doubts tended to harden into adverse perceptions of U.S. intentions in the entire affair. Academician Arbatov said that American handling of the whole matter raised in Moscow "many doubts about the goals of American policy, what the Americans are up to, what do they want, how you can understand this vacillation in their policy, and whether they are partners with whom you can do this tremendously important job of lessening (world) tensions." He stressed that soon after the summit a number of anti-Soviet issues had been raised and efforts made to destroy the return to détente.[45]

After the administration displayed such tenacity in publicly criticizing the Soviet Union for what it conceded was a long-standing arrangement with Cuba that did not pose a threat to the United States, Soviet suspicion that the issue had been devised and pursued for other purposes grew. Soviet press commentary became more critical as the issue dragged on. *Pravda* said of the president's speech that it "confirms that he [Carter] and his entourage intend to use the myth—which they themselves created—about a threat to the United States from the USSR and Cuba to further intensify the policy of building up the arms race, militarizing budgets, and fueling tensions in various regions of the world."[46] The specific measures in the Caribbean were the subject of many commentaries, which depicted the affair as "a pretext for increasing its [U.S] own military presence in the Caribbean" and noted the establishment of the Caribbean Joint Task Force.[47] But most Soviet concern centered on the episode as reflecting growing efforts by opponents of détente to stir up

---

44. As late as October 31 Vance spoke of signs of "not unpleasant" changes in the Soviet military presence in Cuba, but he declined to explain this curious and enigmatic observation and cautioned that people not "leap to optimistic conclusions." John M. Goshko, "Cuba Signs 'Not Unpleasant,'" *Washington Post*, November 1, 1979. Vance does not refer to this statement in his memoir.

45. See Kevin Klose, "Soviets: Cuban Issue Clouds U.S. Ties," *Washington Post*, September 29, 1979, reporting on an interview with Arbatov. I also heard this reaction from Arbatov in mid-September 1979. An American reporter who was in Moscow at the time studying Soviet and American perceptions reported the same reactions; see Murrey Marder, "Soviet Views of Troop Issue Colored by 1962 Debacle," *Washington Post*, October 1, 1979.

46. "Speech of J. Carter," *Pravda*, October 3, 1979.

47. V. Boikov, "Threats and Butterflies," *New Times*, no. 44 (October 1979), p. 8.

anti-Soviet sentiment and work against both SALT and détente.[48] The most uncertainty, and tinged with great suspicion, rested on the role of President Carter himself, or at least of the leading members of his administration, in precipitating and stimulating the issue.

The most revealing commentaries appeared in 1980, after the Carter administration had virtually abandoned U.S.-Soviet détente in response to the occupation of Afghanistan. Then, with fewer constraints and greater certainty with hindsight (whether correctly or not), Carter and his administration were blamed more directly. Arbatov cited on Radio Moscow in May 1980 as one example of U.S.-managed efforts to build a campaign against an alleged "Soviet threat" and "to poison the political environment" the fact that opponents of détente had "started speculation about an unexpected discovery of a Soviet combat brigade in Cuba," even though the Soviet military personnel had been there for years and American officials admitted that they posed no threat to American security.[49] Many commentators noted, among the "purely provocative" efforts to derail détente after the Vienna summit and signing of the SALT II Treaty, "the case of the Cuban 'mini-crisis' fabricated last fall."[50] One interpretation of the episode by some experts on American affairs (but not shared by all) was that the event was "the first volley in President Carter's election campaign. No matter that it missed the target, it did accomplish its main aim: the attention of Americans was for a time distracted from the mess of their daily lives." The same author also saw an attempt "to create the image of a strong president saving America." This effort was reflected not only in the Cuba brigade episode, but more broadly as a "strategy underlying the turn from détente to a new heating up of international tensions,"[51] especially after Afghanistan.

One other aspect of the situation, less noted (although not totally absent) in Soviet commentaries, was a rising concern on the part of Soviet leaders over yet another round of the China card game. On August 27, just three days before the inflammatory announcement on the brigade by Senator Church, Vice President Mondale in Beijing had made his significant statement that the United States and China had "parallel strategic interests," and had equated moves against China as "counter to American interests."[52]

---

48. For example, see A. Soldatov, "Ideological Concoction of Opponents of Détente," *Izvestiya*, October 16, 1979.

49. G. Arbatov, Radio Moscow, May 4, in FBIS, *Soviet Union*, May 5, 1980, p. A2.

50. Vitaly Kobysh, "Observer's Opinion. SALT II—Vocabulary and Semantics," *Literaturnaya gazeta*, March 26, 1980. Kobysh is an important commentator affiliated with the Central Committee.

51. B. R. Izakov, "The President's Pre-Election Strategy," *SShA: Ekonomika, politika, ideologiya* (USA: Economics, Politics, Ideology), no. 5 (May 1980), p. 58.

52. See chapter 22.

President Carter dropped another diplomatic bombshell on October 1, the same day he resolved the Cuba brigade issue by his address and unilateral steps. As will be recalled, they included plans to augment American intelligence monitoring of "Soviet and Cuban military activities—both in Cuba and *throughout the world*," "to further enhance the capacity of our rapid deployment forces" in the context of our *"worldwide* interest in peace and stability," and to reinforce the U.S. military presence in the Indian Ocean.[53] Then, in an off-the-record comment to newsmen, under ground rules specifying that the president not be cited as the source, he said that Secretary of Defense Brown would be visiting Beijing in a few months and hinted that he might discuss transfer of some dual-purpose (military and civilian) technology to China.[54] In fact, the press had been filled in September (and, retrospectively, in October) with leaks and speculation concerning American options for dealing with the brigade issue. Several informed accounts directly or indirectly indicated that Brzezinski had advocated using the China card (especially the provision of dual-purpose technology to China) as negative incentives to reinforce concern over the fate of the SALT II Treaty and to persuade the Soviet leaders to assist the administration in getting out of the predicament it had created with the inflated Cuba brigade issue.[55]

Brzezinski did indeed press a hard line by seeking to use the brigade issue to draw attention to what he saw as a global threat of Soviet and Soviet-supported Cuban interventions. On September 7 he had referred to the Cubans as "puppets" of Moscow and stressed that they were "paid" mercenaries since the Soviet Union supplied their weaponry without charge—points that President Carter himself reiterated on September 25 and again on October 1. Brzezinski had turned to this broader aspect of the Soviet-Cuban global challenge in part as a way to extricate the administration from the brigade problem, which he had recognized from the beginning as being greatly overplayed. He had not favored the position Vance and Carter had taken in declaring the status quo "not acceptable."

In October and November the Cuba brigade issue faded from public attention and as an issue in American-Soviet relations. It left, however, several significant aftereffects. Most important was a serious blow to the prospects for Senate approval of ratification of the SALT II Treaty. The Carter administration, including all principal figures (Vance, Brown, and Brzezinski, as well as Carter himself), continued strongly to support the SALT treaty throughout the brigade crisis and thereafter. But not only was the rhythm of the ratification process thrown off for a crucial month and a half, the mood was

---

53. *Presidential Documents*, vol. 15 (October 8, 1979), p. 1805. Emphasis added.

54. The president was disclosed to be the source for this background revelation by columnist William Safire, "Louder Than Words," *New York Times*, October 4, 1979.

55. In particular, see William Beecher, "US May Use 'China Card' over Cuba," *Boston Globe*, September 22, 1979; and Jack Anderson, "Brzezinski Blueprint Full of Hard Lines," *Washington Post*, October 31, 1979.

also changed. New suspicions and dissatisfactions had stirred up old ones, both with respect to public and congressional views of Soviet policy and with respect to the competence of the Carter administration.

One of the score of understandings and reservations the Senate Foreign Relations Committee appended to the SALT II Treaty on November 2 was sponsored by the tenacious Senator Church. It required that prior to ratification "the President shall affirm that the United States will assure that Soviet military forces in Cuba (1) are not engaged in a combat role, and (2) will not become a threat to any country in the Caribbean or elsewhere in the Western Hemisphere."[56] This understanding was held to be in consonance with President Carter's statements on October 1 and would not require any acknowledgment or acceptance by the Soviet Union. It was a silly provision, accepted merely to assuage Senator Church's need to justify his own action in the affair. It was, therefore, the least important consequence for SALT, even though the only formal action affecting it.

In retrospect, given other subsequent developments it is clear that unless the SALT II Treaty could have been approved by the Senate in 1979, it had no chance. Even apart from such important later developments as the Soviet intervention in Afghanistan at the end of the year, the margin of support for the SALT treaty by the fall of 1979 was so thin that even the modest negative effects of the brigade were possibly enough to kill it. Senator Byrd, who was managing the campaign for ratification, for one believed that before the brigade flap SALT II was all but assured of Senate approval, but that afterwards the outcome was "problematical."[57]

Many others, including senior figures in the Carter administration, concluded retrospectively that all things considered the Cuba brigade issue was responsible for failure to ratify SALT II in 1979.[58] While it is impossible to say for sure that the SALT II Treaty would have been ratified had it not been for the brigade affair, that episode certainly prejudiced the prospect for ratification and ensured its delay until the far greater obstacle of Afghanistan arose.

The other major effect of the brigade issue was its negative impact on both Americans and Soviets in their judgment of the other as partners in a

---

56. *The SALT II Treaty,* Report of the Senate Committee on Foreign Relations, 96 Cong. 1 sess., Executive Report No. 96-14 (Washington, D.C.: Government Printing Office, 1979), p. 47.

57. Cited by Kaiser, *Washington Post,* October 28, 1979. At least one influential and potentially key senator—Russell Long of Louisiana—who had previously supported the SALT II Treaty switched his position at the height of the affair (September 12), explicitly because of Soviet "bad faith" as evidenced in the brigade affair. Robert G. Kaiser, "Long Says He Opposes SALT, Cites Unverifiability, Soviet Troops in Cuba," *Washington Post,* September 13, 1979.

58. For example, among those interviewed for this study and who do not object to attribution one who holds this view is former Secretary of Defense Brown; Brzezinski, on the other hand, does not, and believes the Soviet-Cuban support for Ethiopia in 1978 marked the critical turning point for SALT because it undermined the possibility of maintaining essential public support for it. All conclude that when ratification did not occur by the end of 1979, Afghanistan thereafter made it impossible during the remainder of the term of the Carter administration.

renewal of détente. In the United States the impact was more on the attitudes of Congress and the public, and much less on the leadership (which only hoped for more forthcoming Soviet help in defusing the crisis, once it became clear that the Soviet leaders had done nothing to create or build up the brigade for some years). The impact on the Soviet leaders was more jarring. It raised serious questions about both the desire and the ability of the Carter administration to resume détente. Other developments were soon to increase their suspicions in this respect.

25 European Theater Nuclear Forces, 1977–80

WITH THE DAWN of the era of intercontinental strategic parity between the United States and the Soviet Union, concern grew in Europe over the nuclear balance in the European theater. The Soviet Union, in turn, became concerned over actions by the West that would affect not only the military balance in that theater, but also the global strategic balance. The existence of fears on both sides compounded the issue, as each side took steps to ensure its own security which the other in turn perceived as threatening to its security.

NATO and the Theater Nuclear Force Decision

By the mid-1970s, there was growing concern within the NATO alliance that détente, whatever its other merits, was not a substitute for continuing NATO military programs and that the Soviet Union was steadily building its military power—conventional, tactical nuclear, and long-range theater nuclear forces (LRTNF)—in Europe.[1] By December 1976 a consensus had developed in the Defence Planning Committee (DPC), composed of defense ministers, that NATO needed to mount a concerted effort to assure a tolerable military balance in Europe. By the time of the DPC ministerial meeting in May 1977, the Carter administration, only recently in office, had successfully rallied agreement on a target of at least a 3 percent annual increase in real terms in the defense budgets of all NATO countries. In May 1978, at a summit meeting of the heads of government of NATO countries in Washington, agreement was formally reached on a Long-Term Defense Program

---

1. Some of the discussion in this section appeared earlier in Raymond L. Garthoff, "The NATO Decision on Theater Nuclear Forces," *Political Science Quarterly*, vol. 98 (Summer 1983), pp. 197–214.

(LTDP). It incorporated the goal of a 3 percent annual increase in real terms in military expenditures, but went beyond that in developing a substantial program for improving NATO forces.[2]

The 3 percent increase was adopted mainly as a simple and general rallying benchmark. It was, as its American boosters were especially aware, intended in particular as a tool to use in pressing to raise the U.S. defense budget. It also was intended to signal allied determination to the Soviet Union. Finally, it was also meant to buttress resolve in all NATO countries to step up defense efforts. It soon ran into difficulties—notably in the United States itself, where it contradicted President Carter's own preelection pledge to reduce military expenditures. In other countries of NATO, creative bookkeeping was sometimes necessary, as not all of them met the goal.[3] By all indications, however, for better or worse the Soviet leaders took the matter seriously.

The 3 percent guideline on expenditures was primarily directed toward enhancing concrete defense programs, and the LTDP outlined a number of specific areas for improvement, including conventional forces, reinforcement capabilities, and theater nuclear weapons. As early as 1977 the United States itself moved to build both its short- and longer-term military strength in Europe. In the conventional field, during 1977–78 it increased its forces in Europe by 35,000 men and decided to station two additional combat brigades there and to store full sets of arms and equipment for three more divisions, in addition to the stocks for two divisions and other units that had been in Europe since the late 1960s.

In the nuclear forces area, the United States had quietly changed the assignment of strategic submarine-launched ballistic missiles (SLBM) available to the NATO supreme allied commander, Europe (SACEUR) from five Polaris submarines (with 80 missiles capable of attacking 80 targets) to 400 Poseidon warheads capable of attacking 400 targets. (They are in addition to the entire American strategic force, which serves a deterrent role for NATO and provides contingent war-fighting capabilities.) In addition, in 1977 the number of U.S. F-111 long-range fighter-bombers capable of all-weather delivery of nuclear weapons deep into the Soviet Union based in Europe (in Great Britain) was doubled, from 80 to 164. As noted earlier,[4] in the United States itself the administration decided to move forward with development of

---

2. "Defence Planning Committee Final Communique," May 18, 1977, and "North Atlantic Council Final Communique," *NATO Review*, vol. 25 (June 1977), pp. 24–27, 20–21; and "North Atlantic Council Final Communique," May 31, 1978, *NATO Review*, vol. 26 (August 1978), pp. 28–31. See also Foreign Policy Research Institute (FPRI), *The Three Per Cent Solution and the Future of NATO* (Philadelphia, Pa.: FPRI, 1981); and David Greenwood, "NATO's Three Per Cent Solution," *Survival*, vol. 23 (November–December 1981), pp. 252–60.

3. See FPRI, *The Three Per Cent Solution*, pp. 3–31; and Greenwood, *Survival*, vol. 23 (1981), pp. 254–56.

4. See chapter 22.

both extended range Pershing ballistic missiles and intermediate-range cruise missiles.

Another decision, which leaked into the public domain in June 1977 and stirred up a major controversy, was the plan to produce and deploy neutron weapons.[5] The neutron bomb became a rallying symbol for diverse elements opposing the continued arms buildup and nuclear weapons in general, and those repelled by the idea of reliance on enhanced radiation weapons. It also fed anti-NATO and anti-American sentiment and became the subject of an intensive Soviet propaganda campaign. In important respects the neutron weapon was unfairly characterized: it was not a capitalist weapon to "kill people but not property"; it was not a "bomb." It was a munition intended for delivery by artillery and short-range missiles, especially against tank attacks. While it did rely on enhanced radiation relative to blast, the radiation effects would not be appreciably greater than the munitions it would replace—while the blast damage would be *less*. Some officials had reservations and opposed it as unnecessary and not cost-effective. The broad public opposition that made it a political issue in several countries of Western Europe, above all West Germany, was, however, based on more emotional and less reasoned grounds. The most troubling question raised in the debate was whether such tactical nuclear weapons would bolster the deterrence of war, or make resort to nuclear weapons more feasible, and therefore more likely, if conventional hostilities erupted. There was also some concern over the possible adverse impact on the MBFR and SALT negotiations.

The controversy over the neutron weapon was most pronounced in Western Europe but also became an issue in American politics. And both domestic and alliance politics influenced President Carter in reaching a decision. While arguments were advanced as to the expected good and bad effects on the Soviet Union of a decision to deploy neutron weapons (would it impress the Soviet leaders with U.S. resolve and increased war-fighting capabilities, or would it stimulate alarm over U.S. military and political intentions?), these considerations became secondary to calculations of the political impact, domestic and within the alliance. In July 1977 Carter urged Congress to support funding to initiate production but postponed a decision on deployment.[6] Congress did so in November. The delay in the decision on deployment only prolonged the debate.

---

5. The initial article was by Walter Pincus, "Neutron Killer Warhead Buried in ERDA Budget," *Washington Post*, June 6, 1977; see also further articles by Pincus on June 7, June 9, July 1, July 6, and July 8, 1977. The most comprehensive account of the whole neutron weapons episode is Milton Leitenberg, "The Neutron Bomb—Enhanced Radiation Warheads," *Journal of Strategic Studies*, vol. 5 (September 1982), pp. 341–69. See also Zbigniew Brzezinski, *Power and Principle: Memoirs of the National Security Adviser, 1977–1981* (Farrar, Straus, Giroux, 1983), pp. 301–06.

6. See Walter Pincus, "Carter Urges Production Funds for Neutron A-Weapons," *Washington Post*, July 13, 1977.

In Europe, opposition grew. Chancellor Helmut Schmidt in West Germany faced a particular problem within his own Social Democratic party. Largely in an attempt to defuse the political opposition in Europe, the United States proposed in NATO that an attempt be made in arms limitation talks with the Soviet Union to trade off the neutron weapon—either for the new Soviet intermediate-range SS-20, or in MBFR for a reduction in the Soviet and Warsaw Pact quantitative superiority in tanks.[7] But this idea was contrived and did little to mollify either proponents or opponents of neutron weapons.

Efforts were intensified to resolve the issue before the planned May 1978 summit-level NATO meeting. President Carter first sought public support from the other NATO countries. But he also continued to equivocate, making it very difficult for Chancellor Schmidt, who could only press for a positive decision if it were advanced clearly and strongly as a required measure. As talks on the neutron weapon continued in the alliance, on March 20, 1978, Carter abruptly canceled a planned meeting on the subject by NATO ambassadors in Brussels. Then he dispatched Deputy Secretary of State Warren Christopher to Bonn to explain his plan to cancel the neutron weapon program unless the allies joined promptly in the production decision, while deferring a final decision on deployment. But between the time Christopher left Washington on March 24 and arrived in Bonn on March 30 (after other stops) new instructions had been sent from Washington. Christopher was to tell Schmidt that Carter now had a "strong inclination" to cancel the project. Schmidt, disbelieving, asked Christopher to reconfirm the decision with Carter and also told him that he was prepared to support production of the neutron weapon, and that if Carter did cancel, the president should not justify it on the basis of a lack of support by NATO governments. The West German foreign minister, Hans-Dietrich Genscher, said Schmidt would support production. On April 5 Bonn publicly announced its backing. But on April 4 a press item, based on a leak, had reported Carter's decision not to proceed with production, followed by reports on April 5 and 6 that the president was again reviewing his decision. A storm of protest from congressional and other proponents of the neutron weapon followed. Further leaks disclosed that Secretary of State Vance, Secretary of Defense Brown, and National Security Adviser Brzezinski had all urged Carter to reconsider his intention not to proceed with production of the weapon. Bewilderment and disbelief were expressed in Bonn and several other European capitals. Finally, on April 7 President Carter issued a definitive statement that he had decided "to defer production of weapons with enhanced radiation effects," with "the ultimate decision" to be made later. The nuclear artillery and missile systems concerned (eight-inch guns and the Lance short-

---

7. John Robinson, "Neutron Weapon Deal Proposed," *Washington Post*, March 10, 1978, disclosed this proposal, made in a closed NATO meeting in Brussels on February 24. See also Cyrus Vance, *Hard Choices: Critical Years in America's Foreign Policy* (Simon and Schuster, 1983), pp. 67–69; and Brzezinski, *Power and Principle*, pp. 301–03.

range missile) would be modernized, "leaving open the option of installing the enhanced radiation elements."[8]

President Carter's rather impulsive decision to draw back from a clear-cut decision on production undercut earlier arguments that that step was necessary and important. It was particularly damaging to Chancellor Schmidt, who had expended considerable political capital in supporting the move. There was substantial muted criticism of the decision in alliance countries, and less muted objections from various quarters in the United States itself.

The neutron bomb fiasco was not important in terms of its direct impact on American-Soviet relations. The Soviet leaders and press had mounted a major propaganda campaign against neutron weapons and had criticized not only the weapon but also the U.S. motivation in escalating the arms race. Although the Soviet Union had proposed a ban on neutron weapons on both sides, after Carter's announcement it opposed any attempt to negotiate a trade-off in arms limitations.

The principal effect of the neutron weapon affair was to reduce Western confidence in American leadership in the alliance, and later to lead the United States to seek to undo that effect by another new arms initiative for NATO. But while the rankling effect did not quickly dissipate, it did not interfere with (and may even have rallied some compensating support for) endorsement of the Long-Term Defense Program at the May 1978 NATO summit conference.

Before returning to the LTDP, it is necessary to note another brief eruption and lingering irritant affecting the alliance's confidence that occurred in the midst of the neutron weapon affair. In August 1977 an informed, if distorted, press leak alleged that in a meeting of the Special Coordinating Committee (SCC) on July 28–29, chaired by Brzezinski and meeting to discuss Presidential Review Memorandum (PRM)–10, it was said that given insufficient conventional forces in Europe, the United States would have to plan on the basis that in the event of an attack by the Warsaw Pact on Western Europe, NATO forces would have to adopt a strategy of falling back and trading space for time. Brzezinski was quoted as saying, "We agree there must

---

8. The press from April 4 on was filled with articles and disclosures on the proceedings. See, in particular, Walter Pincus, "Bonn Backs Producing Neutron Arms" and "Congressional Leaders Oppose Cancelling Program," *Washington Post*, April 5 and 6, 1978; Richard Burt, "Carter Is Reported Reconsidering a Ban on the Neutron Bomb" and "Pressure from Congress Mounts to Reverse Ban on Neutron Bomb," *New York Times*, April 5 and 6, 1978; Bernard Gwertzman, "Neutron Policy and Diplomacy," *New York Times*, April 5, 1978; and, reporting from Bonn, John Vinocur, "U.S. Gave a Hint to Bonn of Shift in Policy on Bomb" and "Bonn Says Allied Alarm Caused Carter Weapon Shift," *New York Times*, April 5 and 6, 1978. President Carter's words are cited from the White House press release of April 7, 1978, the text of which also appears in the *New York Times*, April 8, 1978. For the accounts of key U.S. participants, see the memoirs of Vance, *Hard Choices*, pp. 92–96; Brzezinski, *Power and Principle*, pp. 303–06; and, the least frank, Jimmy Carter, *Keeping Faith: Memoirs of a President* (Bantam Books, 1982), pp. 225–29.

be a gap between our declared strategy and our actual capability. We cannot for political reasons announce our strategy." Instead of holding firm on a forward defense in Europe, the United States would retaliate elsewhere.[9] The White House immediately said the report was "misleading," and Brzezinski telephoned Foreign Minister Genscher personally after Bonn expressed concern. The State Department, in words intended to reassure, said the statements attributed to Brzezinski were "partial, inaccurate and deal with only one aspect of the overall defense strategy." All in all this affair—the leak on such a sensitive subject, as well as the reported comment itself—helped to raise further doubts, especially in Bonn, about the competence and steadiness of the Carter administration.[10]

The initial impetus for the LTDP came, as noted, from the United States. The program was focused mainly on conventional arms and reinforcement of conventional forces. But tactical theater nuclear weapons requirements were also to be addressed.[11] As part of the LTDP review, a number of task forces were established, including one on theater nuclear weapons, Task Force 10. The meeting of defense ministers of the NATO Nuclear Planning Group (NPG) in Bari, Italy, in October 1977 decided to convert Task Force 10 into a High Level Group (HLG) to examine the need for NATO theater nuclear force (TNF) modernization and the technical, military, and political implications of alternative NATO TNF postures. It was chaired by U.S. Assistant Secretary of Defense David McGiffert.

The United States initially was not convinced that new long-range theater nuclear forces (LRTNF) were needed in Europe. While some elements of the American military establishment favored new long-range nuclear delivery systems, and research and development was proceeding on several of them (including both intermediate-range land- and sea-based cruise missiles and an extended-range version of the Pershing tactical land missile), in 1977 there was no strong constituency favoring a new deployment in Europe. In October 1977 Secretary of State Vance had stated (in congressional testimony on the SALT negotiations) that the alliance was reviewing its theater nuclear posture but that with existing submarine- and forward-based systems no additional long-range ground- or sea-based systems were required.[12]

---

9. Rowland Evans and Robert Novak, "Conceding Defeat in Europe," *Washington Post*, August 4, 1977. This same SCC meeting also produced the U.S. decision to approve the 3 percent annual increase in defense spending, a point not mentioned in the leak.

10. See Charles Mohr, "Brzezinski Assures Bonn on U.S. Strategy in a War," *New York Times*, August 4, 1977.

11. While not directly referred to in the LTDP in 1977, the principal study underlying a need for theater nuclear force modernization was a special report submitted by Secretary of Defense Schlesinger to Congress in 1975, *The Theater Nuclear Force Posture in Europe*, Report to the U.S. Congress in Compliance with Public Law 93-365 [Washington], 1975.

12. Cited in *The Modernization of NATO's Long-Range Theater Nuclear Force*, Subcommittee on Europe and the Middle East of the House Foreign Affairs Committee, 96 Cong. 2 sess. (Washington, D.C.: Government Printing Office, 1981), p. 19.

Another statement in October 1977 was much more significant in reflecting the considerations that eventually led NATO to make a decision on deployment. Chancellor Schmidt used the occasion of a speech to the International Institute for Strategic Studies to give vent to a rising European concern that one effect of the stabilization of U.S.-Soviet strategic power through SALT would be to leave the military and deterrence balance in Europe unsecured. This concern was widely shared in Europe (although by no means universally or in equal measure), but was intensified in Schmidt's case by his lack of confidence in President Carter. He was also influenced by a group of unofficial but influential American and European defense intellectuals, who had been stirring alarm over a perceived gap in the chain of deterrents between NATO's conventional and short-range tactical nuclear capabilities and U.S. strategic forces. In the eyes of this group, most of whom did not favor SALT I or the emerging SALT II agreement, stabilization of strategic parity was adverse to the extended deterrence umbrella over Europe that traditionally had relied on (or at least had enjoyed) American strategic superiority. In addition, there were rumblings of discontent (and not only on the part of this group or of Schmidt) over the U.S. move in SALT to include limitations on cruise missiles. It was believed that those systems might prove useful or even necessary for defense and deterrence in Europe. At the extreme—and some opponents of SALT chose to accent the extreme—it was said that the Americans not only were settling for strategic arms limitations just on the intercontinental forces of the two superpowers, but were in effect encouraging the Soviet Union to go forward with deployments of its own intermediate-range systems, while agreeing to constraints on U.S. intermediate-range systems that might be important to Europe's security.[13]

Schmidt did not directly raise any of these points in his speech. He only suggested in a few sentences that "changed strategic conditions confront us with new problems. SALT codifies the nuclear strategic balance between the Soviet Union and the United States. To put it another way: SALT neutralizes their strategic nuclear capabilities. In Europe this magnifies the significance of the disparities between East and West in nuclear tactical and conventional weapons." He said "we Europeans" were to blame for not having had a clear enough understanding earlier of the close connection between strategic and European forces. By implication, the United States could not be trusted to make policy with an adequate understanding of European interests. Hence the need for unspecified additional means to support the deterrence strategy of the alliance, because "strategic arms limitations confined to the United States and the Soviet Union will inevitably impair the security of the West European members of the Alliance *vis-à-vis* Soviet military superiority in Europe if we do

---

13. The best account, if perhaps somewhat overdrawn, of the influence of this group of European and American defense intellectuals, headed by Albert Wohlstetter, is an article by Fred Kaplan, "Warring over New Missiles for NATO," *New York Times Magazine*, December 9, 1979, pp. 46ff.

not succeed in removing the disparities of military power in Europe parallel to the SALT negotiations."[14]

Schmidt did not go as far as most members of this cabal of hard-line defense intellectuals. He did not oppose the SALT II Treaty; on the contrary, he supported it. But he was clearly uneasy over the European balance in an era of strategic parity, and untrusting of President Carter's ability to take European interests into account.

There was also rising European concern over the U.S. moves in SALT in 1977 (and continuing in 1978–79) toward accepting limitations on cruise missiles, as noted. This concern corresponded with an intensified campaign in the United States against SALT, in which Paul Nitze publicly disclosed the current SALT positions that had been provided by the administration to Congress on a secret basis. The administration believed that it had protected well the interests of the alliance in cruise missiles by agreeing only to a ban on deployment (but not on development and testing) of ground- and sea-launched cruise missiles with a range greater than 600 kilometers, and that only for the three years of the protocol. But many Europeans (and some Americans) were concerned that that accord could set a powerful precedent and have a strong inertial effect that would tend to prolong the limit after the three years.[15] Moreover, Senator Jackson and others had for some time been urging the Europeans to develop such concerns and to express them to the U.S. administration.

Another strand of concern was based on Soviet modernization (or, as usually described, buildup) of its long-range TNF. The Backfire bomber was being deployed facing Europe, and administration arguments in the SALT debate that Backfire was not a strategic intercontinental bomber implicitly confirmed that it *was* a potent addition to the Soviet LRTNF. But the most significant development, or at least what was perceived to be the most significant development, in the Soviet forces facing Europe was the deployment of the SS-20 missile system.

The SS-20 is a mobile intermediate-range ballistic missile (IRBM) with greater range, more accuracy, and, above all, less vulnerability than its predecessors. It also has three MIRV warheads, increasing its coverage of targets in relation to a comparable number of launchers. The Soviets began to deploy it in 1976, with the first real public notice of the deployment occurring in an uncleared public speech by the hard-line director of the Arms Control and Disarmament Agency in the Ford administration, Fred Iklé, in August 1976. In late 1977 the first unit became operational. Between 1977 and 1979 the SS-20 became the key justification for a new NATO LRTNF program.[16]

---

14. See Helmut Schmidt, "The 1977 Alastair Buchan Memorial Lecture," October 28, 1977, *Survival*, vol. 20 (January–February 1978), pp. 3–4.

15. See chapter 23.

16. The Soviet decision to deploy the SS-20 is discussed later in this chapter. In terms of Western perceptions of the growing threat of the SS-20, Senator Jackson prematurely claimed as early as

In the latter part of 1977 and early in 1978 the U.S. government was cool to the idea that any new NATO LRTNF were needed. In 1977 it dispatched American experts to NATO to brief on the pluses, minuses, and uncertainties of cruise missile technology. But while these presentations were scrupulously fair, the common assumption of many Europeans was that they were designed to cultivate European support of the American SALT position and thus were biased against the potential of cruise missiles.[17] In addition, Brzezinski's deputy, David Aaron, and a Defense Department team consulted quietly in European capitals in late 1977, seeking to place the Soviet threat in perspective and to reassure the allies that American nuclear forces were sufficient and that no additional new systems were needed.[18] Again, while done to allay overwrought concerns, these consultations seemed to some Europeans to be an attempt to pacify their concerns while the United States proceeded on its own arms control path. They did not succeed in providing reassurance, in part because other Americans in the previous administration had been saying the opposite, as were nonofficial voices such as the Committee on the Present Danger.

In December 1977, at the semiannual ministerial-level NATO meetings, Secretary of Defense Brown sought to reassure the allies that SALT II would not curtail any NATO options, informing them that the Soviet Union had now agreed that the three-year protocol would not limit the testing of cruise missiles up to a 1,500-nautical-mile range, and that deployment could not be started before the expiration of the protocol in any case. Secretary of State Vance proposed consideration of multilateral arms limitation talks between East and West on the European LRTNF and discussed with the British, West German, and French foreign ministers a new forum for consultation within NATO. Regrettably, nothing further was done to develop those proposals. Vance had intended his initiative to allow the Europeans to decide

---

February 23, 1977, that 100 were deployed. Charles W. Corddry, "Soviet Said to Deploy 100 SS-20s," *Sun* (Baltimore), February 24, 1977. Official estimates made public showed a gradual but steady increase from 18 at the end of 1977 to 100 by October 1979, 125 by the time of the December 1979 decision, 150 by the time of the June 1980 NATO ministerial meeting, 200 by September 1980, 250 by the time the Defense Department booklet, *Soviet Military Power* (GPO, 1981) was issued (with data as of July 1981), 300 by March 1982 when Brezhnev announced a unilateral moratorium on further deployments in the European USSR, and 351 total (of which 243 were within range of Western Europe) by the time the initial deployment was completed early in 1983. An additional 27 launchers were subsequently deployed in the Asian areas in 1983, for a total of 378 SS-20 launchers when the moratorium ended in late 1983.

17. See Robert J. Art and Stephen E. Ockenden, "The Domestic Politics of Cruise Missile Development, 1970–1980," in Richard K. Betts, ed., *Cruise Missiles: Technology, Strategy, Politics* (Brookings Institution, 1981), pp. 400–01. See also Kaplan, *New York Times Magazine*, December 9, 1979, p. 55. Other American and European participants in these briefings confirmed this belief in interviews with me. Secretary of State Vance, on the other hand, believed the consultations had succeeded in reassuring the allies. See Vance, *Hard Choices*, p. 67.

18. Interviews with David Aaron and others.

whether they would prefer to participate directly in SALT III, which was likely to cover LRTNF, or to have the United States continue to negotiate alone with close consultation. No immediate decision was needed, and none was taken. As a result, events moved on their own.

The High Level Group (HLG) first met in November and then in December 1977. While not much occurred at these initial meetings, at the third one, in Los Alamos, New Mexico, in February 1978, a surprising consensus developed among the representatives of the alliance (who were for the most part from their respective defense ministries) that a new NATO weapons deployment was needed. Assistant Secretary of Defense McGiffert had not been prepared for such a turn of events but was not inclined to oppose it. It was therefore agreed that NATO should modernize, or, as expressed in international bureaucratese, should undertake an "evolutionary upward adjustment" in LRTNF, to include the capability to strike targets in the Soviet Union itself. Some people in the U.S. government who were not yet ready to reach that decision were concerned, and at the March 1978 HLG meeting in Brussels the American delegation, now including a representative of the NSC staff, waffled. At the next meeting, in April, the consensus of the HLG nonetheless continued to roll forward, with the U.S. representatives providing most of the data on possible weapons systems for NATO deployment. Also in April the HLG submitted an interim report to the Nuclear Planning Group. By this time, some senior officials in the White House and Department of State felt that the Defense Department representatives in the HLG had been running far ahead of an American decision on what the alliance needed and that the U.S. position was being decided by default. Moreover, the neutron bomb debacle in April had again drawn attention to the need for better coordination and consideration of all relevant aspects of such problems in the alliance. Accordingly, in May the NSC staff prepared and in early June the president issued PRM-38, "Long-Range Theater Nuclear Capabilities and Arms Control," calling for a review of pros and cons, and alternative options. From June to August the government carried out an intensive review.

The cabinet-level Special Coordinating Committee chaired by Brzezinski met in August and September and finally established a U.S. position that supported in principle a modernization of NATO's long-range nuclear forces (the "evolutionary upward adjustment" of forces, as yet undefined). Following these meetings, Brzezinski, who had been personally engaged with the issue for the first time, traveled to London, Bonn, and Paris to determine views at the political level. The position he expressed was essentially that the U.S. government did not see a military requirement for a new NATO LRTNF deployment but was quite prepared to proceed with one if it would meet European political-military concerns.[19]

---

19. See Brzezinski, *Power and Principle*, pp. 294, 307. Also based on interviews with Brzezinski, Aaron, McGiffert, and European diplomats.

The neutron weapon debacle of April 1978, viewed in retrospect, proved a critical factor in the entire decisionmaking process on the NATO LRTNF. As noted, it reduced European confidence in American competence in decisions on the range of issues involved. Further, the Carter administration itself felt it needed to compensate for its handling of the neutron decision. It sought to do so by responding boldly to a perceived European concern through exercising vigorous leadership in welding an alliance consensus in support of the deployment of long-range nuclear weapons, in that way generating a NATO success in the TNF field. Doubts about the military necessity or even desirability of deploying new LRTNF systems were overwhelmed by a perceived political necessity within the alliance. Thus, the United States did not believe a new LRTNF deployment was necessary to match the SS-20s or for deterrence against the Soviet Union. Rather, it was needed to reassure the NATO allies.[20]

In October the HLG, on the basis of an American technical paper on options for military modernization derived from the PRM-38 review, outlined several alternative LRTNF forces. No specific recommendations were made, but particular attention was focused on ground-launched cruise missiles (GLCM). Consideration was also given to a sea-launched cruise missile (SLCM), but many Europeans favored a land-based system as more politically visible and more demonstrative of resolve. U.S. Defense officials were also undecided on the desirability of a sea-launched nuclear land-attack cruise missile, and favored the GLCM. Other possibilities included an extended-range Pershing ballistic missile or a new mobile IRBM.

A summit meeting of President Carter, Chancellor Schmidt, President Valéry Giscard d'Estaing of France, and Prime Minister James Callaghan of Great Britain in Guadaloupe in January 1979 was the key link in the chain of decisionmaking. Just as the August–September SCC meetings had first really engaged Brzezinski with the issue, so preparation for this alliance summit meeting first directly engaged President Jimmy Carter.[21] At Guadaloupe Chan-

---

20. For example, Brzezinski has since written, "I was personally never persuaded that we needed TNF for military reasons. I was persuaded reluctantly that we needed it to obtain European support for SALT. . . . We felt we were responding to the European desire in shaping the TNF, but we were also very conscious of the fact that Europeans were ambivalent." See "East-West Relations: Strategic Crossroads," *Trialogue*, no. 30/1 (Summer–Fall 1982), p. 21. This was the prevailing attitude in the upper reaches of the Carter administration, as confirmed in a number of interviews.

21. President Carter, in one of the very few references to the TNF issue in his memoir, describes the Guadaloupe discussion in terms that stressed his own advocacy of a NATO deployment as necessary. He characterizes Schmidt as "contentious." He also describes the discussion as "inconclusive," but makes no reference at all to the extensive allied consultations since 1977 or to the subsequent meetings prior to December 1979. See Carter, *Keeping Faith*, pp. 234–35, 535. Brzezinski also states that Schmidt needed some persuasion. See Brzezinski, *Power and Principle*, p. 295.

cellor Schmidt committed West Germany to accept stationing of LRTNF missiles, provided it would not be the only continental European country in which they were deployed.[22] Less crucial, but not insignificant, was the concurrence of Giscard d'Estaing, who could have chosen to assert a differing European view, and of Callaghan, who expressed Great Britain's readiness to participate.

A successful campaign for a NATO consensus on a new LRTNF deployment initiative now became a major goal of American policy. By the end of 1978 the White House, the Defense Department, and the State Department had all come to agree that a TNF success would serve several purposes: it would reestablish domestic U.S. political confidence in the administration's handling of alliance and nuclear weapons affairs; it would reconfirm U.S. readiness to meet European needs and desires; it would demonstrate that SALT was not an impediment to meeting alliance commitments and defense needs; it would signal to the Soviet leaders American resolve to maintain military programs needed to assure parity; and it would reinforce the chain of deterrence and thus serve strategic stability. Accordingly, throughout 1979 the United States actively led the alliance members—and sometimes drove them hard—to make a positive LRTNF decision.

At Guadaloupe Chancellor Schmidt had also pressed for a parallel effort to negotiate arms limitations. He hoped with this track to disarm those in West Germany who would oppose a new missile deployment by providing that it could be obviated if arms limitations could be agreed to. It might also further East-West détente.

Accordingly, in April 1979 NATO set up a Special Group on Arms Control and Related Matters to work out an arms control proposal to accompany the decision on missile deployment. The Special Group was chaired by the director of the Bureau of Politico-Military Affairs in the U.S. State Department (initially Leslie H. Gelb and later Reginald Bartholomew). Again, a basically American position was adopted during meetings in the summer and early fall of 1979.

The fact that the Special Group on Arms Control was not established until April 1979, when most of the thinking of the HLG on deployment had been essentially worked out, meant that such considerations as the destabilizing effects in a crisis of a weapon such as the Pershing II, having only a few

---

Secretary of State Vance was never engaged in the issue fully, as is evident from his very cursory references to the entire TNF issue in his memoir. It appears as only a fleeting concomitant to the neutron weapon affair and to reassurance of the allies on the SALT II negotiations and treaty. See Vance, *Hard Choices*, pp. 64–65, 96–98, 355.

22. The West German position has always been of particular importance, and ultimately crucial. For a detailed account, see David S. Yost and Thomas C. Glad, "West German Party Politics and Theater Nuclear Modernization since 1977," *Armed Forces and Society*, vol. 8 (Summer 1982), pp. 525–60.

minutes flight time to strategic targets deep in the Soviet Union, were barely recognized, and then only after the decision for deployment had virtually been set in train. Similarly, the baffling and significant problem of verifying the limitations on numbers of small cruise missiles (to say nothing of trying to distinguish nuclear from conventionally armed cruise missiles) was not given weight before the enthusiasm for deployment was well-developed. Of course, if a serious threat was perceived (as it was by some) or a political opportunity for alliance "renewal" (as seen by others), those requirements might override arms control considerations. Deciding to undertake arms control negotiations essentially for political reasons—to mobilize support for a deployment program— was almost bound to give arms control considerations a secondary role. Many were hoping that arms control agreements could be reached in order to obviate or limit the need for deployment, as well as for other reasons. But some considered negotiated arms limitations to be futile and were therefore disinclined to be much influenced by arms control considerations, even though they overtly supported an arms control track in order to garner political support for the planned LRTNF deployment. Vance has candidly commented that "the arms control aspect of this so-called two-track approach was politically essential to contain expected internal opposition to the proposed deployments within most of the member countries."[23]

The HLG continued to refine its studies of the most suitable candidates for NATO TNF modernization.[24] By the late spring of 1979, it had decided to support deployment of a mix of Pershing II and GLCM missiles in the range of 200–600 (a range proposed by the United States). Greater numbers, it was deemed, would seem provocative, fewer, too weak. The HLG (and especially the West Germans) did *not* want to attempt to equal the Soviet intermediate missile force in numbers—the purpose was to have a comparable kind of European-based capability to ensure a chain of deterrence so as not to permit a decoupling of the U.S. strategic forces from NATO's conventional and short-range nuclear forces. To equal the Soviet force numerically could, on the other hand, have a decoupling effect, as it could imply that there was no need to escalate to the American strategic forces, and could thus threaten to leave a war limited to Europe. As a result, the HLG decided against attempting to equal the levels of Soviet forces.

The number decided on, 572, comprising 108 Pershing II missiles and 464 GLCMs, was proposed by David Aaron and accepted by the Special

23. Vance, *Hard Choices*, p. 392. Further illustrating the lower priority given to arms control considerations, at least in the U.S. government, Brzezinski devotes only one sentence to arms control in his entire account of the TNF decision, and that is a passing reference to the fact that the December NATO decision included an arms control track as well as a deployment decision. Brzezinski, *Power and Principle*, p. 309.

24. The decision to work out a deployment program in the broader alliance forum in effect ratified the approach already agreed upon by the United States, West Germany, France, and the United Kingdom at Guadaloupe in January 1979.

Coordinating Committee (Brzezinski, Vance, Brown, and JCS Chairman General David C. Jones). President Carter officially adopted it in early July 1979.[25] The decision was really very simple and logical in terms of the cybernetic theory of decisionmaking and "bureaucratic politics" school of political analysis.

The Pershing II had originally been decided on in part to give the U.S. Army a role. Under long-standing guidance, any such medium-range ballistic missile (MRBM) or IRBM would normally belong to the U.S. Air Force. But since the Pershing II was to use the same basic infrastructure and personnel as the Pershing IA, it was kept as an army system and retained the Pershing name, although its extended range and other characteristics completely changed its role. For the same reason, it was easy to decide on the number and the location of deployment: the U.S. Army had 108 Pershing IA launchers in West Germany that would be replaced by 108 Pershing II MRBMs at the same bases.

It has been noted that some American defense officials, as well as some Europeans, had come to favor the GLCM over the SLCM. In order to nudge the decision in the direction of the GLCM, in 1979 the Pentagon quietly reversed the research and development schedules of the two systems so that it would be possible to say to the allies that the GLCM would be available sooner.

The GLCM was a U.S. Air Force system (although not one the Air Force had really shown much interest in). It would need, for alliance political reasons, to be deployed in several countries. The basic unit was a "flight" of sixteen missiles (four each on four launch vehicles). Units of forty-eight were the minimum logical units per major deployment area (hence, forty-eight each were assigned to Belgium and the Netherlands). The total number of GLCMs was set at 464, the next to highest multiple of sixteen that kept the LRTNF total (including the 108 Pershing IIs) under 600, the high side of the recommended range. Thus the figure of 572 LRTNF missiles was reached. It had been assumed in the SCC, incorrectly, that the allies might wish to reduce the number somewhat, and that level was also designed to allow some negotiating room for talks with the Soviet Union as well.[26]

---

25. See Walter Pincus, "Birth of a Euromissile: Arms Decision Stirred a Storm around NATO," *Washington Post*, November 18, 1981, for a useful general account, as well as for an informed and detailed account of the SCC meeting of July 5, 1979, at which the decision on the LRTNF program of 572 missiles was made. See also Brzezinski, *Power and Principle*, p. 308.

   The Defense Nuclear Agency and the JCS had earlier proposed a force of 1,500 warheads on 500 mobile IRBMs with MIRVs—an American SS-20, as it were. But because the congressional review was negative, the development lead time was considered too long, and the cost would be greater, the mobile IRBM was dropped from consideration. In addition, some American and West German officials had expressed concern that a force of that size deployed (mostly in West Germany) for a strike on the Soviet Union could stimulate Soviet alarm, given the force's potential for a first strike.

26. Brzezinski, *Power and Principle*, p. 308.

During 1978 the United States had shifted from uncommitted and even reluctant readiness to consider new LRTNF deployments to ardent advocacy. Throughout 1979 there was an active campaign to persuade and mobilize European support and to seek a unanimous and resounding NATO consensus. A team of high-level representatives from the White House (the NSC), the State Department, and the Defense Department was on the road frequently in Europe on missions of persuasion.[27] By October the basic consensus seemed firm, but with some uncertainty about deployments in the Netherlands and Belgium and some uneasiness in the Scandinavian countries. The consensus was rooted in a two-track approach that envisaged parallel plans and preparations for deployment and efforts to negotiate arms limitations.

By October 1979 both the LRTNF deployment plan and the arms control approach were agreed to at the senior working level.[28] Italy privately agreed (subject to approval by its Parliament, which was granted in November) that it would accept GLCM deployments, thus assuring Chancellor Schmidt that West Germany would not be the only continental country to receive the new weapons. This assurance was important in that neither Belgium nor the Netherlands had finally decided to participate, given certain reservations and political uncertainty, especially in the Netherlands, although both were contingently prepared to do so.

In October the United States prepared a "U.S. Rationale Paper: Modernization and Arms Control for Long-Range Theater Nuclear Forces." Its purpose was to provide a supporting brief for the two-track decision, which was planned to be made at a special joint session of the NATO foreign and defense ministers in December.

Despite this progress, political uneasiness began to emerge in some NATO countries in October, as the project clearly began to move toward a formal and public decision.[29] Some people, particularly in the northern European NATO countries, questioned the need for making a firm decision on deployment before trying to reach agreement on limitations. The United States led a concerted campaign to ensure that a full deployment decision and

27. Dispatching this team was sometimes referred to informally in Washington as "firing our ABM" again—an acronym drawn from the last initials of Aaron, the "godfather" of the group, Bartholomew, who was also chairman of the NATO Special Group on TNF arms control, and McGiffert, also chairman of the NATO HLG on TNF.

28. Both the HLG and the Special Group met separately in Brussels in late September and each approved the deployment plan and a set of guidelines for arms control talks. On September 28 the two groups met together for the only time. Drawing on their two separate reports, the chairman of the HLG prepared a draft Integrated Decision Document on October 4. This draft was submitted to the North Atlantic Council on November 6 and approved by the Permanent Representatives on November 28, 1979.

29. European unease was also stimulated by a curious and remarkable public speech by Kissinger in Brussels in September on the thirtieth anniversary of the founding of NATO, in which he questioned the credibility of the American nuclear guarantee. See Henry A. Kissinger, "NATO: The Next Thirty Years," *Survival*, vol. 21 (November–December 1979), pp. 264–68.

commitment be achieved in December, coupled with agreement to pursue the arms control track.[30]

Throughout the entire two-year development of the decision by NATO to deploy new LRTNF there was virtually no attention in the deliberations either by the U.S. government or by NATO as to the effect on the East-West political relationship—indeed, there was no recognition that it would have an effect. Nor was any account taken either of possible Soviet concerns or of likely Soviet reactions and retaliatory responses. In retrospect it is clear that this was a glaring omission in the NATO deliberation. Consideration of this dimension of the problem was all the more important if and as the alliance decided to carry out the deployment, but it was not undertaken.

Meanwhile, on October 6, in a major speech in East Berlin, Brezhnev proposed to reduce the number of medium-range nuclear delivery systems deployed in the western parts of the Soviet Union, *if* no additional such systems were deployed in the NATO countries. He also denounced the plans for a NATO deployment of new American LRTNF in Western Europe as designed "to upset the balance of forces in Europe and to attempt to secure military superiority for the NATO bloc."[31] Brezhnev thus coupled a strong attack on the NATO LRTNF plan with an offer to reduce Soviet systems in exchange for abandonment of the project.

The Soviet proposal was, however, vague on important details. For example, it did not necessarily involve any curtailment of the deployment of SS-20s, in view of the fact that reductions of the older SS-4 and SS-5 missile systems were already under way and could be extended to effect the promised reduction.[32] Most important, the proposal came at a time when the NATO deployment plan was moving into its final stage of formal approval. Apart from there being insufficient time to explore the vague offer, it would have required substituting the unclear prospect of an agreement with Moscow for the decision on deployment.

Particularly because one of the driving purposes of the LRTNF deployment plan was to rally and demonstrate the solidarity of the NATO

---

30. It would be inaccurate to say, as some in effect have charged, that the United States railroaded its allies onto the deployment track. But it may not be far off the mark to say that it engineered the consensus.

31. L. I. Brezhnev, "Speech at the Ceremonial Meeting in Berlin on the Occasion of the Thirtieth Anniversary of the Founding of the GDR," *Pravda*, October 7, 1979. Brezhnev used the same occasion to reiterate calls for a political conference on "a broad complex" of measures relating to "military détente in Europe" and announced (with the MBFR negotiations in mind) a unilateral Soviet withdrawal from East Germany of 20,000 military personnel and 1,000 tanks over the next year. The Soviet Union did withdraw the Sixth Tank Division in 1979–80.

32. On the other hand, Brezhnev did contend—correctly—that the Soviet modernization of its LRTNF (to be discussed presently) was not an increase but a replacement of missile launchers and medium bombers, and one that decreased the megatonnage. See Raymond L. Garthoff, "Brezhnev's Opening: The TNF Tangle," *Foreign Policy*, no. 41 (Winter 1980–81), pp. 82–94.

alliance, it was unthinkable to abandon the project on the eve of success, especially in exchange for an uncertain and suspect Soviet offer. The United States and most of the principal allied governments thus vigorously overrode such modest interest as the proposal raised. The Soviet offer was seen as an attempt not only to head off the deployment by NATO (which plainly it was), but also to interfere in an internal political decision of the alliance. Moreover, it endangered a needed political shot-in-the-arm for the alliance. Thus the Soviet proposal was seen as a challenge virtually requiring that NATO stick to its guns (in this case missiles).

The Soviet Union conducted an extensive propaganda campaign in Western Europe from October to December, marked by an unusual spate of interviews in the Western media by senior political officials (including key members of the party Central Committee organization). Moreover, these authoritative officials provided data on Soviet forces to buttress their contention that a balance existed, and that not only was a new NATO LRTNF deployment unnecessary, it would be provocative. But Soviet assurances were discounted, the implied threats of an arms race were not persuasive, and the campaign did not succeed. It did, however, lay a foundation for later doubts in Western public opinion about whether NATO had acted precipitately.

The U.S. administration promptly launched a major countercampaign. President Carter led off on October 9 with a rejection of Brezhnev's proposal and a vigorous reaffirmation of the need to proceed with the NATO deployment. (The administration, it will be recalled, was just recovering from a self-inflicted wound in the brouhaha over the Soviet brigade in Cuba—a subject that was raised again at the same news conference). Vice President Mondale, Secretary of Defense Brown, and National Security Adviser Brzezinski all made major statements within a few days. The chief efforts were directed toward intensive diplomatic lobbying with the European allies.

The Nuclear Planning Group approved the deployment at a meeting in The Hague in mid-November. Next the North Atlantic Council foreign and defense ministers, meeting on December 12, 1979, in Brussels, unanimously approved the two-track plan for deployment coupled with arms control limitations. Nevertheless, several members still had reservations. Both the Dutch and Norwegian prime ministers and the Danish foreign minister made special trips to Washington in December before the NATO ministerial meeting to urge strongly a serious effort to negotiate in the hope that deployment would not be necessary. The Netherlands Parliament, in a nonbinding vote preceding that visit, by a narrow margin disapproved the NATO plan. Denmark also urged that the deployment decision be delayed pending arms limitation negotiations, and only reluctantly went along with the general consensus. Finally, all the countries involved acquiesced, although the Netherlands withheld its final decision (initially for two years, then extended) on whether to accept the forty-eight GLCMs projected for deployment there, and Belgium also insisted on the right to review its acceptance of forty-eight GLCMs (initially for six months, later extended until the decision was confirmed in 1985). Thus participation of those countries remained less than certain. (Denmark and Norway do not allow deployment of nuclear weapons on their territories.)

The decision, as noted, was to deploy 108 Pershing II missiles and 464 GLCMs. These 572 missiles (each with a single warhead) would replace the 108 Pershing IA shorter-range missiles already deployed, and the 572 warheads would replace the same number of older nuclear munitions.[33]

As part of the campaign to generate support for the decision, the United States had decided in October (and gained general agreement) also to include in the package unilateral withdrawal of 1,000 nuclear munitions from the 7,000 stocked in Europe since the 1960s.[34]

The LRTNF modernization and arms control efforts were described in the communiqué issued after the ministerial meeting as "two parallel and complementary approaches." It went on, "Success of arms control in constraining the Soviet build-up can enhance Allied security, modify the scale of NATO's TNF modernization requirements, and promote stability and détente in Europe in consonance with NATO's basic policy of deterrence, defense and détente as enunciated in the Harmel Report."[35]

The ministerial meeting also created a new Special Consultative Group (in practice, a renewal of the Special Group under the North Atlantic Council), which began its work in January 1980. The HLG of the Nuclear Planning Group also continued to consult on the deployment program as it proceeded. It was assumed that the arms limitation negotiation would, in the words of the communiqué, be handled "bilaterally in the SALT III framework in a step-by-step approach." While not explicitly urging ratification of the

---

33. The decision actually refers to "108 Pershing II *launchers*" and "464 GLCM," but by also specifying 572 warheads the text makes clear that the plan was not to provide reloads for the 572 launchers, although they are technically capable of rapid reloading and refiring.

34. One purpose of this move was to demonstrate an interest in avoiding an intensified arms race, and perhaps to match the unilateral Soviet withdrawal of a tank division from East Germany. A second purpose was to permit withdrawal of the earlier MBFR proposal for a contingent removal of 1,000 nuclear munitions. Third, but not least, the U.S. Department of Defense had long wanted to remove these obsolete munitions, many of which were warheads for delivery systems no longer in service. Not only were they militarily useless, but the fissionable material in them could be salvaged and reworked for new munitions. The stockpile level of 7,000 nuclear munitions had no military rationale; it existed because the number had been publicly disclosed in 1967 and was now familiar and long accepted. The burden of proof rested with the advocates of any change. There was concern that any reduction might give a wrong signal to the Soviets, or even more to the allies, that the U.S. commitment was eroding. Now a palatable and even exemplary reason existed for recovering this potential asset. This background did not, however, prevent President Reagan, at the time of a later celebrated initiative on TNF arms control (November 18, 1981), from making an irrelevant and misleading comparison of the Soviet deployment of 750 warheads on SS-20s to the U.S. withdrawal of 1,000 warheads.

35. "Special Meeting of Foreign and Defence Ministers," December 12, 1979, in *NATO Review*, vol. 28 (February 1980), pp. 25–26.

SALT II Treaty, then stalled in the U.S. Senate, in the communiqué the ministers did "welcome the contribution which the SALT II Treaty makes," assuming and obviously favoring its ratification.[36] In fact, a number of allied leaders had even conditioned their support for the LRTNF deployment plan on the conclusion of SALT II even before the treaty had been signed in June. The Carter administration had also sought to parlay this allied support for SALT II into an additional argument in its favor in the Senate deliberations.

In December 1979 the NATO LRTNF deployment decision appeared to be the success its authors had worked so hard to bring about. In effect, the United States had got its way on the deployment decision, while the Europeans had got their way on a commitment to talks on arms control. Among professional NATO diplomats and the military, however, few expected (and some did not want) the arms control talks to lead to any constraining agreement. Nevertheless, the second track provided the essential glue to hold the consensus together. Above all, the alliance position seemed to represent a successful political-military response to a perceived Soviet political-military challenge, exemplified in the steady deployment of SS-20s. This missile system increased the vulnerability of NATO military forces and provided greater survivability to Soviet LRTNF. While these facts would not be changed by the NATO deployment, these military effects did not affect significantly the balance of overall capabilities of the two sides. The real threat was perceived to be a Soviet ability to capitalize on what was seen as a weak link in the NATO chain of deterrence to levy political pressure. And this possibility would be countered by the NATO decision. Perhaps even more important, NATO was showing itself that it could get its act together and do something to meet a situation in which the Soviet side was doing something.

In the United States, some (especially Brzezinski) also came to see the LRTNF decision as serving a more subtle purpose in supporting the war-waging options to be unveiled some months later in PD-59. The counterforce strike capabilities of the Pershing II and GLCM would bolster American capabilities in a way that should enhance the political-military leverage of the United States. These were not, however, among the considerations involved in the NATO deliberations and decision.

The Soviet reaction was predictably prompt, strong, and highly negative. The NATO decision was said to have "destroyed the basis for [arms control] talks that had existed,"[37] a position the Soviets were virtually required to take to maintain the credibility of the earlier Soviet offer to negotiate if the NATO decision were not made. Nevertheless, the Soviet Union gradually moderated its stand. Some spokesmen indicated that if NATO would "repeal" its decision, later modified to "suspend" its implementation, talks could still be

---

36. Ibid., p. 25.

37. For example, see TASS political commentators Anatoly Krasikov and Sergei Losev on Radio Moscow, December 14, 1979, in Foreign Broadcast Information Service, *Daily Report: Soviet Union*, December 17, 1979, pp. AA5, AA7.

held. By the end of June 1980, when Chancellor Schmidt was in Moscow, Brezhnev indicated that talks could proceed with no preconditions (either in terms of any change in the NATO LRTNF decision or prior U.S. ratification of the SALT II Treaty).

The Soviet military intervention and occupation of Afghanistan, which occurred very soon after the NATO decision, had several important effects. First, it led to a very strong American reaction cutting off almost all cooperative contact and negotiation with the Soviet Union, and a strongly disapproving but much less far-reaching European response. The United States swiftly became notably more cool to the initiation of the TNF arms control negotiations than most of its European allies. Second, ratification of SALT II, with Senate consent already uncertain, was shelved for an indefinite time— leaving the adjunct TNF question (planned for an early "SALT III" negotiation) in limbo. And third, it became unclear under these unforeseen circumstances whether public and political support for the LRTNF deployment decision in several key European countries would last.

In mid-June, just before Chancellor Schmidt's trip to Moscow (a visit not favored by the U.S. administration on general grounds), President Carter reacted to what he suspected to be a softened position by Schmidt on TNF deployment. Carter sent him a strong personal letter, drafted by Brzezinski. Schmidt himself described the letter as "astonishing."[38] This situation led to a sharp exchange between Schmidt and Carter in a bilateral meeting on the occasion of the Western economic summit session at Venice a few days later.[39]

Although the United States remained cool to resuming negotiations with the Soviet Union, when Secretary of State Edmund S. Muskie met Foreign Minister Gromyko in New York on September 25, they agreed to open talks in mid-October.[40] A preliminary round of TNF arms limitation talks took place from October 16 to November 17, 1980, in Geneva. The two sides were very far apart, not only because of their cautious and conservative opening positions, but also because of their basically different conceptions. The United States stood on a platform worked out in NATO (especially in the Special Consultative Group meetings in mid-September, with subsequent approval by the North Atlantic Council, although the position was based mainly on American proposals). NATO wanted to limit the talks to land-based LRTNF ballistic missile systems—the existing Soviet SS-4, SS-5, and new SS-20 systems, and

---

38. See Bradley Graham, "Schmidt Defends His Missile Proposals; Carter Letter 'Astonishing,' " *Washington Post*, June 21, 1980; and Graham, "U.S., W. Germany Tangle on Issue of Stationing Missiles in Europe," *Washington Post*, June 19, 1980.

39. President Carter's version of the letter and meeting is presented in his memoir, *Keeping Faith*, pp. 536–38. Brzezinski presents his version in some detail, *Power and Principle*, pp. 309–10, 462–63. Chancellor Schmidt's version remains to be heard.

40. Brzezinski has disclosed that Brezhnev took the first step, proposing talks in a letter to Carter on August 21. Carter replied and Brezhnev responded before the Muskie-Gromyko meeting. See Brzezinski, *Power and Principle*, p. 310.

the planned Pershing II and GLCM systems. This approach omitted all sea-based missile systems and all aircraft systems on both sides. It was also limited to U.S. and Soviet systems, omitting any consideration of allied long-range nuclear forces. At the same time, the NATO approach included Soviet forces deployed in the Far East beyond range of Western Europe, on the grounds that the SS-20 was mobile and transferable from one theater to another.

The Soviet side, not surprisingly, found such proposals quite unacceptable. Apart from claiming that their land-based missile systems in Europe were arrayed to counter NATO air and sea systems, allied as well as American, the Soviets would not agree to a proposal that left the United States, as well as its allies, free to deploy unlimited numbers of air- and sea-based systems (for which the West had long shown a preference), while limiting the Soviet land-based missile systems. Even more basic, the Soviet leaders saw LRTNF as the newest element of the American forward-based systems (FBS), relevant not only in a European theater context, but also in the strategic global balance between the United States and the Soviet Union.

The Soviet position, in turn, was not acceptable to the United States or NATO. The Soviet side wished to include all American FBS, including dual-capable tactical fighter-bombers such as F-4s—even though they were capable of delivering nuclear strikes on the Soviet Union only by one-way missions from their operating bases. The Soviet case was more solid on the longer range aircraft, the F-111s based in Great Britain, and those carrier-based A-6 and A-7 attack bombers deployed within range of the Soviet Union. In addition, while prepared to omit limitations on French and British nuclear striking forces, the Soviet side insisted on taking them into account by compensation in setting levels of forces for the United States. Thus it proposed lower levels for the United States than for the Soviet Union on the basis of "equality" and "equal security" for the Soviet Union vis-à-vis not only the American nuclear strike forces based in Europe, but also the French and British forces.[41]

The gap between the positions of the two sides was vast. The NATO rationale for concentrating on land-based missiles was that they were "the most threatening element" in the picture, whereas aircraft would only complicate the negotiation. From the Soviet standpoint, while the proposed future Pershing II and GLCM were indeed seen as "threatening," the existing air- and sea-based NATO forces were also considered as threatening and as an essential element rather than a "complicating" factor.

The TNF arms limitation talks were not resumed by the new American administration that entered office in January 1981 until a year later, and then in a new context.[42] So 1980 ended with an abortive effort on the

---

41. The descriptions of the positions of the two sides are based partly on published accounts, as well as on interviews with members of both delegations.

42. See chapter 28.

promised arms control track of the NATO LRTNF program. And deployment of the Soviet SS-20 continued.

In 1980 substantial popular opposition to the TNF decision grew in a number of European countries. The TNF decision was the precipitating factor (as the neutron weapon decision of 1977–78 had been earlier). But the public debate and political action were often directed more broadly against nuclear weapons of any kind, and in many cases assumed pacifist, anti-NATO, and anti-American tones. The nature and extent of the rising public opposition showed a deeply based fear of nuclear war and doubts that NATO was doing all it could to lessen the arms race. The Soviets for their part maintained a steady and heavy propaganda attack on the NATO decision. Nevertheless, apart from further postponement of the question of participation by the Netherlands and Belgium in the deployment, the NATO consensus held firm and was reaffirmed at the NATO ministerial meeting in December 1980.

The Soviet SS-20 TNF Decision

The NATO TNF decision of December 1979 was essentially framed and justified as a necessary reaction to the Soviet deployment of the SS-20 missile system.[43] It is instructive, in turn, to review the Soviet decision to deploy the SS-20.[44] In the Soviet case, the data that make reconstruction of the NATO process of decisionmaking on TNF rather detailed and clear-cut are of course not available. There is, however, considerable information for analysis, and the main considerations leading to the Soviet decision can be identified, if

---

43. The official NATO communiqué of December 1979 justifies the need to deploy NATO LRTNF systems as a response to an aggravation of the strategic situation "over the last few years by Soviet decisions to implement programs modernizing and expanding their long-range nuclear capability substantially. In particular, they have deployed the SS-20 missile," although the communiqué also mentions the Backfire bomber. *NATO Review*, vol. 28 (1980), p. 25. Secretary of State Muskie later commented, "Now, with respect to TNF, after all, they [the Soviets] began the whole thing with the SS-20." Transcript of Secretary Muskie's news briefing en route to Brussels, May 13, 1980. In the Reagan administration, ACDA Director Eugene Rostow stated in congressional hearings that "the implacable growth of the Soviet SS-20 program gave rise to the NATO two-track decision of December 1979." See *Overview of Nuclear Arms Control and Defense Strategy in NATO*, Hearings before the House Foreign Affairs Committee, February 23, 1982, 97 Cong. 2 sess. (GPO, 1982), p. 17. Secretary of State Haig described the NATO decision as "a response to the massive buildup of Soviet SS-20s targeted on Western Europe." "Peace and Deterrence," April 6, *Department of State Bulletin*, vol. 82 (May 1982), p. 32.

44. The following discussion first appeared in much the same form in Raymond L. Garthoff, "The Soviet SS-20 Decision," *Survival*, vol. 25 (May–June 1983), pp. 110–19.

not the details, with some confidence.[45] The picture that emerges is not the one generally assumed in the West.

The Soviet Union had given priority to deployment of regional strategic forces in the Eurasian theaters over intercontinental forces in its bomber buildup of the mid-1950s and its missile buildup in the late 1950s and early 1960s. This pattern had not been anticipated at the time in Washington, and it contributed (along with both political and institutional factors) to the successive bomber and missile gap alarms of that period. The reasons for the Soviet concentration on Eurasian TNFs included, but were not confined to, military-technical ones. One consideration was that until the early 1960s the United States deployed the bulk of its strategic forces in forward bases around the Eurasian periphery.[46] And the continental Russian outlook had long focused on Europe, the Middle East, and the Far East, a tradition that played its part. Thus from the late 1950s to the mid-1960s the Soviet Union deployed up to 709 SS-4 MRBMs and SS-5 IRBMs around its periphery, all but about 100 of them arrayed against the European theater.

By the late 1970s twenty years had elapsed since these large unwieldy missiles were deployed. The United States deactivated its comparable Thor and Jupiter IRBM missiles two decades ago in 1963. But those U.S. systems had been deployed only as an interim measure while its ICBM and SLBM forces were being built up, and the United States did not see a military requirement to replace them.[47] The Soviet leaders, on the other hand, have

---

45. It is indicative that neither the U.S. government nor NATO analyzed the possible Soviet reaction; they assumed Soviet motivations, rather than even attempting to infer or deduce them from the record analyzed here. The absence of analysis has been confirmed in interviews with many American and European participants in the U.S. and NATO decision. There have been very few other efforts to analyze Soviet motivations and purposes in deploying the SS-20. One useful discussion from the standpoint of Soviet military doctrine is Dennis M. Gormley, "Understanding Soviet Motivations for Deploying Long-Range Theater Nuclear Forces," *Military Review*, vol. 61 (September 1981), pp. 20–34. The most comprehensive analysis is Stephen M. Meyer, *Soviet Theater Forces*, part 1: *Development of Doctrine and Objectives*, Adelphi Paper 187, and part 2: *Capabilities and Implications*, Adelphi Paper 188 (London: IISS, 1984), especially part 2, pp. 25–28.

46. Beginning with the basing of B-29 and B-50 bombers in Great Britain in the late 1940s, the United States in the late 1950s built a network of major air bases for B-47 and B-52 bombers in Spain, Morocco, Libya, Saudi Arabia, Okinawa, and Guam. Aircraft carriers with strategic nuclear bombers had been given a major strategic role in the late 1940s and were deployed in the Atlantic and Pacific oceans and the Mediterranean Sea; Mace IRCMs were deployed in West Germany and Okinawa; and in the late 1950s and early 1960s Thor and Jupiter IRBMs were based in Great Britain, Italy, and Turkey.

47. In political terms, the United States replaced the 105 IRBMs in Europe when it assigned five Polaris submarines to SACEUR in 1963. This was done both to reassure the alliance and to justify to the domestic political constituencies of the governments of Turkey and Italy the U.S. withdrawal of Jupiter missiles deployed only five years earlier. The American decision to remove the Jupiters was made on grounds of strategic and cost-effectiveness, although the timing was influenced by a private statement of his intention to do so from President Kennedy to Khrushchev at the time of the resolution of the Cuban missile crisis in October 1962.

seen a continuing requirement to maintain strategic nuclear forces aimed at a wide range of targets on the Eurasian periphery—including, but not limited to, American forward bases (such as the Polaris-Poseidon submarine bases at Holy Loch, Scotland, and Rota, Spain, and forward-based nuclear delivery aircraft such as the F-111s in Great Britain), British, French, and Chinese strategic nuclear strike forces, and NATO nuclear delivery forces of all ranges. In the 1950s and early 1960s the Soviet political and military leaders had given priority to their regional strategic forces. From the mid-1960s to the mid-1970s, in turn, they gave priority to bringing their intercontinental forces up to parity with the United States.

One reason for Western concern over the deployment of the SS-20 was a misunderstanding of the Soviet purpose in modernizing its intermediate-range missile force. A widespread Western view was that the Soviet deployment of over 700 SS-4 MRBMs and SS-5 IRBMs in the late 1950s and early 1960s had been intended to serve as an interim strategic deterrent to hold Western Europe hostage pending the buildup of a Soviet intercontinental missile force against the United States itself. It was assumed that once the Soviets had built up a large ICBM and SLBM force in the late 1960s and early 1970s, the medium- and intermediate-range missile force would become an anachronism, although it might remain in place because of the well-known Soviet penchant for hanging on to obsolescent weaponry much longer than did the West. The appearance of a new, modern intermediate-range missile force facing Europe was thus unexpected and unexplained, and gave rise to suspicions about its purpose. Western European unease over the implications of the new situation of Soviet-American strategic parity stirred concern that the Soviet leaders must be seeking to use this new deployment of SS-20s to exert pressure aimed at decoupling the security of Europe from that of the United States. Little understood was that the Soviet view of its military requirements had all along posited a full range of capabilities from the battlefield to the intercontinental level. Had the West realized that the Soviets saw their intermediate-range theater strike forces not merely as an interim ersatz strategic deterrent, but as a key continuing element in a comprehensive structure of military forces designed to cover the full range of military requirements, the Soviet purpose in modernization could have been recognized more readily. Although the capabilities of the SS-20 force would have been the same, a clearer understanding of the reason for the Soviet deployment could have affected importantly the nature of the Western response.

The Soviet leaders, seeing a continuing military requirement for long-range theater nuclear systems, had become increasingly concerned over the growing obsolescence and vulnerability of the SS-4 and SS-5 force. As early as the mid-1960s the Soviets formulated a program for possible replacements. Two mobile intermediate-range missile systems were put into development and testing, the SS-14 MRBM and the SS-15 IRBM. They were solid-fuel missiles; the SS-15 was based on two stages of the solid-fuel SS-13 ICBM (a small solid-fuel missile originally intended as the equivalent of the U.S. Minuteman). There was a limited deployment of both these missiles in Asia, but neither (nor the SS-13) was considered satisfactory, and they were not placed into series production and deployment.

The next solution to the problem of replacing the SS-4 and SS-5 force was to adapt the versatile SS-11 missile system. It has had a remarkable career. Originally designed as a naval missile system of very long range, it was selected in the early 1960s to serve as the workhorse basic ICBM in place of the unsuccessful SS-13. In the late 1960s, in addition to its large-scale deployment as an ICBM, the SS-11 was again selected and adapted also to serve as a substitute for some of the SS-4 and SS-5 regional strategic missiles. The Soviets began to test this version, sometimes referred to as a VRBM (variable-range ballistic missile), at IRBM ranges in 1968, and in the same year began to deploy it as a regional missile against potential targets in both China and Europe.[48] Thus some 180 SS-11 VRBMs (the last 60 of which were in fact converted to SS-19s) were deployed at two former SS-4 and SS-5 fields in the European USSR—60 silos were begun in 1968, 60 in 1970, and 60 in 1971. These VRBMs initially supplemented, and then replaced, SS-4 and SS-5 deployments in those fields. Further, in 1969–70 all 70 SS-4 and SS-5 missiles in the Far East were deactivated and replaced in the early 1970s by 120 SS-11s.

A second interim expedient was the Soviet SLBMs, available for continental as well as intercontinental use. It is likely—although the evidence is not conclusive—that a large share of the Soviet SLBM force of the 1970s (comprising SS-N-6 medium-range missiles on Yankee (Y)–class submarines) was considered as available for use in peripheral regional roles.[49]

The SS-11 (and SS-N-6) remained, however, only an interim solution. The SS-11 was more accurate and far less vulnerable than the SS-4 and SS-5 force but did not provide the flexibility and further reduced vulnerability of a mobile solid-fuel missile. Moreover, in addition to the technical limitations, there were new political and military constraints imposed from an unexpected quarter: U.S.-Soviet strategic arms limitations.

The Soviet Union had tried from the outset to gain American recognition of the strategic potential of U.S. forward-based nuclear delivery systems (and of the nuclear delivery forces of its allies) in negotiating limitations on the strategic forces of the two countries. The United States, however, remained firm against any limitation or even consideration of any systems except U.S. and Soviet intercontinental and submarine-launched ballistic missiles. Hence in the SALT I Interim Agreement of 1972 no limitations were placed

48. See Robert P. Berman and John C. Baker, *Soviet Strategic Forces: Requirements and Responses* (Brookings Institution, 1982), especially pp. 13–21, 59–61, 98, 102–03, 109–13, 121–24, for a general discussion of the role of the Soviet regional missile forces and the use of the SS-11 interim solution.

49. The Y-class nuclear-powered submarine carried the SS-N-6 SLBM with a 1,500 nautical mile range; it began operational service in 1968. On the regional theater role, again see Berman and Baker, *Soviet Strategic Forces*, pp. 58–59, 126–30, 136.

on American theater nuclear forces, the strategic forces of the Western allies of the United States, or Soviet theater nuclear forces. But the United States had also insisted, understandably, that any missile *capable* of intercontinental range be included in the interim freeze agreement. Since the 1972 Interim Agreement was only a temporary freeze at existing levels, from the Soviet standpoint it did at least permit accommodating some 300 or more SS-11 VRBMs without leaving the number of Soviet ICBM launchers inferior to the number deployed by the United States.

This problem was exacerbated during the SALT II negotiations. As noted earlier, the Soviet leadership decided at Vladivostok in November 1974 again to set aside its insistence on limiting American forward-based nuclear delivery systems, and this time to accept as well equal levels of intercontinental forces with the United States, despite the reservations of military leaders. Several hundred SS-11 VRBMs (and probably hundreds of SS-N-6 SLBMs) dedicated to the regional strategic role now counted against the existing and future Soviet *intercontinental* force ceiling, thus—contrary to the prevalent Western perception—providing *less* than parity to the Soviet Union in numbers of missile launchers in the intercontinental strategic balance. Any further use of SS-11s or SS-N-6s to replace the obsolescent SS-4 and SS-5 forces would only compound this disadvantage.

The SALT negotiations also placed a cloud over mobile ICBMs. When the SALT I agreements were signed in 1972, the United States—unable to get a Soviet commitment to ban such systems—issued a strong unilateral statement that "the U.S. would consider the deployment of operational land-mobile ICBM launchers during the period of the Interim Agreement as inconsistent with the objectives of that Agreement."[50] Later the U.S. position changed. The Soviet Union also became increasingly concerned about a possible future American counterforce-capable mobile ICBM (the MX), at the same time that it was not entirely satisfied with the performance of the only mobile ICBM it had under development, the SS-16. Accordingly, by 1977 the Soviet Union was prepared to forgo a mobile ICBM in a SALT II agreement.

Just as the SS-15 IRBM had been adapted from two stages of the SS-13 ICBM, the Soviet weapons designers had now adapted a more successful mobile IRBM from the first two stages of the SS-16. That new missile was the SS-20.[51]

As Soviet military and political decisionmakers faced the question of regional strategic forces in the mid-1970s, they traced a chain of interrelated

50. *The ABM Treaty and Interim Agreement and Associated Protocol: Message from the President of the United States,* June 13, 1972, 92 Cong. 2 sess. (GPO, 1972), p. 14.

51. These are all U.S. and NATO, not Soviet, designations. Until a system achieves operational deployment, it is designated with an "X" for experimental, and until 1977 the SS-20 was termed "the SS-X-20." This ephemeral change in designator has been omitted here for simplicity.

considerations along the following lines. First, there remained a military requirement for strong regional theater strategic forces, especially as the British, French, and Chinese strategic nuclear missile forces grew and as powerful American and allied nuclear delivery bomber and fighter-bomber forces were based in Europe (and some other points on the Eurasian periphery, especially the U.S. bases in the Far East). These allied forces had the capability to destroy a wide range of military, transportation, and command and control targets. Moreover, the Soviets wanted a hedge against losses from a possible American first strike and to increase their kill probability, cross-targeting, and residual target coverage for restrike. This hedge took the form of high levels of intermediate-range missiles.

Second, Soviet intermediate-range missile forces needed modernization. As noted, the SS-4 and SS-5 systems, long only of marginal value, were badly in need of replacement. Deployed nearly twenty years earlier, they were large, cumbersome liquid-fueled missiles with very slow reaction times (they required several hours to prepare for firing). They were exceedingly vulnerable: three-fourths of the launchers were unprotected open pads, deployed in close groups of four, and even the 135 in underground silos were grouped in close groups of three. A modern missile or air attack could thus in many cases deliver strikes with sufficient accuracy and payload to destroy three or four SS-4 or SS-5 launchers with one shot. True, these missiles had a very large yield—up to two megatons each for the SS-4 and up to five megatons for the SS-5. But while this high yield made up for the very low accuracy of the missile for some targets, it did not for others. Moreover, such high yields produced a high level of contamination and heavy fallout from ground bursts. Given the prevailing easterly winds, those results were militarily undesirable for the Warsaw Pact, political effects aside. The case for replacement and modernization was overwhelming. (There would be side benefits, too, from modernization, such as greater economy in the use of fissionable materials.)

Third, it was not advantageous to expand, or even to retain, adaptations of VRBMs such as the SS-11 and SS-N-6, since these systems counted against the Soviet intercontinental force levels in SALT and would prevent the Soviet Union from maintaining parity in numbers of launchers under the projected SALT II Treaty. The SS-20 could permit release of SS-11 (and follow-on SS-19) launchers for the strategic intercontinental mission.

Fourth, while the SS-14 and SS-15 had not proved satisfactory, the more successful SS-20 (derived from the SS-16 ICBM) was now available. It would provide mobility, solid fuel, rapid reaction, and accuracy. It even had the bonus of three MIRV warheads on each missile. Moreover, not only was it feasible, but with the decision not to deploy the SS-16, a production line was open and parts having a long lead time already produced for the SS-16 could readily be allocated to the SS-20. An unneeded asset could be disposed of while at the same time meeting another critical need.

The decision on the SS-20 thus fell into place as natural and almost inevitable. Moreover, it was fully compatible with the SALT negotiations. Presidents Nixon and Brezhnev had advised one another in May 1972 that the United States and the Soviet Union were going to go forward with military programs not specifically limited by SALT. The United States had withdrawn its early proposal in SALT to limit Soviet MRBMs and IRBMs (raised in April and dropped in August 1970) and had turned down Soviet proposals to limit the U.S. TNF in Europe. There could be no legitimate basis for an American objection. Moreover, the U.S. JCS and the Soviet General Staff had been in full agreement on the right of modernization except where specifically limited, and this agreement had been specifically affirmed in the SALT I agreement.

Even in the SALT strategic dialogue the American side had stressed as criteria for strategic stability precisely the qualities the SS-20 would bring—mobility, greater reliability, reduced vulnerability, and reductions in throw-weight and megatonnage. Without necessarily agreeing with the Americans on what would constitute strategic stability—a matter on which both sides often changed their positions, depending on military-technological developments—the Soviets could justify their SS-20 decision by criteria earlier articulated by the United States. The Soviets would also be following the U.S. lead in what the Americans termed a "qualitative" improvement that also involved a quantitative increase through MIRV. It was the United States, in SALT, that decided to limit the number of launchers, but not warheads, at equal levels. And the vulnerable, large, slow-reacting, multimegaton SS-5 and SS-4 systems—with a low survivability that limited their value only to a first strike—would be retired. The Soviet force level would also not need to be increased: replacement of the launchers for the older systems could be on a one-for-one basis or even less.

Undoubtedly the military leaders advanced those arguments, and there was no reason for the political leaders to object, since this was a normal modernization program and could be accommodated within the overall budgetary and more specific construction limitations of the established military fiscal allocation. The deployment was thus specifically provided for in the Tenth Five-Year Plan approved in early 1976, confirming plans probably tentatively set sometime between 1972 and 1975.

And so the SS-20 deployment decision was made. By 1976 Western intelligence identified the preparation of deployment sites, and by the end of 1977 the first two complexes became operational. Deployment continued steadily until the beginning of the 1980s, when it began to decline.[52] Deactiva-

---

52. It is possible to extrapolate from the publicly released figures that about nine new deployment bases (each having one regiment of nine launchers) were constructed a year in 1978 and 1979, the peak period. This rate meant that an *average* of one launcher became operational each five to seven days, although in fact groups of nine launchers became operational as each base was completed and activated. In 1980 the number of new bases being started began to decline, and few were begun in 1982.

tion and dismantling of the SS-4 and SS-5 systems proceeded apace on a comparable basis.[53]

Most official, and many unofficial, Western discussions have tended to disparage Soviet claims of modernization as a justification for the decision to deploy the SS-20. Public discussion has been regrettably ill-informed. It seems highly likely that, in the Soviets' place, U.S. and NATO military and political leaders would have considered such a modernization program as fully justified and would have done exactly the same thing. The United States would probably have seen it as a step depriving the *other* side of TNF superiority and thus enhancing deterrence of any initial use by the other side. It is not possible to confirm that this was the Soviet view, but it would logically have fitted their frame of reference and perspective.

Did the Soviet Union also see an opportunity to gain political-military advantage and leverage vis-à-vis Western Europe by deploying the SS-20? This has been the Western assumption, and it as much as the fact of deployment stimulated both Western concern and, as noted, the counter NATO decision on LRTNF in 1979. Certainly the Soviet Union would have preferred a margin of safety or advantage in the theater balance and would have welcomed any inhibitions that situation might have placed on NATO's self-confidence. But there is no evidence to support the idea that the Soviet leaders saw a political option flowing from their decision on the SS-20 or that they even considered such a political purpose in making the decision. To the contrary, there is considerable indirect evidence they did not.

Soviet military doctrine and political pronouncements during this period (and since) have stressed the *inadmissibility* of limited nuclear war in Europe, the existence of a *balance*, and the need for *détente*. Whether these pronouncements are accepted as representing a real Soviet view or not, their propaganda effect undercuts any Soviet ability to gain from an implied theater nuclear threat to Europe decoupled from a challenge to the United States itself. The consistent stress on the inevitability, or at the least very great danger, of escalation to all-out nuclear war that would arise from any attempt at limited use of nuclear weapons of any kind in particular worked against any possible Soviet aim of separating Western Europe from the United States by presenting the former with a theater nuclear threat. The authoritative Soviet public declaratory stance, apart from probably reflecting a genuine concern over escalation, has clearly been directed at dissuading American leaders from

---

53. Many official Western accounts were misleading on this score. For example, see those cited in Garthoff, *Foreign Policy*, no. 41 (1980–81), pp. 84–86. Less prominently publicized official estimates show a decline from 650 (the actual number was 649) launchers in January 1970 to 450 (actually 433) in January 1979, to 400 (actually 391) in January 1980, "over 350" (actually 355) in January 1981, 335 (nearer to 300) in January 1982, 280 by August 1982, 248 by the end of 1982, and 224 by the end of 1983 (all SS-4; no SS-5s remained). The first 100 or so were deactivated from 1968 to 1972, and were replaced by SS-11 VRBMs. The total of SS-4, SS-5, and SS-20 launchers remained at about 600. Official U.S. figures on deactivation tend to lag and are not given much publicity.

contemplating limited nuclear warfare as an option, rather than at pursuing such an option. The Soviet leaders have been quite prepared to forgo the option of threatening a Eurostrategic war as a price for reducing *Western* interest in that option.

As has been seen, there was a compelling military-technical rationale for the SS-20 deployment. And the Soviet decision was almost certainly made on those grounds. It should also be noted—as it is now only belatedly in the West—that the Soviet modernization of intermediate-range missiles has been accompanied by modernization of shorter range missiles (such as the SS-21, 22, and 23) as well as strike aircraft.

Thus the view of Soviet military and political leaders was that they had made a necessary and appropriate decision to modernize TNF, and they did not see this action as creating any TNF gap in their favor. Still less did they see it as creating any military or political option for pressuring Western Europe or the Western alliance that they could exploit. Within that context, the Soviet leaders saw the subsequent NATO campaign against the SS-20, and the NATO TNF decision of 1979, not as a justified (or even as a misguided) response, but as a hostile initiative. The NATO decision was believed to have been engineered by the United States in 1978–79 in pursuit of overall military superiority and to put political pressure on the Soviet Union. The Soviet SS-20 deployment was viewed not as a cause of the NATO decision, but as a pretext to justify NATO's contrived need for a counterdeployment. Moreover, the United States was seen as actively circumventing the limitations imposed by the SALT II Treaty signed only six months before the NATO decision. Using a supposedly European initiative and an alleged European strategic context, the United States was in fact deploying forces with counterforce capabilities directed against strategic military targets in the Soviet Union. This new deployment, together with other American strategic programs, was intended to tip the global strategic balance as well as the Eurostrategic balance against the Soviet Union.

The subsequent public surfacing of PD-59, and its articulation of a war-waging military doctrine,[54] was seen as confirming that the new TNF had a role in a broader U.S. strategic design; it both provided additional capabilities and reflected hostile intentions.

Without repeating here the more detailed analyses of Soviet perceptions of the balance in theater nuclear forces and the threat the Soviets believed the planned NATO LRTNF deployment posed, a few key points need further discussion.[55] First of all, perceptions develop within a frame of

---

54. See chapter 22.

55. Identifying real Soviet perceptions is difficult, as most data involve statements designed to influence opinion either abroad or at home. Propaganda often includes, but may exaggerate, real concerns; sometimes it contrives or uses arguments not reflecting real perceptions. Nonetheless, analysis of Soviet argumentation and public pronouncements, together with consideration of its general patterns of perception of its interests and its actions, can tell a great deal

reference. The Soviet frame of reference assumes conflict and Western hostility and expects the United States to seek advantage and superiority. This was especially true after what the Soviet leaders saw as an American turn toward a harder line after 1977. There is also a parallel tendency in the Soviet Union *not* to appreciate in advance, or to recognize afterwards, the role that *its* own actions may have in bringing about a U.S. action.

Thus there is a strong Soviet tendency to reject the idea that its deployment of the SS-20 was responsible in any way for the NATO decision on LRTNF. Since that effect was not anticipated and is adverse, admitting a causal connection would imply at least that the Soviet action might have been a mistake. Instead, Soviet analysts look for, and find, "proof" that the Western decision would have occurred in any event and that the SS-20 deployment was but a pretext for it. Thus their analysts point out, correctly, that NATO was talking about new theater nuclear forces well before the SS-20 deployment began. Even more telling is that the United States had been funding research and development of Pershing II and GLCM systems since the early and mid-1970s, long before the SS-20 deployment began. The fact of earlier research and development on the systems involved is not only used in propaganda, but almost certainly is believed to indicate a long-standing U.S. plan for deployment. Similarly, Soviet commentators note the great increase in attention devoted to the SS-20 after NATO formally decided on the LRTNF deployments (in the Soviet view the United States had made its decision much earlier).

In fact, the SS-20 deployment *was* a major factor leading to NATO's decision. But it was not the only factor, and some NATO planners had believed that NATO needed a new long-range theater nuclear capability apart from the SS-20 deployment and other Soviet TNF modernization. But NATO studies and even American research and development programs did not mean firm commitment to deploying new weapons. It is, in fact, doubtful that a political decision by NATO to deploy would have been taken without prompting from the very visible new threat seen as posed by the SS-20. But it is easy to see how a different Soviet perception could arise and be sustained.

In the same way, the Western perception that the SS-20 posed a new *political*-military threat, a new option for political pressure, arose because of growing Western European doubt about the credibility of extended U.S. deterrence based on intercontinental strategic forces in a period of acknowledged parity and limitations on such forces. This Western perception, probably quite in error, nonetheless contributed greatly to the conclusion by the alliance that a new TNF deployment was needed to bolster deterrence and to

about Soviet perceptions and views. In the present case, for more detailed analyses see Raymond L. Garthoff, "Soviet Perceptions of Western Strategic Thought and Doctrine," in *The Soviet Military Doctrine and Western Security Policy* (Paris: Atlantic Institute, forthcoming); William V. Garner, *Soviet Threat Perceptions of NATO's Eurostrategic Missiles* (Paris: Atlantic Institute, 1983); and Stephen M. Millett, "Soviet Perceptions of the Theater Nuclear Balance in Europe and Reactions to American LRTNFs," *Naval War College Review*, vol. 34 (March–April 1981), pp. 3–17.

reinforce the coupling of conventional and tactical nuclear forces in Western Europe with the geographically removed U.S. strategic forces in North America and at sea. A need for Western reassurance was cloaked in arguments about a need to reinforce deterrence.

Another element in the conflicting perceptions of the two sides is the question whether a general military balance (and in particular in LRTNF) existed in Europe, and if so, whether the SS-20 deployment or the planned NATO LRTNF deployment would upset that balance.

The Soviet Union, supposedly seeking an exploitable superiority, constantly avows that it does not have and is not attaining that superiority. One of the most self-convincing Western arguments has been that if the Soviets said that a balance existed in 1977, they cannot say one still existed in 1979 or 1983. But that judgment is based on a prevailing Western assessment that the SS-20 deployment was not modernization and that replacement is but a buildup. From the Soviet perspective there is no contradiction in saying there has been a "balance" and that one remains—until a NATO LRTNF deployment threatened to upset it. This is particularly true given the interchangeability between intermediate-range and intercontinental variable-range missile systems.

The Soviet claim that a rough parity in Eurostrategic nuclear weapons has existed and that replacement of the SS-4 and SS-5s with SS-20s was legitimately and properly only modernization probably represents the real Soviet view and is not a conscious dissembling for propaganda. Incidentally, it is an example of the dependence of political leaders on the military for information and judgments of this type. Brezhnev, pointedly identifying himself as chairman of the Defense Council of the USSR at the time he proposed TNF arms limitation talks in October 1979, stated that the number of medium-range nuclear delivery systems in the European USSR had not increased over the past decade. More precisely, the number of medium-range (a Soviet term that includes the Western intermediate-range category) missile launchers, the aggregate yield or megatonnage of these missiles, and the number of medium bombers had even been somewhat reduced. Those claims were largely ignored, and indirectly rebuffed, in official U.S. and NATO statements—but they were correct. One can argue over their significance, but the claims were valid.[56]

Western arguments that the SS-20 deployment was not modernization but an attempt to gain superiority reflect a differing real perception from a different vantage point. (The failure to give any credit to the modernization *aspect* of the change, and the frequent reluctance to acknowledge the parallel Soviet dismantling of the older SS-4 and SS-5 systems, however, was a combination of psychological self-deception and information management.)

Similarly, the Soviet political and especially military leaders know best the capabilities, and limitations, of the SS-20 system. While it does repre-

---

56. See Garthoff, *Foreign Policy*, no. 41 (1980–81), pp. 82–94. The Soviet claim that there is a balance of long-range nuclear forces in Europe is another matter; ultimately, it depends on subjective criteria as to range and other factors.

sent a major improvement over the extremely vulnerable SS-4 and SS-5 systems, the SS-20 system is highly vulnerable to a surprise attack, and it has only limited operational mobility (not unlike the Pershing II and GLCM systems). Further, while the MIRV triples the number of warheads, that does not mean that the system has sufficient operational flexibility to triple the number of targets; it is far from comparable to the ICBM and SLBM systems with MIRVs of both sides in this respect.

The Soviets' reaction to the NATO LRTNF decision was thus formed in the context of their belief—self-serving though it may be—that their own modernization and replacement programs based on the SS-20 missile (and Backfire medium bomber) are consistent with maintaining an existing rough balance between the Soviet Union and the United States, and between the Warsaw Pact and NATO. The United States–led NATO decision was not a response, as claimed, nor a comparable modernization program. It was a major new escalation of the arms race and an attempt, by circumventing SALT, to tip the overall strategic balance as well as the European nuclear balance to the advantage of the United States and NATO.

The Soviets also stressed several qualities of the new NATO weapons: they are precision counterforce first-strike weapons, and they are capable of striking strategic targets deep in the USSR. Many Soviet military and political commentators emphasize that the Pershing II is a strategic first-strike weapon: it has accuracies ten times greater than the shorter range Pershing I and a yield sufficient to destroy ICBM silos and hardened command and control centers. (Soviet commentators do not note publicly, although Soviet specialists are mindful of the fact, that Pershing II is also much more accurate and has a much greater counterforce capability than the SS-20.) Although the Pershing II is being deployed as a single-warhead missile, the Soviets are aware of studies for a possible MIRV warhead and have alluded to this possibility, occasionally incorrectly stating it as a firm future plan.[57] In addition, while the decision by NATO was to deploy 572 missiles, the plan is to deploy them on 572 launchers. If a decision were made (as the Soviets assume it will be) to provide a refire capability, just a single reload would double the number of missiles to more than 1,000.[58]

Of particular strategic significance, as many Soviet commentators stress, the flight time of the Pershing II from target to destination is poten-

---

57. See, in particular, L. Semeyko, "Staking on a First-Strike Potential," *Krasnaya zvezda* [Red Star], August 8, 1980; and Leonid Zamyatin, "The World Needs Military Détente," *Pravda*, December 25, 1979. Colonel Semeyko cited *Strategic Review* as stating that the Pershing II would have MIRVs by 1985.

58. Soviet suspicions and concerns seemed to have been confirmed when it was disclosed in late 1982 that the U.S. Department of Defense had proposed to West German Defense Minister Manfred Woerner plans to deploy in his country 108 Pershing II "spares" in addition to the 108 missiles on launchers—a proposition the Germans quickly rejected and that they later leaked. See Elizabeth Pond, "West Germans Want NATO Missiles—but Not Pentagon's Numbers," *Christian Science Monitor*, November 16, 1982; and Bradley Graham, "Kohl Rejects Deployment of Extra Pershing Missiles," *Washington Post*, November 26, 1982.

tially six to ten minutes, in contrast to the twenty-five to thirty minute flight time for an ICBM from the United States. Some discussions state that Pershing II would even be *more* useful in a first strike than would intercontinental missiles, particularly for the initial wave of "decapitating" strikes on command, control, and communications (C³) targets. Several political commentators, including a prominent member of the Central Committee staff, have noted that the very short flight time would not permit use of the hot line. Some (including, most pointedly, the then chief of the General Staff, Marshal Ogarkov) have hinted at what is one of the principal Soviet military concerns over Pershing II—given its very short flight time, even if promptly detected at the time of launch, there would not be enough time to allow a launch on warning before the missiles struck Soviet ICBM silos or control centers.[59] There is considerable evidence that for the past decade the Soviet Union has adopted the concept of launch on warning or launch under attack in the event of an enemy attack.[60] While the concept of a launch under attack is potentially destabilizing and dangerous, even worse would be resort to a preemptive launch at a time of feared and perceived imminent Western attack, a necessary strategy if the nature of the weapons would not allow waiting even for a launch on warning. Many Soviet discussions describe not only the Pershing II but also the cruise missile (which, although much slower, is designed to evade detection and tracking and is highly accurate) as designed for surprise preemptive or preventive attack.[61] (Incidentally, Vadim Zagladin, the first deputy chief of the International Department of the Central Committee, has cited the Western press as having described the Pershing II and GLCM as first-strike weapons. He then recalled the declassified official U.S. war plan of 1949 against the Soviet Union, "Dropshot." The details were accurately reported, except that Dropshot was described as "a plan for a preventive war against the USSR," rather than as a contingency war plan.)[62] Western first-strike plans are seen not as a theoretical possibility, but as real plans in the past, and therefore possibly again in the present and future.

Soviet commentary on the Pershing II included one anomaly of some interest. Many discussions, including ones by Marshal Ustinov, the minister of defense, have referred to the strategic capabilities and (imputed) strategic purposes of the system. Most Soviet discussions, including the official Soviet

---

59. See Marshal N. V. Ogarkov, "In the Interests of Raising Combat Readiness," *Kommunist vooruzhennykh sil* [Communist of the Armed Forces], no. 14 (July 1980), p. 26; and Major General R. Simonyan, "In Search of a 'New Strategy,'" *Pravda*, March 19, 1979.

60. See the discussion in Raymond L. Garthoff, "Mutual Deterrence, Parity and Strategic Arms Limitation in Soviet Policy," in Derek Leebaert, ed., *Soviet Military Thinking* (London: Allen and Unwin, 1981), pp. 101–03.

61. See Raymond L. Garthoff, "Soviet Perspectives," in Betts, ed., *Cruise Missiles*, pp. 343–48.

62. V. V. Zagladin, "Mr. Zagladin Replies to Minister of National Defense Desmarets," *Le Soir* (Brussels), December 12, 1979. This article was to a letter replying to comments by the Belgian minister of defense in an interview with the newspaper.

Ministry of Defense booklet *Whence the Threat to Peace,* attribute a range of about 2,500 kilometers (about 1,500 miles) to the Pershing II—a range that would include Moscow. Western sources ascribe to it a range of about 1,800 kilometers (a little over 1,000 miles), a range that covers many Soviet strategic targets, but not as many and not Moscow. This is a rare divergence over a question of fact about a U.S. system.[63] The GLCM is generally accorded, in Soviet as in Western commentary, a range of about 2,500–2,600 kilometers.

The context of the NATO TNF decision gave another strategic significance to the deployment. It followed just six months after the signing of the SALT II Treaty that set equal levels of ICBM, SLBM, and heavy bomber systems for the United States and the Soviet Union. The treaty included an undertaking by the parties "not to circumvent the provisions of this Treaty, through any other state or states, or in any other manner" (Article XII).[64] The comments of Soviet political leaders and of other political and military spokesmen place considerable weight on the fact that the deployment of systems not limited by SALT and capable of striking strategic targets in the Soviet Union, and especially the hundreds of such highly sophisticated missiles with counterforce capabilities, would—and was intended to—circumvent the SALT limitations.

If any of the Soviet SALT negotiators or others involved in Soviet decisionmaking had been influenced by the U.S. arguments to downplay the significance of the FBS question in SALT from 1969 to 1979, nothing could have reinforced the Soviet military arguments about its importance more than the NATO TNF deployment decision in December 1979.

The issuance of PD-59 some months after the TNF decision has been cited as creating still further ominous overtones. While one of the principal reasons for the decision by NATO was to avoid Soviet perception of any decoupling in the Western nuclear deterrent, in fact the Soviets ascribe to the United States the aim of decoupling through conjunction of the TNF and

---

63. See *Whence the Threat to Peace* (Moscow: Military Publishing House, USSR Ministry of Defense, 1982), p. 60. From 1979 through 1981 there was an unusual divergence in various Soviet sources in describing the range of the Pershing II system. Of fifteen references from late 1979 through early 1981 that attribute a specific range to the system, one-third give figures on the order of 1,500–1,800 kilometers, the usual range in Western discussions. But the other two-thirds cite ranges of 2,400–2,600 kilometers. Included in the latter group were the three general officers who were commenting, among them the two representatives of the Soviet General Staff. Perhaps the discrepancy comes from a combination of U.S. reticence to provide an official figure, and the Soviets' understanding of plans for tests up to the 2,500-kilometer range, which led the Soviet military to assume the worst on the operational range of the system.

64. The treaty also included in its protocol a provision not to deploy GLCMs of greater than a 600-kilometer range prior to December 31, 1981. While a plan to deploy such GLCMs in 1983 in no way would have violated that provision, the *purpose* of the protocol was to provide negotiating time for talks on further limitations of such weapons. The U.S. and NATO decision to delay the talks until after a deployment decision—and the U.S. delay in ratifying SALT II in the latter part of 1979—cast doubt in Soviet minds about the good faith of the United States.

PD-59 actions. The United States is seen as wishing to make possible a limited nuclear war in Europe that would involve strategic exchanges limited to the Soviet Union and Western Europe, with the territory of the United States sanctuary. The United States is said to have both pressured and cajoled its Western European allies into the deployment decision (and also to have tricked them by promising SALT II ratification in exchange, and then defaulting on that promise). The United States is also said to have used the SS-20 scare and TNF response to test NATO solidarity, to assert its leading role, and to commit the alliance to the new upward swing in the arms race.

NATO proposals for LRTNF arms control (since 1981 termed INF, for intermediate-range nuclear forces) were denounced as a sham, and the evident lack of enthusiasm by the Reagan administration was exploited. The Soviets see the United States as having successfully stymied INF arms limitation from 1979 through 1983, when the INF deployment began. While negotiations occurred from late 1981 to late 1983, the U.S. position was so contrived to give the U.S. and NATO advantage that it was not a genuine negotiation but a stalling tactic.[65]

The INF deployment is thus seen in military terms as both a reinforcement and an augmentation of the U.S. strategic triad, as a super-FBS element, and as strengthening the strategic nuclear component of the so-called NATO Triad (that is, NATO long-range theater nuclear, shorter range tactical nuclear, and conventional forces). In addition, the United States is alleged to have been seeking to make possible a Eurostrategic war that it could hope to wage with immunity for its own territory. The Soviets say they will not permit the United States to achieve superiority or these objectives; they will build countervailing capabilities.

The SS-20s are deployed in three areas: facing the European-Mediterranean theater, facing the East Asian theater, and east of the Urals in a swing position capable of supporting either theater. The initial deployment from 1977 through 1982 comprised 351 launchers, 243 of which (deployed both in Europe and in the swing area) were within range of Western Europe, with the remaining 108 deployed against targets in Asia. In 1982–83 an additional deployment was undertaken in Asia, raising the number there to 135 and the overall total to 378. Then in December 1983, after the first U.S. deployments, the Soviet Union canceled a unilateral moratorium under which no new deployments within range of Western Europe had been initiated after March 1982.[66]

---

65. See chapter 28.

66. The initial decisions on deployment were made in 1972–75, and the basic deployment program was established in the framework of the Tenth Five-Year Plan in 1975–76. The deployment decision was for six armies (with 81 launchers each, in three divisions of 27 launchers, each comprising three regiments of 9 launchers, totaling 486 launchers). In 1979 a decision was made to curtail this deployment to a total of 351 launchers, with three armies in the west (243 launchers) and one in the east (augmented with one extra division, for a total of 108 launchers). (It had become necessary to divide the swing area because launchers located in the

Thus the moratorium on further deployment in the European USSR announced with fanfare by Brezhnev in March 1982 reflected a decision to curtail the initial planned deployment.[67] As Andropov's proposal in December 1982, and its elaboration in 1983, showed, the Soviet leaders would have been prepared to cut sharply back on their own deployed SS-20 force, as well as to deactivate the remaining SS-4 force, in order to head off the American deployment. In the future, if serious negotiations should occur, the Soviet military will be highly reluctant to curtail its SS-20s unless there is substantial constraint not only on the planned Pershing II and GLCM deployment, but also on existing and future allied as well as U.S., sea-based as well as land-based, INF systems. This is the Soviet position even though the Soviet Union has very large ICBM and SLBM forces available for contingent use in the European theater as well as for intercontinental missions.

The SS-20 made its substantial contribution to the generation of an intermediate-range nuclear arms race in the 1970s and 1980s, although this result stemmed from Western misconceptions as well as from Soviet decisions. The Soviet leaders were unwise, from the standpoint of their own interests, to proceed with the SS-20 deployment—despite what they saw as an ample political-military justification and military requirement.[68] They were particularly unwise not to explain what they were doing and why; their explanations on modernization would probably not have been well-received even if well-founded,

---

western portion around Omsk were within range of Western Europe and had to be so counted in arms negotiations; those around Novosibirsk were counted in the eastern area.) In early 1982 the decision was confirmed to limit the western deployments to 243 and to announce a moratorium on further deployment in the west. It was also decided then to add one additional division in the east, raising the total there to 135 launchers, and the overall total to 378. After the NATO INF deployment began in November 1983 and the moratorium was ended, an additional deployment was begun in the west.

67. Some American and NATO officials, including Secretary of Defense Caspar W. Weinberger and SACEUR General Bernard D. Rogers, charged that activation of a few SS-20 groups several months subsequent to the moratorium violated Brezhnev's pledge. "Soviet Adding Nuclear Sites, NATO Chief Says," *Washington Times*, September 3, 1982; and "Soviet Missile Deployment Is Reported," *Washington Post*, October 16, 1982. While the wording of Brezhnev's statement in March (and another in May that confused the issue further) were not precise on the point, it soon became clear that it meant no additional SS-20 sites within range of Western Europe would be deployed beyond those on which construction was already completed or under way. (This procedure corresponded to that used in the completion of construction of Soviet ICBM launchers in progress when the SALT Interim Agreement was signed in 1972.) Despite recurrent Western reports of continuing deployment from 1982 through 1983, as construction was completed on sites begun before March 1982 or in the Far East, no *new* deployment sites within range of central Western Europe were started after the moratorium was announced in March 1982 until after the moratorium was revoked in December 1983.

68. In particular, Chancellor Schmidt warned Brezhnev of Western concern over the SS-20 deployments when they met in Bonn in May 1978. But Brezhnev and his associates did not realize the impact of their action on NATO's decision to undertake what was seen as an offsetting deployment.

but at least there would not have been open-ended uncertainty as to the scope of the program. By the same token, the NATO LRTNF decision, while conceived as a needed and justified reaction and while much better explained, was probably equally unnecessary.

The Soviet and the NATO decisions to deploy long-range theater nuclear forces in the 1970s seemed appropriate and necessary in the context of their respective decisions. Both reflected, however, one-sided evaluations of the strategic situation and differing perspectives of the military balance. Both showed serious failures in recognition of the interaction and effects of the decisions in stimulating adverse counteractions by the other side. The decisions also stemmed from shortcomings in the process of negotiating strategic arms limitations and from the low prospect for meeting perceived security requirements through cooperative rather than unilateral and ultimately confrontational actions. The long-term impact on East-West and American-Soviet relations remains to be seen. But in the context of other developments in the late 1970s and early 1980s, the TNF decisions of the two sides clearly contributed to the deterioration in political relations and to reducing, rather than enhancing, the security of both.

26 Afghanistan: Soviet Intervention and the American Reaction, 1978–80

THE SOVIET military intervention in Afghanistan in December 1979 and the American reaction to it marked a watershed in American-Soviet relations, sharply dividing the previous decade of détente (admittedly, faltering badly by that time) from the ensuing years of containment and confrontation.

Why did events involving that nearly forgotten corner of the world have such an impact on the central relationship in world politics? Before turning to the conditions within and related to Afghanistan in the critical months leading up to the Soviet move, and the way they were interpreted and acted on in Moscow and Washington, it is helpful to review the geopolitical setting in which those developments occurred, both in historical perspective and, in more detail, in the political perspective of the years immediately preceding.

The Setting: The Great Game

Afghanistan, a unified country only since the late eighteenth century, from early in the nineteenth century until the middle of the twentieth owed its continuing existence to its role as a buffer between the Russian and British empires. Each rival empire was driven to fend off expansion by the other as much as to expand its own rule. The Anglo-Russian maneuvers centered on Afghanistan came to be aptly called in the English-speaking world "the Great Game," a phrase coined by a junior British officer and popularized by Rudyard Kipling.[1] A century before Soviet troops entered Kabul in 1979, British troops had preceded them—in 1879, and before that in 1839.

---

1. David Fromkin, "The Great Game in Asia," *Foreign Affairs*, vol. 58 (Spring 1980), pp. 936–51, details the origin of the term and reviews the British conception.

The British seized Peshawar and the Pushtun tribal areas east of the Khyber Pass in 1839. The ruling Amir, Dost Mohammad, thereupon appealed for Russian assistance in recapturing the lost areas. Although St. Petersburg declined to intervene, the British were sufficiently alarmed at this indication of Afghan readiness to turn to the Russians, and fearful of Russian use of that opportunity, that they invaded Afghanistan in what later came to be called the First Afghan War. Although the British occupied Kabul, they could not pacify the Afghan tribes and eventually the British army was decimated in its withdrawal.[2]

In 1878 the Russians sought to put pressure on Great Britain in a diplomatic contest over the Balkans following the Russo-Turkish War by massing troops north of Afghanistan. Moreover, Russia had, independent of that development, established diplomatic relations with Afghanistan. The British, fearing Afghan collusion in a Russian military threat to India, again invaded Afghanistan, launching the Second Afghan War. Amir Sher Ali, like his predecessor Dost Mohammad, appealed for Russian help, but the Russian commander in Central Asia declined to send troops across the Hindu Kush in winter. Again in a sense prefiguring the Soviet intervention a century later, the British in 1879–80 succeeded in bringing about a change of regime, repudiation of Afghan diplomatic relations with Russia, territorial concessions, and the complete surrender of the conduct of Afghan external relations to Great Britain.[3]

British and Russian rivalry continued to dominate developments in the region, although from 1877 to 1907 a series of understandings led the British to agree not to annex any additional portions of Afghanistan, while the Russians agreed to accept the Amu Darya River (the Oxus of classical antiquity) as its border, marking the end of the gradual imperial Russian expansion in Central Asia. The St. Petersburg Convention of 1907 in particular moderated Russian-British rivalry. But it also contributed to the emergence of Afghan nationalism, because many Afghans believed Great Britain and Russia would settle their problems at the expense of Afghanistan.[4]

Afghanistan continued to chafe under British influence. One ruler, Amir Habibullah, tried and failed to regain the lost Pushtun tribal lands and was assassinated. He was succeeded by one of his sons, Amanullah. Amir Amanullah launched the short Third Afghan War in 1919 by attacking the Pushtun areas beyond the Khyber. The British defeated this thrust. But the British had no stomach for a further campaign in Afghanistan, after the cruel travail of the

2. See Henry S. Bradsher, *Afghanistan and the Soviet Union* (Durham, N.C.: Duke University Press, 1983), pp. 9–10.

3. Vartan Gregorian, *The Emergence of Modern Afghanistan: Politics of Reform and Modernization, 1880–1946* (Stanford, Calif.: Stanford University Press, 1969), pp. 108–10; and Bradsher, *Afghanistan and the Soviet Union*, p. 10.

4. See Gregorian, *The Emergence of Modern Afghanistan*, p. 211; Alfred L. Monks, *The Soviet Intervention in Afghanistan* (Washington, D.C.: American Enterprise Institute, 1981), pp. 3–7; and Alvin Z. Rubinstein, *Soviet Policy toward Turkey, Iran, and Afghanistan: The Dynamics of Influence* (Praeger, 1982), pp. 124–25.

Great War and on top of their other embroilments in the Western intervention in Russia and the suppression of an uprising in India. They therefore agreed in August 1919 to renounce their special role in Afghanistan and to recognize the country's full independence in internal and external affairs.[5]

British recognition of the independence of Afghanistan was matched by Soviet recognition that same year. Internal political developments now became the central element in the country, although they were still heavily influenced by the two powers.

In 1921 Amanullah signed a treaty of friendship with Soviet Russia as insurance against the possibility of renewed pressure by the British. The Soviet leaders committed themselves to an annual subsidy (economic aid, in more modern parlance) that Afghanistan needed to redress the difficulties caused by the cessation of the British subsidy that had been provided from 1880 until 1919. Amanullah, who was by no means a Marxist, was also interested in Soviet economic and security assistance, as he initiated a stiffly resisted program of internal reform. His father and grandfather, who had ruled since 1880, had intentionally resisted modernization, but Amanullah began to change that policy.[6]

A local regional rebellion in 1924 was suppressed but gave the Soviet Union a chance to demonstrate its support and friendship—and to gain a foothold of influence—by providing not only economic aid but also military and aviation advisers and the modest beginnings of an Afghan air force.[7] In 1926 the two countries concluded a Non-Aggression Treaty.

Another development in the early 1920s, by contrast, caused reservations and complications in Afghan-Soviet relations. During this period Moscow had consolidated Soviet control over fierce continuing resistance by local insurgents, called *Basmachi*, in the areas of Central Asia formerly under imperial Russia's control. Many of the rebels fled to neighboring Afghanistan where others of the same nationalities and tribes lived. And many used Afghanistan as a sanctuary from which to mount forays into Soviet Central Asia. Amanullah's desire for good relations with the Soviet Union did not prevent his lending tacit support to these *Basmachi*. The Soviet leaders in turn balanced their desire to cultivate good relations with Amanullah and Afghanistan against their determination to stamp out the *Basmachi*.[8] In 1925 the Soviets even sent troops in to occupy a small Afghan island in the Amu Darya River where

---

5. See Anthony Arnold, *Afghanistan: The Soviet Invasion in Perspective* (Stanford, Calif.: Hoover Institution Press, 1981), pp. 1–7; and Rubinstein, *Soviet Policy*, p. 126.

6. For the basic account see Leon B. Poullada, *Reform and Rebellion in Afghanistan, 1919–1929: King Amanullah's Failure to Modernize a Tribal Society* (Ithaca, N.Y.: Cornell University Press, 1973).

7. See Ludwig W. Adamec, *Afghanistan's Foreign Affairs to the Mid-Twentieth Century: Relations with the USSR, Germany, and Britain* (Tucson, Ariz.: University of Arizona Press, 1974), pp. 87–90, 107–08.

8. See Arnold, *Afghanistan*, pp. 8–17; and Thomas T. Hammond, *Red Flag over Afghanistan: The Communist Coup, the Soviet Invasion, and the Consequences* (Boulder, Colo.: Westview, 1984), pp. 10–11, 18.

Basmachi had settled, but they acceded to a ruling by a joint border commission and soon withdrew.[9]

Widespread revolt erupted in 1929 as a result of the growing opposition to Amanullah's reforms. He had returned from a trip abroad (that included Moscow, as well as Egypt, India, and Turkey) inspired to emulate Mustafa Kemal Ataturk, the charismatic ruler of Turkey, in modernizing and secularizing Afghanistan. Before he was able to move far along this path he was forced out. (One source of dissatisfaction had been press photographs of his wife on their travels abroad appearing without her veil.) Amanullah fled Kabul and was succeeded by a semiliterate Afghan Tadzhik bandit known as Bacha-i-Saqao.

In the ensuing disorder the Soviet leaders intervened indirectly in an effort to reestablish Amanullah to the throne. The Afghan ambassador in Moscow, Ghulam Nabi, had three influential brothers who had held high posts under Amanullah (one was the foreign minister, another had been governor in a key northern province). They maintained contact with Amanullah after he fled and went to Moscow to ask for assistance. The Soviets agreed to help, calling on Vitaly Primakov, the Soviet military attaché in Kabul, a veteran officer of the Russian civil war and also an experienced military adviser with the Chinese Nationalists in 1925–26. These men led a mixed Afghan-Soviet (Central Asian) force of a few thousand men into Afghanistan from near Termez, gaining control of Mazar-i-Sharif, the third largest city of the country, by April 1929. But by this time Amanullah and his family had fled to India. The Soviets promptly withdrew their forces and support, and the campaign collapsed. While the Soviets were prepared to support the former legal ruler in his effort to regain control, they were not prepared to attempt to establish a proxy rule themselves.

Bacha-i-Saqao was soon overthrown by Mohammad Nadir Khan, a cousin of Amanullah, who rallied an army from the British-held frontier areas and prevailed, with tacit British aid. He in turn was soon killed by the son of Ghulam Nabi, whom he had executed. Amanullah's own teenage son, Mohammad Zahir Shah, was crowned in 1933 and pursued a generally pro-British policy for most of his forty-year rule.[10]

There followed a number of years of relative quiescence in internal and external affairs. Both Great Britain and the Soviet Union intervened with force in neighboring Iran in 1941 to overthrow the pro-Axis ruler, substituting

---

9. See Hammond, *Red Flag*, pp. 12–13, although he overstates the situation in describing this incursion as "the first small-scale Soviet invasion of Afghanistan." See also Arnold, *Afghanistan*, p. 17.

10. See Hammond, *Red Flag*, pp. 15–18; Arnold, *Afghanistan*, pp. 18–20; and Bradsher, *Afghanistan and the Soviet Union*, pp. 15–16.

Of incidental interest, one of the British intelligence agents active in inciting insurgency in Afghanistan in 1929 was the famous Colonel T. E. Lawrence—"Lawrence of Arabia"—who arrived in Peshawar for this task in 1928 under the pseudonym of Shaw.

his young son, Reza Shah Pahlevi. They also compelled—but by collaborative diplomatic pressure—the expulsion from Afghanistan of all advisers and diplomats from the Axis countries.[11]

After World War II the most important new development directly involving Afghan interests was the British withdrawal from the subcontinent and the creation in 1947 of Pakistan, which inherited ethnically Afghan (Pushtun) tribes and territory east of the Durand Line. The Durand Line had been imposed (and bought, by bribing the Afghan representative) by the British in 1893, although Afghanistan had never really accepted it as representing the national border. Afghanistan was the only country to vote against admission of the new state of Pakistan into the United Nations, in a futile gesture.[12]

The most significant general international development after the war was the rise of the United States and the Soviet Union to predominant political influence and their polarization in the cold war. Because the leaders of Afghanistan saw the Soviet Union as a potential threat, while the United States seemed a distant and disinterested political counterweight, they sought to develop economic, political, and military ties with the latter.[13] For nearly nine years, from 1946 to 1955, Afghanistan sought American aid and support. Finally the United States made clear its commitment to Pakistan and unreadiness to commit itself comparably to Afghanistan. The Afghans thereupon promptly turned to the Soviet Union, which eagerly responded with economic and military aid.[14] A combination of U.S. ideological and political rigidity in support of alliance pacts for containment and of objections to neutralism regrettably coincided with, after years of Stalinist rigidity, greater Soviet flexibility in recognizing nonalignment. Afghanistan was a prime case of the negative impact of this conjunction on American interests.

From 1953 to 1963 Prince Mohammad Daoud Khan, first cousin of King Mohammad Zahir Shah (and previously the lieutenant general commanding the Kabul central command), served as prime minister. From 1955 on, Afghanistan developed its ties with the Soviet Union. While the United States provided some economic aid, it was not influential. Indeed, increasingly

---

11. Arnold, *Afghanistan*, pp. 24–26.

12. Ibid., pp. 27–29; and see Rubinstein, *Soviet Policy*, p. 128.

13. The United States had not recognized any government of Afghanistan until 1934 and did not establish a resident legation until 1942; it was raised to embassy status in 1948. The first Afghan ambassador to the United States was Mohammad Naim Khan, a first cousin of the king (and brother of Prince Mohammad Daoud Khan). See "The United States and Afghanistan," *Department of State Bulletin*, vol. 82 (March 1982), pp. 1–6. (Hereafter *State Bulletin*.)

14. See Bradsher, *Afghanistan and the Soviet Union*, pp. 17–24; and Hammond, *Red Flag*, pp. 23–25.

Secretary of State John Foster Dulles finally made the American position brutally clear to Daoud's brother, Mohammad Naim, who had been sent back to Washington as a special envoy in December 1954. Daoud flew to Moscow only a few weeks later. See Hammond, *Red Flag*, p. 25.

close American-Pakistani ties contributed to a growing Afghan-U.S. estrangement and to increasing Afghan-Soviet ties.[15]

In 1963 the king replaced Daoud and for the succeeding decade
attempted a moderate reform program. During this period relations with the
Soviet Union, and tension with Pakistan over the Pushtun areas, were moderated. Nevertheless, in terms of relations with the Soviet Union and the United
States the situation remained essentially unchanged.[16]

In retrospect, the most significant development within Afghanistan
was the establishment of a communist party (though the term was abjured),
the People's Democratic Party of Afghanistan (PDPA), in 1965; Nur Mohammad Taraki served as its secretary general. Two years later the party split into
several factions, the principal ones being called (after the names of their respective newspapers) the Khalq ("The Masses") and the Parcham ("The Banner").
Taraki headed the Khalq, which was the more militant and drew its members
mainly from the Pushtun tribes. Babrak Karmal headed the Parcham group,
which was closer to Moscow orthodoxy and also more prepared to work within
the existing system; it was mainly drawn from Tadzhik and other non-Pushtun
minorities. At the time neither party nor their leaders seemed likely to have an
important role in Afghan history.[17]

King Zahir's reforms and partial democratization promised more
than it could deliver. In July 1973, while the king was visiting Italy, Daoud
seized power in a nearly bloodless coup d'état. He had retained wide popularity, especially (and most critically important) in the officer corps. One reason
was his continuing support for "Pushtunistan," a Pushtun state to be carved
from Pakistan as a step toward reunification with Afghanistan.[18] Some of the
officers involved in the coup were also close to the Afghan communists, especially, at that time, to the Parcham; they included Major Abdul Qader Dagarwal of the air force, and Captain Mohammad Aslam Watanjar, a capable
junior tank force commander, both of whom would later play important roles.
The Parcham itself supported the coup, and Daoud rewarded it by naming
several of its members and sympathizers to his cabinet and to other posts. (In

---

15. See Rubinstein, *Soviet Policy*, pp. 128–31.

16. See Arnold, *Afghanistan*, pp. 32–46; Bradsher, *Afghanistan and the Soviet Union*, pp. 32–36;
and Rubinstein, *Soviet Policy*, pp. 134–39.

17. See Hammond, *Red Flag*, pp. 29–34; Bradsher, *Afghanistan and the Soviet Union*, pp. 43–52;
Arnold, *Afghanistan*, pp. 47–53; and Suzanne Jolicoeur Katsikas, *The Arc of Socialist Revolutions: Angola to Afghanistan* (Cambridge, Mass.: Schenkman, 1982), pp. 216–21. See also
Beverley Male, *Revolutionary Afghanistan: A Reappraisal* (St. Martin's Press, 1982), pp.
20–51, by a foreign observer strongly supportive of the Khalqist Hafizullah Amin.

18. Daoud had a personal reason for his devotion to the cause of reuniting the Pushtun (or
Pathan) tribes of Pakistan with Afghanistan: his great-great-grandfather had been the last
Afghan ruler in Peshawar before the British seized control in 1834.

addition, whether to reward them or to dissipate their energies, he sent some 160 young Parcham activists out to the countryside to "reform" the civil administration; they became, instead, largely disillusioned and in any case were swallowed up by it.) Thus the Parcham (whom some disdainful Khalq members ironically called "the Royal Communist Party" in the preceding years) carried its pragmatic readiness to work *within* the system (royal or republican) to becoming part *of* the system in 1973. The Khalq, not participating, drew a more radically inclined membership; it also began to recruit, actively and clandestinely, in the armed forces officer corps, an assignment given to one of its leaders, Hafizullah Amin, a teacher trained in the United States.[19]

Before long Daoud began to replace the Parcham members of his government and a number of key leftist officers, a process he carried out from 1974 to 1977. In 1975 he set up his own political party and required all other parties at least nominally to merge with it. By 1977 he had gained approval of a constituent assembly (*loya jirgah*) for a constitution establishing a presidential one-party system. He quashed a series of reported or feared coup plots from the right and the left. One result of the exclusion of the Parcham was an uneasy reunification in mid-1977 of it and the Khalq, a move that was urged by several pro-Soviet Asian communist parties.[20]

One other internal development of future consequence should be noted. Beginning in 1975, a fundamentalist Muslim group called Hizb-i-Islami began armed insurgency, with financial assistance from the Moslem Brotherhood and Pakistan, and also, reportedly, from Libya.[21]

In addition to seeking to consolidate his internal political control, Daoud soon began a significant shift in Afghanistan's international relations.[22] Initially he attempted in 1974 to press the Pushtun issue against Pakistan and made a careful endorsement of the Soviet proposal for an Asian collective security arrangement. Then Daoud turned to seek more balanced relations. While not abruptly changing course, he moved to improve relations with Iran, Pakistan, and China, while diminishing Afghan dependence on the Soviet Union.

---

19. See Hammond, *Red Flag*, pp. 35–37; Bradsher, *Afghanistan and the Soviet Union*, pp. 53–57, 67; Male, *Revolutionary Afghanistan*, pp. 52–61; and Arnold, *Afghanistan*, pp. 55–60.

20. See Arnold, *Afghanistan*, pp. 57–65; Bradsher, *Afghanistan and the Soviet Union*, pp. 57–59, 67–72; Hammond, *Red Flag*, pp. 37–38, 49–50; Louis Dupree, *Red Flag over the Hindu Kush*, pt. 1: *Leftist Movements in Afghanistan*, American Universities Field Staff Report 44 (Hanover, N.H.: AUFSR, 1979); and Hannah Negaran (pseud.), "The Afghan Coup of April 1978: Revolution and International Security," *Orbis*, vol. 23 (Spring 1979), pp. 94–100.

21. "The Rebellion Recruits a Country," *The Economist*, May 23, 1981, p. 36.

22. For a good summary and documented treatment of the events discussed in the remainder of this section, see Bradsher, *Afghanistan and the Soviet Union*, pp. 60–67; and Hammond, *Red Flag*, pp. 38–42.

In December 1974 Daoud sent his brother, Naim, to Beijing to meet with Zhou Enlai and to reassure the Chinese that despite qualified support for the Soviet Asian collective security proposal, Afghanistan would continue to be neutral in the Sino-Soviet dispute. In April 1975 Daoud himself visited the shah in Tehran; in June 1976 President Zulfikar Ali Bhutto of Pakistan visited Kabul; and in August Daoud returned the visit to Islamabad.[23]

There has been some dispute among experts as to the extent of the role played by the shah of Iran in encouraging this shift by Daoud, but there is no question he played a role. Daoud began as early as 1974 to turn to Iran, Saudi Arabia, and Kuwait for economic aid. In 1975 the shah offered up to $2 billion over a ten-year period and, more concretely, early that same year lent $400 million on easy terms. The shah (and the Saudis) also urged, and helped, Afghanistan to improve relations with Pakistan.[24] Daoud, while still heavily dependent on Soviet military as well as economic aid, also began to arrange military cooperation and training with India, Egypt, and Pakistan (and even to increase the number of officers sent to the United States). By early 1978 the cumulative effect of these changes and planned further steps was considerable.

In the spring of 1978 Daoud visited India, Pakistan, Egypt (twice), Libya, Turkey, Yugoslavia, Saudi Arabia, and Kuwait. He and General Mohammad Zia ul-Haq of Pakistan agreed during Daoud's second visit to that country to dampen the Pushtun issue. The shah of Iran was scheduled to visit Afghanistan in June of 1978, while Daoud announced plans to visit President Carter in Washington. In March an economic agreement was signed with China. And Daoud publicly stated that at the forthcoming conference of the nonaligned movement Afghanistan would press for "true non-alignment"— unlike that of Cuba, the host.

Relations with the Soviet Union had become cool—not surprising in view of these developments. Following Daoud's initial friendly visit in 1974, relations had gone downhill. President Podgorny's return visit in December 1975 was said to have involved "frank" (that is, strained) exchanges, and no reference was made to friendship as it had been the previous year. When Daoud visited Moscow in April 1977, according to Afghan diplomatic sources, there was an angry confrontation between Daoud and General Secretary Brezhnev. Daoud reportedly stalked out of the room after reminding Brezhnev that he was the president of an independent country.[25] Nonetheless, on the surface Soviet-Afghan relations continued to be normal.

What this course of policy would have led to is not clear—on April 27, 1978, Daoud was overthrown and killed in a military coup.

---

23. See Rubinstein, *Soviet Policy*, pp. 138–51.

24. Ibid., pp. 146–51. The strongest claim for the shah's role was presented by Selig S. Harrison, "The Shah, Not Kremlin, Touched off Afghan Coup," *Washington Post*, May 13, 1979. See also Katsikas, *Arc of Socialist Revolutions*, pp. 224–26.

25. See Hammond, *Red Flag*, p. 42 and associated footnotes.

The Events: From Coup to Intervention

The trouble began on April 17, 1978, when Mir Akbar Khyber, a leading Parcham intellectual and organizer, was murdered. It is still not known who was responsible. Possibly it was the Daoud government (or someone within it, such as the anticommunist interior minister, General Abdul Qader Nuristani), or possibly rival communists from the Khalq, perhaps Hafizullah Amin.[26] When a remarkably large crowd of some 10,000 to 15,000 Afghani demonstrated at his funeral two days later, shouting anti American slogans, Daoud was alarmed at the unexpected show of communist strength. Six days later he moved, arresting the seven principal Khalq and Parcham leaders and announcing the uncovering of an "anti-Islamic" plot. Among those arrested were Taraki, Amin, and Karmal. Inexplicably, there was a delay of several hours in taking Amin to prison, during which he was simply held under house arrest. That time enabled him to send several relatives to warn other Khalq party members and leftist officers not under arrest.[27]

According to the later Afghan communist history of these events, Amin prepared and dispatched plans for a coup that included assignments for key persons.[28] This account is, however, suspect. The evidence strongly supports the conclusion that key communist sympathizers in the officer corps decided on their own on the spur of the moment to preempt a likely move by Daoud against them by striking first. While these were the same men who had mounted the 1973 coup with Daoud, to varying degrees they had become estranged from him in recent years. Moreover, some had close ties with the arrested leaders of the illegal PDPA, and all, as security risks, were potential targets in a broad Daoud crackdown on the left.

The morning after the arrests, April 27, Major Mohammad Aslam Watanjar, deputy commander of the Fourth Tank Brigade in Kabul, led a force of some 60 tanks and 600 men against the Arg, the walled area containing Daoud's palace residence and offices. (Watanjar, then a captain, had been in the lead tank in the assault in the 1973 coup.) Colonel Abdul Qader Dagarwal, recently reinstated as chief of staff of the air force, several hours later brought in about 20 MiG-21 and Su-7 fighter-bombers that strafed and fired rockets against the palace and its 1,800-man presidential guard. Daoud was meeting with his cabinet at the time the attack began, deciding the fate of the seven arrested communist leaders. The minister of defense, Lieutenant General Ghu-

---

26. See Bradsher, *Afghanistan and the Soviet Union*, pp. 72–73, for a good summary of available information and speculations. As Bradsher notes, Amin was later accused by one of the Parcham survivors of his purges in 1980. He also points out that there had been two other suspicious and probably political murders, shortly before Khyber's.

27. Ibid., pp. 73–74; and Hammond, *Red Flag*, p. 51. Bradsher notes the rumor that Amin had also maintained secret ties with the police.

28. For a sympathetic account crediting Amin's later official version, see Male, *Revolutionary Afghanistan*, pp. 62–67.

lam Heydar Rasuli, was able to leave and tried to rally loyal troops. Although the armed forces had been placed on alert at the time of the arrests, premature celebrations over that event had left some units disorganized. Even though the coup leaders had neglected to take the government communications center, Rasuli was still unable to rally the forces. Moreover, the major army units stood aside to await the outcome, which came with the final surrender of the remaining presidential guard early the next morning. Daoud, most of his ministers, and his family were killed while resisting or after surrendering.[29] A blood purge of the Mohammadzai clan, to which Daoud (and the deposed king) had belonged, followed.

The actions of the coup forces may help explain their purposes. While naturally the principal effort was directed against Daoud and his guard, it is remarkable that such key objectives as the government communications center, the Ministry of Defense headquarters, and Radio Kabul were not priority targets. Moreover, the arrested communist leaders were not freed from prison until six or seven hours after the attack on the presidential palace—during which time they were lucky not to have been disposed of. By the evening of April 27, with victory in sight although not yet secured, Colonel Qader addressed the nation on Radio Kabul to inform it that a "revolutionary council of the armed forces" (later called the Revolutionary Military Council) had assumed "the power of the state." Watanjar was also named. In the initial broadcast, and for three days, there was no reference to Taraki, Amin, Karmal, the PDPA, or any civilians or civilian organizations.[30]

On April 30, Decree No. 1 of the newly named Democratic Republic of Afghanistan announced that the Revolutionary Military Council had been disbanded and succeeded by a Revolutionary Council headed by Taraki and including all the members of the former military council, as well as the Khalq and Parcham PDPA leaders. Taraki was also named prime minister, but no deputies were yet named. Only two days later, in Decree No. 2, Karmal, head of the Parcham, was named vice president of the Revolutionary Council, and both he and Amin were made deputy prime ministers. Amin was also named foreign minister. Qader and Watanjar were the next ranking members of the council and of the cabinet. Qader was promoted to major general and made minister of national defense, while Watanjar was made a deputy prime minister and minister of communications and promoted to lieutenant colonel.[31]

---

29. See Louis Dupree, *Red Flag over the Hindu Kush*, pt. 2: *The Accidental Coup, or Taraki in Blunderland*, American Universities Field Staff Report 45 (Hanover, N.H.: AUFSR, 1979); Bradsher, *Afghanistan and the Soviet Union*, pp. 75–77; and Hammond, *Red Flag*, pp. 52–53.

30. Dupree, *Red Flag over the Hindu Kush*, pt. 2 (1979).

31. These decrees were read on Radio Kabul on April 30 and May 2, 1978. See Bradsher, *Afghanistan and the Soviet Union*, pp. 79–80; and Hammond, *Red Flag*, pp. 58–59. The transition from the military council, announced on April 30, had occurred the previous evening. Later

Clearly there was some initial pulling and hauling as the party leaders persuaded the military that their political expertise was needed to manage the progressive reforms on which Daoud had turned his back since 1973 but which they could achieve. Taraki was held in high standing by the officers, so his selection was easy, but it was evidently more difficult to sort out the distribution of positions to the three groups: the Khalq, the Parcham, and the leftist officers.

The new regime declared itself "nonaligned" and eschewed the label "communist." It did indicate its intention "to further strengthen and consolidate friendly relations and all-around cooperation with the USSR" and to pursue "democratic land reforms" at home. There were many signs of communist organizational forms and terms (for example, leaders were referred to as "comrades," and a Politburo was created), but at least for a time the new regime did not flaunt its communist orientation. One reason was to avoid provoking domestic and international anticommunist sentiment. In addition, the Taraki government hoped to continue to receive some U.S. economic assistance, which would have been barred if the American government were to reach a finding that the new regime was "communist."[32]

The question of a possible Soviet role in instigating the April coup has been largely answered in the negative as more has been learned about the events. Even most of those who believe the Soviet leaders intended to foster a seizure of power at some point by the PDPA concede that the coup was precipitated by Daoud's arrest of its leaders, and that it had not been planned. Moreover, Soviet reactions seem to confirm Moscow's uncertainty even after the coup occurred. Local Soviet military advisers must have learned of what was to happen at some point in the hours before Qader and Watanjar struck, and some may even have participated, accompanying the Afghan units to which they were assigned into action. But there was neither time nor opportunity for Moscow to have decided upon, much less to have masterminded, the coup. From April 27 to April 30 TASS called it a military coup d'état. This is hardly the term it would have used if it were merely concealing an Afghan communist takeover—that would have been called a popular revolution.[33]

Afghan (but not Soviet) accounts provided a spurious rewriting of history, attempting to expunge the existence of the Revolutionary Military Council and place Taraki or Amin, or both, in command of the coup (revolution) and the new regime from the outset. See Bradsher, pp. 79–80.

32. Hammond, *Red Flag*, pp. 59–62, stresses the deception exercised by the Taraki regime and official American receptivity. See also Bradsher, *Afghanistan and the Soviet Union*, p. 85.

33. For an argument in support of Soviet complicity see Rubinstein, *Soviet Policy*, pp. 151–56, but his case is not convincing. Hammond, *Red Flag*, pp. 51–54, is inclined to see a long-term Soviet plan to seize power and to believe that "it is difficult to imagine that the Soviets did not know a coup was being hatched," but he concedes they may have known only a few hours in advance, and this did not mean "that the Soviets planned or stage-managed the coup." Bradsher (and

The initial purge of Daoud's administration, to be expected, was soon followed by a breakdown of the uneasy Khalq-Parcham alliance. Within two months and despite the efforts of a Soviet Communist party official dispatched from Moscow to hold the PDPA factions together, the Parcham leaders were removed from power and six of them were sent abroad as ambassadors. In August Major General Abdul Qader, Major General Shapur Ahmezdai, chief of staff of the army, and the three remaining Parcham cabinet ministers (including Major Mohammad Rafi) were relieved. Several, including Qader, were imprisoned for an "antirevolutionary" conspiracy. By November the Parcham ambassadors were dismissed and ordered home (none was so foolish as to return), and Parcham leader Babrak Karmal was denounced as the head of a Parcham-led plot that General Qader had joined. Within the Khalq party and the government Amin rose to become the deputy to Taraki in both party and government roles. In fact, Taraki was well on the way to becoming a figurehead chief of state.[34]

As the Khalq consolidated its power in the regime and Amin within the Khalq, the leadership increasingly pressed for radical reforms in the country. The communist accession to power in Afghanistan in 1978 came to be a revolution, although not in the way depicted in subsequent Afghan (and Soviet) commentary. The forceful deposition of the Daoud government by a preemptive military coup d'état, and the subsequent turnover of political power by the leftist military coup leaders, in no way constituted a political revolution. The "Great Saur (April) Revolution," as the coup came to be called, was the invention of the communist Khalq leaders once in power. There had been no political or military involvement outside Kabul, and even there only a minority of the military forces participated. Later, however, the Khalq leaders not only purged the ranks of the new leadership of the Parcham and independent leftist military colleagues, but also launched a far-reaching national revolution from above.

---

most other observers) similarly do not see Soviet initiative in the coup. See Bradsher, *Afghanistan and the Soviet Union*, pp. 82–84; and Katsikas, *Arc of Socialist Revolutions*, pp. 225–26.

Both American *and Soviet* diplomats scrambled to find biographical backgrounds on many of the new leaders. Interestingly, of the twenty-one members of the new cabinet, ten had had their advanced education in the United States, including Taraki and Amin; only the three military men had studied in the Soviet Union (of the others, two had studied in Egypt, one each in France and West Germany, and four only in Afghanistan). Eleven, including the three military men (Colonel Qader, Major Watanjar, and Major Rafi), had been serving the Daoud government at the time of the coup, while seven others had just been arrested. See Louis Dupree, "Afghanistan under the Khalq," *Problems of Communism*, vol. 28 (July–August 1979), p. 40.

34. See Dupree, *Problems of Communism*, vol. 28 (1979), pp. 41–43; Bradsher, *Afghanistan and the Soviet Union*, pp. 87–89; and Katsikas, *Arc of Socialist Revolutions*, pp. 227–28. For an account accepting the Khalq charges of a Parcham-military plot, see Male, *Revolutionary Afghanistan*, pp. 127–41.

Among the elements of the regime's revolution were a range of social, political, and economic reforms. Most were not peculiarly communist but involved attempts at modernization similar to those in many other third world countries having a variety of ideological and governmental institutions: land reform, educational reform, secularization, social security, women's liberation, and the like. Again, as in many other cases, the means included attempts at political centralization and the dispatch of eager young officials to modernize the countryside, a decline in administrative efficiency (the result of purging the experienced bureaucrats and officials), and unintended arbitrariness and favoritism. The rapid pace of the attempts at reform was doubly self-defeating: not only was popular opposition aroused, but very often the reforms failed. Moreover, owing to the lack of experience of the young new officials it became necessary to bring in more and more Soviet advisers—not because of Soviet pressure to do so, but simply to help manage the country after the removal of those who had done it for so long.[35] This influx added a further foreign element to the already ideologically foreign approach of the new regime.

The peoples of Afghanistan had always been fiercely independent ("unruly" was the word the British had used) and religious. The fall of the monarchy in 1973 meant little to them, as did the transition from a republic to a people's republic in 1978. Many were initially not sorry to see Daoud go, as he had sought to increase the authority of his rule. But when the new regime also began to attempt to centralize control over the tribes, and to overthrow their traditional social-religious-economic order, many rebelled. The new regime literally waved a red flag at the people when it changed the national standard from Islamic green, black, and red to a red one very similar to those of the Central Asian republics of the USSR. That act was particularly provocative and foolish. But it was not as significant as the *real* reforms: education for girls, and coeducation at that, with the girls exposed (that is, without veils) before male instructors—that was far more a cause of intense opposition. Similarly, the attempt to reduce the bride price dowries, intended to enhance the status of women, undercut their traditional social security (and an integral part of the rural economy). While Taraki said that the new regime would "respect the principles of Islam," he also said that "religion must not be used as a means for those who want to sabotage progress." This policy pitted the whole reform program against the mullahs. Ultimately the land reform had to be cut back sharply (although to hollow claims of success). All in all, the domestic socialist program of the new regime "violated practically every Afghan cultural norm, and strayed far beyond the allowable bounds of deviance in the social, eco-

---

35. The number of Soviet military and civilian advisers in April 1978 was about 350. That number doubled in the next two months, and continued to grow, reaching some 3,000 to 3,500 (including 1,000 military) by May 1979 and 7,200 by December 1979. These estimates were by the U.S. embassy in Kabul.

nomic, and political institutions. It almost appears that [the new leaders] systematically planned to alienate every segment of the Afghan people."[36]

By the summer there was a major armed uprising in Nuristan, in the eastern part of the country, and by the winter of 1978–79 armed resistance had spread to most of the twenty-eight provinces. Whereas some Muslims had engaged in armed opposition to the Daoud regime since 1975, now far wider Muslim-led and local tribal rebellions began to spread in reaction to the reforms of the new government.[37] The Afghan army—comprised largely of conscripted villagers—became less and less reliable and effective in countering the resistance: it had little stomach for fighting and killing other villagers. Desertions began to mount, and with them a flow of arms to the opposition. Resistance also grew as the regime became more closely identified with the Soviet Union and Russian military advisers came in larger numbers and assumed a more obvious role.

In March 1979 a major uprising occurred in Herat, one of the three principal cities of the country. It included the defection to the rebels of the 17th Infantry Division of the Afghan army in garrison there. Several dozen Russian military advisers and their families were hunted down and slaughtered cruelly, their impaled heads brandished on pikes carried through the streets. Local Khalq cadres and officials sent from Kabul were also killed. And there were heavy casualties when Afghan troops, brought from far away, retook the city. Rebellion continued to spread, as did further mutinies of army units.[38]

Among the consequences of the Herat mutiny was an intensification of the internal power struggle. On March 27 Amin became prime minister. But at the same time Assadullah Sarwari—not an associate of Amin, and in some respects a rival—was made head of the secret police. And two other key posts were given to ambitious young officers: Colonel Watanjar became minister of defense, and Major Mazdooryar was named minister of the interior.[39]

Another consequence of the Herat mutiny was a major increase in the number of Soviet military advisers (and the return to the Soviet Union of

---

36. Louis Dupree, *Red Flag over the Hindu Kush,* pt. 3: *Rhetoric and Reforms, or Promises! Promises!* American Universities Field Staff Report 23 (Hanover, N.H.: AUFSR, 1980), p. 4. See also Dupree, *Problems of Communism,* vol. 28 (1979), pp. 34–50; Bradsher, *Afghanistan and the Soviet Union,* pp. 90–96; Hammond, *Red Flag,* pp. 68–75; Katsikas, *Arc of Socialist Revolutions,* pp. 229–36; and David Chaffetz, "Afghanistan in Turmoil," *International Affairs,* vol. 56 (January 1980), pp. 15–36. Again, for a sympathetic account of the PDPA's strategy for reform see Male, *Revolutionary Afghanistan,* pp. 102–26.

37. The Jamaat-i-Islami began underground opposition in 1973, and by 1975 had been joined by the Hizb-i-Islami with sporadic armed resistance to the Daoud government. Covert assistance was received from Pakistan.

38. See Bradsher, *Afghanistan and the Soviet Union,* pp. 100–01; Hammond, *Red Flag,* pp. 74–75; and Dupree, *Problems of Communism,* vol. 28 (1979), p. 44.

39. See Male, *Revolutionary Afghanistan,* pp. 163–65.

wives and other dependents), as well as an increase in the supply of weapons, including armored vehicles and helicopter gunships. Clearly the growing insurgency would require increased military action.

A third consequence was a Soviet and Afghan claim that foreign powers were responsible for instigating the growing unrest and insurgency. A few days after the Herat uprising *Pravda* began to charge that Pakistan, Egypt, China, and "some Western countries" were responsible. The Western countries were soon identified as the United States, Great Britain, and West Germany; Iran was also added to the list. (In fact, the Afghans had blamed Iran from the outset. Herat is near the Iranian border, and some Afghans may have returned there from Iran. But Kabul's charge that 4,000 Iranian soldiers had infiltrated was untrue.)[40] On June 1 *Pravda* also accused the government of Pakistan of complicity in the insurgency and warned that it constituted "a case of actual aggression against a state with which the USSR has a common border." In fact, since the winter of 1978–79 the insurgents had developed a network of guerrilla training camps in Pakistan and supply routes across the border into Afghanistan and were using Pakistan as a sanctuary.[41] More basically, however, and in the broader charges that had less foundation, the Soviet leaders were simply not willing to admit that the uprising in the country *could* have been in response to the Khalq rule or was explicable by any internal political dynamic, given the "people's" Great Saur Revolution. There was a need to blame foreign enemies.

The question of possible external involvement was also of particular significance, since on December 5, 1978, the Soviet Union and Afghanistan had signed a Treaty of Friendship, Good Neighborliness, and Cooperation, thus formalizing and enlarging the Soviet commitment to support the new government, despite its internal difficulties and Soviet reservations about its course.[42] The treaty was ratified in May 1979.

The Soviet leaders also moved to assess, and to change, the political situation within Afghanistan. This was ultimately the most significant consequence of the growing insurgency, exemplified so vividly by the Herat uprising. On April 5 General of the Army Aleksei Yepishev, chief of the political administration in the Soviet armed forces, accompanied by a delegation that in-

---

40. See I. Aleksandrov, "Reactionary Intrigues against Democratic Afghanistan," *Pravda*, March 19, 1979; and A. Petrov, "A Rebuff to the Forces of Reaction and Imperialism," *Pravda*, March 21, 1979. Both names are established pseudonyms for authoritative commentaries by the Soviet leadership. On the Afghan charges see Bradsher, *Afghanistan and the Soviet Union*, p. 101; and Male, *Revolutionary Afghanistan*, pp. 161–62. Male points out that the Afghans were, however, less inclined than the Soviets to blame the Western powers.

41. A. Petrov, "Provocations Continue," *Pravda*, June 1, 1979. See also Bradsher, *Afghanistan and the Soviet Union*, pp. 100, 103.

42. See *Vneshnyaya politika sovetskogo soyuza i mezhdunarodnye otnosheniya, 1978 god* [The Foreign Policy of the Soviet Union and International Relations, 1978] (Moscow: Mezhdunarodnye otnosheniya, 1979), pp. 223–26.

cluded six other generals, arrived for a week-long visit to evaluate the situation and to urge measures to restore discipline, morale, and effectiveness in the Afghan army. The visit had little evident impact.[43]

By far the most important Soviet move was the dispatch in June of a troubleshooter to try to put the Afghan party and government back on track. The Soviet leaders were very unhappy with the way in which the Taraki-Amin leadership was running the country. They opposed the purge of the Parcham and military elements from the leadership and repeatedly and strongly advised against pushing radical social reforms. General Yepishev may have advised that no real improvement in dealing with the insurgency in the field would be possible without changes in Kabul. But with or without that advice the potentially disastrous nature of the course being pursued by the Taraki-Amin leadership was increasingly clear to Moscow, especially after Herat.

As early as May American intelligence reports suggested that "the Soviets are already moving forward with plans to engineer replacement of the present Khalqi leadership," perhaps with Karmal.[44] In June Vasily Safronchuk arrived as a special representative—nominally as a second deputy to Ambassador Aleksandr Puzanov—with the dual mission of urging Taraki and Amin to broaden the political base of the regime and of scouting out alternatives. Safronchuk sought, unsuccessfully, to persuade Taraki and Amin to rehabilitate purged Parcham members and to expand the base of the Communist party, to establish a wide "national front," and to broaden the government itself by bringing in competent noncommunists. In addition, he continued to urge pulling back on radical reforms. But Taraki and, increasingly, Amin declined most of the advice. And instead of the insurgency lessening, it was spreading; instead of the regime gaining popular support, it was losing what little it had; instead of the ruling group broadening its membership, leadership became further concentrated in Amin's hands.

Whether as part of Safronchuk's search for an alternative leadership or coincidentally, by mid-July a spate of underground "night letters" (leaflets secretly distributed at night around Kabul) began to attack Amin—but not Taraki. Some of these leaflets urged a return to the true revolutionary goals espoused by Mir Akbar Khyber, the Parcham leader whose assassination in 1978 had touched off the arrests and the coup, "with the support of the Soviet Union and the other socialist countries." Amin was called a "criminal" supported by a "fascist band of gangsters," and even a secret "CIA agent" whose mission was to destroy the credibility of socialism and the Soviet Union in

---

43. General Yepishev had also made an assessment visit to Czechoslovakia several months before the Soviet military intervention there in 1968, a fact often noted after the December 1979 Soviet intervention in Afghanistan. The later parallel actions were not directly relevant; the fact of assessing a deteriorating situation was. The visit was given normal press coverage.

44. Cited in Bradsher, *Afghanistan and the Soviet Union*, p. 104, from a declassified official U.S. Department of State briefing memorandum of May 24, 1979.

Afghanistan.[45] These were among the charges against Amin later sounded by Karmal—and the Soviet Union—after Amin's death and replacement. Other such leaflets in August purported to be written by disaffected Khalqi members within the government, who even claimed to have taken their complaints (including those over the purges of "loyal revolutionaries") to Taraki, only to be told by him that "Amin is in charge of everything."[46]

In mid-July the American embassy in Kabul was able to send an extraordinary report from a very well placed source confirming that Safronchuk had been given the mission of bringing about a "radical change" in the Afghan government. This source reported that the Soviets were "deeply worried over the worsening situation in Afghanistan," "know the regime has little public support and is losing control of the country," but "are determined to save the revolution." Amin, who "personally runs the entire government," had "blun-

---

45. These reports are cited in cables sent to Washington by the American embassy in Kabul, specifically U.S. Embassy Kabul 5360, Confidential, July 16, 1979, and U.S. Embassy Kabul 5433, Confidential, July 18, 1979. The latter cable noted that any serious attempt to effect a political solution and avoid the need for Soviet military intervention to deal with the insurgency would require "a leadership change [that] would probably have to include the departure, or—better yet—the death of Amin." It went on, "Safronchuk could be the local behind-the-scenes director of this particular drama" ("insuring the future of the revolution, although perhaps without the present composition of the Afghan leadership"). U.S. Embassy Kabul 5433, paras. 10, 15.

These cables are not among those declassified and released by the U.S. government and were not available to Hammond and Bradsher, who used a number of other U.S. Embassy Kabul reporting cables from 1978 and 1979 in their excellent studies. The cables cited here were among a large batch dating from the period January 1978 to November 1979 seized by the Iranian militants who occupied the American embassy in Tehran. They were subsequently published both in Farsi translation and in photo-reproduction of the originals (including a few reconstituted from the shredder) in two books from a series called "Spynest Revelations." Two volumes of that series are called *Afghanistan* (Tehran: Moslem Students Followers Imam [1981]). Volume 1, in English, comprises a 37-page introduction and 195 pages of reproduced official U.S. communications, mostly from early 1978 to early August 1979, including some from the Department of State and other American posts, as well as Embassy Kabul, plus a Farsi translation; and volume 2, 163 pages of reproduced official U.S. communications from August to early November 1979, plus a Farsi translation. The cables cited above appear in volume 1, on pages 167–69 and 170–77, respectively. Further citations to cables from this collection reference both the original document (for example, "U.S. Embassy Kabul . . .") and the pages of the *Afghanistan* (Tehran) collections, volume 1 or 2.

The American embassy in Moscow had reported in May, even before Safronchuk left for Kabul, that he would be going there as "diplomatic adviser" to the Afghan government. It also passed along an unconfirmed Pakistani report that Safronchuk had visited Kabul at about the time of the April 1978 coup. U.S. Embassy Moscow 13169, Confidential, May 24, 1979, in *Afghanistan* (Tehran), vol. 1, pp. 122–23.

Of the later analyses of the situation in Afghanistan in 1979, only Bradsher, *Afghanistan and the Soviet Union*—alerted by anonymous U.S. government officials—has appreciated Safronchuk's role, but he did not have the key documentary sources.

46. See U.S. Embassy Kabul 6605, Confidential, September 2, 1979, quoted in Hammond, *Red Flag*, pp. 81–82, and cited by Bradsher, *Afghanistan and the Soviet Union*, p. 105.

dered badly"; Taraki was well-intentioned but little informed and ineffective. What was needed, in Moscow's view, was a strong new prime minister "not identified with present policies." The source said Safronchuk had been given the task of replacing Amin because "it is not good for the Soviet Ambassador himself to be seen holding these delicate negotiations," and if they fail and "Safronchuk were expelled as persona non grata, that would attract less attention and be less of a diplomatic embarrassment for the Soviet Union than if Ambassador Puzanov were expelled." The source remarked that "we are now seeing the closing chapter of this government" and that "August is going to be hot, and I don't mean the weather." He noted that no such necessary internal radical change in the leadership could occur without Soviet support and that a political solution would have to embrace three elements: "saving the face of the Soviets, saving the face of the Afghan party (PDPA), and saving the face of the Muslims."[47]

Meanwhile, Amin was aware that the Soviets were increasingly dissatisfied with him.[48] On July 27 he moved Colonel Watanjar from the Ministry of Defense (thus removing one of the main coup leaders of 1973 and 1978 from the armed forces) and assumed de facto control of defense himself. He also removed Major Mazdooryar from the Ministry of Interior and shifted several other ministers.[49]

Serious military mutinies continued. One occurred in Jalalabad in April; again Soviet military advisers were killed. An uprising in the Hazara region in June triggered a precautionary alert of an airborne division in the Soviet Union. Finally, in early July a 600-man battalion of the 105th Guards Airborne Division was flown in from the Soviet Union and stationed at Bagram air base near Kabul, the key military communications center.[50] Another serious

---

47. The source of this remarkable revelation was East German Ambassador Hermann Schweisau in a conversation with American Chargé d'Affaires J. Bruce Amstutz, reported in U.S. Embassy Kabul 5459, Secret-Exdis [Exclusive Distribution, a special "close hold" classification], July 18, 1979, in *Afghanistan* (Tehran), vol. 1, pp. 179–84. He had earlier spoken less openly along the same line, reported in U.S. Embassy Kabul 5246, Confidential, July 11, 1979, in ibid., vol. 1, pp. 162–66. There had been a further discussion in which Schweisau admitted it might already be too late to build a genuinely expanded political base, but indicated that the Soviets were building an anti-Amin coalition of non-Pushtuns, whom he named. See U.S. Embassy Kabul 5470, Secret-Exdis, July 19, 1979, in ibid., vol. 1, pp. 185–87. In addition, Safronchuk himself had made clear to Amstutz soon after his arrival in June the Soviet dissatisfaction with the Amin regime and his own role in seeking a broadened political base. See U.S. Embassy Kabul 4888, Confidential, June 25, 1979, in ibid., vol. 1, pp. 127–33.

48. The embassy reported hints by Amin in public remarks that suggested he might be aware of the behind-the-scenes maneuvering and that these hints represented an attempt to warn off the Soviets or rally supporters against any Soviet move. See U.S. Embassy Kabul 5493, Confidential, July 22, 1979, in *Afghanistan* (Tehran), vol. 1, pp. 192–94.

49. See U.S. Embassy Kabul 5683, Confidential, July 28, 1979, and U.S. Embassy Kabul 5736, Confidential, July 30, 1979, in *Afghanistan* (Tehran), vol. 1, pp. 213–14, 222–24.

50. The unit was in fact a 600-man battalion intended as a quick-reaction force to provide security for the growing Soviet advisory element with the Afghan air force, centered at Bagram air base.

military mutiny occurred in early August at the Bala Hissar fortress in Kabul itself.[51] In September insurgents briefly cut off the tunnel in the Salang Pass, a key chokepoint on the main route from the Soviet Union to Kabul.

Soon after the mutiny by the regiment at Bala Hissar was crushed, on August 17 a high-powered Soviet military delegation led by Deputy Defense Minister General of the Army Ivan Pavlovsky, chief of the Soviet ground forces, arrived in Afghanistan for what became a two-month stay. His delegation totaled sixty-three, including twelve other general officers and six colonels. Their tasks involved a new assessment of the military situation and of the prospects for turning the tide against the widespread insurgencies—and probably also an evaluation of the requirements for direct Soviet military participation if that course could not be averted. This latter task would later be expanded.[52]

Meanwhile, on the political front, Safronchuk and his associates were also sounding out alternative noncommunist leaders. There were persistent reports that the Soviets contacted the former prime minister Mohammad Yousouf, the head of King Zahir's government from 1963 to 1965; Nur Ahmad Etemadi, the king's prime minister from 1967 to 1971 (even though he was imprisoned); Abdul Samed Hamed, a deputy prime minister under the king (and also now imprisoned by the Khalq regime); and Mohammad Musa Shafik, Daoud's immediate predecessor as prime minister in 1973.[53] It is clear that the Soviets did not exclude the possibility of a progressive noncommunist, or coalition, government to succeed the Taraki-Amin regime.

Initially this unit was estimated to have 400 men, and this figure was released to the press by U.S. government sources. Most subsequent analyses have therefore referred to it as a 400-man battalion (for example, Bradsher, *Afghanistan and the Soviet Union*, p. 107). For a later and more fully informed account, identifying the battalion at Bagram as "at least 600" men, see U.S. Embassy Kabul 7319, Secret-Exdis-Noforn, October 3, 1979, in *Afghanistan* (Tehran), vol. 2, pp. 111–12.

An embassy assessment in early September referred to the buildup at Bagram as "reminiscent of the pattern of increasing USG [U.S. government] involvement in Vietnam." U.S. Embassy Kabul 6672, Secret, September 6, 1979, in *Afghanistan* (Tehran), vol. 2, p. 53.

51. U.S. Embassy Kabul 5967, Secret, August 6, 1979, in *Afghanistan* (Tehran), vol. 1, pp. 228–32; and see Bradsher, *Afghanistan and the Soviet Union*, pp. 107–08.

52. The composition of the delegation and its initial expectation of remaining about twenty-five days is reported in a CIA evaluation. CIA Headquarters message, Secret, September 19, 1979, in *Afghanistan* (Tehran), vol. 2, p. 162. An embassy report that "trusted Afghan officials" had been told that "fact-finding" was its mission. U.S. Embassy Kabul 5604, Secret-Exdis, September 2, 1979, in ibid., vol. 2, p. 51. The other purposes of the delegation could only be surmised. Unlike the visit in April by General Yepishev, the arrival of General Pavlovsky and his delegation was not mentioned in the press.

53. Based on released State Department and U.S. Embassy Kabul cables. See Bradsher, *Afghanistan and the Soviet Union*, pp. 105–06; and Hammond, *Red Flag*, pp. 80, 83. See also U.S. Embassy Kabul 5448, Confidential, July 18, 1979, and U.S. Embassy Kabul 5470, Secret-Exdis, July 19, 1979, in *Afghanistan* (Tehran), vol. 1, pp. 178, 187.

On August 18, Afghanistan's national day, General Secretary Brezhnev and Prime Minister Kosygin sent congratulations that omitted any reference to the Treaty of Friendship signed the previous December. This omission seemed to reflect uncertainty about whether the Soviet Union was prepared under all contingencies to "save the revolution." But Safronchuk continued to try to influence Amin—and alternatively to build a coalition to dislodge and replace him.[54] And General Pavlovsky was studying military requirements to defeat the insurgency.[55]

At this juncture Taraki went to Havana for the summit meeting of nonaligned countries. En route back to Afghanistan he stopped in Moscow for two days of talks with Brezhnev. Unconfirmed reports have indicated that Taraki agreed to Soviet urging to broaden the political base by bringing members of the Parcham back into the party and government—and to get rid of Amin. (Less credible later rumors also had Taraki meeting with Karmal.) There have been many conflicting accounts of plots by Taraki or by Colonel Watanjar and others against Amin, and vice versa. Brezhnev himself later told a Western visitor that he had warned Taraki against Amin.

Precisely what happened is not clear.[56] Upon his return Taraki was greeted with great fanfare and a demonstrative embrace by Amin. Three days later, on September 14, there was a showdown in which Taraki's security guard attempted to assassinate Amin. In the ensuing shoot-out with Amin's security guard, Amin survived only because the security chief, Major Sayed Daoud Taroun, was standing in front of him and was hit by the bullets intended for Amin. Reportedly Amin had feared a trap and had gone to the presidential palace at Taraki's request only after receiving Ambassador Puzanov's assurances of his safety—and with the precaution of taking Major Taroun as a security escort. Ambassador Puzanov may even have been present.

The immediate cause of the showdown was Amin's decision to purge four key members of his cabinet—to which Taraki objected strongly but

---

54. Ambassador Schweisau returned to East Germany very suddenly on August 16. He was taken by ambulance to an Aeroflot flight with a seriously broken leg. The American embassy later speculated that his abrupt departure might have been related to Amin's objection to his outspoken critical comments to diplomats; they did not also note the possibility that the Soviets were concerned at Schweisau's outspokenness on Soviet dissatisfaction with Amin. U.S. Embassy Kabul 7706, Confidential, October 25, 1979, in *Afghanistan* (Tehran), vol. 2, pp. 124–25. One of those suspicious of the alleged reason for his sudden departure was the American chargé, who reported at the time that on August 12 Schweisau had mentioned to the American deputy chief of mission in an aside at a reception that he wanted to see him "as soon as possible about an urgent matter." When the American called the next day to arrange a meeting, he was told that Ambassador Schweisau had broken his leg the preceding evening and could not receive visitors. Without making any of the customary departure calls Schweisau was medically evacuated three days later. U.S. Embassy Kabul 6309, Secret-Exdis, August 20, 1979, in ibid., vol. 2, p. 38.

55. See Bradsher, *Afghanistan and the Soviet Union*, p. 108.

56. Ibid., pp. 110–11, Hammond, *Red Flag*, p. 82, and Male, *Revolutionary Afghanistan*, pp. 182–85, describe various reports in more detail.

which Amin nonetheless proceeded to do that day. They were Colonel Watan-jar, the minister of the interior; Major Sherjan Mazdooryar, minister of frontier affairs; Lieutenant Colonel Sayed Mohammad Gulabzoy, minister of communications; and Assudullah Sarwari, head of AGSA (the secret police). This purge disposed of the three remaining leftist military men who had led the coups of 1973 and 1978 and the chief of the secret police (who was not an associate of Amin's). But all four escaped arrest and found refuge in the Soviet embassy or other Soviet protection. Meanwhile Amin hastily rounded up some forces, returned, and took Taraki prisoner.[57]

The failure of Taraki's attempt to curb Amin and his own fall from power were a dramatic turn of events in their own right. But even more impor-tant was the near certainty that Taraki had acted at Soviet urging. Ambassador Puzanov's assurances to Amin only confirmed his suspicions that the Soviets were out to get rid of him. The Soviet advice to Taraki to get rid of Amin was reportedly tipped to Amin either by Foreign Minister Shah Wali, a long-time close associate of Amin's who had accompanied Taraki to Moscow, or by Ma-jor Taroun.[58] The next day, September 15, Ambassador Puzanov called on Amin and talked with him for two hours. While there is no confirming evi-dence, it seems likely that he urged Amin to release Taraki.[59] If so, he failed. On September 16 Radio Kabul reported an extraordinary session of the Cen-tral Committee of the People's Democratic Party of Afghanistan, presided over by Shah Wali, at which it was decided to accept Taraki's "request" to be relieved of his party and government positions "due to health reasons and physical incapacitation which render him unable to continue his work." Hafi-zullah Amin succeeded him as general secretary of the party. A secret six-page document circulated among party cadres said that the meeting had adopted a secret resolution on "the unprincipled behavior and terrorist actions of Nur

---

57. The main source is the American embassy reporting on the affair: U.S. Embassy Kabul 6914, September 16, 1979, and U.S. Embassy Kabul 7784, Confidential, October 30, 1979. These and other sources are cited by Bradsher, *Afghanistan and the Soviet Union*, pp. 112–13; and Hammond, *Red Flag*, pp. 84–85. Of particular interest is a further report that was not avail-able to them from the ambassador of a communist country who had discussed the matter with Ambassador Puzanov. See U.S. Embassy Kabul 7281, Secret-Exdis, October 2, 1979, in *Af-ghanistan* (Tehran), vol. 2, pp. 107–10.

Watanjar and Gulabzoy were in the Soviet embassy; Sarwari may also have been there; Mazdooryar may have been under Soviet protection at the Soviet military advisory compound at the Pul-i-Charki tank forces base. See U.S. Embassy Kabul 7784, Confidential, October 30, 1979, in *Afghanistan* (Tehran), vol. 2, pp. 126–27. There is uncertainty over other details, such as whether Amin actually fired the four ministers before the showdown with Taraki or after, but the main events are clear.

Amin gave Major Taroun a hero's funeral and renamed the city of Jalalabad for him. See Bradsher, *Afghanistan and the Soviet Union*, p. 114.

58. See Bradsher, *Afghanistan and the Soviet Union*, p. 112; and Hammond, *Red Flag*, p. 85.

59. U.S. Embassy Kabul 6936, Confidential, September 17, 1979, cited in Bradsher, *Afghanistan and the Soviet Union*, pp. 113–14, and text in *Afghanistan* (Tehran), vol. 2, pp. 72–75.

Mohammad Taraki and the gang of four" (the dismissed ministers and secret police chief), charging them with "conspiracies" against Amin and expelling all five from the party.[60] On October 8 Taraki was killed on Amin's order; two days later the *Kabul Times* reported that Taraki had died of "serious illness."[61]

The Soviet leaders were embarrassed at the sudden fall from power of the man that Brezhnev personally had seen off from Moscow with an embrace only a few days earlier. *Pravda* was still discussing the Taraki visit as late as September 16. But this element of their discomfort was minor. Far more important was that their attempt to get rid of Amin had backfired badly: instead Taraki had been removed, as had the other key leaders on whom the Soviets had banked, and Amin had greatly enhanced his own power. Moreover, Amin's suspicions and hatred of the Soviets had been confirmed and enlarged. What remained to sustain a hollow, forced collaboration were Amin's dependency on Soviet aid and the Soviet stake in Afghanistan. Neither could afford to cut off the other, but their relationship was very bad.

The uneasiness of the alliance was very evident. In late September Kosygin flew back to Moscow from India without stopping over in Kabul or even sending the usual message of greeting while flying over the country (as had been done in March and would be done again the next year).[62] Ambassador Puzanov failed to attend several functions in Kabul that he normally would have. Amin boycotted Puzanov's embassy reception on the sixty-second anniversary of the October Revolution, the Soviet national day.[63] But these were only small surface signs of the underlying strain in relations.

On October 6 Amin's chief deputy, Shah Wali, invited all the ambassadors of communist countries (except China) to a meeting at which he accused Ambassador Puzanov of complicity in an abortive attempt to remove Amin, saying that Puzanov had been in Taraki's office when he assured Amin by telephone that it was safe to accept Taraki's request to come to the palace. He also accused Puzanov of harboring Watanjar, and perhaps the other three fugitives, in the Soviet embassy. Finally, Wali said that Amin had been invited to Moscow to discuss the situation but had refused to go. Safronchuk attended

---

60. U.S. Embassy Kabul 7428, October 11, 1979, cited in Bradsher, *Afghanistan and the Soviet Union*, p. 114.

61. See Bradsher, *Afghanistan and the Soviet Union*, pp. 115–16.

On October 3 a Soviet diplomat told the American chargé that Taraki was then being held prisoner in isolation and confirmed reports that Taraki and the three dismissed ministers had been expelled from the PDPA. Commenting more generally on the difficult political situation, he remarked that "we [the Soviet embassy] never know what tomorrow will bring here." See U.S. Embassy Kabul 7318, Confidential, October 3, 1979, in *Afghanistan* (Tehran), vol. 2, p. 113.

62. Bradsher, *Afghanistan and the Soviet Union*, p. 118.

63. U.S. Embassy Kabul 7444, October 11, 1979, cited in Hammond, *Red Flag*, p. 86; and see Bradsher, *Afghanistan and the Soviet Union*, p. 118.

the meeting in place of Puzanov; while greatly embarrassed by these accusations he did not deny them.[64]

Ambassador Puzanov was declared persona non grata, and Moscow had no choice but to remove him. On November 8 the designation of his successor, Ambassador Fikryat Akhmedzhanovich Tabeyev, a Tatar Muslim by origin, was accepted, although Puzanov did not leave until November 19 and Tabeyev did not arrive until November 28. Safronchuk remained.[65]

Meanwhile, it is highly likely that in mid-September General Pavlovsky was given a new assignment: to assess the requirements for a direct Soviet military intervention under circumstances in which the Afghan government and army could not be counted upon. He completed his mission in mid-October and he and his delegation returned to Moscow.

The possibilities of success with the political track that Safronchuk had been pursuing had virtually collapsed. The disaffected Khalqi and other associates of Taraki had now been purged. Some other alternatives had also been lost (for example, Amin had former prime minister Etemadi, whom the Soviets had consulted in prison, executed on September 16).[66]

Amin, now unchallenged in the leadership, set about trying to bolster his position and that of his regime within the country and abroad. He placed his nephew, Assadullah Amin, at the head of the secret police. Without really changing the oppressive police state he was creating, he did with much fanfare create a new "extraordinary revolutionary court" to review the cases of those imprisoned since April 1978. Some were released—while others continued under arrest. In September Amin appointed a commission to write a new constitution—Afghanistan had had none since the coup. The death sentences earlier imposed after secret trials of General Qader and Sultan Ali Keshtmand in August were reduced to fifteen years imprisonment. Amin also tried to mollify Muslim resentment by promising religious freedom. But these maneuvers did not enhance his regime's popular standing, nor broaden its very narrow political base, nor impress the Soviets that, whatever his other faults, Amin could turn the tide of the descent toward chaos.[67]

---

64. U.S. Embassy Kabul 7444, October 11, 1979, and U.S. Embassy Kabul 7784, October 30, 1979, in *Afghanistan* (Tehran), vol. 2, p. 128; and see Bradsher, *Afghanistan and the Soviet Union*, p. 117 and associated footnotes. When Safronchuk asked Wali how he knew Watanjar was at the embassy (which the Soviets had denied), he was told that Watanjar had phoned the Kabul military commander from there—evidently trying to drum up a coup.

65. See Bradsher, *Afghanistan and the Soviet Union*, pp. 117–18; and Hammond, *Red Flag*, p. 92, note 10.

66. Reported by U.S. Embassy Kabul 7784, Confidential, October 30, 1979, corroborating a Turkish report relayed by U.S. Embassy Ankara 7966, Confidential, October 25, 1979, in *Afghanistan* (Tehran), vol. 2, pp. 128, 122, respectively. Also noted by Bradsher, *Afghanistan and the Soviet Union*, p. 115.

67. See Bradsher, *Afghanistan and the Soviet Union*, pp. 119–21, citing U.S. Embassy Kabul 7876, November 6, 1979; and see Hammond, *Red Flag*, pp. 88–91.

The insurgency continued. A major counterinsurgency offensive in Paktia in late October, with extensive direct Soviet military assistance, was a failure. And in mid-October the 7th Infantry Division near Kabul mutinied.[68] Amin was not winning the campaign to pacify the country either politically or militarily.

On the international scene Amin continued to express rapport with the Soviet Union and continued to receive economic and military assistance. But he also began to seek better ties with other countries, for example, Pakistan and Iran. Nevertheless, President Zia remained wary. By early December, Amin's efforts to get Zia's foreign affairs and national security adviser, Agha Shahi, to visit became increasingly urgent, even frantic. The visit was arranged for December 22, but the flight was canceled because of snow. Because of Shahi's schedule, it had to be set for December 30. By that time Amin was no more.[69] It remains unclear just what Amin hoped a sudden rapprochement with Pakistan could do, but clearly he hoped to become less dependent on the Soviet Union, and he may have thought Pakistan could intercede with the United States to help him if he cut his Soviet connection. On several occasions Amin expressed an interest in improving relations with the United States, but it did not go beyond that.[70] (As will been seen, Soviet and American perceptions on this question were at sharp variance.)

In November Amin declined a Soviet invitation to visit Moscow; he was understandably not prepared to entrust his own security to the Soviet Union.[71] Strained, though normal, Soviet-Afghan relations continued into late December.[72]

---

68. See U.S. Embassy Kabul 7502, October 15, 1979, cited in Hammond, *Red Flag*, p. 90; and see Bradsher, *Afghanistan and the Soviet Union*, p. 120.

69. See Bradsher, *Afghanistan and the Soviet Union*, pp. 121–23, 179; and Hammond, *Red Flag*, p. 91.

70. Amin was notably friendly in a private meeting with the American chargé on September 27; see U.S. Embassy Kabul 7218, Confidential-Exdis, September 27, 1979, in *Afghanistan* (Tehran), vol. 2, pp. 89–91. See also Hammond, *Red Flag*, pp. 86–88; and Bradsher, *Afghanistan and the Soviet Union*, p. 123 and associated notes.

71. According to unconfirmed reports originating with Amin's mistress and nephew after their escape to London via Pakistan, in late November the Soviets also requested, and Amin rejected, establishment of a Soviet air base at Shindand. See Anthony Mascarenhas, "Invasion Born out of Error," *The Age* (London), January 5, 1980, for the originating report. If this report is well grounded, it may have represented a Soviet subterfuge for establishing a pre-attack presence in Shindand for the alleged purpose of surveying the airfield. Certainly the Soviet leaders neither needed nor wanted Amin's approval for a Soviet base when they were already planning to remove him (assuming the late November date for the request is correct). Subsequent Soviet development and use of military facilities at Shindand and elsewhere during the years after the Soviet intervention have all been related to the internal counterinsurgency campaign.

72. See Bradsher, *Afghanistan and the Soviet Union*, pp. 124–25.

The most relevant developments, it later became clear, involved Soviet military measures within the Soviet Union and in Afghanistan from November through December in preparation for the Soviet military intervention that was planned along with a forced change in the Afghan leadership. Military deployments in the central southern region of the USSR have always enjoyed a lower priority, strength, and readiness than the forces deployed in or facing Europe or the Far East. Apart from the single airborne division located in Central Asia, of the eleven divisions there in the summer of 1979 only three could have been considered ready for combat without mobilization of reserves. And those three were not well-situated for commitment in Afghanistan.[73] The 105th Guards Airborne Division in Fergana (the only one located east of the Urals) had been alerted in March and June at the time of the Herat and Hazara uprisings and in mid-September at the time of the Taraki-Amin showdown. As earlier noted, a battalion of the division had been deployed to Bagram air base near Kabul in July, the only Soviet combat unit in Afghanistan (apart from helicopter gunships nominally part of the Afghan air force, and the Soviet military advisers numbering about 1,500 assigned to the 90,000-man Afghan army). This light airborne battalion was for protection of Soviet personnel rather than for combat operations against the rebels.

In November the Soviets began to call up reservists to flesh out two motorized rifle divisions located near Afghanistan, and in late November and December there were further call-ups of reservists to fill out three additional divisions. From November 29 to December 5 two additional battalions of the 105th Airborne were flown to Bagram, raising the total to 2,500 men. A 600-man armored battalion was flown in from December 8 to 10, and in mid-December it moved north from Bagram to secure the key Salang tunnel on the highway to Termez in the Soviet Union. One of the airborne battalions moved south to Kabul airfield. Also in mid-December Soviet military air transports gathered at Moscow and Tashkent, and some tactical air units were moved to bases in Soviet Central Asia near Afghanistan. Two more of the Soviet Union's seven airborne divisions were alerted, the 103rd and 104th. A military command and communications center was established at the Soviet border city of Termez. Then from December 24 to 26 the rest of the 105th Airborne Division landed at Kabul airport, and two other airborne battalions were landed at the air bases at Shindand near Herat in the west and at Qandahar in the south.[74]

Meanwhile, on November 28 Lieutenant General Viktor Paputin, a first deputy minister of the interior, had arrived in Kabul. It has been reported that a KGB general, never identified, also arrived at that time. Paputin's role is still not entirely clear, but presumably he was intended to neutralize the security police whom his ministry, together with the East Germans, had been

---

73. U.S. Embassy Moscow 13083, Secret, May 24, 1979, in *Afghanistan* (Tehran), vol. 1, p. 119.

74. This account is based on official American and British releases; it is reported for the most part in Bradsher, *Afghanistan and the Soviet Union*, pp. 176, 179.

advising since the 1978 coup (replacing West German police advisers who had served previously). He and the shadow KGB general, who presumably was guiding KGB experts attached to the Afghan secret police, were almost certainly involved in planning a security forces coup against Amin. Paputin was reported in the Afghan press to have met with the minister of the interior on November 30, with Prime Minister Amin on December 2, and then to have departed on December 13. He may never have left, or he may have returned clandestinely, but he was probably present at the next stage: what was to have been either the seizure or assassination of Amin on December 17. Amin was reportedly wounded slightly, but his nephew Assadullah Amin, chief of the secret police, was seriously wounded—and taken to the Soviet Union for medical treatment.[75]

Amin was clearly shaken. He moved the prime ministry and revolutionary council (and his residence) to the isolated Tajbeg Palace in the Darulaman complex on the southern outskirts of Kabul and sought to bolster his defenses.[76] All parties continued to play out a strange macabre drama. For example, as late as the afternoon of December 27 Amin received a courtesy call by the visiting Soviet minister of communications, Nikolai V. Talytsin.[77]

A few hours later, on the evening of December 27, an explosion knocked out the Kabul telephone system, and Soviet airborne troops captured the ministry of the interior and attacked the Darulaman complex and the Tajbeg Palace. Even before it had fallen, a radio station identifying itself as Radio Kabul broadcast on the Kabul frequency a tape-recorded message from Babrak Karmal announcing that "the bloody apparatus of Hafizullah Amin . . . has been broken," praising the martyr Taraki, and "rais[ing] the banner of national *jihad*"—a holy war—for "the glorious April Revolution." The real Radio Kabul fell soon after. During the night resistance at Darulaman ended, and Amin was dead.[78]

---

75. Later, after Amin had been killed and Karmal succeeded him, Assadullah Amin was returned to Afghanistan and executed in June 1980. See Bradsher, *Afghanistan and the Soviet Union*, p. 230.

76. As in 1973, the bulk of the Afghan army stood aside. The commander of the 4th Tank Brigade, Lieutenant Colonel Alawoddin, later declared that on the evening of December 26 General Yaqub, the chief of the General Staff, had telephoned the brigade headquarters and ordered it to Darulaman to protect the (Amin) government, but that he and his colleagues had decided to wait and see what was going on, and did not take action as advised. "It was decided to investigate the situation and not to take any steps which might damage the gains of the April revolution." This brigade had been Colonel Watanjar's before the April coup. From an interview in Kabul by Soviet correspondents on Radio Moscow, Domestic Service, January 16, in Foreign Broadcast Information Service, *Daily Report: Soviet Union*, January 17, 1980, p. D8. (Hereafter FBIS, *Soviet Union*.)

77. See Bradsher, *Afghanistan and the Soviet Union*, pp. 177–80; and Hammond, *Red Flag*, p. 99.

Minister Talytsin's delegation, probably not incidentally, had an excellent opportunity to reconnoiter firsthand the entire central Afghan communications system.

78. Bradsher, *Afghanistan and the Soviet Union*, pp. 180–81.

Early on December 28 the real Radio Kabul, now in the hands of the new regime, announced that Babrak Karmal was president of the revolutionary council and general secretary of the PDPA. Also named as vice presidents were Sarwari, the ousted secret police chief reportedly hiding in the Soviet embassy since September, and the imprisoned Keshtmand. Members of the council presidium included the imprisoned General Qader and Colonel Watanjar, also late of the Soviet embassy. Also broadcast was a formal appeal to the Soviet Union for military assistance and the announcement that the Soviets had accepted that request.[79]

That same morning two motorized rifle divisions began crossing the Amu Darya River on pontoon bridges, and two more prepared to follow them. These four divisions headed for Herat, Kabul, and Qandahar to secure the major cities and airfields. Within the next month seven divisions in all, constituting the new 40th Army with its headquarters in Termez and under the direct command of First Deputy Minister of Defense Marshal Sergei Sokolov, had occupied the major centers of the country. Some 85,000 Soviet military personnel were in Afghanistan. Massive Soviet military "assistance" had arrived very promptly.[80]

Several minor mysteries remain. On January 3 *Pravda* reported the death on December 28 of the fifty-three-year-old General Paputin, in an obituary that lacked the usual signatures of senior leaders, photograph, and the like normally accorded a deceased first deputy minister and lieutenant general. There was speculation in Moscow and abroad and reports that he might have been killed in the fighting in Kabul, or that he might have committed suicide after returning to Moscow because of the failure of his mission to dispose of Amin quickly and quietly. The latter seems more likely, especially in view of the obituary.[81]

---

79. Ibid., p. 181.

80. The seven divisions were the 105th Guards Airborne Division and six motorized rifle divisions from the Central Asian Military District: the 357th, the 66th, the 360th, the 201st, and later the 16th and 54th. One battalion each from the 103rd and 104th Guards Airborne Divisions may also have been used initially in December in Herat and Qandahar but were then withdrawn after the infantry divisions arrived a few days later.

   The presence of a very large proportion of ethnic Muslim Uzbek, Turkoman, and Tadzhik soldiers excited speculation in the West. The explanation is very simple—the normally low-strength divisions permanently stationed in Central Asia were filled during November and December with local Central Asian reservists. They were simply the available divisions and soldiers; the Soviet leaders neither sought, nor sought to avert, the large proportion of Central Asians in the initial occupying force.

81. See U.S. Embassy Moscow 94, January 3, 1980, and 1395, January 25, 1980; Bradsher, *Afghanistan and the Soviet Union*, p. 183; Hammond, *Red Flag*, p. 98, and note 6 on pp. 102–03; David Binder, "U.S. Links Afghan Events and Soviet General's Death," *New York Times*, February 3, 1980; and Kevin Klose, "Death of Soviet Official Spurs Rumors," *Washington Post*, March 14, 1980. The speculation that Paputin was sent to arrange a political transition seems very unlikely, given Safronchuk's role, the prior organization of the Karmal team in the Soviet Union, and his unsuitability for the task. See Jiri Valenta, "From Prague to Kabul: The

Soviet military advisers already in Afghanistan with units of the Afghan army are reported to have helped ensure against possible Afghan resistance. Many told the Afghans that all the activity was an exercise. Some Afghan units were instructed to turn in live ammunition for blanks for training; batteries were removed from some tanks for "winterizing," while other tanks were sent to depots supposedly for correction of a "defect"; some communications were cut. A large number of Afghan officers in Kabul were also reported to have been invited to a reception by Soviet officers early in the evening of the assault and then were locked in. While it is not possible to verify all these reports, most if not all are probably true.[82]

Quite apart from such disarming deceptions, the presence of numerous Soviet military advisers and the earlier introduction without opposition of airborne units at the Bagram and Kabul airfields greatly facilitated the final coup assault in Kabul. Subsequently the Soviet military takeover elsewhere also proceeded smoothly. Although usually described as an "invasion," which in a political sense it was, the Soviet military intervention and occupation were largely unopposed. There had been fierce fighting with Amin's guard force, and there was some fighting at Herat and by the 26th Paratroop Regiment of the Afghan army, which refused orders to disarm and was crushed.[83] But all in all there was little resistance, and the Soviet divisions did not even have to assume combat dispersal in their movement. There were reportedly more Soviet casualties from road accidents than from combat.

The direct Soviet military role in deposing Amin was clear, despite Soviet and Karmalist Afghan insistence that Amin had been overthrown, tried, and executed by the Afghans themselves. The concurrent introduction of four Soviet divisions overland (plus two more in January), in addition to the airborne division in the first instance, in the eyes of the world constituted a visible Soviet invasion. However one judged the claimed justification, there had been a massive direct Soviet military intervention concurrent with removal of Amin and installation of Karmal in his stead. Clearly, while the military elimination of Amin and the occupation were quite successful, the political measures intended to manage a transition from Amin to Karmal and to provide legitimacy for the dispatch of Soviet military forces had gone very badly. General Paputin may have been the only one to offer his life in expiation, but he was not alone responsible for the failure.

It is important to note that the basic Soviet political expectation was in error. The Soviet leaders believed that a new political reconciliation of

---

Soviet Style of Invasion," *International Security*, vol. 5 (Fall 1980), pp. 131–32, for such speculation.

82. See Arnold, *Afghanistan*, p. 95; Hammond, *Red Flag*, p. 99; and Bradsher, *Afghanistan and the Soviet Union*, p. 180.

83. See "U.S. Reports Soviet Fights Afghan Army," *New York Times*, January 14, 1980.

good Khalqs—those in the Taraki tradition rather than Amin's—and the return and release of the Parcham leaders and military men would provide a basis, along with liberalized policies, for encouraging a political renewal. Meanwhile, braced by the presence of 85,000 Soviet soldiers in the background, the Afghan army could deal with the insurgency. And the insurgents would be cowed by the presence and availability of the Soviet army. All these assumptions and expectations proved woefully overoptimistic. The surviving Khalq and Parcham leaders remained very suspicious and hostile toward one another. (It was little wonder; for example, one of the rehabilitated Khalqs named deputy prime minister was Sarwari, the secret police chief under Taraki who had personally tortured some of the Parcham prisoners, including his new colleague, the other deputy prime minister, Keshtmand.) The populace was not in the least disposed to accept yet more promises of liberalization, religious freedom, and the like. Karmal appeared in public with some coopted mullahs but to no avail. The traditional Afghan flag replaced the red banner. But it was too late for such palliatives. And the new leadership had the added burden of owing its return to power, and continued exercise of power, to the Russians—who now occupied the country militarily and were becoming more involved in its administration.

The insurgency soon grew enormously over what it had been, as did a mass exodus to Pakistan and Iran, which rose from 100,000–200,000 to 2–3 million in a few years. And the Afghan army was so rent by desertions and defections that it soon numbered only about one-third of the 90,000 it numbered before the intervention. Even that lower level was sustained only by forced conscription. The army's effectiveness was similarly diminished. As a result, the Soviet army had to assume more and more of the counterinsurgency military effort, intensifying the cycle of disaffection and resistance.[84]

The Soviet Perspective and the Decision to Intervene

How did the Soviet leaders perceive these events of April 1978 through December 1979? What were their intentions in seeking to influence and to respond to developments in and affecting Afghanistan?

While the Soviet leaders were quick to welcome the April 1978 military coup and the subsequent assumption of power by the People's Democratic Party of Afghanistan, they were cautious in their evaluation of the new regime. While welcoming a new putative candidate for the socialist camp, they were wary both of the stability and depth of commitment of the Afghan communists to Soviet-style "real socialism" and of their ability to maintain

---

84. See, for example, Bradsher, *Afghanistan and the Soviet Union*, pp. 205–39; and Hammond, *Red Flag*, pp. 148–54.

power and to formulate and carry out a policy attuned to the country. The Soviets were unsure that Afghanistan was ready for socialism and that the undisciplined team of Taraki, Karmal, Amin, and their associates were tried or true Marxist-Leninists. The April 1978 coup was unexpected and was viewed by the Soviets with trepidation and concern. A failed socialist revolution would be worse than none at all.

The Soviet leaders were pleased to see an end to Daoud's shift toward a pro-Western slant of nonalignment but would probably have preferred to see him change rather than leave the scene. When he was ousted, they would probably have preferred a more conservative liberal who would return to the Daoud line of 1973–74, offering apprenticeship in power for PDPA members as Daoud had provided to the Parcham in 1973–75.

Soviet concerns were soon borne out, as the PDPA descended into internecine personal struggles and purges. Karmal and his Parcham faction were frozen out within a few months. Taraki was too detached from reality, blithely assuming that radical and fast-moving changes could be made. He was also too indulgent and dependent on the more practical and efficient, but ambitious and uncontrollable, Amin. The Soviet leaders were alarmed by the growing alienation of the Afghan people as the Taraki-Amin regime pushed its radical reforms with excessive zeal.[85] Nonetheless, by December 1978 they were willing to conclude a treaty of friendship that considerably raised the Soviet commitment to the new regime.[86] Even then the Soviet leaders declined to consider the PDPA a communist party, or the People's Republic of Afghanistan a member of the socialist community (except for one ambiguous reference in May 1979).

As noted earlier, the uprising in Herat (and bloody massacre of Soviet advisers and their families) in March 1979 had jarred the Soviet leaders into their first real consideration of the possibility of a more direct military role. From their standpoint this shift would not necessarily involve Soviet military operations in the country, although if it did, they would be in *support* of the Taraki-Amin government. Nonetheless, the Soviet leaders were well aware of the potential costs and liabilities of directly committing Soviet military

---

85. Soviet writers subsequently have criticized the Afghan leaders for trying in 1978–79 "without justification to accelerate social transformations," and cite Afghanistan as an example of "the damage that can be inflicted on society" by such ultra-leftist zeal. See Nodari Simoniya, "The Contemporary Stage of the Liberation Struggle," *Aziya i Afrika segodnya* [Asia and Africa Today], no. 5 (May 1981), pp. 15–16.

86. For the text of the Treaty of Friendship, Good-Neighborliness and Cooperation signed in Moscow on December 5, 1978, and the communiqué on the attendant Afghan visit, see *Vneshnyaya politika sovetskogo soyuza, 1978 god* [Foreign Policy of the Soviet Union, 1978], Collection of Documents (Moscow: Mezhdunarodnye otnosheniya, 1979), pp. 223–31.

   One reason for the treaty was to bolster the morale and political stability of the Taraki government. In addition, the Soviet leaders considered it prudent in view of the China-Japan peace treaty signed just a few months earlier, which escalated the Soviet and Chinese competition in Asia and efforts to encircle one another.

forces beyond advisers and specialists such as helicopter pilots. But the security situation in the country continued to deteriorate throughout the year.

In the late spring and summer of 1979 the Soviets launched the effort outlined earlier to build a political solution to the problem of security and stability. The approach called for cooler and more careful action by the Afghan leadership, a broadening of the leadership of the party and the government (curtailing, and if possible reversing, the purge of the Parcham wing of the party and also bringing in nonparty, apolitical bureaucrats), broadening public support by less radical programs, and attempting to crush those insurgents who would not desist.

Safronchuk, the emissary sent by Moscow to press this political program, was well aware that the alternative (and fallback) was to seek a military solution with more active Soviet assistance and, if necessary, the introduction of Soviet troops. Soon after his arrival in late June, Safronchuk acknowledged in a remarkably frank conversation with Amstutz, the American chargé, that if Soviet troops were brought in (to help deal with the insurgency), it would have bad repercussions internationally and internally in Afghanistan. He also agreed with the American's observation that Soviet troops would have a difficult time in the rugged terrain of the country. When Amstutz expressed the hope that Afghanistan would not become an area of confrontation between the United States and the Soviet Union, Safronchuk said, "I agree with you completely." He also agreed when warned that if the Soviets did bring troops into the country, it "would very much complicate and harm Soviet-American relations." Safronchuk could hardly have been expected to say the opposite. But if he had really believed then that Soviet troops would or even might be required in Afghanistan, it is highly unlikely that he would have done more than deny that such action was planned, while leaving the possibility open in the future. He certainly did not need to volunteer, as he did, that "it would be bad policy in terms of internal Afghan affairs." Safronchuk also noted that Lenin had declared that "every revolution must defend itself."[87]

Safronchuk was not the only frank and forthright official from the Soviet bloc in Kabul. As noted earlier, the East German ambassador, Schweisau, a few weeks later confirmed that Safronchuk had been sent to find a political solution, and to bring about a "radical change" in the leadership as well as broaden the base for support at all levels. Ambassador Schweisau himself brought up the question of possible Soviet military intervention in an extraordinary conversation with Amstutz on July 18, in which he also said that Amin had to be removed. He noted the speculation in the Kabul diplomatic community that the Soviets might eventually have to intervene militarily. "Were they to do so," he said, "it would solve one problem but create an-

---

87. U.S. Embassy Kabul 4888, Confidential, June 25, 1979, in *Afghanistan* (Tehran), vol. 1, pp. 130–31. Amstutz judged that Safronchuk "genuinely believed" that direct Soviet intervention even to help the Afghan regime "would be more harmful than helpful for Soviet interests, and therefore it would not occur."

other." It could eliminate the present (Amin) government, but the "entire Afghan nation" would turn against the Soviet Union, just as they turned on the British invaders in the nineteenth century.[88]

These evaluations of the consequences of a Soviet military intervention were realistic and prescient. They strongly suggest that at least the Soviet representatives in Kabul recognized the hazards of direct intervention. Beyond that, the fact that these sentiments were voiced further suggests that Moscow at that time had considered a possible direct military role but that it was deemed too costly and clearly less advantageous than internal political manipulation of the leadership and a broader Afghan political program in the country. A political solution incorporating these elements would obviate the need for direct Soviet military intervention.

It also seems clear that at that point there was little concern over possible *American* intervention. The frank Soviet (and undoubtedly Soviet-authorized East German) acknowledgments to the U.S. chargé d'affaires of Soviet dissatisfaction with and desire to remove Amin could only have been intended to prepare the United States to understand and accept the need for that change in the interests of stabilizing the internal situation in Afghanistan. If there had been real concern then over American ties with Amin (let alone the 1980 charge that Amin had long been a CIA agent), it is inconceivable that Safronchuk and Schweisau would have disclosed Soviet desire and intentions to remove Amin. The American chargé concluded that the Soviet leaders intended these statements by Safronchuk and Schweisau "to send us a signal . . . that they are unhappy with the Amin regime, that they are trying to arrange a change, and (I am speculating here) are hoping this will not have a negative impact on us."[89] In addition, the two Soviet bloc officials calculated that if direct intervention or the introduction of Soviet troops became necessary, the U.S. government would know that the Soviets had tried to use political means and had turned to military means only as a last resort.[90]

The Soviet attempt to engineer the removal of Amin and effect a Khalq-Parcham reconciliation under Taraki, and ultimately the whole possibility of a political solution, collapsed. Not only did Taraki fail to remove Amin, but the abortive assassination left Amin in firm control—and highly suspicious and hostile—even though still dependent on Soviet assistance. And the Taraki centrists and reconciliationists were imprisoned or in sanctuary in the Soviet embassy.

From mid-September to late November the Soviet leaders considered the new situation and possible courses of action. From mid-September to

---

88. U.S. Embassy Kabul 5459, Secret-Exdis, July 18, 1979, in *Afghanistan* (Tehran), vol. 1, pp. 181, 183.

89. Ibid., p. 184.

90. This possible purpose of the disclosure was noted by the American embassy in U.S. Embassy Kabul 5627, Secret, July 25, 1979, in *Afghanistan* (Tehran), vol. 1, p. 202.

mid-October General Pavlovsky and his team assessed the military requirements not only to deal with the insurgency but also, if necessary, to support the removal of Amin by force. Because of his direct involvement in falsely assuring Amin's safety on September 16, and his responsibility for the sanctuary given Watanjar and the other former Taraki cabinet ministers, Ambassador Puzanov had to be recalled in response to Amin's demand. But Safronchuk remained.

The Soviet policy deliberation in the fall of 1979 involved a complete strategic reappraisal. Amin was now seen not merely as a burden or obstacle to needed policy corrections; he was seen as an enemy. The Soviet advisers, now several thousand in all, were not only assets but also potential hostages. Some had been wiped out in the Afghan army mutinies of Herat in March and Jalalabad in August, and all were potentially at risk to Amin. Soviet advisers and a pro-Soviet (and possibly long-time KGB collaborator) secret police chief, Assadullah Sarwari, had been unable to stem events in September—and Sarwari was now a fugitive secretly holed up in the Soviet embassy in Kabul. The Soviets had the dubious benefit of the expert advice of the Parcham and Tarakite émigrés and fugitives—some of whom had, for example, since 1967 been accusing Amin of being a CIA agent.[91] Earlier known events took on a newly ominous meaning. Amin, for example, had met with a shadowy Afghan with American citizenship, Zia Nassery, in late 1978—and Zia subsequently met with two of the leading Islamic rebel groups.[92] In November

---

91. See U.S. Embassy Kabul 3511, Secret, May 3, 1978, in *Afghanistan* (Tehran), vol. 1, p. 57. Amin had graduated from Columbia Teachers' College in 1958 and then pursued graduate studies at Columbia University in 1963–65, with support from U.S. government grants. Whether he had any contacts with American intelligence is not known. The Karmal government in 1980 loudly accused Amin of having long been a CIA agent and referred to documentary proof that was never produced; the Soviet media initially picked up and reported these "official" Afghan statements of Amin's alleged CIA ties but soon dropped the accusation. A Soviet official with known KGB intelligence affiliation told me in October 1980 that while Amin might not have been a CIA "agent," he had CIA "connections." High-level CIA officials have stated privately to congressional inquirers that Amin had never been a "CIA agent"; information from a senator who made that inquiry.

92. See U.S. Embassy Islamabad 5531, Secret, May 14, 1979, in *Afghanistan* (Tehran), vol. 1, p. 101. An account of Amin's meetings with Zia Nassery, and the latter's meetings with two leading resistance groups in Peshawar, was provided by a well-connected Afghan exile, who warned the American embassy that Nassery was "probably a double agent." Soon thereafter Nassery visited Iran and met with high-level officials, including the Ayatollah Khomeini himself; he sought increased Iranian aid for the Afghan resistance. (See note 101 below.) He also met with a number of members of the U.S. Congress and others lobbying for support of the insurgents and obtained medical and communications equipment. On his visits to the U.S. embassies in Kabul and Tehran, not only was Nassery not received as a CIA agent, but his overt reception made such a status highly improbable. Still, to the Afghan, Iranian, and Soviet security services he must have appeared to be very suspicious. In 1981 he was reported imprisoned in Iran as a "CIA agent."

Many later Soviet and Afghan accounts stressed Nassery's American contacts and his own published statements in the United States that he had come to obtain financial, materiel, and political support for the Afghan insurgents. He did meet with several U.S. senators and others.

and December 1979 Amin was reportedly in contact with Gulbuddin Hekma-
tyar, the leader of Hizb-i-Islami, one of the main Islamic resistance groups.[93]

The Soviets saw Amin's increasingly desperate attempts to establish
contact with President Zia of Pakistan in November and December as further
confirmation of their suspicions that he was unreliable on socialism and desired
to break away from the Soviet Union. They saw not merely a desire by Amin
to reduce dependence on the Soviet Union, but also a strong indication that
Amin wanted to emulate President Sadat of Egypt by sending the Soviet
advisers home and realigning Afghanistan with the United States, Pakistan,
and China.[94]

In addition, the Soviet leaders may even have begun to nurse suspicions of direct ties between Amin and the United States. As in other respects,
the Soviet reevaluation in the fall of 1979 may have led them to be more
concerned than they had been with respect to Amin's earlier residence in the
United States and current contacts.[95] On the whole, Soviet concerns were prob-

---

See, for example, a detailed account by Vadim Zagladin, first deputy chief of the International
Department of the Central Committee, in an interview with the West German journal *Stern*
(Hamburg, January 31, 1980, p. 2). See also A. Petrov (pseud.), "Attacks by Enemies of the
Afghan People Are Rebuffed," *Pravda*, February 28, 1980; and Nikolai Baratov, Radio Mos-
cow, February 16, in FBIS, *Soviet Union*, February 19, 1980, pp. A1–2. Some of these accounts
note that Nassery's first U.S. visit and appeal for aid shortly preceded the major uprising in
Herat in March 1979.

See also Male, *Revolutionary Afghanistan*, p. 173, and note 19, p. 203.

93. See *Kabul New Times*, January 22 and 27, 1980. This contact has not been confirmed, and it
is unclear whether Soviet intelligence accepted this report or originated it for disinformation.

94. I was struck in conversations with Soviet officials in 1980, including several members of the
Central Committee, with the frequency and weight given this consideration in their explana-
tions of the reasons for the Soviet decision to intervene in Afghanistan. In addition, some
published Soviet accounts later made explicit the parallel between Amin's ambitions and
Sadat's actions. For example, see V. Sidenko, "The Undeclared War against Afghanistan,"
Pravda, February 5, 1980.

95. In Kabul, U.S. Ambassador Theodore L. Eliot, Jr., and his successor Ambassador Adolph
Dubs, had met with Amin on a number of occasions. (Reports that Dubs met Amin fourteen
times between May 1978 and February 1979, when Ambassador Dubs met his tragic end, are,
however, almost certainly an exaggeration.) After Ambassador Dubs's death, in the course of
sharply curtailing all aid, the United States announced that it had decided "to terminate a
military training program that was in the planning stages," raising the curtain on a previously
undisclosed and rather surprising development that had been under way. See "Development
and Military Assistance Programs in Afghanistan," statement by the White House Press Secretary, February 22, *Weekly Compilation of Presidential Documents*, vol. 15 (February 26,
1979), p. 310. (Hereafter *Presidential Documents*.) Amin's few contacts with the U.S. embassy
after September 1979 were not conspiratorial, but Moscow may nevertheless have been suspicious. On September 27, when U.S. Chargé Amstutz met with Amin, as all chiefs of mission
did in ceremonial calls on the new president, he found him friendly and interested in improving relations, but nothing out of the ordinary was said. That meeting lasted nineteen minutes,
in part because Amstutz was under instructions from Washington to keep the meeting short as

ably addressed primarily toward potential moves by Amin and the Americans, rather than at existing contacts, but they were nevertheless real concerns.

In their own assessments earlier in the year the Soviet leaders had understood that the growing armed resistance sprang from general dissatisfac tion by the Afghan populace, even after the Soviet press began in March 1979 to explain away this phenomenon by blaming foreign intrigue and external support for the counterrevolutionary insurgency. By the fall of 1979 two things had changed: first, there *was* increasing foreign assistance, and second, the changed context meant a possible alignment of resistance forces, foreign inter ests—and Amin.

Very little has appeared in published sources on the foreign assis tance to the Afghan insurgents in the period prior to the Soviet military inter vention in late December 1979. While Soviet and Afghan claims must be heavily discounted, they have some foundation. The Soviets may well have believed there was more outside assistance than was in fact the case, particu larly as they (and the Afghan regime) were loath to accept that indigenous popular discontent was rising.

One probable source of external, albeit limited and covert, military assistance that included training as well as arms was China.[96] Indeed, the Chi nese may have given assistance to Tadzhik guerrillas in Badakhshan and to Kazakh guerrillas in the Wakhan Corridor adjoining China even before the 1978 coup.[97] On the other hand, before the Soviet intervention in late 1979 the Chinese refrained from participating in the limited support given by Muslim

---

a sign of continued U.S. coolness. See U.S. Embassy Kabul 7218, Confidential, September 27, 1979, in *Afghanistan* (Tehran), vol. 2, pp. 89–91.

Many Soviet accounts have charged that Amin's "emissaries established secret contacts with representatives of Washington" and that "Amin was in constant contact with the Americans." P. Demchenko, "Afghanistan: In Defense of the People's Achievements," *Kommunist*, no. 5 (March 1980), p. 75; and Ye. Primakov, "When Black Is Presented As White . . . ," *Literatur-naya gazeta* [Literary Gazette], March 12, 1980, p. 14. See also Vadim Kassis, "The CIA's Secret War," *Nedelya* [The Week], no. 11 (March 1980), p. 14.

Male makes a case that Amin had sought to keep open an "American option" in 1978–79, and argues that the United States made a more active attempt to gain Amin's collaboration in the fall of 1979, but on terms Amin could not accept. Male, *Revolutionary Afghanistan*, pp. 142–48, 199–200. This argument is not supported by the evidence.

96. For a general account of Chinese policy toward Afghanistan, see Yaacov Vertzberger, "Af ghanistan in China's Policy," *Problems of Communism*, vol. 31 (May–June 1982), pp. 1–23. Vertzberger refers only briefly to Chinese aid to antiregime insurgents (p. 13). See also Katsi kas, *Arc of Socialist Revolutions*, p. 233. For Soviet claims, see Yu. Agranov, "The Afghan Revolution and Peking's Treacherous Course," *Problemy dal'nego vostoka* [Questions of the Far East], no. 3 (March 1980), pp. 102–03.

97. The terrorists who took Ambassador Dubs hostage in February 1979, and with whom he perished when the Afghan police attacked, had demanded the release of some pro-Chinese Tadzhik guerrilla leaders in custody since before the 1978 coup (and later executed). See Bradsher, *Afghanistan and the Soviet Union*, pp. 99, 275.

countries through Pakistan, and even requested that Pakistan not permit Chinese arms it had received to be sent to the insurgents in Afghanistan.[98] Nonetheless, Soviet suspicion of the Chinese role remained high.[99] Suspicion had also been raised by the completion of the Karakorum Road in 1979 (nominally in 1978), which provided overland access from China to Pakistan near the Wakhan Corridor of eastern Afghanistan.

By mid-1979 Libya was providing financial assistance to Islamic insurgents in Afghanistan, despite Soviet-Libyan ties.[100] Iran under Khomeini also provided assistance to Afghans who fled there and used Iran as a base to mount forays into Afghanistan.[101] Saudi Arabia, Egypt, and Pakistan—all American proxies in Moscow's eyes—were the principal outside sources of support to the insurgents before the Soviet intervention. (This support has been confirmed by secret American diplomatic messages seized in the takeover of the American embassy in Tehran.)[102]

---

98. The United States knew from a reliable confidential source that during the visit to Pakistan by Zhang Caiqian, the deputy chief of the Chinese General Staff in late October 1979, he told President Zia that the Chinese could not provide aid to the insurgents. The reason was that if discovered, "serious international repercussions" would ensue and would affect the Sino-Soviet talks then under way in Moscow. Caiqian reiterated an earlier request by the Chinese ambassador in Islamabad that arms and ammunition of Chinese origin not be provided as part of the covert Pakistani support. General Zia had so instructed his own government in early September, following the first request. CIA message from Islamabad, Secret, October 30, 1979, text in *Afghanistan* (Tehran), vol. 2, pp. 148–49.

99. Commentary in the Soviet press after the intervention was replete with references to a Chinese threat through Afghanistan. One of the more reserved, but because of that tone more credible, indications of Soviet thinking was the following comment by Igor Belyaev, the Middle East correspondent of the *Literary Gazette.* "If the Amin clique had stayed in power in Kabul, the length of the border of the Soviet Union which would have had to be significantly strengthened for security reasons would have increased by 2,500 kilometers. I don't want to say that China would right away have rushed headlong to use this border for anti-Soviet actions. But considering the present course of the Peking leadership and its rapprochement with American imperialism, it would be a mistake to exclude such actions." I. Belyaev, "Dialogue: When Black Is Presented as White . . . ," *Literaturnaya gazeta,* March 12, 1980, p. 11.

100. U.S. Embassy Tripoli 1185, Secret, July 29, 1979, in *Afghanistan* (Tehran), vol. 1, p. 215. The Libyan government had confidentially made this assistance known to the U.S. embassy.

101. For one firsthand report, confirming limited operations from Iran in May 1979, see U.S. Embassy Tehran 5246, Secret, May 21, 1979, *Afghanistan* (Tehran), vol. 1, p. 114. The source was the shadowy Zia Nassery, then seeking additional aid for the insurgents, including a meeting with the Ayatollah Khomeini.

102. Saudi financial support was confirmed by the CIA, reported in Department of State 266505, Secret-Noforn, October 11, 1979, and see U.S. Embassy Jidda 7548, Confidential, October 6, 1979. The texts are in *Afghanistan* (Tehran), vol. 2, pp. 142–43, 114. Official Pakistani covert supplies of arms, munitions, and other support is confirmed in a CIA message from Islamabad, Secret, October 30, 1979, text in ibid., vol. 2, pp. 148–49.

These documents were available to the Soviet Union in 1980 and 1981, but Soviet intelligence had almost certainly been aware in 1979 of the contacts and of U.S. and other external support. Very probably the Soviets estimated that there was more support than they had been able to confirm.

There is also an intriguing implication in cryptic references by Brzezinski in his memoir that the United States supported the Saudi, Egyptian, and Pakistani aid to the insurgents during 1979. He states that in April 1979 he "pushed a decision through the SCC [Special Coordinating Committee] to be more sympathetic to those Afghans who were determined to preserve their country's independence." The decision was supported by Vice President Mondale against "rather timid opposition" from the State Department. And by September, after the Amin coup, Brzezinski also personally "consulted with the Saudis and the Egyptians regarding the fighting in Afghanistan."[103] Later an investigative reporter stated that the CIA covertly began providing field hospitals and communications equipment to the Afghan resistance from Pakistan in November 1979.[104] It is not clear, however, whether the United States provided any direct assistance to the Afghan resistance before the Soviet intervention.[105] Substantial military assistance was later provided, as discussed below, but before January 1980 any such aid was minimal.

External military assistance was thus not a serious factor in the situation prior to the Soviet decision to intervene. Its significance as a political factor and perceived threat in Soviet calculations is, however, another matter that it is more difficult to judge. At the least it contributed to Soviet fears of the desire and readiness of the United States, supported by Muslim allies and coordinated with the separate assistance of the Chinese, to attempt to influence the situation in Afghanistan.

The real Soviet fear was that Amin was neither reliable as a partner nor subject to Soviet guidance, and at the same time was ineffective in controlling the growing resistance. In desperation Amin might turn to the United States as Egyptian President Sadat and Somali General Siad had done. Alternatively, he would likely be swept away by a popular Islamic nationalist movement. In either case the Soviet Union would lose all its cumulative investment in Afghanistan—strategic, political, ideological, and economic. And in either case there was a substantial risk that the United States might to some degree displace the Soviet Union in Afghanistan, acquiring new strategic assets and coming closer to completing a geostrategic encirclement of the Soviet Union, ranging in the west from Norway through Turkey and in the east from Alaska through Japan and China to Pakistan. Politically and ideologically, the loss of socialist Afghanistan on the very border of the Soviet Union itself could not be accepted with the same equanimity as was, for example, the overthrow of

---

103. Zbigniew Brzezinski, *Power and Principle: Memoirs of the National Security Adviser, 1977–1981* (Farrar, Straus, Giroux, 1983), p. 427. At that time he also "urged expanded broadcasts to the Moslems and Ukrainians in the U.S.S.R." Ibid., p. 428.

104. Tad Szulc, "Putting Back the Bite in the C.I.A.," *New York Times Magazine*, April 6, 1980, p. 28.

105. A very senior and knowledgeable member of the Carter administration, who confirmed to me the supply of military assistance after January 1980, declined either to confirm or deny whether the United States had provided any assistance before that date.

Salvador Allende in distant Chile. Afghanistan, which had never been aligned with the West, was, after all, in the Soviet backyard. And the Soviet Union, immediately adjacent, was in a position to intervene readily.

The world, including the United States, had accepted the coming to power of the PDPA after the April 1978 coup and its subsequent more open identification with communism and closer alignment with the Soviet Union. Any Soviet measures to ensure continued communist rule in Afghanistan would but represent consolidation of the established status quo with respect to international geopolitics.

To be sure, since the spring of 1979 some American officials had publicly and privately warned the Soviets of vague, unspecified, adverse consequences for Soviet-American relations of a direct Soviet military intervention. But those warnings had become routine and had recently been shown to mean very little. By October the Soviet leaders could look back on the experience of the Cuba brigade incident, with the odd alarmist warnings by the United States that the continued presence of a Soviet brigade in Cuba was unacceptable, followed by acceptance of the status quo.[106] Throughout the year the Americans had also been warning the Soviets not to use bases in Vietnam but then had acquiesced in their use. The Americans had also been warning the Soviet Union against any intervention in Iran, which it was not contemplating (and where it recognized that the United States, as well as the Soviet Union, had real interests).[107] But in Afghanistan the Soviet Union saw vital interests of its own, and by contrast the United States had no substantial interests. The latter had even curtailed sharply its modest remaining economic aid and declined to send a new ambassador to Kabul after the tragic death of Ambassador Dubs.

What were the Soviet interests in Afghanistan? For one, the two have a common 2,500-kilometer border adjoining the Muslim Central Asian republics of the USSR, which are populated by people of the same ethnic background as those in northern Afghanistan. While Soviet vulnerability from and concern over its own Muslim populations should not be exaggerated, this was one factor in Moscow's thinking. In 1978 there had been a Tadzhik riot against Russians in Dushanbe, just north of Afghanistan.[108] After the Soviet intervention the KGB chief in Muslim Soviet Azerbaidzhan, Major General Zia Yusif-zade, publicly linked the situation in Afghanistan (and Iran) with alleged American intelligence efforts to exploit Islam in the Muslim republics

---

106. See chapter 24.

107. The Soviet Union was in turn warning the United States against intervening in Iran, following the seizure of the American embassy and its occupants and the American buildup of its fleet nearby. See note 125 below.

108. See Bradsher, *Afghanistan and the Soviet Union,* p. 156. Some accounts have alleged a Chinese role in stirring up this 1978 disturbance in Soviet Tadzhikistan.

of the USSR.[109] And a deputy prime minister of the Soviet Republic of Kirgiziya was retired after having stated too bluntly that the Soviet Union had helped combat a locust plague in nearby Afghanistan "that could have spread to us."[110] (It can only be wondered what happened to the hapless editor of a Soviet Uzbek-language literary journal who, after visiting Afghanistan, published in October 1979 a Khalq-inspired account of the Afghan revolution that pictured Amin as a hero and Karmal as an untrustworthy villain.)[111] In 1980 the prime minister of the Soviet Republic of Kirgiziya met an even more drastic end—he was assassinated. After the unsurprising failure of a Soviet-sponsored international Islamic conference in Tashkent in 1980, three of the four Soviet Muslim *muftis* were dismissed.[112] But difficulties or vulnerabilities within Soviet Central Asia, while adding to Soviet concerns, were not central to the decision to intervene.

That decision was the result of cumulative developments and evolving considerations. The unexpected emergence of Amin as the leader and the removal of Taraki and other counterweights from the Afghan leadership, and Amin's demonstrated independence and hostility, compelled the Soviet leaders to consider how to deal with a nominally friendly socialist country headed by an opportunistic and hostile leader, and whether and how to remove that leader.

The rapidly deteriorating security situation in Afghanistan also compelled a search for more effective measures. One option was to reinforce the Afghan army by the direct introduction of Soviet military forces. The Soviet political, and probably military, establishments had resisted this action. The awareness of its heavy risks and costs so readily acknowledged by Safronchuk and Schweisau in June and July were widely shared. But while it was then an easy choice in Moscow to pursue internal political means to change the Afghan leadership and policy, by October that option was exhausted. General Pavlovsky, who returned from Afghanistan on October 22, must have reported that the situation was deteriorating rapidly and that a decision must be

---

109. Major General Zia Yusif-zade, "Protecting the Country and the People," *Bakinskii rabochii* [The Baku Worker], December 19, 1980. See also Geidar Aliyev, *Bakinskii rabochii*, December 25, 1980.

110. Cited by Bradsher, *Afghanistan and the Soviet Union*, p. 157.

111. Mirmuhsin (Mirsaidov), "Chodrali ayal" [Woman with a Veil], *Sharg yulduzi* [Star of the East], no. 10 (October [signed to press September 17] 1979), p. 67. See also a favorable reference to Amin in K. Dudyev, M. Yakovlev, and E. Babenko, "International Review: The World This Week," *Turkmenskaya iskra* [The Turkmen Spark], December 9, 1979.

112. See Kemal Karpat, "Moscow and the 'Muslim Question,'" *Problems of Communism*, vol. 32 (November–December 1983), p. 77; and Alexandre Bennigsen, "Mullahs, Mujahidin, and Soviet Muslims," ibid., vol. 33 (November–December 1984), p. 43. The conference had been scheduled before the Soviet move into Afghanistan. The Soviets closed the conference when a majority appeared ready to support a call for withdrawal of all foreign forces from Muslim countries. No international Islamic conference has been held in the USSR since then.

reached soon either to pull out the Soviet military advisers and let the regime
go under, or to bolster the Afghan army with a large-scale Soviet military
presence as well as increased direct Soviet military support. Continuation of
the current policy had no prospect of success and very real risks of a disastrous
collapse. It has been speculated that the Soviet military advocated intervention, but there is no direct information to that effect. It is possible that the
military had reservations about becoming directly involved in a long counterinsurgency campaign. But as the political calculation moved toward the necessity
of intervention, the military would have become more inclined to think of
ways to meet that challenge.[113]

The two principal problems merged as the Soviets considered a
military solution: Amin would be removed, and a new broadened leadership
with more enlightened policies could build a broadened popular constituency
and thus reduce support for the insurgents, and, braced by the presence of the
Soviet army as well as by a new political climate, the Afghan army would be
reinvigorated to carry out the necessary counterinsurgency campaign. The insurgents would lose popular support at the same time that they came under
more effective military pressure.

While direct information is lacking, it may be surmised that some
questioned whether this scenario was realistic.[114] But there were powerful

---

113. Some have postulated that "Soviet military leaders may also have viewed Afghanistan as an
opportunity to test new weapons, try new tactics, and get combat experience for their troops,
as well as a chance to win medals, promotions, and glory for themselves." Hammond, *Red
Flag*, p. 143. It is highly unlikely that such considerations affected the judgment of the
military leaders more than an evaluation of the difficulties did, or influenced the basic decision of the military and political leaders on whether to intervene. On the other hand, once
that decision was made, the desire to gain combat experience and test weapons and tactics
surely did arise. This consideration would become more important as the Soviet forces became more fully and directly engaged than had initially been contemplated, when the Soviet
role was expected to be more passive. The Soviet military clearly did not have counterinsurgency tactics worked out and ready to test when they entered Afghanistan; they had to be
developed painfully in the months and years following (learning such things as the vulnerability of helicopters in valleys to sniper fire from ridges above). The units initially employed
were standard, below-average, motorized infantry divisions filled in with local (Central Asian)
reservists and with equipment and weapons standardized for the European theater. On the
other hand, the Soviet army did begin almost from the outset a vigorous cycling of generals
and other senior officers for short tours of duty to give them combat command experience.
(In contrast to the U.S. practice in Korea and Vietnam, junior officers and men have not
been similarly rotated—they remain with their units, which are rotated after normal tours.)

114. See, for example, the earlier cited statements by Safronchuk (and East German Ambassador
Schweisau), which reflected the kind of awareness that must have been shared by other Soviet
officials as well, probably including members of the fact-finding missions headed by Generals
Yepishev and Pavlovsky.

A former KGB major, Vladimir Kuzichkin, who served in Iran from 1977 until his defection to the West in June 1982, has said that ever since the coup in 1978 the KGB had been
advising against becoming embroiled in taking over Afghanistan. He may have been aware of
some such sentiment and concern in the KGB. At the same time, his account is riddled with

sources of support for it, not least the political-ideological presumption that if properly led the Afghan people would be *bound* to favor a progressive, socialist order rather than a semifeudal backward one.[115] Moreover, the risks of inaction seemed at least as great as the risks of action.

The strongest argument for intervention (even if a less rational basis for believing it would work) was the absence of an acceptable alternative. The alternative envisaged was seeing a budding socialist Afghanistan succumb either to defection or disintegration. Amin was seen as unscrupulous, unreliable, and hostile, and it was believed that if he retained power, he would eliminate Soviet sympathizers while preparing to reverse alliances. If he did not retain power, a fundamentalist religious-nationalist anti-Soviet regime would probably succeed him. Either of these cases threatened to provide opportunities for the United States and China—increasingly seen as acting in collusion— to inject their own presence and influence.

The Soviet decision to intervene thus rested on a reluctant conclusion that failure to do so would imperil its many long-standing investments in Afghanistan—political, military, economic, and, since 1978, ideological—and their prestige as well.

But even more was involved than retrieving major Soviet interests that were sliding toward loss. The fundamental consideration in the Soviet decision was the need to defend its security interests. For all the rhetoric on aiding a threatened socialist country, the Soviet leaders have been very clear on the issue of security. Brezhnev, in his major statement two weeks after the Soviet intervention, said the Soviet action had been necessary because there

---

demonstrably serious errors and cannot be taken as reliable. See "Coups and Killings in Kabul: A KGB Defector Tells How Afghanistan Became Brezhnev's Viet Nam," *Time*, November 22, 1982, pp. 33–34.

On the other hand, some advisers may have been predisposed to support assessments favoring Soviet intervention. Apart from such directly interested parties as Babrak Karmal and the other Afghans displaced by Amin, the Afghan ambassador in Moscow, Raz Mohammad Pakteen, may have been a proponent of intervention. (After the event, he became a member of Karmal's cabinet and of the PDPA Central Committee.) It is not known what position former Ambassador Puzanov took after his recall to Moscow in mid-November.

There has been speculation as to the possible positions of Brezhnev and other individual Soviet leaders, but no evidence. Commentary—as, for example, "possibly Kosygin and even Brezhnev questioned the wisdom of a military invasion. It cannot be excluded that, because of their failing health, they might not even have been present at the crucial Politburo deliberations"—would best be avoided. Valenta, *International Security*, vol. 5 (Fall 1980), p. 126.

115. The Soviet predisposition to believe that people prefer what Soviet ideology tells them people should prefer—a progressive socialist people's democracy in the Soviet pattern—is perhaps most readily understood by comparing it to the not dissimilar tendency by Americans to assume that people will, when given the choice, prefer the capitalist free enterprise system and political democracy roughly in the American pattern. In both cases this underlying perceptual lens has an impact, notwithstanding a considerable degree of hardheaded, cynical, and sophisticated worldliness about power politics and manipulation of the elements of power.

had been "a real threat that Afghanistan would lose its independence and be turned into an imperialist military bridgehead on our southern border. . . . To have done otherwise would have meant to watch passively the origination on our southern border of a seat of serious danger to the security of the Soviet state."[116] Reporting to the Central Committee plenum six months later, he reiterated that *"the point* is that the plans to draw Afghanistan into the orbit of imperialist policy and to create a threat to our country from the south have collapsed."[117] The Central Committee resolution at that plenum, in appraising the intervention, claimed that it had prevented the establishment of "a pro-imperialist bridgehead of military aggression on the southern borders of the USSR."[118]

The Soviet leaders decided to intervene militarily in Afghanistan not because they were unwilling to keep it as a buffer, but precisely because they saw no other way to ensure that it would remain a buffer. Intervention was not the next in a series of moves to increase Soviet influence, as in Angola, Ethiopia, and South Yemen, nor the first in a new series involving escalation to direct use of Soviet military power in the third world. It was seen as the only solution to a specific situation on their border that was threatening Soviet security. Clearly, there are some circumstances in which the Soviet Union is prepared to use its armed forces when that is considered essential to ensure its security.[119]

Distinctly secondary, although often tied to the articulation of defending Soviet national security, was the rationale of aiding an endangered progressive or socialist regime. Again, in Brezhnev's key speech in January 1980, immediately following his reference to the threat to the Soviet southern bor-

---

116. "Replies of L. I. Brezhnev to Questions of a Correspondent of Pravda," *Pravda,* January 13, 1980.

117. "Address by the General Secretary of the CC of the CPSU Comrade L. I. Brezhnev," June 23, *Kommunist,* no. 10 (July 1980), p. 6. Emphasis added.

118. "On the International Situation and the Foreign Policy of the Soviet Union: A Resolution of the Plenum of the Central Committee of the CPSU, June 23, 1980," *Kommunist,* no. 10 (July 1980), p. 10.

119. Insofar as the Soviet experience in Afghanistan has any effect on future Soviet decisions, it would hardly encourage that sort of involvement—except in extreme cases. The Soviet military intervention has involved a difficult, long-term military-economic burden, with adverse political effects as well. But it did preclude an Afghan defection or disintegration and an advance of the Western presence to the Soviet frontier. The one case that seems to represent a possible parallel is northern Iran—should developments in that country threaten chaos and there be a risk that American military power would fill the vacuum. In that case the most likely course would be a Soviet military occupation of northern Iran and an American military occupation of southern Iran—as in the Russian-British division of spheres of influence in 1907, and the joint Russian and British military interventions and division of the country under occupation from 1941 to 1946. Such an outcome would reflect the fact that the Soviets have a perceived vital interest in the north and the United States in the south. Intervention would still pose considerable risk, not least because the U.S. leaders would probably misconstrue the Soviet aim as a move on the oil of the Persian Gulf and might therefore overreact.

der, came a revealing sentence: "In other words, the time had come when we could no longer fail to respond to the request of the government of friendly Afghanistan." He continued, "To have acted otherwise would have meant leaving Afghanistan prey to imperialism, allowing the forces of aggression to repeat in that country what they had succeeded in doing for example in Chile, where the people's freedom was drowned in blood." That sentence was followed by one cited earlier that "to have acted otherwise would have meant to watch passively the origination on our southern border of a seat of serious danger to the security of the Soviet state."[120]

Western commentary devoted considerable attention to the Soviet move into Afghanistan as an extension of the Brezhnev Doctrine that justified intervention to prevent the overthrow of a socialist regime by internal revolt or subversion. It was the first direct use of Soviet military forces to restore a pro-Soviet regime other than in Warsaw Pact countries (the previous cases being Hungary in 1956 and Czechoslovakia in 1968). The Brezhnev Doctrine, however, was above all the articulation of a rationale for Soviet action in cases where Soviet security needs were perceived as justifying direct action. In other words, it is a rationale to legitimize such action where it is deemed warranted. But it is not a mandate that the Soviets intervene where action is not considered necessary, prudent, and feasible. For example, the Soviet leaders did not feel impelled to undertake quixotic application of the Brezhnev Doctrine in Chile in 1973 or Grenada in 1983 (or to block adverse peaceful change in Jamaica in 1981), where the capacity to do so was lacking. Nor did it act in Poland in 1956, or 1970, or 1980–81, where other measures were feasible and clearly deemed preferable; nor in Yugoslavia in 1948 or any later time, nor—even within the Warsaw Pact—in Romania or Albania. Nor would the Soviets feel obliged to respond militarily in the event of a threat or actual change in rule in Nicaragua or Angola or Ethiopia or South Yemen. Soviet decisions on direct intervention are made on the basis of national security requirements, including political but not ideological ones.[121] The governing considerations are interests, costs, and risks, not doctrine.[122]

---

120. Brezhnev, *Pravda*, January 13, 1980.

121. By the same token, while the Soviets are very cautious about any commitment of their own military power, they do not exclude that under some circumstances they would intervene directly with their own armed forces even in the absence of a friendly progressive or socialist regime. In such a case, however, they might attempt to create such a regime—parallel, in a sense, to the establishment of Karmal's government in December 1979—and the abortive attempt to create an alternative Czech leadership in August 1968, and the Soviet-created "government" headed by the veteran Soviet Finnish leader Otto Kuusinin in Karelia at the time of the Soviet attack on Finland in 1939 (which was, however, dissolved when the military campaign went badly).

122. Heller makes the point well in one of the best early analyses of the Soviet intervention. See Mark Heller, "The Soviet Invasion of Afghanistan," *Washington Quarterly*, vol. 3 (Summer 1980), pp. 36–59.

It is true that one Soviet justification was its internationalist duty. Shortly after the intervention in Afghanistan an editorial in a Soviet journal declared that "at critical moments solidarity with a victorious revolution calls not only for moral support but also for material assistance including, under definite circumstances, military assistance." It continued, "To deny support to the Afghan revolution, to leave it face to face with the forces of international reaction and aggression, would have been to doom it to defeat, which would have been a serious blow to the entire Communist and national liberation movement." Even then, the discussion went on to justify Soviet action "in the given instance" with a security argument—failure to do so would "make ever more dangerous" international tension in the region.[123] It should also be noted that while expressing support for "the Afghan revolution," Soviet leaders continued to characterize Afghanistan as having only a "socialist orientation" and as "nonaligned," while reaffirming that "the revolutionary process in Afghanistan is irreversible."[124]

A collapse of the Amin regime (even though in Soviet eyes Amin was no longer truly socialist) would have meant a defeat for real socialism or communism in the eyes of the world. This belief was a contributory factor in the Soviet decision. That collapse would have reflected badly on the image of an upward and forward revolutionary movement of history, as any setback does, but also more directly on the Soviet ability to support and defend its own satellites and friends. The December 1978 treaty had raised the Soviet commitment of its prestige. But this consideration alone would probably not have been sufficient and was ancillary to Soviet security interests.

In the case of Afghanistan, the risks of direct confrontation were correctly recognized to be nil, while the political costs were probably recognized to be considerable (although still underestimated). But the strength of the Soviet security interest was overriding. Considerations of a negative impact on Soviet relations with the United States and Western Europe, and on Soviet relations with countries of the third world (especially Muslim countries), were not only secondary but were almost certainly considered in terms of how to cushion expected reactions, rather than as factors that weighed in the basic decision on whether to intervene.

Even if the Soviet leaders had known at the time what they later learned about Western and world reactions, they almost certainly would have

---

123. Editorial, "World Communist Solidarity with the Afghan Revolution," *New Times*, no. 3 (January 18, 1980), p. 9.

124. B. N. Ponomarev, "An Unswerving Course of Peace," *Pravda*, February 5, 1980, was the first affirmation by a Politburo (candidate) member of Afghanistan's nonaligned status, a position the Central Committee plenum formally reaffirmed in a resolution in June. See "On the International Situation and the Foreign Policy of the Soviet Union," *Pravda*, June 24, 1980. Brezhnev later reaffirmed Soviet dedication to its internationalist duty and made the statement on irreversibility. "In Friendly Conditions: Speech of L. I. Brezhnev," *Pravda*, October 17, 1980.

made the same decision. Nor would alternative feasible threatened punitive responses by the West have carried greater weight.

The decision to intervene was not motivated, or even influenced, by perceptions of American weakness, vacillation, or distraction. Vacillation in Washington over the handling of the Soviet brigade in Cuba may well have devalued the significance of American "warnings," but beyond that, if anything, it merely reflected that each superpower is especially sensitive to events in its backyard. The fact that the United States did not react more strongly to the Iranian seizure of the embassy and hostages was not yet clear in November 1979 when the decision was made. Indeed, it is possible that the Soviet leaders believed the United States was planning to launch a military attack on Iran. While that consideration might have been expected to mitigate somewhat the world reaction to a Soviet move in Afghanistan parallel in time, and to distract American attention, the Soviets nonetheless sought through public and private warnings to prevent such American action.[125] If the question of possible American action in Iran had any substantial influence on the Soviet decision, it would have been to reinforce the need to act before the United States became more directly committed in Southwest Asia.

Considerations of American military weakness and of a changed strategic military balance between the two superpowers did not enter the picture. It was obvious in Moscow that the United States could not and would not counterintervene militarily in Afghanistan, under any administration and regardless of the strategic balance. Indeed, had the events in and affecting Afghanistan that occurred in 1978–79 taken place in 1968–69, or 1958–59, the Soviet reaction and decision would probably have been the same.

The Soviet leaders did not see their decision to intervene militarily as an opportune option but as a security imperative; not as an opportunity for expansion but as a reluctant necessity to hold on; not as something they were free to do but as something they were regrettably bound to do. It was a decision forced by events, not an opportunity created by them.

This difference is significant. For example, American moves that are designed to show muscle and a readiness to stand up to the Soviets, measures that could usefully influence the Soviet leaders against seizing opportunities, work in the opposite way when the Soviets see the need for defensive actions, required to stave off a perceived threat or to bolster themselves against it. The

---

125. See, in particular, Charles Fenyvesi, "Carter's 'Double-Cross,' " *Washington Post*, April 12, 1981. Soviet warnings to the United States included a public one by Brezhnev in November. See "L. I. Brezhnev's Reply to the Question of a Pravda Correspondent," *Pravda*, November 19, 1979; see also *Pravda*, December 10, 1979.

Shortly before the Soviet decision was finally confirmed, a U.S. government spokesman had specifically declined to rule out resort to force in the hostage crisis, and President Carter had ordered another aircraft carrier task force to augment the large naval force assembled in the Arabian Sea. See Bernard Gwertzman, "Carter Shifts Stand," *New York Times*, November 21, 1979.

Soviet leaders could not afford to let themselves be deterred from defending their own borders. Insofar as the Soviet decision was influenced by their views of the American strategic posture, it was affected not by any perception of American weakness, but by heightened concern over the American buildup of its strength, particularly the Indian Ocean fleet, the quest for new bases in the area, and the development of security ties with China.

Subsequent American actions tended to confirm to the Soviet leaders that they needed to secure Afghanistan. They perceived the Carter Doctrine, intended to deter Soviet advances in the Persian Gulf area, quite differently, particularly because they had never intended to move on the Gulf. Soviet claims of American and Chinese designs on Afghanistan seemed to be confirmed by the coordination of assistance to the Afghan resistance,[126] and more generally by the establishment of a quasi alliance marked by Secretary of Defense Brown's visit to China in January 1980, a visit planned and announced before the Soviet intervention. When American intelligence collection facilities were set up in China in 1980 to monitor strategic missile tests in the central Soviet Union, making up for the major stations lost in Iran, the Soviets felt vindicated in their earlier suspicion that the United States had had designs on Afghanistan for that very purpose.[127]

---

126. For example, in his speech justifying the Soviet intervention, made while Brown was still in China, Brezhnev cited reports that during his talks in Beijing Brown had "colluded with the Chinese leadership on the coordination" of assistance to forces making military forays into Afghanistan. See Brezhnev, *Pravda*, January 13, 1980.

127. P. Demchenko and L. Mironov, "For a Rallying of the People: Report from Kabul," *Pravda*, January 3, 1980, said that "the Pentagon and the U.S. Central Intelligence Agency, having lost their bases in Iran, were counting on stealthily approaching our country through Afghanistan."

   On the American intelligence facilities in China, see chapter 21.

   Nikita Khrushchev, in his memoir, states that one reason the Soviet Union decided in 1955 to undertake an aid program to Afghanistan was to preempt possible American establishment of a military base in that country. See Strobe Talbott, ed., *Khrushchev Remembers: The Last Testament* (Boston, Mass.: Little, Brown, 1974), pp. 298–300.

   In the 1950s the Soviets had been suspicious of U.S. seismic installations for monitoring earthquakes (*and* capable of monitoring Soviet nuclear weapons tests) located briefly in northern Afghanistan. The Afghan government under King Zahir acquiesced in Soviet requests that the facilities be withdrawn. U.S. seismological equipment was again brought into the country under Daoud in 1975. See Bradsher, *Afghanistan and the Soviet Union*, p. 62.

   It has also been reported that the American-built airport at Qandahar, Afghanistan (begun in the mid–1950s and completed in 1962), which seemed a useless white elephant as a civilian airport (its runway was 10,500 feet), had in fact been built as a wartime "recovery base" for American bombers. In case of war, bombers could have used that base to refuel after completing attacks on targets in the Soviet Union when bases from which they had launched the attack were too distant to return to without refueling. See Bradsher, ibid., pp. 29–30, and associated source references, which include declassified official U.S. documents and interviews with knowledgeable American civilian and air force officials.

As many Western observers have noted, American-Soviet relations were already at a low point at the time the Soviet leaders decided to intervene militarily in Afghanistan. The Soviets saw little to lose from any worsening of relations that their action in Afghanistan might provoke. The SALT II Treaty was in trouble; NATO was clearly going to decide to install new missiles in Europe; and the United States was playing the China card to the limit. And there was little under way in prospective areas of cooperation that Washington could curtail if it chose to react. In addition, the Soviet leaders almost certainly underestimated the American reaction.

It would not be correct to draw a conclusion (as some have done) that the Soviet leaders gave priority to Afghanistan over détente. The Soviet leaders, as U.S. and other leaders would do in similar circumstances, gave priority to addressing a perceived threat to their security in Afghanistan, even if it should have costs in terms of the already deteriorated relations with the United States (and the West more generally). It was certainly not seen as a choice between expansionism and détente.

The final Soviet decision was made only in late November, with the decision presented to the Central Committee on November 27. After that date a variety of military preparations were undertaken, as well as a number of preparatory actions in Afghanistan, as noted earlier. The presentation to the Central Committee and discussion are not available, but the decision probably came as a surprise to most members and a shock to some.[128] Brezhnev later stated frankly, "It was no simple decision for us to send Soviet military contingents to Afghanistan."[129] Indeed, as another political spokesman put it, it was in fact "a very difficult decision."[130] In his report to the Central Committee plenum the next June, Brezhnev said, "We had no choice but to send troops. And events have confirmed that this was the only correct decision."[131] And in a candid explanation of Soviet policymaking, Dmitry Polyansky, a former member of the Politburo, mentioned the decision on Afghanistan as an illustration of collective decisionmaking: "Decisions are made collectively, and in no case is a decision made individually. Questions are carefully discussed, but

---

128. A remarkable incidental, or coincidental, impact of the decision was a series of heart attacks. Academician Georgy Arbatov, a member of the Central Committee and director of the Institute of USA and Canada, suffered a heart attack that very night. Only a few hours later one of his deputies, Radomir Bogdanov, similarly had a heart attack. And only a few days later Georgy Kornienko, a first deputy minister of foreign affairs and former head of the American desk, also suffered a heart attack.

Ambassador Anatoly Dobrynin returned from Washington to Moscow on December 10, as the final preparations were under way. There is no indication the advice of these experts on American affairs was even solicited before the November decision.

129. Brezhnev, *Pravda*, January 13, 1980.

130. Aleksandr Bovin, interview in *Corriere della sera* (Milan), April 2, 1980.

131. Brezhnev, *Kommunist*, no. 10 (1980), p. 6. This statement was followed by "prolonged applause," according to the text.

final decisions are made with unanimity. The decision on the dispatch of Soviet troops to Afghanistan was made in accordance with this practice. . . . The debate on this question was not easy. But the final decision was adopted with unanimous approval."[132]

While direct evidence of the Soviet decisionmaking on intervention in Afghanistan is thin, in this case there is no reason to doubt these Soviet statements about its difficult nature. Similarly, although the positions individual leaders may have taken can only be inferred or speculated on, as is true of the arguments advanced by various institutions, it seems quite likely that there were both reservations and final agreement by the leaders as a group. Those most concerned with the international repercussions, such as Gromyko and Suslov, may well have been concerned over the adverse effects in various foreign countries and in the world communist movement—but they were also aware of the need to save the Soviet foreign political investment in Afghanistan. The military no doubt smarted over the Soviet casualties and reverses suffered by the army they had been training, and were highly reluctant to suffer the defeat of withdrawal, but they may have recognized at least the possibility that there would be a long and inconclusive campaign. While the Soviet army could gain useful direct combat experience, the campaign could also be debilitating and drain resources needed for meeting other military requirements. Overall, the Soviet leaders saw the overriding consideration as avoiding a serious political, ideological, and strategic setback that not only would weaken the Soviet security buffer, but could lead to a serious new threat by permitting one or another degree of American and Chinese presence directly at the weakest Soviet border area.

The compelling nature of the motivation to defend Soviet national security probably contributed to the underestimation of the costs and negative consequences of the decision. As the scenario of action was being developed, the sequence of planned events and desired outcomes tended to become a given, and possible failures tended to be obscured. Moreover, the decision in November was not the actual denouement in December. A quiet removal of Amin (for which there were undoubtedly several plans, not initially including the one finally resorted to) and his replacement by Karmal and a reconciliation coalition (including not only Parcham leaders but also Khalq associates of Taraki, as well as the relatively popular military men such as General Qader and Colonel Watanjar) would have as much legitimacy as Amin ever had. Karmal, after all, had been the other vice president along with Amin under Taraki in May 1978, and General Qader was a familiar figure from precommunist days. For such a new government to call for a greater Soviet troop presence in the country would probably provoke some criticism abroad but would not even appear to be an invasion. General Paputin's suicide (or other untimely demise) after the failure to bring about a more smooth removal of Amin in

---

132. Interview by Ambassador D. Polyansky, in *Asahi Shimbun*, Tokyo, March 8, 1980. Cited by Valenta, *International Security*, vol. 5 (1980), p. 127.

mid-December could not, however, make amends for this critical snag in implementing the plans.

Taraki and even Amin may well have asked earlier for more direct Soviet military assistance, including the dispatch of Soviet troops, as the Soviets subsequently claimed. But the Soviet leaders were certainly disingenuous in citing these requests for Soviet troops as justification for their intervention in December. It may be indicative that Amin made no known complaint, and certainly no public one, when the Soviet Union brought in airborne troop units from December 8 to 25. If the Soviet leaders had in fact received earlier Af ghan pleas to send in troops, they evidently chose not to meet them then. This course of events strongly suggests that they were not looking for an opportunity to station their troops in Afghanistan until it became necessary to shore up a regime responsive to Soviet direction. Central Committee official Vadim Zagladin was not being coy when he remarked that "moving troops into the territory of another country is always a difficult matter" requiring careful consideration of "all aspects and interrelationships" of such a measure.[133]

Once the Soviet troops had been introduced in sizable numbers, as the commander of the Turkestan Military District, General Yury Maksimov stated, the Soviet expectation soon after the event was that "the presence of our troops will permit the stabilization of the situation in Afghanistan, will allow the democratic forces to consolidate and the gains of the revolution to be secured, and will permit cooling the ardor of those who initiated military adventures."[134] While this estimate was woefully erroneous, it is not hard to see how Soviet military and political leaders would have been able to convince themselves of this sequence once they had bitten the bullet and decided to take the step.

Moreover, as the Soviet leaders were reaching their decision, they saw no easier alternative. To withdraw and permit the Amin regime to turn to the West or to collapse would but substitute certain great costs and risks for what otherwise remained only possible ones. Things had gone too far for that option in terms of commitment of Soviet prestige, and in any case the strategic consequences of permitting a power vacuum to develop on their border were too great.

Continuation of the course pursued since May 1978 was also no longer a real alternative. Earlier attempts to advise and persuade the Afghani had not succeeded, nor had attempts to bring about a more moderate and responsive leadership. In addition, Amin was increasingly considered likely to turn to the West and perhaps to strike a deal with some of the insurgents. Finally, the several thousand Soviet advisers were only an asset up to a point; they could also become hostages to Amin. The slaughter of Soviet military

133. V. Zagladin, first deputy chief of the International Department of the Central Committee of the CPSU, interview in *Stern* (Hamburg), January 31, 1980.

134. Colonel General Yu. Maksimov, "A Mighty Guard over the Achievements of Socialism," *Pravda vostoka* [Pravda of the East], Tashkent, February 21, 1980.

advisers in Herat and Jalalabad by mutinous Afghan army units was a real, if not primary, consideration to the Soviet military leaders in particular. Amin might be able to place large numbers hostage in a showdown unless he were quickly neutralized. He could even call for an Afghan *jihad* against Soviet invaders. Similarly, the possibility or even probability that Amin would execute the imprisoned Afghan communist leaders and perhaps carry out a wide blood purge was another factor calling for early and decisive action.[135]

These factors, while not basic to the Soviet decision, did add urgency and help sustain the decision to press ahead, despite setbacks such as the failure to eliminate Amin in mid-December and to install Karmal first and have him request Soviet troops before they had to be dispatched.[136] Amin's frantic efforts to establish contact with President Zia of Pakistan in December, even if his precise purpose was unclear, were another reason for urgency. In short, in November and increasingly throughout December the Soviet leaders saw a need to act quickly before Amin took any of a number of possible preemptive actions, both within Afghanistan and internationally: denunciation of the 1978 Soviet-Afghan treaty, taking hostage or expelling the Soviet advisers, entering into a concordat with the Islamic revolutionaries, executing the imprisoned Afghan communists and military leaders, even appealing to the United States for military assistance. In light of those possible hazards, the effective elimination of Amin and simultaneous installation of Karmal and introduction of Soviet troops seemed necessary, prudent, and at acceptable cost.

While it is highly unlikely that the Soviet Union (or the United States) ever considers foreign policy decisions directly in terms of compatibility with the Basic Principles of détente agreed upon in 1972, the Soviet leaders undoubtedly considered their action in Afghanistan as consistent with those principles. It was, as they saw it, a defensive measure to sustain the stability of the status quo by preventing Afghanistan from plunging into chaos and falling

---

135. Many later Afghan and Soviet accounts claim that Amin planned a mass execution of imprisoned communist and military leaders on December 29. For example, see A. Petrov (pseud.), "Captive to Cold War Dogmas," *Pravda*, January 19, 1980; and Vladimir Goncharov, Radio Moscow, January 3, in FBIS, *Soviet Union*, January 4, 1980, p. A2.

   Soviet party officials in Moscow have referred in conversation with evident real feeling to the decimation of Afghan "comrades" by Amin.

136. The attempted coup by the security forces against Amin on December 17 was described earlier. A statement by Sultan Ali Keshtmand, a former PDPA Politburo member, at that time a prisoner and later one of Karmal's closest associates, is quoted in the authoritative Soviet party journal as having said that the (phantom) Afghan party "underground" which allegedly later overthrew Amin had "with the help of the military" planned "several variants" of plans to oust him. Before the successful attempt on December 27, "one of those [variants] had been planned for execution in mid-December." This statement is the closest there is to a Soviet acknowledgment of the December 17 attempt against Amin. See Demchenko, *Kommunist*, no. 5 (March 1980), p. 75.

under hostile external influences. It was intended to preserve, not upset, an existing geopolitical balance. But even if that were not the case, the Soviets saw the Basic Principles as reflecting an implicit acceptance by each of the two powers of the vital interests of the other. And Afghanistan had never been in the American security system. Since April 1978 it had gravitated into the Soviet orbit, and the Soviet Union had the right to ensure that Afghanistan did not become hostile to its interests. The situation was, in the Soviet view, comparable to that involving American interests in the Dominican Republic, where the United States had intervened directly in 1965 without an invitation from a previously recognized government. And before departing, the United States established a responsive government. Soviet commentators did not publicly use that comparison because they did not want to admit that the Soviet Union also resorted to imperialist-style military interventions. But in speaking to foreign audiences they did draw a parallel to the American removals of Ngo Dinh Diem in Vietnam and Allende in Chile.[137] Moreover, the Soviets had warned the United States months earlier that it might become necessary to remove Amin, and they had tried to accomplish that by less extreme political means. The Soviets' perception thus led them to distort their own expectations of the American reaction, which they preferred to hope would be a limited, transient objection for the record. They even believed that such a preposterous allegation as Amin's being a CIA agent would be understood as popular propaganda. It was meant to signify that objectively, if not consciously, Amin was capable of serving American interests by pulling Afghanistan away from the Soviet Union (and by giving socialism a bad name in Afghanistan and the world). At the very least, the American leaders should certainly understand that the Soviet action was limited to Afghanistan.

The Soviet leaders had understood the U.S. warnings, including President Carter's raising the matter at the summit meeting in June 1979, as an attempt to intimidate them from taking measures to defend and retain their position of influence in their primary security zone. After Amin's coup in September they no longer tried to communicate with the U.S. government on this matter. In part the reason was the greater risk that Amin might turn to the United States, in part an understanding that the United States could never directly acquiesce, and in part a belief that the United States was behaving in increasingly unpredictable and unreasonable ways, notably with respect to the Soviet brigade in Cuba. But the most basic reason was that the Soviet leaders conceived of the whole problem as an internal one within a sphere of predominant Soviet security interest and they therefore could not visualize that the U.S. reaction could be keyed to a perceived Soviet challenge to the West and its vital interests.

---

137. For example, see the interview with an anonymous Soviet diplomat in *Die Welt* (Bonn), January 14, 1980. Soviet officials have raised these comparisons in conversations with me.

The American Perspective and Reaction

"The principal US policy goal" in Afghanistan, in the words of an overall assessment of Afghanistan prepared by the U.S. embassy just three months before the 1978 coup overthrowing President Daoud, was "to support Afghanistan's efforts to preserve the largest possible degree of independence from Soviet pressures." In looking back over the preceding year, the embassy concluded that "U.S. interests in the promotion and preservation of regional stability were well served during the year by Daoud's responsible improvement of Afghan relations with Pakistan and Iran. His handling of the difficult and complex relationship with the USSR also continued to be deft and able."[138] The United States had strongly encouraged the Afghans (and the Iranians and Pakistanis) to improve relations and reduce Afghan dependence on the Soviet Union.[139] The shah of Iran did not need coaxing; on a visit to Washington in 1977 "he spent a good portion of his presentation to President Carter . . . expounding the shared American-Iranian interest in protecting Afghanistan's genuine neutrality"—meaning, moving Afghanistan politically closer to the West.[140]

In bilateral relations with Afghanistan the United States had maintained a modest American presence, mainly through economic assistance programs, and in 1977 doubled the funding for a modest U.S. military training program to help offset somewhat the strong preponderance of Soviet military training. The main new initiative had been an American invitation to President Daoud to visit the United States, which he had accepted. The visit was planned for the summer of 1978.[141]

The American objective was not, however, an end to the Soviet presence and its replacement by American, Iranian, and Pakistani influence. Such an aim would have been considered quite unrealistic. The United States hoped to encourage and help Daoud to reduce Afghan dependence on the Soviet Union, to steer Afghanistan on a more pro-Western course, and all the while to contribute to preserving regional stability. These aims stopped well

---

138. U.S. Embassy Kabul 0820, Confidential, January 30, 1978, text in *Afghanistan* (Tehran), vol. 1, pp. 47–50; the passages cited are found on p. 50.

139. When Secretary of State Kissinger visited Afghanistan in August 1976, he expressed "the United States' strong support for the recent initiatives [of Daoud] which have improved relations among the states of the region," a statement that went well beyond his reserved comments on an earlier visit in 1974. See "U.S.-Afghanistan Joint Statement Issued at Kabul, August 8," *State Bulletin*, vol. 75 (September 6, 1976), p. 316.

140. Brzezinski, *Power and Principle*, p. 356.

141. U.S. Embassy Kabul 0820, Confidential, January 30, 1978, in *Afghanistan* (Tehran), vol. 1, pp. 47–48. Secretary of State Vance extended the invitation to Daoud when he met in New York with Afghan Foreign Minister Wahid Abdullah on October 1, 1977.

short of expecting to displace the Soviet Union or even of seeking to do so. The Soviet leaders, on the other hand, were less sure of this limit to American ambition—even though that outcome was dictated by a realistic evaluation of "the correlation of forces." If, unexpectedly, a pro-American coup had led Afghanistan to try to remove the Soviet presence and replace it with an American one, they could not see Washington spurning the appeal.

The United States accordingly reacted to the April 1978 coup and the installation of a Marxist pro-Soviet regime in Afghanistan with equanimity, if disappointment. The main reason it did not become an issue in American-Soviet relations was that, in Secretary of State Vance's later words, "we had no evidence of Soviet complicity in the coup."[142] Indeed, there was mounting evidence that it was a preemptive reaction to Daoud's crackdown on the left. At the same time, the coup was seen as another in a series of actions in the region from which the Soviet Union profited, even if not all were its own doing. As the United States monitored the situation in 1978, the administration "concluded that our interests would best be served by letting Afghanistan continue its traditional balancing act between East and West."[143] The United States believed this balance would continue despite the clear shift to closer relations with the Soviet Union.

From May 1978 to March 1979 the United States sought to retain a limited role by continuing a modest program of economic aid, but with no expectation of more than marginal influence. Under existing legislation this aid could be extended only so long as the United States government did not conclude officially that the new Afghan government was "communist."[144] By continuing its economic assistance the United States in effect accepted the legitimacy of the new regime.[145] By the beginning of 1979, while American-Afghan relations remained very limited, the United States was satisfied that it

---

142. Cyrus Vance, *Hard Choices: Critical Years in America's Foreign Policy* (Simon and Schuster, 1983), p. 384.

143. Ibid., p. 386.

144. The initial State Department reaction had been to hold back from any discussion of economic aid to allow "the dust to settle." But the American embassy in Kabul argued for continued aid and negotiation of further programs, a position that was accepted. See U.S. Embassy Kabul 3805, Confidential, May 10, 1978 (citing also Department of State cable 116319, not available); Department of State 304356, Secret-Limdis, December 1, 1978; Department of State 194166, Secret-Limdis, August 1, 1978; texts in *Afghanistan* (Tehran), vol. 1, pp. 64–67, 73–75, and vol. 2, pp. 20–22. Secretary of State Vance notes that continuing limited aid was the policy from the start, but he does not note the internal divergences before the policy was decided. Vance, *Hard Choices*, p. 385.

145. Hammond notes that a few people opposed this policy. On the basis of interviews, he suggests that in retrospect a number of Carter administration officials, including Brzezinski and Vance's Soviet affairs adviser, Marshall D. Shulman, agree that the United States should have signaled its objection to the new regime more strongly, perhaps by cutting off all aid. *Red Flag*, pp. 62–64.

had "opened new channels to the Afghan Government and had established a quiet, but useful, dialogue concerning developments in Afghanistan."[146]

American policy was jolted by the kidnapping of Ambassador Dubs and his death in an ill-advised rescue attempt by Afghan police (with a Soviet adviser observed present with the police chief) in February 1979.[147] This act, and the failure of the Afghan government to express greater regret and responsibility,[148] led the United States to curtail its economic aid sharply. For their own reasons the Afghans had also been cutting it back.[149] The United States also terminated its small military training program and withdrew the Peace Corps.

Soon after Ambassador Dubs's tragic death, the Herat uprising drew attention to the growing (if still sporadic) armed resistance within Afghanistan. There was a consequent increase in Soviet military advisers and arms. Charges of Western assistance to the counterrevolutionaries also began to appear in the Afghan and Soviet press, as noted earlier. The Herat uprising and mutiny, and growing armed resistance, also had an impact on American policy, although less strong and less direct than it had on Soviet policy.

The American embassies in Kabul and Moscow, and the Department of State, concluded, on the basis of their assessments in the spring, that the Soviet Union was unlikely to commit its own armed forces directly to quell the rising Afghan resistance.[150] The question of possible Soviet intervention to *change* the Afghan leadership did not arise; the only question was the extent of direct Soviet involvement in *support* of the Taraki-Amin regime.

The Carter administration had also been put off balance by the serious setback to American interests in Southwest Asia that accompanied the Iranian revolution. Not only had the United States lost a stalwart regional ally in the shah and imperial Iran, but the arc of crisis seemed to have buckled at its center. Apart from the serious adverse effects on American prestige, the United States had lost concrete assets such as the two important technical intelligence monitoring stations in Iran. Their loss caused a number of influential senators (such as John Glenn of Ohio) to withhold support for the SALT II Treaty.

---

146. "The United States and Afghanistan," *State Bulletin*, vol. 82 (March 1982), p. 12.

147. See Hammond, *Red Flag*, pp. 64–65.

148. In what appeared to be a calculated affront the Afghan foreign minister did not even sign the condolence book at the American embassy in Kabul.

149. See U.S. Embassy Kabul 2052, Confidential, March 18, 1979, in *Afghanistan* (Tehran), vol. 1, pp. 76–80, reporting on a meeting of the U.S. AID director in Kabul with representatives from other Western countries contributing economic aid. All urged continued American participation while expressing understanding of the American cutback under the circumstances. Some also cited evidence of growing Afghan disenchantment with the terms of aid from the Soviet bloc, and Soviet bloc unreadiness to increase its aid to replace Western programs.

150. U.S. Embassy Kabul 3626, Confidential, May 29, 1979, and U.S. Embassy Moscow 13083, Secret, May 24, 1979; texts in *Afghanistan* (Tehran), vol. 1, pp. 91–94, 116–21.

Apart from these losses, the American leaders also feared Soviet gains. Initially many believed that the semifeudal obscurantist religious fundamentalism of the Ayatollah Khomeini could not last and worried that the Soviet Union, through the local Tudeh (communist) party and other leftists, could succeed in inheriting power in Iran. The advent of a leftist, even communist regime in Kabul also seemed more consequential by early 1979 than it had a year before.

In March 1979 Brzezinski began a campaign to raise the issue of the Soviet presence in Afghanistan. He instructed Director of Central Intelligence Stansfield Turner "to generate more information regarding the nature and extent of the Soviet involvement in Afghanistan."[151]

Brzezinski also began in March to bring the matter up on a number of occasions in his daily national security briefings with President Carter. In early May he warned the president that the Soviets could seek to press from Afghanistan through Pakistan and Iran to the Indian Ocean. He informed the president (unintentionally misleadingly) of a Soviet claim to preeminence in the region; allegedly this claim had been made by Vyacheslav Molotov to Adolf Hitler in 1940. This comment led Carter to ask the Department of State to brief all of Afghanistan's neighbors on the situation.[152] Brzezinski relates

---

151. Brzezinski, *Power and Principle*, p. 346.

152. Ibid., p. 427. Brzezinski writes, "I also reminded the President of Russia's traditional push to the south, and briefed him specifically on Molotov's proposal to Hitler in late 1940 that the Nazis recognize the Soviet claim to preeminence in the region south of Batum and Baku."

Brzezinski thus repeated a regrettably widespread misinterpretation of the secret negotiations between Hitler and Foreign Minister Joachim von Ribbentropp, and Soviet Foreign Minister Vyacheslav Molotov, in November 1940. Molotov did *not* "propose" that the Nazis recognize a Soviet claim of preeminence in the region south of Batum and Baku. In those talks, which concentrated chiefly on Eastern Europe and the Balkans, Hitler and von Ribbentropp proposed that "the territorial aspirations of the Soviet Union would presumably be centered south of the territory of the Soviet Union in the direction of the Indian Ocean" and presented a *German* draft protocol to that effect. Not only did Molotov not propose that language, but even after being pressed for "an answer to the question of whether the Soviet Union was in principle sympathetic to the idea of obtaining an outlet to the Indian Ocean," he declined to respond. (The official German Foreign Office memorandum recording the conversation offered the explanation that Molotov "did not know the opinion of Stalin and of his other friends in Moscow in the matter.") *Nazi-Soviet Relations, 1939–1941*, Documents from the Archives of the German Foreign Office, U.S. Department of State (GPO, 1948), pp. 250, 254. Thus it was clearly not a *Soviet* proposal. A few weeks later in Moscow Molotov replied by requesting an amendment of that point "so as to stipulate the focal point of the aspirations of the Soviet Union south of Batum and Baku in the general direction of the Persian Gulf" (ibid., p. 259), as referred to by Brzezinski. But this wording was a Soviet amendment of a German proposal intended to pick up a concession offered by the Germans, while omitting the element of interest to the Germans: setting up a collision course between Russian and British interests. Instead, Molotov asserted an interest in Iran, where the Germans were actively gaining influence with Shah Reza Khan Pahlevi. Von Ribbentropp had not concealed the German aim: "The decisive question was whether the Soviet Union was prepared and in a position to cooperate with us in the great liquidation of the British Empire." Ibid., p. 253. Molotov had replied that "the Germans were assuming the war against England had already been won." While not opposing the delineation of spheres of influence,

that he "continued to press for a more vigorous U.S. reaction and [the Department of] State continued to comply reluctantly." In April he "pushed a decision through the SCC to be more sympathetic to those Afghans who were determined to preserve their country's independence." While Brzezinski does not note what this decision entailed, it clearly went beyond a sympathy card. A few weeks later the American embassy in Islamabad reported a conversation with a representative of the Afghan resistance who said that Saudi Arabia, the United Arab Emirates, and China had all promised assistance.[153] In early September Brzezinski reports that he "consulted with the Saudis and the Egyptians regarding the fighting in Afghanistan."[154]

The first public warning to the Soviets occurred in March. The State Department spokesman said that the United States would regard external involvement in Afghanistan's internal problems as "a serious matter with a potential for heightening tensions and destabilizing the situation in the entire region."[155] Brzezinski also "registered a serious concern" over the growing Soviet involvement in Afghanistan in his occasional meetings with Ambassador Dobrynin.[156] With President Carter's authorization Brzezinski also made a public statement at the beginning of August that was reported in the *New York Times* under the heading, "U.S. Is Indirectly Pressing Russians to Halt Afghanistan Intervention."[157]

---

he clearly regarded doing so as premature. The key Soviet interest remained not the South Asian area that the Germans were pushing, but the Balkans, where the Germans were on the move and where German and Soviet interests were clashing. For this same reason the whole exercise of defining future spheres of influence collapsed in early 1941. Ibid., pp. 260–79.

For an example of the inaccurate historiography underlying Brzezinski's error see Rubinstein, *Soviet Policy*, p. 62. Rubinstein cites Molotov's reply of November 26 in Moscow (and refers to the State Department archival account, but only to pp. 258–59) as though Molotov had taken the initiative and advanced a Soviet proposal and even made it the condition for agreeing on spheres of influence, rather than noting it was a response. See also Ray S. Cline, "No Surprise: Soviets Told Hitler What They Wanted," *Washingtonian*, vol. 15 (April 1980), p. 13. Cline relates the reported Soviet aim to a move into Afghanistan, whereas in fact, as noted above, the Soviets in 1940 rejected the Nazi proposal that would have included Afghanistan as well as British India (Pakistan and India).

In view of the pro-Nazi sympathies of the shah, the Soviet Union and Great Britain jointly occupied Iran on August 25, 1941 (the Soviets the north, the British the rest of the country, with Tehran "neutral"). The shah was also forced to abdicate in favor of his son, Mohammed Reza Shah Pahlevi, who ruled until the end of the Iranian empire in January 1979.

153. U.S. Embassy Islamabad 5531, Secret, May 14, 1979, in *Afghanistan* (Tehran), vol. 1, pp. 99–101.

154. Brzezinski, *Power and Principle*, p. 427.

155. See Stuart Auerbach, "U.S. Cautions Soviets on Interfering in Afghanistan," *Washington Post*, March 24, 1979.

156. Brzezinski, *Power and Principle*, p. 346. It is unclear from Brzezinski's account (see also p. 427) when these private warnings began, sometime between late March and late July.

157. Ibid., p. 427. Brzezinski warned not only that the Soviet Union "abstain from intervention" in the region, without specifically mentioning Afghanistan, but also that it refrain from efforts

At his summit meeting with Brezhnev President Carter included a veiled warning on Afghanistan when he listed a long series of places in which, he contended, the United States had shown restraint or sought peaceful solutions and the Soviet Union had not. He said that "the United States has not interfered in the internal affairs" of Afghanistan (and Iran) and that "we expect the Soviet Union to do the same."[158] Because Carter did not accuse the Soviet Union of having interfered so far in Afghanistan, it was not entirely clear what he was asking the Soviet Union not to do. (The American concern became clearer only much later—the United States did not want a large Soviet military presence in the country.) Brezhnev responded by urging the United States to join the Soviet Union in discouraging attacks on the Afghan government.[159]

During this time the Soviet Union was pushing its political efforts first to influence the policies of Taraki and Amin and then to replace Amin's growing domination. In addition, it will be recalled, in late June and July special Soviet emissary Safronchuk and East German Ambassador Schweisau confidentially and very frankly informed Amstutz, the American chargé, of Soviet dissatisfactions with the Taraki-Amin regime and its policies. Schweisau explicitly disclosed Soviet desire and intention to remove Amin. Brzezinski notes in his memoir, without revealing the original source, that on July 23 he "warned the President that the Soviets would probably unseat Prime Minister Amin" and got Carter to agree to his recommendation that the State Department be instructed to publicize this "analysis."[160]

Brzezinski, Vance, and Carter do not comment at all on why the Soviets chose to inform the United States of their view of the situation and their intentions. Nor did they see that this attempt to explain the Soviet interest and limited nature of Soviet aims followed, and may have been the result of, President Carter's having raised the matter in Vienna. Moreover, subsequent contingency planning on the U.S. reaction to any overt Soviet military intervention in Afghanistan, so far as is known, was all still keyed to Soviet military assistance to the regime rather than its replacement.

"to impose alien doctrines on deeply religious and nationally conscious peoples"—which theoretically could mean within the Soviet Union itself. In any case, the Soviets saw it not as a diplomatic warning but as crass political warfare.

158. Jimmy Carter, *Keeping Faith: Memoirs of a President* (Bantam Books, 1982), p. 254.

159. Ibid., p. 256.

160. Brzezinski, *Power and Principle*, p. 427; and *New York Times*, August 3, 1979. Brzezinski refers to an "analysis" he presented to the president rather than a report from Kabul of a confidential disclosure by the East German ambassador (on July 18). It is clear that Brzezinski thought about this matter only from the standpoint that it was a sign of Soviet interference in Afghanistan that could be exploited, rather than as either an indication of the state of play of political developments in Afghanistan or as a purposeful Soviet communication to the United States.

From September to December, according to his account, Brzezinski continued to press for greater publicity to the growing Soviet involvement in Afghanistan, over the reluctance and objections of the State Department.[161] Nonetheless on September 19 the State Department spokesman declared that "the United States is opposed to any intervention in Afghanistan's internal affairs."[162] State Department officials also expressed concern in congressional testimony and stated that the United States had "repeatedly impressed on the Soviet Government the dangers of more direct involvement in the fighting in Afghanistan."[163] After early November the Iranian seizure of the American embassy and hostages dominated all else in foreign affairs in Washington.

From the American perspective, the United States played no role in influencing Amin or the Afghan internal political scene. From all accounts the U.S. government was virtually oblivious to the frantic signals Amin was sending in November and December. There is no evidence of American efforts to get Amin to defect through contacts such as the Islamic revolutionary insurgents in Pakistan or directly. Where the Soviets may have seen such a pattern—and the subsequent Soviet and Afghan media present alleged contacts as evidence of a major effort to influence and eventually to collude with a receptive Amin—they probably did not have very persuasive evidence, or it would have been presented in 1980.[164] In any case, to whatever extent there may have been real Soviet concerns over such a development—and there probably were—from the American perspective that role was completely absent, and charges to that effect were seen as merely propaganda.

After the Soviets decided to intervene, their preparations for that operation became increasingly evident. While Soviet intentions remained unclear, the increasing possibility of the introduction of armed forces into the country excited a new series of private and public warnings by the United States directed to the Soviet leaders. On December 11, following the first introduction of new airborne troops, Deputy Secretary of State Warren M.

---

161. Brzezinski, *Power and Principle*, p. 428.

162. Cited in *State Bulletin*, vol. 82 (March 1982), p. 12.

163. "South Asia: Situation in Afghanistan," testimony of Assistant Secretary Harold Saunders before the Subcommittee on Asian and Pacific Affairs of the House Foreign Affairs Committee, September 26, *State Bulletin*, vol. 79 (December 1979), p. 53. This statement and a longer passage of several paragraphs of which it is a part were also used verbatim by another Department of State official, Howard Schaffer, in a public address in New York on December 1, 1979, in ibid., vol. 80 (February 1980), p. 62.

164. Neither the Soviet Union nor Afghanistan ever issued a once-promised White Paper documenting their charges of a U.S.-Amin conspiracy, although the press of both countries had many articles charging it. The most authoritative Afghan officials to make such charges were two victims of Amin's September purge, Watanjar and Gulabzoy, in press conferences in Kabul on January 16 and 21, 1980, respectively. Their statements and many others are included in two collections of Soviet propaganda, published in English (and other languages, as well as Russian), *The Undeclared War: Imperialism vs. Afghanistan* (Moscow: Progress Publishers, 1980), pp. 42–63; and *The Truth about Afghanistan: Documents, Facts, Eyewitness Reports* (Moscow: Novosti Press Agency, 1980), pp. 83–96.

Christopher expressed U.S. concern to Soviet Chargé d'Affaires Vladilen Vasev. Beginning December 19, State Department press spokesman Hodding Carter made clear American concern and provided the press with data on the military buildup in the southern USSR. Later he provided data on the introduction of additional Soviet troops into Afghanistan from December 24 to 26. On December 26 Hodding Carter referred to the Soviet action as "blatant military interference into the internal affairs of an independent sovereign state," which was more true than the State Department realized: the major airlift of Soviet troops from December 24 through 26 was still assumed in Washington to be an action to *bolster* Amin's regime against the insurgents.[165]

After the Soviets killed Amin on December 27 and introduced several Soviet divisions into Afghanistan, the United States (and the world) faced this far more objectionable situation. The line between influencing events, and directly intervening to determine them, had been breached. President Carter, in a press conference the next day, referred to the Soviet action not only as a "blatant violation of accepted international rules of behavior," but also as representing "a grave threat to peace," presumably because it was taken to mean that the Soviet Union was more broadly ready to resort to direct use of its own armed forces.[166]

The NSC met on December 28 and again two days later to consider the Soviet military intervention and replacement of the Amin regime. These were but the most prominent in a series of meetings and decisions leading up to a major presidential address to the nation on January 4, 1980, setting forth the American reaction and responses to the Soviet move.

It is instructive to review the process of decisionmaking in late December and early January. Brzezinski stresses that he had been pressing for a tougher stand in publicizing and warning against Soviet preparations for the dispatch of military forces into Afghanistan but that the Department of State had been dragging its heels. The latter point is only partly true, as the record shows, but it is clear that Brzezinski was pushing to go further in challenging the Soviets even before their overthrow of Amin. Indeed, after the beginning of the large-scale entry of Soviet airborne troops on December 25–26, but *before* the attack on Amin, Brzezinski wanted to label the action an "invasion" and to take strong American political countermeasures.[167]

---

165. "Soviet Invasion of Afghanistan," Department Statement, December 26, 1979, *State Bulletin*, vol. 80 (February 1980), p. 65. See also Richard Burt, "U.S. Voices Concern Repeatedly to Moscow over Afghan Buildup," *New York Times*, December 23, 1979, citing, as requested, an anonymous "high-ranking official" (Hodding Carter) and laying out the data on the Soviet military buildup in Central Asia and introduction of some troops into Afghanistan, and also the fact that the United States had several times expressed concern to Soviet officials.

166. "American Hostages in Iran and Soviet Intervention in Afghanistan: Remarks by the President, December 28, 1979," *Presidential Documents*, vol. 15 (December 31, 1979), p. 2287.

167. Brzezinski's account, usually carefully checked with the record, is blurry on the developments of December 25–28. He writes, "During the night of December 25, Soviet forces invaded Afghanistan and occupied Kabul, and a new President was installed to replace the one murdered during the Soviet coup." In fact, Amin was attacked on December 27, and killed only

The Soviet use of armed forces to overthrow Amin, the installation of a new leadership clearly beholden to the Soviet leaders, and the concurrent large-scale introduction of Soviet army forces in what was seen as an invasion represented a serious violation of international law and posed a severe challenge to U.S. policy. Previous differences within the Carter administration were quickly submerged. As Brzezinski puts it, "We all knew that a major watershed had been reached in the American-Soviet relationship," and the NSC met on December 28 in a "grave" mood. Brzezinski writes that "to me, it was a vindication of my concern that the Soviets would be emboldened by our lack of response over Ethiopia."[168]

President Carter saw the action as a sharp blow to his hopes of renewing a policy of détente, and especially to ratification of the SALT treaty. He remarks in his memoir: "The worst disappointment to me personally was the immediate and automatic loss of any chance for early ratification of the SALT II treaty."[169]

Secretary of State Vance recognized that "Afghanistan was unquestionably a severe setback to the policy I advocated." He believed that it made it necessary "promptly to demonstrate to the Soviets that such behavior was not an acceptable part of the East-West competition."[170] There was ready agreement that a strong response was needed, with the aim "to ostracize and condemn the Soviets and to reinforce regional confidence."[171]

As a number of observers have noted, the vigor of the American reaction cannot be attributed to the Soviet intervention alone. Although the move into Afghanistan was regarded as both an affront and a potential threat, even more important was that it triggered the release of tensions that had been growing in Soviet-American relations over Angola, Ethiopia, Shaba, the Yemens, Cambodia, and, most recently, the brigade in Cuba. Perhaps as important were frustrations not even related to the Soviet Union, above all the Iranian hostage crisis. Afghanistan provided a focus and crystallized the consensus that the United States must do something.

---

on the night of December 27–28, while Soviet forces entered overland in strength beginning December 28. This fuzzing of the chronology obscures the significance of the fact that at an SCC meeting on December 26, before the Soviets had resorted to arms or Amin had been ousted, at a point when all that had occurred was a stepped-up airlift of airborne troops to Kabul, Brzezinski had proposed a presidential message to Brezhnev saying that "SALT was now in jeopardy," and flashing the China card by saying "the scope of our relationship with China would be affected." So far as Washington knew then, all that had occurred was a Soviet reinforcement of its existing presence, presumably at the request of the Afghan government, so it is not surprising that Vance and Christopher objected to this proposed course of action. See Brzezinski, *Power and Principle*, pp. 428–29. Vance mentions the series of high-level meetings as having begun on December 27. *Hard Choices*, p. 389. That still would place the initial meeting earlier than the attack on Amin's palace.

168. Brzezinski, *Power and Principle*, p. 429.

169. Carter, *Keeping Faith*, p. 473.

170. Vance, *Hard Choices*, pp. 394, 391.

171. Brzezinski, *Power and Principle*, p. 429.

The objectives of the new consensus, however, remained unclear and inconsistent. Brzezinski is probably correct when he states that the objective was "to ostracize and condemn the Soviets." But is that a goal, or should that have been a means to some end? Vance's account reinforces those of Brzezinski and Carter. He states, "The administration's response ... was strong and calculated to make Moscow pay a price for its brutal invasion. Our fundamental objective was to bring about the withdrawal of Soviet forces."[172] Vance thus did introduce an objective. But was a policy of making them pay consistent with bringing about withdrawal? There probably was no way the American leaders could have brought about a withdrawal, and surely it was necessary to condemn the action. But later actions pointed up a basic inconsistency that proved not helpful to U.S. interests: the more the Soviets had to pay, the more they would be inclined to keep what they had paid for.

Moreover, there was a considerable difference in approach below the surface of the easy early consensus on a punitive policy toward the Soviet Union. It is best seen in divergent comments by Vance and Brzezinski. Vance relates directly to the question of the motive behind the U.S. response "the question of why Moscow had elected to intervene." He notes that two main theories were advanced: the Soviet reaction was essentially local, that is, focused on Afghanistan, and was "related directly to perceived threats to its national security"; or, the Soviets had seen an opportunity to advance their global position. In his view it may well have been both, although he believed that the "immediate aim was to protect Soviet political interests in Afghanistan which they saw endangered."[173] Brzezinski, on the other hand, describes his concern at the time that "the President might be prevailed upon—as he had been earlier in the Cuban [brigade] case—to view the Afghan problem as an isolated issue." All along he had been stressing broader Soviet aims (as, for instance, in his misbegotten history lesson on the Molotov-Hitler talks in 1940). And he emphasized to the president that "the issue was not what might have been Brezhnev's subjective motives in going into Afghanistan but the objective consequences of a Soviet military presence so much closer to the Persian Gulf."[174]

President Carter accepted Brzezinski's approach. As he saw it, "the brutality of the act was bad enough, but the threat of this invasion to the rest of the region was very clear—and [would have] had grave consequences."[175]

Insofar as the local, Afghan aspect was concerned, there is no indication that any attention was given to the Soviet motivation or the political situation within Afghanistan. What the Soviet leaders saw as an acute local political dilemma requiring drastic remedy the U.S. president saw simply, in his

172. Vance, *Hard Choices*, p. 389.

173. Ibid., pp. 387–88.

174. Brzezinski, *Power and Principle*, p. 430.

175. Carter, *Keeping Faith*, p. 471.

words, as "direct aggression by the Soviet armed forces against a freedom-loving people, whose leaders had been struggling to retain a modicum of independence from their huge neighbor."[176] Carter's posthumous promotion of Amin as the leader of a freedom-loving people struggling to retain independence may have been a less calculated rewriting of history than the Soviet claim that the USSR had been invited in by "the government of friendly Afghanistan." Both were, however, equally departures from reality.

In his major address to the nation a few days later on January 4, President Carter used what was to become the standard American formulation: he referred to a Soviet invasion of "the small, nonaligned, sovereign nation of Afghanistan."[177] Whether Afghanistan had been nonaligned was not only questionable, but more to the point, this stance seemed to contradict the earlier administration position that "the course of events unfolding after the Afghan coup of 1978 [had] brought this previously neutralist government into close alignment with the Soviet Union."[178] Nonetheless, in the perception of the American leaders there was a difference between Soviet use of force against straying members of the Warsaw Pact and against other allies and associates of the Soviet Union. President Carter, still rewriting history, also described the Soviet intervention as "the first time they had used their troops to expand their sphere of influence since they had overthrown the government of Czechoslovakia in February 1948 and established a Soviet puppet government there."[179] No Soviet troops had been in Czechoslovakia before or after the internal communist accession to power in 1948. Secretary of State Vance, more accurately but still under the influence of the Warsaw Pact–Brezhnev Doctrine syndrome, characterized the Soviet intervention as "the first time since World War II" that the Soviet Union had "used its own armed forces beyond the Warsaw Pact sphere to impose its authority directly over a Third World coun-

---

176. Ibid., p. 471. Carter notes that the Soviets replaced Amin with "an Afghan leader of their own persuasion, who had been hiding in the Soviet Union"—the only reference in his account to the entire Afghan political drama of 1978-79.

177. President Carter, "Soviet Invasion of Afghanistan: Address to the Nation, January 4, 1980," *Presidential Documents*, vol. 16 (January 14, 1980), p. 25.

178. Marshall Shulman, "An Overview of U.S.-Soviet Relations," Statement before the Subcommittee on Europe and the Middle East of the House Foreign Affairs Committee, October 16, *State Bulletin*, vol. 79 (December 1979), p. 43.

   On September 26 Assistant Secretary Saunders also expressed American "regret" over "the reorientation in Afghanistan's foreign policy away from its traditional genuine nonalignment" since 1978. Saunders, ibid., p. 53.

   Similarly, a State Department release, "Background on Afghanistan," in February 1980 noted that the Soviets had moved quickly after April 1978 "to consolidate their ties" with the new Marxist regime. It further declared, "Since April 1978 Afghanistan has been ruled by a Marxist regime" and stressed the *continuity* of the new regime of Babrak Karmal installed by the Soviets in December 1979 with its predecessors since 1978. See "Background on Afghanistan," ibid., vol. 80 (February 1980), p. 66.

179. Carter, *Keeping Faith*, p. 471.

try."[180] The Soviet action was thus perceived as breaking a constraint followed in the past and even a doctrine, the so-called Brezhnev Doctrine, that the West considered to be limited to the Warsaw Pact—although the Soviet leaders had never conceived the doctrine as applying only to the Warsaw Pact.

The Soviet intervention in Afghanistan was thus seen as a "sharp escalation"[181] in resort to force to serve its interests. Little attention was paid to questions of whether this action was a reluctant recourse or eager seizure of an opportunity; an action to retain, or to expand, the area of Soviet hegemony; and an occasion likely, or unlikely, to be repeated and under what circumstances.

The first decision to emerge from the NSC meeting on December 28 was to send a strong message to Brezhnev on the hot line. Carter describes it as "the sharpest message of my Presidency, telling him that the invasion of Afghanistan was 'a clear threat to the peace' and 'could mark a fundamental and long-lasting turning point in our relations.'. . . unless you draw back from your present course of action, this will inevitably jeopardize the course of United States–Soviet relations throughout the world." He urged prompt withdrawal of Soviet forces and cessation of Soviet interference in the internal affairs of Afghanistan.[182]

Brezhnev's response two days later had a sharply negative impact on President Carter and intensified his initial strong reaction against the Soviet move. Brezhnev argued, as did the Soviets in their public justifications, that the Soviet troops had been sent in response to requests by the Afghan government, necessitated by external armed incursions into Afghanistan. He promised to withdraw the Soviet troops when "the reasons which prompted the Afghan request to the Soviet Union disappear."[183] To Brzezinski, this explanation was "mendacious"; he also describes it as "arrogant."[184] Carter calls it "devious," apparently because it made what he regarded as false claims of an Afghani invitation and external interference. He took it as an insult to his intelligence and was almost apoplectic in his reaction.[185] Whether intended by

---

180. "Meeting the Challenge in Southwest Asia: [Vance's] Statement before the Senate Appropriations Committee, February 1, 1980," *State Bulletin*, vol. 80 (March 1980), p. 35. See also Vance, *Hard Choices*, p. 391.

181. President Carter, "Situation in Iran and Soviet Invasion of Afghanistan: Remarks at a White House Briefing for Members of Congress, January 8, 1980," *Presidential Documents*, vol. 16 (January 14, 1980), p. 40.

182. Carter, *Keeping Faith*, p. 472. Brzezinski notes that the draft message had been prepared by his staff. Brzezinski, *Power and Principle*, p. 429. Vance does not mention the message.

183. Carter, *Keeping Faith*, p. 472.

184. Brzezinski, *Power and Principle*, p. 429.

185. See Carter, *Keeping Faith*, p. 472. My characterization of Carter's reaction is also based on interviews with people in direct contact with the president at the time.

Carter or not, his public charge that Brezhnev was lying to him also implicitly suggested that the Soviet leader was not a fit partner for détente.

President Carter's extreme reaction was evidently stimulated by his belief that a more frank rapport had been established at the summit meeting. In his toast in Vienna on June 16 he had spoken of "continuing cooperation and honesty in our discussions," and in his report to Congress two days later he had proudly referred to the fact that "President Brezhnev and I developed a better sense of each other as leaders and as men."[186] He now felt personally betrayed by an explanation not deemed worthy of a presidential dialogue.

The most striking and most noted sign of President Carter's extraordinary reaction to Brezhnev's reply was an off-the-cuff statement on Afghanistan in a television interview just hours after receiving it. "This action of the Soviets," Carter stated, "has made a more dramatic change in my own opinion of what the Soviets' ultimate goals are than anything they've done in the previous time I've been in office." This statement was quickly and widely interpreted as a sign of Carter's naïveté in understanding the Soviet leaders, a reaction that further spurred him to demonstrate his toughness in responding to the Soviet move.[187]

Even before Carter received Brezhnev's message, a number of responses had been set in train. On December 28 he had begun to call and consult with several foreign leaders, including not only some of the American European allies (to whom he also dispatched Deputy Secretary of State Christopher on December 30), but Presidents Josip Tito of Yugoslavia and Nicolae Ceausescu of Romania, as well as President Zia of Pakistan.[188]

The first direct response was to move for a United Nations condemnation of the blatant Soviet military intervention. By January 5 an emergency meeting of the Security Council had been convened. The Soviets vetoed the measure of condemnation (the vote was 13 to 2). The General Assembly then met and on January 14 condemned the Soviet action by a vote of 104 to 18.[189]

---

186. "Vienna Summit Meeting: Toast at a Working Dinner Hosted by the U.S. Delegation, June 16, 1979," *Presidential Documents*, vol. 15 (June 25, 1979), p. 1049, and "Vienna Summit Meeting: Address Delivered before a Joint Session of the Congress, June 18, 1979," ibid., p. 1092.

187. "Transcript of President's Interview with Frank Reynolds on Soviet Reply," *New York Times*, January 1, 1980. This statement was subsequently considered so embarrassing to Carter that it was not included in the official *Weekly Compilation of Presidential Documents*. Nor does he, Brzezinski, or Vance refer to it in their memoirs, although it drew heavy press attention and was cited by political opponents in the next election campaign as evidence of Carter's naïveté.

188. Carter, *Keeping Faith*, p. 472.

189. There were another eighteen abstentions and twelve countries absent or not voting. Romania was among those choosing to be absent, Nicaragua and Syria among those abstaining. Joining the Soviet Union and Warsaw Pact countries (less Romania) were Afghanistan, Cuba, Vietnam, Mongolia, Laos, Angola, Ethiopia, Mozambique, South Yemen, and Grenada.

Soon after, on January 28, thirty-five countries at an Islamic Conference meeting in Islamabad condemned the Soviet action even more sharply.

Meanwhile, high-level meetings held in Washington from December 30 through January 4 considered a number of punitive sanctions against the Soviet Union. Both the Department of State and the White House NSC staff prepared lists of ongoing U.S.-Soviet activities that could be curtailed. There was a total of some forty possible sanctions. While this list comprised what Brzezinski referred to as a "menu" from which measures could be selected, *most* of the measures were adopted in the end. President Carter and Brzezinski were surprised to find Vance strongly in favor of most of the proposed sanctions—including a grain embargo and even reinstitution of military conscription. As President Carter later commented, the State Department advocacy of stronger measures than the NSC staff was "a reversal of their usual attitudes."[190]

Brzezinski notes that he felt that the United States could have sent an adequate message to the Soviets with just a few substantial measures: limits on grain sales to the Soviet Union and on the provision of further high technology, possibly U.S. transfers of defensive arms to China, and provision of a large aid package to Pakistan.[191] Carter notes that "Brzezinski was remarkably sober, concerned about future relationships with the Soviet Union."[192] Brzezinski, for all his desire to wage a tough geopolitical competition, did see—even better, apparently, than Vance did—the risks of engendering long-term difficulty in relations with the Soviet Union by dismantling virtually the whole range of active relations. But Carter himself was "determined to make them pay for their unwarranted aggression."[193] The risks he saw were not so much in terms of future relations with the Soviet Union, as in terms of domestic U.S. politics. Vice President Mondale strongly objected to the grain embargo and to registration for a draft for domestic political reasons that also troubled Carter, although they did not dissuade him.[194]

The decisions were made in an uneven stream. For example, the idea of a boycott of the international Olympic Games scheduled for Moscow in the summer was discussed very early. On January 4 in his address to the nation President Carter referred to this possibility but withheld a final decision. He stated ambiguously that the United States would "prefer not to withdraw" but that "continued aggressive actions" by the Soviet Union would "endanger" participation by athletes and spectators. Meanwhile, Deputy Secretary of State Christopher, in his consultations with the major allies in which he sought to generate a concerted reaction, had been under instructions to tell

190. Carter, *Keeping Faith*, p. 476.

191. Brzezinski, *Power and Principle*, pp. 430–31.

192. Carter, *Keeping Faith*, p. 476.

193. Ibid.

194. Ibid.

them that the United States was *not* for the time being contemplating withdrawal. When, on January 20, President Carter announced that he had requested the U.S. team not to attend the games, it was too late to organize a fully concerted Western abstention.[195]

On January 2 Carter recalled Ambassador Thomas Watson from Moscow for consultations, a diplomatic euphemism for strong dissatisfaction with another government. This measure had not even been taken after the Soviet attack in Hungary in 1956 or the Soviet occupation of Czechoslovakia in 1968.

On January 3, with evident reluctance and regret, President Carter formally asked the Senate to postpone indefinitely its further consideration of the SALT II Treaty because the Soviet action in Afghanistan had made consideration of the treaty "inappropriate at this time." He did not, however, withdraw the treaty, because it remained "in the national security interest of the United States." Nominally the purpose was to clear the way for consideration of measures to deal with what he called the Afghanistan "crisis." It also represented recognition that the treaty almost certainly would not have been sustained in the Senate at that time.[196] This action was not undertaken as a punitive sanction.

On January 4, in an address to the nation primarily on Afghanistan (but opening with the Iranian hostage situation), President Carter laid out a series of measures intended to show that the United States could not "continue to do business as usual with the Soviet Union" because "the Soviets must understand our deep concern." He announced a series of new measures: a delay in opening any new American or Soviet consular facilities (putting off the planned opening of new consulates-general in Kiev and New York); a deferral of action on "most of the cultural and economic exchanges" under consideration; a sharp curtailment of Soviet fishing privileges in American waters; a directive that "no high technology or other strategic items will be licensed for sale to the Soviet Union until further notice"; and an embargo on sales of grain, including 17 million tons already contracted for over the 8 million tons that the United States was obliged by formal international agreement to sell. He also announced that the United States would provide military and economic assistance to Pakistan to "defend its independence and its national security against the seriously increased threat it now faces from the north" and presaged additional regional measures by stating American readiness "to help other nations in the region in similar ways."[197]

---

195. *Presidential Documents*, vol. 16 (January 14, 1980), p. 27; "Meet the Press," January 20, ibid. (January 28, 1980), pp. 107–08; and see Brzezinski, *Power and Principle*, pp. 433–34.

Many European leaders did not, in any case, regard the Christopher discussions as constituting real consultation, and regarded the whole string of U.S. initiatives as unilateral.

196. "Strategic Arms Limitation Treaty," *Presidential Documents*, vol. 16 (January 7, 1980), p. 12.

197. *Presidential Documents*, vol. 16 (January 14, 1980), pp. 26–27.

A number of other minor or corollary measures were also undertaken but with less fanfare. For example, on January 8 the Soviet airline Aeroflot was limited to two flights weekly. On January 11 the United States suspended all outstanding previously validated export licenses to the USSR pending their review (eventually some $150 million in contracts were canceled). Ten days later licenses already granted for the export of spare computer parts for the Kama River truck plant—a major industrial facility contracted for in 1973—were revoked. In February an embargo was placed on the export of American phosphates (and on reexport by third countries) to the Soviet Union. In March exports of American goods and technology to be used in the Moscow Olympics were barred. Seventeen Soviet diplomats, in New York in connection with the planned consulate there, were sent home (and seven American diplomats in Kiev were recalled). The United States also let it be known that no high-level official visits would take place. Other measures were more indirect; for example, the criteria for denying visas to Soviet officials to visit the United States were tightened, not by directive but by less readiness (by the Department of State) to challenge FBI suspicions of possible intelligence affiliations.

Thus a very considerable number of economic and other sanctions were hastily decided on, with little consideration of their implications and consequences.[198] In addition, as early as January 18 the American press reported that anonymous U.S. intelligence sources had predicted that the Soviet Union "may use" toxic chemical weapons in Afghanistan. This claim was based on sightings of standard decontamination equipment carried by the Soviet divisions entering Afghanistan. The Soviet Union sharply rejected the charge. A week later the Department of State spokesman expressed concern over admittedly unconfirmed reports of the use of such weapons and confirmed the presence of decontamination equipment with Soviet troops.[199] This issue would linger on.

The second main line of American reaction, apart from the punitive sanctions and demonstration that business would not continue as usual, was deterrence of possible Soviet moves of aggrandizement beyond Afghanistan. The first step along this line—the president's declaration that the United

198. For an extended discussion and attempt to assess the impact of these sanctions after about a year, see *An Assessment of the Afghanistan Sanctions: Implications for Trade and Diplomacy in the 1980s*, prepared for the Subcommittee on Europe and the Middle East of the House Foreign Affairs Committee, 97 Cong. 1 sess. (GPO, 1981).

199. The initial reports appeared on the Associated Press and other wire services on January 18, 1980. TASS issued its rebuttal the same day. For the statement by Hodding Carter, State Department spokesman, see "Chemical War Issue Raised on Invasion," *Washington Post*, January 25, 1980. The U.S. indictment of the Soviet Union for unconfirmed use of poison gas was suspect not only because of the evident eagerness to use the charge against the Soviet Union even without proof, but also because of its use to support a new U.S. campaign to acquire additional chemical weapons. See William Safire, "The Other Gas Crisis," *New York Times*, January 28, 1980; and "Military Experts Pressing U.S. to Revive Chemical Weapons," *Washington Star*, February 24, 1980.

States would provide military and other assistance to Pakistan—had been uni-lateral and premature. Two weeks later, when President Zia was offered an aid package of $400 million, he publicly declined it as "peanuts."[200]

The president's annual State of the Union address on January 23 was the occasion for unveiling the Carter Doctrine for the defense of the Persian Gulf region. "An attempt," said President Carter, "by any outside force to gain control of the Persian Gulf region will be regarded as an assault on the vital interests of the United States of America, and such an assault will be repelled by any means necessary, including military force."[201] Brzezinski writes that when President Carter pronounced those words, "For me it was a particularly gratifying moment because for more than a year I had been seek-ing within the U.S. government the adoption of such a policy."[202] Brzezinski had submitted a memorandum to Carter on January 9 proposing a regional security strategy, couched in terms of "coping with the consequences of the Soviet action in Afghanistan." Brzezinski capitalized on the new situation to get his long-urged policy adopted. He was successful, for a week later the president agreed, giving Brzezinski the main responsibility for drafting the policy address. The national security adviser patterned the address on the Tru-man Doctrine of 1947.[203]

President Carter repeated that the Soviet Union must be made to realize the costs of its use of military force in Afghanistan, but the stress was now on preventing possible future moves. Accordingly, further measures were no longer additional sanctions levied on the Soviet Union but new means of strengthening the United States militarily. Carter announced an increase in the defense budget for fiscal year 1981 that amounted to a real increase above inflation of 5 percent. Without specifying, he also referred to improving "the capability to deploy U.S. military forces rapidly to distant areas." And in a controversial move he reinstated mandatory registration of young men for se-lective service. Less directly relevant but clearly intended to reinforce the image of growing strength, he mentioned the recent NATO decision to deploy modern intermediate-range nuclear missiles (without, incidentally, even men-tioning the second track of arms control that was integral to the decision and that was the preferred outcome of most Europeans).

---

200. William Borders, "Pakistani Dismisses $400 Million in Aid Offered by U.S. as 'Peanuts,' " *New York Times*, January 18, 1980.

201. Jimmy Carter, "The State of the Union," January 23, *Presidential Documents*, vol. 16 (Janu-ary 28, 1980), p. 197.

202. Brzezinski, *Power and Principle*, p. 443, and see pp. 446–47. See also chapter 19 of this book.

203. Brzezinski, *Power and Principle*, pp. 444–45.

Incidentally, Brzezinski recounts that before the president made this decision, he, Brzezin-ski, had a conversation at lunch on January 10 with former Secretary of Defense Schlesinger, in which the latter urged Brzezinski to resign in order to jolt President Carter into making the necessary response to the Soviets. Brzezinski states that if Carter had not decided on the course taken, he might have followed Schlesinger's suggestion. Ibid., pp. 447–48.

The United States also brought the China card into play in the Afghan game, especially during the propitiously timed visit by Secretary of Defense Brown to China in January 1980. Secretary of State Vance had strongly supported direct American sanctions against the Soviet Union. Nonetheless, he vigorously—but unsuccessfully—opposed Brzezinski and Brown on abandoning the evenhanded approach to the two great communist powers, on creating a common security platform with China, on gestures toward the supply of militarily related technology to China, and on (in Brzezinski's words) "opening the doors to a U.S.-Chinese defense relationship."[204]

On January 21, on the eve of the State of the Union address, the United States also signaled its new resolve by having B-52 bombers fly over a Soviet naval task force in the Indian Ocean. This was the first of a series of flights to demonstrate the U.S. capability to bring its military power to bear in the region. The buildup of a massive American naval force in the Indian Ocean, already under way in response to the Iranian revolution and seizure of hostages, was now intensified so as to demonstrate—and to have on hand—American naval power.

The new ascendancy of geopolitical over diplomatic considerations in U.S. policy was evident not only in these measures, but even in the atmosphere. President Carter's use of a pointer and maps in his address on January 4 symbolized the change (and was unintentionally reminiscent of early presidential speeches to the nation on Vietnam). It was also evident in the swift shift in policy toward Pakistan. Human rights and nuclear nonproliferation were replaced by military aid and covert cooperation.

As noted earlier, demonstrative sanctions against the Soviet Union were not selected from a "menu," as Brzezinski and many in the State Department had expected. The purpose in compiling the lists, as they understood it, was to canvas the whole range of ongoing activities susceptible to interruption—not to recommend severing all ties or activities. Some, such as the opening of consulates-general in Kiev and New York, were considered more in American than in Soviet interest. But rather than the usual procedure of removing measures objected to by one or another agency and boiling the lists of options down to the common consensus, the lists were simply added one to another and the measures on them treated not merely as available for consideration but as proposed sanctions. Those who had previously argued most strongly for the value of developing ties with the Soviet Union were either too angered at the Soviet action or too fearful of being considered soft to oppose inclusion of any measure. The burden was not on arguing whether or why—for example, would barring the consulates in Kiev and New York be useful, and would that measure cost the Soviet Union more than it would the United States? Rather, it was on anyone willing to appear soft to argue why a measure should *not* be included. As a case in point, in canceling cultural exchanges (such as a planned exhibition of paintings from the Hermitage at the Metro-

---

204. Ibid., p. 431, and see pp. 432–33. See also the discussion in chapter 27.

politan Museum), the burden was on arguing why it should *not* be included. As no one spoke up, the exhibition was canceled.

Not only did the administration go overboard in tossing almost everything movable onto the sacrificial bonfire of sanctions, but it tied the whole to the obviously unattainable maximum aim of getting the Soviets to withdraw from Afghanistan. At the outset of the announcements of the sanctions—in his address of January 4—President Carter had given no indication of how long the measures he was announcing would continue, only that the United States could not conduct business as usual. By January 15 Secretary of State Vance was saying, "The Soviets must recognize that they are going to have to pay a cost as long as their troops stay in Afghanistan." On January 23 Carter too said, "While this invasion continues, we and the other nations of the world cannot conduct business as usual with the Soviet Union." By March 3 the knot was tied: Vance said, "Let me affirm today that the sanctions we have undertaken in response to the Soviet invasion will remain in force until all Soviet troops are withdrawn from Afghanistan." Both Vance and Carter continued in the following month to repeat this stand.[205]

The Carter administration, in particular President Carter and Secretary of State Vance, seem not to have learned an important lesson from the recent painful experience with the Soviet brigade in Cuba: it is self-defeating to term not acceptable a situation that cannot be changed and that must, faute de mieux, be accepted. Yet Carter not only termed the intervention "not acceptable," but said the United States could not "accept Soviet occupation and domination of Afghanistan as an accomplished fact." Without prejudice to the American view of the unacceptability of the Soviet action, the Soviet occupation of Afghanistan *was* "an accomplished fact."[206] Vance still argues in his memoir that the Soviet actions dictated that the United States "demonstrate" to the Soviets that such behavior was not "acceptable."[207]

The question is not one of semantics, but of policy. By tying virtually the whole of U.S. relations with the Soviet Union—everything involved in business as usual, from high-level official contacts to exchange visits of art exhibitions—to the continued Soviet military presence in Afghanistan, the Carter administration in essence mortgaged American policy to this issue. Much of the administration's foreign policy had already been taken hostage

205. " 'New York Times' Interview," *State Bulletin*, vol. 80 (March 1980), p. 38 (and "Excerpts from the Interview with Secretary Vance," *New York Times*, January 16, 1980); *Presidential Documents*, vol. 16 (January 28, 1980), p. 196; Vance, "Afghanistan: America's Course," March 3, *State Bulletin*, vol. 80 (April 1980), p. 12; Vance, "U.S. Foreign Policy: Our Broader Strategy, Statement before the Senate Foreign Relations Committee on March 27, 1980," ibid. (May 1980), p. 18; and Carter, "American Society of Newspaper Editors," April 10, *Presidential Documents*, vol. 16 (April 14, 1980), p. 635.

206. See "The President's News Conference of February 13, 1980," *Presidential Documents*, vol. 16 (February 18, 1980), p. 309; and April 10, ibid. (April 14, 1980), p. 635.

207. Vance, *Hard Choices*, p. 391.

along with the embassy staff in Tehran in November. Now the president chose to make American relations with the Soviet Union and détente hostage to the latter's decision to keep its troops in Afghanistan—even, in a perverse way, to Soviet fortunes in suppressing the Afghan resistance.[208]

Part of the reason for the Carter administration's adamant stand was the president's own concern over the widespread domestic criticism that he had been irresolute on a variety of other issues from the neutron weapon affair to the Iranian hostage problem. But Carter's attempt to redeem the charges of naïveté for believing the Soviets to be benign now involved a naïveté that the Soviet leaders were placing themselves beyond possible diplomatic dealings and would have to capitulate to an unenforceable American demand purchased by giving up U.S. diplomatic flexibility.

Carter's overreaction was evident in his repeated characterization of the Soviet invasion of Afghanistan as "the greatest threat to peace since the Second World War."[209] This was obviously a gross overstatement no matter how heinous or even potentially threatening the action. The most disturbing aspect of this proclaimed evaluation was that the president seemed to believe it. He became emotionally charged—never a good basis for policy decision. Moreover, his moralistic approach came to the fore. Not only did he stress that the Soviet action was morally reprehensible (on which there was universal agreement), but he also took an absolute stance against dealing with the perpetrators of such an evil deed as long as they continued "the invasion" (as he still characterized the continued Soviet occupation months later). Here Carter, and U.S. policy, diverged from the rest of the world, as will be discussed.[210]

Thus the president's personal passion was a key factor in setting American policy. In addition, even if it was not consciously articulated, Carter (and his chief advisers) felt a need to draw the line not only for deterrence of possible further Soviet advances, but also for the American people to see—in short, to provide political reassurance (and to retain political support) at home as well as abroad with respect to U.S. allies.

Secretary of State Vance not only did not seek to restrain Carter, but joined in supporting the U.S. posture of regarding the Soviet actions as unacceptable. He seemed to be the only one—other than Carter on occasion—actually to believe that the Soviet leaders would agree to withdraw—a point on which he remained stubbornly optimistic for the months he remained in office. It is hard to escape the conclusion that Vance also sought to counter an image of himself as having been excessively deferential to maintaining the détente relationship with the Soviet Union. He may even have felt let down by the Soviet leaders. In any event, he not only agreed to but urged the wide range of

---

208. See chapter 27.

209. *Presidential Documents*, vol. 16 (January 14, 1980), p. 40; "Meet the Press," January 20, ibid. (January 28, 1980), p. 108; and "The State of the Union," January 23, ibid., p. 196.

210. See chapter 27.

sanctions in American-Soviet relations—excepting arms control. He did, however, object to the turn toward China on an anti-Soviet platform, and he defended not only SALT but also preservation of the "framework" of détente.[211]

Brzezinski saw Afghanistan as a more blatant Soviet move in a pattern of hard geopolitical competition and welcomed its galvanizing effect in precipitating an American counterstrategy. But he did not press for the suspension of American-Soviet relations and still less to tying them to continued Soviet presence in Afghanistan. He saw the demands for a Soviet withdrawal as a means of keeping attention focused on the Soviet presence and as a support for American, global, and regional reactions. That approach would give the United States a stronger military and political position for waging the continuing competition—but it was not a position that should foreclose future American diplomacy toward the Soviet Union.

Despite these disparate approaches, as has been seen, the administration readily reached a consensus on a policy that *combined* punitive sanctions, a freeze on American-Soviet relations, increasing geopolitical leverage (especially through the new relationship with China), and building regional geopolitical positions of strength (the Carter Doctrine). One reason that this policy consensus was reached—and that it failed to attract more support from U.S. allies—was that it was thrown together hastily to meet a perceived domestic and international need for a quick, striking, and strong reaction to Soviet aggression, without much thought of the implications and consequences. The exception is that the domestic political scene was considered. In the very first days, before the sanctions were unveiled on January 4 but after Carter had confessed publicly to having had his understanding of Soviet policy jarred, there were incipient political attacks for not "doing enough." (Later the politically most costly measures—the grain embargo and draft registration—were criticized by many of these same political opponents as going too far.) But the *basis* for a rational decision on a strategy of action was bypassed.

The administration's strong reaction may also have reflected some unease and self-doubt over whether the leaders had done all that they could to head off the Soviet intervention. Vance comments in his memoir, "In looking back, I think we should have expressed our concerns more sharply at the time of the April coup that brought Taraki to power." He then reviews the still convincing reasons why that was not done.[212] Brzezinski was inclined to fault

---

211. Ibid.

212. Vance, *Hard Choices*, p. 386.

Kissinger criticized the Carter administration—in January 1980, not May 1978—for not telling Moscow after the 1978 coup that the replacement of a nonaligned government with a communist one was "incompatible with the rules of coexistence." He was either ignorant of— or, more likely, ignoring—the fact that the Soviet leaders did not engineer the coup and that such representations would have been futile. See "An Interview with Henry Kissinger," *Wall Street Journal*, January 21, 1980.

the administration for not having taken a stronger stance in Ethiopia and other cases—as he had urged. "Had we been tougher sooner, had we drawn the line more clearly, had we engaged in the kind of consultations that I had so many times advocated, maybe the Soviets would not have engaged in this act of miscalculation."[213] Carter, on the other hand, makes no reference to what might have been done to deal with what he seems to have felt was a somehow arbitrary, outrageous, and inexplicable act by the Soviet leaders.

As Vance noted in his memoir, there were differing views in Washington on why the Soviets intervened. This question was, however, swept aside by mutual consent, with an evident lack of awareness of its relevance to the task of defining effective countermeasures. Even Vance, who acknowledges in his memoir the relevance of the question to "the nature of our response,"[214] failed to pursue it. This failure was crucial, because Vance himself did not know the situation in and relating to Afghanistan.[215] Yet he was the key link in bringing expert knowledge to bear if it was to be taken into account. The kind of professional judgment that was available in the Department of State was never tapped.[216] This is not to say that a detached, historically and politically informed approach was the only element needed in making national decisions, but it could have contributed a great deal.[217]

---

213. Brzezinski, *Power and Principle*, p. 432.

214. Vance, *Hard Choices*, pp. 387–88.

215. Vance's brief account of the development of the situation in Afghanistan in 1978–79 is surprisingly ill-informed and inaccurate. He mentions alleged Soviet dissatisfaction with Taraki (rather than Amin) in the summer of 1979, and Soviet hopes if not expectations that Amin would be better; there are also errors of detail. See ibid., pp. 384–86. His account of the defensive theory of Soviet motivation, even though the one to which he largely subscribed, is very weak and incomplete. It exaggerates the Soviet concern over ethnic religious influences in Soviet Central Asia and neglects the more real security concerns. Ibid., p. 388.

216. A good illustration of historical perspective was given in an address by Under Secretary of State for Political Affairs Newsom to the Council on Foreign Relations in October 1978. "Since Alexander [the Great]'s day," Newsom noted, "other actors from outside have tried to exercise influence or power to the exclusion of others. . . . British and Russian imperialism met across the Hindu Kush [in Afghanistan]. If after the Second World War some players changed, the region was still an area of direct competition between outside powers." "Superpowers and Regional Alliances," Address to the Council on Foreign Relations, October 18, *State Bulletin*, vol. 78 (December 1978), p. 52. President Carter did not want to hear that he had been a player in a "Great Game" without having intended to—nor that the Soviet Union had reason to believe the United States was a player in such a geopolitical contest.

217. Under Secretary Newsom later charged that the Carter Doctrine had been decided upon without adequate interagency consultation. Stung by that charge, Brzezinski has documented *earlier* deliberations, citing the December 4, 1979, NSC meeting before the Soviet invasion of Afghanistan, in which "the President discussed the need for a more sustained American engagement in the region with his principal advisors, of whom Under Secretary Newsom was not one." Brzezinski, *Power and Principle*, pp. 445–46. Brzezinski may have a point; but so does Newsom.

Vance himself, in an interview for the *New York Times* in mid-January, mentioned the same two theories about Soviet motivation that he later notes in his memoir (essentially, whether the Soviet action was intended mainly to achieve a position from which to move further southward, or was intended to prevent further deterioration of the situation in Afghanistan because of concern over its impact in Soviet Central Asia). Both of these were wide of the mark. Belying the recognition in his later memoir of the relevance of Soviet motivations in the selection of American responses, Vance said at the time, "I don't think it does any good to try, at this point, to psychoanalyze which of these was the reason—or what combination of them . . . there must be a sharp and firm response."[218] That certainly capsulized the administration's reaction. On February 1 Vance again commented that "the Soviets' precise motives in attacking Afghanistan may remain unclear" and brushed the question aside.[219] Later, too, on March 3, Vance said in his major speech on Afghanistan, "Not even the most penetrating analysis can determine with certainty Soviet interactions in the region—whether their motives in Afghanistan are limited or part of a larger strategy."[220] On April 10 President Carter gave the same brush-off to the question of Soviet motivations: "We cannot know with certainty the motivations of the Soviet move into Afghanistan, whether Afghanistan is the purpose or the prelude. Regardless of its motives, there can be no doubt that the Soviet invasion poses an increased threat to the independence of nations in the region and to the world's access to vital resources and to vital sealanes."[221] But it *did* make a crucial difference.

The punitive, confrontational-containment approach adopted by the U.S. government, which did not even attempt to weigh the Soviet motivation, led directly if unwittingly to a response keyed to the *least* likely Soviet motivation—pursuit of a relentless expansionist design.

The administration's cop-out on the question of Soviet motivations was underlined by the careful references to the inability to know with "certainty" the "precise" Soviet motives, a defensive formulation. It became increasingly evident at least to those close to the situation that the Soviet motivation had been predominately the shoring up of a slipping existing Soviet hegemony in Afghanistan, rather than control over anyone's oil or vital sea lanes.[222]

---

218. *State Bulletin*, vol. 80 (March 1980), p. 38; and *New York Times*, January 16, 1980.

219. *State Bulletin*, vol. 80 (March 1980), p. 35.

220. *State Bulletin*, vol. 80 (April 1980), p. 12. Vance repeated this same point in his last major statement as secretary of state on March 27. Ibid. (May 1980), p. 17.

221. *Presidential Documents*, vol. 16 (April 14, 1980), p. 635.

222. Most commentators have inclined to the prudent middle view that it must be a combination of defensive and offensive aims; even most adherents of an expansionist explanation, such as Brzezinski, tended to see the Soviets as seizing an opportunity to advance rather than as implementing part of a specific plan to move on the Persian Gulf. But those most versed in

The American response should have taken into account the Soviet motivation. While the Soviet intervention deserved condemnation, and perceived concerns justified a clear and strong statement of American commitment to counter any Soviet move beyond Afghanistan, many aspects of the response should have been based on the best judgment of Soviet purpose. To take but one salient example, should the United States (and other countries) assist the anti-Soviet, anti-Marxist Afghan insurgency? While a number of factors were (and still are) relevant to answering that question, not least among them should have been the Soviet motivation. If the Soviet Union was on the march and would be likely to find a pretext for intervening in Pakistan once Afghanistan had been pacified and Soviet control consolidated, it might have made sense to prolong the period when such control was not achieved by destabilizing the situation within Afghanistan. If, on the other hand, the Soviets were prepared to withdraw once the situation was stabilized, it might have been more advantageous (in the long run even for Afghanistan) not to prolong the conflict.

Given the uncertainty (and lack of consensus) about Soviet aims (which, moreover, could change over time in either direction), a middle course might have been most prudent. Such a course might have sought to bring some combination of contingent pressures and inducements to bear that might have led the Soviets to conclude that their interests would be better served by a compromise that reduced Soviet control but was consistent with preserving Soviet security. Moreover, if the Soviet aim was mainly to preserve its stake in Afghanistan, the extent of the future threat to Pakistan might have hinged importantly on what Pakistan (and the United States, China and others) did in and from Pakistan with respect to support of the insurgency in Afghanistan. External support for the resistance would tend to confirm Soviet suspicions (that perhaps may not theretofore have been universally held in Moscow with the same staunchness) that there was a potential American, American-proxy Muslim, and Chinese threat to Soviet security through Afghanistan. In short, if the Soviet aim was to consolidate a stepping-stone base in Afghanistan for expansion beyond, support of the insurgents might help *deter* a Soviet threat

---

the actual political interplay in and around Afghanistan and in analyzing Soviet policy and actions saw the preservation of the Soviet stake in Afghanistan itself as the overrriding element in the Soviet action. This interpretation of Soviet purpose was not, however, welcome to those such as Brzezinski who wanted to use the occasion to turn American policy toward containment, nor to political leaders such as Carter and Mondale who feared that a complex differentiation would appear irresolute (in addition to Carter's own sense that Brezhnev was playing him for the fool), nor even to Secretary of State Vance's view of the need to stand very firmly on the issue in order not to be vulnerable to charges of softness and to preserve the possibility of later resurrecting SALT and détente. Rather than attempting to argue against the informed professional assessment of Soviet motivations (advanced with some caution by those who saw its political unpopularity), the senior leaders of the administration opted to put aside those unwelcome assessments and to make decisions without them or despite them. Hence the repeated defensive remarks in passing about why Soviet motivations and purposes were not knowable with certainty or were changeable.

to Pakistan. But that same action could increase or even *provoke* a threat to Pakistan if the Soviet aim was to secure Afghanistan itself.

Beginning in January 1980, with a further boost in October (and yet another under President Ronald Reagan in the fall of 1982), the United States, Egypt, and Pakistan, with financial support from Saudi Arabia, and separately from but in parallel with China, began covertly to provide military and other assistance to the insurgents (publicly termed "freedom fighters" by President Carter in February 1980). While the U.S. government did not officially acknowledge its support,[223] some officials have intentionally (as well as others perhaps unintentionally) leaked information on such covert support unofficially. One reason for such leaks was a belief that awareness of the support could be helpful in domestic political terms. Some may have also believed it might put further pressure on the Soviets.[224]

In a revealing, if cryptic, disclosure, Brzezinski notes in his memoir that as early as the first NSC meeting on December 28 after the Soviet invasion of Afghanistan, "plans were also made to further enhance our cooperation with Saudi Arabia and Egypt regarding Afghanistan."[225] On visits to Pakistan and Saudi Arabia in early February Brzezinski negotiated cooperation in providing assistance to the Afghan insurgents—or, as he discreetly puts it, "separate negotiations regarding cooperative responses to the Soviet action in Afghanistan," which, he adds, "yielded tangible results."[226] In September 1981 President Sadat publicly confirmed that immediately after the initial Soviet military occupation the United States had contacted him to request shipments of Soviet-made arms for the insurgents and that he had at once agreed and begun to supply them—as he was still doing.[227]

---

223. Two cabinet-level officials of the Carter administration in interviews with me after leaving office confirmed (though not for attribution) the American provision of military and other assistance to the insurgents in 1980, as well as "consultation" with the Chinese and collaborative efforts with several Muslim governments.

224. See Michael Getler, "U.S. Reportedly Is Supplying Weapons to Afghan Insurgents," *Washington Post*, February 15, 1980; Drew Middleton, "Aides Disagree on Level of U.S. Arms Aid to Afghans," *New York Times*, July 21, 1980; Michael T. Kaufman, "Afghans Said to Get Better Guns after Trip to Egypt," *New York Times*, January 22, 1981; Howell Raines, "Reagan Hinting at Arms for Afghan Rebels," *New York Times*, March 10, 1981; Michael T. Kaufman, "Afghan Rebels Bristle with New Arms," *New York Times*, April 14, 1981; Carl Bernstein, "Arms for Afghanistan," *New Republic*, vol. 185 (July 18, 1981); Leslie H. Gelb, "U.S. Said to Increase Arms Aid for Afghan Rebels," *New York Times*, May 4, 1983; "Helping out the Afghan Rebels," *New York Times*, May 8, 1983; and Bradsher, *Afghanistan and the Soviet Union*, pp. 218–26, who also discusses the various resistance groups among the refugees.

Information on the deliberate nature of some of the disclosures is from news correspondents with firsthand experience.

225. Brzezinski, *Power and Principle*, p. 429.

226. Ibid., p. 449.

227. See "U.S. Flies Weapons to Rebellion in Afghanistan, Sadat Says," *Washington Post*, September 23, 1981.

The initial American aims of making the Russians pay and getting them to withdraw were not only probably inconsistent with each other, but their combination was incompatible with the perceived Soviet security requirements that had led them to undertake the action. Yet this inconsistency was not recognized. At least rhetorically, and apparently politically as well, a third American objective was soon added that further ensured that the Soviet Union would see no alternative to settling down for the duration. While the Soviets would probably have made that decision anyway, U.S. policy and its proclaimed aims further reduced whatever possibility there was for Soviet reconsideration or compromise.

President Carter was first asked at a press conference on February 13, "What kind of regime would be acceptable to you" if the Russians were to withdraw? His reply suggested that the question had been deemed sufficiently remote that it had not been addressed in policy councils. He said, "We would like to have a neutral country" and suggested perhaps a UN or Muslim peace-keeping force for an interim period. "But the prime consideration that I have is to make sure that the Soviets know that their invasion is not acceptable, to marshal as much support from other nations of the world as possible, and to prevent any further threat to peace."[228] By the time of Secretary of State Vance's speech on Afghanistan two weeks later the United States had a new objective. After reaffirming the aims of "impos[ing] a heavy price for this aggression" and full Soviet withdrawal of troops, Vance said the goal was "to restore a neutral, nonaligned Afghan Government that would be responsive to the wishes of the Afghan people."[229] He repeated this aim thereafter, as did President Carter.[230] While a creditable goal, American espousal of a return not to the status quo before the Soviet military intervention but to the status quo before the April 1978 communist accession to power upped the ante. It was an escalation of aim (comparable, in a sense, to General Douglas MacArthur's advance northward in Korea in 1950 after clearing the invaders from the south). It meant that the United States was eliminating the alternative of the Soviets withdrawing their troops to leave a "friendly" government in Kabul. Thus the United States drastically reduced the possibility of a Soviet compromise involving withdrawal of Soviet troops and retraction of the Soviet military presence from Afghanistan. That outcome (if attainable) would have been compatible with the expressed U.S. concern over forward basing of Soviet troops beyond Soviet territory and closer to other potential targets of expansion.[231]

---

228. *Presidential Documents*, vol. 16 (February 18, 1980), p. 309.

229. *State Bulletin*, vol. 80 (April 1980), p. 12.

230. See Vance, March 27, *State Bulletin*, vol. 80 (May 1980), p. 18; and Carter, April 10, *Presidential Documents*, vol. 16 (April 14, 1980), p. 636.

231. It was very clear that the American conception of a nonaligned government in Afghanistan, neutral and "responsive to the wishes of the Afghan people," excluded a formally nonaligned but pro-Soviet coalition communist and noncommunist government of the type that the

This American reaction reflected and was an unintended consequence of the failure to realize that the Soviet decision was a reluctant recourse to defend vital interests. Not only was that the Soviet position, but the Soviets had attempted to convey it to the United States by delineating their aims in Afghanistan fairly clearly in the diplomatic conversations in Kabul in the summer of 1979. At that time they signaled their attempt to meet their needs by political means and sought to elicit a tacit American understanding of their limited aims. The U.S. leadership, however, did not even try to calculate the Soviet purposes—much less to accept or even recall the Soviet explication of them. Thus it failed to recognize this effort.[232] The Soviet dialogue was merely filed away by American diplomatic and intelligence specialists whose views were not even sought by the leadership. Instead, the reluctant Soviet resort to military means to solve the Afghan problem was misread as a military threat to American interests further afield in the region that *were* regarded as vital, and led to an American reliance on military as well as political countermeasures to guard against the perceived post-Afghan Soviet threat to the region. This outcome was precisely what the Soviets had sought, perhaps ineptly and certainly inadequately, to prevent. They did not, however, dare consult with the United States on the matter after September: Amin was restless and suspicious, while the United States was unpredictably challenging and erratic in the Cuba brigade episode and later was enveloped in the charged atmosphere of the Iranian hostage crisis.

The U.S. reaction in turn failed to carry the intended message because the Soviet leaders could not believe that the American leaders meant it. They knew that Afghanistan was not a vital interest of the United States, and yet the American reaction implied it was. Since the Soviet leaders knew they were not threatening real and vital U.S. interests in the Persian Gulf, they did not credit the American explanations for the Carter Doctrine and the wide swath of other sanctions. The American explanation for the U.S. actions lacked credibility to them because the American reaction lacked proportionality. In-

---

Soviet leaders might have been prepared to countenance. Particularly after the Soviet intervention, it became even more unlikely that a pro-Soviet regime could maintain itself in power in Afghanistan without the presence of Soviet troops. Thus in practice the fact of two discordant conceptions of nonalignment may not have been important. On the other hand, it was important in that it reinforced the Soviet belief that the United States was unprepared to recognize Soviet interests even in a country just across its border and, indeed, was intent on drawing tighter a ring of encirclement—precisely the fear that had contributed to the Soviet decision to intervene.

232. It may be quixotic even to note the point, but it is obvious that no one in the American leadership sought to understand the Soviet position by imagining a comparable parallel situation on the southern border of the United States (moreover, with a hostile China and an adversary alliance in place of the Atlantic and Pacific oceans). In such a case it would not have been difficult to visualize an American intervention to save American lives and strategic assets and preemptively to preclude a hostile presence—as, for example, was done in the Dominican Republic and Grenada. The fact that the scale was larger in Afghanistan only underlines the greater stake for their security that the Soviet leaders saw in the situation there.

stead, the Soviet leaders believed (and believe) that the U.S. leadership in 1980 used the Soviet action as a pretext to dismantle détente, gear up the arms race another notch, build American positions of strength in the Persian Gulf, and mount a general anti-Soviet offensive (for example, the boycott of the Olympic Games). The American action was seen not as a response to the Soviet move in Afghanistan, but as the line the U.S. leaders preferred, for which Afghanistan was just a pretext. It was also convenient not to have to recognize and accept blame for bringing on the American reaction—but that was a secondary and unconscious factor. The primary one was the cold calculation that the U.S. leadership, now completely dominated by a Brzezinski hard line, would not have scuttled détente over Afghanistan unless it had wanted to.[233] A serious American misreading of the Soviet purpose thus in turn helped engender a serious Soviet misreading of the U.S. position.

---

233. See the further discussion in chapter 27.

27   After Afghanistan: U.S. Return to Containment, 1980

THE CARTER ADMINISTRATION, as did most of the world, saw the Soviet military occupation of Afghanistan and the bloody installation of a new leadership beholden to the Soviet Union as a dangerous and reprehensible action. President Carter's outrage at what he considered to be a personal affront in General Secretary Brezhnev's response to his protest of the Soviet action intensified the American reaction. While there were some differences of judgment among members of the administration on the question of Soviet aims, there was a consensus that the United States needed to demonstrate forcefully its refusal to accept the Soviet action in Afghanistan and its ability and resolve to prevent further resort to military force to extend Soviet sway.

The End of Détente

The American response to the Soviet occupation of Afghanistan, as discussed in the preceding chapter, involved several elements: first, an extensive program of unilateral and international punitive sanctions that expressed strong opposition and that sought to bring an end to the Soviet intervention in Afghanistan; second, a new Carter Doctrine designed to reassure others of U.S. forcefulness and to dissuade the Soviet leaders from any further such actions in the region; and third, an attempt to build a stronger global system of containment of Soviet expansionism, including an escalation in the use of the China card and a further military buildup in the United States. These lines of action tended to dominate developments over the following year.

Before looking more closely at American-Soviet relations in the final year of the Carter administration, it is necessary to recall and to stress the impact of the Iranian hostage crisis on American policy. While the Afghanistan situation dominated U.S.-Soviet relations, the long agony of the Iranian hostage situation dominated the American political scene even more pervasively—absorbing the attention of the president personally and determining the general mood in the United States—in what was, to boot, an election year. The Iranian crisis overshadowed all other aspects of international affairs, including relations with the Soviet Union, and it also impinged on them by aggravating American feelings of impotence and frustration. In turn, these feelings contributed to a dissatisfaction with the perceived fruits of détente, a heightened uneasiness over Soviet military strength, and a desire to reassert American power and will.

The Soviet occupation of Afghanistan and the American response led to a sharp break from the whole course of U.S.-Soviet relations over the preceding decade. It gave the coup de grâce to the already seriously eroded and weakened mutual policy of détente established in May 1972. One may question whether it should have had that effect, but it did.

In 1980 American relations with the Soviet Union entered a new period—although whether it was a new phase of limited duration or a longer-term era was unclear.

In retrospect, while the first three years of the Carter administration represented basically a continuation of the Nixon-Ford policy of détente (albeit not the ascendant détente of 1972–75), the fourth and last year was a precursor to the Reagan turn toward confrontation, although not recognized as such. From 1977 to 1979, even as relations deteriorated, the *structure* of negotiations and institutions launched in the early 1970s still persisted, as did the *aim* of détente, which the United States frequently reaffirmed. After January 1980 that structure was largely dismantled and the aim subject to such a major condition—Soviet withdrawal from Afghanistan—that détente became inoperative. In many ways January 1980 was a sharper turning point than January 1981, when Ronald Reagan was inaugurated and repudiated détente.

President Carter and his administration did not *wish* to discard détente, but the president never fully appreciated that that was a consequence of his shift in policy. This failure led to the anomaly that the leading hawk in the administration, Brzezinski, who *did* realize to a far greater extent the significance of the shift, was *less* inclined in January 1980 than Carter and Secretary of State Vance to sweep into the ashcan the whole panoply of American-Soviet relations.[1]

The blatant Soviet intervention in Afghanistan clearly called for both a vigorous American response and international condemnation. As perceived at the time, it also called for visible reinforcement of a policy of containment against possible further Soviet expansionist moves in Southwest Asia. But it did not require that the administration make future relations with the Soviet Union hostage to a continued Soviet military presence in Afghanistan. Nor did the Soviet action in Afghanistan, even if it were deemed to reflect an opportunistic attempt to expand the Soviet domain, represent "the greatest threat to

---

1. See chapter 26; and Jimmy Carter, *Keeping Faith: Memoirs of a President* (Bantam Books, 1982), p. 476.

peace since World War II," as Carter repeatedly characterized it,[2] or even conceivably mean that "our own Nation's security was *directly* threatened."[3]

Despite the hyperbole of the Carter administration's reaction (and, in the view of many abroad and of some in the United States, overreaction), it did not mean that Carter or his administration clearly saw détente as ended or wished that outcome. But the prospect and the policy were blurred and unclear. In his State of the Union address on January 23 Carter stressed the central importance of American-Soviet relations to world peace and noted that it "has not been a simple or a static relationship. Between us there has been cooperation, there has been competition, and at times there has been confrontation." But, he went on, the essence of the American purpose was now to lead other nations "in meeting the challenge of mounting Soviet power."[4] Even Secretary of State Vance declared that "our relations with the Soviet Union *have been and will be essentially competitive.*"[5] The United States had moved from the Nixon-Kissinger policy of managing the emergence of Soviet power back to the Truman-Eisenhower-Kennedy policy of containment. Moreover, Carter described the effort involving détente in the past tense: "In the 1970's three American Presidents negotiated with the Soviet leaders in attempts to halt the growth of the nuclear arms race. We sought to establish rules of behavior that would reduce the risk of conflict, and we searched for areas of cooperation." By contrast, in speaking in the present tense, Carter saw but one aim: "While this invasion continues, we and the other nations of the world cannot conduct business as usual with the Soviet Union."[6]

Still, in aspiration if not in policy, Carter sought a return to détente. Eventual ratification of the SALT II Treaty was the one major and stated exception to his moratorium on cooperation. The treaty was for the time being shelved because "consideration of the SALT II Treaty [would be] inappropriate at this time" (and because approval could not possibly have been attained). But Carter reaffirmed that ratification would be pressed when the timing was more appropriate.[7] In effect, Carter's one positive achievement in

---

2. For example, on January 8, 15, and 20. See *Weekly Compilation of Presidential Documents,* vol. 16 (January 14, 1980), p. 40; (January 21, 1980), p. 87, and (January 28, 1980), p. 108. (Hereafter *Presidential Documents.*)

3. *Presidential Documents,* vol. 16 (January 14, 1980), p. 41. Emphasis added.

4. "The State of the Union: Address Delivered before a Joint Session of the Congress, January 23, 1980," *Presidential Documents,* vol. 16 (January 28, 1980), p. 195.

5. "Afghanistan: America's Course," Address before the Council on Foreign Relations, Chicago, March 3, *Department of State Bulletin,* vol. 80 (April 1980), p. 13. Emphasis added. (Hereafter *State Bulletin.*)

6. *Presidential Documents,* vol. 16 (January 28, 1980), p. 196. Carter had first used this formulation in his address to the nation on January 4; see ibid. (January 14, 1980), p. 26.

7. *Presidential Documents,* vol. 16 (January 7, 1980), p. 12. The form was a letter from the president to Senate Majority Leader Robert Byrd on January 3, "requesting a delay in Senate consideration of the Treaty."

arms control and in developing relations with the Soviet Union was being taken out of the line of fire of the administration's own far-ranging barrage, as well as of the now jubilant opponents of SALT and détente. But this one exception only begged the broader question: were détente and arms control "business as usual" to be jettisoned in a display of disapproval and anger over Afghanistan?

Initially some effort was made to distinguish between temporary (pending Soviet withdrawal from Afghanistan) punitive sanctions levied on particular activities, and preserving the underlying structure of the détente accords. Thus, for example, Secretary of State Vance twice in March stated that "it is not in our interest, even during a period of heightened tensions, to dismantle the framework of East-West relations constructed over more than a generation."[8] Nor was this position only Vance's. In March Brzezinski also stated that in the hope of resuming constructive movement toward arms control in particular, the administration had been "careful to preserve the framework of East-West accommodation even though in recent months it has been stripped to the bone as a result of the Soviet aggression against Afghanistan."[9] And the president, in his message to Congress on programs for international cooperation in science and technology, stated that the "administration has recently taken steps to demonstrate that the Soviet Union's invasion of Afghanistan will have an adverse effect on all forms of cooperation including scientific exchanges. I have taken the deliberate decision to focus our restrictive measures against specific activities, not against the framework of the agreements themselves."[10]

The problem was that measures intended to be demonstrative and temporary in fact became governing. While intended to have a more limited (but significant) impact, the whole range of sanctions and other measures predictably—inescapably—dismantled the framework of détente.

The bilateral arms control negotiations with the Soviet Union set in train in 1977 were interrupted in January 1980. Apart from the special case of SALT, the ongoing negotiations over antisatellite weapons (ASAT) were the most important casualty. Arms control remained essentially on hold throughout 1980, along with most other aspects of American-Soviet relations. Arms control was, it seems, part of business as usual—meaning, in 1980, essentially no business. In fact, there was even some pulling back, unannounced and unremarked. After Afghanistan the United States ceased to use the standard Soviet-favored formulation of "equal security" as an aim of arms control—

---

8. "U.S. Foreign Policy: Our Broader Strategy," Statement of Vance before the Senate Foreign Relations Committee on March 27, *State Bulletin*, vol. 80 (May 1980), p. 20; and see ibid., vol. 80 (April 1980), p. 13.

9. "Brzezinski on Aggression and How to Cope with It," *New York Times*, March 30, 1980.

10. "International Science and Technology, Message to the Congress Reporting on U.S. Programs, February 27, 1980," *Presidential Documents*, vol. 16 (March 30, 1980), p. 406. This message was submitted in a routine annual report called for by standing legislation.

a formulation last reaffirmed at the Vienna summit meeting. Arms control was also put under a cloud by reports that the Soviets were using chemical agents in Afghanistan. Moreover, the State Department announced in March that there had been an unexplained outbreak of anthrax near Sverdlovsk a year earlier and that it was suspected that the accident had occurred at a biological weapons research facility.

The American sanctions were relatively ineffective economically, except for the grain embargo, which did cause some dislocation of plans and discomfort to the Soviet Union. But it was also expensive for the United States, costing about $4 billion, most of it borne by the government in order to prevent U.S. farmers from bearing a heavy burden (and to avoid a domestic political backlash). As will be seen, the embargo had a palpable negative effect on Soviet confidence in relying on economic ties with the United States—and no effect at all on Soviet policy toward Afghanistan.[11] Perhaps the most that can be said for the embargo is that it made American policymakers feel they had been resolute.

American trade with the Soviet Union dropped by nearly 60 percent from 1979 to 1980—from $4.45 billion to $1.96 billion—although Soviet exports to the United States remained largely unchanged, including the sale of strategic minerals such as chrome, manganese, palladium, nickel, uranium oxide, and rare earth metals.[12]

The U.S.-USSR cultural exchange agreement was permitted to expire, and the officially estimated drop in government-sponsored scientific and technical exchanges was 80 percent. Even unofficial tourism from the United States, which had reached about 100,000 a year in the 1970s, declined considerably in 1980 and the years following.

The Carter administration continued to show occasional signs of verbal support for détente—once the Soviet leaders learned their lesson and withdrew, chastised and chastened, from Afghanistan. In June, during a visit to Yugoslavia, Carter described the Soviet invasion of Afghanistan as "a major setback to détente and to the prospects for world peace" but said, "We are trying to preserve the essence of détente—that is, to oppose aggression and also to eliminate the threats to world peace."[13] But his policy remained one of

---

11. See Robert L. Paarlberg, "Lessons of the Grain Embargo," *Foreign Affairs*, vol. 59 (Fall 1980), pp. 144–62.

12. Jack Brougher, "1979–82: The United States Uses Trade to Penalize Soviet Aggression and Seeks to Reorder Western Policy," in Joint Economic Committee, ed., *Soviet Economy in the 1980s: Problems and Prospects* (Washington, D.C.: Government Printing Office, 1982), pt. 2, p. 421.

13. "Interview with the President," June 12, 1980, *Presidential Documents*, vol. 16 (June 30, 1980), p. 1207. Similarly, in an interview in March with the *Washington Post*, Carter had said, "We want to maintain as best as we can the principles of détente . . . to alleviate tensions between us." But he explicitly conditioned restoration of "normal trade relationships and other relationships with the Soviets" on their withdrawal from Afghanistan and said that "they have to recognize that we will not accept their invasion of Afghanistan as an accomplished

attempting to return to détente through containment and to get the Soviets to leave Afghanistan by external pressures rather than through a resumption of dialogue and a search for collaborative measures.

The Carter administration, including the president as well as Secretary of State Vance and especially Brzezinski, had often referred to détente as involving a mix of cooperation and competition. They recognized the need to persist with efforts to mitigate the dangers of the American-Soviet rivalry by collaborative efforts as well as by unilateral adversarial moves. Secretary of State Vance, in his major speech on March 3, reiterated this position but with a new emphasis. As earlier noted, he stated that within the mix of competitive and cooperative elements "our relations with the Soviet Union have always been and will be essentially competitive." At the same time he reaffirmed that "our competition must be bounded by restraint and by sensitivity to each other's vital interests. For such a relationship between the two superpowers is central to peace."[14]

President Carter and Brzezinski saw American obligations as a superpower somewhat differently. While not disagreeing with the point Vance emphasized, they interpreted the Soviet action in Afghanistan as a challenge and, in Carter's case, apparently even as a threat to the United States. Accordingly Carter stressed his personal sense of responsibility that a stiff American response was the necessary reaction of "the other super power."[15]

In his action over Afghanistan Carter seemed—especially to the Soviet leaders—to be answering the challenge he had raised when he threw down the gauntlet of a choice between "confrontation or cooperation" in his speech at Annapolis in 1978. The Soviet leaders saw his move toward dismantling virtually the whole structure of détente built up in the 1970s not as a response (even an unjustified one) but as his choice for confrontation. To Carter it likewise seemed that the Soviets had chosen confrontation by their intervention in Afghanistan.

The Carter Doctrine and Containment

President Carter reacted to the Soviet intervention in Afghanistan by adopting a *posture* of confrontation while reaffirming an *aspiration* for détente, and without articulating a consistent *policy* for either. The closest approximation to a policy was the reaffirmation of and attempt to implement containment of Soviet expansionism.

---

fact." See "Jimmy Carter Talking about Himself . . . His Record . . . His Campaign," *Washington Post*, March 29, 1980.

14. *State Bulletin*, vol. 80 (April 1980), p. 13.

15. "Situation in Iran and Soviet Invasion of Afghanistan," Remarks at a White House Briefing for Members of Congress, January 8, *Presidential Documents*, vol. 16 (January 14, 1980), p. 41.

The Carter administration had two principal purposes in its new policy toward the Soviet Union. The first and most spontaneous was punitive—to demonstrate American outrage and opposition to the Soviet intervention in Afghanistan and to seek Soviet withdrawal or, at the least, to make the Soviets pay for their dastardly deed. Achieving this aim took the form of the grain embargo and other economic sanctions, along with curtailment of a wide range of other bilateral relations and efforts to mobilize allied, Islamic, and general world condemnation and sanctions. The initial unilateral American steps, and condemnations by the United Nations and the Islamic Conference, were supplemented by the campaign to boycott the Olympic Games in Moscow (an effort that met with only partial success).[16] But after that demonstrative gesture, little seemed to remain that could be done. The United States had played its full hand of cards in the first days after the Soviet action.

The second line in American policy was more substantial and more directed at preventing future Soviet aggrandizement elsewhere, rather than at registering disapproval and seeking to roll back the Soviet move in Afghanistan itself. Surprisingly little attention or analysis was given to the question whether, or under what circumstances, the Soviet Union would in fact be inclined to expand further. President Carter initially contributed to a rush to that judgment and the conclusion that only the United States could mobilize an effective deterrent by military and political containment. In unprepared remarks to members of Congress on January 8 he gave his own candid—and highly exaggerated—views:

In my own opinion . . . the Soviet invasion of Afghanistan is the greatest threat to peace since the Second World War. It's a sharp escalation in the aggressive history of the Soviet Union. . . . We are the other super power on Earth, and it became my responsibility, representing our great Nation, to take action that would prevent the Soviets from this invasion with impunity. The Soviets had to suffer the consequences. In my judgment our own Nation's security was directly threatened. There is no doubt that the Soviets' move into Afghanistan, if done without adverse consequences, would have resulted in the temptation to move again and again until they reached warm water ports or until they acquired control over a major portion of the world's oil supplies.[17]

This series of judgments no doubt reflected (as well as contributed further to) the prevailing American view. But it did not necessarily—and very likely did not, as the analysis shows—describe the real Soviet motivations.

As some began to question this reading of Soviet motivation, and hence of appropriate response, Carter stood fast on the course of action. He

---

16. In addition to the United States, West Germany, Japan, and China were among the sixty-four countries absenting themselves. On the other hand, teams from Great Britain, France, Italy, most other NATO countries, and India were among the eighty attending.

17. *Presidential Documents*, vol. 16 (January 14, 1980), pp. 40–41. Note the recurring references to an "invasion" rather than the occupation of Afghanistan—a term the president continued to favor for months. It implied an ongoing move that could be reversed, whereas occupation represented the settling down of a situation unlikely to be reversed.

grudgingly allowed that there was some uncertainty as to motivation and intention, but argued on grounds of prudence for the more dangerous assumption. "We cannot be certain," he said a few weeks later in February, ". . . if they seek colonial domination only in Afghanistan, or if they seek other conquests as well. No President of the United States can afford to gamble our peace and security upon wishful thinking about the present or the future intentions of the Soviet Union."[18]

By April Carter was saying that "*if* the invasion of Afghanistan does indeed foreshadow a pattern of Soviet behavior, then . . . we are in for challenging and very difficult times." By this time he had moved from his initial certainty to saying, "We cannot know with certainty the motivations of the Soviet move into Afghanistan, whether Afghanistan is the purpose or the prelude." But he remained sure that "regardless of its motives, there can be no doubt that the Soviet invasion poses an increased threat to the independence of nations in the region and to the world's access to vital resources and to vital sealanes."[19] And two days later he argued in an interview that if the United States and its allies did not stand united in taking "firm actions to show the Soviets that they will suffer" because of their action in Afghanistan, "that *might* lead to increasing encroachment by the Soviet Union against other countries."[20]

Containment as a policy to deter or deal with possible Soviet encroachments called for contingent preparations and warnings. Elements of punitive as well as deterrent action were, however, mixed in the Carter analysis and prescription for remedy. Moreover, containment came to fill the vacuum caused by shelving détente, rather than, as before, being one component in a strategy encompassing competition and cooperation. Containment of Soviet expansion had always remained one element in American policy under a strategy of détente. Now, however, it became the policy itself.

The new policy of containment involved several elements: (1) a pledge of American resolve and commitment to stop any further Soviet advance in the Southwest Asia–Persian Gulf area, buttressed by a series of political and military steps; (2) a more general diplomatic effort to confront Soviet power, including further play of the China card; and (3) a renewed stress on building American military power across the board—strategic forces and general purpose land, air, and seapower, as well as the Rapid Deployment Force. This policy was in part a response to the fall of the shah of Iran and the hostage crisis and in part to the Soviet move into Afghanistan. And it marked a significant shift. It reversed earlier initiatives of the Carter administration,

---

18. "American Legion: Remarks at the Legion's Annual Conference, February 19, 1980," *Presidential Documents*, vol. 16 (February 25, 1980), p. 345.

19. "American Society of Newspaper Editors, Remarks and a Question-and-Answer Session, April 10, 1980," *Presidential Documents*, vol. 16 (April 14, 1980), p. 635.

20. "Interview with the President: Question-and-Answer Session with Foreign Correspondents, April 12, 1980," *Presidential Documents*, vol. 16 (April 21, 1980), p. 673. Emphasis added.

some admittedly moribund by the end of 1979. Negotiations with the Soviet Union on demilitarization of the Indian Ocean and on restraining conventional arms sales to third countries were superseded by further massive buildup of the American naval presence in the Indian Ocean–Persian Gulf region, eager efforts to increase the supply of arms to Pakistan, Egypt, Saudi Arabia, and other friendly states in the region, and a quest for naval and air bases or use of facilities in Oman, Kenya, Somalia, and elsewhere. Other aspects of the administration's policy were also submerged; for example, nuclear nonproliferation and human rights considerations, which had led to curtailing assistance to Pakistan, were overridden.

The new containment approach marked a very fundamental revision of policy. The Carter Doctrine was not only a reaffirmation and extension of the Truman and Eisenhower Doctrines of an earlier political and geopolitical era; it was also in part a repudiation of the post-Vietnam Nixon Doctrine. No longer would the United States expect other countries in the first instance to defend their own security, nor would decisions about commitments by the United States to meet its interests be made on the basis of careful consideration of specific circumstances. For the Persian Gulf area explicitly, in President Carter's words, "An attempt by any outside force to gain control of the Persian Gulf region will be regarded as an assault on the vital interests of the United States of America, and such an assault will be repelled by any means necessary, including military force."[21] In later actions and statements this approach was applied more generally.

While the Carter Doctrine was specifically keyed to and prompted by the Soviet action in Afghanistan, the more specific measures adopted to support this policy had been under way for some time before that event. The Rapid Deployment Force had been proposed by Brzezinski in Presidential Review Memorandum (PRM)–10 in 1977 and approved by President Carter in August 1977. The conflict in the Horn of Africa in 1977–78 led to further attention to the idea, but nothing happened. The fall of the shah in January 1979 (and Saudi alarm over a flare-up of fighting in Yemen soon after)[22] bestirred Washington once again to consider the question. Brzezinski presented a new policy paper on that region to Carter on February 28, 1979, soon after a special visit there by Secretary of Defense Brown. It called for a more active U.S. military role. After Iran seized the American hostages in November, action studies were undertaken, and a study team was sent in December to the area to look into the availability of base facilities in Saudi Arabia, Oman, Somalia, and Kenya. This team returned shortly *before* the Soviet occupation of Afghanistan. So Afghanistan was but the immediately precipitating factor.

In following through on the development of regional security arrangements, in early February Brzezinski and Under Secretary of State Warren M. Christopher visited Pakistan and Saudi Arabia—the new American bastions

---

21. *Presidential Documents*, vol. 16 (January 28, 1980), p. 197.

22. See chapter 19.

in the region. While in Pakistan Brzezinski allowed himself to be photographed at the Khyber Pass with Afghanistan in the background—and in the foreground, in his hand, a Chinese-made AK-47 automatic rifle.[23] As earlier noted, Brzezinski also conducted negotiations in both countries on cooperation in providing assistance to the Afghan insurgents.[24]

While Soviet charges that the Carter administration used Afghanistan as a pretext for an intensified arms race are misplaced, it is true that those in the administration who favored a more rapid military buildup were able to press their case successfully. As Brzezinski subsequently put it, Afghanistan "permitted" politically a needed military buildup.[25] In addition to budget increases, active negotiations to obtain use of military facilities in the Indian Ocean–Persian Gulf area were pressed.

The increased military effort was focused not only on the Rapid Deployment Force and enhancement of conventional capabilities, nor just on substantial increases in military programs designed to enhance American capabilities to contain Soviet expansion, including programs to reinforce the strategic deterrent. As noted earlier, the administration developed a military doctrine that emphasized war-waging concepts. Most notable was the issuance in July, and public revelation in August, of Presidential Directive (PD)-59.[26]

On the diplomatic military-political front, in addition to the active measures in the Southwest Asia area—involving mobilization of unusable U.S. naval power in frustrated reaction to the Iranian hostage crisis—there was the American attempt to gain effective political containment of the Soviet Union. The strong verbal reaction of the thirty-four countries represented at the Islamic Conference in Islamabad marked a clear short-term blow, and less certain longer-term cost, to Soviet efforts to expand its influence in South Asia and the Middle East. Countries beholden to the Soviet Union such as South Yemen and Syria were discomfited, and many others were prepared to depart from neutralist nonalignment to criticize strongly the Soviet line. But this stand was a reaction to the Soviet intervention and not enlistment in an American-Soviet contest. The United States stressed the responsibility of an "atheistic" Soviet Union (President Carter even awkwardly *contrasted* the Soviet action against "deeply religious" Afghanistan with earlier Soviet action against—implicitly less religious—Hungary and Czechoslovakia).[27] Above all the United States attempted to convert Islamic and other third world criticism of the Soviet

---

23. Brzezinski is sensitive about this episode and exaggerated accounts in the U.S. press that had him firing the weapon. See Zbigniew Brzezinski, *Power and Principle: Memoirs of the National Security Adviser, 1977–1981* (Farrar, Straus, Giroux, 1983), p. 449.

24. See chapter 26.

25. George Urban, "A Long Conversation with Dr. Zbigniew Brzezinski," *Encounter* (May 1981), p. 21.

26. See chapter 22.

27. For example, see *Presidential Documents*, vol. 16 (January 14, 1980), p. 41, and (January 21, 1980), p. 91.

Union into a sort of alignment *with the United States* against the other super-power. But these efforts proved counterproductive. Most third world critics of the Soviet Union over Afghanistan remained, and were determined to remain, nonaligned—even if in some cases that meant tempering their expression of anger at the Soviet Union in order not to become tagged as part of an American coalition for containment.

Another specific result of the third world reaction was to quash Cuban aspirations for leadership in the Non-Aligned Movement. Cuba had come very close to obtaining a seat on the UN Security Council as chairman of the Non-Aligned Movement but had to withdraw after the Soviet intervention undermined its position. Initially the Cubans equivocated over whether to support the Soviet action but soon concluded that they had no choice but to fall into line. They cut their losses in the nonaligned world as best they could while becoming more obviously a dependency of the Soviet Union.

A fascinating question is whether the United States could have used this fleeting opportunity to improve relations with Fidel Castro and to reduce Cuban dependency on the Soviet Union. Carter had earlier established a confidential channel of communication with Castro, and in early January he was informed that Havana was interested in discussing the situation in Afghanistan and Iran. Carter hoped, without really expecting it, that Castro would condemn the Soviet action and boycott the Olympic Games in Moscow. Castro made clear to the American emissaries with whom he met in Havana on January 16–17 that he would not "betray" the Soviet leaders after their long support. He also made clear that there was little likelihood of any substantial improvement in Cuban relations with the United States as long as American-Soviet relations were poor. Nonetheless, Castro expressed a desire to move toward a better relationship with the United States and discussed his "problems with the Soviet Union," and his desire to withdraw his troops from Ethiopia.[28] These conversations continued nonstop for eleven hours, with Castro opening up after 3:00 a.m. with his most frank comments. The American participants were amazed to learn that the Soviet leaders had still not briefed Castro on what had happened in Afghanistan and why they had intervened. Castro was most interested in learning more about the situation from the Americans.[29] Subsequently U.S.-Cuban relations coasted until the mass exodus of Cuban emigrants from Mariel a few months later.[30]

The second major pillar of Carter's post-Afghanistan course of containment, paralleling his defense buildup and the Carter Doctrine centered on Southwest Asia, was the attempt to rally the NATO alliance and Western

---

28. This meeting was one of the few new disclosures in Carter's memoir; see *Keeping Faith*, pp. 479–80. The account here also benefited from an interview with Robert Pastor, then the Latin American specialist on the NSC staff and one of the two American emissaries.

29. Interview with Robert Pastor.

30. Meanwhile on February 29 the State Department announced that the Soviet brigade in Cuba was again engaged in a training exercise—rubbing salt into an earlier self-inflicted wound.

world into a punitive policy that would suspend East-West détente. The Europeans disapproved strongly of the Soviet occupation of Afghanistan. All were prepared to demonstrate that disapproval in the United Nations and to send diplomatic signals, for example, instructing the ambassadors of the NATO countries not to attend the Soviet National Day parade in Moscow.[31] Some were willing to join the boycott of the Olympics. But they were not prepared to jettison détente.

The East-West détente in Europe had different origins, wider impact, and deeper roots than the American-Soviet détente of the 1970s had.[32] But it was only after Afghanistan and the U.S. effort to make Soviet behavior a touchstone of East-West relations that the full extent of the difference, and its significance in both East-West and American-European relations, became evident.

While the Europeans saw Soviet behavior in Afghanistan as reprehensible, they saw détente in Europe as working—and working to their benefit. To them, sacrificing their interests by suspending détente in Europe would mean not only giving up something worthwhile, but possibly renewing tensions that had effectively been relaxed. This was a very important difference from the American perspective, and contributed to different reactions—and to an American-European rift on the issue.

In concrete terms the Europeans saw no benefit to themselves or, for that matter, to the Afghans in curtailing trade with the Soviet Union. They certainly were not prepared to make that sacrifice for a punitive policy with no clear purpose. The result was that while American-Soviet trade plummeted by nearly 60 percent in 1980, after the Soviet Union turned to Europe, in that same year Soviet-French trade increased by 100 percent, Soviet–West German trade by 65 percent, and Soviet-Japanese and Soviet-Italian trade by 35 percent each.[33] This eagerness of its allies not only to continue trading but to pick up the slack in American trade was not appreciated in the United States, and contributed to reciprocal U.S.-European unhappiness over the issue.

The Europeans also objected to, and were concerned about, the manner and terms of the swing in U.S. policy, as well as its direction and consequences. The failure of Washington to consult (and when it did to give conflicting signals) before unilaterally announcing the sanctions and the boycott of the Olympic Games further undercut support that might have been rallied for some of these moves (and provided a further excuse for those who would not have concurred in any case). There was little confidence in American leadership. President Carter had put the U.S. government out on a limb over the unacceptability of the continued presence of a Soviet brigade in Cuba a

---

31. The ambassadors of the NATO countries all absented themselves on November 7 of both 1980 and 1981. By 1982 several attended, ending the ambassadorial boycott.

32. See chapters 4 and 14.

33. Data from Kempton Jenkins, president of the U.S.-USSR Trade Council.

few months earlier. He had undercut U.S. support for his own SALT II Treaty before having to back down. The Europeans were certainly not disposed to place *their* détente in jeopardy over the question of the acceptability of continued Soviet presence in Afghanistan, no matter how distasteful that presence was.

Thus a disjunction in both perspective and reaction led to mutual European and American complaints and resentment. A British parliamentary committee commented on "inadequate consultation among alliance members before it was decided to impose sanctions," while a U.S. congressional committee report declared that "the reactions of the allies have been found wanting."[34]

When West German Chancellor Helmut Schmidt and French President Valéry Giscard d'Estaing met in Paris in early 1980, as Washington was—with enthusiasm in some quarters—pronouncing détente dead, they declared that pursuit of détente had become "more difficult" as a result of "the Afghanistan incident." The furthest they would go was to warn the Soviet leaders that "detente would probably not be able to withstand another shock of the same type." In other words, détente *had* withstood *this* shock; its pursuit was more difficult but not impossible *or* undesirable. Détente was very much still alive. After President Carter's initial alarmist statements Schmidt had said, "We will not permit ten years of detente and defense policy to be destroyed." Giscard had spoken of keeping Europe out of U.S.-Soviet "bloc politics" and had said that "the balance of power in Europe is a separate problem."[35] The Europeans also did not, by and large, see the same degree of threat for the future from the Soviet action that the Carter administration (and many, probably most, Americans) did. Finally, in the United States abstaining from détente was not only a less onerous sacrifice, but was also considered more advantageous in domestic political terms—while the opposite was true in Europe.

Some American critics of the European stand regarded it as too insular, too much focused on the European peninsula, with too little attention to the global picture. But many Europeans were looking at the situation across

34. Both are cited by Harry S. Bradsher, *Afghanistan and the Soviet Union* (Durham, N.C.: Duke University Press, 1983), p. 199. See also *East-West Relations in the Aftermath of Soviet Invasion of Afghanistan*, Hearings before the Subcommittee on Europe and the Middle East of the House Foreign Affairs Committee, 96 Cong. 2 sess., January 24 and 30, 1980 (Washington, D.C.: Government Printing Office, 1980); and *An Assessment of the Afghanistan Sanctions: Implications for Trade and Diplomacy in the 1980's*, Report prepared for the Subcommittee on Europe and the Middle East of the House Foreign Affairs Committee (GPO, 1981), pp. 98–110.

35. See James O. Goldsborough, "Europe Cashes in on Carter's Cold War," *New York Times Magazine*, April 27, 1980, pp. 42ff., for a further review of differing European reactions. See also John Vinocur, "Schmidt Still Plans Moscow Trip," Flora Lewis, "How Critical a Crisis?" and James Reston, "The Allies' Doubting Assent," all in *New York Times*, January 18, 1980.

a wide geopolitical horizon and with greater historical experience, and therefore reached different conclusions from the Carter administration.[36]

The American reaction under the Carter administration in 1980 was to deprive the Soviet Union of the fruits of détente as a punishment for its assertiveness in the third world. The Soviet Union was considered to have passed a threshold of tolerance by its direct military intervention in Afghanistan. But détente remained a recourse if and when the Soviet leaders learned their lesson and withdrew from Afghanistan. The Carter approach intended merely to shelve détente, although in practice Carter turned to a policy of containment and even confrontation. Later the Reagan administration would purposefully repudiate and discard détente.

As seen by many in Europe, the new American policy of containment in response to perceived Soviet global challenges in the third world threatened to make Europe—the first and second "worlds"—an arena of reprisal for Soviet actions in Asia and Africa. The United States, in short, was playing a European card in a global game. But the Europeans did not see that their interests were served by being a card for the United States to play over Afghanistan. Moreover, the stakes were theirs, more than the Americans'. Earlier the Europeans had balked at being a card in Kissinger's ill-conceived Year of Europe in the heyday of détente in 1973. They certainly did not want to become hostage to mercurial American and Soviet imperial confrontation in a new cold war.

In April the Europeans gave great attention to the twenty-fifth anniversary of the Austrian State Treaty—the first major step in the post-Stalin détente between East and West in Europe and universally regarded as a solid achievement. On May 19 President Giscard, without advance consultation or even notification, met Brezhnev in Warsaw. At the end of June Chancellor Schmidt visited Moscow, after a consultation between himself and President Carter that involved a partly publicized nasty exchange of nonconfidence. More generally, Carter and some other American spokesmen displayed irritation over the continuation of European détente by the Western allies.[37]

The most evident disarray in the Western position involved economic relations. Not only did the European countries not join in the U.S. economic sanctions, but within a few months France, West Germany, Italy, and Japan held high-level bilateral talks on the *expansion* of trade with the Soviet Union. A number of trade deals previously expected to be concluded with American firms went instead to European firms, including $118 million for offshore oil-drilling rigs (to the French) and expertise for a plant to produce

---

36. For instance, while naturally they did not draw attention to the example, the British could recall their *own* occupations of Afghanistan over a century of geopolitical containment of Russia and place the current event in a broader historical context.

37. In particular, see Carter's comments in a news briefing on April 12, *Presidential Documents*, vol. 16 (April 21, 1980), p. 675. On the June contretemps with Schmidt see chapter 25.

blue jeans (to the Italians). Some contracts with American firms canceled by the U.S. government, including a $353 million specialty steel mill and a $100 million aluminum plant, were later replaced by deals with European firms.

Business as usual, abjured after Afghanistan by the United States but not by the Europeans, did not only mean commerce. Nor was its value to the Europeans only economic and financial. For example, in 1979, 8 million Germans visited back and forth between West and East Germany. A deeply felt issue was that no one in Europe wanted to be responsible for renewed tensions over Berlin because of anything happening in Kabul. Nor did the Europeans see developments elsewhere in the world as simply part of a Soviet-American game of diplomatic-military chess. For example, Western Europeans, especially the Social Democrats in several countries (including the government in West Germany) decided to support the Sandinistas in Nicaragua so that they would not become dependent on Cuba and the Soviet Union. The renewed propensity to draw a line of containment made the United States less prepared to support such a strategy (or to appreciate its pursuit by allies).

In the field of security, NATO concentrated on consolidating the decision to deploy long-range theater nuclear weapons. For some months Soviet objections and equivocation were responsible for a delay in starting the parallel track of arms control negotiations on theater nuclear weapons (TNF). But after mid-year the Soviets were prepared to start, and in October–November preliminary talks were held in Geneva.[38] Similarly, the MBFR talks continued, Afghanistan notwithstanding, with the Soviets submitting proposals in July, no doubt introduced at that juncture to reinforce their image of desire and readiness to continue to develop European security measures under détente. Soon after the Soviets announced completion of the unilateral withdrawal of 20,000 men and 1,000 tanks from Europe.[39] And in November 1980 a new round of Conference on Security and Cooperation in Europe (CSCE) talks opened in Madrid. In December Poland formally proposed, on behalf of the Warsaw Pact, convening a Conference on Military Détente and Disarmament in Europe, while the Soviet Union offered for the first time to apply some confidence-building measures in its own territory. But the American failure to ratify SALT II and the equivocation on TNF talks by both sides contributed to a period in which the various parties did little more than go through the motions in the whole field of arms control and security. Indeed, in the CSCE talks in Madrid the West focused almost exclusively on berating the

---

38. See chapter 25. These talks were resumed as negotiations on intermediate-range nuclear forces (INF) in November 1981; see chapter 28.

39. The net effect of this move was unclear, since the Soviets also carried out some offsetting improvements in the capabilities of existing forces. The Soviet Union did withdraw one tank division, although it was given virtually no public notice in the West. On the MBFR talks see chapter 22.

Soviet Union over Afghanistan and over shortcomings in human rights practices in communist countries.[40]

Late in 1980 events in Poland seemed to pose a threat of Soviet military intervention. NATO and the United States warned the Soviet leaders of the adverse impact on East-West relations of such a move. While intervention did not occur, the developments in Poland had negative effects on East-West relations. They became another subject of debate in the Madrid CSCE talks, and the Soviet Union and several countries in Eastern Europe resumed jamming of Western Russian-language and other Eastern European–language broadcasts.

Meanwhile, the United States continued its sanctions and policy of containment. On February 28 Secretary of State Vance had advised the president of indirect communications from several Soviet leaders—Party Secretary and Politburo candidate member Boris Ponomarev and Foreign Trade Minister Nikolai Patolichev—that hinted at Soviet concessions on Afghanistan in exchange for reconsideration of U.S. sanctions. He also noted that Ambassador Dobrynin had indicated a desire for a formal meeting between Vance and Foreign Minister Gromyko, proposing a date in March. Vice President Mondale and Brzezinski feared, however, that the United States would appear weak or vacillating, and Carter himself was opposed. Vance suggested as an alternative a letter from Carter to Brezhnev, perhaps to be taken to Moscow by his special assistant on Soviet affairs, Marshall Shulman. But after some maneuvering by both Vance and Brzezinski over Carter's approval, the idea was rejected. Vance did write to Gromyko on February 8 (with Carter's agreement, although without Brzezinski's knowledge). In mid-March he asked Dobrynin to tell Gromyko that he hoped to get together with him in April or May.[41] But before that could come about, Vance had left the administration.

While the resignation of Vance as secretary of state in April was keyed directly to the decision by President Carter to attempt to rescue the American hostages in Iran by force, it was also symbolic of the sharp change in American-Soviet relations after Afghanistan. Vance's successor, Edmund S. Muskie, was bound by circumstances as well as the short term remaining (as determined by the election in November) to an interim role. In May and again in September Muskie did meet with Gromyko, but there was little significance to the meetings beyond their occurrence. Late in 1979 Carter had sent a distinguished businessman, Thomas Watson, to be the new ambassador to Moscow

---

40. The American approach to the Madrid meeting had been evident in Carter's selection of Max M. Kampelman to head the U.S. delegation. Kampelman, a neoconservative Democrat, was the first member of the Committee on the Present Danger to be named to a government post. He was sufficiently in tune with the views of the succeeding Reagan administration to become the only official of that rank kept on under that administration.

41. See Brzezinski, *Power and Principle*, pp. 435–37; and Cyrus Vance, *Hard Choices: Critical Years in America's Foreign Policy* (Simon and Schuster, 1983), pp. 394–95.

and to assist in a renewal of détente after the Vienna summit. But Watson had scarcely arrived before being recalled for consultations at the end of the year in a symbolic demonstration of American disapproval of the Soviet intervention in Afghanistan.

The Iranian hostage problem was compounded by the eruption of a war between Iraq and Iran in September, when Iraq escalated from border skirmishes to a large-scale invasion. To the surprise of the Iraqis and many others, Iran did not collapse and after a time stabilized the military situation (and later drove the Iraqis out of the country). From the standpoint of American-Soviet relations, this war further reduced Iraqi confidence in the Soviet Union (although it did not lead, as Brzezinski hoped, to an Iraqi-Soviet break and a sharp Iraqi turn to the West). Both the Soviet Union and the United States were concerned about the effects of that war on the stability of the area, and both saw their interests as best served by not siding with either party and by keeping a low profile. The Soviet leaders were, however, able to use the Iraqi turn to closer ties with Jordan and Egypt to get Syria to accept a Treaty of Friendship and Cooperation in October (just a year after it had signed a similar treaty with South Yemen).

The Vietnamese continued to encounter resistance in their campaign in Kampuchea. The United States characterized that campaign as part of a Soviet expansionist surge in the arc of crisis from the Horn of Africa to Indochina. In March the United States had warned the Soviets that establishment of Soviet military bases in Vietnam would require the United States to take unspecified countermeasures. (At least it finally avoided the term "unacceptable" for something it opposed but could not prevent.) Nonetheless, owing to the greater Vietnamese dependence on the Soviet Union as a result of the Chinese attack the previous year, Vietnam did (despite earlier refusal and reluctance) make naval and air facilities available for Soviet operational use, even if not formally as Soviet "bases."

The final and especially significant element in U.S. global efforts at containment of the Soviet Union (design would be an overstatement) was still closer alignment with China.

The China Card Again

The American policy of developing relations with China had its own momentum. The next stage began with the visit of Secretary of Defense Brown in January 1980. This visit had been scheduled several months earlier, but took on a new significance in light of the sharp downturn in U.S.-Soviet relations.

In Washington a new play of the China card seemed to fit the new mood and turn of policy. That it would provoke the Soviet leaders had been a strong argument *against* any far-reaching military cooperation as late as the November–December preparations for Brown's visit. Now, in the final days before Brown's departure, it appeared to the administration that that effect was a plus. Moreover, at this juncture the United States and China could, it was believed, concert their efforts more effectively to contain the Soviet Union.

It was thought that some demonstrative new action was called for as a sign of U.S. readiness to develop security relations with China.[42] As noted earlier, the decision to open an American-Chinese security relationship on the basis of patently anti-Soviet containment was reached over the strong objection of Secretary of State Vance, but President Carter supported the view of Brzezinski and Brown.[43]

Brzezinski (identified only as "a senior official") told the *New York Times* that the Soviet invasion of Afghanistan had given Secretary of Defense Brown's mission "a new dimension" and that "the Soviets have forced us and the Chinese into a posture in which we both see the world in the same way." He commented that many now saw closer security ties with Peking as "a principal way" the United States could respond to the Soviet actions.[44]

Brown's visit of January 6–13, 1980, was important more for what it symbolized than for its concrete agreements. Nonetheless, it did initiate consideration of a range of areas for political and military cooperation. As a demonstrative gesture the United States made available for purchase a receiving station for the Landsat-D earth satellite, to be used for economic and scientific research surveys of China. Brown also told the Chinese leaders that the United States was prepared to consider authorizing exports of dual-purpose technology and equipment suitable for military as well as civilian uses on a case-by-case basis. But the United States did not modify its ban on the sale of weapons.

The United States proposed, but the Chinese declined, establishment of a hot-line direct communications link. This response was unexpected; the Chinese indicated they regarded it as something more appropriate between

---

42. In addition, it was considered necessary to offset another move that had gone forward under its own momentum. As a concomitant to the termination of the Mutual Defense Treaty with Taiwan on December 31, the United States—on the basis of plans and commitments made long before—resumed sale of military equipment and arms to Taiwan on January 2. China immediately protested this action.

43. See Vance, *Hard Choices*, pp. 390–91; Brzezinski, *Power and Principle*, pp. 431–33; and, in a revealingly naïve passing reference, Carter states that the Soviet action made it "easier" for him now to "strengthen our ties with other countries who were naturally fearful of Soviet aggression, including China." Carter, *Keeping Faith*, p. 475.

44. Richard Burt, "U.S. Looks to China for Aid to Pakistan," *New York Times*, January 3, 1980. Another account, reporting on the same background briefing, said, "In the last 10 days, the Russians have forced us to look at the world the way the Chinese do." Michael Parks, "Brown Trip a Warning to Soviet," *Baltimore Sun*, January 6, 1980. Brzezinski and Brown have both confirmed to me the new significance of the Brown mission after Afghanistan.

adversaries than between friends.[45] Brown also discussed American arms control policy and sought to open a dialogue that the United States hoped might lead to Chinese accession to the Threshold Nuclear Test Ban Treaty.

The most noteworthy element of the Brown visit at the time seemed to be its symbolization of increasing collaboration in opposing the Soviet Union. The Chinese were pleased at the collapse of American-Soviet détente and the much tougher U.S. line. They had also used the rapprochement with the United States as protection in repudiating the Sino-Soviet Treaty of 1950 in 1979. But they were not as ready as the Americans had assumed to join in an alignment with the United States in which *they* would be committed and, given the realities of power, could only be the junior partner. Moreover, they probably regarded this sudden swing in the American policy pendulum as being of uncertain force and duration.

The Carter administration basically misjudged Chinese policy. Intent on playing the China card (enthusiastically in the case of Brzezinski, with considerable reservations in the case of Vance, and with Carter, swept by events, supporting Brzezinski), the administration took the Chinese position at face value as a given—adamantly anti-Soviet and completely receptive to whatever extent of alignment the United States would be prepared to accept. In fact, the Chinese objectives shifted as certain of them were secured.

The highest Chinese priority from 1969 through 1979 had been to prevent a Soviet-American entente and condominium at China's expense— which, in fact, the Soviet leaders had sought and which fitted some elements of American policy.[46] The second objective was to prevent a Soviet-American détente that would permit the Soviet Union to exert effective pressure on China. This aim called for spoiling action to encourage U.S.-Soviet tension, but without a commitment of China to the American side. Their third priority was to build Chinese-American ties not only to counterbalance and limit American-Soviet ties, but also to benefit other Chinese purposes. But along with these objectives, the Chinese intended to maintain an independent stance and to bid for independent influence in the world in competition with the United States as well as the Soviet Union. The U.S. reaction to Afghanistan consolidated the first and second of these objectives and furthered the third, but none of this meant that China would abandon the parallel fourth objective and join an American-led coalition. This stance was not, however, clear to American policymakers in 1980 (or subsequently).

The Chinese had strongly criticized the Soviet military intervention in Afghanistan from the outset. On December 31 they stated that it "poses a direct threat to the security of China." On January 20 they announced that in

---

45. The Chinese had agreed to Soviet proposals to reinstate a telephonic hot line in 1970, after abruptly cutting off that contact when the Soviets tried to use it in March 1969; see chapter 6.

46. In the mid-1960s the U.S. government had, as the Chinese probably knew, considered unilateral action, and even possible tacit collusive action with the Soviet Union, to eliminate Chinese nuclear weapons facilities. I was involved in these internal deliberations.

view of the threat to "world peace and the security of China" posed by the Soviet invasion of Afghanistan, China had decided to cancel the Sino-Soviet negotiations resumed only four months earlier.[47]

Condemnation of the Soviet action was an area of easy Sino Ameri can agreement. En route to Beijing Brown had referred to the Soviet action in Afghanistan "and Chinese and U.S. reactions to it" as "one example of a broader relationship on a global or strategic level in which the United States and China find it in the self-interest of each of us to concert parallel responses to the world situation." On the first day of the visit he stated publicly that the United States and China could respond with "complementary actions in the field of defense as well as diplomacy" if their "shared interests" were threatened. And he proposed exchanging views on how the two countries "might facilitate wider cooperation on security matters."[48] The Chinese, however, preferred to attack Soviet behavior rather than to commit themselves to openended collaboration with the United States.

When Brown proposed concrete measures for cooperation in the supply of American arms to Pakistan, the Chinese were noncommittal, perhaps aware of Pakistani reticence. Brown also proposed direct cooperation in military assistance to Thailand should Vietnam attack that country.

Most topical, but by their nature most sensitive, were talks on possible direct counteractions to the Soviet intervention in Afghanistan, including assistance to the growing anti-Soviet resistance within that country.[49] A press article, citing unnamed administration officials, stated that the Chinese leaders said they were ready to increase the covert flow of Chinese arms to rebels in Afghanistan, which they had earlier been supplying to Afghans in Pakistan.[50] On January 20 Chinese Foreign Minister Huang Hua arrived in Islamabad to discuss with Pakistani leaders the implications of the Soviet intervention in Afghanistan for the security of both countries—and undoubtedly to talk about assistance to the insurgents.

Soon after the Brown visit Secretary of State Vance sought to put the Chinese-American security relationship into perspective. He stated in an interview that both Americans and Chinese would each pursue the courses they considered to be correct. "There may be a degree of parallelism on steps

47. Xinhua [New China News Agency], January 20, in *Foreign Broadcast Information Service, Daily Report: People's Republic of China*, January 21, 1980, p. C1.

48. For the statement en route, see Parks, *Baltimore Sun*, January 6, 1980; and see Fox Butterfield, "Defense Secretary Arrives in China for 8-Day Visit," *New York Times*, January 6, 1980. For the second quotation, see Jay Mathews, "Brown Seeks Chinese Military Cooperation," *Washington Post*, January 7, 1980.

49. Senior members of the Carter administration have confirmed, although not for attribution, that this subject was discussed during the Brown visit and acted upon subsequently, but they declined to disclose details.

50. Richard Halloran, "Peking Reported to Offer More Guns to Afghan Rebels," *New York Times*, January 17, 1980.

that should be taken in connection with Afghanistan. But that does not mean that there is any military alliance or such relationship between the United States and China."[51] The thrust of this statement not only differed from that of the Brown visit, but was also offset by an official public announcement by the Department of Defense eight days later that the United States was ready to sell dual-purpose technology (such as communications equipment and early warning radar) to China.[52] This was the same technology long barred from sale to the Soviet Union.

On January 24, the same day as the Pentagon announcement, Congress approved the U.S.-China Trade Agreement with its grant of most-favored-nation (MFN) status.[53] On October 22 a grain sales agreement was concluded providing for a minimum annual sale of six million tons for each of the next four years.

It should again be remarked that even in the heyday of the post-Afghanistan spurt of American-Chinese rapprochement there were signs of new restraint by China that suggested reservations about too close a relationship. For example, on January 11 China absented itself from the meeting rather than support the United States in a key UN vote on sanctions against Iran for holding the American hostages.

Nonetheless, the course of developing relations continued, including the new element of military contact and security relationships. Numerous visits by officials, members of Congress, and others continued. New York and Beijing officially became "sister cities" on February 28. In all, over 1,000 Chinese delegations visited the United States in 1980, while 5,000 Chinese students (not counting 15,000 from Taiwan) were studying there. Some 60,000 Americans visited China during the year. And trade rose from virtually nothing a decade earlier to about $5 billion in 1980, exceeding U.S. trade with the Soviet Union for the first time (although still a little under half the value of trade with Taiwan).[54]

On the military side, from May 5 to June 18 the Deputy Chief of Staff of the People's Liberation Army (PLA), Liu Huaqing, led a delegation to the United States. It visited industrial and military facilities, including the North American Aerospace Defense Command (NORAD). During that visit Vice Premier Geng Biao (who soon after became minister of national defense) arrived with another high-level PLA group, returning the visit by Secretary of

---

51. *New York Times*, January 16, 1980 (and *State Bulletin*, vol. 80 [March 1980], p. 39).

52. "U.S.-China Discuss Sale of Military Technology," Defense Department Statement, January 24, *State Bulletin*, vol. 80 (March 1980), p. 45.

53. Some in Congress had argued in hearings in November for a parallel decision with respect to the Soviet Union. After Afghanistan that idea evaporated. Approval of the China trade agreement was overwhelming—294–88 in the House and 74–8 in the Senate.

54. Damian T. Gullo, "China's Hard Currency Export Potential and Import Capacity through 1985," *China under the Four Modernizations*, Selected Papers Submitted to the Joint Economic Committee, 97 Cong. 2 sess. (GPO, 1982), pt. 2, pp. 104–08.

Defense Brown. They were received by President Carter, Vice President Mondale, National Security Adviser Brzezinski, and Secretary of State Muskie. They also met military leaders and toured military facilities. By mid-year the United States had quietly changed the Munitions Control List for China, shifting that country out of the same category as Warsaw Pact states and into a category that permitted American firms to build military equipment plants in China. From September 16 to 19 Under Secretary of Defense for Research and Engineering William J. Perry visited China to continue talks on technology transfer and to tour Chinese facilities. He also was able to report approval of export licenses for some 400 items in the area of advanced technology in military support equipment.[55] Immediately after, from September 21 to October 6, a fourteen-man PLA delegation visited the United States to study the U.S. military logistics system. From October 11 to 28 Deputy Minister of National Defense Xiao Ke led a delegation that visited the senior American military academies and war colleges.

The only dispute that arose within the Carter administration, once the question of military sales had been resolved early in the year, was of a different character: whether, in view of the human rights record of China, a request to purchase police equipment should be granted. The decision was deferred.

During Vice Premier Geng Biao's visit in May, Brzezinski, as he has since disclosed, used the occasion to discuss in detail reactions to the Soviet intervention in Afghanistan. He also advanced as his own interpretation that the Soviet leaders were pursuing "a two-pronged offensive strategy, one pointing through Afghanistan at the Persian Gulf and one through Cambodia at the Strait of Malacca." Geng, he notes, "very much liked that analysis, and I was amused to hear him, as well as Deng Xiaoping, repeat it to me as the Chinese view of Soviet strategy when I visited Beijing in 1981." All in all, Brzezinski concludes, "what had started as an exercise in evenhandedness [in U.S. relations with China and the Soviet Union] by 1980 became demonstrably a tilt, driven by stark strategic realities."[56] Brzezinski is perhaps too modest; his own contribution in effecting the shift was considerable.

Some friction remained in American-Chinese relations, particularly over Taiwan. The *Washington Post* published excerpts from a secret Chinese speech in which the Chinese people were told that the American imperialists were as bad as ever and that the Sino-American rapprochement was merely "tactical," a united front against Soviet hegemonism, thus casting doubt on the future of Sino-American relations.[57] If the Chinese authorities were embarrassed by that revelation, so was the U.S. government when the same newspa-

---

55. Brzezinski, *Power and Principle*, p. 424.

56. Ibid., pp. 424–25.

57. Jay Mathews, "Scathing Critique of American Life Surfaces in Peking," *Washington Post*, March 31, 1980.

per later disclosed that American strategic nuclear targeting under PD-59 included about 100 targets in China.[58] This disclosure proved very disturbing to the Chinese leaders.[59]

The Soviet role remained essentially reactive. As one immediate response to the Soviet military intervention in Afghanistan, China declined to resume the bilateral talks with Moscow that had been started only three months earlier after six months of preliminary maneuvering. The Soviet Union thus had no leverage with either the United States or China and could do little but complain about the Brown visit and other moves in the U.S.-Chinese rapprochement, now developing in the military as well as in the political and economic spheres.

The Central Committee of the Communist Party of the Soviet Union at a special session in June devoted to reevaluating the international situation in light of the virtual break in Soviet-American relations stated unequivocally: "The rapprochement between aggressive circles of the West, above all the United States, with the Chinese leadership is taking place on an anti-Soviet basis, hostile to peace. The partnership of imperialism and Peking hegemonism is a dangerous new phenomenon in world politics, dangerous to all mankind, including the American and Chinese peoples."[60]

The development of American-Chinese relations in 1980 was thus distinguished by a conjunction of two developments, each perceived as adverse to Soviet interests and together seen as alarming. A move toward military contact would have been a source of concern in any case, but in the context of the American jettisoning of détente with the Soviet Union and turn to confrontation it appeared even more dangerous.

Even under these circumstances Moscow was divided over the seriousness of the Sino-American rapprochement and its future. While all saw the trend as adverse, some experts on China and America in Moscow continued to predict that American and Chinese interests would remain distinct and would sooner or later lead to an erosion of the newfound partnership and even to a clash of interests.[61] Taiwan was one such potential stumbling block, but not

58. Jack Anderson, "U.S. Strategic Targets Include China," *Washington Post*, October 3, 1980.

59. Chinese officials privately showed real concern over this disclosure and seemed shocked. The seriousness of the matter was also evident in the *absence* of Chinese press criticism or commentary of any kind; to my knowledge the matter was never mentioned in the Chinese press, only in confidential internal Chinese governmental summaries of the foreign press. The Soviet media, as would be expected, did exploit the matter (including broadcasts beamed to China), seeking to stir up Chinese suspicion and to weaken Chinese ties with the United States. See, for example, V. Skvortsov, "Who's Kidding Whom?" *Pravda*, October 5, 1980; broadcast internationally on Radio Moscow, October 5, in Foreign Broadcast Information Service, *Daily Report: Soviet Union*, October 7, 1980, p. AA1. (Hereafter FBIS, *Soviet Union*.)

60. "On the International Situation and the Foreign Policy of the Soviet Union: A Resolution of the Plenum of the Central Committee of the CPSU, June 23, 1980," *Kommunist* [The Communist], no. 10 (July 1980), p. 9.

61. For example, see V. P. Lukin, "Washington-Beijing: 'Quasi Allies?' " *SShA: Ekonomika, politika, ideologiya* [USA: Economics, Politics, Ideology], no. 12 (December 1979), pp. 54–55 (here-

the only one. Moreover, Soviet commentary took note of the fact that a ban on American supply of weapons to China continued in effect, although without publicly giving the Carter administration credit for that restraint. Nonetheless, there had clearly been a shift adverse to Soviet interests, even if not yet dangerous and perhaps not irrevocable. And the Soviets had no means by which to affect the situation.

Some elements in the Soviet leadership gave special emphasis to the potential dangers. The military in particular were prone to see and stress these dangers. Marshal Ogarkov told a large military conference in June: "The strengthening of a military-political rapprochement of the United States, China and Japan, attempts to form a united anti-Soviet front in which the military power of the United States and the European NATO countries in the West would be combined with the manpower resources of China and the industrialization potential of Japan in the East, represents a serious threat to peace [that is, to the Soviet Union]. By widening military contacts with China and increasing its acquisition of military equipment and technology, the Western powers count on pushing Peking into openly aggressive actions against our country and the states of Southeast Asia."[62] The threat of Chinese aggressive actions against the Soviet Union may or may not have been regarded as real; the threat to Soviet interests and allies in Indochina surely was.

As Central Committee official Valentin Falin put it: "The Sino-American rapprochement and cooperation has already produced one war. A year ago, right after Deng Xiaoping's visit to the United States, China perpetrated aggression against Vietnam. Perhaps inspired by U.S. support, which already transcends the forms of mere political support—the United States has said it is ready to supply China with military hardware and technology—China may be encouraged to some other adventures. Who knows?"[63]

Falin also ascribed an important role to China in changing overall U.S. policy from détente to confrontation. "There is no doubt," he said, "that China played an important role in the unfavorable turn of United States policy. China, as the White House expected, offered the United States a chance to change the correlation of forces." He cited a recent statement by Secretary of Defense Brown (in his annual report to Congress) that China formed an important element in the defense of U.S. interests in Asia. And for its part,

after *SShA*); and A. A. Nagorny and A. B. Parkansky, "U.S. Scientific-Technical Contacts with China," *SShA*, no. 8 (August 1980), pp. 36–37. Even some military writers noted the contradictions in Sino-American ties; see Major General D. Volkogonov, "Irreconcilability toward Maoism—The Ideology and Policy of War," *Kommunist vooruzhennykh sil* [Communist of the Armed Forces], no. 9 (May 1980), p. 79. (Hereafter *KVS*.)

62. Speech of Marshal Nikolai Ogarkov, chief of the General Staff and first deputy minister of defense, "In the Interests of Raising Combat Readiness," June 3, *KVS*, no. 14 (July 1980), p. 26. This excerpt was not included in an abbreviated account of Ogarkov's speech published in "Raising the Educational Role of the Soviet Armed Forces," *Krasnaya zvezda* [Red Star] on June 5, 1980.

63. Valentin Falin, Studio 9, Moscow Domestic Television, March 1, in FBIS, *Soviet Union*, March 14, 1980, p. A8.

"China is cooperating with the United States on a temporary basis while it is profitable for China. It uses U.S. overtures and U.S. support to achieve its aims which probably have little in common with U.S. aims."[64]

There is quite a difference in nuance between Ogarkov's and Falin's judgments as to the solidity of the rapprochement in American-Chinese relations—and even of the motivations for it. Nonetheless, both saw the rapprochement and its anti-Soviet basis as a reality. And that view affected the general tone of Soviet commentary. For example, most Soviet accounts in 1980 went much further than in 1979 to allege American approval of the Chinese invasion of Vietnam.[65]

Differences among Soviet observers notwithstanding, within the general context of reevaluating Soviet policy following the serious setback in Afghanistan itself, and the *de facto* U.S. repudiation of the policy of détente, Moscow saw the American-Chinese rapprochement as posing an additional current problem and potential serious threat.[66]

To the extent that the United States sought to heighten Soviet fears, it succeeded. But there is no indication that the Soviet leaders saw their own action in Afghanistan as the real *cause* of the further U.S. turn to China in 1980. Rather, that turn seemed to justify Soviet concern over the vulnerability of the Afghan link in a chain of Sino-American encirclement. As for the Chinese, rather than accepting a role in an American-led grand coalition, they saw both a need and an opportunity, given the collapse of Soviet-American détente, to take a more independent stance in the world. In addition, they saw that they could eventually improve their leverage vis-à-vis both the Soviet Union and the United States in the triangular relationship.

Soviet Policy

While U.S. foreign policy in 1980 was focused above all on the hostages in Iran and on mobilizing a counterreaction to the Soviet occupation of Afghanistan, the Soviet leaders concentrated on the American reaction to Afghanistan and on keeping East-West détente alive, which meant in part frustrating or limiting American moves to bury it. The range of other Soviet

---

64. Ibid., pp. A6, A8.

65. For example, see V. Teplov, "To Uphold the Policy of Detente," *International Affairs*, no. 5 (May 1980), p. 104; V. Andreyev, "The Partnership between Peking and Imperialism—a Threat to Peace and Independence," ibid., no. 11 (November 1980), p. 76; and D. Kapustin, " 'Big Zbig' and His Trump Card," ibid., p. 103.

66. A senior Soviet diplomat privately commented to me that while China would not be a real military threat to the Soviet Union for many years, even with some American military assistance, to Moscow the most seriously disturbing element was that it put the *United States* and its aims in a different light.

policy objectives were for the most part also reactive and closely tied to relations with the United States: in Europe, to roll back the NATO TNF decision of December 1979, as well as to minimize the damage Afghanistan might cause to East-West détente; in the third world, to minimize the negative impact of Afghanistan (and to pressure Cuba and Syria to show support for the Soviet Union); to prevent the United States from building military bases in Southwest Asia and the Indian Ocean area; and with China, while there were no prospects for renewed diplomatic dialogue in the near term, to reaffirm Soviet desire to improve relations.

The Soviet leaders had clearly underestimated the American reaction to their move in Afghanistan. (To the extent that the American response was an overreaction, it may have been a rational estimate even if mistaken.) There was never any possibility that the Carter administration's punitive sanctions would lead the Soviet leaders to withdraw from Afghanistan. While their decision to intervene had been a difficult one, once the action was taken the stakes changed completely; while the world political costs were higher than expected, a withdrawal would be even more costly. On the other hand, the American reaction did lead the Soviets to reconsider and reinterpret U.S. policy, in addition to stimulating new Soviet countermoves.

As early as January 6, 1980, two days after President Carter's Address to the Nation, TASS issued the initial official Soviet reaction. It stressed the "lack of balance" in the American position, which showed "disregard for the fundamental long-term interests of peace, relaxation of international tension, and constructive development of Soviet-American relations." The sanctions involved "violation of agreements." Carter's speech was "permeated with the spirit of the cold war" and "not at all in keeping with the responsibility that the United States, as a great power, is called upon to bear for the maintenance of world peace." Finally, the address "lacks political balance, lacks a realistic consideration of the international situation and overestimates the actual potentialities" of the United States to affect Soviet actions.[67]

On January 13 Brezhnev himself delivered the authoritative position of the Soviet leadership in *Pravda*. He contended that "it has now been evident for some time that ruling circles of the United States . . . have embarked on a course hostile to the cause of détente, a course of spiraling the arms race," and he cited a number of developments beginning with the May 1978 NATO meeting. He gave vent to Soviet suspicions and disappointments when he commented with respect to SALT II that "hardly had the treaty been signed before some in the United States began to discredit it" and opponents began to work against its ratification, "not without the connivance of some U.S. government circles." In addition to defending the Soviet action in Afghanistan, he described the U.S. criticism as hypocritical, given American involvement in Vietnam, and commented that the Americans did not "lift a finger when the Chinese aggressors made their armed intervention in socialist

---

67. "TASS Statement," *Pravda*, January 7, 1980

Vietnam" in 1979. Moreover, the United States had kept a military base in Cuba (Guantánamo Bay) for decades against the will of the Cubans, was attempting to exert military pressures on Iran, and was now colluding with the Chinese in coordinating military assistance to Afghans intervening in Afghanistan from base areas outside the country.

Brezhnev argued, "In a word, the events in Afghanistan are not the real cause of the present worsening of the international situation. If there were no Afghanistan, certain circles in the United States and NATO would surely have found some other pretext to aggravate the world situation." He then criticized the U.S economic sanctions, disruption of scientific, cultural, and human contacts, the other punitive actions, and the breaking of contracts. He accused the United States of "arbitrarily and unilaterally violating a number of treaties, intergovernmental agreements, accords and understandings." He showed particular sensitivity to the American arrogation of the "right" unilaterally to reward or punish other sovereign states. The exasperation of the Soviet leadership was also evident in Brezhnev's charge that "as a result of the Carter administration's actions the entire world increasingly is forming the impression of the United States as a completely unreliable partner in interstate relations, as a state whose leadership, prompted by some whim, caprice or emotional outburst, or by considerations of narrowly conceived immediate advantage, is capable at any moment of violating international treaties and agreements. There is hardly any need to explain what a dangerous destabilizing impact this has on the entire international situation, particularly when it is the leadership of a large, influential power, from which peoples have a right to expect a considered and responsible policy."[68]

Only after President Carter's State of the Union message a week later did the Soviet leadership characterize the whole line of American policy as having changed. Moscow read that message, which set forth the Carter Doctrine, as clearly marking a policy shift: it "sets up an overt U.S. claim to world domination, proclaims a course towards confrontation and renunciation of the achievements of detente, and puts forward a conception of reliance on U.S. military might and force."[69]

In an apparent effort to answer unvoiced questions about why the Soviet leaders had not foreseen the U.S. turn to a hard line, on February 22 Brezhnev asserted that such a move had not been "unexpected." Even if that claim were true, the extent of the shift and its speed had clearly not been anticipated. Brezhnev referred to the present as a time when "the forces of imperialism have gone over to a counteroffensive against détente," but argued

---

68. "Replies by L. I. Brezhnev to Questions from a Correspondent of Pravda," *Pravda*, January 13, 1980.

69. TASS, "Following a Course toward Confrontation," Radio Moscow, January 22, in FBIS, *Soviet Union*, January 23, 1980, p. A1. See also the editorial, "On the Message of the U.S. President," *Pravda*, January 29, 1980.

that "from the very beginning it was clear that reliably to secure peace and détente was possible only in a determined political struggle."[70]

These authoritative early statements clearly established the Soviet position. There was a host of continuing commentaries, ranging from sophisticated analyses by Soviet academic analysts to crude propaganda for internal and external consumption. To some extent the variety in Soviet commentary reflected varying purposes and audiences.

The wide range of Soviet interpretations and reinterpretations of U.S. policy in 1980 also, however, showed that the official Soviet line on relations with the United States under détente in the preceding period had submerged but not eliminated some widely differing Soviet views. Some traditional polemicists, or gunslingers of invective, began to criticize American policy harshly—a phenomenon not without parallel in the United States. In this connection Soviet officials privately have been very critical of what they regarded as a breaking by President Carter and his administration of an early tacit détente understanding not to attack and impugn personally the top national leaders of the other side.[71] On the other hand, some Soviet commentaries by sophisticated supporters of détente argued that the American reaction was an aberration and probably temporary and that "of course" the American leadership had a different assessment of the situation from that of the Soviet leadership.[72] One such commentary in February 1980, in addition to deploring the disproportion between the official U.S. reaction and the precipitating cause (a criticism also made by some Americans and many Western Europeans), called for an understanding of the U.S. perspective. It is worth citing several sentences.

Another element has recently begun to stand out clearly in Washington's conduct: the disproportion between the cause and the reaction to it. It is understandable that Washington is displeased at the entry of a limited contingent of Soviet troops into Afghanistan. One can fully admit that the Soviet reasoning and explanation of the reasons for this action are not represented sufficiently convincingly there. But the important question these days is: Does the reaction by the leaders of the United States accord with the situation? What American national interests are affected by the temporary presence of

70. "Our Course—Peaceful Construction: Speech of L. I. Brezhnev," *Pravda*, February 23, 1980.

71. Interviews with senior Soviet officials. I am independently aware that that understanding had been worked out in exchanges conducted through Ambassador Dobrynin in 1965 and that it had remained in effect until January 1980. It is, however, unlikely that President Carter or his senior advisers were even aware of it, although they probably would not have regarded it as limiting in any event.

72. Fedor Burlatsky, "Remember!" *Literaturnaya gazeta* [The Literary Gazette], February 13, 1980. Burlatsky is head of the Philosophy Department of the Institute of Social Sciences of th Central Committee. Georgy Arbatov, the chief American affairs expert, stressed the conflicting U.S. views and expressed optimism that "the basic foundations of the policy of easing tensions is still intact" and "there are many other indications that Americans will not remain forever in a state of hysteria" but would begin again to analyze the situation seriously. Radio Moscow, July 4, in FBIS, *Soviet Union*, July 8, 1980, pp. A1–2.

Soviet troops in Afghanistan? Can the world be brought to the brink of a return to the Cold War as a result of this? Finally, is it correct to allow a few emotional actions to erase all the achievements built up over a decade of détente?[73]

While clearly addressed to the leaders of the United States, who are seen as having jettisoned détente for a relatively less significant cause, the rhetorical question in the final sentence may also have been intended to remind Soviet readers not to overreact to U.S. actions and not to jeopardize the fruits of a decade of détente that might still be salvaged.

Authoritative commentators saw the U.S. shift as putting Soviet-American relations back by ten or more years.[74] Retorting to Carter's evident exaggeration that the Soviet occupation of Afghanistan was "the greatest threat to world peace" since World War II, they said that the greatest threat to world peace "at least in the last decade" was the new "American shift toward a cold war policy."[75]

Overall the Soviet reaction was to interpret the American shift in policy as reflecting a strong further step in a move away from détente under way since 1977. Many commentaries stressed the continuity of the new elements of policy with earlier developments. Thus the Carter Doctrine was traced to the initial approval of the concept of developing a Rapid Deployment Force in August 1977 and the buildup of naval forces in the Indian Ocean and initiation of a search for new base facilities in 1979; the shelving of the SALT II Treaty was tied to the earlier delays and failures to press for ratification in 1979, in part owing to such things as the artificial crisis over the Soviet brigade in Cuba; the NATO TNF decision was seen as an attempt to circumvent the SALT II limitations on American strategic forces, which preceded Afghanistan; the chain of NATO military increases had begun in 1977; and many other developments had roots in the years preceding Afghanistan. In 1980 some charged, for example, that President Carter had not been sincere about the SALT II Treaty even when he signed it; others argued that he had been but had later given in to pressure from opponents. In general the Carter administration was reinterpreted as having been more hostile from 1977 on, although specialists still stressed contending forces in American politics and depicted Carter as capitulating to antidétente pressures rather than instigating them.[76]

---

73. I. Kremer, "A Policy of Missed Opportunities," *Novoye vremya* [New Times], no. 7 (February 15, 1980), p. 6.

74. Most refer to the early seventies or a decade. Leonid Zamyatin, chief of the International Information Department of the Central Committee, said, however, that bilateral relations had not been so tense in fifteen years and had been "put back by decades." Leonid Zamyatin, "To Restore a Climate of Détente and Trust," *Literaturnaya gazeta*, February 27, 1980.

75. Georgy Arbatov, "On the Threshold of a New Decade: U.S. Foreign Policy," *Pravda*, March 3, 1980.

76. To cite but a few good illustrative sources, on the struggle of Carter with foes of détente, see A. A. Kokoshin, "The Internal Causes of the Change in [U.S.] Foreign Policy," *SShA*, no. 7

The retroactive ascription since 1980 of a containment policy to the Carter administration also affected the official evaluation of Soviet-American relations during the late 1970s. For example, the fourth edition of the authoritative *History of the Foreign Policy of the USSR, 1917–1980,* edited by Politburo members Andrei Gromyko and Boris Ponomarev, contained a passage taken from *Pravda* (March 30, 1980) that cites a statement by President Carter made in June 1977 as evidence of an intention to challenge the Soviet Union aggressively for influence in the world. This reference shows, however, that the Soviets are not always careful about the accuracy of quotations (a shortcoming that unfortunately is also true of many American citations of Soviet statements). What President Carter actually said in 1977, in a question-and-answer comment, was this: "My own inclination, though, is to aggressively challenge, in a peaceful way, of course, the Soviet Union and others for influence in areas of the world that we feel are crucial to us now or potentially crucial 15 or 20 years from now."[77] The *Soviet* version, literally retranslated, is as follows: "I personally would like . . . in an aggressive form to throw down the gauntlet [to challenge] the Soviet Union and other countries . . . in order to gain influence in all regions of the world which, in my opinion, have a decisive [crucial] significance for us today or may acquire such significance in 10 to 15 years."[78] The editors of *Pravda* slanted the statement considerably, and theirs was the version available and used in the official publication. In this and many other cases (in both countries) it is often not possible to determine at what level the distortion entered.[79] In any event, the purpose was clearly to argue, primarily to a Soviet audience, that the United States and not the Soviet Union was responsible for the struggle for influence in the world.

There have been substantial variations in Soviet perceptions and evaluations of American policymaking, although within a general range of consensus. Brezhnev, it will be noted, had referred ambiguously to "certain circles" in the Carter administration as having sought for some time to steer away from détente. Thus, while some experts on the U.S. political system have traced

---

(July 1980), pp. 6–13. On this conflict and on Carter's succumbing to it, and for a detailed retroactive account of the hardening of the Carter administration's line toward the Soviet Union since 1977, see G. Trofimenko, "A Policy without Prospects (On the So-Called Carter Doctrine)," *Mirovaya ekonomika i mezhdunarodnye otnosheniya* [The World Economy and International Relations], no. 3 (March 1980), pp. 17–27. (Hereafter *MEiMO.*) Both authors are leading Soviet experts on the United States.

77. *Presidential Documents,* vol. 13 (June 20, 1977), p. 866 (the remarks were made in a meeting with members of the Magazine Publishers Association, June 10, 1977).

78. A. A. Gromyko and B. N. Ponomarev, *Istoriya vneshnei politiki SSSR, 1917–1980* [History of the Foreign Policy of the USSR, 1917–1980], vol. 2, 1945–1980 (Moscow: Nauka, 1981), p. 605.

79. It is, for example, not clear whether translating "to aggressively challenge" by words meaning "in an aggressive form to throw down the gauntlet" was a directed translation or merely the product of a zealous official translator. Someone obviously deliberately decided to omit "in a peaceful way" but had the compunction to use an ellipsis to indicate the omission. The change from "15 or 20 years" to "10 or 15 years" is hard to explain.

with sophistication (sometimes with insight but sometimes with error) the shifting pressures on and within the Carter administration and on the part of the president himself, some propagandists probably believe and certainly portray the matter as simply imperialist malevolence. They assert that the president can steer public opinion as he wishes in order to make policy shifts—and claim that Carter did so using the Soviet action in Afghanistan as a pretext.[80] While published Soviet commentary from the beginning of 1980 gave vent to heavier retroactive criticism of the Carter administration's actions from 1977 on, the actual perception—reflected in some writings and in oral exchanges— was that in fact the Carter administration had gradually shifted from vacillation to an anti-Soviet and pro-military line. The policy underpinning was perceived to have moved from an assertive balance-of-power version of détente in 1977–78 to a broader containment policy in 1978–79, and then overtly to anti-Soviet containment and a jettisoning of détente at the beginning of 1980. This change in policy was seen in arms control (with a "last gasp" reprieve for SALT in early to mid-1979), in American relations with China, and in American actions and reactions in the third world; in each of these areas the United States went from a moderate position in 1977 to a harder one in 1978 and to a confrontational one in 1980.

There was a corresponding failure in Moscow to appreciate the role of Soviet actions in stimulating the general change and the specific American moves—in part because some of the U.S. perceptions of the Soviet role were highly exaggerated and could not be taken seriously in Moscow (for example, Shaba II in 1978, the Yemen conflict in 1979, the alleged Soviet direction of Vietnamese actions, the interpretations placed on Soviet motives in its military relations with Cuba, the broader geopolitical aims ascribed to the Soviets in Ethiopia and above all in Afghanistan, and so on). The Soviets paralleled the U.S. failure to recognize the legitimate security interests and security concerns of the other side. When they did sometimes attempt to do so, the result was a rebuff by the United States. The most notable instance was Brezhnev's proposal in December 1980 that all the major powers agree to a ban on the use or threat of force in the Persian Gulf region.[81] Thus, the United States, conceiv-

---

80. For a good example, typically but not exclusively by a political officer in the military establishment, see Colonel N. Khmara, "The Chauvinist Platform for the Hegemonic Ambitions of Washington," *KVS*, no. 12 (June 1980), pp. 75–79, and on Carter especially, pp. 76–77.

81. "L. I. Brezhnev's Speech to Indian Parliamentarians," New Delhi, December 10, *Pravda*, December 11, 1980. This proposal did contain other elements clearly to American disadvantage; it called for a ban on military bases and nuclear weapons in the area. But the United States, rather than determining if these aspects were initial propaganda trimmings, rejected the proposal out of hand.

The U.S. rejection did not just reflect skepticism of the Brezhnev offer. It also reflected the desire not only that the Soviet Union not enter the Middle East by force, but that it not enter at all. The United States sought not only to ensure Western access, but to keep the Soviets out.

ing its buildup of military power in Southwest Asia as defensive, could not understand how Moscow could see five attack aircraft carriers deployed in the region and a frantic round of negotiating for new base facilities as threatening. And the Soviet leaders, conceiving their action in Afghanistan as preserving a socialist ally from counterrevolution and potential hostile American and Chinese exploitation, could not accept as real U.S. belief that the Soviets were attempting to cut Persian Gulf oil off from the West.

To the Soviets, the American reaction to the intervention seemed very deliberately designed to repudiate détente, so much so that they could not see that reaction as caused by the Soviet move. For example, Soviet leaders and commentators emphasized the nonratification of SALT, its circumvention through the NATO TNF deployment decision, and the cutting off of the whole range of other arms limitation talks under way since 1977 and even earlier, despite earlier "commitments." The Carter administration in 1980 simply rolled back more than a decade of arms control efforts and "suspended the dialogue on key issues of military détente."[82]

More broadly, the United States is said to have repudiated the Basic Principles and the Final Act signed in Helsinki in 1975. While Americans are quite familiar with Soviet human rights practices that in their view are clearly not in keeping with the Helsinki Accords, they do not consider that when they impose economic sanctions and break signed contracts, they are violating the provision on facilitating trade. The Soviets saw as violations of the provisions on cultural exchanges and sports activities the U.S. decision not to allow visits of Soviet cultural groups or cultural activities such as planned art exhibitions, or to renew the expired cultural exchange agreement, or to participate in the international Olympics. Similarly the cancellation of plans to open consulates in Kiev and New York, and to curtail civil aviation services, was held to violate the call in the Final Act for facilitating movement of peoples. The Helsinki Accords are not in fact binding obligations, so neither side should speak of "violations." But neither—for reasons of state policy—has always conducted itself in ways fully consonant with the intention, direction, and promise of those accords.

The Soviet reaction, apart from propaganda criticizing the United States and seeking support for Soviet positions, affected its ideological and political-military perceptions of the United States. Boris Ponomarev, party secretary and candidate member of the Politburo, interpreted the American shift in policy in the late 1970s and after as reflecting a turn by imperialism toward "undermining détente and toward confrontation" in relation to the Soviet Union, and as pursuing a military buildup designed to forestall an up-

---

82. See V. Israelyan, "Nuclear Arms Race or Disarmament Talks?" *International Affairs*, no. 4 (April 1982), p. 83. Ambassador Israelyan is a senior official in the Ministry of Foreign Affairs long identified with arms control and security matters. See also A. Gromyko, "Leninist Foreign Policy in the Contemporary World," *Kommunist*, no. 1 (January 1981), pp. 18–21.

surge in the world revolutionary process in a vain attempt to stem the progressive march of history.[83] Others, including but not limited to military theoreticians, interpreted U.S. military doctrine both as reflecting Carter's repudiation of détente and as demonstrating a renewed American readiness to place its stakes on military power in its quest for world domination.[84]

In the most authoritative and considered Soviet reaction to the changed international political scene, the Central Committee at a special plenary session in June 1980 stated in a formal decree: "The leaders of the NATO military bloc, the United States above all, have taken a course directed at upsetting the military balance which has been established in the world to their favor and to the detriment of the Soviet Union and the socialist countries, international détente, and the security of nations."[85] Further: "In an effort to impose their will on other countries, ruling circles of the United States have taken the course of economic 'sanctions' and of breaking scientific and technical, cultural and sports relations. They are refusing to honor their obligations and violate accords and agreements they have signed. Anti-Sovietism and anti-communism have become an instrument for stirring up the arms race. . . . The rapprochement of aggressive Western circles, the United States above all, with the Chinese leadership is proceeding on an anti-Soviet basis hostile to the cause of peace."[86]

The purpose of the special Central Committee plenary meeting in June was not merely to criticize the United States. Rather, it was to determine Soviet foreign policy in response to the new American line of confrontation. And the decision was strongly to reaffirm détente. The decree issued by the plenum stated, "The Plenum instructs the Politburo of the Central Committee in the present situation as well, when the intensified activities of the United States and its accomplices have intensified the threat of war, steadfastly to stay the course of the 24th and 25th Congresses of the CPSU"—a course of peaceful coexistence and détente.[87]

The decree specifically expressed confidence in the leadership of Brezhnev and of the collective Politburo: "the Plenum of the CC of the CPSU completely and fully approves the activity of the Politburo of the CC of the CPSU, and of Comrade L. I. Brezhnev, General Secretary of the CC of the CPSU and Chairman of the Presidium of the Supreme Soviet of the USSR, in the implementation of the Leninist political course set by the XXIV and XXV

---

83. B. N. Ponomarev, "Unshakable Policy of Peace," *Pravda*, February 5, 1980.

84. For example, see Colonel T. Kondratkov, "What Is Concealed under the Bourgeois Conception of the Essence of War," *KVS*, no. 20 (October 1980), p. 75.

85. *Kommunist*, no. 10 (July 1980), p. 8.

86. Ibid., pp. 8–9.

87. Ibid., p. 9. The plenum also decided on and announced convocation of the 26th Party Congress in February 1981.

Congresses of the Party."[88] The plenum also "fully approves the measures taken to provide all-round aid to Afghanistan" and called for a "political settlement of the situation which has developed around Afghanistan."[89]

In addition to a ringing endorsement of détente, which had "sunk deep roots into international life," the plenum specifically expressed the confidence of the Central Committee in the existence of "objective possibilities" to prevent "descent into a new 'cold war' " and said that "the path to solution of this task is the path of negotiation, based on strict observance of the principle of equality and equal security. And this fully applies to Soviet-American relations."[90]

Meanwhile, in response to the shelving of SALT II, the NATO TNF deployment decision, and the intensified American military buildup after Afghanistan, the plenum also concluded that the new situation "requires constant vigilance and all-round strengthening of the defense capability of our state, in order to frustrate the plans of imperialism to achieve military superiority and establish worldwide dictate."[91] In fact, Soviet military programs continued on the substantial but reduced basis established in 1976, and the basic weapons acquisition and deployment programs under way were not changed in any perceptible way, leading to some unease among the military. But the Soviet leadership was determined not to permit the United States to attain military superiority. As was seen, parity in an overall military balance was regarded as a foundation of détente. This parity was reaffirmed, as the policy of détente was reconsidered and reendorsed.

"Détente," stated the Central Committee decree, "is the natural result of the correlation of forces in the world arena which has developed over the past decades. The military-strategic balance between the world of socialism and the world of capitalism which has been reached is an achievement of truly historical significance. It serves as a deterrent to the aggressive strivings of

---

88. Ibid., p. 8.

89. Ibid., p. 10. The word translated here as "settlement" is more literally translated as "regulating," but an official Soviet translation also uses the term "settlement." The passage also goes on to refer to "Afghanistan, which is pursuing a policy of nonalignment." This authoritative and possibly significant hint of Soviet desire for a political settlement based on Afghanistan's nonalignment was ignored in the West.

   It would appear that the Soviet leaders were concerned with heading off any questions about the wisdom of the intervention and took special pains to justify their action (and to accept collective responsibility) by the endorsement of the Central Committee plenum. In his report to the plenum Brezhnev commented in remarkably defensive terms, "We had no choice but to send troops. And events have confirmed that this was the only correct decision." "Address by the General Secretary of the CC of the CPSU L. I. Brezhnev," *Kommunist*, no. 10 (July 1980), p. 4.

90. Ibid., p. 9.

91. Ibid., pp. 10–11.

imperialism, and meets the basic interests of all nations. Calculations on over-
turning this balance are doomed to failure."

The aim was to meet the challenge of the U.S. shift to containment
without permitting the changed *American* course to deflect the continuing
Soviet pursuit of a policy of détente. "In this complex international situation,
the Central Committee of the CPSU and the Soviet Government are displaying true Leninist restraint, firmness, and principle, staying with and implementing a course directed at preservation of the peace, insuring the security of the
Soviet people and international security as a whole, not yielding to provocation, and at the same time rebuffing imperialist aspirations."[92]

The impact of the change in American policy affected much more
than bilateral relations and reciprocal perceptions. It also affected some important *internal* Soviet political decisions. In particular, quite apart from the political propaganda, the direct economic consequences of the American grain
embargo, and the cancellation of a number of other previously authorized and
signed economic contracts, the American use of economic sanctions reopened
the internal political-economic debate of the early 1970s over the advisability
of growing Soviet involvement in international economic interdependence. Advocates of economic autarky, vanquished in 1973 only after a hard struggle and
changes in the Politburo itself, gained opportunities to reopen the issue. Advocates of East-West trade were thrown on the defensive and now conceded the
need to avoid becoming "strategically vulnerable," although they continued to
argue for international economic cooperation.[93]

One aspect of readjustment to U.S. sanctions after Afghanistan was
simply to redirect Soviet foreign trade to other Western countries.[94] But the
more basic question remained. Now for the first time in seven years powerful
voices began to argue that "the present situation shows that it is necessary for
us to concentrate our energies on making our country completely independent
of any and all foreign deliveries, especially when this concerns questions of vital
importance for the country."[95]

The renewed debate over economic relations with the West, while
it did not lead to a reversal of Soviet trade patterns, meant that the Soviet
leaders hedged on some arrangements, showed greater caution, and even

---

92. Ibid., p. 9.

93. See in particular, Oleg Bogomolev, "Economic Ties between Socialist and Capitalist Countries," *MEiMO*, no. 3 (March 1980), pp. 41–51. Bogomolev, head of the Institute of the
Economy of the World Socialist System, had been a leading advocate of the shift in 1973; see
chapter 10.

94. The quick shift to Western European and Japanese suppliers of industrial technology has been
noted. Over the next several years, even after the United States lifted the embargo on grain
sales in early 1981, the Soviet Union shifted its sources of supply so that the United States,
which had supplied over three-quarters of the grain imported by the USSR in the 1970s, was
held to less than one-quarter in the early 1980s.

95. Anatoly P. Aleksandrov, president of the USSR Academy of Sciences, address on Soviet Science Day, Radio Moscow, April 18, in FBIS, *Soviet Union*, April 21, 1980, p. U1.

shifted some economic priorities. It also raised the question of a possible change in the domestic consensus in support of détente. Moreover, potentially these concerns could merge with those of the Soviet military to assure the capacity of the Soviet economy to mobilize and shift to a war footing in case of actual hostilities or extreme tension.[96]

By a year later the impact of the January 1980 sanctions was even clearer. In February 1981 Brezhnev himself, at the Twenty-sixth Congress of the CPSU, warned, in a notable shift from the position he had taken at the previous congress five years earlier, against seeking solutions to economic problems by relying on trade with the West. While he reaffirmed Soviet interest in trade and economic relations with the West, he cautioned that "we must also consider the policy of the capitalist states. They not infrequently attempt to use economic ties with us as a means of political pressure."[97] Academician Nikolai Inozemtsev, a strong supporter of détente and interdependence, also stressed that one of the lessons the Soviets had learned from the U.S. sanctions after Afghanistan was not to permit "important sectors of the Soviet economy to become dependent on the import of machinery from the capitalist countries." But he also concluded that the Soviet Union should not forgo the benefits of international economic and scientific-technological collaboration with those capitalist countries ready to proceed on an "equal and mutually advantageous" basis, perhaps implying that the West would continue to be divided over sanctions or other attempts to place pressure on the USSR.[98]

Soviet pronouncements on world affairs after January 1980 included a reassessment of the relative significance of Soviet-American détente and general East-West (mainly European) détente. In 1969–71, when the two superpowers had not yet reached agreement on a common platform of détente, Soviet commentaries naturally stressed the improvement of Soviet–Western European ties. From 1972 through the mid-1970s, pride of place went to Soviet-American relations. This stance was moderated in the late 1970s. Then in 1980 there was a reversal: developments in Europe were explicitly described as the greatest achievement of détente. In his initial post-Afghanistan retort to President Carter, General Secretary Brezhnev focused on Europe as the principal area of concern because "the United States is not content with doing just about everything to poison Soviet-American relations. It would like also to spoil the relations of the Western European countries with the Soviet Union . . . [and] is trying to undermine the spirit and the substance of the Helsinki Final Act, which has become a recognized milestone in strengthening security and developing peaceful cooperation in the continent." He defensively noted that "détente in Europe is needed by the Western states, including the

---

96. Signs of this merging began to appear somewhat later in 1981; see chapter 28.

97. L. I. Brezhnev, "Report of the Central Committee of the CPSU to the XXVI Congress of the Communist Party of the Soviet Union," *Pravda*, February 24, 1981.

98. Academician N. Inozemtsev, "The XXVI Congress of the CPSU and Our Tasks," *MEiMO*, no. 3 (March 1981), pp. 12–13.

United States too, no less than it is needed by the socialist countries including the Soviet Union."[99]

This shift from a priority for Soviet-American relations, now torn asunder, to Soviet–Western European relations was retroactively justified by historical reinterpretation. Pointedly on July 4, 1980, the chief Soviet expert on the United States, Georgy Arbatov, declared, "The seventies went down in history as the decade of reduced international tension with the high point being the signing of the Helsinki accords."[100] On earlier occasions he had cited the Soviet-American summit agreements as the apogee of détente. Other authoritative commentaries also declared that "the process of détente reached its greatest results precisely in Europe."[101]

During 1980 the Soviet Union also exerted strong efforts to maintain the East-West détente in Europe. This policy required attention not only to Soviet relations with the countries of Western Europe, but also to those within Eastern Europe and with the Western European communist parties. In a Declaration of May 15, 1980, and at a meeting of foreign ministers again in October, the Warsaw Pact countries reaffirmed proposals for European cooperation and security. An April conference of European communist parties was only partly successful—the Yugoslav and Romanian parties, and several Western European ones including the Eurocommunist Italian and Spanish parties, did not even attend. But on the whole Soviet relations with Europe and the communist parties there weathered the aftermath of Afghanistan and the sharp turn in American-Soviet relations.

Brief note should also be taken of a crisis that did *not* occur in Europe in 1980. In May Yugoslav President Josip Tito died. Belying the concerns often expressed in earlier years that the Soviet Union might use that occasion to destabilize Yugoslavia, and even to intervene with force, the transition of power evoked no such pressures or actions. Whether in the longer run Yugoslavia would overcome continuing internal national friction and economic difficulties remained to be seen. While in the future a changed internal situation might precipitate Soviet involvement, in 1980 it did not. To the contrary, the Soviets went out of their way to honor Tito, to reaffirm Soviet-Yugoslav friendship, and to broaden economic and other cooperation.

The United States, choosing not to have even a pro forma contact between President Carter and President Brezhnev, sent Vice President Mondale to Tito's funeral. President Carter then visited Yugoslavia in June, reaffirming American support. That support, which was proffered against possible Soviet interference, was welcome in Belgrade but was also an embarrassment, as it was extended too obviously and in the absence of any threat. Indeed, a few weeks *before* Tito's death, in a general statement of U.S. policy toward

---

99. Brezhnev, *Pravda*, January 13, 1980.

100. Radio Moscow, July 4, in FBIS, *Soviet Union*, July 8, 1980, p. A1.

101. V. V. Kortunov, "The CPSU in the Struggle for Detente: The Confrontation of the Two Tendencies in International Affairs," *Voprosy istorii KPSS* [Questions of the History of the CPSU], no. 10 (October 1980), p. 30.

Eastern Europe but in a passage reflecting the new stress on containment, a Department of State spokesman had warned Moscow that "attempts to undermine Yugoslavia's unity, territorial integrity, and independence would be a matter of grave concern to the United States."[102] The Soviet response was that this gratuitous warning "not only cast aspersions on the policy of the USSR, but nearly went as far as threats."[103] As this whole matter illustrates, even developments that did *not* involve a direct clash of Soviet and American interests still became subsidiary points of confrontation.

Internal developments in the Soviet Union, some of which affected external relations directly, also had an impact on Soviet-American relations. On January 22, in response to criticism of the Soviet occupation of Afghanistan by Nobel Laureate Andrei Sakharov, that most distinguished Soviet dissident was compelled to leave Moscow for internal exile in Gorky, a location much less accessible to foreign correspondents and other Russian dissidents. This action led in turn to a protest by many U.S. scientists that further curtailed contact with Soviet counterparts, reinforcing the official American measures to reduce contacts.[104]

Jewish emigration from the Soviet Union, tolerated in the 1970s in part owing to U.S. interest in the subject, dropped sharply in 1980, reaching, by 1981, the lowest level since 1970—less than 10,000 in contrast to the peak of over 50,000 in 1979.[105]

During the last months of 1980 the developing political crisis in Poland dominated Soviet attention. These months were also marked by Soviet concern over the possible direction of U.S. policy under a new or renewed administration. The issue of Afghanistan remained but without the same intensity as earlier in the year. There was also Soviet concern over possible American military moves against Iran, either as a desperate act by the frustrated Carter administration,[106] or by a new administration determined to resolve the issue.

---

102. Deputy Assistant Secretary of State Robert L. Barry, April 22, 1980, *U.S. Policy and Eastern Europe*, Current Policy 139 (Washington, D.C.: Department of State, 1979), p. 4.

103. Yury Kornilov, TASS political analyst, Radio Moscow, April 23, in FBIS, *Soviet Union*, April 24, 1980, p. A13.

104. It may also have contributed to the resignation a few days later of Vladimir Kirillin, the deputy chief of the State Committee on Science and Technology.

105. Jewish emigration had totaled only 8,733 in the six years 1965–70, then rose under détente to 34,733 in 1973, and declined again with the Jackson-Vanik legislation, which sought to demand such emigration as the price for trade normalization. In 1978 and especially 1979, as progress was made toward SALT II and there were hopes for a summit that would renew détente, the Soviets again permitted emigration to rise—to a peak of 51,320 in 1979. The flow was again cut sharply in 1980 when American-Soviet détente was shelved; in 1981 it declined to 9,447, lower than any year since 1970. These data are from the Soviet Jewry Research Bureau, National Conference on Soviet Jewry, Washington, D.C.

106. Soviet concern over a possible American invasion of Iran in the late summer or early fall of 1980 led to military preparations for a possible counterintervention to secure northern Iran and prevent a U.S. military presence on the Soviet southern border. Secret American intelli-

It was in this context that the Polish problem erupted after July 1980. The Soviet response included military troop concentrations and maneuvers late in the year, intended to influence the Polish leaders as well as the Polish public. It was also a contingency preparation for possible intervention if that drastic resort should become necessary. More directly affecting Soviet-American relations, after the Polish labor disturbances in Gdansk in August 1980 the Soviet Union resumed jamming the Voice of America radio broadcasts. That jamming had been stopped in 1974 as a sign and product of the development of détente.

Thus throughout the year, even more than before, Soviet foreign policy was reactive. First there was the internal disintegration of the Soviet position in Afghanistan, to which the reaction was political and military intervention at the end of 1979. Most of 1980 was devoted to responding to U.S., Western, Eurocommunist,[107] Islamic, nonaligned, and other negative world reactions to the intervention in Afghanistan. Within Afghanistan, the Soviet Union was occupied with its persistent inability to establish the legitimacy of the regime of Babrak Karmal or to curb the insurgency. Neither the insurgents nor the Soviet army and Soviet-supported government could defeat the other. Internationally, the Soviet Union contended that its troops would remain in Afghanistan only until the country was secure from an externally supported threat. More broadly, the unexpectedly strong U.S. response to Afghanistan had complicated the defensive Soviet stance, although it had also led to a rift between America and Western Europe. Meanwhile, the Soviets were also reacting to the NATO TNF decision of 1979, seeking to reverse it.

Détente itself had contributed to the development of the crisis in Poland in several ways. Most directly, it had facilitated the unwise practice of the Polish leaders of borrowing more and more Western funds to expand trade without using them to build an economic structure and productivity that would sustain those Western purchases. The result was the postponement of economic reforms and intensification of economic imbalance and debt. In other ways, too, détente encouraged many Poles to believe that with reduced East-West tensions (and in particular the sharp decline in fears of West Germany) the Soviet leaders would be more tolerant of substantial internal political change in Poland. This contributed to Solidarity's escalating political demands in 1980 and 1981 that, in turn, made inevitable the repression of Solidarity and rollback of political liberalization after December 1981.

As the Soviet leaders awaited the outcome of the American presidential election, and then after the election awaited the unfolding of the policy of the Reagan administration, they were guardedly hopeful that there

---

gence on Soviet communications with respect to the preparations for that contingency were later publicly disclosed and cited by Jack Anderson, "U.S. and Soviets Flexed Muscles in '80 Showdown," *Washington Post*, October 23, 1981.

107. The communist parties of Belgium, Britain, Italy, Spain, and Sweden openly criticized the Soviet resort to force in Afghanistan.

would be some degree of "return to realism" in Washington. But they did not see ways in which they could influence that result. Soviet officials, commentators, and academic specialists on U.S. affairs all expressed uncertainty, but also belief that the outcome of the election would probably make relatively little difference. Reagan's harder line was to some extent discounted as election rhetoric, while Carter's policy record was seen as much tougher on the Soviet Union and stronger on military buildup than it was by the public in the United States. A number of Soviet officials and others in private conversation expressed a hope, some even an expectation, that Reagan would be another Nixon—a hard-line conservative who would, once in power, move to negotiate on the basis of hardheaded economic and political interests, while avoiding such gratuitously troublesome areas as human rights. Some, echoing much U.S. sentiment, said that despite important political differences they expected at least to know where things stood—in contrast to the vacillations and reversals of position that marked the Carter administration.[108]

At the same time, while there were hopes for some improvement in relations under a new administration, there was also the expectation that a long period of intensified competition was starting. By the early fall of 1980, even before the presidential election, in response to the increased U.S. military programs the Central Committee requested that Soviet experts on American affairs study what the United States was economically capable of sustaining in the way of military buildup. They did not think it necessary to ask for estimates of American intentions.[109]

The last year of the Carter administration was considered in Moscow to be a time of transition from the weakened détente of the preceding three years to something not yet clearly defined. There was a hope that renewed détente, although probably with a keen competitive edge, would emerge, but also concern over a possible confirmation of the confrontational line of the transitional period.

The U.S. Election Campaign

The American presidential election campaign was in part a referendum on the stewardship of President Jimmy Carter. It also involved an appeal by a genial conservative supported by a new right that sought to repeal both the internal economic and social policy, and the détente foreign policy, of several Republican as well as Democratic administrations.

---

108. These impressions were reinforced in a number of meetings I had with senior Soviet officials and scholars during a visit to Moscow in October 1980, and in other contacts after the election.

109. Soviet officials referred, in conversations with me, to that study, which was later confirmed to have originated with the Central Committee organization.

There were rising economic problems and dissatisfaction. There was also widespread popular uneasiness over the apparent decline in American power and standing, as witnessed by the failure of efforts in Vietnam, the widely reported growing military strength of the Soviet Union, a series of mishaps such as the Cuba brigade episode and the failure of the hostage rescue attempt in Iran, the inability of the United States to do anything about the Soviet occupation of Afghanistan, and, perhaps above all, the year of national travail and frustration over the continuing incarceration of the hostages in Iran. American-Soviet relations, or rather attitudes toward the Soviet Union and doubts about the success of past American policy, were thus mixed with other things in the American consciousness.

The 1980 presidential election campaign was launched at the beginning of the year. In addition to the challenge from the Republicans (and Ronald Reagan effectively defined the challenge long before he was confirmed as the Republican candidate), Carter also initially faced strong criticism from within the Democratic party. Senator Edward M. Kennedy, before fading as a serious contender, countered Carter in a major speech only five days after the State of the Union address in January 1980. Kennedy said that the United States must not "foreclose every opening to the Soviet Union. . . . The task of statesmanship is to convince the Russians that there is reason for fear, but also reason for hope, in their relations with the United States." And he endorsed arms control as well as military power. But overall he tried too hard to bring both détente-minded and hard-line factions of the Democratic party into support of his candidacy, losing credibility with both constituencies.[110] Nevertheless, this challenge from within his own party, even if ambivalent in direction, posed additional difficulties for Carter.

The president's greatest problems, however, were his record of apparent vacillation, the failure to foresee and forestall the Soviet occupation of Afghanistan (which he converted into an even more major event than it was), and above all his inability to deal with the hostage crisis (which, again, he magnified even as he proved unable to resolve it). He thus faced widespread public doubt about his consistency and effectiveness, some of it deserved, some of it not.

Carter had to defend détente if he wished to offer a real alternative to the Reagan challenge. Yet he could not defend the success of *his* policy of détente while arguing strongly, even stridently, that the Soviet intervention in

---

110. "Address by Senator Edward M. Kennedy, Georgetown University, January 28," *Congressional Record*, vol. 126 (January 30, 1980), pp. 5651–53; and *New York Times*, January 29, 1980.

Five days earlier Kennedy had met with a group of Democratic hawks: Senator Henry Jackson, Paul Nitze, Eugene Rostow, Richard Pipes, Henry Fowler, and Max Kampelman. See Rowland Evans and Robert Novak, "Kennedy Dove or Kennedy Hawk?" *Washington Post*, January 28, 1980.

On this occasion and several others Kennedy also suggested that Carter's poor handling of the brigade in Cuba had "invited" the Soviet invasion of Afghanistan.

Afghanistan was an unacceptable violation of détente. And, despite all his efforts, he was unable to obtain a Soviet withdrawal. He was thus in part a victim of this Soviet move, but also in important part a victim of his own interpretation of the meaning of the Soviet move. It should also be recalled that as important as the issue of Afghanistan was, it diminished during the year as public attention and frustration focused even more on the hostage crisis, which bedeviled the Carter administration literally to its last minutes in office. Moreover, domestic economic issues grew in importance.

In discussing his aims in a second term if elected, President Carter said in September, "I would like to see our relationship with the Soviet Union improved." But he went on to reaffirm the condition he had established in January—and to add another: "But I will not base that improvement on [acceptance of] the invasion by the Soviet Union of Afghanistan and their ignoring of the principle of human rights." He also urged as an "important reason" why SALT II should be ratified that he favored "going into SALT III with much greater reductions in nuclear weapons." But then he once again declared as a condition to ratification of SALT II "positive movement by the Soviets to withdraw their occupying troops from Afghanistan."[111]

The collapse of the Carter administration's policy toward the Soviet Union and the abandonment of détente were by no means crucial to his electoral defeat. The failure in 1980 to reconcile his aspirations and his policies toward the Soviet Union did not lead him to question either. But this difficulty over foreign policy was by then symptomatic of a growing ineffectiveness of his administration, which the public perception further magnified.

The first exploratory round of arms limitation talks on European theater nuclear forces was held in Geneva in October–November following the election.[112] Also in November was the opening of the second stage of talks on European security and cooperation under the CSCE Helsinki Accord. They took place in Madrid and were marked by highly confrontational and polemical exchanges.

The most significant development, however, was the growing crisis in Poland, as the Polish workers broadened their challenge to the communist regime, and concern grew over possible Soviet military intervention, concern that prompted American and NATO warnings to the Soviet Union.[113]

---

111. "Independence, Missouri: Remarks and a Question-and-Answer Session at a Townhall Meeting, September 2, 1980," *Presidential Documents*, vol. 16 (September 8, 1980), pp. 1619–20.

112. See chapter 25.

113. In early December the administration received what it believed to be reliable information that the Soviet Union was about to intervene with military forces in Poland. Carter sent a message to Brezhnev warning of serious consequences. (Brezhnev did not even reply.) Prime Minister Indira Gandhi was prevailed upon to register India's strong concern. Going beyond those warnings to Moscow, Brzezinski came perilously close to a direct intervention on his own. In his words, "through my own channels, I arranged for telephone calls to alert the Solidarity leaders in Warsaw, so that they could take personal precautions," and he "phoned

Internal tension in Poland and the threat of external intervention abated, for a time, by January. And the Iranian hostage crisis was finally resolved precisely at the time of transition to a new administration.

The Carter administration left for its successor an unusually blank slate on American-Soviet relations. Containment of feared future Soviet expansionist moves remained the operative policy in governing a wide range of *other* U.S. foreign and defense policy activities, even though that policy was ever more irrelevant to what the Soviet Union was actually doing, as it continued to focus on the European détente. The administration's chief legacies were a hollow aspiration to renew détente that coexisted uneasily with a failed policy keyed to compelling the Soviet Union to withdraw from Afghanistan. The new administration, however, speedily brushed aside both. And while the new administration did not have a strategy for managing relations *with* the Soviet Union, at least it believed it had an alternative—confrontation.

---

the Pope and briefed him on the situation" (in Polish). Carter had approved the call to the pope and in his memoir also takes credit for Brzezinski's message to the Solidarity leaders (calling them "the opposition leaders in Poland"). See Brzezinski, *Power and Principle*, pp. 466–67; and Carter, *Keeping Faith*, pp. 584–85.

28　Adrift after Détente, 1981–84

THE DEVELOPMENT of American-Soviet relations from 1969 through 1980 encompassed the rise and fall of détente. More precisely, there were the tentative moves toward a possible détente from 1969 to 1972, its sudden blossoming from 1972 through 1975, and its decline from 1976 through 1979. The year 1980 marked the beginning of a post-détente relationship, but because it brought the closing of an American administration, 1980 was transitional. What it was transitional toward became evident only with the election of Ronald Reagan, and his clear repudiation of détente. In terms of the substance of relations, however, there was in fact little to distinguish 1980 from the years that followed. Thus the main turning point in many respects, and especially in the Soviet view, was not January 1981 so much as January 1980. That juncture marked the real divide between the 1970s and the 1980s.

As noted at the outset of this study, and as has been evident throughout, the relationship between the United States and the Soviet Union has at all times been a mix of competition and cooperation. Competition was active even at the height of détente, while some elements of cooperation have been present even when confrontation has been dominant.

There is good reason to single out the period 1969 through 1980 for a study of the rise and fall of détente. But those years remain just a slice of a continuing relationship that was influenced by the 1950s and 1960s and that will in turn affect the 1980s and beyond. It is therefore useful to include a brief analysis of the period from 1981 through 1984. This lends perspective to the evolution of the period surveyed. These years mark the attempt in the first Reagan administration to establish a new post-détente relationship. And, finally, they cover a period of Soviet adjustment not only to a new American policy attitude, but also to changes within the Soviet leadership. Brezhnev had staked his policies on détente and was left with no alternative when the United States abandoned it after Afghanistan. His successors, Yury Andropov and then Konstantin Chernenko, had to struggle with the same problem of defining a policy to meet the new situation in Soviet-American relations, changes in the world, and sharpening problems within the Soviet bloc.

This chapter does not provide the same detailed and close-grained look at developments in the first half of the 1980s as was applied to the preceding twelve years. To do so requires another book.[1] The discussion here will draw from the four years of the first Reagan administration and the concurrent Soviet leadership change to outline the main developments in American-Soviet—and Soviet-American—relations as both countries search to develop a post-détente policy. The further development of four main areas of U.S.-Soviet interaction traced throughout the 1970s is also discussed: strategic arms control, the interrelation with détente in Europe, the triangular relationship with China, and the competition in the third world.

U.S. Policy: Containment or Confrontation?

The Reagan administration came to power knowing what it did *not* want—détente. It was less clear, and less unified, in its conception of what it did want. That ambiguity and ambivalence began with President Reagan himself.

Reagan believed that under détente the United States had unduly trusted the Soviet leaders and had been betrayed; had relied on arms control and had been outnegotiated; had let American national military, political, and economic power slide while bemused with internationalism and détente; and, above all, had lost its free enterprise spirit for standing tall in the world. While Reagan had very strong negative attitudes toward communism and the Soviet Union and believed the Soviet leaders had been duplicitous and had taken advantage of the United States, he blamed the preceding (Republican as well as Democratic) administrations for having permitted this erosion of power and prestige at home and abroad.

Reagan believed—and stated frankly and publicly—that the Soviet leaders were "the focus of evil in the modern world," and that "the Soviet Union underlies all the unrest that is going on" in the world.[2] Nevertheless, he

---

1. A sequel to the present study, *In Search of a Policy: American-Soviet Relations, 1981–85* (Brookings Institution, forthcoming), is in preparation, providing a more complete review of these years.

   For a perceptive general analysis of this period, see also Strobe Talbott, *The Russians and Reagan* (Vintage Books, 1984); and for an incisive academic study of the first two years of the Reagan period see Alexander Dallin and Gail W. Lapidus, "Reagan and the Russians: United States Policy Toward the Soviet Union and Eastern Europe," in Kenneth A. Oye, Robert J. Lieber, and Donald Rothchild, *Eagle Defiant: United States Foreign Policy in the 1980s* (Boston, Mass.: Little, Brown, 1983), pp. 191–236.

2. President Reagan, "Remarks at the Annual Convention [of the Evangelicals] in Orlando, Fla., March 8, 1983," *Weekly Compilation of Presidential Documents*, vol. 19 (March 14, 1983), p. 369 (hereafter *Presidential Documents*); and Reagan, campaign address in June 1980, cited in Anthony Lewis, "Reagan on War and Peace," *New York Times*, October 20, 1980.

believed that the principal requirement for meeting the Soviet challenge was to abandon the feckless pursuit of détente and cooperative resolution of conflicts, and to resume a unilateral American reassertion of leadership and a rebuilding of strength (military and economic) and self-reliance. He inclined naturally toward a confrontational *attitude* toward the Soviet Union and the communist system (as the ultimate in big government). He did not necessarily intend a confrontational *policy* aimed at weakening the Soviet system—which he believed combined great military power with great economic and political weakness. On the other hand, it was unclear whether he rejected such a confrontational policy, which was favored and advanced by some members of his administration.

The chief member of the Reagan administration to outline a policy toward the Soviet Union in the first year and a half was Secretary of State Alexander M. Haig, Jr., widely labeled the "vicar" of foreign policy.[3] Haig, who had served his apprenticeship as a member of the staff of Henry Kissinger from 1969 to 1973, was the foremost spokesman for a policy of containment of the Soviet Union. The essence of his approach was pragmatic and geopolitical rather than ideological, although he adopted some confrontational camouflage. He aimed at compelling the Soviet Union to accept "restraint and reciprocity" in its international behavior.[4] Echoing Kissinger's aim of a decade earlier, Haig saw "the task ahead for this vital decade before us," the 1980s, as "the management of global Soviet power."[5] While eschewing the term détente, Haig in essence sought, with a greater stress on the stick than on the carrot, to carry forward what former President Nixon began to call "hard-headed détente."[6]

3. In addition to his speeches and other statements as secretary of state in 1981–82, see his memoir, Alexander M. Haig, Jr., *Caveat: Realism, Reagan, and Foreign Policy* (Macmillan, 1984).

4. Haig cited this theme of "restraint and reciprocity" in many speeches. For one example, in which he called it "the central theme of our foreign policy," see Secretary Haig, "NATO and the Restoration of American Leadership," Commencement Address at Syracuse University, May 9, *Department of State Bulletin*, vol. 81 (June 1981), p. 11. (Hereafter *State Bulletin*.) Occasionally he made what he really meant explicit: the United States wanted "greater *Soviet* restraint and greater *Soviet* reciprocity." Secretary Haig, "A Strategic Approach to American Foreign Policy," Address to the American Bar Association, August 11, *State Bulletin*, vol. 81 (September 1981), p. 11. Emphasis added.

   Haig and most other members of the Reagan administration avoided use of the term containment to describe their policy. One reason was a belief by some, including Haig, that Soviet influence had expanded beyond a clear line that could be drawn around the Soviet Union and its adjacent "satellites." A second reason, not fully consistent with the first, was a belief held by many others ever since the late 1940s that Truman's containment policy was too soft, and that the U.S. aim should be not only to contain communism but to roll it back. I use the term simply as descriptive of a policy aimed at containing Soviet expansion.

5. Haig's address to the Republican National Convention in July 1980, cited in "Sample of Haig's Views," *New York Times*, December 18, 1980.

6. See Richard Nixon, "Hard-Headed Détente," *New York Times*, August 18, 1982, and "A Call for Hard-Headed Détente," *Time*, December 27, 1982, p. 18.

After George P. Shultz replaced Haig in June 1982, Shultz was the main pragmatic voice in the administration. But whereas Haig's chief concern had been geopolitical, focused on containment, Shultz's was political and focused on negotiating limited agreements aimed at a modus vivendi in American-Soviet relations. He therefore placed greater stress on arms control. His theme was "realism, strength, and dialogue" (or negotiation).[7] While both Haig and Shultz were pragmatic rather than ideological, they both took very tough positions. Hardheaded détente was hard, not soft.

Secretary of Defense Caspar W. Weinberger and several key civilian assistants (notably Under Secretary for Policy Fred C. Iklé and Assistant Secretary for International Policy Richard N. Perle) were the most ideological and the most inclined toward a policy of confrontation. Richard H. Allen, the first national security adviser, and several members of the NSC staff, notably Richard Pipes, were well known for their long-standing anti-Soviet fervor. They all pressed for stringent constraints on East-West trade, and for stiff economic sanctions when Soviet actions or other international events made them an option for American policy. They opposed on principle, and when necessary embraced with a kiss of death, negotiations of any arms limitation agreements with the Soviet Union. They fought any political accommodation and supported intensified propaganda and political warfare.

The Reagan administration did not codify any policy guidance on relations with the Soviet Union until December 1982. At that time the president approved National Security Decision Directive (NSDD)–75. The directive was a compromise between the ideological-confrontational tendency of the NSC staff and civilian leadership in the Pentagon, and the pragmatic-geopolitical tendency represented by Haig, Shultz, and the professionals in the Department of State. The directive's main thrust was, however, pragmatic. It established three long-term objectives: (1) to contain Soviet expansion and to moderate Soviet international behavior; (2) to encourage, by the limited means at the disposal of the United States, change in the Soviet system toward greater liberalism over time; and (3) to negotiate agreements that were in the interests of the United States. Thus NSDD-75 confirmed containment, and circumscribed (although it did not eliminate) a confrontational approach. Although important qualifications were placed on the aim of encouraging change in the Soviet system, that goal remained. Negotiation was clearly affirmed, but decisions on whether, when, and what to negotiate remained to be resolved.[8]

To the extent that the president's directive left a degree of ambiguity, it reflected Reagan's own ambivalence. He could usually be persuaded by

---

7. This theme was spelled out in a number of speeches from mid-1983 through 1984. The key one was made in congressional testimony in mid-1983. See Secretary Shultz, "U.S.-Soviet Relations in the Context of U.S. Foreign Policy," Statement before the Senate Foreign Relations Committee, June 15, *State Bulletin*, vol. 83 (July 1983), pp. 65–72.

8. NSDD-75 remains classified, but the positions taken in it have been confirmed in authoritative off-the-record interviews.

someone like Haig or Shultz to take a geopolitical position, although his own inner conviction and inclination were ideological. Reagan was not disposed to take confrontational courses of action that risked a direct clash with the Soviet Union, nor were any of his principal advisers, but he held a confrontational attitude that often found rhetorical expression and that often competed with other considerations in the never-ending process of establishing concrete policy positions.

The Reagan administration gradually moved from intransigence and confrontational rhetoric in 1981–83 to increasing efforts to develop a diplomatic dialogue in 1983–84. Throughout 1984 the president himself devoted several major speeches to the theme of strength and dialogue or negotiation.[9]

The administration's own explanation for its shift toward greater expressed readiness for negotiation and dialogue, even with the untrustworthy leaders of an "evil empire," was the restoration of American strength. The United States was not as weak as President Reagan and others in his administration believed in 1981, nor that much stronger by 1984. But if those were their real perceptions, they provided a sound basis for the shift in stance. Many commentators believed that the shift in policy was attributable to a desire to show moderation during the election year. That consideration was clearly present, but it may not have been the principal one. Certainly during its first term the Reagan administration had pressed ahead with a major military program. Economic recovery had placed the United States in a strong economic position internationally, at the same time that the persistence of Soviet economic problems was evident. And politically the Western alliance had surmounted several crises (in particular the one engendered by the ill-conceived sanctions the Reagan administration levied after the imposition of martial law in Poland) and had overcome strong but fading popular opposition to the deployment of American missiles in Europe. Thus by the time of President Reagan's address to the United Nations General Assembly in September 1984 he could say that "America has repaired its strength. . . . We are ready for constructive negotiations with the Soviet Union."[10]

In short, by the end of 1984, when the Reagan administration was returned to office for another four years by an overwhelming majority, it seemed to have chosen containment and "peace through strength" (a slogan it borrowed from the Ford administration, which had turned to it as a substitute for détente in 1976), and in addition an interest in dialogue and negotiation on arms reductions, rather than confrontation. Nonetheless, whether the second Reagan administration could sustain and implement a policy of negotiation

9. See, in particular, "Peace through Credible Deterrence," January 16, *Presidential Documents*, vol. 20 (January 23, 1984), pp. 41–44; "Center for International and Strategic Studies of Georgetown University: Remarks at the Center's National Leadership Forum, April 6, 1984," ibid. (April 9, 1984), pp. 490–97; and "United Nations: Address before the 39th Session of the General Assembly, September 24, 1984," ibid. (October 1, 1984), pp. 1352–59.

10. *Presidential Documents*, vol. 20 (October 1, 1984), p. 1356.

remained doubtful. In addition, after several years of quasi confrontation, there was also a question of the readiness of the Soviet leaders to negotiate with the United States.

Soviet Policy: Détente or Confrontation?

The Soviet reaction to President Carter's abandonment of détente after Afghanistan was to reaffirm it as Soviet policy and to call for an American return to détente.[11] This approach was maintained after the Reagan administration came to power, as authoritatively confirmed at the Twenty-sixth Party Congress held in February–March 1981. Moreover, at that early stage the Soviets placed the blame on the departed Carter administration,[12] leaving open the possibility that the Reagan administration would take a different course. This was an important early hope of the Soviet leaders, although diminished by the early confrontational rhetoric of President Reagan and other members of his administration. At the Party Congress Brezhnev also urged dialogue and suggested a summit meeting.[13]

Throughout 1981 and 1982 the Soviet leaders continued to advocate dialogue with the American administration. They reiterated this desire not only in public statements but also in private diplomatic contacts. They expected tough negotiations, but negotiation nonetheless. There was, however, a gradual and evidently reluctant conclusion that the Reagan administration did not want to negotiate.

The Soviet leaders understood, even though they did not agree with or welcome, the geopolitical containment message of Secretary of State Haig. They also understood, and even overvalued the significance of, the U.S. pursuit of greater military power to provide greater political power. What they could not understand was whether Reagan and his administration were determined to use enhanced American power to challenge the Soviet Union and the bloc of socialist states in their own sphere, that is, whether the United States was serious about the crusade against socialism over which Reagan waxed eloquent in his rhetoric. Containment and competition had been a continuing reality under détente. But détente had involved American recognition and acceptance of the legitimacy of the Soviet Union and even of its nominal

---

11. See chapter 27.

12. L. I. Brezhnev, "Report of the Central Committee of the CPSU to the Twenty-sixth Congress of the Communist Party of the Soviet Union and the Current Tasks of the Party in the Fields of Domestic and Foreign Policy," *XXVI s'yezd kommunisticheskoi partii sovetskogo soyuza, 28 fevralya–3 marta 1981 goda: Stenograficheskii otchet* [The Twenty-sixth Congress of the Communist Party of the Soviet Union, February 28–March 3, 1981: Stenographic Report] (Moscow: Politizdat, 1981), vol. 1, pp. 39–40.

13. Ibid., p. 40.

parity as a superpower. Now that recognition seemed increasingly to be rejected. While U.S. actions were not all consistent, the most basic political, economic, and military ones supported the more ominous thrust of the rhetoric and seemed to be aimed not merely at competition and containment, but at confrontation and cold war.

The change in the Soviet leadership after Brezhnev died in November 1982 did not entail any major change in policy. Andropov strongly reaffirmed a policy of détente and stressed that it was not "a chance episode" or "a past stage." Rather, he expressed confidence that "the future belongs to it."[14]

Despite Andropov's desire to resuscitate détente with the United States, the main development over the year or so of his active incumbency as seen in Moscow was a steady American military buildup, including the actual deployment of missiles in Europe. At the same time, the United States was conducting a successful political holding action in the arms limitation talks. Moreover, the United States also intensified its ideological and political "crusade." In March 1983 President Reagan described the Soviet leaders as "the focus of all evil" and the Soviet Union as an "evil empire."[15] Two weeks later, he called for developing an impenetrable ballistic missile defense with new technologies, dubbed a "Star Wars" initiative.[16] Thus the United States was seen as intensifying the course of confrontation and military buildup.

By June, Andropov was thus led to describe the present period to a plenary meeting of the Communist party as "marked by confrontation, unprecedented in the entire postwar period by its intensity and sharpness, of the two diametrically opposite world outlooks, the two political courses, socialism and imperialism."[17] This statement was still short of concluding that the Soviet Union and the United States were on a collision course, and was posed in terms of ideological conflict. Nonetheless, it was still a considerable escalation beyond two contending "trends," for and against détente, featured in Brezhnev's Twenty-sixth Party Congress report in 1981 and Andropov's own initial statements as party chief in November 1982.

The most jarring development in Soviet-American relations since Afghanistan was an incident on the night of August 31–September 1, 1983. A Korean civil airliner, KAL 007, flew off course in a deep penetration of Soviet airspace in the Far East and was shot down by a Soviet interceptor. The Soviet Union claimed that the airplane was on an intelligence collection mission for

---

14. "Speech of General Secretary of the CC of the CPSU Yu. V. Andropov to the Plenum of the CC of the CPSU, November 22, 1982," *Kommunist*, no. 17 (November 1982), p. 20. This remark was followed by applause. See also "Speech of Yu. V. Andropov at the Funeral Meeting, November 15, 1982," ibid., pp. 11–12.

15. See *Presidential Documents*, vol. 19 (March 14, 1983), p. 369.

16. See "National Security," March 23, *Presidential Documents*, vol. 19 (March 28, 1983), pp. 442–48.

17. "Speech of General Secretary of the CC of the CPSU Comrade Yu. V. Andropov," *Kommunist*, no. 9 (June 1983), p. 5.

the United States; that allegation was denied by Washington. Evidence to resolve the discrepancy was—and remains—inconclusive.[18]

There was widespread outrage in the world, especially in the United States, over the loss of 269 innocent lives in the tragedy. The Soviet charge was generally not accepted in the West, and was in any case not considered to justify the Soviet action. There was wide public denunciation of the Soviet Union in the United States. The American response, once the passion of outrage had been spent, was moderate in terms of actions, mainly a suspension of Aeroflot flights to the United States. The administration therefore believed it had shown great restraint. The president, the secretary of state, and other American leaders had, however, leapt to unjustified initial assumptions— and public charges—that the Soviets had known the airplane was a civilian airliner when it was shot down. Later it became clear that the evidence did not support those assumptions and charges. In addition, the speed and intensity of official U.S. denunciation made a deeply negative impression on the Soviet leaders and further persuaded them of American hostility, if not indeed provocation, in the whole incident (as did Reagan's successful use of the incident to lobby for his defense program).

The KAL incident demonstrated vividly how deeply relations between the two countries had plunged. Each was only too ready to assume the worst of the other and rush not only to judgment but also to premature indictment. The United States (as evidenced in bipartisan congressional expression, as well as administration statements) seemed almost to welcome in the tragedy an opportunity to belabor the Soviet Union with hasty charges of savage barbarity. The Soviet leaders, in response, and to fend off the charges, not only charged callous recklessness in what they continued to believe had been an illegal reconnaissance intrusion, but also political provocation and hostile exploitation of the tragedy. While Americans focused their outrage on the consequences of the Soviet military action, the Soviets focused on the facts of deep penetration of their sovereign airspace unexplained except as espionage, and of the immediate U.S. seizure of the initiative in using the incident to mount sharp attacks on the Soviet system. Each side thus converted its ready suspicions and worst assumptions about the other into accusations that could not be proved or disproved, but that tended to be believed by its own side and bitterly resented by the other. The upshot was to set American-Soviet and Soviet-American relations considerably further back and undercut tentative steps toward an improvement in relations.

On September 28 an unusual formal statement by Andropov, as chief of state and party, was issued on behalf of the Soviet leadership. It represented the first definitive and authoritative overall evaluation of the policy of the Reagan administration by the Soviet leadership. While precipitated

---

18. For discussions of the KAL incident, including Soviet and other sources, see Alexander Dallin, *Black Box: The KAL Incident and the Superpowers* (Berkeley, Calif.: University of California Press, 1985); and the forthcoming study by Seymour Hersh.

by the KAL incident, the evaluation presented had been building for a long time. The policy of the Reagan administration was described as "a militarist course that represents a serious threat to peace. Its essence is to try to ensure a dominating position in the world for the United States of America without regard for the interests of other states and peoples." While Soviet policy of peaceful coexistence was reaffirmed, the leadership's statement went on to declare, "If anyone had any illusions about the possibility of an evolution for the better in the policy of the present American administration, recent events have dispelled them once and for all."[19] While this did not mean that the Soviet leaders were giving up on any conduct of relations with the United States, it did mean that thereafter they were even less inclined to base their own policy on expectation of the possibility of serious negotiation or agreement with the United States.

Throughout this entire period Soviet party officials, government officials, and academic and media commentators gave varying assessments of American policy. All agreed that the United States had abandoned détente, was pursuing military superiority, and was pressing a broad offensive against the Soviet Union, socialism, and national liberation movements. Where they differed was on the possibility of a return of realists in the capitalist ruling circles who would recognize the futility and risks of a course of confrontation and the common interest the United States and the Soviet Union had in controlling their continuing competition. Increasingly, détente came to embody just the key component of arms limitations and other measures to reduce the risk of war. What had earlier been termed "military détente" began to displace political détente as the core interest.

One important policy issue for the Soviet leaders that continued throughout the entire period under review here was determining the necessary level of resources for defense. The military leaders had stressed the turn by the United States in the late 1970s to seeking military superiority. When the Reagan administration intensified the military buildup, they emphasized that "military preparations" were being "raised to unprecedented levels" and were being accompanied by "military doctrines which stem from the strategy of 'direct confrontation' proclaimed by Washington and are directed at achieving military superiority over the Soviet Union and establishing U.S. world supremacy." And this was all taking place in the context of "the new 'crusade' against communism proclaimed by the president."[20] There was no disagreement in Moscow over these conclusions as to American military-political efforts and aims. There were, however, divided views over the extent of the direct military

---

19. "Statement by Yu. V. Andropov, General Secretary of the CC of the CPSU, Chairman of the Presidium of the Supreme Soviet of the USSR," *Pravda*, September 29, 1983. The statement was read on Soviet radio and television on September 28 and later reprintings give it that date.

20. These statements were made by Minister of Defense Marshal D. F. Ustinov in "Up to the Level of New Tasks: Meeting of the Party Aktiv of the Order of Lenin Moscow Military District," *Krasnaya zvezda* [Red Star], December 8, 1982.

threat and therefore over the readiness posture and other measures the Soviet Union needed to take. All agreed that the Soviet Union must and would see that its own military strength was maintained at the "necessary" or "appropriate" level, but there were divergences over what that level was.

The most consistently alarmist and vocal military leader in the period 1980 through 1984 was Marshal Nikolai Ogarkov, first deputy minister of defense and chief of the General Staff. His standing as the senior professional military man was unchallenged until his sudden removal from those posts in September 1984. While no official explanation was given for his removal, it seems clear that one reason, probably the principal one, was his persistence in demanding that still more needed to be done to meet military requirements for deterrence and defense in the face of the U.S. military buildup.[21]

While the question of military requirements and resource allocations to the military is an important and persisting one for the Soviet leaders, they have seen the U.S. military buildup under the Reagan administration as posing far more basic questions. To the Soviet leaders, a pervasive political-military shift had actually begun in the late 1970s under Carter, with the rise in military programs only one element in a broader policy shift.

---

21. In what is certainly more than coincidence, on the day preceding Ogarkov's removal an editorial in *Pravda*, and on the day of his removal a similar editorial in the armed forces newspaper *Red Star*, strongly suggested that the party leadership had just rejected a proposal to reallocate resources from consumer programs to defense. *Pravda* stated, "Despite the current tense international situation, which requires diverting considerable resources to strengthening the security of the country, even *thinking* about cutting the broad social program laid down by the party at the XXVI Congress is not admissible." "For Soviet Man," *Pravda*, September 5, 1984. Emphasis added. The next day *Red Star* fell into line, repeating almost exactly the same words (changing only "security" to "defense capability" of the country, and dropping the reference to the Party Congress from this sentence, because it appeared in the preceding sentence and was directly linked). "For the Good of the People," *Krasnaya zvezda*, September 6, 1984. The language used in these editorials, which clearly stemmed from a party decision, had an august progenitor. In his March 2 election speech to the Supreme Soviet Chernenko had said that despite defense requirements, "we did not even think of cutting social programs." This statement was again quoted in a *Pravda* editorial on July 30. K. U. Chernenko, *Pravda*, March 3, 1984, and "Party Solicitude in the Sphere of Services," *Pravda*, July 30, 1984. But the new formulation made clear that it was also not admissible for *others*—like Ogarkov—to think of doing so either. Further, Chernenko's reference had been to the past; the September references were in the present tense with a future application.

Ironically, to support a plea for more attention to advanced conventional weaponry, Ogarkov had earlier quoted Chernenko as saying that "military men must . . . resolutely overcome any conservatism and inertia" and take as their slogan "from a correct idea, fully armed with experience—to bold actions!" But he overestimated the permissible limits of bold actions. See interview with Marshal N. V. Ogarkov, "The Defense of Socialism: The Experience of History and the Present Day," *Krasnaya zvezda*, May 9, 1984.

Marshal Ogarkov was not retired or completely disgraced. He was removed from his key position ranking behind the ailing minister of defense, Marshal Ustinov, and in a manner indicating a fall from favor, but he was quietly named commander of a new Western Theater of Military Operations organization, the most important army field command.

First was a decisive change in the *U.S. political line* to an abandonment of détente, following several years of a growing tendency in that direction. President Carter's across-the-board reaction to the Soviet intervention in Afghanistan was, as earlier described, not recognized in Moscow as having been caused by that event. At most the Soviet move was seen as having precipitated the American action, and as serving as a pretext for it. Détente was, in practice, dropped in January 1980. Reagan merely took the next step of disavowing détente explicitly. In the Soviet view, a principal reason for dropping détente was to stir up a more militant anti-Soviet atmosphere in order to gain public and congressional support for a major military buildup. The same purpose was seen behind President Reagan's inflammatory rhetoric about the "evil empire."

Second was the *U.S. military program* launched by President Carter in 1980 and, again, only intensified by Reagan. The U.S. and NATO military buildup was traced to 1978, but the major steps were the decision in December 1979 to deploy intermediate-range missiles in Europe and the large increases in the U.S. military budget and outlays in 1980. Reagan expanded and sustained the arms buildup and added the threat of a new dimension in the arms race through ballistic missile defense with space systems.

Third was the change in *U.S. military doctrine.* The United States abandoned mutual deterrence based on parity and substituted a drive for superiority in war-waging capabilities in order to provide escalation dominance at all levels of nuclear and nonnuclear engagement. Presidential Directive (PD)–59 under Carter in 1980 was the culmination of a process that had begun in 1974 with the Schlesinger Doctrine. Again, the decision by NATO in 1979 to deploy the missiles was seen as related to the war-waging capabilities sought under PD-59. Moreover, the turn by the United States to pursuit of war-waging superiority came after explicit Soviet modification of its military doctrine and renunciation of superiority and belief in the winnability of war in the nuclear age. This American quest for ways to use its nuclear military capabilities was seen as being carried forward by the Reagan administration's Defense Guidance and National Security Decision Directives (NSDD)–13 and –32, approved in the spring of 1982.

Fourth, and rounding out the other three changes, was *U.S. abandonment of arms control.* Carter's shelving of the SALT II Treaty in January 1980 raised serious questions in Moscow about American readiness to proceed not only with the treaty, but with the whole process of negotiated strategic arms limitation. When the Reagan administration later resumed negotiations, first on intermediate-range nuclear forces (INF) in November 1981, and then on strategic arms reductions (START) in June 1982, it was clear that it did so only to head off growing opposition in the West to the arms buildup, and not because of a real interest in reaching agreements on arms limitation. The position the United States took in those talks, until finally broken off by the Soviets in frustration at the end of 1983, only confirmed to the Soviet leaders the lack of U.S. interest in seeking mutually acceptable agreements. Again, after the Soviet Union had developed and demonstrated a serious interest in negotiating strategic arms limitations in the 1970s, the United States had dropped out.

A fifth change was the *U.S. resort to military force* in the third world to block or roll back progressive revolutionary movement. The Carter Doctrine was seen as but the first step in an intensification of American reliance on military means to secure what it termed "vital interests" but that seemed to extend to any area, even where U.S. interests had been minimal. It was a repudiation of the Nixon Doctrine, and reflected an end to the "Vietnam syndrome" and self-imposed restraint in the use of military means in the geopolitical competition.

Increased American readiness to resort to use of military power around the world was seen in El Salvador, Nicaragua, Lebanon, and Grenada. American use of its own military force has been indirect in Central America, and was ineffective in Lebanon. Nonetheless, this return to pre-Vietnam gunboat diplomacy (symbolized, in a way, by the return of the four battleships and exemplified literally when the *New Jersey* bombarded the Shiites and Druze in Lebanon) reflected greater American reliance on military means. It was also seen not only as undercutting Soviet influence at least in the short run, but also as damaging the argument that continued Soviet advocacy of great power détente aids, or is even compatible with, progressive revolutionary change in the world. Finally, the United States and its proxies have been waging a series of scarcely disguised covert wars against Afghanistan, Nicaragua, Kampuchea, Ethiopia, Angola, and Mozambique. The Soviets, too, have reason for wanting "restraint and reciprocity" in superpower behavior in the third world.

Thus, from the Soviet perspective, in the 1980s the United States has chosen across the board not only to give priority to competition over collaboration and negotiations, but to give priority to military power. U.S. policy may be seen, and intended, in Washington as pursuit of a policy of peace through strength, containment of Soviet expansion, restoration of military power that had languished, a peaceful assertion of democratic values in an ideological challenge, and readiness to negotiate (from a strong position). But as seen from Moscow the Reagan administration has sought to acquire military superiority in order to roll back a changing correlation of forces in the world, to negotiate if at all from a position of power to compel one-sided terms, and to press a political-economic-ideological offensive against socialism and the USSR under the shadow of growing military strength and thus to attempt to reassert American dominance in the world.

The Carter administration after vacillation, and then the Reagan administration with undisguised enthusiasm, thus chose confrontation over détente, and the pursuit of military superiority over mutual arms limitation.

How have the Soviet leaders responded to this challenge? Throughout the four years of the first Reagan administration, and throughout two changes in the leadership at home, the Soviet Union continued to advocate détente and arms limitations, while attacking the United States for abandoning the path of détente, arms control, and negotiation. Soviet policy may be described (and is described by the Soviet leaders and media) as pressing peace initiatives against the negative, recalcitrant United States. In fact, it has been very reactive. (In general Soviet policy is, as this study shows, far more reactive than either Moscow or Washington depicts it, and it has been even more reactive than usual in the first half of the 1980s.)

In surveying the alignment of forces in the world, the Soviet leaders have seen few opportunities to advance Soviet influence or to assist the progressive movement of history. They have been on the defensive in relation not only to the United States, but to the world at large. They have been on the defensive in their own camp, with the serious internal challenge in Poland since 1980 only the most critical instance. In those areas where the Soviet Union had most committed itself in the 1970s (in Afghanistan, and in support of Vietnam against Kampuchea) and even in the 1960s (Cuba) it has become heavily overcommitted in terms of economic aid (and in Afghanistan in a drawn-out military campaign as well). Ethiopia, Angola, and Mozambique continue to be weak and threatened, instead of leading a progressive movement in Africa. The Soviets expected a revolutionary surge in Central America during a brief period from mid-1979, after the Sandinista victory in Nicaragua (with minimal Soviet support), until January 1981, when the Salvadoran "final offensive" failed. Even during that period direct Soviet aid was minor. Since that time, the Soviets have not expected early revolution in Central America nor have they given more than minimal aid to revolutionary movements (official American claims and perceptions notwithstanding). They have also not undertaken any initiatives in the Middle East or South Asia. Even in relations with China and in Europe the Soviet role has been passive and defensive. The reactive nature of the Soviet international position does not mean that the Soviet leaders have no ambitions or expectations of change. Rather, they pride themselves on patience and on acting in accordance with objective possibilities that do not always permit forward movement.

The Soviet leaders are led to stress relations with the United States not because they see great promise, but because those relations are of central importance. Even if the prospects for strategic arms limitations are bleak, whatever possibilities may arise (or can be stimulated) are so important as to require continuing efforts. Moreover, American policy in the past has shown wide swings, and internal political or economic constraints may lead to changes in position. There are differences in the Soviet political establishment, and perhaps in the leadership, over the question of the extent and nature of possible shifts in American policy. And so there should be, given differing tendencies within the administration itself and in Congress and public opinion, notwithstanding President Reagan's own strong victory in the 1984 election.

There has been no question in Moscow about whether détente or confrontation is the preferred policy. While, as discussed earlier and illustrated throughout this study, the Soviet and American conceptions of détente have differed, the Soviet leadership has shown persistent support for détente rather than confrontation. While Soviet reactions to perceived American confrontational challenges have involved confrontational responses (for example, the shift to virulent attacks on U.S. policy in the Soviet media), the Soviet leaders clearly would prefer to return to the détente of the 1970s. That is clearly not in prospect in the 1980s, as the Soviet leaders well understand. Thus, in the first half of the 1980s the question in Moscow has been "détente or confrontation," not as a choice they pose to themselves, but as a question about whether the United States has chosen for them and issued a confrontational challenge the Soviet Union cannot refuse.

Arms Control

Strategic arms limitation was in many respects a key element in the development of détente from 1969 to 1972, and the fate of both remained closely tied through 1979. Both were placed in suspension in 1980, and then in effect rejected in 1981, by the United States.

President Reagan decided early in his administration not to ratify what his colleagues called the "fatally flawed" SALT II Treaty, signed by President Carter in June 1979. But he went much further. He also did not try to amend it, and was flagrantly uninterested in resuming the SALT negotiations. Senior members of his administration made clear that priority would be given to building up American military power, and perhaps then to negotiating arms limitations—from a position of strength.

The Soviet leaders had expected the Reagan administration to take a tough stand on SALT II. They braced themselves for expected demands for renegotiation. At first they tried to discourage attempts to amend the treaty by emphasizing that it was already the result of balanced compromises by both sides and that, as a solemnly signed treaty, it should not be reopened. Then they began to stress the value of the treaty without ruling out some additions or minor changes. But they had no response to the lack of interest in *any* SALT treaty displayed by the new administration, even though it decided to take no actions contrary to the unsatisfied treaty (and the expired SALT Interim Agreement of 1972) for the time being.

Throughout most of 1981 Ambassador Dobrynin, in private meetings with Secretary of State Haig, kept urging a resumption of the strategic arms talks. Haig would only repeat the need first for Soviet restraint in the third world (and in Poland).[22] When finally the United States showed an interest in negotiation, it was initially only in the field of intermediate-range nuclear forces (INF), and the reason for that American interest was transparently the rising public opposition in Western Europe to the planned deployment of U.S. missiles. Only by at least appearing to work for arms limitation on the negoti-

---

22. See Haig, *Caveat*, pp. 102–09.

ating "track" could public support in the West be maintained so that NATO could go forward on the second, deployment track of the 1979 NATO alliance decision. And when the United States was ready to resume strategic arms talks (redubbed strategic arms reduction talks, or START, to stress reduction—and to shed the old acronym), it was again obvious that it was attempting to head off rising American public support for a freeze on the deployment of all nuclear weapons.

The INF and START negotiations from 1981 through 1983 have been well-chronicled in detail.[23] The internal policy debates and decisions within the Reagan administration have been more revealing, and ultimately more significant, than the negotiations between the United States and the Soviet Union. Not only has there been constant bureaucratic infighting, but the general policy line of the Reagan administration (at least in its first term) as well as its leadership style ensured that the American position precluded agreement.

In the INF negotiations the Reagan administration opted for the propaganda high ground by proposing a "zero option" for intermediate-range missiles. While this proposal shored up political support in NATO countries for continuing preparations for deployment, the principal purpose of the administration, it also killed the prospect for serious negotiation and agreement. While on the surface the proposition was equitable and admirable (in aiming at "eliminating a whole class of armaments"), it was heavily loaded to Soviet disadvantage. While it would have meant NATO would not proceed with the newly planned deployment of 572 U.S. missiles in Europe, it would have involved the Soviets' not only eliminating all their deployments of SS-20 missiles, but rolling back twenty years of strategic history and dismantling the nearly 600 Soviet intermediate-range missiles deployed since the late 1950s. It would also have limited only land-based missiles, exempting all sea-based missiles and aircraft. Thus the United States would have retained the option of an unlimited increase in those systems capable of striking the Soviet Union. Further, by restricting the proposed constraints to U.S. and Soviet systems, all British and French nuclear strike systems were excluded. Again, not only would their existing missile and bomber systems be untouched, but future expansion would be unlimited. And announced plans of the British and French for deploying MIRV warheads would make their forces larger in number of warheads than the Soviet INF missile forces and give them more than double the number of planned American missile warheads. Finally, the U.S. and NATO proposal called for limiting all Soviet intermediate-range land-based missiles wherever deployed, not just those in or facing Europe. While some SS-20 missiles deployed east of the Ural Mountains were in range of Europe and would reasonably have been included on that basis, the American proposal would also have covered others in the Far East beyond range of Western Europe. In short, on

23. See Strobe Talbott, *Deadly Gambits: The Reagan Administration and the Stalemate in Nuclear Arms Control* (Knopf, 1984).

all counts the proposal was loaded to Western advantage and Soviet disadvantage, and it was clearly not a basis for negotiation aimed at reaching agreement.

The American policy community (with the likely significant exception of President Reagan himself) well understood the nonnegotiability of the zero option. Indeed, some civilian leaders in the Pentagon and hardliners in the White House had successfully pushed its adoption for that very reason.[24]

The reasons for the failure of the INF negotiations, however, went deeper than an American position tailored to be unacceptable to the Soviet Union. The basic interest of NATO in American INF deployments in the first place had been to ensure a coupling of U.S. conventional and tactical nuclear forces in Europe with U.S. intercontinental nuclear forces. For that purpose, *some* U.S. deployment was needed. To be sure, the zero option itself violated that premise, and that fact was troubling to some NATO strategic analysts. But since the real purpose, and the only realistic outcome, of advancing the zero option was to preclude agreement and to ensure deployment, that theoretical inconsistency did not trouble many. But the Soviet aim in INF was to head off *any* deployment of U.S. intermediate-range missiles in Europe. Thus the aims of the two sides were irreconcilable, even if moderate positions had been advanced. The Soviets offered increasingly substantial reductions in their own missile force in exchange for nondeployment of the American missiles, eventually offering to reduce the number of SS-20s facing Europe by nearly half and to reduce the total number of missile launchers to less than one-fourth what it was or had been before the new SS-20 deployments, and to reduce the number of warheads to less than half the current number, a level that again would be lower than before the SS-20 deployment began. But by 1983 the United States was only interested in proceeding with deployment, not in reducing Soviet forces, even if that resulted in a more favorable overall balance.

When the NATO deployment began in November 1983, the Soviet Union broke off the talks. The separate INF arms limitation track was at a dead end.[25] The Soviet and American (and British and French) nuclear forces remained to be taken into account in unilateral decisions and in broader future negotiations. Such negotiations began in March 1985.

START, too, was fated to fail. While each side initially took a position loaded to its advantage, that could have reflected bargaining tactics. There was no fundamental incompatibility in the aims of the two sides compa-

---

24. For the most complete review of the INF negotiations see ibid., pp. 21–206.

   Secretary of State Haig opposed the zero option on the grounds that, as he puts it in his memoir, "proposal of the Zero Option would, as it has, generate the suspicion that the United States was only interested in a frivolous propaganda exercise, or worse, that it was disingenuously engaging in arms negotiations simply as a cover for a desire to build up its nuclear arsenal." Haig, *Caveat*, p. 229.

25. See Raymond L. Garthoff, "Postmortem on INF Talks," *Bulletin of the Atomic Scientists*, vol. 40 (December 1984), pp. 7–10.

rable to that in the INF talks, although there were other heavy impediments to successful negotiation. First, there was the legacy of SALT II. In framing an arms control position, the Reagan administration intentionally ignored the SALT II limitations and set out to do better for the United States. Since the SALT II provisions represented the results of seven years of hard bargaining, it was unlikely that the Soviet Union would make appreciably greater concessions. Nevertheless, the United States proposed deeper reductions, skewed in a fashion that would eviscerate the heart of the Soviet strategic force, as they called for reduction by two-thirds in Soviet large missiles. While proposed overall equal levels would nominally be equitable, the more detailed subceilings bore much more heavily on the Soviet forces. Even more important, none of the planned major improvements to the U.S. strategic force—the large MX missile with MIRVs, the B-1 bomber, the Trident SLBM and submarine force—would have been banned or even reduced. While the Soviet Union was being asked to give up most of its best forces, the United States could modernize its best forces and slough off older systems planned for retirement in any case.[26]

The Soviet approach, while also slanted in its favor, attempted to preserve and build on the foundation of SALT II. In effect, the Soviets attempted to negotiate SALT III, proposing sizable reductions from the SALT II ceilings. (In fact, the basic limit of 1,800 strategic nuclear delivery vehicles was the same as the number proposed by the Carter administration in March 1977—and by the Nixon administration in August 1970—although other terms of the proposal differed.)

START did not begin until mid-1982. By the summer of 1983 both sides had made some modifications in their positions, but the gap remained very great.[27] In particular, the United States was not ready to accept curtailment of its own buildup of counterforce capabilities comparable to the drastic reductions sought in Soviet counterforce capabilities. While the U.S. proposals were nominally equal, they would have applied unequally. For example, the proposed limit of 5,000 missile warheads for each side would have involved a sizable and equitable cut of about one-third in the arsenals of both sides. But a subceiling of 2,500 warheads on land-based missiles, and further sublimits of 210 on MX-sized ICBMs (for example, the Soviet SS-18 and SS-19 and U.S. MX) and of 100 on very large ICBMs (the Soviet SS-18), would have meant a cut of more than half in Soviet ICBM warheads and two-thirds in SS-18 and SS-19 warheads, while the United States could have deployed additional ICBM warheads, including the then planned 200 MX missiles. Moreover, *all*

---

26. See Talbott, *Deadly Gambits*, pp. 233–76.

Haig himself admits that the U.S. START proposal was "a nonnegotiable package . . . a two-faced proposal which was clearly going to fall of its own weight and did." See Roy Gutman, "Bad Tidings: The World According to Haig," an interview with the former secretary of state, *Newsday*, August 12, 1984; and Haig, *Caveat*, p. 223.

27. Ibid., pp. 277–342.

other U.S. strategic modernization programs could have continued as well: Trident II SLBMs, bomber-based ALCMs, submarine-based SLCMs, and the Pershing II and GLCM European-based systems. Overall, while the proposal would have alleviated the vulnerability of American land-based intercontinental missiles, it would have greatly *increased* the vulnerability of Soviet land-based missiles. As a Soviet general remarked to me in 1983, "You [the United States] want to solve *your* vulnerability problem by making *our* forces vulnerable." And he was right.

The natural conservatism on both sides, evident throughout the SALT negotiations of the 1970s, remained. Both tried to get maximum reductions in the forces of the other side, but without being willing to make comparable sacrifices in their own forces and capabilities. Both were wary about constraining future options. In the past that contradiction had been resolved by reaching agreements that did not seriously reduce the strategic forces of either side. Critics of the SALT I Interim Agreement and SALT II Treaty were correct in saying they did not do enough to curb improvements or to achieve reductions in military forces. U.S. attempts to impose drastic changes on the Soviet military force while keeping its own intact and enhanced were obviously unacceptable to the Soviet Union. And Soviet attempts to do the same to the United States, or, failing that, again to make relatively larger but still ineffective cuts on both sides, were not acceptable to the Reagan administration (although they probably would have been to any of its three predecessors).

Indeed, the interest of the Reagan administration as a whole (and it was rent by disagreements among its chief components) in strategic arms limitation remained very uncertain. The argument continued to be made, and perhaps even believed by some (including President Reagan), that only as American military power was "restored" (that is, expanded and enhanced) would the Soviets have an incentive to negotiate seriously (that is, to accede to U.S. terms). This approach was either very naïve or feckless.

When the Soviet leaders decided to break off the INF talks at the end of 1983, they also suspended the START negotiations. The reason was a conviction that, after a year and a half of nonstart START, the United States was not seriously interested in negotiating a mutually acceptable agreement. They also believed that the shock in the West of ending the two negotiations would cause a reappraisal and might jar the United States into undertaking a more serious negotiating effort. Instead, the Reagan administration was able to claim that it remained as interested in arms limitations as ever and that the Soviets were solely to blame for the breakdown caused by their walkout. Whatever the merits of the respective charges, the U.S. position seemed more justified in the West because the Soviet Union had walked out.

An important new element entered the picture in 1983, one that would cast a long shadow over all subsequent strategic arms negotiations and possible limitations. President Reagan, in a dramatic and unexpected embrace of the concept of strategic ballistic missile defense in a speech in March 1983, resurrected a whole additional dimension of the arms race.[28] While both sides had continued to conduct research and development work on antiballistic missile (ABM) systems (now usually referred to as ballistic missile defense, BMD), the ABM Treaty of 1972, of indefinite duration, had for a decade largely removed this key area of strategic defense from the arms equation. Suddenly it was back. While the technology was uncertain and distant, the very idea of "Star Wars," as the president's idea was quickly dubbed, captured wide public attention. It also stirred considerable disquiet. The president's initial idea was to substitute assured defense for deterrence by assured retaliation. Later discussion of his concept, officially termed the strategic defense initiative (SDI), blurred this aim and tended more to stress a high priority research and development of exotic BMD systems that might complement, rather than replace, strategic offensive forces intended to deter. The concept, as well as the concrete technical schemes envisaged, remained uncertain. Nevertheless, the United States soon launched a $26 billion, five-year program.

Many in the United States (and in Western Europe) questioned the desirability, as well as the technical prospect, of a pursuit of strategic defense. The very idea challenged the underpinnings of mutual deterrence, which had been the foundation for U.S. and NATO policy long before SALT. Moreover, while the administration argued (not completely convincingly) that its whole development program would be compatible with the ABM Treaty, no one could dispute that the avowed purpose of SDI was to find effective means of ballistic missile defense (BMD), the deployment of which (and at least some testing) would require amendment or abrogation of the ABM Treaty.

There also arose a new charge not only from hardline critics outside the administration, but from the administration itself, that the Soviets were violating the ABM Treaty. Not everyone saw this action as merely coincidental with the rising interest in some quarters in freeing the United States from the constraints of the treaty.

Soviet reaction was strongly negative. The Soviet leader, Yury Andropov, personally responded to the Star Wars speech with a resounding denunciation of the reopening of the issue of BMD and reaffirmation of mutual deterrence and the ABM Treaty. Soviet scientists, like most American ones, saw no prospect of a truly effective defense against an enemy first strike, as President Reagan had described his goal. What they did see was the possibility of (and likely American lead in) developing a partially effective defense that, while not protection against the full force of an enemy first strike, might be considered adequate against a ragged *retaliatory* strike. Thus the SDI complemented suspiciously well what they already saw as a concerted long-term American plan to develop a first-strike capability.

---

28. President Ronald Reagan, "National Security: Address to the Nation, March 23, 1983," *Presidential Documents*, vol. 19 (March 28, 1983), pp. 442–48.

SDI was thus seen as an ominous alternative to arms control, predicated on removing the most effective existing arms limitation agreement, the ABM Treaty, and prejudicing the prospects for any strategic offensive arms limitation. It also contributed to the Soviet decision to abandon the START charade.

The U.S. program to develop a strategic BMD thus greatly complicates the attainment (and preservation) of any strategic arms limitation. Arguments advanced by President Reagan and his administration that the SDI will facilitate offensive arms reductions are either naïve, as is probably true in his case, or disingenuous.

In the fall of 1984, partly in response to a Soviet initiative to open talks to ban space weaponry, the administration raised the idea of "umbrella talks" to cover a flexible combination of arms limitations on various strategic offensive and defensive arms. The Soviet reaction, to the surprise of many Americans, was favorable—albeit cautious. An umbrella approach could provide a new way not only to resume strategic arms limitation and reduction talks without either side having to back down on the issues that stalemated INF and START, but also to address the SDI and ASAT (antisatellite arms talks) issues. The Soviets are suspicious that the United States may simply be seeking to use threats of SDI to pressure them to agree to disadvantageous one-sided offensive limitations. That outcome they will not accept.

As the year drew to a close, agreement was reached for a meeting in early January 1985 between Secretary of State Shultz and Foreign Minister Gromyko to discuss ways to proceed under the umbrella approach. Agreement was reached to resume negotiations. Nonetheless, the future of strategic arms limitation and reduction, and arms control in general, remained clouded. Ultimately, the prospects for preserving or extending strategic arms limitations and reductions—for the unconsummated START and INF, the expired SALT I Interim Agreement, the unratified but observed SALT II Treaty, and the valid ABM Treaty—depend above all on the political relationship between the United States and the Soviet Union. And as long as the one regards the other as the Evil Empire, and prefers to indict the Soviets for alleged violations rather than work to resolve questions about compliance, the prospects for agreements to enhance their mutual security seem remote indeed.[29]

---

29. The most relevant consideration among various charges by the two sides is compliance with existing arms control agreements. While the process of resolving questions of compliance through the established Standing Consultative Commission (SCC) worked well from 1972 through 1979, as noted in an earlier chapter there have been unofficial charges of violations since 1975. In response to a congressional mandate, the Reagan administration in January 1984 sent a classified report to Congress that charged seven specific "violations and probable violations" by the Soviet Union. (An unclassified summary of the report was made public.) The validity of the charges has been challenged. The Soviet Union denied them and issued its own list of alleged American violations since 1975. In December 1984 a new report to Congress added twelve more alleged violations, and a more complete report, in both classified and unclassified versions, was issued in February 1985.

Europe between the Superpowers

The disjunction between the collapse of American-Soviet détente and the continuation of an East-West détente in Europe intensified in the early years of the 1980s. The first effects were felt, as noted, in 1980, in the wake of the Soviet military intervention in Afghanistan, when the United States abandoned détente and Europe did not.[30] During 1981–82 a similar discrepancy attended the responses of the United States and Western Europe to the Polish suppression of the Solidarity movement in December 1981 and thereafter.

While less clearcut and dramatic, an uneasy compromise was also required in NATO policy statements and in coordinating the positions of the NATO countries for the Conference on Security and Cooperation in Europe (CSCE) follow-through conference in Madrid (1981–83) and the succeeding Conference on Disarmament in Europe (CDE) in Stockholm (1983 and continuing). The most central and politically important issue straining U.S.–West European relations was the internal debate over deployment of American intermediate-range missiles in Europe and attendant concerns over the conduct of the INF arms talks. Least prominent during the years 1981–84, but potentially very important, was a growing divergence over the role of arms control in general as a measure to alleviate the tensions and risks of war between East and West. The Western Europeans have felt much more strongly and positively about arms control than has the American administration. This gap, while muffled, gave rise to doubts in Europe about the U.S. commitment to arms control and to concern over the U.S. preference for a unilateral arms buildup, including the strategic defense initiative. To the Europeans, SDI threatened the ABM Treaty and the whole process of East-West arms control, as well as stirred fears of American strategic decoupling and isolationism. At the same time, there was a growing American sentiment that the Europeans were not doing their share to carry the common defense burden and were too readily inclined to take a soft détente attitude and to be too eager for arms control.

Finally, underlying all these concerns and differences was a growing mutual estrangement over what the tasks, if not the purposes, of the alliance should be. The NATO alliance has withstood and outlived many internal "crises" over its three-and-a-half decades. It overcame the specific issues of the early 1980s reasonably well. Nonetheless, if the United States were to remain on a confrontational-containment track while Western Europe pursued a détente track in relations with the Soviet Union and the Soviet bloc in Eastern Europe, the long-term impact on the alliance could be very great.

While the merits of the charges clearly are important, to date they have not been established. But they have stimulated public doubt about the value of the arms control process. This doubt may become an important factor in debates over any arms limitation agreements reached and submitted for ratification.

30. See chapter 27.

The European allies had not been happy with the United States' unilaterally taking some steps toward détente and arms limitation with the Soviet Union in the early 1970s. That feeling was nothing compared with their unhappiness and concern over a unilateral U.S. pursuit of a course of quasi confrontation in the early 1980s. The harsh rhetoric emanating from the top officials of the Reagan administration, including the hostile remarks about the Soviet system by President Reagan himself, was disquieting to many Europeans. Particularly distressing were remarks criticizing détente itself—to which NATO, including the United States, had solemnly subscribed in December 1967.[31] For example, the Europeans found shocking an off-the-cuff statement by Secretary of Defense Weinberger to a group of NATO defense ministers, a statement reported widely in the European press: "If the movement from cold war to détente is progress, then let me say we cannot afford much more progress."[32]

The meeting of NATO foreign ministers in May 1981 was the first occasion under the new U.S. administration that called for a formal statement of alliance policy. In preparing and negotiating the ministerial communiqué (a process that preceded the actual meeting), the U.S. representatives tried to omit any reference to détente, but the Europeans balked. They all could agree on criticizing the Soviet Union, especially for the occupation of Afghanistan. But the European allies insisted on reaffirming the aim of détente. Finally the United States reluctantly acceded to a formulation that reaffirmed the goal of a "more constructive East-West relationship," and stated that the allies would "maintain a dialogue with the Soviet Union and will work together for genuine detente and the development of East-West relations, whenever Soviet behavior makes this possible." They also agreed "to encourage Soviet restraint and responsibility."[33]

Again in May 1982, at the meeting following the imposition of martial law in Poland, the United States sought to have the aim of détente deleted. Again the allies (led by the West Germans) insisted on its retention. Thus the May 1982 communiqué reaffirmed the aims of "genuine detente" and a "more constructive East-West relationship," to be achieved through "dialogue and negotiation." Moreover, "arms control and disarmament, together with deterrence and defense," were recognized as "integral parts of

---

31. See chapter 4.

32. Cited in Walter Isaacson, "Softly, with a Big Stick," *Time*, April 27, 1981, p. 28. The occasion was a meeting of the Nuclear Planning Group. Weinberger made disparaging comments about détente on other occasions during that same visit to Europe.

33. "Final Communique, May 5, 1981," *State Bulletin*, vol. 81 (July 1981), pp. 39–40.

The term "genuine détente" implied doubt whether current Soviet behavior reflected full adherence to détente, a point on which the European allies agreed after Afghanistan. This phrase was first used in the NATO communiqué in December 1980. But alliance support for détente was reaffirmed.

Alliance security policy."[34] These themes were reiterated in all alliance communiqués through 1984, including a special alliance declaration in May 1984 that reaffirmed the Harmel Report of 1967.[35]

The U.S. agreement to open arms limitation talks on intermediate-range nuclear forces (INF), announced to the allies at the May 1981 ministerial meeting, prevented what otherwise could have become a serious split over the deployment of INF missiles, and consequently over mutual confidence between the United States and its allies. The zero option proposal, while it was initially successful in attracting European praise, increasingly came to be regarded as the nonnegotiable propaganda platform it was. At the same time, the West generally considered the steadfast Soviet objection to any deployment of U.S. missiles as equally intransigent and unacceptable. Thus, despite increasing dissatisfaction at the failure of the INF talks over their two-year life (November 1981–November 1983), by breaking off the talks the Soviet Union took the lion's share of the blame in the eyes of Western publics.

One episode did cause a flare-up of concern in the alliance before it subsided. In July 1982 the American negotiator, Ambassador Paul H. Nitze, had worked out with his Soviet counterpart, Ambassador Yuly Kvitsinsky, a possible compromise agreement. This private negotiation had, however, been undertaken without authorization from Washington, and the would-be compromise was turned down by both Washington and Moscow. As word of the possible compromise leaked out, the U.S. administration was criticized in some quarters in Europe for repudiating the attempt. Serious division within the alliance was spared by the Soviet rejection. Which side had turned the compromise down first was not possible to determine, and the blame was seen as shared.[36]

The INF talks did not lead to an agreement; indeed, they stimulated additional Soviet deployments as an avowed countermeasure. They were, however, successful in another respect. The mere fact that they had taken place was sufficient to reduce to politically manageable levels popular opposition to the NATO deployment. It began on schedule in December 1983, and by the end of 1984 over 100 missiles were in place. It did not appear likely that the process of deployment would be seriously impeded by continuing public opposition.

Despite genuine Soviet concern over the military implications of the short-time-to-target Pershing II missiles in particular, the INF deployment was not strongly supported in Washington, or in NATO, for its military value. Rather, it was seen initially—on both sides of the Atlantic, and in Washington by both the Carter and Reagan administrations—as a step to shore up alliance

---

34. "Final Communique, May 18, 1982," *State Bulletin*, vol. 82 (August 1982), p. 67.

35. "Washington Statement on East-West Relations, May 31, 1984," *State Bulletin*, vol. 84 (July 1984), pp. 11–13. See chapter 4 for discussion of the Harmel Report.

36. Talbott, *Deadly Gambits*, pp. 116–51.

unity. It was also seen, especially in Europe, as a step to reinforce deterrence by "coupling" American conventional and strategic forces. The real European concern was strengthening the American commitment, and the real U.S. interest was demonstrating that commitment. Nonetheless, a measure that had been intended to brace unity became a source of friction and division, especially in Europe.

The widespread popular opposition to the INF deployment in the early 1980s frequently assumed broader antinuclear, anti-American, and anti-alliance overtones. It led the Social Democratic party in Germany, especially after it lost the elections in March 1983, to oppose the INF deployment that to a large extent its leader, Helmut Schmidt, had inspired. At the grass roots all three parties in Germany were affected by the shift in popular opinion against the INF deployment, even though the West German governments under both parties continued to support deployment. In Great Britain, too, the opposition Labour party moved far toward rejecting any nuclear weapons, American or British, in the country. While public opposition tended to subside once the deployment began and the INF talks ended, it did not die.

The NATO governments all supported proceeding with both the negotiation and deployment tracks as they had agreed in 1979. The stronger American interest in deployment and the growing European interest in arms limitation, in response to public pressures, did, however, cause frictions. Moreover, by 1983 the U.S. government had turned a measure originally designed to accede to European desires into an alliance loyalty test administered by Washington. The predominant view in the Reagan administration from the outset was that the INF talks were essentially a matter not of arms control, but of "alliance management."[37] To many Europeans, this approach looked like alliance manipulation by Washington. Moreover, the goal became not the satisfaction of European preferences, but success in deployment despite arms talks, European public disaffection, and—in particular—Soviet opposition.

The Soviet leaders, as noted earlier, undertook a major campaign to influence Western public opinion against deployment. They placed the INF issue in the political forefront and made it a much more important political-military factor than it inherently was. In doing so, they only increased the significance of their failure. By making support for INF deployment a touchstone of political intentions and détente, they damaged East-West political relations (particularly with West Germany, the key country). The Soviets were heavy-handed in their attempt to influence the West German election in 1983, and their efforts backfired. Overall, deployment became a defeat for the Soviet Union of larger political dimensions than it would otherwise have been.

At the same time, INF deployment was less clearly a victory for the United States and NATO. Deployment was not an end in itself, or merely a victory in overcoming Soviet opposition, although both came to predominate

---

37. This phrase has been attributed to Richard Burt, first director of politico-military affairs and then assistant secretary for European affairs in the Department of State. See ibid., p. 62.

as aims in Washington. The purpose of the deployment had been to reinforce deterrence, to reassure the allies, and to enhance allied unity over the long run. All of these aims were, at least to some degree, casualties. The victory was pyrrhic.

The other major political confrontation in Europe occurred within the Soviet bloc. As the Reagan administration was entering office, a potential crisis over Soviet military intervention in Poland, feared in December 1980, was dissipating. The internal political crisis in Poland, however, continued and intensified. During 1981 the Reagan administration, and the NATO allies, continued to issue warnings against Soviet military intervention. As the NATO ministerial communiqué in May 1981 put it, "Poland must be left free to resolve its own problems."[38] Then, on December 13, 1981, General Wojciech Jaruzelski and the Military Committee of National Salvation took over from the Communist party and government in what was virtually a military coup and did act, imposing martial law. Thus when the Poles acted, without direct Soviet action or military intervention, the Western powers suddenly found they had been deterring the wrong contingency. While Soviet responsibility was widely suspected, and the shadow of Soviet power was clearly ever present in the background, the Soviet Union did not, as had been feared, intervene directly.

In response to martial law in Poland, the Western countries called off planned meetings to renegotiate Poland's huge hard-currency debt. They also announced that no new commercial credits would be extended. This action was primarily intended to demonstrate dissatisfaction with the Polish political repression of Solidarity, but it also was a form of economic retrenchment that fell short of calling the Polish debt into default. The United States went further in its demonstrative punitive gestures by banning U.S. government sponsored shipments of agricultural products, denying Polish fishing rights in American waters, and suspending landing rights to the Polish national airline. Most-favored-nation (MFN) trade status for Poland was suspended ten months later, and the United States also blocked Poland from receiving assistance from the International Monetary Fund until late 1984.

The United States, however, also imposed economic sanctions on the Soviet Union, an action in which the European allies did not join. There was an ironic element in the American move. The United States had threatened punitive action *if* the Soviet army moved into Poland. Then, when it did *not* do so, the United States imposed sanctions anyway. Some of the unilateral actions were clearly demonstrative, such as denying landing rights to the Soviet airline Aeroflot and not renewing the scientific exchange agreement. Others were more concrete economic measures: the Kama purchasing commission

---

38. *State Bulletin*, vol. 81 (July 1981), p. 39. While the communiqué went on to say that "any outside intervention would have the gravest consequences for international relations," it was clear that it meant any overt and direct, in particular military, intervention by the Soviet Union.

(which bought parts for a truck factory built in the early 1970s) was closed; negotiations on a new maritime agreement were suspended; and negotiations on a new grain sales agreement were postponed. Most significant, the United States suspended sales of oil and gas technology and validation of export licenses for high technology.

While these actions were authorized by the president as a response to Soviet pressures on Poland, hard-line advocates of a confrontational approach had been urging them for some time for quite different reasons: to place the Soviet economy under greater pressure and to reduce even indirect contributions to Soviet military capacity.

Six months later, in June, the administration—overriding the objections of Secretary of State Haig—expanded its economic sanctions by banning the sale of American equipment and technology for construction of the Soviet gas pipeline to Western Europe. Worse still, this ban included American technology manufactured by Western European firms under U.S. license. Moreover, this action followed only days *after* an alliance summit meeting at Versailles at which the allies had understood that the United States would not seek to impose such extraterritorial restraints on trade, but would accept a general agreement to tighten the terms of credit to the Soviet Union.[39]

The Europeans were incensed, and on other grounds as well, not the least of which was the illegality of the action in their view (and also the view of almost all international lawyers). They saw no relation between the U.S. moves and Poland or any other Soviet action. Finally, to make matters worse, just a month later the United States unilaterally decided to sign a new grain sale agreement with the Soviet Union. It looked as though the United States wanted its European allies to bear the burden of a policy of economic warfare they did not accept, while the United States would retain its own lucrative trade in grain. Again the United States (as in its sanctions against Iran in 1979 and against the Soviet Union after Afghanistan in 1980) gained a reputation for breaking contracts and for unreliability as an economic partner. The main U.S. rationale for seeking to prevent construction of the pipeline was to protect the Europeans from possible Soviet pressure in the form of a potential future threat to withhold gas once the Europeans were (marginally) dependent on it. Yet here was the United States itself exerting very real economic pressure on its Western allies. Moreover, the Western European powers were confident they could understand and defend their own interests against the Russians—or, if need be, the Americans.

Ultimately some Europeans concluded that the Reagan administration was behaving so vehemently over the gas pipeline not because it was concerned about the vulnerability of Western Europe, as it claimed, nor even because it wanted to put economic pressure on the Soviet Union. Rather, the pipeline represented a major East-West economic link that supported Euro-

---

39. For Haig's account of these events see Haig, *Caveat*, pp. 303–16.

pean détente, one not shared by the United States, and it reduced *U.S.* leverage over Western Europe on questions of policy toward the Soviet Union.

Finally, five painful months later the extended trade sanctions of June 1982 were removed. The allies accepted a vague agreement to be vigilant in East-West trade, to keep it economically sound and not one-sidedly to Soviet advantage. In the United States, the administration justified the resolution of the impasse with the allies over sanctions as representing a new consensus on a *tougher* general trade policy toward the Soviet Union, which it was not. Thus ultimately the trade sanctions, rather than modifying Soviet, or West European, behavior, created a problem resolved only by modifying the U.S. position.

No serious new problems in coordinating Western economic relations with the Soviet Union or Eastern Europe arose in 1983–84, but a persisting divergence remained, marked by more restrictive American practice and continuing U.S. pressure on its allies.

On the question of sanctions over Poland, the moderation of the Polish regime and its end to martial law and release of political prisoners gradually led to a partial relaxation of American sanctions in 1984. It should also be noted that even when the United States was pressing for tough economic sanctions against the Soviet Union over Poland in 1982, it did not suspend the INF talks that it had just begun. And the START talks on strategic arms reduction, while delayed by three months, began in mid-1982.

As discussed earlier, START drew relatively less attention, especially in Europe, where the INF talks were in the forefront. The American position in START, while not provoking objection, did not strike most Europeans who followed the subject as likely to lead to agreement.

The main development in the strategic arms field was not, however, arms control, but the major new American program for strategic defense, the SDI or Star Wars program. This initiative disturbed many Europeans for several reasons. First, it was a sudden, unilateral pronouncement by the United States on a subject of long-standing central importance to the alliance, on which the expressed alliance consensus was diametrically the opposite of the president's stand. Second, it represented a direct long-term challenge to the ABM Treaty, strongly endorsed by the alliance on its merits and generally acknowledged as the most significant arms limitation agreement to date. Third, it posed difficult potential problems either if the defense technology were provided to Europe (posing problems of strategy as well as cost), or if it were not. The very idea of such strategic defenses seemed applicable only to the United States. If so, the SDI would potentially decouple the security of the United States from the security of Western Europe. Moreover, it threatened to stir up an arms race that would undercut the British and French nuclear deterrents. Last, but far from least, it seemed to represent a turning away from arms control and reduction of East-West tensions by the United States in favor of unilateral U.S. pursuit of a new military technological will-o'-

the-wisp with isolationist overtones. The absence of consultation only reinforced this impression.

Meanwhile, military détente in Europe itself was sluggish. The mutual and balanced force reductions (MBFR) negotiation in Vienna continued, with minor changes of position by both sides, leading neither to breakdown nor to agreement. The Soviet walkout from START as well as INF talks at the end of 1983 was not carried over to MBFR.

The CSCE review conference in Belgrade in 1977–78 had been dominated by acrimonious exchanges over the question of human rights, but they were mild compared with the strong exchanges at the next review conference in Madrid. Convened in November 1980, it lasted until September 1983—a year longer than the original CSCE negotiation of 1973 to 1975. Its main achievement was agreement on a Conference on Confidence- and Security-Building Measures and Disarmament in Europe (CCSBMDE, usually shortened to CDE).

The CDE opened in Stockholm in January 1984. Its purpose was to build on and extend beyond the modest confidence-building measures in the 1975 Helsinki Final Act. New confidence- and security-building measures were to be designed to reduce the risk of military confrontation and conflict, to be extended to "the whole of Europe" from the Atlantic to the Urals. It quickly became clear that while the West would focus on concrete measures limiting or providing information on military activities, the Soviet bloc would stress nonaggression, no first use of nuclear weapons, nuclear-free zones, a freeze on military budgets, and other such general measures. This phase of the CDE was to conclude by 1986, when the next CSCE review conference is scheduled to be held. A possible later stage of the CDE might address more far-reaching measures including some disarmament.

The main line of European détente was not, however, developed in multilateral forums or focused on security issues. It was the continuation of the development of an organic network of ties through trade, travel, and bilateral contacts of all kinds among the countries and peoples of East, West, and neutral Europe. These ties proved more durable and meaningful than the more dramatic political designs for détente.[40] And, as noted, they contributed to the divergence between the United States and its Western European allies.

Détente in Europe also continued to attenuate to some degree the dependence of the Eastern European countries on the Soviet Union. Not only the fact of Soviet military predominance and the political-military obligations of the Warsaw Pact, but also the realities of continuing economic dependence, ensured the hegemonic role of the Soviet Union in the socialist community. Nonetheless, the area of autonomous decision and the development of a European relationship that transcended the ideological and political division of the two camps continued to develop.

---

40. See chapter 14.

By late 1983 and 1984 this phenomenon of East-West rapprochement of the European countries resting uneasily between the Soviet Union and the United States assumed some unexpected forms. First was the reluctance in Eastern Europe to join the Soviet campaign of stirring up anti-West German sentiment because of German persistence in proceeding with the INF deployment. In addition, the Eastern Europeans, notably the Czechoslovaks and East Germans, were openly unenthusiastic over the Soviet decision to deploy additional missiles in those countries as a countermeasure to the NATO deployment.[41] Finally, with evident reluctance and under clear Soviet pressure, the East German leader, Erich Honecker, and the veteran Bulgarian leader, Todor Zhivkov, postponed plans to visit West Germany in September 1984. That they agreed to postpone the visits was less surprising than that they did not do so until Moscow interceded strongly. Originally the Soviet leaders had strongly pushed the development of East-West détente, and specifically a rapprochement between East and West Germany, in order to influence Western policy. By September 1984, after Moscow had decided to cool that approach, it was clear that even such stalwart and close allies as East Germany and Bulgaria had developed a strong desire to maintain their détente ties.

The rapprochement between the two Germanies, only partially and temporarily arrested by the postponement of the visit, had led to such developments as a West German loan of $683 million to East Germany and East German permission for 33,000 Germans to emigrate to West Germany in the first eight months of 1984.[42] These events all took place in 1984, after the INF missile deployment had begun and the Soviet Union was trying to maintain a stern anti–West German line.

In June 1984 there was a summit meeting of the Council for Mutual Economic Assistance (CMEA, or COMECON), the first since 1969. It did not produce the kind of unity of views the Soviet leaders had hoped for (Chernenko called the exchange of views at the meeting "frank" as well as fruitful, a code word for disagreement).

Neither the NATO alliance nor the Warsaw Pact alliance has been endangered by the trend toward decreased tension and increased East-West contact. Increasingly, however, both have become less than a principal focus in East-West relations. Thus even when the United States adopted a more confrontational stance toward the Soviet Union after Afghanistan, especially under the Reagan administration, and the Soviet Union in turn sought to heighten tensions as a reaction to the NATO INF deployment, the countries of Europe—East and West—continued to pursue a general policy of détente.

---

41. See Bradley Graham, "Soviet Missile Plan Disconcerts Bloc Allies," *Washington Post*, December 20, 1983; and James M. Markham, "East Europe Is Uneasy over Missiles," *New York Times*, December 28, 1983.

42. The two developments were closely related. "E. Germany Lets 33,000 Migrate, Kohl Announces," *Washington Post*, August 18, 1984.

Nevertheless, by 1984, five years of uneasy coexistence between European détente and American-Soviet confrontation had shown Europeans both in the East and the West that to an important extent East-West relations were not divisible. While European détente survived, it was seriously constrained by the continuing tension between the superpowers. The United States continued to press for limits on economic relations by its Western European allies with the countries of the East; the Soviet Union imposed limits on the political relations of its Eastern European allies with the West. As a senior West German official put it: "As long as both superpowers do not improve their relations, Europeans in East and West have only a very small margin [in which] to cooperate." Probably alluding in particular to the postponement of the visit by the East German leader, he added, "We have already experienced just how small our room for manuever really is."[43] Incidentally, this comment reflects a general tendency to see the position of the Europeans as one—when they speak of "our room for maneuver," they mean all Europeans, East and West.

Triangular Diplomacy

The course of triangular diplomacy among the United States, the Soviet Union, and China had entered a new phase in 1980. The processes of adaptation to the post-détente American-Soviet relationship were, however, further affected by a sharp contradiction in the approach of the new Reagan administration.

On the one hand, the administration advocated a continued effort to build American-Chinese relations on the basis of a strategic geopolitical alignment directed against the Soviet Union. This course, essentially a continuation of the policy advanced by Brzezinski and conducted from 1978 through 1980, was energetically pursued by Secretary of State Haig. It also appealed to the anti-Soviet inclination of President Reagan and other members of the administration. But it conflicted head-on with a second course, based on another strongly held feeling of Reagan and a number of his colleagues: a strong sympathy for the Republic of China on Taiwan, and a distaste for close ties with the People's Republic of China at Taiwan's expense. Reagan and many right-wing conservatives had levied that criticism at the Carter administration. The foremost representative of this view within the administration was Reagan himself, encouraged by his national security adviser, Richard V. Allen. At the extreme were those with an ideological aversion to close collaboration with any communist country, even in order to use one against another.

---

43. Cited by William Drozdiak, "Visiting Kohl Seeks Link to Arms Talks," *Washington Post*, November 30, 1984.

Policy toward China was not a priority matter for the new administration. Haig, however, decided to preempt the issue before others could do so. Even in his congressional confirmation hearings before the inauguration, Haig had stressed the "compatibility and . . . convergence" of American and Chinese "strategic" interests.[44] On February 6 he had the Department of State spokesman declare the administration's intention to base its policy on the U.S.-Chinese normalization communiqué of December 15, 1978.[45] This move, unexpected and not cleared, led the White House to make background comments stressing the counterpoint—the president's intention to act in strict accordance with the Taiwan Relations Act. This pattern of public contradiction was repeated frequently.

The Reagan administration on assuming office was surprised to learn the scope and extent of American-Chinese relations, especially the secret collaboration on intelligence.[46] The momentum of developing relations was evident in increasing contacts. During 1981, 80,000 Americans visited China, and 16,000 Chinese visited the United States; by mid-1982, 8,000 Chinese students were at American universities, and 1,500 Americans were resident in China.[47]

A major problem quickly intruded, one that would plague American-Chinese relations for most of the next two years. Taiwan, eager to determine if the Reagan administration would change course, pressed for new advanced combat aircraft from the first days of the new administration.[48] Although the administration did not deal with the problem for some time, it was plainly there. Both Taiwan and China wanted to learn where they stood with the new administration.

Haig, with some support from Vice President Bush, who had served as the U.S. representative in Beijing for a time in the Ford administration, persuaded Reagan to authorize him to visit China. In mid-June Haig went to Beijing to set American policy firmly on course and to strengthen American-Chinese ties as a weapon in maneuvering with the Soviet Union. He also hoped to overcome Chinese doubts and quiet the Taiwan issue.

Haig's visit to Beijing was generally regarded as a step toward improving relations and moving beyond early frictions over the status to be accorded Taiwan by the United States. Haig naturally treated the trip as a success. And in one indirect respect it was. As Haig puts it in his memoir, "The trip was an opportunity to drive the bureaucracy and the Administration

44. "Major Points in the Senate Foreign Relations Committee's Questioning of Haig," *New York Times*, January 11, 1981.

45. See Bernard Gwertzman, "Reagan and the World," *New York Times*, February 8, 1981.

46. See Jonathan D. Pollack, *The Lessons of Coalition Politics: Sino-American Security Relations*, R-3133-AF (Santa Monica, Calif.: Rand Corp., 1984), p. 74.

47. See Allen S. Whiting, "Sino-American Relations: The Decade Ahead," *Orbis*, vol. 26 (Fall 1982), p. 697.

48. Pollack, *The Lessons of Coalition Politics*, p. 74.

toward the policy I had been struggling to establish."[49] In advance of the visit, Haig had succeeded in getting the president to approve a change in the trade status accorded China: it was placed in the category of a friendly but not allied country. This change permitted the transfer of somewhat more advanced technology and dual-use items having military as well as civilian applications, and allowed China to request the purchase of items on the munitions list, including defensive weapons, from commercial U.S. sources.[50] (In 1980 Secretary of Defense Brown had held out the possibility of that status, and Minister of National Defense Geng Biao had submitted a list of desired items, but no action had been taken on the requests.)

In Beijing Haig publicly announced with great éclat the U.S. readiness to sell defensive weapons to China. His statement annoyed both the Chinese leaders and the White House and Pentagon. Haig had been authorized to tell the Chinese of the decision but not to announce it publicly. For their part, Deng and other Chinese leaders did not want to appear to have agreed to a strategic relationship with the United States while the Taiwan issue remained unresolved. This impression and the Chinese unhappiness were enhanced when Haig also announced a forthcoming visit by General Liu Huaqing, deputy chief of staff of the Chinese army, to discuss arms purchases. Again, this announcement had not been authorized by the Chinese, and when they did confirm the planned visit, they studiously omitted any reference to possible arms purchases. Haig fails to note the Chinese dissatisfaction in his memoir. When he complains of the White House reaction, including President Reagan's reference at a press conference to carrying out the Taiwan Relations Act, made on the last day of the secretary of state's visit, Haig also fails to note that the president's statement was prompted by his own public overexuberance about arms sales to China. Reagan, like Deng, did not want a domestic constituency to think the unsettled Taiwan issue had been cast aside.[51]

Overall, Haig's visit was a failure. He had played a major card, arms sales, at the wrong time. The Chinese, rather than being impressed, saw the United States as trying to bind them into an anti-Soviet alignment under American direction and on American terms, including the Taiwan issue. Deng Xiaoping was moved to say, "The United States thinks that China is seeking its favor. In fact, China is not seeking any country's favor." While expressing the hope that Sino-American relations would develop further, he even felt it necessary to say, "If worst comes to worst and the relations retrogress to those prior to 1972, China will not collapse. . . . The Chinese people . . . will never bow and scrape and beg for help. . . . When U.S. Secretary of State Alexander

---

49. Haig, *Caveat*, p. 205.

50. Ibid., pp. 204–05.

51. Ibid., pp. 205–08; and Pollack, *The Lessons of Coalition Politics*, pp. 83–88.

Haig came to China, I told him the same thing. . . . China and the United States should cooperate on an equal footing."[52]

Haig had thought the Chinese would be so tempted by the prospect of American arms sales and strategic cooperation against the Soviet Union that they would acquiesce in American arms sales to Taiwan. He was wrong, as he should have known from soundings taken when former President Ford visited China in March and from Chinese reaction to speculation in the U.S. press after leaks that the United States intended to permit the sales.[53]

The Soviet leaders observed both the American effort to build a stronger strategic cooperation with China and the growing Chinese restraint. They drew conclusions for Soviet policy on both counts, as discussed later.

Over the next year American relations with China continued to be strained over Taiwan. The main question became whether the United States would supply the advanced FX fighter-bomber (F-5G) to Taiwan, but as A. Doak Barnett has pointed out, the FX served as a symbol of broader concerns.[54] The Chinese postponed indefinitely the planned visit by General Liu Huaqing. Even after the United States decided in January 1982 not to supply the F-5G, it reaffirmed continued coproduction of the F-5E and supply of some used F-104 Gs. Only on August 17, 1982, was agreement reached in a joint U.S.-Chinese communiqué that settled the Taiwan arms sales issue for a time. And even then the two sides immediately interpreted the joint statement differently.[55]

By that time Secretary of State Haig, who had struggled to advance U.S. relations with China in pursuit of alignment against the Soviet Union, had left the scene. After nearly two years under the Reagan administration, the United States was more or less back to the point it had been at in terms of relations with China when the administration had assumed office. Haig attributed great significance to the role of China in the world alignment of political forces, in particular as a major factor in containing Soviet expansion.[56] He had not, however, been successful in establishing American policy toward China on

---

52. Interview with Deng Xiaoping, Ming Bao (Hong Kong), August 25, in Foreign Broadcast Information Service, *Daily Report: People's Republic of China*, August 25, 1981, p. W6. (Hereafter FBIS, *China*.)

53. Pollack notes that a Chinese Foreign Ministry spokesman explicitly rejected this proposal on June 10, shortly before Haig's visit, and also notes earlier rejections. *The Lessons of Coalition Politics*, pp. 81–83. General Brent Scowcroft, who accompanied Ford, has confirmed to me that soundings were taken on that visit, and that Deng Xiaoping took the initiative in raising and rejecting the idea of U.S. supply of arms to both China and Taiwan.

54. A. Doak Barnett, *U.S. Arms Sales: The China-Taiwan Tangle* (Brookings Institution, 1982), p. 28. Barnett's study gives an excellent review of the problem in its broader context, through the spring of 1982.

55. Pollack, *The Lessons of Coalition Politics*, pp. 94–95.

56. See Haig, *Caveat*, pp. 194–95.

the line he sought, although he did help to prevent a greater worsening of American-Chinese relations.

American policy and diplomatic communication with China developed more regularly in 1983 and 1984. Secretary of State Shultz visited Beijing in February 1983; Secretary of Commerce Malcolm Baldrige in May; the president's science adviser, George A. Keyworth, also in May; and Secretary of Defense Weinberger in September 1983. Minister of Foreign Affairs Wu Xueqian visited the United States in October 1983 and Minister of National Defense Zheng Aiping in June 1984. The most important political visits were those by Premier Zhao Ziyang to Washington in January and by President Reagan to Beijing in April 1984, to which the discussion will turn shortly.

Although no major issue comparable to the question of arms sales to Taiwan arose in 1983–84, the effects of that divergence remained and lesser new irritants arose. For example, in the first three months of 1983 there arose a conflict of interests over trade, in particular over U.S. curbs on imports of textiles, an important issue when Shultz visited Beijing in February.[57] Soon after, in April 1983, a Chinese tennis star defected to the United States, leading China to curtail sharply cultural contacts for about a year.[58] In May 1983 the editor of a Hong Kong communist newspaper was sentenced to ten years imprisonment as a U.S. spy.[59]

On the other hand, there were some steps forward. In May 1983 the United States further relaxed constraints on technology transfer. China was raised to the same general category (category V) as the Western European countries, Australia, Japan, and India. Each sale still needed to be decided case by case, but the symbolic significance was considerable, and the change permitted greater leeway in trade.[60] And Secretary of Defense Weinberger's visit in September restored a low-key military security relationship (despite unrequited efforts by Weinberger to stir up a more militant anti-Soviet stance). Both the United States and China made some efforts and compromises to improve relations in 1983–84.

The visit by President Reagan to China was of particular importance. He seemed to marvel at his discovery that China was a multicolored tapestry and not merely a sea of red. Indeed, on his return trip President Reagan—who had expressed vehement hostility to "Red China" for over thirty years—spoke about his experience in "so-called Communist China" (and, based on his rather constricted observations, he expressed optimism that the

57. Michael Weisskopf, "Chinese Trade Issues Seen Snagging Shultz," *Washington Post*, January 31, 1983; and Christopher S. Wren, "China, Upset by U.S. Trade Curb, Halting Import of 3 Commodities," *New York Times*, January 20, 1983.

58. See "19 Events with U.S. Canceled by China," *New York Times*, April 8, 1983.

59. Christopher S. Wren, "China Jails a Hong Kong Editor as a Spy for U.S.," *New York Times*, May 16, 1983.

60. Pollack, *The Lessons of Coalition Politics*, p. 108.

Chinese were embracing capitalist principles in their economic reform).[61] He also seemed not to have noticed that his efforts to forge an anti-Soviet alliance, which he (and his immediate advisers) assumed would be a bond, were in fact rebuffed and his anti-Soviet statements censored by the Chinese. The principal achievement, rushed for the summit visit, was an agreement on cooperation on peaceful uses of nuclear energy that included American assistance in the development of Chinese nuclear power reactors.[62] On closer inspection and following further discussions after the summit meeting, the agreement turned out not to provide the minimum necessary assurances against nuclear proliferation to third powers and was so unacceptable that it could not be submitted to Congress. Yet Reagan, in terms approaching the enthusiasm of Nixon over his summitry with the communist powers, described the developing relationship between China and the United States as "one of the principal events of postwar diplomacy," and he expressed the hope that "this important, new friendship of ours will mature and prosper."[63]

U.S.-China relations in 1983–84 were back on a track of normal development, although still plagued by occasional eruptions of the basically unsettled differences over Taiwan. They did not, however, return to the situation that had prevailed from 1978 into 1980. For one thing, China did not occupy so central a place in the thinking of the U.S. leaders from 1981 on (with the exception of Haig during his tenure, and he was frustrated in his attempt to set policy). In different ways Kissinger, with his image of a flexible triangular balance of power, and Brzezinski, with his aim of a more active American-Chinese collaboration against the Soviet Union, had both given a more salient role to China than did the Reagan administration. Reagan's own belated enthusiasm that attended his visit in the spring of 1984, and Shultz's, also largely derived from his visit, were not rooted in any geopolitical conception of world politics and were in no way as important as Nixon's and Carter's. Moreover, the Reagan administration (including Haig) implicitly assumed that China had a greater stake in improving relations than did the United States, and that the United States could therefore dangle arms sales but otherwise ignore Chinese interests, including Taiwan.

One sign of the changed American view of the role of China was a statement by Secretary of State Shultz a month after his visit. In it he ascribed

---

61. Cited in Robert G. Kaiser, "Another Western 'Barbarian' Honors the Middle Kingdom," *Washington Post*, May 6, 1984. Deng Xiaoping could scarcely have appreciated this compliment, which supported the charges of his Chinese political opponents, not all of whom had been removed from the party leadership.

62. Three other minor agreements were concluded on a series of cultural exchanges, an extension of an American course in management techniques, and a guarantee against double taxation of American corporations operating in China.

63. "Remarks at a Ceremony for the Signing of Four Agreements between the United States and China for the President's Departure from Beijing, April 30, 1984," *Presidential Documents*, vol. 20 (May 7, 1984), p. 613.

to China a regional role more than a global one, as well as a role in "resisting Soviet aggression." The Chinese did not take kindly to either characterization, especially because in the same speech Shultz made clear the far more important role of Japan in American thinking, and also reiterated that "progress in U.S.-China relations need not come at the expense of relations with our other friends . . . including . . . the people of Taiwan."[64]

The second important new element in the situation in the 1980s was Chinese policy. Third was a changed Sino-Soviet relationship, which stemmed mainly from the Chinese reevaluation of the triangular relationship.

During 1981, Deng Xiaoping, the key Chinese leader despite his modest formal post as vice premier, and the driving force in the rapprochement with the United States from 1978 on, strengthened his position. Nonetheless, powerful elements wary of the turn toward the United States remained in the Chinese political system.

China also continued its move toward greater independence and reassertion of its position in areas that diverged or contradicted U.S. positions. In June a prominent article revived the "three worlds" theory, in which China—while pursuing an "independent and self-reliant" foreign policy—identified itself with the third world as distinct from, and to an important extent in opposition to, both the Western and Soviet worlds.[65] Soon thereafter another article continued this theme, directly attacking U.S. policy toward the third world, and in particular the Reagan administration's support for Israel, South Africa, South Korea, and Taiwan.[66] At the Cancún summit meeting of North-South leaders, Premier Zhao Ziyang lumped the two superpowers together and said that in their rivalry they were menacing international security.[67]

Other differences emerged. China did not support the Solidarity movement in Poland. Chinese concern over uncontrolled spontaneous political movements in communist countries overrode its satisfaction at seeing the Soviet Union further burdened. And when the United States instituted sanctions against Poland and the Soviet Union after the Poles instituted martial law and suppressed Solidarity, China not only did not join in, but on the contrary boosted its trade with Poland, recognizing that General Jaruzelski was not a Soviet puppet, and wishing to aid him to maintain power.

---

64. "The U.S. and East Asia: A Partnership for the Future," Address before the World Affairs Council, San Francisco, on March 5, 1983, *State Bulletin*, vol. 83 (April 1983), p. 33, and see pp. 31–34.

65. "Resolution on Certain Questions in the History of Our Party since the Founding of the People's Republic of China," Xinhua [The New China News Agency, NCNA], June 30, in FBIS, *China*, July 1, 1981, pp. K7, K32.

66. Mei Zhenmin, "U.S. Relationship with the Third World," Xinhua, July 8, in FBIS, *China*, July 9, 1981, pp. B1–2.

67. Xinhua, October 27, in FBIS, *China*, October 27, p. J3.

President Reagan was reported to have been unhappy that Zhao labeled the United States an "imperialist" power. Information from a member of the U.S. delegation.

In February 1982 Vice Premier Li Xiannian commented in an interview that "the United States is not a friendly country."[68] Usually the Chinese simply stressed the hegemonic rivalry of the two superpowers and did not identify China with either, but rather with the third world. In August Foreign Minister Huang Hua said, "China will never cling to any superpower. China will never play the 'U.S. card' against the Soviet Union, nor the 'Soviet card' against the United States. We will also not allow anyone to play the 'Chinese card.' "[69] And at the Twelfth National Congress of the Communist Party of China on September 1 General Secretary Hu Yaobang stressed that China "never attaches itself to any big power or group of powers, and never yields to pressure from any big power."[70] He was also highly critical of both the United States and the Soviet Union.

Clearly, by the time of the Party Congress in 1982 the Chinese leadership had decided to move to a detached independent position between the United States and the Soviet Union. In theory, they would remain equidistant. In practice, they would probably continue to be closer to the United States or at least more wary of the Soviet Union. But ties with the Soviet Union would soon be reactivated, as discussed presently. The Chinese soon chose to distance themselves more from the United States than they had in the period from 1978 to 1980, above all to avoid becoming a dependency within a U.S.-led coalition. When the Chinese had sought a united front against the Soviet Union from 1971 through 1979, their primary purpose had been to prevent a Soviet-American coalition against them. That accomplished as a result of the collapse of the Soviet-American détente, China could now afford independence. Moreover, the Chinese believed that the Reagan administration in the early 1980s was overdoing confrontation with the Soviet Union, just as they believed the United States had overdone détente in the 1970s.[71]

In addition to the change in American-Soviet relations there was a difference in the Chinese perception of the balance of power between the two superpowers. In the second half of the 1970s the Chinese saw a trend toward growing Soviet military power. In the first half of the 1980s they saw the United States as again becoming the stronger. They also concluded that there was a generally stable balance between the two. This view also provided a better base for China to maneuver without its having to lean to one side or the other to help ensure the balance.

---

68. Allen S. Whiting, "Reading Tea Leaves: China-Soviet Détente," *New York Times*, May 18, 1982.

69. Xinhua, August 20, in FBIS, *China*, August 23, 1982, p. A1.

70. Hu Yaobang, "Create a New Situation in All Fields of Socialist Modernization: Report to the 12th National Congress of the Communist Party of China, September 1, 1982," *Beijing Review*, vol. 25 (September 13, 1982), p. 29.

71. This opinion was not publicly stated by the Chinese, but it is frequently implied and was explicitly told to me by a senior Chinese official in 1984.

The Chinese shift may also have reflected differences among the leaders. Hu Yaobang, whose influence had grown, may have given a less central role to the United States in his conception of China's balanced policy than did Deng Xiaoping. It is, however, often difficult to tell, since Deng's own position on triangular diplomacy had certainly changed by the early 1980s from what it had been in the late 1970s.

As noted earlier, one of the main areas of divergence and conflict in Chinese and American policy after 1980 concerned the third world. Moreover, as the Chinese restored more normalcy to their relationship with the Soviet Union and sought to establish greater identification with the third world, they stated their position in terms designed to make their policy clear. An article in October 1982, shortly after the Party Congress, explicitly noted that China stood with the United States in opposition to the Soviet Union on the issues of Afghanistan and Kampuchea, while it stood with the Soviet Union in opposition to the United States on Israeli aggression and South African apartheid. But, the article concluded, "This does not mean that China 'allies' with the United States under some circumstances or becomes a Soviet partner under other circumstances. This precisely proves that . . . China is independent of all [both] the superpowers."[72] Similarly, in 1981 China voted with the United States on only 10 percent of the votes in the United Nations General Assembly (in contrast with 33 percent in 1979), and with the Soviet Union on 76 percent. As the Chinese correctly argue, this did not reflect a turn to a pro-Soviet alignment, but a turn to a more third world position. For example, China initially took a line similar to that of the United States in warning that the Soviet Union and Cuba were seeking to use the situation in El Salvador to advance their influence. But as early as March 1981 China had switched to support the position of the Salvadoran guerrillas (and throughout supported Nicaragua) against efforts by the United States to use the situation to advance *its* interests.[73]

One reason for the Chinese decision in 1982 to resume direct talks with the Soviet Union was to enhance its position in triangular diplomacy while maintaining its independence. In the 1970s the Chinese had wanted a more confrontational relationship between the United States and the Soviet Union and had therefore opposed détente between them. One important reason was to reduce the ability of the Soviet Union to place pressure on China.

---

72. *Liaowang*, quoted by Xinhua, October 20, in FBIS, *China*, October 21, 1982, pp. A1–2. Cited by Harry Harding, ed., *China's Foreign Relations in the 1980s* (Yale University Press, 1984), p. 199, and see his discussion on pp. 195–201.

For a study stressing the historical roots of Chinese foreign policy independence as adapted to the ideology of Marxism-Leninism and to current geopolitical realities, see Mark Mancall, *China at the Center: 300 Years of Foreign Policy* (Macmillan Free Press, 1984), especially pp. 445-502.

73. This shift is well-documented by Pollack, *The Lessons of Coalition Politics*, pp. 79–80.

Another was precisely to increase the opportunity for China to play a more active role in triangular diplomacy, and that aim required improving Sino-Soviet relations in order to gain increased leverage with both superpowers. Finally, this changed triangle would permit China to pursue a more independent policy in the third world.

By 1981–82 the time to do this had arrived. China's intention became crystal clear when it called for renewed Sino-Soviet border talks within three days of the conclusion of Secretary of State Haig's visit in June 1981.[74] The Chinese had, however, outlined three conditions for any serious improvement in relations with the Soviet Union: Soviet withdrawal from Afghanistan, Vietnamese withdrawal from Kampuchea, and a rollback of the Soviet military buildup along the Chinese borders since the end of the 1960s (including withdrawal of Soviet forces from Mongolia). These were evidently stiff terms, and the Soviets saw them as precluding real improvement, unless the Chinese were in practice to modify their stance. In September 1982 Hu Yaobang continued to stress that normalization of relations with the Soviet Union was dependent on the Soviets' taking "practical steps to lift their threat to the security of our country."[75] But by October the Chinese, while maintaining the three conditions in principle, set them aside in practice to the extent of agreeing to hold "consultations" on normalization at the deputy ministerial level. After a hiatus of many years the Chinese also began again to refer to the Soviet Union as a socialist country (following a Soviet concession on the same point).

It should be noted that these Chinese moves to improve relations with the Soviet Union accompanied steps to improve relations with the United States (the Taiwan arms communiqué, it will be recalled, had been signed on August 17, 1982). China was not shifting from the United States to the Soviet Union. It was applying the Nixon-Kissinger strategy of gaining leverage in triangular diplomacy by improving relations (albeit on a restrained basis) with both the other powers.

Chinese relations with the Soviet Union developed unevenly in 1983–84. The Chinese may have expected greater concessions from the post-Brezhnev leaders. Irritants continued. A squabble in the press over alleged Chinese claims to Soviet territory occurred in January 1983, spurred by a Soviet article.[76] The talks on normalization got under way at a two-week session in the first half of March 1983, but little was accomplished beyond the renewal of contact and dialogue. The Chinese raised, and the Soviets rejected, the three conditions.

---

74. Littuichan, *Renmin ribao* [People's Daily], in FBIS, *China*, June 17, 1981, pp. C1–7.

75. Hu Yaobang, *Beijing Review*, vol. 25 (1982), p. 31.

76. Observer, "What Is the Purpose?" *New Times*, no. 3 (January 1983), pp. 12–14. The Chinese promptly rebutted the charges. "A Reply to the 'Observer' of the Soviet New Times Weekly," *Shijie zhishi* [World Affairs], no. 3 (January 1983), in FBIS, *China*, January 23, 1983, pp. C1–3.

In separate but parallel talks, the two countries agreed to increase trade. From 1983 to 1984, trade doubled, reaching some $1.2 billion (about one-fourth of the amount of Sino-U.S. trade). One reason for the increase was Chinese recognition that its industrial plant and economic planning system remained largely geared to the Soviet system. But the Chinese also continued to turn to Japan and the West for new technology, while for their part the Soviets held back on advanced technology, awaiting an improvement in overall relations.

Further rounds of talks continued in March and October 1983, and March and October 1984, but without major advances. A visit by Soviet First Deputy Prime Minister Ivan V. Arkhipov, scheduled for May 1984, was postponed because of a renewed Vietnamese-Chinese border battle in April—and perhaps because of pique at President Reagan's visit to Beijing. The Chinese and Soviet foreign ministers, Wu Xueqian and Andrei Gromyko, did meet for six hours in New York in September 1984 to carry the dialogue forward. And in December 1984 Arkhipov did visit Beijing, the highest ranking contact since Nikolai Kosygin's meeting with Zhou Enlai at the Beijing airport in 1969, and further economic agreements were reached.

Soviet policy toward China, evidently, was also moving. The Soviets took the initiative on several occasions in 1981 and 1982 in attempting to resume the Sino-Soviet dialogue broken off in early 1980 (soon after it had begun) after Afghanistan. The Soviets proposed concrete talks on confidence-building measures in March 1981 and border talks in September 1981.

In February 1982 Prime Minister Nikolai Tikhonov warily said that the Soviet Union would not "walk away from concrete steps directed toward improving relations" if talks were held "on the basis of equality and in the spirit of mutual understanding," but stressed "this process must not be one-sided."[77] The next month in Tashkent Brezhnev went much further in a conciliatory direction, saying, "We have never considered normal the state of hostility and estrangement between our countries," and "We are prepared to come to terms, without preconditions, on mutually acceptable measures to improve Soviet-Chinese relations on the basis of mutual respect for each other's interests." He also said that the Soviets did not "deny the existence of a socialist system in China," a point that had not been conceded for years, even though Brezhnev then went on to criticize Beijing's "association with the policy of the imperialists around the world" that "contradicts the interests of socialism."[78] In a speech in Baku in September Brezhnev repeated the Soviet interest in improving relations, as he did at a meeting with military leaders in Moscow in October shortly before his death. On this latter occasion he linked Soviet

---

77. "Replies of Chairman of the Council of Ministers of the USSR N. A. Tikhonov to Questions from the Editors of the Newspaper 'Asahi' (Japan)," *Pravda*, February 17, 1982.

78. "Speech of L. I. Brezhnev," *Pravda*, March 25, 1982. Brezhnev also emphasized that the Soviet Union had always supported the Chinese position on Taiwan, in an attempt to rub salt in the Sino-American wound over this issue.

interest in improving relations with China to the deterioration in Soviet relations with the United States.[79]

Brezhnev's successors continued to urge improvement in relations. Foreign Minister Huang Hua was received briefly by Andropov and spent ninety minutes with Gromyko on the occasion of Brezhnev's funeral in November 1982. Andropov, in his first major address as the new party leader, referred to his predecessor's speeches in Tashkent and Baku and, as if to deny speculation about differences in Moscow, stressed "the convictions of *all* our party, its striving to look forward" in seeking improved relations. He also noted, "We pay close attention to every positive response to this from the Chinese side."[80] In August 1983 Andropov referred to "certain positive trends . . . perceptible in our relations recently." But, as noted, while the actual course of Sino-Soviet relations in 1983–84 remained on a more normal basis than was the case before 1982, they still involved little more than semiannual exchanges at the level of deputy foreign ministers and modestly improved trade.

The Soviets tried to keep relations with both China and the United States from deteriorating, in part to prevent a return to closer Sino-American ties. They also sought to prevent China from succeeding in its effort to consolidate a position at the apex, or balance, of the triangle, but they had little leverage. One small sign of their tandem approach with the other two powers can be seen in the fact that the senior specialists on China and the United States in the Foreign Ministry in Moscow were both raised to deputy minister rank at the same time in December 1982.[81]

On the whole the Soviets took with equanimity the gradual improvement in Sino-American relations in 1983–84, although clearly they had hoped to keep their own relations with China on a par with those of the United States. They had not, however, been prepared to take the drastic actions sought by China with respect to any of the three conditions posed earlier. Soviet analysts of both American and Chinese affairs continued in their assessments to stress the basic long-term stresses in the Sino-American relationship, while other Soviet observers varied in their judgments. From the standpoint of Soviet-American relations, the China factor continued to trouble the Soviet leaders, but much less so in 1981–84 than it had in 1978–80.

The general outcome of the shift in triangular diplomacy from the 1970s to the 1980s was thus the American loss of its position as the balancing element. Nixon and Kissinger had improved U.S. relations with both of the

---

79. "Kremlin Meeting of Military Leaders," *Pravda*, October 28, 1982.

80. Andropov, *Kommunist*, no. 17 (November 1982), p. 20.

81. This double promotion—of Viktor G. Komplektov, head of the USA Department, and Mikhail S. Kapitsa, head of the First Far Eastern (China) Department—occurred on December 17, 1982.

   Soon after, China also promoted the head of its Soviet and East European Affairs Department, Yu Hongliang, to vice foreign minister.

other powers and gained leverage with both. Carter and Brzezinski lost much of this leverage by aligning with China. Reagan exacerbated relations with both and lost leverage with both, in particular in the first two years (despite Haig's efforts to sustain Brzezinski's approach). By 1983–84 the United States was seeking to ameliorate relations with China and, by the end of the period, to some extent with the Soviet Union as well. But the heyday of triangular diplomacy, at least for the United States, had passed.

Competition in the Third World

President Reagan entered office with the conviction that "the Soviet Union underlies all the unrest that is going on" in the world.[82] Secretary of State Haig, while far more knowledgeable about world politics, also had a simplified and magnified image of the Soviet role in exploiting circumstances and situations around the world for its own advantage. Haig placed the subject of Soviet involvement and expansion of influence in the third world at the very center of American-Soviet relations. He saw Soviet pursuit of forceful expansion of its influence as aimed at securing strategic gains: "When the Soviet Union exploits local conditions for its own strategic aims, the problem is no longer local but a strategic threat to our own survival. We cannot ignore this threat." Consequently, he said, "Illegal Soviet intervention calls into question the whole range of our relations with Moscow. It violates the restraint and reciprocity we seek in our relations."[83]

While stressing a key Soviet role, Haig and others in the administration also put particular stress on Soviet use of proxy and surrogate forces. In speeches and other statements in 1981 and 1982, and in his memoir, Haig repeatedly refers to Cuba, Libya, the PLO, Vietnam, and Nicaragua as Soviet "proxies," "surrogates," or "clients." This lumping together of communist allies of the Soviet Union such as Cuba and Vietnam (each, incidentally, with its *own* regional interests and aims) with noncommunist independent actors on the world scene such as Libya and the PLO was an egregious error.[84] President Reagan, too, referred to "Qadhafi in Chad, Cuba in Angola, Cuba and East Germans in Ethiopia, in South Yemen, and of course, now the attempt here in our own Western Hemisphere" as actions involving "surrogates" of the Soviet

---

82. Ronald Reagan, in a campaign address in June 1980, cited in Anthony Lewis, "Reagan on War and Peace," *New York Times*, October 20, 1980.

83. Secretary Haig, "Peaceful Progress in Developing Nations," Commencement Address at Fairfield University, May 24, *State Bulletin*, vol. 81 (July 1981), p. 9.

84. For example, see Haig, *Caveat*, pp. 96, 109, 110, 172, 220, and his statements of February 23, March 13, March 29, April 24, May 24, June 28, and October 29, 1981. See *State Bulletin*, vol. 81 (April 1981), p. 15; (May 1981), pp. 1–2; (May 1981), p. 5; (June 1981), p. 6; (July 1981), pp. 8–9; (August 1981), pp. 51–52; and (December 1981), p. 28.

Union. He also spoke of Cuba, Libya, the PLO, "and others in the Communist bloc nations" suggesting that he did not realize that Qaddafi and the PLO were not communists.[85]

The blurring of Soviet *support* for various third world countries and imputed *control* of those countries and direction of their actions was facilitated by a tendency on the part of both Haig and Reagan to see the national liberation struggle in various countries only as a device that served Soviet geopolitical and strategic expansion. Haig was aware that there were serious problems in the third world that gave rise to revolutionary situations. But once there was Soviet, Soviet-aligned, or local communist involvement or prospective gain (even if only by diminished Western influence), he saw the situation as converted into a Soviet offensive threat to the United States that must be countered. Thus, for example, "grave though its plight might be, El Salvador was not merely a local problem. It was also a regional problem that threatened the stability of all of Central America, including the Panama Canal and Mexico and Guatemala with their vast oil reserves. And it was a global issue because it represented the interjection of the war of national liberation into the Western Hemisphere."[86] Such a contorted view of the "interjection" of a civil war from another hemisphere was possible only because Haig (and Reagan) saw the whole phenomenon as a "*Soviet strategy* of wars of liberation,"[87] rather than as Soviet support for—and exploitation for its own benefit of—indigenous conflicts.

Soviet involvements and interventions in the third world in the latter 1970s, from Angola through Afghanistan, had been widely regarded in the United States as behavior not in keeping with détente. The Reagan administration not only shared this view but saw these Soviet actions as a challenge to the security of a Free World and especially to American influence and security. Secretary of State Haig in particular, but also President Reagan and other leading administration figures, frequently reiterated that view and listed up to six or eight situations that they saw as a snowballing series of interventions by the Soviet Union or its proxies in the Free World (that is, in countries beyond the acknowledged Soviet bloc). Haig's list, which he recited with minor variation on more than a dozen occasions in 1981, comprised seven cases of Soviet or Soviet-sponsored direct or indirect aggression from 1975 through 1979: Angola (in 1975–76, mainly through the Cuban proxy), Ethiopia (in 1977–78, mainly through the Cuban proxy but with direct Soviet military participation), South Yemen (local communist coup in 1978), North Yemen (South Yemeni–supported incursions in 1979), Afghanistan (local communist coup in 1978), Kampuchea (Vietnamese invasion in late 1978), and finally Afghanistan

85. "Interview with the President: Question-and-Answer Session with Walter Cronkite of CBS News, March 3, 1981," in *Presidential Documents*, vol. 17 (March 9, 1981), pp. 229, 233.

86. Haig, *Caveat*, p. 118.

87. Ibid., p. 106. Emphasis added.

again (direct Soviet military intervention in December 1979). All these cases have been reviewed, most in detail, in this study.[88] In fact, the list was mixed up: it included some cases of local action in which no Soviet role was demonstrated or even likely (the coups in South Yemen and Afghanistan in 1978), and others in which the initiative was by Soviet friends on their own (the South Yemeni–sponsored push into North Yemen, the Vietnamese invasion of Kampuchea, and even the initial Cuban aid to the MPLA in Angola). The only cases of clear Soviet involvement were its support of the independent Angolan regime, aid to the Ethiopian government after it came under attack from Somalia, and the quite different case of Afghanistan—the only one involving direct Soviet military intervention.[89] The Soviet Union did see, and seize, several opportunities in the latter half of the 1970s to extend its influence. These moves did not, however, constitute a coordinated Soviet expansionist drive that was gathering momentum. Increasingly, however, that was the perception in the United States. This perception was not accompanied by any recognition of the considerable efforts and successes of the United States in expanding *its* geopolitical influence in the 1970s, for example, with China and Egypt.

The important point is that the main *impression* of the Reagan administration (as of the Carter administration in its last years), and of the American public, was one of the Soviet Union and its associates "on the move." And this seemed to represent a threatening pattern of expansion not in keeping with détente. Haig described it as "an increasing [Soviet] proclivity to

---

88. See chapter 15 on Angola, chapter 19 on most of the other cases, and chapter 26 on Afghanistan in 1978 and 1979.

89. Curiously, Haig omitted the North Vietnamese takeover of South Vietnam in 1975, the two émigré Katangan incursions into the Shaba province of Zaire in 1977 and 1978 (which were comparable to the Kampuchean and North Yemeni cases), and even the Sandinista takeover in Nicaragua in mid-1979, although some other members of the administration did not.

Haig was the best informed on foreign affairs of the senior members of the Reagan administration, but this was a relative matter. Haig displayed abysmal ignorance when he attempted to do more than list the cases he confidently cited. For example, in referring to the 1978 military coup in Afghanistan, Haig said that it was a *Soviet* intervention, in which the Soviets moved "to install a puppet leader a year before the actual invasion," and that "the step from that, unchallenged [by the West], to the massive intervention of Soviet forces a year later is a very small step to take." "Secretary [Haig] Participates in St. Louis Town Hall Forum," May 29, *State Bulletin*, vol. 81 (July 1981), p. 15. Compare that statement with the actual course of events in 1978 and 1979 discussed in detail in chapter 26. And Haig depicts the harassing border incursions into North Yemen, where even direct South Yemeni participation was never clear and where the Soviet preference was against the action, as an effort "to overthrow the government in Northern Yemen by the use of Southern Yemen forces and proxy forces shipped over from Ethiopia—Cubans and perhaps Ethiopians as well." Secretary Haig, "Death of Egyptian President Sadat," October 6, ibid., vol. 81, (November 1981), p. 70. There were Cuban advisers in South Yemen, but no forces were sent over from Ethiopia or involved in the incursions. As to the 1978 coup (one of a series by factional rivals) in South Yemen, as Haig's memory registered it, "We saw a very heavy hand of Soviet activity in the original overthrow of the Southern Yemen regime." Ibid., p. 70. Compare with the account in chapter 19.

support change—either directly or indirectly—by rule of force, by bloodshed, terrorism, so-called wars of liberation." Haig continued, "At long last the American people have decided that this is no longer acceptable Soviet activity."[90] Haig also argued, "Only the United States has the pivotal strength to convince the Soviets—and their proxies—that violence will not advance their cause." American strength and determination would cause the Soviets to "respect reciprocity."[91]

This view underlay the stress the Reagan administration, and above all Haig, placed on disciplining the Soviet Union to respect the American conception of "restraint and reciprocity" within existing spheres of interest and hegemony, and on containing Soviet expansionist designs using force, locally and usually indirectly, but backed by a relentless Soviet military buildup.

Haig was genuinely concerned about what he saw as the Soviet expansionist threat to vulnerable strategic areas of the third world. He also saw a U.S. military buildup and militant containment as most effective to "discipline" and contain the Soviets. In addition, Haig was aware that some elements within the Reagan administration, and still more among its constituents and supporters around the country, did not share his desire for a hardheaded détente, but preferred a clean, hard line of confrontation and tended to be suspicious of negotiation. By taking the offensive, and if possible achieving early successes, through a policy of opposing Soviet expansionism, Haig hoped not only to stop the Soviets, but also to build his credentials as a tough and effective anticommunist strategist. Then, as both American power and Soviet awareness of the risks of pursuit of unilateral gains grew, he could deal from a position of strength in negotiation.

An arena for early engagement in opposing Soviet expansion presented itself, and Haig seized it: Soviet-sponsored, Cuban-managed, Nicaraguan-supplied, communist-led terrorist-guerrilla insurgency in El Salvador. By no means did all agree with that picture of the civil war in El Salvador, but such a characterization both reflected Haig's own perception and fitted his purpose. El Salvador was in America's backyard and far from the Soviet Union; it seemed possible at minimal risk and cost to win a victory that would demonstrate to all—to the Soviet leaders, to U.S. allies, to others in the world, and to the American people—that American will and strength, reasserted, were effective in countering continuing Soviet efforts around the world to advance at American expense.

---

90. "Secretary Haig Interviewed for *The Wall Street Journal*," *State Bulletin*, vol. 81 (September 1981), p. 25. Haig also criticizes President Carter not only for failing to react more vigorously to these Soviet actions in the third world, but also for failing to comprehend the threat from "wars of liberation." See Haig, *Caveat*, p. 122.

91. "A New Direction in U.S. Foreign Policy," Address to the American Society of Newspaper Editors, April 24, *State Bulletin*, vol. 81 (June 1981), p. 6. Note Haig's repeated identification of national liberation movements with terrorism.

Haig launched a major campaign to highlight and attack the role of the Soviet Union and Cuba. The State Department issued a hastily prepared White Paper entitled "Communist Interference in El Salvador" that termed the situation there "a textbook case of indirect armed aggression by Communist powers through Cuba."[92] Diplomatic "truth squads" were sent to Western Europe to persuade America's allies of the Soviet and other communist role, although without notable success. Haig testified in open hearings in Congress that the Soviet Union had "major responsibility" for the spread of international terrorism and had a "hit list" for the "takeover of Central America"—Nicaragua, El Salvador, Honduras, and Guatemala.[93] He threatened unspecified American retaliation at "the source" of these eruptions, identified sometimes as Cuba and sometimes as the Soviet Union itself.[94]

This focal American counterchallenge in Central America also served Haig's general policy not only of containment of Soviet expansion but also of developing American relations with the Soviet Union on the basis of "restraint and reciprocity."

In actuality, throughout the 1970s the Soviet Union—and to a lesser extent even Cuba—had shown great restraint in supporting revolutionary movements of the left in Latin America. Both Moscow and Havana primarily provided discreet training, including paramilitary training in Cuba and the Soviet Union, for some Latin American (as well as Arab and African) revolutionaries. Only their verbal support, and such political support as that entailed, was unsparing. Considering the strong declaratory stand of the Soviet Union and Cuba in support of national liberation and progressive change, this assistance was unsurprising except perhaps in its limited scope.

After the overthrow of the Allende government in Chile in 1973 and the suppression of local terrorists in Argentina and Uruguay, the situation in most of Latin America became relatively stabilized until opposition to repressive right-wing dictatorships in several countries of Central America and

---

92. "Communist Interference in El Salvador," Department of State Special Report 80 (February 23, 1981), p. 8; reprinted in *State Bulletin*, vol. 81 (March 1981), p. 7. The report was filled with errors and misuse of captured documents cited as sources. The press soon pointed them out. The key articles were Jonathan Kwitny, "Tarnished Report? Apparent Errors Cloud U.S. 'White Paper' on Reds in El Salvador," *Wall Street Journal*, June 8, 1981; Robert G. Kaiser, "White Paper on El Salvador Is Faulty," *Washington Post*, June 9, 1981; and Juan de Onis, "U.S. Officials Concede Flaws in Salvador White Paper but Defend Its Conclusion," *New York Times*, June 10, 1981.

93. See Bernard Gwertzman, "Haig Cites 'Hit List' for Soviet Control of Central America," *New York Times*, March 19, 1981.

94. After earlier references in congressional testimony and in private interviews, Haig made public statements on reacting "at the source," identifying Cuba as the subject, on February 23 and 27. Later he identified the Soviet Union as "the source of the problem." See "Secretary Haig Interviewed for French Television," *State Bulletin*, vol. 81 (April 1981), p. 15; "Secretary Haig Discusses Foreign Assistance," ibid., p. 22; and "Interviews at Breakfast Meetings," ibid. (May 1981), p. 15.

the Caribbean basin erupted into armed struggle late in the decade. The most significant was the left-to-moderate liberal coalition led by the Sandinistas that eventually overthrew the Somoza regime in Nicaragua in July 1979. Even there, greater external support was given by such noncommunist countries as Panama, Costa Rica, Venezuela, and Mexico than by the Soviet Union and Cuba. The Soviets remained very guarded in their support even after the Sandinista-led victory. Moreover, it has been reported that Castro himself counseled the Sandinistas *not* to adopt too radical a course and not to alienate American support, as he had done. Castro's own regime in Cuba survives only owing to Soviet support amounting to some $8 million a day by the end of the decade. Moscow did not desire to subsidize Nicaragua in addition to Cuba (and Vietnam).

The turn to violence next in El Salvador led to a reformist *coup d'état* in October 1979. Within a few months, however, right-wing military elements within the ruling junta gained a predominant role, and most of the liberal and moderate political elements left the government, some eventually joining the guerrilla opposition. Through the 1970s the small Communist party of El Salvador had, on Soviet advice, declined to join other groups in armed resistance. Only in 1980 did they begin to participate, and even then they remained one of the smallest components. The United States continued to support the junta and to encourage economic reform, although violence from the extreme right and left led to increasing polarization that united the moderate opposition with the radical left.

On the eve of the change of American administrations in January 1981, the Soviet Union and Cuba shifted course and began to supply arms on a more substantial scale to the Salvadoran revolutionaries. This shift did not occur because the Soviet leaders had decided to abandon détente; they were trying, at the very same time, though presumably without high expectations, to restore a measure of détente into relations with the incoming American administration. One reason for the shift was simply that the Soviet leaders believe progressive revolutions are morally right and historically inevitable under conditions of rising popular dissatisfaction with repressive authoritarian rule and economic exploitation. Given that this reason applied earlier, it could not have been the cause for a change in policy. Still, it deserves note because, while it should be obvious, it is rarely recognized. A second reason is that the Soviet leaders believed that the prospects for the revolution in El Salvador succeeding, even if not imminent, were nonetheless on the rise. Moscow (and Havana) wanted to be seen by potential revolutionaries everywhere, and especially in the immediate region, as ready to support progressive change, especially in contrast to the United States. This was an important changed factor in the situation: American policy was clearly swinging to support the existing authoritarian regimes in Central America. By channeling arms through Nicaragua to El Salvador the Soviets and Cubans could probably ensure American identification with efforts at forcible repression in El Salvador—and perhaps also lead the United States to develop closer ties with the authoritarian regimes in

Guatemala and Honduras. Such U.S. actions would alienate many in such countries as Mexico and Costa Rica, as well as in Western Europe, who favored progressive change. The United States, as it ostentatiously set aside the banner of human rights, would again be cast in the role of external Yanqui policeman in a region with a long history of resentment against American intervention. Meanwhile, the Soviet and Cuban role was indirect and could even be denied. There were no Soviet or even Cuban soldiers with the revolutionary forces, while American military men had resumed instruction in internal military policing and suppression operations in El Salvador.

Very soon after the failure of the Salvadoran guerrilla "final offensive" in January 1981, the Soviet leaders began to revert to their skepticism over whether there was a revolutionary situation in Central America. This outlook reinforced their caution and contributed to their low-key involvement thereafter.

There may also have been a more subtle additional consideration in the Soviet decision. The Soviet leaders may have wished to demonstrate to Washington that just as the United States and its friends such as Egypt were quietly supplying arms (including weapons of Soviet origin) to the resistance in Afghanistan in the Soviet Union's backyard, so too could the Soviet Union and its friends such as Cuba quietly supply arms (including American-made M-16 rifles acquired in Vietnam) to the revolutionaries in El Salvador. This action would, in addition to serving the other purposes noted earlier, at a minimum show Washington that two can play the same game and might even lead to a tacit agreement by both to curtail or cease such actions. That would be a deal Moscow was only too ready to make, despite its principled support for the cause of progressive revolutionary change in Central America. It would not acknowledge such a deal publicly, but that would not be necessary, since it had not acknowledged supply of arms in the first place.

The Soviets also hoped the elected leftist government in Jamaica represented a sign of progressive movement in those countries having democratic processes. The left-wing coup in Grenada in 1979 by the pseudo-Marxist New Jewel movement of Maurice Bishop had also been welcomed, but warily. The Soviets only cautiously supported Castro's efforts to bring Grenada into the outer circle of Soviet-aligned progressive states and carefully refrained from close identification or commitment. Contrary to later U.S. claims, the evidence later acquired on Grenadan contacts with the Soviets shows how little support the Soviets gave to Grenada (and how little confidence they had in its leaders). Moscow did not attempt to use Grenada as a base to expand communist rule in the area. Similarly, the Soviets welcomed warily the leftward turn of Colonel Desi Bouterese, the dictator in Suriname who took power in a coup in 1980, and kept him at arm's length.

The United States, for its part, in parallel with its support for the government of El Salvador, took an increasingly hostile position toward Nicaragua. On April 1, 1981, the United States cut off aid to Nicaragua. From August to November Assistant Secretary of State Thomas Enders negotiated with the Nicaraguans over terms to secure a halt to Nicaraguan support for the guerrillas in El Salvador. But increasingly the administration shifted its objective to one of bringing pressure on the Sandinistas to share power within Nicaragua and to curtail their ties with Cuba and the Soviet Union.

As early as March 9, 1981, President Reagan had issued a secret "Presidential Finding on Central America" that instituted a covert action program to interdict arms supply via Nicaragua to the guerrillas in El Salvador. After a key National Security Council (NSC) meeting on November 16, he issued NSDD-17, authorizing a considerable expansion in covert support for paramilitary Nicaraguan forces (popularly called the "contras," a diminutive of "contrarevolutionarios") and providing an initial $19 million. The CIA armed, trained, and supported a force of contras that grew from a few hundred in 1981 to some 12,000–15,000 troops in the field in 1984. They operated into Nicaragua from bases in Honduras (and to a lesser extent Costa Rica).

An NSC document of April 1982 that later leaked into the public domain defined the American objectives for these covert operations and a much wider range of political, economic and other activities. The objectives were much broader than interdicting arms supply into El Salvador, the initial public justification, and applied in varying ways to the whole of Central America. Basically the unpublicized U.S. aim was "to eliminate Cuban/Soviet influence in the region." Moreover, this was to be accomplished "in the short run." In the longer run the aim was to "build politically stable governments able to withstand such influences." This action program was predicated on the conclusion that the United States has "a vital interest in not allowing the proliferation of Cuba-model states" in the region.[95]

The burgeoning U.S. covert action program and support to antigovernment insurgents being sent into Nicaragua gradually became publicly known and proved controversial. President Reagan defended support to the contras, whom he called "freedom fighters."[96] But congressional support waned. Meanwhile, throughout 1983 and 1984 the anomaly of a widely publicized and openly debated and funded "covert" operation to overthrow the recognized government of a country with which the United States was not at war became ever more bizarre. The turning point leading to a congressional cutoff of funding was the mining of Nicaraguan ports, with deaths and damage to ships of other countries.[97] The Senate voted 84 to 12 to condemn the

---

95. The leaked NSC Planning Group document, "U.S. Policy in Central America and Cuba through F.Y. '84, Summary Paper," April 1982, was printed in full in "National Security Council Document on Policy in Central America and Cuba," *New York Times*, April 7, 1983. This document included references and details on the Presidential Finding of March 9, 1981, and NSDD-17 of November 1981. A second Presidential Finding followed on December 1, 1981.

96. Lou Cannon, "Reagan Defends Nicaragua Role," *Washington Post*, May 5, 1983.

97. Bob Woodward and Fred Hiatt, "CIA Views Minelaying Part of Covert 'Holding Action': Stepped-Up Role Seen after U.S. Elections," *Washington Post*, April 10, 1984; and Fred Hiatt and Joanne Omang, "CIA Helped to Mine Ports in Nicaragua," ibid., April 7, 1984.

mining, and the House soon followed, 281 to 111.[98] Although that action was not binding on the administration, Congress also soon moved to cut off all funds for covert support for the contras.[99] The final blow was the revelation that the CIA had prepared for the contras a manual on the conduct of operations that included but thinly veiled language to urge selective terrorism and assassination.[100] The contras continued their operations with other sources of support, including large sums from unofficial U.S. sources.[101]

In El Salvador, while the guerrillas had suffered a major setback in their premature offensive on the eve of the Reagan administration, they had sufficiently broad popular support to maintain a continuing insurrection. Although Haig's plans for an early victory also failed, continuing U.S. support and military assistance kept the Salvadoran government in control. A military stalemate developed in El Salvador over the period 1982–84 and prospectively well beyond: neither the government nor the guerrillas could defeat the other.

In 1982 the administration announced a "Caribbean initiative," intended as an economic-aid carrot to rally countries in the region to American policy, as well as to enhance their viability and resistance to leftist revolution. In 1983 the administration appointed a prestigious commission chaired by former Secretary of State Kissinger, primarily in order to rally the support of the American public for the policy of resisting communist encroachment in the region. Neither device was notably successful in deflecting attention from the internal conflict in El Salvador and the incursions into Nicaragua.

While El Salvador, and in time Nicaragua, were the focus of action in the region, the principal target of American concern at the outset was Cuba. Many members of the Reagan administration shared an animosity toward Castro's Cuba. Moreover, Cuba was seen not only as a tool of successful Soviet expansion of influence in Africa, but also as the potential source of expanded communist influence in the Western Hemisphere, especially the Caribbean basin. As noted, both Reagan and Haig frequently referred to Cuba as a Soviet proxy.

Haig early in the administration recommended to President Reagan that, in his own words, the president "lay down a marker on the question

98. Joanne Omang and Don Oberdorfer, "Senate Votes, 84–12, to Condemn Mining of Nicaraguan Ports: Administration Tries to Defend Its Position," *Washington Post*, April 11, 1984; and T. R. Reid and Joanne Omang, "CIA Funds Run Short for Covert Operations: House Joins Senate to Condemn U.S. Participation in Minelaying," ibid., April 13, 1984.

99. Martin Tolchin, "Senators, 88 to 1, Drop Money to Aid Nicaragua Rebels," *New York Times*, June 26, 1984; Philip Taubman, "White House Quits Rebel Aid Battle," ibid., July 25, 1984; and Taubman, "House Votes to Deny Help to Nicaraguan Insurgents," ibid., August 3, 1984.

100. "C.I.A. Said to Produce Manual for Anti-Sandinistas," *New York Times*, October 15, 1984; "Excerpts from Primer for Insurgents," ibid., October 17, 1984; Joel Brinkley, "C.I.A. Primer Tells Nicaraguan Rebels How to Kill," ibid., October 17, 1984.

101. Lou Cannon, Don Oberdorfer, and George Lardner, Jr., "Private U.S. Groups Raise Funds for Contras," *Washington Post*, September 10, 1984; and Fred Hiatt, "Private Groups Press 'Contra' Aid: Millions Raised in U.S.," ibid., December 10, 1984.

of Cuba."[102] When the president did not do so, Haig himself did. Several times in February he referred, as noted, to the need to deal with the problem of external assistance to the guerrillas in El Salvador "at the source"—and "clearly it's Cuba."[103] Not only did Haig's strident stance alarm the Cubans and give Moscow concern, but Secretary of Defense Weinberger and the JCS also did not want to become needlessly involved in a war with Cuba. Haig's proposal to consider a naval blockade of any shipments of arms from Cuba was rejected by the president after strong objections from the Pentagon. As Haig said later, he was "virtually alone" in the administration on this issue.[104]

The incoming Reagan administration had been surprised to learn of a secret diplomatic channel of communication that the Carter administration had developed to Castro. In February the Cubans quietly sought to continue it but were turned down. By November 1981, however, Haig availed himself of an offer by the Mexican government and met with Cuban Vice President Carlos Rafael Rodriguez. This contact was followed by a secret visit to Havana by General Vernon Walters, the former deputy chief of the CIA and now a special roving ambassador, who met with Castro. These exchanges did not, however, lead to any improvement in relations.[105]

Cuban aid to Nicaragua, including some military assistance, remained at a level that annoyed Washington without provoking it. There was, however, continuing concern and displeasure in the administration over increased Soviet supply of arms to Cuba, recurrently expressed publicly. In 1981 the general volume of arms rose substantially, and in early 1982 included a second squadron of MiG-23 fighters—again stirring up the question of a possible violation of the 1962/1970 understanding, as had the delivery of the first squadron in 1978.[106] CIA Director William J. Casey in 1982, and President Reagan himself in 1983, both made casual (and unwarranted) charges that the Soviets had violated the 1962 understanding by supplying these arms to Cuba.[107] These were, however, only offhand statements reflecting a general assumption of Soviet violation rather than considered charges, and they were not followed up.

Haig charged that the arms in Cuba "far exceeds" what Cuba needed for defense against "any potential threat emanating from this hemi-

102. Haig, *Caveat*, p. 98.

103. *State Bulletin*, vol. 81 (April 1981), p. 15.

104. Haig, *Caveat*, p. 129, and see pp. 123–31.

105. Ibid., pp. 132–37. See also Don Oberdorfer, "Nicaraguan Leader Blasts U.S. at U.N., Offers Negotiations: Diplomacy Up, but Optimism on Result Is Not," *Washington Post*, March 26, 1982; and John M. Goshko, "U.S. and Cuba Open Official Negotiations," ibid., July 13, 1984.

106. See chapter 18.

107. Interview with CIA Director William J. Casey, "The Real Soviet Threat in El Salvador—and Beyond," *U.S. News and World Report*, vol. 92 (March 8, 1982), pp. 23–24; and Francis X. Clines, "President Accuses Soviet on '62 Pact," *New York Times*, September 15, 1983.

sphere."[108] That assertion could only be true if he meant the United States would never go to war against Cuba—a veiled threat he himself had made. From the standpoint of both Moscow and Havana, the buildup of arms in Cuba did reinforce deterrence of a possible American attack. Moreover, the Soviet leaders were not prepared to commit themselves to come to Cuba's aid if it were attacked, and from their standpoint the supply of arms was a politically useful reassurance to Castro as well as a way of making that extreme eventuality less likely.

While El Salvador and Cuba were most directly in the limelight in 1981, the administration also devoted considerable attention to the other very prominent alleged Soviet proxy, Qaddafi's Libya.[109] In May the United States closed the Libyan mission in Washington because of links to suspected terrorism. On August 19 two U.S. Navy F-14 interceptors shot down two Su-22 Libyan jet fighters that had unwisely attacked them over the Gulf of Sidra, some sixty nautical miles from the coast in an area claimed by Libya. President Reagan triumphantly announced, "Let friend and foe alike know that America has the muscle to back up its words."[110] Also in August and again in October reports appeared of a U.S. plan to "destabilize" Qaddafi's rule in Libya.[111] In November and December 1981 there was, in turn, a scare prompted by reports that Qaddafi had sent a hit team to assassinate President Reagan or some other senior American leader.[112] No substantiation for the report was found.

The Reagan administration also addressed the Soviets directly with its concerns over what it saw as Soviet proxies. Haig constantly raised this subject with Dobrynin in the early months of 1981 in his quest for Soviet acceptance of "restraint and reciprocity" in the third world. As Haig himself notes in his memoir, Dobrynin told him, "All I ever hear from you . . . is Cuba, Cuba, Cuba!"[113] Haig sought to ensure that the Soviet leaders would get the message of U.S. seriousness by seeing to it that "every official of the State Department, in every exchange with a Soviet official, emphasized American determination that the U.S.S.R. and its clients—especially Fidel Castro and Qaddafi—must moderate their interventionist behavior."[114] Dobrynin, for his

108. "The Secretary: Question-and-Answer Session Following ABA Address," August 11, *State Bulletin*, vol. 81 (September 1981), p. 15.

109. For example, see Haig's repeated references in *Caveat*, pp. 96, 109, 110, 172, 220.

110. "U.S.S. Constellation: Remarks during a Visit to the Aircraft Carrier in the Pacific Ocean off the Coast of California, August 20, 1981," *Presidential Documents*, vol. 17 (August 24, 1981), p. 891.

111. See Don Oberdorfer, "U.S. Has Sought to Pressure Qaddafi," *Washington Post*, August 20, 1981.

112. Philip Taubman, "U.S. Officials Say F.B.I. Is Hunting Terrorists Seeking to Kill President," *New York Times*, December 4, 1981.

113. Haig, *Caveat*, p. 107, and see pp. 108–10.

114. Ibid., p. 110.

part, denied knowledge of any untoward behavior by Castro. As for Qaddafi, as Haig notes, "Dobrynin made it clear that Libya was an American problem," not a Soviet responsibility.[115]

Haig's efforts to impress American concern on the Soviets reinforced their calculations that the time was not ripe for encouraging revolution in the Caribbean basin. Haig acknowledges that the United States "began to receive signals in return . . . that the Soviets were telling their friends to slow down support to insurgencies and urging restraint in their dealings with the United States." Although Haig does not identify the friends, he had in mind Nicaragua in particular. But although those signals were indeed being sent, for some reason in his memoir Haig refers to this intelligence as "rumors, which I did not altogether credit."[116] The reason is that he did not want to acknowledge this restraint, as it did not jibe with his ongoing and strident campaign on a Soviet threat to the region.

Beginning with Haig's conversations in 1981, but especially in 1982–83, with talks at the assistant secretary of state level, several rounds of unpublicized U.S.-Soviet diplomatic exchanges took place that dealt with regional issues and potential crises in southern Africa, the Middle East (in particular the Iran-Iraq war), and Afghanistan. These quiet diplomatic discussions were one of the most successful aspects of American diplomacy with the Soviet Union in the early 1980s. One main reason was their confidentiality. Another was the interest on both sides in pragmatically probing "rules of engagement" in the regional geopolitical competition. To cite an example, both the United States and the Soviet Union not only warned the other not to exploit the Iran-Iraq war, but also used the opportunity to explain some of their own activities in the region (including U.S. military preparations for contingent action to ensure world access to the Persian Gulf), as those actions might have been subject to misinterpretation by the other side.[117]

Higher-level exchanges on key regional issues occasionally served the same purpose. The hotline was used in the Lebanese situation to help prevent misinterpretations. And most important, in October 1982 Secretary of State Shultz warned Foreign Minister Gromyko of serious adverse consequences if MiG aircraft were delivered to Nicaragua. Despite many earlier signs that the Soviet bloc had intended to provide such aircraft, they were not sent.[118]

The United States also undertook actions that were not directly related to the Soviet Union but that would advance American, while curtailing Soviet, influence. Briefly noted earlier were some of the U.S. programs in Central America and the Caribbean basin. The Middle East was the other prime

---

115. Ibid., p. 109.

116. Ibid., p. 108.

117. Information from informed U.S. officials on a background basis.

118. Ibid.

area of attention. Initially, the administration had a curiously naïve belief in the possibility of creating a "strategic consensus" that would weld Israel, Egypt, Jordan, and Saudi Arabia together. This completely unreal scheme was predicated on the fact that all were America's friends and all shared a desire not to see Soviet influence in the region expand. So far, so good. But the conception completely ignored the sharp divisions over the Palestinian issue and the exigencies of the internal and external relationships and imperatives of the countries. The proposition collapsed of its own weight, but not before causing difficulties, including a bitter battle in Congress over the sale of the AWACS surveillance system and other air defense systems to Saudi Arabia. That issue also adversely affected U.S.-Israeli relations. So, in reverse, did the Israeli bombing of the Iraqi nuclear reactor in June 1981.

The Israeli invasion of Lebanon in June 1982, on a very thin pretext of retaliation for a terrorist action in London (by an anti-PLO Arab splinter group, it soon turned out), opened a wide range of new problems for Israel, Syria, the PLO, Lebanon, the United States, and the Soviet Union. Secretary of State Haig had, whether knowingly or not, given what the Israelis considered a green light to proceed with their plan. But he was removed from office almost immediately after the Israeli invasion began, and the administration took an increasingly negative attitude toward the deep Israeli thrust all the way to Beirut.[119]

The United States landed marines to help arrange the evacuation of the PLO from Beirut in August, after a cease-fire was arranged, and then withdrew them. But after the Lebanese right-wing Christian Phalange massacred Palestinian refugees in the Shatila and Sabra camps in September and evident Israeli failure to provide security, despite a written American pledge to the PLO based on firm Israeli assurances to the United States, the U.S. Marines (together with French and Italian contingents) were brought in.[120] Unlike the European contingents, however, the United States began, through naval gunfire and air action in the interests of local security, to participate haphazardly in the Lebanese civil war.

The Soviets, for their part, provided Syria with extensive replacements of arms to make up for the losses suffered in the Syrian-Israeli fighting in Lebanon, but they made clear to Syria that their commitment did not include any direct Soviet action to assist the Syrians beyond the borders of Syria. While the Soviet Union lost standing by not assisting the PLO in any way, it avoided any direct involvement even after the United States intervened.

The Soviet leaders were quite concerned in 1982 over the U.S. military involvement in Lebanon because of what they believed it meant. They could not imagine that the United States would commit the U.S. Marines

---

119. For a perceptive analysis, see George W. Ball, *Error and Betrayal in Lebanon: An Analysis of Israel's Invasion of Lebanon and the Implications for U.S.-Israeli Relations* (Washington, D.C.: Foundation for Middle East Peace, 1984).

120. Ibid., pp. 55–59.

unless Washington had decided to use force as necessary to meet a broader American aim: establishment of a satrapy in Lebanon. The later U.S. military withdrawal after the tragic and humiliating loss of 241 marines in a terrorist truck-bombing in October 1983 was ascribed not to American goodwill or even prudence, but to domestic repercussions in the United States.

The American invasion of Grenada that same month, on the other hand, was seen as evidence of a continuing U.S. readiness, even eagerness, to use military power to roll back progressive revolutionary change where that could be done expeditiously.

From the Soviet perspective, in the first half of the 1980s the United States had turned to a broad policy of more active use of counterrevolutionary insurgent forces in its attempt to roll back history. Thus, beginning in 1981 the Reagan administration stepped up U.S. assistance to insurgents in Afghanistan, stimulated a new insurgency in Nicaragua, and indirectly supported other reactionary powers in aiding the insurgencies in Kampuchea, Angola, Mozambique, and Ethiopia. In short, virtually all the gains by revolutionary forces in the latter half of the 1970s were being subjected to a vigorous counterattack in the first half of the 1980s. Moreover, the Soviet Union itself was overextended and not in a favorable position to aid those regimes (except in Afghanistan, where the Soviet Union had a direct and dominant role, although it was still unable to suppress the insurgency effectively).

The Soviet evaluation of the moral and historical role of the governments in these six countries was subjective. But its evaluation that the wheel of fortune had turned against these movements once in power was objectively founded. So was the perception of the U.S. role, although with some exaggeration in terms of Soviet assessments and much more in terms of its propaganda.

The absence of Soviet support to new progressive revolutions was in the first instance based on the lack of new indigenous revolutionary situations. In addition, the Soviet Union was overextended as a result of its direct commitment in Afghanistan and its support to Vietnam and Cuba and, to a much lesser extent, Ethiopia (and scarcely at all in Nicaragua, Angola, and Mozambique). Soviet preoccupation with Poland, the issue of INF missile deployment in Europe, internal economic problems, and a double transition in the Soviet leadership itself further reduced any inclination to wider involvement in the geopolitical competition in the third world.

1981–84: A Summing-Up

The conjunction of leadership changes in the United States and the Soviet Union in the early 1980s combined with an urgent need in both countries to redefine their relationship after the collapse of the détente of the 1970s. The particular combination was inauspicious. The new president in

January 1981 was vigorous and ideological, had clear authority, believed in the need for a more assertive stand, and had very little awareness of international politics. The Soviet leadership, by contrast, was old and weak (Kosygin and Suslov died and Brezhnev was dying as the new leadership came into office in Washington, and then Andropov lasted barely a year and a half before passing away, to be replaced by Chernenko) and was bureaucratically constrained, transitional, and ideologically ossified and set in its ways with respect to international politics. While this combination might seem to give the United States an advantage, that conclusion is doubtful. Its main effect was to preclude constructive negotiation and collaboration. Moreover, while the posture of the Reagan administration from 1981 through 1983 was confrontational, and not only in terms of rhetoric, its policy was much more equivocal and fragmented.

U.S. actions from 1981 through 1983 were not sufficiently aggressive to be described as a policy of confrontation (which is not to say that the results would have been desirable if it had been). Yet it was too gratuitously hostile to serve usefully a policy of competition. It was neither a policy of combining the carrot and the stick, as in the early and mid–1970s, nor even of applying the stick while offering the carrot as in the late 1970s (and as Haig sought to do). Rather, it was a provocative brandishing of a stick that was enough to annoy and alarm the Soviet bear but not enough to cage him. (Moreover the United States is not a trainer, nor is the Soviet Union its bear to tame.) Nor did the United States offer any positive incentives to the Soviet leaders no matter what they did.

Even on the basis of its own apparent objectives, the Reagan administration, at least in its first three years, dissipated many of its advantages. It lost much of the consensus of the American public on the need for a defense buildup by a mindless spending spree. The administration reduced, rather than rebuilt, allied confidence. The gap between the United States and Western Europe increased, despite a conservative swing in West Germany and Great Britain (and in the policies of France), and the successful weathering of the issue of the deployment of INF missiles. In 1984, however, the Reagan administration began to recoup its losses on many of these fronts and was well-placed by the start of the second term to move on to a more constructive path—should the president decide to do so and firmly to lead in that direction.

While the Reagan administration did launch U.S. policy, and especially policy toward the Soviet Union, on a new path, it also borrowed much from other approaches. Even its slogans (which were, unexpectedly, often the best guide to policy) were largely borrowed. "Peace through strength" was the term Ford had turned to after shelving the word détente (in his primary contest with Reagan in 1976). "Reciprocity" was borrowed from Carter and Brzezinski; "dialogue" from Nixon and Kissinger. The confrontational rhetoric was the most original, but also the least useful for any purpose except to satisfy internal political-psychological drives and to mollify a hard-line constituency. It created a new barrier that could only be partly dispelled by its abandonment in 1984.

Most of the other foreign policy successes of the administration involved the later neutralization of problems the administration itself had generated. China policy, for example, got back on track by 1983–84 after travails largely caused by the Reagan administration's own agitation of the Taiwan issue in 1980–81. Relations with the West Europeans were restored in 1983–84 after being aggravated by U.S. assaults on European détente and economic interests in 1981–82. The United States disentangled itself and withdrew its surviving marines from Lebanon after entangling itself there in the first place. The involvements in Central America were less clearly on a path toward resolution by the end of 1984, but Congress was keeping the administration from excessive commitments to covert warfare.

Relations with the Soviet Union itself remained uncertain at the beginning of 1985. Renewed consideration of arms control (which had stalemated by the end of 1983 after two years of disproving the thesis that if two powers stand firm they are negotiating) at least suggested a willingness on both sides to see whether there was any basis for dialogue and negotiation. President Reagan, Secretary of State Shultz, and National Security Adviser McFarlane seemed interested even after the election in pursuing a dialogue with the Soviet leaders. Moscow saw this stance as positive, although by itself as no more than keeping open a possibility.

As the Soviet leaders assess the possibilities for improving relations with the United States, still a Soviet aim, they are skeptical. The one element they regard as potentially the most significant but still quite uncertain is that political realities in the United States and the world may lead "realists" in U.S. ruling circles to shift back to a policy akin to what Nixon now calls hardheaded détente, represented most closely by the positions held first by Haig and later Shultz, and at least rhetorically by Reagan in 1984. The Soviets are acutely aware of their own very limited ability to influence U.S. realities. But some among them do see at least a possibility that internal American economic and political constraints, and what they firmly believe remain the long-term trends in the world historical process, will compel realists in Washington to see—as Nixon and Kissinger did—a better prospect in swinging with the historical trend than attempting to buck it. At the same time, they themselves have a more sober and less optimistic evaluation of the pace of change in the global correlation of forces, and so they do not expect early or far-reaching change in American policy. Moreover, advocates of a more confrontational policy have continued to have a role in the administration and to have a powerful voice in U.S. policy.

The Soviet leaders have undoubtedly been disturbed by the ability of the Reagan administration to pursue its policy as successfully as it has. While American critics may point to some signal failures and many uncertain or untoward results (some have been noted earlier), in many cases these judgments stem from disagreements with the administration over aims, and not over an assessment of achievements in terms of the Reagan administration's own goals. Here the Soviet analyst approaches the subject from a standpoint paradoxically closer to that of the administration. Thus, for example, whether one sees a failure of arms control, or a success of arms buildup, depends on perspective. And both the Soviet observer and at least important elements in the Reagan administration see a sustained U.S. military buildup and the deployment of the Pershing II and GLCM missiles in Europe as signal successes of the Reagan policy—not as failures of arms control. The ability to revive the American economy while carrying out this tremendous military program is again seen as a success by the administration and by the alarmed Soviet observer—rather than as a failure in which wasteful expenditures intensify an arms race and contribute to an enormous deficit.

The Soviet leaders, as they look to the second half of the 1980s and beyond, do not expect a "Détente II," a return to the relationship of the 1972–74 period. They do, however, believe that the imperatives of coexistence and the need to reduce the risks of nuclear war remain a paramount interest of the United States as well as of themselves. While not anticipating that the United States would choose resort to war, the Soviet leaders do see increased dangers of situations getting out of control. They seek a more regulated, predictable, and risk-resistant relationship. For that reason, as well as because of economic pressures and resource constraints, the Soviet leaders have been seriously interested in negotiated arms limitations and what they term military détente. But they are also determined not to accept unequal limitations, above all not under pressure from a United States intent on gaining and using military advantage precisely in order to compel Soviet acceptance of inferiority. Hence they are on guard not to appear weak and not to encourage the imperialists by seeming to be overeager for (or in) arms control negotiations. While seeking arms limitations on what they would regard as equal terms, they are also determined not to settle for less.

The debate over arms control in Moscow in the 1980s is no longer, as it was in the 1960s and early 1970s, whether arms control and mutual arms limitation are in its interests. That battle was decided in the 1970s in favor of arms control. Today the question is whether there is any real prospect of U.S. interest in arms limitations on a mutually advantageous basis. It is not the advisability of arms control but its attainability that is now in serious doubt.

The Soviet leaders are also prepared to deal with the United States on the geopolitical issues of "reciprocity and restraint" in the competition in the third world. Their view of the problems in this respect, and of both the American role and their own, differ greatly from those held in Washington. These differences in perception, as well as clashes in interests and competition for influence, will not make agreement easy or far-reaching. But some points can be negotiated or, more often, clarified and ameliorated by less formal but authoritative and concrete dialogue. Thus, for example, while the situation may change in the future, during the period from 1981 through 1984 the Soviet Union did not provide MiG fighters to Nicaragua, despite clear earlier indications they had planned to do so. Similarly, while the United States and several Muslim countries provided arms to the anticommunist guerrillas in Afghanistan via Pakistan, the quantities and types of weapons were kept below a threshold that could have provoked Soviet retaliation or interdiction attacks in Pakistan.

Dialogue on the range of political and geopolitical interests of the two powers continued intermittently through the first half of the 1980s, but on an erratic basis. Whether it will become more effective remains to be seen.

Soviet hegemony in the Eastern European Warsaw Pact area, and American commitment to the NATO countries, represent well-defined and respected limits to any use of military power by the other side.

The years 1981 through 1984, as was also true in large measure of 1980, marked a period of transition for policy adrift after détente. That time of transition had not ended at the close of 1984. Whether the years following would prolong it or mark the start of a new course in one or another direction could not be said at the time. The year 1984 itself could, in retrospect, mark the start of a new approach on the U.S. side. If so, 1985 could find the two countries resuming a path of mixed competition and cooperation. A policy of confrontation seemed likely in 1981–83. Given that such a policy had not been established by the end of the Reagan administration's first term, it was not likely to be the administration's choice in the second. The Soviet turn to a confrontational response to the INF issue in Europe, and to some other aspects of the Reagan approach, was also clearly not the preferred general course in Moscow. Nonetheless, a turn to confrontation cannot be ruled out if events precipitate a new and direct clash of a kind fortunately absent in the first half of the decade.

In oversimplified dialectical terms, it may be said that dissatisfaction with the thesis of détente in the 1970s led to its antithesis in confrontation in the early 1980s, but that a new synthesis may follow, perhaps as early as the last half of the 1980s.

29   The Failure of American-Soviet Détente in the 1970s

THE DÉTENTE of the 1970s did not succeed, in the view of most Americans, because of Soviet actions that contravened what the *United States* understood détente to mean. Either the Soviet leaders abused détente, or if they did act in accordance with it, détente itself was flawed. Both the Soviet Union *and détente itself* were thus seen as sharing the blame for a mounting series of disquieting developments.

In the Soviet view, the joint détente effort of the 1970s has been willfully abandoned by the United States. The leaders of the United States have, since the late 1970s, preferred to seek advantages from a policy of confrontation, renewed an American quest for military superiority, and been unwilling to accept strategic and political parity. In the avowed Soviet view, however, détente remains an objective, continues to be Soviet policy, and can be a common policy again if and when the United States returns to it.

This difference in perspective—like so many differences in American and Soviet perspective and perception—makes it difficult for Americans and Soviets even to conduct parallel assessments of the détente effort of the 1970s in order to diagnose the causes of its failure. Indeed, such assessments are scarcely deemed necessary in either Washington or Moscow. On each side, the actions of the other are virtually taken for granted as having been responsible for the breakdown of détente. Finally, the present climate of mutual hostility and suspicion does not encourage detached and dispassionate consideration.

There is a misleading, even dangerous, tendency in the United States by both advocates and opponents of efforts to improve relations to consider "détente" an entity in its own right and to assume that there is a single policy of détente. This tendency leads to judgments that "détente was tried and failed" or that "détente was betrayed," or, alternatively, that "détente was never really tried." Such oversimplified approaches only mislead. The subject is the concrete historical experience of the two rival superpowers from 1969 through 1979 to increase the range of cooperation and negotiation of

1068

differences, while regulating competition and reducing instances and intensities of confrontation.

American fears have been that the United States was providing more than its share of cooperation, while the Soviet Union was more vigorously devoting itself to competition. This view is, as this book shows, one-sided. So, too, on the other hand, is the Soviet belief that American leaders have consciously chosen to abandon détente for confrontation and that American disenchantment with détente was not seriously influenced by Soviet actions.

This chapter identifies and examines—from a detached perspective—the main causes of the failure of the American-Soviet détente experience of the 1970s.

Differences in Basic Conceptions

Foremost among the causes of the ultimate failure of détente in the 1970s was a fatal difference in the conception of its basic role by the two sides. The American leaders saw it (in Kissinger's words) as a way of "managing the emergence of Soviet power" into world politics in an age of nuclear parity. The Soviet leaders envisaged it as a way of managing the transition of the United States from its former superiority to a more modest role in world politics in an age of nuclear parity. Thus each saw itself as the manager of a transition of the other. Moreover, while the advent of parity ineluctably meant some decrease in the ability of the United States to manage world affairs, this fact was not sufficiently appreciated in Washington. And while it meant a relatively more important role for the Soviet Union, it did not mean acquisition of the kind of power the United States wielded. Finally, both had diverging images of the world order, and although that fact was well enough understood, its implications were not. Thus, underlying the attempts by each of the two powers to manage the adjustment of the other to a changing correlation of forces in the world there were even more basic parallel attempts by both to modify the fundamental world order—in different directions.

The Soviet leaders, conditioned by their Marxist-Leninist ideology, believe that a certain historical movement will ultimately lead to the replacement of capitalism (imperialism) in the world by socialism (communism). But this transition must now occur in a world made incalculably more dangerous by massive arsenals of nuclear weapons. Peaceful coexistence and détente are seen as offering a path to neutralize this danger by ruling out war between states, permitting historical change to occur, as the Soviets believe it must, through fundamental indigenous social-economic-political processes. While Marxist-Leninists do not shun the use of military force (or any other instrument of power) if it is expedient, they do not see military power as the fundamental moving force of history. On the contrary, they see it as a possible ultimate recourse of the doomed capitalist class ruling the imperialist citadels of the

West. There is, therefore, no ideological barrier to or reservation about pursuing a policy of détente aimed at preventing nuclear war. Quite the contrary—détente represents a policy aimed at providing stability to a world order that allows progressive historical change.

The American leadership and the American people, not holding a deterministic ideology, have been much less sure of themselves and of the trend of history. Insofar as they hold an ideology for a global order, it is one of pluralism. That ideology does not assume the whole world will choose an American-style democratic and free enterprise system. The world order is seen as one that should provide stability and at least protect the democratic option for peoples. Occasionally there have been crusades to extirpate communism in the world; a fringe represented, for example, by Norman Podhoretz today when he criticizes the Reagan administration for failing wholeheartedly to rally a new assault on communism and against the Soviet Union. But the dominant American aim has been to contain and deter Soviet or Soviet-controlled communist expansion at the expense of a pluralistic and, in that sense, free world order. What has varied and what periodically has been at issue is the relative weight to be placed, on the one hand, on containment achieved by building positions of counterposing power, and on the other, on cooperation, pursued by seeking common ground for mutual efforts to reduce tension and accommodate the differing interests of the two sides. There have been varied judgments in both countries about whether objective circumstances permit the latter approach or require the former, and therefore about whether détente or confrontation is desirable or feasible.

When Nixon and Kissinger developed a strategy of détente to replace a strategy of confrontation, the underlying expectation was that as the Soviet Union became more and more extensively engaged in an organic network of relations with the existing world order, it would gradually become reconciled to that order. Ideological expectations of global revolutionary change would become attenuated and merely philosophical rather than actively political. Avoidance of the risks of nuclear war was essential; hence there was acceptance of peaceful coexistence and of efforts at strategic arms limitations and other negotiations to reduce the risks.

The common American and Soviet recognition of the need to avert war was (and is) of fundamental significance. But there remained radically different visions of the course world history would follow and, therefore, of the pattern of world politics. This divergence in their worldviews naturally affected the policies of the two powers. The difference was well-known in a general way; its implications for the two superpowers' respective actions, and therefore for their mutual relations and for détente, were not, however, sufficiently understood. And this gap led to unrealistic expectations that were not met and that undermined confidence in détente.

The pursuit of absolute security by any state is not only unattainable but is based (whether recognized or not) on an unacceptable premise: absolute security for one state can only mean absolute insecurity for others.

The fact that absolute security is not attainable in today's world because of geopolitics and the nuclear threat is not sufficiently reassuring to those who fear that their adversaries seek it. While no doubt sincerely denying such an absolute aim, both the United States and the Soviet Union do pursue their own military security in ways that give rise to real concern on the part of the other. Whether in pursuit of military superiority or not, the natural dynamic of military planning is to resolve conservatively the unavoidable uncertainties in measuring the military balance and the outcomes of hypothetical military conflicts. Each side always gives the advantage in such cases to the other side— a situation that then requires unilateral efforts by each to overcome that advantage. Equally important, each is led to see the other side as seeking superiority, domination, and absolute security.

American perceptions of a Soviet drive for world domination are rooted in the U.S. image of the ideological expectations of the Soviets for the future. The United States sees a relentless, inexorable Soviet drive for world communism under the leadership and control of Moscow, and military means as the most—some would say only—successful Soviet instrumentality and therefore the key. The Soviet leaders in turn see, since the late 1970s, a reborn American pursuit of military superiority as the basis for a policy of intimidation (in U.S. terms, an aggressive use of "escalation dominance"). The ultimate aim is world domination in a Pax Americana. Rather than attributing to Americans an underlying ideological expectation for the future, they see a nostalgia for the past, an atavistic reaching back for a time when imperialism ruled the world and, more proximately, for a time when the United States had nuclear superiority and, in the Soviet view, *did* carry out a policy of intimidation (for example, compelling the withdrawal of Soviet missiles from the territory of an ally, Cuba, in 1962).

The United States has not even begun to analyze critically the underlying postulates of either American or Soviet conceptions—nor, indeed, could that be done before they were more clearly articulated. For example, consider the Soviet proposition that "the class struggle" and "national liberation struggle" are not and cannot be affected by détente. With the exception of a minuscule minority that accepts the Soviet line uncritically, virtually any American sees that proposition as communist mumbo jumbo being used as a transparently self-serving argument to excuse pursuit of Soviet interests. In fact, a Soviet leader considers that proposition to be a self-evident truth: détente is a policy, while the class struggle is an objective phenomenon in the historical process that cannot be abolished by policy decision, even if the Soviet leaders wanted to do so. While there *is* a self-serving dimension to the Soviet proposition, it is not cynical artifice. To the contrary, it is sincerely believed. On a logical plane, to whatever extent the Soviet premise is true, it is crystal clear that any inevitable historical process cannot be stopped by any state's policy or agreement between the two states.

It is not necessary to assume a prior meeting of the minds of the leaders of the two powers on ideological conceptions as a prerequisite to agreements based on calculated mutual advantage. While ideological conditioning and belief do influence policy, they do not determine it. Questions about the historical process can and should be left to history. The critical question is not whether there is a global class struggle or national liberation struggle, as defined by Marxism-Leninism, but what the Soviet leadership is going to do about it. While the Soviet leadership accepts a moral commitment to aid the world revolutionary process, it is also ideologically obliged to do so only in ways that do not weaken or risk the attainments of socialism in the USSR. Moreover, the ideology also holds that world revolutionary processes are indigenous. Revolution cannot be exported. Neither can counterrevolution. But both can be aided by external forces. Here the Soviet prescription naturally stresses the ultimate failure but present danger of an imperialist export of counterrevolution (for example, American support to the authorities in El Salvador, its destabilizing covert action against Nicaragua, and the invasion of Grenada). And while the Soviet Union expresses support for genuine revolutions and national liberation movements, it is careful and selective in what support it provides, as ideologically sanctioned prudence requires.

In approaching the question of what is a proper and consistent code of conduct with respect to Soviet—and American—behavior in the third world, each side needs to understand the perspective of the other. Each, naturally, will retain its own view of the historical process, as well as its own national interests. Differences of concrete interests will remain to be reconciled, but failure to understand each other's viewpoint seriously compounds the problem.

Failure to Use Collaborative Measures

A second cause of the collapse of détente was the failure to turn to greater use of collaborative measures to meet the requirements of security. National military power is bound to remain a foundation of national security in the foreseeable future. But it need not be the first, or usual, or sole, recourse. The American-Soviet détente involved efforts to prevent and to manage crises, and to regulate the military balance through arms control and arms limitation. In the final analysis, however, those efforts—while useful and potentially significant—were almost entirely dependent on the political relationship, and in large measure withered with it.

The effort to achieve strategic arms limitations marked the first, and the most daring, attempt to follow a collaborative approach in meeting military security requirements. It involved an unprecedented joint consideration of ways to control the most vital (or fatal) element of national power— the arsenals of strategic nuclear weaponry. Early successes held great promise— but also showed the limits of readiness of both superpowers to take this path. SALT generated problems of its own and provided a focal point for objection by those who did not wish to see either regulated military parity or political détente. The final lesson of the failure to ratify SALT II was that arms control cannot stand alone nor sustain a political détente that does not support itself. Even the early successes of SALT I, which contributed to an upsurge of détente and were worthwhile on their own merits, became a bone of contention as détente came under fire.

The widely held American view that SALT tried to do too much is, in my view, a misjudgment: the real flaw was the failure of SALT to do enough. There were remarkable initial successes in the agreement on parity as an objective and on stability of the strategic arms relationship as a necessary condition, and the control imposed on strategic defensive competition in ABM systems. But there was insufficient political will (and perhaps political authority) to bite the bullet and ban or sharply limit MIRVs—the key to controlling the strategic offensive arms race. Both sides share the blame for this failure, but especially the United States. It led a new round of the arms competition when it could safely have held back (in view of the ABM Treaty) long enough to make a real effort to ban MIRVs. The failure to control MIRVs was ultimately the key to the essential failure in the 1970s to stabilize the military dimension of parity, and it contributed indirectly to the overall fall of détente.

Too little attention has been paid to the efforts in the 1970s to devise a regime of crisis management and crisis avoidance. Paradoxically, the relatively more successful steps in this direction are rarely remembered because they do not seize attention as do political frictions. The agreements of 1971 on averting war by accident or miscalculation and on upgrading the hot line, the agreement of 1972 on avoiding incidents at sea between the U.S. and Soviet navies, and the agreement of 1973 on prevention of nuclear war have played a positive role. (In addition, there were multilateral confidence-building measures in the European security framework.) The one instance sometimes charged to have been a failure of collaboration was in fact, if anything, a success: the defusing of the pseudocrisis between the two superpowers in October 1973 at the climax of the fourth Arab-Israeli war.

Failure to Define a Code of Conduct

A third cause of the failure of American-Soviet détente in the 1970s was the inability of the superpowers to transform the recognition of strategic parity into a common political standard to govern their competitive actions in the world. The divergent conceptions of détente and of the world order underlay this failure, but these were compounded by other factors. One was the unreadiness of the United States, in conceding nominal strategic parity, also to concede political parity. Another was a reciprocated hubris in which each superpower applied a one-sided double standard in perceiving, and judging, the behavior of the other. The basic principles of mutual relations and a code of conduct were never thrashed out with the necessary frank discussion of differing views, a failure that gave rise to a facade of agreement that not only affected public, but to some extent even leadership, expectations. Expectations based on wishful thinking about the effects of the historical process, or based on overconfidence about a country's managerial abilities to discipline the behavior of the other side, were doomed to failure. Paradoxically, these inflated expectations coexisted—on both sides—with underlying excessive and projected fears and imputations of aggressive hostility, which resurfaced when the expectations were not met. That this process influenced wider political constituencies (a much wider body politic in the United States) only compounded a situation that affected the leadership as well.

The United States applied a double standard to Soviet behavior in occupying Afghanistan (and earlier to a series of Soviet moves in the third world). President Carter's pained confession of having learned more about Soviet intentions from that action than from anything else only illustrated the fact. The Soviet intervention in Afghanistan was *not* justified by the standards of a world order endorsed by the community of nations and in principle by the Soviet Union as well as by the United States. But this fact does not alter (although it has effectively obscured) that in practice the United States and the Soviet Union each apply fundamentally different standards to their behavior than they do to that of the rival superpower (and others). There also was an important failure in the case of Afghanistan (as well as in many other cases) by both the United States and the Soviet Union to recognize the perceptions, and motivations, and security interests, of the other side, whether accepting them or not.

The dominant American perception of the motive behind the Soviet intervention in Afghanistan was that it was an egregious example of aggressive expansionism, unprovoked unless perhaps by a temptation that arose from declining American military power. The Soviets were seen as unaffected by détente unless they were using that policy to cover expansionist moves. The occupation of Afghanistan was seen as dangerous to American interests because it represented a stepping-stone for Soviet advancement toward a vital Western interest—assured access to oil from the Persian Gulf.

The official public Soviet justification for its move involved several elements: to assist the Afghan people and government in resisting indirect armed interference by external powers via Pakistan; to respond to the invitation of the Afghan government, with which the Soviet Union had a treaty of friendship and assistance; and to counter the machinations of the traitorous President Amin, who, they claimed, was a CIA agent. This justification is hardly credible or even consistent.

The actual Soviet perception of the situation, as best it can be established, was as follows. First, Amin was personally ambitious and not reliable or responsive (from the Soviet standpoint). He was a potential Sadat who was already actively seeking contact with other powers. He had even lived for some time in the United States and had American contacts. Moreover, Amin was known to be highly suspicious of Moscow since the failure of an attempt to remove him from power in September 1979. Second, Amin was pursuing too radical a course of reforms and was antagonizing and alienating the people of Afghanistan. He had disregarded Soviet advice against this course and was objectively weakening and discrediting communist authority. Third, there was external encouragement and support for the growing tribal resistance, which operated from a sanctuary in Pakistan. Even more important, the United States and China, increasingly operating in anti-Soviet collusion, could be expected to seek to fill any political vacuum that developed. Afghanistan threatened to become another link in a grand U.S.-NATO-Japan-China encirclement of the Soviet Union. Fourth, a fragmented nationalistic, religious regime in Afghanistan (as well as in Iran) would constitute a hostile and chaotic belt along the border adjoining the Muslim south of the Soviet Union. Fifth, decades of Soviet economic and political investment, and since the April 1978 Marxist coup and the December 1978 Treaty of Friendship with the Soviet Union, an ideological-political stake as well, would be lost unless the Soviets acceded to the repeated appeals of the Afghan leaders for Soviet military forces to bolster their position. Sixth, with Soviet military support and a change in command as Amin was eased out, a more reliable socialist regime could restore order. Seventh, *without* Soviet intervention, there would be no escape from a humiliating Soviet withdrawal and defeat. Finally, Soviet vital interests were at stake in this adjoining communist state, while the vital interests of the United States were not. The West had, moreover, accepted the accession of communist rule in Afghanistan in 1978, and the subsequent incorporation of Afghanistan into the Soviet security system, with scarcely a murmur. Soviet military forces were already present in the country; criticism in the Western and third worlds of a larger Soviet military presence would be ephemeral. Nonetheless, the Soviet decision to escalate to direct intervention was most reluctant—the Soviet leaders did not see themselves as seizing an opportunity, but as reluctantly turning to a last resort in order to prevent a serious loss and potential threat.

The Soviet leaders, given their perception of events, saw the attribution to them of offensive purposes and threats to the Persian Gulf region, stressed in the prevailing American perception, not merely as incorrect, but as not representing a real assessment by the American leadership, and indeed as a hostile act. That view seemed to be borne out by the official American response, which included not only a new containment strategy (the Carter Doctrine) and a quasi alliance with China, but also the dismantling of virtually the entire set of American-Soviet relations developed over a decade of détente. The Soviet leaders concluded that this reaction represented the *preferred* American policy. The American administration was using Afghanistan as a pretext for doing what it desired: to mobilize American (and to some extent world) opinion in support of an intensified arms race and an anti-Soviet political line of confrontation. This interpretation fitted the Soviet evaluation of the trend in American policy. It also conveniently removed the Soviet action in Afghanistan as a cause of the collapse of détente.

In the Soviet perception, it was the United States that was acting in a manner inconsistent with the implicit code of conduct of détente. The United States was not respecting vital Soviet interests in its security sphere, as the Soviets had done with respect to Chile and Portugal, where their criticism of American action had not been permitted to interfere with state relations. On the contrary, the United States was directly challenging them and unnecessarily converting the Afghanistan affair into a broad global political challenge, while discarding the achievements of détente.

In the Soviet perception, moreover, the United States was ignoring Soviet parity as a superpower and applying a double standard. The United States had, for example, introduced its own military forces, and changed the leadership, in the Dominican Republic—a country on the American periphery and in the American political, economic, and security sphere. (How, the Soviets might have asked, is the Monroe Doctrine essentially different from the Brezhnev Doctrine?) While voicing criticism, the Soviet Union had not made that or other comparable American actions, including intervention in Vietnam, a touchstone of Soviet-American relations. Indeed, it had not done so even on the occasion of the American escalation in bombing Hanoi and mining Haiphong in May 1972. Those events had not been permitted to derail the first Brezhnev-Nixon summit meeting and the signing of SALT I.[1] Now the United States was putting the signed SALT II Treaty on the shelf and cutting economic, consular, and even cultural and sports relations, and in addition was mounting a strident propaganda campaign and pressing its allies and others to join in a wide range of anti-Soviet actions.

Indeed, the United States was applying a double standard to Soviet actions not only as compared with U.S. actions, but as compared with those of China as well. After all, only months before the United States had, while nominally expressing disapproval, done nothing when China invaded a neighboring smaller communist country. The United States even proceeded with a planned visit to China by its secretary of the treasury, who while there signed an agreement for broadened bilateral economic relations that provided most-favored-nation status—while Chinese troops remained engaged in Vietnam.

The Soviet perception in this case is little understood in the United States. For their part, the Soviets have failed to recognize American perceptions in this whole episode.

The example of Afghanistan also illustrates Soviet difficulty in recognizing that Western actions are often reactions to things the Soviets have done, rather than part of a hostile design that would have led to those same actions under any circumstances. The reverse is also true—the West has difficulty recognizing Soviet perceptions of a threat (one that it does not see itself)

---

1. The American decision also reflected a decision by the Nixon administration to give priority to prosecuting the war in Vietnam over détente with the Soviet Union, if necessary, a decision consciously taken by President Nixon, who anticipated that the Soviet leaders would probably cancel the summit. See chapter 3.

as the cause of some Soviet actions. Further, the West does not recognize that the Soviets often do not perceive sufficiently the reactive motive for Western countermeasures.

The consistent failure of each side to sense and recognize the different perspectives and perceptions of the other has been strongly detrimental to the development of their relations, compounding their real differences. The dangers of the failure of each side to recognize the effects of its own misperceptions are also too little appreciated, as are the dangers of its failure to perceive the implications of differing perceptions and misperceptions. Frequently during the 1970s and 1980s it has been unconsciously assumed that the other side was bound to see something in a certain way. That belief has led to serious errors or distortions in assessing the *intentions* and motivations of the other side. Rather than recognize a differing perception, judging it to be a valid alternative perception, or misperception, both sides typically ascribe a different and usually malevolent purpose to each other. This tendency has, for example, characterized the assessments each has made of the military programs of the other, as well as of many of its political moves. Even when an attempt is made to take account of different ways of thinking, on each side the usual approach is to apply respective stereotypes of "communist" or "imperialist" modes of calculation to the other side, but in a superficial way that stresses the expansionist or aggressive image of the adversary. The result is usually no more than to provide a self-satisfying illusion that the perceptual factor has been taken into account.

In the United States, many in the 1970s saw a cumulative series of Soviet interventions, involving military means, often with proxies—Angola, Ethiopia, Kampuchea, Afghanistan—that they believed formed a pattern of Soviet expansion and aggrandizement inconsistent with the Basic Principles and détente. Moreover, many have believed that these expansionist moves were encouraged by détente, or were at least induced by a weakness of U.S. will and military power. Hence the need to rebuild that power and reassert that will; hence the heightened suspicion of détente.

In fact, the history of diplomatic, political, and interventionist activity during the last decade is much more extensive and complex—and much less one-sided. Certainly from the Soviet perspective, not only has the Soviet role been more limited and more justified than the United States would concede, but the American role has been more active and less benign. For example, in Soviet eyes, during the decade of the 1970s the U.S. policy toward China moved from triangular diplomacy to active alignment on an anti-Soviet platform. The United States came to offer military assistance to China and has established intelligence collection facilities there directed at the Soviet Union. The United States coordinates hostile activities, for example in Afghanistan, with China. And it encouraged China to invade Vietnam and to arm the Cambodian forces of Pol Pot.

In the Middle East, the United States arranged the defection of Sadat's Egypt—and of the Sudan, Somalia, and to some degree Iraq. It effectively squeezed the Soviet Union out of a role in the Middle East peace process, despite repeated assurances that it would not do so. The United States used the Iranian hostage crisis to mobilize a major new military presence in Southwest Asia, which it maintained subsequently. In Africa, U.S. allies and proxies repeatedly and blatantly intervened with military force—Portugal before 1974; France in numerous cases; France, Belgium, Morocco, and Egypt in Zaire; Zaire, South Africa and others in Angola in 1975–76, albeit unsuccessfully; and so forth. Using covert operations, the United States assisted in the overthrow of an elected Marxist, Allende, in Chile and, with European assistance, of the Marxist-supported Gonçalves in Portugal. America was silent when Indonesia suppressed the revolt of former Portuguese Timor. A number of Southeast Asian mountain peoples were used as American proxies in that region. In South Vietnam, the United States used South Korean and Thai proxy troops, and Australian, Philippine, and other support contingents, along with its own armed forces. It encouraged anti-Soviet activity in Poland and Afghanistan, in the latter case with covert military assistance to the rebels and with Pakistani assistance and Egyptian arms paid for by Saudi Arabia. More recently, the United States has provided military assistance to El Salvador and has orchestrated covert operations against Sandinista Nicaragua, ostentatiously permitting that country's exiles to train in military and paramilitary operations in California, Texas, and Florida, and arranging for them to mount active operations from Honduras and Costa Rica. And the United States itself invaded Grenada and established a friendly nonsocialist regime there.

The deterioration of relations during the latter half of the 1970s not only reflected some of these developments but also contributed to them. For the most part the actions of the two powers stemmed not from Soviet or American initiatives, but as responses to local events.

But there also were conscious policies of assertive competition by both powers throughout the period of nominal détente. Recall, for example, the U.S. policy initiatives in the immediate aftermath of the first summit meeting in Moscow in 1972, the summit that launched détente. President Nixon flew directly from the Soviet Union to Iran. One purpose of his visit was to establish the shah as, in effect, American proconsul in the region, in keeping with the Nixon Doctrine. The shah was promised virtually any American arms he wanted. A contributory reason for the shah's deputation that was not apparent was to follow through on some conversations with the Chinese and to signal to them U.S. intention to build regional positions of strength around the Soviet Union, détente notwithstanding. In addition, while in Tehran the president accepted the shah's proposal covertly to arm the Iraqi Kurds. (Iraq had just signed a Treaty of Friendship with the Soviet Union.) Thus the Kurds became proxies of the United States and Iran (and of Israel, which joined in providing support in order to tie the Iraqi army down). And there was a later chapter to this American initiative: the shah persuaded and induced President Mohammad Daoud of Afghanistan in 1975–78 to move away from his previous close alignment with the Soviet Union, to improve relations with Pakistan, and to crack down on Afghan leftists. It was Daoud's arrest of Taraki, Karmal, Amin, and others in April 1978—not some plot concocted in Moscow—that led the Khalq military faction to mount a coup and depose him, turning the government over to the People's Democratic party and setting in train the developments within Afghanistan that culminated in the Soviet intervention.

From Iran President Nixon flew to Poland, where he was greeted by stirring public acclaim, demonstratively showing not only that the United States would support more or less nonaligned communist regimes (Nixon had visited Romania in 1969 and Yugoslavia in 1970, as well as China in 1972), but also that no part of the Soviet alliance was out of bounds to American interest under détente.

As a direct result of the U.S. handling of the Middle East question at the détente summit meeting, Sadat—who was already secretly in touch with the United States—six weeks later expelled the 20,000 Soviet military advisers (and Soviet reconnaissance aircraft) from Egypt.

Only a few months later, in September 1972, China and Japan—with American encouragement—renewed diplomatic relations. And in December new armed clashes occurred on the Sino-Soviet border.

Further, upon President Nixon's return to Washington from the summit he urged not only ratification of the SALT I agreements, but also an increase in strategic arms. Secretary of Defense Laird even conditioned his support for SALT on congressional approval of new military programs, which he justified as necessary so as to be able to negotiate "from a position of strength," wittingly or not invoking a key symbol of the cold war.

It is not the purpose of this brief recapitulation of some examples of vigorous American competitive activity to argue either that the *Soviet* perception of American responsibility for the decline and fall of détente is justified, or that the United States was wrong to compete with the Soviet Union (individual actions have been wise or unwise on their merits, and good or bad in their consequences—as is true of various Soviet actions). But Americans need to recognize that not only the Soviet Union but also the United States was "waging détente" in the 1970s—and that it is not justified in concluding that the Soviet Union was violating some agreed, clear, and impartial standard to which the United States in practice adheres. With respect to a Soviet readership, this same point about the application of a double standard equally needs to be recognized.

Both sides have in fact sought advantages. Surely Nixon and Kissinger, and Brezhnev and Gromyko, never believed that the other side, or that *either* side, would fail to seek advantages at the expense of the other just because they had agreed, in a document on Basic Principles on Mutual Relations, that "efforts to obtain unilateral advantage at the expense of the other, directly or indirectly, are inconsistent with these objectives" (those objectives being "reciprocity, mutual accommodation and mutual benefit").

Moreover, on the whole, since 1972 the leaders of the United States have probably been at least as inclined as those of the Soviet Union to ignore the further elaboration of that same basic principle—"the recognition of the security interests of the Parties based on the principle of equality." Some Americans, including leaders, have spoken and acted as though the Soviet Union had *no* legitimate security interests. Under the confrontational approach of the Reagan administration the very legitimacy of the Soviet system has been repeatedly challenged by the president himself, at least during the years 1981–83.

The United States and the Soviet Union must each recognize the need to take into account the other's interests, not from altruism but in its own self-interest. Restraint and reciprocity can be useful guidelines, but they must be applied by both sides, and by each to its *own* actions as well as to its expectations of the other. The United States, under all administrations in the 1970s and 1980s, has sought to encourage or to impose greater restraint on Soviet behavior in the third world. Yet few here have recognized that the Soviet Union also seeks greater *American* restraint and reciprocity—and that it has a basis for seeing a lack of American restraint.

While both sides throughout the decade recognized their continuing competitive and even adversarial relationship (although the image of that relationship was distorted), they publicly muted this fact—until serious differences emerged. Then both sanctimoniously accused the other of violating an agreed code of conduct. Especially in the United States, this disjunction between private appreciation by its leadership of the political competition, and failure to acknowledge it publicly, contributed to later disillusionment with the détente process itself. In the Soviet Union it has been easier to advocate détente while blaming the other side for renewing tensions.

Both the United States and the Soviet Union have acted in ways contrary to the spirit and letter of a code of conduct for détente as set forth in the Basic Principles to which both committed themselves in 1972. Each has seen its own actions as compatible with pursuit of a *realistic* policy of détente. Each, however, has sought to hold the other side to its own *idealized* view of détente. As a result, each has been disappointed in and critical of the actions of the other. The Soviet leaders, however, adjusted their expectations more realistically, seeing no better alternative than to continue an imperfect détente. This was the Soviet judgment even though the United States was seen as taking advantage of détente in the continuing competition, and even though détente proved less of a restraint on the United States than the Soviets had hoped and expected. Hence Soviet advocacy of détente even after the U.S. repudiation of détente in January 1980 and the subsequent election of Reagan. In the United States, on the other hand, dissatisfaction with the failure of détente to restrain Soviet behavior as expected, and to provide as much leverage on Soviet internal affairs as some had hoped it would, eroded public support for détente. Moreover, it was believed that some other course, containment (under Carter from 1978 on, above all in 1980) or even confrontation (under the Reagan administration from 1981 through 1983), was a possible and preferable alternative. In practice, containment alone, or laced with confrontation, proved—as had an idealized détente—not to be "the answer," or even a viable policy.

The essence of détente, as a practical proposition, was an agreement on mutual accommodation to a political competition in which each side would limit its actions in important (but unfortunately not well-defined) ways in recognition of the common shared interest in avoiding the risks of uncontrolled confrontation. Détente called for political adjustments, both negotiated and unilateral. It did not involve a classical division of the world into spheres of hegemonic geopolitical interests. Rather, it was a compact calling for self-restraint on each side in recognition of the interests of the other to the extent necessary to prevent sharp confrontation. While this general concept and approach were accepted by both sides, regrettably each side had differing conceptions of the proper restraint it—and the other side—should assume. This discrepancy led later to reciprocal feelings of having been let down by the other side. From the outset there was insufficient recognition of the need for more frank exchanges of views and collaboration in dealing with differences of interest. With time, these efforts collapsed. Both sides showed that they were not ready to accommodate the interests of the other. An additional complicating factor was the inability of the U.S. leadership to manage and control its own policy. But more important, on both sides there was a serious gap, even inability, to perceive the viewpoint and interests of the other. This gap grew, rather than lessened, with time and experience. As a consequence, trust—which was never very great—declined.

Both sides also showed themselves guilty of myopia. One additional broad and significant example illustrates this point well. Too little attention has been paid, on both sides, to the important interrelationships that derive from the interplay of their political *strategies*. The Carter and Reagan administrations have seen rapprochement with China as contributing to the containment of the Soviet Union, and therefore as reinforcement in restraining Soviet policy. They have failed to consider whether the tightening noose of a grand encirclement (the United States, NATO, China, and Japan), as seen in Moscow, may have *impelled* the Soviet Union toward more active measures to prevent that encirclement (as in Afghanistan and potentially in Iran) and to leapfrogging to accomplish a counterencirclement (as in Vietnam against China, and in Syria, Yemen, and Ethiopia in the Middle East). The Soviet Union in turn has underestimated the extent to which actions it may have regarded as defensive and counterencircling (largely the same list) have in fact—and not just in propaganda—been perceived in the West and China as offensive moves and thus contributed to the development of the very coalition of encirclement they were intended to counter.

One important change in the American strategy of global competition exacerbated this inattention to the interplay of strategies. The transition from Kissinger's strategy of détente in the period from 1969 to 1976 to that of Brzezinski in 1978–79 (continued in the post-détente strategies of 1980 and 1981–84) was characterized by a shift from a contest of maneuver in a system with two predominant powers to a positional conflict of two sides. Relations with China can illustrate. Kissinger avoided aligning the United States with either the Soviet Union or China against the other and secured a balancing position in triangular diplomacy. Under this approach, the United States could improve relations with both powers and improve its overall position in the process. After 1978 the United States shifted to a relationship with China designed to place pressure on the Soviet Union by aligning China with the United States in a coalition the latter would dominate. Thereafter, if the United States improved relations with either power, it would make its relations with the other worse. Moreover, the Chinese, once freed of the fear of American-Soviet alignment, reasserted their own independence from alignment with the United States and to an extent gained the balancing position in a reordered triangle.

Intentions, Perceptions, and Perspectives

Many developments during the period under review bear witness to the importance of evaluating correctly the intentions, and not merely the capabilities or ambitions, of the other power. As noted, close study suggests that in 1979 the Soviet leaders saw a real threat to their own security in Afghanistan. Judgment of the intentions of the Americans and Chinese, coupled with the internal vulnerability of the Amin regime in Afghanistan itself, led them reluctantly to decide to intervene militarily to replace the Amin leadership and bolster socialist rule within the country, while preventing the United States, China, and Islamic fundamentalists from gaining from the collapse or defection of the Amin regime. The Carter administration's evaluation of the Soviet motivation for intervention, one widely shared in the West, imputed expansionism and a threat to the Gulf and its oil. Therefore the United States stressed the need to deter further Soviet movement by strong punitive retaliation. This reaction merely reinforced the Soviet belief that a real threat had existed, and it did not deter further moves that had not been planned.

If one side is in fact motivated by an expansionist impulse, then a forceful advance stand in opposition or retaliatory response *is* called for and can sometimes be effective. If, however, the action—no matter how reprehensible and forcible—is motivated by fear of a threat or loss, a vigorous show of strength and threats of counteraction may in fact *contribute* to the perceived threat and hence to the very moves that the other side wants to deter. By contrast, measures to allay the unfounded fears might have been a more effective course. It thus becomes highly important to assess, and assess correctly, the intentions and motivations of the other side.

The importance of assessment is that it not only applies to a specific situation, but also affects the lessons drawn from that experience. The easy conclusion often reached about Soviet moves adverse to American interests (especially by critics but sometimes also by incumbent administrations) has been to question whether the United States possessed sufficient strength and had demonstrated clearly enough its readiness to use it. Sometimes that may be the question. But the record suggests that often it has been not American strength and resolve that Soviet leaders have doubted, but American restraint and recognition of Soviet interests.

If international tension is seen as the product of perceived threats, détente can be characterized as the reduction of threat perceptions. In the latter half of the 1970s both sides perceived growing threats from the military programs, and political actions, of the other. Afghanistan in 1979 appeared to the Soviet leaders as a threat, not an opportunity. But the American leadership did not recognize that perception, despite earlier attempts by the Soviet side to indicate to the American government its aims in Afghanistan.

Both powers have also been reluctant to acknowledge, even to recognize, failures of their own political systems. Instead, they have been only too ready to project responsibility onto the other side. Thus, for example, Soviet claims of American responsibility for internal opposition in Afghanistan and Poland serve (among other purposes) as an alibi for failures of Soviet-style socialism. American charges of Cuban and Soviet responsibility for revolution in Central America are similarly more convenient than acknowledging failures of reactionary regimes to provide for needed peaceful change. In addition to reflecting genuine fears based on perceived vulnerabilities, it is simply easier to project hostile intervention than to admit failures to facilitate or permit peaceful change within respective areas of predominant influence.

Thus, apart from differing conceptions of détente, there have been very important differences in perceptions not only of the motivations of the other side, but of the very reality of world politics. Détente, if it is revived, must be recognized as one complex *basis* for a competitive relationship, not as an alternative to competition. That has been the reality, and the fact must be recognized.

During much of the 1970s (and since) American perceptions of what was occurring in the world failed to reflect reality. One example was the failure of the United States to see that it was waging a vigorous competition along with the Soviet Union. And the U.S. leadership to varying degrees was more aware of the realities than the public (Nixon was the most aware, Carter the least). But even the practitioners of hardheaded détente often failed to recognize the whole reality. Political critics also either did not see, or did not wish to acknowledge, reality. The desire to sustain public support for policy by using a myth of détente (and of conformity with idealistic goals) also inhibited public awareness that the United States was competing as much as the Soviet Union. The result was a shift of public opinion as détente *seemed* not to be safeguarding and serving American interests. Ronald Reagan's challenge to President Ford in 1976 marked the first significant political manifestation of this shift. Although the challenge did not succeed, it did lead Ford to shelve SALT and to jettison the very word détente. By 1980 this shift contributed (along with domestic economic and other concerns, and President Carter's ineptness and plain bad luck) to Reagan's victory and open American renunciation of détente.

Naïveté was charged to the advocates of détente. But while some may have had unrealistic aims and expectations, the American leaders and practitioners of détente (Nixon, Ford, Kissinger, Brzezinski, and Vance) were not as naïve as were the critics and challengers who preferred to remain blind both to the strength and vigor of U.S. global competition and to the limits on Soviet power and policy. The critics of détente saw both American and Soviet power and its exercise from opposite ends of a telescope—a greatly exaggerated image of relentless Soviet buildup and use of power in a single-minded offensive expansionist policy, and a grossly distorted image of U.S. passivity and impotence in the world.

This U.S. perspective contributed to American-European differences and frictions. The European powers (and most other countries in the world as well) had a much more balanced perception. Although they still exaggerated the Soviet threat, at least they recognized more accurately the active American role in competition—often they were concerned over what they saw as excessive competition. For the Europeans had (and have) a very different view of the cooperative element in détente, valuing more highly than most Americans the potential for economic, political, social, and arms control gains and the realities of cooperation under détente. Hence, when the United States threw much of the substance of détente overboard after Afghanistan in favor of a policy of containment, and then, after the election of the Reagan administration, jettisoned even the aim of détente for a confrontational crusade, the Europeans balked, and East-West détente in Europe survived. Further U.S. attempts to push and pull its Western European allies off détente and onto a course of confrontation through such means as attempting to compel economic sanctions only intensified the gap. Even as such key European countries as Britain and West Germany turned to conservative governments in the early 1980s, support for East-West détente (and criticism of American confrontational policies, for example in the Caribbean basin) continued, to the perplexity, dismay and sometimes anger of leaders in Washington.

An additional reason for European satisfaction with détente, and a diverging American view, is that one important but little remarked consequence of détente in Europe from 1969 through 1979 was that the focus of U.S.-Soviet and general East-West competition shifted from Europe to the third world. The Europeans welcomed this shift, which they correctly (if not usually articulately) perceived as a fruit of détente. The United States, with little European support in the third world competition, was less grateful to détente.

The principal gap in perceptions is the broader and deeper one between the Soviet Union and the United States, and more generally between East and West. Much of the gap is likely to remain for a long time. The inability to empathize with the other side or to consider the perceptions of the other side as real (even if not necessarily valid) is an important perceptual failing. Nonetheless, in addition to improving the American perception of reality it is also clearly desirable to seek to reduce Soviet and Western misperceptions of one another.

There has also been a strong tendency to attribute to the other side exaggerated *strength*, *control* over events, and *consistency* both in purpose and in implementation of policy. What makes this irony dangerous is that each side acts on its perceptions of the intentions and power of its adversary in ways that tend to make these perceptions self-fulfilling prophecies.

The Arms Race and the Military Balance

A fourth cause of the decline in confidence in détente in the 1970s was the view widely held on both sides that the other side was acquiring military capabilities in excess of what it needed for deterrence and defense, and therefore was not adhering to détente. This is a complex question. For example, the limits under SALT reduced some previously important areas of concern and uncertainties in projecting the military balance—notably with respect to ABMs. But another effect was that the rather complex *real* strategic balance was artificially simplified in the general understanding (and not just of the general public) to certain highlighted indexes, thereby increasing sensitivity to a symbolic arithmetical "balance." And national means of intelligence, which are given high credibility when it comes to identifying a threat, are regarded with a more jaundiced eye when called upon to monitor and verify compliance with an arms limitation agreement.

In any event, during the latter half of the 1970s concern mounted in the United States over why the Soviet Union was engaged in what has been termed a relentless continuing arms buildup. At the same time U.S. military programs were justified as meeting that buildup. In turn the Soviet Union saw the American buildup as designed to restore the United States to a position of superiority.

Throughout the preceding two decades of cold war and cold peace, the United States had maintained a clear strategic nuclear superiority. As the Soviet Union continued to build its strategic forces, despite earlier agreed strategic arms limitations, new fears and suspicions arose in the United States. Unfortunately, the actual consolidation of parity in the latter 1970s was not in synchronization with the political acceptance and public impression of parity in the early 1970s. What the Soviets saw as finally closing the gap through programs of weapons deployment, which they saw as fully consonant both with the terms of the SALT agreement and with achievement of parity, many in the United States saw as a Soviet pursuit of advantages that violated at least the spirit, if not the letter, of SALT and that threatened to go beyond parity to superiority. The real inconsistency was between the continuing Soviet deployments and the American public's *expectation* derived from SALT. The interim freeze of 1972 had set a level with respect to the deployment of forces, including some construction under way that had not yet been completed by the Soviet Union. In addition, it had limited only the level of strategic missile launchers, not of warheads, and the Soviets, who were behind in terms of arming their strategic missile force with MIRVs, sought to catch up in the years following. If the Soviet strategic deployments had occurred more nearly at the time of American deployment, and both countries had agreed to accept parity and stop at the same time (and not merely at the same level), the public perception would have been quite different.

While a desire to influence public opinion played a part in inflating presentations of the military threat posed by the other side, there were real buildups on both sides. In part, then, perceptions on both sides of a hostile arms buildup were genuine. But both sides were unduly alarmist in exaggerating the military capabilities—and imputed intentions—of the other.

The U.S. misestimate of the pace of Soviet military outlays in the period from 1977 to 1983 also contributed to the exaggerated impression of a relentless Soviet buildup. The fact of a deliberate cut in Soviet military expenditure from an annual real increase of 4–5 percent in the first half of the 1970s to only 2 percent from 1976 until 1983, with a stagnation at zero percent annual increase in military procurement for those seven years, was not recognized until 1983. While the Soviet military program continued at a high level, the significance of this Soviet reduction of their military outlays was missed. And from the Soviet standpoint, the U.S. public insistence that there was a continuous Soviet increase, and use of that allegation to justify a real American and NATO buildup in the late 1970s and early 1980s, was perceived as a malevolent design rather than a mistaken intelligence assessment.[2]

The Soviet Union did not serve its own best interests or the interests of détente by continuing to be so secretive about its military forces and programs. The case of the U.S. misestimate of Soviet military spending is one clear illustration. To cite but one other significant example, the argument of the USSR that its SS-20 intermediate-range ballistic missile deployment represented only modernization of a long-standing theater missile force, and timely indication that it would replace a like number of older, larger-yield weapons, might have convinced some in the West who were uncertain and fearful as to the purpose behind the Soviet deployment. A strategic dialogue before rather than after NATO decided on a counterdeployment might have permitted some preventive arms control without the heightened tension and less promising ex post facto attempt at arms limitations on intermediate-range nuclear forces (INF).

The INF deployments and the failed attempt at INF arms control in the late 1970s and early 1980s illustrate the close connection between arms control and political as well as military relationships. The INF situation be-

---

2. See chapter 22.

came a major political issue between East and West, and also within the West. What the Soviet leaders had intended to be military modernization was perceived instead as a political-military challenge, and it spurred a Western counteraction. The NATO counteraction, which in turn was intended to reassure Western opinion and to ensure deterrence, instead was perceived in Moscow as an American threat that tied Western Europe more closely into U.S. designs to regain overall military superiority with which to intimidate the Soviet Union. This perception of the American purpose led the Soviet leaders to attempt to head off the NATO deployment altogether—and when that attempt failed, to mount demonstrative military countermeasures through new deployments. The alliance maintained the consensus to proceed with deployment, defeating the Soviet attempts to head it off. But it was a pyrrhic victory, as the issue weakened the basic social-political support for the alliance, while the resulting renewed Soviet buildup did not allay the concerns that had led to the NATO deployment. Neither side added to its security, only to the strain on political relations.

Failures in Relating Détente to Internal Politics

In addition to major gaps in mutual understanding of such key elements of détente as behavior in international politics and in managing the arms race, a fifth cause of the decline of détente was a failure to understand its crucial relationship to the internal politics of the two countries. In part this failure was reflected in errors, in particular by the Soviet Union, in comprehending the domestic political processes and dynamics of the other country. There was also some failure by political leaders, especially in the United States, to gauge the degree of their own authority. The Soviet leaders also put too much trust in the ability of an American president to carry out policy. This situation was true in the whole matter of normalization of trade and repeatedly with SALT II from 1975 to 1980. While Nixon, Kissinger, and Ford were careful to relate linkages to foreign policy issues, Congress attempted to make its own linkages with Soviet internal affairs. It failed in the effort, creating in the process new issues in U.S.-Soviet relations and reducing support for détente in the United States. The Soviet leaders also had difficulty understanding the sudden changes and discontinuities between (and occasionally within) administrations. On the other hand, American leaders, especially Presidents Carter and Reagan, have had little understanding of the Soviet political leadership or of Soviet political processes. President Carter was especially insensitive to the necessary limits on détente as a medium for influencing the internal political affairs of the Soviet Union.

Leaders on both sides, especially the Soviet leaders, have frequently and seriously underestimated the impact of their own actions on the perceptions and policy of the other side, and the extent to which the actions of one side have been responses to real or perceived challenges. And again, Soviet secrecy, and self-serving justifications on both sides, have compounded this problem.

Finally, the failure in the United States to sustain a political consensus in support of détente also ranks as a major cause of its collapse. This conclusion is particularly clear when the role of domestic political factors in the United States in torpedoing the attempt at détente is considered. Most blatant, but far from unique, was the attempt to tie trade, and thus the whole economic dimension of détente, to what amounted to interference in the internal affairs of the Soviet Union. The approach was all the more tragic but no less lethal because of the high moral motivations of many of the supporters of the effort. In this respect, the Soviet leaders were more successful in the less difficult, though not easy, task of maintaining a consensus in their quite different political process.

One reason for the disintegration of the consensus in favor of détente in the United States was the failure of the leadership to explain its limits as well as its promises to the public. To the extent that the leaders themselves failed to gauge the differences in conceptions about détente and were prisoners of their own view of the world order, they could not make this limitation clear to others. But Nixon and Kissinger did understand very well at least that there was a continuing active competition—not only in the Soviet conception, but in their own policy—a competition that was, however, masked by too much talk about a new structure of peace. When the expectations of the public, aroused by the hyperbole about the benefits of peace and détente, were not met, disillusion set in—and so did a natural temptation to blame the other side. This reaction against détente, based on disillusionment (in the pure meaning of the term), was thus in part engendered by both Nixon's and Kissinger's overestimation of their ability to manipulate and manage both international and national affairs. It should also be noted that the public (including the broader congressional and active political constituencies) has been little aware of or prepared to understand the subtleties of international politics, or even the basic idea of a political relationship of mixed cooperation and competition with the Soviet Union. In addition, the political process in the United States not only does not provide a tradition of continuity or cushion against sudden changes in foreign policy, but invites domestic political exploitation of apparent and actual adversities in the course of international relations.

Conclusion

The decade of détente in American-Soviet relations was in fact one of mixed confrontation and détente, of competition and cooperation, with a remarkable if ill-starred attempt to build—too rapidly—a structure for peaceful coexistence between powerful adversaries. Détente is not an entity. Détente has not been tried and failed. Nor was détente betrayed by one side or one action. Whether or not new terms can be found to express the reality, the United States and the Soviet Union will continue to coexist in a mixed relationship of cooperation and competition. As the 1980s succeeded the 1970s, a period of renewed confrontation began. Yet as should be amply evident by the mid-1980s, a policy of confrontation is no easier or more successful in serving American interests than one of détente. What then, can be said about the future?

30   Confrontation and Détente: Looking to the Future

AMERICAN-SOVIET relations stand in need of a redefinition of goals and means. Anyone who in the heyday of détente a decade ago may have forgotten or misjudged the continuation of competition and of an adversarial relationship has been sharply reminded of it since Afghanistan. The fragility of the structure of cooperation erected early in the 1970s was evident in its collapse at the end of the decade. The absence of mutual trust is, in the mid-1980s, stark and clear. Dispelling illusions about détente can be useful. What is not useful—indeed is dangerous—is to resurrect in their place cold war myths and misperceptions. A misreading by one side of the motivation and intentions of the other, and action on that basis, is akin to Don Quixote's charge against windmills of imagined threatening and evil strength. But the danger is much greater than misapplied chivalry and energy. It is the risk of giving substance to a sharper and deeper conflict than would have been justified by a sound understanding and sober evaluation of real conflicts of interest and the real requirements for competition—and, equally important, of the opportunities still available to realize areas of cooperation in serving mutual interests, including, above all, survival in a nuclear world.

The imperative of coexistence and the reality of competition remain. So do the problems of reconciling them. Thoughtful study of the experience of the 1970s is of the highest importance in order to learn as much as possible about the requirements and conditions for—and limitations on—cooperation, and about the nature and forms of competition. That knowledge can contribute to the design of policies and a policy process for the future that can help to work toward a world order that, while short of the ideal or preference of any one ideology or nation, will nevertheless preserve the essential peace. Without that peace, no idea or people in our day can survive.

Some proponents have mistakenly suggested that détente provides the only alternative to war. What needs to be carefully weighed is what course of action, among many, best serves peace and security. Some opponents of détente, on the other hand, have attempted to counterpose it to security. But détente is one possible (and, under favorable circumstances, preferable) means of contributing to security. Again, what is needed is a sober consideration of the range of possible combinations of political strategies, defense programs, arms control, and other policy measures. The true antipode to détente is not security or hardheaded national interest, but tension. And tension serves neither of those objectives. Critics of détente, arms control, negotiation, engagement, and contact should recognize that the antipodes are tension, an uncontrolled arms race, confrontation, containment, and isolation. While confrontation may seem a better course of action, that judgment is counterintuitive, and the burden of proof rests on its proponents. Opponents of détente, who ascribe to the Soviet leaders hardheaded pursuit of their interests and a very high degree of success and skill, do not explain why, if détente, arms control, negotiation, engagement, and contact are necessarily soft policies, a hardheaded Soviet Union pursues them. They do not adequately explain why they believe the United States cannot pursue such a policy while the Soviet Union can. There are, to be sure, systemic differences that do make at least some tactics of manipulation much easier for Soviet leaders to pursue. And there may be more of a tendency in American opinion to build excessive expectations. But there are also fundamental systemic strengths in an open society.

The experiment with punitive containment within a policy of nominal suspended détente, pursued in the last year of the Carter administration, and the avowed repudiation of détente and pursuit of a more confrontational policy in the first three years of the Reagan administration, both proved ineffective and counterproductive. A confrontational approach, designed and intended to place pressure on the Soviet Union, results in reduced support, in particular from U.S. allies, for American policies and provides the Soviet Union with enhanced opportunities. Even at home, the American public, while wary of détente, is not eager to assume the avoidable additional burdens and risks of choosing confrontation.

The preceding chapter has drawn some conclusions from the American-Soviet experience with détente in the 1970s. In applying these conclusions and other considerations to the future, one contribution to the effort would be to abandon the term détente. Not only is its meaning unclear, it is now politically charged.

Whether a new sobriquet can be devised or will simply evolve, U.S. understanding will have to include recognition of the reality that American-Soviet relations in the 1980s and beyond will remain an amalgam of competition and cooperation. Whether some term such as "competitive coexistence" or "controlled competition" (shaded, respectively, toward détente or confrontation) will find acceptance is much less important than recognition and acceptance of the realities that constitute a limiting *framework* for policy. The other essential ingredients are the formulation of policy *objectives*, the selection of *instrumentalities* for the realization of those policy objectives, and *consistent implementation* of policy.

In framing U.S. policy toward the Soviet Union, it is necessary not only to examine both U.S. and Soviet objectives and courses of action, but also what may be termed courses of interaction. Reactions of the other side to any U.S. action obviously should be considered, although in reality they are not always weighed. But far too little attention is paid to a further chain of interactions. Similarly, effects on others, including unintended effects, should be anticipated to the extent possible. The perceptions of the other side (and of others) should be part of such evaluations. Finally, the extent of unity and consistency of one's own objectives and policy course, and of the course of interaction with the other side, should be calculated.

As this study has made clear, the interactions of U.S. and Soviet policy have overlapped with complex interactions in East-West European relations, in the triangle of relations involving China, and in many situations and some conflicts born of local developments around the world. In short, it is necessary to think in terms of developing a strategy of U.S. policy in terms of the interplay of U.S. and Soviet strategies in a broad context of world politics.

Regrettably, the record indicates a progressive decline in such strategic policymaking in the United States from the early 1970s to the mid-1980s. While the Nixon-Kissinger leadership showed lamentable miscalculation in a number of cases, it did proceed from an understanding of the need for a strategy of policy. It exaggerated its own ability to control and manage events, but at least it sought to do so in pursuit of a purposeful strategy. While the Reagan administration certainly has had aims, it has had a much less coherent strategy. Moreover, by misconstruing many aspects of both Soviet policy and world politics, it has had much less success in meeting its own aims then it could otherwise have had, to say nothing of failing to set and reach other aims that would have been in the interest of the United States.

One necessary condition is to discard illusory aims of either a comprehensive settlement of differences and achievement of a complete accommodation of U.S. and Soviet interests on the one hand, a goal sometimes misattributed to détente, or a U.S. victory in a contest with the Soviet Union, an aspiration of proponents of confrontation. The real question is how best to manage the relationship of mixed competition and cooperation between rivals.

It is not easy to deal with the dialectical relationship between competition and cooperation. This relationship is a reality, but it is difficult to articulate in terms that command the necessary public support. It is also, for that and other reasons, very difficult to manage without competition getting out of hand and leading to confrontation. Yet that undesirable outcome is not necessary.

American relations with the Soviet Union cover many areas. Three principal areas of specific policy are of salient importance: *national security, geopolitical conduct,* and *economic relations.*

National security in its broadest sense clearly embraces political competition and economic relations. Nonetheless, it seems the best term to characterize in particular the amalgam of defense and deterrence requirements involved in both unilateral military programs and negotiated arms control measures. Military security is too narrow a focus; so, too, is arms control. Both unilateral and negotiated measures affecting American (and Soviet) military power must be considered as complementary means to achieve desired objectives of enhanced stability, reduced arms competition, assured deterrence, and maintenance of military forces needed to defend other interests and meet other commitments in the world.

Geopolitical conduct is a term that can represent in abbreviated form behavior by the Soviet Union and the United States in pursuing their interests around the world. A major source of difficulty is that both countries have shown a strong tendency not only to judge the behavior of the other by a politically motivated standard, but to fail even to recognize—let alone accept—the different perspective of the other. Both have applied a double standard. Shortcomings in the behavior of the other side are often exaggerated and sometimes judged unfairly—certainly without applying the same standards to one's *own* behavior. Both sides call for restraint and reciprocity, but do not apply reciprocity in international behavior, and expect restraint from the *other* side while rarely exercising it where one's own advantage is seen as attainable at low cost and risk.

Economic relations, although of lesser significance than the first two areas, are important in themselves and as a reflection of the political relationship, especially to the Soviet Union. The dominant American approach, both in détente and in confrontation over the period under review, has been to regard economic relations as either a carrot (under détente) or a stick (in confrontation), rather than as an aspect of relations that deserves to stand on its own on the traditional basis of mutual benefit as determined by a policy of laissez-faire. This tendency stems from the perception of an American advantage in the economic sphere that can be used for leverage against Soviet policy in other areas (for example, to encourage arms control or internal liberalization, or to increase pressures to cause economic-military-political strains in the Soviet system).

National Security

National security is at the core of the interests and concerns of every country and is salient in both American and Soviet policy. While readily understood by Americans as applying to the United States, it is less often made explicit in American discussion of the Soviet Union.

Soviet policy is made on the basis of Soviet interests, of which security is preeminent. In their pronouncements, and in their actions, the Soviet leaders recognize national security as fundamental. It underlies such basic lines of policy as the prevention of nuclear war. At the same time, the Soviet leaders are not pacifists; they believe they must be prepared to defend their vital interests if those interests are attacked—just as the leaders of the United States do.

Deterrence of attack by the other side is a principal aim of both sides. The role of deterrence in American thinking has been enlarged to such an extent that it tends to dominate both defense and foreign policy. While it is a necessary element of policy, it is not central; that is, it does not deal with the main range of problems involved in managing relations with an adversary. It does not even deal with the main lines of Soviet efforts to expand its influence and reduce that of the United States. More broadly, while the role of military power is essential, it is not central to most of the action of world politics. The shadow of military power influences a great deal of political maneuvering, but it is not its only source.

Deterrence provides insurance and reinforcement of other disincentives against attack by the other side. It is, if only because of its value as reassurance, an essential continuing element in both Western and Soviet policy. Indeed, the main *real* role of most military programs and deployments seen as buttressing deterrence may have been reassurance rather than deterrence of temptations to attack. But deterrence does not prevent and need not impede collaborative military détente, to use the Soviet-coined term.

Each side influences the definition of the security requirements as seen by the other. In many cases such influence makes itself felt in ways not intended or controlled or even recognized. Moreover, the effects of one of the superpower's actions or policies on the other side are often not those sought or desired—they may result in consequences opposite to those intended. For example, the reciprocal failures to recognize the intentions involved in the deployments of intermediate-range missiles in Europe in the latter 1970s led to an arms race and political confrontation not intended or desired by either side. Ultimately it did not serve the security interests of either side, although both *perceived* their decisions and actions as necessary for security reasons.

The fact that deterrence is designed above all to influence the perceptions of the other side is generally recognized, but the implications of the fact are not adequately appreciated. Particularly in the United States, this question, *essentially* one of political perception, has come to be addressed almost exclusively in military-technical terms. Excruciatingly antiseptic computations of residual theoretical force capabilities after n number of strategic "exchanges" are substituted for the commonsense thinking of political leaders evaluating national interests. Moreover, even in dealing with the human element of the equation, failure to consider the perceptions of the other side leads to grave political error. Intended displays of firm resolve for defensive deterrence may be (and, alas, often are) seen by leaders on the other side as offensive intimidation requiring a reciprocal display of firm resolve. If a fraction of the effort given to calculating technical deterrence requirements were devoted to raising political awareness of the perceptions of the other side, there might be a substantial increase in security for both sides.

Deterrence is predicated on denying or reducing the expected *gains* to a putative attacker from a premeditated attack. In more sophisticated calculations it may be intended to reduce the chance of choice of war in a crisis situation. But by far the greatest risk of war lies not in decisions by one side or the other in which it sees a choice and possible gain, but from action under circumstances in which it sees no real choice except whether to seize the initiative before an expected imminent attack by the other side. Military programs and actions intended to enhance deterrence by reducing assumed enemy "incentives" to attack not only may be irrelevant, but may in fact increase risks rather than reduce them. Finally, the prevention of nuclear war requires a much wider range of political efforts than deterrence alone, to say nothing of the still wider range of actions to manage and mitigate the political and geopolitical competition.

During the late 1960s and early 1970s security concerns on both sides initially gave impetus to arms control negotiations. Wariness and caution on both sides led to only modest achievements in this area. Later, increasing security concerns led to decreased use of cooperative security approaches and increased reliance on unilateral pursuit of military security, spurring the arms race and raising fears. Paradoxically, the shortcomings of arms control measures such as the SALT I Interim Agreement and the SALT II Treaty in meeting perceived security requirements tended to be blamed on the process of negotiated arms limitations. The real blame stemmed from the fact that both sides had been too reluctant to give up promising military "options," and too cautious to agree on more effective and far-reaching constraints. In addition, the fact that the Soviet Union, still overcoming its inferiority, continued to build its strategic forces (in accordance with the provisions of the SALT agreements and, at least from the Soviet perspective, also consistent with maintaining parity) was widely perceived in the United States as either violation or circumvention of the agreements. What it really contravened was the expectation the agreements had created in American eyes.

Arms control is never an end in itself. It is a tool of policy, and in particular of security policy, as are unilateral military programs (or "arms uncontrolled"). Both the Soviet Union and the United States always judge possible negotiated arms control limitations and reductions from this perspective. Arms control may provide specific constraints designed to enhance stability and reduce the risk of war. Arms control agreements (or the mere pursuit or conduct of arms control negotiations) may also, or alternately, be intended to serve broader political and public relations effects. Finally, arms control limitations may be sought to reduce requirements for resource allocations in an unlimited arms competition. For arms control to have more than modest impact, it must be seen by the parties as making a contribution to security that outweighs the constraints it imposes on military tools of policy.

This analysis points to two lessons that must be applied in the future:

1. *Arms control can play an important part in stabilizing a strategic military balance, and can contribute to improved political relations as well, only if it is given the chance to do so.* The experience of SALT does not demonstrate the limitations of arms control or its failure, but rather the failure

of the United States and the Soviet Union in the 1970s to give arms limitation a chance to do more.

2. *A stable strategic balance under negotiated arms control must be defined in sufficiently concrete terms to provide a common framework for permitted unilateral military programs for the two sides.* SALT defined clear constraints on strategic arms, and those limits were adhered to. But they were so excessively permissive that new unilateral strategic programs pursued by both sides, as allowed by the agreements, were perceived by the other side as threatening the balance. There must be stronger limitations—at whatever level—and an agreed conception of what constitutes the balance.

Both sides have couched their arguments in the strategic dialogue of SALT in the 1970s, and especially START and INF in the early 1980s, in self-serving terms. To take but one example, in SALT in 1969 the United States was neutral and noncommittal on the question of whether mobile land-based ICBMs should be permitted. From 1970 through the SALT I agreements in 1972 the United States strongly opposed mobile ICBMs on the grounds of unverifiability. In May 1972, when it could not get the Soviets to agree to a ban on mobile ICBMs, the United States reluctantly agreed to defer the issue. But it issued a strong unilateral statement that "the U.S. would consider any deployment of operational land-mobile ICBM launchers during the period of the Interim Agreement as inconsistent with the objectives of that Agreement." Yet by 1977 the United States had decided it wanted the option of deploying a mobile ICBM. And by 1979, at the time SALT II was signed, it insisted that deployment was necessary. It agreed only reluctantly in June 1979 to include in a protocol to SALT II, with duration limited to three years, an agreement not to deploy mobile ICBMs during that period. The Soviet Union had similarly changed its position—from refusing a ban in 1972 to pressing for one in 1979. These shifts reflected current or prospective unilateral military programs, and efforts to curb programs of the other side. But these positions were formulated in terms of the "stabilizing" or "destabilizing" effect of ICBM mobility. Many other examples could be cited of how each side fashioned its strategic rationales in the negotiations on this basis.

Another problem in defining a balance was caused by the great reluctance on the Soviet side to provide data or to discuss the numbers, characteristics, or even designations of its weaponry. There was a considerable change over the ten years from 1969 to 1979, with the Soviets becoming increasingly willing to provide the data. But a wide gap between what is published and known in the West and in the Soviet Union about such matters remains, reflecting the difference in openness of the two societies.[1] The standard should

---

1. The prevailing openness on military matters in the United States is not, however, the standard by which Soviet practice should be judged. Many Western democracies, and most of the world, are much more restrictive in this respect than is the United States.

An interesting example of the increasing openness of the Soviet Union in making public information about the military balance, including information on numbers and types of Soviet

be, and now generally is accepted to be, to provide that information which is necessary for negotiation of particular limitations.

Another problem is far more serious: the difference in the perspectives of the United States and the Soviet Union on what military forces are to be counted in measuring any balance (and, correlatively, in determining limitations or reductions). The United States has contended that only American and Soviet forces should be considered. Moreover, it has argued that only American forces designated as strategic should be included: ICBMs, SLBMs and heavy bombers in SALT/START, and land-based intermediate-range missiles in INF. The Soviet Union, on the other hand, has contended that the valid criterion should be nuclear delivery forces capable of striking the Soviet Union or the United States, regardless of where they are deployed or by whom they are operated. The Soviets thus argue that American forward-based systems (aircraft at bases around the periphery of the USSR, including on aircraft carriers) must be taken into account, and also strategic systems of American allies, especially the British and French strategic nuclear forces. This issue is complex, especially because there are strong arguments to be made on both sides. But it must be faced. It is not the purpose here to address possible solutions, but to note the importance of the issue when looking ahead at the prospects and problems facing arms control in the last half of the 1980s.

During the period since 1969, a recurring question has been posed about the proper relationship of negotiations on arms limitation and reductions to political relations. Clearly any arms limitation agreement presented for congressional approval at times of heightened American-Soviet tensions is not likely to be endorsed. SALT II was in trouble even before the Soviet intervention in Afghanistan required that it be shelved for the remainder of the Carter administration. Other political circumstances have also dictated arms control policy. In early 1976 President Ford, despite the prospects for a SALT II accord and his desire to achieve one, felt compelled to set SALT aside in the face of a conservative challenge in the presidential election campaign. Even the Reagan administration, if belatedly and with patently nonnegotiable proposals, did resume START and INF negotiations, despite its general confrontational posture, skepticism about arms control, and announced intention first to arm

---

weapons, is the issuance, and domestic circulation, of the Ministry of Defense publication *Whence the Threat to Peace*. This is the Soviet counterpart of, and counterpublication to, the U.S. Department of Defense publication *Soviet Military Power*. Each appeared in three editions during 1981–84. The Soviet publication was issued in English, French, German, Italian, Spanish—and Russian. The circulation of the Russian-language version of the first edition was, however, limited to 5,870 copies. By the time the second edition appeared about eight months later in 1982, the Russian-language version was printed in 100,000 copies (as was the third edition in 1984). See *Otkuda izkhodit ugroza miru* [Whence the Threat to Peace] (Moscow: Voyenizdat, Ministerstvo Oborony SSSR, 1st ed. January 1982; 2d ed. August 1982; 3d ed. July 1984). The 100,000 circulation is more or less standard for major Soviet publications on military affairs such as the *Soviet Military Encyclopedia* (1976–79) and a series of booklets by Marshals Ustinov, Ogarkov, Kulikov, Sokolov and General of the Army Yepishev published in late 1982.

in order to parley from a position of strength. Arms limitation should not be regarded as a reward for good relations: arms control negotiations are only needed between rivals or adversaries, not between allies or others.

Some American opponents of arms control have tended to equate its pursuit with American altruism and naïveté and Soviet manipulation and lack of serious interest. In fact, it is clear that the Soviet leaders, as hardheaded realists, have been interested in the prevention of nuclear war as the highest aim of national security policy. From that point of departure, they developed a real interest in arms control in the early 1970s as a possible element in furthering the national security of the Soviet Union through negotiated agreements with the United States, based on parallel interests. Regrettably, by the 1980s they came to see little prospect for arms control because of the shifting American stand. The United States has ratified none of the arms limitation treaties it has signed since 1974, it repudiated the SALT II Treaty signed in 1979, and in the START and INF talks of 1981–83 it took positions that the Soviet leaders saw as not intended to lead to agreements. The question in Moscow in the 1980s is not whether arms control can serve the security interests of the Soviet Union (as well as of the United States), but whether the United States is prepared to curb its unilateral military pursuits in negotiated, mutually acceptable constraints.

At the present writing, in early 1985, new strategic arms limitation talks on strategic offensive arms and strategic defensive space arms have begun. The substantive problems and differences in approach of the two sides are formidable. Nonetheless, there is an opportunity for both sides to enhance their security through negotiated arms constraints. Arms control has returned to center stage in relations between the two powers because it derives from the central aspect of relations in which there is an underlying common interest: national security and survival.

The basic issue remains whether arms control is recognized to be of sufficient value for the superpowers to make a serious negotiating effort, and to forgo linkage with other issues that preclude successful outcomes. If arms control is really important and in the interests of both sides, it is self-defeating to link it to other issues such as internal human rights or external behavior (for example, the role of the United States in Vietnam, or the Soviet Union in Angola or even Afghanistan). Those who do not really see mutual benefit in arms control are naturally the most eager to press for linkages to political concessions by the other side.

Another aspect of cooperative pursuit of security is crisis prevention and crisis management. Many aspects of geopolitical conduct, to be discussed presently, involve prevention or avoidance of crises. Crisis management, however, is best considered as a complement to unilateral (and alliance) military preparation and to negotiated arms control constraints and arms limitations or reductions. Early in détente, in 1971–73, a number of agreements were reached on avoidance of incidents at sea between the American and Soviet navies, on curbing the risk of war by accident or miscalculation, on improving the direct communication link (hot line), and most ambitiously on seeking to prevent the eruption of nuclear war. On the whole these steps were useful, but clearly they were no substitute for effective political consultation. Moreover, efforts at crisis management were almost invariably subordinated to pursuit of political advantages. The advance consultation provisions of the Prevention of Nuclear War agreement did not lead the Soviet leaders to inform Washington when they learned two days in advance of the planned Egyptian-Syrian attack on Israel in October 1973. Nor did the American leaders advise or consult Moscow after Deng Xiaoping had disclosed to them plans for an attack on Vietnam in early 1979. Nonetheless, crisis management should be pursued. *Particularly* when relations are bad and normal contacts are strained, it is vitally important to both countries to avoid any outbreak of war by mistake.

More attention needs to be paid to developing a strategic dialogue. Such a dialogue may seem to some to be only a matter of verbal exchanges without relevance to "hard" military realities. Confidence in what the other side says about its strategic intentions or interests may be low. Yet a better reciprocal understanding of the strategic thinking, concerns, and intentions of the two sides can be of great importance and can be enhanced by dialogue. One example is dealing with questions about compliance with arms control agreements. Another is the opportunity to clarify both one's own intentions in pursuing particular military programs and those of the other side. Even general discussion of conceptions of parity, deterrence, and stability can be meaningful and not mere abstractions.

During the period from 1967 to 1969, the United States contributed through quiet, partly unofficial, dialogue in influencing a significant change in Soviet views of the strategic offensive-defensive relationship that, in turn, made agreement possible on the ABM Treaty.[2] In 1985 the United States administration wants to persuade the Soviet leaders of the opposite view, that strategic defenses would be stabilizing rather than destabilizing. Whatever the merits of this position (I continue to believe the conclusions held in the 1960s and 1970s remain valid), it is useful to discuss the issue with the Soviet Union. Even if the two sides do not reach agreement, a bona fide discussion could be useful.

Particularly in the areas of averting crises and the prevention of war by accident or by miscalculation, a more serious and sustained dialogue is necessary, as noted above. One aim can be specific agreements on confidence-building or crisis-moderating measures, or even curtailment of certain military deployments or exercise practices. Even without such concrete agreements, however, better understanding can be reached and risks reduced.[3]

2. See Raymond L. Garthoff, "BMD and East-West Relations," in Ashton B. Carter and David N. Schwartz, eds., *Ballistic Missile Defense* (Brookings Institution, 1984), pp. 286–314.

3. The most comprehensive analysis is Alexander L. George, ed., *Managing U.S.-Soviet Rivalry: Problems of Crisis Prevention* (Boulder, Colo.: Westview, 1983). See John Borawski, ed., *Arms Control and Crisis Stability: Confidence-Building Measures* (Cambridge, Mass.: Ballinger, forth-

In the final analysis, if the United States and the Soviet Union are to conduct a useful dialogue on security issues and negotiate arms limitations and confidence-building measures, they must each recognize that the only sound basis is for each to accept the right of the other to define its security interests and determine its strategic requirements. The United States and its allies cannot determine or dictate the security requirements for the Soviet Union and the Warsaw Pact, and vice versa. But each can seek to meet its own deterrence and defense requirements to the greatest extent feasible in ways that are not provocative to the other. Determining ways to meet that aim would be a particularly useful area for dialogue and possible negotiation, as well as an important consideration in unilateral decisions.

Geopolitical Conduct

Concern over the strategic balance was important in raising American suspicions and fears of the Soviet Union, as was, to a much lesser extent, unease over the continuation of repressive internal Soviet activities. Probably the chief cause of U.S. public and political disillusionment with détente, however, was the growing impression that the Soviets were pursuing an expansionist policy in the world that involved both actions and objectives not consistent with détente—or at least not consistent with American expectations of Soviet behavior under détente, a significant but little appreciated difference. The widespread impression of an energetic Soviet pursuit of a policy of aggrandizement was perceived in the United States as standing in contrast to a much more restrained American policy. Americans saw the vigorous Soviet intervention or support for the successful expansion of communist rule in Angola, Ethiopia, South Yemen, Afghanistan, and Kampuchea as taking advantage both of American restraint and of a decline in American power, and as reflecting both a growing Soviet strength and a growing readiness to use that strength in ways that advanced Soviet interests and contravened American interests. Empirical evidence and logical arguments in support of this view were powerfully reinforced by psychological considerations. The United States seemed to be increasingly impotent—from the fall of Vietnam in 1975 through the humiliating failure for over a year to obtain the release of the hostage embassy staff in Iran. That neither of these (or many other) developments was due to Moscow's machinations was given little weight. Many Americans simply felt the United States was being pushed around. The fact that changes in the strategic nuclear balance were irrelevant not only to those events, but also to

coming), for a broad review of confidence-building measures in the past and discussion of possible future measures. See also the discussion in *Managing East-West Conflict: A Framework for Sustained Engagement*, Statement of the Aspen Institute International Group (Aspen Institute for Humanistic Studies, 1984), pp. 12–18.

the Soviet advances in Africa and Afghanistan, did not prevent a gut feeling that the United States was becoming weaker and the Soviet Union stronger. And these changes were associated with the period of détente.

Many in the United States quickly seized upon these and other developments to argue that the American administrations of the 1970s, and the policy of détente and of arms control negotiations, were to blame, along with the Soviet Union, for this sorry state of affairs. The Soviet Union was depicted as taking advantage of détente and of American military and political restraint to build its own military and political power and more boldly to advance in the world.

This American (and, to a much lesser extent, more general Western) image of Soviet behavior is far removed from the picture the Soviet leaders hold of their own actions, and of those of the United States. Not only do the Soviets see their moves as justified and restrained, but from their perspective their geopolitical gains were much less. Indeed, gains were more than offset by a chain of geopolitical losses (Soviet influence in Egypt, Sudan, Somalia, Guinea, and Chile), to say nothing of the growing American-Chinese politico-military tie and potential encirclement of the USSR by the United States, NATO, China, and Japan. From the Soviet standpoint, while Angola and Ethiopia were carefully selected cases of local situations permitting legal and limited Soviet involvement and expanded influence, Afghanistan (like Poland) was not an opportunity for advance, but a reluctantly accepted necessity to hold a critical defensive line. Finally, the Soviets saw the decline and fall of Soviet-American détente as engineered by cold warrior opponents of détente in the United States, abetted by China and Israel. While claiming that their purpose was to stop Soviet expansion, these cold warriors manipulated both events and their interpretation in order to effect a return to a confrontational line and to gain public support for a major arms buildup aimed at reacquiring strategic military superiority. Their purpose was to conduct a more far-reaching political offensive against the Soviet Union and the socialist community (Soviet bloc) not only on its periphery, but even within the socialist countries.

In the United States, the general impression has been one of Soviet activism, indeed adventurism, in pursuing an expansionist course. In fact, Soviet policy has been active, but selective and cautious, not adventuristic. While the general impression has been exaggerated, it is less in error in seeing an active Soviet role than in failing also to recognize an active U.S. role. There is also a tendency to give much more attention to alarming developments than to favorable ones. Soviet advances are given a great deal of attention; Soviet reverses are scarcely noted. The result is a very skewed picture in the minds not only of the public but of many American political leaders as well. The image of Soviet expansion of influence in the third world in the 1970s was blown up out of all proportion. Moreover, this situation has then often been ascribed to weakness of U.S. resolution or military capabilities. One consequence has been to misdirect American countermeasures to military programs rather than to diplomacy in the third world. Another consequence was to make the détente in

American-Soviet relations appear to be responsible for a trend that was not only overstated, but not caused by that policy. Détente clearly did not prevent continuing competition, but it did not create it. Nor did it disarm or disable the United States from pursuing the competition very actively and much more sucessfully than has been generally recognized. Ironically, a U.S. course of policy that seemed weak to most Americans has seemed excessively strong to the Soviet leaders.

Rivalry and competition for influence and power have characterized American-Soviet relations since 1945. What was unique in the détente of the 1970s was the first attempt to devise basic principles to govern the conduct of the two powers. The purpose was, ostensibly, to constrain and limit the risks of competition—to establish a code of conduct or rules of the game. These two unofficial slogans, however, encapsulate two somewhat different aspects of the experiment. A code of conduct (especially one formulated in appropriately idealized terms) implies acceptance of a common high standard of behavior. Rules of the game, on the other hand, implies a common set of guidelines for carrying out a competitive exercise such as a sport—hitting below the belt may be banned, but other continuing blows and parries are expected and accepted.

As has been seen, from the outset it was relatively easy to agree on broad guidelines—partly because they were not examined closely to determine if there was *real* acceptance of a common standard or even of agreed rules for regulating the competition. Indeed, it was quite evident to those involved that there was no common standard or agreed rules. But the leaders on both sides believed they would be able to justify their *own* behavior by their unilateral interpretation of the rules, and that they could use the rules to constrain the other side marginally. In addition, in adopting high rhetorical standards, both leaderships were playing for popular support from their own domestic political constituencies, as well as from the world's peoples. This tactic was in keeping with long-standing practice in world public diplomacy. The first effect, however, was to create excessively high public expectations about the behavior of the other side, especially in the United States. Leaders who themselves assumed *Realpolitik* as the prevailing political reality failed, especially in the United States, to recognize their inability to control popular expectations that they themselves did not for the most part share. Moreover, the Soviet leaders seriously underestimated the way in which these nominal rhetorical commitments, especially the Helsinki Final Act, could be held against them by both domestic dissidents and Western opponents of close relations with the Soviet Union. And the American leaders failed to recognize that while they could manage their own interpretations of and applications to Soviet behavior, they could not control more far-reaching applications by domestic political opponents, in particular those opposed to close American relations with the Soviet Union. Adopting rhetoric with excessively demanding ideal standards of conduct did not curb either side's actions, but it did disorient those who accepted the rhetoric at face value. And it gave a weapon to those who wanted to strike at the less-than-ideal reality of relations under détente.

The establishment of general lofty basic principles, hastily and secretly negotiated in the context of a summit meeting arranged and played for domestic political impact (especially in the United States), as well as for the furtherance of American-Soviet relations, did not permit clarification of the expectations of any *real* rules of the game even to the leaders on either side. The leaders were immune to the kind of credulity with which the manifestos were accepted by many in the general public (with a large assist from the official praise for their achievement and optimistic talk of building a structure for peace). But the leaders themselves on *both* sides were still influenced to some extent by the principles as a charter for détente.

The Soviet leaders saw the American leadership as representing a conservative capitalist class whose interests in internal and foreign affairs were unchanged but who were more realistic in recognizing a new era marked by a reduced capability of the United States (political and economic, as much as military) to manage events in the world. In their terms, Nixon and Kissinger were "sober realists" who were prepared to acknowledge the changed "correlation of forces" in the world and to accept the fact of budding strategic parity and even nominal political equality for the Soviet Union.[4] The Soviets were well aware from the history of relations from 1969 to 1972 that the United States under this same leadership would continue very vigorously to use its still massive resources to support American interests in the world and to oppose many Soviet moves. But the Soviet leaders were elated when in 1972 this tough but realistic leadership was ready to endorse peaceful coexistence, equality, and strategic parity.

The American leaders, Nixon and Kissinger, were well aware that competition would remain keen and that détente was a strategy for managing competition rather than an alternative based only on cooperation. But they also believed that as cooperative relationships with the Soviet Union were built, the Soviet leaders would develop and be influenced by a growing stake in preserving détente. This consideration would in turn lead them to forgo temptations to press for opportunistic gains. Moreover, these U.S. policymakers intended under the strategy of détente to wield sticks and proffer carrots to help steer the Soviet Union along cooperative paths and away from expansionist engagements. Their approach was reinforced when, as has been seen, they misread developments such as the Syrian-Jordanian crisis of 1970 and the Indo-Pakistani War of 1971 in such a way that they got an exaggerated impression of their ability to discipline Soviet involvement in third world conflicts.

For their part, Brezhnev and his colleagues to some extent misread the meaning for the future of the American disengagement from Vietnam, the Nixon Doctrine, and U.S. readiness to accept the SALT I agreements. The

---

4. The assessment by the Soviets of the correlation of forces in the early and mid-1970s was basically sound, but it included an overestimation of Western difficulties (economic, Vietnam, Watergate) and an underestimation of their own (economic, Eastern Europe, third world entanglements).

Soviet leaders also overestimated the consistency and continuity of American policy. They assumed President Nixon could deliver on his promises on economic relations and later did not foresee (or, then, comprehend) the impact of Watergate in weakening American advocacy of détente. They also did not believe, in the early and mid-1970s, that the United States would apply in its policy (as distinct from propaganda) a double standard for the code of conduct and treat Soviet support for national liberation and progressive movements in the third world (which the Soviet leaders had always made very clear they considered fully consistent with Soviet-American détente) as a touchstone of that détente. They expected continuing vigorous American competition in the third world, but not serious reverberations on Soviet-American relations in other spheres. But when Kissinger negotiated the Basic Principles in April 1972, as he has revealed in his memoir, he ignored Nixon's only explicit guidance: to gain Soviet agreement not to aid national liberation wars. Kissinger did not even make that American position clear. While this omission may not have vitiated the Basic Principles, it undercut later American arguments that Soviet actions—from Angola through Afghanistan—contravened Soviet acceptance of an agreed code of conduct. And the unmet American expectations in turn certainly weakened American support for détente.

Underlying the failure to reach a common understanding on rules of the game, and underlining the significance of that fact, was the more basic failure to develop a common conception of détente. The United States interpreted the Basic Principle not to seek "unilateral gain" as involving at least a rough Soviet commitment not to intervene to disrupt the status quo of the global political balance. The Soviet leaders interpreted it as meaning nonintervention by the United States to stem a progressively changing correlation of forces in the world. They also believed that American acceptance of parity meant a readiness to accept a degree of shared and equal power by the two superpowers, which carried implications of cooperation—if not condominium—in avoiding challenges to each other's vital interests.

The American leaders, as they have since made clear, were counting less on Soviet restraint from taking advantages, and more on active American efforts to ensure that the Soviets could not do so. The United States would manage Soviet behavior through linkages and a manipulation of incentives and penalties.

The subsequent failure of the code of conduct stemmed more from the failure of this détente strategy of Nixon and Kissinger to do what they expected than from Soviet violation of the code. Kissinger, with some justification (although less than he claims), blames this failure on congressional refusal to provide key carrots (such as most-favored-nation trade status) and key sticks (banning further covert aid in Angola, or, unconvincingly, renewed arms supply to South Vietnam in 1975).

While U.S. attention was focused on the several cases of clear Soviet and Cuban direct or indirect military intervention (in Angola, Ethiopia, and Afghanistan), Americans have been oblivious to the much longer list of local crises and conflicts in which Western powers or other associates of the United States became involved and in which the Soviet Union and its allies chose not to be involved—the Katangan incursions into Zaire; the continuing conflict in the Western Sahara, the Rhodesian internal conflict; Namibia; the externally aided changes of regime in Equatorial Guinea, the Central African Republic, Uganda, and Chad; the Indonesian occupation and bloody suppression of East Timor; the division of Cyprus; and many others. The Soviets, for their part, see these and many other Western interventions as inspired and supported by the United States and its allies, along with such other cases of direct and indirect U.S. intervention as the reversal of unwanted progressive change by the overthrow of Allende in Chile in 1973, the counterrevolution in Portugal in 1975, the invasion of Grenada in 1983, and the attempt since 1981 to destabilize Nicaragua.

There is a strong tendency on each side to draw attention only to those situations in which it wants to criticize the other side, and to interpret the facts as well as justifications from its own perspective, as well as to manipulate facts and arguments for propaganda and political justification of its own preferences and actions and to discredit the arguments and actions of its adversary. Both sides apply double standards.

Americans are well enough aware of the Soviet uses of a double standard (and vice versa). Sometimes American critics of administration policies recognize its application. But generally Americans are little inclined to see matters from other perspectives. The Soviets also not only see things from a different perspective, but tend to see and interpret (and still more to present) matters from a completely one-sided standpoint. Unless one seeks the facts and reviews the history in some detail, one is often not even aware of the bases for other viewpoints.

Leaders (and publics) on both sides apply double standards of judgment not only because this approach is self-serving, but also because it stems from one-sided perceptions of reality.[5] Such discrepant perception, and in part also biased depiction, is not conscious and is therefore extremely difficult to change. And it affects not only how particular events and developments are perceived but also the whole frame of reference and selection of events. Thus while, as noted, Americans have tended to look only at Soviet and Cuban involvements in Angola, Ethiopia, South Yemen, and Afghanistan, and the Vietnamese in Kampuchea, the Soviets have seen the American efforts to exclude the Soviet Union from the Middle East (to "expel" them, to use

---

5. In theoretical terms, there are two alternative standards, either of which may be applied. They may be termed the "realist-geopolitical" and the "moral-ideological." The behavior of the United States and the Soviet Union may be judged by either standard, but it is not proper (or wise) to judge one's own actions by one standard and the other side's by the other. In practice, each side usually judges the other with a slanted moral-ideological standard, while accepting only for itself the justification of realist motivations (reconciled with its own subjective moral assumptions). This practice makes for lively propaganda but ill serves the policy and diplomatic processes.

Kissinger's apt statement of the U.S. objective), including Egypt, the Sudan, Somalia, and to a degree Iraq; the playing of the China card against the Soviet Union; and U.S. involvements in a wide series of third world situations, also including Angola, Somalia, North Yemen, Oman, Zaire, Chile, El Salvador, Grenada, and Nicaragua. The Soviets also see as related the many interventions by American allies or proxies noted earlier.

As détente crumbled, the Soviet leaders were especially concerned that American moves violated not only a code of conduct for competition in the third world, but also the tacit restraint both sides had observed in the 1970s in not intervening in the traditional spheres of influence of the other (with American restraint in Eastern Europe and Soviet restraint in Western Europe and Latin America). While the Soviet leaders were clearly limited in their ability to influence events in the latter areas, they also showed restraint in the face of certain opportunities, such as Portugal in 1974–75, Chile in 1971–73, Nicaragua, Guatemala, and (despite later American claims) El Salvador.

The extent to which the controversies and conflicting involvements of the two powers in those situations were permitted to affect their bilateral relationship is another important question. Here the Soviet record clearly is more restrained, beginning with the Soviet decision in April–May 1972 to go ahead with the first Nixon summit meeting, despite the escalation of U.S. military action against North Vietnam on the eve of that meeting. In judging the lack of U.S. restraint in this respect, it is, of course, necessary to recognize that the area of control by the leadership over decisions is limited by the workings of an open society and free press. Even had he wished to do so, President Carter could not have gained ratification of the SALT II Treaty in the aftermath of the Soviet intervention in Afghanistan. There are, however, many cases where such linkage is a matter of policy choice.

It is also necessary to consider what is called in international law the rule of proportionality—retaliation, even when justified, should be proportional to the offense. Many in the West (more in Western Europe than in the United States itself) have regarded American reactions to even such clear Soviet transgressions as the occupation of Afghanistan and support for the suppression of Solidarity in Poland as disproportionate—as well as damaging to *Western* interests. The Soviets have complained that the U.S. responses were disproportionate. More important, they have concluded that the responses must have been more than reactive—they must have reflected a desire for pretexts to discard détente. One Soviet writer, in a very unusual published admission, explicitly addressed "the disproportion between the cause and the reaction" in the American response to Afghanistan. "It is understandable that Washington is displeased at the entry of a limited contingent of Soviet troops into Afghanistan. It is quite possible that the Soviet reasoning and explanation of the reasons for this action are not represented sufficiently convincingly there. But the important question these days [February 1980] is this: Does the reaction of the American leaders accord with the situation? Which of that country's *national interests* are affected by the temporary presence of Soviet troops in Afghanistan? *Can the world be brought to the brink of a return to the cold war as a result of this?* Finally, is it correct to *allow a few emotional reactions to wipe out all the achievements the people have built up over a decade of détente?* . . . the events in Afghanistan could have been no more than a pretext for the implementation of a political line for which the foundation had earlier been laid."[6] This judgment is profoundly in error, but it is a natural one from the Soviet perspective.

There are no easy answers to questions on the divisibility of détente (or of any other general pattern of relationship, including confrontation). Clearly an open and internally competitive political system such as that of the United States imposes severe limits on the feasibility of isolating and compartmentalizing relations with another power by simultaneously advancing cooperative and collaborative relations in one sphere while offering confrontation in another, even if that approach is considered desirable. Yet all partial agreements between adversaries involve some such balance. The question is not whether geopolitical rivalry can be ignored or suspended, but what kinds of tacit or explicit agreements on geopolitical conduct can be reached and carried out under conditions of competitive coexistence.

The first rule appears to be simple but involves a very difficult process: *each side must seek to understand the perspective, and the interests, of the other.* This approach will not remove or even reduce the conflicts of interest, but it will help to reduce the frictions caused or exacerbated by the failure even to recognize the perspective and interests of the other.

Second, *there must be reciprocity in agreed standards of conduct: reciprocity in commitments of the two sides, in their own actions, and in their judgments about the behavior of the other side.* This rule seems self-evident and is often advanced by both sides as a requirement—but it is rarely applied in practice by either. For example, any agreement not to intervene militarily in third party conflicts, apart from clearly specifying what actions would be covered, cannot succeed without a real understanding of the conditions and situations to which it is expected to apply. The Soviet Union cannot expect to retain the right to arm insurgents, say, in El Salvador, on the grounds that they are national liberation forces, and expect the United States not to aid the Salvadoran authorities. Nor can the United States expect to end external arms supply to El Salvador while arming and dispatching insurgents to Nicaragua or Afghanistan.

Is the Soviet Union prepared to apply to itself (and to the extent it can, to its allies and clients) the same restraints on the export of revolution that it wishes to apply to American and other exporters of counterrevolution? Is the United States prepared to apply to itself (and to the extent it can, to its allies and clients) the same restraints on military intervention and arms supply

---

6. I. Kremer, "A Policy of Missed Opportunities," *Novoye vremya* [New Times], no. 7 (1980), p. 6. Emphasis added. Note that the basic argument is couched entirely in terms of national interests.

that it wishes to apply to Soviet and other communist countries? These are both large and difficult questions. And even when the answer is affirmative, difficult issues remain. How would situations be handled in which the Soviet Union and the United States could not control clients they had armed—for example, Cuba or Vietnam on the one hand, and Israel or Pakistan on the other? Or how would they handle attacks on friends by other third powers— should the Soviet Union be expected not to aid Vietnam if invaded again by China, or Ethiopia by Somalia? Or the United States not to aid Egypt if attacked by Libya, or Bahrain if attacked by Iran? The United States and the Soviet Union each have a variety of relationships with many countries ranging from close alliances to loose friendships, as well as geopolitical interests apart from formal or implied commitments that may be affected. Neither the Soviet Union nor the United States could remain indifferent to a military intervention by the other against Iran, for example, no matter how it came about and notwithstanding the currently strained relations each has with that country.

The relativity of relationships and their change over time are also important factors, a point readily illustrated by just a few of many examples. In the 1950s the Soviet Union gave the late Kurdish chieftain, Mustapha Barzani, refuge and covertly armed and supported him as a fighter for national liberation. That same man, leading the same people in the same cause, was also covertly armed and supported by the United States (and Iran and Israel) in the 1970s as a freedom fighter, and later was given refuge in the United States. In the early 1970s the Soviet Union supported the genocidal Kampuchean leader of the Khmer Rouge, Pol Pot, whom U.S.-armed Vietnamese reviled and fought. A decade later Pol Pot was being championed by the United States at the United Nations as the legitimate leader of his people, while his forces, with Western and Chinese arms, were battling Soviet-armed Vietnamese. The United States, which had introduced Cuban anticommunist mercenary pilots into the Congo in the mid-1960s, was by the late 1970s arguing that armed Cubans had no place in Africa. The number of countries that have been armed by the United States and later rearmed by the Soviet Union (Ethiopia, Iraq, Libya, India, Vietnam, Cuba, and Nicaragua) is probably equaled by the number armed first by the Soviet Union and later by the United States (Yugoslavia, Indonesia, Morocco, Egypt, Sudan, and Somalia). Insurgencies have been "transferred" with changes of alignment (for example, Eritrea and the Iraqi Kurds). Allies and clients, pursuing their own interests, have formed strange coalitions (for example, in Angola the MPLA was supported by many pro-Western African states as well as by the Soviet Union and Cuba, while the FNLA was armed and trained by China and North Korea as well as by the United States and Zaire). Today Cuban troops provide perimeter security for Gulf Oil in Angola against guerrillas receiving Western arms.

The limits on the ability, or political readiness, of the United States and the Soviet Union to pressure their allies and clients are real and not a subterfuge. For example, the Soviet Union could not make final decisions for Libya or Syria or even Vietnam; the United States obviously could not for

Israel or France. (Note, for example, the French decision to supply arms to Nicaragua, and the covert Israeli supply of military equipment to Iran, over U.S. objections.) Such limits also apply to other groups and even individuals. Neither the Soviet Union nor the United States controls everyone it has trained for covert operations (especially the Arabs and Cubans, respectively, but not even its own nationals—for example, former CIA officers Edwin P. Wilson and Francis E. Terpil, who trained terrorists in Libya).

In looking to the future, it is important to begin by recognizing that any meaningful rules of the game will only be possible to the extent that attempts to establish guidelines for the conduct of the superpowers are seen to accord with their interests, are clearly understood and accepted by them, and are seen as remaining in their best interests. It would be futile to believe that either the Soviet Union or the United States would accept restraints *imposed* by any document. Apart from the fact that virtually any obligation contained in the Basic Principles, for example—or the Helsinki Final Act—can be variously interpreted, there is no authority that can compel Soviet or American acquiescence in any application of a code that the superpower regards as unjustified or unacceptable. Sanctions in the form of negative incentives may or may not be effective (usually they are not). Sanctions such as "punishment" for a transgression as *judged* by the adversary are bound to be unacceptable—indeed, to be seen as a hostile act, rather than as a meting out of justice by a self-appointed and by definition not disinterested judge. Nor will world opinion, as reflected in UN votes, for example, be a decisive influence when it contravenes perceived national interests (witness the Soviet reaction to the UN opposition to the occupation of Afghanistan, or—while admittedly not comparable in important respects—the American refusal to accept the overwhelming world consensus on a Law of the Sea regime or the judgment of the World Court on U.S. support of covert military operations against Nicaragua).

This fundamental limitation does not mean there cannot be useful agreed restraints. But they must be clear, they must be accepted, there must be a common standard, and there must be reciprocity in their application. Above all, both sides must believe it is in their interests to abide by the restraints so that the other side will also do so. To the extent one side does not, the other will not either.

There must also be an essential degree of reciprocity in not challenging the legitimacy, internal affairs, or global vital interests of the other side. Nothing has galled Soviet leaders more than attempts by American leaders to arrogate to themselves the right to pass judgment on the Soviets, and then to use that judgment as a basis for determining American-Soviet relations. They object strongly to the idea that the United States can claim the right to reward or punish its equal, the USSR. In reacting to the American stand on Afghanistan, authoritative Soviet commentators stress that "irrespective of assessments of this action (the White House, of course, has an assessment that differs from those of the USSR or Afghanistan), the method of linking these events with American-Soviet relations and in general with the American line in the world arena is in itself fallacious. . . . The talk to the effect that the USSR must be 'punished' is simply ludicrous. . . . Why does the United States arrogate to itself the right to punish anyone, *especially a great power such as the Soviet Union?* And how can it do this? This logic of 'punitive action' was refuted quite recently in China's relations with Vietnam. As Western experts acknowledge, China came out of Vietnam with a bloody nose. *This logic is still more inappropriate, even absurd, in relations between the two thermonuclear giants.*"[7]

Many Soviet commentaries in the period since the collapse of détente have stressed the responsibility, as they see it, not only of American policy itself, but of American attempts to impose its own preferred code of conduct, for the failure of U.S.-Soviet détente.[8] The United States is accused not only of attempting to fashion a code of conduct for others that fits its own aims and purposes, but of attempting to impose it "in its role of world policeman."[9] Moreover, at least since 1981, it has built up its military forces as a means of compelling others (including even the Soviet Union) to accept this code.[10] Finally, the United States is said to have abandoned détente at the beginning of the 1980s because the Soviet Union and socialist community had refused to accept the imposition of that code of conduct. To do so would have meant subordinating their foreign policies and permitting interference in their internal affairs.[11]

Despite these Soviet objections to the U.S. version of a code of conduct in the latter 1970s and early 1980s, the Soviet leaders have accepted the idea of a code, based on the UN Charter, the Helsinki Final Act, and the bilateral U.S.-USSR Basic Principles of Mutual Relations of 1972. The problem is one of determining the content of a code based on "restraint and reciprocity" (to use the term favored by former Secretary of State Haig, and by Brzezinski before him).

The key questions are as follows. Is the Soviet Union willing and able to apply the same standards to itself as to the United States? And, no less important, is the United States willing and able to apply the same standards to itself as to the Soviet Union? To what extent is each willing, and able, to apply

---

7. Fedor Burlatsky, "Remember!" *Literaturnaya gazeta* [The Literary Gazette], February 13, 1980. Emphasis added.

8. For example, see V. Petrovsky, "The Main Path to Peace," *Literaturnaya gazeta*, October 1, 1980; A. Bovin, "The Lasting Significance of Leninist Ideas," *Kommunist* [The Communist], no. 10 (July 1980), p. 80; S. Beglov, *Novosti Daily Review*, February 17, 1981, p. 4; and V. Kobysh, "Once Again on the Benefit of Doctoring," *Literaturnaya gazeta*, April 1, 1981.

9. Beglov, *Novosti Daily Review*, February 17, 1981, p. 4.

10. Kobysh, *Literaturnaya gazeta*, April 1, 1981.

11. V. Baranovsky, "A Strategy Leading to a Dead End," *Mirovaya ekonomika i mezhdunarodnye otnosheniya* [The World Economy and International Relations], no. 2 (February 1981), p. 133.

the same standards to its allies and clients with respect to the other superpower's allies and clients? This last is an even more difficult matter than when the United States or the Soviet Union undertakes obligations for itself. The reality is that despite loose charges on both sides of proxies, puppets, and satellites, the friends and allies of *both* superpowers have varying but often significant independence of decision and action. How can this reality be accommodated without obtaining the consent of these other powers—or without leaving major loopholes for surrogate interventions? To what extent and under what conditions would the Soviet Union, or the United States, be prepared to bring its influence to bear to curb an uncontrolled associate—or even be capable of doing so? The Soviet Union could strive to control some action by Syria, or North Korea, or Vietnam, or Cuba without being able to do so. In other cases, control could not be exercised at an acceptable political cost. The limitations on U.S. ability to control actions by its allies, or by other friends such as Israel, is evident (in some cases even to the Soviets). But leaving that important question aside, is the United States, and is the Soviet Union, ready to accept the same objective standards that it would apply to the other?

Is the United States willing and able to grant rewards as well as punishments—and to *accept* punishments as well as rewards—if such are to be linked to behavior? Recent history suggests serious practical questions about the limits that the American political system in particular imposes on the ability (to say nothing of its consistent willingness) to do so. A carrot-and-stick approach as an agreed *reciprocal* policy seems highly impractical.

It may be useful to consider a few possible desiderata for a U.S.-USSR code of conduct in the third world:

1. Nonintervention in the affairs of other states.
2. No military intervention by forces of the two powers or their allies in any third world country.
3. No supply of arms to insurgents.
4. No military bases without the consent of the host country.
5. No support of any kind to any country that attacks any other country.
6. No military threats against any country.

The first of these desiderata is virtually meaningless as a restraint and unenforceable as a constraint, given the wide range of political communication, economic, and other transactions and the difficulty in defining "intervention." It could, for example, mean that the United States would be intervening in Soviet internal affairs if it requested an increase in Jewish emigration. If a request is not intervention, what about legislation that deprives the other side of normal trade status unless a certain action is taken? Is that not intervention (or at least an attempt at intervention) by economic pressure? What about U.S. economic sanctions against the Soviet Union unless the government of Poland releases its own imprisoned citizens? Suppose the Soviet Union were to condition economic or some other aspect of its bilateral relations on a change in American immigration laws? Or to tie its implementation of signed economic contracts to the lifting of martial law in Turkey, the Philippines, or El Salvador, and to the release of those detained under their laws?

Military intervention seems a more manageable restraint. But what is admissible? (For example, friendly naval visits certainly are—but what about an offshore show of force?) The United States would wish to rule out such things as the Soviet intervention in Afghanistan, or the rule would be meaningless. But would the United States be prepared to forgo the kind of parallel intervention it mounted in the Dominican Republic in 1965? Or in Vietnam? Or in Grenada in 1983? To be sure, every case is unique, but the United States was not invited into the Dominican Republic or Grenada by any recognized government, and it participated at least passively in the physical elimination of Diem in South Vietnam before a successor government asked it to intervene. (One reason given for massive military intervention in Vietnam in 1965 was to protect the small U.S. military forces already there, which had come under attack at Pleiku; one reason for the Soviet intervention in Afghanistan was the threat raised by insurgent attacks that killed Soviet military personnel already in the country. How would the rule apply in those instances?)

What about arms supply to insurgents? As best as the tangled tale in Angola in 1974–75 can be sorted out, a key turning point was probably the *Chinese* supply of arms to the FNLA in June–July 1974, followed by the Soviet supply to the MPLA in October 1974, and the American supply to the FNLA in January and July 1975. Then the first foreign troops to enter Angola were pro-Western Zairians. But leaving them aside, after South African troops made an incursion into Angola in August 1975, about 1,500 Cuban troops arrived in late September 1975 (without Soviet initiative, transport, or other assistance), a move that led in turn to a South African drive deep into the country in October–November, followed by large-scale Cuban troop arrivals by Soviet air transport from late November 1975 to March 1976. All these countries and many others had been involved in supporting their favored factions for some time.

The Soviet Union would have to forswear supplying arms to revolutionaries such as the insurgents in El Salvador. But it has supplied none directly. If allies were included, the Cubans and Nicaraguans would also have to desist. But so would the United States—it would have to stop supplying arms to Nicaraguan insurgents based in Honduras, and to Afghans in Pakistan, and to Cambodians (Khmer Serei) in Kampuchea. Would the Egyptians and others also be barred from supplying arms to Afghan insurgents via Pakistan? Would the Chinese stop supplying arms to the Khmer Rouge in Kampuchea and to Meo tribesmen in Laos?

One thing is clear: no distinction could ever be agreed on that was based on a differentiation between legal, or good, and bad insurgents. What one side terms terrorists another sees as national liberation fighters or freedom fighters. Both sides employ a double standard in judging state-sponsored terrorism.

A ban on military bases without the consent of the host government would certainly not be a proposal the United States would advance. But
it would be one it could have to face, and it is difficult to argue against except
on legalistic grounds based on treaty rights. The only current relevant case is
the American naval base at Guantánamo Bay in Cuba.

No support of any kind to any country that attacks another country
is a proposition that might offer a concrete way for the superpowers to discourage third parties from military intervention. But the proposal would not survive longer than the time it takes to read these lines. The United States would
never agree if for no other reason than its open commitment to Israel.

No military threats against any country is another proposition that
would be extremely difficult to apply. Moreover, any attempt to show support
for an ally or friend in the third world implies a threat to its opponent. Deterrence, after all, is a form of threat, and the distinction between defensive
deterrence and offensive compellence often resides in the perspective of the
parties, not in anything objectively identifiable.

The purpose of this brief illustrative review is to demonstrate that
many attractive and desirable restraints in any proposed code of conduct are
too loose—or too tight—to provide a standard. But some *could* be devised—if
both the Soviet Union and the United States were prepared to deprive themselves of some options to which they might resort (and have in the past resorted). That condition is the main obstacle, but it deserves further reflection
on both sides.

The main reliance, in any case, should be placed not on a written
code, which requires interpretation and application and is unenforceable, but
on mutual recognition of the benefits of reciprocal restraint and the practice of
close political consultation. Soviet and American restraint from intervention in
some local or civil war or crisis in the third world *may* result from consultation.
It will not result from either side's trying to pursue its own advantage while
applying a different standard in futile attempts to prevent the other side from
doing so.

Early in the Reagan administration Secretary of State Haig tried to
revive the idea of a code of conduct, to the accompaniment of charges of
Soviet violations of the 1972 Basic Principles. This confrontational approach
did not serve any constructive purpose and prejudiced the possibility at that
juncture for negotiating a code. Nonetheless, even after that episode the Soviet leaders kept open the possibility of further negotiations. The real problem
is not that both sides object in principle to a code, but that they differ over its
content and above all its evenhanded application.

When considering the future, one needs to bear in mind Soviet, as
well as U.S., perspectives and aims. *Reciprocity should extend to constraints
on both sides not to take actions that would be unacceptable to the other.*
The obverse of this proposition is that each side must be very rigorous and
restrained in establishing (in advance) what behavior by the other side would

really be unacceptable, as contrasted with actions that are merely unpalatable and even unjustifiable. Real consideration of reciprocity goes a long way in trimming down what any party really wants to designate as beyond the pale of acceptability. For example, in 1979, contrary to the administration's initial statements, the continued presence of a Soviet combat brigade of 2,600 men in Cuba was not really "unacceptable" to the United States after all. Nor, for that matter, is the continued presence of over 100,000 Soviet troops in Afghanistan, or Soviet suppression of public dissent or refusal to permit emigration of its citizens—no matter how unjustified or unjust those practices are. The United States may vigorously oppose those actions, and certainly should not condone them. But they are not unacceptable, nor should their resolution be a prior condition to agreement on other measures to defuse tensions that risk Soviet-American conflict and nuclear war. U.S. actions in Vietnam in the 1960s and 1970s were abhorrent to the Soviet leaders and were vigorously opposed, but they were not considered unacceptable or an obstacle to embarking on the détente of the early 1970s. The Reagan administration, for all its confrontational posture, did not repeat the unwise stance of the Carter administration in declaring that the presence of Soviet troops in Afghanistan was unacceptable and that their removal was a precondition to resumption of a range of arms control negotiations, as well as many other aspects of U.S.-Soviet relations.

How far are the United States and the Soviet Union prepared to go in reciprocal restraint in the geopolitical competition? It may be asking too much to seek a Soviet repudiation of the Brezhnev Doctrine or an American renunciation of the Monroe Doctrine. But both powers should seek mutual benefit in restraint from direct involvement in furthering, or combating, national liberation wars and local wars in the third world. They have stayed out of the Iran-Iraq war. They have avoided direct interventions in Namibia. They would both have been better off to have exercised greater restraint and to have supported a coalition government in Angola. The Soviet Union should have sought other ways to ensure its own legitimate security interests in Afghanistan without becoming embroiled in a direct military intervention and occupation. The United States could have ensured its legitimate security interests in preventing Nicaragua from becoming a military base threatening other countries without generating an external intervention. Neither power is going to become a passive onlooker at events that it believes affect its interests, but there are various means of serving one's interest. Both should be prepared to forgo opportunities for new military bases and alliances in favor of neutrality and non-alignment in almost all third world areas. And, without their exercise of condominium, cooperation in moderating threatening situations in areas such as the Middle East can serve the interests of both powers as well as the general interest.

It is not easy for either power to accept the norms of behavior it sets for the other. Yet "restraint and reciprocity," given political realities, must indeed apply to both sides. If the United States wishes to draw the Soviet

Union into accepting norms of behavior and an existing international order, it too must observe those norms itself. The Soviet leaders are naturally more influenced by what Americans do than by what they say, especially when the two diverge. Yet the United States, under all administrations, has routinely acted on the Eurasian periphery of the Soviet Union in ways that it would not accept in Soviet behavior in the Western Hemisphere. And the Soviet leaders have to give up the idea that support for "progressive" revolutions is acceptable while support for "reactionary" counterrevolutions is not. The fact is that most guerrilla insurrections in the mid-1980s are in communist or other leftist-ruled countries aligned with the Soviet Union: Afghanistan, Cambodia, Angola, Ethiopia, Mozambique, and Nicaragua. All were the scene of leftist accession to power in the 1970s, but the wheel has turned.

This discussion of geopolitical conduct has concentrated on the roles of the Soviet Union and the United States in the third world. That focus takes as its point of departure that perceived American concern over Soviet actions in the third world poses a serious problem for relations between the two countries, and then considers as well the Soviet perspective and the need in the future to take both perspectives into account. The geopolitical arena has two other highly important elements that affect American-Soviet relations: Europe and China.

The European-centered East-West détente that began in the latter 1960s, somewhat earlier than the American-Soviet one, was assumed by many during most of the 1970s to be concomitant with the American-Soviet détente of that period. The fact that it had different roots and a different impact on the political relationship was not evident to many until the sharp decline and collapse of American-Soviet détente by the end of the decade. The disjunction between American and Western European attitudes toward détente in relations with the Soviet Union has become most evident in American-European friction over economic relations, but it has extended to other aspects of policy as well. To be sure, there is no identity of view among or within the Western countries, but as a whole Western and Eastern Europe have maintained a détente relationship that underlies the differences between the United States and its Western allies (including Japan). While the Soviet Union has preferred détente with both Western Europe and the United States, when that has no longer been possible, it has sought to play upon internal Western differences to its own benefit.

In conducting its relations with the Soviet Union—and with the Western Europeans—the United States should not exacerbate Western differences and thereby serve Soviet interests. To the extent that the United States and its NATO allies do not agree on aspects of their relations with the East, the United States should not seek to compel its allies to follow its preferred course of action. It is better to recognize and accept differences on some issues than to enlarge or deepen the areas of divergence in the name of demanding unity. More broadly, the United States must consider the whole range of East-

West European relations on their own merits, as well as in conjunction with American-Soviet relations.

The other major element has been, and will be, the triangular relationship among the United States, China, and the Soviet Union. The American rapprochement with China that paralleled the development of American-Soviet détente in the early 1970s significantly boosted the U.S. role. Later in the decade, when the United States moved into an alignment with China against the Soviet Union, a shift that was made at a time of sharp deterioration in American-Soviet relations, the U.S. role was seriously reduced. The Chinese naturally sought to improve their own position. By the early 1980s they no longer needed to curry American favor to ensure against a Soviet-American détente and could afford to improve their relations with the Soviet Union. Both countries, especially China, thus increased their leverage in the triangle vis-à-vis the United States.

In the future, the United States should return to seeking more of a balancing role, above all by not committing itself to alignment with either China or the Soviet Union in a way that inhibits improving relations with the other.

Economic Relations

In view of the adversarial relationship between the United States and the Soviet Union, the long-standing American and general Western refusal to export weaponry and strategic goods to the Soviet Union and its allies has not been at issue and will no doubt continue. Questions have arisen over the strategic significance of some high-technology items, such as certain computers and high-precision drilling tools. These questions on the margin will continue to be resolved on a practical basis after case-by-case review. Although opinions on individual decisions may vary, the purpose and the process will remain. The range of economic policies and strategies that the United States (and the Western European countries) may consider would all incorporate this element.

What has become a political issue in the United States, and to some extent between the United States and its European (and Japanese) allies, is whether the West should seek not only to deny advanced technology directly useful for Soviet military industry, but also to deny access to a much wider range of goods important to the Soviet economy. The question of terms of trade, in particular credits (and especially at concessional rates), is a related issue.

Advocacy of a broad policy of economic denial by the Reagan administration met widespread Western disagreement, highlighted by the ill-starred attempt by the United States in 1982 to impose sanctions on European subsidiaries of American firms and on European licensees (and even to apply those sanctions retroactively to prevent deliveries of goods under signed contracts). There was something ironic in the argument that the United States must impose economic pressures and sanctions on Western Europe in order to protect it from growing dependence and possible future imposition of economic pressures and sanctions by the Soviet Union. It also went against the grain for the United States to insist that Europe make economic sacrifices involving the gas pipeline, while the United States permitted, indeed encouraged, the Soviets to purchase its grain.

A policy of confrontation, consistently prosecuted, would include as one element in its strategy far-reaching constraints on trade intended to increase economic—and political—tensions within the Soviet bloc and the Soviet Union itself. That approach would involve a much longer-term American policy of sharp competition than would economic sanctions related to particular Soviet behavior with respect, say, to Afghanistan or Poland. A challenge to the Soviet system presumes either a preference for, or prejudgment of the inevitability of, a continuing and intensifying cold war.

An alternative range of economic strategies would use trade constraints to affect particular Soviet *policies*, rather than to wage economic war as a way to challenge the Soviet economic and political *system*. A "hard headed detente," as advocated recently by former President Nixon and as favored by Kissinger, Brzezinski, and Haig, would relate economic constraints to Soviet foreign political behavior. The key difference with a confrontational strategy is the readiness to lift trade constraints if Soviet actions eschewed the particular behavior to which the United States objected. In most variants such a strategy of manipulated trade relations also offers inducements—carrots—as well as sanctions—sticks—to help move Soviet policy in the preferred directions.

Throughout the 1970s American trade relations were gradually expanded and developed, with limited use of economic incentives. But the ability to pursue this strategy was severely limited when in 1974 Congress linked trade normalization and credits to changes in internal Soviet policy. This move and the use of economic sanctions by the Carter and Reagan administrations have cut U.S.-Soviet trade sharply. But the sanctions have not achieved their political purposes. By the mid-1980s the Reagan administration had reduced its use of economic sanctions, but had not developed a new economic policy.

In looking to the future, the United States must first of all seek to develop whatever policy it adopts on economic relations as an integral part of its broader overall policy toward the Soviet Union. This policy may include encouraging trade with minimal strategic constraints and maximum normalization (for example, granting most-favored-nation status and eliminating predetermined credit limits). Or the United States may seek to tie some steps in the development of economic relations to improvement in political relations (as was the general design in the 1970s). Particularly if an understanding is reached on reciprocal restraints in global competition, that could be accompanied by agreements on more open economic ties.

Decisions on economic policy toward the Soviet Union should remain a subject of serious consultation among the Western allies, even when they cannot reach full agreement. This approach should apply above all to any consideration of sanctions. On the whole, sanctions appear to be of limited economic or political efficacy. On the one hand they should be considered only in serious situations, but on the other hand they are not likely to be effective in moving the Soviet Union in such situations. Perhaps the most that can be said is that economic sanctions are not a useful tool in most cases, although they are a possible resort if an appropriate situation arises. And the effectiveness of sanctions is highly dependent on substantial Western unity—but should not in turn be permitted to become a cause of increasing Western disunity.

Developing Reciprocal Understanding

The need for a better understanding in the United States of the political processes, perceptions, thinking, and aims of the Soviet Union, and for a better Soviet understanding of the United States, should be evident from this study. Understanding should not be taken to mean agreement or concord; both sides, as adversaries, need to understand their differences and conflicting interests, as well as common interests. Improved reciprocal understanding involves at least three important categories of people: experts (academic and other nongovernmental analysts and commentators, as well as government specialists), political leaders, and publics. The roles of these categories vary between the two countries; in particular, the need for public understanding is far greater in the United States.

The requirement that U.S. policy be sustainable by the public is indeed critical. Studies have stressed the need to educate the public on the complexity of world politics and the reality of both competition and cooperation in U.S.-Soviet relations.[12] Too often in the past, however, this need has been given lip service but has been granted only a patronizing attitude in practice. Political leaders, above all the president, must lay it on the line rather than gloss over complex political issues and attempt to manipulate rather than to inform public opinion.

In order to inform and rally public opinion, leaders must of course themselves first understand the real situation. Regrettably, through the administrations of the 1970s and 1980s there has been a steady decline, rather than an improvement, in presidential understanding of the Soviet Union and of the interrelationships between the two powers. Not unrelated to that fact, both as partial cause and as one effect, has been the decline in the role of expertise on

12. For example, several of the contributors to a recent study of U.S. policymaking on Soviet affairs stress this need. See the discussions by William Schneider, Stanley Hoffman, Samuel P. Huntington, and Joseph S. Nye, Jr., in Joseph S. Nye, Jr., ed., *The Making of America's Soviet Policy* (New Haven, Conn.: Yale University Press, 1984), pp. 11–36, 262–63, 288–89, 352–53.

Soviet affairs in the making of policy. Expertise must not only be solid, and available, but must also be used by policymakers.

The need remains to develop and exercise expertise, within both the government and the broader academic and analytical communities. In the United States attention to the study of Soviet affairs has experienced fluctuation over the years. The challenge of learning more about a new adversary boosted academic study and professional employment during the cold war, but academic attention has not kept pace with developments over the last two decades. This is even more true of the wider public. For example, there are today fewer *students* of the Russian language in the United States than there are *teachers* of English in the Soviet Union. Nonetheless, cumulatively there has developed a substantial number of scholars and government analysts who professionally study the Soviet Union.

The Soviet Union has made a more consistent and larger-scale effort to study the United States. In 1967 a separate Institute of the USA (later broadened to include Canada) was established under the framework of the Academy of Sciences of the USSR. It engages several hundred researchers. The professional journal *USA (SShA)* has a current circulation of about 30,000 (down by some 10,000 from its peak in 1979 and a return to the 1972 level). The Ministry of Foreign Affairs, and presumably the KGB, have a large corps of American experts. Dozens of professional books and monographs on the politics and policy of the United States, apart from mass propaganda, are published in the Soviet Union each year.

It is much more difficult to assess the levels of competence, and of real understanding, found in American studies of the Soviet Union and in Soviet studies of the United States. I shall not attempt to do so here. It is of course even more difficult to assess the quality of unpublished internal studies and analyses prepared within (or on contract for) the U.S. and Soviet governments. Enough, however, is known to conclude that the general nature of *analysis* of the adversary does not vary greatly between published and unpublished official sources. (*Policy* studies are another matter, and unofficial published studies may vary greatly from official internal deliberations. Classified secret intelligence information may make an important difference in some analyses, but not in general understanding.)

Political science in the United States in recent years has made considerable strides in opening up new approaches to understanding the workings of the Soviet policymaking system. Apart from studies of Soviet foreign policy that analyze case studies, improved methodologies of political analysis have begun to be applied to the study of Soviet policymaking—and of *American* policymaking toward the Soviet Union. For example, the traditional approach has been to study policymaking as if policy were made on the basis of a simple rational decision based on national interest. To have a "rational actor" interpreting a clear "national interest" is not only an oversimplification, but such an approach omits from consideration many factors that have demonstrably influenced policy decisions in history. Political scientists have therefore developed an alternative approach using various decisionmaking models, centering on internal bureaucratic interests, personal power rivalries, conflicting institutional interests, and the like. Most productive is analysis based on testing and using whichever approaches prove most suitable in any given instance, depending on the nature of the problem, availability of data, and other considerations. Differing approaches can complement one another. Information is usually incomplete to one or another degree, and analysts differ in their judgments on the weight that should be given to various factors, but this kind of approach is far superior to one that ignores the multiplicity of factors affecting decisions.[13]

Applying such an approach to Soviet affairs is even more difficult than applying it to American policymaking. But the application is equally valid, even if the mix of factors differs and the lacunae in information loom larger. Those who assume that the Soviet political system is monolithic would not accept this approach, but virtually all serious students of Soviet affairs recognize at least some diversity of views and interests in the Soviet body politic, and most believe that such differences affect Soviet policymaking. Western specialists differ over the nature and roles of various viewpoints in Soviet policymaking, but such differences are best resolved by empirical inquiry. A number of Western specialists on Soviet affairs have in recent years been clarifying the methodology and advancing the state of understanding in their studies.[14] Analysis of Soviet policymaking in the United States, and indeed U.S. policy itself, has tended to reflect three schools of thought that have been termed the "essentialist," "mechanistic," and "interactionist" approaches.[15]

The essentialist approach focuses not on what the Soviet Union does, but on what it is. It sees Soviet policy as a relentless attempt to attain immutable Soviet objectives, including a communist world, and the Soviet challenge as basically ideological, although relying heavily on military power. The sources of Soviet behavior are regarded as the very nature of its ideology and system, and as inherently not only expansionist but evil. An essentialist

---

13. The pathbreaking study was an analysis of American decisionmaking in the Cuban missile crisis of 1962, employing several models. See Graham T. Allison, *Essence of Decision: Explaining the Cuban Missile Crisis* (Boston, Mass.: Little, Brown, 1971).

14. A particularly useful discussion of this whole subject, including a valuable survey of relevant Western studies, is found in Alexander Dallin, "The Domestic Sources of Soviet Foreign Policy," in Seweryn Bialer, ed., *The Domestic Context of Soviet Foreign Policy* (Boulder, Colo.: Westview, 1981), pp. 335–408, including its bibliographical references.

15. Again, while there is a rich literature by many scholars, a useful recent discussion that both articulates these schools and discusses the wider literature is found in Alexander Dallin and Gail W. Lapidus, "Reagan and the Russians: United States Policy toward the Soviet Union and Eastern Europe," in Kenneth A. Oye, Robert J. Lieber, and Donald Rothchild, eds., *Eagle Defiant: United States Foreign Policy in the 1980s* (Boston, Mass.: Little, Brown, 1983), pp. 191–236, including its bibliographical references. The account here draws greatly on this discussion, including the distinction among the three schools of thought.

approach sees inevitable continuing conflict and risk of war, no real possibility of accommodation, and little if any positive value in negotiation. The appropriate American policy is therefore confrontation.

The mechanistic approach is concerned with Soviet behavior, not with the essence of the system and its ideology. While regarding the Soviet Union as an adversary, mechanists perceive the Soviet threat as primarily geopolitical. Although they see a Soviet aim to expand Soviet influence in the world, they also regard the Soviet Union as prudent and opportunistic, and as responsive to incentives and to risks and costs. Hence, while skeptical of accommodation, mechanists see opportunities for U.S. policy to use both American power and negotiation to influence and even to "manage" Soviet foreign policy behavior.

The interactionist approach sees the sources of Soviet-American conflict not only as rooted in conflicting aims and ambitions, and in geopolitical more than ideological terms, as do the mechanists, but also as stemming from the dynamics of the competition itself and from mutual perceptions and misperceptions as well as conflicts of interest. Adherents of this approach vary among themselves in assessments of Soviet intentions and capabilities, but they tend to find an important reactive element in Soviet policy and interactive element in Soviet-American relations. Interactionists agree with mechanists that Soviet behavior is subject to external influence, but see much wider possibilities for change and for American influence. They tend to find greater diversity in internal Soviet politics and therefore greater potential for evolution of the Soviet system. They also believe there is a greater learning process and feedback in foreign relations and greater interaction between the actions and policies of the two sides. While the mechanists rely on linkage and leverage with sticks and carrots (incentives and penalties) orchestrated by the United States to manage Soviet behavior, the interactionists see less efficacy in attempts by the United States to manipulate Soviet policy and more need to deal with the Soviets directly. Soviet policy is viewed not only as pursuing Soviet aims and objectives, but also as being realistic and reactive and influenced by experience. Interactionists see possibilities, and a need, for negotiation of common constraints, arms control, and rules of the game or a code of conduct to contain geopolitical competition, and both less opportunity and greater risks in attempts by unilateral American actions to impose constraints on the Soviet Union from a position of strength.

While in practice many variations exist within these approaches, clearly the détente policy of Nixon and Kissinger, the diluted détente policy of Brzezinski, and the post-détente policy advocated by Haig and Shultz are all within the mechanistic school. In the Carter administration, policy controversy stemmed from tension between the mechanistic geopolitical approach of Brzezinski and the interactionist approach of Vance. In the Reagan administration, Reagan himself set a confrontational tone with his essentialist declarations about the Soviet system as the focus of evil, although he proved less consistent in practice and the tension of his administration has shifted to a tug of war between mechanists and essentialists. Haig and Shultz have been the main exponents of the mechanist approach, and William P. Clark, Richard Pipes, Richard Perle, and Jeane Kirkpatrick have been among the most prominent essentialists.[16] In the 1980s essentialists are back, and interactionists are absent, for the first time in two decades.

The present study has not been undertaken to test the validity of any of these approaches, and the inquiry allowed the possibility of supporting any of the three. But my own view, based on past study and experience, has been most closely in line with the interactionist approach. That is why this study has focused on both American and Soviet policy and relations between the two countries. The findings of the study, in my judgment, provide powerful support for an interactionist interpretation of Soviet policy. The narrative account has, however, been presented without reference to any particular interpretation, and the reader may give his or her own interpretation to the record of American-Soviet relations set forth in it.

It is also useful to note that in the Soviet Union there are roughly parallel divisions and schools of thought about the policy of the United States. Most available data come from the writings of political analysts and writers in the Soviet political establishment—academic analysts at institutes, commentators, foreign affairs officials, military men, and party officials in the departments of the Central Committee—but also from the speeches and writings of the political leaders. In the Soviet Union, as in the United States, one sees a spectrum of views ranging from ideological essentialists to pragmatic interactionists. And in the Soviet Union, too, there was a rise of mechanists and to a lesser extent interactionists in the 1970s, and a parallel sharp decline in the political influence of interactionists and partial resurgence of essentialists with the collapse of détente.[17]

Analytical and historical studies, especially those that deal with the real interplay between the two countries, can contribute to better understanding. Further studies of Soviet policymaking, and of American policymaking toward the Soviet Union,[18] can also contribute. So can studies of the role of different perspectives and perceptions on the two sides. A few such studies have appeared,[19] but more work is needed. Clearly, there is also need for much

---

16. For a prescriptive study from an essentialist standpoint that advocates confrontation, see Richard Pipes, *Survival Is Not Enough: Soviet Relations and America's Future* (Simon and Schuster, 1984).

17. The most complete analysis is Franklyn Griffiths, "The Sources of American Conduct: Soviet Perspectives and Their Policy Implications," *International Security*, vol. 9 (Fall 1984), pp. 3–50. See also Jerry Hough, *The Struggle for the Third World: Soviet Debate and American Options* (Brookings Institution, 1985); and Robert Legvold, *The Soviet Union and the Other Superpower: Soviet Policy toward the United States* (forthcoming).

18. In particular, see Nye, *The Making of America's Soviet Policy*.

19. For example, see Ralph K. White, *Fearful Warriors: A Psychological Profile of U.S.-Soviet Relations* (Free Press, 1984).

greater efforts to develop understanding of the United States in the Soviet Union. No one writing in the West can hope to advise the Soviets on how to improve their understanding.While a need clearly exists for *reciprocal* improved understanding, whatever advances can be made on each side help. Each side will serve its own interests through improved understanding, whether the other makes parallel progress or not. Many possibilities for improved relations will of course depend on increased mutual understanding, but even in its absence some other steps may be taken.

In concluding this discussion, it is useful to reaffirm the importance of a U.S. dialogue with the Soviet leaders and others in the political establishment at all levels. Both sides can benefit from increasing and enhancing communication. This includes official and unofficial contact of a kind that exists on a wider basis than is generally recognized, but that still needs development.

Conclusions

This look at the future has pointed to three salient areas of bilateral U.S.-Soviet relations: national security, global geopolitical competition, and economic relations. American interest in Soviet internal affairs was omitted not because developments in that sphere are not important to the United States, or ultimately relevant to its policy, but because they are not intrinsically a matter of American relations with the Soviet Union. The conflicts in ideological worldviews and values between the Soviet Union and the United States are profound, but they are a reality to which policy must be geared. The problems, and potential dangers, in relations between the two states make the containment of competition a sine qua non. Global competition involves risks of precipitating direct conflict between the two powers, as well as many limited shifts in power relationships. Efforts to contain the continuing competition are difficult enough to manage, and important enough on their own merits, not to be further weighted by other matters. Economic relations are, for the United States, more open to unilateral management. But experience confirms that manipulating economic relations has very limited potential for influencing Soviet behavior. To the contrary, direct attempts to wield an economic stick are more likely to reduce than to increase U.S. influence on Soviet internal practices.

Successive American administrations, through détente and confrontation, have had to address the way to handle human rights practices in the Soviet Union. A confrontational policy prescribes a confrontational approach to this subject. But any policy of mixed competition and cooperation, whether the mix leans toward détente or containment, poses a question of how to deal with a problem of concern to Americans but one that involves Soviet internal affairs. Basically, there are three possible approaches. One is to make clear the American viewpoint and do nothing more. Some critics have accused the

Nixon and Ford administrations of taking this course. The second course is not only to make the American view clear but also to seek to persuade the Soviet leaders to alleviate the situation. This approach can include incentives, but not punitive sanctions. The third approach is to vilify the Soviet system and place pressure on the Soviet leaders in an attempt to compel changes in their internal practices or at least penalize them for not making them. It seeks to do so by establishing linkage with other aspects of American-Soviet relations of interest to the Soviet leaders, for example, trade or arms control, for leverage to effect such internal changes. The record strongly supports the conclusion that while the Soviet leaders object even to any American expression of judgment on such matters, they are prepared to take that consideration into account and make some accommodation. If, on the other hand, they are faced with attempts at intimidation and coercion, they will react strongly and not yield. Above all, attempts to link demands for internal changes with important arms control or trade agreements are likely only to sacrifice those security or economic interests and worsen political relations without moderating Soviet internal practices. The real "linkage" is often a matter of internal *American* political gamesmanship rather than one that affects positively internal Soviet affairs. The case of the Jackson-Vanik amendment is a prime example; by 1984 Jewish emigration from the Soviet Union was down to 896, the lowest figure since 1970 and more than 50,000 below the peak reached in 1979 when the Carter administration had promised to seek cancellation of the amendment. Ultimately, while the American people and their government are not indifferent to human rights and other aspects of internal affairs in the Soviet Union (and other states), those concerns should not be made central to state relations.

The United States should not expect, or seek to rely on, a codification of rules of international conduct. Instead, what is required is a commitment by both sides to a *process* of diplomatic consultation and adjustment to prevent rivalry and competition from leading to uncontrolled confrontation. Deterrence remains necessary, and as such requires that a military balance be maintained, preferably one stabilized by agreed arms control measures that include arms limitations and reductions. But deterrence and military security are just one necessary element. Active diplomacy between the United States and the Soviet Union and with others is also needed, since the most dangerous crises can evolve from situations in which neither the United States nor the Soviet Union has the initiative or controls the actions of third parties. Moreover, diplomacy must be directed not only at crisis management, but at crisis prevention, and more broadly at facilitating peaceful change so that crises do not erupt.

American-Soviet relations must be firmly grounded in the interests of both powers. It is not a question of trust, or persuasion, but of meeting the interests of the two sides through reciprocal recognition that there is greater advantage in establishing and maintaining particular agreements or understandings than in not doing so. (This is an argument that essentialists are not prepared to accept; both mechanists and interactionists accept it, although they differ over the extent policy objectives can be achieved through manipulation of the behavior of the other side or require accord in making any given understanding meet a balance of interests of the two sides.) It is possible to build not only on common interests, but on divergent or even conflicting interests, if both are balanced and served by any particular reciprocal understanding. In order to build on interests, one must above all be clear about what one's own real interests are, and the priorities among them. Moreover, these priorities are not absolute; a fundamental interest in avoiding nuclear war, which both sides share, does not preclude many conflicting interests that must be contested or resolved by means that do not provoke risks of war. Priorities of interest mean giving higher attention to security requirements than to ideological preferences, as both sides constantly demonstrate in practice. It is particularly difficult, and particularly necessary, for the United States to articulate its interests and priorities because the changing political agenda and political leadership in this country place more of a premium on innovation than on continuity. Yet one must have a clear understanding of one's own interests before one can fruitfully communicate and negotiate with the other side. And some degree of consistency and continuity is also required.

One difficulty in managing relations between the two powers applies particularly in the United States. A political democracy of the American pattern poses a certain inner tension and practical political difficulty in managing a consistent and purposeful central control over the levers of policy, given the independence of the executive and legislative branches of government. Nixon and Kissinger recognized this problem and actively sought to overcome it through a combination of secrecy and executive control, but they were neither entirely successful, nor was their approach fully acceptable. Difficulties stemming from the problem of democracy have plagued all administrations. Ultimately the citizenry must realize the need for and accept a sufficient delegation of authority in the implementation of strategy. Clearly that strategy must be understood and accepted by them.

One aspect of the internal Soviet scene that may come to affect the range of possible American-Soviet relations is the change in leadership. Mikhail Gorbachev and his colleagues face a number of internal problems, as well as some in foreign affairs, that require difficult decisions. The problems are not new—nor are the Soviet leaders newcomers. Still, there is an important element of change. The deaths in the span of just a few years of Mikhail Suslov, Aleksei Kosygin, Leonid Brezhnev, Yury Andropov, Dmitry Ustinov, and Konstantin Chernenko represent a generational change. The United States cannot expect, and should not attempt, to influence these decisions of the Soviet leadership except in one important way: to reaffirm U.S. readiness to support and defend its interests, while at the same time clearly indicating readiness to improve relations if the Soviet leaders are prepared to seek that improvement on the basis of mutual benefit, restraint, and reciprocity. Neither the United States nor the Soviet Union should expect unilateral concessions. But to the extent that both show a readiness to resume a common effort to contain the risks in their continuing competition, and even to resume efforts to build areas of cooperation, it should be possible to apply some lessons from the path of the 1970s that can help achieve greater success in the second half of the 1980s and beyond.

In President Reagan's words, "It takes two to tango."[20] Quite so. Particularly given the intensification of mutual suspicion in recent years, it will be even more difficult to determine that both sides are indeed ready to seek an improvement in relations and to work constructively to that end. But such an outcome can occur.

---

20. An equivalent Russian saying may be more felicitous: "It takes two hands to applaud."

Index